Mobil 1998
TRAVEL GUIDE ®

On the Road
with your Pet

**More than 4,000 Mobil-Rated Lodgings
in North America for Travelers with
Dogs, Cats, and Other Pets**

**Introduction, Pet-Travel Tips,
and Resources by Andrea Arden**

Fodor's Travel Publications, Inc.
New York • Toronto • London • Sydney • Auckland
www.fodors.com/

Andrea Arden is founder and director of the Manhattan Dog Training & Behavior Center. She's authored several books on dog training and has been the on-air animal trainer and field correspondent for Fox Cable Network's daily national pet show, "The Pet Department," since its inception in June of 1994. Andrea lives in Manhattan with her two dogs, Oliver and Meggie.

Mobil Travel Guide Staff
General Manager: Diane E. Connolly
Editorial/Inspection Coordinators: Sara D. Hauber, Doug Weinstein
Inspection Assistant: Brenda Piszczek
Editorial Assistants: Korrie Klier, Julie Raio, Kathleen Rose, Kristin Schiller, Elizabeth Schwar
Creative Director: Fabrizio La Rocca
Designer: Alison Saltzman

Acknowledgments
We gratefully acknowledge the help of our more than 100 field representatives for their efficient and perceptive inspection of hotels and restaurants; the proprietors of these establishments for their cooperation in showing their facilities and providing information about them; and our many friends and users of the Mobil Travel Guide for their time and information.

Published in 1998 by
Fodor's Travel Publications, Inc.
201 E. 50th St.
New York, NY 10022

ISBN 0-679-03548-6
ISSN on file and available from the Library of Congress

Printed in the United States of America

10 9 8 7 6 5 4 3 2

Contents

Welcome

For 40 years the *Mobil Travel Guide* has provided travelers in North America with reliable advice on finding good value, quality service, and the attractions that give a destination its special character. During this time, our teams of culinary and hospitality experts have worked hard to develop objective and exacting standards. In so doing, they seek to fully meet the desires and expectations of a broad range of customers.

At Mobil, we demonstrate the energy to make a difference through a commitment to excellence that allows us to bring the best service and products to the people we serve. We believe that the ability to respond to and anticipate customers' needs is what distinguishes good companies from truly great ones.

It is our hope, whether your travels are for business or leisure, over a long distance or a short one, that this book will be your companion, dependably guiding you to quality and value in lodging and dining.

Finally, I ask that you help us improve the guides. Please contact us on the Internet at www.mobil.com/travel.

Lucio A. Noto
Chairman and
Chief Executive Officer
Mobil Corporation

A Word to Our Readers

Since 1958 the *Mobil Travel Guide* has worked to serve the needs of travelers in North America. The trusted Mobil quality One- to Five-Star Rating System has guided many a weary voyager to a clean, safe room and a good, hot meal. Over the years, our in-house staff and teams of industry experts have kept us on the cutting edge of industry developments. From in-room modem links to business services, health club privileges and exercise equipment, we've given you the latest in lifestyle, technology and hospitality trends.

In this all-new edition, the *Mobil Travel Guide* team has endeavored to satisfy the information needs of people traveling with their pets. Indeed, more people are traveling with pets than ever before, and more establishments—of every type, from country inns to resorts and spas—will accept and even welcome them.

All of the more than 4,000 properties listed in this guide accept pets. For obvious reasons, only lodgings are included. An introduction covering the dos and don'ts of traveling with pets and appendices on first-aid and pet resources are provided to help you plan and prepare for your trip.

Of course, the passage of time means that some establishments will close, change hands, remodel, improve or go downhill. Though every effort has been made to ensure the accuracy of all information when it was printed, change is inevitable. Always call and confirm that a place is open and that it has the features you want. Whatever your experiences at any of the establishments we list—and we hope they're terrific—or if you have general comments about our guide, we'd love to hear from you. Drop us a line at Mobil Travel Guide, Fodor's Travel Publications, Inc., 4709 W. Golf Road, Suite 803, Skokie, IL 60076.

Whether you're traveling with the family dog and a car full of kids, or a friend, two cats and a cooler, we wish you a safe voyage and fond memories!

Bon voyage and happy "tails!"

THE EDITORS

Introduction

by Andrea Arden

Animals have been an important part of our family life for ages, so it's no surprise more and more people are making their pets a part of their travels. If your pet is a good companion around the house, he can also be good companion away from home. Actually, animals can be such a great source of comfort that some people can't even conceive of a vacation without their dog or cat.

Pets can add to your travel adventures in many ways. Traveling with your pet can open the door to meeting new people. Animals are great conversation starters, and animal lovers are everywhere! While hours spent leisurely dining are usually ruled out when your pet is with you, you can enjoy a picnic in a park or an outdoor barbecue. Instead of shopping you can go for a walk in town or explore a hiking trail.

In return for companionship and fun, your pet will require much of your time, just as he does at home. In fact, if you elect to include him, your pet will probably be a major focus of your trip. Even the most adaptable pet will require your attention throughout your trip. Days must be planned keeping the pet's needs in mind. Often, this means you aren't as free to spend leisurely hours shopping or eating. If these activities are your idea of a vacation, you should consider hiring a pet-sitter or finding a good kennel. Sending your dog to a doggie camp or bringing a dog sitter along on your trip are other good options. If you are planning a "get-away-from-it-all" sort of trip, bringing along your pet may not be a good idea.

Making travel plans can be time-consuming and tedious, even more so when you are taking your pet. While the number of travelers accompanied by animals is growing, some within the travel industry are still cautious to put out the welcome mat. In some areas of the country finding decent accommodations that accept you and your pet can be a daunting task.

Most important, if you don't think your pet will enjoy traveling, it is unfair to both him and you to make him do so needlessly. While most pets do have a remarkable ability to adapt to new situations, those that don't can become highly stressed and in some cases even ill. Remember, always try to see things from your pet's point of view.

Take Your Pet or Leave Him?

Deciding to travel with your pet can be a difficult decision. Try not to let your emotions take precedence over practical concerns, such as your pet's age, temperament and health. Consider your aspirations for the trip and how you will handle the responsibility of taking care of your pet on the road. If you think it will greatly hamper your enjoyment, then it may be unfair to both you and your pet to take him along.

The most important consideration is, of course, your pet. The best candidates for travel are pets that are even-tempered, well-behaved, sociable and in good health. If your pet is anxious, aggressive, or is likely to be highly stressed, it is probably in his best interest to make alternative plans, such as boarding or pet-sitting in your home.

While it is legal to transport an eight-week-old kitten or puppy by plane, it is advisable to wait until he or she is at least 12 weeks old. At eight weeks animals are susceptible to many more diseases because their immune systems are not fully developed. It's also important to control the environment of very young puppies and kittens so they don't have experiences that may frighten them. This is difficult to do while traveling.

Some trips are inappropriate for pets because of the environment, time of year and nature of the journey. A friend of mine chose to take her six-year-old lab on a cross-country drive from New York to Arizona. She left at the end of June. By the time she reached the Grand Canyon it was mid-July. The heat was tough on her but almost unbearable for her dog. As a result she spent a lot of time worrying about her dog rather than sightseeing. If she had made the trip at a different time of year, it might have been a more pet-friendly adventure.

WHO SHOULD STAY AND WHO SHOULD GO?

Bring	Leave
Calm pets	Anxious pets
Well-behaved pets	Pets who are noisy, boisterous or not housetrained
Friendly pets	Unfriendly pets
Pets who enjoy new experiences	Fearful pets
Pets over 12 weeks old	Pets under 12 weeks old
If your travel plans are pet-friendly	If your travel plans are not pet-friendly
If weather permits	If weather will be uncomfortable for your pet

Types of Travel with Pets

Around home. Most of the travel we do with our pets is around our hometown and often isn't pleasant for them. The destination is almost always a place they don't like, such as the veterinarian, groomer or kennel. Try to make it a habit to take your pet on short trips and to places he likes around town. You can take your dog to the local park for a walk, or take your cat in its carrier to run an errand to the bank. When you get to your destination, give the animal a few treats, or better yet have a friendly person give a treat to your pet. This teaches your pet to enjoy travel by making it a more common and pleasant occurrence, and it will help the animal to be more comfortable with lots of different people and things in environments outside of your home.

Human destination. Pets require a good part of your attention each day. If you are traveling to a place where there will be a lot of people, be sure you are willing to devote your time and attention to your pet. Trips to visit friends, relatives or resorts can be fun, but often at these destinations your pet is likely to play second fiddle. If you are planning to do a lot of socializing, you may not want to devote your attention to your pet.

Doggie holiday. Camping sites can be very pet-friendly. Trips to this sort of destination are fun for both you and your pet and are relatively easy to plan.

Doggie destination. There are vacations you can take with your dog that will be as much of an adventure for him as for you. Dog camps, seminars and workshops are a terrific way to have fun with your pet and learn more about your canine companion. Some of the best sources for information on these sorts of trips are The Association of Pet Dog Trainers, Camp Gone to the Dogs and Whiz Kid Dog Camp. For more information on these sources, refer to APPENDIX B.

Tips for Traveling Happily with Your Pet

BEFORE YOU GO/PREPARING TO TRAVEL

Preparation is the key to successfully traveling with your pet. As when making any travel plans, the farther in advance you begin the better. This includes training your pet for travel and making reservations for accommodations.

Due to the fast-changing nature of the lodging industry, it is important to call ahead and confirm the pet-friendly status of your lodgings a few days prior to your departure. It's not uncommon for the policies of accommodations to change on short notice. It can take just one irresponsible visitor with his or her pet to convince a manager that pets just aren't worth the trouble.

When confirming your reservation be sure to double-check the fees and restrictions of each lodging. Accommodations often have restrictions on the size and age of animals (puppies are often discouraged). Be prepared to leave a deposit (usually refundable) in case your animal damages the property.

Try to have a confirmation mailed or faxed to you prior to your departure. At the very least, take down the name and title of a contact person for each of your lodgings.

WHAT TO PACK

The following list may seem a bit daunting, but my friends with young children insist their lists are much longer when they pack for their kids! It's usually best to keep all of your pet's items in one easy-to-reach bag. You want to avoid fumbling around for something for your pet in an overhead bin or the back seat of your van.

One of the most important safety concerns when traveling with your pet is to make sure your animal is wearing clear identification, in case she gets lost. The more methods of identification, the better the chance of recovery. The most common and traditional method is an ID tag. Your pet should wear two tags when traveling: one with your permanent address and telephone number and another with a way to contact you on the road. A trick is to staple a matchbook from your lodging to your pet's collar. You can also buy tags that can be changed by slipping in a new piece of paper. Also, keep a current photo of your pet on hand while traveling. Visual images are extremely helpful in locating lost pets. Consider having your pet tattooed or microchipped in addition to wearing traditional ID tags. Both processes are humane and effective for tracking pets. For more information on microchipping and tattooing, talk to your vet and/or refer to APPENDIX B.

1. **Identification and Health Records**
   - A leash and collar or harness with ID tags (an extra set is advisable).
   - Health and vaccination records.
   - A lost-pet packet. Taking every imaginable precaution doesn't guarantee your pet won't get lost on your trip. As a safety measure bring some current photos and a description of your pet in case you need to put up signs.
   - A bell to attach to your pet's collar. This is a great backup safety measure if she gets loose in the woods.

2. **Food and Water**
   - Bowls (paper plates and a collapsible water bowl are light to carry and easy to dispose of).
   - Your pet's food. If it isn't a national brand and you suspect it may be difficult to find while traveling, be sure to bring enough for the whole trip. A sudden change in your dog's food could cause an upset stomach. If you usually add a bit of moist food to the dry food but prefer not to take heavy cans with you, bring a few packets of a mild dry soup mix. Sprinkle a bit over the kibble and mix with warm water to make a tasty gravy.

- If you choose to bring canned food, don't forget an opener and a spoon.
- A container of water from your home. This is especially advisable if your pet has a sensitive stomach and may be affected by drinking new water.
- A spray bottle—to squirt water in your pet's mouth if necessary.

3. **Cleanup Stuff**
   - Plastic bags.
   - A lint and hair remover for yourself and to tidy up your lodgings.
   - Room deodorizer.
   - Baby wipes or towelettes for quick and easy clean ups of paws and hands.
   - Old cloths and/or paper towels for lining the carrier and cleanup. Also, bring a supply of plastic bags for soiled towels and a spray bottle of cleaner.
   - If you are traveling with a cat, don't forget a litter box, litter, a plastic bag to slip over the box and a couple of large rubber bands to hold the bag in place.
   - Grooming tools to keep your pet clean (and therefore more likely to be welcome).

4. **Sleeping**
   - A bed, towel or piece of carpet sample for your pet to sleep on (see What Should My Pet Be Trained to Do?).
   - A relaxation tape (see Relaxing to Music).

5. **Toys**
   - Sterilized white bones to stuff with meat, cheese, kibble or peanut butter.
   - Kong toys to stuff with meat, cheese, kibble or peanut butter.
   - Cat toys. The easiest and cheapest is a piece of crumpled paper or a square of cardboard tied to string. Pet stores sell all sorts of inexpensive, intriguing, safe toys.

6. **Medical Stuff**
   - Any medication prescribed by your veterinarian.
   - A first-aid kit (ask your vet for assistance or contact Pet Pak, Inc. See APPENDIX B).
   - A slip-on muzzle, in case your pet or a stray has a medical emergency.
   - Honey or hard candy to help alleviate car sickness (be sure to consult your vet first).
   - Tweezers and scissors (for removing burs, ticks and other things).

7. **Extras**
   - Flashlight (for nighttime walks).
   - A clip-on minifan for the hotel room or the car.

Travel Petiquette

A well-trained pet is the most important component of an enjoyable travel experience. Training is what determines whether traveling with your pet will be easy and enjoyable or no fun at all. The best travel companion, whether two- or four-legged, is a well-behaved one. A calm, well-mannered pet is sure to be invited back for a second visit and will help to pave the way for future visits from pets. Whether at home or on the road, an animal who likes to be around people and is calm and under control is a joy to be with. Dogs and cats are social animals who relish communication with their pack. Training helps your pet to communicate with you by putting human words to dog and cat behaviors. If you think your pet needs some travel training, plan on starting at least a few weeks before your trip to give both of you ample time. Have a travel prep party to help train your dog or cat to be an ambassador for canines and felines. Invite friends over to help your pet practice meeting people and coping in a hectic environment. One of the best sources for training books, audios and videos for both cats and dogs is available from James and Kenneth Publishers (see APPENDIX B).

WHERE TO TRAIN

Most people just train their dogs at home and at a training club. It's important to train your pet in a variety of places to optimize your pet's exposure to different people, places and things. Visit local buildings and hotels where dogs are welcome. These buildings often have good parking, are climate controlled and have carpeting, which makes for good traction. Think of this training as getting your pet ready at the "home game" before the big "away game."

STRESS AND TRAVELING

Traveling is stressful for people, but for an animal it can be even more so. The best ways to alleviate stress for your pet are to teach her what you want and to control her environment. Most stress comes from not knowing how to act. Be considerate of your pet's stress levels. Don't expect her to meet and greet too many people in one day, especially when under the stress of traveling. Even the most social animals can be overwhelmed if too many people say hello at once or if they are overtired from meeting too many new people. You should control who comes into contact with your pet and how often. Watch your pet for signs of stress (yawning, excessive panting, avoiding eye contact) and give her a place to relax quietly if she needs to. A crate or blanket is great for this purpose. Follow the guidelines set by the Delta Society (listed in APPENDIX B), an organization that facilitates pet therapy programs in hospitals and nursing homes. They suggest that when an animal and owner team goes on a visit, they stay no more than one hour. Most pets should have no more than one hour of meeting and greeting a day.

What Should My Pet Be Trained to Do?

Both cats and dogs should know how to be friendly with people and how to relax and calmly accept travel. They should know how to settle down in different situations. They should also be housetrained or litterbox trained. Dogs should know how to come to you when you call (cats can learn this too!), to walk politely on a leash and to stop barking when asked.

GREETING PEOPLE

Start teaching your pet at home that meeting people is a safe and fun thing to do. The more good experiences your pet has with people, the more comfortable he will be around people. Take him to meet people all over town: at the local shopping mall, in the park and on the streets. You should also teach him to sit to greet people. To do this invite friends over and have each of them ready with a handful of treats. Have your dog on a leash and when they approach to greet him ask him to sit. While he is sitting they can give him a bit of food. He will learn that saying hello to people while sitting is a rewarding experience. For your cat, you can have people gently hold him and offer him a treat.

SETTLING DOWN

Your dog should be able to settle down at the drop of a hat. Start in your calm home environment by teaching him that the word *down* means to lay down and relax until you release him. Have a blanket, towel or piece of scrap rug as the dog's settle-down spot. Ask him to lay down on it and use a bit of food in your hand to guide his head down, in which case his body will follow. When he is laying down, give him the treat and praise him. Let him know when he can get up by saying a word or phrase such as *all done* or *free dog*. By repeating this you will be teaching him that laying quietly on that spot is the best way to get two of the things he likes most: your attention and a treat. Be sure to practice in different places—by your side, at the dinner table, while you're watching television or reading a book. Practice with the dog out of site in a different room to prepare him for if you ever need to leave him alone in his carrier while traveling.

When your dog will lay quietly in your home for a few moments, you should begin to use the settle-down command on walks. Stop every 25 yards or so to train him to quickly lay down and relax even when he is excited (most dogs are when going for a walk). Use praise and food the same way you did in your home. Offer him a bit to get him into the "down" position by using your hand with the food in it to guide his head to the floor. When he is laying down, give him the treat and praise him.

CARRIER/CRATE TRAINING

Crating allows you to relax while your pet is safe and secure. It also allows your pet to relax in a familiar place. The first step is to teach your pet to accept and even enjoy time spent in his carrier. I can't think of a better investment of a pet owner's time. If used properly, a carrier is a fantastic tool for training and helping your pet to feel at home anywhere. To begin, place the carrier near your pet's feeding and/or resting area. Let him investigate it on his own. A great little trick is to put a piece of food or your pet's dinner inside the crate and close the door with him outside the crate. When he shows a strong interest in the food, open the door and let him go in to get it. Then begin to have him spend time in the carrier by gently placing him in it and offering a food treat. Slowly increase the time your pet spends in the crate, from a few seconds to a few minutes. Make sure every encounter is a pleasant one and never use the carrier to punish your pet. Continue to have your pet spend time in his carrier doing things he enjoys (such as eating). To ensure that your pet sees his carrier as a safe place, don't let people bother him when he is in it.

How long should this take? Training puppies takes very little time. Older dogs and cats usually require a little more time. But it depends on your pet's temperament. The more laid back your pet, the quicker it will be. On average, it should take no more than a few weeks to teach your pet that his carrier is a pleasant place to spend a little time.

Choosing and maintaining the carrier. There are three main considerations to keep in mind when choosing a carrier: size, quality and comfort. The carrier should be big enough for your pet to stand up, turn around and lay down in. Don't make the mistake of choosing one that gives your pet too much extra room. Animals are more likely to be injured in a carrier that is too big. There are many different brands of carriers on the market. Airline-approved carriers are a wise choice, because they can be used for both air and car travel and offer the best assurance of durability. For most pets you should line the carrier with a mat, towels or shredded newspaper. However, if you are still house-training your dog, a liner may make him more likely to use the crate as a toilet. So, until he is house-trained, keep the carrier floor bare.

RELAXING TO MUSIC

At home, play a tape of music every time you feed, stroke or massage your pet. After a while she will begin to associate this tape with positive and calm experiences. Then you can bring the tape with you when you travel to help calm your pet. It's like bringing a bit of home with you.

SPEAKING AND SHUSHING

To teach your dog to be quiet on command you first will have to get him to bark. Set up a situation that will get him to do so. Say "speak" and have a friend ring the doorbell. Praise him for barking once or twice, tell him to "shush" and waggle a treat in front of his nose. He will stop barking to sniff the treat. When he is quiet for just a moment give him the treat. Repeat this process a few times a day and he will start to understand that being quiet when you ask him to means he will get a reward.

WALKING ON A LEASH

Your dog should be able to walk calmly by your side, even in crowded areas. To teach this, start by walking her first in relatively quiet areas around your home and garden. Praise and encourage when she pays attention to you. If she gets distracted go in another direction. When she catches up with you, praise her again and maybe offer a food treat. Most people think cats can't be trained to walk on leash, but they can. If you plan on traveling with your cat it is a good idea to get her used to wearing a harness and leash. You can teach your cat to enjoy wearing her harness by slowly acclimating her to it. To begin, put it on her for short periods of time. Each time she wears it give her a special food treat. In a short while she will associate wearing her harness with something great—food.

COMING WHEN CALLED

Make sure you've taught your dog to come to you when called. This is the most valuable emergency safety command. Imagine he's gotten loose and is headed toward a road. It's imperative that he knows to respond immediately when you call him. Unlike when training at home, where the objective is to phase out lures and rewards for obedience, it is a sound policy not to attempt this when on the road. Let your dog know he is highly likely to get a couple of treats and lots of praise when he comes when called. It is dangerous to have a dog who won't come when called while at home, but it is disastrous to lose your dog in an unfamiliar setting. Start teaching him to come when called by having your dog on a leash in a calm environment without too many distractions. Call him to you. When he turns your way, praise him and give him a treat when he gets to you. If he doesn't come to you, use the leash to gently get his attention and encourage him to you. When he responds reliably at home, start to take him to new areas to train, but always keep him on a leash. You can use a longer leash and practice having him come when you call from a farther distance. With this reward system, your dog will learn that coming to you always results in something great: your praise and/or a treat. This means you shouldn't call your dog to you when you are going to do something to him he doesn't like, such as give him a bath. In those cases, go and get him. Teaching a dog to respond to a silent dog whistle is a great idea. The sound carries much farther than your voice. Teach this in the same way you teach your dog to come to you when you use your voice to call him. However, please try to keep your dog on leash as much as possible when traveling. Remember, his attention and obedience will probably not be as reliable in unfamiliar places.

ELIMINATING

Whether you want your dog to go outside or on paper inside, training him to go on cue will make traveling much easier. "Pit stops" often are meant to be fast, and waiting for your dog to find just the right spot can delay your trip. With a small dog who goes on paper, the act of placing the paper on the floor usually is enough to get her to go. But larger dogs who eliminate outside are often taught to go for a long walk before they eliminate. Change things around: When you take your dog out, wait for her to eliminate before you walk around the block. When she begins to eliminate say something like "go potty" in a happy tone and praise her. This way she'll learn to go immediately and see the walk as the reward. For the first week or two this training may seem tedious (just standing in one spot), but it will be well worth the effort when you are on the road or when you must take your dog out on a rainy night.

SOCIALIZING

Take your pet out into the world and let him become accustomed to new sights, sounds and people. Introduce him to people at your home, then take him with you on errands around town. Never push your pet into a situation where he feels uncomfortable. Bring along some treats and offer them as a way of praising your pet for calmly accepting new experiences. He will soon associate new experiences with good things.

CAR TRAVEL TRAINING

Most pets only travel when going to the veterinarian, groomer or kennel, all of which are not much fun for your pet. In fact most pets, especially cats, only make three trips in the car (to the vet) before they are five months old. These experiences are not conducive to your pet enjoying travel. If your pet hasn't traveled much, you should dedicate at least a few weeks before your trip to getting him accustomed to car travel and carrier training. When your pet is calm and relaxed in the carrier at home, you can repeat the training process with the carrier placed in your car. After a few days take short trips in the car and make the destination a place that will please your pet. Most dogs will learn to love car rides if they believe they will sometimes bring them to play ball in the local park.

On the Road

CAR SAFETY

Travel by car is a far better option with your pet than travel by airplane. It is safer and less stressful for your pet. There are two major safety concerns for pets: overheating and restraint.

Overheating. Leaving your pet in the car unsupervised is a dangerous proposition. Even in mild temperatures a car can heat up in minutes to a level that can cause heatstroke and even death. Opening the windows and parking in the shade will not prevent this from happening. Dogs and cats do not have good cooling systems, because they don't sweat very much through their skin, rather they rely on panting. In warm weather a damp towel draped over the carrier will help to cool the air circulating through the crate while you are in the car with your dog, but it will not do much good in a car that isn't moving.

Restraint. A loose animal in the car is a danger to himself and everyone else in the car. If you make a short stop or are involved in an accident, the animal could be badly injured or killed. In a 30-mile-an-hour collision, an animal becomes a lethal weapon to all the passengers. When loose, an animal is also likely to distract you and may get caught under the accelerator or brake pedal. Make sure your pet is restrained to avoid accidents and injury. Options for restraint are a carrier, a harness attached to a seatbelt or a regular leash tied to a stationary part of the car. If you choose to use a crate, make sure it is secured so it won't tip over if you make a sharp turn or stop. Don't allow your pet to keep his head out of the window when you are driving. It's common for animals to need veterinary care as a result of debris becoming embedded in their eyes. You can open the windows a bit to allow fresh air to circulate, but not enough to allow your pet to put his head out. If you want to open your windows fully, consider installing window guards.

CAR SICKNESS

Consult your vet if your pet has a history of severe car sickness. She may recommend medication. An holistic approach might also work well for your pet. Many people have had success with Rescue Remedy, which is a mix of flower essences. This option should also be discussed with your vet. Never give your pet any drugs, especially tranquilizers, without your veterinarian's approval.

LOSS OF APPETITE

Many animals suffer from a lack of appetite when they are traveling or under stress in general. It may be due to an existing chronic illness, in which case you should talk to a vet. But in most cases it is simply due to stress caused by travel. If you plan ahead you can train your pet to eat in the car and/or his crate. Feed him in his crate in and out of the car for at least a few weeks prior to your trip. By doing so, you will train your pet to think of his crate as his portable dining room.

LEAVING YOUR PET IN THE CAR

It is dangerous to leave your pet unsupervised in the car. Animals are suscepti-ble to heatstroke (even in mild weather) and are a target for theft. If you are traveling alone and must leave your pet in the car when you go to the restroom, an option is to leave the car running with the air-conditioning on (in warm weather). You'll need to have two sets of car keys with you so you can leave one in the ignition. Be sure to keep your pet secured and away from the car's control panels, and remember that leaving your pet alone for even a moment leaves him susceptible to thieves. If you don't have air-conditioning, leave two windows open for circulation. But—this point cannot be made often enough—if you leave your pet unsupervised in the car, you are taking an enormous risk with his life. If you want to stop and have a day of sightseeing in an area that does not allow pets, contact the local vet or boarding kennels and negotiate a day-rate for boarding.

BATHROOM ROUTINE

When on the road try to keep as close to your pet's normal routine as possible. When you stop for yourself, always be considerate of your pet and allow him time to stretch and relieve himself as well. How often you should stop depends on your pet's age and temperament. For very young or old animals, stops should be more frequent. Traveling can be stressful for even the calmest animal, and stress will make your pet more likely to need to eliminate. So allow your pet a few more opportunities to get out and eliminate than you would at home. At each rest stop offer your pet some water from home. Allowing him to exercise for a bit before you head off will make him more likely to sleep. Many rest stops have grassy areas appropriate for pets, but no matter how well trained your pet is, be sure to keep him on a leash at all times. You will find that pit stops will be much quicker if you've taught your dog to eliminate on command.

In the Air

Air travel can be a very stressful and sometimes dangerous experience for pets. This is especially true if they are in the excess baggage or cargo holds instead of in the cabin with you. The International Air Transport Association (IATA), which governs air travel for pets along with the United States Department of Agriculture (USDA), estimates half a million dogs and cats travel on commercial airlines in the United States each year. Of those, a reported 99 percent arrive at their destination without incident. However, that leaves approximately 5,000 airline mishaps a year—enough to make any pet owner very cautious of this mode of transportation. The best way to ensure your pet's safety is to ask lots of questions and be sure to get answers that sound right to you before you proceed. Just remember that each person you speak with is in some way responsible for the care of your pet, so be considerate!

Each airline has its own guidelines for travel. Reconfirm your plans 24 to 48 hours before flight departure, especially during peak flying times. If possible, get written confirmation of your arrangements from the airline. Most airlines have information regarding pet travel on their Web sites (see IMPORTANT TOLL-FREE NUMBERS).

AIR TRAVEL GUIDELINES

Pets who can fly by plane. Healthy animals over eight weeks old who have been issued a health certificate no more than ten days prior to flying are legally allowed to fly. However, it is advisable to wait until they are 12 weeks old. If your pet is under the care of a veterinarian for an existing medical condition, you should consult your vet on the pros and cons of air travel.

Pets who shouldn't travel by plane. If your pet is pregnant, ill or under 12 weeks old she should not fly, because the stress can cause serious complica-tions. According to the Animal Welfare Act, dogs and cats must be at least eight weeks old to travel by plane, but 12 weeks is a much safer age. Keep in mind that pug-nosed animals (such as Bulldogs, Pugs and Boston Terriers and Himalayan and Persian cats) may have difficulty breathing at high altitudes because of their short nasal passages. You should also consider an alternative method of travel or consult your vet if your pet does not handle new and stressful situations well.

Requirements to travel. To travel by plane, your pet will need a health certificate that has been issued no more than ten days prior to the flight and an airline-approved carrier.

WHEN TO TRAVEL
- **Best days to travel.** Weekday flights are usually less hectic than weekend flights. Both you and your pet are more likely to receive attentive service during the week.
- **Best months to travel.** If you must travel in the summer months, book flights only in the early morning or late evening when the temperatures are lowest. In the winter, midday flights are best because temperatures are usually higher than in the morning or evening.
- **Best routes to travel.** Direct and nonstop flights are the best. Avoid bringing your pet on a flight with a stopover, especially flights that require passengers to change planes. These are the situations in which a mishap is most likely to occur because of scheduling changes or simple human error. If you are making a flight connection to a different airline, you will have to recheck your animal and pay another fee for excess baggage.
- **Weather requirements.** Most airlines use the following guidelines regarding temperatures in which animals may be flown: No less than 32°F and no more than 85°F.

Cost. The cost of flying your pet is determined by the individual airline and may be based on the size and weight of your animal as well as where and how (cabin, baggage or cargo) it is to be flown. If you do not have your own carrier, some airlines sell them, but they're usually quite a bit more expensive than carriers from a pet-supply catalog or store.

Crate requirements. A crate must be big enough for your pet to stand up, turn around and lay down in comfortably. It must be sturdy and well-ventilated and contain two plastic food and water dishes (these usually come with the crate). If your pet is traveling in the cabin with you, he can be carried in a Sherpa bag, which is airline-approved. If you're traveling with two cats, you might consider using a slightly larger crate and letting the cats travel together.

Tranquilizers. Most vets do not recommend tranquilizers because they can have adverse effects at high altitudes and may make the animal less able to right himself if his carrier is mishandled. Also, tranquilizers can adversely affect your pet's body temperature-regulation process. It is best to discuss this matter with your vet, who will consider your pet's age and temperament as well as the duration of the flight before advising you on the use of tranquilizers.

Exercise. Try to exercise your pet a bit before departure so he will be more likely to relax or even sleep.

Feeding. In most cases it is advisable to avoid feeding your pet a large meal within two hours of departure time. It is usually best to feed dogs a small meal before you leave and then a larger meal upon arrival at your destination at the end of the day. Cats usually won't eat when they see you packing anyway, so when you get to your destination be sure to set up a quiet spot for your cat to eliminate and eat.

Airline Travel Options

FLYING YOUR PET IN THE CABIN WITH YOU
Some airlines permit animals to travel in the cabin as long as they are kept in their carriers and the carrier fits under the seat. Usually, no more than two pets

are allowed in a cabin per flight, so make reservations well in advance and double check the airline's regulations. As a general rule, pets permitted to travel in the cabin can weigh no more than ten pounds. Most airlines charge between $50 and $75 one way for a pet in the cabin. When you arrive at the security gate, you will be required to remove your pet from its carrier and send the carrier through the X-ray machine. Be sure to have a collar or harness and leash attached to your pet. Most airlines have approved soft-sided carriers, such as the Sherpa bag, for cabin travel. To avoid delays, be sure to have your pet's health certificate and boarding pass ready when you approach the security gate.

CABIN NUMBER REQUIREMENTS

Airline	Animals allowed in 1st class/Main cabin
American	2/5
Continental	1/2
Delta	No/No
Northwest	1/1
TWA	1/2
United	1/2
USAir	1/1

FLYING YOUR PET AS BAGGAGE

To travel on your flight as excess baggage, the total weight of your pet and its carrier must not exceed 100 pounds. If the weight of the animal and carrier combined is greater than that, most airlines will only allow the pet to be shipped as cargo.

FLYING YOUR PET AS CARGO

If your pet and its carrier exceeds the maximum weight allowed to fly as excess baggage (100 pounds in most cases), she may have to fly as cargo. When flying as cargo, airlines do not guarantee that your pet will be on the same flight as you. Pricing also changes: It will be based on the weight and/or the measurements of the kennel. Flying as cargo is one of the most hazardous ways to transport your pet. If it is your only option, you must be even more careful to question the airline on every aspect of your pet's journey.

CHECKING YOUR PET AS BAGGAGE OR CARGO

- The checking-in process can take a bit of time, so get to the airport at least 1 1/2 hours before flight time. Make sure you have all of your paperwork ready and be friendly to everyone at the airline—remember, they will be taking care of your pet.
- Bring a health certificate that has been issued no more than ten days before the flight.
- Have a carrier that is airline-approved and properly fitted to your pet. Approved crates will be marked as such, and appropriately sized crates should be big enough for your pet to stand up, turn around and lay down in with ease. If it is too large, your animal could be hurt because too much movement means he is more likely to be banged around. Don't include toys because they increase the possibility of choking. A piece of your old clothes or a blanket or towel from home may help to relax your pet a bit.
- Make sure the carrier is clearly identified and boldly marked so you can spot it from a distance. Tape a friendly note on the top of the crate with all relevant information regarding your pet. A sample might be: HI MY NAME IS..... I AM A .....-YEAR-OLD ....I AM GOING TO.......ON FLIGHT..... ON.....AIRLINE. THIS IS MY .....FLIGHT SO I AM A LITTLE NERVOUS. THANK YOU FOR TAKING GOOD CARE OF ME.
- After you check your pet in, go to your gate and watch to make sure your pet is safely loaded (a brightly marked carrier will make it easy to spot your

animal). If possible ask one of the airline employees to reconfirm with baggage personnel that your pet is aboard.

- If you must change plans at a stopover, check with airline personnel again to make sure your pet has made the connection. If there will be a long delay in the second flight departure, claim your pet, take him for a quick walk, etc. and then reboard him.
- After arrival your pet will be delivered to the baggage-claim area. Pick your pet up there.

TRAVEL ABROAD

Make plans well in advance. Regulations vary from country to country. Your travel agent should be consulted as well as your airline and local embassy. For Canada, the rabies vaccination must be no more than three years old. For Mexico, the animal's health certificate must be verified by the Mexican Consulate in advance.

When You Arrive at Your Lodging

Allowing pets to stay is a courtesy offered by lodgings. Many places roll out the red carpet for travelers with pets, but they are also quick to roll the carpet up and put it away after just one or two bad encounters! You and your pet act as ambassadors for every person who travels with his or her pet, so please be on your best behavior. Make sure to adhere to some basic rules, such as cleaning up after your pet, as well as any specific rules posted by the manager. If no rules are posted, ask about them and follow them. Be understanding of people's concerns about pets.

Use the following general guidelines while in lodgings:
- Always clean up after your pet.
- Also, please clean up any other pet messes you see lying around. It is the only proper thing to do (anyway, someone might think your dog did it!).
- Walk your dog in areas away from flower beds and other public areas. Ask the manager where he would prefer you to walk your dog.
- Always keep your pet on a leash or in its carrier.
- Never leave your pet alone in your room unless he is in his carrier and you are sure he will not disturb other guests. This is for the safety of your pet and the lodging employees. An employee might enter the room to clean and accidentally let your pet slip out of the room. For the safety of lodging employees, if you must leave your pet alone in a room, it is best to hang the DO NOT DISTURB sign.
- If your pet damages any hotel property, immediately discuss the situation with the manager and agree to cover the cost.
- Request a ground-floor room, which is much more convenient for late-night potty runs.
- Be sure to wipe your dog's feet when you enter the room after a walk, and bring an extra towel or sheet if you intend to allow the dog on the furniture (which you shouldn't do anyway!).
- Bring a relaxation tape for your pet. Before you leave on your trip, play a music tape every time you feed him. He will begin to associate the tape with pleasant, calm experiences. When traveling, playing this tape will be like bringing a little bit of home with you.
- Cats should be secured on a leash and harness or in a carrier when transporting them from your room to the car. Put some newspaper under the litter box and put the box in the bathroom or in the bathtub so the cat is less likely to track litter on the carpet. If you know your cat has a tendency to scatter litter out of the box, be sure to clean it up.
- Control who comes into contact with your pet. Allowing too many people to say hello to him may add to his stress (and yours!). The stress of traveling can make even the most friendly animal behave abnormally.

POISONS

Be aware that many public areas and lodgings use poisons to get rid of insects and rodents. These are also poisonous to pets. When you register ask if any poisons are used, and always keep your pet leashed when in public areas.

Health and Safety Precautions

Health problems and emergencies when traveling with your pet are not much different from problems at home. If anything goes wrong, take your pet to the vet. If you have any questions or concerns about your pet's health, contact a vet. Following are some general tips on things to do before you leave.

KNOW YOUR PET'S "NORMALS"

You should know all your animal's normal vital signs, including temperature, heart rate, respiration rate and the frequency of eating, drinking, urinating and defecating. Consult your vet to help compile this list.

Any variation in your pet's normal heart rate, pulse, temperature, or urination or defecation may be an indication that something isn't right. Furthermore, you should take your pet to the vet in the case of persistent loose stool, vomit, blood in the stool or vomit, shortness of breath, excessive slobbering, abnormal body posture, loss of appetite, runny nose or eyes or shaking.

COMPLETE PHYSICAL

Take your pet for a complete physical before you leave on your trip. The stress of travel can cause even the most minor health concern to turn into a more serious condition. Keep in mind that entry regulations for certain states require certain health certificates. A complete physical for your animal will identify any preexisting conditions, ascertain your pet's "normals" and give you an opportunity to discuss your travel plans and concerns with your vet.

GET VET REFERRALS BEFORE YOU TRAVEL

Before you leave home ask your vet for veterinary referrals in any areas you plan to travel to. Alternatively contact the American Animal Hospital Association or the American Veterinary Medical Association (see APPENDIX B).

FIRST-AID KIT

You should always have a first-aid kit whether at home or traveling. You can buy a pre-packed kit or make one on your own. At a minimum a first-aid kit should contain scissors, blunt tweezers, cotton gauze, antibiotic ointment, rectal thermometer, 3 percent hydrogen peroxide, cotton swabs, panalog ear drops, pepto-bismol, kaopectate, and activated charcoal tablets.

BREED-SPECIFIC TRAVEL PROBLEMS

Breeds of animals with pug noses such as Boston Terriers, Pugs and Bulldogs, and Himalayan and Persian cats often have difficulty breathing at high altitudes, and some airlines advise against these animals being transported by air.

Understanding the Listings

All of the more than 4,000 properties listed in this guide accept pets. For obvious reasons, only lodgings are included. The following section fully explains the elements of a *Mobil Travel Guide* listing, allowing you to find a lodging that will not only accept your pet, but offer you the other amenities you desire as well.

The Listings

ORGANIZATION

When a property is in a town that does not have its own heading, the listing appears under the town nearest its location with the address and town in parentheses immediately after the establishment name. In large cities, lodgings located within 5 miles of major, commercial airports are listed under a separate "Airport" heading, following the city listings.

LODGING CLASSIFICATIONS

Each property is classified by type according to the characteristics below. Because the following features and services are found at most motels, lodges, motor hotels, and hotels, they are not shown in those listings:

- Year-round operation with a single rate structure unless otherwise quoted
- European plan (meals not included in room rate)
- Bathroom with tub and/or shower in each room
- Air-conditioned/heated, often with individual room control
- Cots
- Daily maid service
- Phones in rooms
- Elevators

Motels and Lodges. Accommodations are in low-rise structures with rooms easily accessible to parking (usually free). Properties have outdoor room entry and small, functional lobbies. Service is often limited, and dining may not be offered in lower-rated motels and lodges. Shops and businesses are found only in higher-rated properties, as are bellhops, room service, and restaurants serving three meals daily.

Lodges differ from motels primarily in their emphasis on outdoor recreational activities and in location. They are often found in resort and rural areas rather than in major cities or along highways.

Motor Hotels. Offering the convenience of motels along with many of the features of hotels, motor hotels range from low-rise structures offering limited services to multistory buildings with a wide range of services and facilities. Multiple building entrances, elevators, inside hallways, and parking areas (generally free) near access doors are some of the features of a motor hotel. Lobbies offer sitting areas and 24-hour desk and switchboard services. Often bellhop and valet services as well as restaurants serving three meals a day are found. Expanded recreational facilities and more than one restaurant are available in higher-rated properties.

The distinction between motor hotels and hotels in metropolitan areas is minor.

Hotels. To be categorized as a hotel, an establishment must have most of the following facilities and services: multiple floors, a restaurant and/or coffee shop, elevators, room service, bellhops, a spacious lobby, and recreational facilities.

In addition, the following features and services not shown in listings are also found:

- Valet service (one-day laundry/cleaning service)
- Room service during hours restaurant is open
- Bellhops
- Some oversize beds

Resorts. These specialize in stays of three days or more and usually offer American Plan and/or housekeeping accommodations. Their emphasis is on recreational facilities, and a social director is often available. Food services are of primary importance, and guests must be able to eat three meals a day on the premises, either in restaurants or by having access to an on-site grocery store and preparing their own meals.

Inns. Frequently thought of as a small hotel, an inn is a place of homelike comfort and warm hospitality. It is often a structure of historic significance, with an equally interesting setting. Meals are a special occasion, and refreshments are frequently served in late afternoon. Rooms are usually individually decorated, often with antiques or furnishings representative of the locale. Phones, bathrooms, and TVs may not be available in every room.

Guest Ranches. Like resorts, guest ranches specialize in stays of three days or more. Guest ranches also offer meal plans and extensive outdoor activities. Horseback riding is usually a feature; there are stables and trails on the ranch property, and trail rides and daily instruction are part of the program. Many guest ranches are working ranches, ranging from casual to rustic, and guests are encouraged to participate in ranch life. Eating is often family-style and may also include cookouts. Western saddles are assumed; phone ahead to inquire about English saddle availability.

Cottage Colonies. These are housekeeping cottages and cabins that are usually found in recreational areas. Any dining or recreational facilities are noted in our listing.

QUALITY RATINGS

The *Mobil Travel Guide* has been rating lodgings and restaurants on a national basis since the first edition was published in 1958.

All listed establishments were inspected by experienced field representatives or evaluated by a senior staff member. Ratings are based upon their detailed inspection reports of the individual properties, on written evaluations of staff members who stay and dine anonymously, and on an extensive review of comments from our readers.

You'll find a key to the rating categories, ★ through ★ ★ ★ ★ ★, on page xxiii. All establishments in the book are recommended. Even a ★ place is above average, usually providing a basic, informal experience. Rating categories reflect both the features the property offers and its quality in relation to similar establishments.

For example, lodging ratings take into account the number and quality of facilities and services, the luxury of appointments, and the attitude and professionalism of staff and management. A ★ establishment provides a comfortable night's lodging. A ★★ property offers more than a facility that rates one star, and the decor is well planned and integrated. Establishments that rate ★★★ are professionally managed and staffed and often beautifully appointed; the lodging experience is truly excellent and the range of facilities is extensive. Properties that have been given ★★★★ not only offer many services but also have their own style and personality; they are luxurious, creatively decorated, and superbly maintained. The ★★★★★ properties are among the best in the United States, superb in every respect and entirely memorable, year in and year out.

Each rating is reviewed annually and each establishment must work to maintain its rating (or improve it). Every effort is made to assure that ratings are fair and accurate; the designated ratings are published purely as an aid to travelers.

In general, properties that are very new or have recently undergone major management changes are considered difficult to assess fairly and are often listed without ratings.

Good Value Check Mark. In all locales, you'll find a wide range of lodging establishments with a ✔ in front of a star rating. This indicates an unusually good value at economical prices as follows:

In Major Cities and Resort Areas

Average $105–$125 per night for singles; average $115–$140 per night for doubles

Local Area Listings

Average $50–$60 per night for singles; average $60–$75 per night for doubles

LODGINGS

Each listing gives the name, address, directions (when there is no street address), neighborhood and/or directions from downtown (in major cities), phone number (local and 800), fax number, number and type of rooms available, room rates, and seasons open (if not year-round). Also included are details on recreational and dining facilities on property or nearby, the presence of a luxury level, and credit-card information. A key to the symbols at the end of each listing is on page xxiii. (Note that Mobil Corporation credit cards cannot be used for payment of meals and room charges.)

All prices quoted in the *Mobil Travel Guide* publications are expected to be in effect at the time of publication and during the entire year; however, prices cannot be guaranteed. In some localities there may be short-term price variations because of special events or holidays. Whenever possible, these price changes are noted. Certain resorts have complicated rate structures that vary with the time of year; always confirm listed rates when you make your plans.

Symbols and Abbreviations

The definitions and explanations that follow will help you navigate the listings with ease. For definitions of property types and broader descriptions of the rating designations, see pages xx-xxii.

Symbols At End of Listings

D	Facilities for the disabled
	Pets allowed
	Fishing
	Horseback riding
	Snow skiing nearby
	Golf, 9-hole minimum, on premises or privileges within 10 miles
	Tennis court(s) on premises or privileges within 5 miles
	Swimming
	Exercise equipment or room
	Jogging
	Major commercial airport within 2 miles
	No-smoking rooms
	Smoke detector and/or sprinkler system
SC	Senior citizen rates
	Business center

Quality Ratings

★ ★ ★ ★ ★	One of the best in the country
★ ★ ★ ★	Outstanding—worth a special trip
★ ★ ★	Excellent
★ ★	Very good
★	Good, better than average
✔	In addition, an unusually good value, relatively inexpensive

Terms and Abbreviations in Listings

The following terms and abbreviations are used consistently throughout the listings:

AP	American plan (lodging plus all meals).
Bar	Liquor, wine, and beer are served in a bar or cocktail lounge and usually with meals unless otherwise indicated (e.g., "wine, beer").
Business center	The property has a designated area accessible to all guests with business services.

Business servs avail	The property can perform/arrange at least two of the following services for a guest: audiovisual equipment rental, binding, computer rental, faxing, messenger services, modem availability, notary service, obtaining office supplies, photocopying, shipping, and typing.
Cable	Standard cable service; "premium" indicates that HBO, Disney, Showtime, or similar services are available.
Ck-in, ck-out	Check-in time, check-out time.
Coin lndry	Self-service laundry.
Continental bkfst	Usually coffee and a roll or doughnut.
Cr cds:	A, American Express; C, Carte Blanche; D, Diners Club; DS, Discover; ER, enRoute; JCB, Japanese Credit Bureau; MC, MasterCard; V, Visa.
D	Followed by a price, indicates room rate for a "double"—two people in one room in one or two beds (the charge may be higher for two double beds).
Downhill/x-country ski	Downhill and/or cross-country skiing within 20 miles of property.
Each addl	Extra charge for each additional person beyond the stated number of persons at a reduced price.
Exc	Except.
Exercise equipt	Two or more pieces of exercise equipment on the premises.
Exercise rm	Both exercise equipment and room, with an instructor on the premises.
Fax	Facsimile machines available to all guests.
Golf privileges	Privileges at a course within 10 miles.
Hols	Holidays.
In-rm modem link	Every guest room has a connection for a modem that's separate from the phone line.
Kit. or kits.	A kitchen or kitchenette that contains stove or microwave, sink, and refrigerator and that is either part of the room or a separate room. If the kitchen is not fully equipped, the listing will indicate "no equipt" or "some equipt."
Luxury level	A special section of a hotel, covering at least an entire floor, that offers increased luxury accommodations. Management must provide no less than three of these four services: separate check-in and check-out, concierge, private lounge, and private elevator service (key access). Complimentary breakfast and snacks are commonly offered.
MAP	Modified American plan (lodging plus two meals).
Movies	Prerecorded videos are available for rental.
No cr cds accepted	No credit cards are accepted.
No elvtr	In lodgings with more than two stories, it's assumed there are elevators; only their absence is noted.
No phones	Phones, too, are assumed; only their absence is noted.
Parking	There is a parking lot on the premises.

Private club	A cocktail lounge or bar available to members and their guests. In motels and hotels where these clubs exist, registered guests can usually use the club as guests of the management; the same is frequently true of restaurants.
S	Followed by a price, indicates room rate for a "single," i.e., one person.
Tennis privileges	Privileges at tennis courts within 5 miles.
TV	Indicates color television; B/W indicates black-and-white television.
Under certain age free	Children under that age are not charged for if staying in room with a parent.
Valet parking	An attendant is available to park and retrieve a car.
VCR	VCRs in all guest rooms.
VCR avail	VCRs are available for hookup in guest rooms.

Special Information for Travelers with Disabilities

The *Mobil Travel Guide* symbol [D] shown in accommodation listings indicates establishments that are at least partially accessible to people with mobility problems.

The *Mobil Travel Guide* criteria for accessibility are unique to our publication. Please do not confuse them with the universal symbol for wheelchair accessibility. When the [D] symbol appears following a listing, the establishment is equipped with facilities to accommodate people using wheelchairs or crutches or otherwise needing easy access to doorways and rest rooms. Travelers with severe mobility problems or with hearing or visual impairments may or may not find facilities they need. Always phone ahead to make sure that an establishment can meet your needs.

All lodgings bearing our [D] symbol have the following facilities:

- ISA-designated parking near access ramps
- Level or ramped entryways to building
- Swinging building entryway doors minimum 3'0"
- Public rest rooms on main level with space to operate a wheelchair; handrails at commode areas
- Elevators equipped with grab bars and lowered control buttons
- Restaurants with accessible doorways; rest rooms with space to operate wheelchair; handrails at commode areas
- Minimum 3'0" width entryway to guest rooms
- Low-pile carpet in rooms
- Telephone at bedside and in bathroom
- Bed placed at wheelchair height
- Minimum 3'0" width doorway to bathroom
- Bath with open sink—no cabinet; room to operate wheelchair
- Handrails at commode areas; tub handrails
- Wheelchair accessible peephole in room entry door
- Wheelchair accessible closet rods and shelves

In general, the newest properties are apt to impose the fewest barriers.

To get the kind of service you need and have a right to expect, do not hesitate when making a reservation to question the management in detail about the availability of accessible rooms, parking, entrances, restaurants, lounges, or any other facilities that are important to you, and confirm what is meant by "accessible." Some guests with mobility impairments report that lodging establishments' housekeeping and maintenance departments are most helpful in describing barriers. Also inquire about any special equipment, transportation, or services you may need.

Important Toll-Free Numbers

and On-Line Information

HOTELS AND MOTELS

Adam's Mark 800/444–2326
Web www.adamsmark.com
Best Western .... 800/528–1234, TDD 800/528–2222
Web www.bestwestern.com
Budgetel Inns 800/428–3438
Web www.budgetel.com
Budget Host 800/283–4678
Clarion 800/252–7466
Web www.clarioninn.com
Comfort 800/228–5150
Web www.comfortinn.com
Courtyard by Marriott 800/321–2211
Web www.courtyard.com
Days Inn 800/325–2525
Web www.travelweb.com/daysinn.html
Doubletree 800/528–0444
Web www.doubletreehotels.com
Drury Inns 800/325–8300
Web www.drury-inn.com
Econo Lodge 800/446–6900
Web www.hotelchoice.com
Embassy Suites 800/362–2779
Web www.embassy-suites.com
Exel Inns of America 800/356–8013
Fairfield Inn by Marriott 800/228–2800
Web www.marriott.com
Fairmont Hotels 800/527–4727
Forte 800/225–5843
Four Seasons 800/332–3442
Web www.fourseasons.com
Friendship Inns 800/453–4511
Web www.hotelchoice.com
Hampton Inn 800/426–7866
Web www.hampton-inn.com
Hilton .... 800/445–8667, TDD 800/368–1133
Web www.hilton.com
Holiday Inn .... 800/465–4329, TDD 800/238–5544
Web www.holiday-inn.com
Howard Johnson .... 800/654–4656, TDD 800/654–8442
Web www.hojo.com
Hyatt & Resorts 800/233–1234
Web www.hyatt.com
Inns of America 800/826–0778
Inter-Continental 800/327–0200
Web www.interconti.com
La Quinta .... 800/531–5900, TDD 800/426–3101
Web www.laquinta.com
Loews 800/235–6397
Web www.loewshotels.com

Marriott 800/228–9290
Web www.marriott.com
Master Hosts Inns 800/251–1962
Meridien 800/225–5843
Motel 6 .... 800/466–8356
Nikko International 800/645–5687
Web www.hotelnikko.com
Omni 800/843–6664
Web www.omnirosen.com
Park Inn 800/437–7275
Web www.p-inns.com/parkinn.html
Quality Inn 800/228–5151
Web www.qualityinn.com
Radisson 800/333–3333
Web www.radisson.com
Ramada .... 800/228–2828, TDD 800/228–3232
Web www.ramada.com/ramada.html
Red Carpet/Scottish Inns 800/251–1962
Red Lion 800/547–8010
Web www.travelweb.com/travelweb/rl/common/redlion.html
Red Roof Inn 800/843–7663
Web www.redroof.com
Renaissance 800/468–3571
Web www.niagara.com/nf.renaissance
Residence Inn by Marriott 800/331–3131
Web www.marriott.com
Ritz-Carlton 800/241–3333
Web www.ritzcarlton.com
Rodeway 800/228–2000
Web www.rodeway.com
Sheraton 800/325–3535
Web www.sheraton.com
Shilo Inn 800/222–2244
Signature Inns 800/822–5252
Web www.signature-inns.com
Sleep Inn 800/221–2222
Web www.sleepinn.com
Super 8 .... 800/848–8888
Web www.super8motels.com/super8.html
Susse Chalet 800/258–1980
Web www.sussechalet.com
Travelodge/Viscount 800/255–3050
Web www.travelodge.com
Vagabond 800/522–1555
Westin Hotels & Resorts 800/937–8461
Web www.westin.com
Wyndham Hotels & Resorts 800/822–4200
Web www.travelweb.com

AIRLINES
Air Canada 800/776–3000
Web www.aircanada.ca
Alaska 800/426–0333
Web www.alaska-air.com/home.html
Aloha 800/367–5250
American 800/433–7300
Web www.americanair.com/aahome/aahome.html
America West 800/235–9292
Web www.americawest.com

British Airways 800/247–9297
Web www.british-airways.com
Canadian 800/426–7000
Web www.cdair.ca
Continental 800/525–0280
Web www.flycontinental.com
Delta 800/221–1212
Web www.delta-air.com
Hawaiian 800/367–5320
IslandAir 800/323–3345
Mesa 800/637–2247
Northwest 800/225–2525
Web www.nwa.com
SkyWest 800/453–9417
Southwest 800/435–9792
Web www.iflyswa.com
TWA 800/221–2000
Web www.twa.com
United 800/241–6522
Web www.ual.com
USAir 800/428–4322
Web www.usair.com

TRAINS
Amtrak 800/872–7245
Web www.amtrak.com

BUSES
Greyhound 800/231–2222
Web www.greyhound.com

CAR RENTALS
Advantage 800/777–5500
Alamo 800/327–9633
Web www.goalamo.com
Allstate 800/634–6186
Avis 800/331–1212
Web www.avis.com
Budget 800/527–0700
Web www.budgetrentacar.com
Dollar 800/800–4000
Web www.dollarcar.com
Enterprise 800/325–8007
Web www.pickenterprise.com
Hertz 800/654–3131
Web www.hertz.com
National 800/328–4567
Web www.nationalcar.com
Payless 800/237–2804
Rent-A-Wreck 800/535–1391
Web www.rent-a-wreck.com
Sears 800/527–0770
Thrifty 800/367–2277
Web www.thrifty.com
Ugly Duckling 800/843–3825
U-Save 800/272–8728
Value 800/327–2501
Web www.go-value.com

Alabama

Alexander City

Motel

★ ★ **JAMESON INN.** *4335 US 280. 205/234-7099; FAX 205/234-9807; res: 800/541-3268.* 60 rms, 2 story. S, D $48; each addl $5; suites $53-$58; under 13 free. Crib free. Pet accepted, some restrictions. TV; cable (premium). Pool. Complimentary continental bkfst. Restaurant nearby. Ck-out 11 am. Meeting rms. Exercise equipt; bicycle, weight machine. Some refrigerators. Cr cds: A, C, D, DS, MC, V. 🇩 🖘 🖘 🛪 🖎 🖎 SC

Anniston *(See also Gadsden)*

Motel

(Higher rates Talladega race weekends)

✔ ★ ★ **BEST WESTERN RIVERSIDE INN.** *(11900 US 78, Pell City 35125) I-20 exit 162 & US 78. 205/338-3381; FAX 205/338-3183.* 70 rms, 2 story. S $35-$40; D $45-$55; each addl $6; under 12 free; race wkends 4-day min. Crib $2. Pet accepted, some restrictions. TV. Pool; wading pool. Restaurant 6 am-2 pm, 5-9 pm. Ck-out 11 am. Coin lndry. Meeting rms. Boating; waterskiing. Pier. On Logan-Martin Lake. Cr cds: A, C, D, DS, MC, V. 🇩 🖘 🖘 🖎 🖎 🖎 SC

Athens *(See also Huntsville)*

Motels

★ **BEST WESTERN.** *PO Box 816, 2 mi E via I-65, at US 72 exit 351. 205/233-4030; FAX 205/233-4551.* 88 rms, 2 story. S $36; D $44; each addl $4; under 12 free. Crib free. Pet accepted, some restrictions. TV; cable (premium). Pool. Complimentary continental bkfst. Restaurant opp 6 am-midnight. Ck-out noon. Picnic tables. Cr cds: A, C, D, DS, MC, V. 🇩 🖘 🖘 🖎 🖎 SC

✔ ★ **WELCOME INN.** *1101 US 31 S, 1 mi S on US 31 at jct US 72. 205/232-6944; FAX 205/232-8019; res: 800/824-6834.* 80 rms, 1-2 story. S $38-$39; D $44-$45; each addl $5; under 12 free. Crib free. Pet accepted. TV; cable (premium). Pool. Restaurant 6 am-9 pm; Sun to 2 pm. Rm serv. Ck-out noon. Meeting rms. Valet serv. Sundries. Cr cds: A, C, D, DS, JCB, MC, V. 🇩 🖘 🖘 🖎 🖎 SC

Auburn *(See also Opelika; also see Columbus, GA)*

Motel

✔ ★ ★ **QUALITY INN.** *1577 S College St, I-85 exit 51. 334/821-7001.* 122 rms, 3 story. S, D $42-$64; each addl $5; suites $64-$84; under 18 free; higher rates Auburn Univ football games (2-day min). Crib free. Pet accepted. TV; cable (premium). Pool. Complimentary continental bkfst. Restaurant hrs vary. Bar 4 pm-1 am. Ck-out 11 am. Meeting rms. Business servs avail. In-rm modem link. Sundries. Refrigerators in suites. Cr cds: A, C, D, DS, JCB, MC, V. 🇩 🖘 🖘 🖎 🖎 SC

Hotel

★ ★ ★ **AUBURN UNIVERSITY HOTEL & CONFERENCE CENTER.** *241 S College St. 334/821-8200; FAX 334/826-8755; res: 800/228-2876.* 248 rms, 6 story. S, D $59-$125; each addl $10; suites $165-$250; under 18 free; higher rates football games. Crib free. Pet accepted. TV; cable. Pool. Restaurants 6 am-11 pm. Bar 11:30 am-11 pm. Ck-out noon. Business servs avail. In-rm modem link. Convention facilities. Gift shop. Exercise equipt; bicycles, treadmill. Located on eastern edge of campus opp Samford Hall, university library. Cr cds: A, C, D, DS, MC, V. 🇩 🖘 🖘 🛪 🖎 🖎 SC

Birmingham *(See also Cullman)*

Motels

(Rates are generally higher during race & football seasons)

✔ ★ **BUDGETEL INN.** *513 Cahaba Park Circle (35242), I-459 and US 280, south of downtown. 205/995-9990; FAX 205/995-0563.* 102 rms, 3 story. S $41.95; D $47.95; each addl $7; suites $55.95-$62.95; under 18 free. Crib free. Pet accepted, some restrictions. TV; cable (premium). Complimentary continental bkfst. Ck-out noon. Meeting rm. Business servs avail. In-rm modem link. Cr cds: A, C, D, DS, MC, V. ⓓ 🖎 ⋈ 🖎 🖎 SC

★ ★ **HAMPTON INN.** *(2731 US 280, Mountain Brook 35223) S on I-65, NE on Oxmoor Rd to US 280.* 205/870-7822; FAX 205/871-7610. 131 rms, 5 story. S $62; D $62-$67; under 18 free. Crib free. Pet accepted, some restrictions. TV; cable. Pool. Complimentary continental bkfst. Restaurant adj 6 am-11 pm. Ck-out noon. Meeting rm. Business servs avail. In-rm modem link. Cr cds: A, C, D, DS, MC, V. ⓓ 🖎 ⋈ 🖎 🖎 SC

★ ★ **LA QUINTA MOTOR INN.** *905 11th Court W (35204), near jct I-20, US 78, north of downtown.* 205/324-4510; FAX 205/252-7972. 106 rms, 3 story. S, D $57-$77; each addl $10; under 18 free. Crib free. Pet accepted, some restrictions. TV; cable. Pool. Complimentary continental bkfst. Restaurant adj open 24 hrs. Ck-out noon. Meeting rms. Cr cds: A, C, D, DS, MC, V. ⓓ 🖎 ⋈ 🖎 🖎 SC

★ ★ **MOTEL BIRMINGHAM.** *7905 Crestwood Blvd (35210), I-20 Montevallo Rd exit, east of downtown.* 205/956-4440; FAX 205/956-3011; res: 800/338-9275. 242 rms, 1-2 story, 18 kits. (no equipt) S $48-$63; D, kit. units $58-$68; suites $95-$250; under 16 free. Crib free. Pet accepted, some restrictions; $15. TV; cable (premium). Pool. Playground. Complimentary continental bkfst. Restaurant adj open 24 hrs. Ck-out noon. Meeting rms. Business center. In-rm modem link. Valet serv. Health club privileges. Cr cds: A, C, D, DS, MC, V. ⓓ 🖎 ⋈ 🖎 🖎 SC 🖎

★ ★ **RESIDENCE INN BY MARRIOTT.** *3 Greenhill Pkwy (35242), at US 280, south of downtown.* 205/991-8686; FAX 205/991-8729. 128 kit. suites, 2 story. Kit. suites $104-$129; wkly, monthly rates. Crib free. Pet accepted; $165-$215. TV; cable. Pool; whirlpool. Complimentary continental bkfst. Ck-out noon. Coin lndry. Meeting rms. Business servs avail. Valet serv. Sport court. Gas grills. Cr cds: A, C, D, DS, JCB, MC, V.
ⓓ 🖎 ⋈ 🖎 🖎 SC

Motor Hotel

★ ★ **RAMADA INN-AIRPORT.** *5216 Airport Hwy (35212), I-20/I-59, Airport exit, near Municipal Airport, east of downtown.* 205/591-7900; FAX 205/592-6476. 193 rms, 4 story. S, D $69-$75; each addl $8; suites $100-$140. Crib free. Pet accepted, some restrictions; $25. TV; cable (premium). Pool. Coffee in rms. Restaurant 6 am-10 pm; Sat, Sun from 7 am. Rm serv from 7 am. Bar 2 pm-2 am; entertainment. Ck-out noon. Meeting rms. Business servs avail. In-rm modem link. Bellhops. Valet serv. Free airport transportation. Exercise equipt; weight machine, bicycle. Cr cds: A, C, D, DS, JCB, MC, V.
ⓓ 🖎 ⋈ 🏋 ✈ 🖎 🖎 SC

Hotel

★ ★ ★ **PICKWICK.** *1023 20th St S (35205), downtown.* 205/933-9555; FAX 205/933-6918; res: 800/255-7304. 63 rms, 8 story, 28 suites. S, D $86-$89; each addl $10; suites $109; under 12 free; wkend rates. Crib free. Pet accepted, some restrictions; $50. TV. Complimentary continental bkfst. Ck-out noon. Business servs avail. In-rm modem link. Shopping arcade. Barber, beauty shop. Free covered parking. Health club privileges. Some refrigerators. In historical area. Art-deco decor. Cr cds: A, C, D, MC, V. ⓓ 🖎 🖎 🖎 SC

Clanton *(See also Montgomery)*

Motels

★ ★ **HOLIDAY INN.** *2000 Holiday Inn Dr, 3 mi SE at jct US 31, AL 22 & I-65.* 205/755-0510; FAX 205/755-0510, ext. 116. 100 rms, 2 story. S, D $45-$56; each addl $5; under 19 free. Crib free. Pet accepted. TV. Pool; wading pool. Restaurant 6 am-2 pm, 5-10 pm. Rm serv. Bar 4-11 pm, closed Sun. Ck-out noon. Meeting rms. Business servs avail. In-rm modem link. Valet serv. Free airport transportation. Cr cds: A, C, D, DS, MC, V.
🖎 ⋈ 🖎 🖎 SC

✔ ★ **KEY WEST INN.** *2045 7th St S, I-65 exit 205.* 205/755-8500; FAX 205/280-0044; res: 800/833-0555. 43 rms, 2 story. S $42; D $46; each addl $5; under 18 free; higher rates fishing tournaments. Crib free. Pet accepted. TV; cable. Complimentary coffee in lobby. Restaurant nearby. Ck-out noon. Coin lndry. Business servs avail. In-rm modem link. Totally nonsmoking. Cr cds: A, C, D, DS, MC, V. ⓓ 🖎 🖎 🖎 SC

Cullman (See also Birmingham)

Motels

✔ ★ **DAYS INN.** *1841 4th St SW (35055), jct I-65 & US 278.* 205/739-3800; FAX 205/739-3123. 117 rms, 2 story. S, D $36-$40; each addl $4; family, wkly rates. Crib free. Pet accepted; $3. TV; cable (premium). Pool. Playground. Restaurant 6 am-8 pm. Ck-out noon. Meeting rms. Business servs avail. In-rm modem link. Sundries. Picnic tables. Cr cds: A, C, D, DS, MC, V. 🖉 🌊 🐾 🔊 🔥 SC

★ ★ **RAMADA INN.** *PO Box 1204 (35056), I-65 & AL 69W, ¼ mi E of I-65 Cullman-Good Hope exit.* 205/734-8484; FAX 205/739-4126. 126 rms, 1-2 story. S, D $40-$60; each addl $5; under 18 free. Crib free. Pet accepted. TV; cable (premium). Indoor pool; whirlpool. Restaurant 6 am-2 pm, 5-10 pm. Rm serv. Ck-out noon. Coin lndry. Meeting rms. In-rm modem link. Cr cds: A, C, D, DS, JCB, MC, V. D 🖉 🌊 🔊 🔥 SC

Demopolis

Motels

★ **BEST WESTERN-MINT SUNRISE.** *1034 US 80 SE.* 334/289-5772; FAX 334/289-5772, ext. 100. 70 rms. S $40.95; D $44.95; each addl $2; under 12 free; wkly rates. Crib free. Pet accepted. TV; cable, VCR avail (movies $6). Pool. Complimentary continental bkfst. Ck-out 11 am. Meeting rms. Business center. In-rm modem link. Exercise equipt; weights, bicycles. Refrigerators. Cr cds: A, C, D, DS, ER, JCB, MC, V.

D 🖉 🌊 🍴 🔊 🔥 SC 🛠

✔ ★ **WINDWOOD INN.** *628 US 80 E.* 334/289-1760; FAX 334/289-1768; res: 800/233-0841. 90 units, 2 kits. S $29-$32; D $31-$35; each addl $5; kit. units $34-$43; under 12 free. Crib free. Pet accepted. TV; cable (premium). Pool. Restaurant adj 5 am-10 pm. Ck-out 11 am. Meeting rm. Business servs avail. Some refrigerators. Cr cds: A, C, D, DS, MC, V. 🖉 🌊 🔊 🔥 SC

Dothan

Motels

★ ★ ★ **COMFORT INN.** *3593 Ross Clark Circle NW (36304).* 334/793-9090; FAX 334/793-4367. 122 rms, 5 story. S $50-$70; D $55-$89; each addl $5; suites $60-$89; under 18 free. Crib free. Pet accepted. TV; cable (premium), VCR avail (movies). Pool. Continental bkfst. Restaurant open 24 hrs. Ck-out 1 pm. Meeting rm. Business servs avail. In-rm modem link. Exercise equipt; weights, bicycles. Many refrigerators. Near shopping centers. Cr cds: A, C, D, DS, ER, JCB, MC, V. D 🖉 🌊 🍴 🔊 🔥 SC

✔ ★ ★ **DAYS INN.** *2841 Ross Clark Circle SW (36301).* 334/793-2550; FAX 334/793-7962. 120 units, 2 story. S $31-$38; D $36-$48; each addl $5; family rates; some wkend rates. Crib free. Pet accepted; $5. TV; cable (premium). Pool. Coffee in rms. Restaurant adj open 24 hrs. Ck-out noon. Business servs avail. In-rm modem link. Cr cds: A, D, DS, MC, V. D 🖉 🌊 🔊 🔥 SC

★ ★ **HOLIDAY INN-SOUTH.** *2195 Ross Clark Circle SE (36301).* 334/794-8711; FAX 334/671-3781. 144 rms, 2 story. S $50-$56; D $56-$62; each addl $6; under 18 free; suites $64-$74. Pet accepted. TV; cable. Pool. Complimentary full bkfst. Complimentary coffee in lobby. Restaurant 6 am-9:30 pm; Sun from 7 am. Rm serv (limited hrs). Bar 2:30 pm-2 am. Ck-out noon. Meeting rms. Business servs avail. In-rm modem link. Cr cds: A, C, D, DS, JCB, MC, V. D 🖉 🌊 🔊 🔥 SC

★ ★ **HOLIDAY INN-WEST.** *3053 Ross Clark Circle (36301).* 334/794-6601; FAX 334/794-9032. 102 rms, 2 story, 44 suites. S, D $57-$62; suites $66-$71; under 18 free; wkend rates. Crib free. Pet accepted. TV; cable (premium). Pool; wading pool. Restaurant 6 am-9 pm. Rm serv. Bar 5 pm-1 am. Ck-out noon. Meeting rms. Business center. In-rm modem link. Bellhops. Valet serv. Refrigerators avail. Cr cds: A, C, D, DS, MC, V.

D 🖉 🌊 🔊 🔥 SC 🛠

✔ ★ **MOTEL 6.** *2907 Ross Clark Circle SW (36301).* 334/793-6013; FAX 334/793-2377. 102 rms, 2 story. S, D $28.99-$34.99; each addl $5-$6; under 17 free. Crib free. Pet accepted. TV; cable. Pool. Coffee in lobby. Ck-out noon. In-rm modem link. Cr cds: A, C, D, DS, MC, V. D 🖉 🌊 🔊 🔥

★ ★ ★ **RAMADA INN.** *3011 Ross Clark Circle SW (36301).* 334/792-0031; FAX 334/794-3134. 159 rms, 2 story. S $50; D $56; each addl $6; suites $75-$105; under 18 free; wkly rates; some wkend rates. Crib free. Pet accepted. TV; cable (premium), VCR avail (movies). Pool; wading pool. Complimentary bkfst. Restaurant 6 am-9 pm. Rm serv. Bar; entertainment. Ck-out noon. Meeting rms. Business center. Valet serv. Free airport transportation. Cr cds: A, C, D, DS, JCB, MC, V. [D] ⬤ ⬤ ⬤ ⬤ ⬤ [SC] ⬤

Eufaula

Motel

★ ★ **HOLIDAY INN.** *US 82 at Riverside. 334/687-2021.* 96 rms, 2 story. S $44.50-$55; D $49.50-$66.50; each addl $5; suites $61.50-$65.50; under 18 free; golf plans. Crib free. Pet accepted. TV; cable (premium). Pool. Restaurant 6 am-10 pm. Rm serv. Bar 4 pm-midnight. Ck-out noon. Meeting rms. Business servs avail. In-rm modem link. Bellhops. On lake. Cr cds: A, C, D, DS, JCB, MC, V. [D] ⬤ ⬤ ⬤ ⬤ [SC]

Evergreen

Motels

🗸 ★ ★ **COMFORT INN.** *1 blk W on AL 83 Business, I-65 exit 96. 334/578-4701; FAX 334/578-3180.* 58 rms, 2 story. S $38; D $50; each addl $5. Crib $5. Pet accepted; $5. TV; cable (premium). Pool. Restaurant adj open 24 hrs. Ck-out 11 am. Business servs avail. In-rm modem link. Cr cds: A, C, D, DS, JCB, MC, V. [D] ⬤ ⬤ ⬤ ⬤ [SC]

★ **DAYS INN.** *Rte 2, Box 38, I-65 & US 83, exit 96. 334/578-2100.* 40 rms, 2 story, 4 suites. Mid-June-Labor Day: S, D $48; each addl $5; suites $55-$60; under 12 free; lower rates rest of yr. Crib free. Pet accepted, some restrictions; $5. TV; cable (premium). Complimentary continental bkfst. Ck-out 11 am. Cr cds: A, DS, MC, V. [D] ⬤ ⬤ [SC]

Florence

Motels

🗸 ★ **BEST WESTERN EXECUTIVE INN.** *504 S Court St. 205/766-2331; FAX 205/766-3567.* 120 rms, 2 story. S, D $51-$56; each addl $5; under 12 free. Crib free. Pet accepted, some restrictions. TV; cable (premium), VCR avail (movies avail). Pool; poolside serv. Restaurant 6 am-10 pm; Sat, Sun from 7 am. Rm serv. Bar 4 pm-1 am; closed Sun. Ck-out noon. Coin lndry. Meeting rms. Business servs avail. Cr cds: A, C, D, DS, MC, V. ⬤ ⬤ ⬤ ⬤ [SC]

★ **DAYS INN.** *(2700 Woodward Ave, Muscle Shoals 35661) S on US 43, then E on AL 133. 205/383-3000.* 79 rms, 2 story. S $44; D $50; each addl $5; under 16 free; wkly rates. Pet accepted. TV; cable (premium). Pool. Complimentary continental bkfst. Coffee in rms. Restaurant opp 6-1 am. Bar 11-2 am. Ck-out noon. Valet serv. Exercise equipt; bicycle, treadmill. Cr cds: A, C, D, DS, MC, V. [D] ⬤ ⬤ ⬤ ⬤ ⬤ [SC]

Fort Payne *(See also Gadsden)*

Motel

★ ★ **QUALITY INN.** *1412 Glenn Blvd SW. 205/845-4013; FAX 205/845-2344.* 79 rms, 2 story. S $38-$42; D $42-$45; each addl $5; under 16 free; higher rates hols. Crib free. Pet accepted, some restrictions. TV; cable (premium), VCR avail. Pool; wading pool. Complimentary coffee in lobby. Ck-out 11 am. Coin lndry. Meeting rms. Business servs avail. Cr cds: A, C, D, DS, ER, MC, V. [D] ⬤ ⬤ ⬤ ⬤ [SC]

Gadsden *(See also Anniston, Fort Payne, Guntersville)*

Motel

★ **KEY WEST INN.** *(410 E Mill Ave, Boaz 35957) 20 mi N on US 431. 205/593-0800; FAX 205/593-9100.* 41 rms, 2 story. Oct-Dec: S, D $46.50-$51.50; each addl $5; under 18 free; lower rates rest of yr. Crib free. Pet accepted, some restrictions; $5. TV; cable (premium). Complimentary continental bkfst. Restaurant opp 11 am-4 pm. Ck-out 11 am. Meeting rm. Some refrigerators. Cr cds: A, C, D, DS, MC, V. [D] ⬤ ⬤ ⬤ [SC]

Greenville *(See also Montgomery)*

Motel

★ ★ **HOLIDAY INN.** *941 Fort Dale Rd, jct AL 185, I-65, E off Greenville exit 130, on Fort Dale Rd. 334/382-2651.* 96 rms, 2 story. S $44.50; D $50.50; each addl $6; under 19 free. Crib free. Pet accepted. TV; cable. Pool. Restaurant 6 am-10 pm. Rm serv. Bar 4-11 pm. Ck-out noon. Meeting rms. Business servs avail. In-rm modem link. Cr cds: A, C, D, DS, JCB, MC, V. [D] 🐾 ➡ ≈ 🛏 🛅 SC

Gulf Shores *(See also Mobile; also see Pensacola, FL)*

Motels

★ ★ **BEST WESTERN ON THE BEACH.** *337 AL 182E. 334/948-2711; FAX 334/948-7339.* 113 units, 6 story, 50 kits. May-Labor Day: S, D $99-$225; under 12 free; wkly rates; lower rates rest of yr. Crib $5. Pet accepted, some restrictions; $20. TV; cable, VCR (movies). 2 pools; whirlpools. Restaurant open 24 hrs. Ck-out 11 am. Meeting rms. Business servs avail. Refrigerators. On Gulf beach. Cr cds: A, C, D, DS, MC, V.
[D] 🐾 ➡ ≈ ≈ 🛏 🛅 SC

✔ ★ **LIGHTHOUSE.** *455 E Beach Blvd (36547). 334/948-6188.* 219 rms, 1-5 story, 136 kits. May-Labor Day: S, D $69-$149; kit. units $76-$149; wkly rates; lower rates rest of yr. Crib $3. Pet accepted, some restrictions; $60. TV; cable (premium). 4 pools, 2 heated, 1 indoor; whirlpool. Restaurants nearby. Ck-out 11 am. Business servs avail. Game rm. Refrigerators. Private patios, balconies. On Gulf beach. Cr cds: A, D, DS, MC, V.
[D] 🐾 ➡ ≈ 🛅

Guntersville *(See also Gadsden, Huntsville)*

Motels

✔ ★ ★ **BEST WESTERN BOAZ OUTLET CENTER.** *(751 US 431S, Boaz 35957) Jct US 431 & AL 168. 205/593-8410; FAX 205/593-8410, ext. 300.* 116 rms, 2 story. S $39-$46; D $48-$60; each addl $5; under 12 free. Crib free. Pet accepted. TV; cable. Pool; wading pool. Ck-out 11 am. Business servs avail. Cr cds: A, C, D, DS, MC, V.
[D] 🐾 ≈ 🛏 🛅 SC

★ **MAC'S LANDING.** *7001 Val-Monte Dr. 205/582-1000; FAX 205/582-1385.* 53 units, 2 story. Apr-Oct: S, D $47-$56; each addl $5; suites, kit. units $78-$93; under 19 free; lower rates rest of yr. Crib $5. Pet accepted. TV; cable (premium). Pool. Complimentary continental bkfst. Restaurant adj 11 am-10 pm. Bar 3:30 pm-1 am; Thurs-Sat noon-2 am. Ck-out 11 am. Coin lndry. Meeting rms. Business servs avail. Gift shop. Balconies. Picnic tables, grills. On lake; swimming. Cr cds: A, C, D, DS, MC, V. 🐾 ➡ ≈ 🛏 🛅 SC

Huntsville *(See also Athens)*

Motels

★ ★ **BUDGETEL INN.** *4890 University Dr NW (35816). 205/830-8999; FAX 205/837-5720.* 102 rms, 3 story. S $39.95; D $41.95-$48.95; each addl $7; under 18 free. Crib free. Pet accepted. TV. Pool. Complimentary continental bkfst. Restaurant adj open 24 hrs. Ck-out noon. Meeting rm. Business servs avail. In-rm modem link. Cr cds: A, C, D, DS, MC, V. [D] 🐾 ≈ 🛏 🛅

✔ ★ **ECONO LODGE.** *3772 University Dr NW (35816). 205/534-7061.* 82 rms, 2 story. S $27-$49; D $30-$49; suites $39-$59; under 18 free. Crib free. Pet accepted, some restrictions; $12.50. TV; cable (premium), VCR avail (movies). Pool. Complimentary coffee in lobby. Restaurant nearby. Ck-out 11 am. Refrigerator in suites. Cr cds: A, C, D, DS, JCB, MC, V. [D] 🐾 ≈ 🛏 🛅 SC

★ ★ **HOLIDAY INN-SPACE CENTER.** *3810 University Dr (35816), W on US 72 at jct AL 53. 205/837-7171; FAX 205/837-7171, ext. 301.* 112 rms, 2 story. S, D $65; under 12 free; some wknd rates. Crib free. Pet accepted, some restrictions; $50 refundable. TV; cable (premium). Pool. Coffee in rms. Restaurant 6:30 am-2 pm, 5:30-10 pm. Rm serv. Bar 4 pm-2 am. Ck-out noon. Coin lndry. Meeting rms. Business servs avail. In-rm modem link. Bellhops. Valet serv. Sundries. Free airport transportation. Health club privileges. Cr cds: A, C, D, DS, ER, JCB, MC, V. 🐾 ≈ 🛏 🛅 SC

★ ★ **LA QUINTA.** *3141 University Dr NW (35816). 205/533-0756; FAX 205/539-5414.* 130 rms, 2 story. S $52; D $58; each addl $6; under 18 free. Crib free. Pet accepted, some restrictions. TV; cable. Pool. Complimentary continental bkfst. Restaurant adj open 24 hrs. Ck-out noon. Meeting rms. Business servs avail. In-rm modem link. Refrigerators avail. Health club privileges. Cr cds: A, C, D, DS, MC, V. [D] 🐾 ≈ 🛏 🛅 SC

★ ★ **RESIDENCE INN BY MARRIOTT.** *4020 Independence Dr (35816). 205/837-8907; FAX 205/837-5435.* 112 kit. suites, 1-2 story. Suites $75-$105; some wknd rates. Crib free. Pet accepted, some restrictions; $50. TV; cable (premium), VCR avail. Pool; whirlpool. Complimentary continental bkfst. Ck-out noon. Business servs avail. Valet serv

Mon-Fri. Airport transportation. Sports court. Health club privileges. Fireplaces. Private patios, balconies. Picnic tables. Cr cds: A, C, D, DS, MC, V. D ✦ ≋ ⊠ ⊠ SC

Hotels

★ ★ ★ **HILTON.** *401 Williams Ave (35801), at Freedom Plaza. 205/533-1400.* 279 rms, 4 story. S $95-$103; D $105-$113; each addl $10; suites $130-$295. Crib free. Pet accepted. TV; cable. Pool; whirlpool, poolside serv. Restaurant 6 am-10 pm. Bars 11 am-midnight; entertainment exc Sun. Ck-out noon. Convention facilities. Business servs avail. In-rm modem link. Free airport transportation. Health club privileges. Wet bar in suites. Civic Center, city park opp. Luxury level. Cr cds: A, C, D, DS, ER, MC, V. D ✦ ≋ ⊠ ⊠ SC

★ ★ **MARRIOTT.** *5 Tranquility Base (35805), at Space Center. 205/830-2222; FAX 205/895-0904.* 290 rms, 7 story. S, D $69-$120; suites $275; under 18 free; wknd rates. Crib free. Pet accepted, some restrictions. TV; cable (premium). Indoor/outdoor pool; whirlpool, poolside serv. Restaurants 7 am-10 pm. Bar 5 pm-2 am; dancing. Ck-out noon. Convention facilities. Business center. In-rm modem link. Concierge. Airport transportation. Exercise equipt; weights, bicycles, sauna. Game rm. Space & Rocket Museum adj. Cr cds: A, C, D, DS, JCB, MC, V. D ✦ ≋ 🏃 🏋 ⊠ ⊠ SC 🏌

Jasper *(See also Birmingham, Cullman)*

Motel

✔ ★ **TRAVEL-RITE INN.** *200 Mallway Dr, opp mall. 205/221-1161.* 60 rms, 2 story. S $25-$28; D $32; each addl $3; under 12 free. Crib $4. Pet accepted. TV. Restaurant adj 6 am-11 pm. Ck-out 11 am. Meeting rm. Cr cds: A, C, D, DS, MC, V. D ✦ ⊠ ⊠

Mobile *(See also Gulf Shores)*

Motels

(Rates may be higher during Mardi Gras)

★ **DAYS INN AIRPORT.** *3650 Airport Blvd (36608), at I-65. 334/344-3410; FAX 334/344-8790.* 162 rms, 6 story. Mar-Aug: S $47-$55; D $52-$60; each addl $5; under 12 free; wkly rates; lower rates rest of yr. Crib free. Pet accepted; $25. TV; cable (premium). VCR (movies). Pool. Complimentary continental bkfst. Restaurant 5:30-9 pm. Bar. Ck-out noon. Meeting rms. Business servs avail. In-rm modem link. Valet serv. Some refrigerators. Cr cds: A, C, D, DS, MC, V. D ✦ ≋ ⊠ ⊠ SC

★ ★ **DRURY INN.** *824 S Beltline Hwy (36609). 334/344-7700.* 110 rms, 4 story. S $55-$63; D $63-$71; each addl $8; under 18 free. Crib free. Pet accepted, some restrictions. TV; cable. Pool. Complimentary continental bkfst; afternoon refreshments. Restaurant adj open 24 hrs. Business servs avail. In-rm modem link. Ck-out noon. Meeting rms. Valet serv. Cr cds: A, C, D, DS, MC, V. D ✦ ≋ ⊠ ⊠ SC

★ ★ **LA QUINTA.** *816 S Beltline Hwy (36609). 334/343-4051; FAX 334/343-2897.* 122 units, 2 story. S, D $53-$61; each addl $8; under 18 free. Crib free. Pet accepted. TV; cable (premium). Pool. Complimentary continental bkfst. Restaurant adj open 24 hrs. Ck-out noon. Meeting rms. Business servs avail. In-rm modem link. Cr cds: A, C, D, DS, MC, V. D ✦ ≋ ⊠ ⊠ SC

✔ ★ **RED ROOF INN.** *5450 Coca Cola Rd (36619). 334/666-1044; FAX 334/666-1032.* 108 rms, 2 story. S $34-$41; D $39.99-$47; each addl $7; under 18 free. Crib free. Pet accepted, some restrictions. TV; cable. Complimentary coffee in lobby. Restaurant nearby. Ck-out noon. Business servs avail. Cr cds: A, C, D, DS, MC, V. D ✦ ⊠ ⊠ SC

★ **SHONEY'S INN.** *5472-A Tillman's Corner Pkwy (36619), at I-10 exit 15B. 334/660-1520; FAX 334/666-4240; res: 800/222-2222.* 120 rms, 3 story, 15 suites. S $50; D $54; each addl $6; suites $60; under 18 free; golf plan. Crib free. Pet accepted; $5. TV; cable. Pool. Complimentary coffee in lobby. Restaurant adj 6 am-midnight. Ck-out noon. Business servs avail. Some refrigerators. Cr cds: A, C, D, DS, MC, V. D ✦ ≋ ⊠ ⊠ SC

Motor Hotel

★ ★ **HOLIDAY INN.** *6527 90W (36619), AL 90 & I-10 exit 15B. 334/666-5600; FAX 334/666-2773.* 160 units, 5 story. S, D $61-$80; suites $81-$95; under 18 free. Crib free. Pet accepted. TV; cable. Pool; whirlpool. Restaurant 6 am-2 pm, 5-10 pm. Rm serv. Bar 5 pm-2 am. Ck-out noon. Coin lndry. Meeting rms. Business center. Bellhops. Valet serv. Free airport transportation. Luxury level. Cr cds: A, C, D, DS, JCB, MC, V. D ✦ ≋ ⊠ ⊠ SC 🏌

Hotel

★ ★ ★ **CLARION.** *3101 Airport Blvd (36606), I-65 Airport Blvd exit. 334/476-6400; FAX 334/476-9360.* 250 rms, 20 story. S, D $69-$89; each addl $10; suites $150-$200; under 18 free. Crib free. Pet accepted, some restrictions. TV; cable (premium), VCR avail. Pool; whirlpool. Restaurant 6:30-2 am. Bar. Ck-out noon. Convention facilities. Business servs avail. In-rm modem link. Some refrigerators. Some balconies. Cr cds: A, C, D, DS, MC, V. ▣ 🖛 ≈ ⊠ 🐾 SC

Montgomery

Motels

✔ ★ **DAYS INN.** *2625 Zelda Rd (36107), I-85 exit 3. 334/269-9611.* 120 rms, 2 story. S, D $55-$60; each addl $5; under 12 free. Crib free. Pet accepted; $5. TV; cable. Pool. Complimentary continental bkfst. Coin lndry. Ck-out noon. Business servs avail. In-rm modem link. Cr cds: A, C, D, DS, MC, V. 🖛 ≈ ⊠ 🐾 SC

★ ★ ★ **HOLIDAY INN-EAST.** *1185 Eastern Bypass (36117). 334/272-0370; FAX 334/270-0339.* 213 rms, 2 story. S, D $71.95-$79.95; each addl $10; suites $160; under 16 free; golf plan. Crib free. Pet accepted. TV. Indoor pool; whirlpool. Restaurant 6:30-9:30 am, 5:30-9:30 pm. Rm serv. Bar 4 pm-1 am. Ck-out noon. Meeting rms. Business servs avail. In-rm modem link. Bellhops. Valet serv. Sundries. Putting green. Exercise equipt; weights, bicycles, sauna. Game rm. Rec rm. Cr cds: A, C, D, DS, JCB, MC, V.
▣ 🖛 ≈ 🏋 ⊠ 🐾 SC

✔ ★ ★ **LA QUINTA.** *1280 Eastern Blvd (36117). 334/271-1620; FAX 334/244-7919.* 130 rms, 2 story. S $50.40; D $60; each addl $6; under 18 free. Crib free. Pet accepted. TV; cable (premium), VCR avail (movies). Pool. Complimentary continental bkfst. Restaurant adj 6 am-10 pm; Fri, Sat to 11 pm. Ck-out noon. Meeting rms. Business servs avail. In-rm modem link. Cr cds: A, C, D, DS, MC, V. ▣ 🖛 ≈ ⊠ 🐾 SC

Motor Hotel

★ ★ **HOLIDAY INN SOUTH/AIRPORT.** *1100 W South Blvd (36105), I-65 exit 168. 334/281-1660.* 150 rms, 4 story. S, D $51-$56; suites $67-$72; under 10 free. Crib free. Pet accepted, some restrictions. TV; cable (premium). Pool. Restaurant 6 am-10 pm. Rm serv. Bar 4-11 pm. Ck-out noon. Coin lndry. Meeting rms. Business servs avail. In-rm modem link. Bellhops. Free airport transportation. Cr cds: A, C, D, DS, ER, MC, V.
▣ 🖛 ≈ ⊠ 🐾 SC

Opelika (See also Auburn; also see Columbus, GA)

Motels

★ ★ **BEST WESTERN MARINER INN.** *1002 Columbus Pkwy, jct I-85 & US 280. 334/749-1461; FAX 334/749-1468.* 95 rms, 2 story. S $29-$34; D $36-$46; each addl $7; under 12 free; wkly rates. Crib $7. Pet accepted. TV; cable. Indoor pool; whirlpool. Complimentary coffee in lobby. Restaurant nearby. Bar 3 pm-2 am, Sat to midnight. Business center. In-rm modem link. Cr cds: A, C, D, DS, MC, V. ▣ 🖛 ≈ ⊠ 🐾 SC

★ ★ **DAYS INN.** *1014 Anand Ave. 334/749-5080.* 43 rms, 2 story. S $38-$45; D $42-$50; each addl $5; suites $65-$80; under 12 free; higher rates special events. Crib free. Pet accepted; $5. TV; cable (premium). Indoor pool; wading pool, whirlpool. Complimentary continental bkfst. Restaurant opp open 24 hrs. Ck-out 11 am. Refrigerators. Cr cds: A, C, D, DS, MC, V. ▣ 🖛 ≈ ⊠ 🐾 SC

Scottsboro (See also Huntsville)

Motel

★ **DAYS INN.** *1106 John T. Reid Pkwy. 205/574-1212; FAX 205/574-1212, ext. 253.* 84 rms, 2 story. S $39-$60; D $42-$60; each addl $5; under 18 free; higher rates June Jam. Crib free. Pet accepted. TV; cable (premium). Pool. Complimentary continental bkfst, coffee. Restaurant adj 11 am-9 pm. Ck-out 11 am. Business servs avail. In-rm modem link. Cr cds: A, C, D, DS, MC, V. ▣ 🖛 ≈ ⊠ 🐾 SC

Selma (See also Montgomery)

Motel

✔ ★ ★ **HOLIDAY INN.** *US 80 W, 3 mi W on US 80. 334/872-0461.* 165 rms, 2 story. S $50-$53; D $55-$60; each addl $5; under 19 free. Crib free. Pet accepted. TV; cable. Pool;

wading pool. Complimentary bkfst. Restaurant 6 am-2 pm, 5-10 pm. Rm serv. Bar 5 pm-1 am. Ck-out noon. Meeting rms. Business servs avail. In-rm modem link. Valet serv. Cr cds: A, C, D, DS, JCB, MC, V. 🈳 🈴 🈵 🈶 SC

Sheffield (See also Florence)

Motel

★ **KEY WEST INN.** (1800 US 72W, Tuscumbia 35674) 3 mi S. 205/383-0700. 41 rms, 2 story. S $43-$60; D $48-$60; each addl $5; under 18 free. Crib free. Pet accepted, some restrictions; $5. TV; cable (premium). Complimentary continental bkfst. Restaurant nearby. Ck-out noon. Coin lndry. Meeting rm. Business servs avail. Some refrigerators. Cr cds: A, C, D, DS, MC, V. D 🈳 🈴 🈵 🈶 SC

Motor Hotels

★ ★ ★ **HOLIDAY INN.** 4900 Hatch Blvd. 205/381-4710; FAX 205/381-4710, ext. 403. 204 units, 3 story. S, D $69-$83; each addl $6; suites $203-$281; under 18 free. Crib free. Pet accepted, some restrictions. TV; cable. Pool; whirlpool. Coffee in rms. Restaurant 6:30 am-2 pm, 5:30-10 pm. Rm serv. Bar 4 pm-2 am; entertainment exc Sun. Ck-out noon. Coin lndry. Meeting rms. Business servs avail. In-rm modem link. Bellhops. Free airport transportation. Tennis privileges. Golf privileges. Exercise equipt; weight machine, bicycle. Some refrigerators. Cr cds: A, C, D, DS, JCB, MC, V. D 🈳 🈴 🈵 🈶 🈷 🈸 🈹 🈺 SC

✓ ★ **RAMADA INN.** 4205 Hatch Blvd. 205/381-3743; FAX 205/381-2838. 150 rms, 2 story. S $42-$57; D $42-$64; each addl $7; suites from $125; under 18 free. Crib free. Pet accepted; $10. TV; cable (premium). Pool; whirlpool, poolside serv. Coffee in rms. Restaurant 6 am-10 pm. Rm serv. Bar 4 pm-1 am; entertainment. Ck-out noon. Meeting rms. Business servs avail. Free airport transportation. Golf privileges. Some in-rm whirlpools, refrigerators. Cr cds: A, C, D, DS, JCB, MC, V.
D 🈳 🈴 🈵 🈶 🈷 🈸 SC

Troy (See also Montgomery)

Motel

✓ ★ **ECONO LODGE.** 1013 US 231. 334/566-4960; FAX 334/566-5858. 69 rms, 2 story. S $38-$43; D $43-$51; each addl $5; under 18 free; higher rates football wkends. Crib free. Pet accepted. TV; cable (premium). Pool. Complimentary continental bkfst. Ck-out 11 am. Business servs avail. Cr cds: A, C, D, DS, MC, V. D 🈳 🈴 🈵 🈶 SC

Tuscaloosa

Motel

(Rates are generally higher during football season)

✓ ★ ★ **RAMADA INN.** 631 Skyland Blvd E (35405). 205/759-4431; FAX 205/758-9655. 108 rms, 2 story. S $39-$63; D $47-$85; each addl $5; under 18 free. Crib free. Pet accepted. TV; cable. Pool. Restaurant 6 am-2 pm, 5-10 pm. Rm serv. Bar 5 pm-1 am; Fri, Sat to 2 am; entertainment exc Sun. Ck-out noon. Meeting rms. Business servs avail. Valet serv. Cr cds: A, C, D, DS, JCB, MC, V. D 🈳 🈴 🈵 🈶 SC

Arizona

Bullhead City *(See also Kingman)*

Motels

★ ★ **BEST WESTERN BULLHEAD CITY INN.** *2360 4th St (86430). 520/754-3000; FAX 520/754-5234.* 88 rms, 2 story. S, D $45-$75; higher rates special events. Crib free. Pet accepted; $5. TV; cable (premium). Pool; whirlpool. Complimentary continental bkfst. Restaurant nearby. Ck-out noon. Business servs avail. Refrigerators; microwaves avail. Cr cds: A, C, D, DS, ER, JCB, MC, V. [D] [⟲] [≈] [⤢] [⊼] [SC]

★ **LAKE MOHAVE RESORT & MARINA.** *Katherine Landing (86430), 6 mi NE, 3¹/₂ mi N of AZ 68, N of Davis Dam. 520/754-3245; FAX 520/754-1125; res: 800/752-9669.* 51 rms, 1-2 story, 14 kits. S, D $60; each addl $6; kit. units $83; under 5 free. Crib $6. Pet accepted, some restrictions; $5. Restaurant 7 am-9 pm mid-Apr-Nov. Bar 4-10 pm. Ck-out 11 am. Business servs avail. In-rm modem link. Water sports; houseboats, boat moorings, boat rental, fishing supplies. Private patios, balconies. Spacious grounds. View of lake. Cr cds: DS, MC, V. [D] [⟲] [⤢] [≈] [⊼] [SC]

Carefree *(See also Chandler, Mesa, Phoenix, Scottsdale, Tempe)*

Resort

★ ★ ★ ★ **BOULDERS RESORT & CLUB.** *34631 N Tom Darlington Dr. 602/488-9009; FAX 602/488-4118; res: 800/553-1717.* Web www.slh.com/slh. Dramatic architecture using indigenous materials and Native American art and furnishings make this large resort, with golf and tennis clubs and a spa, blend into a desert landscape dotted with massive granite boulders. Accommodations are in spacious adobe casitas with wood-burning, kiva-style fireplaces. 160 casitas, 1-2 story; also patio homes. Mid-Jan-Apr & late Dec: S, D $525; each addl $25; under 13 free; MAP avail; lower rates rest of yr. Serv charge $16/day. Crib free. Pet accepted, some restrictions; $50. TV; cable (premium), VCR. 2 heated pools; whirlpool, poolside serv. Dining rms (public by res) 7-10:30 am, noon-2:30 pm, 6-9:30 pm. Box lunches, snack bar. Rm serv. Bar 11-1 am. Ck-out noon, ck-in 4 pm. Grocery, package store 2 blks. Coin lndry 2 mi. Meeting rms. Business center. In-rm modem link. Gift shop. Airport transportation. Tennis, pro. 36-hole golf, greens fee $155, pro, putting green, driving range. Entertainment. Exercise rm; instructor, weights, bicycles, sauna, steam rm. Massage. Refrigerators, fireplaces. Private patios. Cr cds: A, C, D, MC, V.
[D] [⟲] [🏌] [🏃] [≈] [🎿] [⛷] [⤢] [⊼] [🛶]

Chandler *(See also Mesa, Phoenix, Scottsdale, Tempe)*

Resort

★ ★ ★ **SHERATON SAN MARCOS GOLF RESORT & CONFERENCE CENTER.** *1 San Marcos Pl (85224), S of Arizona Ave, 1 blk W on Buffalo. 602/963-6655; FAX 602/963-6777.* 295 rms, 45 air-cooled, 4 story. Jan-May: S, D $235; each addl $10; under 18 free; wkend, hol rates; golf plans; lower rates rest of yr. Crib free. Pet accepted; $50 deposit. TV; cable (premium). Complimentary coffee in rms. Restaurant 6:30 am-10 pm. Box lunches, snack bar, picnics. Rm serv 24 hrs. Bar 11-1:30 am. Ck-out noon, ck-in 3 pm. Grocery 1 blk. Coin lndry 2 blks. Package store 1 blk. Convention facilities. Business center. Bellhops. Valet serv. Concierge. Shopping arcade. Barber, beauty shop. Airport transportation. Sports dir. Lighted tennis, pro. 18-hole golf, greens fee $85, pro, putting green, driving range. Bicycle rentals. Exercise equipt; weight machines, bicycles. Health club privileges. Pool; wading pool, whirlpool, poolside serv. Many balconies. Cr cds: A, C, D, DS, ER, JCB, MC, V. [D] [⟲] [🏌] [🏃] [≈] [⛷] [⤢] [⊼] [SC] [🛶]

Flagstaff *(See also Sedona, Williams, Winslow)*

Motels

(Rates higher Native American Powwow)

★ **ARIZONA MOUNTAIN INN.** *685 Lake Mary Rd (86001), near Pulliam Field Airport. 520/774-8959.* 18 units, 1-4 story, 15 kit. cottages, 3 suites. No A/C. No elvtr. No rm phones. S, D $75-$105; each addl $10; suites $80-$120; under 3 free; wkly rates. Pet accepted, some restrictions. Playground. Ck-out 11 am. Coin lndry. Business servs avail.

Downhill/x-country ski 14 mi. Fireplaces. Balconies. Picnic tables, grills. Rustic atmosphere. Cr cds: DS, MC, V. [D] 🐾 ⊠ ⊠ 🐾

★ ★ **COMFORT INN.** *914 S Milton Rd (86001), 1 mi N of I-40 exit 195B. 520/774-7326.* 67 rms, 2 story. June-Aug: S, D $69-$93; each addl $5; under 19 free; lower rates rest of yr. Crib $2. Pet accepted, some restrictions. TV; cable (premium). Heated pool. Complimentary coffee. Restaurant nearby. Ck-out 11 am. Downhill ski 15 mi. Cr cds: A, C, D, DS, ER, MC, V. [D] 🐾 ⊠ ⊠ ⊠ 🐾 SC

★ ★ **DAYS INN-HIGHWAY 66.** *1000 W US 66 (86001). 520/774-5221.* 157 rms, 2 story. Mid-June-mid-Sept: S, D $72-$82; under 12 free; higher rates: hols, special events; lower rates rest of yr. Crib free. Pet accepted, some restrictions. TV; cable (premium). Complimentary coffee in lobby. Restaurant 6-10 am, 5-9 pm. Bar from 5 pm. Ck-out 1 pm. Meeting rms. Business servs avail. Bellhops. Valet serv. Sundries. Gift shop. Coin lndry. Health club privileges. Pool. Cr cds: A, C, D, DS, ER, JCB, MC, V. [D] 🐾 ⊠ ⊠ 🐾 SC

★ **RAMADA LIMITED SUITES.** *2755 Woodland Village Blvd (86001). 520/773-1111; FAX 520/774-1449.* 90 suites, 2 story. May-Sept: S, D $59-$100; under 17 free; lower rates rest of yr. Crib free. Pet accepted; $25 refundable. TV; cable (premium), VCR avail. Heated pool; whirlpool. Complimentary continental bkfst. Restaurant nearby. Ck-out 11 am. Coin lndry. Meeting rms. Business servs avail. Sundries. Exercise equipt; weight machine, bicycles, sauna. Refrigerators, microwaves. Cr cds: A, C, D, DS, ER, JCB, MC, V. [D] 🐾 ⊠ 🏃 ⊠ 🐾 SC

✔ ★ **SUPER 8.** *3725 N Kasper (86004), I-40 exit 201. 520/526-0818; FAX 520/526-8786.* 90 rms, 2 story. Apr-Oct: S $65; D $70; each addl $5; lower rates rest of yr. Crib free. Pet accepted. TV; cable. Complimentary coffee in lobby. Restaurant adj 6 am-midnight. Ck-out 11 am. Business servs avail. Downhill ski 15 mi. Cr cds: A, C, D, DS, MC, V. [D] 🐾 ⊠ ⊠ 🐾 SC

Motor Hotels

★ ★ **AMERISUITES.** *2455 S Beulah Blvd (86001), I-40 exit 195B. 520/774-8042; FAX 520/774-5524; res: 800/833-1516.* Web www.canyon-country.com. 118 kit. suites, 5 story. May-Sept: S $109; D $119; each addl $10; under 18 free; ski plans; lower rates rest of yr. Crib free. Pet accepted; $10. TV; cable (premium), VCR (movies). Complimentary continental bkfst. Complimentary coffee in rms. Ck-out noon. Coin lndry. Meeting rms. Business center. In-rm modem link. Valet serv. Free airport, RR station, bus depot transportation. Downhill/x-country ski 15 mi. Exercise equipt; weight machine, treadmill. Cr cds: A, C, D, DS, ER, JCB, MC, V. [D] 🐾 ⊠ 🏃 ⊠ 🐾 SC 🏃

★ ★ ★ **EMBASSY SUITES.** *706 S Milton Rd (86001). 520/774-4333; FAX 520/774-0216.* E-mail embassyflagstaff@thecanyon.com; web www.thecanyon.com/embassyflagstaff. 119 suites, 3 story. Mid-Apr-mid-Sept: suites $99-$154; Each addl $10; ski, hol rates; lower rates rest of yr. Pet accepted, some restrictions. TV; cable (premium). Heated pool; whirlpool. Complimentary full bkfst. Coffee in rms. Restaurant adj 11:30 am-10 pm. Rm serv 5-9 pm. Ck-out 1 pm. Meeting rms. Business servs avail. In-rm modem link. Gift shop. Game rm. Downhill ski 12 mi. Exercise equipt; weights, stair machine. Refrigerators, microwaves. Picnic tables. Cr cds: A, C, D, DS, ER, JCB, MC, V. [D] 🐾 ⊠ ⊠ 🏃 ⊠ 🐾 SC

★ ★ **HOLIDAY INN.** *2320 Lucky Lane (86004). 520/526-1150; FAX 520/779-2610.* 157 rms, 5 story. Mid-May-mid-Oct: S, D $69-$150; each addl $10; under 18 free; lower rates rest of yr. Crib free. Pet accepted. TV; cable (premium). Heated pool; whirlpool. Restaurant 6-10 am, 5-10 pm. Rm serv. Bar 4 pm-1 am. Ck-out noon. Coin lndry. Meeting rms. In-rm modem link. Bellhops. Valet serv. Downhill ski 11 mi. Cr cds: A, C, D, DS, JCB, MC, V. [D] 🐾 ⊠ ⊠ ⊠ 🐾 SC

★ **HOWARD JOHNSON.** *2200 E Butler Ave (86004), I-40 exit 198. 520/779-6944; FAX 520/774-3990.* Web www.traveler.net/htio/cus tom/service/0430.html. 100 rms, 3 story. June-Oct: S, D $79-$119; under 18 free; ski plans; higher rates special events; lower rates rest of yr. Crib free. Pet accepted; $50 deposit. TV; cable, VCR avail. Indoor pool; whirlpool, sauna. Coffee in rms. Restaurant open 24 hrs. Rm serv 7 am-10 pm. Bar 4:30 pm-1 am. Ck-out noon. Business servs avail. Bellhops. Sundries. Free airport, RR station, bus depot transportation. Downhill/x-country ski 15 mi. Game rm. Some refrigerators. Some balconies, patios. Cr cds: A, C, D, DS, ER, JCB, MC, V. [D] 🐾 ⊠ ⊠ ⊠ 🐾 SC

Florence

Inn

✔ ★ ★ **INN AT RANCHO SONORA.** *9198 N AZ 79. 520/868-8000; res: 800/205-6817; FAX 520/868-8000.* 9 rms, 5 with shower only, 2 suites. Some rm phones. Oct-Apr: S, D $59-$69; suites $95; under 5 free; lower rates rest of yr. Pet accepted, some restrictions;

$10. TV; VCR avail (free movies). Complimentary continental bkfst. Restaurant nearby. Ck-out 11 am, ck-in 2 pm. Business servs avail. Coin Indry. Pool; whirlpool. Some refrigerators, microwaves. Picnic tables, grills. Built in 1930. Original adobe, western and traditional decor. Courtyard. Totally nonsmoking. Cr cds: A, MC, V.

Gila Bend

Motel

✔★★ **BEST WESTERN SPACE AGE LODGE.** *401 E Pima. 520/683-2273; FAX 520/683-2273.* 41 rms. Jan-Apr: S $60-$70; D $65-$85; each addl $4; under 17 free; lower rates rest of yr. Crib free. Pet accepted. TV; cable (premium). Pool; whirlpool. Coffee in rms. Restaurant open 24 hrs. Ck-out noon. Some refrigerators. Cr cds: A, C, D, DS, MC, V.

Glendale *(See also Litchfield Park, Mesa, Phoenix, Scottsdale, Tempe)*

Motel

★★ **WINDMILL INN-SUN CITY WEST.** *(12545 W Bell Rd, Surprise 85374) Approx 7 mi E on Bell Rd. 602/583-0133; FAX 602/583-8366.* 127 rms, 3 story. Mid Jan-mid-Apr: S, D $116-$145; each addl $6; under 18 free; lower rates rest of yr. Crib free. Pet accepted, some restrictions. TV; cable (premium). Heated pool; whirlpool. Complimentary continental bkfst. Restaurant adj 6 am-10 pm. Ck-out 11 am. Coin Indry. Meeting rms. Business servs avail. Microwaves avail. Cr cds: A, C, D, DS, MC, V.

Globe

Motel

✔★ **CLOUD NINE.** *PO Box 1043, at jct US 60 & 70. 520/425-5741; res: 800/256-8399.* 80 rms, 2 story. S $47-$62; D $53-$72; each addl $7; under 14 free. Crib free. Pet accepted, some restrictions. TV; cable. Heated pool; whirlpool. Ck-out noon. Meeting rm. Business servs avail. Refrigerators. Picnic tables. Cr cds: A, C, D, ER, MC, V.

Grand Canyon National Park

Motel

★ **RED FEATHER LODGE.** *AZ 64 & US 180. 520/638-2414; FAX 520/638-9216; res: 800/538-2345.* Web www.gcanyon.com. 234 rms, 2- & 3-story. May-Oct: S, D $100-$175; each addl $10; under 18 free; lower rates rest of yr. Crib free. Pet accepted; $45. TV; cable. Restaurant adj 6 am-10 pm. Ck-out 11 am. Business servs avail. Exercise equipt: rower, bicycle. Cr cds: A, C, D, MC, V.

Greer

Lodge

★ **GREER LODGE.** *AZ 373, 1/2 mi S of post office. 520/735-7216; FAX 520/735-7720.* 8 rms in main lodge, 3 story, 9 kit. cabins (1-2 bedrms), little lodge with kit. (4 bedrms, 3 baths), 2 story; 2-night min wkends, 3-night min hols. No A/C. No elvtr. No rm phones. S $90; D $120; each addl $15; kit. units $75-$110; each addl (after 2nd person) $15; little lodge $280; each addl (after 8th person) $15; #10 cabin (6 people) $210; each addl (after 6th person) $15; fly-fishing school package. Crib avail. Pet accepted in cabins; $10/day. TV in lobby & lounge. Restaurant (public by res) 7-10 am, 11:30 am-2:30 pm, 5-8:30 pm. Bar 10 am-10 pm. Ck-out 11 am. Meeting rm. X-country ski 5 mi. Ice-skating; skates provided. Sleigh rides. Stocked trout pond. Picnic tables, grills. Sun deck. Fireplace, piano in living room. On 9 acres; overlooks Little Colorado River. Cr cds: A, DS, MC, V.

Holbrook *(See also Winslow)*

Motels

★★ **BEST WESTERN ARIZONIAN INN.** *2508 E Navajo Blvd. 520/524-2611.* 70 rms, 2 story. June-Aug: S $52-$64; D $56-$70; each addl $4; under 17 free; lower rates rest of yr. Crib $5. Pet accepted, some restrictions. TV; cable (premium). Heated pool. Complimentary coffee in lobby. Restaurant open 24 hrs. Ck-out 11 am. Some refrigerators, microwaves. Cr cds: A, C, D, DS, MC, V.

★ ★ **COMFORT INN.** *2602 E Navajo Blvd.* 520/524-6131; *FAX 520/524-2281.* 60 rms, 2 story. May-Sept: S $60; D $65; each addl $5; under 18 free; wkly, wkend rates; lower rates rest of yr. Crib free. Pet accepted, some restrictions. TV; cable (premium). Pool. Complimentary coffee in lobby. Restaurant adj open 24 hrs. Ck-out 11 am. Coin lndry. Some refrigerators, microwaves. Cr cds: A, C, D, DS, MC, V. 🅓 🐾 ⊠ ⧖ 🐾 SC

★ ★ **ECONO LODGE.** *2596 E Navajo Blvd, I-40 exit 289.* 520/524-1448; *FAX 520/524-2281.* 63 rms, 2 story. June-Aug: S $44; D $50; each addl $5; under 18 free; lower rates rest of yr. Crib free. Pet accepted. TV; cable (premium). Heated pool. Complimentary coffee in lobby. Restaurant adj open 24 hrs. Ck-out 11 am. Coin lndry. Some refrigerators. Picnic table. Cr cds: A, C, D, DS, MC, V. 🅓 🐾 ⊠ ⧖ 🐾 SC

★ ★ **HOLIDAY INN EXPRESS.** *1308 E Navajo Blvd, I-40 exit 286.* 520/524-1466; *FAX 520/524-1788.* Web www.cybertrails.com/ nazguide. 59 rms, 2 story. Late May-late Aug: S $59; D $63; each addl $4; suites $69-$83; under 17 free; lower rates rest of yr. Crib $4. Pet accepted. TV; cable. Indoor pool; whirlpool. Complimentary continental bkfst. Restaurant nearby. Ck-out 11 am. Coin lndry. Meeting rm. Refrigerator, microwave in suites. Cr cds: A, C, D, DS, JCB, MC, V. 🅓 🐾 ⊠ ⧖ 🐾 SC

Kayenta

Motel

★ ★ **GOULDING'S MONUMENT VALLEY LODGE.** *(Monument Valley 84536)* in UT just N of AZ border, 2 mi W of US 163. 801/727-3231; *FAX 801/727-3344.* 19 rms in lodge, 41 rms in 2-story motel; 2 cabins. S, D $102; each addl $6; cabins $114. Pet accepted; fee. TV, VCR (movies). Indoor pool. Restaurant 7 am-9 pm. Ck-out 11 am. Coin lndry. Sundries. Gift shop. Refrigerators. Private patios, balconies. Guided jeep tours. 1 bldg is old trading post; now museum. John Wayne movies filmed here. Navajo Tribal Park 5 mi. Earth Spirit multimedia show. Cr cds: A, C, D, DS, JCB, MC, V. 🐾 ⊠ ⧖ 🐾

Kingman (See also Bullhead City, Lake Havasu City)

Motels

★ ★ **BEST WESTERN-A WAYFARER'S INN.** *2815 E Andy Devine Ave.* 520/753-6271; *FAX 520/753-9608.* 100 rms, 2 story. May-Sept: S $66-$77; D $66-$96; each addl $5; suites $88-$104; under 12 free; lower rates rest of yr. Crib $5. Pet accepted. TV; cable (premium). Heated pool. Ck-out noon. Coin lndry. Refrigerators, microwaves. Cr cds: A, C, D, DS, ER, JCB, MC, V. 🐾 ⊠ ⧖ 🐾 SC

★ **DAYS INN.** *3023 Andy Devine Ave.* 520/753-7500; *FAX 520/753-4686.* 60 rms, 2 story, 40 kit. units. May-Sept: S, D $55-$75; kit. units $60; higher rates hols; lower rates rest of yr. Crib free. Pet accepted; $3. TV; cable (premium). Heated pool; whirlpool. Coffee in lobby. Restaurant opp 6 am-11 pm. Coin lndry. Business servs avail. In-rm modem link. Microwaves avail. Cr cds: A, C, D, DS, ER, JCB, MC, V. 🅓 🐾 ⊠ ⧖ 🐾 SC

✔ ★ **HILL TOP.** *1901 E Andy Devine Ave.* 520/753-2198; *FAX 520/753-5985.* 29 rms. May-Sept: S $25-$36; D $32-$44; each addl $5; higher rates hol wkends; lower rates rest of yr. Crib $5. Pet accepted, some restrictions. TV; cable (premium). Heated pool. Restaurant nearby. Ck-out 11 am. Coin lndry. Business servs avail. Refrigerators avail. Cr cds: DS, MC, V. 🐾 ⊠ ⧖ 🐾 SC

★ **HOLIDAY INN.** *3100 E Andy Devine Ave.* 520/753-6262; *FAX 520/753-7137.* 116 rms, 2 story. S, D $49-$89; each addl $5; under 12 free. Crib free. Pet accepted, some restrictions. TV; cable. Pool. Restaurant 6 am-10 pm. Rm serv 6 am-10 pm. Bar 5 pm-1 am. Ck-out noon. Coin lndry. Meeting rms. Business servs avail. Valet serv. Sundries. Cr cds: A, C, D, DS, ER, JCB, MC, V. 🅓 🐾 ⊠ ⧖ 🐾 SC

✔ ★ **QUALITY INN.** *1400 E Andy Devine Ave.* 520/753-4747. 98 rms, 1-2 story. June-Aug: S, D, kit. units $54-$69; each addl $10; under 18 free; lower rates rest of yr. Crib free. Pet accepted. TV; cable (premium). Pool; whirlpool. Complimentary continental bkfst. Complimentary coffee in rms. Ck-out noon. Meeting rm. Business servs avail. Free airport transportation. Exercise equipt; treadmill, bicycle, sauna. Cr cds: A, C, D, DS, ER, JCB, MC, V. 🅓 🐾 ⊠ 🏃 ⧖ 🐾 SC

Lake Havasu City (See also Kingman)

Motor Hotels

✔ ★ **HOLIDAY INN.** *245 London Bridge Rd.* 520/855-4071; *FAX 520/855-2379.* 162 rms, 4 story. Feb-Nov: S $49-$78; D $57-$84; each addl $8; suites $97-$135; under 18 free; wkly rates; golf plan; higher rates: hols, special events; lower rates rest of yr. Crib free. Pet accepted, some restrictions. TV; cable (premium). Heated pool. Restaurant 6 am-10 pm. Rm serv. Bar 11-1 am; Sun from noon. Ck-out noon. Coin Indry. Meeting rms. Business servs avail. In-rm modem link. Free airport transportation. Game rm. Refrigerators. Balconies. On lake; state park adj. Cr cds: A, C, D, DS, ER, JCB, MC, V.

★ ★ **LONDON BRIDGE RESORT.** *1477 Queens Bay Rd, near Municipal Airport. 520/855-0888; FAX 520/855-5404; res: 800/238-8808.* 65 rms, 3 story. S, D $75-$150; suites $125-$250; under 12 free. Pet accepted, some restrictions; $10/day. TV; VCR avail. 3 heated pools; whirlpool. Restaurants 7 am-2 pm, 5-9 pm. Bar 11-1 am. Meeting rms. Business servs avail. Shopping arcade. Airport transportation. Lighted tennis. 9-hole golf, pro, putting green. Some bathrm phones, refrigerators; microwaves avail. Private patios, balconies. Picnic tables. On lake. Cr cds: A, C, D, DS, MC, V.

Litchfield Park *(See also Glendale, Mesa, Phoenix, Scottsdale, Tempe)*

Motel

★ ★ **HOLIDAY INN EXPRESS.** *(1313 Litchfield Rd, Goodyear 85338) I-10 W exit 128. 602/535-1313; FAX 602/535-0950.* 90 rms, 3 story. Jan-May: S, D $129-$149; each addl $10; family rates; higher rates special events; lower rates rest of yr. Crib free. Pet accepted. TV; cable (premium). Complimentary continental bkfst. Restaurant adj 6:30 am-10 pm. Ck-out noon. Meeting rms. Business servs avail. In-rm modem link. Bellhops. Valet serv. Coin Indry. Exercise equipt; weight machine, treadmill. Pool; whirlpool. Game rm. Many in-rm whirlpools, refrigerators, microwaves, wet bars. Cr cds: A, C, D, DS, MC, V.

Resort

★ ★ ★ ★ ★ **THE WIGWAM.** *Litchfield & Indian School Rds, 2½ mi N of I-10 Litchfield Rd exit. 602/935-3811; FAX 602/935-3737; res: 800/327-0396.* E-mail wigwamresort@worldnet.att.net; web www.wigwamresort .com. This resort on 75 landscaped acres is known for its world-class golf. Spacious casitas and guest rooms in desert tones have large bathrooms. 331 units in 1-2 story casitas. Jan-Apr: S, D $296-$356; each addl $25; suites $356-$1,800; under 18 free; golf plan; AP & MAP avail; family rates avail hol seasons; lower rates rest of yr. Crib free. Pet accepted, some restrictions. TV; cable (premium). 2 pools; whirlpool, poolside serv. Playground. Supervised child's activities (June-Sept & hols); ages 5-12. Dining rms (public by res) 6:30-10:30 am, 11:30 am-2:30 pm, 5-10 pm. Rm serv 24 hrs. Box lunches, bkfst rides, steak fries. Bar 11-1 am. Ck-out 1 pm, ck-in 4 pm. Meeting rms. Business center. Concierge. Valet serv. Gift shop. Barber, beauty shop. Airport transportation. Lighted tennis, pro. 54-hole golf, greens fee $85-$95 (incl cart), pro, putting greens. Stagecoach, hayrides. Bicycles. Skeet, trapshooting. Indoor, outdoor games. Soc dir; entertainment, dancing; special hol programs for families. Exercise equipt; weights, bicycles, sauna, steam rm. Some refrigerators, minibars, wet bars, fireplaces. Library. Private patios. Cr cds: A, C, D, DS, ER, JCB, MC, V.

Marble Canyon *(See also Page)*

Motel

✔ ★ **MARBLE CANYON LODGE.** *US 89A, at Navajo Bridge. 520/355-2225; res: 800/726-1789.* 58 rms, some kits. May-Aug: S $45; D $55-$60; suites $125; kit. units $55; under 12 free; some lower rates rest of yr. Crib free. Pet accepted. Complimentary coffee in rms. Restaurant 6 am-9 pm; Dec-Mar from 6:30 am. Bar 6 am-9 pm. Ck-out 11 am. Coin Indry. Meeting rms. Business servs avail. Sundries. Hiking. 4,500-ft paved landing strip. Shuttle serv for river rafting. Cr cds: DS, MC, V.

Mesa *(See also Chandler, Phoenix, Scottsdale, Tempe)*

Resort

★ ★ ★ **ARIZONA GOLF RESORT & CONFERENCE CENTER.** *425 S Power Rd (85206), 1 mi N of Superstition Fwy. 602/832-3202; FAX 602/981-0151; res: 800/528-8282 (US).* E-mail azgolfresort@earthlink.net; web www.arizonaguide.com/arizona.golf. 186 kit. units, 1-2 story. Jan-Apr: S, D $185-$205; each addl $15-$25; suites $215-$440; under 16 free; golf package; lower rates rest of yr. Crib free. Pet accepted. TV; cable (premium), VCR avail. Heated pool. Coffee in rms. Dining rm 6 am-9 pm. Bar 10 am-midnight; entertainment Wed-Sat. Ck-out noon, ck-in 3 pm. Coin Indry. Meeting rms. Business servs avail. Valet serv. Lighted tennis. 18-hole golf, pro, putting green, driving range. Exercise equipt; stair machine, weights. Refrigerators, microwaves. Private patios, balconies. Picnic tables, grill. Cr cds: A, C, D, DS, ER, JCB, MC, V. [icons]

Nogales *(See also Patagonia, Tucson)*

Motel

★ **AMERICANA.** *639 N Grand Ave. 520/287-7211; FAX 520/287-5188; res: 800/874-8079.* 97 rms, 2 story. Nov-May: S $45-$55; D $55-$70; each addl $5; under 12 free; lower rates rest of yr. Crib $5. Pet accepted, some restrictions; $5. TV; cable. Pool; poolside serv. Restaurant 6:30 am-10 pm. Rm serv. Bar 11-1 am; Sun from noon. Ck-out noon. Meeting rms. Valet serv. Business servs avail. Barber, beauty shop adj. Some refrigerators. Cr cds: A, C, D, DS, MC, V. [icons] SC

Resort

★ ★ **RIO RICO.** *1069 Camino Caralampi, 12 mi N on I-19, exit 17. 520/281-1901; FAX 520/281-7132; res: 800/288-4746.* 196 units, 2-3 story. No elvtr. S, D $130-$140; each addl $15; suites $155-$700; under 18 free; golf, tennis, horseback riding plans; lower rates mid-Apr-mid-Oct. Crib $10. Pet accepted. TV; cable (premium). Heated pool; whirlpool, poolside serv. Dining rm 6 am-3 pm, 5-10 pm. Box lunches, picnics. Rm serv. Bar 11-1 am; entertainment wkends. Ck-out noon, ck-in 4 pm. Grocery 1/2 mi. Meeting rms. Business servs avail. Valet serv. Gift shop. Beauty shop. Airport transportation. Lighted tennis. 18-hole golf $55 with cart, pro, putting green, driving range. Stables. Exercise equipt; weight machine, bicycles, sauna. Lawn games. Private patios, balconies. Western cook-outs. On mesa top with scenic view. Cr cds: A, C, D, DS, MC, V.

[icons] SC

Page *(See also Marble Canyon)*

Motels

★ ★ ★ **BEST WESTERN.** *716 Rimview Dr. 520/645-2466; FAX 520/645-2466, ext. 501; res: 800/826-2718.* 103 units, 3 story. Apr-Oct: S $62-$92; D $79-$92; each addl $5; suites $125; under 18 free; lower rates rest of yr. Crib free. Pet accepted. TV; cable, VCR (movies). Pool; whirlpool. Restaurant 6 am-10 pm. Bar. Ck-out noon. Meeting rm. Business servs avail. Airport transportation. Overlooking Glen Canyon Dam & Lake Powell. Cr cds: A, C, D, DS, MC, V. [icons]

★ **LAKE POWELL.** *Box 1597, 4 mi NW of Glen Canyon Dam on US 89 at Wahweap jct. 520/645-2477; res: 800/528-6154 (exc AZ).* 24 rms, 2 story. May-Oct: S, D $74; each addl $7; under 18 free; lower rates rest of yr. Crib free. Pet accepted. TV. Pool privileges. Ck-out 11 am. Free airport transportation. View of canyon, cliffs, Lake Powell. Cr cds: A, C, D, DS, MC, V. [icons]

★ **WESTON'S EMPIRE HOUSE.** *107 S Lake Powell Blvd. 520/645-2406; res: 800/551-9005.* 69 rms, 2 story. Apr-Oct: S $58; D $70; each addl $5; under 12 free with 2 adults; some lower rates rest of yr. Crib $4. Pet accepted. TV; cable. Pool. Restaurant 5:30 am-9 pm. Bar 3 pm-1 am; closed Dec-Mar. Ck-out 11 am. Gift shop. Free airport transportation. Balconies. Cr cds: MC, V. [icons]

Motor Hotels

★ ★ **HOLIDAY INN.** *287 N Lake Powell Blvd. 520/645-8851; FAX 520/645-2523.* 130 rms, 3 story. Mid-Apr-Oct: S, D $85-$106; each addl $7; under 18 free; lower rates rest of yr. Crib free. Pet accepted. TV; cable. Heated pool. Restaurant 6 am-10 pm (summer); 6:30 am-2 pm, 5-9 pm (winter). Rm serv from 7 am. Bar 4 pm-1 am in summer. Ck-out 11 am. Coin lndry. Meeting rms. Business servs avail. Bellhops. Sundries. Gift shop. Free airport transportation in summer. Private patios, balconies. Picnic tables, grills. Cr cds: A, C, D, DS, MC, V. [icons]

★ ★ ★ **WAHWEAP LODGE & MARINA.** *Box 1597, 5 mi NW of Dam at Glen Canyon Recreation Area, 2 1/2 mi SE of US 89. 520/645-2433.* 350 rms in 8 bldgs, 2 story. May-Oct: S, D $119-$130.50; each addl $10; suites $200; under 18 free; lower rates rest of yr. Crib free. Pet accepted. TV; cable. 2 pools; whirlpool, poolside serv. Restaurants 6 am-10 pm. Bar 11-1 am; Sun from noon. Ck-out 11 am. Coin lndry. Meeting rms. Business servs avail. Bellhops. Concierge. Sundries. Gift shop. Free airport transportation. Golf privileges. Exercise equipt; weight machine, stair machine. Private patios, balconies. On lake. Boats, motorboats, scenic boat trips. Host for national bass fishing tounaments. Cr cds: A, C, D, DS, MC, V. [icons]

Patagonia (See also Nogales, Sierra Vista)

Motel

✔ ★ **STAGE STOP INN.** *303 W McKeown, 1 blk S of AZ 82.* 520/394-2211; FAX 520/394-2211; res: 800/923-2211. 43 rms, 2 story, 11 kits. S $45; D $59; each addl $10; suites, kit. units $65-$99; under 6 $5; wkly, group rates; golf plan. Pet accepted. TV; cable. Heated pool. Restaurant 7 am-9 pm; Fri, Sat to 10 pm; Ck-out noon. Meeting rms. Business servs avail. Sun deck. Frontier atmosphere. Cr cds: A, D, DS, MC, V. 🖭 🌊 🐾

Payson (See also Phoenix)

Motels

✔ ★ ★ **BEST WESTERN PAYSONGLO LODGE.** *1005 S Beeline Hwy.* 520/474-2382; FAX 520/474-1937. 47 rms, 2 story. Late May-Aug: S, D $72-$102; each addl $10; family rates; hols (2-day min); higher rates special events; lower rates rest of yr. Crib $10. Pet accepted, some restrictions. TV; cable (premium). Complimentary continental bkfst. Restaurant nearby. Ck-out noon. Business servs avail. Coin lndry. Pool; whirlpool. Refrigerators; some fireplaces. Cr cds: A, D, DS, MC, V. 🖪 🌊 🐾 SC

★ ★ **RAMADA INN.** *801 N Beeline Hwy (85547), (AZ 87), ¼ mi N of AZ 260.* 520/474-3241; FAX 520/472-6564; res: 800/247-9477. 103 rms, 2 story. May-Sept: S, D $89-$159; each addl $10; apt (2-bedrm) $149; under 17 free; lower rates rest of yr. Crib $10. Pet accepted; $10/day. TV; cable (premium). Heated pool (summer). Complimentary continental bkfst. Complimentary coffee in rms. Ck-out noon. Meeting rm. Business servs avail. Refrigerators; some in-rm fireplaces, whirlpools. Private patios. Cr cds: A, D, DS, JCB, MC, V. 🖪 🌊 🐾 SC

Phoenix

Motels

★ ★ **HAMPTON INN.** *8101 N Black Canyon Hwy (85021), I-17 exit Northern Ave on frontage rd.* 602/864-6233; FAX 602/995-7503. 149 rms, 3 story. Jan-mid-Apr: S, D $100-$110; under 18 free; higher rates special events; lower rates rest of yr. Crib free. Pet accepted, some restrictions. TV; cable (premium). Heated pool; whirlpool. Complimentary continental bkfst. Ck-out noon. Meeting rms. Business servs avail. In-rm modem link. Cr cds: A, C, D, DS, MC, V. 🖪 🌊 🐾 SC

★ ★ **HOMEWOOD SUITES.** *2001 E Highland Ave (85016).* 602/508-0937; FAX 602/508-0854. 124 kit. suites, 4 story. Jan-Apr: S $169-$179; D $179-$189; each addl $10; under 18 free; wkly, wkend, hol rates; lower rates rest of yr. Crib free. Pet accepted, some restrictions. TV; cable (premium). Complimentary continental bkfst. Complimentary coffee in rms. Restaurant adj 11 am-11 pm. Ck-out noon. Meeting rm. Business center. In-rm modem link. Valet serv. Sundries. Coin lndry. Exercise equipt; weights, bicycle. Health club privileges. Pool. Refrigerators, microwaves; some fireplaces. Grills. Cr cds: A, C, D, DS, MC, V. 🖪 🌊 🍴 🐾 SC

★ ★ **LA QUINTA-COLISEUM WEST.** *2725 N Black Canyon Hwy (85009), I-17 exit Thomas Rd.* 602/258-6271; FAX 602/340-9255. Web www.laquinta.com. 139 rms, 2 story. Jan-Apr: S, D $95-$110; each addl $10; under 18 free; lower rates rest of yr. Crib free. Pet accepted, some restrictions. TV; cable. Heated pool. Complimentary continental bkfst. Coffee in rms. Restaurant adj open 24 hrs. Ck-out noon. Coin lndry. Business servs avail. In-rm modem link. Valet serv. Some refrigerators. Cr cds: A, C, D, DS, MC, V. 🖪 🌊 🐾 SC

✔ ★ **PREMIER INN.** *10402 N Black Canyon Hwy (85051), at I-17 Peoria Ave exit.* 602/943-2371; FAX 602/943-5847; res: 800/786-6835. 253 rms, 2 story. Jan-Apr: S, D $59.95-$89.95; suites $129.95; lower rates rest of yr. Crib $3. Pet accepted, some restrictions. TV; cable (premium). 2 pools, 1 heated; wading pool. Ck-out noon. Coin lndry. Meeting rms. Bathrm phone in suites. Some refrigerators. Some private patios. Cr cds: A, C, D, DS, MC, V. 🌊 🍴 🐾 SC

Motor Hotels

★ ★ **BEST WESTERN INNSUITES.** *1615 E Northern Ave (85020).* 602/997-6285; FAX 602/943-1407. E-mail esphoenix@attmail.com; web www.arizonaguide.com/innsuites. 123 rms, 2 story, 4 kits. Jan-mid-Apr: S, D $119-$129; kit. suites $149-$169; under 19 free; lower rates rest of yr. Crib free. Pet accepted, some restrictions; $25 refundable. TV; cable (premium). Heated pool; whirlpool. Complimentary continental bkfst. Complimentary coffee in rms. Ck-out noon. Coin lndry. Meeting rms. Business servs avail. In-rm modem link.

Exercise equipt; stair machine, bicycle. Playground. Refrigerators, microwaves. Picnic tables, grills. Cr cds: A, C, D, DS, MC, V. D ⭐ 🏊 🏋 🛏 🐾 SC

✔★ **QUALITY INN SOUTH MOUNTAIN.** *5121 E La Puente Ave (85044). 602/893-3900; FAX 602/496-0815.* 193 rms, 4 story. Jan-Apr: S, D $99-$119; suites $135-$155; under 17 free; lower rates rest of yr. Crib free. Pet accepted; $15. TV; cable. Heated pool; whirlpool. Coffee in rm. Restaurant 6:30-11 am, 5-9 pm. Rm serv. Ck-out 11 am. Coin lndry. Meeting rms. Business servs avail. Valet serv. Health club privileges. Some refrigerators. Microwaves avail. Cr cds: A, C, D, DS, ER, JCB, MC, V. D ⭐ 🏊 🏋 🐾 SC

★ ★ ★ **WYNDHAM GARDEN HOTEL.** *2641 W Union Hills Dr (85027), at I-17 & Union Hills. 602/978-2222; FAX 602/978-9139.* 166 rms, 2 story. Jan-Apr: S $139; D $149; each addl $10; under 18 free; lower rates rest of yr. Pet accepted, some restrictions; $25. TV; cable. Heated pool; whirlpool; poolside serv. Full bkfst. Coffee in rms. Restaurant 6:30 am-10 pm. Rm serv 5-10 pm. Bar 4:30-11 pm. Ck-out noon. Coin lndry. Meeting rms. Business servs avail. Valet serv. Sundries. Some refrigerators. Some private patios. Cr cds: A, C, D, DS, ER, JCB, MC, V. D ⭐ 🏊 🏋 🐾 SC

Hotels

★ ★ **LEXINGTON HOTEL & CITY SQUARE SPORTS CLUB.** *100 W Clarendon Ave (85013). 602/279-9811; FAX 602/631-9358.* 180 rms, 3 & 7 story. Jan-May: S, D $149-$169; under 18 free; wkend rates; lower rates rest of yr. Crib free. Pet accepted, some restrictions. TV; cable (premium). Heated pool; whirlpool. Restaurant 6:30 am-10:30 pm; closed Sun. Bar. Ck-out noon. Business servs avail. Barber, beauty shop. Gift shop. Free valet parking. Exercise rm; instructor, weights, bicycles, steam rm, sauna. Aerobics. Basketball. Racquetball. Some microwaves. Some balconies. Cr cds: A, C, D, DS, ER, MC, V. ⭐ 🏊 🏋 🛏 🐾

★ ★ **QUALITY HOTEL & RESORT.** *3600 N Second Ave (85013). 602/248-0222; FAX 602/265-6331.* Web www.getawayla goon.com. 280 rms, 8 & 10 story, 33 suites. Jan-Apr: S $109; D $119; each addl $10; suites $150-$185; under 18 free; lower rates rest of yr. Crib free. Pet accepted. TV; cable (premium) VCR avail. Complimentary coffee in rms. Restaurant 6 am-10 pm. Bar 4 pm-midnight; entetainment Tues-Sat. Ck-out noon. Meeting rms. Business center. Gift shop. Grocery store. Coin lndry. Free garage parking. Exercise equipt; bicycle, stair machine. Health club privileges. Pool; wading pool, whirlpool, poolside serv. Playground. Game rm. Lawn games. Refrigerators avail. Picnic tables. Cr cds: A, C, D, DS, ER, JCB, MC, V. D ⭐ 🏊 🏋 🛏 🐾 SC 🎿

✔★ **SAN CARLOS.** *202 N Central Ave (85004). 602/253-4121; FAX 602/253-6668; res: 800/528-5446.* 132 rms, 7 story. Jan-Apr: S, D $99-$109; each addl $10; suites $129-$159; under 12 free. Crib free. Pet accepted, some restrictions. TV; cable (premium). Heated pool. Complimentary continental bkfst. Complimentary coffee in rms. Restaurant 11 am-11 pm. Ck-out noon. Meeting rms. In-rm modem link. Valet. Health club privileges. Refrigerators; microwaves avail. Cr cds: A, C, D, DS, MC, V. ⭐ 🏊 🏋 🐾 SC

★ ★ **SHERATON CRESCENT.** *2620 W Dunlap Ave (85021), at I-17. 602/943-8200; FAX 602/371-2857.* Web www.arizonaguide.com/ sheratoncrescent/. 342 rms, 8 story. Early Jan-mid-May: S, D $165-$239; suites $275-$650; some wkend rates; lower rates rest of yr. Crib free. Pet accepted, some restrictions; $100 ($75 refundable). TV; cable (premium), VCR avail. Heated pool; whirlpool, poolside serv. Complimentary coffee in rms. Restaurant 6 am-11 pm. Bar 11-1 am; entertainment. Ck-out noon. Convention facilities. Business center. Gift shop. Free covered parking. Lighted tennis. Exercise rm; instructor, weights, bicycles, sauna, steam rm. Lawn games. Refrigerators, minibars. Balconies. Some fireplaces. Luxury level. Cr cds: A, C, D, DS, ER, JCB, MC, V. D ⭐ 🏊 🏋 🛏 🐾 🎿

Prescott

Motel

★ ★ **BEST WESTERN PRESCOTTONIAN.** *1317 E Gurley St (86301), at jct US 89, AZ 69. 520/445-3096; FAX 520/778-2976.* 121 rms, 2-3 story. No elvtr. Apr-Oct: S $59-$93; D $79-$95; each addl $7; suites $125-$200; higher rates special events; lower rates rest of yr. Crib free. Pet accepted. TV; cable. Pool; whirlpool. Complimentary continental bkfst. Coffee in rms. Restaurant 11 am-9:30 pm. Bar 11 am-9:30 pm. Ck-out noon. Coin lndry. Business servs avail. Refrigerators. Some private patios, balconies. Cr cds: A, C, D, DS, ER, MC, V. D ⭐ 🏊 🏋 🐾 SC

Hotel

★ ★ ★ **FOREST VILLAS.** *3645 Lee Circle (86301), E on AZ 69 to Lee Blvd. 520/717-1200; FAX 520/717-1400; res: 800/717-1200.* 61 rms, 2 story, 16 suites. Apr 15-Oct 31: S

$79-$99; D $89-$109; each addl $10; suites $129-$179; under 13 free; wkly rates; lower rates rest of yr. Crib free. Pet accepted, some restrictions; $150 refundable. TV; cable (premium), VCR avail. Heated pool; whirlpool. Complimentary continental bkfst. Complimentary coffee in rms. Ck-out noon. Meeting rms. Business servs avail. Free garage parking. 18-hole golf privileges, greens fee $44 (incl cart), pro, putting green, driving range. Balconies. European decor with grand staircase. Cr cds: A, C, D, DS, MC, V. [D] 🛱 🌊 🐾 [SC]

Inn

★★ **LYNX CREEK FARM.** *(86302). mile-marker 291 (Onyx Rd), call for directions.* 520/778-9573. 6 rms, 2 story, 2 kit. rms. No rm phones. Mar-Dec: S, D $75-$145; each addl $15-$20; wkly rates; higher rates hols; single Sat; lower rates rest of yr. Crib free. Pet accepted, some restrictions; $10/day/pet. TV rm; VCR (movies avail). Heated pool; whirlpool. Complimentary full bkfst. Complimentary coffee in rms. Concierge serv. Free airport transportation. Lighted tennis privileges, pro. Balconies. Picnic tables. Totally nonsmoking. Cr cds: A, DS, MC, V. 🛱 🏇 🌊 🎿 🐾

Scottsdale *(See also Chandler, Glendale, Mesa, Phoenix, Tempe)*

Motels

★★ **HOSPITALITY SUITE RESORT.** *409 N Scottsdale Rd (85257).* 602/949-5115; FAX 602/941-8014; res: 800/445-5115. E-mail reservations@hospitalitysuites.com; web www.hospitalitysuites.com. 210 kit. suites (1-2 rm), 2-3 story. Mid-Jan-mid-Apr: S, D $169-$199; under 18 free; lower rates rest of yr. Crib $10. Pet accepted, some restrictions; $100 refundable. TV; cable (premium). 3 heated pools; whirlpool, poolside serv. Complimentary full bkfst. Coffee in rms. Restaurant 6:30 am-10 pm. Rm serv. Bar 11-1 am; entertainment (seasonal). Ck-out 11 am. Coin lndry. Meeting rms. Business servs avail. Bellhops. Valet serv. Free airport transportation. Lighted tennis. Lawn games. Health club privileges. Refrigerators, microwaves. Picnic tables; grills. Cr cds: A, C, D, DS, ER, MC, V. [D] 🛱 🏇 🌊 🎿 🐾 [SC]

★★ **LA QUINTA INN & SUITES.** *8888 E Shea Blvd (85260).* 602/614-5300; FAX 602/614-5333. 140 rms, 3 story. Jan-Apr: S, D $134-$144; each addl $10; under 17 free; lower rates rest of yr. Crib $10. Pet accepted, some restrictions. TV; cable (premium). Complimentary continental bkfst. Complimentary coffee in rms. Restaurant adj 7 am-11 pm. Ck-out noon. Meeting rms. Business servs avail. Coin lndry. Exercise equipt; weight machine, bicycle. Pool; whirlpool. Some refrigerators, microwaves. Cr cds: A, C, D, DS, MC, V. [D] 🛱 🏇 🌊 🎿 🐾 [SC]

★ **SAFARI RESORT.** *4611 N Scottsdale Rd (85251).* 602/945-0721; FAX 602/946-4703; res: 800/845-4356. 188 rms, 2 story, 64 kits. Jan-mid-Apr: S $92-$150; D $102-$160; each addl $10; kit. units $130-$160; under 18 free; golf plans; lower rates rest of yr. Crib free. Pet accepted; $50 refundable. TV; cable, VCR avail (movies). 2 heated pools; whirlpool. Complimentary continental bkfst. Restaurant 11 am-11 pm. Rm serv. Bar 11-1 am. Ck-out noon. Coin lndry. Meeting rms. Business servs avail. Bellhops. Valet serv. Gift shop. Health club privileges. Lawn games. Many private patios, balconies. Cr cds: A, C, D, DS, MC, V. [D] 🛱 🌊 🎿 🐾

Motor Hotel

★★★ **DOUBLETREE LA POSADA RESORT.** *4949 E Lincoln Dr (85253).* 602/952-0420; FAX 602/840-8576. 252 rms, 10 suites. Jan-May: S, D $245; each addl $20; suites $375-$750; under 18 free; package plan; lower rates rest of yr. Crib free. Pet accepted, some restrictions. TV; cable (premium). 2 heated pools; whirlpool, poolside serv. Complimentary coffee in rms. Restaurant 6 am-10 pm; Fri, Sat to 11 pm. Rm serv. Bar noon-1 am. Ck-out noon. Convention facilities. Business servs avail. Bellhops. Valet serv. Sundries. Gift shop. Barber, beauty shop. Lighted tennis, pro, pro shop. Golf privileges, 2 putting greens. Exercise equipt; weights, bicycles, sauna. Lawn games. Some refrigerators, minibars. Private patios. Multiple cascading waterfalls; lagoon-like pool. At foot of Camelback Mountain. Cr cds: A, C, D, DS, ER, JCB, MC, V. [D] 🛱 🏇 🏇 🌊 🎿 🎿 🐾 [SC]

Inn

★★★ **INN AT THE CITADEL.** *8700 E Pinnacle Peak Rd (85255), at Inn at the Citadel Complex.* 602/585-6133; FAX 602/585-3436; res: 800/927-8367. 11 suites. Mid-Jan-May: S, D $295-$335; under 12 free; lower rates rest of yr. Crib free. Pet accepted. TV; cable. Complimentary continental bkfst. Coffee in rms. Dining rm 7 am-10 pm. Rm serv. Ck-out noon, ck-in 3 pm. Business servs avail. Golf privileges. Some balconies, minibars. Each rm individually decorated with antiques, artwork. View of Sonoran Desert, city. Cr cds: A, C, D, DS, MC, V. [D] 🛱 🏇 🎿 🐾

Resorts

★ ★ ★ ★ ★ **MARRIOTT'S CAMELBACK INN RESORT GOLF CLUB & SPA.** *5402 E Lincoln Dr (85253), Paradise Valley, northeast of downtown. 602/948-1700; FAX 602/951-8469; res: 800/24-CAMEL.* Web www.camelbackinn.com. A southwestern-style lobby and large hilltop spa stand out at this vintage desert oasis on 125 beautifully landscaped acres. The spacious guest rooms have scenic views. 454 rms in 1-2-story casitas. Jan-May: S, D $339-$365; suites $600-$2,000; AP addl $64/person; MAP addl $48/person; Camelback plan (bkfst, lunch) addl $29/person; under 18 free; wkend rates; golf, tennis, spa plan; lower rates rest of yr. Crib free. Pet accepted. TV; cable (premium), VCR avail. 3 pools; whirlpool, poolside serv, lifeguards. Supervised child's activities (June-Aug; also some wkends & hols); ages 3-12. Dining rms 6:30 am-10 pm. Rm serv to midnight. Box lunches. Bars 11-1 am. Ck-out noon, ck-in 4 pm. Coin lndry. Business center. In-rm modem link. Valet serv. Concierge. Barber, beauty shop. Gift & sport shops. Lighted tennis, pro. 36-hole golf, greens fee $105 (incl cart), pros, putting greens, driving range, golf school. Bicycle rental. Lawn games. Soc dir; entertainment; movies winter & spring hols. Extensive exercise rm; instructor, weights, treadmills, sauna, steam rm. Spa. Refrigerators, minibars. Wet bar, microwave; fireplace, private pool in some suites. Private patios; many balconies. Cr cds: A, C, D, DS, ER, JCB, MC, V.

★ ★ ★ **RENAISSANCE COTTONWOODS.** *6160 N Scottsdale Rd (85253). 602/991-1414; FAX 602/951-3350.* Web www.renaissanceho tels.com. 107 suites, 64 rms. Jan-May: S, D $245-$260; each addl $10; suites $285-$315; kit. units $345-$355; under 18 free; package plans; lower rates rest of yr. Crib free. Pet accepted, some restrictions. TV; cable (premium), VCR avail (movies). 3 heated pools; whirlpools, poolside serv. Complimentary continental bkfst in rms. Restaurant 7 am-10:30 pm. Rm serv 24 hrs. Bar noon-1 am. Ck-out noon. Meeting rms. Business center. Bellhops. Concierge. Valet serv. Airport transportation. Lighted tennis, pro. Golf privileges, putting green. Health club privileges. Lawn games. Bicycle rentals. Refrigerators, minibars; some bathrm phones, fireplaces; microwaves avail. Whirlpool on patios. Adj to Borgata shopping complex. Cr cds: A, C, D, DS, ER, JCB, MC, V.

★ ★ ★ **SCOTTSDALE PLAZA.** *7200 N Scottsdale Rd (85253). 602/948-5000; FAX 602/998-5971; res: 800/832-2025.* E-mail res@tspr.com; web www.tspr.com. 404 rms, 2 story, 180 suites. Jan-May: S, D $275-$290; each addl $10; suites $300-$3,500; under 17 free; wkend rates; lower rates rest of yr. Crib free. Pet accepted, some restrictions; $100 ($50 refundable). TV; cable (premium), VCR avail. 5 heated pools; poolside serv. Dining rms 6 am-11 pm. Rm serv. Bar 11-1 am; entertainment. Ck-out noon, ck-in 3 pm. Valet serv. Convention facilities. Business center. Concierge. Sundries. Gift shop. Beauty shop. Lighted tennis, pro. Racquetball. Bike rentals. Lawn games. Exercise equipt; treadmill, bicycle, sauna. Refrigerators, minibars; many wet bars; microwaves avail. Spanish colonial-style buildings on 40 acres; waterfall. Cr cds: A, C, D, DS, ER, JCB, MC, V.

Sedona *(See also Flagstaff)*

Motels

★ ★ **BEST WESTERN.** *1200 W AZ 89A. 520/282-3072; res: 800/292-6344; FAX 520/282-7218.* 110 rms, 3 story. Mar-May, Sept-Oct: S, D $115-$135; each addl $10; under 12 free; hols (2-day min); lower rates rest of yr. Crib free. Pet accepted; $10. TV; cable (premium). Complimentary continental bkfst. Complimentary coffee in rms. Restaurant adj 11 am-9 pm. Ck-out 11 am. Meeting rms. Business servs avail. Bellhops. Exercise equipt; treadmill, stair machine. Pool; whirlpool. Many refrigerators; some fireplaces. Balconies. Cr cds: A, C, D, DS, JCB, MC, V.

✔ ★ ★ **DESERT QUAIL INN.** *6626 AZ 179 (86351). 520/284-1433; FAX 520/284-0487; res: 800/385-0927.* E-mail quail@sedona.net; web www.desertquailinn.com. 32 rms, 9 suites, 2 story. S, D $54-$89; suites $100-$150; each addl $5; under 12 free; golf plan; higher rates hols (2-day min), special events. Crib free. Pet accepted, some restrictions; $15. TV; cable (premium). Pool. Complimentary coffee in rms. Restaurant nearby. Ck-out 11 am. Guest lndry. Business servs avail. 18-hole golf privileges, greens fee $55-$85, putting green, driving range. Health club privileges. Jeep, bicycle rentals. Refrigerators; microwaves avail. Cr cds: A, C, D, DS, JCB, MC, V.

★ ★ **HOLIDAY INN EXPRESS.** *6175 AZ 179 (86351). 520/284-0711; FAX 520/284-3760.* 104 rms, 2 story, 12 suites. Mar-July, Sept-Dec: S, D $89-$114; each addl $10; suites $129-$143; under 19 free; golf plans; lower rates rest of yr. Crib free. Pet accepted; $25. TV; cable (premium), VCR avail (movies). Complimentary continental bkfst. Restaurant nearby. Ck-out 11 am. Meeting rms. Business servs avail. 18-hole golf privi-

leges, greens fee $75, pro, putting green, driving range. Pool; whirlpool. Microwaves avail.
Cr cds: A, D, DS, JCB, MC, V.   D ⮕ 🏌 ⩰ ⊠ 🐾 SC

Lodge

★ ★ **SKY RANCH LODGE.** *Airport Rd (86339), S on AZ 89A to Airport Rd, 1 mi to
lodge. 520/282-6400; FAX 520/282-7682.* E-mail skyranch@sedona.net. 94 rms, 1-2 story,
20 kit. units, 2 cottages. No A/C. S, D, kit. units $75-$125; each addl $8; cottages $155;
under 12 free. Crib free. Pet accepted, some restrictions; fee. TV; cable. Heated pool;
whirlpool. Complimentary coffee in lobby. Restaurant nearby. Ck-out 11 am. Coin lndry.
Business servs avail. Gift shop. Some refrigerators. Cr cds: MC, V.   D ⮕ ⩰ ⊠ 🐾

Show Low

Motel

★ **DAYS INN.** *480 W Deuce of Clubs (US 60W). 520/537-4356; FAX 520/537-
8692.* 122 rms, 2 story. S $51-$65; D $59-$74; each addl $5; higher rates special events.
Crib free. Pet accepted, some restrictions; $50 deposit & $5/day. TV; cable (premium).
Heated pool. Restaurant 6 am-10 pm. Ck-out noon. Coin lndry. Meeting rms. Business servs
avail. Beauty shop. Free airport transportation. Refrigerators, microwaves. Cr cds: A, C, D,
DS, MC, V.   D ⮕ ⩰ ⊠ 🐾 SC

Sierra Vista *(See also Patagonia)*

Motor Hotel

★ ★ **WINDEMERE.** *2047 S AZ 92. 520/459-5900; FAX 520/458-1347; res:
800/825-4656.* 149 rms, 3 story. S $68-$78, D $68-$86; each addl $8; suites $125-$250;
under 16 free; golf plans. Crib free. Pet accepted, some restrictions; $50 refundable. TV;
cable. Heated pool; whirlpool. Coffee in rms. Complimentary bkfst buffet. Restaurant 6 am-2
pm, 4:30-9 pm. Rm serv. Bar 4-11 pm, Fri & Sat to 1 am; entertainment. Ck-out 11 am. Coin
lndry. Meeting rms. Business servs avail. Valet serv. Free airport transportation. Health club
privileges. Refrigerators avail. Cr cds: A, C, D, DS, ER, JCB, MC, V.
D ⮕ ⩰ ⊠ 🐾 SC

Tempe *(See also Chandler, Glendale, Mesa, Phoenix, Scottsdale)*

Motels

★ ★ **COUNTRY SUITES BY CARLSON.** *1660 W Elliot Rd (85283). 602/345-8585;
FAX 602/345-7461.* 139 kit. suites, 3 story. Jan-mid-May: kit. suites $99-$149, each addl
$10; under 16 free; golf plans; lower rates rest of yr. Crib free. Pet accepted, some
restrictions; $50. TV; cable (premium), VCR avail. Pool; wading pool, whirlpool. Complimen-
tary continental bkfst. Complimentary coffee in rms. Restaurant nearby. Ck-out noon. Coin
lndry. Meeting rms. Business servs avail. Valet serv. Free airport transportation. Health club
privileges. Refrigerators, microwaves. Cr cds: A, C, D, DS, MC, V.   D ⮕ ⩰ ⊠ 🐾 SC

✔ ★ ★ **HOLIDAY INN EXPRESS.** *5300 S Priest Dr (85283). 602/820-7500; FAX
602/730-6626.* 160 rms, 4 story. Jan-Apr: S $80-$120; D $90-$130; each addl $5; under 21
free; lower rates rest of yr. Crib free. Pet accepted. TV; cable (premium). Pool; whirlpool.
Complimentary continental bkfst. Ck-out noon. Meeting rm. Business servs avail. Free
airport transportation. Cr cds: A, C, D, DS, ER, JCB, MC, V.   ⮕ ⩰ ⊠ 🐾 SC

★ ★ **LA QUINTA.** *911 S 48th St (85281), near Sky Harbor Intl Airport. 602/967-
4465; FAX 602/921-9172.* Web www.laquinta.com/la quinta.html. 129 rms, 3 story. Jan-Apr:
S, D $109-$119; each addl $10; suites $149; under 18 free; lower rates rest of yr. Crib free.
Pet accepted, some restrictions. TV; cable (premium). Heated pool. Complimentary continental bkfst. Restaurant adj open 24 hrs. Ck-out noon. Coin lndry. Business servs avail. Free
airport transportation. Putting green. Cr cds: A, C, D, DS, MC, V.
D ⮕ ⩰ ✕ ⊠ 🐾 SC

✔ ★ **TRAVELODGE-TEMPE/UNIVERSITY.** *1005 E Apache Blvd (85281).
602/968-7871; FAX 602/968-3991.* 93 rms, 2 story. Jan-Apr: S, D $59-$89; each addl $10;
under 16 free; lower rates rest of yr. Crib free. Pet accepted, some restrictions; $4/day. TV;
cable (premium), VCR avail (movies). 2 pools. Complimentary continental bkfst. Complimentary coffee in rms. Restaurant nearby. Ck-out noon. Coin lndry. Business servs avail.
Refrigerators, microwaves avail. Cr cds: A, C, D, DS, ER, MC, V.   D ⮕ ⩰ ⊠ 🐾 SC

Motor Hotels

★ ★ **HOLIDAY INN-PHOENIX-TEMPE/ASU.** *915 E Apache Blvd (85281).
602/968-3451; FAX 602/968-6262.* E-mail hitempe@world net.att.net; web www.amdest

.com/az/tempe/hi/hol. 190 rms, 4 story. Jan-Apr: S $144; D $154; suites, studio rms $172; under 19 free; lower rates rest of yr. Crib free. Pet accepted. TV; cable (premium), VCR avail. Heated pool; whirlpool, poolside serv. Complimentary coffee in rms. Restaurant 6 am-10 pm. Rm serv. Bar 11-1 am. Ck-out 1 pm. Free lndry facilities. Meeting rms. Business servs avail. Bellhops. Valet serv. Gift shop. Free airport transportation. Tennis privileges. Golf privileges. Exercise equipt; weights, stair machine. Health club privileges. Refrigerators; microwaves avail. Some private patios, balconies. Cr cds: A, C, D, DS, JCB, MC, V.

★ ★ INNSUITES. *1651 W Baseline Rd (85283), at I-10.* 602/897-7900; FAX 602/491-1008; res: 800/842-4242. *170 rms, 2-3 story, 81 kits. Jan-Apr: S, D $89-$119; suites, kit. units $99-$139; under 18 free; lower rates rest of yr. Crib free. Pet accepted; $25. TV; cable (premium). Heated pool; whirlpool. Playground. Complimentary continental bkfst. Complimentary coffee in rms. Restaurant 6 am-2 pm, 4-10 pm; Oct-Apr 6 am-10 pm. Ck-out noon. Coin lndry. Meeting rms. Business center. In-rm modem link. Valet serv. Free airport transportation. Lighted tennis. Exercise equipt; weight machine, bicycle. Health club privileges. Refrigerators, microwaves. Some private patios, balconies. Grills. Cr cds: A, C, D, DS, MC, V.*

Tombstone

Motel

✔ ★ ★ BEST WESTERN LOOKOUT LODGE. *Box 787, ¹/₂ mi NW on US 80.* 520/457-2223; FAX 520/457-3870. *40 rms, 2 story. S $53-$63; D $58-$73; each addl $5; under 12 free; higher rates special events. Crib free. Pet accepted, some restrictions; $50 & $5/day. TV; cable. Heated pool. Complimentary continental bkfst. Restaurant nearby. Ck-out 11 am. Business servs avail. Cr cds: A, C, D, DS, MC, V.*

Tucson (See also Nogales)

Motels

★ ★ BEST WESTERN INNSUITES-CATALINA FOOTHILLS. *6201 N Oracle Rd (85704), in Foothills.* 520/297-8111; FAX 520/297-2935. *159 rms, 2 story, 74 kit. suites. Jan-mid-Apr: S, D $109-$129; 2-rm suites $129-$179; under 19 free; wkend, wkly rates; higher rates special events; lower rates rest of yr. Crib free. Pet accepted, some restrictions; $25 refundable. TV; cable (premium). Heated pool; whirlpool. Complimentary bkfst buffet. Coffee in rms. Restaurant adj 6 am-midnight. Rm serv. Ck-out noon. Coin lndry. Meeting rms. Business servs avail. Valet serv. Lighted tennis. Exercise equipt; weight machine, treadmill. Refrigerators; some in-rm whirlpools. Some private patios, balconies. Grills. Cr cds: A, C, D, DS, MC, V.*

★ ★ ★ CLARION HOTEL-AIRPORT. *6801 S Tucson Blvd (85706), near Intl Airport, south of downtown.* 520/746-3932; FAX 520/889-9934. Web mmm.arizonaguide.com/clarion-tucson. *191 rms, 2 story. Jan-Mar: S $95-$120; D $105-$135; each addl $10; suites $210-$250; under 18 free; wkend rates; lower rates rest of yr. Crib free. Pet accepted, some restrictions; $30 refundable. TV; cable (premium). Heated pool; whirlpool, poolside serv. Restaurant 6 am-11 pm; Fri, Sat to midnight. Rm serv. Bar. Ck-out noon. Coin lndry. Meeting rms. Business servs avail. In-rm modem link. Bellhops. Valet serv. Sundries. Free airport transportation. 18-hole golf privileges. Exercise equipt; weight machine, bicycles. Some refrigerators. Picnic tables, grills. Cr cds: A, C, D, DS, ER, JCB, MC, V.*

★ ★ LA QUINTA. *6404 E Broadway (85710), in Midtown.* 520/747-1414; FAX 520/745-6903. *140 rms, 2 story. Jan-Apr: S, D $92-$99; under 18 free; lower rates rest of yr. Crib free. Pet accepted, some restrictions. TV; cable (premium). Heated pool; whirlpool. Complimentary continental bkfst. Coffee in rms. Restaurant adj open 24 hrs. Ck-out noon. Coin lndry. Meeting rms. Business servs avail. Health club privileges. Some private patios, balconies. Cr cds: A, C, D, DS, MC, V.*

★ RAMADA INN FOOTHILLS. *6944 E Tanque Verde Rd (85715), in Tanque Verde.* 520/886-9595; FAX 520/721-8466. E-mail ramadafoothills@juno.com; web desert.net/ramada/. *113 units, 2 story. Jan-Apr: S, D $100-$120; each addl $10; suites $110-$140; under 18 free; lower rates rest of yr. Crib free. Pet accepted, some restrictions; $10. TV; cable (premium). Heated pool; whirlpool, sauna. Continental bkfst. Restaurant adj 6 am-10 pm. Ck-out noon. Coin lndry. Meeting rms. Business servs avail. Health club privileges. Some refrigerators. Cr cds: A, C, D, DS, ER, JCB, MC, V.*

★ RODEWAY INN-NORTH. *1365 W Grant Rd (85745), north of downtown.* 520/622-7791; FAX 520/629-0201. *146 rms, 2 story. Jan-Apr: S, D $60-$130; each addl $6;*

under 19 free; summer rates. Crib free. Pet accepted; $10/day. TV; cable (premium). Heated pool, whirlpool. Coffee in rms. Restaurant 6 am-2 pm, 5-9 pm. Rm serv. Bar 3 pm-midnight. Ck-out noon. Coin lndry. Meeting rms. Business servs avail. Valet serv. Some refrigerators. Cr cds: A, C, D, DS, JCB, MC, V. ☐ ☐ ☐ ☐ ☐ SC

★ **TRAVELODGE FLAMINGO.** *1300 N Stone (85705), just north of downtown. 520/770-1910; FAX 520/770-0750.* 80 rms, 2 story, 20 suites. Feb-Apr: S, D $72-$76; suites $82-$86; under 18 free; higher rates gem show; lower rates rest of yr. Crib free. Pet accepted, some restrictions; $50 deposit. TV; cable (premium). Heated pool; whirlpool. Complimentary continental bkfst. Complimentary coffee in rms. Restaurant nearby. Ck-out 11 am. Coin lndry. Meeting rms. Business servs avail. Health club privileges. Game rm. Refrigerator in suites. Cr cds: A, C, D, DS, ER, JCB, MC, V. ☐ ☐ ☐ ☐ ☐ SC

✔ ★ ★ **WAYWARD WINDS LODGE.** *707 W Miracle Mile (85705), north of downtown. 520/791-7526; FAX 520/791-9502; res: 800/791-9503.* Web www.arizonaguide.com/wallward.winds. 41 rms, 19 kits. Dec-Apr: S $69-$74; D $74-$79; each addl $5; kit. suites $76-$84; apts $84-$89; under 18 free; wkly, monthly rates, golf plans, summer family plans; lower rates rest of yr. Crib free. Pet accepted. TV; cable, VCR avail. Heated pool. Complimentary continental bkfst. Restaurant nearby. Ck-out noon. Coin lndry. Business servs avail. Covered parking. Rec rm. Lawn games. Golf privileges. Microwaves avail. Picnic tables, grill. Spacious grounds. Cr cds: C, D, DS, JCB, MC, V. ☐ ☐ ☐ ☐ ☐ ☐ SC

Motor Hotels

★ ★ ★ **DOUBLETREE.** *445 S Alvernon Way (85711), in Midtown. 520/881-4200; FAX 520/323-5225.* 295 rms, 2-9 story. Mid-Jan-mid-Apr: S, D $129-$159; each addl $15; suites $290-$475; under 17 free; lower rates rest of yr. Crib free. Pet accepted, some restrictions; $50 refundable. TV; cable (premium), VCR avail. Heated pool; whirlpool, poolside serv. Restaurant 6 am-11 pm. Rm serv. Bars 11-1 am, Sun from noon. Ck-out noon. Meeting rms. Business servs avail. Bellhops. Valet serv. Gift shop. Beauty shop. Lighted tennis. 36-hole golf privileges. Exercise equipt; weight machine, stair machine. Some minibars. Some private patios. Cr cds: A, C, D, DS, ER, JCB, MC, V. ☐ ☐ ☐ ☐ ☐ ☐ ☐ ☐ SC

★ ★ ★ **EMBASSY SUITES BROADWAY.** *5335 E Broadway (85711), in Midtown. 520/745-2700; FAX 520/790-9232.* Web www.em bassy-suites.com. 142 suites, 3 story. No elvtr. Jan-Apr: S $89-$159; D $99-$169; each addl $10; under 12 free; lower rates rest of yr. Crib free. Pet accepted, some restrictions. TV; cable (premium). Heated pool; whirlpool. Complimentary full bkfst; evening refreshments. Coffee in rms. Restaurant opp 8 am-10 pm. Rm serv. Ck-out noon. Coin lndry. Meeting rms. Business servs avail. Bellhops. Gift shop. Valet serv. Sundries. Health club privileges. Refrigerators, microwaves. Grills. Cr cds: A, C, D, DS, JCB, MC, V. ☐ ☐ ☐ ☐ ☐ SC

★ ★ **WINDMILL INN AT ST PHILIP'S PLAZA.** *4250 N Campbell Ave (85718), in Foothills. 520/577-0007; FAX 520/577-0045; res: 800/547-4747.* Web www.mind.net/wind mills. 122 suites, 3 story. Oct-Apr: suites $115-$395; each addl $10; under 18 free; lower rates rest of yr. Pet accepted, some restrictions. TV; cable (premium); VCR avail. Heated pool; whirlpool. Complimentary continental bkfst. Complimentary coffee in lobby. Restaurant adj 11 am-11 pm. Ck-out 11 am. Coin lndry. Meeting rms. Business servs avail. Bathrm phones, refrigerators, microwaves, wet bars. Bicycles. Library. Cr cds: A, D, DS, MC, V. ☐ ☐ ☐ ☐ ☐ SC

Hotels

★ ★ **DOUBLETREE GUEST SUITES.** *6555 E Speedway Blvd (85710), in Midtown. 520/721-7100; FAX 520/721-1991.* 304 suites, 5 story. Jan-mid-May: suites $105-$160; under 17 free; honeymoon, wkend rates; lower rates rest of yr. Crib free. Pet accepted, some restrictions; $25. TV; cable (premium); VCR avail. Heated pool; whirlpool, poolside serv. Complimentary continental bkfst. Restaurant 6 am-11 pm. Bar. Ck-out noon. Coin lndry. Convention facilities. Business center. Gift shop. Indoor tennis privileges. Golf privileges. Exercise equipt; treadmill, bicycles. Health club privileges. Refrigerators; microwaves avail. Balconies. Picnic tables, grill. Cr cds: A, C, D, DS, JCB, MC, V. ☐ ☐ ☐ ☐ ☐ ☐ ☐ ☐

★ ★ **EMBASSY SUITES HOTEL & CONFERENCE CENTER.** *7051 S Tucson Blvd (85706), near Intl Airport, south of downtown. 520/573-0700; FAX 520/741-9645.* 204 kit. suites, 3 story. Jan-mid-May: S, D $139-$159; each addl $10; under 12 free; wkend rates; lower rates rest of yr. Crib free. Pet accepted. TV; cable (premium), VCR avail. Heated pool; whirlpool, poolside serv. Complimentary full bkfst. Coffee in rms. Restaurant 11 am-10 pm; Fri, Sat to 11 pm. Bar 11-1 am; Sun from 11 am. Ck-out 1 pm. Coin lndry. Meeting rms. Business servs avail. Gift shop. Free airport transportation. Exercise equipt; weight machines, rower. Wet bars, refrigerators. Grills. Cr cds: A, C, D, DS, ER, MC, V. ☐ ☐ ☐ ☐ ☐ ☐ ☐ SC

✔★★ **HOLIDAY INN-CITY CENTER.** *181 W Broadway (85701), downtown.* *520/624-8711; FAX 520/623-8121.* 309 rms, 14 story. Jan-mid-May: S $89-$135; D $99-$135; each addl $10; suites $185; under 18 free; lower rates rest of yr. Crib free. Pet accepted, some restrictions; $25 refundable. TV; cable (premium). Heated pool; poolside serv. Complimentary coffee in rms. Restaurant 6 am-2 pm, 5-10 pm. Bar 2:30 pm-midnight; wkends to 1 am. Ck-out noon. Convention facilities. Business servs avail. Concierge. Gift shop. Free garage parking. Exercise equipt; weight machine, stair machine. Health club privileges. Microwaves avail. Adj to Tucson Convention Center, music hall, theater, government offices. Cr cds: A, C, D, DS, ER, JCB, MC, V. ⒹⓇ🏊🏋️‍♂️↕️💆 SC

Resorts

★★★★ **SHERATON EL CONQUISTADOR RESORT & COUNTRY CLUB.** *10000 N Oracle Rd (85737), 15 mi N, in Foothills.* *520/544-5000; FAX 520/544-1224; res: 800/325-7832.* Web www.arizonaguide.com/sheraton_tucson. A huge copper mural filled with cowboys and cacti, as well as a wide-window view of one of the pools set against a backdrop of the rugged Santa Catalina Mountains, set the mood of this Southwestern resort. 428 rms. Jan-May: S, D $220-$290; suites, studio rms $265-$600; under 17 free; golf, tennis plans; lower rates rest of yr. Crib free. Pet accepted, some restrictions. TV; cable (premium), VCR avail. Pools; whirlpools, poolside serv. Supervised child's activities; ages 5-12. Coffee in rms. Dining rms 6 am-11 pm. Rm serv to 2 am. Bar to 1 am; Sun from 10:30 am; entertainment. Ck-out noon, ck-in 4 pm. Convention facilities. Business center. Bellhops. Valet serv. Concierge. Shopping arcade. Beauty shop. Pro shop. Sports dir. Lighted tennis, pro. 45-hole golf, greens fee (incl cart) $95-$135 ($48-$60 in summer), pro, putting green, driving range. Bicycles. Bkfst & evening horseback rides; hayrides. Exercise rm; instructor, weights, bicycles, sauna. Massage. Lawn games. Basketball. Hiking & nature trails. Minibars; some bathrm phones, wet bars, fireplaces; microwaves avail. Private patios, balconies. Cr cds: A, C, D, DS, ER, JCB, MC, V. ⒹⓇ🚴🏋️‍♂️🏊🏋️🧖↕️💆 SC

★★★ **WESTWARD LOOK.** *245 E Ina Rd (85704), in Foothills.* *520/297-1151; FAX 520/297-9023; res: 800/722-2500.* Web www.west wardlook.com. 244 rms, 2 story. Mid-Jan-Apr: S, D $169-$369; each addl $10; under 16 free; golf plans; hol rates; higher rates special events; lower rates rest of yr. Crib free. Pet accepted, some restrictions; $75 deposit. TV; cable (premium). 3 heated pools; whirlpools. Complimentary coffee in rms. Restaurants 7 am-2 pm, 5:30-10 pm. Rm serv. Box lunches, snacks, picnics. Bar 4 pm-1 am; entertainment Thurs-Sat. Ck-out noon, ck-in 4 pm. Coin lndry 6 mi. Gift shop. Grocery 1/4 mi. Bellhops. Valet serv. Concierge. Meeting rms. Business servs avail. In-rm modem link. Sports dir. Lighted tennis, pro. 18-hole golf privileges, greens fee $50-$150, pro, putting green, driving range. Lawn games. Exercise equipt; weights, bicycles. Massage. Some refrigerators, minibars. Some balconies. Bicycles. Cr cds: A, C, D, DS, MC, V.

ⒹⓇ🚴🏋️‍♂️🏊🏋️🧖↕️💆 SC

Tumacacori National Historical Park
(See also Nogales, Patagonia, Tucson)

(Exit 29 on I-19, 48 mi S of Tucson, 18 mi N of Nogales)

Motel

★★ **TUBAC GOLF RESORT.** *(Box 1297, Tubac 85646) On I-19, exit 40, 2 mi S on E Frontage Rd.* *520/398-2211; res: 800/848-7893.* 32 rms, 9 kits. Mid-Jan-mid-Apr: S, D $125; each addl $10; suites $155; lower rates rest of yr. Crib free. Pet accepted, some restrictions. TV. Heated pool. Complimentary coffee in rms. Restaurant 7 am-9 pm. Bar to 10 pm, Sun from 10 am. Ck-out noon. Coin lndry. Meeting rm. Tennis. 18-hole golf, greens fee $50 (incl cart), pro, putting green, pro shop. Refrigerators. Many fireplaces. Many private patios. Mexican decor. Pool area has mountain view. Cr cds: A, MC, V.

Ⓡ🏋️‍♂️🏋️🧖↕️💆 SC

Wickenburg *(See also Phoenix)*

Motel

✔★★ **BEST WESTERN RANCHO GRANDE.** *293 E Wickenburg Way (85390).* *520/684-5445; FAX 520/684-7380.* 80 rms, 1-2 story, 24 kits. Nov-Apr: S $61-$75; D $65-$79; each addl $3; suites $86-$99; higher rates special events; lower rates rest of yr. Crib $3. Pet accepted. TV; cable, VCR avail (movies). Heated pool; whirlpool. Playground. Complimentary coffee in rms. Restaurant nearby. Ck-out noon. Meeting rms. Business servs avail. Bellhops. Valet serv. Free airport transportation. Tennis. Golf privileges. Refrigerators; some bathrm phones, microwaves. Some private patios, balconies. Cr cds: A, C, D, DS, ER, JCB, MC, V. ⒹⓇ🏋️‍♂️🏋️🏊🧖↕️💆 SC

Willcox

Motels

✔ ★ ★ **BEST WESTERN PLAZA INN.** *1100 W Rex Allen Dr, I-10, exit 340.* 520/384-3556; FAX 520/384-2679. 92 rms, 2 story. S, D $59-$99; each addl $8; under 12 free. Crib free. Pet accepted, some restrictions; fee. TV; cable. Heated pool; whirlpool. Complimentary full bkfst. Coffee in rms. Restaurant 6 am-10 pm. Rm serv. Bar 4 pm-1 am. Ck-out noon. Coin lndry. Meeting rms. Business center. Many refrigerators. Cr cds: A, C, D, DS, MC, V.

✔ ★ ★ **DAYS INN.** *724 N Bisbee Ave.* 520/384-4222; FAX 520/384-3785. 73 rms, 2 story. June-Aug & Nov-Feb: S $38-$48; D $46-$56; each addl $5; under 18 free; higher rates Rex Allen Days; lower rates rest of yr. Crib free. Pet accepted, some restrictions. TV; cable. Heated pool. Complimentary coffee. Restaurant opp open 24 hrs. Ck-out 11 am. Coin lndry. Business servs avail. In-rm modem link. Cr cds: A, C, D, DS, ER, JCB, MC, V.

Williams (Coconino Co) *(See also Flagstaff)*

Motels

★ **MOTEL 6.** *831 W Bill Williams Ave.* 520/635-9000; FAX 520/635-2300. 52 rms, 2 story. June-Sept: S, D $45-$69; each addl $6; under 18 free; higher rates hols; lower rates rest of yr. Crib free. Pet accepted. TV, cable. Indoor pool; whirlpool. Restaurant opp 11 am-9 pm. Ck-out 11 am. Coin lndry. Business servs avail. Cr cds: A, C, D, DS, MC, V.

★ **RAMADA INN-CANYON GATEWAY.** *642 E Bill Williams Ave.* 520/635-4431; FAX 520/635-2292. E-mail ramada@thegrandcan yon.com. 96 rms, 2 story. Apr-Oct: S, D $95-$125; each addl $10; under 18 free; 2-day min stay hols; lower rates rest of yr. Crib free. Pet accepted. TV, cable. Heated pool; whirlpool. Restaurant 6 am-2 pm, 4-10 pm. Rm serv (evening only). Bar. Ck-out noon. Gift shop. Downhill ski 4 mi. Microwaves avail. Picnic tables. Cr cds: A, C, D, DS, MC, V.

Motor Hotel

★ ★ **HOLIDAY INN.** *950 N Grand Canyon Blvd.* 520/635-4114; FAX 520/635-2700. 120 rms, 2 story, 12 suites. S, D $79-$99; each addl $10; suites $99-$119; under 19 free; higher rates hols; lower rates rest of yr. Crib free. Pet accepted. TV; cable. Complimentary coffee in lobby. Restaurant 6-10 am, 5-10 pm; summer hrs 6 am-10 pm. Rm serv. Bar from 5 pm. Ck-out 11 am. Meeting rm. Business servs avail. Bellhops. Gift shop. Coin lndry. Downhill ski 5 mi. Indoor pool; whirlpool. Game rm. Some refrigerators. Wet bars in suites. 1 mi to lake. Cr cds: A, D, DS, MC, V.

Winslow *(See also Holbrook)*

Motels

★ ★ **BEST WESTERN ADOBE INN.** *1701 N Park Dr.* 520/289-4638; FAX 520/289-5514. 72 rms, 2 story. June-Aug: S $50-$56; D $54-$58; suites $68; under 18 free; lower rates rest of yr. Crib $4. Pet accepted, some restrictions. TV; cable (premium), VCR avail. Indoor pool; whirlpool. Restaurant 6 am-2 pm, 4-10 pm; Sun to 9 pm. Rm serv. Bar 4-11 pm, Sun to 10 pm. Ck-out 11 am. Coin lndry. Meeting rms. Business servs avail. Free airport, RR station, bus depot transportation. Cr cds: A, C, D, DS, MC, V.

✔ ★ **ECONO LODGE.** *1706 N Park Dr, N Park Dr & I-40 exit 253.* 520/289-4687; FAX 520/289-9377. 72 rms, 2 story. Late May-Sept: S, D $45-$59; under 18 free; lower rates rest of yr. Pet accepted; $5/day. TV; cable (premium), VCR avail. Pool. Complimentary coffee in rms. Ck-out 11 am. Coin lndry. Business servs avail. Some refrigerators, microwaves. Cr cds: A, C, D, DS, JCB, MC, V.

Yuma

Motels

★ ★ **BEST WESTERN INNSUITES.** *1450 Castle Dome Ave (85365).* 520/783-8341; FAX 520/783-1349. E-mail isyuma@attmail.com; web www.innsuites.com. 166 rms. Jan-Apr: S $84-$99; D $89-$119; 2-rm suites $94-$139; under 20 free; higher rates opening wk dove season; lower rates rest of yr. Crib free. Pet accepted. TV; cable (premium), VCR avail. Heated pool; whirlpool. Coffee in rm. Complimentary continental bkfst. Ck-out noon. Coin lndry. Business center. In-rm modem link. Valet serv. Lighted tennis. Exercise equipt;

stair machine, weights. Refrigerators, microwaves. Library. Cr cds: A, C, D, DS, JCB, MC, V. 🅳 👋 🛌 ≈ 🍴 🚳 🐾 SC 🏃

✔ ★ **INTERSTATE 8 INN.** *2730 S 4th Ave (85364). 520/726-6110; res: 800/821-7465; FAX 520/726-7711.* 120 rms, 2 story. Jan-Mar: S $33.95; D $52.95; each addl $6; under 13 free; higher rates special events; lower rates rest of yr. Crib free. Pet accepted, some restrictions. TV; cable (premium), VCR avail (movies). Complimentary coffee in lobby. Restaurant adj 6 am-11 pm. Ck-out 11 am. Business servs avail. Coin lndry. Pool; whirlpool. Refrigerators; microwaves avail. Picnic tables, grills. Cr cds: A, C, D, DS, ER, JCB, MC. 👋 ≈ 🚳 🐾

★ ★ **RADISSON SUITES INN.** *2600 S 4th Ave (85364). 520/726-4830; FAX 520/341-1152.* Web www.radisson.com. 164 suites, 3 story. Oct-Apr: S $106; D $116; each addl $10; under 16 free; lower rates rest of yr. Crib free. Pet accepted. TV; cable (premium). Heated pool; whirlpool. Complimentary continental bkfst. Complimentary coffee in rms. Restaurant adj open 24 hrs. Ck-out noon. Meeting rms. Business servs avail. Bellhops. Valet serv. Free airport, RR station, bus depot transportation. Health club privileges. Refrigerators, microwaves, wet bars. Cr cds: A, C, D, DS, ER, JCB, MC, V. 🅳 👋 ≈ 🚳 🐾 SC

✔ ★ ★ **TRAVELODGE-AIRPORT.** *711 E 32nd St (85365). 520/726-4721; FAX 520/344-0452.* 80 rms, 2 story. S $54; D $62; each addl $5; suites $78; under 17 free; higher rates special events (2-day min); lower rates rest of yr. Crib free. Pet accepted, some restrictions; $25 deposit. TV; cable (premium), VCR avail (movies). Complimentary continental bkfst. Complimentary coffee in rms. Restaurant 11 am-10 pm. Bar. Ck-out noon. Business servs avail. Coin lndry. Health club privileges. Pool; whirlpool. Refrigerators; microwaves avail. Wet bar in suites. Picnic tables, grills. Cr cds: A, C, D, DS, JCB, MC, V. 🅳 👋 ≈ 🚳 🐾 SC

Motor Hotel

★ ★ ★ **SHILO INN.** *1550 S Castle Dome Rd (85365), off I-8 exit 16th St. 520/782-9511; FAX 520/783-1538.* 134 rms, 4 story, 15 kits. S, D $85-$139; each addl $12; kit. units $105-$250; patio-side rms $105-$110; under 12 free; higher rates dove season. Crib free. Pet accepted. TV; cable (premium), VCR avail. Heated pool; whirlpool, poolside serv. Complimentary continental bkfst. Coffee in rm. Restaurant 6 am-10 pm. Rm serv. Bar to midnight. Ck-out noon. Coin lndry. Meeting rms. Business servs avail. Valet serv. Exercise equipt; weight machines, bicycles, sauna, steam rm. Bathrm phones, refrigerators. Microwave avail. Private patios, balconies. Cr cds: A, C, D, DS, ER, JCB, MC, V. 🅳 👋 ≈ 🍴 🚳 🐾 SC

Arkansas

Arkadelphia *(See also Hot Springs)*

Motels

★ ★ **BEST WESTERN CONTINENTAL INN.** *I-30 & US 67. 870/246-5592; FAX 870/246-3585.* 59 rms, 2 story. S, D $52; each addl $5; family rates; higher rates hols. Crib free. Pet accepted. TV; cable (premium), VCR avail. Complimentary coffee in rms. Restaurant 6 am-10 pm. Rm serv. Ck-out 11 am. Coin lndry. Pool. Playground. Cr cds: A, C, D, DS, MC, V. 🄳 🐾 ⚱ 🏋 🐾 SC

✔ ★ **QUALITY INN.** *Jct AR 7, I-30. 870/246-5855; FAX 870/246-8552.* 63 rms, 2 story. S, D $40-$59; under 16 free. Crib $1. Pet accepted. TV; cable (premium). Pool. Coffee in lobby. Ck-out noon. Coin lndry. Some in-rm whirlpools; microwaves avail. Cr cds: A, C, D, DS, ER, JCB, MC, V. 🐾 🐾 ⚱ 🏋 🐾 SC

Batesville *(See also Greers Ferry Lake Area, Mountain View, Newport)*

Motel

★ ★ **RAMADA INN.** *1325 N St Louis, Hwy 167 N. 870/698-1800.* 124 units, 2 story. S $53; D $59; each addl $6; suites $95; under 18 free. Crib free. Pet accepted. TV; cable (premium). Pool; whirlpool. Coffee in rms. Restaurant 6 am-2 pm, 5-9:45 pm; Sun 6 am-2 pm. Rm serv. Private club 4 pm-midnight. Ck-out noon. Coin lndry. Meeting rms. Some refrigerators; microwaves avail. Cr cds: A, C, D, DS, ER, JCB, MC, V.

🄳 🐾 ⚱ 🏋 🐾 SC

Benton *(See also Hot Springs, Little Rock)*

Motel

★ **DAYS INN.** *17701 I-30, exit 118. 501/776-3200; FAX 501/776-0906.* 117 rms, 2 story. S $42; D $50; each addl $5; under 18 free. Crib free. Pet accepted; $5. TV; cable (premium), VCR avail. Pool. Complimentary coffee in lobby. Restaurant adj 6-1 am. Ck-out 11 am. Coin lndry. Meeting rms. Business servs avail. Valet serv. Sundries. Cr cds: A, C, D, DS, MC, V. 🄳 🐾 ⚱ 🏋 🐾 SC

Bentonville *(See also Fayetteville, Rogers, Springdale)*

Motels

★ **BEST WESTERN.** *2307 SE Walton Blvd, US 71 exit 65. 501/273-9727; FAX 501/273-1763.* 54 rms, 2 story. S $43-$47; D $47; each addl $5; suite $85; under 12 free; higher rates special events. Crib $5. Pet accepted, some restrictions; $5. TV; cable (premium). Pool. Complimentary coffee in lobby. Restaurant adj 6 am-10 pm. Ck-out 11 am. Business servs avail. In-rm modem link. Many refrigerators; microwaves avail. Cr cds: A, C, D, DS, MC, V. 🐾 ⚱ 🏋 🐾 SC

★ **SUPERIOR INN.** *2301 SE Walton Blvd, US 71W, exit 62. 501/273-1818; FAX 501/273-5529.* 52 rms, 2 story. S $47.60; D $52.73; suite $77.70; higher rates special events. Crib avail. Pet accepted. TV; cable (premium). Pool. Complimentary continental bkfst. Restaurant adj 6 am-11:30 pm. Ck-out 11 am. Free airport transportation. Picnic tables. Cr cds: A, DS, MC, V. 🄳 🐾 ⚱ 🏋 🐾 SC

Blytheville

Motels

★ **ECONO LODGE.** *301 Access Rd, ¹/₂ mi NE of jct AR 18, I-55 exit 67. 870/763-5220.* 87 rms, 2 story. S $41.50; D $45.50; each addl $4; under 12 free. Crib free. Pet accepted. TV; cable (premium). Pool. Complimentary continental bkfst. Restaurant 10 am-9 pm. Ck-out noon. Microwaves avail. Cr cds: A, C, D, DS, MC, V.
🄳 🐾 ⚱ 🏋 🐾 SC

★ ★ **HOLIDAY INN.** *AR 18E & I-55, E Main St. 870/763-5800; FAX 870/763-1326* 153 rms, 2 story. Mar-mid-Sept: S, D $65; under 19 free; wkend rates; lower rates rest of y Crib free. Pet accepted. TV; cable (premium). 2 pools, 1 indoor; whirlpool, steam poolside serv. Restaurant 5:30 am-11 pm. Rm serv. Bar 4 pm-1 am, closed Sun; entertainment. Ck-out noon. Coin lndry. Meeting rms. Holidome. Cr cds: A, C, D, DS, MC, V.

[D] [⊷] [≊] [⊠] [⋈] [SC]

Bull Shoals Lake Area (See also Harrison, Mountain Home)

Motel

★ **THEODOSIA MARINA RESORT.** *(Lake Rd 160-25, Theodosia MO 65761) 417/273-4444; FAX 417/273-4263.* 20 rms, 7 kit. cottages. Mar-Sept: S $35-$45; D $50-$55; each addl $5; under 6 free; hols 3-day min; lower rates rest of yr. Crib $5. Pet accepted; $2. TV; cable. Restaurant 7 am-9 pm. Ck-out 2 pm. Meeting rms. Coin lndry. Lighted tennis. Pool. Playground. Refrigerators; some microwaves. Balconies. Picnic tables, grills. On lake. Cr cds: A, DS, MC, V. [D] [⊷] [≊] [ᴈ] [⋈] [≊] [⋈] [SC]

Resort

★ ★ ★ **GASTON'S WHITE RIVER RESORT.** *(1777 River Rd, Lakeview 72642) 3 mi SE of dam, 2 mi off AR 178.* 870/431-5202; FAX 870/431-5216. 74 cottages (1-10 bedrm), 1-2 story, 47 kits. (with boat). S, D $69-$83; each addl $14; suites $98-$146; cottages $83-$805; kits. $83.25; under 6 free; fishing rates. Crib free. Pet accepted. TV; cable. Pool. Playground. Dining rm 6:30 am-10 pm. Box lunches, shore lunches, picnics, cookouts. Bar. Ck-out 11 am. Grocery. Meeting rms. Business center. In-rm modem link. Gift shop. Airport, bus depot transportation. Tennis. 9, 18-hole golf privileges, greens fee $9, $12.50. Boats, motors. Dock. Lawn games. Rec rm. Fishing guides; clean, store area. Hiking trail; riverside walk. 3,200-ft private landing strip. Refrigerators, fireplaces. Private patios, balconies. Picnic tables. On river. Cr cds: MC, V. [D] [⊷] [⊷] [ᴈ] [ᴈ] [≊] [⋈] [⋈] [⋈]

Cottage Colony

↙ ★ **SHADY OAKS.** *(HC 62, Box 128, Flippin 72634) 5 mi S on AR 178, on Jimmie Creek arm of Bull Shoals Lake.* 870/453-8420; FAX 870/453-7813; res: 800/467-6257. 11 kit. cottages (1, 2 & 4 bedrm). Cottages $60-$75. Crib free. Pet accepted. TV, VCR avail. Pool. Playground. Restaurant 4¹/₂ mi, 6 am-10 pm. Ck-out 10 am, ck-in 3 pm. Coin lndry. Grocery 5 mi. Package store 7 mi. Airport transportation. Boats, motors; lighted dock. Game rm. Rec rm. Lawn games. Fishing guides; clean, store. Refrigerators, microwaves. Private patios. Picnic tables, grills. Lake swimming, waterskiing, scuba diving. Nature walks. Cr cds: DS, MC, V. [⊷] [⊷] [≊] [⋈] [SC]

Conway (See also Morrilton)

Motels

↙ ★ ★ **BEST WESTERN.** *Box 1619 (72032), Jct I-40, US 64E at exit 127.* 501/329-9855; FAX 501/327-6110. 70 rms, 2 story. S $39-$59; D $46-$69; each addl $7; suites $66-$76; under 17 free. Crib $5. Pet accepted. TV; cable (premium). Pool. Restaurant open 24 hrs. Ck-out noon. In-rm modem link. Coin lndry. Valet serv. Microwaves avail. Cr cds: A, C, D, DS, MC, V. [D] [⊷] [≊] [⋈] [⋈] [SC]

★ **COMFORT INN.** *150 AR 65 (72032), I-40 & US 65N, exit 125.* 501/329-0300; FAX 501/329-8367. 60 rms, 2 story. May-Oct: S $47-$52; D $59-$69; each addl $5; suites $59; under 12 free; lower rates rest of yr. Crib $5. Pet accepted, some restrictions. TV; cable (premium). Pool. Complimentary continental bkfst. Restaurant opp 11 am-10 pm. Ck-out 11 am. Meeting rm. Business servs avail. Microwaves avail. Cr cds: A, C, D, DS, ER, JCB, MC, V. [D] [⊷] [≊] [⋈] [⋈] [SC]

★ ★ **RAMADA INN.** *815 E Oak St, US 64 at I-40, exit 127.* 501/329-8392; FAX 501/329-0430. 78 rms, 2 story. S $46-$60; D $52-$66; each addl $6; under 18 free. Crib free. Pet accepted, some restrictions. TV; cable (premium). Heated pool. Restaurant 6 am-9 pm. Rm serv. Ck-out noon. Meeting rms. Business servs avail. In-rm modem link. Airport transportation. Sundries. Some refrigerators. Cr cds: A, C, D, DS, ER, JCB, MC, V.

[D] [⊷] [≊] [⋈] [⋈] [SC]

?umas

★ **RAMADA LIMITED.** *722 Hwy 65S, 1 mi S on US 65.* 870/382-2707. 52 rms. S $36; D $40; each addl $4. Crib $2. Pet accepted. TV; cable. Pool. Complimentary ... tal bkfst. Ck-out noon. Coin lndry. Some refrigerators; microwaves avail. Cr cds: A, MC, V. [D] [⊷] [≊] [⋈] [⋈] [SC]

El Dorado *(See also Camden, Magnolia)*

Motel

✓★★ **COMFORT INN.** *2303 Junction City Rd, AR 167 exit 82. 870/863-6677; FAX 870/863-8611.* 70 units, 2 story. S, D $57-$63; each addl $7; under 12 free. Crib free. Pet accepted. TV; cable (premium). Pool; whirlpool. Complimentary continental bkfst. Ck-out noon. Coin lndry. In-rm modem link. Free airport transportation. Balconies. Cr cds: A, C, D, DS, MC, V. [D] [icons]

Motor Hotel

★★ **BEST WESTERN KINGS INN CONFERENCE CENTER.** *1920 Junction City Rd, AR 167 exit 82B. 870/862-5191; FAX 870/863-7511.* 131 rms, 2 story. S $59-$65; D $65-$71; each addl $7; wkend rates. Crib free. Pet accepted. TV; cable (premium). 2 pools, 1 indoor; wading pool, whirlpool, sauna. Playground. Restaurant 6 am-2 pm, 5-9 pm. Rm serv. Private club 4-11 pm. Ck-out noon. Coin lndry. Meeting rms. Business servs avail. Valet serv. Sundries. Airport transportation. Lighted tennis. Refrigerators; microwaves avail. Balconies. Picnic tables. On 8 acres. Cr cds: A, C, D, DS, ER, JCB, MC, V. [icons]

Eureka Springs *(See also Harrison, Rogers)*

Motels

★★ **1876 INN.** *Rte 6, Box 247, US 62E & AR 23S. 501/253-7183; res: 800/643-3030.* E-mail inn1876@ipa.net; web www.eureka-usa.com/ac/1876.html. 72 rms, 3 story. Mid-June-Sept: S $59.50-$62; D $60-$65; each addl $6; under 15 free; higher rates Oct; lower rates Mar-mid-June. Closed rest of yr. Crib free. Pet accepted, some restrictions; $10. TV; cable. Heated pool; whirlpool. Complimentary morning coffee. Restaurant 6:30-11 am, 5-8 pm. Ck-out 11 am. Business servs avail. In-rm modem link. Gift shop. Balconies. Cr cds: A, DS, MC, V. [D] [icons]

★★ **ALPEN-DORF.** *Rte 4, Box 580, 3½ mi E on US 62. 501/253-9475; res: 800/771-9876; FAX 501/253-2928.* E-mail alp dorf@ipa.net; web www.eureka-usa.com. 30 rms, 2 story. Mid-May-late Oct: S $38-$42; D $42-$59; each addl $5; suites $79-$99; kit. units $65-$75; under 18 free; lower rates rest of yr. Pet accepted. TV; cable. Pool. Playground. Restaurant nearby. Ck-out 11 am. Cr cds: A, DS, MC, V. [icons]

✓★★★ **BEST WESTERN INN OF THE OZARKS.** *Box 431, 1 mi W on US 62. 501/253-9768; res: 800/552-3785.* 122 rms, 2 story. S $32-$69; D $38-$73; each addl $5; suites $85-$125; under 18 free; higher rates: some hol wkends, War Eagle festival. Crib free. Pet accepted. TV; cable (premium), VCR avail. Heated pool. Restaurant 6:30 am-9 pm. Serv bar. Ck-out 11 am. Coin lndry. Meeting rms. Business servs avail. In-rm modem link. Lighted tennis. Golf privileges, greens fee $20. Rec rm. Some bathrm phones; wet bar in suites. Some balconies. Picnic tables. Cr cds: A, C, D, DS, MC, V. [icons]

★★ **COLONIAL MANSION INN.** *AR 23S. 501/253-7300; FAX 501/523-7149; res: 800/638-2622.* 30 rms, 2 story. Apr-Nov: S, D $24-$75; each addl $6-$8; suites (up to 6 persons) $95-$120; package plans; higher rates special events; lower rates rest of yr. Crib $5. Pet accepted, some restrictions. TV; cable. Pool. Complimentary continental bkfst. Restaurant nearby. Ck-out 11 am. Business servs avail. In-rm whirlpool in suite. Cr cds: A, DS, MC, V. [icons]

★★ **DOGWOOD INN.** *AR 23S, ¼ mi S of US 62. 501/253-7200; res: 800/544-1884.* 33 rms, 2 story. June-Oct: S $42-$48; D $48-$56; each addl $5; higher rates special events; lower rates rest of yr. Crib $5. Pet accepted; $10. TV; cable (premium). Pool; whirlpool. Playground. Complimentary continental bkfst. Restaurant nearby. Ck-out 11 am. Business servs avail. In-rm modem link. Cr cds: A, DS, MC, V. [icons]

✓★ **ROADRUNNER INN.** *RR 2 Box 158. 501/253-8166; res: 888/253-8166.* 12 kit. units, shower only, 2 story. June-Aug & Oct: S $32-$36; D $36-$40; each addl $6; higher rates special events; lower rates rest of yr. Closed mid-Nov-mid Mar. Crib free. Pet accepted. TV. Complimentary coffee in rms. Restaurant nearby. Ck-out 11 am. Refrigerators; microwaves avail. Picnic tables, grills. Overlooks lake. Cr cds: A, D, MC, V. [icons]

★★ **SWISS VILLAGE.** *Rte 6, Box 5, ½ mi SE on US 62. 501/253-9541; res: 800/447-6525.* 55 rms, 2 story. Mid-May-Aug, Oct: S, D $55-$72; suites $77-$150; lower rates Mar-mid-May, Sept, Nov. Closed rest of yr. Crib free. Pet accepted. TV; cable (premium), VCR avail. Heated pool; whirlpool. Complimentary continental bkfst. Restaurant nearby. Ck-out 11 am. Some in-rm whirlpools. Balconies. Sun decks. Picnic tables. Cr cds: A, DS, MC, V. [D] [♦] [≈] [⊠] [🐾] [SC]

✔★ **TRADEWINDS.** *77 Kings Hwy, on US 62. 501/253-9774; res: 800/242-1615.* 17 units, 1 kit. Apr-Nov: S $24-$52; D $28-$56; each addl $6; suites $45-$80; higher rates special events. Closed rest of yr. Crib $4. Pet accepted, some restrictions. TV; cable. Pool. Complimentary coffee. Restaurant nearby. Ck-out 11 am. Microwaves avail. Picnic tables. Cr cds: A, DS, MC, V. [♦] [≈] [⊠] [🐾]

Hotel

✔★ **BASIN PARK.** *12 Spring St. 501/253-7837; FAX 501/253-6985; res: 800/643-4972.* E-mail www.pimps.com/eureka/hotel/basinprk.html. 61 rms, 6 story. S, D $66-$81; suites $90-$175; under 12 free; higher rates Blues Fest. Crib free. Pet accepted. TV; cable, VCR avail (movies). Complimentary continental bkfst. Restaurant 11 am-9 pm. Bar. Ck-out 11 am. Meeting rms. Business servs avail. Some in-rm whirlpools; microwaves avail. Historic hotel built 1905. Overlooks Basin Park and Spring. Cr cds: A, DS, MC, V. [D] [♦] [⊠] [🐾] [SC]

Fayetteville *(See also Rogers, Springdale)*

Motels

(Prices are generally higher on football wkends)

★★ **BEST WESTERN WINDSOR SUITES.** *1122 S Futrall Dr (72701), at US 71 & 62. 501/587-1400.* 68 rms, 2 story, 37 suites. S $55-$70; D $60-$75; each addl $5; suites $65-$105; under 18 free; higher rates special events. Crib free. Pet accepted, some restrictions. TV; cable (premium), VCR avail. Complimentary continental bkfst. Complimentary coffee in rms. Restaurant nearby. Ck-out 11 am. Meeting rms. Business center. In-rm modem link. Coin lndry. Exercise equipt; weights, bicycle. Indoor pool; whirlpool. Bathrm phone, in-rm whirlpool in suites. Some refrigerators, wet bars; microwaves avail. Cr cds: A, C, D, DS, JCB, MC, V. [D] [♦] [≈] [🏃] [⊠] [🐾] [SC] [⚓]

✔★★ **DAYS INN.** *2402 N College Ave (72703). 501/443-4323.* 150 rms, 2 story, 6 suites. S, D $45-$72; each addl $5; suites $80-$115. Crib free. Pet accepted; some restrictions, $50 deposit. TV; cable (premium), VCR avail. Pool. Complimentary continental bkfst. Ck-out noon. Coin lndry. Meeting rms. Business servs avail. Cr cds: A, C, D, DS, MC, V. [♦] [≈] [⊠] [🐾] [SC]

✔★ **INN OF FAYETTEVILLE.** *1000 US 71 (72701). 501/442-3041; FAX 501/442-0744.* 105 units, 2 story. S, D $43-$48; each addl $5; suites $69; under 16 free; wkly rates. Pet accepted; $10. TV; cable. Pool. Complimentary continental bkfst. Coffee in rms. Ck-out noon. Microwaves avail; refrigerator in suites. Cr cds: A, C, D, DS, MC, V. [D] [♦] [≈] [⊠] [🐾] [SC]

★★ **RAMADA INN.** *3901 N College Ave (72703). 501/443-3431; FAX 501/443-1927.* 120 rms, 2 story. S $49-$59; D $55-$65; each addl $6; under 18 free. Crib free. Pet accepted. TV; cable (premium). Pool. Playground. Restaurant 6 am-9 pm. Rm serv. Private club 5 pm-1 am. Ck-out noon. Meeting rms. Business servs avail. Valet serv. Tennis. Health club privileges. Cr cds: A, C, D, DS, MC, V. [♦] [🏃] [≈] [⊠] [🐾] [SC]

★★ **HILTON.** *70 N East Ave (72701). 501/442-5555; FAX 501/442-2105.* 235 rms, 15 story. S $61-$92; D $69-$100; each addl $8; suites $150-$299. Crib free. Pet accepted. TV; cable (premium), VCR avail. Indoor/outdoor pool. Restaurant 6 am-9 pm; wkends from 6:30 am. Bar 3 pm-midnight. Meeting rm. Business servs avail. Gift shop. Free parking. Free airport, bus depot transportation. Exercise equipt; weights, bicycles. Microwaves avail. Cr cds: A, C, D, DS, ER, MC, V. [D] [♦] [≈] [🏃] [⊠] [🐾] [SC]

Forrest City *(See also Helena)*

Motel

★★ **BEST WESTERN-BRINKLEY.** *(1306 N AR 17, Brinkley 72021) approx 20 mi W on I-40, exit 216. 870/734-1650; FAX 870/734-1657.* 100 rms, 2 story. S $54.50; D $59.50; each addl $5; under 12 free; higher rates duck season. Crib $3. Pet accepted, some restrictions. TV; cable. Complimentary full bkfst. Restaurant 6 am-9 pm. Ck-out noon. Exercise equipt; weights, treadmill. Pool. Playground. Some-in rm whirlpools. Picnic tables, grills. Cr cds: A, C, D, DS, ER, JCB, MC, V. [D] [♦] [≈] [🏃] [⊠] [🐾] [SC]

Fort Smith

Motels

↙★ **BEST WESTERN.** *101 N 11th St (72901). 501/785-4121; FAX 501/785-0316.* 129 rms, 2 story. S $43-$47; D $48; each addl $5; suites $63-$100; under 12 free. Crib free. Pet accepted. TV; cable (premium). Pool. Restaurant 6 am-2 pm, 4-9 pm. Rm serv. Private club Mon-Thurs 3 pm-5 am; Fri-Sun from 7 pm; entertainment. Ck-out noon. Meeting rms. Business servs avail. Free airport, bus depot transportation. Wet bar, microwave in suites. Cr cds: A, C, D, DS, ER, JCB, MC, V. D ⊶ ☰ ⊠ ⊠ SC

★★ **FOUR POINTS BY SHERATON.** *5711 Rogers Ave (72901), I-540 (AR 22) exit 8. 501/452-4110; FAX 501/452-4891.* 151 rms, 2 story. S, D $59.95; each addl $10; suites $160. Crib $10. Pet accepted. TV; cable (premium). Pool; wading pool. Complimentary full bkfst. Coffee in rms. Restaurant 6-9:30 am, 11 am-2 pm, 5-9:30 pm. Rm serv. Private club 5 pm-2 am. Ck-out noon. Meeting rms. Business servs avail. In-rm modem link. Airport transportation. Refrigerators; microwaves avail. Grills. Cr cds: A, C, D, DS, MC, V. D ⊶ ☰ ✕ ⊠ ⊠ SC

Hotel

★★ **HOLIDAY INN CIVIC CENTER.** *700 Rogers Ave (72901). 501/783-1000; FAX 501/783-0312.* E-mail fsm@tjqh@ibm.net. 255 units, 9 story. S, D $91; each addl $10; suites $97.50-$130; under 18 free; wkend rates. Crib free. Pet accepted, some restrictions. TV; cable (premium). Indoor pool; whirlpools. Restaurant 6 am-2 pm, 5-10 pm. Private club 3 pm-1 am; entertainment. Ck-out noon. Convention facilities. Business servs avail. In-rm modem link. Gift shop. Valet parking. Free airport, bus depot transportation. Exercise equipt; bicycles, treadmills, sauna. Some refrigerators. Cr cds: A, C, D, DS, JCB, MC, V. D ⊶ ☰ ✕ ⊠ ⊠ SC

Greers Ferry Lake Area *(See also Batesville, Mountain View)*

Motel

↙★ **BUDGET INN.** *(616 W Main St, Heber Springs 72543) At jct AR 25B, 110. 501/362-8111; res: 888/297-7955.* 25 rms. S $36; D $42; each addl $5; suites, studio rms $47. Crib $5. Pet accepted. TV; cable. Pool. Complimentary coffee. Restaurant nearby. Ck-out 11 am. Cr cds: A, D, DS, MC, V. ⊶ ☰ ⊠ ⊠ SC

Harrison *(See also Bull Shoals Lake Area, Eureka Springs)*

Motels

↙★ **RAMADA INN.** *1222 N Main St. 870/741-7611; FAX 870/741-7610.* 100 rms, 2 story. June-Oct: S $49-$55; D $56-$58; each addl $7; under 18 free; higher rates: some hol wkends, War Eagle wkend; lower rates rest of yr. Crib free. Pet accepted; some restrictions. TV; cable (premium). Pool; wading pool. Playground. Ck-out noon. Meeting rms. Business servs avail. Sundries. Lighted tennis. Game rm. Cr cds: A, C, D, DS, MC, V. D ⊶ ⊼ ☰ ⊠ ⊠ SC

★★ **SUPER 8.** *1330 US 62/65N. 870/741-1741; FAX 870/741-8858.* 50 units, 2 story. June-Oct: S $50; D $55; under 12 free; lower rates rest of yr. Crib free. Pet accepted; some restrictions. TV; cable (premium), VCR avail (movies). Pool. Continental bkfst. Restaurant nearby. Ck-out 11 am. Business servs avail. Game rm. Some in-rm whirlpools. Cr cds: A, C, D, DS, MC, V. D ⊶ ☰ ⊠ ⊠ SC

Helena *(See also Forrest City)*

Motel

↙★ **DELTA INN.** *(1207 US 49N, West Helena 72390) 3 mi N on US 49. 870/572-7915; FAX 870/572-3757; res: 800/748-8802.* 100 rms. S $37; D $42; each addl $5; kit. units $48; under 16 free. Crib $5. Pet accepted. TV; cable (premium). Pool. Complimentary continental bkfst. Restaurant nearby. Ck-out 11 am. Business servs avail. Cr cds: A, D, DS, MC, V. D ⊶ ☰ ⊠ ⊠ SC

Hope *(See also Texarkana, TX)*

Motels

★ **BEST WESTERN.** *I-30 & AR 4, exit 30.* 870/777-9222; FAX 870/777-9077. 75 rms, 2 story. S $38-$42; D $48-$52; under 12 free. Crib $10. Pet accepted. TV; cable (premium). Pool. Coffee in rms. Restaurant adj 6 am-10 pm. Ck-out noon. Coin lndry. Bathrm phones, refrigerators. Cr cds: A, C, D, DS, ER, MC, V. 🄳 📮 ⛖ 🇽 🐾

✔ ★ **SUPER 8.** *2000 Holiday Dr, jct I-30, AR 4.* 870/777-8601; FAX 870/777-3142. 100 rms, 2 story. S $26.88; D $35.88; each addl $7; under 12 free. Crib free. Pet accepted. TV; cable (premium). Pool. Playground. Complimentary continental bkfst. Coffee in rms. Ck-out noon. Coin lndry. Meeting rms. Business servs avail. Tennis. Lawn games. Some refrigerators; microwaves avail. Landscaped grounds; bridges. Cr cds: A, C, D, DS, MC, V. 🄳 📮 🏃 ⛖ 🇽 🐾 SC

Hot Springs & Hot Springs National Park

Motels

(All prices are considerably higher during the Thoroughbred racing season, Jan-Apr)

★ ★ **AVANELLE MOTOR LODGE.** *(1204 Central Ave, Hot Springs National Park 71902)* 501/321-1332; res: 800/225-1360. 88 rms, 2 story, 16 kits. S $44-$50; D $49-$54; each addl $5; suites from $62; kit. units $54-$58; under 12 free. Crib $2. Pet accepted. TV; cable (premium). Heated pool. Restaurant 6 am-2 pm; 6-10 pm. Rm serv. Ck-out 11 am. Meeting rms. Cr cds: A, C, D, DS, MC, V. 📮 ⛖ 🇽 🐾 SC

★ ★ **HAMPTON INN.** *(151 Temperance Hill Rd., Hot Springs 71913)* 501/525-7000; FAX 501/525-7626. 83 rms, 4 story, 17 suites. S $72-$89; D $81-$99; suites $114-$124; under 18 free. Crib free. Pet accepted, some restrictions. TV; cable (premium). Complimentary continental bkfst. Restaurant nearby. Ck-out noon. In-rm modem link. Valet serv. Sundries. Coin lndry. Health club privileges. Pool. Some bathrm phones, in-rm whirlpools. Refrigerator, microwave, wet bar in suites. Cr cds: A, C, D, DS, MC, V. 🄳 📮 ⛖ 🇽 🐾 SC

★ **QUALITY INN.** *(1125 E Grand Ave, Hot Springs 71901)* 501/624-3321; FAX 501/624-5814. 138 rms, 2 story. S, D $45-$65; each addl $5; under 18 free. Crib $4. Pet accepted; $5. TV; cable (premium). Pool; whirlpool. Playground. Restaurant 6 am-2 pm, 5-9 pm; Sun to 2 pm. Rm serv. Bar. Ck-out 11 am. Meeting rm. In-rm modem link. Game rm. Refrigerators, microwaves avail. Cr cds: A, C, D, DS, MC, V. 🄳 📮 ⛖ 🇽 🐾 SC

Hotels

★ ★ **CLARION RESORT ON THE LAKE.** *(4813 Central Ave, Hot Springs 71913)* 501/525-1391; FAX 501/525-0813. 149 rms, 7 story. May-Sept: S $79.95-$125.95; D $89-$135.95; each addl $10; under 12 free; lower rates rest of yr. Crib avail. Pet accepted. TV; cable (premium). Pool. Continental bkfst. Restaurant 11 am-10 pm. Bar 5 pm-1 am. Ck-out 11 am. Coin lndry. Meeting rms. Business servs avail. Tennis. Golf privileges. Health club privileges. Boat rentals, waterskiing. Playground. Some refrigerators. Microwaves avail. Balconies. Cr cds: A, C, DS, MC, V. 🄳 📮 📮 🏃 ⛖ 🇽 🐾

★ ★ **RAMADA INN TOWER.** *(218 Park Ave, Hot Springs 71901)* 501/623-3311; FAX 501/623-8871. 191 rms, 9 story. S $69-$79; D $79-$89; each addl $10; suites $89-$250; under 18 free. Crib free. Pet accepted. TV; cable (premium). Heated pool; wading pool. Restaurant 6 am-2 pm, 5-10 pm. Bar 4:30 pm-1 am; entertainment. Ck-out noon. Meeting rms. Business servs avail. In-rm modem link. Golf privileges. Balconies. Cr cds: A, C, D, DS, MC, V. 🄳 📮 🏃 ⛖ 🇽 🐾 SC

Resort

★ ★ **LAKE HAMILTON RESORT.** *(2803 Albert Pike, Hot Springs 71913) 3 mi W on US 270.* 501/767-5511; FAX 501/767-8576; res: 800/426-3184. E-mail lhresort@dire clynx.net; web www.cabotar .com/hamilton/resort.htm. 104 suites, 3 story. Jan-Oct: suites $79-$94; under 18 free; lower rates rest of yr. Closed Dec. Crib free. Pet accepted. TV; cable. 2 pools, 1 indoor; whirlpool, sauna. Playground. Restaurant 7 am-9 pm. Box lunches. Picnics. Rm serv. Bar 4 pm-1 am. Ck-out noon, ck-in 2 pm. Coin lndry. Convention facilities. Business servs avail. In-rm modem link. Valet. Grocery, package store ½ mi. Airport transportation. Lighted tennis. Private swimming beach. Boat dock, launching ramp, rentals; motorboats; waterskiing. Entertainment. Exercise equipt; bicycle, treadmill. Game rm. Fishing guides. Refrigerators. Microwaves avail. Balconies. Picnic tables, grills. Scenic view from all rms. 10 acres on Lake Hamilton; elaborate landscaping. Fountain; duck pond; lakeside gazebo. Cr cds: A, C, D, DS, MC, V. [symbols]

Cottage Colonies

★★ **BUENA VISTA RESORT.** *(201 Aberina St, Hot Springs 71913) 4 mi S on AR 7, then* $1/2$ *mi SE. 501/525-1321; res: 800/255-9030 (exe AR); FAX 501/525-8293.* 50 kit. units, 1-2 story. June-Aug: S, D $69-$101; each addl $5; suites $120; under 5 free. Crib $5. Pet accepted, some restrictions. TV; cable. Pool. Playground. Ck-out 11 am, ck-in 3 pm. Coin lndry. Package store $1^1/2$ mi. Conference center. Business servs avail. Lighted tennis. Miniature golf. Lawn games. Rec rm. Game rm. Fishing; clean, store area. Refrigerators. Balconies. Picnic tables, grills. 10 acres on Lake Hamilton. Cr cds: MC, V.

[symbols]

★ **SHORECREST RESORT.** *(360 Lakeland Dr, Hot Springs 71913) 501/525-8113; res: 800/447-9914.* 25 kit. cottages. Feb-early Sept: S $45; D $51-$60; each addl $4; lower rates rest of yr. Crib free. Pet accepted. TV; cable. Pool. Ck-out 11 am, ck-in 2 pm. Grocery $1^1/2$ blks; package store $1/4$ mi. Private beach. Complete marina nearby. Lawn games. Fishing guides; clean, store area. Refrigerators. Private patios. Picnic tables; grills. Scenic, wooded location on Lake Hamilton. Cr cds: DS, MC, V. [symbols]

Jonesboro *(See also Walnut Ridge)*

Motels

✔★ **DAYS INN.** *2406 Phillips Dr, E off Caraway at Ark 63. 870/932-9339; res: 800/227-9345; FAX 870/931-5289.* 46 rms. S, D $31.95; each addl $5; suites $37.95-$40.95; under 12 free. Crib free. Pet accepted. TV; cable (premium). Complimentary continental bkfst. Restaurant opp 6 am-10 pm. Ck-out 11 am. Sundries. Cr cds: A, DS, MC, V. [symbols]

★★ **HOLIDAY INN.** *3006 S Caraway Rd, N off US 63 Bypass. 870/935-2030; FAX 870/935-3440.* 179 rms, 2 story. S, D $65; each addl $7; suites $65-$100. Crib free. Pet accepted. TV; cable (premium). Indoor pool; whirlpool. Restaurant 6 am-10 pm. Rm serv. Bar 4 pm-midnight, Sat from 5 pm; entertainment exc Sun. Ck-out noon. Coin lndry. Meeting rms. Business servs avail. Airport transportation. Exercise equipt; weights, bicycles. Game rm. Rec rm. Cr cds: A, C, D, DS, JCB, MC, V. [symbols]

Motor Hotels

★★ **HOLIDAY INN EXPRESS.** *2407 Phillips Dr. 870/932-5554; FAX 870/932-2586.* 102 rms, 4 story. S, D $55; each addl $7; suites $65; under 18 free. Pet accepted, some restrictions. TV; cable (premium). Complimentary continental bkfst. Restaurant nearby. Ck-out noon. Meeting rms. In-rm modem link. Coin lndry. Health club privileges. Microwaves avail. Cr cds: A, C, D, DS, MC, V. [symbols]

★★ **WILSON INN.** *2911 Gilmore Dr, off US 63. 870/972-9000.* 108 rms, 5 story, 31 suites, 59 kits. S, D $39.95-$44.95; each addl $5; suites $54.95; under 19 free. Crib free. Pet accepted. TV; cable (premium), VCR avail. Complimentary continental bkfst. Restaurant adj 11 am-10 pm. Ck-out noon. Meeting rms. Business servs avail. Health club privileges. Refrigerators; microwaves avail. Wet bar in suites. Cr cds: A, C, D, DS, MC, V.

[symbols]

Little Rock & North Little Rock

Motels

★★ **COMFORT INN.** *(3200 Bankhead Dr, Little Rock 72206) 8 mi E on I-440, near Little Rock Airport. 501/490-2010; FAX 501/490-2229.* 115 rms, 2 story, 12 kits. S, D $48-$53; each addl $5; kits. $58-$63; under 18 free. Crib free. Pet accepted. TV; cable (premium), VCR avail (movies). Pool. Complimentary continental bkfst. Coffee in rms. Restaurant adj open 24 hrs. Ck-out noon. Coin lndry. Business servs avail. In-rm modem link. Sundries. Free airport transportation. Some refrigerators. Cr cds: A, D, DS, MC, V.

[symbols]

★★ **LA QUINTA.** *(11701 I-30 & I-430, Little Rock 72209) 501/455-2300; FAX 501/455-5876.* 145 rms, 3 story. S $61-$77; D $69-$77; each addl $7; suites $139-$147; under 18 free. Crib free. Pet accepted, some restrictions. TV; cable (premium), VCR avail. Pool; whirlpool. Complimentary continental bkfst. Restaurant 11 am-2 pm, 5-10 pm; Sat from 5 pm; Sun to 2 pm. Bar 4 pm-midnight. Ck-out noon. Coin lndry. Meeting rms. Business servs avail. In-rm modem link. Valet serv. Cr cds: A, C, D, DS, JCB, MC, V.

[symbols]

★ **LA QUINTA.** *(2401 W 65th St, Little Rock 72209) I-30 exit 135.* 501/568-1030; *FAX* 501/568-5713. 112 rms, 2 story. S $54-$61; D $61-$68; each addl $7; suites $77; under 18 free. Crib free. Pet accepted, some restrictions. TV; cable (premium). Pool. Complimentary continental bkfst. Restaurant adj open 24 hrs. Ck-out noon. Business servs avail. In-rm modem link. Cr cds: A, C, D, DS, MC, V. 🄳 ☞ 🏊 🔀 🐾 SC

★ **MOTEL 6.** *(7501 I-30, Little Rock 72209) exit 134.* 501/568-8888; *FAX* 501/568-8355. 130 units, 3 story. S $31.99, D $37.99; each addl $3; suites $41.79; under 17 free. Crib free. Pet accepted, some restrictions. TV; cable (premium). Pool. Coffee in lobby. Restaurant adj open 24 hrs. Ck-out noon. Coin lndry. In-rm modem link. Patios. Cr cds: A, C, D, DS, MC, V. 🄳 ☞ 🏊 🔀 🐾 SC

★ **RED ROOF INN.** *(7900 Scott Hamilton Dr, Little Rock 72209) I-30 exit 134.* 501/562-2694; *FAX* 501/562-1723. Web www.red roofinns.com. 108 rms, 2 story. S $30-$35; D $36-$46; under 18 free. Crib free. Pet accepted. TV; cable (premium). Restaurant adj open 24 hrs. Ck-out noon. Business servs avail. In-rm modem link. Cr cds: A, C, D, DS, MC, V. 🄳 ☞ 🔀 🐾

Motor Hotels

★ ★ ★ **HOLIDAY INN WEST.** *(201 S Shackelford Rd, Little Rock 72211) jct I-430 & I-630.* 501/223-3000; *FAX* 501/223-2833. 261 rms, 5 story. S, D $88-$99; each addl $8; suites $135-$299; under 18 free; wkly, wkend rates. Crib avail. Pet accepted. TV; cable (premium). Indoor/outdoor pool; poolside serv. Complimentary coffee in rms. Restaurant 6 am-10 pm. Rm serv 5 pm-midnight. Bar 5 pm-midnight; entertainment. Ck-out noon. Meeting rms. Business servs avail. In-rm modem link. Bellhops. Valet serv. Concierge. Coin lndry. Free airport, RR station transportation. Exercise equipt; weights, treadmill, sauna. Game rm. Cr cds: A, C, D, DS, MC, V. 🄳 ☞ 🏊 🏋 🔀 🐾 SC

★ **WILSON INN.** *(4301 E Roosevelt, Little Rock 72206) I-440 exit 3, at Little Rock Airport.* 501/376-2466; *FAX* 501/376-0253. 110 units, 5 story, 13 suites, 18 kit. units. S, D $47.95-$69.95; suites $64.95-$69.95; kit. units $45.95-$55.95; under 18 free. Crib free. Pet accepted, some restrictions. TV; cable (premium), VCR. Whirlpool. Complimentary continental bkfst. Ck-out noon. Meeting rm. Business servs avail. In-rm modem link. Bellhops. Free airport transportation. Refrigerators. Cr cds: A, C, D, DS, MC, V. 🄳 ☞ 🏋 🔀 🐾 SC

Magnolia *(See also El Dorado)*

Motel

✔★★ **BEST WESTERN COACHMAN'S INN.** *420 E Main St.* 870/234-6122; *FAX* 870/234-1254. E-mail magnoliaplace@world net.att.net; web www.bbonline.com/ar/magno lia. 84 rms, 2 story. S $49-$55; D $49-$59. Crib free. Pet accepted, some restrictions. TV; cable (premium). Pool. Complimentary continental bkfst. Restaurant 11 am-9 pm. Ck-out noon. Meeting rms. Business servs avail. In-rm modem link. Refrigerators. Balconies. Cr cds: A, C, D, DS, MC, V. 🄳 ☞ 🏊 🔀 🐾 SC

Morrilton *(See also Conway, Russellville)*

Motel

★ ★ **BEST WESTERN.** *356 Hwy 95 & I-40, exit 107.* 501/354-0181; *FAX* 501/354-1458. 55 rms, 2 story. S, D $38-$52; each addl $4; under 12 free; higher rates special events. Crib free. Pet accepted, some restrictions. TV; cable (premium). Pool. Complimentary coffee in lobby. Restaurant adj 6 am-9 pm. Ck-out noon. Meeting rms. Business servs avail. Some refrigerators, microwaves. Cr cds: A, D, DS, MC, V. ☞ 🏊 🔀 🐾 SC

Mountain Home *(See also Bull Shoals Lake Area)*

Motels

✔★★ **BEST WESTERN CARRIAGE INN.** *963 US 62E.* 870/425-6001. 82 rms, 2 story. S $43-$57; D $50-$62; each addl $6; under 12 free. Pet accepted. TV; cable (premium). Pool. Restaurant 5-9 pm. Rm serv. Private club from 4:30 pm, closed Sun. Ck-out noon. Meeting rms. Cr cds: A, C, D, DS, JCB, MC, V. ☞ 🏊 🔀 🐾 SC

★ **HOLIDAY INN.** *1350 Hwy 62 SW, 1 mi SW on US 62.* 870/425-5101; *FAX* 870/425-5101, ext. -300. 100 rms, 2 story. S $49; D $52; each addl $7; under 18 free. Crib free. Pet accepted. TV; cable (premium), VCR avail. Pool. Restaurant 6 am-10 pm. Rm serv. Private club 5 pm-1 am, closed Sun; entertainment. Ck-out noon. Coin lndry. Meeting rms. Business servs avail. In-rm modem link. Airport transportation. Health club privileges. Cr cds: A, C, D, DS, JCB, MC, V. 🄳 ☞ 🏊 🔀 🐾 SC

Cottage Colony

★ **TEAL POINT.** *715 Teal Point Rd, 6 mi E on US 62, then* $^1/_2$ *mi N on AR 406.* *870/492-5145.* 17 kit. cottages. No rm phones. June-Sept: cottages $57-$129; each addl $5; family rates; lower rates rest of yr. Crib free. Pet accepted; $7/day. TV; cable. Pool. Playground. Restaurant 1 mi. Ck-out 9 am, ck-in 3 pm. Grocery. Coin lndry. Package store 2.5 mi. Boats, rentals. Game rm. Lawn games. Fishing guides. Microwaves. Private patios. Picnic tables, grills. On Lake Norfork. Cr cds: MC, V. D ⬚ ⬚ ⬚ ⬚ SC

Mountain View (See also Batesville, Greers Ferry Lake Area)

Motel

★ **DOGWOOD.** *AR 14 E, 1 mi E of downtown. 870/269-3847; FAX 870/269-3088.* 30 rms. Apr-Oct: S, D $42-$60; lower rates rest of yr. Pet accepted, some restrictions. TV; cable. Pool. Complimentary coffee in lobby. Ck-out 11 am. Gift shop. Picnic table, grill. Cr cds: A, DS, MC, V. D ⬚ ⬚ ⬚ ⬚ SC

Newport (See also Batesville)

Motel

✔ ★ ★ **PARK INN INTERNATIONAL.** *901 US 367N. 870/523-5851; FAX 870/523-9890.* 58 rms. S $42-$49; D $48-$58; each addl $3; under 18 free. Crib free. Pet accepted. TV; cable (premium), VCR avail (movies). Pool. Coffee in lobby. Restaurant 5 am-9 pm. Bar 4-11 pm. Ck-out noon. Coin lndry. Meeting rms. Business servs avail. Valet serv. Health club privileges. Sundries. Some refrigerators; microwaves avail. Some rms with cathedral ceiling. Cr cds: A, C, D, DS, JCB, MC, V. D ⬚ ⬚ ⬚ ⬚ SC

Pine Bluff

Motel

★ **THE INN.** *210 N Blake (71601), jct US 65, US 79. 870/534-7222; FAX 870/534-5705.* 90 units, 2 story. S, D $45; each addl $5; suites from $53; under 12 free. Pet accepted. TV; cable (premium). Pool. Complimentary continental bkfst. Restaurant adj 6 am-midnight. Ck-out noon. Meeting rms. Business servs avail. Exercise equipt; weights, weight machine. Microwaves avail. Picnic tables, grills. Cr cds: A, C, D, DS, MC, V. D ⬚ ⬚ ⬚ ⬚ ⬚ ⬚ SC

Hotel

★ ★ ★ **HOLIDAY INN.** *2 Convention Center Plaza (71601), S off Main St behind Convention Center. 870/535-3111; FAX 870/534-5083.* 200 units, 5 story, 84 suites. S, D $69; each addl $5; suites $79-$89; under 18 free. Crib free. Pet accepted, some restrictions. TV: cable. Indoor pool; whirlpool, sauna. Restaurant 6:30 am-10 pm. Bar 4-10 pm. Ck-out 11 am. Business servs avail. In-rm modem link. Meeting rm. Beauty shop. Gift shop. Indoor putting green. Exercise equipt; weights, bicycles. Game rm. Refrigerators; microwave, wet bar in suites. Atrium, balconies. Cr cds: A, C, D, DS, JCB, MC, V. D ⬚ ⬚ ⬚ ⬚ ⬚ SC

Rogers (See also Bentonville, Eureka Springs, Fayetteville, Springdale)

Motels

★ **BEAVER LAKE LODGE.** *100 Dutchman Dr, 4 mi E on AR 12 (RR 7), then* $^1/_4$ *mi N. 501/925-2313; res: 800/367-4513; FAX 501/925-1406.* 23 kit. units in motel, 2 duplex kit. cottages. May-Sept: S, D $54-$59; under 12 free; wkly rates; lower rates rest of yr. Crib free. Pet accepted, some restrictions; $10. TV; cable (premium). Pool. Complimentary coffee. Restaurant nearby. Ck-out 11 am. Microwaves. Picnic tables, grills. Cr cds: A, MC, V. ⬚ ⬚ ⬚ ⬚ SC

✔ ★ ★ **RAMADA INN.** *1919 US 71B, jct 94E. 501/636-5850.* 127 rms, 2 story. S $44-$52; D $49-$59; each addl $6; under 18 free. Crib free. Pet accepted. TV; cable (premium). Pool. Complimentary bkfst buffet. Restaurant 6 am-10 pm. Private club 11-2 am. Ck-out noon. Meeting rms. Business servs avail. Airport transportation. Microwaves avail. Cr cds: A, C, D, DS, JCB, MC, V. D ⬚ ⬚ ⬚ ⬚ SC

Russellville *(See also Morrilton)*

Motel

★ ★ **HOLIDAY INN.** *AR 7, jct I-40. 501/968-4300.* 149 units, 2 story. S $53-$63; D $63-$73; each addl $10; under 18 free. Crib free. Pet accepted, some restrictions. TV; cable (premium). Pool. Complimentary coffee in rms. Restaurant 6 am-2 pm, 4-10 pm; Sun from 7 am. Rm serv. Private club 4:30 pm-midnight; closed Sun. Ck-out noon. Meeting rms. Business servs avail. In-rm modem link. Airport transportation. Health club privileges. Microwaves avail. Cr cds: A, C, D, DS, ER, JCB, MC, V. 🔲 🐾 ≋ ⊠ 🐾 SC

Searcy *(See also Greers Ferry Lake Area, Little Rock)*

Motels

✔ ★ **COMFORT INN.** *107 S Rand St, 1 blk off US 67/167, exit 46. 501/279-9100.* 60 rms, 2 story. S $50; D $60; under 14 free. Crib $5. Pet accepted. TV; cable (premium). Pool. Complimentary continental bkfst. Restaurant nearby. Ck-out 11 am. Cr cds: A, C, D, DS, ER, JCB, MC, V. 🔲 🐾 ≋ ⊠ 🐾 SC

★ ★ **HAMPTON INN.** *3204 E Race St, 1 blk W off US 67/167, exit 46. 501/268-0654; FAX 501/278-5546.* E-mail tn009670@psinet.com. 106 units, 2 story. S, D $60-$70; suites $100-$150; under 18 free. Crib free. Pet accepted. TV; cable (premium), VCR avail (movies). Indoor/outdoor pool; whirlpool. Complimentary continental bkfst. Restaurant 6 am-midnight. Rm serv 7 am-10 pm. Ck-out noon. Coin lndry. Meeting rm. Business center. Valet serv. Exercise equipt; weights, bicycles, sauna. Many refrigerators; microwaves avail. Balconies. Atrium glassed area near pool. Cr cds: A, C, D, DS, ER, MC, V. 🔲 🐾 ≋ 🏋 ⊠ 🐾 SC 🚶

Springdale *(See also Bentonville, Fayetteville, Rogers)*

Motel

✔ ★ ★ **EXECUTIVE INN.** *2000 S US 71B (72764), jct 412E, downtown. 501/756-6101; FAX 501/756-6101, ext. 295; res: 800/544-6086.* 101 rms, 2 story. S, D $44-$50; each addl $6; under 18 free; higher rates football wknds. Crib free. Pet accepted. TV; cable. Pool. Complimentary coffee in rms. Restaurant 6:30 am-2 pm, 5-9 pm; Sat, Sun 7 am-9 pm. Bar 4 pm-2 am; Sat, Sun from 6 pm. Ck-out noon. Coin lndry. Meeting rms. Some refrigerators, microwaves. Cr cds: A, C, D, DS, MC, V. 🔲 🐾 ≋ ⊠ 🐾 SC

Hotel

★ ★ **HOLIDAY INN.** *1500 S 48th St (72762). 501/751-8300; FAX 501/751-4640.* 206 units, 8 story, 22 suites. S, D $99; suites $135; under 18 free; higher rates: U of A athletic events, War Eagle craft show. Crib free. Pet accepted. TV; cable (premium), VCR avail (movies). Indoor pool; whirlpool. Complimentary coffee. Restaurant 6 am-2 pm, 5-10 pm. Bar 4-11 pm. Ck-out noon. Coin lndry. Business center. In-rm modem link. Gift shop. Free airport transportation. Exercise equipt; weights, bicycles, sauna. Microwaves avail. Cr cds: A, C, D, DS, JCB, MC, V. 🔲 🐾 ≋ 🏋 ⊠ 🐾 SC 🚶

Stuttgart *(See also Pine Bluff)*

Motel

★ ★ **BEST WESTERN DUCK INN.** *704 W Michigan. 870/673-2575.* 72 rms, 2 story. Mid-Nov-mid-Jan: S $55-$75; D $60-$85; each addl $5; suites $85; family rates; lower rates rest of yr. Crib free. Pet accepted, some restrictions. TV; cable (premium), VCR. Complimentary coffee in rms. Restaurant adj 6 am-10 pm. Ck-out noon. Meeting rm. Indoor pool. Some refrigerators. Cr cds: A, D, MC, V. 🔲 🐾 ≋ ⊠ 🐾 SC

Walnut Ridge *(See also Jonesboro)*

Motel

✔ ★ **ALAMO COURT.** *US 67S, 1 mi N of jct US 63, 67. 870/886-2441; FAX 870/886-6007; res: 800/541-5590.* E-mail snapps@intel linet.com. 35 rms. S $38; D $43; each addl $4; under 12 free. Crib $4. Pet accepted. TV; cable. Playground. Coffee in lobby. Restaurant 6 am-9 pm. Ck-out noon. Meeting rms. Sundries. RV parking, electric hookups. Refrigerators, microwaves avail. Cr cds: A, C, D, DS, MC, V. 🔲 🐾 ⊠ 🐾 SC

California

Alturas

Motels

★ ★ **BEST WESTERN TRAILSIDE INN.** *343 N Main St.* 916/233-4111; FAX 916/233-3180. 39 rms, 2 story, 4 kits. May-Oct: S $50; D $50-$60; each addl $5; kit. units $10 addl; lower rates rest of yr. Crib $5. Pet accepted, some restrictions. TV; cable (premium). Pool. Complimentary coffee. Restaurant nearby. Ck-out 11 am. Business servs avail. In-rm modem link. Downhill/x-country ski 10 mi. Cr cds: A, C, D, DS, MC, V.

✔ ★ **HACIENDA.** *201 E 12th St.* 916/233-3459. 20 rms, 2 kits. S $29; D $31-$49; each addl $3; kit. units $5 addl; under 8 free. Pet accepted; $3. TV; cable (premium). Complimentary coffee in rms. Restaurant nearby. Ck-out 11 am. Downhill/x-country ski 10 mi. Refrigerators. Microwaves avail. Cr cds: A, C, D, DS, MC, V.

Anaheim (See also Buena Park, Corona, Los Angeles)

Motel

★ ★ **RAMADA LIMITED.** *800 S Beach Blvd (92804).* 714/995-5700; FAX 714/826-6021. 72 rms, 3 story. S $65-$100; D $70-$105; under 12 free. Crib $7. Pet accepted, some restrictions; $10/day. TV; cable (premium). Complimentary continental bkfst. Restaurant opp open 24 hrs. Ck-out noon. Meeting rm. Business servs avail. Coin lndry. Free Disneyland transportation. Pool; whirlpool. Some in-rm whirlpools, refrigerators, microwaves. Cr cds: A, D, DS, JCB, MC, V.

Motor Hotel

★ ★ **QUALITY HOTEL MAINGATE.** *616 Convention Way (92802),* Anaheim Convention Center adj; 2 blks S of Disneyland. 714/750-3131; FAX 714/750-9027. 284 rms, 9 story. S $69.95-$109.95; D $79.95-$139.95; each addl $10; suites $99.95-$259.95; under 18 free. Crib free. Parking $7. Pet accepted. TV; cable. Heated pool; poolside serv. Coffee in rms. Restaurants 6:30 am-2 pm; dining rm 5-10 pm. Rm serv. Bar 2 pm-midnight. Ck-out noon. Coin lndry. Convention facilities. Business servs avail. In-rm modem link. Bellhops. Free Disneyland transportation. Valet serv. Health club privileges. Gift shop. Barber/beauty shop. Game rm. Some balconies. Cr cds: A, C, D, DS, ER, JCB, MC, V.

Hotel

★ ★ ★ **HILTON HOTEL & TOWERS.** *777 Convention Way (92802),* 2 blks S of Disneyland. 714/750-4321; FAX 714/740-4460. Web www.hilton.com. 1,576 units, 14 story. S $130-$280; D $160-$310; each addl $30; suites $650-$1,125; family rates. Crib free. Pet accepted. Covered parking: valet $11, garage in/out $6. TV; cable (premium). 2 heated pools, 1 indoor; whirlpools, poolside serv. Supervised child's activities. Coffee in rms. Restaurants 6 am-midnight. Rm serv. Bars from 11 am; entertainment. Ck-out noon. Convention facilities. Business center. Concierge. Shopping arcade. Barber, beauty shop. Exercise rm; instructor, weights, bicycles, saunas, steam rms. Game rm. Some refrigerators. Some private patios, balconies. Luxury level. Cr cds: A, C, D, DS, ER, JCB, MC, V.

Arcadia (See also Los Angeles, Pasadena)

Motels

★ ★ **HAMPTON INN.** *311 E Huntington Dr (91006).* 626/574-5600; FAX 626/446-2748. 131 rms, 4 story. S $69-$85; D $79-$95; under 18 free; higher rates Rose Bowl (3-day min). Crib free. Pet accepted; $5/day. TV; cable (premium). Heated pool. Complimentary continental bkfst. Complimentary coffee in rms. Restaurant adj 11-1 am. Ck-out noon. Meeting rm. Business servs avail. Valet serv. Microwaves avail. Cr cds: A, C, D, DS, MC, V.

★ ★ **RESIDENCE INN BY MARRIOTT.** *321 E Huntington Dr (91006).* 626/446-6500; FAX 626/446-5824. 120 kit. suites, 2 story. Kit. suites $145-$175; higher rates Rose Bowl (4-day min). Crib free. Pet accepted; $50-$75. TV; cable (premium). VCR avail. Heated pool; whirlpool. Complimentary continental bkfst. Complimentary coffee in rms. Restaurant nearby. Ck-out noon. Coin lndry. Meeting rms. Business servs avail. Valet serv. Free airport transportation. Refrigerators, microwaves; some fireplaces. Some balconies. Picnic tables, grills. Cr cds: A, C, D, DS, JCB, MC, V. 🅳 📞 ≋ ⛷ 🐾 SC

Motor Hotel

★★ **HOLIDAY INN MONROVIA.** *(924 W Huntington Dr, Monrovia 91016) 626/357-1900; FAX 626/359-1386.* 173 rms, 10 story. S, D $109-$119; wkly, wkend rates; higher rates Rose Parade. Crib free. Pet accepted; $50. TV; cable (premium). Complimentary continental bkfst. Complimentary coffee in rms. Restaurant 6 am-10 pm. Rm serv. Bar 3-11 pm. Ck-out noon. Meeting rms. Business servs avail. Bellhops. Valet serv. Sundries. Coin lndry. Health club privileges. Pool; whirlpool. Microwaves avail. Cr cds: A, C, D, DS, JCB, MC, V. 🅳 📞 ≋ ⛷ 🐾 SC

Auburn (See also Grass Valley, Sacramento)

Motel

✔★★ **BEST WESTERN GOLDEN KEY.** *13450 Lincoln Way, I-80 at Foresthill exit. 916/885-8611; FAX 916/888-0319.* 68 rms, 2 story. S $55-$62; D $60-$68; each addl $4; wkly rates. Crib $4. Pet accepted, some restrictions. TV; cable. Heated pool. Complimentary continental bkfst. Coffee in rms. Restaurant nearby. Ck-out noon. Coin lndry. Meeting rm. Some refrigerators. Cr cds: A, C, D, DS, MC, V. 🅳 📞 ≋ ⛷ 🐾 SC

Bakersfield

Motels

★★ **BEST WESTERN HILL HOUSE.** *700 Truxtun (93301), near civic center. 805/327-4064; FAX 805/327-1247.* 99 rms, 2 story. S $50-$60; D $55-$65; each addl $5; under 12 free. Crib $5. Pet accepted; $3. TV; cable. Pool. Complimentary continental bkfst. Restaurant 6:30 am-8 pm. Bar. Ck-out noon. Meeting rms. Exercise equipt; weight machine, bicycles. Refrigerators. Balconies. Cr cds: A, C, D, DS, MC, V. 📞 ≋ 🏋 ⛷ 🐾 SC

★ **LA QUINTA.** *3232 Riverside Dr (93308). 805/325-7400; FAX 805/324-6032.* 129 rms, 3 story. S $53-$60; D $61-$68; suites $66; under 18 free. Crib free. Pet accepted. TV; cable (premium), VCR avail. Heated pool. Complimentary continental bkfst. Restaurant adj 5:30 am-10 pm. Ck-out noon. Meeting rms. Business servs avail. Free airport transporation. Cr cds: A, C, D, DS, MC, V. 🅳 📞 ≋ ⛷ 🐾 SC

✔★★ **OXFORD INN.** *4500 Pierce Rd (93308). 805/324-5555; FAX 805/325-0106; res: 800/822-3050 (CA).* 208 rms, 3 story. S $39-$48; D $46-$58; each addl $5; suites, kit. units $56-$64; under 18 free. Pet accepted; $6. TV; cable. Pool; sauna. Ck-out 1 pm. Coin lndry. Meeting rms. Business servs avail. Valet serv. Sundries. Free airport, RR station, bus depot transportation. Refrigerator in suites. Some balconies. Cr cds: A, C, D, DS, MC, V. 🅳 📞 ≋ ⛷ 🐾 SC

Barstow

Motel

✔★ **DAYS INN.** *1590 Coolwater Lane. 760/256-1737.* 113 rms, 2 story. S $24; D $29-$33; wkly rates. Pet accepted. TV; cable. Heated pool. Complimentary coffee in lobby. Restaurant adj. Ck-out 11 am. Cr cds: A, D, MC, V. 🅳 📞 ≋ ⛷ 🐾 SC

Beverly Hills (See also Hollywood, Los Angeles)

Hotels

★★★ **BEVERLY HILTON.** *9876 Wilshire Blvd (90210). 310/274-7777; FAX 310/285-1313.* 581 rms, 8 story. S, D $285-$315; each addl $20; suites $500-$1,500; family rates. Crib free. Pet accepted. Garage, valet parking $17. TV; cable (premium), VCR avail. Heated pool; wading pool, poolside serv. Restaurant 6:30-10 pm; dining rm 5:30 pm-midnight. Rm serv 24 hrs. Bars 11:30-2 am. Ck-out noon. Meeting rms. Business center. In-rm modem link. Concierge. Shopping arcade. Barber, beauty shop. Complimentary transportation to nearby shopping. Exercise equipt; weight machines, bicycles. Some bathrm phones; refrigerators. Patio, balconies. Lanai rms around pool. Cr cds: A, C, D, DS, ER, JCB, MC, V. 🅳 📞 ≋ 🏋 ⛷ 🐾 SC 🍸

✔★★★ **PLAZA BEVERLY HILLS.** *10300 Wilshire Blvd (90024). 310/275-5575; FAX 310/275-3257; res: 800/800-1234.* 116 suites, 5 story. S, D $135-$385. Crib avail. Pet accepted. TV; cable (premium), VCR avail. Heated pool; whirlpool, poolside serv. Restaurant 7 am-10 pm. Bar. Ck-out noon. Meeting rm. Business servs avail. In-rm modem link. Gift shop. Exercise equipt; weight machine, treadmill. Refrigerators, minibars. Many balconies. Garden; tropical plants. Cr cds: A, C, D, DS, JCB, MC, V. ⊡ ⊡ ⊡ ⊡ ⊡

★ ★ ★ ★ **REGENT BEVERLY WILSHIRE.** *9500 Wilshire Blvd (90212). 310/275-5200; FAX 310/274-2851; res: 800/545-4000.* Web www.rih.com. Sited at the south end of Rodeo Drive, this hotel is often home to visiting celebrities. 275 rms, 10 & 12 story, 69 suites. S, D $285-$425; suites $450-$4,500; under 16 free. Pet accepted. Covered parking, valet $20. TV; cable (premium), VCR avail (movies). Pool; whirlpool, poolside serv. Restaurant 6:30 am-2:30 pm, 6-10 pm. Rm serv 24 hrs. Bar 11-2 am; entertainment. Ck-out noon. Convention facilities. Business center. In-rm modem link. Concierge. Gift shops. Beauty shop. Exercise rm; instructor, weights, bicycles, sauna, steam rm. Massage. Bathrm phones, refrigerators. Some balconies. Cr cds: A, C, D, DS, ER, JCB, MC, V.

⊡ ⊡ ⊡ ⊡ ⊡ ⊡ ⊡

Big Bear Lake *(See also Lake Arrowhead, San Bernardino)*

Motels

★ ★ **ROBINHOOD INN.** *40797 Lakeview Dr, center of Big Bear Lake Village. 909/866-4643; FAX 909/866-4645; res: 800/990-9956.* 21 rms, 2 story. S, D $49-$110; suite $69-$149; higher rates hols; under 12 free. Pet accepted; some restrictions. TV; cable, VCR avail (free movies). Restaurant opp 6 am-11 pm. Ck-out 11 am. Meeting rm. Business servs avail. Downhill/x-country ski ½ mi. Whirlpool. Massage. Many refrigerators, some fireplaces. Grill, picnic table, sun deck. Cr cds: A, MC, V. ⊡ ⊡ ⊡ ⊡ ⊡

✔ ★ ★ **WILDWOOD RESORT.** *40210 Big Bear Blvd (CA 18), ½ mi W of Big Bear Lake Village. 909/878-2178; FAX 909/878-3036; res: 888/294-5396.* 5 rms in main bldg, 2 story, 14 kit. cottages. S, D $49-$90; kit. cottages $70-$190; weekly rates. Crib free. Pet accepted, $10/night. TV; cable, VCR avail. Heated pool; whirlpool. Playground. Complimentary coffee in rms/cottages. Restaurant nearby. Ck-out 11 am. Downhill/x-country ski 3 mi. Many fireplaces. Lawn games. Picnic tables, grills. Cr cds: A, DS, MC, V.

⊡ ⊡ ⊡ ⊡ ⊡ ⊡

Inn

★ ★ ★ **EAGLE'S NEST.** *41675 Big Bear Blvd, E of Big Bear Lake Village. 909/866-6465; FAX 909/866-8025.* 5 rms, 2 story, 5 cottages. S, D $75-$150; wkly rates. Pet accepted, some restrictions. TV in cottages. Full bkfst. Ck-out 11 am, ck-in 2 pm. Ski area transportation. Downhill/x-country ski ¼ mi. Refrigerators, microwaves in cottages. Fireplaces. Western decor; antiques. Horse & carriage rides avail (fee). Totally nonsmoking. Cr cds: A, MC, V. ⊡ ⊡ ⊡ ⊡ ⊡

Bishop

Motels

★ ★ **BEST WESTERN HOLIDAY SPA LODGE.** *1025 N Main St. 760/873-3543; FAX 760/872-4777.* 89 rms, 1-2 story. May-Oct: S $56-$87; D $78-$87; each addl $5; higher rates hols; lower rates rest of yr. Crib $10. Pet accepted, some restrictions. TV; cable. Pool; whirlpool. Complimentary coffee in rms. Ck-out 11 am. Coin lndry. X-country ski 20 mi. Fish cleaning, freezer facilities. Refrigerators. Cr cds: A, C, D, DS, JCB, MC, V.

⊡ ⊡ ⊡ ⊡ ⊡ ⊡ ⊡

★ **COMFORT INN.** *805 N Main St. 760/873-4284; FAX 760/873-8563.* 52 rms, 2 story. S $60-$75; D $70-$75; each addl $5; suites $72-$90; higher rates hols. Crib $5. Pet accepted. TV; cable (premium). Heated pool; whirlpool. Complimentary coffee in rms. Complimentary continental bkfst. Restaurant nearby. Ck-out 11 am. Coin lndry. Fish cleaning, freezer facilities. Refrigerators; some wet bars. Picnic tables, grill. Cr cds: A, C, D, DS, MC, V. ⊡ ⊡ ⊡ ⊡ ⊡ ⊡

✔ ★ **THUNDERBIRD.** *190 W Pine St. 760/873-4215; res: 800/82-T-BIR.* 23 rms, 2 story. S $34-$44; D $40-$60; each addl $4. Crib $2. Pet accepted, some restrictions.. TV; cable. Coffee in rms. Restaurant nearby. Ck-out 11 am. X-country ski 20 mi. Refrigerators. Cr cds: A, C, D, DS, MC, V. ⊡ ⊡ ⊡ ⊡ ⊡

Blythe

Motels

(Rates may be higher for dove-hunting season in early Sept; res necessary, 3-day min.)

★ ★ **BEST WESTERN SAHARA.** *825 W Hobson Way. 760/922-7105; FAX 760/922-5836.* 47 rms. S $49-$66; D $54-$70; each addl $5; under 12 free; higher rates special events. Crib free. Pet accepted. TV; cable, (premium), VCR. Pool; whirlpool. Complimentary continental bkfst. Complimentary coffee in rms. Restaurant opp 5 am-11 pm. Ck-out noon. Refrigerators, microwaves. Cr cds: A, C, D, DS, ER, MC, V.

D ✦ ≈ ⊠ 🖈 SC

✔★ **COMFORT INN.** *903 W Hobson Way. 760/922-4146; FAX 760/922-8481.* 48 rms, 2 story. S $48-$58; D $52-$65; each addl $5; under 18 free; higher rates special events. Crib free. Pet accepted. TV; cable (premium). Pool. Complimentary continental bkfst in lobby. Restaurant opp 5 am-11 pm. Ck-out noon. Refrigerators; microwaves avail. Cr cds: A, C, D, DS, ER, MC, V. ✦ ≈ ⊠ 🖈 SC

★★ **HAMPTON INN.** *900 W Hobson Way. 760/922-9000; FAX 760/922-9011.* 59 rms, 2 story. Jan-May: S $60-$95; D $68-$105; under 18 free; higher rates special events; lower rates rest of yr. Crib free. Pet accepted, some restrictions. TV; cable (premium), VCR. Complimentary continental bkfst. Restaurant nearby. Ck-out 11 am. Meeting rm. Business servs avail. In-rm modem link. Coin lndry. Exercise equipt; weight machine, treadmill. Pool; whirlpool. Bathrm phones, refrigerators, microwaves. Cr cds: A, C, D, DS, MC, V.

D ✦ ≈ 🏋 🖈 ⊠ 🖈

★ **TRAVELODGE.** *850 W Hobson Way. 760/922-5145; FAX 760/922-8422.* 50 rms, 34 with shower only, 2 story. S, D $46-$58; each addl $4; under 14 free; wkly rates. Crib free. Pet accepted, some restrictions; $25 deposit. TV; cable (premium). Pool. Complimentary coffee in rms. Complimentary continental bkfst. Restaurant adj 5 am-11 pm. Ck-out 11 am. Refrigerators; microwaves avail. Picnic tables, grills. Cr cds: A, C, D, DS, ER, JCB, MC, V. D ✦ ≈ ⊠ 🖈 SC

Bridgeport *(See also Coleville)*

Motels

✔★ **SILVER MAPLE.** *310 Main St. 619/932-7383.* 20 rms. No A/C. No rm phones. S $50-$55; D $55-$65; each addl $10. Pet accepted. TV; cable (premium). Complimentary coffee in rms. Restaurant opp 6 am-10 pm. Ck-out 11 am. Lawn games. Picnic tables. Grills. Cr cds: A, C, D, DS, MC, V. D ✦ ⊠ 🖈 SC

★★ **WALKER RIVER LODGE.** *US 395. 619/932-7021; FAX 619/932-7914; res: 800/688-3351.* 36 rms, 1-2 story. Mid-Apr-Oct: S $65-$120; D $75-$120; each addl $10; kit. units $95-$200; lower rates rest of yr. Crib free. Pet accepted. TV; cable (premium). Heated pool; whirlpool. Complimentary coffee in rms. Restaurant opp 6 am-2 pm. Ck-out 11 am. Business servs avail. Gift shop. Refrigerators. Some balconies. Picnic tables, grills. Fish freezer. Cr cds: A, C, D, DS, MC, V. D ✦ ≈ ⊠ 🖈 SC

Buena Park *(See also Anaheim, Long Beach, Whittier)*

Hotel

★★★ **SHERATON CERRITOS AT TOWNE CENTER.** *(12725 Center Court Dr, Cerritos 90703) 4 mi W on CA 91, Bloomfield Ave exit S. 562/809-1500; FAX 562/403-2080.* 203 rms, 8 story. S, D $85-$160; each addl $15; suites $160-$400; under 18 free. Crib free. Pet accepted, some restrictions; $25. TV; cable (premium). Heated pool; whirlpool, poolside serv. Coffee in rms. Restaurant 6:30 am-10 pm. Bar noon-1 am. Ck-out noon. Meeting rms. Business center. In-rm modem link. Concierge. Gift shop. Free Disneyland transportation. Exercise equipt; weight machine, bicycles. Refrigerators; some bathrm phones. Atrium. Cr cds: A, C, D, DS, ER, JCB, MC, V. D ✦ ≈ 🏋 ⊠ 🖈 SC 🏌

Burbank

Hotel

★★ **HILTON-BURBANK AIRPORT.** *2500 Hollywood Way (91505), I-5 Hollywood Way exit S 1 1/2 mi, opp Burbank Airport. 818/843-6000; FAX 818/842-9720.* E-mail bur hilton@aol.com; web www.hilton.com/hotels/bura hhf/index.html. 486 rms, 8-9 story. S $120-$180; D $130-$190; each addl $10; suites $140-$480; family, wkend rates. Crib free. Pet accepted. TV; cable (premium). 2 heated pools; whirlpool, poolside serv. Complimentary coffee in rms. Restaurant 6 am-11 pm. Rm serv 24 hrs. Bar 11-1 am. Ck-out noon. Coin lndry. Convention facilities. Business center. Concierge. Gift shop. Free local airport transportation. Exercise equipt; weight machine, bicycles, sauna. Health club privileges. Microwaves avail; refrigerator in suites. Cr cds: A, C, D, DS, ER, JCB, MC, V.

D ✦ ≈ 🏋 ✈ ⊠ 🖈 SC 🏌

Cambria *(See also Morro Bay, San Simeon)*

Motel

★ **CAMBRIA SHORES.** *6276 Moonstone Beach Dr. 805/927-8644; FAX 805/927-4070; res: 800/433-9179 (CA).* Web www.ernestallen.com/tr/ ca/cambriashores inn/. 24 rms. No A/C. Memorial Day-Labor Day, wkends, hols: S, D $75-$110; lower rates rest of yr. Crib free. Pet accepted, some restrictions; $5. TV; cable. Complimentary continental bkfst. Complimentary coffee in rms. Ck-out 11 am. Business servs avail. Refrigerators. Microwaves avail. Ocean view; beach opp. Cr cds: A, DS, MC, V. 🐾 🐾 🖼 🐾

Carlsbad *(See also Escondido, La Jolla, San Diego, San Juan Capistrano)*

Motel

🔹★ **INNS OF AMERICA.** *751 Raintree Dr (92009), W of I-5, Poinsettia Ln exit. 760/931-1185; FAX 760/931-0970.* 126 rms, 3 story. June-mid-Sept: S $51.90; D $56.90; lower rates rest of yr. Crib free. Pet accepted. TV; cable (premium). Heated pool. Complimentary continental bkfst. Restaurant adj 11:30 am-midnight. Sun brunch 9 am-1 pm. Ck-out 11 am. Coin lndry. Business servs avail. Cr cds: A, MC, V. 🅳 🐾 🖼 🖼 🐾 SC

Resort

FOUR SEASONS AVIARA. *(Too new to be rated) 7100 Four Seasons Point (92009). 760/931-6672; res: 800/332-3442; FAX 760/931-0390.* Web www.fourseasons .com. 331 rms, 3 story, 44 suites. S, D $275-$375; suites $475-$1,200; under 17 free; golf plans. Crib free. Pet accepted. TV; cable (premium). VCR avail. Pool; wading pool, whirlpool, poolside serv. Complimentary coffee in rms. Restaurants 6 am-2:30 pm, 5:30-10 pm. Rm serv 24 hrs. Bar to midnight; entertainment. Ck-out noon, ck-in 2 pm. Convention facilities. Business center. In-rm modem link. Bellhops. Valet serv. Concierge. Shopping arcade. Barber, beauty shop. Airport transportation. Sports dir. 6 lighted tennis courts, pro. 18-hole golf, greens fee $130, pro, putting green, driving range. Exercise rm; instructor, weight machine, bicycles, sauna, steam rm. Massage. Bathrm phones, mimibars. Balconies. Located on the north shore of Batiquitos Lagoon. Cr cds: A, D, MC, V.

🅳 🐾 🏋 🏃 🖼 🏃 🖼 🐾 🏃

Carmel *(See also Carmel Valley, Monterey, Pebble Beach)*

Motels

(Higher rates on holidays and during special events)

★ ★ **CARMEL MISSION INN.** *3665 Rio Rd (93923), 1 blk E of CA 1. 408/624-1841; FAX 408/624-8684.* 165 rms, 4 story. S, D $99-$179; each addl $10; suites $289-$359; under 13 free. Crib free. Pet accepted; $15. TV; cable. Heated pool; whirlpools, poolside serv. Restaurant 7-10 am; wkends to 11 am, 5:30-9:30 pm. Rm serv. Bar. Ck-out noon. Meeting rms. Business servs avail. Bellhops. Valet serv. Refrigerators. Many balconies. Picnic sites. Cr cds: A, C, D, DS, JCB, MC, V. 🅳 🐾 🖼 🖼 🐾 SC

★ ★ **WAYSIDE INN.** *7th Ave & Mission St (93921). 408/624-5336; FAX 408/626-6974; res: 800/433-4732.* E-mail concierge@carmelinns.com; web www.webdzine.com/ inns. 21 rms, 2 story, 10 kits. No A/C. Mid-June-mid-Oct, wkends: S, D $99-$165; each addl $15; suites $219-$249; 2-day min wkends; lower rates rest of yr. Pet accepted. TV; cable. Complimentary continental bkfst in rms. Coffee in rms. Restaurant nearby. Ck-out noon. Ck-in 3 pm. Business servs avail. Refrigerators; many fireplaces; microwaves avail. Some balconies. Colonial Williamsburg decor. Cr cds: A, DS, JCB, MC, V. 🐾 🖼 🐾 SC

Inn

★ ★ **CYPRESS.** *Lincoln St & 7th Ave (93921). 408/624-3871; FAX 408/624-8216; res: 800/443-7443.* E-mail hollace@cypress-inn.com. 34 rms, 2 story. S, D $110-$285; each addl $15; lower rates Dec-Jan. Pet accepted; $17. TV; cable (premium). Complimentary continental bkfst. Complimentary refreshments in rms. Bar 7 am-11 pm. Ck-out noon, ck-in 3 pm. Business servs avail. Bellhops. Some refrigerators, fireplaces. Some verandas. Mediterranean facade; set in heart of Carmel Village. Cr cds: A, DS, JCB, MC, V.

🐾 🖼 🐾

Resort

★ ★ ★ ★ **QUAIL LODGE RESORT & GOLF CLUB.** *8205 Valley Greens Dr (93923), 3 mi E of CA 1 on Carmel Valley Rd. 408/624-1581; FAX 408/624-3726; res: 800/538-9516 (exc CA), 800/682-9303 (CA).* Set amid 850 acres of impeccably landscaped grounds, Quail is known for its gardens and its golf facilities. Guest rooms are done in rustic California style with rattan armchairs, glass-topped tables and floral drapes and spreads. 100 units. S, D

$225-$285; each addl $25; suites $325-$705; under 12 free; golf plan Sun-Thurs. Pet accepted. TV; cable. 2 heated pools; whirlpool, poolside serv. Supervised child's activities by request (July-Sept). Complimentary afternoon refreshments. Complimentary coffee in rms. Restaurants 6:30-10 pm. Rm serv 7 am-11 pm. Bars 11 am-midnight; entertainment. Ck-out 1 pm. Meeting rms. Business servs avail. Bellhops. Concierge. Airport transportation. Tennis, pro. 18-hole golf, greens fee $105, putting greens, driving range. Bicycles. Health club privileges. Lawn games. Some fireplaces, wet bars. Private patios, balconies. Cr cds: A, C, D, JCB, MC, V.

Carmel Valley *(See also Carmel, Monterey)*

Motel

✓★ **CARMEL VALLEY INN.** *Carmel Valley Rd, at Los Laureles Grade. 408/659-3131; res: 800/541-3113; FAX 408/659-0137.* E-mail sales@carmelval leyinn.com; web www.carmelvalleyinn.com. 47 rms, 11 with shower only, 1 story. Apr-Oct: S, D $80-$125; under 12 free; wkends, hols (2-3-day min); higher rates special events; lower rates rest of yr. Crib $10. Pet accepted; $10. TV; cable. Complimentary coffee in lobby. Restaurant 7 am-9 pm. Bar. Ck-out noon. Meeting rms. Business servs avail. Concierge. Tennis, pro. Pool; whirlpool, poolside serv, lifeguard. Some balconies. Totally nonsmoking. Cr cds: A, C, D, DS, MC, V.

Inn

★★ **VALLEY LODGE.** *Carmel Valley Rd at Ford Rd. 408/659-2261; FAX 408/659-4558; res: 800/641-4646.* Web www.gp.infohut.com. 31 units, 1-2 story, 8 kits. No A/C. S, D $99-$119; each addl $15; studios $139; kit. units, cottages $159-$249; higher rates: hols, special events; 2- or 3-day min wkends, hols. Crib free. Pet accepted; $10/day. TV; cable, VCR avail. Heated pool; whirlpool. Complimentary continental bkfst. Complimentary coffee in rms. Ck-out noon, ck-in after 2 pm. Meeting rm. Business servs avail. Exercise equipt; bicycle, rowing machine, sauna. Fireplace in suites, cottages; some wet bars. Private patios, balconies. Cr cds: A, MC, V.

Chico *(See also Oroville)*

Motel

✓★ **VAGABOND INN.** *630 Main St (95928). 530/895-1323; FAX 530/343-2719.* 42 rms, 2 story. S $34-$50; D $45-$75; higher rates special events; each addl $5; kit. units $8 addl; under 16 free. Crib free. Pet accepted. TV; cable (premium). Pool. Complimentary continental bkfst. Complimentary coffee in rms. Restaurant adj open 24 hrs. Ck-out 11 am. Meeting rm. Business servs avail. Health club privileges. Cr cds: A, C, D, DS, MC, V.

Motor Hotel

★★ **HOLIDAY INN.** *685 Manzanita Court (95926). 530/345-2491; FAX 530/893-3040.* 172 rms, 5 story. S, D $59-$75; each addl $6; suites $100-$160; under 19 free. Crib free. Pet accepted, some restrictions. TV; cable (premium). Pool; whirlpool. Restaurant 6 am-10 pm. Rm serv. Bar from 2 pm; entertainment. Ck-out 11 am. Coin lndry. Meeting rms. Business servs avail. In-rm modem link. Bellhops. Valet serv. Free airport, bus depot transportation. Health club privileges. Refrigerator in suites. Microwaves avail. Cr cds: A, C, D, DS, JCB, MC, V.

Chula Vista

Motel

✓★★ **GOOD NITE INN.** *225 Bay Blvd (91910), I-5, E St exit. 619/425-8200; FAX 619/426-7411.* 118 rms, 2 story. Mid-May-mid-Sept: S $41, D $49; each addl $6; under 12 free; lower rates rest of yr. Crib free. Pet accepted, some restrictions. TV; cable (premium). Heated pool. Restaurant 6 am-8 pm. Ck-out 11 am. Some refrigerators, microwaves. Cr cds: A, C, D, DS, MC, V.

Claremont *(See also Ontario, Pasadena)*

Motel

★★ **RAMADA INN & TENNIS CLUB.** *840 S Indian Hill Blvd, I-10 Indian Hill Blvd exit, 1 blk S. 909/621-4831; FAX 909/621-0411.* Web www.ramada clar.com. 122 rms, 2 story. S, D $80; each addl $8; under 12 free. Crib free. Pet accepted. TV; cable (premium). Heated pool; wading pool; whirlpool. Complimentary continental bkfst. Restaurant opp 9

am-11 pm. Ck-out noon. Coin lndry. Meeting rms. Business servs avail. Valet serv. Free local transportation. Lighted tennis. Refrigerators. Grill. Cr cds: A, C, D, DS, JCB, MC, V.
🅳 ⛷ ⛷ ≋ ⊠ 🐾 SC

Coleville (See also Bridgeport)

Motel

✔★ **ANDRUSS.** *(106964 CA 395, Walker) 5 mi S on US 395. 916/495-2216.* 12 air-cooled rms, 4 kits. No rm phones. S $36-$42; D, kit. units $42-$52; each addl $4. Pet accepted; $5. TV; cable. Heated pool. Playground. Complimentary coffee in rms. Restaurant opp 6 am-10 pm. Ck-out 11 am. Picnic tables, grill. Fish cleaning, freezing facilities. Cr cds: MC, V. 🖼 ⛷ ≋ 🔥 🐾

Corona (See also Ontario)

Motel

✔★★ **DYNASTY SUITES.** *1805 W Sixth St (91720). 909/371-7185; res: 800/842-7899; FAX 909/371-0401.* Web www.dynasty suites.com. 56 rms, 2 story. S, D $44.95-$59.95; each addl $5. Crib free. Pet accepted, some restrictions; $10/day. TV; cable (premium), VCR avail (movies). Complimentary continental bkfst. Restaurant adj 5-1 am. Ck-out noon. Meeting rms. Business servs avail. Valet serv. Health club privileges. Pool; whirlpool. Bathrm phones, refrigerators, microwaves; some in-rm whirlpools. Cr cds: A, C, D, DS, MC, V. 🅳 ⛷ ≋ ⊠ 🐾 SC

Coronado

Motel

★ **CROWN CITY INN.** *520 Orange Ave. 619/435-3116; FAX 619/435-6750; res: 800/422-1173.* 33 rms, 2 story. Mid-June-mid-Sept: S, D $85-$125; under 18 free; higher rates hols (3-day min); lower rates rest of yr. Crib $5. Pet accepted. TV; cable (premium). Heated pool. Complimentary coffee in rms. Restaurant 8 am-2 pm, 5-9 pm. Rm serv. Ck-out 11 am. Coin lndry. Business servs avail. Health club privileges. Refrigerators, microwaves. Cr cds: A, D, DS, MC, V. ⛷ ≋ ⊠ 🔥

Resort

★★★★ **LOEWS CORONADO BAY.** *4000 Coronado Bay Rd. 619/424-4000; FAX 619/424-4400; res: 800/235-6397.* Located on a 15-acre peninsula, this full-service resort has a New England seaside ambience with sweeping views and an 80-slip marina. 440 rms, 3 story. S, D $195-$275; each addl $20; suites $395-$1,500; under 18 free; tennis plans. Crib free. Pet accepted. TV; cable, VCR avail. 3 pools; whirlpools, poolside serv. Supervised child's activities. Restaurant 6-10 pm. Box lunches. Rm serv 24 hrs. Bar 11-2 am; entertainment. Ck-out noon, ck-in 3 pm. Grocery. Free lndry. Package store. Convention facilities. Business center. In-rm modem link. Bellhops. Valet serv. Concierge. Gift shop. Barber, beauty shop. Sports dir. 5 lighted tennis courts, pro. Beach, boats, water skiing, swimming. Bicycle rentals. Lawn games. Game rm. Exercise rm; instructor, weight machine, treadmill, sauna. Massage. Bathrm phones, minibars; some wet bars; refrigerators, microwaves avail. Balconies. Cr cds: A, C, D, DS, JCB, MC, V.
🅳 ⛷ ⛷ ≋ 🎿 🛶 ⊠ 🐾 SC 🏃

Costa Mesa (See also Irvine, Newport Beach)

Motels

★★ **BEST WESTERN NEWPORT MESA INN.** *2642 Newport Blvd (92627), CA 55, exit Fair Dr. 714/650-3020; FAX 714/642-1220.* 97 rms, 3 story. S, D $54-$74; each addl $6; suites $99; under 17 free; package plans. Crib free. Pet accepted. TV; cable (premium). Heated pool; whirlpool, sauna. Complimentary continental bkfst. Ck-out noon. Coin lndry. Meeting rms. Business servs avail. Free airport transportation. Some bathrm phones; some in-rm whirlpools. Wet bars. Refrigerators, microwaves avail. Balconies. Cr cds: A, C, D, DS, ER, JCB, MC, V. 🅳 ⛷ ≋ ⊠ 🐾 SC

★★ **RAMADA LIMITED.** *1680 Superior Ave (92627), Newport Blvd (CA 55) at 17th St. 714/645-2221; FAX 714/650-9125.* E-mail RamadaLimited @NewportBeach.com; web www.newportbeach.com/RamadaLimited. 140 rms, 3 story. Mid-May-mid-Sept: S $84; D $89; each addl $5; suites $99-$149; under 17 free; lower rates rest of yr. Crib free. Pet accepted. TV; cable (premium). Pool; whirlpool. Complimentary continental bkfst. Restaurant nearby. Ck-out noon. Meeting rm. Valet serv. Coin lndry. Free airport transportation.

Exercise equipt; bicycles, weight machine. Some refrigerators; microwaves avail. Cr cds: A, C, D, DS, JCB, MC, V. [D] 🐾 ⊠ 🍴 ⊠ 🐾 [SC]

✔★ **VAGABOND INN.** *3205 Harbor Blvd (92626), I-405 exit Harbor Blvd S. 714/557-8360; FAX 714/662-7596.* 127 rms, 2 story. May-Sept: S, D $45-$70; each addl $5; suites $60-$110; under 18 free; lower rates rest of yr. Pet accepted; some restrictions; $5/day. TV; cable (premium); VCR avail (movies). Pool; whirlpool. Complimentary continental bkfst. Coffee in rms. Restaurant opp 24 hrs. Ck-out noon. Meeting rm. Business servs avail. Valet serv. Free airport transportation. Exercise equipt; weights, bicycles. Health club privileges. Refrigerators, microwaves avail. Some balconies. Mission-style building. Cr cds: A, C, D, DS, MC, V. 🐾 ⊠ 🍴 ⊠ 🐾 [SC]

Motor Hotel

★ ★ ★ **DOUBLETREE-ORANGE COUNTY AIRPORT.** *3050 Bristol St (92626), I-405 exit Bristol St S. 714/540-7000; FAX 714/540-9176.* Web www.doubletreehotels.com. 484 rms, 7 story. S, D $119-$149; each addl $15; suites $450-$650; under 18 free. Crib free. Pet accepted. Valet parking $8. TV; cable (premium). Heated pool; whirlpool, poolside serv. Coffee in rms. 2 restaurants 6 am-midnight. Rm serv. Bar from 11 am; entertainment Fri-Sun. Ck-out noon. Convention facilities. Business center. In-rm modem link. Concierge. Gift shop. Barber, beauty shop. Free airport transportation. Tennis privileges. Golf privileges. Exercise equipt; weights, treadmill, sauna. Masseur. Game rm. Refrigerators. Many private patios, balconies. Atrium lobby. Luxury level. Cr cds: A, C, D, DS, ER, JCB, MC, V.

[D] 🐾 🏋 🛏 ⊠ 🍴 ✈ ⊠ 🐾 [SC] 🏃

Hotels

★ ★ ★ **THE WESTIN SOUTH COAST PLAZA.** *686 Anton Blvd (92626), I-405 exit Bristol St N. 714/540-2500; FAX 714/662-6695.* Web westin.com. 390 rms, 16 story. S, D $179-$205; each addl $20; suites $285-$960; under 18 free; wkend package plans. Crib free. Pet accepted, some restrictions. Parking $6, valet $12. TV; cable (premium). Heated pool; poolside serv. Complimentary coffee in rms. Restaurant 6:30 am-10 pm. Rm serv 24 hrs. Bar noon-1 am; entertainment wkends. Ck-out 1 pm. Convention facilities. Business center. In-rm modem link. Gift shop. Free local airport transportation. Lighted tennis. Exercise equipt; weight machine, stair machine. Health club privileges. Minibars; wet bar in some suites. South Coast Plaza Retail Center & Village adj. Cr cds: A, C, D, DS, ER, JCB, MC, V. [D] 🐾 🏋 ⊠ 🍴 🏃 🐾 [SC] 🏃

★ ★ **WYNDHAM GARDEN-ORANGE COUNTY AIRPORT.** *3350 Ave of the Arts (92626), I-405 exit Bristol St, N to Anton Blvd. 714/751-5100; FAX 714/751-0129.* 238 rms, 6 story. S, D $109-$119; each addl $10; suites $119-$149; under 12 free; wkly, wkend rates; higher rates special events. Pet accepted, some restrictions; $25. TV; cable (premium). Heated pool; whirlpool. Coffee in rms. Restaurant 6:30 am-2:30 pm, 5-10 pm. Bar 4:30 pm-midnight. Ck-out noon. Coin lndry. Meeting rms. Business servs avail. Free garage parking. Free airport transportation. Exercise equipt; weights, stair machine. Refrigerators, microwaves avail. Some bathrm phones. Private patios, balconies. Fireplace in lobby; marble floors. Pool area overlooks lake. Cr cds: A, C, D, DS, JCB, MC, V.

[D] 🐾 ⊠ 🍴 🛐 ⊠ 🐾 [SC]

Death Valley National Park

(70 mi E of Lone Pine on CA 190)

Motel

✔★ **STOVE PIPE WELLS VILLAGE.** *CA 190 (92328). 619/786-2387; FAX 619/786-2389.* 82 rms, 5 buildings. No rm phones. S, D $53-$76; each addl $10; under 12 free. Crib $5. Pet accepted, some restrictions; $10-$25 refundable. Heated pool. Restaurant 7 am-2 pm, 6:30-10 pm. Bar 4:30-11 pm. Ck-out 11 am. Sundries. Landing strip. Panoramic view of mountains, desert, dunes. Cr cds: A, DS, MC, V. [D] 🐾 ⊠ 🛐 🐾

Dunsmuir

Motel

✔★ **CEDAR LODGE.** *4201 Dunsmuir Ave. 916/235-4331.* 18 rms, 6 kits. S $32-$34; D $36-$50; each addl $4; kit. units $10 addl; family rooms from $55. Crib $4. Pet accepted. TV; cable. Complimentary coffee in rms. Restaurant nearby. Ck-out 11 am. Downhill/x-country ski 16 mi. Private patios. Picnic tables, grill. Large exotic bird aviary. Near Sacramento River. Cr cds: A, DS, MC, V. 🐾 ⊠ ⊠ 🐾 [SC]

El Centro

Motels

✔★ **EXECUTIVE INN.** *725 State St. 760/352-8500; FAX 760/352-1322.* 42 rms, 2 story, 5 kits. S, D $20-$40; kit. units $30-$45; each addl $2; suites $40-$55. Crib $5. Pet accepted, some restrictions. TV; cable. Pool. Complimentary continental bkfst. Restaurant nearby. Ck-out 11 am. Coin lndry. Some free covered parking. Some refrigerators; microwaves avail. Grills. Cr cds: MC, V. 🖚 🏊 🕸 🐾 SC

★★ **RAMADA INN.** *1455 Ocotillo Dr, I-8 & Imperial Ave. 760/352-5152; FAX 760/337-1567.* 147 rms, 2 story. S, D $52-$75; each addl $6; suites $75-$90; under 19 free. Crib free. Pet accepted. TV; cable (premium), VCR avail. Heated pool, whirlpool. Restaurant open 24 hrs. Rm serv 6 am-2 pm, 5-10 pm. Bar 3:30 pm-midnight. Ck-out noon. Coin lndry. Meeting rms. Free airport, bus depot transportation. Exercise rm: weight machine, bicycles. Microwaves avail. Cr cds: A, C, D, DS, JCB, MC, V. 🖚 🏊 🏋 🕸 🐾 SC

★★ **TRAVELODGE.** *1464 Adams Ave. 760/352-7333.* 72 rms, 2 story, 6 kit. units. S, D $36-$45; each addl $4; kits. $38-$47; under 12 free; wkly rates. Pet accepted. TV; cable (premium). Pool. Complimentary continental bkfst. Restaurant adj 7 am-midnight. Ck-out 11 am. Free airport, bus depot transportation. Some refrigerators. Cr cds: A, C, D, DS, MC, V. 🖚 🏊 🕸 🐾 SC

★★ **VACATION INN.** *2015 Cottonwood Circle. 760/352-9523; FAX 760/353-7620; res: 800/328-6289.* 190 rms, 2 story. S, D $60-$65; suites $75-$95; higher rates special events. Crib free. Pet accepted; $25 deposit. TV; cable (premium). 2 heated pools; whirlpool, poolside serv. Restaurant 5:30 am-10 pm. Bar from 7 am. Ck-out noon. Coin lndry. Meeting rms. Business servs avail. In-rm modem link. Some refrigerators; microwaves avail. 31-space RV park adj. Cr cds: A, C, D, DS, MC, V. D 🖚 🏊 🕸 🐾 SC

Escondido *(See also Carlsbad, La Jolla, San Diego)*

Motor Hotel

✔★★★ **QUAILS INN.** *(1025 La Bonita Dr, San Marcos 92069)* W on CA 78 to San Marcos. *760/744-0120; FAX 760/744-0748; res: 800/447-6556.* 140 rms, 2 story. S, D $85-$150; each addl $10; suites, kit. cottages $175-$300; under 12 free; golf packages. Crib $10. Pet accepted, some restrictions; $10. TV; cable (premium), VCR avail. 2 heated pools; whirlpool. Restaurant adj 6:30 am-10 pm. Rm serv. Ck-out noon. Meeting rms. Tennis privileges. Golf privileges. Exercise equipt: weight machines, bicycle. Boat rental. Microwaves avail. Many private patios, balconies. On Lake San Marcos. Extensive grounds. Cr cds: A, D, DS, MC, V. D 🖚 🏋 🖚 🏊 🏋 🕸 🐾 SC

Resort

★★★ **WELK RESORT CENTER.** *8860 Lawrence Welk Dr (92026). 760/749-3000; FAX 760/749-5263; res: 800/932-9355.* 132 rms, 2-3 story. S, D $160-$190; each addl $10; suites $180-$255; golf plans. Pet accepted. TV; cable, VCR avail (movies $6). 2 heated pools; whirlpool. Supervised child's activities. Coffee in rms. Dining rm 7 am-9 pm. Bar 11 am-midnight. Ck-out noon. Meeting rms. In-rm modem link. Concierge. Shopping plaza. Beauty shop. Massage. 3 lighted tennis courts. 3 18-hole golf courses, putting green. Exercise equipt; bicycles, stair machine. Dinner theater. Semi-private patios, balconies. Some refrigerators. Cr cds: A, C, D, DS, ER, MC, V. D 🖚 🏋 🖚 🏊 🏋 🕸 🐾 SC

Eureka

Motels

★★ **CARSON HOUSE INN.** *1209 4th St. 707/443-1601; FAX 707/444-8365; res: 800/772-1622.* 60 rms, 2 story. No A/C. June-mid-Oct: S, D $75-$150; each addl $10; suites $100-$200; lower rates rest of yr. Crib $5. Pet accepted. TV; cable (premium). Heated pool; wading pool, whirlpool, sauna. Complimentary contintental bkfst. Complimentary coffee in rms. Restaurant opp 7 am-11 pm. Ck-out noon. Meeting rms. Business servs avail. Cr cds: A, C, D, DS, JCB, MC, V. D 🖚 🏊 🕸 🐾 SC

✔★ **TRAVELODGE.** *4 Fourth St. 707/443-6345; FAX 707/443-1486.* 46 rms, 2 story. No A/C. S $37-$55; D $38-$73; each addl $5; under 18 free. Crib free. Pet accepted. TV; cable (premium). Heated pool. Complimentary continental bkfst. Coffee in rms. Restaurant nearby. Ck-out 11 am. Business servs avail. Sundries. Cr cds: A, C, D, DS, ER, JCB, MC, V. 🖚 🏊 🕸 🐾 SC

Motor Hotel

★ ★ ★ **RED LION INN.** *1929 4th St. 707/445-0844; FAX 707/445-2752.* 178 rms, 3-4 story. S, D $78; suites $125-$175; under 18 free; wkend rates. Crib free. Pet accepted. TV; cable, VCR avail. Heated pool; whirlpool. Coffee in rms. Restaurant 6 am-10 pm. Rm serv. Bar; entertainment Fri, Sat, jazz Sun. Ck-out noon. Meeting rms. Business servs avail. In-rm modem link. Bellhops. Valet serv. Sundries. Free airport transportation. Balconies. Cr cds: A, C, D, DS, ER, JCB, MC, V. ▢ ⬚ ⬚ ⬚ ⬚ SC

Hotel

★ ★ ★ **EUREKA INN.** *518 7th St. 707/442-6441; FAX 707/442-0637; res: 800/862-4906.* 105 rms, 4 story. No A/C. S, D $100-$150; each addl $10; suites $155-$250; under 16 free. Crib free. Pet accepted. TV; cable. Heated pool; whirlpool, saunas. Restaurant 6:30 am-11 pm. Bar 4 pm-2 am; entertainment. Ck-out noon. Meeting rms. Business servs avail. Free airport, bus depot transportation. Some bathrm phones. Fireplace in lobby. Historic Tudor-style building (1922). Cr cds: A, C, D, DS, MC, V. ▢ ⬚ ⬚ ⬚ ⬚ SC

Fremont *(See also Oakland, San Jose, Santa Clara)*

Motels

★ ★ **BEST WESTERN.** *5400 Mowry Ave (94538). 510/792-4300; FAX 510/792-2643.* 122 rms, 2-3 story. S $75-$80; D $80-$90; each addl $10; under 14 free; lower rates wkends. Crib free. Pet accepted, some restrictions; $50. TV; cable (premium). Pool; whirlpool, sauna. Complimentary continental bkfst. Restaurant noon-2 pm, 5-10 pm. Bar 5 pm-1 am. Ck-out noon. Meeting rms. Business servs avail. Valet serv. Health club privileges. Some private patios, balconies. Cr cds: A, C, D, DS, MC, V. ▢ ⬚ ⬚ ⬚ ⬚ SC

★ ★ **RESIDENCE INN BY MARRIOTT.** *5400 Farwell Place (94536), E of I-880, Mowry Ave exit. 510/794-5900; FAX 510/793-6587.* 80 kit. suites, 2 story. Kit. suites $149-$169; wkly, monthly rates. Pet accepted, some restrictions; $75 & $10 per day. TV; cable (premium). Heated pool; whirlpool. Complimentary continental bkfst. Restaurant adj 6 am-midnight. Ck-out noon. Coin lndry. Meeting rms. Business servs avail. Valet serv. Airport transportation. Health club privileges. Private patios, balconies. Picnic tables, grills. Cr cds: A, C, D, DS, JCB, MC, V. ▢ ⬚ ⬚ ⬚ ⬚ SC

Fresno

Motel

✔ ★ **ECONOMY INNS OF AMERICA.** *2570 S East St (93706). 209/486-1188; FAX 209/486-2743.* 121 rms, 2 story. S $26; D $33.90-$40.90; each addl $5. Pet accepted. TV; cable. Heated pool. Restaurant nearby. Ck-out 11 am. Cr cds: A, MC, V.
▢ ⬚ ⬚ ⬚ ⬚ SC

Hotel

★ ★ ★ **HILTON.** *1055 Van Ness (93721). 209/485-9000; FAX 209/485-7666.* 192 rms, 9 story. S $74-$109; D $79-$129; each addl $10; suites $179-$525; under 18 free; wkend rates. Crib free. Pet accepted, some restrictions. TV; cable. Heated pool; whirlpool, poolside serv. Restaurant 11 am-11 pm. Bar. Ck-out noon. Meeting rms. Gift shop. Free airport transportation. Health club privileges. Cr cds: A, C, D, DS, MC, V.
▢ ⬚ ⬚ ⬚ ⬚ SC

Fullerton *(See also Anaheim, Buena Park)*

Hotel

★ ★ ★ **MARRIOTT AT CALIFORNIA STATE UNIVERSITY.** *2701 E Nutwood Ave (92831), CA 57, Nutwood Ave exit, 1 blk W. 714/738-7800; FAX 714/738-0288.* Web www.marriott.com/marriott/laxel. 224 rms, 6 story. S, D $119; suites $275. Crib avail. Pet accepted. TV; cable (premium). Heated pool; whirlpool, poolside serv. Restaurant 6:30 am-11 pm. Bar from 11 am. Ck-out noon. Meeting rms. Business servs avail. In-rm modem link. Exercise equipt; weight machine, stair machine, sauna. Health club privileges. Bathrm phone, refrigerator in suites. Microwaves avail. Cr cds: A, C, D, DS, JCB, MC, V.
▢ ⬚ ⬚ ⬚ ⬚ ⬚ SC

Garberville

Motel

★ ★ **SHERWOOD FOREST.** *814 Redwood Dr. 707/923-2721; FAX 707/923-3677.* 32 rms. May-Oct: S $56; D $60-$62; each addl $5; suites, kit. units $80-$88; lower rates rest of yr. Crib $6. Pet accepted. TV; cable (premium). Heated pool; whirlpool. Coffee in rms. Restaurant adj 6 am-3 pm. Ck-out 11 am. Coin lndry. Business servs avail. Free local airport transportation. Many refrigerators. Picnic tables, grills. Fish cleaning, fish storage facilities. Cr cds: A, DS, JCB, MC, V.

Glendale

Motel

★ **VAGABOND INN.** *120 W Colorado St (91204), I-5 exit Colorado St, 1 mi E. 626/240-1700; FAX 626/548-8428.* 52 rms, 3 story. S $53-$63; D $58-$70; each addl $5; under 18 free; higher rates: special events, Rose Bowl (3-day min). Crib $5. Pet accepted, some restrictions; $5/day. TV; cable (premium). Heated pool. Complimentary continental bkfst. Restaurant adj. Ck-out noon. Some refrigerators; microwaves avail. Cr cds: A, C, D, DS, MC, V.

Grass Valley

Motel

✔★ **HOLIDAY LODGE.** *1221 E Main St (95945). 916/273-4406; res: 800/742-7125 (CA).* 36 rms, 1-2 story. Mid-Apr-mid-Oct: S $38; D $46-$50; each addl $6; gold panning, hol rates; lower rates rest of yr. Crib $6. Pet accepted, some restrictions; $10. TV; cable. Pool. Continental bkfst. Restaurant nearby. Ck-out 11 am. Meeting rm. Some balconies. Cr cds: A, C, D, DS, MC, V.

Guerneville (See also Healdsburg, Santa Rosa)

Inn

★★ **HIGHLAND DELL INN.** *(21050 River Blvd, Monte Rio 95462) S on Bohemian Hwy, cross river, then left on River Blvd. 707/865-1759; res: 800/767-1759.* E-mail highland @netdex.com; web www.netdex.com/~highland. 8 units, 3 story, 4 suites. No A/C. May-Oct: S, D $90-$110; suites $130-$160; lower rates rest of yr. Adults only. Pet accepted, some restrictions; $100 deposit. TV; cable, VCR (free movies). Pool. Complimentary full bkfst; afternoon refreshments. Ck-out 11 am, ck-in 4-8 pm. Business servs avail. In-rm modem link. Refrigerators in suites. Grills. Built 1906, this was the first lodging in Sonoma County to have hot & cold running water. Overlooks Russian River. Stained-glass windows; fireplace in lobby; heirloom antiques and collection of historic local photos. Cr cds: A, DS, JCB, MC, V.

Half Moon Bay (See also San Mateo)

Motel

★ **HOLIDAY INN EXPRESS.** *230 S Cabrillo Hwy. 650/726-3400; FAX 650/726-1256.* 52 rms, 2 story. Feb-Oct: S, D $95-$125; each addl $10; under 18 free; higher rates: hols, special events; lower rates rest of yr. Crib free. Pet accepted; $10. TV. Complimentary continental bkfst. Restaurant nearby. Ck-out noon. Business servs avail. In-rm modem link. Cr cds: A, C, D, DS, JCB, MC, V.

Inn

★★ **ZABALLA HOUSE.** *324 Main St. 650/726-9123.* Web www.whis tlere.com/zaballa.rooms.html. 9 rms, 2 story, 3 suites. No rm phones. S, D $140-$275; each addl $10. Pet accepted; $10. TV; cable in some rms. Complimentary bkfst buffet; afternoon refreshments. Restaurant nearby. Ck-out 11 am, ck-in 3-7 pm. Business servs avail. Oldest building in town still standing (1859); some antiques. Some fireplaces, in-rm whirlpools. Totally nonsmoking. Cr cds: A, DS, MC, V.

Hanford

Inn

★★ **IRWIN STREET.** *522 N Irwin St. 209/583-8000; FAX 209/583-8793; 800 888/583-8080.* 30 rms in 4 Victorian-style buildings, 2 story, 3 suites. S, D $69-$79; suites $99; under 14 free. Pet accepted; $50. TV; cable (premium). Pool; poolside serv. Continental bkfst. Restaurant 7 am-2 pm; 5-9 pm. Ck-out noon, ck-in 2 pm. Balconies. Historic buildings (late 1800s), restored; many antiques. Cr cds: A, C, D, DS, MC, V.

Hayward *(See also Fremont, Oakland, San Francisco Airport Area)*

Motel

★ ★ **EXECUTIVE INN.** *20777 Hesperian Blvd (94541), 2 blks W of I-880, A St exit at Heperian.* 510/732-6300; FAX 510/783-2265; res: 800/553-5083. 145 rms, 3 story, 23 suites. S, D $74-$79; each addl $5; suites $84-$88; under 12 free; wkend rates. Pet accepted, some restrictions. TV; cable (premium). Heated pool. Complimentary coffee in rms. Complimentary continental bkfst. Restaurant nearby. Ck-out noon. Coin lndry. Meeting rms. Business center. Valet serv. Sundries. Free airport transportation. Exercise equipt: treadmill, stair machine. Bathrm phone, refrigerator in suites. Some balconies. Cr cds: A, C, D, DS, JCB, MC, V. 🄳 💺 ⚲ ⌧ 🐾 SC 🏃

Healdsburg *(See also Guerneville, Santa Rosa)*

Motel

✓★ ★ **BEST WESTERN DRY CREEK INN.** *198 Dry Creek Rd.* 707/433-0300; FAX 707/433-1129. Web www.sonoma.com/lodging/dry creek/. 102 rms, 3 story. Apr-Oct: S, D $89-$94; each addl $10; under 12 free; lower rates rest of yr. Crib free. Pet accepted; $10. TV; cable (premium). Heated pool; whirlpool. Complimentary continental bkfst. Restaurant adj. Ck-out noon. Guest lndry. Business servs avail. In-rm modem link. Exercise equipt: weight machine, stair machine. Some refrigerators. Cr cds: A, C, D, DS, ER, JCB, MC, V. 🄳 💺 ⚲ ⌧ ⚲ 🐾

Hemet *(See also Palm Springs)*

Motels

✓★ ★ **BEST WESTERN.** *2625 W Florida Ave (92545), I-215 exit CA 74, E 13 mi.* 909/925-6605; FAX 909/925-7095. 68 rms, 2 story, 29 kits. S $44; D $52-$58; each addl $6; suites $66; kit. units $52-$60; wkly, monthly rates; higher rates Ramona Pageant. Crib $4. Pet accepted, some restrictions; $10. TV; cable (premium). Heated pool; whirlpool. Continental bkfst, coffee in rms. Restaurant adj open 24 hrs. Ck-out 11 am. Coin lndry. Business servs avail. Health club privileges. Lawn games. Refrigerators; microwaves avail. Grills. Cr cds: A, C, D, DS, ER, MC, V. 💺 ⚲ ⌧ 🐾 SC

✓★ **SUPER 8.** *3510 W Florida Ave (92545).* 909/658-2281; FAX 909/925-6492; res: 800/769-6346. 70 rms, 3 story. Oct-Apr: S $38.88; D $46.88; each addl $4; suites $54.88; under 12 free; lower rates rest of yr. Crib free. Pet accepted. TV; cable (premium), VCR avail. Pool; whirlpool. Complimentary continental bkfst. Restaurant nearby. Ck-out 11 am. Business servs avail. Health club privileges. Refrigerators; microwaves avail. Cr cds: A, C, D, DS, JCB, MC, V. 🄳 💺 ⚲ ⌧ 🐾 SC

✓★ ★ **TRAVELODGE.** *1201 W Florida Ave (92543).* 909/766-1902. 46 rms, 2 story. S $38; D $43; suites $38-$43. Crib $5. Pet accepted; some restrictions, $5. TV; cable (premium), VCR avail. Pool; whirlpool. Complimentary continental bkfst. Restaurant opp 6 am-10 pm. Ck-out noon. Meeting rms. Coin lndry. Health club privileges. Refrigerators; microwaves avail. Cr cds: A, C, D, DS, JCB, MC, V. 🄳 💺 ⚲

Hollywood (L.A.) *(See also Los Angeles)*

Motel

✓★ ★ **BEST WESTERN HOLLYWOOD HILLS.** *6141 Franklin Ave (90028), US 101 Gower St exit to Franklin Ave, then 1 blk W.* 213/464-5181; FAX 213/962-0536. 86 units, 3-4 story, 47 kits. S $50-$70; D $70-$85; each addl $5; kit. units $10 addl; under 12 free; wkly rates; higher rates Rose Bowl. Crib $5. Pet accepted, some restrictions; $10. Heated pool. TV; cable (premium). Restaurant 7 am-10 pm; Sun, Mon to 4 pm. Rm serv. Ck-out noon. Business servs avail. Sundries. Health club privileges. Refrigerators; microwaves avail. Cr cds: A, C, D, DS, MC, V. 💺 ⚲ ⌧ 🐾 SC

Hotel

★ ★ ★ **LE MONTROSE SUITE HOTEL DE GRAN LUXE.** *(900 Hammond St, Los Angeles 90069) US 101 exit Sunset Blvd, W 4 mi to Hammond St.* 213/855-1115; FAX 213/657-9192; res: 800/776-0666. Web www.travel2000 .com. 128 kit. suites, 5 story. Suites $220-$500; under 12 free. Crib free. Covered parking $14. Pet accepted. TV; cable (premium), VCR avail. Pool; whirlpool, poolside serv. Restaurant 5 am-10:45 pm. Rm serv 24 hrs. Ck-out noon. Meeting rm. Business servs avail. In-rm modem link. Concierge. Lighted tennis, pro. Exercise rm; instructor, weight machine, stair machine, sauna. Massage. Bathrm phones, refrigerators, fireplaces; many wet bars; microwaves avail. Some balconies. Art nouveau decor. Cr cds: A, C, D, ER, JCB, MC, V.

D ⟦icons⟧ SC

Idyllwild *(See also Palm Desert, Palm Springs)*

Inn

✔ ★ ★ **FIRESIDE.** *54540 N Circle Dr. 909/659-2966.* Web www .idyl.com. 8 rms, 4 with shower only, 2 suites, 1 cabin, 6 kit. units. 1 A/C rm. No rm phones. S, D $55-$75; each addl $10; suites $85; cabin $100; under 5 free. Pet accepted, some restrictions. TV; cable (premium), VCR. Complimentary coffee in rms. Restaurant nearby. Ck-out 11 am, ck-in 2 pm. Refrigerators; microwaves avail. Picnic tables. In wooded area near village center. Cr cds: A, DS, MC, V. ⟦icons⟧ SC

Indio *(See also Idyllwild, Palm Desert, Palm Springs)*

Motel

★ ★ **BEST WESTERN DATE TREE.** *81-909 Indio Blvd (92201). 760/347-3421; FAX 760/347-3421; res: 800/292-5599.* Web www.bestwestern. com/thisco/bw/05215_b .html. 121 rms, 2 story. Jan-Apr: S, D $59-$98; each addl $6; suites, kit. units $79-$165; under 18 free; wkly rates; higher rates special events; lower rates rest of yr. Crib $10. Pet accepted, some restrictions. TV; cable. Heated pool; whirlpool. Playground. Complimentary continental bkfst. Restaurant adj open 24 hrs. Ck-out noon. Coin lndry. Business servs avail. In-rm modem link. Exercise equipt; weight machine, treadmill. Game rm. Lawn games. Refrigerators; microwaves avail. Balconies. Picnic tables, grills. Surrounded by palm trees, cactus gardens. Cr cds: A, C, D, DS, ER, JCB, MC, V. D ⟦icons⟧ SC

Inverness *(See also San Rafael)*

Inn

★ ★ ★ **MANKA'S INVERNESS LODGE.** *30 Callendar Way. 415/669-1034; FAX 415/669-1598; res: 800/585-5634.* 14 rms, 4 with shower only, 2 story, 4 kit. cabins. No A/C. Rm phone in 3 cottages. S, D $115-$325; under 12 free; wkly rates; 2-day min stay wkends; lower rates winter wkdays. Crib free. Pet accepted, some restrictions; $50. TV; cable, VCR. Restaurant 5:30-8:30 pm. Ck-out 11 am, ck-in 4 pm. Business servs avail. In-rm modem link. Hiking. Some refrigerators, some balconies, some fireplaces; microwaves avail. Turn-of-the-century hunting lodge & cabins. Totally nonsmoking. Cr cds: MC, V. ⟦icons⟧

Irvine *(See also Costa Mesa, Laguna Beach, Newport Beach)*

Hotels

★ ★ **HOLIDAY INN SELECT-ORANGE COUNTY AIRPORT.** *17941 Von Karman Ave (92614), I-405 MacArthur Blvd exit, near Orange County Airport. 714/863-1999; FAX 714/474-7236.* Web www.holiday-inn.com. 335 rms, 14 story. S, D $169-$189; each addl $10; suites $179-$289; family rates; lower rates wkends. Crib free. Pet accepted, some restrictions. TV; cable (premium). Indoor pool; whirlpool, poolside serv. Coffee in rms. Restaurant 6 am-10 pm. Bar 11:30 am-midnight. Ck-out noon. Coin lndry. Convention facilities. Business center. In-rm modem link. Gift shop. Free airport transportation. Exercise equipt; weight machine, treadmill, sauna. Health club privileges. Refrigerators avail. Sun deck. Luxury level. Cr cds: A, C, D, DS, JCB, MC, V. D ⟦icons⟧ SC

★ ★ **MARRIOTT.** *18000 Von Karman Ave (92612), in Koll Business Center, near Orange County Airport. 714/553-0100; FAX 714/261-7059.* Web www.marriott.com. 485 rms, 17 story. S, D $89-$178; suites $250-$650. Crib free. Pet accepted, some restrictions. Parking $5, valet $8. TV; cable (premium). Indoor/outdoor pool; whirlpool, poolside serv. Restaurants 6 am-midnight. Bars 11-2 am; entertainment. Ck-out noon. Coin lndry. Convention facilities. Business center. Concierge. Barber, beauty shop. Free airport, local transportation. Lighted tennis; pro. Exercise equipt; weights, bicycles. Health club privileges. Massage. Game rm. Refrigerators; microwaves avail. Some balconies. Luxury level. Cr cds: A, C, D, DS, ER, JCB, MC, V. D ⟦icons⟧ SC

Jackson *(See also Sacramento)*

Motel

✔ ★ **JACKSON HOLIDAY LODGE.** *850 N CA 49. 209/223-0486; FAX 209/223-2905.* 36 rms, 2 story, 8 kits. S $40-$65; D $46-$75; each addl $5; kit. units $70. Crib $5.

Pet accepted, some restrictions. TV; cable. Pool. Complimentary continental bkfst. Complimentary coffee in rms. Ck-out 11 am. Cr cds: A, D, DS, MC, V.

Joshua Tree National Park (See also Indio, Palm Desert)

(Entrances: 25 mi E of Indio on I-10 or S of Joshua Tree, Yucca Valley and Twentynine Palms on CA 62)

Motel

★ ★ OASIS OF EDEN INN & SUITES. *(56377 Twentynine Palms Hwy, Yucca Valley 92284) W on CA 62. 760/365-6321; FAX 760/365-9592; res: 800/606-6686.* Web www.desertgold.com/eden.html. 39 rms, 1-2 story, 20 suites, 6 kit. units. Jan-May: S $44.75-$54.75; D $64.75-$106.75; each addl $5; suites, kit. units $54.75-$95.75; family, wkly, monthly rates; lower rates rest of yr. Crib free. Pet accepted, some restrictions; $10. TV; cable (premium), VCR (movies $3). Heated pool; whirlpool. Complimentary coffee in lobby. Complimentary continental bkfst. Restaurant opp 7 am-10 pm. Ck-out 11 am. Meeting rms. Business servs avail. Golf privileges. Refrigerators; microwaves avail. Theme rms with in-rm whirlpools avail. Cr cds: A, D, DS, MC, V. [D]

Inn

★ ★ JOSHUA TREE. *(61259 Twentynine Palms Hwy, Joshua Tree 92252) 760/366-1188; FAX 760/366-3805; res: 800/366-1444.* 10 rms, shower only, 1 with A/C, 2 suites. Oct-mid-June: S $55-$85; D $85-$95; suites $125-$150; each addl $10; under 10 free; wkly, monthly rates; lower rates rest of yr. Pet accepted, some restrictions; $10. TV; cable (premium), VCR avail. Pool. Playground. Complimentary full bkfst; afternoon refreshments. Dining rm by res. Ck-out noon, ck-in 2 pm. Business servs avail. In-rm modem link. Concierge serv. Luggage handling. Airport transportation. Lawn games. Some refrigerators; microwaves avail. Picnic tables. Cr cds: A, C, D, DS, MC, V.

King City

Motel

★ ★ COURTESY INN. *4 Broadway Circle, off US 101 Broadway exit. 408/385-4646; FAX 408/385-6024; res: 800/350-5616.* 63 rms, 35 suites. S $54-$85; D $59-$89; each addl $6; suites $59-$135; under 14 free. Crib free. Pet accepted, some restrictions; $10. TV; cable (premium), VCR (movies $2.50). Pool; whirlpool. Complimentary continental bkfst. Coffee in rms. Restaurant adj open 24 hrs. Ck-out noon. Coin lndry. Meeting rm. Business servs avail. In-rm modem link. Refrigerators, microwaves; whirlpool suites avail. Grill. Cr cds: A, D, DS, MC, V. [D]

Laguna Beach (See also Costa Mesa, Irvine, Newport Beach, San Juan Capistrano)

Motor Hotel

★ VACATION VILLAGE. *647 S Coast Hwy (92652). 714/494-8566; FAX 714/494-1386; res: 800/843-6895.* 133 rms in 5 buildings, 3-5 story, 70 kits. July-Labor Day (2-day min): S, D $80-$215; each addl $10; suites $175-$295; kit. units $95-$205; family, wkly rates Sept-Memorial Day; winter wkends (2-day min); some lower rates rest of yr. Crib free. Pet accepted, some restrictions. TV; cable. Heated pool; whirlpool. Complimentary coffee in rms. Restaurant 8 am-10 pm. Bar. Ck-out 11 am. Meeting rm. Bellhops. Some covered parking. Game rm. Refrigerators; microwaves avail. Some balconies. Sun deck. On beach. Cr cds: A, C, D, DS, MC, V.

Inn

★ CASA LAGUNA INN. *2510 S Coast Hwy (92651). 714/494-2996; FAX 714/494-5009; res: 800/233-0449.* 20 rms, 3 story, 5 kit. suites. S, D $105-$120; each addl $20; suites $175-$225; under 13 free; wkly rates. Crib $5. Pet accepted. TV; cable, VCR avail. Heated pool. Complimentary continental bkfst; evening refreshments. Ck-out 11 am, ck-in 2 pm. Health club privileges. Some refrigerators; microwaves avail. Balconies. Elaborate grounds; garden. Spanish architecture, individually decorated rms. Panoramic ocean views. Cr cds: A, C, DS, MC, V.

La Jolla (San Diego) (See also San Diego)

Motel

★ ★ RESIDENCE INN BY MARRIOTT. *8901 Gilman Dr. 619/587-1770; FAX 619/552-0387.* 287 kit. suites, 2 story. Kit. suites $180-$299; wkly rates. Crib free. Pet accepted; $50 & $6/day. TV; cable (premium), VCR avail (movies). 2 heated pools; 5 whirlpools. Complimentary continental bkfst. Restaurant nearby. Ck-out noon. Coin lndry.

Meeting rms. Business servs avail. In-rm modem link. Valet serv. Airport transportation. Lawn games. Refrigerators, microwaves, fireplaces. Grills. Cr cds: A, C, D, DS, JCB, MC, V. [D] [icons] SC

Hotel

★ ★ ★ MARRIOTT. 4240 La Jolla Village Dr. 619/587-1414; FAX 619/546-8518. Web www.marriott.com. 360 rms, 15 story. S, D $109-$159; suites $275-$650; under 18 free; wkend rates. Crib free. Pet accepted. Covered parking $8/day, valet $12. TV; cable (premium), VCR avail. Indoor/outdoor pool; whirlpool. Restaurant 6:30 am-10:30 pm. Bar. Ck-out noon. Coin lndry. Convention facilities. Business servs avail. In-rm modem link. Exercise rm; instructor, weights, rower, sauna. Game rm. Refrigerators avail. Private patios, balconies. Luxury level. Cr cds: A, C, D, DS, JCB, MC, V. [D] [icons] SC

Lake Arrowhead (See also Big Bear Lake)

Motel

✔ ★ TREE TOP LODGE. 27992 Rainbow Dr, at jct CA 173, near Lake Arrowhead Village. 909/337-2311; res: 800/358-8733. 20 rms, 1-2 story, 7 kits. S, D $59-$108; suites, kit. units $80-$139; fireplace units $74-$129. Pet accepted, some restrictions. TV; cable, VCR avail (movies $2). Heated pool. Complimentary coffee in lobby. Ck-out 11 am. Refrigerators; some fireplaces. Picnic tables, grill. Private nature trail. Cr cds: A, C, D, DS, JCB, MC, V. [icons] SC

Lancaster

Motel

★ ★ BEST WESTERN ANTELOPE VALLEY INN. 44055 N Sierra Hwy (93534). 805/948-4651. 148 units, 1-3 story. S $63; D $69; each addl $7; suites $125; under 12 free. Crib free. Pet accepted. TV; cable. Heated pool; poolside serv. Playground. Restaurant 5 am-11 pm. Rm serv 6 am-10 pm. Bar 5 pm-1:30 am; entertainment Fri, Sat. Ck-out 1 pm. Meeting rms. Business servs avail. In-rm modem link. Valet serv. Barber, beauty shop. Health club privileges. Lawn games. Cr cds: A, C, D, DS, MC, V. [icons] SC

Lompoc (See also Solvang)

Motor Hotel

✔ ★ ★ QUALITY INN AND SUITES. 1621 North H St. 805/735-8555; FAX 805/735-8566. 219 rms, 4 story, 93 kits. S, D $56-$73; suites $77-$138; each addl $6; under 18 free. Crib free. Pet accepted; $18. TV; cable (premium). Heated pool; whirlpool. Full bkfst buffet. Coffee in rms. Ck-out noon. Coin lndry. Meeting rm. Business servs avail. Valet serv. Driving range. Health club privileges. Massage. Many refrigerators. Cr cds: A, C, D, DS, ER, JCB, MC, V. [D] [icons]

Lone Pine

Motel

✔ ★ ★ DOW VILLA. 310 S Main St. 619/876-5521; FAX 619/876-5643; res: 800/824-9317 (CA). 39 rms, 2 story. S, D $74; each addl $5; suites $80; golf packages. Crib free. Pet accepted, some restrictions. TV; cable, VCR avail. Heated pool; whirlpool. Complimentary coffee in rms. Restaurant open 24 hrs. Ck-out noon. Refrigerators. Some in-rm whirlpools. Motel for motion picture casts since the early 1920s. Cr cds: A, C, D, DS, MC, V. [D] [icons] SC

Long Beach (See also Anaheim, Buena Park, Los Angeles)

Hotels

★ ★ HILTON. Two World Trade Center (90831), adj World Trade Center. 562/983-3400; FAX 562/983-1200. 393 rms, 15 story. S $120-$170; D $140-$190; each addl $25; suites $450-$1,400; family rates; higher rates Grand Prix. Crib free. Pet accepted, some restrictions. Garage parking $8, valet $10. TV; cable (premium). Pool; whirlpool. Restaurant 6 am-midnight. Bar 4 pm-2 am. Ck-out noon. Convention facilities. Business center. In-rm modem link. Concierge. Gift shop. Beauty shop. Airport transportation. Exercise rm; instructor, weight machine, bicycles, steam rm. Minibars; some wet bars; refrigerators avail. Balconies. Opp ocean; most rms have ocean view. Cr cds: A, C, D, DS, ER, JCB, MC, V. [D] [icons] SC

★ ★ ★ **SHERATON.** *333 E Ocean Blvd (90802).* 562/436-3000; FAX 562/436-9176. 460 rms, 16 story. S, D $135-$175; each addl $20; suites $265-$1000; under 17 free; wkend rates; higher rates Grand Prix. Crib free. Pet accepted. Garage $6, valet parking $9. TV; cable (premium), VCR avail. Heated pool; whirlpool, poolside serv. Complimentary coffee in rms. Restaurant 6:30 am-10:30 pm. Rm serv 24 hrs. Bar 11-2 am. Ck-out noon. Convention facilities. Business center. In-rm modem link. Concierge. Gift shop. Airport transportation. Exercise equipt; weight machine, bicycles, sauna. Minibars; some bathrm phones. Opp ocean. Cr cds: A, C, D, DS, ER, JCB, MC, V. 🄳 🛎 🏊 🏃 🖂 🐾 SC 🚶

Los Angeles

Motel

★ ★ **RESIDENCE INN BY MARRIOTT.** *(1700 N Sepulveda Blvd, Manhattan Beach 90266)* CA 405 to Rosecrans exit. 310/546-7627; FAX 310/545-1327. 176 kit. suites, 2 story. S $99-$178; D $150-$198; each addl $10; under 12 free; wkly, monthly rates. Crib free. Pet accepted, some restrictions. TV; cable (premium). Heated pool; whirlpool. Complimentary continental bkfst. Restaurant nearby. Ck-out noon. Meeting rm. Business servs avail. In-rm modem link. Valet serv. Free airport transportation. Microwaves. Balconies. Cr cds: A, C, D, DS, JCB, MC, V. 🄳 🛎 🏊 🖂 🐾 SC

Hotels

★ ★ **CHATEAU MARMONT.** *8221' Sunset Blvd (90046), in West Hollywood.* 213/656-1010; FAX 213/655-5311. E-mail chateaula@aol.com. 63 rms, 7 story, 54 kits. S, D $190; suites $240-$1,200; cottages, kits. $260; villas $600; monthly rates. Pet accepted. TV; cable (premium), VCR. Heated pool; poolside serv. Restaurant 6-2 am. Rm serv 24 hrs. Ck-out noon. Meeting rm. Business servs avail. In-rm modem link. Garage, valet parking. Exercise equipt; weight machines, treadmill. Refrigerators, minibars. Private patios, balconies. Neo-Gothic chateau-style building; old Hollywood landmark. Cr cds: A, C, D, MC, V.
🄳 🛎 🏊 🏃 🐾

✔ ★ ★ **HOLIDAY INN BRENTWOOD-BEL AIR.** *170 N Church Lane (90049), I-405 Sunset Blvd exit, west of downtown.* 310/476-6411; FAX 310/472-1157. E-mail hibelair @deltanet.com. 211 rms, 17 story. S, D $109-$149; each addl $10; suites $210; under 12 free; hol, wkend, wkly rates; higher rates special events; some lower rates in winter. Crib free. Pet accepted, some restrictions. TV; cable (premium), VCR avail. Pool; whirlpool. Restaurant 6:30 am-11 pm. Bar 11 am-midnight. Ck-out noon. Coin lndry. Meeting rms. Business servs avail. In-rm modem link. Concierge. Exercise equipt; treadmill, bicycles. Refrigerators avail. Balconies. Cr cds: A, C, D, DS, JCB, MC, V. 🄳 🛎 🏊 🏃 🖂 🐾 SC

★ ★ **HOLIDAY INN-CITY CENTER.** *1020 S Figueroa St (90015-1392), opp Convention Center, downtown.* 213/748-1291; FAX 213/748-6028. Web www.socalcol.com/la. 195 rms, 9 story. S, D $89-$169; each addl $10; under 18 free. Crib free. Pet accepted, some restrictions. TV; cable (premium), VCR avail. Heated pool. Restaurant 6:30 am-1 pm, 5-10 pm. Bar noon-midnight. Ck-out noon. Coin lndry. Meeting rms. Business servs avail. Gift shop. Exercise equipt; treadmill, stair machine, sauna. Cr cds: A, C, D, DS, JCB, MC, V. 🄳 🛎 🏊 🏃 🖂 🐾 SC

★ ★ ★ ★ **HOTEL BEL-AIR.** *701 Stone Canyon Rd (90077), I-405 to Sunset Blvd exit, in Bel Air.* 310/472-1211; res: 800/648-4097; FAX 310/476-5890. Set among 12 acres of exotic gardens and a lake, this vintage resort offers serenity, seclusion and a family of resident swans. Unique guest rooms are decorated with peach and earth tones in a Mediterranean style. 92 rms, some kits. S, D $325-$435; suites $525-$2,500. Pet accepted; $250. TV; cable (premium), VCR (movies). Pool; poolside serv. Restaurant 7 am-2:30 pm, 6:30-10:30 pm. Rm serv 24 hrs. Bar 10-2 am; entertainment. Ck-out 1 pm. Meeting rms. Business servs avail. In-rm modem link. Concierge. Valet parking. Airport transportation. Exercise equipt; stair machines, treadmills. Massage. Health club privileges. Bathrm phones; some wood-burning fireplaces. Private patios. Cr cds: A, C, D, JCB, MC, V.
🄳 🛎 🏊 🏃 🖂 🐾

★ ★ ★ **HOTEL NIKKO AT BEVERLY HILLS.** *465 S La Cienega Blvd (90048), N of Wilshire Blvd, at Burton Way, west of downtown.* 310/247-0400; FAX 310/247-0315. This contemporary hotel, located on Restaurant Row, is marked by bold American architecture and traditional Japanese simplicity. Hotel Nikko offers a state-of-the-art health club and nightly entertainment as well as a wealth of business services. 296 units, 7 story. S $270-$310; D $295-$395; each addl $25; suites $600-$1,800; under 12 free. Crib $25. Pet accepted. Valet parking $16. TV; cable (premium), VCR avail. Pool. Complimentary coffee in rms. Restaurants 6 am-10 pm. Rm serv 24 hrs. Bar 3 pm-1 am; entertainment. Ck-out 1 pm. Business center. In-rm modem link. Concierge. Gift shop. Exercise equipt; weight machine, bicycles. Massage. Bathrm phones, Japanese soaking tubs, minibars. Balconies. Cr cds: A, C, D, DS, JCB, MC, V. 🄳 🛎 🏊 🏃 🖂 🐾 🚶

★ ★ **SUMMERFIELD SUITES.** *1000 Westmount Dr (90069), I-405 exit Santa Monica Blvd.* 310/657-7400; FAX 310/854-6744; res: 800/833-4353. E-mail sshholly wood@attmail.com. 95 kit. suites, 4 story. S, D $210-$255; under 12 free; monthly rates. Crib free. Pet accepted. Covered parking $9. TV; cable (premium), VCR (movies $5). Pool. Complimentary continental bkfst. Ck-out noon. Coin lndry. Meeting rm. In-rm modem link. Exercise equipt; weight machine, bicycle, sauna. Health club privileges. Refrigerators, microwaves, fireplaces. Balconies. Cr cds: A, C, D, DS, JCB, MC, V.

D ⊷ ≋ 🕇 ⤢ 🐾

Los Angeles Intl Airport Area
(See also Los Angeles)

Motels

✔ ★ ★ **HAMPTON INN.** *(10300 La Cienega Blvd, Inglewood 90304) ³/₄ mi E on Century Blvd, then S on La Cienega Blvd.* 310/337-1000; FAX 310/645-6925. Web www.hampton-inn.com. 148 rms, 7 story. S, D $66-$86; under 18 free. Crib free. Pet accepted, some restrictions. TV; cable (premium). Complimentary continental bkfst. Restaurant nearby. Ck-out noon. Meeting rms. In-rm modem link. Valet serv. Free airport transportation. Exercise equipt; stair machine, bicycles. Cr cds: A, C, D, DS, MC, V.

D ⊷ 🕇 ⤢ ⤢ 🐾 SC

✔ ★ ★ **TRAVELODGE-LAX.** *(5547 W Century Blvd, Los Angeles 90045) ¹/₂ mi W off I-405, at Century Blvd & Aviation Blvd.* 310/649-4000; FAX 310/649-0311. E-mail aci@chms.net; web www.chms.net. 147 rms, 2 story. S $64-$74; D $69-$88; each addl $8; under 18 free. Pet accepted. TV; cable (premium), VCR. Pool. Coffee in rms. Restaurant open 24 hrs. Rm serv 6 am-10 pm. Bar 10-2 am. Ck-out noon. Coin lndry. Bellhops. Valet serv. Gift shop. Free airport transportation. Exercise equipt; bicycle, rower. Some private patios, balconies. Cr cds: A, C, D, DS, ER, JCB, MC, V.   ⊷ ≋ 🕇 ⤢ ⤢ 🐾

Hotels

★ ★ **EMBASSY SUITES.** *(1440 E Imperial Ave, El Segundo 90245) ¹/₂ mi S on Sepulveda Blvd, then 1 blk W on Imperial Ave.* 310/640-3600; FAX 310/322-0954. Web www.embassy-suites.com. 350 suites, 5 story. S, D $119-$169; each addl $15; under 18 free; wknd rates. Pet accepted, some restrictions. Parking $6. TV; cable (premium), VCR avail. Indoor pool; whirlpool. Complimentary full bkfst. Restaurant 11 am-10 pm. Bar to 2 am. Ck-out noon. Meeting rms. Business center. In-rm modem link. Gift shop. Free airport transportation. Exercise equipt; weight machine, bicycles. Refrigerators, microwaves. Balconies. Sun deck. Spanish mission architecture. Near beach. Cr cds: A, C, D, DS, ER, JCB, MC, V.   D ⊷ ≋ 🕇 ⤢ ⤢ 🐾 SC 🐾

★ ★ ★ **HILTON & TOWERS-LOS ANGELES AIRPORT.** *(5711 W Century Blvd, Los Angeles 90045) ³/₄ mi W of I-405.* 310/410-4000; FAX 310/410-6250. 1,234 rms, 17 story. S $109-$169; each addl $20; suites $150-$900; family, wknd rates. Valet parking $13, garage $9. Pet accepted. TV; cable (premium), VCR avail. Heated pool; whirlpools, poolside serv (seasonal). Restaurants open 24 hrs. Bar 11-2 am. Ck-out noon. Convention facilities. Business center. In-rm modem link. Drugstore. Coin lndry. Free airport transportation. Exercise rm; instructor, weights, bicycles, sauna. Some bathrm phones; refrigerators, microwaves avail. Some private patios. Luxury level. Cr cds: A, C, D, DS, ER, JCB, MC, V.

D ⊷ ≋ 🕇 ⤢ ⤢ 🐾 SC 🐾

★ ★ **MARRIOTT-AIRPORT.** *(5855 W Century Blvd, Los Angeles 90045) I-405 exit Century Blvd W.* 310/641-5700; FAX 310/337-5358. 1,010 rms, 18 story. S, D $135-$160; suites from $189; family, wknd rates. Crib free. Pet accepted, some restrictions. Parking $10, valet $12. TV; cable (premium), VCR avail. Heated pool; whirlpool, poolside serv. Restaurants 6 am-midnight. Rm serv 24 hrs. Bars; entertainment. Ck-out 1 pm. Coin lndry. Convention facilities. Business center. In-rm modem link. Concierge. Shopping arcade. Beauty shop. Free airport transportation. Exercise equipt; weights, bicycles. Some bathrm phones, refrigerators. Balconies. Luxury level. Cr cds: A, C, D, DS, JCB, MC, V.

D ⊷ ≋ 🕇 ⤢ ⤢ 🐾 SC 🐾

✔ ★ ★ **QUALITY HOTEL-LOS ANGELES AIRPORT.** *(5249 W Century Blvd, Los Angeles 90045) I-405 exit Century Blvd W.* 310/645-2200; FAX 310/641-8214. 278 rms, 10 story. S, D $89-$119; each addl $10; under 18 free; wknd rates. Pet accepted. TV; cable (premium), VCR avail. Pool; poolside serv. Restaurant 6 am-10 pm. Bar 5-11 pm. Ck-out noon. Convention facilities. Business center. Free airport transportation. Exercise equipt; bicycles, treadmill. Cr cds: A, C, D, DS, ER, JCB, MC, V.   D ⊷ ≋ 🕇 ⤢ ⤢ 🐾 SC 🐾

★ ★ ★ **WESTIN-L.A. AIRPORT.** *(5400 W Century Blvd, Los Angeles 90045) 1 mi E on Century Blvd.* 310/216-5858; FAX 310/645-8053. Web www.westin.com. 723 rms, 12 story. S, D $129-$159; each addl $20; suites $275-$1,500; under 18 free; wkend rates.

Covered parking $8. Pet accepted. TV; cable (premium). Heated pool; whirlpool. Restaurant 6 am-11 pm. Rm serv 24 hrs. Bar 10-2 am; entertainment. Ck-out noon. Convention facilities. Business center. In-rm modem link. Gift shop. Free airport transportation. Guest lndry. Exercise equipt; weight machine, bicycles, sauna. Minibars; bathrm phones in suites; microwaves avail. Balconies. Luxury level. Cr cds: A, C, D, DS, ER, JCB, MC, V.

D ✔ ≈ 🏋 ✈ ⊠ 🐾 SC 🏌

Madera (See also Fresno)

Motel

✔★ **ECONOMY INNS OF AMERICA.** *1855 W Cleveland Ave. 209/661-1131; FAX 209/661-0224.* 80 rms, 2 story. S $29.90-$35.90; D $36.90-$44.90. Pet accepted. TV. Heated pool. Restaurant adj 6 am-10 pm. Ck-out 11 am. Cr cds: A, MC, V.

D ✔ ≈ ⊠ 🐾 SC

Mammoth Lakes (See also Bishop)

Motels

(Wkend, holiday rates are usually higher in this area)

✔★ **ECONO LODGE WILDWOOD INN.** *Box 568, 1/4 mi W of Old Mammoth Rd on Main St (CA 203). 619/934-6855; FAX 619/934-3626; res: 800/845-8764.* 32 rms, 2 story. No A/C. Nov-Apr: S $49-$99; D $59-$99; ski plans; lower rates rest of yr. Pet accepted. TV; cable (premium). Heated pool; whirlpool. Continental bkfst. Coffee in rms. Restaurant nearby. Ck-out 10 am. Business servs avail. Downhill/x-country ski 3 mi. Some refrigerators. Mountain view from some rms. Cr cds: A, C, D, DS, MC, V. D ✔ ✈ ≈ ⊠ 🐾 SC

★★ **SHILO INN.** *2963 Main St (CA 203). 619/934-4500; FAX 619/934-7594.* 70 rms, 4 story. Mid-Nov-mid-Apr: S, D $79-$129; under 12 free; lower rates rest of yr. Crib free. Pet accepted, some restrictions; $7. TV; cable (premium), VCR avail. Indoor pool. Complimentary continental bkfst. Restaurant opp 5 am-10 pm. Ck-out noon. Coin lndry. Meeting rms. Business servs avail. Garage parking. Free airport transportation. Downhill/x-country ski 5 mi. Exercise equipt; weight machine, bicycles, whirlpool, sauna. Bathrm phones, refrigerators. Cr cds: A, C, D, DS, ER, JCB, MC, V. D ✔ ✈ ≈ 🏋 ⊠ 🐾 SC

Marysville (See also Oroville)

Motel

✔★ **VADA'S.** *(545 Colusa Ave, Yuba City 95991) On CA 20 in Yuba City. 916/671-1151; res: 800/593-4666.* 38 rms, 1-2 story, 7 kits. S $33-$45; D $36-$70; kit. units $5 addl. Pet accepted; $50 deposit. TV; cable. Complimentary continental bkfst, coffee in rms. Restaurant adj open 24 hrs. Ck-out 11 am. Refrigerators avail. Cr cds: A, DS, MC, V.

✔ ⊠ 🐾

Mendocino (See also Willits)

Inn

★★★ **STANFORD INN BY THE SEA.** *S on CA 1. 707/937-5615; FAX 707/937-0305; res: 800/331-8884.* 33 rms, 2-3 story, 2 kits. No A/C. S, D $175-$225; kit. suites $200-$325. Crib $5. Pet accepted. TV; cable (premium), VCR (movies $4). Indoor pool; whirlpool, sauna. Complimentary full bkfst. Coffee in rms. Ck-out noon, ck-in 4 pm. Business servs avail. In-rm modem link. Bellhops. Concierge. Free airport transportation. Exercise equipt; stair machine, bicycle. Refrigerators, fireplaces. Private patios, balconies. Antiques. Big River llamas on grounds. Tropical greenhouse. Organic gardens, nursery. On 10 acres of meadow, forest overlooking ocean, river. Totally nonsmoking. Cr cds: A, C, D, DS, ER, JCB, MC, V. D ✔ ✔ ≈ ⊠ 🐾

Merced

Motel

✔★ **BEST WESTERN SEQUOIA INN.** *1213 V Street (95340). 209/723-3711; FAX 209/722-8551.* 98 rms, 2 story. S $54-$59; D $59-$64; each addl $5. Crib $5. Pet accepted. TV. Pool. Restaurant 6 am-11 pm. Rm serv. Bar noon-11 pm, wkends to midnight. Ck-out noon. Meeting rm. Cr cds: A, C, D, DS, MC, V. D ✔ ≈ ⊠ 🐾 SC

Monterey *(See also Carmel, Pebble Beach, Salinas)*

Motels

(Rates are often higher holidays, special events, some wkends)

★ ★ **BAY PARK.** *1425 Munras Ave. 408/649-1020; FAX 408/373-4258; res: 800/338-3564.* E-mail baypark@montereybay.com. 80 rms, 3 story. No elvtr. June-Sept: S, D $99-$150; each addl $10; under 18 free; lower rates rest of yr. Crib free. Pet accepted; $5 per day. TV, cable. Heated pool; whirlpool. Restaurant 7 am-9 pm. Rm serv. Bar 4-10 pm; entertainment Sat. Ck-out noon. Meeting rms. Business servs avail. Sundries. Some refrigerators, microwaves. Cr cds: A, C, D, DS, ER, MC, V. 🛌 ≈ 🖎 🐾 SC

★ ★ **CYPRESS GARDENS INN.** *1150 Munras Ave. 408/373-2761; FAX 408/649-1329; res: 800/433-4732.* E-mail concierge@carmelinns.com; web www.innsbythesea.com. 46 rms, 2 story. No A/C. Late June-Oct: S, D $89-$115; each addl $10; suite $195; under 13 free; lower rates rest of yr. Crib free. Pet accepted. TV; cable (premium). Heated pool; whirlpool. Complimentary continental bkfst. Ck-out noon. Business servs avail. Microwaves avail. Private patios, balconies. Fireplace in suite. Cr cds: A, DS, JCB, MC, V.
🛌 ≈ 🖎 🐾 SC

★ **EL ADOBE INN.** *936 Munras Ave. 408/372-5409; FAX 408/375-7236; res: 800/433-4732.* E-mail concierge@camelinn.com; web www.innsby thesea.com. 26 rms, 2 story. No A/C. Late June-Oct: S, D $85-$115; each addl $10; under 13 free; lower rates rest of yr. Crib free. Pet accepted. TV; cable (premium). Complimentary continental bkfst. Ck-out noon. Business servs avail. Whirlpool. Sun deck. Cr cds: A, DS, JCB, MC, V.
🛌 🖎 🐾 SC

Motor Hotels

★ ★ **BEST WESTERN MONTEREY BEACH.** *2600 Sand Dunes Dr, near Monterey Peninsula Airport. 408/394-3321; FAX 408/393-1912.* 196 rms, 4 story. June-Oct: S, D $99-$199; under 13 free; lower rates rest of yr. Crib free. Pet accepted; $25. TV; cable (premium). Pool; whirlpool. Restaurant 7 am-9:30 pm. Rm serv. Bar 4-11 pm. Ck-out noon. Meeting rms. Business servs avail. Bellhops. Exercise equipt; treadmills, stair machines. Some refrigerators; microwaves avail. Ocean view; beach access. Cr cds: A, C, D, DS, JCB, MC, V. D 🛌 ≈ 🏋 🖎 🐾 SC

★ ★ **BEST WESTERN VICTORIAN INN.** *487 Foam St. 408/373-8000; FAX 408/373-4815; res: 800/232-4141.* 68 rms, 3 story. S, D $99-$289; each addl $10; under 13 free. Pet accepted; $100 deposit, $25 fee. TV; cable, VCR (movies). Complimentary continental bkfst. Ck-out noon. Meeting rms. Business servs avail. Whirlpool. Bathrm phones, refrigerators, fireplaces. Private patios, balconies. Victorian furnishings. 2 blks from bay. Cr cds: A, C, D, DS, JCB, MC, V. D 🛌 🖎 🐾 SC

Morro Bay *(See also Atascadero, Pismo Beach, San Luis Obispo)*

Motels

✔ ★ ★ ★ **BEST WESTERN EL RANCHO.** *2460 Main St. 805/772-2212; FAX 805/772-2212.* 27 rms. Easter-Labor Day: S, D $59-$99; each addl $7; under 12 free; lower rates rest of yr. Crib $5. Pet accepted; $5. TV; cable, VCR (free movies). Heated pool. Restaurant 7 am-10 pm. Ck-out 11 am. Coin lndry. Business servs avail. Refrigerators. Microwaves avail. Grill. Redwood lobby, etched glass door. Ocean view. Cr cds: A, C, D, DS, MC, V.
🛌 ≈ 🖎 🐾 SC

★ ★ **HARBOR HOUSE INN.** *1095 Main St. 805/772-2711; res: 800/247-5076.* 46 rms, 2 story. No A/C. Memorial Day wkend-Sept: S $60-$80; D $60-$110; lower rates rest of yr. Pet accepted, some restrictions; $6. TV; cable (premium); VCR avail (movies). Complimentary coffee in rms. Restaurant opp open 24 hrs. Ck-out 11 am. Business servs avail. Whirlpool. Some refrigerators. Patios, balconies. Bay 3 blks. Cr cds: A, DS, MC, V.
D 🛌 🖎 🐾 SC

✔ ★ **TRAVELODGE SUNSET.** *1080 Market Ave. 805/772-1259; FAX 805/772-8967.* 31 rms, 1-2 story. No A/C. S, D $45-$98; each addl $6; under 16 free; higher rates wkend, hols, special events. Crib free. Pet accepted; deposit required. TV; cable (premium), VCR avail. Heated pool. Complimentary continental bkfst. Coffee in rms. Restaurant nearby. Ck-out 11 am. Business servs avail. In-rm modem link. Refrigerators. Microwaves avail. Sundeck. 1 blk from ocean. Cr cds: A, C, D, DS, ER, JCB, MC, V. 🛌 ≈ 🖎 🐾 SC

Mountain View *(See also Palo Alto, Santa Clara)*

Motel

★ ★ **RESIDENCE INN BY MARRIOTT.** *1854 El Camino Real W (94040). 650/940-1300; FAX 650/969-4997.* 112 kit. suites, 2 story. S, D $139-$163; wkly, wkend, monthly rates. Pet accepted; $50-$75 nonrefundable and $6 per day. TV; cable (premium). Heated pool; whirlpool. Complimentary continental bkfst. Restaurant nearby. Ck-out noon. Coin lndry. Meeting rm. Business servs avail. Valet serv. Health club privileges. Refrigerators. Picnic tables, grills. Cr cds: A, C, D, DS, JCB, MC, V. D ✦ ⛱ ◪ 🔥 SC

Mt Shasta *(See also Dunsmuir, Redding)*

Motel

✔ ★ **SWISS HOLIDAY LODGE.** *S Mt Shasta Blvd, 2 mi S at jct CA 89, I-5 McCloud exit. 916/926-3446.* 21 air-cooled rms, 2 story. S, D $40.95-$60.95; each addl $4; suite $90. Crib $5. Pet accepted. TV; cable (premium). Heated pool (seasonal); whirlpool. Complimentary coffee in rms. Complimentary continental bkfst. Ck-out 11 am. Downhill/x-country ski 10 mi. Refrigerators avail. Free community kitchen. Picnic tables, grills. View of Mt Shasta. Cr cds: A, D, DS, MC, V. ✦ ⛱ ◪ 🔥 SC

Newport Beach *(See also Irvine, Laguna Beach, Long Beach)*

Hotels

★ ★ ★ ★ **FOUR SEASONS.** *690 Newport Center Dr (92660). 714/759-0808; FAX 714/759-0568.* A short stroll from the Fashion Island shopping mall, this high-rise luxury hotel features a soaring marble lobby and pale, elegant guest rooms with views of the ocean and harbor. 285 rms, 20 story. S, D $295-$335; each addl $30; suites $420-$2,500; under 18 free; wkend rates; golf plans. Pet accepted. Valet parking $13.50. TV; cable (premium), VCR avail (movies). Pool; whirlpool, poolside serv. Restaurants 6:30 am-10 pm. Rm serv 24 hrs. Bar 11-1 am; entertainment. Ck-out noon. Convention facilities. Business center. In-rm modem link. Concierge. Gift shop. Beauty shop. Airport transportation. Lighted tennis, pro. Golf privileges. Bicycles. Exercise rm; instructor, weights, bicycles, sauna. Massage. Bathrm phones, refrigerators; microwaves avail. Balconies. Cr cds: A, C, D, ER, JCB, MC, V. D ✦ 🏋 🏃 ⛱ 🏃 ◪ 🔥 SC 🎿

★ ★ ★ **MARRIOTT HOTEL & TENNIS CLUB.** *900 Newport Center Dr (92660), at Fashion Island. 714/640-4000; FAX 714/640-5055.* 570 rms, 16 story. S, D $135-$180; 1-2-bedrm suites $250-$600; under 12 free; wkend, tennis package plans. Crib free. Pet accepted. TV; cable (premium). 2 heated pools; whirlpool, poolside serv. Restaurant 6:30 am-10 pm. Bar 4 pm-2 am. Ck-out noon. Coin lndry. Convention facilities. Business center. In-rm modem link. Gift shop. Valet parking avail. Free airport transportation. 8 lighted tennis courts, pro, tennis club. Exercise rm; instructor, weights, bicycles. Health club privileges. Refrigerators avail. Private patios, balconies. Beautiful landscaping. Shopping center opp. Luxury level. Cr cds: A, C, D, DS, JCB, MC, V. D ✦ 🏃 ⛱ 🏃 ◪ SC 🎿

Resort

★ ★ ★ **HYATT NEWPORTER.** *1107 Jamboree Rd (92660). 714/729-1234; FAX 714/644-1552.* Web www.hyattnewporter.com. 410 rms, 3 story, four 3-bedrm villas. S, D $145-$225; each addl $25; suites $350-$500; villas for 1-6 $750-$900; under 18 free. Crib free. Pet accepted, some restrictions. TV; cable (premium). 3 pools, 1 heated; whirlpool, poolside serv. Supervised child's activities (Fri, Sat evenings Memorial Day-Labor Day); ages 3-15. Dining rm 6 am-10:30 pm. Rm serv to midnight. Bar 11-2 am; entertainment Thurs-Sat. Ck-out noon, ck-in 4 pm. Convention facilities. Business center. In-rm modem link. Valet serv. Concierge. Gift shop. Barber, beauty shop. Free airport transportation. Lighted tennis privileges, pro. 18-hole golf privileges, 9-hole golf. Exercise equipt; weights, bicycles. Health club privileges. Bicycle rentals. Lawn games. Boating nearby. Wet bar in suites. Villas have fireplaces, private pool. Private patios, balconies. 26 acres, beautiful landscaping, lush gardens, overlooking bay and harbor. Ocean 1 mi. Cr cds: A, C, D, DS, MC, V. D ✦ 🏋 🏃 ⛱ 🏃 ◪ 🔥 SC 🎿

Oakland *(See also Hayward, San Francisco, San Francisco Airport Area, San Mateo)*

Hotel

★ ★ **CLARION SUITES LAKE MERRITT.** *1800 Madison (94612), at Lakeside Dr. 510/832-2300; FAX 510/832-7150.* 50 units, 6 story, 41 suites. S, D $109; each addl $10; suites $149-$179; under 17 free. Valet parking $9. Pet accepted; $150. TV; cable (premium), VCR avail. Complimentary continental bkfst. Complimentary coffee in rms. Restaurant 11 am-10 pm; Sat, Sun by res. Bar. Ck-out 11 am. Meeting rms. Business servs avail. In-rm modem link. Concierge. Health club privileges. Refrigerators, microwaves, minibars. Restored Mediterranean/art deco landmark (1927) offers views of Lake Merritt. Cr cds: A, D, DS, MC, V. ⮐ ⊠ ⊠ SC

Ojai *(See also Santa Barbara, Ventura)*

Resort

★ ★ ★ **OJAI VALLEY INN.** *Country Club Rd. 805/646-5511; FAX 805/646-7969; res: 800/422-6524.* 211 units, 3 story. S, D $195-$260; suites, cottages $345-$850; family rates. Pet accepted; $10. TV; cable (premium). 2 heated pools; whirlpool, poolside serv. Playground. Supervised child's activities; ages 3-12. Coffee in rms. Restaurant (public by res): 6:30 am-10 pm. Box lunches, snack bar, picnics. Rm serv 24 hrs. Bar 11:30 am-midnight. Ck-out noon, ck-in 4 pm. Meeting rms. Business center. In-rm modem link. Concierge. Sports dir. Lighted tennis, pro. 18-hole golf, greens fee from $80, pro, putting green, driving range. Bicycles. Lawn games. Hiking, horseback riding, mountain biking. Aviary. Children's petting zoo. Soc dir; entertainment. Exercise rm; instructor, weights, stair machine, sauna, steam rm. Refrigerators, minibars; some fireplaces. Many private patios, balconies. On 220 acres. Mountain views. Cr cds: A, D, DS, MC, V. D ⮐ ⇟ ⅋ ⇞ ⇟ ⇟ ⇞ ⇟ ⊠ ⊠ SC

Ontario *(See also Claremont)*

Motels

★ ★ **BEST WESTERN AIRPORT.** *209 N Vineyard Ave (91764), I-10 Vineyard Ave exit S, near Intl Airport. 909/983-9600; FAX 909/395-9219.* 150 rms, 2 story. S $55-$60; D $60-$70; each addl $5; under 12 free. Crib free. Pet accepted. TV; cable (premium). Heated pool; whirlpool. Complimentary continental bkfst. Complimentary coffee in rms. Restaurant adj open 24 hrs. Ck-out noon. Coin lndry. Meeting rms. Valet serv. Free airport transportation. Some refrigerators; microwaves avail. Cr cds: A, C, D, DS, MC, V.

D ⮐ ⇟ ✈ ⊠ ⊠ ⊠ SC

★ ★ **RESIDENCE INN BY MARRIOTT.** *2025 Convention Center Way (91764), I-10 Vineyard Ave exit S, near Intl Airport. 909/983-6788; FAX 909/983-3843.* Web www.csz.com/residence-inn. 200 kit. units, 2 story. Kit. units $79-$149; under 16 free. Pet accepted; $35-$50 and $6/ day. TV; cable (premium), VCR avail. Heated pool; whirlpool. Complimentary continental bkfst. Coffee in rms. Restaurant nearby. Ck-out noon. Coin lndry. Meeting rm. Business servs avail. Valet serv. Free airport transportation. Exercise equipt; treadmills, bicycle. Paddle tennis. Refrigerators, microwaves; some fireplaces. Some balconies. Picnic tables, grills. Cr cds: A, C, D, DS, ER, MC, V.

D ⮐ ⇟ ⇞ ✈ ⊠ ⊠ SC

Motor Hotel

★ ★ **HOLIDAY INN.** *3400 Shelby St (91764), I-10 Haven Ave exit N, near Intl Airport. 909/466-9600; FAX 909/941-1445.* 150 kit. suites, 3 story. Suites $95-$110; 1-bedrm suites $110-$130; each addl $10; wkly rates. Crib free. Pet accepted, some restrictions. TV; cable (premium), VCR avail. Heated pool; whirlpool. Complimentary continental bkfst. Complimentary coffee in rms. Restaurant 6:30-10 am, 11 am-2 pm, 6-10 pm; Sat, Sun 7:30 am-2 pm, 6-10 pm. Rm serv. Bar 5-10 pm. Ck-out noon. Coin lndry. Meeting rms. Business servs avail. Valet serv. Sundries. Gift shop. Free airport transportation. Exercise equipt; bicycles, rowers, sauna. Game rm. Microwaves. Some patios. Grill. Cr cds: A, C, D, DS, MC, V. D ⮐ ⇟ ✈ ⊠ ⊠ ⊠ SC

Orange *(See also Anaheim)*

Motel

★ ★ **RESIDENCE INN BY MARRIOTT.** *201 N State College Blvd (92868), off I-5 Chapman Ave exit. 714/978-7700; FAX 714/978-6257.* 104 kits, 2 story. S, D $99-$218; family, wkly rates. Crib free. Pet accepted, some restrictions; $75. TV; cable (premium), VCR avail. Heated pool; whirlpool. Complimentary continental bkfst. Complimentary coffee in rms. Restaurant nearby. Ck-out noon. Coin lndry. Meeting rms. Business servs avail. Valet serv. Airport, RR station, bus depot transportation. Free Disneyland transportation. Health club privileges. Basketball, volleyball. Microwaves. Some balconies. Picnic tables, grills. Anaheim Stadium 1/2 mi N. Cr cds: A, C, D, DS, JCB, MC, V. D ⮐ ⇟ ⊠ ⊠ SC

Oroville *(See also Chico, Marysville)*

Motel

★ ★ **BEST WESTERN GRAND MANOR INN.** *1470 Feather River Blvd. 916/533-9673; FAX 916/533-5862.* 54 rms, 3 story. S, D $64-$84; suites $87-$125; under 12 free. Crib $6. Pet accepted, some restrictions. TV; cable. Pool; whirlpool. Complimentary continental bkfst. Complimentary coffee in rms. Restaurant nearby. Ck-out 11 am. Coin lndry. Meeting rm. Business servs avail. In-rm modem link. Exercise equipt; weight machine, bicycles, sauna. Refrigerators. Many balconies. Cr cds: A, C, D, DS, MC, V.

[D] [✦] [≋] [⊠] [⊠] [SC]

Inn

★ ★ ★ **LAKE OROVILLE BED AND BREAKFAST.** *(240 Sunday Dr, Berry Creek 95916) CA 70 to CA 162, E 1¹/₂ mi to Olive, S to Bell Rd, W to Sunday Dr. 916/589-0700; res: 800/455-5253; FAX 916/589-5313.* E-mail lakeinn@dfci.net; web www.now2000.com /lakeoroville. 6 rms. S, D $75-$135; each addl $10; hols (2-3 day min). Pet accepted, some restrictions. TV avail; VCR avail (movies). Complimentary full bkfst. Restaurant nearby. Ck-out 11:30 am, ck-in 3-6 pm. Business servs avail. Luggage handling. 18-hole golf privileges. Bicycles avail. Game rm. Rec rm. Many in-rm whirlpools; microwaves avail. Some balconies. Picnic tables, grills. Lake view. Hiking trails. On 40 acres. Totally nonsmoking. Cr cds: A, D, MC, V. [✦] [🎿] [⊠] [⊠] [SC]

Palm Desert

Motel

★ **DEEP CANYON INN.** *74470 Abronia Trl. 760/346-8061; res: 800/253-0004; FAX 760/341-9120.* 32 rms, 2 story, 13 kit. units. Mid-Dec-May: S, D $69-$119; kit. units $109-$129; wkly rates, golf plans; lower rates rest of yr. Crib free. Pet accepted, some restrictions; $20 deposit. TV; cable. Complimentary continental bkfst. Complimentary coffee in rms. Restaurant nearby. Ck-out noon. Business servs avail. Golf privileges. Pool. Refrigerators. No cr cds accepted. [D] [✦] [🎿] [≋] [⊠] [⊠]

Resort

★ ★ ★ **RENAISSANCE ESMERALDA.** *(44-400 Indian Wells Lane, Indian Wells 92210) 1 blk S of CA 111. 760/773-4444; FAX 760/773-9250.* This 350-acre golf resort is nestled in the foothills of the Santa Rosa Mountains. 560 units, 7 story. Jan-May: S, D $300-$400; each addl $25; suites $600-$2,500; under 18 free; tennis, golf, honeymoon plans; lower rates rest of yr. Crib free. Pet accepted, some restrictions. TV; cable (premium). 2 pools; whirlpool, wading pool, poolside serv. Supervised child's activities; ages 3-12. Dining rms 6:30 am-10 pm. Rm serv 24 hrs. Bar noon-2 am; entertainment. Ck-out noon, ck-in 3 pm. Coin lndry. Meeting rms. Business center. In-rm modem link. Bellhops. Valet serv. Concierge. Gift shops. Airport transportation. Sports dir. Lighted tennis, pro. 36-hole golf, greens fee $100-$110, pro, putting green, driving range. Tennis & golf clinics; equipt rentals. Private beach. Hiking. Bicycle rentals. Lawn games. Game rm. Extensive exercise rm; instructor, weight machines, bicycles, sauna, steam rm. Massage. Bathrm phones, minibars; some wet bars. Some suites with woodburning fireplace. Balconies. Cr cds: A, C, D, DS, ER, JCB, MC, V. [D] [✦] [🎿] [🎿] [≋] [🎿] [⊠] [⊠] [SC] [🎿]

Palm Springs

Motels

★ **CHANDLER INN.** *1530 N Indian Canyon Dr (92262). 760/320-8949; res: 888/386-7869; FAX 760/323-2121.* 21 rms, 2 story, 3 kit. units. Nov-May: S, D $79-$89; kit. units $98; wkly rates; golf plans; wkends, hols (2-, 3-day min); lower rates rest of yr. Pet accepted, some restrictions; $20 deposit. TV; cable, VCR avail (movies). Complimentary continental bkfst. Restaurant nearby. Ck-out 11 am. Business servs avail. Golf privileges. Pool; whirlpool. Refrigerators. Cr cds: A, C, D, JCB, MC, V. [✦] [🎿] [≋] [⊠] [⊠] [SC]

✔ ★ **MOTEL 6.** *660 S Palm Canyon Dr (92264). 760/327-4200; FAX 760/320-9827.* 148 rms, shower only, 3 story. Sept-mid-Apr: S $34.99; D $40.99; each addl $3; under 17 free. Crib free. Pet accepted, some restrictions. TV; cable (premium). Heated pool. Restaurant nearby. Ck-out noon. Coin lndry. Business servs avail. Cr cds: A, C, D, DS, MC, V. [D] [✦] [≋] [⊠] [⊠] [SC]

★ ★ **PLACE IN THE SUN.** *754 San Lorenzo Rd (92264). 760/325-0254; FAX 760/237-9303; res: 800/779-2254.* 16 kit. units, 3 with shower only, 11 suites. Mid-Dec-May: S, D $59-$79; each addl $12; suites $99-$149; higher rates hols (2-day min); lower rates rest of yr. Crib $10. Pet accepted, some restrictions; $10. TV; cable. Heated pool. Restaurant nearby. Ck-out noon. Coin lndry. Meeting rms. Free airport transportation. Health club privileges. Lawn games. Refrigerators, microwaves. Cr cds: A, MC, V. 🐾 ⩟ ⬚ 🐾 SC

✔ ★ ★ **SUPER 8.** *1900 N Palm Canyon Dr (92262). 760/322-3757; FAX 760/323-5290.* Web www.super8motels.com. 61 rms, 2 story. Late Dec-May: S $68; D $73; each addl $5; suites $90-$110; under 12 free; lower rates rest of yr. Crib $4. Pet accepted; $10. TV; cable. Heated pool; whirlpool. Complimentary continental bkfst. Restaurant nearby. Ck-out 11 am. Coin lndry. Business servs avail. Refrigerators. Cr cds: A, C, D, DS, MC, V.
D 🐾 ⩟ ⬚ 🐾 SC

Motor Hotel

★ ★ ★ **RIVIERA RESORT AND RACQUET CLUB.** *1600 N Indian Canyon Dr (92262). 760/327-8311; FAX 760/327-4323; res: 800/444-8311.* 477 rms, 2-3 story. Mid-Jan-mid-May: S, D $139-$189; each addl $20; suites $215-$860; under 18 free; lower rates rest of yr. Crib free. Pet accepted. TV; cable. 2 heated pools; whirlpools, poolside serv. Restaurant 6:30 am-10 pm. Rm serv. Bar 11-2 am; entertainment. Ck-out noon. Convention facilities. In-rm modem link. Bellhops. Valet serv. Concierge. Sundries. Gift shop. Beauty shop. Free valet parking. Free airport transportation. Lighted tennis. Golf privileges. Exercise equipt; weight machine, bicycles. Massage. Health club privileges. Bicycle rentals. Lawn games. Bathrm phones, refrigerators; microwaves avail. Some wet bars. Balconies. Cr cds: A, C, D, DS, JCB, MC, V. D 🐾 🏃 🏌 ⩟ 🏊 ⬚ 🐾 SC

Hotels

★ ★ ★ **HILTON.** *400 E Tahquitz Canyon Way (92262), near Municipal Airport. 760/320-6868; FAX 760/320-2126.* E-mail pshilton@aol.com; web www.desertresorts.com. 260 rms, 3 story. Dec-May: S, D $205-$305; each addl $20; suites $265-$685; studio rms $155; kit. condos $235-$345; under 18 free; lower rates rest of yr. Crib free. Pet accepted. TV; cable (premium), VCR avail (movies). Heated pool; 2 whirlpools, poolside serv. Child's activities (Sept-May & some hols); ages 3-12. Coffee in rm. Restaurant 6 am-10 pm. Bar 4 pm-2 am. Ck-out noon. Convention facilities. Business center. In-rm modem link. Concierge. Gift shop. Barber, beauty shop. Valet parking. Free airport transportation. Exercise equipt; weight machines, treadmill, sauna. 6 lighted tennis courts, pro, pro shop. Golf privileges. Refrigerators, minibars; microwaves avail. Private patios, balconies. Cr cds: A, C, D, DS, ER, JCB, MC, V. D 🐾 🏃 🏌 ⩟ 🏊 ⬚ 🐾 SC 🎿

★ ★ **RAMADA RESORT.** *1800 E Palm Canyon Dr (92264), at Sunrise Way. 760/323-1711; FAX 760/322-1075; res: 800/245-6907 (exc CA), 800/245-6904 (CA).* 254 rms, 3 story. Feb-May: S, D $79-$139; each addl $15; suites $125-$200; under 18 free; higher rates: wkends, hols; lower rates rest of yr. Crib free. Pet accepted. TV. Heated pool; whirlpools, poolside serv. Coffee in rms. Restaurant 7 am-10 pm. Bar 11 am-midnight; entertainment wkends. Ck-out noon. Coin lndry. Meeting rms. In-rm modem link. Gift shop. Free airport transportation. Tennis privileges. Golf privileges. Exercise equipt; weights, bicycles, sauna. Refrigerators; wet bar in suites. Microwaves avail. Balconies. Cr cds: A, C, D, DS, MC, V. D 🐾 🏃 🏌 ⩟ 🏊 ⬚ 🐾 SC

★ ★ ★ **WYNDHAM.** *888 E Tahquitz Canyon Way (92262), near Municipal Airport. 760/322-6000; FAX 760/322-5351.* Web www.travelweb.com. 410 units, 5 story, 158 suites. Jan-June: S, D $210-$240; each addl $25; suites $230-$250; under 17 free; lower rates rest of yr. Crib free. Pet accepted; $25. TV; cable. Pool; wading pool, whirlpool, poolside serv. Coffee in rms. Restaurant 6:30 am-11 pm. Bar 11-1:30 am. Ck-out noon. Convention facilities. Business center. In-rm modem link. Concierge. Gift shops. Barber, beauty shop. Free valet parking. Free airport transportation. Tennis privileges. Golf privileges. Exercise equipt; weight machines, bicycles, sauna. Private patios, balconies. Covered walkway to convention center. Cr cds: A, C, D, DS, ER, JCB, MC, V.
D 🐾 🏃 🏌 ⩟ 🏊 🏊 ⬚ 🐾 SC 🎿

Inns

★ ★ **CASA CODY.** *175 S Cahuilla Rd (92262). 760/320-9346; FAX 760/325-8610; res: 800/231-2639.* 23 rms, 21 kit. suites. Late Dec-late Apr: S, D $79-$199; each addl $10; monthly, wkly rates; lower rates rest of yr. Crib $10. Pet accepted. TV; cable, VCR avail (free movies). 2 heated pools; whirlpool. Complimentary continental bkfst. Restaurant nearby. Ck-out 11 am, ck-in 2 pm. Business servs avail. Health club privileges. Refrigerators, microwaves; many fireplaces. Many private patios. Cr cds: A, C, D, DS, MC, V.
🐾 ⩟ 🐾

★ ★ **ESTRELLA INN.** *415 S Belardo Rd (92264). 760/320-4117; FAX 760/323-3303; res: 800/237-3687.* E-mail estrella@ix.netcom.com; web www.palm-springs.org/es trella.html. 62 rms, 6 with shower only, 2 story, 8 suites. Jan-Apr: S, D $150; each addl $15; suites $225-$275; villas $250-$275; under 12 free; wkly rates; tennis, golf plans; lower rates rest of yr. Crib free. Pet accepted; $10. TV; VCR avail. 3 heated pools. Complimentary coffee in rms. Complimentary bkfst. Restaurant nearby. Ck-out noon, ck-in 3 pm. Business servs avail. Luggage handling. Concierge serv. Free airport transportation. Health club privileges. Lawn games. Refrigerators, microwaves. Patios, balconies. Built 1929. Cr cds: A, C, D, MC, V. 🐾 ≈ ⊠ 🐾 SC

Resorts

★ ★ ★ ★ **MARRIOTT'S RANCHO LAS PALMAS.** *(41000 Bob Hope Dr, Rancho Mirage 92270) SE on CA 111. 760/568-2727; FAX 760/568-5845.* E-mail rlpbus@earth link.com; web www.marriott.com/marriott /pspca. Set on spacious grounds with a garden, this resort offers large, luxurious guest rooms and a variety of sports. 450 rms, 2 story. Jan-Apr: S, D $225-$245; suites $330-$1,000; under 18 free; golf, tennis plans; lower rates rest of yr. Pet accepted, some restrictions. TV; cable (premium), VCR avail (movies). 2 pools; whirlpool, wading pool, poolside serv. Playground. Supervised child's activities; under age 12. Restaurants 6-10 pm. Rm serv; limited serv midnight-6 am. Box lunches, snack bar. Bar 11-2 am. Ck-out noon, ck-in 4 pm. Convention facilities. Business center. In-rm modem link. Concierge. Gift shop. Barber, beauty shop. Lighted tennis, pro. Tennis school. 27-hole golf, greens fee $90-$100, pro, putting green, driving range. Bicycle rentals. Soc dir. Exercise equipt; weight machines, bicycles. Health club privileges. Some refrigerators, minibars; microwaves avail. Private patios, balconies. Cr cds: A, C, D, DS, ER, JCB, MC, V. D 🐾 🏃 ≈ 🚣 🐾 SC 🏌

★ ★ ★ ★ **THE WESTIN MISSION HILLS.** *(71333 Dinah Shore Dr, Rancho Mirage 92270) at Bob Hope Dr. 760/328-5955; FAX 760/321-2955.* Web www.westin.com. This 360-acre resort is landscaped with lagoons, waterways and lush vegetation. Most guest rooms afford panoramic views of the golf course fairways and mountains. 512 units in 16 bldgs, 2 story. Jan-May: S, D $240-$360; each addl $25; suites $430-$1,250; under 18 free; golf, tennis plans; lower rates rest of yr. Crib free. Pet accepted, some restrictions. TV; cable (premium), VCR avail (movies). 3 pools; whirlpool, poolside serv, lifeguard (main pool); 60-ft waterslide. Playground. Supervised child's activities; ages 4-12. Dining rms 6 am-11 pm. Box lunches, snack bar. Rm serv 24 hrs. Bars 10-2 am; entertainment. Ck-out noon, ck-in 4 pm. Convention facilities. Business center. In-rm modem link. Bellhops. Valet serv. Concierge. Shopping arcade. Beauty shop. Sports dir. 7 lighted tennis courts, pro, pro shop. Pete Dye & Gary Player championship 18-hole golf courses, pro, 6 putting greens, 2 double-sided practice ranges, pro shop. Bicycle rentals. Lawn games. Soc dir. Game rm. Exercise equipt; weight machines, treadmills, steam rm. Health and fitness center. Massage. Refrigerators, minibars; microwaves avail. Cr cds: A, C, D, DS, ER, JCB, MC, V. D 🐾 🏃 🏃 🚣 ≈ 🐾 SC 🏌

Palo Alto *(See also Fremont, Santa Clara)*

Hotel

★ ★ **HYATT RICKEYS.** *4219 El Camino Real (94306). 650/493-8000; FAX 650/424-0836.* 344 units, 1-6 story. S $150-$180; D $175-$205; suites $230-$305; under 18 free; wkend rates. Crib free. Pet accepted, some restrictions; $50 deposit. TV; cable (premium). Pool; poolside serv. Coffee in rms. Restaurant 6:30 am-10 pm. Bar 11-1:30 am. Ck-out noon. Convention facilities. Business center. In-rm modem link. Exercise equipt; weights, stair machine. Lawn games. Putting green. Fireplace in many suites. Refrigerators avail. Some balconies. On 22 acres with gardens, pond. Cr cds: A, C, D, DS, JCB, MC, V. D 🐾 ≈ 🚣 🐾 SC 🏌

Pasadena *(See also Claremont, Glendale, Los Angeles, Pomona, San Marino)*

Motor Hotel

(Rates are usually higher late Dec-early Jan, Rose Parade and Festival)

★ ★ ★ **HOLIDAY INN.** *303 E Cordova St (91101), I-210 exit Marengo Ave S. 626/449-4000; FAX 626/584-1390.* 318 rms, 5 story. S $99-$139; D $114-$154; each addl $15; suites $295-$350; under 19 free; Rose Parade (4-day min); wkend rates. Pet accepted, some restrictions. Garage $4. TV; cable (premium). Heated pool; poolside serv. Coffee in rms. Restaurant 6 am-2 pm, 5-10 pm. Rm serv. Bar 2 pm-1 am. Ck-out noon. Convention facilities. Business servs avail. Bellhops. Gift shop. Lighted tennis. Some patios, balconies. Cr cds: A, C, D, DS, JCB, MC, V. D 🐾 🏃 ≈ ⊠ 🐾 SC

Hotel

★ ★ **HILTON.** *150 S Los Robles Ave (91101), ¹/₂ mi S of I-210. 626/577-1000; FAX 626/584-3148.* E-mail pasphhh@hilton.com; web www.hilton. com/hotels/pasphhh/index .html. 291 rms, 13 story. S $120-$180; D $135-$195; each addl $15; suites $200-$500; family, wkend rates; Rose Parade (4-day min). Crib free. Pet accepted. Garage $6/day. TV;

cable (premium), VCR avail. Heated pool; whirlpool. Coffee in rms. Restaurant 6 am-10 pm. Bar 11-1 am. Ck-out noon. Convention facilities. Business center. Gift shop. Barber, beauty shop. Garage parking. Exercise equipt; weight machine, stair machine. Minibars; some bathrm phones. Some balconies. Cr cds: A, C, D, DS, ER, JCB, MC, V.

🄳 🔣 🔣 🄺 🔣 🔣 SC 🔣

Pebble Beach *(See also Carmel, Monterey)*

Resort

★ ★ ★ ★ **THE LODGE AT PEBBLE BEACH.** *Seventeen Mile Dr, 3 mi N of Carmel on Seventeen Mile Dr. 408/624-3811; FAX 408/625-8598; res: 800/654-9300.* Web www.pebble-beach.com. This lavish resort on Carmel Bay, with guest rooms overlooking a beach and golf course, includes an equestrian center with 34 miles of trails. 161 rms, 1-3 story. S, D $350-$575; suites $700-$1,800; under 18 free. Serv charge $15/day. Crib free. Pet accepted. TV; cable (premium), VCR avail. Heated pool; wading pool, whirlpool, poolside serv. Supervised child's activities (June-Aug). Restaurants 7 am-3:30 pm, 6:30-10 pm. Afternoon tea. Box lunches, snacks. Rm serv 24 hrs. Bar 11-1 am. Ck-out noon, ck-in 4 pm. Convention facilities. Business servs avail. In-rm modem link. Valet serv. Concierge. Shopping arcade. Barber, beauty shop. Valet parking. Free airport transportation. Tennis. 4 golf courses, par-3 golf, greens fee $150-$275, putting green, 2 driving ranges. Private beach. Exercise rm; instructor, weights, bicycles, sauna, steam rm. Massage. Fireplaces; refrigerators, microwaves avail; some wet bars. Private patios, balconies. Cr cds: A, C, D, DS, JCB, MC, V. 🔣 🔣 🔣 🔣 🔣 🔣 🔣 🔣

Pismo Beach *(See also San Luis Obispo)*

Motor Hotels

★ ★ ★ **OXFORD SUITES RESORT.** *651 Five Cities Dr. 805/773-3773; FAX 805/773-5177; res: 800/982-7848.* E-mail jomaac@ccaccess.net; web www.oxfordsuitesresort.com. 133 suites, 2 story. S, D $69-$102; each addl $6; under 10 free. Crib free. Pet accepted; $6. TV; cable, VCR (movies $3). Heated pool; wading pool, whirlpool. Complimentary full bkfst. Ck-out noon. Coin lndry. Meeting rms. Business servs avail. Valet serv. Gift shop. Refrigerators, microwaves. Cr cds: A, C, D, DS, ER, JCB, MC, V. 🄳 🔣 🔣 🔣 🔣 SC

★ ★ ★ **SPYGLASS INN.** *2705 Spyglass Dr. 805/773-4855; FAX 805/773-5298; res: 800/824-2612 (CA).* 82 rms, 1-2 story. S, D $59-$139; each addl $6; suites, kit. units $89-$159; under 12 free; higher rates wkends. Pet accepted; $10 fee. TV; cable, VCR (movies $3). Pool; whirlpool. Coffee in rms. Restaurant 7 am-2 pm, 4-9:30 pm. Bar 10-2 am; entertainment Thurs-Sat. Ck-out 11 am. Meeting rm. Business servs avail. Refrigerators. Many private patios, balconies with ocean view. Cr cds: A, C, D, DS, ER, JCB, MC, V.

🄳 🔣 🔣 🔣 🔣 SC

Pleasanton *(See also Fremont, Hayward, Oakland)*

Hotels

✔ ★ ★ ★ **HILTON AT THE CLUB.** *7050 Johnson Dr (94588), at jct I-580, I-680, Hopyard exit off I-580. 510/463-8000; FAX 510/463-3801.* 294 rms, 5 story. S, D $95-$155; each addl $10; suites $200-$500; family, wkend rates. Crib free. Pet accepted, some restrictions; $15. TV; cable (premium), VCR avail. Heated pool; poolside serv. Restaurant 6:30 am-10:30 pm. Bar 11-1:30 am. Ck-out noon. Meeting rms. Business center. Gift shop. Barber, beauty shop. Valet parking. Indoor tennis, pro. Exercise rm; instructor, weights, bicycles, sauna. Bathrm phones. Luxury level. Cr cds: A, C, D, DS, ER, JCB, MC, V.

🄳 🔣 🔣 🔣 🄺 🔣 🔣 SC 🔣

★ ★ ★ **HOLIDAY INN SELECT.** *11950 Dublin Canyon Rd (94588), just W of jct I-580, I-680, Foothill Rd exit. 510/847-6000; FAX 510/463-2585.* 244 rms, 6 story. S $112-$119; D $122-$129; each addl $10; under 18 free; wkend rates. Crib free. Pet accepted, some restrictions; $15 deposit. TV; cable (premium). Heated pool; whirlpool. Complimentary coffee in rms. Restaurant 6 am-10 pm. Bar noon-midnight. Ck-out noon. Coin lndry. Convention facilities. Business servs avail. Gift shop. Exercise equipt; weight machine, bicycle. Refrigerators avail. Cr cds: A, C, D, DS, JCB, MC, V. 🄳 🔣 🔣 🄺 🔣 🔣 SC

Rancho Cordova *(See also Sacramento)*

Motels

★ **COMFORT INN.** *3240 Mather Field Rd (95670), S of jct US 50 & Mather Field Rd. 916/363-3344; FAX 916/362-0903.* 110 rms, 4 story. S $57; D $62; suites $65-$75; under 14 free. Pet accepted; $100. TV; cable. Pool; whirlpool. Coffee in rms. Complimentary continental bkfst. Restaurant adj 7 am-9 pm. Ck-out noon. Coin lndry. Meeting rms. Airport transportation. Some refrigerators. Mather AFB ¹/₂ mi. Cr cds: A, C, D, DS, ER, JCB, MC, V. [D] 🏷 ⛱ 🚫 🐾 [SC]

✔★ **ECONOMY INNS OF AMERICA.** *12249 Folsom Blvd (95670), SW of jct US 50 & Hazel Ave. 916/351-1213; FAX 916/351-1817.* 124 rms, 2 story. S $36.90; D $44.90-$51.90; each addl (up to 4) $7. Pet accepted. TV; cable. Pool. Complimentary continental bkfst. Restaurant adj open 24 hrs. Ck-out 11 am. Cr cds: A, MC, V. [D] 🏷 ⛱ 🚫 🐾 [SC]

Rancho Santa Fe

Resorts

★ ★ ★ **THE INN AT RANCHO SANTA FE.** *5951 Linea del Cielo, 4 mi E of I-5 Lomas Santa Fe Dr, Solana Beach. 619/756-1131; FAX 619/759-1604; res: 800/843-4661.* 89 units in lodge, cottages. S, D $95-$210; each addl $20; suites $275-$520. Crib $20. Pet accepted. TV; VCR avail. Heated pool; poolside serv. Restaurant 7:30-10:30 am, noon-2:30 pm, 6:30-9:30 pm. Rm serv. Box lunches. Bar 11 am-11 pm. Ck-out noon, ck-in 3 pm. Grocery 2 blks. Meeting rms. Business servs avail. Bellhops. Tennis. 18-hole golf privileges. Exercise equipt; weights, stair machine. Massage. Lawn games. Some refrigerators, fireplaces, wet bars. Some in-rm whirlpools. Microwaves avail. Many private patios. On 20 acres of landscaped grounds. Beach house in Del Mar avail for day use. Cr cds: A, C, D, MC, V.
🏷 🏋 🏃 ⛱ 🎿 🐾

★ ★ ★ **MORGAN RUN RESORT & CLUB.** *5690 Cancha de Golf (92091). 619/756-2471; FAX 619/756-3013; res: 800/378-4653.* 70 rms, 14 suites, 2 story. May-Oct: S, D $148-$159; each addl $20; suites $219-$229; golf plans; lower rates rest of yr. Crib free. Pet accepted. TV; cable (premium). Pool; poolside serv. Complimentary coffee in rms. Restaurant 6:30 am-10 pm. Bar 10 am-midnight. Ck-out noon, ck-in 3 pm. Gift shop. Meeting rms. Valet serv. Lighted tennis, pro. 27-hole golf course, greens fee $75, pro, putting green, driving range. Exercise equipt; bicycles, weight machine. Some refrigerators; microwaves avail. Some balconies. Cr cds: A, D, MC, V. 🏷 🏋 🏃 ⛱ 🎿 🚫 🐾 [SC]

★ ★ ★ **RANCHO VALENCIA.** *5921 Valencia Circle. 619/756-1123; FAX 619/756-0165; res: 800/548-3664.* The Spanish architecture at this luxury tennis resort recalls early California haciendas. The spacious, secluded suites occupy red tile-roofed casitas and have private terraces. 43 suites. S, D $395-$535; 2-bedrm suites $860-$970; 3-bedrm hacienda from $3,000; tennis clinic, golf plans. Crib free. Pet accepted; $75/day. TV; cable (premium), VCR. Pool; poolside serv. Complimentary coffee in rms. Restaurant 7 am-2:30 pm, 6-9:30 pm. Box lunches, picnics. Bar from 10 am. Ck-out noon, ck-in 4 pm. Guest lndry. Meeting rms. Business servs avail. In-rm modem link. Bellhops. Valet serv. Gift shop. 18 tennis courts, pro. 18-hole golf privileges adj. Bicycle rentals. Lawn games. Soc dir. Exercise equipt; weights, treadmill. Massage. Bathrm phones, refrigerators, minibars, wet bars, fireplaces; microwaves avail. Cr cds: A, C, D, MC, V.
[D] 🏷 🏋 🏃 ⛱ 🎿 🚫 🐾

Redding (See also Mt Shasta)

Motel

✔★ ★ **RIVER INN.** *1835 Park Marina Dr (96001). 530/241-9500; FAX 530/241-5345; res: 800/995-4341.* 79 rms, 2-3 story. No elvtr. S from $43; D from $48; each addl $5; under 12 free. Crib $5. Pet accepted. TV; cable, VCR avail (movies). Pool; whirlpool, sauna. Coffee in rms. Restaurant 7 am-9 pm. Bar 11-2 am. Ck-out 11 am. Business servs avail. Refrigerators; some wet bars. Private patios, balconies. Picnic tables. Cr cds: A, C, D, DS, MC, V.
[D] 🏷 🏊 ⛱ 🚫 🐾 [SC]

Motor Hotels

★ ★ **LA QUINTA.** *2180 Hilltop Dr (96002). 530/221-8200; FAX 530/223-4727.* 140 rms, 3 story. S $59-$69; D $69-$79; each addl $10; suites $126; under 18 free. Crib free. Pet accepted, some restrictions. TV; cable. Pool; whirlpool. Complimentary continental bkfst. Restaurant 5 pm-midnight. Rm serv. Ck-out noon. Coin lndry. Meeting rms. Business servs avail. In-rm modem link. Valet serv. Private patios, balconies. Cr cds: A, C, D, DS, ER, MC, V. [D] 🏷 ⛱ 🚫 🐾 [SC]

★ ★ **RED LION HOTEL.** *1830 Hilltop Dr (96002). 530/221-8700; FAX 530/221-0324.* 194 rms, 2 story. May-Sept: S $90-$130; D $105-$145; each addl $15; suites $250; under 18 free; package plans; lower rates rest of yr. Crib free. Pet accepted. TV; cable, VCR avail (movies). Pool; wading pool, whirlpool, poolside serv. Complimentary coffee in rms. Restaurant 6 am-11 pm; dining rm 11:30 am-1:30 pm, 5-10 pm; Fri, Sat to 11 pm. Rm serv. Bar 11-2 am; entertainment, dancing Thurs-Sat. Ck-out 1 pm. Meeting rms. Business servs avail. In-rm modem link. Bellhops. Valet serv. Sundries. Free airport, RR station, bus depot transportation. Putting green. Health club privileges. Private patios, balconies. Cr cds: A, C, D, DS, ER, MC, V. [D] [♦] [≈] [⊠] [🔥] [SC]

Roseville (See also Rancho Cordova, Sacramento)

Motor Hotel

★ ★ **FIRST CHOICE INNS.** (4420 Rocklin Rd, Rocklin 95677) W on I-80 exit Rocklin Rd N. 916/624-4500; FAX 916/624-5982; res: 800/462-2400. 90 rms, 3 story. May-Sept: S, D $60-$95; each addl $5; suites, kit. units $85-$125; under 12 free; lower rates rest of yr. Crib free. Pet accepted; $25/wk. TV; cable (premium), VCR avail. Pool; whirlpool. Complimentary full bkfst; afternoon refreshments. Complimentary coffee in rms. Restaurant adj open 24 hrs. Bar 5:30-8:30 pm. Ck-out noon. Coin lndry. Meeting rms. Business center. In-rm modem link. Valet serv. Refrigerators; minibar in suites. Picnic tables. Cr cds: A, C, D, DS, MC, V. [D] [♦] [≈] [⊠] [🔥] [SC] [🚶]

Sacramento (See also Rancho Cordova)

Motels

(All rates are generally higher during conventions, state fair and other special events)

✔ ★ **LA QUINTA.** 200 Jibboom St (95814). 916/448-8100; FAX 916/447-3621. 170 rms, 3 story. S $54-$60; D $58-$70; each addl $5; under 18 free. Pet accepted, some restrictions. TV; cable (premium). Pool. Complimentary continental bkfst. Restaurant nearby. Ck-out noon. Guest lndry. Meeting rms. Business servs avail. In-rm modem link. Free airport, RR station, bus depot transportation. On Sacramento River. Cr cds: A, C, D, DS, MC, V. [D] [♦] [≈] [⊠] [🔥] [SC]

★ ★ **LA QUINTA.** 4604 Madison Ave (95841), at I-80. 916/348-0900; FAX 916/331-7160. 127 rms, 3 story. S, D $59-$74; each addl $5; suites $94; under 18 free. Crib free. Pet accepted, some restrictions. TV; cable (premium). Pool. Continental bkfst. Restaurant adj open 24 hrs. Ck-out noon. Coin lndry. Meeting rms. Business servs avail. In-rm modem link. Fireplace in lobby. Cr cds: A, C, D, DS, MC, V. [D] [♦] [≈] [⊠] [🔥] [SC]

✔ ★ **VAGABOND INN.** 1319 30th St (95816), at N Street. 916/454-4400; FAX 916/736-2812. 83 rms, 3 story. S,D $40-$60; each addl $5; under 18 free. Crib free. Pet accepted, some restrictions; $5/day. TV; cable. Pool. Coffee in lobby. Restaurant adj open 24 hrs. Ck-out noon. Cr cds: A, C, D, DS, MC, V. [♦] [≈] [⊠] [🔥] [SC]

★ **VAGABOND INN.** 909 3rd St (95814). 916/446-1481; FAX 916/448-0364. 107 rms, 3 story. S $63-$67; D $70-$75; each addl $5; under 17 free. Crib free. Pet accepted, some restrictions; $5/day. TV; cable. Heated pool. Complimentary continental bkfst. Restaurant adj open 24 hrs. Ck-out noon. Meeting rm. Valet serv. Free airport, RR station, bus depot transportation. Cr cds: A, C, D, DS, ER, JCB, MC, V. [D] [♦] [≈] [⊠] [🔥] [SC]

Motor Hotels

★ ★ ★ **DOUBLETREE.** 2001 Point West Way (95815). 916/929-8855; FAX 916/924-4913. 448 rms, 4 story. S $119-$144; D $134-$159; each addl $15; suites $200-$500; under 18 free. Crib free. Pet accepted, some restrictions. TV; VCR avail. Pool; poolside serv. Complimentary full bkfst. Restaurant 6 am-midnight. Rm serv. Bar 11-2 am; dancing. Ck-out noon. Meeting rms. Business center. In-rm modem link. Bellhops. Valet serv. Gift shop. Free airport, RR station, bus depot transportation. Exercise equipt; weight machine, stair machine. Bathrm phone, refrigerator, minibar, whirlpool in suites. Balconies. Cr cds: A, C, D, DS, ER, JCB, MC, V. [D] [♦] [≈] [🏋] [⊠] [🔥] [SC] [🚶]

★ ★ ★ **RADISSON.** 500 Leisure Lane (95815), off CA 160 Canterbury Rd exit. 916/922-2020; FAX 916/649-9463. 309 rms, 2 story. S, D $89-$139; each addl $10; suites $139-$395; under 18 free; wkend rates. Crib avail. Pet accepted, some restrictions; $100. TV; cable, VCR avail. Pool; poolside serv. Complimentary coffee in rms. Restaurant 6 am-11 pm. Rm serv 24 hrs. Bar 11-2 am; entertainment. Ck-out noon. Convention facilities. Business center. Bellhops. Valet serv. Concierge. Sundries. Gift shop. Free valet parking. Free airport, RR station, bus depot transportation. Exercise equipt; weight machine, stair machine, whirlpool. Some refrigerators. Balconies. On small, private lake. Cr cds: A, C, D, DS, ER, JCB, MC, V. [D] [♦] [≈] [🏋] [🏃] [⊠] [🔥] [SC] [🚶]

★ ★ ★ **RED LION SACRAMENTO INN.** 1401 Arden Way (95815). 916/922-8041; FAX 916/922-0386. 376 rms, 2-3 story. S $89-$109; D $104-$124; each addl $15; suites $150-$445; under 18 free. Crib free. Pet accepted, some restrictions; $25 deposit. TV; cable. 3 pools; wading pool, poolside serv. Restaurant 6 am-10 pm. Rm serv. Bar 11-2 am; entertainment Tues-Sat. Ck-out 1 pm. Coin lndry. Meeting rms. Bellhops. Sundries. Gift shop. Free airport, RR station, bus depot transportation. Putting green. Exercise equipt; weights, bicycles. Some bathrm phones, in-rm whirlpools, refrigerators. Private patios, balconies. Cr cds: A, C, D, DS, JCB, MC, V. ⓓ ⓦ ⓧ ⓧ ⓧ ⓧ sc

Hotel

★ ★ ★ **HILTON INN-SACRAMENTO.** *2200 Harvard St (95815). 916/922-4700; FAX 916/922-8418.* 325 rms, 12 story. S $86-$136; D $96-$146; each addl $10; suites $250-$425; wkend rates. Crib free. Pet accepted, some restrictions; $25 deposit. TV; cable (premium), VCR avail. Heated pool; poolside serv. Coffee in rms. Restaurant 6 am-11 pm. Bar 11-2 am; dancing. Ck-out noon. Convention facilities. Business servs avail. In-rm modem link. Gift shop. Free airport, RR station, bus depot transportation. Exercise equipt; weights, bicycles, whirlpool, sauna. Refrigerator in suites. Some minibars. Some balconies. Cr cds: A, C, D, DS, ER, JCB, MC, V. ⓓ ⓦ ⓧ ⓧ ⓧ ⓧ

St Helena *(See also Santa Rosa, Yountville)*

Motel

★ ★ **EL BONITA.** *195 Main St. 707/963-3216; FAX 707/963-8838; res: 800/541-3284.* E-mail elbonita@aol.com; web www.napavalley.com/napaval ley/lodgings/hotels/el bonita/index.html. 42 rms, 27 kits. Apr-Oct: S, D $99-$160; suites $140-$195; lower rates rest of yr. Crib $5. Pet accepted, some restrictions; $8. TV; cable (premium). Pool; whirlpool, sauna. Complimentary coffee in rms. Restaurant nearby. Ck-out 11:30 am. Business servs avail. Refrigerators; some in-rm whirlpools. Cr cds: A, C, D, DS, MC, V. ⓓ ⓦ ⓧ ⓧ

Inn

★ ★ **HARVEST.** *1 Main St. 707/963-9463; FAX 707/963-4402; res: 800/950-8466.* E-mail innkeeper@harvestinn.com; web www.harvestinn.com. 54 rms, 1-2 story. May-Nov: S, D $175-$290; each addl $20; suites $290-$366; 2-night min wkends; lower rates rest of yr. Crib free. Pet accepted, some restrictions; $20. TV; cable, VCR avail (movies). 2 heated pools; whirlpools. Complimentary coffee in rms. Complimentary continental bkfst, snacks. Ck-out 11 am, ck-in after 4 pm. Meeting rms. Business servs avail. In-rm modem link. Refrigerators, bathrm phones, fireplaces, wet bars. Some private patios, balconies. Overlooks vineyards. Award-winning landscaping. Cr cds: A, D, DS, MC, V. ⓦ ⓧ ⓧ

Salinas *(See also Carmel, Monterey)*

Motel

(Rates may be higher, no single rms avail during rodeo, special events)

✔ ★ **VAGABOND INN.** *131 Kern St (93905). 408/758-4693; FAX 408/758-9835.* 70 rms, 2 story. S $52-$65; D $62-$85; each addl $5; under 18 free. Crib free. Pet accepted, some restrictions; $5. TV; cable (premium). Heated pool. Complimentary continental bkfst. Restaurant adj. Ck-out noon. Cr cds: A, C, D, DS, ER, MC, V. ⓦ ⓧ ⓧ ⓧ sc

San Bernardino *(See also Anaheim, Lake Arrowhead)*

Motel

★ ★ **LA QUINTA.** *205 E Hospitality Lane (92408), I-10 exit Waterman Ave N. 909/888-7571; FAX 909/884-3864.* 153 rms, 3 story. S $58-66; D $66-$74; suites $110-$138; each addl $8; under 18 free. Pet accepted, some restrictions. TV; cable (premium). Heated pool. Complimentary continental bkfst. Coffee in rms. Restaurant adj 11 am-midnight. Ck-out noon. Business servs avail. Valet serv. Health club privileges. Refrigerators, microwaves avail. Cr cds: A, C, D, DS, MC, V. ⓓ ⓦ ⓧ ⓧ ⓧ sc

San Clemente *(See also Anaheim, Laguna Beach, San Juan Capistrano)*

Motor Hotel

★ ★ **HOLIDAY INN.** *111 S Ave de Estrella. 714/361-3000; FAX 714/361-2472.* 72 rms, 3 story, 19 suites. S, D $79-$89; suites $119-$139; under 12 free; wkly, monthly rates. Crib free. Pet accepted; $10. TV; cable (premium), VCR avail. Heated pool. Restaurant 7 am-2 pm, 5-10 pm. Rm serv. Bar. Ck-out noon. Meeting rms. Business servs avail. In-rm modem link. Bellhops. Free garage parking. Health club privileges. Massage. Refrigerators; some wet bars; microwaves avail. Balconies. Cr cds: A, C, D, DS, JCB, MC, V.

ⓓ ⓦ ⓧ ⓧ ⓧ sc

San Diego

Motels

✔★ **GOOD NITE INN.** *4545 Waring Rd (92120), NE of downtown. 619/286-7000; FAX 619/286-8403; res: 800/648-3466.* Web www.good-nite.com. 94 rms, 2 story. S, D $35-$45; each addl $6; under 18 free. Crib free. Pet accepted. TV; cable (premium). Heated pool. Restaurant adj 10 am-9 pm; Fri-Sun from 7 am. Ck-out 11 am. Coin lndry. Meeting rm. Refrigerator, microwaves avail. Private patios, balconies. Cr cds: A, D, DS, MC, V.

D ✔ ⩯ ⬳ 🐾 SC

★★ **LA QUINTA.** *10185 Paseo Montril (92129), north of downtown. 619/484-8800; FAX 619/538-0476.* 120 rms, 4 story. S, D $58-$66; each addl $6; under 18 free. Crib free. Pet accepted. TV; cable (premium). Heated pool. Complimentary continental bkfst. Restaurant adj 6 am-midnight. Ck-out noon. Cr cds: A, C, D, DS, MC, V. D ✔ ⩯ ⬳ 🐾 SC

★ **OLD TOWN INN.** *4444 Pacific Hwy (92110), near Lindbergh Field Intl Airport, north of downtown. 619/260-8024; FAX 619/296-0524; res: 800/643-3025.* 84 rms (41 with shower only), 1-3 story, 69 with A/C. June-Sept: S, D $36-$58; each addl $5; suites $92-$109; kit units $56-$72; under 12 free; wkly rates; higher rates hols (3-day min); lower rates rest of yr. Crib $5. Pet accepted; $5. TV; cable (premium). Complimentary continental bkfst. Restaurant nearby. Ck-out 11 am. Coin lndry. Refrigerators avail. Cr cds: A, C, D, DS, MC, V. D ✔ ⬳ 🐾 SC

✔★ **VAGABOND INN.** *625 Hotel Circle S (92108), north of downtown. 619/297-1691; FAX 619/692-9009.* 88 rms, 2 story. Mid-May-mid-Sept: S, D $63-$90; each addl $5; under 18 free; lower rates rest of yr. Crib free. Pet accepted; $10. TV; cable (premium). 2 heated pools; whirlpool. Complimentary continental bkfst. Restaurant adj open 24 hrs. Ck-out noon. Business servs avail. In-rm modem link. Cr cds: A, C, D, DS, MC, V.

✔ ⩯ ⬳ 🐾 SC

Hotels

★★ **BEST WESTERN HANALEI.** *2270 Hotel Circle N (92108), downtown. 619/297-1101; FAX 619/297-6049.* 416 rms, 8 story. June-Sept: S, D $79-$169; suite $175-$350; under 18 free; 2-day min hols; lower rates rest of yr. Crib free. Pet accepted, some restrictions; $50 deposit. TV; cable (premium). Pool; whirlpool, poolside serv. Restaurant 6:30 am-10 pm; Sat, Sun to 11 pm. Bar. Ck-out noon. Coin lndry. Meeting rms. Business servs avail. In-rm modem link. Concierge. Tennis privileges. Health club privileges. Lawn games. Some refrigerators. Balconies. Cr cds: A, C, D, DS, JCB, MC, V.

D ✔ ⩯ 🏃 ⬳ 🚶 🐾 SC

★★★ **DOUBLETREE MISSION VALLEY.** *7450 Hazard Center Dr (92108), Mission Valley. 619/297-5466; FAX 619/297-5499.* 300 rms, 11 story. S, D $210; each addl $15; under 18 free. Crib free. Pet accepted. TV; cable. 2 pools, 1 indoor; whirlpool, poolside serv. Complimentary coffee in rms. Restaurant 6 am-11 pm. Bar 5 pm-2 am; entertainment. Ck-out noon. Convention facilities. Business servs avail. In-rm modem link. Gift shop. Garage parking; valet. Free airport, RR station, bus depot transportation. Lighted tennis. Exercise equipt; weight machine, stair machine, sauna. Health club privileges. Minibars. Microwaves avail. Some bathrm phones, wet bars in suites. Some balconies. Luxury level. Cr cds: A, C, D, DS, JCB, MC, V. D ✔ 🏃 ⩯ 🚶 ⬳ 🐾 SC

★★★ **HILTON BEACH AND TENNIS RESORT.** *1775 E Mission Bay Dr (92109), in Mission Bay. 619/276-4010; FAX 619/275-8944.* E-mail contact@ hiltonsandiego.com. 357 rms, 8 story. S $155-$260; D $175-$280; each addl $20; suites $400-$650; family, wkend rates. Crib free. Pet accepted; $50. TV; cable (premium), VCR avail. Heated pool; wading pool, whirlpool, poolside serv. Playground. Supervised child's activities; ages 6-12. Complimentary coffee in rms. Restaurant 6:30 am-10 pm. Bar 10:30-1 am; entertainment. Ck-out noon. Coin lndry. Convention facilities. Business center. In-rm modem link. Gift shop. Beauty shop. Valet parking. Lighted tennis, pro. Putting greens. Exercise rm; instructor, weights, bicycles, sauna. Massage. Rec rm. Lawn games. Many bathrm phones, refrigerators, minibars; microwaves avail. Private patios, balconies. Dock; boats. On beach. Cr cds: A, C, D, DS, ER, JCB, MC, V. D ✔ 🏃 ⩯ 🚶 ⬳ 🐾 SC 🚣

★★★ **HILTON-MISSION VALLEY.** *901 Camino del Rio S (92108), off I-8 Mission Center Rd exit. 619/543-9000; FAX 619/543-9358.* Web www.hilton. com. 350 rms, 14 story. S $179-$189; D $189; each addl $10; suites $200-$400; under 18 free. Crib free. Pet accepted, some restrictions; $25. TV; cable (premium). Heated pool; whirlpool, poolside serv. Coffee in rms. Restaurant 6:30 am-10:30 pm. Bar 11-1 am. Ck-out noon. Convention facilities. In-rm modem link. Some covered parking. Exercise equipt; weight machine, bicycles, sauna. Health club privileges. Refrigerators. Large entrance foyer. Cr cds: A, C, D, DS, MC, V. D ✔ ⩯ 🚶 ⬳ 🐾 SC

★ ★ **HOLIDAY INN ON THE BAY.** *1355 N Harbor Dr (92101), downtown. 619/232-3861; FAX 619/232-4924.* 600 rms, 14 story. S, D $169.95-$189.95; each addl $10; suites $250-$800; under 19 free. Crib free. Pet accepted, some restrictions. Parking $10/day. TV; cable (premium). Heated pool. Coffee in rms. Restaurant 6:30 am-11 pm. Bar 11-2 am. Ck-out noon. Convention facilities. Business servs avail. In-rm modem link. Shopping arcade. Free airport transportation. Exercise equipt; bicycle, treadmill. Some bathrm phones, refrigerators. Balconies. Many bay view rms. Outside glass-enclosed elvtr. Cruise ship terminal opp. Cr cds: A, C, D, DS, JCB, MC, V. 🄳 ✦ ≋ ✗ ⊠ 🐾 SC

★ ★ ★ **MARRIOTT HOTEL & MARINA.** *333 W Harbor Dr (92101), adj to Seaport Village & Convention Center, downtown. 619/234-1500; FAX 619/234-8678.* Web www.sdmarriott.com. 1,355 rms, 26 story. S, D $255-$275; each addl $20; suites from $400; under 18 free. Crib free. Pet accepted. TV; cable (premium). Pool; whirlpool, poolside serv. Restaurant 6:30 am-11 pm. Rm serv 24 hrs. Bar 11-2 am; entertainment. Ck-out noon. Coin lndry. Meeting rms. Business center. In-rm modem link. Concierge. Shopping arcade. Barber, beauty shops. 6 lighted tennis courts, pro. Exercise equipt; weight machines, treadmill, sauna. Game rm. Bathrm phones, minibars; some refrigerators. Some balconies. Luxurious; large chandeliers in lobby. Bayside; marina. Luxury level. Cr cds: A, C, D, DS, ER, JCB, MC, V. 🄳 ✦ 🏌 ≋ ✗ ⊠ 🐾 SC 🚶

★ ★ ★ **MARRIOTT SUITES-DOWNTOWN.** *701 A Street (92101), downtown. 619/696-9800; FAX 619/696-1555.* 264 suites, 27 story. S, D $199-$209; under 18 free. Crib free. Pet accepted, some restrictions; $50. Garage $10, valet parking $15. TV; cable (premium). Indoor pool; whirlpool. Coffee in rms. Restaurant 6:30 am-10 pm. Bar 11:30 am-midnight. Ck-out noon. Meeting rms. In-rm modem link. Gift shop. Exercise equipt; weight machine, bicycles, sauna. Health club privileges. Refrigerators, minibars; microwaves avail. Cr cds: A, C, D, DS, ER, JCB, MC, V. 🄳 ✦ ≋ ✗ ⊠ 🐾 SC

★ ★ ★ **RADISSON SUITE.** *11520 W Bernardo Court (92127), north of downtown. 619/451-6600; FAX 619/592-0253.* 174 suites, 3 story. S, D $79-$170; each addl $10; under 12 free; golf plans. Crib free. Pet accepted, some restrictions. TV; cable (premium), VCR (movies). Heated pool; whirlpool. Complimentary full bkfst. Complimentary coffee in rms. Restaurant 6-9:30 am, 5-11 pm. Bar 5-11 pm. Ck-out noon. Coin lndry. Meeting rms. Business servs avail. In-rm modem link. Tennis privileges. Golf privileges. Exercise equipt; weight machine, bicycles. Minibars, microwaves. Cr cds: A, C, D, DS, ER, JCB, MC, V. 🄳 ✦ 🏌 🏌 ≋ ✗ ⊠ 🐾 SC

★ ★ ★ **U. S. GRANT.** *326 Broadway (92101), downtown. 619/232-3121; FAX 619/232-3626; res: 800/237-5029.* 280 rms, 11 story, 60 suites. S, D $155-$195; each addl $20; suites $275-$1,500. Crib free. Pet accepted. Valet parking $11. TV; cable (premium), VCR avail. Cafe 6:30-10:30 pm. Bar 11-2 am; entertainment Fri, Sat. Ck-out noon. Business center. Concierge. Gift shop. Free airport transportation. Exercise equipt; weights, bicycles. Massage. Bathrm phones, minibars. Antiques, artwork, period chandeliers and fixtures. 1910 landmark has been restored to its original elegance. Luxury level. Cr cds: A, C, D, DS, MC, V. 🄳 ✦ ✗ ⊠ 🐾 SC 🚶

Resorts

★ ★ ★ **DOUBLETREE CARMEL HIGHLAND GOLF & TENNIS RESORT.** *14455 Penasquitos Dr (92129), north of downtown. 619/672-9100; FAX 619/672-9187.* E-mail carmel@highland.doubletreehotels.com; web www. highlanddoubletreehotels.com. 172 rms, 3 story, 6 suites. S, D $119-$179; each addl $10; suites $179; under 12 free; golf, tennis, fitness plans. Crib free. Pet accepted, some restrictions; $150. TV; cable (premium). 2 pools; whirlpool, poolside serv, lifeguard (summer). Supervised child's activities (June-early Sept); ages 6-12. Complimentary coffee in rms. Dining rms 6:30 am-10 pm. Rm serv. Bar 11-1 am. Ck-out noon, ck-in 3 pm. Convention facilities. Business servs avail. Bellhops. Beauty salon. 5 lighted tennis courts, pro. 18-hole golf, greens fee $45-$58, pro, putting green. Exercise rm; instructor, weights, bicycles, saunas, steam rm. Microwaves avail. Private patios, balconies. On 130 acres. Cr cds: A, C, D, DS, JCB, MC, V. 🄳 ✦ 🏌 🏌 ≋ ✗ ⊠ 🐾 SC

★ ★ **SAN DIEGO PRINCESS.** *1404 W Vacation Rd (92109), on island in Mission Bay. 619/274-4630; FAX 619/581-5929; res: 800/542-6275.* Web www.princessresort .com/princess. 462 cottage rms, 153 kits. May-Aug: S, D $180-$230; each addl $15; suites $245-$375; kit. units $190-$220; lower rates rest of yr. Crib free. Pet accepted. TV; cable (premium). 5 pools, 2 heated; wading pool, whirlpool, poolside serv. Supervised child's activities (June-Aug); ages 3-18. Complimentary coffee in rms. Dining rms 7 am-11 pm. Rm serv. Bars 11-2 am; entertainment Tues-Sun. Ck-out noon, ck-in 4 pm. Coin lndry. Convention facilities. Business servs avail. In-rm modem link. Valet serv. Concierge. Gift shop. Lighted tennis, pro. Putting green. Exercise rm; instructor, weights, stair machine, sauna, steam rm. Bicycles. Game rm. Lawn games. Boats. Some bathrm phones, refrigerators; microwaves avail. Private patios. On beach. Botanical walk. Cr cds: A, DS, ER, MC, V.

D ⬧ ⬧ ⬧ ⬧ ⬧ ⬧ ⬧ SC

San Francisco

Hotels

★ **BERESFORD.** *635 Sutter St (94102), north of Union Square. 415/673-9900;* FAX 415/474-0449; res: 800/533-6533. E-mail beresfordsfo@ delphi.com; web www.beresford.com. 114 rms, 7 story. No A/C. S $99; D $109; each addl $10; family units $119-$129; under 12 free. Crib free. Pet accepted, some restrictions. Garage parking $15 in/out. TV; cable, VCR avail. Complimentary continental bkfst. Restaurant 7 am-2 pm, 5:30-10 pm; Sun, Mon to 2 pm. No rm serv. Bar 7-1 am, Sun to 2 pm. Ck-out noon. Business servs avail. In-rm modem link. Health club privileges. Refrigerators, minibars. Cr cds: A, C, D, DS, JCB, MC, V. ⬧ ⬧ ⬧ SC

★ ★ **BERESFORD ARMS.** *701 Post St (94109), west of Union Square. 415/673-2600;* FAX 415/533-5349; res: 800/533-6533. E-mail beresfordsfo @delphi.com; web www.beresford.com. 96 rms, 8 story, 40 kit. units. No A/C. S, D $99-$109; each addl $10; suites $125-$160, under 12 free. Crib free. Pet accepted, some restrictions. Valet parking $15 in/out. TV; cable, VCR (movies $5). Complimentary continental bkfst. Ck-out noon. Business servs avail. In-rm modem link. No rm serv. Health club privileges. Refrigerators; some bathrm phones, in-rm whirlpools, minibars; microwaves avail. Cr cds: A, C, D, DS, JCB, MC, V. D ⬧ ⬧ ⬧ SC

★ ★ ★ **CAMPTON PLACE.** *340 Stockton St (94108), on Union Square. 415/781-5555;* FAX 415/955-5536; res: 800/235-4300. E-mail reserve@camp ton.com. Uniformed doormen greet you outside a simple brownstone facade with a white awning, but inside the small luxury hotel is lavish decor punctuated with antiques and artwork. Rooms are done with Asian touches in subtle tones of gold and brown. 117 rms, 7-17 story. S, D $230-$355; suites $450-$1,000; under 18 free. Pet accepted, some restrictions; $25. Valet parking $25. TV; cable, VCR avail (movies). Restaurant 7 am-2 pm, 6-10 pm. Rm serv 24 hrs. Bar 10 am-11 pm; Fri, Sat to midnight. Ck-out noon. Meeting rms. Business servs avail. In-rm modem link. Concierge. Butler serv. Health club privileges. Massage. Bathrm phones, minibars; microwaves avail. Cr cds: A, C, D, JCB, MC, V. D ⬧ ⬧ ⬧

★ ★ ★ **THE CLIFT.** *495 Geary St (94102), at Taylor St, west of Union Square. 415/775-4700;* FAX 415/441-4621. 329 rms, 17 story. S $245-$400; D $250-$450; each addl $30; suites $395-$700; under 18 free; wknd rates. Crib free. Pet accepted. Valet parking $25. TV; cable (premium), VCR avail. Restaurant 6:30-10:30 am, 5:30-10 pm. Rm serv 24 hrs. Bar 11-2 am; pianist 5:30 pm-1:30 am. Ck-out 1 pm. Valet serv 24 hrs. Concierge. Business center. In-rm modem link. Exercise equipt; bicycles, treadmill. Bathrm phones, refrigerators, minibars; microwaves avail. Cr cds: A, C, D, DS, JCB, MC, V.
D ⬧ ⬧ ⬧ ⬧ ⬧

★ ★ ★ **HOTEL TRITON.** *342 Grant Ave (94108), east of Union Square. 415/394-0500;* FAX 415/394-0555; res: 800/433-6611. Web www.tritonsf.com. 140 rms, 7 story. S, D $139-$229; suites $245-$295; under 16 free. Crib free. Valet, in/out parking $22. Pet accepted; $15. TV; cable, VCR avail. Complimentary morning, afternoon refreshments. Restaurants 6:30 am-10 pm. Bar from 11 am. Ck-out noon. Meeting rm. Business servs avail. Concierge. Exercise equipt: stair machine, bicycle. Health club privileges. Minibars. Whimsical sophisticated design; showcase for local artists. Cr cds: A, C, D, DS, ER, JCB, MC, V. D ⬧ ⬧ ⬧ ⬧ SC

★ ★ ★ **PAN PACIFIC.** *500 Post St (94102), west of Union Square. 415/771-8600;* FAX 415/398-0267; res: 800/533-6465. E-mail vulrich@sfo.pan-pacific.com; web www.panpac.com. This centrally located hotel features a third-floor atrium lobby, decorated mostly in marble (with commissioned sculpture) and highlighted by a spectacular 17-story skylight. 330 units, 21 story. S, D $280-$390; suites $550-$1,700; under 18 free; wknd rates. Crib free. Garage, in/out $25; valet parking. Pet accepted, some restrictions. TV; cable (premium), VCR avail. Restaurant 6:30 am-10:30 pm. Rm serv 24 hrs. Bar 11 am-11:30 pm; pianist. Ck-out noon. Meeting rms. Business center. In-rm modem link. Personal valet serv. Concierge. Exercise equipt; weight machines, bicycles. Health club privileges. Minibars, bathrm phones. Cr cds: A, C, D, DS, JCB, MC, V. D ⬧ ⬧ ⬧ ⬧ ⬧

★ ★ ★ **PARK HYATT.** *333 Battery St (94111), at Clay St, in Financial District. 415/392-1234;* FAX 415/421-2433. Situated in Embarcadero Center, this hotel is designed with neoclassical formality. 360 rms, 24 story, 37 suites. S, D $265-$320; each addl $25; suites $350-$2,500; under 18 free; wknd rates. Crib free. Pet accepted, some restrictions. Covered valet parking, in/out $24. TV; cable (premium), VCR avail (movies). Afternoon refreshments. Restaurant 6:30 am-9:30 pm. Rm serv 24 hrs. Bar 11-1 am; entertainment. Ck-out noon. Meeting rms. Business center. Concierge. Exercise equipt for in-rm use. Health club privileges. Bathrm phones, minibars; microwaves avail. Some balconies. Reference library with national and international publications. Cr cds: A, C, D, DS, ER, JCB, MC, V. [D] [✦] [⊠] [⛿] [SC] [✈]

★ ★ ★ ★ **THE WESTIN ST FRANCIS.** *335 Powell St (94102), on Union Square.* *415/397-7000; FAX 415/774-0124. Web www.westin.com.* An impeccably restored, 93-year-old hotel, the Westin St Francis offers luxury and elegance in the heart of downtown San Francisco. The opulent lobby is appointed with gold and crystal chandeliers, lush Oriental carpets and elaborate gold-leafed ceilings. Extensive crown moldings and 19th-century sleigh beds decorate rooms in the main building. 1,192 rms in hotel & tower, 12 & 32 story. S $199-$355; D $209-$385; each addl $30; suites $295-$2,100; under 18 free. Crib free. Pet accepted, some restrictions. Garage in/out, valet parking $24. TV; cable, VCR avail. Restaurants 6 am-midnight. Rm serv 24 hrs. Bars 11-2 am; entertainment. Ck-out 1 pm. Convention facilities. Business center. In-rm modem link. Concierge. Shopping arcade. Barber, Beauty shop. Exercise equipt; weight machines, bicycles. Refrigerators, minibars; microwaves avail; bathrm phone in suites. Cable car stop. Cr cds: A, C, D, DS, JCB, MC, V. [D] [✦] [✗] [⊠] [⛿] [SC] [✈]

Inn

★ ★ **MANSIONS HOTEL.** *2220 Sacramento St (94115), in Pacific Heights.* *415/929-9444; FAX 415/567-9391; res: 800/826-9398.* 21 rms, 3 story. No A/C. S, D $129-$350; suites $189-$350. Pet accepted. Complimentary full bkfst. Dining rm (res required) dinner only. Rm serv 7:30 am-midnight. Ck-out noon, ck-in 3 pm. Business servs avail. Luggage handling. Airport transportation. Game rm. Music rm. Evening magic concerts. Some balconies. Built in 1887; Victorian memorabilia, antiques, art. Presidential letter collection. Jack London's typewriter used to write "Call of the Wild." Cr cds: A, C, D, DS, MC, V. [✦] [⊠] [⛿]

San Francisco Airport Area
(See also Hayward, Oakland, San Francisco, San Mateo)

Motel

★ ★ **RAMADA HOTEL AIRPORT NORTH.** *(245 S Airport Blvd, South San Francisco 94080)* 2 mi N on US 101, off S Airport Blvd exit. 650/589-7200; FAX 650/588-5007. 175 rms, 2 story. S $80-$110; D $85-$115; each addl $10; under 18 free; wkend rates. Crib free. Pet accepted, some restrictions. TV; cable (premium). Pool. Restaurant 6:30 am-1:30 pm, 5-10 pm. Rm serv. Bar 4-midnight; Sat, Sun 11-1 am. Ck-out noon. Coin lndry. Meeting rms. Business servs avail. Bellhops. Gift shop. Barber shop. Free airport transportation. Health club privileges. Cr cds: A, C, D, DS, ER, JCB, MC, V. [✦] [≋] [✈] [⊠] [⛿] [SC]

Motor Hotel

★ ★ **BEST WESTERN EL RANCHO INN.** *(1100 El Camino Real, Millbrae 94030)* 1 mi SE on US 101, then 1/2 mi W on Millbrae Ave to El Camino Real (CA 82), then 1 mi NW. 650/588-8500; FAX 650/871-7150. 300 rms, most A/C, 1-3 story. S $94-$104; D $99-$109; each addl $10; kit. units, suites $135-$160; under 18 free. Crib free. Pet accepted, some restrictions. TV; cable (premium), VCR avail. Heated pool. Coffee in rms. Restaurant 6:30 am-10 pm. Rm serv. Bar. Ck-out 1 pm. Coin lndry. Meeting rms. Business servs avail. In-rm modem link. Bellhops. Valet serv. Free airport transportation. Exercise equipt; weights, bicycles, whirlpool. Some refrigerators. Cr cds: A, C, D, DS, ER, JCB, MC, V. [D] [✦] [≋] [✗] [✈] [⊠] [⛿] [SC]

Hotels

★ ★ **DOUBLETREE.** *(835 Airport Blvd, Burlingame 94010)* 2 mi S on US 101. 650/344-5500; FAX 650/340-8851. 292 rms, 8 story. S $99-$129; D $109-$139; each addl $10; suites $169-$300; under 17 free. Crib free. Pet accepted, some restrictions; $20. TV; cable, VCR avail. Coffee in rms. Restaurant 6:30 am-10 pm. 24 hr rm serv. Bar 11 am-11:30 pm. Ck-out noon. Meeting rms. Business center. In-rm modem link. Gift shop. Free airport transportation. Exercise equipt; weight machine, bicycles. Refrigerator, wet bar in suites. Cr cds: A, C, D, DS, ER, JCB, MC, V. [D] [✦] [✗] [✈] [⊠] [⛿] [SC] [✈]

★ ★ ★ **MARRIOTT-AIRPORT.** *(1800 Old Bayshore Hwy, Burlingame 94010)* 1 mi SE on US 101, then E on Millbrae Ave to Old Bayshore Hwy, then SE on San Francisco Bay. 650/692-9100; FAX 650/692-8016. 684 rms, 11 story. S, D $179; suites $450-$600; under 18 free; wkend, wkly rates. Crib free. Pet accepted, some restrictions. Valet parking $10. TV; cable (premium), VCR avail. Indoor pool; whirlpool, poolside serv. Restautant 6 am-11 pm. Rm serv 24 hrs. Piano bar. Ck-out noon. Coin lndry. Convention facilities. Business servs avail. In-rm modem link. Concierge. Gift shop. Free airport transportation. Exercise equipt;

treadmills, stair machines, sauna. Some bathrm phones, refrigerators. Luxury level. Cr cds: A, C, D, DS, ER, JCB, MC, V. [D] [icons]

★ ★ **PARK PLAZA.** *(1177 Airport Blvd, Burlingame 94010) 1¹/₂ mi S on US 101 to Broadway exit, then E to Airport Blvd.* 650/342-9200; FAX 650/342-1655; res: 800/411-7275. 301 rms, 10 story. S, D $150-$195; each addl $10; suites $195-$350; under 18 free; wkend rates. Crib free. Pet accepted. TV; cable (premium), VCR avail. Indoor/outdoor pool; whirlpool. Restaurant 6 am-11 pm. Bar; entertainment. Ck-out 1 pm. Coin lndry. Convention facilities. In-rm modem link. Gift shop. Barber, beauty shop. Free airport transportation. Free covered parking. Exercise equipt; weights, bicycles. Cr cds: A, C, D, DS, ER, MC, V. [D] [icons]

★ ★ ★ **THE WESTIN-SAN FRANCISCO AIRPORT.** *(1 Old Bayshore Hwy, Millbrae 94030) 1 mi SE on US 101, then E on Millbrae Ave to Old Bayshore Hwy.* 650/692-3500; FAX 650/872-8111. 390 rms, 7 story. S, D $175-$195; each addl $20; suites $340-$390; under 18 free; wkend rates. Crib free. Pet accepted, some restrictions. Valet parking $8. TV; cable (premium), VCR avail. Indoor pool; whirlpool, poolside serv. Restaurant 6 am-10 pm. Rm serv 24 hrs. Bar noon-1 am; entertainment. Ck-out 1 pm. Convention facilities. Business center. Concierge. Gift shop. Free airport transportation. Exercise equipt; stair machines, treadmill. Refrigerators, minibars. Luxury level. Cr cds: A, C, D, DS, ER, JCB, MC, V. [D] [icons]

San Jose *(See also Fremont, Santa Clara)*

Motels

✓ ★ ★ **BEST WESTERN GATEWAY INN.** *2585 Seaboard Ave (95131), near Intl Airport.* 408/435-8800; FAX 408/435-8879. 146 rms, 2 story. S $80-$99; D $85-$104; each addl $5; under 12 free; higher rates special events. Crib free. Pet accepted, some restrictions; $20. TV; cable (premium), VCR avail (movies). Pool; whirlpool. Complimentary continental bkfst. Ck-out noon. Meeting rms. Business servs avail. Valet serv. Sundries. Free airport transportation. Refrigerators. Cr cds: A, C, D, DS, MC, V. [D] [icons]

★ ★ **RESIDENCE INN BY MARRIOTT.** *(2761 S Bascom Ave, Campbell 95008) Off I-880 exit Camden Ave.* 408/559-1551; FAX 408/371-9808. 80 kit. suites, 2 story. Kit. suites $129-$154. Crib free. Pet accepted, some restrictions. TV; cable (premium), VCR (movies). Heated pool; whirlpool. Complimentary continental bkfst. Ck-out noon. Coin lndry. Meeting rm. Business servs avail. Free airport transportation. Health club privileges. Refrigerators, fireplaces. Balconies. Grills. Cr cds: A, C, D, DS, JCB, MC, V. [D] [icons]

★ ★ **SUMMERFIELD SUITES.** *1602 Crane Ct (95112), off US 101, 1st St exit, then right on Brokaw Rd, ¹/₄ mi NE to Bering Dr, then S to Crane Ct, near Intl Airport.* 408/436-1600; FAX 408/436-1075; res: 800/833-4353. 98 kit. units, 2-3 story. S, D $170-$210. Pet accepted, some restrictions; $75 and $10/day. TV; cable (premium), VCR (movies). Heated pool; whirlpool. Complimentary continental bkfst. Complimentary coffee in rms. Restaurant nearby. Ck-out noon. Coin lndry. Meeting rms. Business servs avail. Valet serv. Sundries. Free airport transportation. Exercise equipt; stair machine, treadmill. Some fireplaces. Picnic tables, grills. Cr cds: A, C, D, DS, JCB, MC, V. [D] [icons]

Motor Hotel

★ ★ ★ **CAMPBELL INN.** *(675 E Campbell Ave, Campbell 95008) W off I-880, CA 17 at Campbell Ave.* 408/374-4300; FAX 408/379-0695; res: 800/582-4449. 95 rms, 2 story, 8 suites. S, D $115; suites $140-$225; under 12 free; lower rates wkends. Pet accepted, some restrictions; $10 per night. TV; VCR (free movies). Heated pool; whirlpool. Complimentary full buffet bkfst. Ck-out noon. Business center. Valet serv. Free airport, RR station, bus depot transportation. Lighted tennis. Bathrm phones, refrigerators. Health club privileges. Steam bath, fireplace in suites. Private patios, balconies. Cr cds: A, C, D, DS, MC, V. [D] [icons]

Hotels

★ ★ ★ **DOUBLETREE.** *2050 Gateway Pl (95110), off US 101, 1st St exit/Brokaw Rd, near Intl Airport.* 408/453-4000; FAX 408/437-2898. 505 rms, 10 story. S $99-$175; D $109-$205; each addl $20; suites $450-$650; under 18 free; wkly rates. Pet accepted, some restrictions; $15 refundable. TV; cable, VCR avail. Heated pool; poolside serv. Restaurants 6 am-midnight. Rm serv. Bar to 1:30 am; entertainment, dancing. Ck-out 1 pm. Convention facilities. Business servs avail. In-rm modem link. Concierge. Gift shop. Barber, beauty shop. Free airport, RR station transportation. Exercise equipt; weights, stair machines, sauna. Refrigerator in suites. Balconies. Cr cds: A, C, D, DS, ER, JCB, MC, V. [D] [icons]

★★ **HYATT.** *1740 N 1st St (95112), near Intl Airport. 408/993-1234; FAX 408/453-0259.* 474 rms, 2-3 story. S $129; D $154; each addl $25; suites $199-$599; under 18 free; wkend rates. Pet accepted, some restrictions; $100 refundable. TV; cable (premium), VCR avail. Heated pool; poolside serv. Restaurant 5:30 am-midnight. Bar 11-2 am. Ck-out noon. Meeting rms. Business center. In-rm modem link. Gift shop. Barber, beauty shop. Free airport transportation. Exercise equipt; weight machine, bicycle, stair machine, whirlpool. Some refrigerators; wet bar in suites. Many private patios, balconies. Cr cds: A, C, D, DS, JCB, MC, V. 🅳 ⟨icons⟩

San Juan Capistrano *(See also Anaheim, Laguna Beach, San Clemente)*

Motel

★★ **BEST WESTERN CAPISTRANO INN.** *27174 Ortega Hwy. 714/493-5661; FAX 714/661-8293.* 108 rms, 2 story. Mar-Sept: S, D $69-$78; each addl $6; kit. units $74-$79; under 12 free; lower rates rest of yr. Crib $5. Pet accepted, some restrictions. TV; cable (premium). Heated pool; whirlpool. Complimentary full bkfst (Mon-Fri). Complimentary coffee in rms. Restaurant adj open 24 hrs. Ck-out noon. Meeting rm. Business servs avail. In-rm modem link. Health club privileges. Microwaves avail. Some balconies. Cr cds: A, C, D, DS, ER, JCB, MC, V. 🅳 ⟨icons⟩

San Luis Obispo *(See also Morro Bay, Pismo Beach)*

Motels

★★ **BEST WESTERN OLIVE TREE INN.** *1000 Olive St (93405). 805/544-2800; FAX 805/772-8967.* 38 rms, 2 story, 6 kits. Some A/C. S $55-$58; D $62-$95; each addl $6; suites $85-$125; kits. $85-$95. Crib free. Pet accepted. TV; cable (premium). Heated pool; sauna. Complimentary continental bkfst. Restaurant 7 am-9 pm; Mon, Tues to 2 pm. Ck-out 11 am. Coin lndry. Business servs avail. In-rm modem link. Sundries. Many refrigerators. Microwaves avail. Balconies. Cr cds: A, C, D, DS, MC, V. ⟨icons⟩

★★ **BEST WESTERN ROYAL OAK.** *214 Madonna Rd (93405). 805/544-4410; FAX 805/544-3026.* 99 rms, 2 story. No A/C. May-mid-Nov: S, D $59-$89; each addl $7; under 12 free; higher rates special events, some hols; lower rates rest of yr. Crib free. Pet accepted, some restrictions. TV; cable (premium). Heated pool; whirlpool. Complimentary continental bkfst. Complimentary coffee in rms. Restaurant 6 am-10 pm. Rm serv. Ck-out noon. Coin lndry. Meeting rms. Business servs avail. In-rm modem link. Valet serv. Airport, RR station transportation. Some refrigerators. Balconies. Cr cds: A, C, D, DS, ER, JCB, MC, V. 🅳 ⟨icons⟩

★★ **SANDS.** *1930 Monterey St (93401). 805/544-0500; FAX 805/544-3529; res: 800/441-4657.* 56 rms, 1-2 story, 14 suites. May-Sept: S, D $59-$99; each addl $7; suites $69-$129; under 12 free; higher rates: special events, hols; lower rates rest of yr. Crib $5. Pet accepted, some restrictions; $5. TV; cable, VCR avail (free movies). Heated pool; whirlpool. Complimentary continental bkfst. Restaurant adj 6-1 am. Ck-out 11 am. Coin lndry. Meeting rms. Business servs avail. In-rm modem link. Sundries. Some covered parking. Free airport, RR station, bus depot transportation. Refrigerators. Some private patios, balconies. Picnic tables, grill. Delicatessen. Cr cds: A, C, D, DS, MC, V.
🅳 ⟨icons⟩

San Mateo *(See also San Francisco Airport Area)*

Motor Hotels

★ **DUNFEY.** *1770 S Amphlett Blvd (94402), at jct US 101, CA 92W. 650/573-7661; FAX 650/573-0533; res: 800/843-6664 (exc CA), 800/238-6339 (CA).* 270 rms, 3 story. S, D $130; each addl $10; suites $180-$350; under 18 free; wkend rates. Crib free. Pet accepted; $75 refundable. TV. Heated pool. Restaurant 6:30 am-9 pm; Fri, Sat to 10 pm. Rm serv. Bar 4 pm-midnight. Ck-out 1 pm. Meeting rms. Coin lndry. Valet serv. Gift shop. Free airport transportation. Game rm. Some refrigerators; wet bar in suites. Cr cds: A, C, D, DS, MC, V. 🅳 ⟨icons⟩

★★ **VILLA HOTEL-AIRPORT SOUTH.** *4000 S El Camino Real (94403). 650/341-0966; FAX 650/573-0164.* 300 rms, 2-5 story. S $79-$99; D $79-$109; each addl $10; suites $115-$225; under 18 free. Crib free. Pet accepted, some restrictions. TV; cable (premium), VCR avail. Pool; poolside serv. Complimentary coffee in rms. Restaurant open 24 hrs. Rm serv. Bar 10-2 am. Ck-out 1 pm. Convention facilities. Business servs avail. Bellhops. Gift shop. Barber, beauty shop. Free airport transportation. Exercise equipt; weight machine, stair machine. Some refrigerators. Some balconies. Cr cds: A, C, D, DS, ER, JCB, MC, V.
🅳 ⟨icons⟩

San Pedro (L.A.) *(See also Los Angeles)*

Hotel

★ ★ **HILTON.** *2800 Via Cabrillo Marina (90731). 310/514-3344; FAX 310/514-8945.* 226 rms, 3 story. S $89-$139; D $89-$149; each addl $10; suites $180-$325; under 18 free; wkend rates. Crib free. Pet accepted. TV; cable (premium). Pool; whirlpool. Restaurant 6:30 am-11 pm. Bar. Ck-out noon. Meeting rms. Business center. Gift shop. Barber, beauty shop. Free parking. Lighted tennis. Exercise equipt; weight machine, bicycles, sauna. Refrigerators avail. On marina. Cr cds: A, C, D, DS, ER, JCB, MC, V.

[D] [✦] [♫] [≈] [🍴] [🛋] [≋] [🔥] [SC] [🚶]

San Rafael *(See also San Francisco)*

Inn

★ ★ ★ **GERSTLE PARK INN.** *34 Grove St (94901). 415/721-7611; res: 800/726-7611; FAX 415/721-7600.* E-mail gerstle@wenet.net; web www.wenet. net/~gerstle. 12 rms, 2 with shower only, 4 kit. units. No A/C. S, D $129-$189; each addl $15; kit. units $169-$189; wkly rates; wkends, hols (2-day min). Pet accepted, some restrictions. TV; VCR (free movies). Complimentary full bkfst. Restaurant nearby. Ck-out noon, ck-in 3 pm. Business servs avail. In-rm modem link. Concierge serv. Free bus, ferry transportation. Tennis privileges. Some in-rm whirlpool. Balconies. Picnic tables. Built in 1895. Elegant decor with garden, antiques. Totally nonsmoking. Cr cds: A, MC, V. [D] [✦] [🛋] [≋] [🔥]

San Simeon *(See also Cambria, Morro Bay)*

Motels

★ ★ ★ **BEST WESTERN CAVALIER OCEANFRONT RESORT.** *9415 Hearst Dr. 805/927-4688; FAX 805/927-6472.* Web www.cavalierresort.com. 90 rms, 2 story. No A/C. May-Oct: S, D $75-$159; each addl $6; lower rates rest of yr. Crib free. Pet accepted, some restrictions. TV; cable (premium), VCR (movies avail). 2 heated pools; whirlpool. Restaurant 7 am-10 pm; summer to 11 pm. Rm serv. Serv bar. Ck-out noon. Coin lndry. Meeting rms. Business servs avail. In-rm modem link. Shopping arcade. Exercise equipt; bicycle, rowing machine. Refrigerators, minibars; many wet bars, fireplaces. Many private patios, balconies. On ocean. Cr cds: A, C, D, DS, ER, JCB, MC, V. [➤] [➤] [≈] [🍴] [≋] [🔥] [SC]

★ ★ **BEST WESTERN COURTESY INN.** *9450 Castillo Dr. 805/927-4691; FAX 805/927-1473.* 117 rms, 2 story. Mid-May-Sept: S, D $69-$114; each addl $10; family units $79-$134; suites $95-$189; lower rates rest of yr. Crib free. Pet accepted; $10. TV; cable (premium). Indoor pool; whirlpool. Complimentary continental bkfst. Restaurant adj 7 am-9 pm. Ck-out noon. Coin lndry. Meeting rm. Business servs avail. Lighted tennis. Game rm. Rec rm. Cr cds: A, C, D, DS, ER, JCB, MC, V. [D] [✦] [🛋] [≈] [≋] [🔥] [SC]

Santa Barbara *(See also Ojai, Solvang, Ventura)*

Motel

★ ★ **CASA DEL MAR INN.** *18 Bath St (93101). 805/963-4418; FAX 805/966-4240; res: 800/433-3097.* 21 rms, 2 story, some kits. June-Sept: S, D $79-$129; each addl $10; suites $114-$199; under 13 free; lower rates rest of yr. Pet accepted, some restrictions; $10/day. TV; cable. Complimentary continental bkfst; evening refreshments. Ck-out noon. Business servs avail. In-rm modem link. Whirlpool. Many fireplaces. Near ocean. Cr cds: A, D, DS, MC, V. [D] [✦] [≋] [🔥] [SC]

Motor Hotel

★ ★ ★ **HOLIDAY INN.** *(5650 Calle Real, Goleta 93117) US 101, Patterson exit. 805/964-6241; FAX 805/964-8467.* 160 rms, 2 story. May-Oct: S $119-$149; D $129-$159; each addl $10; under 18 free; higher rates special events; lower rates rest of yr. Crib free. Pet accepted; $25. TV; cable. Complimentary coffee in lobby. Restaurant 6:30 am-9 pm. Rm serv. Ck-out noon. Meeting rms. Business servs avail. In-rm modem link. Bellhops. Shopping arcade. Free airport transportation. Pool. Cr cds: A, C, D, JCB, MC, V.

[D] [✦] [≈] [≋] [🔥] [SC]

Hotels

★ ★ ★ **FESS PARKER'S DOUBLETREE RESORT.** *633 E Cabrillo Blvd (93103). 805/564-4333; FAX 805/564-4964.* 360 rms, 3 story. S, D $229-$359; each addl $15; suites $429-$849; under 18 free; package plans. Pet accepted, some restrictions. TV; cable (premium), VCR avail (free movies). Heated pool; poolside serv. Coffee in rms. Restaurants 6:30 am-11 pm. Rm serv 24 hrs. Bar 11-1 am; entertainment. Ck-out noon. Coin lndry.

Convention facilities. Business servs avail. In-rm modem link. Valet serv. Concierge. Barber, beauty shop. Valet parking. Free airport transportation. Lighted tennis, pro. Exercise equipt; weight machines, stair machine. Massage. Game rm. Lawn games. Microwaves avail. Minibars. Private patios, balconies. Atrium lobby. On 24 acres; ocean opp. Cr cds: A, C, D, DS, ER, JCB, MC, V. [icons]

★ ★ ★ **FOUR SEASONS BILTMORE.** *1260 Channel Dr (93108). 805/969-2261; FAX 805/969-4682.* Web www.fshr.com. Guest rooms at this 23-acre hotel have views of the ocean, mountains or gardens. 234 rms, 1-2 story. No A/C. S, D $250-$450; suites from $500; under 18 free. Crib free. Pet accepted. Valet parking $14. TV; cable (premium), VCR. 2 heated pools; wading pool, whirlpool, poolside serv. Supervised child's activities (June-Aug, rest of yr wkends); ages 5-12. Restaurants 7 am-10 pm. Rm serv 24 hrs. Bar 11:30 am-midnight; Fri, Sat to 2 am; entertainment. Ck-out noon. Meeting rms. Business center. In-rm modem link. Concierge. Gift shop. Beauty salon. Free airport transportation. Lighted tennis, pro. Golf privileges, putting green. Exercise rm; instructor, stair machine, treadmill, sauna. Massage. Bicycles. Lawn games. Bathrm phones, minibars; many fireplaces. Many private patios, balconies. Cr cds: A, C, D, ER, JCB, MC, V.

[icons]

Guest Ranch

★ ★ ★ **SAN YSIDRO RANCH.** *900 San Ysidro Lane (93108). 805/969-5046; FAX 805/565-1995; res: 800/368-6788.* 38 cottages units. S, D $335-$625; suites $750-$2,500. Crib free. Pet accepted; $75. TV; cable (premium), VCR (movies). Heated pool; wading pool, poolside serv. Playground. Coffee in rms. Dining rm 8 am-9:30 pm. Rm serv 24 hrs. Box lunches. Bar 5 pm-midnight, wkends to 1 am; entertainment Thurs, Fri. Ck-out noon, ck-in 3 pm. Grocery 1 mi. Meeting rms. Business servs avail. In-rm modem link. Bellhop. Gift shop. Tennis. Driving range. Summer activities. Exercise rm; instructor, bicycle, stair machine. Massage. Lawn games. Refrigerators, fireplaces; some in-rm whirlpools; microwaves avail. 550 acres in mountains. Cr cds: A, D, MC, V. [icons]

Santa Clara *(See also Fremont, San Jose)*

Motels

★ **ECONO LODGE SILICON VALLEY.** *2930 El Camino Real (95051). 408/241-3010; FAX 408/247-0623.* 70 units, 2 story. 17 kits. S $65-150; D $65-$150; each addl $5; kit. units $100-$150; under 17 free. Crib $5. Pet accepted; $5. TV; cable, VCR (movies). Heated pool. Complimentary continental bkfst. Complimentary coffee in rms. Restaurant nearby. Ck-out 11:30 am. Business servs avail. In-rm modem link. Valet serv. Refrigerators. Some balconies. Cr cds: A, C, D, DS, JCB, MC, V. [icons]

✔ ★ **VAGABOND INN.** *3580 El Camino Real (95051), at jct CA 82, Lawrence Expy. 408/241-0771; FAX 408/247-3386.* 70 rms, 2 story. S $59-64; D $69; each addl $5; under 18 free. Crib free. Pet accepted; $5. TV; cable (premium). Heated pool. Complimentary continental bkfst. Restaurant nearby. Ck-out noon. Coin lndry. Business servs avail. In-rm modem link. Valet serv. Cr cds: A, C, D, DS, ER, MC, V. [icons]

Hotels

★ ★ ★ **MARRIOTT.** *2700 Mission College Blvd (95052), 5 mi N, 1/2 mi E of US 101 at Great America Pkway exit. 408/988-1500; FAX 408/727-4353.* 754 rms, 2-14 story. S, D $149; suites $400; under 18 free; wkend plans. Crib free. Pet accepted, some restrictions. TV; cable (premium), VCR avail. Indoor/outdoor pool; whirlpool, poolside serv. Restaurants 6 am-11 pm. Rm serv to midnight. Bar 11:30-2 am. Ck-out 11 am. Convention facilities. Business center. Gift shop. Free airport transportation. Lighted tennis. Exercise equipt; weight machines, bicycles. Game rm. Some refrigerators; bathrm phone in suites. Some private patios, balconies. Luxury level. Cr cds: A, C, D, DS, ER, JCB, MC, V.

[icons]

★ ★ ★ **WESTIN.** *5101 Great America Pkwy (95054), near Great America Theme Park. 408/986-0700; FAX 408/980-3939.* 500 rms, 14 story. S $199; D $214; each addl $15; suites $350-$500; under 18 free; wkend, hol rates. Crib free. Pet accepted, some restrictions. Valet parking $7. TV; cable (premium). Heated pool; whirlpool, poolside serv. Restaurant 6 am-10:30 pm; Sat & Sun 6:30 am-10 pm. Rm serv 24 hrs. Bar 11 am-11 pm. Ck-out noon. Convention facilities. Business center. In-rm modem link. Concierge. Gift shop. Tennis privileges adj. Exercise equipt; weight machines, treadmill, sauna. Health club privileges. Some minibars. Refrigerators avail. Balconies. Picnic tables. Near airport. Cr cds: A, C, D, DS, ER, JCB, MC, V. [icons]

Santa Monica
(Sea also Beverly Hilles, Buena Park, Fullerton, Los Angeles)

Hotels

★ **GEORGIAN.** *1415 Ocean Ave (90401). 310/395-9945; res: 800/538-8147; FAX 310/451-3374.* E-mail sales@georgianhotel.com; web www.georgianhotel.com. 84 rms, 8 story, 32 suites. No A/C. July-Aug: S $165-$200; D $200-$235; each addl $25; suites $285-$350; family, wkly rates; lower rates rest of yr. Crib free. Pet accepted; $250 ($50 nonrefundable). Valet parking $10. TV; cable (premium), VCR avail. Complimentary coffee in rms. Restaurant 6:30-10:30 am. Ck-out noon. Meeting rms. Business servs avail. In-rm modem link. Concierge. Health club privileges. Minibars. Opp ocean. Cr cds: A, D, JCB, MC, V. ⅅ 🐾 ⩘ ⩘ 🐾 SC

★ **HOLIDAY INN.** *120 Colorado Ave (90401). 310/451-0676; FAX 310/393-7145.* 132 rms, 7 story. Apr-Oct: S $159-$189; D $174-$204; each addl $15; under 18 free; higher rates Rose Bowl, other special events; lower rates rest of yr. Crib free. Pet accepted; $50 deposit. Valet parking $6.60, in/out $6.60. TV; cable (premium), VCR avail (movies). Pool. Restaurant 6:30-11 am, 5-10 pm. Ck-out noon. Coin lndry. In-rm modem link. Concierge. Gift shop. Health club privileges. Some refrigerators. Cr cds: A, C, D, DS, JCB, MC, V. ⅅ 🐾 ⩘ ⩘ 🐾 SC

Santa Nella

Motels

★ ★ **BEST WESTERN ANDERSEN'S INN.** *12367 S CA 33, at jct I-5, CA 33. 209/826-5534.* 94 rms, 2 story. S $56-$64; D $62-$68; each addl $7; under 18 free. Crib free. Pet accepted, some restrictions; $10. TV; cable. Heated pool. Complimentary continental bkfst. Restaurant adj 7 am-10 pm. Ck-out noon. Private patios, balconies. Cr cds: A, C, D, DS, MC, V. ⅅ 🐾 ⩘ ⩘ 🐾 SC

✔ ★ **RAMADA INN.** *13070 S CA 33, jct I-5. 209/826-4444; FAX 209/826-8071.* 159 rms, 2 story. S $39.95-$59.95; D $49.95-$64.95; each addl $10; under 13 free. Pet accepted; $10. TV; cable. Heated pool; whirlpool. Playground. Restaurant 6:30 am-10 pm. Rm serv. Bar 2 pm-2 am; dancing Fri, Sat. Ck-out noon. coin lndry. Meeting rms. Sundries. Some private patios, balconies. Cr cds: A, C, D, DS, JCB, MC, V. ⅅ 🐾 ⩘ ⩘ 🐾 SC

Santa Rosa *(See also Healdsburg, Sonoma)*

Motels

★ ★ **BEST WESTERN GARDEN INN.** *1500 Santa Rosa Ave (95404), off US 101. 707/546-4031.* 78 rms. June-Oct: S, D $65-$89; suites $136-$145; each addl $6; under 12 free; lower rates rest of yr. Crib free. Pet accepted, some restrictions; $10. TV; cable (premium). 2 pools. Coffee in rms. Restaurant 6:30-11 am. Coin lndry. Business servs avail. Health club privileges. Some refrigerators. Some patios. Cr cds: A, C, D, DS, MC, V. ⅅ 🐾 ⩘ ⩘ 🐾 SC

★ **LOS ROBLES LODGE.** *1985 Cleveland Ave (95401). 707/545-6330; FAX 707/575-5826; res: 800/255-6330.* 104 units, 2 story. May-Oct: S $75-$90; D $85-$105; each addl $8; under 16 free; lower rates rest of yr. Crib free. Pet accepted, some restrictions. TV; cable, VCR avail. Heated pool; wading pool, whirlpool, poolside serv. Complimentary coffee in rms. Restaurant 6 am-10 pm. Rm serv. Bar 11 am-midnight; entertainment. Ck-out noon. Coin lndry. Meeting rms. Business servs avail. In-rm modem link. Valet serv. Free airport transportation. Exercise equipt; treadmill, stair machine. Refrigerators; microwaves avail. Private patios, balconies; many overlook pool. Cr cds: A, C, D, DS, JCB, MC, V. ⅅ 🐾 ⩘ 🐾 ⩘ ⩘ SC

San Ysidro (San Diego)

Motels

✔ ★ **ECONOMY INNS OF AMERICA.** *230 Via de San Ysidro (92073). 619/428-6191.* 122 rms, 2 story. S, D $25-$45. Pet accepted. TV; cable (premium). Heated pool. Restaurant adj open 24 hrs. Ck-out 11 am. Cr cds: A, MC, V. ⅅ 🐾 ⩘ ⩘ 🐾 SC

★ ★ **INTERNATIONAL MOTOR INN.** *190 E Calle Primera (92173). 619/428-4486; FAX 619/428-3618.* 92 rms, 2 story, 35 kit. units. S, D $46-$49; each addl $3; kit. units $51-$57; under 18 free. Crib free. Pet accepted. TV; cable (premium), VCR avail. Complimentary coffee in rms. Restaurant adj open 24 hrs. Ck-out 11 am. Business servs avail.

Sundries. Coin lndry. Pool; whirlpool. Refrigerators; microwaves avail. Cr cds: A, C, D, DS, MC, V. [D] [✦] [⟰] [⊠] [🐾] [SC]

Solvang *(See also Lompoc, Santa Barbara)*

Motel

(Rates are generally higher during special celebrations)

★ ★ ★ **DANISH COUNTRY INN.** *1455 Mission Dr, 3 mi E of jct CA 246, I-101.* 805/688-2018; FAX 805/688-1156; res: 800/447-3529. 82 rms, 3 story, 9 suites. S, D $148-$158; each addl $10; suites $185; under 12 free; golf plans. Crib free. Pet accepted; $25. TV; cable, VCR (movies $4). Heated pool; whirlpool. Complimentary full bkfst. Restaurant 6-9:30 am; Sat, Sun from 7 am. Ck-out noon. Meeting rms. Business servs avail. In-rm modem link. Garage parking. Refrigerators. Balconies. Country inn elegance. Sitting rm. Antiques. Cr cds: A, C, D, DS, JCB, MC, V. [D] [✦] [⟰] [⊠] [🐾] [SC]

Sonoma *(See also St Helena, Santa Rosa)*

Motel

★ ★ **BEST WESTERN SONOMA VALLEY INN.** *550 2nd St W.* 707/938-9200; FAX 707/938-0935. E-mail svi-wine@pacbell.net; web www. sonoma.com.svi. 75 rms, 2 story. S, D $85-$184; each addl $10; under 12 free; golf plans. Crib free. Pet accepted; $10/day. TV; cable (premium). Pool; whirlpool. Complimentary continental bkfst in rms. Restaurant nearby. Ck-out noon. Lndry facilities. Business center. Valet serv. Exercise equipt; bicycles, treadmills. Refrigerators; many fireplaces; some in-rm whirlpools. Microwaves avail. Private patios, balconies. Totally nonsmoking. Cr cds: A, C, D, DS, ER, JCB, MC, V. [D] [✦] [⟰] [⊁] [⊠] [🐾] [SC] [⚓]

Sonora

Inn

★ ★ **NATIONAL HOTEL.** *(PO Box 502, Jamestown 95327) On Main St, 3 mi W on CA 108.* 209/984-3446; FAX 209/984-5620; res: 800/894-3446 (CA); 800/446-1333, ext 286 (US). 11 rms, 6 with shower only, 2 story. No rm phones. S, D $65-$80; each addl $8. Children over 10 yrs only. Pet accepted, some restrictions; $50 deposit. TV avail. Complimentary bkfst. Dining rm 11 am-10 pm; Sun 9 am-9 pm. Rm serv. Ck-out noon, ck-in 2 pm. Free airport transportation. Balconies. Continuously operated since 1859. Cr cds: A, C, D, DS, MC, V. [✦] [🐾]

South Lake Tahoe (Lake Tahoe Area)

Motels

✔ ★ **MATTERHORN.** *2187 Lake Tahoe Blvd (96150).* 530/541-0367; FAX 530/541-0367. 18 rms, 2 story. No A/C. Mid-June-mid-Sept, wkends, hols: S, D $49-$79; kit. units $10 addl; lower rates rest of yr. Pet accepted; $10 per day. TV; cable. Pool; whirlpool. Complimentary coffee in lobby. Ck-out 11 am. Business servs avail. Downhill ski 3 mi; x-country ski 10 mi. Microwaves avail. Near marina. Cr cds: A, C, D, DS, MC, V. [✦] [⟰] [⊠] [🐾] [SC]

★ **QUALITY INN & SUITES.** *3838 Lake Tahoe Blvd (96150).* 530/541-5400; FAX 530/541-7170. 121 rms, 2 story. S, D $58-$88; kits. $110-$130; under 12 free; higher rates: wkends, hols. Crib free. Pet accepted, some restrictions. TV; cable. Pool. Complimentary coffee in rms. Restaurant. Bar. Ck-out 11 am. Coin lndry. Meeting rms. Business servs avail. Downhill ski 3 mi; x-country ski 13 mi. Local transportation. Lake 4 blks. Cr cds: A, C, D, DS, ER, JCB, MC, V. [D] [⊁] [⟰] [⊠] [🐾] [SC]

✔ ★ **TAHOE COLONY INN.** *3794 Montreal Rd (96150).* 530/544-6481; res: 800/338-5552; FAX 530/544-2775. E-mail colony@tahoe.net.com; web www.americana inns.com. 86 rms, 2 story. No A/C. Mid-June-Sept: S, D $59; wkend rates; hols (2-day min); lower rates rest of yr. Crib free. Pet accepted, some restrictions. TV; cable. Complimentary continental bkfst. Restaurant opp open 24 hrs. Ck-out noon. Meeting rms. Business servs avail. Pool; whirlpool. Some balconies. Grills. Cr cds: A, D, MC, V. [✦] [⟰] [⊠] [🐾] [SC]

Sunnyvale (See also Santa Clara)

Motels

✓★★MAPLE TREE INN. *711 E El Camino Real (94087). 408/262-2624; FAX 408/738-5665; res: 800/262-2624 (CA); 800/423-0243 (exc CA).* 181 rms, 2-3 story. S $55-$105; D $60-$115; each addl $10; suites, kit. unit $99-$150; under 12 free; wknd, hol rates; higher rates Stanford graduation. Crib free. Pet accepted, some restrictions. TV; cable (premium). Pool. Complimentary continental bkfst. Restaurant nearby. Ck-out noon. Coin lndry. Meeting rm. Business servs avail. In-rm modem link. Valet serv. Health club privileges. Some refrigerators. Cr cds: A, C, D, DS, ER, JCB, MC, V. [D] [★] [≈] [≥] [♠] [SC]

★★RESIDENCE INN BY MARRIOTT-SILICON VALLEY I. *750 Lakeway (94086). 408/720-1000; FAX 408/737-9722.* 231 kit. units, 2 story. S $99-$139; D $139-$159. Pet accepted; $8/day. TV; cable (premium), VCR avail (movies $6). Pool; 2 whirlpools. Complimentary continental bkfst. Restaurant nearby. Ck-out noon. Coin lndry. Meeting rm. Business servs avail. Valet serv. Free airport transportation. Tennis. Exercise equipt; bicycle, weight machine. Lawn games. Picnic tables, grills. Small lake. Cr cds: A, C, D, DS, JCB, MC, V. [D] [★] [★] [≈] [ﾊ] [≥] [♠] [SC]

★★SUMMERFIELD SUITES. *900 Hamlin Ct (94089), just E of US 101 Mathilda Ave (N) exit. 408/745-1515; FAX 408/745-0540; res: 800/833-4353.* 138 kit. suites, 2-3 story. S $160; D $200; wknd rates. Crib free. Pet accepted, some restrictions; $10 daily. TV; cable (premium), VCR (movies $3). Pool; whirlpool. Complimentary coffee in rms. Complimentary bkfst buffet. Restaurant nearby. Ck-out noon. Coin lndry. Meeting rms. Business servs avail. In-rm modem link. Valet serv. Sundries. Free airport transportation. Exercise equipt; weight machine, stair machine. Health club privileges. Some fireplaces. Grills. Cr cds: A, C, D, DS, JCB, MC, V. [D] [★] [≈] [ﾊ] [≥] [♠] [SC]

Tehachapi (See also Bakersfield)

Lodge

★★SKY MOUNTAIN RESORT. *18100 Lucaya, 15 mi W on CA 202 to Cummings Valley, then follow signs to Stallion Springs. 805/822-5581; FAX 805/822-4055; res: 800/244-0864.* 63 rms in main bldg, 2 story, 21 kit. cottages (1-2 bedrms). S, D, suites $70-$185; each addl $10; kit. cottages $155-$185; golf plans. Crib $10. Pet accepted. TV; cable. Heated pool; whirlpool. Playground. Supervised child's activities (seasonal). Dining rm 7:30 am-1:30 pm, 6-8:30 pm. Bar 4-10 pm, wkend hrs vary; entertainment. Ck-out noon, ck-in 3 pm. Meeting rms. Sports dir. Lighted tennis, pro. 18-hole golf, greens fee $22-$32, pro, putting green, driving range. Hiking. Bicycle rentals. Lawn games. Exercise equipt; bicycles, weight machine, sauna. Balconies. Situated atop hill; overlooks golf course, lakes, forests. Cr cds: A, DS, MC, V. [D] [★] [▬] [⊁] [⅄] [⤋] [★] [≥] [♠] [SC]

Three Rivers

Motels

★★BEST WESTERN HOLIDAY LODGE. *40105 Sierra Dr, 8 mi W of Sequoia & Kings Canyon National parks' entrance, on CA 198. 209/561-4119; FAX 209/561-3427.* 54 rms, 1-2 story. S $61-$82, D $69-$82; each addl $4; suites $72-$84. Crib $4. Pet accepted. TV; cable. Pool; whirlpool. Playground. Continental bkfst 7-10 am. Complimentary coffee in rms. Ck-out 11 am. Refrigerators; some fireplaces. Balconies. Grills. Cr cds: A, C, D, DS, JCB, MC, V. [D] [★] [▬] [≈] [≥] [♠]

★★LAZY J RANCH. *39625 Sierra Dr, on Hwy 198. 209/561-4449; res: 800/341-8000.* 18 rms, 14 with shower only, 1 story. S $42-$52; D $58-$80; suites $140-$170; kit. units $80-$92; wkly rates; higher rates hols (3-day min). Crib free. Pet accepted, some restrictions. TV; cable. Pool. Playground. Complimentary coffee in rms. Ck-out 11 am. Coin lndry. X-country ski 20 mi. Picnic tables. Refrigerators. On river. Cr cds: A, C, D, DS, MC, V. [D] [★] [▬] [≈] [≈]

✓★SIERRA LODGE. *43175 Sierra Dr. 209/561-3681; FAX 209/561-3264; res: 800/367-8879.* 22 units, 3 story, 5 kit. suites. No elvtr. May-Sept: S, D $52-$70; each addl $3; suites $85-$165; lower rates rest of yr. Pet accepted. TV; cable (premium). Pool. Complimentary continental bkfst. Complimentary coffee in rms. Restaurant nearby. Ck-out 11 am. Meeting rm. Business servs avail. Refrigerators; some fireplaces. Balconies. Cr cds: A, C, D, DS, JCB, MC, V. [★] [≈] [≥] [♠]

Torrance

Motel

★★ **SUMMERFIELD SUITES.** *19901 Prairie Ave (90503), I-405 to Redondo Beach Blvd. 310/371-8525; FAX 310/542-9628; res: 800/833-4353.* 144 kit. suites, 3 story. Kit. suites $148-$178; under 12 free. Crib avail. Pet accepted. TV; cable. Heated pool; whirlpool. Complimentary continental bkfst. Complimentary coffee in rms. Restaurant nearby. Ck-out noon. Coin lndry. Meeting rm. Airport transportation. Exercise equipt; treadmill, bicycles. Microwaves. Lawn games. Picnic tables, grills. Cr cds: A, C, D, DS, JCB, MC, V. D ⊯ ≈ ✗ ⊠ ⊠ SC

Valencia *(See also Los Angeles)*

Motel

★★★ **HILTON GARDEN INN-SIX FLAGS.** *27710 The Old Road, opp Six Flags California. 805/254-8800; FAX 805/254-9399.* 152 rms, 2 story. S $89-$129; D $99-$139; each addl $10; suites $198-$250. Crib free. Pet accepted, some restrictions. TV; cable (premium). Heated pool; poolside serv. Complimentary coffee in rms. Restaurant 6:30 am-10 pm. Rm serv 5:30-10:30 pm. Bar 5-10:30 pm. Ck-out noon. Coin lndry. Meeting rms. Business center. In-rm modem link. Exercise equipt; bicycle, stair machine. Some bathrm phones; refrigerators, microwaves avail. Some balconies. Cr cds: A, C, D, DS, ER, JCB, MC, V. D ⊯ ≈ ✗ ⊠ ⊠ SC ⚐

Vallejo *(See also Oakland)*

Motel

★★ **BEST WESTERN HERITAGE INN.** *(1955 E 2nd St, Benicia 94510) 6 mi E off I-780 2nd St exit. 707/746-0401; FAX 707/745-0842.* 100 rms, 3 story. S, D $60-$80; each addl $5; suites $85-$100; kit. units $75-$85; under 12 free; wkly, monthy rates. Crib free. Pet accepted, some restrictions; $50 refundable. TV; cable (premium). Pool; whirlpool. Complimentary continental bkfst. Coffee in rms. Restaurant nearby. Ck-out 11 am. Meeting rms. Business servs avail. Valet serv. In-rm whirlpools; some refrigerators, wet bars; microwaves avail. Cr cds: A, C, D, DS, MC, V. D ⊯ ≈ ⊠ ⊠ SC

Ventura *(See also Ojai, Santa Barbara)*

Motel

✔★ **VAGABOND INN.** *756 E Thompson Blvd (93001). 805/648-5371; FAX 805/648-5613.* 82 rms, 2 story. S $45-$68; D $50-$80; each addl $5; higher rates special events. Crib free. Pet accepted. TV; cable (premium). Heated pool; whirlpool. Complimentary continental bkfst. Complimentary coffee in rms. Restaurant open 5 am-10 pm. Ck-out noon. Business servs avail. Cr cds: A, C, D, DS, MC, V. ⊯ ≈ ⊠ ⊠ SC

Walnut Creek *(See also Oakland)*

Hotels

★★ **EMBASSY SUITES.** *1345 Treat Blvd (94596), I-680 to Treat exit. 510/934-2500.* Web www.embassy-suites.com. 249 suites, 8 story. S $129-$179; D $144-$194; each addl $15; under 13 free. Crib free. Pet accepted; $50. In/out parking $5. TV; cable (premium), VCR avail. Complimentary full bkfst. Complimentary coffee in rms. Restaurant 11:30 am-2:30 pm, 5-10 pm. Rm serv 11 am-11 pm. Bar 11 am-midnight. Ck-out 1 pm. Meeting rms. Business servs avail. In-rm modem link. Gift shop. Coin lndry. Exercise equipt; weight machine, bicycle. Heated indoor pool; whirlpool. Refrigerators, microwaves, wet bars. Cr cds: A, C, D, DS, JCB, MC, V. D ⊯ ≈ ✗ ⊠ ⊠ SC

★★★ **MARRIOTT-SAN RAMON.** *(2600 Bishop Dr, San Ramon 94583) I-680 exit Bollinger Canyon Rd, 5 mi N of I-580 interchange at Bishop Ranch. 510/867-9200; FAX 510/830-9326.* Web www.marriott.com. 368 rms, 6 story. S, D $149; suites $300-$600; under 18 free; wkend rates. Crib free. Pet accepted. TV; cable (premium), VCR avail. Pool; whirlpool. Restaurant 6:30 am-10 pm. Bar 11:30 am-midnight. Ck-out noon. Coin lndry. Convention facilities. Business servs avail. Concierge. Sundries. Exercise equipt; weights, stair machines, sauna. Microwaves avail; wet bar in suites. View of Mt Diablo. Luxury level. Cr cds: A, C, D, DS, ER, JCB, MC, V. D ⊯ ≈ ✗ ⚑ ⊠ ⊠ SC

West Covina

Motel

★ ★ **HAMPTON INN.** *3145 East Garvey Ave N (91791), I-10 exit Barranca Ave N. 626/967-5800; FAX 626/331-8819.* Web www.hamp ton-inn.com. 126 rms, 5 story. S $54-$64; D $59-$69; under 18 free. Crib free. Pet accepted. TV; cable (premium). Heated pool. Complimentary continental bkfst. Restaurant adj 11 am-11 pm. Ck-out noon. Meeting rms. Business servs avail. Valet serv. Cr cds: A, C, D, DS, MC, V. [D] ✦ ☒ ☒ ☒ SC

Westwood Village (L.A.)

Motel

★ ★ **HOTEL DEL CAPRI.** *10587 Wilshire Blvd (90024). 310/474-3511; FAX 310/470-9999; res: 800/44-HOTEL.* 80 units, 2-4 story, 46 kit. suites. S $90; D $100-$110; each addl $10; kit. suites $115-$145. Crib $10. Pet accepted, some restrictions. TV; cable (premium), VCR avail. Heated pool. Complimentary continental bkfst. Restaurants nearby. Ck-out noon. Guest lndry. Business servs avail. Bellhops. Valet serv. Health club privileges. Bathrm phones, refrigerators; many in-rm whirlpools. Cr cds: A, C, D, MC, V.

✦ ☒ ☒ ☒ SC

Hotel

★ ★ ★ **WESTWOOD MARQUIS HOTEL & GARDEN.** *930 Hilgard Ave (90024). 310/208-8765; FAX 310/824-0355; res: 800/421-2317.* E-mail padavis@earthlink.net. 257 suites (1-3 bedrm), 16 story. S, D $235-$650; wkend rates. Crib free. Pet accepted. Garage; valet parking, in/out $18. TV; cable (premium), VCR avail (movies). 2 heated pools. Restaurants 6:30 am-11 pm. Rm serv 24 hrs. Bar 10-2 am; entertainment Fri-Sun. Ck-out noon. Meeting rms. Business servs avail. In-rm modem link. Concierge. Maid serv 24 hrs. Gift shop. Exercise equipt; weights, bicycles. Massage. Health club privileges. Refrigerators, minibars; microwaves avail. Cr cds: A, C, D, DS, JCB, MC, V. [D] ✦ ☒ ⊀ ☒ ☒

Whittier *(See also Anaheim, Buena Park, West Covina)*

Motel

✔ ★ **VAGABOND INN.** *14125 E Whittier Blvd (90605), I-605 exit Whittier Blvd E. 562/698-9701; FAX 562/698-8716.* 49 rms, 3 story. S $45-$55; D $55-$65; each addl $5; under 18 free. Crib free. Pet accepted, some restrictions; $5/day. TV; cable. Heated pool. Complimentary continental bkfst. Restaurant opp 7 am-11 pm. Ck-out noon. Meeting rm. Refrigerators avail. Cr cds: A, C, D, DS, MC, V. ✦ ☒ ☒ ☒ SC

Willits *(See also Mendocino)*

Motel

★ ★ **BAECHTEL CREEK INN.** *101 Gregory Lane (95496). 707/459-9063; FAX 707/459-0226.* 46 rms, 2 story. June-Oct: S, D $65-$105; each addl $3; under 12 free; lower rates rest of yr. Crib free. Pet accepted. TV; cable; VCR avail (movies). Pool; whirlpool. Complimentary continental bkfst. Restaurant adj 6 am-11 pm. Ck-out 11 am. Meeting rms. Some refrigerators. Cr cds: A, DS, MC, V. ✦ ☒

Willows

Motels

✔ ★ **CROSS ROADS WEST.** *452 N Humboldt Ave. 916/934-7026; res: 800/814-6301.* 41 rms, 2 story. S $30.30-$32.50; D $37.80-$41; each addl $6; under 6 free. Pet accepted. TV; cable. Pool. Complimentary morning coffee. Restaurant adj 7 am-9 pm. Ck-out 11 am. Cr cds: A, DS, MC, V. ✦ ☒ ☒ ☒ SC

★ **WOODCREST INN.** *(400 C St, Williams 95987) Approx 30 mi S on I-5. 916/473-2381; FAX 916/473-2418; res: 800/856-4496.* 61 rms, 2 story. S $45; D $49; each addl $5; under 18 free. Crib free. Pet accepted. TV; cable. Pool; whirlpool. Complimentary continental bkfst. Restaurant nearby. Ck-out noon. Business servs avail. Refrigerators avail. Cr cds: A, C, D, DS, ER, MC, V. [D] ✦ ☒ ☒ ☒ SC

Woodland Hills (L.A.)

Motels

★ ★ ★ **COUNTRY INN AT CALABASAS.** *(23627 Calabasas Rd, Calabasas 91302) 2 mi W on US 101, Pkwy Calabasas exit. 818/222-5300; FAX 818/591-0870; res: 800/447-3529.* 122 rms, 3 story. S, D $130-$160; each addl $10; kit. suites $275-$300; under 12 free. Crib free. Pet accepted; $50. TV; VCR (movies $4). Heated pool; whirlpool. Complimentary full bkfst. Restaurant nearby. Ck-out noon. Coin lndry. Meeting rm. Business servs avail. In-rm modem link. Valet serv. Health club privileges. Refrigerators, microwaves, wet bars. Cr cds: A, C, D, DS, JCB, MC, V. 🅓 🖐 🏊 🔌 🐾 SC

★ **VAGABOND INN.** *20157 Ventura Blvd (91364), US 101, Winnetka Ave exit, S to Ventura Blvd. 818/347-8080; FAX 818/716-5333.* 99 rms, 3 story. S $60-$75; D $65-$85; each addl $5; under 19 free. Crib free. Pet accepted, some restrictions; $5. TV; cable (premium). Heated pool; whirlpool. Complimentary continental bkfst. Restaurant adj open 24 hrs. Ck-out noon. Meeting rm. Business servs avail. Valet serv. Cr cds: A, C, D, DS, MC, V. 🅓 🖐 🏊 🔌 🐾 SC

Yosemite National Park

Motel

(Note: All accommodations within Yosemite National Park are operated by the Yosemite Park & Curry Co, under supervision of the National Park Service. Reservations are advised and should be made through the central reservations office, 209/252-4848. The company maintains a wide variety of accommodations here. Riding horses, pack trips. Grocery, drugstore, barber, coin lndry, other facilities are at a central area in Yosemite Valley. Accommodations outside the park are privately operated.)

★ **MARIPOSA LODGE.** *(Box 733, 5052 CA 140, Mariposa 95338) At jct CA 140, CA 49. 209/966-3607; FAX 209/742-7038; res: 800/341-8000.* 44 rms, 31 rms with shower only. Apr-Oct: S,D $65-$70; each addl $6; lower rates rest of yr. Crib $6. Pet accepted, some restrictions; $6. TV; cable (premium), VCR avail. Heated pool; whirlpool. Complimentary coffee. Restaurant adj 7 am-9 pm. Ck-out 11 am. Free local airport transportation. Gazebo. Cr cds: A, C, D, DS, MC, V. 🅓 🖐 🏊 🔌

Lodge

★ ★ ★ **TENAYA LODGE AT YOSEMITE.** *(Box 159, Fish Camp 93623) 2 mi S of Yosemite Natl Park south gate on CA 41, near Fish Camp. 209/683-6555; FAX 209/683-8684; res: 800/635-5807.* 244 rms, 3 story, 20 suites. Mid-May-mid-Sept: S, D $189-$219; suites $250-$350; under 18 free; lower rates rest of yr. Crib free. Pet accepted, some restrictions. TV; cable (premium), VCR avail. 2 pools, 1 indoor; whirlpool. Supervised child's activities; ages 3-12. Dining rm 7-11 am, 6-10 pm. Deli 7 am-11 pm. Rm serv. Ck-out noon, ck-in 3 pm. Coin lndry. Convention facilities. Business center. In-rm modem link. Bellhops. Valet serv. Concierge. Gift shops. X-country ski on site. Exercise equipt; bicycles, treadmill, saunas, steam rm, massage. Game rm. Guided hikes and tours. Bicycle rentals. Bathrm phones. Wet bar in suites. On river; water sports. Southwest, Indian decor; rustic with an elegant touch. Jun-Sept wester jamboree cookouts, wagon rides. Cr cds: A, C, D, DS, JCB, MC, V.

🅓 🖐 🖐 ⛷ 🏊 🏊 ✈ 🎿 🔌 🐾 SC 🏇

Yountville *(See also St Helena)*

Motor Hotel

★ ★ ★ **VINTAGE INN.** *6541 Washington St. 707/944-1112; FAX 707/944-1617; res: 800/351-1133.* 80 rms in 9 buildings, 1-2 story. S, D $175-$250; each addl $25; suites, villas $225-$275; under 12 free. Crib $25. Pet accepted; $25. TV; cable, VCR avail (movies). Heated pool; whirlpool. Complimentary continental bkfst with champagne. Afternoon refreshments. Coffee in rms. Restaurant adj 11:30 am-10 pm. Bar 10 am-10 pm. Ck-out noon. Meeting rms. Business servs avail. Concierge. Bellhops. Valet serv exc Sun. Napa airport transportation. Tennis. Health club privileges. Refrigerators, in-rm whirlpools, fireplaces. Verandas. Vineyard, mountain views. Stream on property. Cr cds: A, C, D, MC, V. 🅓 🖐 🎾 🏊 🔌 🐾 SC

Colorado

Alamosa (See also Monte Vista)

Motel

★ ★ **HOLIDAY INN.** *333 Santa Fe Ave, just E on US 160. 719/589-5833; FAX 719/589-4412.* 127 rms, 2 story. June-Aug: S $64-$74; D $84-$94; each addl $10; suites $115; under 18 free; lower rates rest of yr. Crib free. Pet accepted. TV; cable, VCR avail (movies $6). Indoor pool; whirlpool, sauna. Restaurant 6 am-10 pm. Rm serv. Bar 5 pm-2 am, Sun to midnight. Ck-out noon. Coin lndry. Meeting rms. Business center. In-rm modem link. Gift shop. Free airport, bus depot transportation. Holidome. Game rm. Rec rm. Microwaves avail. Cr cds: A, C, D, DS, MC, V. 🄳 👷 🏊 🛌 🔥 SC 🏃

Aspen (See also Snowmass Village)

Motels

(Because of the altitude, air conditioning is rarely necessary. Hours and dates open may vary during off-season, making it advisable to call ahead.)

★ **THE BEAUMONT.** *1301 E Cooper Ave. 970/925-7081; FAX 970/925-1610; res: 800/344-3853.* E-mail beaumont@sopris.net. 31 rms, 2 story. No A/C. Late Nov-early Apr: S, D $170-$255; each addl $20; higher rates winter hols; lower rates rest of yr. Pet accepted, some restrictions. $20/day. TV; cable, VCR avail (movies). Pool; whirlpool. Complimentary full bkfst. Restaurant nearby. Ck-out 11 am. Coin lndry. Meeting rm. Business servs avail. In-rm modem link. Downhill/x-country ski 7 blks. Health club privileges. Lounge with fireplace. Cr cds: A, C, D, DS, MC, V. 🄳 👷 🏊 🛌 🔥 🗽

✔ ★ ★ **LIMELITE LODGE.** *228 E Cooper. 970/925-3025; FAX 970/925-5120; res: 800/433-0832.* 63 rms, 34 A/C, 29 air-cooled, 1-3 story. No elvtr. Dec-Mar: S, D $68-$178; each addl $10; under 12 free; ski package; higher rates hols; varied lower rates rest of yr. Pet accepted. TV; cable (premium), VCR avail. 2 heated pools; whirlpool, sauna. Playground opp. Complimentary continental bkfst. Restaurant nearby. Ck-out 10:30 am, noon in summer. Coin lndry. Business servs avail. In-rm modem link. Downhill ski 3 blks. Refrigerators. Cr cds: A, C, D, DS, MC, V. 🄳 👷 🏊 🛌 🔥 SC

Hotels

★ ★ ★ **HOTEL JEROME.** *330 E Main St. 970/920-1000; FAX 970/925-2784; res: 800/331-7213.* E-mail hjerome@aol.com; web www.aspen.com/jerome. One of Colorado's grand hotels since 1889, the Jerome is strikingly Victorian. The sumptuous public areas sport five kinds of wallpapers; guest rooms are individually decorated with period pieces. 93 rms, 3-4 story. Mid-Nov-mid-Mar: S, D $255-$510; suites $355-$1,470; lower rates rest of yr. Pet accepted. Garage $10. TV; cable (premium), VCR (movies $6). Heated pool; whirlpools, poolside serv. Restaurant 7 am-10 pm. Rm serv 24 hrs. Bar noon-2 am. Ck-out 11 am. Meeting rms. Business servs avail. In-rm modem link. Concierge. Gift shop. Free airport transportation. Downhill/x-country ski 4 blks. Exercise equipt; weight machines, treadmill. Massage. Bathrm phones, refrigerators; some in-rm whirlpools. Cr cds: A, C, D, MC, V. 🄳 👷 🏊 🏋 🛌 🗽 SC

★ ★ ★ ★ **LITTLE NELL.** *675 E Durant Ave. 970/920-4600; FAX 970/920-4670; res: 800/843-6355.* Aspen's only true ski-in, ski-out hotel has upscale, mountain chalet decor: stripped-pine gateleg tables and oatmeal carpet in the guest rooms, and luxurious bathrooms. Atmosphere is noticeably warm thanks to an unusually helpful, friendly staff. 92 rms, 4 story, 14 suites. S, D $275-$375; suites $550-$1,825; higher rates winter. Crib free. Pet accepted. Garage; valet parking $14. TV; cable (premium), VCR (movies). Heated pool; whirlpool, poolside serv. Restaurant 7 am-2:30 pm, 6-10 pm. Bar 3 pm-midnight; entertainment Thurs-Sat. Ck-out noon. Meeting rms. Business servs avail. In-rm modem link. Concierge. Shopping arcade. Free airport transportation. Downhill ski on site. Exercise rm; instructor, weights, bicycles, steam rm. Massage. Bathrm phones, refrigerators, minibars, gas fireplaces; microwaves avail. Cr cds: A, C, D, DS, JCB, MC, V. 🄳 👷 🏊 🏋 🛌 🗽

LUXURY COLLECTION. *(New management, therefore not rated)* *315 E Dean St. 970/920-3300; FAX 970/925-8998.* 257 rms, 6 story. Early Jan-late Mar & early June-early Oct: S, D $259-$349; each addl $25; suites $349-$595; under 18 free; ski plans; lower rates rest of yr. Crib free. Pet accepted. Valet parking $17. TV; cable (premium), VCR avail (movies). Heated pool; whirlpools, poolside serv (summer). Supervised child's activities (Nov-mid-Apr); ages 3-16. Restaurants 6:30 am-11 pm. Rm serv 24 hrs. Bar 11-1 am; entertainment. Ck-out noon. Convention facilities. Business center. In-rm modem link. Concierge. Gift shop. Beauty shop. Golf privileges. Downhill ski/x-country ski 2 mi; rental equipt. Hiking. Bicycle rentals. Exercise rm; instructor, weight machine, bicycles, saunas, steam rms. Massage. Bathrm phones, minibars; microwaves avail. Some balconies. Luxury level. Cr cds: A, C, D, DS, ER, JCB, MC, V. [D] 🐾 🏊 🍴 ≈ 🏃 ⊠ 🐾 🔥

Boulder *(See also Denver, Longmont)*

Motel

★ ★ **RESIDENCE INN BY MARRIOTT.** *3030 Center Green Dr (80301), Foothills Pkwy at Valmont.* 303/449-5545; FAX 303/449-2452. 128 kit. suites, 2 story. Kit. suites $115-$179; wkly rates. Pet accepted; $5/day; $50 min. TV; cable (premium). Heated pool; whirlpool. Complimentary continental bkfst. Ck-out noon. Coin lndry. Meeting rms. Business servs avail. In-rm modem link. Valet serv. Health club privileges. Microwaves. Picnic tables, grills. Playground. Cr cds: A, C, D, DS, MC, V. [D] 🐾 ≈ ⊠ 🐾 SC

Motor Hotel

★ ★ ★ **BROKER INN.** *555 30th St (80303).* 303/444-3330; FAX 303/444-6444; res: 800/338-5407. E-mail B93385@aol.com; web www.bldr.broker_inn. 116 rms, 4 story. May-Sept: S, D $98-$108; each addl $6; suites $160-$195; under 18 free; wkend rates; lower rates rest of yr. Crib free. Pet accepted. TV; cable (premium). Heated pool; whirlpool, poolside serv. Complimentary bkfst. Restaurant 6:30-10:30 am, 11 am-2 pm, 5-10 pm. Rm serv. Bar 11-2 am, Sun to midnight; entertainment. Ck-out noon. Meeting rms. Business center. In-rm modem link. Bellhops. Valet serv. Health club privileges. Airport, bus depot transportation. Some bathrm phones, in-rm steam baths. Cr cds: A, C, D, DS, MC, V.
[D] 🐾 ≈ ⊠ 🐾 SC 🔥

Buena Vista

Motel

✔ ★ **TOPAZ LODGE.** *Box 596, 115 N US 24, ¹/₄ blk N of jct US 24, CO 306.* 719/395-2427. 18 rms (fans in each unit), 3 2-bedrms apts. No A/C. Mid-May-mid-Sept: S $40-$55; D $55-$76; each addl $4; 2-bedrm apts $100; wkly rates off-season; lower rates rest of yr. Crib $4. Pet accepted; some restrictions, $5. TV; cable. Playground opp. Complimentary coffee in rms. Restaurant nearby. Ck-out 10 am. Tennis opp. X-country ski 7 mi. Cr cds: A, C, D, DS, MC, V. 🐾 🏊 ⊠ 🐾

Burlington

Motel

✔ ★ **BUDGET HOST CHAPARRAL MOTOR INN.** *405 S Lincoln, I-70 exit 437 & US 385.* 719/346-5361; FAX 719/346-8502. 39 rms. June-Sept: S $33-$43; D $34-$44; each addl $4; under 12 free; lower rates rest of yr. Crib $5. Pet accepted, some restrictions. TV; cable (premium). Heated pool; whirlpool. Playground. Restaurant adj 6 am-11 pm. Ck-out 11 am. Cr cds: A, C, D, DS, MC, V. 🐾 ≈ ⊠ 🐾 SC

Cañon City *(See also Colorado Springs, Cripple Creek)*

Motel

★ ★ ★ **CAÑON INN.** *3075 E US 50.* 719/275-8676; FAX 719/275-8675; res: 800/525-7727 (CO). Web www.canoninn.com. 152 rms, 2 story. May-Sept: S $65-$90; D $80-$100; each addl $7; under 16 free; lower rates rest of yr. Crib free. Pet accepted; $50. TV; cable (premium). Heated pool; whirlpools. Restaurant 5:30 am-10 pm. Rm serv. Bar 4 pm-2 am. Ck-out 11 am. Coin lndry. Meeting rms. Business servs avail. Valet serv. Free airport, bus depot transportation. Some bathrm phones, refrigerators; microwaves avail. Cr cds: A, C, D, DS, MC, V. [D] 🐾 🏊 ⊠ 🐾

Colorado Springs *(See also Cañon City, Cripple Creek, Manitou Springs)*

Motels

★ ★ **DRURY INN.** *8155 N Academy Blvd (80920), I-25 exit 150A.* 719/598-2500. Web www.drury-inn.com. 118 rms, 4 story. May-early Sept: S, D $74-$109; each addl $10; under 18 free; lower rates rest of yr. Crib free. Pet accepted, some restrictions. TV; cable, VCR avail. Heated indoor/outdoor pool; whirlpool. Complimentary bkfst. Restaurant adj open 24 hrs. Ck-out noon. Coin lndry. Meeting rms. Business servs avail. In-rm modem link.

Valet serv. Exercise equipt; bicycles, stair machine. Some refrigerators; microwaves avail. Cr cds: A, C, D, DS, MC, V. ⬛ 🐾 〰️ 🍴 〰️ 🐾 SC

★ ★ **HOLIDAY INN EXPRESS.** *8th & Cimarron (80905). 719/473-5530; FAX 719/473-8763.* 207 rms, 2 story. Mid-May-mid-Sept: S, D $89-$105; each addl $10; suites $225; under 19 free; family, wkly rates; lower rates rest of yr. Crib free. Pet accepted; $75 ($25 nonrefundable). TV; cable (premium). Complimentary continental bkfst. Restaurant opp 11 am-10 pm. Ck-out noon. Meeting rms. Business servs avail. In-rm modem link. Heated pool. Cr cds: A, C, D, DS, ER, JCB, MC, V. ⬛ 🐾 〰️ 〰️ 🐾 SC

★ ★ **RAMADA INN.** *3125 Sinton Rd (80907). 719/633-5541; FAX 719/633-3870.* 220 rms, 2 story. S $49; D $105; suites $175-$225; under 18 free. Crib free. Pet accepted; $25 deposit. TV; cable (premium), VCR avail. Complimentary coffee in lobby. Restaurant 6 am-2 pm, 5-10 pm. Rm serv. Bar 5 pm-midnight. Ck-out noon. Meeting rms. In-rm modem link. Valet serv. Coin lndry. Indoor pool. Game rm. Cr cds: A, C, D, DS, ER, JCB, MC, V. ⬛ 🐾 〰️ 〰️ 🐾 SC

★ ★ **RESIDENCE INN BY MARRIOTT.** *3880 N Academy Blvd (80917). 719/574-0370; FAX 719/574-7821.* 96 kit. suites, 2 story. S, D $127-$165; each addl $10; under 18 free. Pet accepted; $15/day. TV; cable (premium), VCR avail. Heated pool; whirlpool. Complimentary continental bkfst. Ck-out noon. Meeting rms. Business servs avail. In-rm modem link. Coin lndry. Valet serv. Free airport transportation. Health club privileges. Refrigerators. Some fireplaces. Microwaves avail. Balconies. Grills. Cr cds: A, D, DS, JCB, MC, V. 🐾 〰️ 〰️ 🐾 SC

★ ★ **RESIDENCE INN-SOUTH.** *2765 Geyser Dr (80906). 719/576-0101; FAX 719/576-4848.* 72 units, 3 story. May-Oct: S $119-$139; D $165-$195; lowr rates rest of yr. Crib free. Pet accepted, some restrictions; $50. TV; cable (premium). Complimentary continental bkfst. Complimentary coffee in rms. Restaurant adj 4-11 pm. Ck-out noon. Meeting rms. Business servs avail. In-rm modem link. Valet serv. Coin lndry. Lighted tennis. Exercise equipt; treadmill, stair machine. Indoor pool; whirlpool. Refrigerators, microwaves; some fireplaces. Grills. Cr cds: A, C, D, DS, JCB, MC, V. ⬛ 🐾 🎿 〰️ 🍴 〰️ 🐾 SC

Motor Hotels

★ ★ ★ **DOUBLETREE WORLD ARENA.** *1775 E Cheyenne Mountain Blvd (80906), I-25 exit 138. 719/576-8900; FAX 719/576-4450.* E-mail dtcswa@aol. com. 299 rms, 5 story. S, D $155-$170; each addl $15; suites $425-$525; under 18 free; wkend rates. Crib free. Pet accepted. TV; cable (premium). Indoor pool; whirlpool. Coffee in rms. Restaurant 6 am-10 pm. Rm serv. Bar 11-2 am; entertainment Tues-Sat. Ck-out noon. Convention facilities. Business servs avail. In-rm modem link. Bellhops. Valet serv. Gift shop. Free airport transportation. Exercise equipt; weights, bicycles, sauna. Some bathrm phones. Private patios, balconies. Cr cds: A, C, D, DS, ER, MC, V. ⬛ 🐾 〰️ 🍴 〰️ 🐾 SC

★ ★ ★ **RADISSON AIRPORT.** *1645 Newport Dr (80916), near airport. 719/597-7000; FAX 719/597-4308.* E-mail highplainsmgmt@msn.com web www.radisson.com/colora dosprings-airport. 155 rms, 2 story. S, D $120; each addl $15; suites $160; under 18 free; wkly rates. Crib free. Pet accepted, some restrictions; $50. TV; cable (premium). Indoor pool; whirlpool, poolside serv. Complimentary coffee in rms. Complimentary bkfst. Restaurant 11 am-10 pm. Rm serv 24 hrs. Bar. Ck-out noon. Coin lndry. Meeting rms. Business center. In-rm modem link. Bellhops. Concierge. Gift shop. Free airport transportation. Exercise equipt; weight machine, rowers. Game rm. Microwaves avail. Cr cds: A, C, D, DS, ER, JCB, MC, V. ⬛ 🐾 〰️ 🍴 〰️ 〰️ 🐾 SC 🎣

★ ★ ★ **RADISSON INN.** *8110 N Academy Blvd (80920), I-25 exit 150A. 719/598-5770; FAX 719/598-3434.* 200 rms, 2-4 story. May-Sept: S, D $124-$144; each addl $10; suites $159-$259; under 18 free; wkend rates; lower rates rest of yr. Crib free. Pet accepted, some restrictions. TV; cable (premium), VCR avail. Indoor pool; whirlpool, sauna. Coffee in rms. Restaurants 6:30 am-10 pm. Rm serv. Bar from 11 am. Ck-out noon. Meeting rms. Business servs avail. In-rm modem link. Gift shop. Coin lndry. Free airport transportation. Exercise equipt; weight machine, stair machine. Microwaves avail. Near USAF Academy. Cr cds: A, C, D, DS, ER, JCB, MC, V. ⬛ 🐾 〰️ 🍴 〰️ 🐾 SC

★ ★ ★ **SHERATON.** *2886 S Circle Dr (80906), off I-25 exit 138. 719/576-5900; FAX 719/576-7695.* 500 rms, 2-4 story. Mid-May-mid-Sept: S, D $105-$155; suites $175-$325; under 18 free; wkend rates; some lower rates rest of yr. Crib $5. Pet accepted. TV; cable (premium), VCR avail (free movies). 2 pools, 1 indoor; wading pool, whirlpool. Playground. Coffee in rms. Restaurant 6 am-10 pm. Rm serv. Bars 11-2 am; entertainment Fri, Sat. Ck-out 11 am. Convention facilities. Business center. In-rm modem link. Bellhops. Valet. Concierge. Gift shop. Airport transportation. Lighted tennis. Putting green. Exercise equipt;

weight machine, bicycles, steam rm, sauna. Game rm. Some refrigerators. Microwaves avail. Private patios, balconies. Cr cds: A, C, D, DS, JCB, MC, V.

Hotel

✔★★★ **DOUBLETREE ANTLERS.** *4 S Cascade Ave (80903), Pikes Peak Ave & Cascade Ave; I-25 Bijou exit. 719/473-5600; FAX 719/389-0259.* E-mail jan@autlers.com web www.antlers.com. 290 rms (some with shower only), 13 story. S $79-$176; D $89-$176; each addl $15; suites $200-$825; under 18 free; wkend rates. Crib free. Pet accepted, some restrictions. Garage $5. TV; cable (premium), VCR avail. Indoor pool; whirlpool, poolside serv. Complimentary coffee in rms. Restaurants 6:30 am-midnight; Fri & Sat to 1 am. Bars 11-1 am, Sun to midnight. Ck-out noon. Convention facilities. Business servs avail. Concierge. Gift shop. Valet parking. Exercise equipt; weights, treadmill. Microwaves avail. Cr cds: A, C, D, DS, ER, JCB, MC, V.

Cortez

Motels

★ **ANASAZI.** *640 S Broadway. 970/565-3773; FAX 970/565-1027; res: 800/972-6232 (exc CO).* 87 rms, 1-2 story. June-Sept: S $57; D $69-$71; each addl $6; under 18 free; lower rates rest of yr. Crib free. Pet accepted. TV; cable, VCR avail. Heated pool; whirlpool. Restaurant 6 am-9 pm. Rm serv 7 am-9 pm. Bar; entertainment Fri, Sat. Ck-out noon. Meeting rms. Business servs avail. Gift shop. Free airport transportation. Cr cds: A, D, DS, MC, V.

★★ **BEST WESTERN TURQUOISE.** *535 E Main St. 970/565-3778; FAX 970/565-3439.* E-mail tqmi@frontier.net web www.cortez.bestwestern. com. 77 rms, 2 story, 31 suites. June-Sept: S $73-$95; D $92-$125; each addl $5; lower rates rest of yr. Crib free. Pet accepted, some restrictions. TV; cable (premium). Heated pools; whirlpool. Complimentary continental bkfst. Coffee in rms. Ck-out 11 am. Coin lndry. Business servs avail. In-rm modem link. Free airport transportation. Refrigerators, microwaves in suites. Cr cds: A, C, D, DS, MC, V.

★★ **COMFORT INN.** *2321 E Main, at Hawkins Dr. 970/565-3400; FAX 970/564-9768.* 148 rms, 3 story. Memorial Day-Labor Day: S $89; D $99; each addl $6; under 18 free; ski plans; lower rates rest of yr. Crib $4. Pet accepted. TV; cable (premium). Complimentary continental bkfst. Restaurant nearby. Ck-out noon. Meeting rms. In-rm modem link. Coin lndry. Indoor pool; whirlpool. Some in-rm whirlpools. Cr cds: A, C, D, DS, JCB, MC, V.

✔★★ **HOLIDAY INN EXPRESS.** *2121 E Main St. 970/565-6000; FAX 970/565-3438.* 100 rms, 3 story. S $48-$90; D $55-$96; each addl $6; under 18 free. Crib free. Pet accepted, some restrictions. TV; cable (premium). Indoor pool; whirlpool. Complimentary continental bkfst. Restaurant nearby. Ck-out 11 am. Business center. In-rm modem link. Valet serv. Free airport transportation. Exercise equipt; weight machines, ski machine. Cr cds: A, C, D, DS, JCB, MC, V.

Craig *(See also Steamboat Springs)*

Motel

★★ **HOLIDAY INN.** *300 S CO 13, 1 mi SW. 970/824-4000; FAX 970/824-3950.* E-mail hicraig@cmn.net. 152 rms, 2 story. S $59-$65; D $69-$75; each addl $6; suites $84-$109; under 19 free. Crib free. Pet accepted. TV; cable (premium), VCR avail. Indoor pool; whirlpool, poolside serv. Restaurant 6 am-2 pm, 5-10 pm. Rm serv. Bar 4 pm-midnight. Coin lndry. Meeting rms. Business servs avail. Valet serv. Holidome. Exercise equipt: stair machine, bicycle. Game rm. Microwaves avail. Cr cds: A, C, D, DS, JCB, MC, V.

Cripple Creek *(See also Cañon City, Colorado Springs, Manitou Springs)*

Inn

★★ **VICTOR HOTEL.** *(4th St & Victor Ave, Victor 80860) 6 mi S on CO 67. 719/689-3553; FAX 719/689-3979; res: 800/748-0870.* Web www.indra.com/fallline/vh/vh.htm. 30 air-cooled rms, 4 story. Mid-May-mid-Oct: S $89; D $99; under 12 free; lower rates rest of yr. Pet accepted. TV; cable (premium). Complimentary continental bkfst. Restaurant May-Sept 11 am-2 pm; Fri-Sat to 9 pm; Sun brunch 8 am-2 pm. Rm serv. Ck-out 11 am. Business servs avail. Former bank; bird-cage elevator. Cr cds: A, DS, MC, V.

Delta *(See also Montrose)*

Motel

✔★ **BEST WESTERN SUNDANCE.** *903 Main St, 5 blks S on US 50. 970/874-9781; FAX 970/874-5440; res: 800/626-1994.* 41 rms, 2 story. June-Sept: S $45-$55; D $55-$65; each addl $10; under 13 free; lower rates rest of yr. Pet accepted. TV; cable (premium). Heated pool; whirlpool. Complimentary full bkfst. Complimentary coffee. Restaurant 6:30 am-9 pm. Rm serv. Bar 11-2 am. Ck-out 11 am. Coin lndry. Meeting rm. Business servs avail. In-rm modem link. Exercise equipt; weight machine, treadmill. Cr cds: A, C, D, DS, JCB, MC, V. 🐾 ⚊ 🏂 ⊠ 🔥 SC

Denver

Motels

★★ **LA QUINTA AIRPORT.** *3975 Peoria St (80239), I-70 exit 281, east of downtown. 303/371-5640; FAX 303/371-7015.* Web www.laquinta.com. 112 rms, 2 story. S, D $69-$89; each addl $10; under 18 free. Crib free. Pet accepted, some restrictions. TV; cable (premium). Heated pool. Complimentary continental bkfst in lobby. Restaurant adj open 24 hrs. Ck-out noon. Coin lndry. Business servs avail. In-rm modem link. Valet serv. Free airport transportation. Health club privileges. Refrigerators, microwaves avail. Cr cds: A, D, DS, MC, V. [D] 🐾 ⚊ ⊠ 🔥 SC

✔★★ **LA QUINTA DOWNTOWN.** *3500 Park Ave W (80216), I-25 exit 213, west of downtown. 303/458-1222; FAX 303/433-2246.* Web www.laquinta.com. 105 rms, 3 story. S, D $70-$80; each addl $10; under 18 free. Crib free. Pet accepted. TV; cable (premium), VCR avail. Pool. Complimentary bkfst. Complimentary coffee in lobby. Restaurant adj open 24 hrs. Ck-out noon. Business servs avail. In-rm modem link. Valet serv. Cr cds: A, C, D, DS, MC, V. [D] 🐾 ⚊ ⊠ 🔥 SC

★★ **QUALITY INN SOUTH.** *6300 E Hampden Ave (80222), I-25 exit 201, east of downtown. 303/758-2211; FAX 303/753-0156.* 185 rms, 1-2 story. S, D $75-$120; each addl $10; under 18 free. Crib free. Pet accepted; $5/day. TV; cable (premium). Pool; whirlpool, sauna, poolside serv. Complimentary coffee in rms. Restaurant 6 am-11 pm. Rm serv. Bar from 4 pm. Ck-out 11 am. Coin lndry. Meeting rms. Business servs avail. In-rm modem link. Health club privileges. Lawn games. Some refrigerators. Private patios, balconies. Picnic tables. Cr cds: A, C, D, DS, ER, JCB, MC, V. [D] 🐾 ⚊ ⊠ 🔥 SC

✔★ **QUALITY INN WEST.** *(12100 W 44th Ave, Wheat Ridge 80033) off I-70 to 44th Avenue. 303/467-2400; FAX 303/467-0198.* 107 rms, 5 story. May-Aug: S $54-$59; D $64-$79; under 18 free; lower rates rest of yr. Crib free. Pet accepted, some restrictions; $25 deposit. TV; cable (premium). Complimentary coffee in lobby. Restaurant 6 am-10 pm. Rm serv. Bar. Ck-out 11 am. Meeting rms. Business center. Exercise equipt; bicycles, weight machine. On lake. Cr cds: A, D, DS, MC, V. [D] 🐾 🏂 ⊠ 🔥 SC 🎿

★★ **RESIDENCE INN BY MARRIOTT-DOWNTOWN.** *2777 Zuni (80211), jct Speer Blvd N, I-25 exit 212B, west of downtown. 303/458-5318.* 156 kit. suites, 2 story. S $89-$119; D $109-$145. Crib free. Pet accepted; $10. TV; cable, VCR avail. Heated pool; whirlpool. Complimentary continental bkfst. Restaurant nearby. Ck-out 11 am. Meeting rms. Business servs avail. Valet serv. Free grocery shopping serv. RR station, bus depot transportation. Exercise equipt; weights, bicycles. Refrigerators, microwaves; many fireplaces. Private patios, balconies. Cr cds: A, D, DS, JCB, MC, V. [D] 🐾 ⚊ 🏂 ⊠ 🔥 SC

Motor Hotels

✔★ **QUALITY INN AND SUITES.** *4590 Quebec St (80216), just N of I-70 exit 278, east of downtown. 303/320-0260; FAX 303/320-7595.* 182 rms, 5 story. May-Sept: S $65-$75; D $70-$75; each addl $7; suites $115-$135; under 17 free; lower rates rest of year. Crib free. Pet accepted; $25. TV; cable (premium). Pool; whirlpool. Complimentary coffee in rms. Restaurant 6-9:30 am, 5:30-10 pm; Sat-Sun 6-11 am, 5:30-10 pm. Rm serv. Bar 4 pm-midnight, Sat & Sun from 5 pm. Ck-out noon. Coin lndry. Meeting rms. Business servs avail. In-rm modem link. Valet serv. Gift shop. Free airport transportation. Exercise equipt; weight machine, bicycles. Cr cds: A, C, D, DS, MC, V. [D] 🐾 ⚊ 🏂 ⊠ 🔥 SC

★★ **RAMADA INN-AIRPORT.** *3737 Quebec St (80207), east of downtown. 303/388-6161; FAX 303/388-0426.* 148 rms, 4 story. S, D $74-$99; each addl $10; under 18 free; wkend rates. Crib free. Pet accepted. TV; cable. Heated pool. Complimentary coffee in rms. Restaurant 6 am-10 pm. Rm serv. Bar 2 pm-2 am, Sun to midnight. Ck-out noon. Meeting rms. Business servs avail. In-rm modem link. Bellhops. Valet serv. Gift shop. Free airport transportation. Exercise equipt; weight machine, bicycle. Health club privileges. Some refrigerators. Cr cds: A, C, D, DS, ER, MC, V. [D] 🐾 ⚊ 🏂 ⊠ 🔥 SC

Hotels

★ ★ ★ **ADAM'S MARK.** *1550 Court Place (80202), on 16th St Mall.* 303/893-3333; *FAX 303/623-0303.* E-mail sales@denver.adamsmark.com. 1,225 rms, 2 bldgs, 8 & 22 story. S, D $150-$190; each addl $15; suites $375-$1,000; under 18 free; wknd rates. Crib free. Garage $14; in/out privileges. Pet accepted, some restrictions; $100 deposit. TV; cable (premium). Pool; poolside serv (seasonal). Restaurants 6:30 am-11 pm. Rm serv 24 hrs. Bar 11-2 am; entertainment. Ck-out noon. Coin lndry. Convention facilities. Business center. In-rm modem link. Concierge. Barber, beauty shop. Airport transportation. Exercise equipt; stair machine, bicycles, steam rm, sauna. Health club privileges. Microwaves avail. Luxury level. Cr cds: A, C, D, DS, ER, JCB, MC, V. ⬛ 🦶 ≈ 🏃 🎿 🐾 SC 🏋

★ ★ ★ **BURNSLEY.** *1000 Grant St (80203), downtown.* 303/830-1000; *FAX 303/830-7676; res: 800/231-3915 (exc CO).* 82 kit. suites, 16 story. Suites $159-$180; each addl $15. Pet accepted, some restrictions; $50. TV; cable (premium). Pool. Complimentary bkfst. Complimentary coffee in rms. Restaurant 6:30 am-2 pm, 6-9 pm. Rm serv to 11 pm. Bar from 11 am. Ck-out noon. Meeting rms. Business center. Garage parking. Health club privileges. Microwaves. Balconies. Converted apartment building in residential area, near State Capitol. Cr cds: A, C, D, MC, V. 🦶 ≈ 🐾 🐾 SC 🏋

★ ★ ★ **EMBASSY SUITES-AIRPORT.** *4444 N Havana St (80239), N of I-70 at exit 280, east of downtown.* 303/375-0400; *FAX 303/371-4634.* 212 suites, 7 story. Suites $124-$145; each addl $12; under 12 free; ski plans, wkend package. Crib free. Pet accepted, some restrictions; $150 deposit. TV; cable (premium), VCR avail. Indoor pool; whirlpool, poolside serv. Complimentary full bkfst. Coffee in rms. Restaurant 6 am-11 pm. Bar to 1 am. Ck-out 1 pm. Coin lndry. Meeting rms. Business servs avail. In-rm modem link. Valet serv. Gift shop. Free airport transportation. Exercise equipt; weights, bicycles, steam rm, sauna. Refrigerators, microwaves, wetbars; some minibars. Cr cds: A, C, D, DS, MC, V. ⬛ 🦶 ≈ 🏃 🐾 🐾 SC

★ ★ **EXECUTIVE TOWER.** *1405 Curtis St (80202), downtown.* 303/571-0300; *FAX 303/825-4301; res: 800/525-6651.* E-mail sales @exec towerhotel.com; web www.exec towerhotel.com. 337 rms, 16 story. S $147-$174; D $157-$182; each addl $10; suites $180-$340; under 16 free; wknd rates. Crib free. Pet accepted, some restrictions. TV; cable (premium), VCR avail. Indoor pool; whirlpool. Restaurants 6:30 am-9 pm; wkends to 10 pm. Bar 4 pm-midnight. Ck-out noon. Coin lndry. Meeting rms. Business servs avail. In-rm modem link. Garage. Valet serv. Tennis. Exercise equipt; weights, stair machine, sauna, steam rm. Rec rm. Cr cds: A, C, D, DS, MC, V. ⬛ 🦶 🎾 ≈ 🏃 🏃 🐾 🐾 SC

★ ★ **HOLIDAY INN.** *(10 E 120th Ave, Northglenn 80233) 6 mi N on I-25, exit 223.* 303/452-4100; *FAX 303/457-1741.* 235 rms, 6 story. Apr-Sept: S, D $89-$125; each addl $10; suites $150-$175; under 17 free; wknd rates; lower rates rest of yr. Crib avail. Pet accepted. TV; cable. Indoor pool; whirlpool, poolside serv. Restaurant 6 am-11 pm. Bar 11 am-11 pm. Ck-out noon. Convention facilities. Business center. In-rm modem link. Gift shop. Airport transportation. Exercise equipt; bicycle, treadmill. Health club privileges. Cr cds: A, C, D, DS, JCB, MC, V. ⬛ 🦶 ≈ 🏃 🏃 🐾 SC 🏋

★ ★ ★ **LOEWS GIORGIO.** *4150 E Mississippi Ave (80222), N of I-25, south of downtown.* 303/782-9300; *FAX 303/758-6542.* E-mail elar son@loew shotels.com; web www.loewshotels.com. A modern steel-and-glass facade conceals an Italian Renaissance-style interior distinguished by magnificent frescoes. Guest rooms are spacious and elegant. 183 rms, 11 story. S $199-$229; D $219-$249; each addl $20; suites $259-$900; under 18 free; wkend rates. Crib free. Pet accepted, some restrictions. TV; cable (premium), VCR avail (movies). Complimentary coffee in lounge. Restaurant 6 am-10 pm. Bar noon-1 am. Ck-out 11 am. Meeting rms. Business center. Concierge. Gift shop. Valet parking. Exercise equipt; treadmills, stair machines. Health club privileges. Bathrm phones, minibars; some refrigerators; microwaves avail. Library. Cr cds: A, C, D, DS, JCB, MC, V. ⬛ 🦶 🏃 🐾 🐾 SC 🏋

✔ ★ ★ **MARRIOTT DENVER TECH CENTER.** *4900 South Syracuse (80237), off I-25 exit 199, south of downtown.* 303/779-1100; *FAX 303/740-2523.* 626 rms, 2-10 story. S, D $87-$149; suites $260-$500; under 17 free; wknd plans. Crib free. Pet accepted. TV; cable (premium), VCR avail. 2 pools, 1 indoor; whirlpool. Restaurant open 24 hrs. Bar 11 am-midnight. Ck-out noon. Convention facilities. Business center. In-rm modem link. Shopping arcade. Valet parking. Exercise equipt; weights, bicycles, steam rm, sauna. Health club privileges. Rec rm. Refrigerators. Some balconies. Cr cds: A, C, D, DS, JCB, MC, V. ⬛ 🦶 ≈ 🏃 🐾 🏋

★ ★ **MARRIOTT-CITY CENTER.** *1701 California St (80202), downtown.* 303/297-1300; *FAX 303/298-7474.* 615 rms, 19 story. S $164-$174; D $180-$195; each addl $10; suites $225-$825; under 12 free; wknd plans. Crib free. Valet parking; fee. Pet accepted, some restrictions. TV; cable (premium), VCR avail. Indoor pool; whirlpool. Restaurant 6:30

am-10 pm. Rm serv to midnight. Bar 11-2 am. Ck-out noon. Convention facilities. Business center. In-rm modem link. Concierge. Shopping arcade. Exercise equipt; weight machine, stair machine, sauna. Health club privileges. Game rm. Some bathrm phones, refrigerators; microwaves avail. Luxury level. Cr cds: A, C, D, DS, ER, JCB, MC, V.

★ ★ ★ **MARRIOTT-SOUTHEAST.** *6363 E Hampden Ave (80222), I-25 exit 201, south of downtown. 303/758-7000; FAX 303/691-3418.* 595 rms, 11 story. S, D $82-$154; suites $150-$350; under 18 free; wkend package plan. Crib free. Pet accepted, some restrictions. TV; cable (premium), VCR avail. 2 pools, 1 indoor; whirlpool, poolside serv. Complimentary coffee. Restaurant 6 am-11 pm. Bar 11 am-midnight. Ck-out 1 pm. Coin lndry. Convention facilities. Business center. In-rm modem link. Concierge. Shopping arcade. Barber, beauty shop. Covered parking. Airport transportation. Exercise equipt; weight machine, bicycles. Game rm. Some bathrm phones, refrigerators. Balconies; some private patios. Luxury level. Cr cds: A, C, D, DS, ER, JCB, MC, V.

★ ★ ★ **THE WARWICK.** *1776 Grant St (80203), downtown. 303/861-2000; FAX 303/839-8504; res: 800/525-2888.* 194 rms, 15 story. S, D $165-$175; each addl $20; suites $200-$800; under 18 free; wkend package plan. Crib free. Garage $10. Pet accepted. TV; cable (premium). Rooftop pool (in season); poolside serv. Complimentary continental bkfst. Restaurant 6:30 am-2 pm, 6-10 pm; Fri, Sat 7-11 am, 6-10 pm. Rm serv 24 hrs. Bar 11 am-midnight. Ck-out 1 pm. Meeting rms. Business servs avail. In-rm modem link. Concierge. Valet serv. Airport transportation. Free RR station, bus depot transportation. Health club privileges. Bathrm phones, refrigerators; many wet bars; microwaves avail. Many balconies. Cr cds: A, C, D, DS, JCB, MC, V.

★ ★ ★ **WESTIN HOTEL TABOR CENTER.** *1672 Lawrence St (80202), in Tabor Center, downtown. 303/572-9100; FAX 303/572-7288.* 420 rms, 19 story. S $222; D $237; each addl $15; suites $350-$900; under 18 free. Crib free. Pet accepted, some restrictions. Garage $8-$14. TV; cable (premium), VCR avail. Indoor/outdoor pool; whirlpool, poolside serv. Restaurant 6 am-11 pm. Rm serv 24 hrs. Bar 5 pm-1:30 am; pianist Tues-Sat. Ck-out 1 pm. Convention facilities. Business center. In-rm modem link. Shopping arcade. Exercise equipt; bicycles, stair machine, sauna, steam rm. Health club privileges. Refrigerators, minibars; some bathrm phones. Some balconies. Luxury level. Cr cds: A, C, D, DS, ER, JCB, MC, V.

Inn

✔ ★ ★ **HOLIDAY CHALET.** *1820 E Colfax Ave (80218), east of downtown. 303/321-9975; FAX 303/377-6556; res: 800/626-4497.* 10 kit. suites, 3 story. S, D $72.50-$104; each addl $5; under 12 free; wkly rates. Crib free. Pet accepted; $50 deposit. TV; VCR avail. Garage parking $5/day. Complimentary bkfst. Complimentary coffee in rms. Restaurant nearby. Ck-out noon. Concierge. Microwaves avail. Restored brownstone built in 1896. Library; 1880 salt water fish prints. Totally nonsmoking. Cr cds: A, D, DS, MC, V.

Denver International Airport Area *(See also Denver)*

Motor Hotel

★ ★ **BEST WESTERN EXECUTIVE.** *(4411 Peoria St, Denver 80239) N of I-70. 303/373-5730; FAX 303/375-1157.* 199 rms, 2-3 story. Apr-Sept: S, D $85-$89; each addl $10; suites $129; under 18 free; lower rates rest of yr. Crib avail. Pet accepted; $10. TV; cable (premium), VCR avail. Heated pool. Complimentary coffee in rms. Restaurant 6 am-midnight. Rm serv. Bar. Ck-out noon. Coin lndry. Meeting rms. Business servs avail. In-rm modem link. Valet serv. Bellhops. Concierge. Free airport transportation. Exercise equipt; bicycles, treadmill. Balconies. Cr cds: A, D, DS, MC, V.

Hotel

★ ★ **DOUBLETREE.** *(3203 Quebec St, Denver 80207) 303/321-3333; FAX 303/329-5233.* 571 rms, 9 story. S, D $159; suites $300-$500; each addl $10; under 18 free; wkend rates. Crib free. Pet accepted. TV; cable, VCR avail. Indoor pool; whirlpool. Coffee in rms. Restaurant 6 am-11 pm. Rm serv 24 hrs. Bar 5 pm-2 am, Sun to midnight. Ck-out noon. Convention facilities. Business center. In-rm modem link. Free airport transportation. Exercise equipt; weight machine, stair machine, sauna. Refrigerators avail. Some balconies. Sun deck. Cr cds: A, C, D, DS, ER, MC, V.

Dillon

Motels

(Because of the altitude, air conditioning is rarely necessary)

★ ★ **BEST WESTERN PTARMIGAN LODGE.** *652 Lake Dillon Drive, 3 blks S of US 6, on Lake Dillon Dr.* 970/468-2341; FAX 970/468-6465. E-mail ptarmiganlodge@colo rado.net. 69 rms, 1-2 story, 3 kits. No A/C. Late Dec-early Apr: S, D $110-$130; each addl $5-$10; kit. units $10 addl; lower rates rest of yr. Crib free. Pet accepted; $15. TV; cable (premium). Complimentary continental bkfst. Restaurant adj 7 am-10 pm. Ck-out 11 am. Meeting rm. Business servs avail. Free ski area transportation. Downhill/x-country ski 5$^1/_2$ mi. Whirlpool, sauna. Boating. Microwaves avail. Some balconies. On lake. Cr cds: A, C, D, DS, JCB, MC, V. 🅳 ⬚ ⬚ ⬚ ⬚ SC

✔ ★ **DAYS INN SUMMIT COUNTY.** *(580 Silverthorne Lane, Silverthorne 80498) jct US 6, CO 9, I-70 exit 205.* 970/468-8661. 73 rms, 4 story, 30 kits. Nov-Apr: S $80-$90; D $110-$115; suites, kit. units $85-$150; under 13 free; lower rates rest of yr. Crib free. Pet accepted; $10. TV; cable. Wading pool, whirlpool, sauna. Complimentary continental bkfst. Restaurant nearby. Ck-out 11 am. Coin lndry. Business servs avail. Downhill/x-country ski 6 mi. Some fireplaces. Microwaves avail. Cr cds: A, C, D, DS, JCB, MC, V. 🅳 ⬚ ⬚ ⬚ ⬚ SC

★ **NEW SUMMIT INN.** *(1205 N Summit Blvd, Frisco 80443) I-70 exit 203.* 970/668-3220; FAX 970/668-0188; res: 800/745-1211. 31 rms, 2 story. S $34; D $39; under 18 free; higher rates late-Dec-early Jan. Crib $5. Pet accepted; $5. TV; cable. Complimentary continental bkfst. Whirlpool. Restaurant adj 7 am-9 pm. Ck-out 10 am. Coin lndry. Exercise equipt; bicycle, rowing machine, sauna. Microwaves avail. Cr cds: A, C, D, DS, MC, V. 🅳 ⬚ ⬚ ⬚ ⬚ SC

Inn

★ ★ **LARK MOUNTAIN.** *(109 Granite St, Frisco 80443) W on I-70, exit 201.* 970/668-5237; res: 800/668-5275. E-mail lark-inn@toski.com; web www.toski.com/lark. 7 air-cooled rms, 2 shared bath, 2 with shower only, 2 story. No rm phones. Mid-Feb-Apr: S, D $120-$150; family, wkend, wkly rates; ski, golf plans; higher rates hols (3-day min); lower rates rest of yr. Children over 8 yrs only. Pet accepted. TV; cable; VCR avail (movies). Complimentary full bkfst. Restaurant adj 6 am-11 pm. Ck-out 11 am, ck-in 3-9 pm. Business center. Luggage handling. Gift shop. Coin lndry. 18-hole golf privileges. Downhill ski 7 mi; x-country ski 2 mi. Whirlpool. Lawn games. Some balconies. Microwaves avail. Picnic tables,grills. Log timber inn with over 400 hand-stripped rails used in the porch. Totally nonsmoking. Cr cds: MC, V. 🅳 ⬚ ⬚ ⬚ ⬚ ⬚ ⬚ SC ⬚

Durango *(See also Cortez)*

Motels

✔ ★ **ALPINE.** *3515 N Main Ave, 2$^1/_2$ mi N on US 550.* 970/247-4042; FAX 970/385-4489; res: 800/818-4042. 25 rms, 1 & 2 story. Mid-May-mid-Oct: S $68-$74; D $78-$84; ski rates; lower rates rest of yr. Crib free. Pet accepted, some restrictions. TV; cable (premium). Restaurant nearby. Ck-out 11 am. Microwaves avail. Cr cds: A, D, DS, MC, V. 🅳 ⬚ ⬚ ⬚ SC

★ **BEST WESTERN PURGATORY.** *49617 US 550.* 970/247-9669; FAX 970/247-9681. E-mail lodge-at-purgatory@toski.com; web www.iski.com. 31 air-cooled rms, 25 kit. units, 2 story, 21 suites. Late Nov-Mar: S $95-$100; D $95-$120; suites $135-$175; under 13 free (summer); higher rates Christmas hols; lower rates rest of yr. Crib free. Pet accepted; $6/day. TV; cable (premium), VCR avail (movies). Indoor pool; whirlpool. Complimentary continental bkfst (summer). Restaurant 5-9 pm. Bar. Ck-out 11 am. Meeting rms. Business servs avail. Downhill/x-country ski adj. Exercise equipt; treadmill, bicycles. Picnic tables. Cr cds: A, C, D, DS, MC, V. 🅳 ⬚ ⬚ ⬚ ⬚ ⬚ ⬚ SC

✔ ★ **IRON HORSE INN.** *5800 N Main Ave, 4 mi N on US 550.* 970/259-1010; FAX 970/385-4791; res: 800/748-2990. 141 bi-level rms. S, D $60-$100; each addl $5; under 12 free. Crib $6. Pet accepted. TV; cable (premium). Indoor pool; whirlpool, sauna. Restaurant 6:30-10 am, 5-10 pm. Ck-out 11 am. Coin lndry. Meeting rms. Business servs avail. Free airport transportation. Game rm. Lawn games. Fireplaces. Cr cds: A, C, D, DS, MC, V. ⬚ ⬚ ⬚ ⬚ SC

✔ ★ **RODEWAY INN.** *2701 N Main Ave.* 970/259-2540; FAX 970/247-9642; res: 800/752-6072. 31 rms, 2 story. Mid-May-Sept: S $58-$85; D $68-$90; each addl $5; under 17 free; lower rates rest of yr. Pet accepted, some restrictions. TV; cable (premium). Indoor pool; whirlpool. Complimentary continental bkfst. Restaurant nearby. Ck-out 11 am. Coin Indry. Business servs avail. Microwaves avail. Cr cds: A, D, DS, ER, JCB, MC, V.

[icons] SC

Motor Hotel

★ ★ ★ **DOUBLETREE.** *501 Camino Del Rio. 970/259-6580; FAX 970/259-4398.* 159 rms, 4 story. Mid-May-mid-Oct: S, D $129-$164; each addl $15; suites $300; under 18 free; ski plans; higher rates late Dec; lower rates rest of yr. Crib free. Pet accepted. TV; cable (premium). Indoor pool; whirlpool, poolside serv. Coffee in rms. Restaurant 6 am-10 pm. Rm serv. Bar 11:30 am-10 pm. Ck-out noon. Coin Indry. Meeting rms. Business servs avail. In-rm modem link. Bellhops. Valet serv. Gift shop. Beauty shop. Free airport transportation. Exercise equipt; weight machines, bicycles, sauna. Private patios, balconies. Cr cds: A, C, D, DS, ER, MC, V. [icons] SC

Inn

★ ★ ★ **ROCHESTER HOTEL.** *726 N 2nd Ave. 970/385-1920; FAX 970/385-1967; res: 800/664-1920.* E-mail lelaud@frontier.net; web www.crea tivelinks.com/rochester. 15 rms, 2 story, 2 suites, 1 kit. unit. June-Oct: S, D $125-$185; each addl $15; suites $165-$185; kit. unit $185; ski plans; lower rates rest of yr. Pet accepted, some restrictions; $15. TV; cable (premium), VCR avail (free movies). Complimentary full bkfst. Restaurant opp 11 am-10 pm. Ck-out 11 am. Meeting rms. Business servs avail. Luggage handling. Some refrigerators. Restored hotel originally built in 1892. Each room is named and decorated for a movie that was filmed in the area. Totally nonsmoking. Cr cds: A, C, D, DS, MC, V. [icons] SC

Englewood (See also Denver, Lakewood)

Motels

✔ ★ ★ **HAMPTON INN-SOUTHEAST.** *9231 E Arapahoe Rd (80112), just E of I-25 exit 197. 303/792-9999; FAX 303/790-4360.* 152 rms, 5 story. S, D $79-$89; under 18 free. Crib free. Pet accepted. TV; cable (premium), VCR avail. Heated pool. Complimentary continental bkfst. Complimentary coffee in rms. Restaurant nearby. Ck-out noon. Coin Indry. Meeting rms. Business servs avail. In-rm modem link. Valet serv. Exercise equipt; weight machine, bicycles. Health club privileges. Microwaves avail. Cr cds: A, D, DS, MC, V.

[icons] SC

★ ★ **RESIDENCE INN BY MARRIOTT-SOUTH.** *6565 S Yosemite (80111), just W of I-25 exit 197. 303/740-7177; FAX 303/741-9426.* 128 kit. suites, 1-2 story. S, D $129-$165; each addl free; wkend, wkly, monthly rates. Crib free. Pet accepted; $10. TV; cable (premium). Heated pool; whirlpool. Complimentary continental bkfst; refreshments. Restaurant nearby. Ck-out noon. Coin Indry. Business servs avail. In-rm modem link. Valet serv. Health club privileges. Refrigerators, microwaves; many fireplaces. Private patios, balconies. Picnic tables, grills. Cr cds: A, C, D, DS, JCB, MC, V. [icons] SC

Motor Hotel

✔ ★ ★ ★ **HILTON-DENVER SOUTH.** *7801 E Orchard Rd (80111), I-25 exit 198, 1 blk W on Orchard Rd. 303/779-6161; FAX 303/689-7080.* 305 rms, 6 story. S $117-$165; D $127-$175; suites $195-$275; under 18 free; wkend rates. Crib free. Pet accepted. TV; cable (premium), VCR avail. Indoor/outdoor pool. Coffee in rms. Restaurant 6 am-10 pm. Rm serv 24 hrs. Bars 11-midnight. Ck-out noon. Convention facilities. Business servs avail. In-rm modem link. Bellhops. Valet serv. Gift shop. Exercise equipt; weight machine, bicycles, sauna. Microwaves avail. Balconies. Cr cds: A, C, D, DS, ER, JCB, MC, V.

[icons] SC

Estes Park (See also Fort Collins, Granby)

Hotel

★ ★ **THE STANLEY.** *333 Wonderview. 970/586-3371; res: 800/976-1377; FAX 970/586-3673.* Web www.grandheritage.com. 134 rms, 4 story. Mid-May-mid-Oct: S $129-$249; D $159-$299; each addl $20; under 18 free. Crib $10. Pet accepted, some restrictions. TV; cable (premium). Heated pool. Playground. Complimentary coffee. Restaurant 7 am-10 pm. Bar 11-midnight; entertainment Fri-Sun. Ck-out 11 am. Meeting rm. Concierge. Gift shop. Tennis. Exercise equipt; weight machines, treadmill. Health club privileges. Some refrigerators. Built in 1909 by automaker F.O. Stanley. Totally nonsmoking. Cr cds: A, C, D, DS, MC, V. [icons] SC

Cottage Colony

★ ★ **MACHIN'S COTTAGES IN THE PINES.** *2450 Eagle Cliff Rd (Box 2687), 2 mi W on US 36, 1/2 mi S on CO 66, then follow signs. 970/586-4276.* Web www.estes park.com/machins. 17 kit. cottages, 4 one-bedrm, 9 two-bedrm, 4 three-bedrm. Kit. cottages $75-$167; each addl $12; wkly rates. Closed Oct-late May. Crib $3. Pet accepted, some restrictions. TV; cable (premium). Playground. Ck-out 10 am, ck-in 3 pm. Grocery, coin lndry, package store 1 1/2 mi. Gift shop. Hiking trails. Microwaves. Patios. Picnic tables, grills. On 14 acres. Cr cds: A, MC, V. 🐾 🗶

Fort Collins (See also Greeley)

Motor Hotel

✔ ★ ★ **HOLIDAY INN.** *3836 E Mulberry St (80524), 1 mi E on CO 14 at I-25. 970/484-4660; FAX 970/484-2363.* 180 rms, 2-4 story. Mid-May-mid-Sept: S, D $69-$89; each addl $5; under 18 free; higher rates: graduation, special events; lower rates rest of yr. Crib free. Pet accepted. TV; cable, VCR avail. Indoor pool; wading pool, whirlpool, saunas. Restaurant 6 am-2 pm, 5:30-10 pm. Rm serv. Bar 11-2 am; Sun to 10 pm. Ck-out noon. Coin lndry. Meeting rms. Business servs avail. Gift shop. Exercise equipt; weight machines, bicycles. Holidome. Rec rm. Game rm. Sun deck. Some balconies. Cr cds: A, C, D, DS, JCB, MC, V. 🄳 🐾 🏊 🗷 🔥 ㏛

Fort Morgan (See also Sterling)

Motels

★ ★ **BEST WESTERN PARK TERRACE.** *725 Main St, I-76 exit 80. 970/867-8256.* 24 rms, 2 story. Mid-May-Sept: S $46-$52; D $56-$59; each addl $5; lower rates rest of yr. Crib $3. Pet accepted; $25. TV; cable (premium). Pool; whirlpool. Coffee in rms. Restaurant adj 6 am-9 pm; summer hrs vary. Ck-out 11 am. In-rm modem link. Picnic tables. Cr cds: A, C, D, DS, MC, V. 🐾 🏊 🗷 🔥 ㏛

✔ ★ **CENTRAL.** *201 W Platte Ave, I-76 exit 80. 970/867-2401.* 19 rms. May-Sept: S $36.95-$42.95; D $42.95-$49.95; each addl $5; suites from $49.95; under 10 free; lower rates rest of yr. Pet accepted, some restrictions. TV; cable (premium), VCR avail. Complimentary coffee. Restaurant nearby. Ck-out 11 am. Refrigerators, microwaves. Cr cds: A, C, D, DS, MC, V. 🄳 🐾 🗷 🔥 ㏛

Glenwood Springs (See also Aspen, Snowmass Village)

Motels

✔ ★ **GLENWOOD MOTOR INN.** *141 W 6th St. 970/945-5438; res: 800/543-5906.* 45 rms, 3 with shower only, 32 with A/C, 2 story. June-mid-Sept: S $45-$53; D $49-$57; each addl $4; wkly rates; higher rates hols (2-day min); lower rates rest of yr. Crib free. Pet accepted, some restrictions; $20 deposit. TV; cable (premium). Complimentary coffee in lobby. Restaurant opp 7 am-noon; also wkends 5-10 pm. Ck-out 11 am. Coin lndry. Business servs avail. In-rm modem link. Free RR station transportation. Downhill/x-country ski 10 mi. Whirlpool, sauna. Microwaves avail. Balconies. Cr cds: A, D, DS, MC, V. 🄳 🐾 🗷 🔥 ㏛

✔ ★ **RUSTY CANNON.** *(701 Taughenbaugh, Rifle 81650) 28 mi W off I-70 exit 90. 970/625-4004; FAX 970/625-3604; res: 800/341-8000.* 88 rms, 2 story. S $38; D $55-$60; each addl $8. Crib free. Pet accepted, some restrictions; $20 deposit. TV; cable. Heated pool; sauna. Complimentary coffee in lobby. Restaurant adj 6:30 am-10 pm. Ck-out 11 am. Coin lndry. Valet serv. Cr cds: A, C, D, DS, MC, V. 🄳 🐾 🏊 🗷 🔥

Motor Hotel

✔ ★ ★ **REDSTONE INN.** *(82 Redstone Blvd, Redstone 81623) 10 mi SE on CO 82 to Carbondale, then 18 mi S on CO 133. 970/963-2526; res: 800/748-2524.* 35 air-cooled rms, 3 story, 5 suites. No elvtr. S, D $49-$175; suites $90-$175; Crib $5. Pet accepted, $25. TV. Heated pool; whirlpool. Restaurant 7 am-9:30 pm. Bar. Ck-out 11 am. Meeting rms. Business servs avail. Beauty shop. Street parking. Tennis. X-country ski 1/4 mi. Exercise equipt; rowing machine, bicycles. Pool table. Built in 1902; antiques, fireplace, clocktower. Cr cds: A, DS, MC, V. 🐾 🛫 🏊 🎿 🏊 🏃 🍴 🗷 🔥

Cottage Colony

★ **AVALANCHE RANCH.** *(12863 CO 133, Redstone 81623) 15 mi S on CO 82, 13 mi S on CO 133. 970/963-2846; FAX 970/963-3141.* 12 kit. cabins. No A/C. No rm phones. S, D, cabins $95-$155; each addl under 8 free; min stay hols, wkends. Crib free.

Pet accepted, some restrictions; $10. TV in main rm, VCR avail. Playground. Complimentary coffee, tea in rms. Ck-out 11 am, ck-in 3 pm. Business servs avail. Rec rm. Lawn games. Picnic tables, grills. On Crystal River. Renovated 1913 farmhouse with antiques; rustic log cabins. Totally nonsmoking. Cr cds: DS, MC, V. 🐾 💳 📶 🔥 🎿

Golden (See also Denver)

Motel

✔ ★ ★ **LA QUINTA.** 3301 Youngfield Service Rd, I-70 exit 264. 303/279-5565; FAX 303/279-5841. 129 rms, 3 story. S, D $79-$99; under 18 free. Crib free. Pet accepted. TV; cable (premium). Pool. Complimentary continental bkfst 6-10:30 am. Restaurant nearby. Ck-out noon. Coin lndry. Meeting rms. Business servs avail. In-rm modem link. Valet serv. Health club privileges. Cr cds: A, C, D, DS, MC, V. D 🐾 📶 📶 🔥 SC

Granby (See also Grand Lake, Winter Park)

Motel

★ **TRAIL RIDERS.** 215 E Agate Ave. 970/887-3738. 11 rms, 5 suites. S $32, D $42; suites $45-$65; wkly rates. Crib avail. Pet accepted, some restrictions. TV; cable (premium). Coffee in rms. Restaurant adj 11 am-10 pm. Ck-out 10 am. Free airport, RR station transportation. Refrigerators, microwaves. Cr cds: A, DS, MC, V. 🐾 📶 🔥 SC

Resort

★ ★ **INN AT SILVER CREEK.** (62927 US Hwy 40, Silver Creek) 2 mi S on US 40. 970/887-2131; FAX 970/887-2350; res: 800/926-4386. 342 rms, 3 story, 252 kits. No A/C. Feb-Mar: S, D $89; kit. units $119-$229; ski plan; higher rates late Dec; lower rates rest of yr. Crib free. Pet accepted; $12/day. TV; cable (premium). Pool; whirlpool. Bar 4-11 pm, Fri, Sat to 1 am. Ck-out 10 am, ck-in 4 pm. Coin lndry. Convention facilities. In-rm modem link. Shopping arcade. Lighted tennis. Downhill ski 1 mi. Ski rentals. Fishing. Sleigh rides. Racquetball. Whitewater rafting. Mountain bikes. Hot-air balloon rides. Exercise equipt; weight machine, bicycles, sauna. In-rm whirlpools; many refrigerators, fireplaces. Private patios, balconies. Cr cds: A, C, D, DS, MC, V. D 🐾 💳 📶 🏃 📶 🎿 📶 🔥 SC

Grand Junction

Motels

★ ★ **HOWARD JOHNSON LODGE.** 752 Horizon Dr (81506), near Walker Field Airport. 970/243-5150; FAX 970/242-3692. 100 rms, 2 story. S, D $40-$69; each addl $5; under 18 free. Crib free. Pet accepted; $10. TV; cable (premium), VCR avail (movies). Heated pool. Restaurant 6 am-10 pm. Ck-out noon. Coin lndry. Meeting rms. Business servs avail. In-rm modem link. Bellhops. Free airport, RR station, bus depot transportation. Microwaves avail. Private patios, balconies. Cr cds: A, C, D, DS, MC, V.
D 🐾 📶 🎿 📶 📶 SC

✔ ★ **WEST GATE INN.** 2210 US 6 & 50 (81505), I-70 exit 26. 970/241-3020; FAX 970/243-4516; res: 800/453-9253. E-mail wgi@gj.net; web www. gj.net/wgi. 100 rms, 2 story. S $36-$60; D $46-$70; each addl $6; under 11 free. Crib free. Pet accepted. TV; cable (premium). Heated pool. Restaurant 6 am-10 pm. Bar 3 pm-2 am. Ck-out 11 am. Coin lndry. Meeting rms. Business servs avail. Cr cds: A, C, D, DS, MC, V. D 🐾 📶 📶 🔥 SC

Motor Hotels

★ ★ **GRAND VISTA.** 2790 Crossroads Blvd (81506), $1/2$ mi NE from I-70 exit 31, near Walker Field Airport. 970/241-8411; res: 800/800-7796; FAX 970/241-1077. 158 rms, 6 story. S $75; D $85; each addl $10; suites $85-$105; under 18 free; wkend rates. Pet accepted. TV; cable (premium). Indoor pool; whirlpool. Complimentary coffee. Restaurant 6 am-2 pm, 5-10 pm. Rm serv. Bar 11-1 am, Sun to midnight. Ck-out noon. Business servs avail. In-rm modem link. Gift shop. Free airport, RR station, bus depot transportation. Health club privileges. Cr cds: A, C, D, DS, MC, V. D 🐾 📶 🎿 📶 🔥 SC

★ ★ **HOLIDAY INN.** 755 Horizon Dr (81502), N off I-70 airport exit 31, near Walker Field Airport. 970/243-6790; FAX 970/243-6790. E-mail holiday inn@gj.net web www.holidayinn.com. 292 rms, 2 story. S $62; D $68-$72; each addl $6; suites $83-$89; under 20 free. Crib free. Pet accepted. TV; cable (premium), VCR avail. 2 pools, 1 indoor; whirlpool. Coffee in rms. Restaurant 6 am-10 pm. Rm serv. Bar 5 pm-1:30 am, Sun to midnight; entertainment. Ck-out 11 am. Coin lndry. Meeting rms. Bellhops. Gift shop. Free airport, RR station, bus depot transportation. Putting green. Exercise equipt; weight machine, bicycles, sauna. Game rm. Cr cds: A, C, D, DS, JCB, MC, V. D 🐾 📶 🎿 📶 📶 🔥 SC

Hotel

★ ★ ★ HILTON. *743 Horizon Dr (81506), near Walker Field Airport. 970/241-8888; FAX 970/242-7266.* Web www.hilton.com. 264 units, 8 story. May-Oct: S $89-$139; D $99-$149; each addl $10; suites $119-$295; family, wkend rates; golf, ski plans; lower rates rest of yr. Crib free. Pet accepted; $50. TV; cable (premium). Heated pool; whirlpool, poolside serv. Playground. Seasonal supervised children activities. Restaurant 6 am-11 pm. Bar 11-2 am. Ck-out noon. Convention facilities. Business servs avail. Gift shop. Free airport, RR station, bus depot transportation. Lighted tennis. Exercise equipt; weight machine, bicycles. Game rm. Lawn games. Bathrm phones. Luxury level. Cr cds: A, C, D, DS, ER, MC, V. 🄳 🐾 🏃 ≈ 🏋 ✈ 🖎 🖎 🐾 SC

Greeley *(See also Fort Collins)*

Motor Hotel

★ ★ BEST WESTERN RAMKOTA INN. *701 8th St. 970/353-8444; FAX 970/353-4269.* 148 rms, 3 story. S $52-$63; D $60-$71; each addl $8; suites $120-$150; under 18 free. Crib free. Pet accepted. TV; cable. Indoor pool; poolside serv. Complimentary coffee in rms. Restaurant 6 am-10 pm. Rm serv. Bar 11 am-12 am. Ck-out noon. Meeting rms Business center. Health club privileges. Game rm. Balconies. Cr cds: A, C, D, DS, MC, V. 🄳 🐾 ≈ 🖎 🐾 SC 🏊

Gunnison

Cottage Colony

✔ ★ CHAR-B RESORT. *(Box 279MG, Almont 81210) 10 mi N on CO 135, 7 mi NE on Taylor River Rd (County 742), then 2 mi N on Spring Creek Rd (County 744). 970/641-0751; res: 806/259-2073 (winter).* 16 kit. cottages (1-5 bedrm). No A/C. May-Nov: cottages $69-$110; each addl $6; wkly rates. Closed rest of yr. Crib $4. Pet accepted, some restrictions. TV in rec rm. Playground. Restaurant nearby. Ck-out 10 am, ck-in 2 pm. Grocery. Coin lndry. Airport, bus depot transportation. Lawn games. Rec rm. Whirlpool. Refrigerators; some fireplaces. Picnic tables, grills. Rustic decor. Scenic location on Spring Creek. Cr cds: MC, V. 🐾 💌 🐾

La Junta

Motels

✔ ★ ★ BEST WESTERN BENT'S FORT INN. *(E US 50, Las Animas 81054) 20 mi E on US 50 at jct CO 194. 719/456-0011; FAX 719/456-2550.* 38 rms, 2 story. S $49; D $59; each addl $6; under 12 free. Pet accepted, some restrictions. TV; cable. Pool. Restaurant 6 am-8 pm. Rm serv. Bar 5-10 pm. Ck-out noon. Meeting rms. Business servs avail. Free airport, bus depot transportation. Cr cds: A, C, D, DS, MC, V. 🐾 ≈ 🖎 🐾 SC

★ ★ QUALITY INN. *1325 E 3rd St. 719/384-2571; FAX 719/384-5655.* E-mail Quality@iguana.Ruralnet.Net; web www.iguana .ruralnet.net/~quality. 76 rms, 2 story. S $44-$58; D $52-$70; each addl $4; suites $79; under 18 free. Crib $5. Pet accepted, some restrictions. TV; cable (premium), VCR avail (movies). Heated indoor/outdoor pool; whirlpool, poolside serv. Coffee in rms. Restaurant 6 am-9 pm. Rm serv. Bar. Meeting rms. Business servs avail. Free airport, RR station transportation. Exercise equipt; bicycle, treadmill. Refrigerator in suites. Cr cds: A, C, D, DS, ER, JCB, MC, V. 🄳 🐾 ≈ 🏋 🖎 🐾 SC

✔ ★ STAGECOACH INN. *905 W 3rd St, 1 mi W on US 50. 719/384-5476; FAX 719/384-9091.* 31 rms, 2 story. S $35-$40; D $48-$50; each addl $4. Crib $4. Pet accepted. TV; cable (premium). Pool. Restaurant nearby. Ck-out 11 am. In-rm modem link. Cr cds: A, C, D, DS, MC, V. 🐾 ≈ 🖎 🐾 SC

Lake City

Lodge

★ ★ CRYSTAL LODGE. *CO 149, 2 mi S on CO 149. 970/944-2201; FAX 970/944-2504; res: 800/984-1234.* E-mail crylodge@rmi.net. 18 rms, 1-2 story, 5 suites, 4 cottages. No A/C. No rm phones. Memorial Day-Sept (2-day min): S, D $55; each addl $10; suites, cottages $75-$105; under 2 free; ski rates; lower rates rest of yr. Crib free. Pet accepted, some restrictions; $25. TV; VCR avail. Whirlpool. Restaurant 8 am-2 pm, 5:50-8:30 pm. Bar. Ck-out 10 am. Meeting rms. Business servs avail. X-country ski 1 mi. Many refrigerators. Surrounded by San Juan Mountains. Totally nonsmoking. Cr cds: A, MC, V. 🐾 ≈ 🖎 🐾

Lakewood (See also Denver, Englewood, Golden)

Motel

✔ ★ ★ **COMFORT INN-SOUTHWEST DENVER.** 3440 S Vance St (80227), near jct Hampden Ave (US 285) & Wadsworth Blvd (CO 121). 303/989-5500; FAX 303/989-2981. 123 rms, 2 story, 4 suites. S $68; D $76; each addl $10; suites $110; under 18 free; wkly, wkend rates. Crib free. Pet accepted; $50 refundable. TV; cable (premium). Heated pool; whirlpool. Complimentary continental bkfst; afternoon refreshments. Restaurant opp open 24 hrs. Ck-out noon. Coin lndry. Meeting rm. Business servs avail. Bellhops. Valet serv. Airport transportation. Exercise equipt; bicycles, rower. Health club privileges. Some refrigerators. Microwaves avail. Cr cds: A, C, D, DS, ER, MC, V. 🄳 🐾 ≈ 🏋 🖾 🐾 SC

Hotels

★ ★ **FOUR POINTS BY SHERATON.** 137 Union Blvd (80228). 303/969-9900; FAX 303/989-9847. 170 rms, 6 story. S, D $98-$130; each addl $10; under 18 free; wkend rates. Crib free. Pet accepted, some restrictions; $10. TV; cable (premium), VCR avail. Heated pool; whirlpool. Complimentary full bkfst. Complimentary coffee in rms. Restaurant 6 am-2 pm, 4:30-10 pm. Bar. Ck-out noon. Meeting rms. Business servs avail. In-rm modem link. No bellhops. Exercise equipt; bicycle, stair machine, sauna. Health club privileges. Some refrigerators. Cr cds: A, C, D, DS, MC, V. 🄳 🐾 ≈ 🏋 🖾 🐾 SC

★ ★ **SHERATON DENVER WEST.** 360 Union Blvd (80228), at Simms St, near Denver Federal Center. 303/987-2000; FAX 303/969-0263. Web www.ittsheraton.com. 242 rms, 12 story. S, D $140-$175; each addl $15; under 18 free; package plans; wkend rates. Crib free. Pet accepted, some restrictions; $50 deposit. TV; cable (premium). Indoor pool; whirlpool. Coffee in rms. Restaurant 6:30 am-9:30 pm. Bar 11-2 am, Sun to midnight. Ck-out 1 pm. Convention facilities. Business center. In-rm modem link. Concierge. Valet serv. Gift shop. Barber, beauty shop. Exercise rm; instructor, weight machine, bicycles, steam rm, sauna. Health club privileges. Massage. Some refrigerators. Luxury level. Cr cds: A, C, D, DS, JCB, MC, V. 🄳 🐾 ≈ 🏋 🏃 🖾 🔥 SC 🚶

Lamar

Motels

★ ★ **BEST WESTERN COW PALACE INN.** 1301 N Main St. 719/336-7753; FAX 719/336-9598. 102 rms, 2 story. June-Aug: S $75-$90; D $80-$95; each addl $5; lower rates rest of yr. Crib free. Pet accepted. TV; cable (premium), VCR avail. Indoor pool; whirlpool, poolside serv. Coffee & tea in rms. Restaurant 5 am-10 pm. Rm serv. Bar 11-2 am, Sun to midnight. Ck-out 11 am. Meeting rms. Business servs avail. Gift shop. Barber, beauty shop. Free airport, RR station, bus depot transportation. Golf privileges, greens fee $4, driving range. Enclosed courtyard; tropical gardens. Cr cds: A, C, D, DS, MC, V. 🄳 🐾 🙀 ≈ 🖾 🐾 SC

✔ ★ **BLUE SPRUCE.** 1801 S Main St, 1 mi S on US 287, 385. 719/336-7454; res: 800/835-6323; FAX 719/336-4729. 30 rms. S $30; D $36-$38; each addl $4. Crib free. Pet accepted. TV; cable (premium). Pool. Complimentary continental bkfst. Restaurant nearby. Ck-out 11 am. Free airport, RR station, bus depot transportation. Cr cds: A, C, D, DS, MC, V. 🐾 ≈ 🖾 🔥 SC

Limon

Motels

✔ ★ ★ **BEST WESTERN.** 925 T Ave, jct I-70 & US 24. 719/775-0277; FAX 719/775-2921. 48 rms, 2 story. S $50-$65; D $65-$75; each addl $5; under 13 free; family rates. Crib $6. Pet accepted; $10. TV; cable (premium). Complimentary continental bkfst. Restaurant opp 6 am-11 pm. Ck-out 11 am. In-rm modem link. Indoor pool. Cr cds: A, DS, MC, V. 🄳 🐾 ≈ 🖾 🐾 SC

★ **PREFERRED MOTOR INN.** 158 E Main St. 719/775-2385; FAX 719/775-2901. 57 rms. S $28-$38; D $46-$62; each addl $4; suites $65-$100. Crib $4. Pet accepted; $4. TV; cable (premium). Indoor pool; whirlpool. Restaurant nearby. Ck-out 10 am. Meeting rms. Free airport, bus depot transportation. Balconies. Cr cds: A, D, DS, MC, V. 🄳 🐾 ≈ 🖾 🐾 SC

✔ ★ **SAFARI.** 637 Main St. 719/775-2363. 28 rms, 1-2 story. June-Sept: S $36-$42; D $52-$58; each addl $4; suites $62; lower rates rest of yr. Pet accepted; $5. TV; cable (premium). Pool. Playground. Complimentary coffee in rms. Restaurant opp. Ck-out 10 am. Coin lndry. In-rm modem link. Private patios. Cr cds: A, D, DS, MC, V. 🐾 ≈ 🖾 🐾

Longmont *(See also Boulder, Denver)*

Motor Hotel

★ ★ **RAINTREE PLAZA.** *1900 Ken Pratt Blvd (80501). 303/776-2000; FAX 303/682-2195; res: 800/843-8240.* 211 rms, 2 story. S $94; D $104; each addl $10; suites $130-$250; under 18 free. Crib free. Pet accepted. TV; cable. Heated pool. Complimentary bkfst buffet. Coffee in rms. Restaurant 6 am-2 pm, 5 pm-10 pm; Sat 6-10 am, 5-10 pm. Rm serv. Bar. Ck-out noon. Free lndry facilities. Meeting rms. Business center. Bellhops. Valet serv. Airport transportation. Exercise equipt; weight machine, bicycles, sauna. Wet bars, refrigerators. Cr cds: A, C, D, DS, MC, V. 🅳 🐾 ➿ ✈ ⊠ ⊠ 🐾 SC 🏃

Manitou Springs *(See also Colorado Springs)*

Motel

✔ ★ **RED WING.** *56 El Paso Blvd. 719/685-5656; res: 800/733-9547.* 27 rms, 2 story, 11 kits. S $49-$55; D $59-$65; kit. units $10 addl. Crib free. Pet accepted. TV; cable. Heated pool. Playground. Complimentary coffee in rms. Restaurant nearby. Ck-out 10 am. Some refrigerators; microwaves avail. Cr cds: A, C, D, DS, MC, V. 🐾 ➿ ⊠ 🐾 SC

Mesa Verde National Park *(See also Cortez, Durango)*

Motel

★ ★ **FAR VIEW LODGE.** *(Mancos 81328) At Navajo Hill, in park 15 mi from entrance. 970/529-4421; res: 800/449-2288.* 150 rms, 1-2 levels. No A/C. No rm phones. Late Apr-late Oct: D $73-$94; each addl $8; under 12 free. Closed rest of yr. Crib $4. Pet accepted, some restrictions. Restaurant 6:30 am-9 pm; dining rm 5-9:30 pm. Bar 4-11 pm. Ck-out 11 am. Coin lndry. Gift shop. Private balconies. Picnic tables. Hiking trails. Mesa Verde tours avail. Educational programs. View of canyon, Shiprock. Camping sites, trailer facilities. Park concession. General store, take-out serv, coin showers. Cr cds: A, D, DS, MC, V. 🅳 🐾 ⊠ 🐾

Monte Vista *(See also Alamosa)*

Motels

★ ★ **BEST WESTERN MOVIE MANOR.** *2830 US 160. 719/852-5921; FAX 719/852-0122.* 60 rms, 2 story. May-Labor Day: S $72-$82; D $76-$90; each addl $5; lower rates rest of yr. Pet accepted. TV; cable (premium). Playground. Restaurant 6 am-2 pm, 5-10 pm. Bar from 5 pm. Ck-out 11 am. Business servs avail. Exercise equipt; weight machines, bicycle. Drive-in movies visible from rms; speakers in most rms. Cr cds: A, C, D, DS, MC, V. 🅳 🐾 ✈ ⊠ 🐾 SC

★ ★ **COMFORT INN.** *1519 Grande Ave. 719/852-0612; FAX 719/589-4316.* 43 rms, 2 story. May-mid-Oct: S $60-$70; D $75-$85; each addl $5; under 12 free; lower rates rest of yr. Crib free. Pet accepted. TV; cable (premium). Indoor pool; whirlpool. Complimentary continental bkfst. Restaurant nearby. Ck-out 11 am. Business servs avail. In-rm modem link. Cr cds: A, D, DS, JCB, MC, V. 🅳 🐾 ➿ ⊠ 🐾 SC

Montrose *(See also Delta)*

Motels

★ ★ **BLACK CANYON.** *1605 E Main. 970/249-3495; FAX 970/249-0990; res: 800/348-3495.* E-mail blkcanyn@rmi.net; web www.innfinders. com/blackcyn. 49 rms, 1-2 story. May-Sept: S, D $45-$75; each addl $5; suites $95; under 12 free; lower rates rest of yr. Crib $5. Pet accepted, some restrictions. TV; cable (premium). Heated pool; whirlpool. Complimentary continental bkfst. Complimentary coffee in rms. Restaurant nearby. Ck-out 11 am. Meeting rms. Business servs avail. Microwaves avail. Cr cds: A, C, D, DS, MC, V. 🅳 🐾 ➿ ⊠ 🐾 SC

★ **SAN JUAN INN.** *1480 US 550 S. 970/249-6644; FAX 970/249-9314.* 51 rms, 2 story. June-mid-Nov: S $48-$53; D $56-$61; each addl $5; under 13 free; lower rates rest of yr. Crib free. Pet accepted. TV; cable. Indoor pool; whirlpool. Playground. Complimentary coffee in lobby. Restaurant adj 6 am-10 pm. Ck-out 11 am. Free airport transportation. Microwaves avail. Cr cds: A, C, D, DS, MC, V. 🐾 ➿ ⊠ 🐾

Pagosa Springs

Motel

★ ★ **PAGOSA SPRINGS INN.** *3565 US 160 W. 970/731-8400; res: 888/221-8088; FAX 970/731-3402.* 97 rms, 3 story. May-Sept: S $70; D $75-$105; golf, ski plans; lower rates rest of yr. Crib free. Pet accepted. TV; cable (premium). Complimentary coffee in lobby. Restaurant nearby. Ck-out 11 am. Meeting rms. Business servs avail. X-country ski 3 mi. Indoor pool; whirlpool. Game rm. Bathrm phones, refrigerators; some in-rm whirlpools; microwaves avail. Cr cds: A, C, D, DS, MC, V. 🅳 💺 📶 🏊 🚫 🔥

Silverton (See also Durango)

Inn

★ **ALMA HOUSE.** *220 E 10th St. 970/387-5336; FAX 970/387-5974; res: 800/267-5336.* E-mail almahouse@aol.com. 10 air-cooled rms, 2½ story, 6 with bath, 4 share bath. No rm phones. May-Sept: S, D $60-$80; suites $90-100. Closed Nov-Apr. Pet accepted, some restrictions. TV; cable (premium). Complimentary full bkfst. Ck-out 10 am, ck-in noon. Business servs avail. Built 1898. Victorian furnishings. Totally nonsmoking. Cr cds: A, MC, V. 💺 🚫 🔥

Snowmass Village (See also Aspen, Glenwood Springs)

Motor Hotels

(Hours and dates open may vary during off-season, making it advisable to call ahead)

★ ★ ★ **SILVERTREE.** *100 Elbert Ln, in Snowmass Village Mall. 970/923-3520; FAX 970/923-5192; res: 800/525-9402.* E-mail reservations @silvertreehotel.com. 261 rms, 2-7 story. No A/C. Late Nov-early Apr: S, D $130-$375; each addl $25; suites $295-$2,000; under 12 free; family rates in summer; higher rates mid-late Dec; varied lower rates rest of yr. Crib free. Pet accepted. TV; cable (premium). 2 heated pools; whirlpool, poolside serv. Playground. Supervised child's activities. Coffee in rms. Restaurant 7 am-10 pm. Rm serv. Bar 11:30-1 am; entertainment. Ck-out 10 am. Coin lndry. Meeting rms. Business center. In-rm modem link. Valet serv. Concierge. Shopping arcade. Beauty shop. Free local airport transportation. Downhill/x-country ski on site. Ski rentals. Exercise equipt; weight machine, bicycles, steam rm. Massage. Bicycle rentals. Lawn games. Refrigerators. Private patios, balconies. Cr cds: A, C, D, DS, MC, V. 🅳 💺 📶 🏊 🚫 🏃 🚫 🔥 SC 🏌

★ ★ **WILDWOOD LODGE.** *40 Elbert Ln, overlooks Snowmass Village Mall. 970/923-3550; FAX 970/923-5192; res: 800/525-9402.* E-mail silver tree@rof.net. 148 rms, 3-4 story. Nov-Mar: S, D $88-$225; each addl $25; suites $175-$600; under 12 free; ski plans; higher rates hols; lower rates rest of yr. Crib free. Pet accepted. TV; cable (premium), VCR avail. Heated pool; whirlpool, poolside serv. Supervised child's activities in ski season. Complimentary continental bkfst (winter). Complimentary coffee in rms. Restaurant 5-10 pm. Rm serv. Bar. Ck-out 10 am. Coin lndry. Meeting rms. Business servs avail. In-rm modem link. Bellhops. Valet serv. Concierge. Free airport transportation. Downhill/x-country ski 1 blk. Health club privileges. Refrigerators; microwaves avail. Patios, balconies. Cr cds: A, C, D, DS, MC, V. 🅳 💺 📶 🚫 🔥 SC

South Fork (See also Monte Vista)

Lodge

✔ ★ **WOLF CREEK SKI.** *31042 US 160W. 719/873-5547; res: 800/874-0416.* 49 air-cooled rms, 1-2 story, 18 kit. units. S $45-$50; D $51-$58; kit. units $50-$68; ski plans; wkly rates. Crib free. Pet accepted. TV; cable. Playground. Dining rm 6-10:30 am, 5-9 pm. Bar. Ck-out 10 am. Meeting rms. Business servs avail. Downhill ski 18 mi; x-country ski 3 mi. Snowmobiling. Hiking. Whirlpool. Microwaves avail. Cr cds: A, C, D, DS, MC, V. 🅳 💺 📶 🚫 🔥 SC

Steamboat Springs

Motel

(Rates may be higher during Winter Carnival. Hours and dates open may vary during off-season, making it advisable to call ahead.)

✔ ★ **ALPINER.** *424 Lincoln Ave. 970/879-1430; FAX 970/879-0054; res: 800/538-7519.* 33 rms, 2 story. Mid-Nov-Mar: S, D $70-$100; each addl $10; under 12 free; lower rates rest of yr. Crib free. Pet accepted. TV; cable (premium). Complimentary coffee in rms.

Restaurant opp 6 am-10 pm. Ck-out 10 am. Business servs avail. In-rm modem link. Downhill ski 1 mi; x-country ski 1/2 mi. Microwaves avail. Cr cds: A, C, D, DS, MC, V.

☞ ⊁ ⋈ 🐾 SC

Lodge

★ ★ **SKY VALLEY.** *PO Box 3132, E US 40, 8 mi S. 970/879-7749; FAX 970/879-7752; res: 800/499-4759.* 24 rms, 3 story. No A/C. No elvtr. Late Nov-mid-Apr: S, D $85-$150; each addl $10; under 12 free; higher rates Christmas; lower rates rest of yr. Crib free. Pet accepted, some restrictions. TV; cable, VCR avail. Complimentary bkfst. Dining rm 7-10 am, noon-2 pm, 5-8 pm (in season). Bar 3-11 pm. Ck-out 11 am. Meeting rms. Business servs avail. In-rm modem link. Downhill ski 7 mi; x-country ski 5 mi. Whirlpool, sauna. Totally nonsmoking. Cr cds: A, C, D, DS, MC, V. ☞ ⊁ ⋈ 🐾 SC

Motor Hotels

★ ★ **BEST WESTERN PTARMIGAN INN.** *2304 Apres Ski Way, 2 mi E, 1 mi NE of US 40. 970/879-1730; FAX 970/879-6044; res: 800/538-7519.* E-mail steamboat-lodging @toski.com; web www.steamboat-lodging .com. 77 rms, 47 A/C, 3-4 story. Late Nov-mid-Apr: S, D $89-$209; each addl $10; under 12 free; higher rates late Dec; ski, package plans; varied lower rates rest of yr. Closed early Apr-late May. Crib free. Pet accepted. TV; cable. Heated pool; whirlpool, sauna. Complimentary coffee. Restaurant. Rm serv. Bar 4-10 pm. Ck-out 10 am. Coin lndry. Business servs avail. In-rm modem link. Valet serv. Downhill/x-country ski on site. Ski rentals, storage. Refrigerators. Balconies. View of Mt Werner, valley. Cr cds: A, C, D, DS, ER, JCB, MC, V. D ☞ ⊁ ⋈ ⋈ 🐾 SC

★ ★ ★ **HOLIDAY INN.** *3190 S Lincoln Ave, 2 mi E on US 40. 970/879-2250; FAX 970/879-0251.* 82 rms, 2 story. Late Jan-Mar: S, D $99-$159; each addl $10; under 19 free; higher rates late Dec-early Jan; lower rates rest of yr. Crib free. Pet accepted, some restrictions; $25 deposit. TV; cable (premium), VCR avail. Heated pool; wading pool; whirlpool. Restaurant 6 am-11 pm. Rm serv. Bar 4-11 pm. Ck-out 11 am. Coin lndry. Meeting rm. Business servs avail. In-rm modem link. Valet serv. Downhill/x-country ski 1 mi. Exercise equipt; weights, bicycles. Game rm. Lawn games. Some refrigerators; microwaves avail. Cr cds: A, C, D, DS, JCB, MC, V. D ☞ ⊁ ⋈ 🏋 ⋈ 🐾 SC

Sterling

Motels

★ ★ ★ **BEST WESTERN SUNDOWNER.** *Rte 1, Overland Trail St, 1 blk W of I-76 exit 125B. 970/522-6265.* 29 rms. S $70; D $79; each addl $7; under 12 free. Pet accepted. TV; cable (premium), VCR avail. Heated pool; whirlpool. Complimentary continental bkfst. Restaurant nearby. Ck-out 11 am. Coin lndry. Business servs avail. In-rm modem link. Exercise equipt; weight machine, bicycles. Balconies. Picnic tables, grills. Cr cds: A, C, D, DS, MC, V. ☞ ☞ ⋈ 🏋 ⋈ 🐾 SC

★ **COLONIAL.** *915 S Division Ave. 970/522-3382.* 14 rms. S $28; D $32-$34; each addl $3; under 10 free; wkly rates in winter. Pet accepted; $8. TV; cable (premium). Coffee in rms. Playground. Ck-out 10 am. Some refrigerators. Microwaves avail. Cr cds: A, DS, MC, V. D ☞ ⋈ 🐾

✔ ★ ★ **RAMADA INN.** *I-76 exit 125A & US 6, 1/2 mi E on US 6. 970/522-2625; FAX 970/522-1321.* 102 rms, 2 story. S $50-$72; D $57-$81; each addl $7; under 18 free. Crib free. Pet accepted, some restrictions. TV; cable (premium). Indoor pool; whirlpool. Complimentary coffee in rms. Restaurant 6 am-10 pm. Bar 3:30-10 pm. Ck-out noon. Meeting rms. Business servs avail. Exercise equipt; bicycle, treadmill, sauna. Game rm. Cr cds: A, C, D, DS, ER, JCB, MC, V. D ☞ ⋈ 🏋 ⋈ 🐾 SC

Telluride *(See also Norwood)*

Resort

★ ★ ★ **THE PEAKS RESORT AND SPA.** *136 Country Club Dr, S on CO 145 to Mtn Village Blvd, then 1/2 mi E to Country Club Dr, near Municipal Airport. 970/728-6800; FAX 970/728-6175; res: 800/789-2220.* E-mail telluride@gate way.com. 177 air-cooled units, 6 story, 28 suites. Jan-Mar: S, D $350-$440; suites $475-$550; under 18 free; golf, ski plans; higher rates Dec hols; lower rates rest of yr. Crib free. Pet accepted, some restrictions. TV; cable (premium), VCR (free movies). 2 pools, 1 indoor; whirlpools, poolside serv. Supervised child's activities. Complimentary coffee in lobby. Dining rm 7 am-11 pm. Box lunches. Rm serv 7 am-11 pm. Bar. Ck-out noon, ck-in 4 pm. Meeting rms. Business servs avail. In-rm modem link. Bellhops. Valet serv. Concierge. Gift shop. Covered valet parking. Free airport transportation. Sports dir. Tennis, pro. 18-hole golf, greens fee $80-$110 (incl cart), pro, putting green, driving range. Downhill/x-country ski on site; rentals. Snowmobiles, sleighing. Hiking. Exercise rm; instructor, weight machine, bicycles, sauna. Microwaves avail. Refrigerators, minibars. Some balconies. Cr cds: A, MC, V.

🇩 💱 🏊 🎿 ⛷ 🏂 🚶 ✈ 🛷 🔥

Trinidad *(See also Walsenburg; also see Raton, NM)*

Motels

✔★ **BUDGET HOST.** *10301 Santa Fe Trail Dr, off I-25 exit 11. 719/846-3307; FAX 719/846-2215.* 26 rms. June-mid-Sept: S $39.95-$59.95; D $49.95-$69.95; wkly rates; lower rates rest of yr. Crib $3. Pet accepted; $3. TV. Complimentary coffee in rms. Restaurant nearby. Ck-out 11 am. Free airport, RR station, bus depot transportation. Lawn games. Microwaves avail. Picnic tables, grills. Features 107-ft oil derrick. Located along the Mountain Branch of the Santa Fe Trail. Cr cds: A, C, D, DS, MC, V. 💱 🛷 🔥 SC

★ **BUDGET SUMMIT INN.** *9800 Santa Fe Trail Dr. 719/846-2251.* 44 rms (21 with shower only), 2 story. Memorial Day-Labor Day: S $40-$60; D $45-$70; each addl $6; lower rates rest of yr. Pet accepted; $3. TV; cable. Whirlpool. Complimentary continental bkfst. Restaurant adj open 24 hrs. Ck-out 11 am. Coin lndry. Meeting rm. Business servs avail. In-rm modem link. Gift shop. Rec rm. Lawn games. Some refrigerators; microwaves avail. Cr cds: A, C, D, DS, MC, V. 🇩 💱 🛷 🔥 SC

Motor Hotel

✔★★ **HOLIDAY INN.** *9995 County Road 69.1, I-25 exit 11. 719/846-4491; FAX 719/846-2440.* 113 rms, 2 story. June-Sept: S $69-$89; D $79-$89; each addl $10; under 18 free; lower rates rest of yr. Crib free. Pet accepted, some restrictions. TV; cable (premium), VCR avail. Indoor pool; poolside serv. Coffee in rms. Restaurant 6 am-10 pm. Rm serv from 7 am. Bar 5 pm-midnight. Ck-out noon. Coin lndry. Meeting rms. Business servs avail. Gift shop. Game rm. Lawn games. Some bathrm phones, refrigerators; microwaves avail. Cr cds: A, C, D, DS, JCB, MC, V. 🇩 💱 🏊 🛷 🔥 SC

Walsenburg *(See also Trinidad)*

Motel

✔★★ **BEST WESTERN RAMBLER.** *1½ mi N of Walsenburg I-25 exit 52. 719/738-1121; FAX 719/738-1093.* 32 rms. Mid-May-early Sept: S $62-$77; D $77-$87; under 18 free; lower rates rest of yr. Crib free. Pet accepted, some restrictions. TV; cable (premium), VCR avail. Heated pool. Coffee in lobby. Restaurant 6 am-9 pm. Ck-out 11 am. Free bus depot transportation. Cr cds: A, C, D, DS, MC, V. 🇩 💱 🏊 🛷 🔥 SC

Winter Park *(See also Granby, Idaho Springs)*

Lodge

★ **HIGH MOUNTAIN.** *County Rd 50, W on US 40 to County Rd 5, then S on County Rd 50. 303/726-5958; res: 800/772-9987.* 12 air-cooled rms, 2 story. Mid-Dec-early Apr: S $100; D $160; each addl $80; wkly rates; higher rates special events; lower rates rest of yr. Crib avail. Pet accepted, some restrictions. TV in rec rm; cable, VCR avail. Complimentary full bkfst. Restaurant nearby. Bar. Ck-out 10 am. Concierge. Coin lndry. RR station transportation. Downhill/x-country ski 9 mi. Exercise equipt; weights, treadmill, sauna. Indoor pool; whirlpool. Game rm. Lawn games. Refrigerators, microwaves, fireplaces. Some balconies. Picnic tables, grills. Opp stream. Cr cds: MC, V. 🇩 💱 🛷 🏊 🎿 ⛷ 🚶 🔥

Hotel

★★ **THE VINTAGE.** *100 Winter Park Dr. 970/726-8801; FAX 970/726-9230; res: 800/472-7017.* 118 air-cooled rms, 5 story, 90 kit. units. Mid-Nov-mid-Apr: S, D $89-$180; suites $245-$535; higher rates Dec 20-Jan 4; lower rates rest of yr. Crib free. Pet accepted. TV; cable (premium). Heated pool; whirlpool. Continental bkfst. Complimentary coffee in rms. Restaurant 7 am-10 pm. Rm serv (seasonal). Bar 3 pm-midnight; entertainment some wkends, winter. Ck-out 11 am. Coin lndry. Meeting rms. Business servs avail. In-rm modem link. Gift shop. Free RR station, bus depot transportation. Downhill/x-country ski. Exercise equipt; rower, bicycles, sauna. Game rm. Picnic tables. Cr cds: A, C, D, DS, MC, V.

🇩 💱 🏊 🚶 🛷 🔥 SC

Connecticut

Avon *(See also Farmington, Hartford, Wethersfield)*

Motel

★ ★ ★ **AVON OLD FARMS HOTEL.** *E at jct US 44 & CT 10. 860/677-1651; FAX 860/677-0364.* 160 rms, 3 story. S, D $89-$129; suites $160-$260; under 18 free. Crib free. Pet accepted, some restrictions. TV; cable, VCR avail. Pool. Complimentary continental bkfst. Restaurant 6:30-10 am, 11:30 am-2 pm, 5-9 pm; Sun 7 am-1 pm. Rm serv. Ck-out noon. Meeting rms. Business servs avail. Valet serv. Beauty shop. Exercise equipt; weights, bicycles, sauna. Cr cds: A, C, D, DS, MC, V. 🅳 💺 🏊 🏋 🚭 🐾

Branford

Motel

★ ★ **DAYS INN.** *375 E Main St (US 1). 203/488-8314; FAX 203/483-6885; res: 800/255-9296.* 74 rms, 2 story. S $75-$80; D $90-$99; each addl $10; suites $245; under 16 free. Crib free. Pet accepted; $10. TV; cable (premium), VCR avail. Pool. Complimentary continental bkfst. Coffee in rms. Restaurant 7 am-2 pm; Sat, Sun to noon. Ck-out 11 am. Valet serv. Meeting rms. Business center. Gift shop. Barber, beauty shop. Refrigerators avail. Cr cds: A, C, D, DS, ER, JCB, MC, V. 🅳 💺 🏊 🚭 🐾 SC 🏃

Bridgeport

Hotel

★ ★ **HOLIDAY INN.** *1070 Main St (06604). 203/334-1234; FAX 203/367-1985.* 234 rms, 9 story. S $79-$119; D $89-$129; each addl $10; suites $179-$450; under 16 free; family, wkend rates. Crib free. Pet accepted, some restrictions. TV; cable. Indoor/outdoor pool. Restaurant 6 am-10 pm. Bar 4 pm-midnight. Ck-out noon. Meeting rms. Business center. In-rm modem link. Free covered parking. Free airport, RR station, bus depot transportation. Exercise equipt; weight machine, bicycles. Refrigerator in some suites. Atrium; waterfall. Beach 4 blks. Cr cds: A, C, D, DS, JCB, MC, V.

🅳 💺 🏊 🏋 🚭 🐾 SC 🏃

Cornwall Bridge

Inn

★ **CORNWALL INN.** *270 Kent Rd (US 7). 860/672-6884; res: 800/786-6884.* 13 rms, 2 story, 1 suite. No rm phones. S, D $50-$110; each addl $10; suite $150; under 5 free. Crib free. Pet accepted, some restrictions. TV in some rms, also in sitting rm. Pool. Complimentary continental bkfst. Dining rm 6-9 pm Thurs-Mon; res required. Ck-out 11 am, ck-in 2 pm. Bellhop. Bus depot transportation. Downhill ski 5 mi; x-country ski ¼ mi. Picnic tables. Restored 19th-century country inn; antiques. Cr cds: A, DS, MC, V.

🅳 💺 🏊 🏊 🐾

Danbury

Motel

★ ★ **RAMADA INN.** *exit 8 on I-84 (06810), 1½ mi NE at exit 8. 203/792-3800; FAX 203/730-1899.* 181 rms, 2-5 story. S $69-$129; D $84-$144; each addl $15; under 16 free; wkend rates. Pet accepted, some restrictions. TV; cable (premium). Indoor/outdoor pool. Coffee in rms. Restaurant 6:30 am-10:30 pm; Fri to 11 pm; hrs vary wkends. Rm serv. Bar 11-1 am. Ck-out noon. Coin lndry. Meeting rms. Business servs avail. Valet serv. Free local transportation. Health club privileges. Microwaves, refrigerators avail. Cr cds: A, C, D, DS, ER, JCB, MC, V. 🅳 💺 🏊 🚭 🐾 SC

Motor Hotel

★ ★ **HOLIDAY INN.** *80 Newtown Rd (06810), I-84 exit 8. 203/792-4000; FAX 203/797-0810.* 114 rms, 4 story. Apr-Dec: S, D $99-$109; suites $104-$109; under 18 free; lower rates rest of yr. Crib free. Pet accepted. TV; cable (premium), VCR avail (movies). Pool; poolside serv. Complimentary coffee in rms. Restaurant 6 am-midnight. Rm serv 24 hrs. Bar noon-2 am. Ck-out noon. Meeting rms. Business servs avail. In-rm modem link.

Bellhops. Valet serv. Shopping arcade. Free airport transportation. Health club privileges. Some refrigerators. Microwaves avail. Cr cds: A, C, D, DS, JCB, MC, V.

D ⬚ ⬚ ⬚ ⬚ SC

Hotel

★ ★ ★ **HILTON AND TOWERS.** *18 Old Ridgebury Rd (06810), I-84 E, exit 2.* *203/794-0600; FAX 203/798-2709.* 242 rms, 10 story. S $110-$155; D $124-$175; each addl $15; family, wkend rates. Crib free. Pet accepted, some restrictions. TV; cable (premium), VCR (movies). Indoor pool; whirlpool, poolside serv. Restaurant 6:30 am-10 pm. Bar 11-2 am; entertainment. Ck-out noon. Meeting rms. Business center. In-rm modem link. Coin lndry. Lighted tennis. Exercise equipt; stair machine, bicycles, sauna. Health club privileges. Microwaves avail. Cr cds: A, C, D, DS, ER, JCB, MC, V.

Enfield *(See also Windsor Locks; also see Holyoke & Springfield, MA)*

Motel

✔ ★ **RED ROOF INN.** *5 Hazard Ave. 860/741-2571; FAX 860/741-2576.* 109 rms, 2 story. S $34.99-$42.99; D $39.99-$46.99; under 18 free. Crib free. Pet accepted. TV; cable (premium). Restaurant adj 6:30-12:30 am. Ck-out noon. Business servs avail. In-rm modem link. X-country ski 15 mi. Cr cds: A, C, D, DS, MC, V. D ⬚ ⬚ ⬚ ⬚

Farmington *(See also Hartford, New Britain, Wethersfield)*

Motels

★ ★ **CENTENNIAL INN.** *5 Spring Lane. 860/677-4647; FAX 860/676-0685; res: 800/852-2052.* 112 kit. suites, 2 story. S, D $85-$210; family, wkend rates. Crib free. Pet accepted. TV; cable (premium), VCR (movies avail $4). Pool; whirlpool. Complimentary continental bkfst. Complimentary coffee in rms. Ck-out noon. Coin lndry. Meeting rms. Business center. In-rm modem link. Downhill ski 15 mi. Exercise equipt; bicycles, rowers. Fireplaces. Balconies. Grills. On 12 wooded acres. Cr cds: A, C, D, MC, V.

D ⬚ ⬚ ⬚ ⬚ ⬚ ⬚ SC ⬚

★ ★ **FARMINGTON INN.** *827 Farmington Ave, I-84 exit 39 to CT 4 west. 860/677-2821; FAX 860/677-8332, ext. 232; res: 800/648-9804.* 72 rms, 2 story. S, D $89-$119; each addl $10; suites $99-$119; under 16 free. Crib free. Pet accepted. TV; cable (premium), VCR avail. Complimentary continental bkfst. Restaurant. Ck-out noon. Meeting rms. Business servs avail. In-rm modem link. Sundries. Tennis privileges. Golf privileges. X-country ski 1 1/2 mi. Health club privileges. Cr cds: A, C, D, DS, MC, V.

D ⬚ ⬚ ⬚ ⬚ ⬚ ⬚ SC

Hartford *(See also Avon, Farmington, Wethersfield)*

Motor Hotels

★ ★ **HOLIDAY INN.** *363 Roberts St (06108), I-84, exit 58, east of downtown. 860/528-9611; FAX 860/289-0270.* 130 rms, 5 story. S, D $65-$85; under 18 free; wkend rates. Crib free. Pet accepted. TV; cable (premium). Indoor pool. Complimentary coffee in rms. Restaurant 6 am-10 pm. Rm serv. Bar 4 pm-midnight. Ck-out noon. Coin lndry. Meeting rms. Business servs avail. In-rm modem link. Valet serv. Exercise equipt; bicycle, treadmill. Some refrigerators. Cr cds: A, C, D, DS, ER, JCB, MC, V. D ⬚ ⬚ ⬚ ⬚ ⬚ SC

★ ★ **RAMADA INN.** *(100 East River Dr, East Hartford 06108) S via I-91 exit 3 to Pitkin, I-84 exit 53. 860/528-9703; FAX 860/289-4728.* 199 rms, 8 story. S $59-$99; D $65-$114; each addl $10; suites $150-$175; under 18 free; wkend rates. Crib free. Pet accepted. TV; cable (premium). Indoor pool. Playground. Restaurant 6:30 am-2 pm, 5-10 pm. Rm serv. Bar. Ck-out 11 am. Coin lndry. Meeting rms. Business servs avail. In-rm modem link. Valet serv. Cr cds: A, C, D, DS, ER, JCB, MC, V. D ⬚ ⬚ ⬚ ⬚ SC

Hotels

★ ★ **HOLIDAY INN-DOWNTOWN.** *50 Morgan St (06120), at jct I-84 exit 52 & I-91 exit 32, in Civic Center District. 860/549-2400; FAX 860/527-2746.* 342 rms, 18 story. S $79.95-$119.95; D $89.95-$129.95; each addl $10; suites $225; under 18 free; wkend rates. Crib free. Pet accepted. TV; cable (premium), VCR avail. Pool; poolside serv. Restaurant 6:30 am-10 pm. Bar 4 pm-2 am. Ck-out noon. Convention facilities. Business center. In-rm modem link. Free airport transportation. Exercise equipt; weights, stair machine. Cr cds: A, C, D, DS, JCB, MC, V. D ⬚ ⬚ ⬚ ⬚ ⬚ SC ⬚

★ **RAMADA INN-CAPITOL HILL.** *440 Asylum St (06103), opp State Capitol Building, in Civic Center District. 860/246-6591; FAX 860/728-1382.* 96 rms, 9 story. S

$49-$65; D $55-$65; each addl $10. Crib free. Pet accepted, some restrictions. TV; cable (premium). Ck-out noon. Business servs avail. Free valet parking. Cr cds: A, C, D, DS, MC, V. [D] 🐾 🏊 🏋 🔥 [SC]

Lakeville *(See also Cornwall Bridge)*

Motel

🏃 ★ ★ **INNE AT IRON MASTERS.** *229 Main St, on US 44, 1/2 mi W of CT 41. 860/435-9844; FAX 860/435-2254.* 26 rms. Apr-Nov: S $59-$95; D $65-$135; each addl $6-$12; under 12 free; higher rates special events; lower rates rest of yr. Crib $6. Pet accepted, some restrictions. TV; cable. Heated pool. Continental bkfst. Coffee in rms. Restaurant 11 am-9 pm; Thurs-Sat to 10 pm. Bar. Ck-out 11 am. Cr cds: A, D, DS, MC, V. 🐾 🏊 🏋 🔥

Inn

★ ★ **WAKE ROBIN.** *1/4 mi S on CT 41. 860/435-2515.* 39 rms, 2 story. Apr-Nov: S, D $95-$250; each addl $10; lower rates rest of yr. Crib free. Pet accepted. TV in most rms; cable (premium). Ck-out noon, ck-in 2 pm. Former girls school (1898); antiques. Library, sitting rm. On hill. Cr cds: A, MC, V. 🐾 🔥

Resort

★ ★ ★ **INTERLAKEN INN.** *74 Interlaken Rd, 21/2 mi SW on CT 112. 860/435-9878; FAX 860/435-2980.* 80 rms, 2 story. May-Oct: S, D $99-$165; each addl $15; suites $265; higher rates special events; lower rates rest of yr. Crib $10. Pet accepted. TV; cable (premium), VCR (movies). Heated pool. Restaurant 7 am-9 pm; Fri, Sat to 10 pm. Rm serv. Ck-out noon, ck-in 3 pm. Meeting rms. Business servs avail. In-rm modem link. Valet serv. Tennis. 9-hole golf, pro. Rowboats, canoes, sailboats, paddleboats. Lawn games. Rec rm. Exercise equipt; weights, treadmill, sauna. Refrigerator avail. Balconies. Cr cds: A, MC, V. 🐾 ⛷ 🎿 🏊 🏋 🔥 🔥

Litchfield *(See also Cornwall Bridge)*

Inn

★ ★ **TOLLGATE HILL.** *Rte 202, Box 1339, at Tollgate Rd, 21/2 mi NE of the Green on US 202. 860/567-4545; FAX 860/563-8397; res: 800/445-3903.* 20 rms. Mid-May-Dec: S, D $110-$175; each addl $15; lower rates rest of yr. Pet accepted. TV; cable (premium). Complimentary continental bkfst. Restaurant. Rm serv. Bar; entertainment Sat, Sun. Ck-out 11 am. Business servs avail. Airport transportation. Some fireplaces. Restored historic mansion (1745) originally a way station for travelers, relocated to present site. 18th-century paneled walls, corner cupboards, antique furniture, fireplace. Re-creation of colonial ballroom with fiddler's loft. Cr cds: A, D, DS, MC, V. 🐾 🔥

Manchester *(See also Hartford, Windsor)*

Motels

★ ★ **CLARION SUITES INN.** *191 Spencer St. 860/643-5811; FAX 860/643-5811.* 104 kit. suites, 2 story. S, D $99-$139; under 16 free; wkend rates. Crib free. Pet accepted; $250 refundable and $10/day. TV; cable, VCR. Heated pool; whirlpool. Complimentary full bkfst. Complimentary coffee in rms. Restaurant adj 6:30 am-midnight. Ck-out noon. Coin lndry. Meeting rms. Business servs avail. Sundries. Gift shop. Grocery store. Drug store. Valet serv. Free airport, RR station transportation. Downhill/x-country ski 10 mi. Exercise equipt; weight machine, bicycles. Lawn games. Balconies. Cr cds: A, C, D, DS, ER, JCB, MC, V. [D] 🐾 ⛷ 🏊 🏋 🔥 🔥 [SC]

★ **MANCHESTER VILLAGE MOTOR INN.** *100 E Center St. 860/646-2300; FAX 860/649-6499; res: 800/487-6499.* 44 rms, 2 story. S $39.95-$49.50; D $49.50-$57.50; each addl $5; under 18 free. Crib free. Pet accepted. TV; cable (premium), VCR (movies). Complimentary coffee in lobby. Restaurant opp 6:30 am-9 pm. Ck-out 11 am. Business servs avail. Sundries. Balconies. Picnic tables. Cr cds: A, C, D, DS, MC, V. 🐾 🏋 🔥 [SC]

Middletown *(See also Hartford)*

Motel

★ ★ **COMFORT INN.** *(111 Berlin Rd (CT 372), Cromwell 06416) 4 mi N on CT 372, E of I-91 exit 21. 860/635-4100; FAX 860/632-9546.* 77 rms, 4 story. S $54; D $61; each addl $6; under 18 free. Crib free. Pet accepted; $75 refundable. TV; VCR avail. Swimming privileges. Complimentary continental bkfst. Restaurant opp 5:30 am-10 pm. Ck-out 11 am. Health club privileges. Cr cds: A, C, D, DS, ER, JCB, MC, V.

Motor Hotel

★ ★ ★ **RADISSON HOTEL & CONFERENCE CENTER.** *(100 Berlin Rd, CT 372, Cromwell 06416) 4 mi N on CT 72, E of I-91 exit 21. 860/635-2000; FAX 860/635-6970.* 212 rms, 4 story. S $69-$99; D $79-$109; suites $195-$350; under 18 free; wkend rates. Crib free. Pet accepted, some restrictions. TV; cable, VCR avail. Indoor pool; whirlpool, poolside serv. Coffee in rms. Restaurants 6:30 am-10:30 pm. Rm serv. Bar noon-1 am; entertainment Sat. Ck-out noon. Meeting rms. Business servs avail. In-rm modem link. Gift shop. Exercise equipt; bicycles, treadmill, sauna. Some bathrm phones. Cr cds: A, C, D, DS, ER, JCB, MC, V.

Mystic *(See also New London, Norwich)*

Inn

★ **APPLEWOOD FARMS.** *(528 Colonel Ledyard Hwy, Ledyard 06339) I-95, exit 89, N to CT 184, W to Col Ledyard Hwy. 860/536-2022; res: 860/536-4019; FAX 860/536-6015.* 5 rms (3 with shower only), 2 story, 1 suite. No rm phones. S, D $115-$250; each addl $25; suite $250; wkly rates; 2-day min wkends, 3-day min hols. Children over 8 yrs only. Pet accepted, some restrictions. Complimentary full bkfst; tea, coffee, sherry in common rm. Ck-out 11 am, ck-in 3 pm. Luggage handling. Picnic tables. House built 1826, once used as town hall; many fireplaces, Colonial atmosphere. Totally nonsmoking. Cr cds: A, MC, V.

New Britain *(See also Hartford, Wethersfield)*

Motor Hotel

✔ ★ ★ **RAMADA INN.** *65 Columbus Blvd (06051). 860/224-9161; FAX 860/224-1796.* 119 rms, 6 story. S, D $45-$70; each addl $10; suites $125; under 19 free; wkend plans. Crib free. Pet accepted, some restrictions; $10. TV; cable (premium), VCR avail. Restaurant 7 am-9 pm; Sun to 1 pm. Rm serv. Bar. Ck-out noon. Coin lndry. Meeting rms. Business servs avail. Airport transportation. Garage parking. Downhill ski 5 mi. Cr cds: A, C, D, DS, JCB, MC, V.

New London *(See also Mystic, Norwich)*

Motels

✔ ★ **CONNECTICUT YANKEE.** *(Niantic 06357) 6 mi S on I-95 exit 74, at jct CT 161. 860/739-5483; FAX 860/739-4877; res: 800/942-8466.* 50 rms, 2 story. July-Labor Day: S $38-$85; D $42-$85; each addl $7; under 17 free; lower rates rest of yr. Crib free. Pet accepted, some restrictions; $100 refundable. TV; cable (premium). Pool; sauna. Complimentary bkfst. Restaurant 11:30-1 am. Rm serv. Bar. Ck-out 11 am. Meeting rms. Business servs avail. In-rm modem link. Valet serv. Game rm. Beach privileges. Cr cds: A, C, D, DS, MC, V.

★ **RED ROOF INN.** *707 Colman St, I-95, exit 82A. 860/444-0001; FAX 860/443-7154.* 108 rms, 2 story. May-Oct: S $39.99-$57; D $34.99-$77; each addl $5; under 18 free; higher rates special events; lower rates rest of yr. Crib free. Pet accepted. TV; cable (premium), VCR avail. Complimentary coffee in lobby. Restaurant nearby. Ck-out noon. Meeting rms. Business servs avail. In-rm modem link. Cr cds: A, C, D, DS, MC, V.

★ **STARLIGHT MOTOR INN.** *(256 Flanders Rd, Niantic 06357) 6 mi S on I-95 exit 74, at jct CT 161. 860/739-5462.* 48 rms, 2 story. May-Sept: S, D $46-$64; lower rates rest of yr. Pet accepted; $6. TV; cable (premium), VCR avail. Pool. Restaurant 11 am-10 pm. Bar 11:30-1 am. Ck-out 11 am. Cr cds: A, DS, MC, V.

Norwich *(See also New London)*

Motor Hotel

★ ★ **RAMADA HOTEL.** *10 Laura Blvd. 860/889-5201; FAX 860/889-1767.* 127 rms, 6 story. Mid-May-mid-Oct: S $95-$145; D $105-$165; each addl $10-$15; suites $200; under 18 free; package plans; lower rates rest of yr. Pet accepted, some restrictions. TV; cable (premium). Indoor pool. Restaurant 6:30 am-10 pm. Rm serv. Bar 4 pm-1 am, Fri, Sat to 2 am; entertainment Fri, Sat. Ck-out 11 am. Meeting rms. Business center. In-rm modem link. Valet serv. Sundries. Some bathrm phones. Private patios, balconies. Cr cds: A, C, D, DS, MC, V. [D] [icons]

Old Lyme *(See also New London)*

Inn

★ ★ ★ **OLD LYME.** *85 Lyme St. 860/434-2600; FAX 860/434-5352; res: 800/434-5352.* 13 rms, 2 story. S $86-$133; D $99-$158. Closed 1st 2 wks Jan. Pet accepted. TV; VCR avail. Complimentary continental bkfst. Restaurant. Bar. Ck-out noon, ck-in 3-11 pm. Business center. Built 1850, former farm; antiques, murals. Ocean 1/2 mi. Cr cds: A, C, D, DS, MC, V. [D] [icons]

Plainfield *(See also Norwich, Putnam)*

Motel

✔ ★ **PLAINFIELD.** *(Box 101, RR 2, Moosup 06354) On CT 14 at I-395 exit 89. 860/564-2791; FAX 860/564-4647.* 35 rms. S, D $42-$59; each addl $10. Crib $10. Pet accepted, some restrictions; $7. TV; cable (premium). Pool. Restaurant adj 5:30 am-9 pm; wkends 24 hours. Ck-out noon. Coin lndry. Business servs avail. Sundries. Picnic tables, grills. Cr cds: A, C, D, DS, MC, V. [D] [icons]

Putnam *(See also Plainfield)*

Motel

★ ★ **KING'S INN.** *5 Heritage Rd, I-395 exit 96. 860/928-7961; FAX 860/963-2463; res: 800/541-7304.* 41 rms, 1-2 story. S $62-$72; D $68-$78; each addl $8; under 12 free; wkly rates. Crib free. Pet accepted. TV; cable (premium), VCR avail. Pool. Complimentary continental bkfst. Restaurant 5-10 pm; Fri, Sat to 10:30 pm. Bar. Ck-out 11 am. Meeting rms. Business servs avail. On pond; gazebo. Cr cds: A, C, D, DS, MC, V.

[icons]

Simsbury *(See also Avon, Farmington, Hartford)*

Motels

✔ ★ **IRON HORSE INN.** *969 Hopmeadow St. 860/658-2216; FAX 860/651-0822; res: 800/245-9938 (CT).* 27 kit. units (no ovens), 2 story. S $69; D $79; under 12 free; wkly rates. Crib free. Pet accepted; $1/day. TV; cable (premium). Pool. Restaurant nearby. Ck-out 11 am. Coin lndry. In-rm modem link. Bathrm phones, refrigerators. Balconies. Picnic tables. Cr cds: A, MC, V. [icons]

★ ★ ★ **SIMSBURY INN.** *397 Hopmeadow St. 860/651-5700; FAX 860/651-8024; res: 800/634-2719.* 98 rms, 4 story. S, D $129; suites $175-$375; under 18 free; wkend rates. Crib free. Pet accepted, some restrictions. TV; cable, VCR avail. Indoor pool; whirlpool. Complimentary continental bkfst. Restaurant 6:30 am-9:30 pm. Bar. Ck-out noon. Meeting rms. Business servs avail. In-rm modem link. Bellhops. Free airport, RR station transportation. Tennis. 18-hole golf privileges, pro, putting green. Downhill/x-country ski 15 mi. Exercise equipt; treadmill, bicycles, sauna. Lawn games. Refrigerators. Picnic tables. Traditional New England country inn atmosphere. Cr cds: A, D, DS, MC, V.

[icons]

Inn

★ ★ **SIMSBURY 1820 HOUSE.** *731 Hopmeadow St. 860/658-7658; FAX 860/651-0724.* 32 rms, 3 story. S, D $95-$140; each addl $10. Pet accepted. TV. Complimentary continental bkfst. Restaurant 11:30 am-2 pm, 6-9:30; Fri, Sat to 10 pm. Rm serv. Ck-out 11 am, ck-in 3 pm. Business servs avail. Private patios, balconies. Built 1820; antiques. Veranda. Cr cds: A, C, D, DS, MC, V. [D] [icons]

Wethersfield *(See also Avon, Hartford, Windsor)*

Motor Hotel

✔ ★ ★ **RAMADA INN.** *1330 Silas Deane Hwy. 860/563-2311.* 112 rms, 4 story. S, D $42-$59; under 18 free. Crib free. Pet accepted. TV; cable (premium), VCR avail. Complimentary continental bkfst. Restaurant adj 11 am-10 pm. Bar; entertainment Fri, Sat. Ck-out noon. Coin lndry. Meeting rms. Business servs avail. In-rm modem link. Downhill ski 20 mi. Health club privileges. Some in-rm whirlpools. Cr cds: A, C, D, DS, MC, V.

[D] [icons]

Windsor *(See also Enfield, Hartford, Manchester)*

Motel

★ ★ **RESIDENCE INN BY MARRIOTT.** *100 Dunfey Lane. 860/688-7474.* 96 kit. suites, 2 story. S, D $115-$145. Crib avail. Pet accepted; $50. TV; cable (premium), VCR avail, in-rm movies avail. Pool; whirlpool. Complimentary continental bkfst. Complimentary coffee in rms. Ck-out noon. Coin lndry. Meeting rms. Business servs avail. In-rm modem link. Valet serv. Free airport transportation. Some fireplaces. Picnic tables, grill. Cr cds: A, C, D, DS, JCB, MC, V. [D] [⊁] [≋] [⊠] [⚓] [SC]

Windsor Locks *(See also Enfield, Hartford, Windsor; also see Springfield, MA)*

Motel

★ ★ **HOMEWOOD SUITES.** *65 Ella Grasso Tpke, near Hartford Bradley Intl Airport. 860/627-8463; FAX 860/627-9313.* 132 kit. suites, 2-3 story. S, D $99-$140. Crib free. Pet accepted, some restrictions; $10. TV; cable, VCR (movies). Pool. Complimentary continental bkfst. Complimentary coffee in rms. Restaurant nearby. Ck-out noon. Coin lndry. Business center. In-rm modem link. Valet serv. Sundries. Gift shop. Free airport, RR station transportation. Exercise equipt; weight machine, bicycles. Lawn games. Picnic tables. Cr cds: A, C, D, DS, MC, V. [D] [⊁] [≋] [⫪] [✈] [⊠] [⚓] [SC] [⫪]

Hotel

★ ★ ★ **SHERATON.** *1 Bradley Intl Airport, at Hartford Bradley Intl Airport. 860/627-5311; FAX 860/627-9348.* 237 rms, 8 story. Sept-June: S, D $85-$153; each addl $15; suites $225-$300; under 5 free; lower rates rest of yr. Crib free. Pet accepted, some restrictions. Free garage parking. TV; cable (premium), VCR avail. Indoor pool. Complimentary coffee in rms. Restaurant 6:30 am-10 pm. Bar 11 am-midnight; entertainment Tues-Thurs. Ck-out noon. Meeting rms. Business servs avail. Concierge. Free RR station transportation. Exercise equipt; weight machine, bicycle, sauna. Cr cds: A, D, MC, V.

[D] [⊁] [≋] [⫪] [⊠] [⚓] [SC]

Delaware

Newark *(See also New Castle, Wilmington)*

Motels

✔★★ **COMFORT INN.** *1120 S College Ave (DE 896) (19713), Exit 1- I95 to DE 896 N.* 302/368-8715; FAX 302/368-6454. 102 rms, 2 story. S $50-$54; D $56-$60; each addl $6; under 18 free. Crib free. Pet accepted. TV; cable, VCR avail (movies). Pool; lifeguard. Complimentary continental bkfst. Ck-out 11 am. Meeting rm. Business servs avail. In-rm modem link. Some refrigerators. Cr cds: A, C, D, DS, JCB, MC, V.
🄳 👷 ≈ 🚫 🐾 SC

★★ **HOWARD JOHNSON.** *1119 S College Ave (DE 896) (19713).* 302/368-8521; FAX 302/368-9868. 142 rms, 2 story. S $55; D $70; each addl $10; under 18 free. Crib free. Pet accepted. TV; cable. Pool. Complimentary continental bkfst. Ck-out noon. Meeting rms. Business servs avail. In-rm modem link. Valet serv. Private patios, balconies. Cr cds: A, C, D, DS, ER, JCB, MC, V. 🄳 👷 ≈ 🚫 🐾 SC

New Castle *(See also Newark, Wilmington)*

Motels

★★ **RAMADA INN.** *I-295 & Rte 13, Manor Branch, 1 mi S of DE Memorial Bridge at jct US 13, I-295.* 302/658-8511; FAX 302/658-3071. 131 rms, 2 story. S $67-$75; D $69-$85; each addl $6; under 18 free. Crib free. Pet accepted. TV; cable. Pool; poolside serv, lifeguard. Restaurant 6:30 am-10 pm; Sun to 9 pm. Rm serv from 7 am. Bar 4:30 pm-midnight. Ck-out noon. Meeting rms. Business servs avail. In-rm modem link. Valet serv. Sundries. RR station, bus depot transportation. Cr cds: A, C, D, DS, MC, V. 🄳 👷 ≈ 🚫 🐾 SC

✔★ **RODEWAY INN.** *US 13/40/301.* 302/328-6246; FAX 302/328-9493. 40 rms. S $49-$59; D $55-$69; each addl $5; under 18 free. Crib $5. Pet accepted. TV; cable. Restaurant adj 11 am-10 pm. Ck-out noon. Business servs avail. Some refrigerators. Cr cds: A, C, D, DS, MC, V. 👷 🚫 🐾 SC

Wilmington *(In PA see also Kennett Square, Philadelphia)*

Motels

✔★★ **BEST WESTERN BRANDYWINE VALLEY INN.** *1807 Concord Pike (US 202) (19803), I-95 exit 8.* 302/656-9436; FAX 302/656-8564. E-mail info@brandywinevalley.com; web www.brandywinevalley .com. 95 rms, 2 story, 12 kit. suites. S $77; D $92; each addl $5; kit. suites $105; under 18 free. Crib $5. Pet accepted. TV; cable (premium), VCR avail. Pool; wading pool, whirlpool, lifeguard. Complimentary coffee in rms. Restaurant adj 7 am-11 pm. Ck-out noon. Meeting rms. Business servs avail. In-rm modem link. Bellhops. Valet serv. Sundries. Gift shop. Exercise equipt; bicycles, stair machine. Microwaves avail. Cr cds: A, C, D, DS, MC, V. 🄳 👷 ≈ 🏋 🚫 🐾 SC

★★ **HOLIDAY INN-NORTH.** *4000 Concord Pike (US 202) (19803), I-95 exit 8.* 302/478-2222; FAX 302/479-0850. Web www.holidayinn.com. 138 rms, 2 story. S, D $79; each addl $6; under 18 free; wknd rates. Crib free. Pet accepted, some restrictions. TV; cable (premium), VCR avail. Pool; lifeguard. Restaurant 6 am-10 pm. Rm serv. Bar 4 pm-1 am. Ck-out noon. Coin lndry. Meeting rms. Business servs avail. In-rm modem link. Bellhops. Sundries. Health club privileges. Cr cds: A, C, D, DS, JCB, MC, V.
🄳 👷 ≈ 🚫 🐾 SC

Hotels

★★★ **HILTON.** *I-95 & Naamans Rd (19703), I-95N exit 11, or I-495S exit 6.* 302/792-2700; FAX 302/798-6182. 193 rms, 7 story. S, D $119-$159; each addl $10; suites $150-$275; under 12 free; wknd rates. Pet accepted; $60. TV; cable (premium). Pool. Playground. Coffee in rms. Restaurant 6:30 am-11 pm. Bar 3:30 pm-1 am. Ck-out noon. Meeting rms. Business center. In-rm modem link. Valet serv. Concierge. Free airport transportation. Exercise equipt; weights, bicycles. Some refrigerators; microwaves avail. Cr cds: A, C, D, DS, MC, V. 🄳 👷 ≈ 🏋 🚫 🐾 SC 🚶

✔ ★ ★ ★ **HOLIDAY INN-DOWNTOWN.** *700 King St (19801). 302/655-0400; FAX 302/655-5488.* 217 rms, 9 story. S $79-$119; D $89-$129; each addl $10; suites $275-$395; under 18 free; wkend rates. Parking $6 wkdays; $2 wkends. Pet accepted, some restrictions. TV; cable (premium), VCR avail. Indoor pool; whirlpool. Coffee in rms. Restaurant 6:30 am-midnight; Sat, Sun from 7 am. Bar 11:30-1 am. Ck-out noon. Meeting rms. Business servs avail. In-rm modem link. Beauty shop. Exercise equipt; rower, bicycles. Some rms overlook pool. Cr cds: A, C, D, DS, JCB, MC, V. [D] [✆] [≋] [✕] [↘] [🖐] [SC]

District of Columbia

Washington

Hotels

★ ★ ★ **ANA.** *2401 M St NW (20037), west of downtown. 202/429-2400; FAX 202/457-5010; res: 800/262-4683.* 415 rms, 10 story. S, D $280-$310; each addl $30; suites $695-$1,650; under 18 free; wkend, summer rates. Crib free. Covered parking; valet $19. Pet accepted, some restrictions. TV; cable (premium), VCR avail. Indoor pool; whirlpool. Restaurant 6:30 am-11 pm. Rm serv 24 hrs. Bar 4 pm-midnight; entertainment. Ck-out 1 pm. Convention facilities. Business center. In-rm modem link. Concierge. Gift shop. Local shopping transportation. Exercise rm; instructor, weight machines, bicycles, sauna, steam rm. Massage. Squash, racquetball courts. Bathrm phones, refrigerators, minibars. Some balconies. Luxury level. Cr cds: A, C, D, DS, JCB, MC, V. 🄳 🌊 🏊 🏋 🛋 🏃 🆂🅲 🏊

★ ★ ★ **THE CARLTON.** *923 16th St NW (20006), downtown. 202/638-2626; FAX 202/638-4231.* Web www.sheraton.com. 192 rms, 8 story. S $260-$310; D $285-$350; each addl $25; suites $550-$2,100; under 18 free; wkend rates. Crib free. Pet accepted, some restrictions. Covered valet parking $22. TV; cable (premium), VCR avail. Pool privileges. Restaurant 7-10:30 am, noon-2 pm, 6-10 pm. Afternoon tea 3-5:30 pm. Rm serv 24 hrs. Bar. Ck-out 1 pm. Meeting rms. Business servs avail. In-rm modem link. Concierge. Gift shop. Tennis privileges. Exercise equipt; bicycles, treadmill. Health club privileges. Bathrm phones, refrigerators, minibars; microwaves avail. Italian Renaissance mansion with courtyard terrace. Cr cds: A, C, D, DS, ER, JCB, MC, V. 🄳 🌊 🏊 🏋 🛋 🏃 🆂🅲

✔ ★ **DAYS PREMIER-CONVENTION CENTER.** *1201 K St NW (20005), downtown. 202/842-1020; FAX 202/289-0336.* E-mail 10545. 2452@compuserve.com. 219 rms, 9 story. Mar-May, Aug-Oct: S, D $75-$175; each addl $10; family, wkend rates; higher rates Cherry Blossom Festival; lower rates rest of yr. Crib free. Garage $12. Pet accepted, some restrictions. TV; cable (premium). Pool; lifeguard. Restaurant 7 am-10 pm; Sat, Sun 7-10:30 am, 5-10 pm. Bar. Ck-out noon. Coin lndry. Meeting rms. Business servs avail. In-rm modem link. Sundries. Exercise equipt; weight machines, treadmill. Microwaves avail. Cr cds: A, C, D, DS, JCB, MC, V. 🄳 🌊 🏋 🏃 🆂🅲

★ **DOUBLETREE GUEST SUITES.** *2500 Pennsylvania Ave NW (20037), in Foggy Bottom. 202/333-8060; FAX 202/338-3818.* Web www.double tree.com. 123 kit. suites, 10 story. S $109-$169; D $109-$184; each addl $15; under 18 free. Crib free. Pet accepted, $12/day. Garage $15. TV; cable (premium). Coffee in rms. Restaurant adj 11 am-midnight. Ck-out noon. Business servs avail. In-rm modem link. Health club privileges. Microwaves. Cr cds: A, C, D, DS, MC, V. 🌊 🏃 🆂🅲

★ ★ ★ ★ **FOUR SEASONS.** *2800 Pennsylvania Ave NW (20007), in Georgetown. 202/342-0444; FAX 202/944-2076.* E-mail seasons@erols.com; web www.fshr.com. This highly efficient, midsize hotel on the edge of Georgetown has a strong dedication to guest service. Rooms, some of which have park views, are comfortably furnished and well-lighted. 196 rms, 6 story. S $320-$365; D $350-$395; each addl $30; suites $750-$2,400; under 18 free; wkend rates. Crib free. Pet accepted. Valet parking $22. TV; cable (premium), VCR avail (movies). Indoor pool. Restaurant 7-2 am. Rm serv 24 hrs. Afternoon tea. Bar from 11 am. Ck-out noon. Meeting rms. Business center. In-rm modem link. Concierge. Exercise rm; instructor, weight machine, bicycles, steam rm. Spa. Bathrm phones, minibars; microwaves avail. Some balconies. Cr cds: A, C, D, ER, JCB, MC, V. 🄳 🌊 🏋 🏃 🆂🅲

★ ★ ★ **HAY-ADAMS.** *800 16th St NW (20006), opp White House, downtown. 202/638-6600; FAX 202/638-2716; res: 800/424-5054.* 143 rms, 8 story. S, D $275-$475; each addl $30; suites $550-$2,250; under 13 free; wkend rates. Pet accepted, some restrictions. TV; cable (premium). Restaurant 6:30 am-2 pm, 5-10 pm. Rm serv 24 hrs. Bar 4:30 pm-midnight; Fri, Sat to 1 am. Ck-out noon. Business servs avail. In-rm modem link. Meeting rms. Concierge. Valet parking $20. Health club privileges. Bathrm phones; some refrigerators, minibars, fireplaces; microwaves avail. Some balconies. Cr cds: A, C, D, ER, JCB, MC, V. 🌊 🏃

✔ ★ ★ **HOLIDAY INN ON THE HILL.** *415 New Jersey Ave NW (20001), on Capitol Hill. 202/638-1616; FAX 202/638-0707.* 342 rms, 10 story. Feb-May, Sept-Nov: S, D $99-$169; each addl $10; suites $198-$475; under 18 free; wkend rates; lower rates rest of yr. Crib free. Pet accepted, some restrictions. TV; cable (premium). Rooftop pool; poolside serv, lifeguard. Supervised evening child's activities (Memorial Day-Labor Day); ages 4-14. Restaurant 6:30 am-midnight. Bar 11-2 am. Ck-out noon. Business servs avail. In-rm modem link. Sundries. Covered parking. Exercise equipt; bicycles, stair machine. Cr cds: A, C, D, DS, JCB, MC, V. ⟦D⟧ ⟦⟧ ⟦⟧ ⟦⟧ ⟦⟧ ⟦⟧ ⟦SC⟧

✔★ **HOTEL HARRINGTON.** *11th & E Sts NW (20004), downtown. 202/628-8140; res: 800/424-8532; FAX 202/343-3924.* E-mail reservations @hotel-harrington.com; web www.hotel-harrington.com. 260 rms, 11 story, 29 suites. Mar-Oct: S $72-$78; D $78-$88; each addl $5; suites $109; under 16 free; family, wknd, wkly, hol rates; lower rates rest of yr. Crib free. Pet accepted, some restrictions. Garage $6.50/day. TV; cable (premium). Restaurants 7 am-midnight. Bar from 11 am. Ck-out noon. Meeting rm. Business servs avail. Gift shop. Barber. Coin lndry. Refrigerators avail. Cr cds: A, D, DS, JCB, MC, V. ⟦D⟧ ⟦⟧ ⟦⟧ ⟦⟧ ⟦SC⟧

★★★ **HOTEL SOFITEL.** *1914 Connecticut Ave NW (20009), in Kalorama area. 202/797-2000; FAX 202/462-0944; res: 800/424-2464.* 144 units, 9 story, 40 suites. S $225-$245; D $245-$265; each addl $20; suites $275; under 12 free; wknd rates. Crib free. Pet accepted; $50 deposit. Garage parking; valet $15. TV; cable (premium). Restaurant 6:30 am-10:30 pm. Rm serv 24 hrs. Bar noon-11:30 pm; Fri, Sat to 1 am; pianist. Meeting rms. Business servs avail. In-rm modem link. Concierge. Exercise equipt; rower, treadmill. Bathrm phones, minibars; microwaves avail. Refurbished apartment building; built 1904. Cr cds: A, C, D, JCB, MC, V. ⟦⟧ ⟦⟧ ⟦⟧ ⟦⟧ ⟦SC⟧

★★★★ **LOEWS L'ENFANT PLAZA.** *480 L'Enfant Plaza SW (20024), south of downtown. 202/484-1000; FAX 202/646-4456.* Web www.loewshotels.com/ lenfanthome.html. The center piece of L'Enfant Plaza, this is an upscale hotel with a pretty lobby and pleasant rooms. The hotel is popular with travelers doing business with nearby government agencies. 370 rms on floors 11-15. S, D $190-$250; each addl $20; suites $370-$1,200; under 18 free; wknd rates. Crib free. Pet accepted. Valet parking $18. TV; cable (premium), VCR (movies avail). Pool; poolside serv, lifeguard. Restaurant 6:30 am-midnight. Bar from 11:30 am. Ck-out 1 pm. Convention facilities. Business center. In-rm modem link. Concierge. Underground shopping arcade with Metro subway stop. Gift shop. Extensive exercise rm; instructor, weights, bicycles. Refrigerators, minibars; microwaves avail. Many balconies. Cr cds: A, C, D, DS, MC, V. ⟦D⟧ ⟦⟧ ⟦⟧ ⟦⟧ ⟦⟧ ⟦⟧ ⟦SC⟧ ⟦⟧

★★ **OMNI SHOREHAM.** *2500 Calvert St NW (20008), north of downtown. 202/234-0700; FAX 202/332-1373.* 771 rms, 8 story. S $215, D $245; each addl $30; suites $400-$1,600; under 18 free; wknd, hol rates. Crib free. Pet accepted, some restrictions. Garage $14. TV; cable (premium), VCR avail. Pool; wading pool, poolside serv, lifeguard. Restaurant 6:30 am-11 pm. Rm serv. Bar 11-2 am; entertainment. Ck-out noon. Meeting rms. Business center. Shopping arcade. Lighted tennis, pro. Exercise equipt; weight machines, bicycles, sauna. Lawn games. Microwave avail in suites. Cr cds: A, C, D, DS, JCB, MC, V. ⟦D⟧ ⟦⟧ ⟦⟧ ⟦⟧ ⟦⟧ ⟦⟧ ⟦SC⟧ ⟦⟧

★★★ **RENAISSANCE WASHINGTON.** *999 9th St NW (20001), near Convention Center & MCI Arena, downtown. 202/898-9000; FAX 202/289-0947.* E-mail sales@ren hotels.com; web www.renaissance.com. 801 rms, 16 story. Apr-June, Sept-Nov: S, D $219-$260; each addl $25; suites $500-$2,000; under 18 free; wknd rates; lower rates rest of yr. Crib free. Pet accepted, some restrictions. Garage $15. TV; cable (premium), VCR avail. Indoor pool; whirlpool. Complimentary coffee in rms. Restaurant 6:30 am-11 pm. Rm serv 24 hrs. Bar 11-1 am. Ck-out 1 pm. Convention facilities. Business center. In-rm modem link. Concierge. Shopping arcade. Exercise rm; instructor, weight machines, bicycles, sauna. Minibars; some bathrm phones; microwaves avail. Luxury level. Cr cds: A, C, D, DS, ER, JCB, MC, V. ⟦D⟧ ⟦⟧ ⟦⟧ ⟦⟧ ⟦⟧ ⟦⟧ ⟦SC⟧ ⟦⟧

★★ **RIVER INN.** *924 25th St NW (20037), 2 blks from Kennedy Center, in Foggy Bottom. 202/337-7600; FAX 202/337-6520; res: 800/424-2741.* E-mail Riverinn@erols.com. 126 kit. suites. S $125-$175; D $140-$190; each addl $15; under 18 free; wknd rates; higher rates Apr-May, Sept-Oct. Crib free. Pet accepted, some restrictions; $100. Parking $15. TV; cable (premium). Restaurant 7-10 am, 11:30 am-2 pm, 5-10 pm; Sat 8-10 am, 11 am-2 pm, 5:30-11:30 pm; Sun 8-10 am, 11 am-2 pm, 5-10 pm. Bar. Ck-out noon. Meeting rm. Business servs avail. In-rm modem link. Health club privileges. Microwaves. Cr cds: A, C, D, MC, V. ⟦D⟧ ⟦⟧ ⟦⟧ ⟦⟧ ⟦SC⟧

★★★ **SHERATON.** *2660 Woodley Rd NW (20008), north of downtown. 202/328-2000; FAX 202/234-0015.* Web www.ittsheraton.com. 1,505 rms, 10 story. Mar-June: S, D $167-$220; each addl $30; suites $250-$2,250; under 12 free; lower rates rest of yr. Crib free. Pet accepted. Valet parking $17; garage $15. TV; cable (premium), VCR avail. Heated pool. Complimentary coffee in rms. Restaurants 6:30 am-11 pm. Bar 11-2 am. Ck-out noon. Convention facilities. Business center. Valet serv. Concierge. Gift shop. Barber. Exercise equipt; weight machines, bicycles, sauna. Some refrigerators. Balconies. Cr cds: A, D, DS, JCB, MC, V. ⟦D⟧ ⟦⟧ ⟦⟧ ⟦⟧ ⟦⟧ ⟦⟧ ⟦⟧

★ ★ **WASHINGTON.** *515 15th St NW (20004), at Pennsylvania Ave, 1 blk from White House, downtown. 202/638-5900; FAX 202/638-4275; res: 800/424-9540.* 344 rms, 11 story. S $170-$235; D $185-$235; each addl $18; suites $430-$668; under 14 free; wkend rates. Crib free. Pet accepted, some restrictions. TV; cable (premium). Restaurant 7 am-10 pm. Bar 11-1 am. Ck-out 1 pm. Meeting rms. Business center. In-rm modem link. Gift shop. Exercise equipt; weight machine, bicycles, sauna. Bathrm phones. Original Jardin D'Armide tapestry (1854). One of the oldest continuously-operated hotels in the city. Cr cds: A, C, D, DS, JCB, MC, V. [D] [✦] [✕] [✕] [✕] [SC] [✕]

★ ★ ★ **THE WASHINGTON COURT ON CAPITOL HILL.** *525 New Jersey Ave NW (20001), on Capitol Hill. 202/628-2100; FAX 202/879-7918; res: 800/321-3010.* 264 rms, 15 story. S, D $175-$250; each addl $25; suites $360-$1,500; under 16 free; wkend rates. Crib free. Pet accepted, some restrictions. Valet parking $15. TV; cable (premium), VCR avail. Restaurant 6:30 am-11 pm. Bar; pianist. Ck-out noon. Meeting rooms. Business servs avail. In-rm modem link. Concierge. Exercise equipt; weight machines, bicycles, sauna. Gift shop. Bathrm phones, refrigerators. Large atrium lobby. Cr cds: A, C, D, DS, MC, V.
[D] [✦] [✕] [✕] [✕] [SC]

★ ★ ★ **WASHINGTON HILTON AND TOWERS.** *1919 Connecticut Ave NW (20009), in Kalorama. 202/483-3000; FAX 202/265-8221.* Web www.hilton .com. 1,123 rms, 10 story. S $200-$265; D $225-$285; each addl $20; suites $444-$1,400; wkend rates. Crib free. Pet accepted, some restrictions. Garage $12. TV; cable (premium), VCR avail (movies). Heated pool; poolside serv, lifeguard (in season). Supervised child's activities (May-Sept). Restaurants 6:30 am-11 pm. Bar 11:30-2 am; entertainment. Ck-out noon. Convention facilities. Business center. In-rm modem link. Gift shop. Lighted tennis, pro. Exercise rm; instructor, weight machines, bicycles, steam rm. Minibars. Resort atmosphere; on 7 landscaped acres. Luxury level. Cr cds: A, C, D, DS, JCB, MC, V. [D] [✦] [✕] [✕] [✕] [✕] [✕] [SC] [✕]

★ ★ ★ **THE WATERGATE.** *2650 Virginia Ave NW (20037), adj Kennedy Center, in Foggy Bottom. 202/965-2300; FAX 202/337-7915; res: 800/424-2736.* 231 rms, 13 story. S $275-$410; D $300-$435; each addl $25; suites $400-$1,885; under 18 free; wkend, hol rates. Crib free. Pet accepted, some restrictions. Valet parking $25. TV; cable (premium), VCR avail (movies). Indoor pool; whirlpool, lifeguard. Restaurant 7 am-2:30 pm, 5:30-10:30 pm. Rm serv 24 hrs. Bar 11:30-1 am; pianist. Ck-out noon. Meeting rms. Business center. In-rm modem link. Concierge. Shopping arcade. Barber, beauty shop. Complimentary downtown & Capitol transportation. Exercise rm; instructor, weight machines, bicycles, sauna, steam rm. Massage. Health club privileges. Bathrm phones, minibars; microwaves avail. Many balconies. Kennedy Center adj. Overlooks Potomac River. Cr cds: A, C, D, DS, JCB, MC, V. [D] [✦] [✕] [✕] [✕] [✕] [✕]

★ ★ ★ **WILLARD INTER-CONTINENTAL.** *1401 Pennsylvania Ave NW (20004), 2 blks E of White House, downtown. 202/628-9100; FAX 202/637-7326.* This opulent Beaux Arts hotel was host to every president from Franklin Pierce to Dwight D. Eisenhower on the eve of their inaugurations. A faithful renovation has returned elegance to the stately columns, mosaic floors and turn-of-the-century decor. Guest rooms are furnished with mahogany Queen Anne-style reproductions. 341 units, 12 story, 35 suites. S $335-$450; D $365-$480; each addl $30; suites $800-$3,600; under 14 free; wkend rates. Crib free. Pet accepted, some restrictions. Covered parking, valet $20. TV; cable (premium), VCR avail. Restaurant 6:30 am-11 pm. Rm serv 24 hrs. Bar 11-1 am; Sun 11:30 am-midnight; entertainment. Ck-out noon. Convention facilities. Business center. In-rm modem link. Concierge. Shopping arcade. Exercise equipt; weight machine, treadmill. Bathrm phones, minibars; some microwaves avail. Cr cds: A, C, D, DS, JCB, MC, V. [D] [✦] [✕] [✕] [✕] [SC] [✕]

Florida

Altamonte Springs (See also Orlando, Winter Park)

Motels

✔★★ **CROSBY'S MOTOR INN.** *(1440 W Orange Blossom Trail, Apopka 32712) 12 mi W on Orange Blossom Trail (FL 441). 407/886-3220; res: 800/821-6685.* 61 rms, 2 story, 14 kit. units. Oct-Mar: S $46-$99; D $56-$109; suites $99-$125; kit. units $15 addl; higher rates: Daytona 500, golf tournaments, special events; lower rates rest of yr. Crib $6. Pet accepted, some restrictions. TV. Pool. Playground. Complimentary coffee in lobby 7-10 am. Ck-out 11 am. Coin lndry. In-rm modem link. Some refrigerators. Picnic tables. Cr cds: A, DS, MC, V. 🅳 🏖 🗲 🏋 🐾 SC

★★ **HAMPTON INN.** *151 N Douglas Ave (32714), I-4 exit 48. 407/869-9000; FAX 407/788-6746.* 210 rms, 2 story. Jan-late Apr: S, D $79-$99; under 18 free; wkend rates; higher rates special events; lower rates rest of yr. Crib free. Pet accepted, some restrictions; $50. TV; cable (premium). Heated pool; whirlpool. Complimentary continental bkfst. Restaurant nearby. Ck-out noon. Coin lndry. Meeting rms. Business center. Valet serv. Exercise equipt; weight machine, bicycles. Refrigerators. Cr cds: A, C, D, DS, MC, V.

🅳 🏖 🏃 🗲 🐾 SC 🛪

✔★★ **LA QUINTA.** *150 S Westmonte Dr (32714), 3 blks W of I-4 exit 48. 407/788-1411; FAX 407/788-6472.* 115 rms, 2 story, 11 suites. S $84; D $94; each addl $10; suites $24 addl; under 18 free. Crib free. Pet accepted. TV; cable (premium). Heated pool. Complimentary continental bkfst. Restaurant adj open 24 hrs. Ck-out noon. Meeting rms. Business servs avail. Valet serv. Cr cds: A, C, D, DS, ER, JCB, MC, V.

🅳 🏖 🗲 🐾 SC

★★★ **RESIDENCE INN BY MARRIOTT.** *270 Douglas Ave (32714), I-4 exit 48W. 407/788-7991; FAX 407/869-5468.* 128 kit. suites, 1-2 bedrm, 2 story. Suites $109-$189; wkly, monthly rates. Crib free. Pet accepted; $150. TV; cable (premium). Heated pool; whirlpools. Complimentary continental bkfst; afternoon refreshments. Ck-out noon. Business servs avail. Coin lndry. Meeting rm. Valet serv. Health club privileges. Microwaves, fireplaces. Private patios, balconies. Grills. Cr cds: A, C, D, DS, MC, V.

🅳 🏖 🗲 🐾 SC

Amelia Island (See also Jacksonville)

Motel

★★ **SHONEY'S INN.** *(2707 Sadler Rd, Fernandina Beach) 904/277-2300.* E-mail shoneysameliaisland@travelbase.com. 135 rms, 2 story, 8 kits. Mar-Sept: S $76; D $104; kit. units $98; under 18 free; lower rates rest of yr. Crib free. Pet accepted, some restrictions. TV; cable (premium). Pool; whirlpool. Restaurant 6 am-10 pm; Fri, Sat to 11 pm. Ck-out 11 am. Coin lndry. Meeting rms. Business servs avail. Beauty shop. Lighted tennis. Microwaves avail. Cr cds: A, C, D, DS, MC, V. 🅳 🏖 🏃 🗲 🐾 SC

Apalachicola

Inn

✔★ **GIBSON INN.** *51 Ave C. 850/653-2191.* 30 rms, 3 story. S, D $70-$85; suite $115; higher rates hols. Crib $5.30. Pet accepted; $5.30. TV; cable. Restaurant 7:30 am-3 pm, 6-9 pm. Ck-out 11 am, ck-in 3 pm. Luggage handling. Built in 1907; served as an officer's club in WW II. Cr cds: A, MC, V. 🗲 🐾 SC

Arcadia (See also Port Charlotte)

Motel

✔★ **BEST WESTERN ARCADIA INN.** *504 S Brevard Ave (33821), on US 17S. 941/494-4884; FAX 941/494-2006.* 35 rms. Jan-June: S $50; D $60; each addl $5; under 12 free; lower rates rest of yr. Crib $5. Pet accepted, some restrictions. TV; cable. Pool. Complimentary continental bkfst. Ck-out 10 am. Business servs avail. Gift shop. Cr cds: A, C, D, DS, MC, V. 🅳 🏖 🗲 🐾 SC

Bartow *(See also Winter Haven)*

Motel

✔★ DAVIS BROS. *1035 N Broadway Ave. 941/533-0711; FAX 941/533-0924; res: 800/424-0711.* 102 rms, 2 story. Jan-mid-Apr: S $42; D $50-$55; each addl $4; under 16 free; lower rates rest of yr. Crib $4. Pet accepted. TV; cable, VCR avail (movies $3.50). Pool; wading pool. Restaurant adj open 24 hrs. Ck-out noon. Meeting rm. Coin lndry. Cr cds: A, C, D, DS, MC, V. 🇩 ⬥ ≈ ⬛ ⬛

Boca Raton *(See also Fort Lauderdale)*

Motor Hotel

★★ DOUBLETREE GUEST SUITES. *701 NW 53rd St (33487), in Arvida Park of Commerce. 561/997-9500; FAX 561/994-3565.* 182 suites, 4 story. Mid-Dec-Apr: suites $129-$169; under 12 free; monthly rates; lower rates rest of yr. Crib free. Pet accepted, some restrictions; $50. TV; cable (premium). Heated pool; whirlpool. Complimentary coffee in rms. Restaurant 6 am-10 pm. Rm serv. Ck-out noon. Coin lndry. Meeting rms. Business servs avail. In-rm modem link. Bellhops. Sundries. Health club privileges. Refrigerators, microwaves. Cr cds: A, C, D, DS, ER, MC, V. 🇩 ⬥ ≈ ⬛ ⬛ SC

Hotels

★★ RADISSON SUITE. *7920 Glades Rd (33434), at Arvida Pkwy Ctr. 561/483-3600; FAX 561/479-2280.* 200 suites, 7 story. Dec-Apr: S, D $169-$380; each addl $10; lower rates rest of yr. Crib free. Pet accepted, some restrictions; $100. TV; cable (premium), VCR avail (movies $5). Heated pool; whirlpool. Complimentary full bkfst. Coffee in rms. Restaurants 11:30 am-10:30 pm. Bars. Ck-out noon. Coin lndry. Meeting rms. Business servs avail. In-rm modem link. Gift shop. Exercise equipt; bicycles, treadmill. Health club privileges. Minibars; refrigerators, microwaves avail. Private patios, balconies. Lake adj. Cr cds: A, C, D, DS, ER, JCB, MC, V. 🇩 ⬥ ≈ 🍴 ⬛ ⬛ SC

★ RAMADA INN. *2901 Federal Hwy (33431). 561/395-6850; FAX 561/368-7964.* 95 rms, 4 story, 32 suites. Mid-Dec-mid-Apr: S, D $95-$125; each addl $10; suites $115-$125; family rates; wkly rates, lower rates rest of yr. Crib free. Pet accepted, some restrictions; $25 deposit. TV; cable, VCR avail. Pool; whirlpool. Complimentary continental bkfst. Complimentary coffee in rms. Restaurant 5-10 pm. Bar. Ck-out noon. Meeting rms. Business servs avail. No bellhops. Refrigerators, microwaves avail. Balconies. Cr cds: A, C, D, DS, ER, MC, V. 🇩 ⬥ ≈ ⬛ ⬛ SC

Boynton Beach
(See also Boca Raton, Palm Beach, West Palm Beach)

Motel

✔★ SUPER 8. *(1255 Hypoluxo Rd, Lantana 33462) N on I-95 exit 45. 561/585-3970; FAX 561/586-3028.* 129 units, 13 kits. Jan-Apr: S $50-$57; D $52-$59; each addl $3; kits. $62-$75; under 18 free; lower rates rest of yr. Crib free. Pet accepted. TV; cable (premium). Pool. Complimentary continental bkfst. Restaurant adj 6 am-11 pm; wkends to 1 am. Ck-out noon. Business servs avail. Cr cds: A, C, D, DS, ER, MC, V. ⬥ ≈ ⬛ ⬛ SC

Bradenton *(See also St Petersburg, Sarasota)*

Motels

★★ BEST WESTERN INN-ELLENTON. *(5218 17th St E, Ellenton 34222) Off I-75 exit 43. 941/729-8505; FAX 941/729-1110.* 73 rms, 2 story, 11 kits. Feb-Apr: S $95-$120; D $95-$145; each addl $5; kits. $110-$150; under 12 free; lower rates rest of yr. Crib free. Pet accepted, some restrictions; $10. TV; cable (premium). Heated pool; whirlpool. Complimentary continental bkfst. Restaurant nearby. Ck-out 11 am. Coin lndry. Meeting rm. Business servs avail. Cr cds: A, C, D, DS, MC, V. 🇩 ⬥ ≈ ⬛ ⬛ SC

✔★ HOWARD JOHNSON EXPRESS. *6511 14th St W (US 41) (34207), near Sarasota-Bradenton Airport. 941/756-8399; FAX 941/755-1387.* 49 units, 2 story, 12 kits. Jan-Apr: S $65; D $85; kits. $75-$95; under 18 free; wkly rates in summer; lower rates rest of yr. Crib free. Pet accepted; $5. TV; cable (premium). Heated pool. Complimentary full bkfst. Restaurant nearby. Ck-out 11 am. Coin lndry. Some refrigerators. Cr cds: A, C, D, DS, MC, V. 🇩 ⬥ ≈ ⬛ ⬛ SC

★ ★ **PARK INN CLUB & BREAKFAST.** *4450 47th St W (34210).* 941/795-4633; FAX 941/795-0808. 128 rms, 3 story, 28 suites. Mid-Jan-Easter: S, D $109-$119; each addl $8; suites $139; under 18 free; lower rates rest of yr. Crib free. Pet accepted, some restrictions. TV; cable. Heated pool; whirlpool. Complimentary continental bkfst. Restaurant adj 11 am-9 pm. Ck-out noon. Meeting rms. Business servs avail. Health club privileges. Bathrm phones. Cr cds: A, C, D, DS, ER, JCB, MC, V. D ⬚ ⬚ ⬚ ⬚ SC

Brooksville *(See also Homosassa Springs)*

Motel

★ ★ **HOLIDAY INN.** *(6172 Commercial Way, Weeki Wachee 34606) 12 mi W on FL 50.* 352/596-2007; FAX 352/596-0667. 122 rms, 2 story. Late Dec-May: S, D $66-$75; each addl $6; under 18 free; lower rates rest of yr. Crib free. Pet accepted, some restrictions. TV; cable (premium). Pool; wading pool. Complimentary coffee in lobby. Restaurant 6:30 am-10 pm. Rm serv. Bar noon-1 am. Ck-out 11 am. Meeting rms. Business servs avail. Lawn games. Picnic tables. Cr cds: A, C, D, DS, JCB, MC, V. D ⬚ ⬚ ⬚ ⬚ SC

Cape Coral *(See also Fort Myers, Sanibel & Captiva Islands)*

Motel

★ **QUALITY INN.** *1538 Cape Coral Pkwy.* 941/542-2121; FAX 941/542-6319. 142 rms, 5 story. Feb-Apr: S, D $80-$100; each addl $10; under 18 free; lower rates rest of yr. Crib free. Pet accepted; $5-$10/day. TV; cable. Pool; poolside serv. Restaurant adj open 24 hrs. Ck-out 11 am. Coin lndry. Meeting rm. Business servs avail. Cr cds: A, C, D, DS, ER, JCB, MC, V. D ⬚ ⬚ ⬚ ⬚ SC

Clearwater *(See also Clearwater Beach, St Petersburg, Tampa, Tarpon Springs)*

Motels

★ ★ **HOLIDAY INN EXPRESS.** *13625 ICOT Blvd (34620), in ICOT Ctr.* 813/536-7275; FAX 813/530-3053. E-mail holidayexpress@travelbase.com. 128 rms, 3 story, 26 suites. S $65-$85; D $75-$95; each addl $5; suites $80-$95; under 18 free. Crib free. Pet accepted, some restrictions. TV; cable (premium), VCR avail. Heated pool; whirlpool. Complimentary continental bkfst. Restaurant opp 11 am-11 pm. Ck-out noon. Meeting rms. Business servs avail. In-rm modem link. Health club privileges. Bathrm phones. Cr cds: A, C, D, DS, ER, JCB, MC, V. ⬚ ⬚ ⬚ ⬚ SC

★ ★ **LA QUINTA.** *3301 Ulmerton Rd (34622), off I-275 at FL 688 exit, near St Petersburg/Clearwater Intl Airport.* 813/572-7222; FAX 813/572-0076. Web www .laquinta.com. 115 units. Jan-May: S $79; D $89; suites $100-$120; under 18 free; lower rates rest of yr. Crib free. Pet accepted, some restrictions. TV; cable (premium). Heated pool; whirlpool. Coffee in rms. Restaurant adj 6 am-10 pm. Ck-out noon. Coin lndry. Meeting rms. Business servs avail. In-rm modem link. Valet serv Mon-Fri. Free airport transportation. Exercise equipt; weight machine, bicycles, sauna. Refrigerators; microwaves avail. Cr cds: A, C, D, DS, MC, V. D ⬚ ⬚ ⬚ ⬚ ⬚ ⬚ SC

★ ★ **RESIDENCE INN BY MARRIOTT.** *5050 Ulmerton Rd (34620), at 49th St, 1 mi E of US 19 on FL 688.* 813/573-4444; FAX 813/572-4446. 88 kit. suites, 2 story. Kit. suites $129-$189; wkly, monthly rates. Pet accepted, some restrictions; $125 & $250 deposit. TV; cable (premium). Heated pool; whirlpool. Continental bkfst. Ck-out noon. Meeting rms. Business servs avail. In-rm modem link. Valet serv. Health club privileges. Lawn games. Microwaves, fireplaces. Some private patios, balconies. Grill. Cr cds: A, C, D, DS, MC, V. D ⬚ ⬚ ⬚ ⬚ SC

Clearwater Beach *(See also Clearwater, St Petersburg, Tampa, Tarpon Springs)*

Motel

✔★ **AEGEAN SANDS.** *421 S Gulfview Blvd (33767), on Clearwater Beach.* 813/447-3464; FAX 813/446-7169; res: 800/942-3432. E-mail info @travelbase.com; web www.travelbase.com/aegean. 68 rms, 4 story, 57 kits. Feb-Apr: S, D $60-$90; each addl $10; kit. units $75-$145; varied lower rates rest of yr. Crib $5. Pet accepted, some restrictions; $15. TV. Heated pool. Ck-out noon. Coin lndry. Business servs avail. Gift shop. Sundries. Lawn games. Refrigerators. Bicycle rental. Many balconies. Beach opp. Cr cds: A, D, DS, MC, V. ⬚ ⬚ ⬚ SC

Cocoa (See also Cocoa Beach, Titusville)

Motels

✔★★ **BEST WESTERN-COCOA INN.** *4225 W King St (32926), I-95 exit 75.* 407/632-1065; FAX 407/631-3302. Web www.bestwestern.com/thisco/bw/10150/10150b .hml. 120 rms, 2 story. Jan-Apr: S, D $45-$65; under 12 free; higher rates: special events, hols; lower rates rest of yr. Crib $4. Pet accepted; $4. TV; cable. Pool. Bar 4 pm-midnight. Complimentary coffee in lobby. Ck-out 11:30 am. Coin lndry. Meeting rms. Game rm. Picnic tables, grills. Cr cds: A, C, D, DS, MC, V. [D] 🐾 🏊 🛏 🐾 **SC**

★ **DAYS INN.** *5600 FL 524 (32926), at I-95 exit 76.* 407/636-6500; FAX 407/631-0513. 115 rms, 2 story. Jan-Mar: S, D $49-$70; each addl $10; under 12 free off-season; wkly rates; higher rates special events; lower rates rest of yr. Crib free. Pet accepted; $5. TV; cable (premium). Pool. Complimentary coffee in lobby. Ck-out 11 am. Some refrigerators; microwaves avail. Cr cds: A, D, DS, MC, V. 🐾 🏊 🛏 🐾 **SC**

★★ **RAMADA INN.** *900 Friday Rd (32926), I-95 exit 76.* 407/631-1210; FAX 407/636-8661. E-mail ramada@iu.net; web www.ln.com/ramada. 150 rms, 2 story. Early Jan-Apr: S, D $49-$69; each addl $7; package plans; higher rates special events; lower rates rest of yr. Crib free. Pet accepted; $25 deposit. TV; cable (premium). Heated pool; poolside serv. Restaurant 6 am-10 pm. Rm serv. Bar 4 pm-2 am. Ck-out noon. Coin lndry. Meeting rms. Lawn games. Microwaves. Private lake. Cr cds: A, C, D, DS, ER, JCB, MC, V. [D] 🐾 🐾 🏊 🍴 🛏 🐾 **SC**

Cocoa Beach (See also Cocoa, Titusville)

Motels

✔★★ **BEST WESTERN-OCEAN INN.** *5500 N Atlantic Ave (FL A1A), near ocean pier.* 407/784-2550; FAX 407/868-7124. 103 rms, 2 story. S $56-$82; D $64-$90; each addl $8; kit. units $74-$90; under 18 free. Crib free. Pet accepted, some restrictions. TV; cable. Pool. Complimentary coffee in lobby. Restaurant adj. Ck-out 11 am. Coin lndry. In-rm modem link. Exercise equipt; bicycle, stair machine. Refrigerators avail. Cr cds: A, C, D, DS, ER, JCB, MC, V. [D] 🐾 🏊 🍴 🛏 🐾 **SC**

★ **SURF STUDIO.** *1801 S Atlantic Ave (FL A1A), FL A1A S of FL520.* 407/783-7100; FAX 407/783-2695. 11 rms, 9 with kit. Mid-Jan-Apr: S, D $70-$75; each addl $10; kit. units $95-$140; under 10 free; wkly rates; min stay hols; lower rates rest of yr. Crib free. Pet accepted; $10. TV; cable (premium), VCR avail. Pool. Ck-out 11 am. Coin lndry. Refrigerators, microwaves. On beach. Cr cds: A, C, D, DS, MC, V. 🐾 🐾 🏊 🐾

Crystal River (See also Homosassa Springs)

Motels

★★ **BEST WESTERN CRYSTAL RESORT.** *614 NW US 19, 1 mi N of FL 44.* 352/795-3171; FAX 352/795-3179. 96 rms, 2 story. Dec-Easter: S $64-$67; D $69-$72; each addl $5; kit. units $70-$79; under 18 free; lower rates rest of yr. Crib free. Pet accepted; $3/day. TV; cable (premium), VCR avail (movies). Heated pool. Bar from 4 pm. Ck-out noon. Coin lndry. Business servs avail. Sundries. Gift shop. Exercise equipt: weight machine, rower. Refrigerators avail. Some balconies. Picnic tables, grill. On Crystal River; dock, launching ramp, boats, guides; scuba diving. Cr cds: A, C, D, DS, JCB, MC, V. [D] 🐾 🐾 🏊 🍴 🛏 🐾 **SC**

✔★★ **COMFORT INN.** *4486 N Suncoast Blvd (US 19/98).* 352/563-1500; FAX 352/563-5426. 66 rms, 2 story. Jan-Apr: S $44.95-$57.95; D $49.95-$67.95; each addl $5; under 18 free; higher rates some hols; lower rates rest of yr. Crib $7. Pet accepted; $5 per day. TV; cable (premium). Pool. Complimentary continental bkfst. Ck-out 11 am. Coin lndry. Business servs avail. In-rm modem link. Lighted tennis. Picnic tables. Cr cds: A, D, DS, ER, MC, V. [D] 🐾 🎾 🏊 🛏 🐾 **SC**

Dania (See also Fort Lauderdale)

Hotel

★★ **WYNDHAM.** *1825 Griffin Rd, at Fort Lauderdale Intl Airport.* 954/920-3500; FAX 954/920-3571. 250 rms, 12 story. Dec-Apr: S $145-$189; D $155-$209; suites $275-$475; under 12 free; lower rates rest of yr. Crib free. Pet accepted, some restrictions; $50. TV; cable (premium). Pool; whirlpool, poolside serv. Restaurant 6:30 am-10:30 pm. Bar 11 am-midnight. Ck-out noon. Convention facilities. Business servs avail. In-rm modem link.

Gift shop. Free airport transportation. Lighted tennis. Golf privileges. Exercise equipt; weights, sauna, steam rm. Health club privileges. Some refrigerators. 2-story atrium lobby. Cr cds: A, C, D, DS, ER, MC, V.

Daytona Beach *(See also DeLand, Ormond Beach)*

Motor Hotels

★ **CASTAWAYS.** *(2043 S Atlantic Ave, Daytona Beach Shores 32118) 2 mi S on FL A1A. 904/254-8480; FAX 904/253-6554; res: 800/407-0342.* Web www.visitdaytona .com. 152 rms, 7 story, 58 kit. units. Feb-Apr, June-Aug: S, D $79-$99; suites $135-$178; kit. units $87-$107; under 18 free; special events (5-day min); lower rates rest of yr. Crib free. Pet accepted, some restrictions; $10. TV; cable (premium), VCR avail. Pool; sauna. Supervised child's activities (mid-June-mid-Aug); ages 5-9. Restaurant 7 am-10 pm. Rm serv. Ck-out 11 am. Coin lndry. Meeting rms. Business servs avail. Game rm. Lawn games. Refrigerators. Balconies. Picnic tables. On beach. Cr cds: A, C, D, DS, MC, V.

★ ★ ★ **HOLIDAY INN SUNSPREE.** *600 N Atlantic Ave (32118). 904/255-4471; FAX 904/253-7543.* Web visitdaytona.com/holidayinn. 323 rms, 14 story, 50 kits. Feb-mid-Apr, mid-June-mid-Sept: S, D $99-$240; under 18 free; golf plans; lower rates rest of yr. Crib free. Pet accepted. TV; cable (premium). Heated pool; poolside serv. Free supervised child's activities (mid-May-Aug); ages 4-12. Complimentary coffee in rooms. Restaurant 7 am-11 pm. Rm serv. Bar from 11 am; entertainment. Ck-out noon. Coin lndry. Convention facilities. Business servs avail. In-rm modem link. Bellhops. Valet serv. Sundries. Golf privileges. Exercise equipt; weights, bicycle. Game rm. Lawn games. Refrigerators, microwaves. Balconies. On beach. Cr cds: A, C, D, DS, JCB, MC, V.

Deerfield Beach
(See also Boca Raton, Dania, Fort Lauderdale)

Motel

★ **COMFORT SUITES.** *1040 E Newport Center Dr (33442). 954/570-8887; FAX 954/570-5346.* 101 suites, 4 story. Jan-Mar: suites $130-$150; under 18 free; golf plans; lower rates rest of yr. Crib free. Pet accepted, some restrictions. TV; cable (premium), VCR avail (movies). Heated pool; whirlpool. Complimentary continental bkfst. Restaurant adj 6:30 am-10 pm. Bar 5-10 pm. Ck-out noon. Coin lndry. Business servs avail. In-rm modem link. Sundries. Gift shop. 18-hole golf privileges, greens fee $30-$100, pro, putting green. Health club privileges. Refrigerators. Cr cds: A, C, D, DS, ER, JCB, MC, V.

Motor Hotel

★ ★ **QUALITY SUITES.** *1050 E Newport Center Dr (33442). 954/570-8888; FAX 954/570-5346.* 107 suites, 5 story. Jan-Mar: suites $146-$160; under 18 free; golf plans; lower rates rest of yr. Crib free. Pet accepted. TV; cable (premium), VCR (movies). Heated pool; whirlpool. Complimentary bkfst buffet. Restaurant 6:30 am-10 pm. Bar from 5 pm. Ck-out noon. Coin lndry. Meeting rms. Business servs avail. In-rm modem link. Valet serv. Gift shop. 18-hole golf privileges, greens fee $30-$100, pro, putting green, driving range. Health club privileges. Refrigerators, microwaves, wet bars. Balconies. Cr cds: A, C, D, DS, ER, JCB, MC, V.

DeLand *(See also Daytona Beach, Winter Park)*

Motel

✓ ★ ★ **QUALITY INN.** *2801 E New York (32724), off I-4 exit 56. 904/736-3440.* 112 rms, 2 story. Mid-Dec-Apr: S, D $44.99-$69.99; each addl $5; under 16 free; higher rates: special events, Daytona 500, July 4; lower rates rest of yr. Crib free. Pet accepted, some restrictions; $5. TV; cable (premium), VCR avail (movies $5). Pool; wading pool. Complimentary continental bkfst. Coffee in rms. Restaurant 6:30 am-10 pm. Rm serv. Bar noon-midnight; entertainment. Ck-out 11 am. Coin lndry. Meeting rms. Microwaves avail. Cr cds: A, C, D, DS, ER, JCB, MC, V.

Hotel

★ ★ **HOLIDAY INN.** *350 International Speedway Blvd (32724), on US 92. 904/738-5200; FAX 904/734-7552.* 149 rms, 6 story. S, D $69-$90; each addl $10; suites $89-$145; higher rates special events. Crib free. Pet accepted, some restrictions. TV; cable (premium), VCR avail. Pool; whirlpool. Complimentary coffee in rms. Restaurant 6:30 am-10 pm. Bar 4 pm-1:30 am. Ck-out noon. Meeting rms. Business servs avail. In-rm modem link. Health club privileges. Some refrigerators. Cr cds: A, C, D, DS, JCB, MC, V.

Englewood *(See also Port Charlotte, Punta Gorda, Venice)*

Motels

✔ ★ **DAYS INN.** *2540 S McCall Rd (FL 776) (34224).* 941/474-5544; FAX 941/475-2124. 84 rms, 2 story, 48 kits. Feb-mid-Apr: S, D $48-$95; each addl $4; under 13 free; lower rates rest of yr. Crib free. Pet accepted, some restrictions; $4. TV; cable. Heated pool. Playground. Restaurant 6 am-2 pm. Ck-out noon. Business servs avail. Microwaves avail. Private patios; some balconies. Cr cds: A, D, DS, MC, V. 🅳 ✔ ➡ ➘ 🐾 SC

★ **VERANDA INN OF ENGLEWOOD.** *2073 S McCall Rd (FL 776) (34224).* 941/475-6533; res: 800/633-8115. 38 rms, 3 story. Feb-mid-Apr: S, D $85-$90; each addl $6; under 16 free; lower rates rest of yr. Crib free. Pet accepted; $10. TV, cable; VCR avail (movies). Pool. Complimentary coffee in lobby. Restaurant adj 11 am-9 pm. Ck-out 11 am. Coin lndry. Business servs avail. Microwaves avail. On creek. Cr cds: A, D, DS, MC, V. 🅳 ✔ ➡ ➘ 🐾 SC

Fort Lauderdale *(See also Boca Raton, Dania)*

Motels

★ ★ ★ **RESIDENCE INN BY MARRIOTT.** *(130 N University Dr, Plantation 33324)* approx 3 mi W on FL 842. 954/723-0300; FAX 954/474-7385. 138 suites, 4 story. Mid-Dec-mid-Apr: suites $179-$249; family, wkly rates; lower rates rest of yr. Crib free. Pet accepted; $200. TV; cable (premium). Pool; whirlpool. Complimentary continental bkfst. Complimentary coffee in rms. Restaurant adj 11:30 am-10 pm. Rm serv. Bar. Ck-out noon. Coin lndry. Meeting rms. Business servs avail. In-rm modem link. Valet serv. Sundries. Exercise equipt; weight machine, bicycle. Health club privileges. Lawn games. Refrigerators, microwaves. Cr cds: A, C, D, DS, ER, JCB, MC, V. 🅳 ✔ ➡ 🏃 ➘ 🐾 SC

✔ ★ ★ **WELLESLEY INN.** *(13600 NW 2nd St, Sunrise 33325)* Approx 10 mi W on I-595, 2 mi N on FL 869. 954/845-9929; FAX 954/845-9996. 104 rms, 4 story, 10 suites. Dec-Mar: S, D $109.99; suites $129.99; lower rates rest of yr. Crib free. Pet accepted, some restrictions; $10. TV; cable (premium). Heated pool. Complimentary continental bkfst. Complimentary coffee in rms. Ck-out 11 am. Meeting rms. Sundries. Some refrigerators. Cr cds: A, D, DS, MC, V. 🅳 ✔ ➡ ➘ 🐾 SC

Hotels

★ **DOUBLETREE GUEST SUITES.** *2670 E Sunrise Blvd (33304).* 954/565-3800; FAX 305/561-0387. Web www.dbltree.com/suites/fll/galeria. 229 kit. suites (1-2 bedrm), 14 story. Mid-Dec-mid-Apr: kit. suites $119-$209; under 18 free; monthly rates; lower rates rest of yr. Crib free. Parking $5; valet $8. Pet accepted; $10. TV; cable (premium). Heated pool; poolside serv. Complimentary coffee, tea. Restaurant 7 am-11 pm. Rm serv 24 hrs. Bar 11 am-midnight. Ck-out noon. Coin lndry. Business servs avail. Concierge. Gift shop. Tennis privileges. Golf privileges. Exercise equipt; stair machine, bicycles; whirlpool, sauna. Microwaves, wet bars; balconies. Overlooks Intracoastal Waterway; dockage. Cr cds: A, C, D, DS, JCB, MC, V. 🅳 ✔ 🏋 🏌 ➡ 🏃 ➘ 🐾 SC

★ ★ ★ **THE WESTIN, CYPRESS CREEK.** *400 Corporate Dr (33334),* I-95 & Cypress Creek Rd. 954/772-1331; FAX 954/772-6867. 293 rms, 14 story, 33 suites. Dec-Apr: S, D $159-$249; each addl $15; suites $299-$460; under 18 free; lower rates rest of yr. Crib free. Valet parking $8. Pet accepted, some restrictions. TV; cable (premium). Pool; whirlpool, poolside serv. Restaurant 6:30 am-10 pm. Rm serv 24 hrs. Bar 11 am-midnight. Ck-out 1 pm. Convention facilities. Business servs avail. In-rm modem link. Concierge. Airport transportation. Tennis privileges. Golf privileges. Exercise equipt; weights, bicycles, sauna. Minibars; microwaves avail. Some private patios, balconies. Blue-mirrored tile building surrounded by palm trees; 20-ft poolside waterfall, 5-acre lake. Paddleboats. Cr cds: A, C, D, DS, ER, JCB, MC, V. 🅳 ✔ 🏋 🏌 ➡ 🏃 🎣 ➘ 🐾 SC

Fort Myers *(See also Cape Coral, Punta Gorda, Sanibel & Captiva Islands)*

Motels

✔ ★ **BUDGETEL INN.** *2717 Colonial Blvd (33907).* 941/275-3500; FAX 941/275-5426. 122 rms, 4 story. Jan-Apr: S, D $69-$98; lower rates rest of yr. Crib free. Pet accepted, some restrictions; fee. TV; cable (premium). Pool. Complimentary continental bkfst. Complimentary coffee in rms. Ck-out 11 am. Meeting rm. Business servs avail. In-rm modem link. Cr cds: A, C, D, DS, MC, V. 🅳 ✔ ➡ ➘ 🐾 SC

★ **COMFORT INN.** *11501 S Cleveland Ave (33907).* 941/936-3993; FAX 941/936-7234. 80 rms, 2 story. Feb-Apr: S $90-$95, D $95-$100; each addl $10; under 18 free; wkend rates; lower rates rest of yr. Crib free. Pet accepted, some restrictions. TV; cable (premium). Heated pool. Complimentary continental bkfst. Restaurant adj 11 am-11 pm. Ck-out 11 am. Meeting rms. Refrigerators. Cr cds: A, C, D, DS, ER, JCB, MC, V.

D ✦ ⩰ ⊠ ⚒ SC

★ **DAYS INN-NORTH.** *13353 N Cleveland Ave (US 41) (33903). 941/995-0535; FAX 941/656-2769.* 127 rms, 2 story. Mid-Dec-Apr: S $85; D $99; each addl $6; under 18 free; wkly rates off season; lower rates rest of yr. Crib free. Pet accepted; $10/day. TV; cable. Pool. Complimentary coffee in lobby. Restaurant adj open 24 hrs. Ck-out noon. Coin lndry. Business servs avail. Lawn games. Cr cds: A, C, D, DS, ER, JCB, MC, V.

D ✦ ⩰ ⊠ ⚒ SC

★ **LA QUINTA.** *4850 Cleveland Ave (33907). 941/275-3300; FAX 941/275-6661.* Web www.travelweb.com/laquinta.html. 130 rms, 2 story. Jan-Apr: S, D $94-$111; each addl $10; under 18 free; lower rates rest of yr. Crib free. Pet accepted, some restrictions. TV; cable (premium); VCR avail (movies). Heated pool. Complimentary continental bkfst. Restaurant nearby. Ck-out 11 am. Meeting rms. Business servs avail. In-rm modem link. Health club privileges. Cr cds: A, C, D, DS, JCB, MC, V.

D ✦ ⩰ ⊠ ⚒ SC

★ ★ **RADISSON INN SANIBEL GATEWAY.** *20091 Summerlin Rd (33908). 941/466-1200; FAX 941/466-3797.* Web www.radisson.com. 156 rms, 3 story. Mid-Jan-Apr: S, D $129-$179; under 16 free; lower rates rest of yr. Crib free. Pet accepted, some restrictions; $50. TV; cable (premium). Heated pool; whirlpool. Restaurant 6:30 am-10 pm. Rm serv. Bar 11 am-11pm; Fri, Sat to midnight. Ck-out noon. Coin lndry. Meeting rm. Business servs avail. In-rm modem link. Refrigerators. Cr cds: A, C, D, DS, ER, JCB, MC, V. D ✦ ⩰ ⊠ ⚒ SC

✔ ★ **TA KI-KI.** *2631 First Street (33916). 941/334-2135; FAX 941/332-1879.* E-mail nshippas@peganet.com; web www.cyberstreet.com/takiki. 23 rms, 5 kits. Mid-Dec-Apr: S, D $58-$62; each addl $5; kit. units $380-$405/wk; varied lower rates rest of yr. Crib free. Pet accepted, some restrictions. TV; cable. Heated pool. Complimentary coffee. Restaurant nearby. Ck-out 11 am. Business servs avail. Picnic tables, grill. On river; boat dock. Cr cds: A, C, D, DS, MC, V. ✦ ➡ ⩰ ⊠ ⚒

✔ ★ ★ **WELLESLEY INN AND SUITES.** *4400 Ford St (33916). 941/278-3949; FAX 941/278-3670; res: 800/444-8888.* 106 rms, 4 story, 15 suites. Mid-Dec-mid-Apr: S, D $60-$110; each addl $10; suites $70-$120; lower rates rest of yr. Pet accepted; some restrictions. TV; cable (premium). Heated pool. Complimentary continental bkfst. Coffee in rms. Restaurant nearby. Ck-out 11 am. Coin lndry. Meeting rm. Business servs avail. Health club privileges. Some refrigerators. Cr cds: A, C, D, DS, MC, V. D ✦ ⩰ ⊠ ⚒ SC

Fort Myers Beach *(See also Cape Coral, Fort Myers, Naples)*

Motor Hotel

★ ★ **BEST WESTERN BEACH RESORT.** *684 Estero Blvd. 941/463-6000; FAX 941/463-3013.* E-mail info@bwbeachresort.com; web www.bw beachresort.com. 75 kit. units, 5 story. Feb-Apr, mid-Dec: S, D $129-$229; under 18 free; lower rates rest of yr. Crib free. Pet accepted, some restrictions. TV; cable (premium). Heated pool. Playground. Complimentary continental bkfst. Restaurant nearby. Ck-out 11 am. Coin lndry. Business servs avail. Game rm. Lawn games. Microwaves. Balconies. Picnic tables, grills. On gulf. Cr cds: A, C, D, DS, MC, V. D ✦ ➡ ⩰ ⊠ ⚒ SC

Fort Pierce *(See also Stuart, Vero Beach)*

Motels

★ **DAYS INN.** *6651 Darter Ct (34945), W off I-95 exit 65, just S of Okeechobee Rd. 561/466-4066; FAX 561/468-3260.* 125 rms, 2 story. Jan-Apr: S, D $65-$70; each addl $5; under 18 free; lower rates rest of yr. Pet accepted; $10. TV; cable (premium). Heated pool. Coffee in rms. Restaurant 6 am-11 pm; Fri, Sat to 1 am. Ck-out 11 am. Coin lndry. Meeting rms. Business servs avail. Sundries. Some refrigerators. Cr cds: A, C, D, DS, JCB, MC, V. D ✦ ⩰ ⊠ ⚒ SC

✔ ★ ★ **HOLIDAY INN EXPRESS.** *7151 Okeechobee (34945), W off I-95 exit 65. 561/464-5000; FAX 561/461-9573.* 100 rms, 2 story. Jan-mid-Apr: S, D $89-$95; under 18 free; lower rates rest of yr. Crib free. Pet accepted, some restrictions. TV; cable (premium). Pool; wading pool. Complimentary continental bkfst. Ck-out noon. Coin lndry. Meeting rms. Sundries. Cr cds: A, C, D, DS, ER, JCB, MC, V. D ✦ ⩰ ⊠ ⚒ SC

Gainesville *(See also Starke)*

Motels

(Rates may be higher during special university events)

✔ ★ **ECONO LODGE.** *2649 SW 13th St (32608). 352/373-7816.* 53 rms, 2 story. S $36; D $39; each addl $5; under 18 free. Crib free. Pet accepted, some restrictions. TV; cable (premium), VCR (movies). Complimentary coffee in lobby. Ck-out 11 am. Cr cds: A, D, DS, MC, V.

★ ★ **RESIDENCE INN BY MARRIOTT.** *4001 SW 13th St (32608). 352/371-2101; FAX 352/371-2101, ext. 66.* 80 suites, 3 story. 1 & 2 bedrm $95-$165. Crib free. Pet accepted, some restrictions; $50. TV; cable (premium), VCR avail (movies). Pool; whirlpool. Complimentary continental bkfst buffet. Ck-out noon. Coin lndry. Meeting rms. Business servs avail. Valet serv. Free airport transportation. Picnic tables, grill. Cr cds: A, C, D, DS, MC, V.

Homestead *(See also Miami)*

Motels

★ **DAYS INN.** *51 S Homestead Blvd (33030). 305/245-1260; FAX 305/247-0939.* 110 rms, 2 story. Mid-Dec-mid-Apr: S $72; D $86-$99; each addl $10; suite $120; under 16 free; higher rates auto races; lower rates rest of yr. Crib free. Pet accepted, some restrictions. TV; cable (premium). Pool. Complimentary continental bkfst. Restaurant 6:30 am-10:30 pm. Rm serv. Bar 3 pm-2 am; entertainment Thurs-Sat. Ck-out 11 am. Coin lndry. Business servs avail. Cr cds: A, C, D, DS, JCB, MC, V.

★ ★ **HAMPTON INN.** *(124 E Palm Dr, Florida City 33034) 305/247-8833; FAX 305/247-6456.* 122 rms, 2 story. Nov-mid-Apr: S, D $79.95-$95.95; each addl $5; under 18 free; higher rates auto races; lower rates rest of yr. Crib free. Pet accepted, some restrictions. TV; cable (premium). Pool. Complimentary continental bkfst. Restaurant opp 11 am-10 pm. Ck-out noon. Business servs avail. In-rm modem link. Bellhops. Tennis and golf privileges. Cr cds: A, C, D, DS, MC, V.

✔ ★ **HOLIDAY INN EXPRESS.** *990 Homestead Blvd (33030). 305/247-7020.* 148 rms, 2 story. S $49.95-$69.95; D $59.95-$79.95; each addl $10; family rates; higher rates auto races. Crib free. Pet accepted, some restrictions. TV; cable (premium). Pool; poolside serv. Complimentary continental bkfst. Ck-out noon. Coin lndry. Meeting rms. Business servs avail. Bellhops. Some refrigerators. Cr cds: A, C, D, DS, JCB, MC, V.

Homosassa Springs *(See also Brooksville, Crystal River)*

Motel

★ ★ **HOWARD JOHNSON RIVERSIDE INN RESORT.** *(5297 S Cherokee Way, Homosassa 34487) 3 mi W on FL 490, 3 mi W of US 19/98. 352/628-2474; FAX 352/628-5208; res: 800/442-2040.* 81 rms, 2 story, 8 kits. S, D $80-$115; each addl $10; kit. units $115; under 14 free; wkly rates. Crib $10. Pet accepted; $5. TV; cable. Pool. Restaurant 7 am-9 pm. Bar; entertainment, dancing Fri & Sat. Ck-out 11 am. Coin lndry. Meeting rms. Tennis. Lawn games. Marina; charters, boat tours, guides; free dockage for guests. Cr cds: A, C, D, DS, ER, MC, V.

Jacksonville *(See also St Augustine)*

Motels

(Rates may be higher and there may be a minimum stay on football wkends)

✔ ★ **BEST INNS OF AMERICA.** *8220 Dix Ellis Trail (32256), I-95 exit 100. 904/739-3323.* 109 rms, 2 story. S $41.88-$47.88; D $48.88-$54.88; each addl $7; under 18 free; wkly rates. Crib free. Pet accepted, some restrictions. TV; cable (premium). Pool. Complimentary continental bkfst. Restaurant nearby. Ck-out 1 pm. Business servs avail. Picnic tables. Cr cds: A, D, DS, JCB, MC, V.

✔ ★ **BEST WESTERN ORANGE PARK.** *(300 Park Ave, Orange Park 32073) S on US 17, at I-295 Bypass. 904/264-1211; FAX 904/269-6756.* 201 rms, 2 story. S $60; D $65; each addl $5. Crib free. Pet accepted; $25. TV; cable (premium). Pool; wading pool. Complimentary coffee in rms. Restaurant 6-11 am, 5-10 pm. Rm serv. Bar. Coin lndry.

Meeting rms. Business servs avail. Valet serv. Golf privileges. Some refrigerators, microwaves. Health club privileges. Cr cds: A, C, D, DS, MC, V. ⓓ ⟵ ≋ ✕ ⚒ SC

✔★ **ECONOMY INNS OF AMERICA.** *4300 Salisbury Rd (32216), in Baymeadows.* 904/281-0198. 124 rms, 3 story. S $42.90; D $49.90. Pet accepted. TV; cable (premium). Heated pool. Complimentary continental bkfst. Ck-out 11 am. Business servs avail. Cr cds: A, MC, V. ⓓ ⟵ ≋ ✕ ⚒ SC

★★ **HOMEWOOD SUITES.** *8737 Baymeadows Rd (32256), in Baymeadows.* 904/733-9299; FAX 904/448-5889. 116 kit. suites, 2-3 story. Suites $112-$165; wkly, monthly rates; higher rates special events. Crib free. Pet accepted, some restrictions; $75. TV; cable (premium), VCR (movies $5.50). Pool; whirlpool. Complimentary continental bkfst. Complimentary coffee in rms. Ck-out noon. Coin lndry. Meeting rms. Business center. In-rm modem link. Valet serv. Exercise equipt; weights, stair machine. Microwaves. Balconies. Grills. Cr cds: A, C, D, DS, MC, V. ⓓ ⟵ ≋ ⚳ ✕ ⚒ SC ⚓

★★ **LA QUINTA.** *8555 Blanding Blvd (32244), south of downtown.* 904/778-9539; FAX 904/779-5214. 122 rms, 2 story. S $58; D $65; each addl $7; under 18 free. Crib free. Pet accepted, some restrictions. TV. Pool. Complimentary continental bkfst. Restaurant adj open 24 hrs. Ck-out noon. Meeting rms. Business servs avail. In-rm modem link. Health club privileges. Microwaves avail. Cr cds: A, D, DS, MC, V. ⓓ ⟵ ≋ ✕ ⚒ SC

★★ **LA QUINTA-BAYMEADOWS.** *8255 Dix Ellis Trail (32256), in Baymeadows.* 904/731-9940; FAX 904/731-3854. 106 rms, 2 story. S $59-$70; D $66-$77; under 18 free. Crib free. Pet accepted. TV; cable (premium). Pool. Complimentary continental bkfst. Restaurant nearby. Ck-out noon. Guest lndry. Business servs avail. In-rm modem link. Valet serv. Health club privileges. Microwaves avail. Cr cds: A, C, D, DS, JCB, MC, V. ⓓ ⟵ ≋ ✕ ⚒ SC

★★ **RAMADA INN-MANDARIN CONFERENCE CENTER.** *3130 Hartley Rd (32257), in Mandarin.* 904/268-8080; FAX 904/262-8718. 150 rms, 2 story. S, D $52-$69; each addl $5; suites $115; family rates. Crib free. Pet accepted, some restrictions. TV; cable. Pool; wading pool. Complimentary full bkfst Mon-Fri; continental bkfst wkends. Restaurant 6:30 am-2 pm, 5-9 pm; Fri, Sat to 10 pm. Rm serv. Bar 4 pm-midnight; pianist, comedy Tues-Sat. Ck-out noon. Meeting rms. Valet serv. Large stone fireplace in lobby. Cr cds: A, C, D, DS, MC, V. ⓓ ⟵ ≋ ✕ ⚒ SC

✔★ **RED ROOF INN.** *6099 Youngerman Circle (32244), south of downtown.* 904/777-1000; FAX 904/777-1005. 108 rms, 2 story. S, D $39-$49; each addl $6; under 18 free. Crib free. Pet accepted, some restrictions. TV; cable. Complimentary coffee in lobby. Ck-out noon. Business servs avail. In-rm modem link. Cr cds: A, C, D, DS, MC, V. ⓓ ⟵ ✕ ⚒

★★ **RESIDENCE INN BY MARRIOTT.** *8365 Dix Ellis Trail (32256), in Baymeadows.* 904/733-8088; FAX 904/731-8354. 112 kit. suites, 2 story. Kit. suites $119-$160. Crib free. Pet accepted; $50. TV; cable (premium), VCR avail (movies $6). Heated pool; whirlpools. Complimentary continental bkfst. Restaurant nearby. Ck-out noon. Coin lndry. Meeting rms. Business servs avail. In-rm modem link. Health club privileges. Microwaves. Grills. Cr cds: A, C, D, DS, JCB, MC, V. ⓓ ⟵ ≋ ✕ ⚒ SC

Motor Hotel

★★★ **HOLIDAY INN-AIRPORT NORTH.** *PO Drawer 18409 (32229), 12 mi N on Airport Rd, at I-95, near Intl Airport, north of downtown.* 904/741-4404; FAX 904/741-4907. Web www.travelbase.com/destinations/jacksonville/holi day-airport. 489 rms, 2-6 story. S, D, studio rms $70-$92; under 18 free. Crib free. Pet accepted. TV; cable (premium), VCR avail. 3 pools, 1 indoor/outdoor; poolside serv. Restaurant 6 am-10 pm. Rm serv. Bar 11-2 am. Ck-out noon. Coin lndry. Convention facilities. Business center. In-rm modem link. Bellhops. Sundries. Gift shop. Free airport transportation. Lighted tennis. Exercise equipt; weights, bicycles. Game rm. Microwaves avail. Luxury level. Cr cds: A, C, D, DS, JCB, MC, V. ⓓ ⟵ ⚳ ≋ ✕ ✕ ⚒ SC ⚓

Key West *(See also Marathon)*

Motels

★★ **HAMPTON INN.** *2801 N Roosevelt Blvd (US 1).* 305/294-2917; FAX 305/296-0221. 157 rms, 2 story. Jan-Apr: S, D $159-$179; under 18 free; higher rates: hols, some special events; lower rates rest of yr. Crib free. Pet accepted, some restrictions. TV; cable (premium). Pool; whirlpool. Complimentary continental bkfst. Bar noon-11 pm. Ck-out noon. Coin lndry. Gift shop. Some covered parking. Two-level sun deck overlooking bay. Cr cds: A, C, D, DS, MC, V. ⓓ ⟵ ≋ ✕ ⚒ SC

★ **KEY LODGE.** *1004 Duval St. 305/296-9915; res: 800/458-1296.* 24 rms, 7 kit. units. Mid-Dec-Apr: S, D $140-$163; each addl $15; kit. units $145-$163; higher rates: hols, special events; lower rates rest of yr. Pet accepted; $10/day. TV; cable. Heated pool. Restaurant nearby. Ck-out 11 am. Refrigerators. Cr cds: A, DS, MC, V.

Resort

★ **SUGAR LOAF LODGE.** *(Box 148, Sugar Loaf Key 33044) 13 mi NE on Overseas Hwy (US 1), at mile marker 17. 305/745-3211; FAX 305/745-3389.* 55 rms. 11 kits. Mid-Dec-Apr: S $105; D $110; each addl $10; kit. units $120; under 12 free; lower rates rest of yr. Crib $5. Pet accepted; $10/day. TV; cable. Pool. Restaurant 7:30 am-10 pm. Rm serv. Box lunches. Bar; entertainment Fri-Sat. Ck-out 11 am, ck-in 1 pm. Grocery. Coin lndry. In-rm modem link. Tennis. Miniature golf. Lawn games. Balconies. Dolphin show. Marina; charter boats. Cr cds: A, C, D, DS, MC, V.

Kissimmee (See also Orlando, Winter Haven)

Motels

★ ★ **HOLIDAY INN.** *5678 Irlo Bronson Memorial Hwy (34746). 407/396-4488; FAX 407/396-8915.* Web www.familyfunhotel.com. 614 rms, 2 story, 110 suites. Mid-Dec-early Jan, Mar-Apr, June-Aug: S, D $109-$130; suites $175-$225; under 18 free; Easter, Dec 25 (3-4 day min stay); higher rates Daytona 500; lower rates rest of yr. Crib free. Pet accepted, some restrictions. TV; cable, VCR (movies). Restaurant 6:30 am-10 pm. Rm serv. Ck-out 11 am. Business servs avail. In-rm modem link. Bellhops. Valet serv. Concierge. Sundries. Gift shop. Coin lndry. Lighted tennis. Exercise equipt; weight machine, stair machine. Pool; wading pool, whirlpool, poolside serv. Playground. Supervised child's activities ages 3-12. Game rm. Refrigerators, microwaves. Cr cds: A, C, D, DS, ER, JCB, MC, V.

✔ ★ **HOWARD JOHNSON.** *2323 E Irlo Bronson Memorial Hwy (US 192) (34744). 407/846-4900; FAX 407/846-4900, ext. 333.* 200 rms, 2 story. Mid-Feb-mid-Apr, mid-June-mid-Aug, mid-Dec-Jan 1: S, D $49-$84; each addl $5; under 18 free; lower rates rest of yr. Crib free. Pet accepted, some restrictions; $5. Pool. Restaurant 7 am-10 pm. Ck-out noon. Coin lndry. Business servs avail. In-rm modem link. Game rm. Microwaves avail. Cr cds: A, C, D, DS, ER, JCB, MC, V.

★ **INNS OF AMERICA-MAINGATE.** *2945 Entry Point Blvd (34747). 407/396-7743; FAX 407/396-6307.* 117 rms, 3 story. Late May-mid-Aug: S, D $55-$70; suites $69-$90; higher rates wk of Easter & Christmas; lower rates rest of yr. Pet accepted, some restrictions. TV; cable (premium). Heated pool. Complimentary continental bkfst. Restaurant adj 7 am-11 pm. Ck-out 11 am. Coin lndry. Refrigerator in suites. Cr cds: A, MC, V.

Lakeland (See also Zephyrhills)

Motel

★ ★ **WELLESLEY INN AND SUITES.** *3520 N US 98 (33805). 941/859-3399; FAX 941/859-3483.* 106 rms, 6 story, 24 suites. Jan-Apr: S, D $99.99-$109.99; each addl $10; suites $104.99-$159.99; under 18 free; wkend rates. Crib free. Pet accepted; $10. TV; cable (premium). Heated pool. Complimentary continental bkfst. Complimentary coffee in rms. Restaurant nearby. Ck-out 11 am. Coin lndry. Meeting rms. Business servs avail. Health club privileges. Refrigerator in suites; microwaves avail. Cr cds: A, C, D, DS, MC, V.

Longboat Key (& Lido Beach) (See also Bradenton, Sarasota)

Motel

★ **AZURE TIDES RESORT.** *(1330 Ben Franklin Dr, Sarasota 34236) 1 mi SW of St Armands Circle Dr in Lido Beach. 941/388-2101; FAX 941/388-3015; res: 800/326-8433.* 65 units, 2 & 3 story. Late Dec-mid-Apr: S, D $135-$150; kit. suites $165-$225; wkly rates; lower rates rest of yr. Crib free. Pet accepted, some restrictions; $50 refundable. TV; cable, VCR avail. Heated pool. Restaurant nearby. Bar. Ck-out 11 am. Coin lndry. Business servs avail. In-rm modem link. Some microwaves. Balconies. On gulf. Cr cds: A, C, D, DS, ER, MC, V.

Marathon

Motel

★ **RAINBOW BEND RESORT.** *Rte 1, Box 159, On Grassy Key, 5 mi NE on Overseas Hwy (US 1), at mile marker 58.* 305/289-1505; FAX 305/743-0257; res: 800/929-1505. 24 units, 1-2 story, 20 kits. Mid-Dec-mid-Apr: S, D, kit. units $120-$210; each addl $17.50; lower rates rest of yr. Crib free. Pet accepted. TV; cable (premium), VCR avail (movies). Pool; whirlpool. Complimentary full bkfst. Restaurant 7:30-9:30 am, 5-11 pm. Ck-out noon. Coin lndry. Business servs avail. Picnic tables, grills. On Beach; fishing pier; Boston whaler boats, sailboats, canoes. Cr cds: A, DS, MC, V. 🐾 🐾 ⛱ 🔥 SC

Marco Island *(See also Naples)*

Motel

★ ★ **THE BOATHOUSE.** *1180 Edington Place (34145), in Old Marco Village.* 941/642-2400; FAX 941/642-2435; res: 800/528-6345. E-mail boat housem@aol.com. 20 rms, 2 story. S, D $82.50-$137.50; each addl $15. TV; cable. Pool. Restaurant nearby. Ck-out 11 am. Coin lndry. Business servs avail. Some microwaves. Balconies. Picnic tables. Built 1883; French doors, antiques. On entrance to Collier Bay; dockage. Cr cds: MC, V.

🐾 🐾 ⛱ 🔥

Marianna

Motel

★ **COMFORT INN.** *Box 1507 (32447), On FL 71N, at jct I-10 exit 21.* 850/526-5600; FAX 850/482-7899. 80 rms, 2 story. S $48-$60; D $52-$60; each addl $4; under 18 free. Crib free. Pet accepted. TV; cable (premium). Pool. Complimentary continental bkfst. Restaurant nearby. Ck-out 11 am. Coin lndry. Business servs avail. Cr cds: A, C, D, DS, MC, V. D 🐾 ⛱ 🔄 🔥 SC

Miami

Motels

(Rates are usually higher during football, Bowl games)

★ **HAMPTON INN.** *2500 Brickell Ave (33129), I-95 exit 1, south of downtown.* 305/854-2070; FAX 305/856-5055. 69 rms, 3 story. Jan-Apr & Dec: S $82.95-$89.95; D $89.95; under 18 free; lower rates rest of yr. Crib free. Pet accepted. TV; cable. Pool. Complimentary continental bkfst. Bar 3-11 pm. Ck-out noon. Meeting rms. Business servs avail. In-rm modem link. Valet serv. Cr cds: A, C, D, DS, MC, V. D 🐾 ⛱ 🔄 🔥 SC

✔ ★ ★ **QUALITY INN SOUTH.** *14501 S Dixie Hwy (33176), south of downtown.* 305/251-2000; FAX 305/235-2225. 100 rms, 2 story, 14 kits. Dec-Apr: S $73-$90; D $79-$96; each addl $5; kit. units $96; under 18 free; varied lower rates rest of yr. Crib free. Pet accepted. TV; cable (premium). Heated pool. Restaurant 6:30 am-10 pm; Fri & Sat to 11 pm. Rm serv. Ck-out 11 am. Coin lndry. Cr cds: A, C, D, DS, JCB, MC, V.

🐾 ⛱ 🔄 🔥 SC

Motor Hotel

★ ★ **AMERISUITES.** *11520 SW 88th St (33176), south of downtown.* 305/279-8688; FAX 305/279-7907. 67 suites, 5 story. Dec-Apr: suites $129-$149; under 16 free; wkend rates; higher rates Boat Show, Grand Prix; lower rates rest of yr. Crib avail. Pet accepted, some restrictions. TV; cable (premium), VCR. Complimentary continental bkfst. Complimentary coffee in rms. Restaurant nearby. Rm serv 11 am-10 pm. Ck-out 11 am. Meeting rms. Business center. In-rm modem link. Bellhops. Valet serv. Concierge. Coin lndry. 18-hole golf privileges, greens fee $30-$50, pro, putting green, driving range. Pool. Refrigerators, microwaves, wet bar. Cr cds: A, C, D, DS, MC, V.

D 🐾 🎿 ⛱ 🔄 🔥 SC 🏌

Hotel

★ ★ ★ **GROVE ISLE CLUB & RESORT.** *4 Grove Isle Dr (33133), in Coconut Grove.* 305/858-8300; FAX 305/858-5908; res: 800/88GROVE. 50 rms, 5 story, 9 suites. Oct-mid-Apr: S $295; D $315; suites $420-$550; under 14 free; lower rates rest of yr. Crib free. Pet accepted, some restrictions. TV; cable (premium), VCR. Pool; whirlpool, poolside serv. Playground. Complimentary coffee in rms. Restaurant 7:30 am-10 pm.

Bar. Ck-out noon. Meeting rms. Business servs avail. Concierge. Gift shop. Barber, beauty shop. Lighted tennis, pro. Exercise equipt; weights, bicycles. Refrigerators. Balconies. On Biscayne Bay. Cr cds: A, D, MC, V. 🄳 💤 💤 🏋 ⛤ 🏃 ⛤ ⬜ 🔥

Miami Intl Airport Area (See also Miami)

Motor Hotels

★ ★ **AMERISUITES.** (3655 NW 82nd Ave, Miami 33166) 305/718-8292; FAX 305/718-8295. 126 suites, 6 story. Jan-Mar: suites $129-$149; under 18 free; wkly, wkend, hol rates; higher rates Grand Prix Doral Ryder; lower rates rest of yr. Crib free. Pet accepted, some restrictions; $10. TV; cable (premium), VCR. Complimentary continental bkfst. Complimentary coffee in rms. Restaurant adj 9 am-midnight. Ck-out 11 am. Meeting rms. Business center. In-rm modem link. Coin lndry. Free airport transportation. Exercise equipt; weight machine, bicycle. Pool. Refrigerators, micro-waves. Cr cds: A, C, D, DS, MC, V. 🄳 💤 🏊 🏃 ⛤ ⬜ 🔥 SC 🏊

★ ★ **HAMPTON INN.** (3620 NW 79th Ave, Miami 33166) 305/513-0777; FAX 305/513-9019. 129 rms, 6 story. Dec-Apr: S $99-$109; D $109-$119; under 18 free; wkend, hol rates; golf plans; higher rates Doral Open, Boat Show; lower rates rest of yr. Crib free. Pet accepted, some restrictions. TV; cable (premium), VCR avail. Complimentary continental bkfst. Restaurant adj 7 am-10 pm. Ck-out 11 am. Meeting rms. Business center. In-rm modem link. Valet serv. Free airport transportation. Pool. Some refrigerators; microwaves avail. Cr cds: A, C, D, DS, MC, V. 🄳 💤 🏊 ⛤ ⬜ 🔥 SC 🏊

Hotels

★ ★ **CLUB HOTEL BY DOUBLETREE.** (1101 NW 57th Ave, Miami 33126) Jct FL 836 & Red Rd exit (57th Ave). 305/266-0000; FAX 305/266-9179. 266 rms, 10 story. Jan-Mar: S $95-$125; D $105-$135; suites $190-$215; under 18 free; higher rates Boat Show; lower rates rest of yr. Crib free. Pet accepted. TV; cable (premium). Pool; wading pool. Complimentary coffee in rms. Restaurant 6 am-11 pm. Bar 4-11 pm. Ck-out noon. Coin lndry. Meeting rms. Business center. Free airport transportation. Refrigerators avail. Cr cds: A, C, D, DS, JCB, MC, V.
🄳 💤 🏊 🏃 ⛤ ⬜ 🔥 SC 🏊

★ ★ ★ **MARRIOTT-AIRPORT.** (1201 NW LeJeune Rd, Miami 33126) SW of FL 836. 305/649-5000; FAX 305/642-3369. 365 rms, 10 story. Dec-Apr: S, D $139-$169; family, wkend rates; lower rates rest of yr. Crib free. Pet accepted, some restrictions. TV; cable (premium). Pool. Restaurant 6-1 am. Bars 11-2 am. Meeting rms. Business center. In-rm modem link. Gift shop. Barber, beauty shop. Free airport transportation. Lighted tennis, pro. Exercise equipt; weights, bicycles, whirlpool. Rec rm. Private patios. Luxury level. Cr cds: A, C, D, DS, ER, JCB, MC, V. 🄳 💤 🏋 🏊 🏃 ⛤ ⬜ 🔥 SC 🏊

★ ★ ★ **SOFITEL.** (5800 Blue Lagoon Dr, Miami 33126) S of East-West Expy (Dolphin Expy, FL 836) via Red Rd (FL 959), W on Blue Lagoon Dr. 305/264-4888; FAX 305/262-9049. 281 rms, 15 story, 27 suites. S, D $179-$225; each addl $30; suites $219-$599; under 17 free; wkend packages. Crib free. Pet accepted, some restrictions. Valet parking $5. TV; cable (premium). Pool. Restaurant 6 am-11 pm. Bar 11-2 am; entertainment. Ck-out noon. Meeting rms. Business servs avail. In-rm modem link. Concierge. Gift shop. Lighted tennis. Exercise equipt; weights, bicycles. On lagoon. Cr cds: A, C, D, DS, MC, V.
🄳 💤 🏋 🏊 🏃 ⛤ ⬜ 🔥 SC

Miami Beach (See also Miami)

Hotels

★ ★ ★ **FONTAINEBLEAU HILTON RESORT AND TOWERS.** 4441 Collins Ave (33140). 305/538-2000; FAX 305/531-9274. Web www.hilton.com. 1,206 rms, 17 story. Mid-Nov-May: S $205-$325; D $235-$395; each addl $25; suites $500-$800; family rates; package plans; lower rates rest of yr. Crib free. Pet accepted, some restrictions. TV; cable (premium). Saltwater pool, 1/2-acre heated lagoon pool; whirlpool, poolside serv. Supervised child's activities. Restaurant 6:30-2 am. Bars; entertainment. Ck-out 11 am. Convention facilities. Business center. In-rm modem link. Concierge. Shopping arcade. Barber, beauty shop. Airport transportation. 7 lighted tennis courts, pro. Exercise rm; instructor, weights, bicycles, steam rm, sauna. Rec rm. Lawn games. Some refrigerators, minibars; microwaves avail. Balconies. Tropical gardens, rocky waterfall into pool. On ocean; dockage, catamarans, jet skis, paddle boats, para-sailing. Luxury level. Cr cds: A, C, D, DS, ER, JCB, MC, V.
🄳 💤 🏋 🏊 🏃 ⛤ ⬜ 🔥 🏊

★ ★ **SEACOAST SUITES.** 5101 Collins Ave (33140). 305/865-5152; FAX 305/868-4090; res: 800/523-3671 (exc FL), 800/624-8769 (FL). E-mail seacoast@sobe.com. 73 kit.

suites (1-2 bedrm), 16-17 story. Early Dec-Apr: kit. suites $185-$425; 7-day min special events, hols; lower rates rest of yr. Crib $5. Pet accepted. TV; cable (premium). Complimentary coffee in rms. Bar. Ck-out noon. Beauty shop. Coin lndry. Valet parking. Heated pool. Lighted tennis. Exercise equipt; bicycles, treadmills. Health club privileges. Game rm. Rec rm. Minibars. Balconies. On ocean, private beach; marina. Cr cds: A, D, DS, MC, V.

★ ★ ★ **SHERATON-BAL HARBOUR.** *(9701 Collins Ave, Bal Harbour 33154) 5 mi N on FL A1A.* 305/865-7511; FAX 305/864-2601. 668 rms, 15 story. Mid-Dec-mid-Apr: S, D $289-$389; suites $550-$1,500; lower rates rest of yr. Crib free. Pet accepted, some restrictions. Valet parking $12. TV; cable (premium), VCR avail (movies). 2 heated pools; wading pool. Supervised child's activities. Coffee in rms. Restaurants 6:30 am-10 pm. Bars 11-1:30 am. Ck-out noon. Convention facilities. Business center. In-rm modem link. Concierge. Lighted tennis, pro shop. Golf privileges. Exercise equipt; weights, bicycles. Massage. Game rm. Minibars. Refrigerators avail. Many balconies. Tropical gardens. On 10 acres at oceanfront; boat rental, water sports. Cr cds: A, C, D, DS, ER, JCB, MC, V.

Inn

✔ ★ ★ ★ **BAY HARBOR INN.** *(9660 E Bay Harbor Dr, Bay Harbor Islands 33154) N via Collins Ave, near Broad Causeway.* 305/868-4141; FAX 305/867-9094. 38 rms, 2 story, 12 suites. Dec-Apr: S $90; D $130; each addl $25; suites $120-$130; under 12 free; higher rates hols (3-day min); lower rates rest of yr. Crib free. Pet accepted, some restrictions. TV; cable. Heated pool. Complimentary continental bkfst. Restaurant 10:30 am-11 pm. Ck-out 11 am, ck-in 3 pm. Business servs avail. Some refrigerators. Inn (1948) located on scenic Indian Creek. Cr cds: A, C, D, MC, V.

Naples *(See also Marco Island)*

Motels

★ **HOWARD JOHNSON.** *221 9th St S (US 41) (34102).* 941/262-6181; FAX 941/262-0318. E-mail napleshojo@sprintmail.com. 101 rms, 2 story. Mid-Dec-mid-Apr: S, D $80-$155; under 18 free; lower rates rest of yr. Crib free. Pet accepted, some restrictions; $25. TV; cable (premium). Heated pool; poolside serv. Playground. Restaurant adj. Ck-out noon. Business servs avail. Lawn games. Bicycle rentals. Some refrigerators. Microwaves avail. Private patios, balconies. Cr cds: A, C, D, DS, ER, JCB, MC, V.

✔ ★ ★ **RED ROOF.** *1925 Davis Blvd (34104).* 941/774-3117; FAX 941/775-5333. E-mail jchizmar@redroofinn.com. 156 rms, 3 story, 29 kits. Dec-Apr: S, D $69-$79; each addl $10; kit. suites $109-$119; under 18 free; lower rates rest of yr. Crib free. Pet accepted, some restrictions. TV; cable (premium). Pool; whirlpool. Restaurant adj 6 am-midnight. Ck-out 11 am. Guest lndry. Business servs avail. Lawn games. Refrigerators; microwaves avail. Private patios. Picnic tables, grills. Marina adj. Beach 1 mi. Cr cds: A, C, D, DS, MC, V.

★ ★ **WELLESLEY INN.** *1555 5th Ave S (34102).* 941/793-4646; FAX 941/793-5248. 105 rms, 3 story. Late Dec-Apr: S, D $69-$129; under 18 free; lower rates rest of yr. Crib free. Pet accepted, some restrictions; $5. TV; cable (premium). Pool. Complimentary continental bkfst. Coffee in rms. Restaurant adj 11 am-10 pm. Ck-out 11 am. Business servs avail. Some refrigerators; microwaves avail. Cr cds: A, C, D, DS, MC, V.

Resort

★ ★ **WORLD TENNIS CENTER & RESORT.** *4800 Airport-Pulling Rd (34105).* 941/263-1900; FAX 941/649-7855; res: 800/292-6663 (US), 800/621-6665 (CAN). 148 2-bedrm apts, 2 story. Feb-Apr: 1-4 persons $175; wkly, monthly rates; lower rates rest of yr. Pet accepted; some restrictions. Maid serv avail (fee). TV; cable. Heated pool; whirlpool, poolside serv. Ck-out 11 am, ck-in 3 pm. Grocery 1 mi. 16 tennis courts, 10 lighted, pro. Microwaves avail. Private patios, balconies. Mediterranean village atmosphere on 82½ acres. Tennis stadium. Cr cds: A, DS, MC, V.

New Port Richey *(See also Brooksville, Clearwater)*

Motel

✔ ★ **DAYS INN AND LODGE.** *(11736 US 19N, Port Richey 34668) On US 19, ⅛ mi S of FL 52.* 813/863-1502. E-mail aol@daysinn.com; web gminet.com/dayspr. 156 rms, 2 story, 35 apts. Feb-Apr: S, D $55-$75; each addl $5; apts $65-$90; under 13 free; monthly rates; lower rates rest of yr. Crib free. Pet accepted; $5 per day. TV; cable (premium).

Heated pool. Complimentary continental bkfst. Ck-out 11 am. Coin lndry. Business servs avail. Refrigerators, microwaves avail. Cr cds: A, C, D, DS, JCB, MC, V.

D ✔ ≈ ⊠ ⋌ SC

Ocala *(See also Silver Springs)*

Motel

✔★★ **HOLIDAY INN.** *3621 W Silver Springs Blvd (34475).* 352/629-0381; FAX 352/629-0381, ext. 42. 272 rms, 2 story. Jan-Apr: S, D $55-$65; under 18 free; lower rates rest of yr. Crib free. Pet accepted, some restrictions. TV; cable (premium). Heated pool. Restaurant 6 am-10 pm. Rm serv. Bar 1 pm-2 am; entertainment. Ck-out noon. Meeting rms. Business servs avail. In-rm modem link. Bellhops. Free RR station, bus depot transportation. Cr cds: A, C, D, DS, MC, V. D ✔ ≈ ⊠ ⋌ SC

Okeechobee

Motels

✔★ **BUDGET INN.** *201 S Parrott Ave (34974).* 941/763-3185. 24 units, 5 kits. Nov-Apr: S $35-$65; D $45-$75; each addl $5; kit. units $7 addl; under 12 free; higher rates special events; lower rates rest of yr. Crib $8. Pet accepted; $3. TV; cable (premium). Pool. Complimentary coffee. Restaurant adj. Ck-out 11 am. Business servs avail. In-rm modem links. Microwaves avail. Cr cds: A, DS, MC, V. ✔ ≈ ⊠ ⋌ SC

★ **ECONOMY INN.** *507 N Parrott Ave (34972).* 941/763-1148; FAX 941/763-1149. 24 rms. Feb-Mar: S $49; D $59; Apr-Jan: S $29, D $39; each addl $5; lower rates rest of yr. Pet accepted. TV; cable. Restaurant nearby. Ck-out 11 am. Business servs avail. Cr cds: A, DS, MC, V. ✔ ⊠ ⋌ SC

Orlando *(See also Altamonte Springs, Kissimmee, Walt Disney World, Winter Park)*

Motels

★ **ECONO LODGE.** *5859 American Way (32819), in International Drive Area.* 407/345-8880; FAX 407/363-9366. 192 rms, 4 story. Mid-Feb-mid-Apr, June-early Sept, late Dec: S, D $59-88; each addl $6; under 18 free; lower rates rest of yr. Crib $6. Pet accepted, some restrictions. TV; cable. Heated pool. Complimentary coffee in lobby. Restaurant adj open 24 hrs. Ck-out 11 am. Coin lndry. Business servs avail. Gift shop. Free transportation to area attractions. Game rm. Cr cds: A, C, D, DS, ER, JCB, MC, V. ✔ ≈ ⊠ ⋌ SC

★★ **GATEWAY INN.** *7050 Kirkman Rd (32819), east of I-4, in International Drive Area.* 407/351-2000; FAX 407/363-1835; res: 800/327-3808. 354 rms, 2 story. Feb-mid-Apr, early June-early Sept, mid-Dec-early Jan: S, D $74-94; each addl $6; under 18 free; lower rates rest of yr. Crib $3. Pet accepted, some restrictions. TV; cable. 2 pools, heated; wading pool, poolside serv. Playground. Restaurant 7 am-10 pm. Bar 11:30-2 am; entertainment. Ck-out 11 am. Coin lndry. Meeting rm. Business servs avail. Bellhops. Sundries. Gift shop. Free transportation to area attractions. Miniature golf. Game rm. Lawn games. Picnic tables. Cr cds: A, C, D, ER, MC, V. ✔ ≈ ⊠ ⋌ SC

★★ **RESIDENCE INN BY MARRIOT ORLANDO INTL DRIVE.** *7975 Canada Ave (32819), south of downtown.* 407/345-0117; FAX 407/352-2689. E-mail riorlando@bell south.net; web marriottresidence inn.com. 176 kit. suites (1-2 bedrm). S, D $104-$199; wkly, monthly rates. Crib free. Pet accepted; some restrictions. Heated pool; whirlpools. Complimentary continental bkfst. Restaurant nearby. Ck-out 11 am. Coin lndry. Meeting rms. Business servs avail. Valet serv. Many fireplaces; microwaves avail. Balconies. Grills. Lighted sports court. Cr cds: A, C, D, DS, JCB, MC, V. D ✔ ≈ ⊠ ⋌ SC

Motor Hotels

★★★ **DELTA ORLANDO RESORT.** *5715 Major Blvd (32819), jct FL 435 & I-4 exit 30B at entrance of Universal Studios, south of downtown.* 407/351-3340; FAX 407/351-5117; res: 800/634-4763. E-mail deltaor@magic net.net; web www.intpro.com /delta. 800 units, 4 story. Mid-Feb-Apr, mid-June-Aug, late Dec: S, D $118-$158; suites $175-$475; under 18 free; lower rates rest of yr. Crib free. Pet accepted, some restrictions; $25. TV; cable (premium). 3 pools, heated; wading pools, whirlpools, sauna, poolside serv. Playground. Free supervised child's activities; ages 4-12. Restaurants 6:30 am-midnight. Child's meals. Rm serv. Bar 11:30-2 am; entertainment. Ck-out 11 am. Coin lndry. Convention facilities. Business servs avail. Bellhops. Valet serv. Airport transportation. Free transportation to area attractions. Concierge. Sundries. Gift shop. Lighted tennis. Golf privileges. Miniature golf. Game rm. Lawn games. Microwaves avail. Private balconies. Cr cds: A, C, D, DS, ER, JCB, MC, V. D ✔ ⋔ ⌇ ≈ ⊠ ⋌ SC

✔ ★ **QUALITY INN-PLAZA.** *9000 International Dr (32819), in International Drive Area. 407/345-8585; FAX 407/352-6839.* 1,020 rms, 4-10 story. S, D $34-$79. Crib free. Pet accepted, some restrictions; $5. TV; cable. 3 pools, heated. Restaurant 6:30-10:30 am, 5:30-9:30 pm. Bar 4 pm-2 am. Ck-out 11 am. Coin lndry. Business servs avail. Gift shop. Health club privileges. Game rm. Cr cds: A, C, D, DS, ER, JCB, MC, V.

✔ ★ **RODEWAY INN INTERNATIONAL.** *6327 International Drive (32819), in International Drive Area. 407/351-4444; FAX 407/352-5806.* 315 rms, 4-9 story. Mid Dec-Jan 1, June-Sept: S, D $59.95; lower rates rest of yr. Crib free. Pet accepted, some restrictions. TV; cable, VCR (movies). Heated pool. Restaurant 6:30-10:30 am, 5:30-9 pm. Bar 6 pm-midnight. Ck-out 11 am. Coin lndry. Meeting rm. Valet serv. Sundries. Gift shop. Health club privileges. Game rm. Refrigerators avail. Cr cds: A, C, D, DS, ER, JCB, MC, V.

Ormond Beach *(See also Daytona Beach, DèLand)*

Motels

(Rates may be higher during race week)

✔ ★ **BUDGET HOST INN.** *1633 N US 1 (32074), I-95 exit 89. 904/677-7310; FAX 904/677-7310, ext. 310.* 64 rms, 2 story. Jan-Apr: S, D $40-$125; each addl $6; under 18 free; higher rates: hols, special events; lower rates rest of yr. Crib free. Pet accepted, some restrictions. TV; cable. Pool; wading pool. Playground. Complimentary continental bkfst. Ck-out 11 am. Coin lndry. Private patios; some balconies. Cr cds: A, DS, MC, V.

★ **COMFORT INN INTERSTATE.** *1567 N US 1 (32174), I-95 exit 89. 904/672-8621; FAX 904/672-8621.* 75 rms, 2 story. Feb-Apr: S, D $69.95-$89.95; under 18 free; higher rates: Daytona races, spring break; lower rates rest of yr. Crib free. Pet accepted. TV; cable. Pool. Complimentary continental bkfst. Restaurant adj open 24 hrs. Ck-out noon. Coin lndry. Business servs avail. Lawn games. Cr cds: A, C, D, DS, ER, JCB, MC, V.

★ **COMFORT INN ON THE BEACH.** *507 S Atlantic Ave (FL A1A) (32176). 904/677-8550; FAX 904/673-6260.* 49 units, 4 story, 26 kits. Feb-Apr, June-Labor Day: S, D $60-$90; each addl $5; kit. units $65-$95; under 18 free; higher rates: Easter, July 4, special events; lower rates rest of yr. Crib $5. Pet accepted, some restrictions; $5. TV; cable. Heated pool; wading pool. Ck-out 11 am. Complimentary continental bkfst. Restaurant adj. Golf privileges. Lawn games. Many private patios, balconies. On ocean, beach. Cr cds: A, C, D, DS, ER, JCB, MC, V.

★ **TOPAZ.** *(1224 S Ocean Shore Blvd, Flagler Beach 32136) 12 mi N, I-95 exit 91. 904/439-3301; res: 800/555-4735.* 58 rms, 2 story. Feb-Apr: S, D $96-$170; each addl $5-$10; kit. units $71-$91; under 12 free; wkly, monthly rates; higher rates: special events, hols; lower rates rest of yr. Crib $5. Pet accepted, some restrictions; $10. TV; cable, VCR (free movies). Pool. Restaurant 5:30-9:30 pm. Ck-out 11 am. Coin lndry. Some balconies. Swimming beach. Cr cds: A, DS, MC, V.

Palm Beach *(See also West Palm Beach)*

Hotels

★ ★ ★ ★ **CHESTERFIELD HOTEL.** *363 Cocoanut Row. 561/659-5800; FAX 561/659-6707; res: 800/243-7871.* With a little pretense, a lot of chintz and brass and a superabundance of service, this hotel may be a Mizner copy, but it has an English-country-style elegance all its own. 55 rms, 3 story, 11 suites. Mid-Dec-Apr: S, D $185-$280; suites $375-$800; lower rates rest of yr. Crib free. Pet accepted; $150 deposit. TV; cable, VCR avail. Pool; whirlpool, poolside serv. Restaurant 7 am-11 pm. Afternoon refreshments. Rm serv 24 hrs. Bar 11-1 am; pianist. Ck-out noon. Meeting rms. Business center. In-rm modem link. Concierge. Free valet parking. Health club privileges. Cigar rm. Library/reading rms. Ocean 3 blks. Cr cds: A, C, D, DS, ER, MC, V.

★ ★ ★ ★ **THE FOUR SEASONS.** *2800 S Ocean Blvd. 561/582-2800; FAX 561/547-1557.* Web www.fshr.com. This beachside property combines contemporary design with the luxurious detailing of a traditional Floridian resort. There are views of the Atlantic Ocean from many rooms. 210 rms, 4 story. Mid-Dec-mid-Apr: S, D $335-$575; suites $850-$2,000; under 17 free; lower rates rest of yr. Crib free. Pet accepted. Valet parking $10. TV; cable (premium), VCR avail (movies). Heated pool; whirlpool, poolside serv. Free supervised child's activities; from age 3. Restaurants 7 am-10 pm. Rm serv 24 hrs. Bar 4 pm-midnight;

pianist. Ck-out noon. Meeting rms. Business center. In-rm modem link. Concierge. Barber, beauty shop. Airport transportation. Tennis, pro. 18-hole golf privileges, greens fee $50, pro. Exercise rm; instructor, weight machine, bicycles, sauna, steam rm. Massage. Bathrm phones, minibars. Refrigerators, microwaves avail. Balconies. On beach; water sports avail. Cr cds: A, C, D, DS, JCB, MC, V. 🅳 📞 💼 🏋 ≈ 🕴 🏃 ⬚ 🐾 🏄

★★ **HEART OF PALM BEACH.** *160 Royal Palm Way.* 561/655-5600; FAX 561/832-1201; res: 800/523-5377. 88 rms, 2-3 story. Mid-Dec-Apr: S, D $129-$199; each addl $15; suites $275; under 18 free; lower rates rest of yr. Crib free. Pet accepted. TV; cable (premium), VCR (movies). Heated pool; poolside serv. Restaurant 7 am-11 pm. Bar from 11 am. Ck-out noon. Business center. In-rm modem link. Valet serv. Free underground parking. Refrigerators. Bicycle rentals. Private patios, balconies. Cr cds: A, C, D, MC, V. 📞 ≈ ⬚ 🏃 ⬚ 🐾 SC 🏄

Inn

★★★ **PLAZA.** *215 Brazilian Ave.* 561/832-8666; FAX 561/835-8776; res: 800/233-2632. E-mail plazainn@aol.com. 50 rms, 3 story. Mid-Dec-Apr: S, D $125-$215; each addl $15; lower rates rest of yr. Crib free. Pet accepted. TV. Heated pool; whirlpool, poolside serv. Complimentary full bkfst. Dining rm 7:30-10 am. Ck-out noon, ck-in 2 pm. Business servs avail. Bellhops. Health club privileges. Picnic tables. Art deco building (1939) near ocean. Cr cds: A, MC, V. 📞 ≈ 🏃 ⬚ 🐾

Pensacola *(See also Fort Walton Beach; also see Mobile, AL)*

Motels

★★ **RAMADA INN BAYVIEW.** *7601 Scenic Hwy (32504).* 850/477-7155. 150 rms, 2 story. May-Aug: S $64; D $72; each addl $6; under 18 free; hols (3-day min); lower rates rest of yr. Crib free. Pet accepted, some restrictions. TV; cable. Complimentary coffee in rms. Restaurant 6 am-1 pm, 5-10 pm. Rm serv. Bar 5 pm-1 am; entertainment Tues-Sat. Ck-out noon. Meeting rms. Business servs avail. In-rm modem link. Valet serv. Exercise equipt; weight machine, stair machine, sauna. Pool. Some balconies. Cr cds: A, C, D, DS, JCB, MC, V. 🅳 📞 ≈ 🏃 ⬚ 🐾 SC

✔★ **RED ROOF INN.** *7340 Plantation Rd (32504), at University Mall.* 850/476-7960; FAX 850/479-4706. 108 rms, 2 story. S, D $41.99-$63.99; each addl $5-$7; under 18 free. Crib free. Pet accepted. TV; cable. Complimentary coffee in lobby. Restaurant nearby. Ck-out noon. Business servs avail. Cr cds: A, C, D, DS, MC, V. 🅳 📞 ⬚ 🐾

Hotel

★★ **PENSACOLA GRAND HOTEL.** *200 E Gregory St (32501).* 850/433-3336; FAX 850/432-7572; res: 800/348-3336. 212 rms, 15 story. S, D $90-$100; each addl $10; suites $175-$408; family rates; package plans. Crib free. Pet accepted, some restrictions; $50. TV; cable (premium). Heated pool. Complimentary coffee in rms. Restaurant 6:30-10 pm. Bars 2 pm-2 am. Ck-out 1 pm. Meeting rms. Business servs avail. In-rm modem link. Shopping arcade. Free airport transportation. Exercise equipt; weight machine, bicycles. Lobby is restored 1912 Louisville & Nashville Railroad Depot. Cr cds: A, C, D, DS, MC, V. 🅳 📞 ≈ 🏃 ⬚ 🐾 SC

Port Charlotte *(See also Arcadia, Punta Gorda)*

Motels

✔★★ **DAYS INN.** *1941 Tamiami Trail (33948).* 941/627-8900; FAX 941/743-8503. Web www.daysinn.com/daysinn.html. 126 rms, 3 story. Jan-Mar: S $79-$99; D $84-$104; each addl $5; under 17 free; lower rates rest of yr. Crib free. Pet accepted, some restrictions. TV; cable (premium). Heated pool. Complimentary coffee in lobby. Restaurant adj 7-1 am. Rm serv. Ck-out 11 am. Coin lndry. Business servs avail. Exercise equipt; bicycle, stair machine. Health club privileges. Refrigerators; microwaves avail. Cr cds: A, C, D, DS, MC, V. 🅳 📞 ≈ 🏃 ⬚ 🐾 SC

★★ **QUALITY INN.** *3400 Tamiami Trail (US 41) (33952).* 941/625-4181; FAX 941/629-1740. 105 rms, 2 story. S, D $75-$110; each addl $6; under 12 free; higher rates special events. Crib free. Pet accepted, some restrictions; $6. TV; cable. Pool. Complimentary continental bkfst. Bar. Ck-out noon. Coin lndry. Meeting rms. Business servs avail. Lawn games. Some refrigerators. Cr cds: A, C, D, DS, JCB, MC, V. 🅳 📞 ≈ ⬚ 🐾 SC

Punta Gorda (See also Fort Myers, Port Charlotte)

Motor Hotel

★ ★ **BEST WESTERN WATERFRONT.** *300 Retta Esplanade (33950). 941/639-1165; FAX 941/639-8116.* 183 rms, 2-5 story. Jan-Apr: S, D $87-$97; each addl $10; suites $115-$225; under 19 free; lower rates rest of yr. Crib free. Pet accepted, some restrictions; $15. TV; cable (premium). Heated pool. Restaurant 6:30 am-10 pm. Rm serv. Bar; entertainment. Ck-out noon. Coin lndry. Meeting rms. Business servs avail. Valet serv. Sundries. Gift shop. Microwaves avail. Private patios, balconies. On harbor; boat dock. Wilderness tours. Cr cds: A, C, D, DS, JCB, MC, V. 🅓 🐾 🖋 ⚓ 🎿 🐾 SC

St Augustine (See also Jacksonville)

Motel

✔★ **DAYS INN.** *2800 N Ponce de Leon Blvd (32084), in Historical District. 904/829-6581; FAX 904/824-0135.* Web daysinn@aug.com. 124 rms, 2 story. S $45-$105; D $50-$105; each addl $5; under 18, $2; under 12 free; higher rates: hols, special events. Crib free. Pet accepted, some restrictions; $10. TV. Pool. Playground. Restaurant 6-11:30 am. Ck-out noon. Business servs avail. Sundries. Patios. Picnic tables. Cr cds: A, C, D, DS, JCB, MC, V. 🅓 🐾 🖋 ⚓ 🎿 🐾 SC

St Augustine Beach (See also St Augustine)

Motels

★ **BEST WESTERN OCEAN INN.** *3955 FL A1A S. 904/471-8010; FAX 904/460-9124.* Web www.bestwestern.com/best.html. 34 rms, 2 story. Feb-early Sept: S, D $59-$79; each addl $6; under 12 free; higher rates major hols; lower rates rest of yr. Crib $6. Pet accepted, some restrictions; $5/day. TV; cable (premium). Pool. Complimentary continental bkfst. Restaurant adj 7:30 am-10 pm. Ck-out 11 am. Business servs avail. Microwaves avail. 2 blks to beach. Cr cds: A, C, D, DS, MC, V. 🅓 🐾 ⚓ 🎿 🐾 SC

★ ★ **HOLIDAY INN OCEANFRONT.** *860 A1A Beach Blvd. 904/471-2555; FAX 904/461-8450.* 151 rms, 5 story. Feb-mid-Sept: S, D $100-$130; under 18 free; lower rates rest of yr. Crib free. Pet accepted, some restrictions. TV; cable VCR (movies). Pool; poolside serv. Restaurant 7-11:30 am, 5-10 pm. Rm serv. Bar 4 pm-midnight. Ck-out 11 am. Coin lndry. Valet serv. Meeting rms. Business servs avail. Balconies. On beach; ocean views. Cr cds: A, C, D, DS, JCB, MC, V. 🅓 🐾 ⚓ 🎿 🐾 SC

St Petersburg (See also Bradenton, Clearwater, Tampa)

Motels

★ ★ **DAYS INN.** *2595 54th Ave N (33714), I-275, exit 14. 813/522-3191.* 155 rms, 2 story. Feb-mid-Apr: S $45-$55; D $49-$65; each addl $5; under 12 free; lower rates rest of yr. Crib free. Pet accepted; $8 per day. TV; cable (premium). Pool; wading pool. Restaurant 6 am-10 pm; Sun 6 am-8:30 pm. Ck-out 11 am. Coin lndry. Meeting rm. Business servs avail. In-rm modem link. Lawn games. Microwaves avail. Picnic tables. Cr cds: A, C, D, DS, JCB, MC, V. 🅓 🐾 ⚓ SC

★ **LA MARK CHARLES.** *(6200 34th St N, Pinellas Park 33781) I-275, exit 15. 813/527-7334; FAX 813/526-9294; res: 800/448-6781.* 93 rms, 1-2 story, 35 kits. Feb-Apr: S, D $60; each addl $5; suites $65-$70; kit. units $65-$75; under 12 free; lower rates rest of yr. Crib $3. Pet accepted; $35 ($25 refundable). TV. Heated pool; whirlpool. Restaurant 7-10 am. Ck-out 11 am. Meeting rm. Business servs avail. Coin lndry. Sundries. Cr cds: A, DS, MC, V. 🐾 ⚓ 🐾 SC

★ ★ **LA QUINTA INN.** *4999 34th St N (33714), I-275, exit 14. 813/527-8421; FAX 813/527-8851.* 120 rms, 2 story. Mid-Jan-Apr: S $79; D $89; each addl $10; lower rates rest of yr. Pet accepted, some restrictions. TV; cable (premium). Heated pool. Complimentary continental bkfst. Ck-out 11 am. Coin lndry. Meeting rm. Business servs avail. In-rm modem link. Exercise equipt; weights, bicycles, stair machine. Cr cds: A, C, D, DS, MC, V. 🐾 ⚓ 🏋 🎿 🐾 SC

✔★ **VALLEY FORGE.** *6825 Central Ave (33710). 813/345-0135; FAX 813/384-1671.* 27 rms, 8 kits. Mid-Jan-mid-Apr: S, D $45-$65; lower rates rest of yr. Crib $5. Pet accepted; $3-$5. TV; cable (premium), VCR avail. Pool. Restaurant nearby. Ck-out 11 am. Business servs avail. Lawn games. Refrigerators; microwaves avail. Private patios. Cr cds: A, DS, MC, V. 🐾 ⚓ 🐾

Sanibel & Captiva Islands (See also Fort Myers)

Motel

★ ★ 'TWEEN WATERS INN. *(15951 Captiva Dr, Captiva Island 33924) 941/472-5161; FAX 941/472-0249; res: 800/223-5865.* E-mail resv@tween- waters.com. 117 rms, 2 story, 66 kit. units. Dec-Apr: S, D $145-$485; each addl $20; suites $260-$285; kit. units $175-$255; under 12 free; lower rates rest of yr. Crib free. Pet accepted, some restrictions; $10 per day. TV; cable (premium). Heated pool; wading pool, poolside serv. Complimentary coffee in rms. Restaurant 7:30 am-10 pm. Bar 11-2 am; entertainment. Ck-out noon. Coin lndry. Meeting rms. Business servs avail. Bellhops. Concierge. Gift shop. Lighted tennis; pro. Lawn games. Game rm. Exercise rm; instructor, weight machine, stair machine. Balconies. On ocean, swimming beach. Cr cds: A, DS, MC, V.

Sarasota (See also Bradenton, Longboat Key & Lido Beach, Siesta Key, Venice)

Motels

★ ★ BEST WESTERN MIDTOWN. *1425 S Tamiami Trail (34239). 941/955-9841; FAX 941/954-8948.* E-mail bestwestern@earthlink.net; web www.travelweb.com/thisco /bw/10227_b.html. 100 rms, 2-3 story. Jan-Mar: S, D $99-$109; each addl $6; under 18 free; lower rates rest of yr. Crib free. Pet accepted, some restrictions. TV; cable (premium). Heated pool. Complimentary continental bkfst. Ck-out 11 am. Business servs avail. Microwaves avail. Cr cds: A, C, D, DS, ER, MC, V.

✔★ COMFORT INN. *4800 N Tamiami Trail (34234), near Sarasota-Bradenton Airport. 941/355-7091; FAX 941/359-1639.* 73 rms, 2 story, 16 kit. units. Jan-mid-Apr: S $89; D $99; kits. $99-$109; under 18 free; lower rates rest of yr. Crib $5. Pet accepted, some restrictions; $5. TV; cable (premium). Heated pool; whirlpool. Complimentary continental bkfst. Restaurant nearby. Ck-out 11 am. Coin lndry. Gift shop. Cr cds: A, C, D, DS, ER, JCB, MC, V.

★ ★ HOLIDAY INN-AIRPORT/MARINA. *7150 N Tamiami Trail (34243), near Sarasota-Bradenton Airport. 941/355-2781; FAX 941/355-1605.* 177 rms, 2 story. Jan-early Apr: S, D $89-$97; suites $100-$110; under 18 free; lower rates rest of yr. Crib free. Pet accepted. TV; cable (premium). Pool; poolside serv. Restaurant 6:30 am-10 pm. Rm serv. Bar; entertainment. Ck-out 11 am. Coin lndry. Meeting rms. Business center. Bellhops. Valet serv. Free airport transportation. Marina; dockage. Cr cds: A, C, D, DS, JCB, MC, V.

★ ★ RAMADA INN-SARASOTA SOUTH. *(1660 S Tamiami Trail, Osprey 34229) S on US 41. 941/966-2121; FAX 941/966-1124.* 148 rms, 2 story, 18 kits. Feb-Mid-Apr: S $85-$95; D $85-$95; kit. units $130-$150; under 18 free; lower rates rest of yr. Crib free. Pet accepted; $25. TV; cable. Heated pool; sauna, poolside serv. Restaurant 6:30 am-2 pm, 5-9 pm. Bar 4 pm-1 am; entertainment Fri, Sat. Ck-out noon. Coin lndry. Meeting rms. Business servs avail. Exercise equipt; weight machines, bicycles. Sundries. Cr cds: A, C, D, DS, MC, V.

Motor Hotel

★ ★ WELLESLEY INN. *1803 N Tamiami Trail (34234), near Sarasota-Bradenton Airport. 941/366-5128; FAX 941/953-4322; res: 800/444-8888.* 106 rms, 4 story, 13 suites. Late Dec-early May: S $100, D $110; each addl $10; suites $120-$130; under 18 free; lower rates rest of yr. Crib $5. Pet accepted, some restrictions; $10. TV; cable (premium). Heated pool. Complimentary continental bkfst. Coffee in rms. Restaurant nearby. Ck-out 11 am. Business servs avail. Valet serv. Free airport transportation. Refrigerator, wet bar in suites. Cr cds: A, C, D, DS, MC, V.

Sebring

Motor Hotel

★ ★ INN ON THE LAKES. *3100 Gulfview Rd (33872), at US 27. 941/471-9400; FAX 941/471-9400, ext. 195; res: 800/531-5253.* 161 rms, 3 story, 14 suites. Jan-mid-Apr: S, D $55-$80; suites $85-$135; wkly, monthly rates; package plans; higher rates special events; lower rates rest of yr. Crib free. Pet accepted, some restrictions. TV; cable (premium), VCR avail. Pool; poolside serv. Restaurant 6:30 am-11 pm. Rm serv. Bar noon-11 pm. Ck-out noon. Coin lndry. Meeting rms. Business servs avail. In-rm modem link. Sundries. 18-hole golf privileges, greens fee $30, putting green, driving range. Exercise equipt; weight machines, bicycles. Health club privileges. Refrigerator, microwaves in suites. Overlooks Little Lake Jackson. Cr cds: A, C, D, DS, MC, V.

Siesta Key (See also Bradenton, Sarasota, Venice)

Inn

★★TURTLE BEACH RESORT. *9049 Midnight Pass. 941/349-4554; FAX 941/918-0203.* E-mail grubi@ix.netcom.com; web www.sarasota-online.com-/turtle. 5 kit. units, 4 with shower only. Mid-Dec-Apr (7-day min): $1,100-$1,600/wk; 5th addl $15; wkend, nightly rates; lower rates rest of yr. Crib free. Pet accepted. TV; cable, VCR avail. Pool. Complimentary coffee in rms. Restaurant adj 5-10 pm. Ck-out 11 am, ck-in 1 pm. Microwaves, in-rm whirlpools. Patios. Picnic tables. View of bay; gazebo. Totally nonsmoking. Cr cds: A, D, DS, MC, V. 🐾 🏊 ⊠ 🔥

Silver Springs (See also Ocala)

Motels

✔★DAYS INN OCALA EAST. *5001 E Silver Springs Blvd (FL 40) (34488). 352/236-2891; FAX 352/236-3546.* 56 rms, 2 story. Mid-Jan-mid-Apr & mid-June-early Sept: S $40-$60; D $45-$60; each addl $5; under 18 free; lower rates rest of yr. Crib free. Pet accepted; $3. TV; cable, VCR avail (movies). Pool. Playground. Complimentary coffee in lobby. Restaurant adj 6 am-2 pm. Ck-out 11 am. Coin lndry. Some refrigerators. Ocala National Forest nearby. Cr cds: A, C, D, DS, JCB, MC, V. 🐾 🏊 ⊠ 🔥 SC

★HOWARD JOHNSON. *PO Box 475 (34488), 5565 E Silver Springs Blvd (FL 40). 352/236-2616; FAX 352/236-1941.* 40 rms, 2 story. Feb-Mar & June-Aug: S $40-$45; D $45-$50; each addl $5; under 18 free; higher rates: races, hols, football wkends, special events; lower rates rest of yr. Crib free. Pet accepted; $10. TV; cable (premium). Pool. Playground. Restaurant adj 7 am-10 pm. Ck-out noon. Lawn games. Some refrigerators. Patios, balconies. Cr cds: A, C, D, DS, JCB, MC, V. 🐾 🏊 ⊠ 🔥 SC

✔★SUN PLAZA. *PO Box 216 (34489), 5461 E Silver Springs Blvd (FL 40). 352/236-2343; FAX 352/236-1214.* 47 rms, 9 kits. Late Dec-Apr, June-Labor Day: S $30; D $35-$50; each addl $5; kit. units $35-$50; lower rates rest of yr. Crib free. Pet accepted; $5. TV. Pool. Playground. Restaurant adj 6 am-11 pm. Ck-out 11 am. Lawn games. Picnic tables, grill. Cr cds: A, C, D, DS, MC, V. 🐾 🏊 🔥

Starke (See also Gainesville)

Motel

★BEST WESTERN. *1290 N Temple Ave (US 301). 904/964-6744; FAX 904/964-3355.* 53 rms, 2 story. S $38-$48; D $45-$55; under 12 free; higher rates special events. Crib free. Pet accepted, some restrictions. TV; cable. Pool. Complimentary continental bkfst, coffee. Restaurant nearby. Ck-out 11 am. Business services avail. In-rm modem link. Some refrigerators. Cr cds: A, C, D, DS, MC, V. 🐾 🏊 ⊠ 🔥 SC

Stuart (See also Fort Pierce)

Motel

★★HOWARD JOHNSON. *950 S Federal Hwy (US 1) (34994). 561/287-3171; FAX 561/220-3594.* 80 rms, 2 story. Jan-Mar: S, D $60-$85; under 18 free; lower rates rest of yr. Crib free. Pet accepted, some restrictions. TV; cable (premium). Pool. Complimentary continental bkfst. Restaurant 11 am-10 pm. Rm serv. Bar to 11 pm. Ck-out noon. Coin lndry. Meeting rms. Business servs avail. Sundries. Health club privileges. Cr cds: A, C, D, DS, MC, V. D 🐾 🏊 ⊠ 🔥 SC

Sun City Center (See also Bradenton, St Petersburg, Tampa)

Motel

★★SUN CITY CENTER INN. *1335 Rickenbacker Drive (33573). 813/634-3331; FAX 813/634-2053; res: 800/237-8200 (exc FL), 800/282-8040 (FL).* 100 rms, 1-2 story. Dec-early May: S $79; D $82; each addl $5; under 17 free; golf plans; lower rates rest of yr. Crib free. Pet accepted, some restrictions; $7.50. TV; cable. Pool. Restaurant 7 am-8 pm. Bar; entertainment. Ck-out 11 am. Meeting rms. Business servs avail. 45-hole golf privileges, putting green. Health club privileges. Some private patios. Some balconies. Cr cds: A, DS, MC, V. D 🐾 ⛳ 🏊 ⊠ 🔥

Tallahassee

Motels

(Rates may be higher university special events)

★ ★ **LA QUINTA MOTOR INN.** *2905 N Monroe (32303). 850/385-7172; FAX 850/422-2463.* 154 units, 3 story. S $59-$69; D $66-$76; each addl $7; under 18 free. Crib avail. Pet accepted, some restrictions. TV; cable (premium). Pool. Complimentary continental bkfst. Restaurant adj 7 am-11 pm. Ck-out noon. Meeting rms. Business servs avail. In-rm modem link. Cr cds: A, D, DS, MC, V. 🄳 🐾 🏊 📶 🐾 SC

✔ ★ **RED ROOF INN.** *2930 Hospitality St (32303). 850/385-7884; FAX 850/386-8896.* 108 rms, 2 story. S, D $39.99-$46.99; each addl $7; under 18 free. Crib free. Pet accepted, some restrictions. TV. Complimentary coffee in lobby. Ck-out noon. Business servs avail. In-rm modem link. Cr cds: A, C, D, DS, MC, V. 🄳 🐾 📶 🐾

Tampa *(See also Clearwater, St Petersburg)*

Motels

(Rates may be higher during state fair, Gasparilla Festival)

✔ ★ **BUDGETEL INN.** *9202 N 30th St (33612), north of downtown. 813/930-6900; FAX 813/930-0563.* 150 rms, 3 story. Jan-mid-Apr, late June-early Sept: S, D $69.95-$77.95; each addl $7; suites $90.95-$97.95; under 18 free; wkly rates; lower rates rest of yr. Crib free. Pet accepted, some restrictions; $10 deposit. TV; cable (premium). Complimentary continental bkfst. Complimentary coffee in rms. Restaurant opp noon-midnight. Ck-out noon. Business servs avail. Shopping arcade. Coin lndry. Pool. Some refrigerators, microwaves. Cr cds: A, C, D, DS, MC, V. 🄳 🐾 🏊 📶 🐾 SC

✔ ★ **DAYS INN-BUSCH GARDENS NORTH.** *701 E Fletcher Ave (33612), near Busch Gardens. 813/977-1550; FAX 813/977-6556.* 235 rms, 3 story. Jan-Apr: S $42-$62; D $48-$85; each addl $6; wkly, monthly rates; lower rates rest of yr. Crib free. Pet accepted, some restrictions. TV; cable (premium). Pool. Complimentary full bkfst. Restaurant 6-10 am; Sat, Sun 7-11 am. Ck-out noon. Coin lndry. Meeting rms. Business servs avail. Gift shop. Cr cds: A, D, DS, MC, V. 🐾 🏊 📶 🐾 SC

✔ ★ **ECONOMY INNS OF AMERICA.** *6606 E Dr Martin Luther King Blvd (33619), I-4 exit 4, east of downtown. 813/623-6667; FAX 813/623-1495.* 128 rms, 2 story. Jan-mid-Apr: S $54.90; D $59.90; lower rates rest of yr. Pet accepted. TV; cable (premium). Heated pool. Complimentary coffee in lobby. Restaurant nearby. Ck-out 11 am. Coin lndry. Cr cds: A, MC, V. 🄳 🐾 🏊 🐾 SC

★ ★ **HOLIDAY INN BUSCH GARDENS.** *2701 E Fowler Ave (33612), I-275 exit 34. 813/971-4710; FAX 813/977-0155.* 400 rms, 2 story. Jan-Apr: S, D $89-$99; each addl $10; under 18 free; lower rates rest of yr. Crib free. Pet accepted, some restrictions. TV; cable (premium). Pool; poolside serv. Restaurant 6:30-1 am. Bar 11-2 am. Ck-out noon. Coin lndry. Meeting rms. Business servs avail. In-rm modem link. Bellhops. Free Busch Gardens transportation. Tropical garden. Opp shopping mall. Sundries. Cr cds: A, C, D, DS, JCB, MC, V. 🄳 🐾 🏊 📶 🐾 SC

★ ★ **HOLIDAY INN EXPRESS-STADIUM.** *4732 N Dale Mabry Hwy (33614), north of downtown. 813/877-6061; FAX 813/876-1531.* 235 rms, 1-2 story, 35 suites. Late Dec-early Apr: S, D $79-$84; each addl $10; suites $95-$125; under 18 free; lower rates rest of yr. Pet accepted; $20. TV; cable (premium). Pool. Complimentary continental bkfst. Restaurant 11 am-11 pm. Ck-out noon. Meeting rms. Business center. In-rm modem link. Bellhops. Valet serv. Free airport transportation. Exercise equipt; treadmills, stair machine. Game rm. Microwaves avail. Cr cds: A, C, D, DS, JCB, MC, V. 🄳 🐾 🏊 🏃 📶 🐾 SC 🏋

✔ ★ ★ **LA QUINTA INN.** *2904 Melbourne Blvd (33605), I-4 exit 3, east of downtown. 813/623-3591; FAX 813/620-1375.* Web www.travelweb.com/ laquinta.html. 128 rms, 3 story. S $44-$64; D $51-$71; each addl $7; suites $78-$100; under 18 free. Crib free. Pet accepted, some restrictions. TV; cable (premium). Pool. Complimentary continental bkfst. Ck-out noon. Guest lndry. Meeting rms. In-rm modem link. Sundries. Cr cds: A, C, D, DS, MC, V. 🄳 🐾 🏊 📶 🐾

★ **RED ROOF INN.** *5001 N US 301 (33610), near I-4 exit 6A, east of downtown. 813/623-5245; FAX 813/623-5240.* 108 rms, 2 story. Jan-Apr: S, D $69.99-$95.99; under 18 free; lower rates rest of yr. Pet accepted, some restrictions. TV; cable (premium). Complimentary coffee. Restaurant adj open 24 hrs. Ck-out noon. Cr cds: A, C, D, DS, MC, V. 🄳 🐾 📶 🐾

★ ★ **RESIDENCE INN BY MARRIOTT.** *3075 N Rocky Point Dr (33607), near Intl Airport, west of downtown, off FL 60.* 813/281-5677; FAX 813/281-5677. E-mail notin show@aol.com; web www.marriott.com. 176 kit. units, 1-2 story. Jan-Apr: S, D $125-$200; family rates; lower rates rest of yr. Crib free. Pet accepted; $100 and $6/day. TV; cable (premium). Pool; whirlpool. Complimentary continental bkfst. Ck-out noon. Coin lndry. Meeting rms. Business servs avail. In-rm modem link. Bellhops. Valet serv Mon-Fri. Free airport transportation. Golf nearby. Health club privileges. Microwaves. Some balconies. Dock; watersports, para-sailing, fishing. On Tampa Bay. Cr cds: A, C, D, DS, MC, V.
D ✦ ➚ ≋ ✕ ⊠ ⊠ SC

✔ ★ ★ **TAHITIAN INN.** *601 S Dale Mabry Hwy (33609), West Shore.* 813/877-6721; FAX 813/877-6218; res: 800/876-1397. 79 rms, 18 with shower only, 2 story. Mid-Jan-mid-Apr: S $46-$52; D $46-$61; each addl $5; suites $65-$75; under 12 free; higher rates football games; lower rates rest of yr. Crib $5. Pet accepted; $25. TV; cable (premium). Heated pool. Restaurant 7 am-2:30 pm; Tues-Thur also 5-8:30 pm; Sat, Sun 8 am-1:30 pm. Rm serv. Ck-out noon. Meeting rm. Business servs avail. In-rm modem link. Bellhops. Sundries. Microwaves avail. Balconies. Cr cds: A, C, D, DS, MC, V. D ✦ ≋ ⊠ ⊠

Motor Hotel

★ ★ **AMERISUITES.** *11408 N 30th St (33612), north of downtown.* 813/979-1922; FAX 813/979-1926. 128 suites, 6 story. Jan-Apr: S $119; D $129; under 17 free; wkend rates; lower rates rest of yr. Crib free. Pet accepted, some restrictions; $50/day. TV; cable (premium), VCR. Complimentary continental bkfst, coffee in rms. Restaurant nearby. Ck-out 11 am. Business center. In-rm modem link. Valet serv. Coin lndry. Exercise rm; instructor, weight machine, treadmill. Pool. Refrigerators, microwaves, wet bars. Picnic table. Cr cds: A, C, D, DS, JCB, MC, V. D ✦ ≋ ✕ ⊠ ⊠ ⊠ SC ✦

Hotels

★ ★ **AMERISUITES.** *4811 W Main St (33607), near Intl Airport.* 813/282-1037; FAX 813/282-1148. Web www.travelbase.com/destinations/ tampa/amerisuites-airport. 126 suites, 6 story. Jan-Apr: S, D $99-$139; each addl $10; family, wkly, monthly rates; 3-day min hols; lower rates rest of yr. Crib free. Pet accepted, some restrictions. TV; cable (premium), VCR. Heated pool. Complimentary continental bkfst. Complimentary coffee in rms. Restaurant adj 5-11 pm. Bar. Ck-out 11 am. Coin lndry. Meeting rms. Business center. Free airport transportation. Exercise equipt; weight machine, bicycle. Refrigerators, microwaves. Picnic tables. Cr cds: A, D, DS, JCB, MC, V. D ✦ ≋ ✕ ✕ ⊠ SC ✦

★ ★ ★ **EMBASSY SUITES-TAMPA AIRPORT/WESTSHORE.** *555 N Westshore Blvd (33609), near Intl Airport, in West Shore.* 813/875-1555; FAX 813/287-3664. 221 kit. suites, 16 story. Jan-Apr: S, D $159-$179; under 18 free; wkly, monthly, wkend rates; lower rates rest of yr. Crib free. Pet accepted, some restrictions; $15/day. TV; cable (premium). Heated pool; whirlpool, poolside serv. Complimentary full bkfst. Coffee in rms. Restaurant 6:30 am-2 pm, 5-10 pm. Rm serv 6 am-11 pm. Bar noon-midnight. Ck-out noon. Coin lndry. Meeting rms. Business servs avail. In-rm modem link. Gift shop. Free covered parking; valet. Free airport transportation. Exercise equipt; bicycles, stair machine, sauna. Microwaves avail. Balconies. Cr cds: A, C, D, DS, ER, JCB, MC, V. D ✦ ≋ ✕ ✕ ⊠ ⊠ SC

★ ★ ★ **FOUR POINTS BY SHERATON.** *7401 E Hillsborough Ave (33610), I-4 exit 5, east of downtown.* 813/626-0999; FAX 813/622-7893. 276 rms, 6 story. Jan-Apr: S, D $139-$149; each addl $10; suites $189-$400; under 17 free; wkend rates; lower rates rest of yr. Crib free. Pet accepted; $35. TV; cable (premium), VCR avail (movies). Pool; whirlpool. Restaurant 6:30 am-10:30 pm. Bar 11-2 am. Ck-out noon. Convention facilities. Business center. In-rm modem link. Gift shop. Airport transportation. Exercise equipt; weights, bicycles. Microwaves avail. Private patios, balconies. Cr cds: A, C, D, DS, JCB, MC, V. D ✦ ≋ ✕ ⊠ ⊠ SC ✦

Tarpon Springs <small>(See also Clearwater, St Petersburg, Tampa)</small>

Motels

★ ★ **BEST WESTERN TAHITIAN RESORT.** *(2337 US 19N, Holiday 34691) ¹/₂ mi N of jct US 19A.* 813/937-4121; FAX 813/937-3806. 140 rms, 2 story, 18 kits. Feb-mid-Apr: S, D, kit. units $69-$89; each addl $5; under 12 free; lower rates rest of yr. Crib $5. Pet accepted, some restrictions. TV; cable. Heated pool. Restaurant 6 am-9 pm. Rm serv. Bar 11-2 am; entertainment Fri, Sat evening. Ck-out 11 am. Coin lndry. Business servs avail. Cr cds: A, C, D, DS, MC, V. ✦ ≋ ⊠ ⊠ SC

★ **KNIGHTS INN.** *(34106 US 19N, Palm Harbor 34684) S on US 19, 1 blk N of Nebraska Ave.* 813/789-2002; FAX 813/784-6206. 114 rms, 12 kits. Jan-Apr: S $64.95; D $69.95; kit. units $76.95; under 18 free; wkly rates; lower rates rest of yr. Crib avail. Pet accepted, some restrictions; $5/day. TV; cable (premium). Heated pool. Coffee in lobby.

Restaurant adj 7 am-8 pm. Ck-out 11 am. Lndry facilities. Meeting rm. Business servs avail. Cr cds: A, C, D, DS, MC, V. [D] 🏃 ⛱ 🖃 🔥 SC

Titusville (See also Cocoa, Cocoa Beach)

Motels

✔★ **DAYS INN-KENNEDY SPACE CENTER.** *3755 Cheney Hwy (32780), I-95 exit 79. 407/269-4480; FAX 407/383-0646.* 150 rms, 2 story. S $59; D $65; each addl $6; kit. units $64-$69; under 17 free; higher rates special events. Crib free. Pet accepted. TV; cable (premium). Pool; wading pool. Complimentary continental bkfst. Ck-out 11 am. Coin lndry. Meeting rms. Lawn games. Refrigerators avail. Cr cds: A, C, D, DS, ER, JCB, MC, V.
[D] 🏃 ⛱ 🖃 🔥 SC

★ **TRAVELODGE.** *3480 Garden St (32796), I-95 exit 80. 407/269-9310; FAX 407/267-6859; res: 800/267-3297.* 115 rms, 2 story. Feb-Apr: S, D $50-$95; each addl $5; under 12 free; higher rates special events; lower rates rest of yr. Crib free. Pet accepted; $5. TV; cable. Pool. Restaurant 11:30 am-10 pm. Ck-out 11 am. Cr cds: A, C, D, DS, MC, V.
🏃 ⛱ 🖃 SC

Venice (See also Sarasota)

Motel

★★ **INN AT THE BEACH RESORT.** *101 The Esplanade S (34285). 941/484-8471; FAX 941/484-0593; res: 800/255-8471.* 45 units, 2 story, 15 suites, 13 kits. Jan-Apr: S, D $140-$175; suites $200-$265; kits. $160-$200; under 12 free; higher rates special events; lower rates rest of yr. Crib free. Pet accepted, some restrictions; $20. TV; cable (premium). Heated pool. Complimentary coffee in lobby. Ck-out 11 am. Coin lndry. Business servs avail. Lawn games. Microwaves avail. Picnic tables, grills. Opp beach. Cr cds: A, C, D, DS, MC, V. 🏃 ⛱ 🖃 🔥 SC

Vero Beach (See also Fort Pierce)

Motels

★ **DAYS INN.** *8800 20th St (32966), I-95 exit 68, East FL 60. 561/562-9991; FAX 561/562-0716.* 115 rms, 2 story. Feb-Apr: S $62; D $67; each addl $5; wkly rates; lower rates rest of yr. Pet accepted; $5. TV; cable. Pool. Restaurant 6 am-9 pm; Sun to 2 pm. Ck-out 11 am. Meeting rms. Business servs avail. In-rm modem links. Cr cds: A, C, D, DS, MC, V. 🏃 ⛱ 🇫 🖃 🔥 SC

★ **HoJo INN.** *1985 90th Ave (32966), I-95 exit 68. 561/778-1985; FAX 561/778-1998.* 62 rms, 2 story. Feb-Mar: S $69; D $74; each addl $5; under 18 free; wkly rates; lower rates rest of yr. Pet accepted, some restrictions; $5. TV; cable, VCR avail (movies). Complimentary bkfst. Restaurant opp open 24 hrs. Ck-out noon. Coin lndry. Business servs avail. In-rm modem links. Refrigerators avail. Cr cds: A, C, D, DS, MC, V. [D] 🏃 🖃 🔥 SC

★★ **HOLIDAY INN-COUNTRYSIDE.** *8797 20th St (32966), I-95 exit 68 (FL 60). 561/567-8321; FAX 561/569-8558.* 117 rms, 2 story. Feb-mid-Apr: S $65-$70; D $73-$78; lower rates rest of yr. Crib free. Pet accepted, some restrictions. TV; cable (premium). Heated pool; wading pool. Playground. Restaurant 7-10:30 am, 5-9 pm. Rm serv. Bar 4 pm-1 am. Ck-out noon. Coin lndry. Meeting rms. Business servs avail. In-rm modem link. Health club privileges. Lawn games. Cr cds: A, DS, MC, V.
[D] 🏃 ⛱ 🇫 🖃 🔥 SC

Walt Disney World
(See also Altamonte Springs, Kissimmee, Orlando, Winter Park)

Motor Hotels

✔★ **COMFORT INN.** *(8442 Palm Pkwy, Lake Buena Vista 32830) at Vista Ctr. 407/239-7300; FAX 407/239-7740.* 640 rms, 5 story. Feb-mid-Apr, June-Aug: S, D up to 4, $59-$85; family rates; lower rates rest of yr. Crib free. Pet accepted; $6. TV; cable (premium). 2 pools, 1 heated. Restaurant 6:30-10:30 am, 5:30-9 pm. Bar 5:30 pm-2 am. Ck-out 11 am. Coin lndry. Business servs avail. Valet serv. Sundries. Gift shop. Free Walt Disney World transportation. Game rm. Cr cds: A, C, D, DS, ER, JCB, MC, V.
[D] 🏃 ⛱ 🖃 🔥 SC

★ **DAYS INN.** *(12799 Apopka-Vineland Rd, Orlando 32836) I-4 exit 27. 407/239-4441; FAX 407/239-0325.* 203 rms, 8 story. S, D $139; higher rates special events. Crib free. Pet accepted, some restrictions; $10. TV; cable (premium), VCR (movies avail). Restaurant

6-11 am, 5-10 pm. Ck-out noon. Business servs avail. Gift shop. Coin lndry. Pool. Playground. Game rm. Balconies. Cr cds: A, C, D, DS, MC, V.

Resort

★ ★ **RESIDENCE INN BY MARRIOTT.** *(8800 Meadow Creek Dr, Orlando 32821) 1 mi S, I-4 exit 27.* 407/239-7700; FAX 407/239-7605. 688 kit. villas, 2 story. Mid-Dec-early Jan, mid-Feb-Apr, mid-June-mid-Aug: S, D $179-$219; wkly, monthly rates; lower rates rest of yr. Crib free. Pet accepted, some restrictions. TV; cable (premium), VCR (movies). 3 heated pools; poolside serv. Complimentary coffee in rms. Ck-out 11 am, ck-in 4 pm. Grocery. Coin lndry. Meeting rms. Bellhops. Gift shop. Walt Disney World transportation. Lighted tennis. Golf privileges. Health club privileges. Balconies. Cr cds: A, C, D, DS, JCB, MC, V.

West Palm Beach *(See also Boynton Beach, Palm Beach)*

Motels

★ ★ **DAYS INN.** *(2700 Ocean Dr, Singer Island 33404) 3 mi N on I-95, exit on Blue Heron Blvd, 4 mi E to Ocean Dr, on Singer Island.* 561/848-8661; FAX 561/844-0999. E-mail daysinger@travelbase.com; web www.travelbase.com/daysinger. 164 rms, 2 story. Feb-Apr: S, D $109-$169; kit. units $109-$199; under 12 free; lower rates rest of yr. Crib free. Pet accepted; $10. TV; cable (premium). Heated pool; whirlpool. Restaurant 6 am-10 pm. Bar 11 am-dusk. Ck-out noon. Business servs avail. Lawn games. Some refrigerators, microwaves. On ocean beach; cabanas. Cr cds: A, C, D, DS, MC, V.

✔ ★ **DAYS INN AIRPORT NORTH.** *2300 45th St (33407), 2 mi N on I-95, exit 54.* 561/689-0450; FAX 561/686-7439. 234 rms, 2 story. Jan-mid-Apr: S, D $79-$109; each addl $10; under 12 free; wkly, monthly rates; lower rates rest of yr. Crib free. Pet accepted; $10; TV; cable (premium). Heated pool; whirlpool. Restaurant 6-10 pm. Ck-out 11 am. Coin lndry. Meeting rms. Business servs avail. Sundries. Cr cds: A, D, DS, MC, V.

★ **DAYS INN TURNPIKE/AIRPORT.** *6255 Okeechobee Blvd (33417).* 561/686-6000; FAX 561/687-0415. 154 rms, 2 story. Mid-Dec-Apr: S, D $66-$99; each addl $6; under 12 free; wkly, monthly rates; lower rates rest of yr. Crib free. Pet accepted; $10. TV; cable (premium), VCR avail (movies). Heated pool; wading pool. Restaurant 7 am-9 pm. Bar 3-11 pm. Ck-out 11 am. Coin lndry. Meeting rms. Business servs avail. Exercise equipt; weights, bicycles; whirlpool. Refrigerators avail. Cr cds: A, C, D, DS, JCB, MC, V.

✔ ★ **FAIRFIELD INN BY MARRIOTT.** *5981 Okeechobee Blvd (33417), FL Tpke exit 99.* 561/697-3388; FAX 561/697-2834. 114 rms, 4 story. Jan-mid-Apr: S, D $75-$119; each addl $7; under 18 free; lower rates rest of yr. Crib free. Pet accepted; $10. TV; cable (premium). Heated pool. Complimentary continental bkfst. Coffee in rms. Ck-out noon. Meeting rm. Business servs avail. In-rm modem link. Free airport transportation. Some refrigerators. Cr cds: A, C, D, DS, ER, JCB, MC, V.

Motor Hotel

★ ★ **COMFORT INN.** *1901 Palm Beach Lakes Blvd (33409), near Intl Airport.* 561/689-6100; FAX 561/686-6177. 157 rms, 6 story. Jan-mid-Apr: S, D $79-$104; each addl $5; under 18 free; lower rates rest of yr. Crib free. Pet accepted, some restrictions. TV; cable (premium). Heated pool. Complimentary continental bkfst. Restaurant 11 am-10 pm. Ck-out noon. Meeting rms. Business servs avail. Valet serv. Refrigerators avail. Health club privileges. Some private patios, balconies. Cr cds: A, D, DS, MC, V.

Hotel

★ ★ **EMBASSY SUITES.** *(4350 PGA Blvd, Palm Beach Gardens 33410) N on I-95, PGA Blvd exit.* 561/622-1000; FAX 561/626-6254. 160 suites, 10 story. Jan-Apr: suites $175-$285; under 17 free; monthly, wkly rates; golf plan; lower rates rest of yr. Crib free. Pet accepted; $50. TV; cable (premium). Heated pool; wading pool, whirlpool. Complimentary full bkfst. Complimentary coffee in rms. Restaurant 5 am-11 pm. Bars 11-1 am. Ck-out noon. Coin lndry. Meeting rms. Business servs avail. In-rm modem link. Gift shop. Beauty shop. Free garage parking. Tennis. 18-hole golf privileges. Exercise equipt; weights, bicycles, sauna. Game rm. Refrigerators. Cr cds: A, C, D, DS, ER, MC, V.

Winter Haven *(See also Lakeland)*

Motels

★ **BUDGET HOST DRIFTWOOD MOTOR LODGE.** *970 Cypress Gardens Blvd (FL 540) (33880).* 941/294-4229; FAX 941/293-2089. 22 rms, 2 kits. Dec-Apr: S, D $42-$62; each addl $6; kit. units $8 addl; lower rates rest of yr. Crib $4. Pet accepted. TV; cable. Heated pool. Complimentary continental bkfst. Restaurant adj 11 am-10 pm. Ck-out 11 am. Lawn games. Some refrigerators. Cr cds: A, DS, MC, V. 🐾 🏊 🎾 🐴 SC

★ ★ **HOLIDAY INN.** *1150 3rd St SW (33880).* 941/294-4451; FAX 941/293-9829. 225 rms, 2 story. Jan-mid-Apr: S, D $69-$119; each addl $10; under 18 free; lower rates rest of yr. Crib free. Pet accepted. TV; cable (premium). Pool; wading pool. Coffee in rms. Restaurant 6 am-10 pm. Rm serv. Bar 3 pm-2 am. Ck-out noon. Coin lndry. Meeting rms. Business servs avail. In-rm modem link. Some refrigerators; microwaves avail. Cr cds: A, C, D, DS, JCB, MC, V. D 🐾 🏊 🎾 🐴 SC

★ **HOWARD JOHNSON.** *1300 3rd St SW (US 17S) (33880).* 941/294-7321; FAX 941/299-1673. 98 rms, 2 story. Dec-Apr: S, D $74-$95; each addl $7; under 18 free; lower rates rest of yr. Crib free. Pet accepted. TV; cable (premium). Heated pool; wading pool. Complimentary continental bkfst. Restaurant 11 am-9 pm. Bar 1 pm-2 am. Ck-out noon. Coin lndry. Valet serv. Miniature golf. Game rm. Lawn games. Some refrigerators; microwaves avail. Private patios, balconies. Picnic table. Cr cds: A, C, D, DS, ER, JCB, MC, V. D 🐾 🏊 🎾 🐴 SC

Winter Park *(See also Altamonte Springs, Orlando)*

Motel

★ **DAYS INN.** *901 N Orlando Ave (32789).* 407/644-8000; FAX 407/644-0032. 105 rms, 2 story. Feb-mid-Apr: S $69; D $79; each addl $6; under 12 free; higher rates: Daytona 500, art show; lower rates rest of yr. Crib free. Pet accepted, some restrictions; $35. TV; cable (premium). Pool. Meeting rm. Business servs avail. Some refrigerators, microwaves. Cr cds: A, C, D, DS, ER, MC, V. D 🐾 🏊 🎾 🐴 SC

Motor Hotel

★ ★ **LANGFORD.** *300 E New England Ave (32789).* 407/644-3400; FAX 407/628-1952. 218 rms, 2-7 story, 10 suites, 82 kits. S, D $39.50-$95; each addl $10; suites $200; kits. addl $10; under 17 free; monthly rates; higher rates art show. Crib free. Pet accepted, some restrictions; $25. TV; cable (premium). Heated pool; sauna, steam rm, poolside serv. Restaurant 7 am-10 pm. Rm serv. Bar 10-1 am; entertainment. Ck-out 11 am. Coin lndry. Meeting rms. Business servs avail. In-rm modem link. Bellhops. Valet serv. Sundries. Beauty shop. Game rm. Balconies. Cr cds: A, D, MC, V. D 🐾 🏊 🎾 🐴 SC

Georgia

Adel *(See also Tifton, Valdosta)*

Motels

★ **DAYS INN.** *I-75 exit 10.* 912/896-4574. 78 rms, 2 story. S, D $34.99-$37.99; each addl $5; under 12 free. Crib avail. Pet accepted. TV; cable (premium), VCR avail (movies). Pool. Complimentary continental bkfst. Restaurant open 24 hrs. Ck-out 11 am. Meeting rm. Business servs avail. Cr cds: A, C, D, DS, MC, V. 🄳 👷 ≋ ⊠ 🐾 SC

★ **HoJo INN.** *I-75 exit 10.* 912/896-2244. 70 rms, 2 story. S $27.99-$30.99; D $31.99-$34.99; each addl $4; suites $59.99; under 17 free; wkly rates. Crib free. Pet accepted; $4. TV; cable. Heated pool. Complimentary coffee in lobby. Restaurant nearby. Ck-out noon. Cr cds: A, C, D, DS, MC, V. 🄳 👷 ≋ ⊠ 🐾 SC

✔ **SUPER 8.** *I-75 exit 10.* 912/896-4523; FAX 912/896-4524. 50 rms, 2 story. S $27.99-$30.99; D $31.99-$34.99; each addl $4; under 12 free; wkly rates. Crib $4. Pet accepted; $4. TV; cable. Pool. Complimentary coffee in lobby. Restaurant nearby. Ck-out 11 am. Cr cds: A, C, D, DS, MC, V. 🄳 👷 ≋ ⊠ 🐾 SC

Albany *(See also Americus, Cordele)*

Motel

★ ★ **RAMADA INN.** *2505 N Slappey Blvd (31701-1095).* 912/883-3211; FAX 912/883-3211, ext. 113. 158 rms, 2 story. S $54; D $60; each addl $7; suites $65-$90; under 18 free; wkend rates. Crib free. Pet accepted. TV; cable (premium), VCR avail. Pool; wading pool. Coffee in rms. Restaurant 6:30 am-2 pm, 5-10 pm; Sun 7 am-2 pm. Rm serv 7 am-9 pm. Bar 5 pm-2 am. Ck-out noon. Meeting rms. Business servs avail. In-rm modem link. Bellhops. Valet serv. Free airport transportation. Sundries. Cr cds: A, C, D, DS, ER, JCB, MC, V. 🄳 👷 ≋ ⊠ 🐾 SC

Americus *(See also Albany, Cordele)*

Inn

✔ ★ ★ ★ **PATHWAY INN.** *501 S Lee St.* 912/928-2075; res: 800/889-1466. 5 rms, 2 with shower only, 2 share bath, 2 story. S $60-$70; D $67-$77; each addl $20. Pet accepted, some restrictions. TV; cable (premium), VCR avail (movies). Complimentary full bkfst. Complimentary coffee in rms. Ck-out 11 am, ck-in 4 pm. Luggage handling. Concierge serv. Southern mansion built in 1906. Totally nonsmoking. Cr cds: A, DS, MC, V. 🄳 👷 ⊠ 🐾

Athens *(See also Commerce, Madison, Winder)*

Motel

✔ ★ ★ **BEST WESTERN COLONIAL INN.** *170 North Milledge (30601).* 706/546-7311; FAX 706/546-7959. Web www.bestwestern.com/best.html. 69 rms, 2 story. S $54; D $59; each addl $5; under 12 free; higher rates: univ football games, graduation. Crib free. Pet accepted; $10. TV; cable (premium). Pool. Complimentary continental bkfst. Restaurant opp 11 am-11 pm. Ck-out 11 am. In-rm modem link. Refrigerators. Cr cds: A, C, D, DS, MC, V. 👷 ≋ ⊠ 🐾 SC

Motor Hotel

★ ★ **RAMADA INN.** *513 W Broad St (30601), US 29, 78, 129, 441.* 706/546-8122; FAX 706/546-1722, ext. 586. 160 rms, 5 story. S $61-$67, D $67-$73; suites $110; under 18 free; wkend rates; higher rates: graduation, football wkends. Crib free. Pet accepted; some restrictions. TV; cable (premium), VCR avail. Pool. Complimentary coffee in rms. Restaurant 6:30 am-9:30 pm. Rm serv. Bar 4:30 pm-1 am; entertainment, dancing Tues-Sat. Ck-out noon. Bellhops. Valet serv. Meeting rms. Business servs avail. In-rm modem link. Sundries. Cr cds: A, C, D, DS, ER, JCB, MC, V. 🄳 👷 ≋ ⊠ 🐾 SC

Atlanta

Motels

✔★ **RED ROOF INN-DRUID HILLS.** *1960 N Druid Hills Rd (30329), I-85 exit 31, north of downtown.* 404/321-1653; FAX 404/248-9774. 115 rms, 3 story. S, D $48-$65; under 18 free. Crib free. Pet accepted, some restrictions. TV; cable (premium). Complimentary coffee in lobby. Restaurant nearby. Ck-out noon. In-rm modem link. Health club privileges. Cr cds: A, C, D, DS, MC, V. 🄳 ⧉ ⧉ ⧉

★★ **RESIDENCE INN BY MARRIOTT-DUNWOODY.** *1901 Savoy Dr (30341), I-285 at Chamblee-Dunwoody exit, north of downtown.* 770/455-4446; FAX 770/451-5183. 144 kit. suites, 2 story. S, D $99-$119; wkend rates. Crib free. Pet accepted, some restrictions; $82.50-$125. TV; cable (premium), VCR avail. Heated pool; whirlpools. Complimentary continental bkfst. Ck-out noon. Coin lndry. Meeting rms. Business servs avail. In-rm modem link. Valet serv. Health club privileges. Many fireplaces; microwaves avail. Private patios, balconies. Picnic tables, grills. Cr cds: A, D, DS, MC, V. 🄳 ⧉ ⧉ ⧉ ⧉ SC

★★ **SUMMERFIELD SUITES.** *760 Mt Vernon Hwy (30328), north of downtown.* 404/250-0110; FAX 404/250-9335; res: 800/833-4353. 122 kit. suites, 2-3 story. 1-bedrm $159; 2-bedrm $199; wkend rates. Crib free. Pet accepted; some restrictions. TV; cable (premium), VCR (movies $6). Heated pool. Complimentary continental bkfst. Complimentary coffee in rms. Ck-out 11 am. Coin lndry. Meeting rms. Business servs avail. In-rm modem link. Sundries. Exercise equipt; treadmill, bicycles, whirlpool. Microwaves avail. Picnic tables, grills. Cr cds: A, C, D, DS, JCB, MC, V. 🄳 ⧉ ⧉ ⧉ ⧉ ⧉ SC

★★ **SUMMERFIELD SUITES.** *505 Pharr Rd NE (30305), in Buckhead.* 404/262-7880; FAX 404/262-3734. 88 suites, 3 story. No elvtr. S, D $179-$219; wkend rates. Crib free. Pet accepted, some restrictions. TV; cable (premium), VCR (movies $6). Heated pool. Complimentary continental bkfst. Complimentary coffee in rms. Restaurant opp 11 am-midnight. Ck-out 11 am. Coin lndry. Meeting rms. In-rm modem link. Valet serv. Sundries. Exercise equipt; bicycle, treadmill, whirlpool. Refrigerators, microwaves. Balconies. Picnic tables, grills. Cr cds: A, C, D, DS, JCB, MC, V. 🄳 ⧉ ⧉ ⧉ ⧉ ⧉ SC

Hotels

★★★★ **FOUR SEASONS.** *75 Fourteenth St (30309), Grand Bldg, in Midtown/Piedmont Park.* 404/881-9898; FAX 404/873-4692. Occupying the first 20 floors of the Grand Building, this luxury hotel combines Old World traditions with New South hospitality. A fifth-floor terrace provides skyline views, while the fourth floor boasts a grand ballroom. 244 rms, 19 story. S, D $195-$225; each addl $25; suites $450-$1,500; under 16 free; wkend rates. Crib free. Pet accepted. Garage parking, valet $15. TV; cable (premium), VCR avail. Indoor pool; whirlpool, poolside serv. Restaurant 6 am-11 pm. Rm serv 24 hrs. Bar 11:30-1 am; entertainment. Ck-out noon. Meeting rms. Business center. In-rm modem link. Concierge. Gift shop. Barber, beauty shop. Exercise rm; instructor, weight machine, bicycles, sauna, steam rm. Spa. Refrigerators, minibars. Cr cds: A, C, D, ER, JCB, MC, V. 🄳 ⧉ ⧉ ⧉ ⧉ ⧉ ⧉ ⧉

★★★ **HOLIDAY INN SELECT.** *4386 Chamblee Dunwoody Rd (30341), I-285, exit 22, north of downtown.* 770/457-6363; FAX 770/936-9592. 250 rms, 5 story. S $129; D $139; each addl $10; suites $225-$400; under 18 free; wkend rates. Crib free. Pet accepted; some restrictions. TV; cable (premium). Heated pool. Complimentary coffee in rms. Restaurant 6 am-2 pm, 5-10 pm; wkends 7 am-2 pm. Bar 4 pm-midnight. Ck-out noon. Coin lndry. Meeting rms. Business servs avail. In-rm modem link. Exercise equipt; treadmill, bicycle. Microwaves avail. Cr cds: A, C, D, DS, ER, JCB, MC, V. 🄳 ⧉ ⧉ ⧉ ⧉ ⧉ SC

★★★ **TERRACE GARDEN INN.** *3405 Lenox Rd NE (30326), in Buckhead.* 404/261-9250; FAX 404/848-7391; res: 800/241-8260. 361 rms, 10 story. S $135-$175; D $150-$190; suites $275-$495; under 14 free; wkend rates. Crib free. Covered parking $8. Pet accepted, some restrictions. TV; cable (premium), VCR avail. 2 pools, 1 indoor; whirlpool, wading pool, poolside serv. Restaurant 6:30 am-2 pm, 5-10 pm. Bars noon-2 am. Ck-out noon. Convention facilities. Business center. In-rm modem link. Concierge. Gift shop. Exercise equipt; weight machines, bicycles, sauna. Raquetball courts. Some refrigerators, wet bars; bathrm phone in suites. Some balconies. Luxury level. Cr cds: A, C, D, DS, MC, V. 🄳 ⧉ ⧉ ⧉ ⧉ ⧉ SC ⧉

★★★ **THE WESTIN PEACHTREE PLAZA.** *210 Peachtree St (30303), at International Blvd, downtown.* 404/659-1400; FAX 404/589-7424. Web www.westin.com. 1,068 rms, 73 story. S $185-$205; D $235-$255; each addl $25; suites $385-$1,450; under 18 free; wkend rates. Crib free. Pet accepted, some restrictions. Garage $16; valet, in/out $15. TV; cable (premium), VCR avail. Indoor pool; poolside serv. Restaurants 6 am-11 pm. Rm serv 24 hrs. Bars (1 revolving rooftop) 11-2 am; entertainment. Ck-out 1 pm. Convention facilities.

Business center. In-rm modem link. Concierge. Shopping arcade. Exercise equipt; weights, bicycles, sauna. Massage. Health club privileges. Many bathrm phones; refrigerators avail. 73-story circular tower built around 8-story atrium. Luxury level. Cr cds: A, C, D, DS, ER, JCB, MC, V. [D] 🐾 🏊 🍴 ⚲ 🔥 🏃

Inn

✔ ★ ★ **BEVERLY HILLS INN.** *65 Sheridan Dr (30305), in Buckhead. 404/233-8520; FAX 404/233-8659; res: 800/331-8520.* Web www.beverlyhillsinn.com. 18 kit. suites, 3 story. S, D $90-$120; each addl $10-$15; wkly, monthly rates. Crib avail. Pet accepted, some restrictions. TV; cable. Pool privileges. Complimentary continental bkfst. Restaurant nearby. Ck-out noon, ck-in 2 pm. Valet serv. Business servs avail. In-rm modem link. Health club privileges. Microwaves avail. Balconies. European-style hotel restored to 1929 ambience. Cr cds: A, C, D, DS, JCB, MC, V. 🐾 🔥

Atlanta Hartsfield Airport Area (See also Atlanta)

Hotels

★ ★ ★ **SHERATON GATEWAY.** *(1900 Sullivan Rd, College Park 30337) S on I-85, exit 18. 770/997-1100; FAX 770/991-5906.* Web www.ittsheraton.com-access. 395 rms, 12 story. S $159; D $169; each addl $10; suites $350; under 17 free; wkend rates. Crib $10. Pet accepted, some restrictions. TV; cable (premium). 2 pools, 1 indoor; whirlpool, poolside serv. Complimentary coffee in rms. Restaurant 6 am-10 pm. Rm serv 24 hrs. Bar 11-2 am; entertainment. Ck-out noon. Convention facilities. Business center. In-rm modem link. Concierge. Gift shop. Free airport transportation. 18-hole golf privileges, pro, putting green, driving range. Exercise equipt; weights, bicycle. Microwaves avail; refrigerator in suites. Cr cds: A, C, D, DS, ER, JCB, MC, V. [D] 🐾 🏌 🏊 🏃 ✈ ⚲ 🔥 SC 🏃

★ ★ ★ **WESTIN.** *(4736 Best Rd, Atlanta 30337) S on I-85, exit Riverdale Rd W. 404/762-7676; FAX 404/763-4199.* 495 units, 10 story. S $170; D $185; each addl $15; suites $175-$600; wkend plans. Crib free. Pet accepted, some restrictions. TV; cable (premium). VCR avail. Indoor/outdoor pool; whirlpool, poolside serv. Complimentary coffee in rms. Restaurant 6:30 am-2:30 pm, 5:30-11 pm. Rm serv 24 hrs. Bar 11-2 am. Ck-out noon. Convention facilities. Business center. In-rm modem link. Gift shop. Exercise equipt; weights, bicycles, sauna. Minibars; some bathrm phones; microwave in suites. Luxury level. Cr cds: A, C, D, DS, ER, JCB, MC, V. [D] 🐾 🏊 🍴 🏃 ⚲ 🔥 SC 🏃

Augusta

Motels

(Rates are higher Masters Golf Tournament week)

✔ ★ **KNIGHT'S INN.** *210 Boy Scout Rd (30909), I-20, exit 65. 706/737-3166; FAX 706/731-9204.* 109 rms, 10 kits. S $21.95, D $26.95; kits. $32.95-$50.95; wkly rates. Pet accepted. TV; cable. Pool. Complimentary coffee. Restaurant nearby. Ck-out 11 am. Coin lndry. Cr cds: A, C, DS, JCB, MC, V. [D] 🐾 🏊 ⚲ 🔥 SC

★ **VALU-LODGE.** *1365 Gordon Hwy (30901). 706/722-4344; FAX 706/724-4437.* 146 rms, 2 story. S $36.95-$42.95; D $39.95-$45.95; each addl $3; under 17 free; wkend, wkly rates. Crib free. Pet accepted. TV; cable (premium). Pool. Restaurant 6 am-10 pm. Rm serv. Bar 4 pm-1 am. Ck-out 11 am. Some refrigerators; microwaves avail. Cr cds: A, C, D, DS, MC, V. [D] 🐾 🏊 ⚲ 🔥 SC

Motor Hotels

★ ★ **AMERISUITES.** *1062 Claussen Rd (30907), I-20, exit 66 off Clausen Road. 706/733-4656; FAX 706/736-1133.* 111 suites, 6 story. S $59; D $64; each addl $5; under 12 free; wkend rates. Pet accepted. TV; cable (premium), VCR avail. Pool; whirlpool. Complimentary bkfst. Complimentary coffee in rms. Restaurant nearby. Ck-out noon. Coin lndry. Meeting rms. Business center. Health club privileges. Exercise equipt; weight machines, bicycles. Refrigerators, microwaves. Picnic table. Business suites avail. Cr cds: A, C, D, DS, JCB, MC, V. [D] 🐾 🏊 🍴 ⚲ 🔥 SC 🏃

★ ★ ★ **RADISSON SUITES INN.** *3038 Washington Rd (30907), at I-20. 706/868-1800; FAX 706/868-9300.* 176 units, 4 story, 152 suites. S $59-$99; D $69-$109; each addl $10; under 18 free. Crib free. Pet accepted; $25. TV; cable (premium). Pool. Complimentary bkfst. Coffee in rms. Restaurant 6:30-9:30 am, 5 pm-9 pm; Sat & Sun from 7 am. Rm serv. Bar 5-7 pm. Ck-out noon. Coin lndry. Meeting rms. Business center. In-rm modem link. Health club privileges. Some wet bars. Bathrm phone, refrigerator, microwave in suites. Cr cds: A, C, D, DS, MC, V. [D] 🐾 🏊 ⚲ 🔥 SC 🏃

Hotels

★ ★ ★ **RADISSON RIVERFRONT.** *2 Tenth St (30901). 706/722-8900; FAX 706/823-6513.* 237 rms, 11 story. S, D $119; suites $135-$475. Crib free. Pet accepted, some restrictions. TV; cable (premium). Pool. Complimentary coffee in rms. Restaurant 6:30 am-2 pm, 5:30-11 pm. Bar 11-1 am; Sun 12:30 pm-midnight. Ck-out noon. Meeting rms. Business servs avail. In-rm modem link. Golf privileges, greens fee $40-$60, putting green, driving range. Exercise equipt; weight machine, bicycle, saunas. Health club privileges. Some refrigerators. On Savannah River. Cr cds: A, C, D, DS, ER, JCB, MC, V.

⬛ 🏌 ≋ 🏋 ⊠ 🐾 SC

★ ★ ★ **SHERATON.** *2651 Perimeter Pkwy (30909), I-520 Wheeler Rd exit. 706/855-8100; FAX 706/860-1720.* 179 rms, 6 story, 27 suites. S, D $104; each addl $10; suites $159; under 17 free. Crib free. Pet accepted, some restrictions. TV; cable (premium), VCR in suites. 2 pools, 1 indoor. Complimentary coffee in rms. Restaurant 6:30 am-10:30 pm. Bars. Ck-out noon. Coin lndry. Convention facilities. Business center. In-rm modem link. Concierge. Gift shop. Free airport transportation. Exercise equipt; weight machine, bicycles, whirlpool, sauna. Refrigerator, microwave in suites. Cr cds: A, C, D, DS, JCB, MC, V.

⬛ 🏌 ≋ 🏋 ⊠ 🐾 SC 🚶

Bainbridge *(See also Tallahassee, FL)*

Motel

✓★ **BEST WESTERN.** *751 W Shotwell St. 912/246-0015; FAX 912/246-9972.* 53 rms, 2 story. S $39-$45; D $44-$45; each addl $5; suites $66; under 19 free; wkly rates; higher rates Bass Fishing Tournament. Crib free. Pet accepted; $42. TV; cable. Heated pool; whirlpool. Complimentary continental bkfst. Restaurant nearby. Ck-out 11 am. Meeting rms. Business servs avail. Refrigerator, wet bar in suites. Cr cds: A, C, D, DS, JCB, MC, V.

⬛ 🏌 ≋ ⊠ 🐾 SC

Brunswick

Motels

✓★ ★ **BEST WESTERN INN.** *5323 New Jesup Hwy (31523). 912/264-0144; FAX 912/262-0992.* 143 rms, 2 story. S $43-$53; D $47-$57; each addl $4; under 12 free. Crib free. Pet accepted. TV; cable. Pool; wading pool. Complimentary continental bkfst. Restaurant nearby. Ck-out 11 am. Coin lndry. Picnic tables. Cr cds: A, D, DS, MC, V.

🏌 ≋ ⊠ 🐾 SC

★ ★ **COMFORT INN.** *5308 New Jesup Hwy (US 341) (31525), at I-95 Jesup exit 7B. 912/264-6540; FAX 912/264-9296.* 118 rms, 5 story. S $49-$79; D $59-$99; each addl $6; under 18 free. Crib $2. Pet accepted. TV; cable (premium). Pool. Complimentary continental bkfst. Restaurant adj open 24 hrs. Ck-out noon. Meeting rms. Business servs avail. In-rm modem link. Cr cds: A, C, D, DS, JCB, MC, V. ⬛ 🏌 ≋ ⊠ 🐾 SC

★ **SLEEP INN.** *5272 New Jesup Hwy (31523), I-95, exit 7B. 912/261-0670; FAX 912/264-0441.* 93 rms (90 with shower only), 2 story. S $49-$79; D $59-$89; under 18 free. Crib $2. Pet accepted. TV; cable. Pool. Complimentary continental bkfst. Restaurant adj open 24 hrs. Ck-out noon. Business center. In-rm modem link. Valet serv. Cr cds: A, C, D, DS, ER, JCB, MC, V. ⬛ 🏌 ≋ ⊠ 🐾 SC 🚶

Hotel

★ ★ **EMBASSY SUITES.** *500 Mall Blvd (31525), I-95 exit 8, near Glynco Jet Port Airport. 912/264-6100; FAX 912/267-1615.* 130 suites, 5 story. S, D $99; each addl $10; under 16 free. Crib free. Pet accepted. TV; cable (premium). Pool. Complimentary full bkfst. Complimentary coffee in rms. Ck-out noon. Meeting rms. Business servs avail. In-rm modem link. Free airport transportation. Exercise equipt; weight machine, stair machine. Health club privileges. Refrigerators, microwaves, wet bars; some in-rm whirlpools. Skylit atrium lobby. Cr cds: A, C, D, DS, MC, V. ⬛ 🏌 ≋ 🏋 ⊠ 🐾 SC

Calhoun *(See also Dalton, Rome)*

Motels

✓★ **DAYS INN.** *742 GA 53 SE, at I-75 exit 129. 706/629-8271.* 120 rms, 2 story. S $30-$42; D $35-$49; each addl $5; suites $65; under 12 free; lower rates May & Sept. Crib free. Pet accepted; $4. TV; cable. Pool. Playground. Ck-out noon. Coin lndry. Business servs avail. Some refrigerators. Cr cds: A, C, D, DS, ER, MC, V. 🏌 ≋ ⊠ 🐾 SC

★ ★ **HOWARD JOHNSON.** *Redbud Rd, On Redbud Rd, I-75 exit 130. 706/629-9191; FAX 706/629-0873.* 99 rms, 2 story. S $49; D $54; each addl $5; under 18 free. Crib free. Pet accepted. TV; cable (premium). Pool; poolside serv. Restaurant 6:30 am-2 pm, 5-10 pm. Rm serv. Ck-out 11 am. Meeting rms. Business servs avail. In-rm modem link. Bellhops. Valet serv. Exercise equipt; bicycle, weight machine. Cr cds: A, C, D, DS, JCB, MC, V. [D] 🐾 ≋ 🕊 🏋 🐾 SC

✔ ★ **QUALITY INN.** *915 GA 53 E, E off I-75 exit 129. 706/629-9501; FAX 706/629-9501.* 100 rms, 2 story. S $30-$60; D $42-$100; each addl $4; under 18 free. Crib $4. Pet accepted, some restrictions; $4. TV; cable (premium). Pool. Complimentary continental bkfst. Restaurant 9 am-10 pm. Rm serv. Bar 4 pm-midnight. Ck-out 11 am. Coin lndry. Meeting rms. Business servs avail. In-rm modem link. Cr cds: A, C, D, DS, JCB, MC, V. [D] 🐾 ≋ 🕊 🐾 SC

Cartersville *(See also Atlanta, Marietta, Rome)*

Motels

✔ ★ **BUDGET HOST INN.** *851 Cass/White Rd, I-75N exit 127. 770/386-0350.* 92 rms, 2 story. S $21.95-$49.95; D $26.95-$89.95; each addl $5. Crib $4. Pet accepted; $2. TV; cable. Pool. Restaurant 6 am-2 pm, 5-9 pm. Ck-out 11 am. Coin lndry. Business center. Cr cds: A, DS, MC, V. 🐾 ≋ 🕊 🐾 SC 🏋

★ ★ **HOLIDAY INN.** *(00306). jct US 411N & I-75 exit 126. 770/386-0830; FAX 770/386-0867.* 150 rms, 2 story. S $61; D $66; each addl $6; under 19 free. Crib free. Pet accepted. TV; cable (premium). Pool. Coffee in lobby. Restaurant 6 am-11 pm, Fri & Sat to midnight. Rm serv. Bar 4 pm-midnight. Ck-out noon. Meeting rms. Business servs avail. In-rm modem link. Valet serv. Sundries. Exercise equipt; weight machine, bicycles, whirlpool. Cr cds: A, C, D, DS, JCB, MC, V. [D] 🐾 ≋ 🏋 🕊 🐾 SC

Columbus

Motels

✔ ★ **BUDGETEL INN.** *2919 Warm Springs Rd (31909). 706/323-4344; FAX 706/596-9622.* 102 rms, 3 story, 10 suites. S $39.95-$43.95; D $46.95-$50.95; suites $47.95-$56.95; under 18 free. Crib free. Pet accepted, some restrictions. TV; cable. Pool. Complimentary continental bkfst. Complimentary coffee in rms. Restaurant opp 11 am-10 pm. Ck-out noon. Meeting rm. Business servs avail. In-rm modem link. Valet serv. Refrigerator in suites. Cr cds: A, C, D, DS, MC, V. [D] 🐾 ≋ 🕊 🐾

★ **COMFORT INN.** *3443 Macon Rd (31907), I-185 exit 4. 706/568-3300.* 66 rms, 3 story. S $49.95; D $55.95; each addl $6; suites $99.95; under 18 free. Crib free. Pet accepted, some restrictions. TV; cable. Pool. Complimentary coffee in rms. Complimentary continental bkfst. Restaurant opp open 24 hrs. Ck-out noon. Business servs avail. Valet serv. Exercise equipt; weights, bicycles, whirlpool. Refrigerators. Near airport. Cr cds: A, C, D, DS, ER, JCB, MC, V. [D] 🐾 ≋ 🏋 🕊 🐾 SC

✔ ★ **LA QUINTA.** *3201 Macon Rd (31906), I-185 exit 4. 706/568-1740; FAX 706/569-7434.* 122 rms, 2 story. S $51-$57; D $57-$64; each addl $6; suites $74; under 18 free. Crib free. Pet accepted. TV; cable (premium), VCR avail (movies). Pool. Complimentary continental bkfst. Restaurant adj open 24 hrs. Ck-out noon. Coin lndry. Meeting rms. Business servs avail. In-rm modem link. Valet serv. Some refrigerators. Grills. Cr cds: A, C, D, DS, MC, V. [D] 🐾 ≋ 🕊 🐾 SC

Commerce *(See also Athens, Gainesville)*

Motels

★ ★ **HOLIDAY INN EXPRESS.** *30741 US 441, S at I-85, exit 53. 706/335-5183; FAX 706/335-6588.* 96 rms, 2 story. S, D $52-$85; under 18 free; higher rates special events. Crib free. Pet accepted, some restrictions. TV; cable (premium). Pool. Complimentary continental bkfst. Ck-out noon. Coin lndry. Meeting rm. Business servs avail. In-rm modem link. Exercise equipt; weight machine, bicycle. Microwaves avail. Cr cds: A, D, DS, MC, V. [D] 🐾 ≋ 🏋 🕊 🐾 SC

✔ ★ **HOWARD JOHNSON.** *30591 US 441, 3 mi N at I-85. 706/335-5581; FAX 706/335-7889.* 120 rms, 2 story. S $40-$55; D $45-$74; each addl $5; under 18 free. Crib free. Pet accepted. TV; cable (premium), VCR avail (movies). Pool; wading pool. Complimentary continental bkfst. Restaurant 6 am-10 pm. Ck-out noon. Microwaves avail. Cr cds: A, C, D, DS, MC, V. [D] 🐾 ≋ 🕊 🐾 SC

Cordele (See also Albany, Perry)

Motel

★ ★ **HOLIDAY INN.** *1711 16th Ave E, at jct US 280, I-75 exit 33. 912/273-4117; FAX 912/273-1344.* 187 rms, 2 story. S, D $50; golf plans. Crib free. Pet accepted. TV; cable (premium). Pool. Restaurant 6 am-10 pm. Rm serv. Ck-out noon. Meeting rms. Business servs avail. In-rm modem link. Valet serv. Sundries. Cr cds: A, C, D, DS, JCB, MC, V.

🅓 🛉 ≋ ⊠ 🐾 SC

Dalton (See also Calhoun; also see Chattanooga, TN)

Motels

✓★ ★ **BEST WESTERN.** *2106 Chattanooga Rd (30720), at I-75 Rocky Face exit 137. 706/226-5022.* 99 rms, 2 story. S $39; D $44; each addl $4; under 12 free. Crib $4. Pet accepted. TV; cable. Heated pool. Playground. Restaurant 6 am-9:30 pm. Rm serv. Bar 4 pm-midnight; entertainment Fri, Sat. Ck-out noon. Coin lndry. Meeting rms. Business servs avail. In-rm modem link. Sundries. Cr cds: A, C, D, DS, MC, V. 🅓 🛉 ≋ ⊠ 🐾 SC

★ ★ **HOLIDAY INN.** *515 Holiday Dr (30720), I-75 exit 136. 706/278-0500; FAX 706/226-0279.* 199 rms, 2 story. S $59-$69; D $64-$72; under 19 free; wkend rates; higher rates special events. Crib free. Pet accepted. TV; cable (premium). Pool; wading pool, poolside serv. Coffee in rms. Restaurant 6:30 am-1:30 pm, 5:30-10 pm. Rm serv. Bar 4:30 pm-midnight, closed Sun; entertainment. Ck-out noon. Coin lndry. Meeting rms. Business servs avail. In-rm modem link. Valet serv. Exercise equipt; weight machine, bicycles. Cr cds: A, C, D, DS, JCB, MC, V. 🅓 🛉 ≋ 🕱 ⊠ 🐾 SC

Douglas

Motels

★ **DAYS INN.** *907 N Peterson Ave. 912/384-5190.* 70 rms, 2 story. S, D $36-$45; each addl $5; under 12 free. Crib free. Pet accepted. TV; cable (premium), VCR (movies). Pool. Complimentary continental bkfst. Restaurant adj 6 am-midnight. Ck-out noon. Health club privileges. Microwaves avail. Cr cds: A, C, D, DS, MC, V.

🛉 ≋ ⊠ 🐾 SC

★ ★ **HOLIDAY INN.** *US 441S. 912/384-9100.* 100 rms, 2 story. S $54; D $59; each addl $5; under 18 free. Crib free. Pet accepted, some restrictions. TV; cable (premium). Pool. Restaurant 6-10 am, 11 am-2 pm, 5-10 pm. Rm serv. Bar 4 pm-midnight. Ck-out noon. Meeting rms. Business servs avail. In-rm modem link. Free airport transportation. Some refrigerators; microwaves avail. Picnic tables. Cr cds: A, C, D, DS, MC, V.

🅓 🛉 ≋ ⊠ 🐾 SC

✓★ ★ **SHONEY'S INN.** *1009 N Peterson Ave. 912/384-2621.* 100 rms, 2 story. June-Aug: S $42-$49; D $47-$54; each addl $5; lower rates rest of yr. Crib free. Pet accepted. TV; cable (premium). Pool. Restaurant 6 am-midnight. Bar 4 pm-2 am; entertainment. Ck-out noon. Meeting rms. Grills, picnic tables. Cr cds: A, C, D, DS, MC, V.

🅓 🛉 ≋ ⊠ 🐾 SC

Dublin

Motel

✓★ ★ **HOLIDAY INN.** *(31021). 3 mi S on US 319/441 at jct I-16. 912/272-7862; FAX 912/272-1077.* 124 rms, 2 story. S $54; D $59; each addl $5; suites $79; under 18 free; wkly rates. Crib free. Pet accepted. TV; cable (premium). Pool. Complimentary bkfst. Restaurant 6:30-9:30 am, 11:30 am-2 pm, 6-9 pm. Rm serv. Bar 5 pm-1 am; entertainment. Ck-out noon. Meeting rms. Business servs avail. In-rm modem link. Valet serv. Airport transportation. Exercise equipt; weight machines, bicycles. Health club privileges. Cr cds: A, C, D, DS, JCB, MC, V. 🅓 🛉 🖐 ≋ 🕱 🕱 ⊠ 🐾 SC

Forsyth (See also Macon)

Motels

✓★ ★ **HAMPTON INN.** *520 Holiday Circle, at I-75 exit 61. 912/994-9697; FAX 912/994-3594.* 124 rms, 4 story. S $46; D $51; under 18 free. Crib free. Pet accepted. TV; cable (premium). Pool privileges. Complimentary continental bkfst. Ck-out noon. Meeting rm. In-rm modem link. Health club privileges. Cr cds: A, C, D, DS, MC, V.

🅓 🛉 ⊠ 🐾 SC

★ ★ **HOLIDAY INN.** *480 Holiday Circle, at I-75 exit 61, Tift College Dr & Juliette Rd. 912/994-5691; FAX 912/994-3254.* 120 rms, 2 story. S, D $59-$64; each addl $5. Crib free. Pet accepted, some restrictions. TV; cable (premium). Pool; wading pool. Restaurant 6 am-10 pm. Rm serv. Bar 4 pm-midnight, closed Sun. Ck-out noon. Coin lndry. Meeting rms. Business center. In-rm modem link. Exercise equipt; weights, bicycles. Game rm. Chapel on premises. Cr cds: A, C, D, DS, JCB, MC, V. 🄳 ⮕ ≈ 🏃 ⊠ 🔥 SC ⛷

Gainesville

Motel

✔ ★ ★ **HOLIDAY INN.** *726 Jesse Jewell Pkwy (30501). 770/536-4451; FAX 770/538-2880.* 132 rms, 2-3 story. S $63-$100; D $68-$105; each addl $5; under 19 free. Crib free. Pet accepted. TV; cable (premium), VCR avail. Pool. Restaurant 6:30 am-9 pm. Rm serv. Bar. Ck-out noon. Coin lndry. Meeting rms. In-rm modem link. Bellhops. Valet serv. Free RR station, bus depot transportation. Cr cds: A, C, D, DS, JCB, MC, V. 🄳 ⮕ ≈ ⊠ 🔥 SC

Hiawassee

Lodge

✔ ★ **SALALE.** *1340 Palmer Place US 76E, 1½ mi S on US 76E. 706/896-3943; FAX 706/896-4773.* 4 rms, 2 story. July-Oct: S $29-$69; D $34-$74; each addl $5; under 12 free; higher rates: country music season, fall foliage; lower rates rest of yr. Pet accepted, some restrictions. TV; cable (premium). Restaurant nearby. Ck-out 11 am. Refrigerators, microwaves. On lake; swimming. Cr cds: A, DS, MC, V. ⮕ 🖐 ⮕ ≈ 🔥

Jekyll Island

Motel

★ ★ **COMFORT INN ISLAND SUITES.** *711 Beachview Dr (31527). 912/635-2211; FAX 912/635-2381.* Web www.motelproperties.com. 188 suites, 2 story, 78 kits. Mid-May-mid-Aug: S, D $109-$179; each addl $10; kits. $159-$189; under 18 free; wkly rates; lower rates rest of yr. Crib $4. Pet accepted; $5. TV; cable. Pool; wading pool, whirlpools. Playground. Complimentary continental bkfst. Restaurant 6 am-11 pm. Ck-out 11 am. Coin lndry. Meeting rms. Sundries. Airport transportation. Tennis privileges. Golf privileges, pro, putting green, driving range. Refrigerators, microwaves; some in-rm whirlpools. Private patios, balconies. On ocean. Cr cds: A, C, D, DS, MC, V.
🄳 ⮕ ⮕ 🏃 ⛷ ≈ 🐟 ⊠ 🔥 SC

Motor Hotel

✔ ★ ★ ★ **HOLIDAY INN BEACH RESORT.** *200 S Beachview Dr (31527). 912/635-3311; FAX 912/635-2901.* 205 units, 2-4 story. May-mid-Sept: S, D $119-129; each addl $10; lower rates rest of yr; under 18 free. Crib free. Pet accepted; $8. TV; cable (premium). Pool; wading pool, poolside serv (in season). Playground. Restaurant 7 am-2 pm, 5:30-10 pm. Rm serv. Bar 5 pm-1 am; entertainment. Ck-out 11 am. Lndry facilities. Meeting rms. Business servs avail. In-rm modem link. Bellhops. Sundries. Tennis. Bicycles. Private patios, balconies. On beach. Cr cds: A, C, D, DS, ER, MC, V.
🄳 ⮕ ⮕ ⛷ ≈ ⊠ 🔥 SC

Resort

★ ★ **VILLAS BY THE SEA.** *1175 N Beachview Dr (31527). 912/635-2521; FAX 912/635-2569; res: 800/841-6262.* Web www.jekyllisland.com. 166 kit. villas, 1-2 story. Late Mar-early Sept: 1-bedrm $99-$154, 2-bedrm $174-$189, 3-bedrm $224-$239; wkly: 1-bedrm $594-$924, 2-bedrm $1,044-$1,134; 3-bedrm $1,344-$1,434; wkend, tennis, golf, honeymoon plans avail; lower rates rest of yr. Crib $7. Pet accepted, fee. TV; cable, VCR avail. Pool; whirlpool, wading pool, poolside serv. Playground. Dining rm 7 am-2 pm, 5-10 pm. Bar. Ck-out 11 am, ck-in 4 pm. Grocery 3 mi. Coin lndry. Package store 3 mi. Convention facilities. Business servs avail. Gift shop. Lighted tennis privileges, pro. Golf privileges, pro, putting green. Bicycle rentals. Private beach. Microwaves, some fireplaces. Private patios, balconies. Picnic tables, grills. On 17 acres. Cr cds: A, C, D, DS, MC, V.
🄳 ⮕ ⮕ 🏃 ⛷ ≈ ⊠ 🔥 SC

Macon

Motels

✔ ★ ★ **HAMPTON INN.** *3680 Riverside Dr (31210), I-75 exit 55A. 912/471-0660; FAX 912/471-2528.* 151 rms, 2 story. S, D $57-$68; under 18 free. Crib free. Pet accepted;

$10. TV; cable. Pool. Complimentary continental bkfst. Ck-out noon. Business servs avail. In-rm modem link. Valet serv. Health club privileges. Cr cds: A, C, D, DS, MC, V.

🄳 ⮐ ≋ ⊠ 🔥 SC

✔★ **RODEWAY INN.** *4999 Eisenhower Pkwy (31206), I-475 exit 1. 912/781-4343; FAX 912/784-8140.* 56 rms, 2 story. S $38-$42; D $48-$54; each addl $4; under 18 free; higher rates Cherry Blossom Festival. Crib $4. Pet accepted. TV; cable (premium), VCR avail (movies). Pool. Complimentary continental bkfst. Restaurant nearby. Ck-out 11 am. Coin lndry. Business servs avail. Refrigerators, microwaves. Cr cds: A, C, D, DS, MC, V.

🄳 ⮐ ≋ ⊠ 🔥 SC

Motor Hotel

✔★★ **HOLIDAY INN EXPRESS.** *2720 Riverside Dr (31298), I-75 exit 54. 912/743-1482; FAX 912/745-3967.* 93 rms, 6 story. S, D $51-$69; each addl $6; suites $69; under 18 free. Crib free. Pet accepted. TV; cable (premium). Pool. Complimentary continental bkfst. Coffee in lobby. Ck-out noon. Meeting rm. Business servs avail. In-rm modem link. Valet serv. Health club privileges. Cr cds: A, C, D, DS, MC, V. 🄳 ⮐ ≋ ⊠ 🔥 SC

Madison *(See also Athens, Eatonton)*

Motels

✔★★ **DAYS INN.** *2001 Eatonton Hwy, 2 mi S at jct US 129/441, I-20 exit 51. 706/342-1839; FAX 706/342-1839, ext. 100.* 77 rms, 2 story. S, D $49.95; each addl $5; under 18 free; higher rates special events. Crib free. Pet accepted; $10. TV; cable (premium). Pool; wading pool. Restaurant 6:30-9:30 am, 11 am-3 pm, 5-8:30 pm. Ck-out noon. Cr cds: A, C, D, DS, MC, V. 🄳 ⮐ ≋ ⊠ 🔥 SC

★★ **HOLIDAY INN EXPRESS.** *(10111 Alcovy Rd, Covington 30209) 27 mi on I-20 exit 45A. 770/787-4900; FAX 770/385-9805.* E-mail hie@mind spring.com. 50 rms, 2 story, 25 suites. S, D $62; each addl $5; suites $67; under 18 free. Crib $5. Pet accepted, some restrictions; $25. TV; cable (premium). Complimentary continental bkfst, coffee in rms. Restaurant adj 11 am-10 pm. Ck-out noon. Meeting rms. Business servs avail. In-rm modem link. Valet serv. Coin lndry. Exercise equipt; bicycle, stair machine. Pool. Refrigerators, microwaves. Cr cds: A, C, D, DS, JCB, MC, V. 🄳 ⮐ ≋ 🕴 ⊠ 🔥 SC

Marietta *(See also Atlanta, Norcross)*

Motels

★★ **HAWTHORN SUITES-ATLANTA NORTHWEST.** *(1500 Parkwood Circle, Atlanta 30339) I-75 exit 110, north of downtown. 770/952-9595; FAX 770/984-2335.* Web www.hawthorne.com. 280 rms, 2-3 story. S, D $99; suites $135-$195; wkend, monthly rates. Crib free. Pet accepted. TV; cable (premium). Heated pool; whirlpool. Complimentary full bkfst. Restaurant nearby. Ck-out noon. Coin lndry. Meeting rms. In-rm modem link. Valet serv. Lighted tennis. Exercise equipt; stair machines, bicycles. Health club privileges. Refrigerators, microwaves. Private patios, balconies. Picnic tables, grills. Elaborate landscaping, flowers. Cr cds: A, C, D, DS, JCB, MC, V. 🄳 ⮐ ≋ 🕴 ⊠ 🔥 SC

★★ **LA QUINTA.** *2170 Delk Rd (30067), I-75 N Delk Rd exit 111. 770/951-0026; FAX 770/952-5372.* 130 rms, 3 story. S $65-$72; D $72-$79; each addl $6; under 18 free. Crib free. Pet accepted, some restrictions. TV; cable (premium). Pool. Complimentary continental bkfst. Restaurant adj 6 am-10 pm; wkends to 11 pm. Ck-out noon. Meeting rm. In-rm modem link. Valet serv. Some microwaves. Cr cds: A, C, D, DS, MC, V.

🄳 ⮐ ≋ ⊠ 🔥 SC

Norcross *(See also Atlanta, Winder)*

Motel

✔★ **RED ROOF INN.** *5171 Brook Hollow Pkwy (30071), I-85 exit 38. 770/448-8944; FAX 770/448-8955.* 115 rms, 3 story. S $39.99; D $55.99-$59.99; each addl $7; under 18 free. Crib free. Pet accepted, some restrictions. TV; cable (premium). Complimentary coffee in lobby. Restaurant nearby. Ck-out noon. In-rm modem link. Sundries. Cr cds: A, C, D, DS, MC, V. 🄳 ⮐ ⊠ 🔥

Hotel

★★★ **MARRIOTT GWINNETT PLACE.** *(1775 Pleasant Hill Rd, Duluth 30136) Approx 6 mi NE via I-85 exit 40, then NW on Pleasant Hill Rd, adj to Gwinnett Mall. 770/923-1775; FAX 770/923-0017.* 426 rms, 8-17 story. S, D $149-$179; suites $225-$325; wkend rates. Crib free. Pet accepted, some restrictions. TV; cable (premium). Indoor/outdoor pool; whirlpool, poolside serv. Restaurant 6:30 am-11 pm. Bar 5 pm-2 am, Sun to midnight; entertainment. Ck-out noon. Convention facilities. Business center. In-rm modem link. Lndry facilities. Gift shop. Covered parking. 18-hole golf privileges, greens fee $45-$70. Exercise equipt; weights, bicycles, sauna. Health club privileges. Some balconies. On 11 landscaped acres. Luxury level. Cr cds: A, C, D, DS, ER, JCB, MC, V.

[D] [symbols]

Perry (See also Cordele, Macon)

Motel

✓★★ NEW PERRY. 800 Main St. 912/987-1000; res: 800/877-3779. 39 hotel rms, 3 story, 17 motel rms. S $26-$42; D $37-$44; each addl $2. Crib $2. Pet accepted; $5/day. TV; cable. Pool. Restaurant 7 am-2:30 pm, 5:30-9 pm. Ck-out noon. Meeting rms. Built in 1925; landscaped grounds. Cr cds: A, MC, V. [symbols]

Rome (See also Calhoun, Cartersville)

Motor Hotel

★★ HOLIDAY INN-SKYTOP. US 411E, 2 mi E of town center. 706/295-1100; FAX 706/291-7128. 200 rms, 2 story. S $56.50; D $62.50; each addl $6; under 18 free. Crib free. Pet accepted. TV; cable (premium). Indoor/outdoor pool; whirlpool, sauna, poolside serv. Restaurant 6:30 am-1:30 pm, 5:30-10 pm. Rm serv. Bar noon-1:30 am, Sat to midnight; entertainment Tues-Sat, dancing. Ck-out noon. Coin lndry. Meeting rms. Business center. Bellhops. Valet serv. Sundries. 18-hole golf privileges, pro. Holidome. Cr cds: A, C, D, DS, ER, JCB, MC, V. [D] [symbols]

Savannah

Motels

(Rates may be higher St Patrick's Day)

✓★ BUDGETEL INN. 8484 Abercorn St (31406). 912/927-7660; FAX 912/927-6392. 103 rms, 3 story. S $39.95; D $44.95; under 18 free. Crib free. Pet accepted, some restrictions. TV; cable (premium). Pool. Complimentary continental bkfst. Complimentary coffee in rms. Restaurant nearby. Ck-out noon. Coin lndry. Meeting rm. In-rm modem link. Valet serv. Some refrigerators. Cr cds: A, C, D, DS, MC, V. [symbols]

★★ HOMEWOOD SUITES. 5820 White Bluff Rd (31405). 912/353-8500; FAX 912/354-3821. 106 kit. suites, 2-3 story. S, D $99-$139; under 18 free; wkend rates. Crib free. Pet accepted; $70. TV; cable, VCR. Pool; whirlpool. Complimentary continental bkfst. Complimentary coffee in rms. Restaurant adj 11 am-11 pm. Ck-out 11 am. Coin lndry. Meeting rms. Business center. In-rm modem link. Valet serv. Sundries. Exercise equipt; weight machine, bicycle. Sports court. Microwaves. Cr cds: A, C, D, DS, MC, V.
[D] [symbols]

✓★ TRAVELODGE. 390 Canebrake Rd (31419), I-95 exit 16. 912/927-2999; FAX 912/927-9830. 56 rms, 2 story. S $45-$50; D $55-$60; each addl $5; under 17 free. Crib $5. Pet accepted, some restrictions; $5. TV; cable (premium). Pool. Complimentary continental bkfst. Complimentary coffee in rms. Restaurant opp 6 am-midnight. Ck-out 11 am. Cr cds: A, D, DS, MC, V. [D] [symbols]

Inns

★★★ BALLASTONE. 14 E Oglethorpe Ave (31401). 912/236-1484; FAX 912/236-4626; res: 800/822-4553. 18 rms, 4 story. S, D $145-$275; each addl $20; suites $235-$275. Children over 14 yrs only. Pet accepted, some restrictions. TV; cable, VCR (free movies). Complimentary continental bkfst. Restaurant nearby. Bar. Ck-out 11 am, ck-in 3 pm. Concierge. Health club privileges. Some in-rm whirlpools, fireplaces. Victorian mansion (1838) with period antiques. Courtyard garden with fountain. Cr cds: A, MC, V. [symbols]

✓★★ BED AND BREAKFAST INN. 117 W Gordon St (31401). 912/238-0518; FAX 912/233-2537. 14 rms, 11 with bath, 4 story. No elvtr. S, D $35-$90; each addl $12; garden apts $85-$90. Crib $8. Pet accepted; $10. TV; cable. Complimentary full bkfst. Restaurant nearby. Ck-out 11 am, ck-in 2 pm. Some refrigerators. Restored 1853 Federal town house in the Historic District. Totally nonsmoking. Cr cds: A, DS, MC, V. [symbols]

★★★ EAST BAY INN. 225 E Bay St (31401). 912/238-1225; FAX 912/232-2709; res: 800/500-1225. 28 rms, 3 story. S, D $109-$129; each addl $10; under 12 free. Pet accepted, some restrictions; $25. TV; cable. Complimentary continental bkfst. Dining rm 11 am-3 pm; dinner hrs vary; closed Sun. Ck-out 11 am, ck-in 3 pm. Business servs avail. In-rm modem link. Bellhop. Built in 1853; formerly a cotton warehouse. Antiques. Opp historic waterfront of Savannah River. Cr cds: A, C, D, DS, JCB, MC, V. 🖘 ⬚ ⬚ SC

★ ★ **OLDE HARBOUR.** *508 E Factors Walk (31401). 912/234-4100; FAX 912/233-5979; res: 800/553-6533.* 24 kit. suites, 3 story. S, D $120-$180; each addl $10; under 12 free; wkly, monthly rates; package plans. Crib free. Pet accepted, some restrictions; $25. TV; cable (premium). Complimentary continental bkfst; refreshments. Business servs avail. Balconies. Antiques. Built in 1892, originally housed offices and warehouse of an oil company. Cr cds: A, D, DS, MC, V. 🖘 ⬚ SC

★ ★ **RIVER STREET INN.** *115 E River St (31401). 912/234-6400; FAX 912/234-1478; res: 800/253-4229.* 44 rms, 5 story. S $79-$139; D $89-$149; each addl $10; under 18 free; higher rates wkend closest to Mar 17. Crib free. Pet accepted, some restrictions. TV; cable (premium). Complimentary bkfst buffet; afternoon refreshments. Dining rms 7 am-10 pm, Sat, Sun 8 am-11 pm. Ck-out noon, ck-in 4 pm. Business servs avail. Luggage handling. Valet serv. Concierge serv. Health club privileges. Microwaves avail. Balconies. On river. Converted cotton warehouse (1817); variety of decors & furnishings; canopy beds, Oriental rugs. Cr cds: A, C, D, MC, V. D 🖘 ⬚ SC

Statesboro

Motels

✔ ★ **DAYS INN.** *461 S Main St. 912/764-5666; FAX 912/489-8193.* 44 rms, 1-2 story. S $36-$52; D $38-$64; each addl $5; under 17 free. Crib free. Pet accepted. TV; cable (premium), VCR avail (movies). Pool. Complimentary continental bkfst. Restaurant adj 11 am-10 pm. Ck-out 11 am. Cr cds: A, C, D, DS, JCB, MC, V. 🖘 ⬚ ⬚ ⬚ SC

✔ ★ ★ **RAMADA INN.** *230 S Main St (US 25/301). 912/764-6121; FAX 912/764-6121, ext. 509.* 129 rms, 2 story. S, D $50; each addl $3; under 18 free. Crib free. Pet accepted, some restrictions. TV; cable (premium). Pool; wading pool. Complimentary bkfst buffet. Restaurant 6:30 am-2 pm, 5-10 pm. Rm serv. Bar 5 pm-midnight. Ck-out noon. Coin lndry. Meeting rms. Business servs avail. In-rm modem link. Valet serv. Cr cds: A, C, D, DS, MC, V. D 🖘 ⬚ ⬚ ⬚ SC

Tifton (See also Adel)

Motel

★ ★ **COMFORT INN.** *1104 King Rd, I-75 exit 19. 912/382-4410; FAX 912/382-4410, ext. 102.* 91 rms, 2 story. S $49; D $57; each addl $5; suites $89-$98; under 18 free; wkend rates; higher rates Agricultural Expo. Crib free. Pet accepted; $2. TV; cable. Indoor/outdoor pool; whirlpool. Complimentary continental bkfst. Restaurant opp open 24 hrs. Ck-out 11 am. Meeting rm. Business servs avail. Refrigerator, wet bar in suites. Cr cds: A, D, DS, MC, V. D 🖘 ⬚ ⬚ ⬚ SC

Toccoa (See also Commerce, Gainesville)

Motel

★ ★ **SHONEY'S INN.** *(14227 Jones St, Lavonia 30553) 20 mi SE on GA 17 exit 58. 706/356-8848; FAX 706/356-2951.* 60 rms, 2 story. S $40-$53; D $45-$64; each addl $5; under 18 free; higher rates special events. Crib free. Pet accepted; $10. TV; cable (premium). Pool. Coffee in lobby. Restaurant adj 6 am-midnight. Ck-out noon. Meeting rms. Business servs avail. In-rm modem link. Some refrigerators; microwave in suites. Cr cds: A, D, DS, MC, V. D 🖘 ⬚ ⬚ ⬚ SC

Valdosta (See also Adel)

Motels

✔ ★ ★ **BEST WESTERN KING OF THE ROAD.** *1403 N St Augustine Rd (31601), 1 blk W of jct GA 94, I-75 exit 5. 912/244-7600; FAX 912/245-1734.* 137 units, 3 story. S $34-$44; D $39-$49; each addl $3; under 12 free. Crib $2. Pet accepted. TV; cable. Pool. Playground. Restaurant 5 am-9 pm. Rm serv. Bar 4 pm-midnight, closed Sun; entertainment. Ck-out 11 am. Meeting rms. Business servs avail. Sundries. Airport transportation. Some refrigerators. Cr cds: A, C, D, DS, MC, V. D 🖘 ⬚ ⬚ ⬚ SC

✔ ★ ★ **QUALITY INN-SOUTH.** *1902 W Hill (31601), I-75 at US 84, exit 4. 912/244-4520.* 48 rms, 2 story. S $35.95; D $37.95; each addl $4; under 17 free. Crib $4. Pet accepted. TV; cable. Pool. Playground. Complimentary continental bkfst. Restaurant 11 am-2 pm, 5-10 pm. Bar 2 pm-2 am, Sat to midnight, closed Sun. Ck-out noon. Business servs avail. Sundries. Cr cds: A, C, D, DS, MC, V. ◻D◻ ▣ ▨ ▨ ▨ **SC**

★ ★ **RAMADA INN.** *2008 W Hill Ave (31601), Jct US 84, I-75 exit 4. 912/242-1225; FAX 912/247-2755.* 102 rms, 2 story. S $44; D $49; under 18 free. Crib free. Pet accepted; $5. TV; cable. Pool. Restaurant 6 am-10 pm. Rm serv. Bar 4 pm-1 am; closed Sun; entertainment. Ck-out noon. Meeting rms. Business servs avail. Valet serv. Cr cds: A, C, D, DS, JCB, MC, V. ▣ ▨ ▨ ▨ **SC**

★ **TRAVELODGE.** *1330 N St Augustine Rd (31601), I-75 exit 5. 912/242-3464.* 88 rms, 2 story. S $34-$41; D $38-$51; each addl $4; under 18 free. Crib free. Pet accepted. TV; cable (premium). Pool. Complimentary coffee in rms. Restaurant. Bar. Ck-out noon. Business servs avail. Valet serv. Some refrigerators. Balconies. Cr cds: A, C, D, DS, ER, JCB, MC, V. ◻D◻ ▣ ▨ ▨ ▨ **SC**

Waycross

Inn

🛏 ★ ★ ★ **POND VIEW INN.** *(4200 Grady St, Blackshear 31516) 10 mi NE on US 84, W on GA 121. 912/449-3697; res: 800/585-8659; FAX 912/449-5624.* 5 rms, 2 story, 1 suite. No rm phones. S $45-$55, D $55-$95; each addl $10; suites $95. Pet accepted; $10. TV in common rm; cable (premium). Complimentary continental bkfst; afternoon refreshments. Restaurant nearby. Ck-out 11 am, ck-in 2 pm. Luggage handling. Located in pines of S Georgia. Cr cds: A, MC, V. ▣ ▣ ▨

Winder *(See also Athens, Atlanta)*

Motel

🛏 ★ **DAYS INN.** *(802 N Broad St, Monroe 30655) US 11 N at US 78. 770/267-3666; FAX 770/267-7189.* 45 rms, 2 story. S, D $45-$55; each addl $5; under 17 free; wkly rates. Crib free. Pet accepted, some restrictions; $5. TV; cable (premium). Complimentary continental bkfst. Restaurant nearby. Meeting rms. Business servs avail. In-rm modem link. Pool. Some refrigerators, microwaves. Cr cds: A, DS, MC, V. ◻D◻ ▣ ▨ ▨ ▨ **SC**

Idaho

Boise *(See also Nampa)*

Motels

★ ★ **BEST REST.** *8002 Overland Rd (83709), near Air Terminal Airport. 208/322-4404; FAX 208/322-7487; res: 800/733-1418.* 86 rms, 2 story. June-mid-Sept: S $50; D $56; under 18 free; ski plans; lower rates rest of yr. Crib free. Pet accepted. TV; cable (premium), VCR (movies). Pool; whirlpool. Restaurant adj open 24 hrs. Ck-out 11 am. Business servs avail. Sundries. Gift shop. Barber, beauty shop. Cr cds: A, C, D, DS, MC, V.
D ⤢ ⩭ ⩬ ⩙ ⩏ SC

★ ★ **HOLIDAY INN.** *3300 Vista Ave (83705), near Air Terminal Airport. 208/344-8365; FAX 208/343-9635.* 265 rms, 2 story. S, D $75-$105; each addl $5; under 18 free; wkend rates. Crib free. Pet accepted. TV; cable (premium), VCR avail. 2 pools, 1 indoor. Restaurant 6 am-11 pm. Rm serv. Bar 11-1 am. Ck-out noon. Coin lndry. Valet serv. Meeting rms. Business servs avail. Bellhops. Sundries. Free airport transportation. Downhill ski 20 mi. Exercise equipt; bicycles, stair machine. Cr cds: A, C, D, DS, JCB, MC, V.
D ⤢ ⩭ ⩬ ⩚ ⩛ ⩙ ⩏ SC

★ **QUALITY INN AIRPORT SUITES.** *2717 Vista Ave (83705), near Air Terminal Airport. 208/343-7505; FAX 208/342-4319.* 79 suites, 2 story, 50 kit. units. May-Oct: suites, kit. units $57-$64; under 18 free; wkly rates; lower rates rest of yr. Crib $2. Pet accepted, some restrictions; $10. TV; cable (premium), VCR avail. Pool. Complimentary continental bkfst. Restaurant nearby. Ck-out noon. Coin lndry. Free airport transportation. Refrigerators. Cr cds: A, C, D, DS, ER, JCB, MC, V. ⤢ ⩭ ⩛ ⩙ ⩏ SC

★ ★ **RESIDENCE INN BY MARRIOTT.** *1401 Lusk Ave (83707), Yale at Capitol Blvd. 208/344-1200; FAX 208/384-5354.* 104 rms, 2 story. S $120; D $120-$150; family rates. Crib free. Pet accepted, some restrictions; $10/day. TV; cable (premium), VCR avail. Pool; whirlpool. Restaurant nearby. Ck-out noon. Coin lndry. Meeting rms. Business servs avail. Free airport, RR station, bus depot transportation. Downhill/x-country ski 20 mi. Lawn games. Refrigerators. Private patios, balconies. Picnic tables, grills. Cr cds: A, D, DS, MC, V. ⤢ ⩭ ⩬ ⩙ ⩏ SC

★ **RESTON.** *1025 S Capitol Blvd (83706), opp Boise State Univ. 208/344-7971; FAX 208/345-6846.* 126 rms, 2 story. S $69; D $77; each addl $5; suites $85-$160; under 18 free. Crib free. Pet accepted; $50. TV; cable (premium), VCR avail (movies). Heated pool; whirlpool, sauna, poolside serv. Complimentary continental bkfst. Bar 5 pm-2 am; entertainment Fri, Sat. Ck-out noon. Meeting rms. Business servs avail. Free airport transportation. Downhill ski 20 mi. Health club privileges. Cr cds: A, C, D, DS, MC, V.
D ⤢ ⩭ ⩬ ⩙ ⩏ SC

★ ★ **SHILO INN AIRPORT.** *4111 Broadway (83705), near Air Terminal Airport. 208/343-7662; FAX 208/344-0318.* 126 rms, 4 story, 88 suites. S, D $70-$75; each addl $10; suites $75-$85; under 13 free; higher rates NCAA events. Pet accepted; $7. TV; cable (premium), VCR avail (movies). Pool; whirlpool. Complimentary continental bkfst. Restaurant adj open 24 hrs. Ck-out noon. Coin lndry. Meeting rms. Business servs avail. Valet serv. Free airport, RR station, bus depot transportation. Exercise equipt; weight machine, bicycles, sauna. Bathrm phones; some refrigerators, wet bars. Cr cds: A, C, D, DS, ER, JCB, MC, V. D ⤢ ⩬ ⩚ ⩛ ⩙ ⩏ SC

★ ★ **SHILO INN RIVERSIDE.** *3031 Main St (83702). 208/344-3521; FAX 208/384-1217.* 112 rms, 3 story. S, D $55-$79; each addl $10; under 12 free. Crib free. Pet accepted; $7. TV; cable (premium), VCR avail (movies). Indoor pool; whirlpool. Complimentary continental bkfst. Restaurant nearby. Ck-out noon. Coin lndry. Meeting rms. Business servs avail. Valet serv. Free airport, RR station, bus depot transportation. Downhill/x-country ski 15 mi. Exercise equipt; weights, bicycles, sauna, steam rm. Refrigerators. Private patios, balconies (many overlook river). Cr cds: A, C, D, DS, ER, JCB, MC, V. ⤢ ⤢ ⩭ ⩬ ⩚ ⩛ ⩙ ⩏ SC

✔ ★ **SUPER 8 LODGE-BOISE AIRPORT.** *2773 Elder St (83705), near Air Terminal Airport. 208/344-8871; FAX 208/344-8871, ext. 444.* 110 rms, 3 story. S $45.88; D $49.88-$58.88; each addl $2. Crib free. Pet accepted, some restrictions; $20. TV; cable (premium), VCR avail. Heated pool. Restaurant opp 6 am-10 pm. Ck-out 11 am. Business servs avail. Cr cds: A, C, D, DS, MC, V. D ⤢ ⩭ ⩛ ⩙ SC

Motor Hotels

★ ★ ★ **DOUBLETREE-RIVERSIDE.** *2900 Chinden Blvd (83714). 208/343-1871; FAX 208/344-1079.* 304 rms, 2 story. S $104-$114; D $119-$129; each addl $15; suites $165-$395; under 18 free. Crib $10. Pet accepted, some restrictions. TV; cable. Heated pool; wading pool, whirlpool, poolside serv. Restaurant 6 am-11 pm. Rm serv. Bar. Ck-out noon. Convention facilities. Business servs avail. In-rm modem link. Bellhops. Valet serv. Sundries. Free airport, RR station, bus depot transportation. Downhill ski 16 mi. Exercise equipt; weight machine, bicycles. Some bathrm phones, refrigerators. Private patios, balconies. Beautifully landscaped grounds; on Boise River. Cr cds: A, C, D, DS, ER, JCB, MC, V.
[D] [icons]

★ ★ ★ **OWYHEE PLAZA HOTEL.** *1109 Main St (83702). 208/343-4611; FAX 208/336-3860; res: 800/233-4611 (exc ID), 800/821-7500 (ID).* 100 rms, 3 story. S $65-$107; D $75-$117; each addl $10; suites $200-$375; under 18 free. Crib free. Pet accepted. TV; cable (premium), VCR avail. Heated pool; poolside serv. Restaurants 6 am-10 pm. Rm serv. Bars; entertainment. Ck-out noon. Meeting rms. Business servs avail. In-rm modem link. Bellhops. Valet serv. Sundries. Beauty shop. Free airport transportation. Downhill/x-country ski 20 mi. Balconies. Built 1910. Cr cds: A, MC, V. [icons] [SC]

Bonners Ferry (See also Sandpoint)

Motel

✔ ★ **SUNSET.** *(2705 Hwy 3E (Canyon St), Creston BC CAN V0B 1G0) 33 mi N via US 2/95 to ID 1, then 7 mi N. 250/428-2229; FAX 250/428-2251; res: 800/663-7082.* 24 rms, 2 story, 7 kit. units. June-mid-Sept: S $45; D $50-$54; each addl $4; kit. units $5 addl; lower rates rest of yr. Crib $4. Pet accepted. TV; cable (premium), VCR avail (free movies). Heated pool. Complimentary coffee in rms. Ck-out 11 am. Business servs avail. In-rm modem link. Refrigerators. Cr cds: A, C, D, DS, ER, MC, V. [D] [icons]

Burley (See also Twin Falls)

Motor Hotel

★ ★ **BEST WESTERN BURLEY INN.** *800 N Overland Ave, I-84 exit 208. 208/678-3501; FAX 208/678-9532.* 126 rms, 2 story. S $58-$68; D $64-$74; each addl $6; suites $88; under 18 free. Crib free. Pet accepted. TV; cable (premium). Heated pool. Playground. Restaurant 6-1:30 am. Rm serv. Bar 4 pm-1 am. Ck-out noon. Coin lndry. Meeting rms. Business servs avail. Lawn games. Trailer facilities. Cr cds: A, C, D, DS, ER, MC, V.
[D] [icons] [SC]

Caldwell (See also Boise, Nampa)

Motel

★ ★ **COMFORT INN.** *901 Specht Ave. 208/454-2222; FAX 208/454-9334.* 65 rms, 3 story. Mid-May-mid-Sept: S $58-$79; D, kit. units $68-$89; each addl $8; suites $89-$130; under 18 free; lower rates rest of yr. Crib free. Pet accepted. TV; cable. Indoor pool; whirlpool. Complimentary continental bkfst. Restaurant adj open 24 hrs. Ck-out 1 pm. Coin lndry. Meeting rms. Sundries. Gift shop. Exercise equipt; weight machine, bicycles, sauna. Health club privileges. Some refrigerators, minibars. Picnic tables, grills. Cr cds: A, C, D, DS, ER, JCB, MC, V. [D] [icons] [SC]

Challis

Motel

✔ ★ **VILLAGE INN.** *Box 6, 6 blks NW on US 93. 208/879-2239.* 54 rms, 6 kits. S $30-$42; D $42-$52; each addl $2; kit. units $2 addl; under 3 free. Pet accepted. TV; cable (premium). Restaurant 6 am-10 pm. Ck-out 11 am. Meeting rm. Downhill ski 7 mi; x-country ski 10 mi. Some refrigerators. Cr cds: A, C, D, DS, MC, V. [icons] [SC]

Coeur d'Alene (See also Kellogg; also see Spokane, WA)

Motels

★ ★ **COMFORT INN.** *280 W Appleway. 208/765-5500; FAX 208/664-0433.* 51 rms, 2 story, 7 suites, 21 kit. units. May-Oct: S $94; D $104-$115; each addl $10; suites $174-$205; kit. units $104-$115; under 19 free; higher rates special events; lower rates rest of yr. Crib free. Pet accepted. TV; cable (premium), VCR avail. Pool; wading pool, whirlpool, sauna. Playground. Complimentary continental bkfst. Restaurant adj open 24 hrs. Ck-out noon. Coin lndry. Meeting rm. Valet serv. Gift shop. Lawn games. Refrigerator, minibar in suites. Picnic tables. Cr cds: A, C, D, DS, ER, JCB, MC, V. [D] 🐾 🏊 🏊 🏊 SC

★ ★ **DAYS INN.** 2200 Northwest Blvd. 208/667-8668; FAX 208/765-0933. 61 rms, 2 story. June-Aug: S $75; D $80; each addl $5; under 13 free; lower rates rest of yr. Crib free. Pet accepted. TV; VCR avail. Complimentary continental bkfst. Ck-out noon. Meeting rms. Valet serv. Sundries. Exercise equipt; bicycles, stair machine, whirlpool, sauna. Cr cds: A, C, D, DS, JCB, MC, V. [D] 🐾 🏋 🏊 🏊 SC

★ **SUNTREE INN.** (W 3705 5th Ave, Post Falls 83854) 10 mi W via I-90 exit 2, then E on 5th Ave. 208/773-4541; FAX 208/773-0235; res: 800/888-6630. 100 rms, 2-4 story. June-Sept: S $59.90; D $64.90; each addl $5; under 15 free; package plans; lower rates rest of yr. Crib $5. Pet accepted, some restrictions; $35. TV; cable (premium), VCR avail. Indoor pool; whirlpool. Complimentary continental bkfst. Restaurant opp open 24 hrs. Ck-out 1 pm. Game rm. Cr cds: A, D, DS, MC, V. 🐾 🏊 🏊 🏊 SC

Motor Hotel

★ ★ ★ **BEST WESTERN TEMPLIN'S.** (414 E 1st Ave, Post Falls 83854) W via I-90, exit 5. 208/773-1611; FAX 208/773-4192. 167 rms, 2-3 story. May-mid-Sept: S $93-$112; D $100-$121; each addl $7; suites $125-$350; under 12 free; lower rates rest of yr. Crib $7. Pet accepted, some restrictions. TV; cable (premium). Indoor pool; whirlpool. Restaurant 6 am-10 pm. Rm serv. Bar 10-1 am; entertainment. Ck-out noon. Meeting rms. Business servs avail. In-rm modem link. RR station, bus depot transportation. Tennis. Exercise equipt; weights, bicycles, sauna. Lawn games. Some refrigerators; bathrm phone in suites. Private patios, balconies. Picnic tables. On river; marina, guest docking, boat rentals. Cr cds: A, C, D, DS, ER, JCB, MC, V. [D] 🐾 🐾 🏊 🏊 🏊 SC

Driggs (See also Rexburg)

Motels

✔ ★ **BEST WESTERN TETON WEST.** 476 N Main St. 208/354-2363; FAX 208/354-2962. 42 rms, 2 story, 2 kits. S $50; D $60-$63; each addl $4; kit. units $100; under 12 free; ski plans. Crib $4. Pet accepted; $25 deposit. TV; cable (premium). Indoor pool; whirlpool. Complimentary continental bkfst. Restaurant nearby. Ck-out noon. Meeting rm. Downhill ski 10 mi; x-country ski 5 mi. Cr cds: A, C, D, DS, MC, V. 🐾 🏊 🏊 🏊 SC

★ **TETON MOUNTAIN VIEW LODGE.** (510 Egbert Ave, Tetonia 83452) 7 mi N. 208/456-2741; res: 800/625-2232; FAX 208/456-2232. E-mail tmvl@axxess.net. 24 rms, 10 with shower only, 2 story. July-Sept: S $79.95; D $89.95; each addl $5; suite $109.95; under 16 free; wkly rates; lower rates rest of yr. Crib free. Pet accepted, some restrictions. TV; cable. Complimentary coffee in lobby. Restaurant nearby. Ck-out noon. Whirlpool. Cr cds: DS, MC, V. 🐾 🏊

Guest Ranch

★ ★ ★ **TETON RIDGE RANCH.** (200 Valley View Rd, Tetonia 83452) N on ID 33, then 1.7 mi E on unnumbered road toward Leigh Creeks, then turn at first left going N to Dry Ridge, follow signs to ranch. 208/456-2650; FAX 208/456-2218. 6 units. July-Aug, AP: S $350; D $475; each addl $100; lower rates rest of yr. Closed Nov-mid-Dec, Apr-May. Children over 12 yrs only. Pet accepted, some restrictions. TV in public rms; cable (premium). Box lunches. Setups. Ck-out, ck-in noon. Grocery. Guest lndry. Package store 9 mi. Meeting rms. Airport transportation. Downhill ski 20 mi; x-country ski on site. Sleighing. Horse stables. Hiking. Mountain bikes (rentals). Rec rm. Fishing/hunting guides, clean & store. Balconies. Secluded mountain valley ranch situated on west side of Grand Tetons. No cr cds accepted. 🐾 🐾 🏊 🏊 🏊 🏊

Idaho Falls (See also Pocatello, Rexburg)

Motel

★ ★ **COMFORT INN.** 195 S Colorado (83402), I-15, exit 118, near Fanning Field Airport. 208/528-2804. 56 rms, 2 story, 14 suites. June-Sept: S $56; D $61; each addl $7; suites $65-$120; under 12 free; lower rates rest of yr. Crib free. Pet accepted, some restrictions. TV; cable. Indoor pool; whirlpool. Complimentary continental bkfst. Restaurant nearby. Ck-out 11 am. Refrigerators. Cr cds: A, D, DS, MC, V. [D] 🐾 🏊 🏊 🏊 SC

Motor Hotel

★ ★ **SHILO INN.** 780 Lindsay Blvd (83402). 208/523-0088; FAX 208/522-7420. 161 suites, 4 story. S, D $89-$120; each addl $12; under 12 free. Crib free. Pet accepted, some restrictions; $7. TV; cable (premium). Indoor pool; whirlpool. Complimentary full bkfst. Coffee in rms. Restaurant 6 am-10 pm. Rm serv. Bar 11-1 am. Ck-out noon. Coin lndry.

Meeting rms. Business servs avail. Bellhops. Valet serv. Sundries. Free airport transportation. Exercise equipt; weight machine, bicycles, sauna. Bathrm phones, refrigerators, microwaves. Balconies. On river. Cr cds: A, C, D, DS, ER, MC, V. 🄳 📶 🏊 🏋 ⛷ 🔥 SC

Jerome *(See also Twin Falls)*

Motel

★ ★ **BEST WESTERN SAWTOOTH INN & SUITES.** *3057 S Lincoln. 208/324-9200; FAX 208/324-9292.* 57 rms, 2 story. June-Sept: S $59; D $69; each addl $5; suites $69-$79; under 18 free; higher rates: Jerome County Fair, 1st wk July; lower rates rest of yr. Crib free. Pet accepted, some restrictions. TV; cable (premium). Complimentary continental bkfst. Restaurant nearby. Ck-out noon. Meeting rms. Business servs avail. Bellhops. Coin lndry. Exercise equipt; treadmill, stair machine. Indoor pool; whirlpool. Some refrigerators, microwaves. Cr cds: A, C, D, DS, JCB, MC, V. 🄳 📶 🏊 🏋 ⛷ 🔥 SC

Kellogg *(See also Coeur d'Alene, Wallace)*

Motel

★ **SILVERHORN.** *699 W Cameron. 208/783-1151; FAX 208/784-5081; res: 800/437-6437.* 40 rms. S $52; D $56-$61; each addl $4; under 12 free. Crib $3. Pet accepted. TV; cable. Restaurant 5 am-11 pm. Rm serv. Ck-out noon. Business servs avail. Valet serv. Free lndry facilities. Gift shop. Downhill/x-country ski 3 mi. Whirlpool. Cr cds: A, C, D, DS, MC, V. 🄳 📶 🏊 ⛷ 🔥 SC

Lewiston *(See also Moscow)*

Motels

★ ★ **HOWARD JOHNSON.** *1716 Main St. 208/743-9526; FAX 208/746-6212; res: 800/634-7669.* 66 rms, 1-2 story, 4 kit. units. S $56.50-$61.50; D $60.50-$65.50; each addl $5; under 12 free. Pet accepted. TV; cable. Complimentary continental bkfst. Heated pool. Ck-out noon. Free lndry facilities. Airport, bus depot transportation. Refrigerators. Cr cds: A, C, D, DS, ER, MC, V. 📶 🏊 ⛷ 🔥 SC

★ ★ **RIVERVIEW.** *1325 Main St. 208/746-3311; FAX 208/746-7955; res: 800/806-7666.* 75 rms, 4 story. S $35.50; D $47.50-$51.50; each addl $6; under 12 free. Crib $5. Pet accepted. TV; cable (premium). Heated pool. Complimentary continental breakfast. Coffee in rms. Restaurant nearby. Ck-out noon. Meeting rm. Cr cds: A, D, DS, MC, V. 📶 🏊 ⛷ 🔥 SC

★ ★ **SACAJAWEA SELECT INN.** *1824 Main St, near Nez Perce County Regional Airport. 208/746-1393; FAX 208/743-3620; res: 800/333-1393.* 90 rms, 2 story. S $42-$45; D $49-$52; each addl $2; suites $65. Crib $3. Pet accepted, some restrictions; $2/day. TV; cable. Heated pool; whirlpool. Restaurant 6 am-10 pm. Bar 11-1 am; closed Sun. Ck-out noon. Coin lndry. Meeting rms. Valet serv. Airport transportation. Exercise equipt; bicycles, stair machine. Refrigerators. Cr cds: A, D, DS, MC, V. 🄳 📶 🏊 🏋 ⛷ 🔥

McCall

Motel

★ ★ **BEST WESTERN.** *415 3rd St. 208/634-6300; FAX 208/634-2967; res: 800/528-1234.* 77 rms, 2 story. Mid-June-mid-Sept: S $70-$120; D $75-$125; under 18 free; higher rates Winter Carnival; lower rates rest of yr. Crib $3. Pet accepted, some restrictions. TV; cable (premium), VCR avail. Indoor pool; whirlpool. Complimentary coffee in lobby. Ck-out 11 am. Coin lndry. Meeting rms. Business servs avail. In-rm modem link. Downhill ski 10 mi. Exercise equipt; weight machine, bicycles. Refrigerators. Cr cds: A, C, D, DS, ER, JCB, MC, V. 🄳 📶 🏊 🏋 ⛷ 🔥 SC

Montpelier

Motel

★ **BEST WESTERN CREST.** *243 N 4th St. 208/847-1782; FAX 208/847-3519.* 65 rms, 2 story. May-Oct: S $53; D $58-$63; each addl $6; suites $80; under 12 free; lower rates rest of yr. Crib $6. Pet accepted, some restrictions. TV; cable (premium), VCR avail (movies). Restaurant opp 6 am-10 pm. Ck-out 11 am. Meeting rm. Business servs avail. In-rm modem link. Exercise equipt; stair machine, weights. Whirlpool. Some refrigerators. Cr cds: A, C, D, DS, JCB, MC, V. 🄳 📶 🏋 ⛷ 🔥 SC

Moscow

Motel

★ ★ ★ **BEST WESTERN-UNIVERSITY INN.** *1516 Pullman Rd. 208/882-0550; FAX 208/883-3050.* 173 units, 2 story. S $63-$79; D $70-$86; each addl $7; suites $150-$350; under 18 free. TV; cable (premium). Pet accepted. Indoor pool; wading pool, whirlpool, sauna. Restaurant open 24 hrs. Rm serv. 2 bars 11-2 am; entertainment. Ck-out noon. Meeting rms. Business servs avail. Valet serv. Airport, bus depot transportation. Some refrigerators. Cr cds: A, C, D, DS, MC, V. 🄳 👶 ≋ 🏋 🖎 🔥 SC

Nampa *(See also Boise)*

Motels

(Rates may be higher Snake River Stampede)

★ ★ **SHILO INN.** *617 Nampa Blvd (83687). 208/466-8993; FAX 208/465-3239.* 61 rms, 3 story. No elvtr. S, D $53-$75; each addl $8; under 13 free. Crib free. Pet accepted. TV; cable. Heated pool; whirlpool, sauna, steam rm. Complimentary continental bkfst. Ck-out noon. Coin lndry. Valet serv. Free airport transportation. Cr cds: A, C, D, DS, ER, JCB, MC, V. 👶 ≋ 🖎 🔥 SC

★ ★ **SHILO INN.** *1401 Shilo Dr (83687). 208/465-3250; FAX 208/465-5929.* 83 suites, 4 story, 8 kits. S, D $59-$73; each addl $10; kit. suites $85; under 13 free. Crib free. Pet accepted. TV; cable. Indoor pool; whirlpool. Complimentary coffee in lobby. Restaurant adj 6 am-10 pm. Rm serv. Ck-out noon. Coin lndry. Meeting rms. Sundries. Free airport, RR station, bus depot transportation. Exercise equipt; weight machine, bicycles, sauna. Bathrm phones, refrigerators; many wet bars. Cr cds: A, C, D, DS, ER, JCB, MC, V.
🄳 👶 ≋ 🏋 🖎 🔥 SC

Pocatello *(See also Idaho Falls)*

Motels

✔ ★ ★ **COMFORT INN.** *1333 Bench Rd (83201). 208/237-8155.* 52 rms, 2 story, 14 suites. June-Sept: S $59; D $69; suites $74; under 18 free; lower rates rest of yr. Crib free. Pet accepted. TV; cable (premium). Indoor pool; whirlpool. Complimentary continental bkfst. Restaurant nearby. Ck-out 11 am. Microwaves avail. Cr cds: A, C, D, DS, ER, MC, V.
🄳 👶 ≋ 🖎 🔥

★ ★ **HOLIDAY INN.** *1399 Bench Rd (83201). 208/237-1400; FAX 208/238-0225.* 202 rms, 2 story. S, D $69; each addl $6; suites $139; under 18 free; wkly, wkend, hol rates. Crib free. Pet accepted, some restrictions; $25 deposit. TV; cable (premium), VCR avail. Complimentary continental bkfst. Complimentary coffee in rms. Restaurant 6 am-2 pm, 5-10 pm. Rm serv 6 am-10 pm. Bar 5 pm-1 am. Ck-out noon. Meeting rms. Business servs avail. Bellhops. Sundries. Coin lndry. Free airport transportation. Indoor putting green. Exercise equipt; bicycle, stair machine, sauna. Indoor pool; whirlpool. Game rm. Cr cds: A, C, D, DS, JCB, MC, V. 👶 ≋ 🏋 🖎 🔥 SC

★ **SUPER 8.** *1330 Bench Rd (83201). 208/234-0888; FAX 208/232-0347.* 80 rms, 3 story, 8 suites. S $42.88; D $46.88-$50.88; each addl $4; suites $64.88; under 12 free. Crib free. Pet accepted, some restrictions; $2. TV; cable. Complimentary continental bkfst. Ck-out 11 am. Microwaves avail. Cr cds: A, C, D, DS, MC, V. 🄳 👶 🖎 🔥 SC

Motor Hotels

★ ★ ★ **BEST WESTERN COTTONTREE INN.** *1415 Bench Rd (83201). 208/237-7650; FAX 208/238-1355.* 149 rms, 3 story. No elvtr. S $63; D $69; studio rms $78-$84; each addl $6; suites $110-$150; under 18 free. Crib free. Pet accepted. TV; cable (premium). Indoor pool; whirlpool. Restaurant 6 am-11 pm. Rm serv. Bar 3:30 pm-1 am. Ck-out noon. Coin lndry. Meeting rms. Business servs avail. Bellhops. Valet serv. Free airport transportation. Some refrigerators; microwaves avail. Cr cds: A, C, D, DS, MC, V.
🄳 👶 ≋ 🖎 🔥 SC

★ ★ **QUALITY INN POCATELLO PARK.** *1555 Pocatello Creek (83201), at jct I-15 & I-86. 208/233-2200; FAX 208/234-4524.* 152 rms, 2 story. S, D $69; suites $125; each addl $5; under 18 free. Crib free. Pet accepted, some restrictions; $10. TV; cable. Indoor pool; wading pool, whirlpool. Coffee in rms. Restaurant open 24 hrs. Rm serv. Bar. Ck-out noon. Coin lndry. Meeting rms. Business center. Valet serv. Free airport transportation. Exercise equipt; weight machine, bicycle, sauna. Microwaves avail. Some balconies. Cr cds: A, C, D, DS, MC, V. 🄳 👶 ≋ 🏋 🖎 🔥 SC 🛠

Priest Lake Area (See also Sandpoint)

Resorts

★ **ELKIN'S.** *(W Shore Priest Lake, Priest Lake 83848)* W shore of Priest Lake. 208/443-2432. 30 air-cooled kit. cottages. July-Aug (1-wk min), Sept-June (2-day min): S, D $80-$235; wkly rates; higher rates hol wkends; lower rates rest of yr. Crib free. Pet accepted. Restaurant 8 am-9 pm; closed Mar & Apr. Box lunches, picnics. Bar. Ck-out 11 am, ck-in 4 pm. Gift shop. Grocery. Coin lndry 2 mi. Meeting rms. Game rm. Private beach. Boats. X-country ski on site. Picnic tables. Cr cds: MC, V. 🅳 🐾 🚭 🎿 🌊 🔥

★ ★ **HILL'S.** *(HCR 5, Box 162A, Priest Lake 83856)* W shore of Priest Lake via ID 57 to Luby Bay Rd. 208/443-2551; FAX 208/443-2363. 50 kit. chalets, cabins, 1-2 story. No A/C. Last wk June-Labor Day: $700-$1,750/wk; each addl $10; lower rates rest of yr. Crib $5. Pet accepted. Dining rm 8 am-9:30 pm. Box lunches. Bar 1 pm-1 am. Ck-out 11 am. Grocery. Coin lndry. Meeting rms. Business servs avail. Tennis. Golf privileges, putting green, driving range. Private beach, boats, rowboats, canoes, waterskiing. X-country ski on site. Sleighing, tobogganing, snowmobiles. Bicycles (rentals). Lawn games. Entertainment, dancing, movies. Game rm. Housekeeping units. Fireplaces. Balconies. Picnic tables, grills. Cr cds: DS, MC, V. 🅳 🐾 🚭 🎿 🏃 🏃 🌊 🔥

Rexburg (See also Idaho Falls)

Motels

★ ★ **BEST WESTERN COTTONTREE INN.** *450 W Fourth St S.* 208/356-4646; FAX 208/356-7461. 101 rms, 2 story. S $64; D $69-74; each addl $5; suite $195; under 18 free. Crib free. Pet accepted. TV; cable. Indoor pool; whirlpool. Restaurant adj 7 am-10 pm. Ck-out noon. Coin lndry. Meeting rms. Business servs avail. Health club privileges. Some refrigerators, microwaves. Balconies. Cr cds: A, C, D, DS, MC, V. 🐾 🌊 🎿 🔥 SC

★ ★ **COMFORT INN.** *1513 W Main St.* 208/359-1311; FAX 208/359-1387. 52 rms, 2 story. June-mid-Sept: S $50-$84; D $60-$84; suites $94; under 18 free; lower rates rest of yr. Crib $5. Pet accepted. TV; cable. Indoor pool; whirlpool. Complimentary continental bkfst. Ck-out 11 am. Meeting rms. Business servs avail. Exercise equipt; bicycle, treadmill. Refrigerator, microwave in suites. Cr cds: A, C, D, DS, JCB, MC, V. 🅳 🐾 🌊 🏃 🎿 🔥 SC

Sandpoint (See also Priest Lake Area)

Motel

★ **LAKESIDE INN.** *106 Bridge St.* 208/263-3717; FAX 208/265-4781; res: 800/543-8126. 60 units, 2-3 story, 10 kits. No elvtr. July-Aug: S $68; D $68-$84; each addl $5; suites $125; kits. $105; under 12 free; ski, golf plans; higher rates major hols; lower rates rest of yr. Crib free. Pet accepted, some restrictions; $5/day. TV; cable. Complimentary continental bkfst. Restaurant nearby. Ck-out 11 am. Coin lndry. Free airport, RR station transportation. Whirlpool, sauna. Lawn games. Balconies. Picnic tables, grills. On Lake Pend Oreille. Cr cds: A, C, D, DS, MC, V. 🅳 🐾 🚭 🎿 🔥 SC

Sun Valley Area

Motel

✔ ★ ★ **HEIDELBERG INN.** *(1908 Warm Springs Rd (PO Box 5704), Ketchum 83340)* N on ID 75, then W on Warm Springs Rd. 208/726-5361; FAX 208/726-2084; res: 800/284-4863. 30 rms, 2 story, 14 kits. S, D $80-$95; kit. units $80-$90; each addl $8. Crib free. Pet accepted; $5. TV; cable. VCR (movies $2). Heated pool; whirlpool. Complimentary continental bkfst. Complimentary coffee in rms. Restaurant nearby. Ck-out 11 am. Coin lndry. Downhill ski 1 mi; x-country ski adj. Sauna. Refrigerators, microwaves; some fireplaces. Picnic tables, grills. Cr cds: A, C, D, DS, MC, V. 🅳 🐾 🎿 🌊 🎿 🔥 SC

Inn

★ ★ ★ **RIVER STREET INN BED & BREAKFAST.** *(100 Rivers St W, Sun Valley 83353)* 208/726-3611; FAX 208/726-2439; res: 800/954-8585. 8 rms, 2 story. Dec-Mar, July-Sept: S $120-$175; D $130-$185; each addl $25; lower rates rest of yr. Pet accepted, some restrictions; $10. TV; cable (premium). Complimentary full bkfst; afternoon refreshments. Ck-out 11 am, ck-in 4 pm. Downhill/x-country ski 1/4 mi. Refrigerators. Japanese soaking tubs in all rms. Totally nonsmoking. Cr cds: A, DS, MC, V. 🐾 🎿 🎿 🎿 🔥 SC

Resort

★ ★ ★ **ELKHORN RESORT & GOLF CLUB.** *(Elkhorn Rd, Sun Valley 83354) 208/622-4511; FAX 208/622-3261; res: 800/355-4676.* 139 rms, 4 story; 48 condo units, 2 story. No A/C. Mid-Dec-Mar, June-Sept: S, D $119-$219; each addl $10; condos $120-$320; under 17 free; ski, golf plans; lower rates rest of yr. Crib free. Pet accepted, some restrictions. TV; cable, VCR. Pools; whirlpool, lifeguard. Supervised child's activities (June-Aug); ages 6-12. Dining rms 7 am-11 pm. Rm serv. Bars 11-1 am. Ck-out 10 am-noon, ck-in 4 pm. Meeting rms. Business servs avail. In-rm modem link. Valet serv. Shopping arcade. Free airport transportation. Tennis, pro. 18-hole golf, greens fee (incl cart) $76, pro, putting green, driving range, golf school. Downhill ski on site. Bicycles, bike trails. Lawn games. Entertainment. Music concerts in summer. Exercise equipt; weights, bicycles, sauna, steam rm. Massage. Fishing/hunting guides. Fly fishing lessons. Luxury level. Cr cds: A, D, DS, MC, V. ⒹⓇⒼⒶⓀⒶⓌⒶⒻⓃⓀⓈⒸ

Twin Falls *(See also Burley, Jerome)*

Motels

✔★ ★ **COMFORT INN.** *1893 Canyon Springs Rd. 208/734-7494.* 52 rms, 2 story, 15 suites. S $52.99; D $59.99; each addl $7; suites $67.99; under 18 free. Crib free. Pet accepted. TV; cable (premium). Indoor pool. Complimentary continental bkfst. Ck-out 11 am. Health club privileges. Cr cds: A, D, DS, MC, V. ⒹⓇⓌⓃⓀⒸ

★ ★ **SHILO INN.** *1586 N Blue Lakes Blvd. 208/733-7545; FAX 208/736-2019.* 128 rms, 4 story. May-Sept: S, D $95-$99; each addl $10; kit. units $99-$125; under 12 free; family rates; wkly rates; lower rates rest of yr. Crib free. Pet accepted, some restrictions; $7. TV; cable (premium), VCR (movies). Complimentary continental bkfst. Complimentary coffee in rms. Restaurant adj 6 am-midnight. Ck-out noon. Meeting rms. Business servs avail. In-rm modem link. Bellhops. Sundries. Coin lndry. Exercise equipt; weight machine, stair machine, sauna. Indoor pool; whirlpool. Bathrm phones, refrigerators, microwaves, wet bars. Cr cds: A, C, D, DS, ER, JCB, MC, V. ⒹⓇⓌⓀⓃⓀⒸ

Wallace *(See also Coeur d'Alene, Kellogg)*

Motel

✔★ **STARDUST.** *410 Pine St. 208/752-1213; FAX 208/753-0981; res: 800/643-2386.* 42 rms, 22 A/C, 2 story. S $44.50; D $52.50; each addl $8; under 12 free. Pet accepted; $25. TV; cable (premium). Restaurant nearby. Ck-out noon. Meeting rms. Airport transportation. Sundries. Downhill ski 10 mi; x-country ski 11 mi. Cr cds: A, C, D, DS, MC, V. ⓇⓀⓃⓀⒸ

Illinois

Altamont (See also Effingham, Vandalia)

Motel

✔★ **SUPER 8.** Rte 2, Box 296, ¹/₄ mi S on IL 128, 1 blk S of I-70 exit 82. 618/483-6300; FAX 618/483-3323. 25 rms, 2 story. S $40.88; D $50.88; each addl $4; under 12 free. Crib $6. Pet accepted; $8. TV; cable (premium). Playground. Restaurant adj 6 am-9 pm. Ck-out 11 am. Coin lndry. Cr cds: A, C, D, DS, MC, V. 🅳 ✎ ➳ ✕ 🐾 SC

Alton (See also Collinsville, Edwardsville)

Motel

★★ **HOLIDAY INN.** 3800 Homer Adams Pkwy. 618/462-1220; FAX 618/462-0906. 137 rms, 4 story. S $72.90-$82.50; D $82.90-$92.50; each addl $10; under 18 free. Crib free. Pet accepted. TV; cable (premium), VCR (movies). Indoor pool; whirlpool. Restaurant 6 am-2 pm, 5-10 pm; Sun from 7 am. Rm serv. Bar 11-1 am; Sun noon-10 pm; entertainment. Ck-out noon. Meeting rms. Business servs avail. In-rm modem link. Bellhops. Free RR transportation. Exercise equipt; weight machine, stair machine, sauna. Game rm. Balconies. Cr cds: A, C, D, DS, JCB, MC, V. 🅳 ✎ ➳ 🏃 ✕ 🐾 SC

Antioch (See also Gurnee, Waukegan)

Motel

★★ **BEST WESTERN REGENCY INN.** 350 IL 173. 847/395-3606. 68 rms, 3 story, 24 suites. May-Sept: S, D $74-$104; suites $94-$114; under 18 free; lower rates rest of yr. Crib $7. Pet accepted, some restrictions; $25 deposit. TV; cable (premium), VCR avail. Complimentary continental bkfst. Restaurant nearby. Bar 3 pm-1 am. Ck-out 11 am. Meeting rms. Business servs avail. In-rm modem link. Health club privileges. Indoor pool; whirlpool. Refrigerator, wet bar in suites. Cr cds: A, C, D, DS, ER, MC, V. 🅳 ✎ ➳ ✕ 🐾 SC

Arlington Heights (See also Chicago O'Hare Airport Area, Wheeling)

Motel

★★ **LA QUINTA.** 1415 W Dundee Rd (IL 68) (60004), E off IL 53. 847/253-8777; FAX 847/818-9167. 123 rms, 4 story. S $78-$88; D $84-$91; suites $114; under 18 free. Crib free. Pet accepted, some restrictions. TV; cable (premium), VCR avail. Heated pool. Complimentary continental bkfst. Complimentary coffee in rms. Restaurant adj 11-1 am. Ck-out noon. Meeting rms. Business servs avail. In-rm modem link. Valet serv. Sundries. Cr cds: A, C, D, DS, MC, V. 🅳 ✎ ➳ ✕ 🐾 SC

Motor Hotel

★★ **AMERISUITES.** 2111 S Arlington Heights Rd (60005), 1 mi N of I-90, exit Arlington Heights Rd N. 847/956-1400; FAX 847/956-0804. 113 suites, 6 story. S $96; D $106; each addl $10; under 12 free; wkend packages. Crib free. Pet accepted. TV; cable (premium). Complimentary buffet bkfst. Complimentary coffee in rms. Restaurant opp open 24 hrs. Ck-out noon. Meeting rms. Business center. Valet serv Mon-Fri. Exercise equipt; weight machine, treadmill. Health club privileges. Whirlpool. Refrigerators. Some theme suites. Cr cds: A, C, D, DS, MC, V. 🅳 ✎ 🏃 ✕ 🐾 SC 🚶

Hotels

★★ **ARLINGTON PARK HILTON CONFERENCE CENTER.** 3400 W Euclid Ave (60005). 847/394-2000; FAX 847/394-2095. 420 rms, 13 story. S $105-$195; D $125-$215; each addl $15; suites $250-$675; family, wkend rates. Crib free. Pet accepted, some restrictions. TV; cable (premium). Indoor pool; whirlpool. Complimentary coffee in rms. Restaurant 6:30 am-10 pm. Bar 11-2 am; Sun from noon. Ck-out 11 am. Convention facilities. Business center. In-rm modem link. Gift shop. Tennis. Exercise rm; instructor, weight machines, bicycles, sauna. Massage. Some bathrm phones. Luxury level. Cr cds: A, C, D, DS, ER, JCB, MC, V.

🅳 ✎ 🏌 ➳ 🏃 ✕ 🐾 SC 🚶

★★★ **RADISSON.** 75 W Algonquin Rd (60005). 847/364-7600; FAX 847/364-7665. 201 rms, 6 story. S, D $109-$149; each addl $10; suites $195-$350; under 18 free; wkend rates. Crib free. Pet accepted, some restrictions. TV; cable (premium), VCR avail. Indoor pool; whirlpool. Coffee in rms. Restaurant 6:30 am-11 pm; Sun to 9 pm. Bar 11-1 am; entertainment Tues-Sat. Ck-out noon. Meeting rms. Business servs avail. In-rm modem link. Gift shop. Free airporttransportation. Exercise equipt; weight machine, bicycles, sauna. Bathrm phone, refrigerator in suites. Cr cds: A, C, D, DS, ER, JCB, MC, V.

D 🐾 ⊠ 🏋 🏃 ⊠ 🔥 SC

Belleville

Motor Hotel

✔★ **TOWN HOUSE.** *400 S Illinois (62220). 618/233-7881; FAX 618/233-7885.* 55 rms, 2 story. S $39.45; D $42.45; each addl $5; under 12 free. Crib free. Pet accepted, some restrictions. TV; cable (premium). Restaurant 6 am-9 pm. Rm serv from 8 am. Bar 5 pm-2 am; entertainment. Whirlpool. Ck-out noon. Meeting rms. Business servs avail. In-rm modem link. Health club privileges. Refrigerators, microwaves avail. Cr cds: A, C, D, DS, MC, V. 🐾 ⊠ ⊠ 🔥 SC

Benton

Motel

✔★ **DAYS INN.** *711 W Main. 618/439-3183.* 55 rms, 2 story. S $39.88; D $48.88; each addl $5; suite $90-$95; under 12 free; higher rates special events. Crib avail. Pet accepted. TV; cable, VCR avail (movies). Restaurant 6 am-10 pm. Bar 3-10 pm; entertainment. Ck-out noon. Meeting rms. Business servs avail. Refrigerators, microwaves avail. Picnic tables. Cr cds: A, C, D, DS, MC, V. D 🐾 ⊠ 🔥 SC

Bloomington *(See also Peoria)*

Motels

✔★★ **BEST INNS OF AMERICA.** *1905 W Market St (61701), 1 blk E of I-55/74 exit 160A. 309/827-5333; FAX 309/827-5333, ext. 113.* 107 rms, 2 story. S $35-$41; D $43-$50; each addl $7; under 18 free. Crib free. Pet accepted. TV; cable (premium). Pool. Complimentary continental bkfst. Restaurant adj 10 am-midnight. Ck-out 1 pm. Business servs avail. In-rm modem link. Cr cds: A, C, D, DS, MC, V. D 🐾 ⊠ ⊠ 🔥 SC

★ **BEST WESTERN UNIVERSITY INN.** *(6 Traders Circle, Normal 61761) Off Main St (US 51), 1/4 mi S of I-55 exit 165A. 309/454-4070; FAX 309/888-4505.* 102 rms, 2 story. S $55-$61; D $61-$68; each addl $7; kit. units $61; under 12 free. Crib free. Pet accepted. TV; cable (premium). Sauna. Heated pool. Complimentary continental bkfst. Restaurant nearby. Ck-out 11 am. Meeting rms. Business servs avail. Valet serv. Free airport, RR station, bus depot transportation. Cr cds: A, C, D, DS, MC, V. D 🐾 ⊠ ⊠ 🔥 SC

★★ **RAMADA INN.** *1219 Holiday Dr (61704), Veterans Pkwy & Empire St (IL 9). 309/662-5311; FAX 309/663-1732.* 209 rms, 2 story. S $49-$68; D $58-$77; under 18 free. Crib free. Pet accepted. TV; cable (premium). Indoor pool; whirlpool. Restaurant 6:30 am-1 pm, 5:30-9 pm. Rm serv. Bar 4:30 pm-midnight. Ck-out noon. Coin lndry. Meeting rms. Business servs avail. Bellhops. Sundries. Free airport, RR station, bus depot transportation. Exercise equipt; stair machine, treadmill, sauna. Miniature golf. Game rm. Cr cds: A, C, D, DS, JCB, MC, V. D 🐾 ⊠ 🏋 ⊠ 🔥 SC

Motor Hotel

★★ **HOLIDAY INN.** *(8 Traders Circle, Normal 61761) Near jct US 55, IL 51. 309/452-8300; FAX 309/454-6722.* 160 rms, 5 story. S $64-$74; D $78-$83; each addl $9; under 18 free. Crib free. Pet accepted. TV; cable (premium), VCR avail (movies). Indoor pool; whirlpool. Complimentary coffee in lobby. Restaurant 6:30 am-2 pm, 5-10 pm. Rm serv. Bar 3 pm-midnight. Ck-out noon. Meeting rms. Business center. Bellhops. Valet serv. Free airport, RR station, bus depot transportation. Exercise equipt; weights, bicycles, sauna. Game rm. Cr cds: A, C, D, DS, MC, V. D 🐾 ⊠ 🏋 ⊠ 🔥 SC 🏄

Hotel

★★★ **JUMER'S CHATEAU.** *1601 Jumer Dr (61704), off Veterans Pkwy, near Bloomington-Normal Airport. 309/662-2020; FAX 309/662-2020, ext. 617.* 180 rms, 5 story, 26 suites. S $85-$100; D $94-$103; each addl $9; suites $107-$154; under 18 free; wkend rates; golf plans. Crib free. Pet accepted. TV; cable (premium). Indoor pool; whirlpool. Coffee in lobby. Restaurant 6:30 am-10 pm; Fri, Sat to 11 pm; Sun 7 am-10 pm. Bar 11:30-1 am, Sun noon-midnight; entertainment, dancing exc Sun. Ck-out noon. Meeting rms. Business servs avail. Gift shop. Free airport, RR station, bus depot transportation. Exercise equipt; weight machine, stair machine, sauna. Game rm. Rec rm. Refrigerator, minibar in suites. French decor. Library, antiques. Cr cds: A, C, D, DS, JCB, MC, V.

D ⊬ ⊵ 𝕏 ✕ ⊠ 🐾 SC

Carbondale *(See also Marion)*

Motels

✔ ★ **BEST INNS OF AMERICA.** *1345 E Main St, jct University Mall & Frontage Rd. 618/529-4801.* 86 rms, 2 story. S $38.88; D $49.88; each addl $6; under 18 free; higher rates special university events. Crib free. Pet accepted. TV; cable. Pool. Complimentary continental bkfst. Restaurant adj 3 pm-midnight. Ck-out 1 pm. Cr cds: A, C, D, DS, MC, V.

D ⊬ ⊵ ⊠ 🐾 SC

★ **SUPER 8.** *1180 E Main St, 1¹/₂ mi E on IL 13. 618/457-8822; FAX 618/457-4186.* 63 rms, 3 story. No elvtr. S $36.88-$42.88; D $39.88-$55.88; under 12 free. Crib free. Pet accepted. TV; cable. Restaurant adj 6 am-midnight. Ck-out 11 am. Cr cds: A, C, D, DS, MC, V. D ⊬ ⊠ 🐾 SC

Champaign/Urbana *(See also Danville)*

Motels

(Rates may be higher for special university wkends)

★ ★ **BEST WESTERN CUNNINGHAM PLACE.** *(1907 Cunningham Ave, Urbana 61801) 217/367-8331; FAX 217/384-3370.* 105 rms, 2 story, 48 suites. S $59-$65; D $69-$78; each addl $7; suites $85-$120; under 18 free. Crib free. Pet accepted, some restrictions. TV; cable (premium), VCR avail. Indoor pool. Complimentary full bkfst. Bar 5-10 pm, closed Sat, Sun. Ck-out noon. Meeting rms. Business servs avail. Bellhops. Valet serv. Free airport transportation. Exercise equipt; weight machines, bicycles, sauna. Some refrigerators, microwaves. Private patios, balconies. Cr cds: A, C, D, DS, JCB, MC, V.

D ⊬ ⊵ 𝕏 ⊠ 🐾 SC

✔ ★ **BEST WESTERN PARADISE INN.** *(1001 N Dunlap, Savoy 61874) 3¹/₂ mi S, near University of Illinois-Willard Airport. 217/356-1824; FAX 217/356-1824, ext. 190.* 62 rms, 1-2 story. S $43-$49; D $53-$63; each addl $4; under 12 free. Crib $4. Pet accepted, some restrictions; $2/day. TV; cable (premium). Heated pool; wading pool. Playground. Complimentary continental bkfst. Complimentary coffee in rms. Restaurant nearby. Ck-out 11 am. Coin lndry. Meeting rm. Business servs avail. In-rm modem link. Free airport transportation. Cr cds: A, C, D, DS, MC, V. ⊬ ⊵ 𝕏 ⊠ 🐾 SC

★ ★ **COMFORT INN.** *(305 W Marketview Dr, Champaign 61821) ¹/₂ mi N of jct I-74 & N Neil St exit. 217/352-4055; FAX 217/352-4055, ext. 329.* 67 rms, 2 story. Mar-Oct: S $54.99; D $60.99; each addl $6; suites $64.99-$70.99; under 18 free; lower rates rest of yr. Crib free. Pet accepted, some restrictions. TV; cable (premium). Indoor pool; whirlpool. Complimentary continental bkfst. Restaurant nearby. Ck-out 11 am. Meeting rm. Business servs avail. Refrigerators in suites; microwaves avail. Cr cds: A, C, D, DS, ER, JCB, MC, V.

D ⊬ ⊵ ⊠ 🐾 SC

★ ★ **LA QUINTA.** *(1900 Center Dr, Champaign 61820) 1 blk N of I-74 Neil St exit. 217/356-4000; FAX 217/352-7783.* 120 rms, 2 story. S $50-$57; D $57-$64; each addl $7; under 18 free. Crib free. Pet accepted, some restrictions. TV; cable (premium). Heated pool. Complimentary continental bkfst. Restaurant adj open 24 hrs. Ck-out noon. Coin lndry. Meeting rms. In-rm modem link. Valet serv. Cr cds: A, DS, MC, V. D ⊬ ⊵ ⊠ 🐾 SC

✔ ★ **RED ROOF INN.** *(212 W Anthony Dr, Champaign 61820) 217/352-0101; FAX 217/352-1891.* 112 rms, 2 story. June-Oct: S $31.99-$47.99; D $39.99-$54.99; each addl $7-$9; under 18 free; lower rates rest of yr. Crib avail. Pet accepted. TV; cable. Complimentary coffee in lobby. Restaurant nearby. Ck-out noon. Business servs avail. Picnic table. Cr cds: A, C, D, DS, MC, V. D ⊬ SC

Hotels

★ ★ **CHANCELLOR.** *(1501 S Neil St, Champaign 61820) 2 mi S of I-74 Neil St exit. 217/352-7891; FAX 217/352-8108.* 225 rms, 4-7 story. S $61-$71; D $69-$79; each addl $8; suites $100-$200; under 18 free. Crib free. Pet accepted. TV; cable. 2 pools, 1 indoor; wading pool, whirlpools. Supervised child's activities. Complimentary continental bkfst. Restaurant 6 am-11 pm; to 2 am wkends. Bar 4 pm-1 am, closed Sun. Ck-out 1 pm. Meeting rms. Business servs avail. In-rm modem link. Gift shop. Free airport, RR, bus transportation. Game rm. Exercise equipt; weight machines, stair machines, saunas. Microwaves avail. Dinner theater. Cr cds: A, C, D, DS, MC, V. D ⊬ ⊵ 𝕏 ✕ 🐾 SC

★ ★ ★ **JUMER'S CASTLE LODGE.** *(209 S Broadway, Urbana 61801) Lincoln Square, 1¹/₂ mi S of I-74 Lincoln exit.* 217/384-8800; FAX 217/384-9001; res: 800/285-8637. 130 rms, 4 story. S $82-$127; D $92-$127; each addl $10; suites $107-$154; under 18 free; wkend rates. Crib free. Pet accepted, some restrictions; $25 deposit. TV; cable (premium). Saunas. Indoor pool; whirlpool. Complimentary coffee in lobby. Restaurant 6:30 am-10 pm; Fri, Sat to 11 pm. Rm serv. Bar 4 pm-1 am; entertainment. Ck-out noon. Meeting rms. Business servs avail. In-rm modem link. Shopping arcade. Free airport transportation. Some fireplaces. Cr cds: A, C, D, DS, ER, JCB, MC, V. ▢ ▨ ▨ ▨ ▨ ▨

Charleston *(See also Mattoon)*

Motel

✔ ★ **ECONO LODGE.** *810 W Lincoln Hwy.* 217/345-7689; FAX 217/345-7697. 52 rms, 2 story. S $38-$79; D $42-$85; under 12 free. Crib $5. Pet accepted; $10 deposit. TV; cable (premium), VCR avail. Complimentary continental bkfst. Restaurant nearby. Ck-out 11 am. Business servs avail. Refrigerators, microwaves avail. Cr cds: A, C, D, DS, JCB, MC, V. ▢ ▨ ▨

Motor Hotel

✔ ★ ★ **BEST WESTERN WORTHINGTON INN.** *920 W Lincoln Hwy, 3 mi W on IL 16 exit I-57.* 217/348-8161; FAX 217/348-8165. Web www.bestwestern.com/thisco/bw/14144 /14144_b.html. 67 rms, 1-2 story. S, D $59-$74; each addl $3; suites $114-$124; under 12 free; wkly rates. Crib free. Pet accepted, some restrictions. TV; cable, VCR avail. Complimentary coffee in lobby. Restaurants 6:30 am-2 pm, 5-9 pm (also see TAPESTRIES). Ck-out 11 am. Meeting rms. Business servs avail. Free airport transportation. Health club privileges. Heated pool. Some refrigerators, microwaves. Cr cds: A, D, DS, MC, V. ▢ ▨ ▨ ▨

Chicago

Motor Hotel

★ **RAMADA INN LAKE SHORE.** *4900 S Lake Shore Dr (60615), Hyde Park.* 773/288-5800; FAX 773/288-5745. 182 rms, 2-4 story. S $89; D $94; each addl $10; suites $155; under 19 free; wkend rates. Crib free. Pet accepted, some restrictions. TV; cable (premium). Pool; poolside serv. Restaurant 6:30 am-10 pm. Rm serv. Bar 11-1 am. Ck-out 11 am. Meeting rms. Business center. Bellhops. Valet serv. Many rms with view of Lake Michigan. Cr cds: A, C, D, DS, MC, V. ▢ ▨ ▨ ▨ ▨ ▨ ▨

Hotels

✔ ★ **CITY SUITES.** *933 W Belmont Ave (60657), Lakeview.* 773/404-3400; res: 800/248-9108; FAX 773/404-3405. Web www.cityinns.com. 45 rms, 4 story, 29 suites. S $85; D $95; each addl $10; suites $99; under 12 free; wkly rates. Crib free. Pet accepted, some restrictions; $200 deposit. Garage parking $7. TV; cable (premium), VCR avail. Complimentary continental bkfst. Restaurant adj 7 am-10 pm. Ck-out noon. Coin lndry. Health club privileges. Refrigerator in suites. Microwaves avail. Cr cds: A, C, D, DS, ER, MC, V. ▨ ▨ ▨ ▨

★ ★ **CLARIDGE.** *1244 N Dearborn Pkwy (60610), Gold Coast.* 312/787-4980; FAX 312/266-0978; res: 800/245-1258. E-mail claridge-hotel@att.net; web www.claridge.com. 168 rms, 14 story. S $119-$175; D $135-$190; each addl $15; suites $250-$450; under 18 free; wkend packages. Crib free. Pet accepted, some restrictions. Valet parking $20.25. TV. Complimentary continental bkfst. Restaurant 6:30 am-10:30 pm. Bar noon-2 am. Ck-out noon. Meeting rms. Business servs avail. Concierge. Airport transportation. Health club privileges. Minibars. Fireplace in some suites. Library. In historic residential area. Cr cds: A, C, D, DS, JCB, MC, V. ▢ ▨ ▨ ▨ ▨

★ ★ ★ **FOUR SEASONS.** *120 E Delaware Place (60611), at 900 N Michigan Ave complex, north of the Loop.* 312/280-8800; FAX 312/280-1748. E-mail fourtiff@aol.com; web www.fourseasonsregent.com. From the spacious English country manor-style lobby of this sparkling hotel, it's easy to forget that you're on the seventh floor of a 66-story skycraper, just above a chic shopping mall on Chicago's fashionable North Michigan Avenue. Many of the guest rooms, which begin on floor 30, have spectacular views of the city and/or Lake Michigan and all the necessities and comforts for work or relaxation. 343 rms, 66 story bldg, guest rms on floors 30-46, 157 suites. S $325-$445; D $365-$485; each addl $30; suites $690-$995; wkend rates; special packages. Crib free. Pet accepted. Self-park adj, in/out $15.25. TV; cable (premium), VCR avail (movies). Indoor pool; whirlpool. Restaurant 6:30-9:30 am, 11:30 am-2 pm, 6-10 pm. Rm serv 24 hrs. Bar 11:30-1 am; entertainment. Ck-out noon. Convention facilities. Business center. In-rm modem link. Concierge. Shopping access to 900 North Michigan Mall. Barber, beauty shop. Extensive exercise rm; instructor, weight machine, stair machine, sauna, steam rm. Massage. Bathrm phones, minibars; some wet bars. Lake 3 blks. Cr cds: A, C, D, DS, ER, JCB, MC, V.

★ ★ **HOLIDAY INN-MART PLAZA.** *350 N Orleans St (60654), atop Apparel Center, adj Merchandise Mart, River North. 312/836-5000; FAX 312/222-9508.* 526 rms, 23 story; guest rms on floors 16-23. S $119-$219; D $134-$244; each addl $16; suites $325-$525; under 18 free; wkend rates; package plans. Crib free. Pet accepted, some restrictions. Garage $13/day. TV. Indoor pool. Restaurant 6:30 am-2 pm, 5-10:30 pm. Bars noon-2 am. Ck-out noon. Coin lndry. Convention facilities. Shopping arcade. Barber, beauty shop. Airport transportation. Exercise equipt; bicycles, treadmill. Refrigerator in suites. Cr cds: A, C, D, DS, JCB, MC, V.

★ ★ **MARRIOTT.** *540 N Michigan Ave (60611), at Ohio St, north of the Loop. 312/836-0100; FAX 312/836-6139.* 1,172 rms, 46 story. S $159-$249; D $189-$299; suites $590-$1,150; under 18 free; wkend rates. Crib free. Pet accepted. Valet parking $23.25. TV; cable (premium), VCR avail. Indoor pool; whirlpool, poolside serv. Coffee in rms. Restaurant 6:30 am-midnight. Bar 11-2 am. Ck-out noon. Convention facilities. Business center. In-rm modem link. Concierge. Shopping arcade. Barber, beauty shop. Exercise rm; instructor, weight machines, bicycles, sauna. Massage. Basketball courts. Game rm. Bathrm phone in suites; microwaves avail. Luxury level. Cr cds: A, C, D, DS, ER, JCB, MC, V.

★ ★ **PALMER HOUSE HILTON.** *17 E Monroe St (60603), at State St, the Loop. 312/726-7500; FAX 312/263-2556.* 1,639 rms, 23 story. S $175-$300; D $200-$325; each addl $25; suites from $650; family, wkend rates. Crib free. Pet accepted. Garage $15, valet $21.25. TV; cable (premium), VCR avail. Indoor pool; whirlpool. Complimentary coffee in rms. Restaurants 6:30-2 am. Bars 11:30-2 am; entertainment. Ck-out noon. Convention facilities. Business center. In-rm modem link. Concierge. Shopping arcade. Barber, beauty shop. Airport transportation. Exercise rm; instructor, weights, bicycles, sauna, steam rm. Massage. Minibars. Refrigerator in suites. Luxury level. Cr cds: A, C, D, DS, ER, JCB, MC, V.

✔ ★ **PARK BROMPTON INN.** *528 W Brompton Ave (60657), in Lakeview. 773/404-3499; res: 800/727-5108; FAX 773/404-3495.* Web www.cityinns.com. 52 rms, 4 story, 22 kit. suites. S $85; D $95; each addl $10; suites $99; under 12 free; wkend rates (2-day min). Crib free. Pet accepted, some restrictions; $200 deposit. Garage parking $7. TV; cable (premium). Complimentary continental bkfst. Restaurant nearby. Ck-out noon. No bellhops. Coin lndry. Health club privileges. Refrigerator, microwave, wet bar in suites. Cr cds: A, C, D, DS, ER, MC, V.

★ ★ ★ **RADISSON.** *160 E Huron (60611), north of the Loop. 312/787-2900; FAX 312/787-5158.* E-mail radchgo@ix.netcom.com. 341 rms, 40 story, 96 suites. Apr-Dec: S $139-$199; D $134-$209; each addl $15; suites $179-$259; under 17 free; wkend rates; lower rates rest of yr. Crib free. Pet accepted, some restrictions. Valet parking $21. TV; cable (premium), VCR avail. Pool; poolside serv. Complimentary coffee in rms. Restaurant 6 am-11 pm. Rm serv 24 hrs. Bar noon-midnight. Ck-out noon. Convention facilities. Business center. In-rm modem link. Concierge. Gift shop. Barber. Exercise equipt; weight machine, bicycle. Minibars; some refrigerators; microwaves avail. Cr cds: A, C, D, DS, ER, JCB, MC, V.

★ ★ ★ **RENAISSANCE.** *1 W Wacker Dr (60601), on the Chicago River, north of the Loop. 312/372-7200; FAX 312/372-0093.* Web www.renaissancehotels.com. The interior of this white-stone-and-glass lodging evokes a grand 19th-century hotel with its multiple fountains, crystal chandeliers, marble accents and grand staircase. All guest rooms have sitting areas and many offer dramatic river views. 553 units, 27 story. S $270-$350; D $290-$370; each addl $20; suites $500-$900; under 18 free; wkend plans. Crib free. Pet accepted, some restrictions. Garage; valet parking in/out $26. TV; cable (premium), VCR avail. Indoor pool; whirlpool, poolside serv. Restaurants 6 am-midnight. Rm serv 24 hrs. Bar 11-2 am; pianist, jazz trio. Ck-out 1 pm. Convention facilities. Business center. In-rm modem link. Concierge. Shopping arcade. Tennis privileges. Exercise rm; instructor, weight machine, bicycles, sauna. Massage. Minibars; bathrm phone in suites. Luxury level. Cr cds: A, C, D, DS, ER, JCB, MC, V.

★ ★ **RESIDENCE INN BY MARRIOTT.** *201 E Walton Place (60611), north of the Loop. 312/943-9800; FAX 312/943-8579.* 221 kit. suites, 19 story. Suites $169-$325; wkend, wkly, monthly rates. Crib free. Pet accepted, some restrictions; $5. Valet parking, in/out $22. TV; cable (premium). Pool privileges. Complimentary continental bkfst; afternoon refreshments. Complimentary coffee in rms. Restaurant adj 6:30 am-10 pm. Ck-out noon. Coin lndry. Meeting rms. Business servs avail. In-rm modem link. Exercise equipt; weight machine, bicycles. Health club privileges. Microwaves. One blk from Oak St beach. Cr cds: A, C, D, DS, JCB, MC, V. ⬛ 🏃 🎿 🛏 🐾 SC

★ ★ ★ ★ **THE RITZ-CARLTON.** *160 E Pearson St (60611), at Water Tower Place, north of the Loop.* 312/266-1000; FAX 312/266-1194; res: 800/621-6906 (exc IL). Magnificent flower arrangements, a fountain, wicker and palms set the tone in the two-story greenhouse lobby here. The guest rooms upstairs are spacious with mahogany furniture, cherry-wood armoires and wingback chairs. 429 rms, 31 story, 84 suites. S, D $315-$395; each addl $30; suites $415-$1,050; under 12 free; wkend rates, special packages. Crib free. Pet accepted. Parking in/out $25.50/day. TV; cable (premium), VCR avail. Heated pool $10; whirlpool. Restaurant 6:30-1 am. Rm serv 24 hrs. Bar from 11 am; Fri, Sat to 2 am. Ck-out 1 pm. Convention facilities. Business center. In-rm modem link. Concierge. Tennis privileges. Exercise rm; instructor, weights, bicycles, sauna, steam rm. Massage. Bathrm phones, minibars; refrigerators avail. Kennels avail. Cr cds: A, C, D, DS, ER, JCB, MC, V. ⬛ 🏃 🎿 🛏 🎿 🛏 🐾 🏃

★ ★ ★ **SHERATON CHICAGO HOTEL & TOWERS.** *301 E North Water St (60611), Columbus Dr at Chicago River, north of the Loop.* 312/464-1000; FAX 312/464-9140. Web www.sheraton.com. 1,204 rms, 34 story, 54 suites. S $199-$269; D $219-$289; each addl $25; suites $350-$3500; under 17 free. Pet accepted, some restrictions. Garage, in/out $24. TV; cable (premium), VCR avail. Indoor pool. Complimentary coffee in rms. Restaurant 6-1 am. Rm serv 24 hrs. Bar 11-1:30 am; pianist. Ck-out noon. Convention facilities. Business center. In-rm modem link. Concierge. Gift shop. Tennis privileges. Exercise equipt; weight machines, bicycles, sauna. Massage. Minibars. On Chicago River, near Navy Pier. Views of Lake Michigan and skyline. Luxury level. Cr cds: A, C, D, DS, ER, JCB, MC, V. ⬛ 🏃 🎿 🛏 🎿 🛏 🐾 SC 🏃

✔★ **SURF.** *555 W Surf St (60657), Lakeview.* 773/528-8400; res: 800/787-3108; FAX 773/528-8483. Web www.cityinns.com. 55 rms, 4 story. S $79-$89; D $99-$129; each addl $10; suites $99-$129; under 12 free; wkends (2-day min). Crib free. Pet accepted; $200 deposit. Garage parking $8. TV; cable. Complimentary continental bkfst. Restaurant nearby. No rm serv. Ck-out 11 am. In-rm modem link. No bellhops. Concierge. Health club privileges. Cr cds: A, C, D, DS, ER, JCB, MC, V. 🏃 🛏 🐾 SC

★ ★ **SUTTON PLACE.** *21 E Bellevue Place (60611), Gold Coast.* 312/266-2100; FAX 312/266-2103; res: 800/606-8188. E-mail info@chi.suttonplace.com; web www.travelweb.com/sutton.html. 246 rms, 22 story, 40 suites. S $245-$270; D $260-$285; each addl $25; suites $315-$725; under 16 free; wkend rates. Crib free. Pet accepted, some restrictions; $200 refundable. Valet parking $24. TV; cable (premium), VCR (movies). Restaurant 7 am-11 pm. Rm serv 24 hrs. Bar 11:30-1 am; Fri, Sat to 2 am. Ck-out noon. Meeting rms. Business center. In-rm modem link. Concierge. Airport transportation. Exercise equipt; stair machine, treadmill. Health club privileges. Bathrm phones, minibars. Penthouse suites with garden terrace. Cr cds: A, C, D, DS, JCB, MC, V. ⬛ 🏃 🎿 🛏 🐾 SC 🏃

★ ★ ★ **TREMONT.** *100 E Chestnut St (60611), north of the Loop.* 312/751-1900; FAX 312/751-8691; res: 800/621-8133. 129 rms, 16 story. S, D $225-$245; suites $345-$925; under 18 free; wkend rates. Crib free. Pet accepted, some restrictions. Parking $23. TV; cable (premium), VCR (movies). Coffee in rms. Restaurant 6:30 am-11 pm. Rm serv 24 hrs. Bar 11-midnight. Ck-out noon. Meeting rms. Business servs avail. In-rm modem link. Concierge. Bathrm phones, minibars; microwaves avail. Cr cds: A, C, D, DS, JCB, MC, V. ⬛ 🏃 🛏 🐾

★ ★ ★ **WESTIN.** *909 N Michigan Ave (60611), at Delaware Place, north of the Loop.* 312/943-7200; FAX 312/649-7447. Web www.westin.com. 740 rms, 27 story. S, D $269-$329; each addl $20; suites $350-$1,500; under 18 free; package plans. Crib free. Pet accepted, some restrictions. Valet parking, in/out $25. TV; cable (premium). Restaurant 6:30 am-10 pm. Rm serv 24 hrs. Bar 11-1:30 am. Ck-out noon. Convention facilities. Business center. In-rm modem link. Concierge. Gift shop. Exercise equipt; weights, bicycles, sauna. Massage. Minibars; many bathrm phones; microwaves avail. Luxury level. Cr cds: A, C, D, DS, ER, JCB, MC, V. ⬛ 🏃 🎿 🛏 🐾 SC 🏃

★ ★ ★ **WESTIN RIVER NORTH CHICAGO.** *320 N Dearborn St (60610), River North.* 312/744-1900; FAX 312/527-2650. The polished granite, black lacquer and mahogany interior of this hotel has an understated elegance. Floor-to-ceiling windows look out on a rock garden. Guest rooms are furnished in either contemporary or traditional style. 422 rms, 20 story. S $275-$315; D $270-$310; each addl $25; suites $450-$2,500 under 18 free; special packages. Crib free. Pet accepted, some restrictions. Valet parking $26 in/out. TV; cable (premium), VCR avail. Coffee in rms. Restaurant 6:30 am-11 pm. Rm serv 24 hrs. Bar 11-1:30 am; pianist 6 days. Ck-out noon. Convention facilities. Business center. In-rm modem link. Concierge. Exercise rm; instructor, weights, bicycles, sauna. Massage. Bathrm phones, minibars. Cr cds: A, C, D, DS, ER, JCB, MC, V.

[D] [✔] [✗] [◢] [◣] [SC] [✦]

Chicago O'Hare Airport Area

(See also Arlington Heights, Chicago, Elmhurst, Schaumburg)

Motels

★ ★ **EXEL INN.** *(2881 Touhy Ave (IL 72), Elk Grove Village 60007) 847/803-9400; FAX 847/803-9771.* 123 rms, 3 story. S $52.99-$60.99; D $62.99-$64.99; under 18 free. Crib avail. Pet accepted, some restrictions. TV; cable. Complimentary continental bkfst. Coffee in rms. Restaurant nearby. Ck-out noon. Coin lndry. Business servs avail. In-rm modem link. Free airport transportation. Exercise equipt; bicycle, treadmill. Refrigerators avail. Cr cds: A, C, D, DS, MC, V. [D] [✔] [✗] [◢] [◣] [SC]

✔ ★ ★ **LA QUINTA.** *(1900 Oakton St, Elk Grove Village 60007) 2 mi NW on I-90 to Elmhurst Rd, then N to Oakton St. 847/439-6767; FAX 847/439-5464.* 142 rms, 4 story. S $79-$84; D $84-$91; each addl $7; under 18 free. Crib free. Pet accepted, some restrictions. TV; cable. Heated pool. Complimentary continental bkfst. Restaurant opp 7 am-11 pm. Ck-out noon. Meeting rms. Business servs avail. In-rm modem link. Valet serv. Free airport transportation. Health club privileges. Some refrigerators. Cr cds: A, C, D, DS, MC, V. [D] [✔] [≋] [✗] [◢] [◣] [SC]

★ ★ **RESIDENCE INN BY MARRIOTT.** *(9450 W Lawrence, Schiller Park 60176) 847/725-2210; FAX 847/725-2211.* 169 kit. suites, 3-6 story. 1-bedrm $129-$179; 2-bedrm $149-$179; 3-bedrm $450; monthly rates. Crib free. Pet accepted; $100. TV; cable (premium). Pool, whirlpool. Complimentary continental bkfst. Coffee in rms. Restaurant adj. Ck-out noon. Coin lndry. Meeting rms. Business center. In-rm modem link. Valet serv. Free airport transportation. Health club privileges. Refrigerators, microwaves. Balconies. Picnic tables, grills. Cr cds: A, C, D, DS, JCB, MC, V. [D] [✔] [≋] [✗] [◢] [◣] [SC] [✦]

Hotels

★ ★ **HOLIDAY INN.** *(5440 N River Rd, Rosemont 60018) on US 45, 1 mi E of O'Hare Intl Airport. 847/671-6350; FAX 847/671-5406.* 507 rms, 14 story. S $159; D $169; each addl $10; suites $175-$200; under 18 free; wkend package. Crib free. Pet accepted. TV; cable (premium). 2 pools, 1 indoor; whirlpool. Restaurant 6:30 am-midnight. Bars 11-2 am; wkends to 4 am; entertainment exc Sun. Ck-out noon. Coin lndry. Meeting rms. Business center. In-rm modem link. Free airport transportation. Exercise equipt; weight machine, stair machine, sauna. Game rm. Refrigerators avail. Minibars. Cr cds: A, C, D, DS, MC, V. [D] [✔] [≋] [✗] [✗] [◢] [◣] [SC] [✦]

★ ★ ★ **HOTEL SOFITEL.** *(5550 N River Rd, Rosemont 60018) 2 blks S of I-90 exit River Rd S. 847/678-4488; FAX 847/678-4244.* 304 rms, 10 story. S $205-$215; D $225-$235; each addl $10; suites $305-$325; under 18 free. Crib free. Pet accepted, some restrictions. Valet parking $12. TV; cable (premium). Indoor pool. Restaurants 6:30-12:30 am. Rm serv 24 hrs. Bar 11-1 am. Ck-out noon. Convention facilities. Business center. In-rm modem link. Concierge. Gift shop. Free airport transportation. Exercise equipt; weights, bicycles, sauna. Bathrm phones, minibars; refrigerators avail. Traditional European-style hotel. Cr cds: A, C, D, DS, ER, JCB, MC, V. [D] [✔] [≋] [✗] [✈] [◢] [◣] [SC] [✦]

★ ★ ★ **MARRIOTT.** *(8535 W Higgins Rd, Chicago 60631) on IL 72, 1¹/₂ mi E of O'Hare Intl Airport at Kennedy Expy, Cumberland Ave N exit. 773/693-4444; FAX 773/714-4297.* 681 rms, 12 story. S, D $149-$204; suites $179-$450; under 18 free; wkend plans. Crib free. Pet accepted. TV; cable (premium). 2 pools, 1 indoor/outdoor; wading pool, whirlpool, poolside serv. Restaurants 6:30 am-10 pm. Rm serv to midnight. Bars 11:30-1:30 am. Ck-out noon. Coin lndry. Convention facilities. Business center. In-rm modem link. Concierge. Gift shop. Valet parking. Free airport transportation. Exercise equipt; weights, bicycles. Refrigerators, microwaves avail. Private patios, balconies. Luxury level. Cr cds: A, C, D, DS, ER, JCB, MC, V. [D] [✔] [≋] [✗] [✈] [◢] [◣] [SC] [✦]

★ ★ ★ **MARRIOTT SUITES.** *(6155 N River Rd, Rosemont 60018) I-190E exit River Rd N. 847/696-4400; FAX 847/696-2122.* 256 suites, 11 story. S $189; D $199; wkend rates. Crib free. Pet accepted. TV; cable (premium), VCR avail. Indoor pool; whirlpool. Coffee in rms. Restaurant 6:30 am-10:30 pm. Bar 11:30 am-midnight. Ck-out 1 pm. Meeting rms. Business servs avail. In-rm modem link. Gift shop. Free airport transportation. Exercise equipt; bicycles, stair machine, sauna. Health club privileges. Refrigerators, wet bars; microwaves avail. Cr cds: A, C, D, DS, ER, JCB, MC, V. [D] [✔] [≋] [✗] [✗] [◢] [◣] [SC]

★ ★ ★ **SHERATON GATEWAY SUITES.** *(6501 N Mannheim Rd, Rosemont 60018) ¹/₂ mi N of I-190 exit Mannheim Rd N. 847/699-6300; FAX 847/699-0391.* Web www.shera

ton.com/sheraton/html/properties/hotel_and_resorts/040.html. 297 suites, 11 story. Sept-Dec: S, D $200-$245; each addl $10; under 18 free; wkend rates; lower rates rest of yr. Crib free. Pet accepted. TV; cable (premium), VCR avail. Indoor pool; whirlpool. Complimentary coffee in rms. Restaurant 11 am-2 pm, 5-10 pm. Rm serv 24 hrs. Bar 11-2 am. Ck-out noon. Convention facilities. Business center. In-rm modem link. Gift shop. Free airport transportation. Exercise equipt; treadmills, stair machine, sauna. Health club privileges. Refrigerators; some microwaves. Cr cds: A, C, D, DS, ER, JCB, MC, V.

⬛ 🏌 ≋ 🏋 🏹 ⇘ 🐾 SC 🛶

★ ★ SHERATON SUITES. *(121 NW Point Blvd, Elk Grove Village 60007) 847/290-1600; FAX 847/290-1129.* 255 rms, 7 story. Apr-June & mid-Sept-mid-Nov: S, D $159-$169; under 18 free; wkend rates; lower rates rest of yr. Crib free. Pet accepted, some restrictions; $50. TV; cable (premium), VCR avail. 2 pools, 1 indoor; whirlpool. Complimentary coffee in rms. Restaurant 6:30 am-10 pm. Bar 11:30 am-midnight. Ck-out 1 pm. Coin lndry. Meeting rms. Business servs avail. In-rm modem link. Gift shop. Free airport transportation. Exercise equipt; treadmills, rower, sauna. Game rm. Refrigerators; some microwaves. Cr cds: A, C, D, DS, ER, JCB, MC, V. ⬛ 🏌 ≋ 🏋 ⇘ 🐾 SC

Collinsville *(See also Belleville, Edwardsville)*

Motels

✔ ★ BEST WESTERN BO-JON INN. *Jct I-55/70 exit 15B & IL 159. 618/345-5720; FAX 618/345-5721.* 40 rms, 2 story. Apr-early Sept: S, D $50-$60; each addl $5; lower rates rest of yr. Pet accepted, some restrictions. TV; cable (premium), VCR avail (movies). Pool. Complimentary continental bkfst. Restaurant nearby. Ck-out 11 am. Business servs avail. In-rm modem link. Picnic tables, grills. Cr cds: A, C, D, DS, MC, V. 🏌 ≋ ⇘ 🐾 SC

✔ ★ HOWARD JOHNSON. *301 N Bluff Rd, I-55/70 exit 11. 618/345-1530; FAX 618/345-1321.* 87 rms, 2 story. June-Aug: S $40-$50; D $55-$65; each addl $5; under 10 free; lower rates rest of yr. Crib free. Pet accepted, some restrictions. TV; cable (premium). Pool; wading pool. Restaurant adj 10 am-10 pm. Bar noon-1 am; Sat to 2 am. Ck-out noon. Coin lndry. Business servs avail. Private patios. Cr cds: A, C, D, DS, MC, V.

🏌 ≋ ⇘ 🐾 SC

Inn

✔ ★ MAGGIE'S. *2102 N Keebler Rd. 618/344-8283.* 5 rms, 3 story. No rm phones. S $35-$75; D $45-$85; each addl $10. Pet accepted, some restrictions. TV; cable, VCR (movies). Complimentary full bkfst. Ck-out noon, ck-in 4-6 pm. Indoor pool; whirlpool. Built in 1900; former boarding house. Totally nonsmoking. No cr cds accepted. 🏌 🐾

Danville *(See also Champaign/Urbana)*

Motels

✔ ★ COMFORT INN. *383 Lynch Drive, I-74 & Lynch Dr exit 220. 217/443-8004.* 56 rms, 2 story, 14 suites. S $43.99-$51.99; D $48.99-$58.99; each addl $5; suites $52.99-$70.99; under 18 free; higher rates special events. Crib free. Pet accepted. TV; cable (premium). Indoor pool; whirlpool. Complimentary continental bkfst. Ck-out 11 am. Business servs avail. In-rm modem link. Game rm. Cr cds: A, C, D, DS, ER, MC, V.

⬛ 🏌 ≋ ⇘ 🐾 SC

★ ★ RAMADA INN. *388 Eastgate Dr, I-74 exit 220. 217/446-2400; FAX 217/446-3878.* 131 rms, 2 story. S $60-$64; D $62-$68; each addl $6; suites $98; under 18 free; wkend rates. Crib free. Pet accepted, some restrictions. TV; cable (premium). Pool. Complimentary continental bkfst. Complimentary coffee in rms. Restaurant 6 am-9 pm. Rm serv. Bar 11-1 am, Sun 1-11 pm. Ck-out noon. Coin lndry. Meeting rms. Business servs avail. Valet serv. Sundries. Free local airport transportation. Exercise equipt; weight machine, bicycles. Minibar in suites. Cr cds: A, C, D, DS, JCB, MC, V. ⬛ 🏌 ≋ 🏋 ⇘ 🐾 SC

Decatur *(See also Lincoln, Springfield)*

Motel

✔ ★ ★ BUDGETEL INN. *5100 Hickory Point (Frontage Rd) (62526), I-72 exit 141B. 217/875-5800; FAX 217/875-7537.* 105 rms, 2 story. S $39.95-$42.95; D $43.95-$46.95; each addl $7; under 18 free. Crib free. Pet accepted. TV; cable, VCR avail. Complimentary continental bkfst. Complimentary coffee in rms. Restaurant nearby. Ck-out noon. Meeting rms. Business servs avail. In-rm modem link. Some refrigerators, microwaves. Cr cds: A, C, D, DS, MC, V. ⬛ 🏌 ⇘ 🐾 SC

Motor Hotel

★ ★ ★ **HOLIDAY INN SELECT CONFERENCE HOTEL.** *Wyckles Rd (62522), 3 mi W on US 36.* 217/422-8800; FAX 217/422-9155. 383 rms, 2-4 story. S, D $85-$95; each addl $10; suites $110-$250; under 19 free. Crib free. Pet accepted; $25 deposit. TV; cable, VCR avail. Indoor pool; wading pool, whirlpool. Playground. Restaurants 6 am-11 pm; Fri, Sat to 1 am. Rm serv. Bar noon-1 am, Sun to 10 pm; entertainment exc Sun. Ck-out noon. Convention facilities. Business center. In-rm modem link. Bellhops. Gift shop. Free airport transportation. Lighted tennis. Exercise equipt; bicycles, treadmill, sauna. Holidome. Game rm. Picnic tables, fishing pond. Cr cds: A, C, D, DS, JCB, MC, V.

D ⊠ ⊠ ⊠ ⊠ ⊠ ⊠ ⊠ SC ⊠

De Kalb

Motel

★ ★ **UNIVERSITY INN.** *1212 W Lincoln Hwy, ³⁄₄ mi W on IL 38.* 815/758-8661; FAX 815/758-2603. 114 rms, 2 story. S, D $40; each addl $5; under 18 free. Crib free. Pet accepted, some restrictions. TV; cable (premium). Heated pool. Complimentary continental bkfst. Ck-out noon. Coin lndry. Meeting rms. Business servs avail. Near Northern Illinois Univ campus. Cr cds: A, C, D, DS, MC, V. D ⊠ ⊠ ⊠ ⊠ SC

Downers Grove (See also Hinsdale, Oak Brook)

Motels

✔ ★ **RED ROOF INN.** *1113 Butterfield Rd, off I-88, Highland Ave exit.* 630/963-4205; FAX 630/963-4425. 135 rms, 2 story. S $45.99; D $51.99-$58.99; under 18 free. Crib free. Pet accepted. TV; cable (premium). Complimentary coffee in lobby. Restaurant nearby. Ck-out 11 am. Meeting rm. Business servs avail. In-rm modem link. Cr cds: A, C, D, DS, MC, V. D ⊠ ⊠ ⊠ SC

Hotels

★ ★ **MARRIOTT SUITES.** *1500 Opus Place, off I-88, Highland Ave exit to Butterfield Rd, then S on Finley Rd.* 630/852-1500; FAX 630/852-6527. 254 suites, 7 story. S $109-$125; D $109-$139; wkend rates. Crib free. Pet accepted. TV; cable (premium), VCR avail (movies $6). Indoor/outdoor pool; whirlpool. Coffee in rms. Restaurant 7 am-10 pm. Bar from 11:30 am. Ck-out noon. Meeting rms. Business servs avail. In-rm modem link. Gift shop. Exercise equipt; weight machine, stair machine, sauna. Refrigerators. Balconies. Cr cds: A, C, D, DS, ER, JCB, MC, V. D ⊠ ⊠ ⊠ ⊠ ⊠

Edwardsville (See also Alton, Belleville, Collinsville)

Motel

★ **COMFORT INN.** *3080 S IL 157.* 618/656-4900; FAX 618/656-0998. 71 rms, 3 story. S $65-$70; D $70-$85; each addl $5; under 18 free; higher rates special events. Crib free. Pet accepted. TV; cable (premium). Complimentary continental bkfst. Coffee in rms. Ck-out noon. Meeting rms. Business servs avail. Indoor pool. Game rm. Cr cds: A, C, D, DS, MC, V. D ⊠ ⊠ ⊠ ⊠ SC

Effingham (See also Altamont, Mattoon)

Motels

★ **BEST INNS OF AMERICA.** *1209 N Keller Dr, off I-57/70 exit 160.* 217/347-5141. 83 rms, 2 story. Mid-May-Oct: S $36.88-$43; D $39-$46; each addl $7; under 18 free; lower rates rest of yr. Crib free. Pet accepted, some restrictions. TV; cable. Pool. Complimentary continental bkfst. Restaurant adj open 24 hrs. Ck-out 1 pm. Cr cds: A, C, D, DS, MC, V. D ⊠ ⊠ ⊠ ⊠ SC

✔ ★ **BEST WESTERN RAINTREE INN.** *Fayette Ave, I-57 & I-70 exit 159.* 217/342-4121. 65 rms, 2 story. May-Oct: S $39.95-$52; D $48-$59; each addl $5; under 12 free; higher rates special events; lower rates rest of yr. Crib $1. Pet accepted, some restrictions. TV; cable (premium). Complimentary continental bkfst. Restaurant nearby. Ck-out 11 am. Business servs avail. Pool. Some balconies. Cr cds: A, C, D, DS, MC, V. ⊠ ⊠ ⊠ ⊠ ⊠

★ **BUDGETEL.** *1103 Ave of Mid America.* 217/342-2525; FAX 217/347-7341. 122 rms, 4 story, 14 suites. S $46.95-$52.95; D $52.95-$55.95; suites $58.99-$65.99; under 18 free; wkly rates; higher rates special events. Crib free. Pet accepted, some restrictions. TV; cable. Complimentary continental bkfst. Complimentary coffee in rms.

Restaurant adj 6 am-10 pm. Ck-out noon. Meeting rms. Business servs avail. Coin lndry. Health club privileges. Indoor pool. Cr cds: A, C, D, DS, MC, V. 〔D〕〔🖐〕〔≋〕〔🏋〕〔🔥〕〔SC〕

★ ★ **COMFORT SUITES.** *1310 W Fayette, 3 bks E off I-57 & I-70 exit 159.* *217/342-3151; FAX 217/342-3555.* 65 rms, 3 story. S $59-$65; D $65-$75; each addl $6; under 18 free; higher rates special events. Crib avail. Pet accepted. TV; cable (premium). Complimentary continental bkfst. Restaurant adj 6-2 am. Ck-out 11 am. Business center. In-rm modem link. Coin lndry. Health club privileges. Indoor pool. Refrigerators, microwaves avail. Cr cds: A, C, D, DS, MC, V. 〔D〕〔🖐〕〔≋〕〔🏋〕〔🔥〕〔SC〕〔🚶〕

✔ ★ **DAYS INN.** *W Fayette Rd, 2 blks E of I-57 & I-70, exit 159.* 217/342-9271. 122 rms, 2 story. Apr-mid-Sept: S $38.88; D $49.95; each addl $5; under 13 free; lower rates rest of yr. Crib free. Pet accepted. TV; cable. Pool. Complimentary continental bkfst. Restaurant adj 6-2 am. Bar 11-1 am. Ck-out noon. Health club privileges. Microwaves avail. Cr cds: A, C, D, DS, MC, V. 〔🖐〕〔≋〕〔🏋〕〔🔥〕〔SC〕

✔ ★ ★ **HAMPTON INN.** *1509 Hampton Dr.* 217/342-4499; FAX 217/347-2828. 60 rms, 2 story. S $49-$59; D $54-$64; suites $79; under 18 free; higher rates special events. Crib avail. Pet accepted. TV; cable (premium). Complimentary continental bkfst. Restaurant nearby. Ck-out noon. Business servs avail. In-rm modem link. Health club privileges. Indoor pool. Refrigerators, microwaves avail. Cr cds: A, D, DS, MC, V. 〔D〕〔🖐〕〔≋〕〔🏋〕〔🔥〕〔SC〕

★ ★ **HOLIDAY INN.** *1600 W Fayette Ave.* 217/342-4161. 135 rms, 2 story. S $45-$60; D $50-$65; each addl $5; suites $95; under 17 free. Crib free. Pet accepted. TV; cable. Pool. Restaurant 6 am-9 pm; Fri, Sat to 10 pm. Rm serv. Bar 3 pm-1 am, Sun to 10 pm. Ck-out noon. Meeting rms. Business servs avail. Airport, RR station, bus depot transportation. Health club privileges. Cr cds: A, C, D, DS, JCB, MC, V. 〔D〕〔🖐〕〔≋〕〔🏋〕〔🔥〕〔SC〕

★ ★ **RAMADA KELLER.** *At jct IL 32/33 & I-57/70, exit 160.* 217/342-2131; FAX 217/347-8757. 169 rms, 2 story, 8 condo units. S $52-$89; D $60-$89; each addl $7; suites $89-$129; condos $109-$129; under 18 free. Crib free. Pet accepted, some restrictions. TV; cable. 2 pools, 1 indoor; whirlpool. Playground. Complimentary continental bkfst. Restaurant 6 am-10 pm. Rm serv. Bar noon-midnight; entertainment. Ck-out noon. Meeting rms. Valet serv. Gift shop. Free RR station, bus depot transportation. Exercise equipt; weights, bicycles, sauna, steam rm. Bowling alley. Miniature golf. Game rm. Some in-rm whirlpools. Balconies. Cr cds: A, C, D, DS, MC, V. 〔D〕〔🖐〕〔≋〕〔🏃〕〔🏋〕〔🔥〕〔SC〕

Elmhurst (See also Chicago O'Hare Airport Area, Hillside, Oak Brook)

Motel

★ ★ **HOLIDAY INN.** *624 N York Rd.* 630/279-1100; FAX 630/279-4038. 229 rms, 4 story. S $80-$90; D $90-$100; under 17 free; wknd rates. Crib free. Pet accepted, some restrictions. TV; cable (premium). Indoor pool; whirlpool. Restaurant 7 am-2 pm, 5-10 pm. Rm serv. Bar 11 am-midnight. Ck-out 11 am. Coin lndry. Meeting rms. Business servs avail. In-rm modem link. Valet serv. Free O'Hare Airport transportation. Putting green. Exercise equipt; weight machine, bicycle, sauna. Holidome. Game rm. Balconies. Cr cds: A, C, D, DS, JCB, MC, V. 〔D〕〔🖐〕〔≋〕〔🏃〕〔🏋〕〔🔥〕〔SC〕

Freeport (See also Rockford)

Motel

★ ★ **GUEST HOUSE INN.** *1300 E South St.* 815/235-3121; FAX 815/235-4946. 85 rms, 2 story. S $61; D $67; each addl $6; under 19 free. Crib free. Pet accepted. TV; cable (premium). Heated pool; poolside serv. Complimentary coffee in rms. Restaurant 6 am-2 pm, 5-10 pm. Rm serv. Bar 4 pm-1 am. Ck-out noon. Meeting rms. Business servs avail. Exercise equipt; stair machine, weight machine. Game rm. Cr cds: A, C, D, DS, JCB, MC, V. 〔D〕〔🖐〕〔≋〕〔🏃〕〔🏋〕〔🔥〕〔SC〕

Galena (See also Platteville, WI)

Motels

★ ★ **BEST WESTERN QUIET HOUSE SUITES.** *9923 W US 20.* 815/777-2577; FAX 815/777-0584. 42 suites, 3 story. S $91-$180; D $91-$190; each addl $10; higher rates: special events, wkends. Pet accepted, some restrictions; $15. TV; cable (premium). Indoor/outdoor pool; whirlpool. Complimentary coffee in lobby. Restaurant adj 7 am-11 pm.

Ck-out 11 am. Business servs avail. Exercise equipt; weights, treadmill. Downhill/x-country ski 12 mi. Some balconies. Cr cds: A, C, D, DS, ER, JCB, MC, V.

[D] [♥] [≋] [≈] [⛷] [🐾] [SC]

✓ ★ **PALACE.** *11383 US 20 W, 2 mi W on US 20, IL 84.* 815/777-2043; FAX 815/777-2625. 51 rms in motel, guest houses, 1-2 story. Some rm phones. S $30; D $55; suites $110-$200; rms in Ryan & Bedford houses $85-$175. Crib $4. Pet accepted, some restrictions. TV. Indoor whirlpool. Complimentary coffee in lobby. Restaurant nearby. Ck-out 11 am. Downhill ski 9 mi; x-country ski 6 mi. Complex consists of motel; Ryan House (1876), a 24-rm Italianate/Victorian mansion with antiques; and Bedford House (1850), an Italianate structure with original chandeliers, leaded glass and walnut staircase. Cr cds: A, DS, MC, V.

[♥] [≋] [🐾] [SC]

Galesburg (See also Moline, Monmouth)

Motel

✓ ★ ★ **COMFORT INN.** *907 W Carl Sandburg Dr (US 150 E).* 309/344-5445. 46 rms, 2 story. May-Sept: S $50.95-$65.95; D $55.95-$70.95; each addl $5; under 18 free; higher rates: Railroad Days, Stearman Fly-in wknd; lower rates rest of yr. Crib free. Pet accepted. TV; cable (premium), VCR avail. Complimentary continental bkfst. Complimentary coffee in lobby. Restaurant nearby. Ck-out 11 am. Meeting rm. Business servs avail. Cr cds: A, C, D, DS, ER, MC, V. [D] [♥] [≈] [🐾] [SC]

Motor Hotels

★ ★ ★ **JUMER'S CONTINENTAL INN.** *E Main St, at I-74.* 309/343-7151; FAX 309/343-7151, ext. 264; res: 800/285-8637. 148 rms, 2 story. S $63-$71; D $69-$77; each addl $6; suites $130; under 18 free; wknd rates. Crib free. Pet accepted. TV; cable (premium), VCR avail. Indoor pool; whirlpool, sauna. Complimentary coffee in lobby. Restaurant 6:30 am-10 pm. Rm serv. Bar 11-midnight; Sun from noon; entertainment. Ck-out noon. Coin lndry. Meeting rms. Business servs avail. Bellhops. Valet serv. Sundries. Gift shop. Free airport, RR station transportation. Golf privileges. Health club privileges. Putting green. Many private patios. In-rm whirlpool. Cr cds: A, C, D, DS, MC, V.

[D] [♥] [🍴] [≈] [⛷] [≋] [🐾] [SC]

★ **RAMADA INN.** *29 Public Sq, just off Main St.* 309/343-9161; FAX 309/343-0157. 96 rms, 7 story. S $50-$55; D $55-$60; each addl $5. Crib free. Pet accepted. TV; cable (premium), VCR avail (movies $6). Indoor pool; whirlpool. Complimentary coffee in lobby. Restaurant. Ck-out noon. Meeting rms. Business servs avail. In-rm modem link. Health club privileges. Game rm. Balconies. Near Knox College campus. Cr cds: A, C, D, DS, JCB, MC, V. [D] [♥] [≈] [≋] [🐾] [SC]

Glen Ellyn

Motor Hotel

★ ★ **HOLIDAY INN.** *1250 Roosevelt Rd (IL 38), E of I-355 exit Roosevelt Rd, E.* 630/629-6000; FAX 630/629-0025. 120 rms, 4 story. S $55-$69; D $61-$75; under 18 free. Crib free. Pet accepted, some restrictions. TV; cable (premium), VCR avail. Heated pool. Complimentary coffee in lobby. Restaurant 6:30 am-2 pm, 5-10 pm. Rm serv. Bar. Ck-out 1 pm. Coin lndry. Meeting rms. Business servs avail. In-rm modem link. Health club privileges. Cr cds: A, C, D, DS, MC, V. [D] [♥] [≈] [≋] [🐾] [SC]

Glenview (See also Northbrook, Skokie, Wheeling)

Motel

★ **BUDGETEL INN.** *1625 Milwaukee Ave (IL 21).* 847/635-8300; FAX 847/635-8166. 150 rms, 3 story. S $46.95-$53.95; D $52.95-$54.95; each addl $7; under 18 free. Crib free. Pet accepted, some restrictions. TV; cable (premium); VCR avail. Complimentary continental bkfst. Coffee in rms. Restaurant opp open 24 hrs. Ck-out noon. Coin lndry. Meeting rm. Business servs avail. In-rm modem link. Valet serv. Some refrigerators, microwaves. Cr cds: A, C, D, DS, MC, V. [D] [♥] [≈] [🐾] [SC]

Greenville (See also Vandalia)

Motel

✓ ★ **BEST WESTERN COUNTRY VIEW INN.** *RR 4, Box 163, Jct I-70, IL 127.* 618/664-3030. 83 rms, 2 story. May-Sept: S $39-$43; D $47-$53; each addl $4; under 18 free; lower rates rest of yr. Crib $2. Pet accepted, some restrictions; $2. TV; cable. Heated pool. Complimentary continental bkfst. Restaurant adj 6 am-10 pm. Ck-out noon. Meeting rm. Microwaves avail. Cr cds: A, C, D, DS, ER, MC, V. [D] 🖢 🖢 🖢 🖢 SC

Gurnee (See also Libertyville, Waukegan)

Motel

★ ★ **BUDGETEL INN.** *5688 N Ridge Rd. 847/662-7600; FAX 847/662-5300.* 106 rms, 4 story. Memorial Day-Labor Day: S, D $99.95; suites $109.95; lower rates rest of yr. Crib free. Pet accepted. TV; cable (premium). Complimentary continental bkfst. Complimentary coffee in rms. Restaurant adj 7 am-10 pm. Ck-out noon. Business servs avail. In-rm modem link. Coin lndry. Meeting rm. Refrigerator, microwave in suites. Cr cds: A, C, D, DS, MC, V. [D] 🖢 🖢 🖢 SC

Hillside (See also Elmhurst, Hinsdale)

Motel

★ ★ **HOLIDAY INN.** *4400 Frontage Rd, at I-290W, exit Wolf Rd. 708/544-9300; FAX 708/544-9310.* 248 rms, 3 story. S, D $89; wkend rates. Crib free. Pet accepted. TV; cable (premium). Heated pool. Restaurant 6 am-2 pm, 5-10 pm. Rm serv. Bar 11:30-2 am; dancing. Ck-out noon. Coin lndry. Meeting rms. Business servs avail. In-rm modem link. Valet serv. Golf privileges. Health club. Exercise equipt; stair machine, weight machine. Cr cds: A, C, D, DS, JCB, MC, V. [D] 🖢 🖢 🖢 🖢 🖢 🖢 SC

Hinsdale (See also Downers Grove, Oak Brook)

Motel

✔ ★ **RED ROOF INN.** *(7535 IL 83, Willowbrook) S on IL 83. 630/323-8811; FAX 630/323-2714.* 109 rms, 3 story. S $39.99-$46.99; D $46.99-$53.99; under 18 free. Crib free. Pet accepted, some restrictions. TV; cable (premium). Complimentary coffee in lobby. Restaurant adj 8 am-10 pm. Ck-out noon. Business servs avail. In-rm modem link. Cr cds: A, C, D, DS, MC, V. [D] 🖢 🖢 🖢

Motor Hotels

★ ★ **BUDGETEL INN.** *(855 79th St, Willowbrook) 4 mi SW on IL 83. 630/654-0077; FAX 630/654-0181.* 137 rms, 3 story. S $47-$58; D $54-$65; under 18 free. Crib free. Pet accepted, some restrictions. TV; cable (premium), VCR avail (movies). Complimentary continental bkfst. Restaurant nearby. Ck-out noon. Meeting rm. Business servs avail. Some refrigerators. Cr cds: A, C, D, DS, MC, V. [D] 🖢 🖢 🖢 SC

★ ★ ★ **HOLIDAY INN.** *(7800 S Kingery Hwy, Willowbrook) On IL 83, just N of I-55. 630/325-6400; FAX 630/325-2362.* 220 rms, 3 story. S $89; D $99; suites $95-$115; studio rms $85; under 19 free; wkend rates. Crib free. Pet accepted, some restrictions. TV; cable (premium), VCR avail (movies). Heated pool; lifeguard. Restaurant 6:30 am-2 pm, 5-10 pm. Rm serv. Bar 11-1 am; Fri, Sat to 2 am. Ck-out 1 pm. Meeting rms. Business servs avail. In-rm modem link. Valet serv. Gift shop. Free Midway Airport transportation. Exercise equipt; weight machine, stair machine, sauna. Luxury level. Cr cds: A, C, D, DS, JCB, MC, V. [D] 🖢 🖢 🖢 🖢 🖢 SC

Homewood

Motel

★ **BUDGETEL INN.** *(17225 Halsted St, South Holland 60473) Just N of jct I-80, I-294, on IL 1. 708/596-8700; FAX 708/596-9978.* 102 rms, 2 story. S $46.95; D $55.95; each addl $7; under 18 free. Crib free. Pet accepted. TV, cable (premium). Complimentary continental bkfst. Restaurant adj open 24 hrs. Ck-out noon. Business servs avail. In-rm modem link. Valet serv. Cr cds: A, C, D, DS, MC, V. [D] 🖢 🖢 🖢 SC

Jacksonville (See also Springfield)

Motel

★ ★ **HOLIDAY INN.** *1717 W Morton Ave. 217/245-9571; FAX 217/245-0686.* 114 rms, 2 story. S, D $56-$69; under 19 free. Crib free. Pet accepted. TV; cable (premium), VCR avail. Indoor pool; whirlpool. Complimentary coffee in lobby. Restaurant 6:30 am-2 pm, 5-10 pm. Rm serv. Bar 3:30 pm-1 am. Ck-out noon. Meeting rms. Business servs avail. In-rm modem link. Valet serv. Health club privileges. Game rm. Some refrigerators, microwaves. Cr cds: A, C, D, DS, JCB, MC, V. [D] 🖢 🖢 🖢 🖢 SC

Joliet *(See also Morris)*

Motels

★ **COMFORT INN-NORTH.** *3235 Norman Ave (60435). 815/436-5141.* 64 rms, 3 story. May-Sept: S $64.95; D $69.95; each addl $6; suites $69.95; under 18 free; higher rates special events; lower rates rest of yr. Crib free. Pet accepted. TV; cable (premium). Indoor pool; whirlpool. Complimentary continental bkfst. Restaurant nearby 6 am-11 pm. Ck-out 11 am. Game rm. Refrigerators avail. Health club privileges. Cr cds: A, C, D, DS, MC, V.

★ ★ **COMFORT INN-SOUTH.** *135 S Larkin Ave (60436), I-80 exit 130B. 815/744-1770; FAX 815/744-1770, ext. 303.* 67 rms, 2 story. S $54.95-$89.95; D $64.95-$89.95; each addl $6; under 18 free. Crib free. Pet accepted. TV; cable (premium). Indoor pool. Complimentary continental bkfst. Restaurant nearby. Ck-out 11 am. Meeting rm. Business servs avail. Sauna. Health club privileges. Some refrigerators. Cr cds: A, C, D, DS, MC, V.
✔ ★ **MANOR.** *(23926 W Eames Rd, Channahon 60410) 6 mi W on I-55, at jct US 6, exit 248, 1 mi so on I-80. 815/467-5385; FAX 815/467-1617.* 77 rms, 1-2 story. S, D $32-$42; each addl $6; under 12 free; wkly, monthly rates. Crib $6.30. Pet accepted. TV; cable (premium). Pool. Complimentary coffee in lobby. Restaurant opp. Ck-out 11 am. Business servs avail. Cr cds: A, C, D, MC, V.
✔ ★ **MOTEL 6.** *1850 McDonough St (60436), off I-80 exit 130B. 815/729-2800; FAX 815/729-9528.* 132 rms, 2 story. S $33.99; D $39.99; each addl $6; under 18 free. Pet accepted, some restrictions. TV; cable (premium). Complimentary coffee in lobby. Restaurant opp 6 am-10 pm. Ck-out noon. Business servs avail. Cr cds: A, C, D, DS, MC, V.

Kewanee

Motel

✔ ★ **KEWANEE MOTOR LODGE.** *400 S Main St. 309/853-4000; FAX 309/853-4000, ext. 401; res: 800/853-4007.* 28 rms, 2 story. S $38.75-$40.75; D $45; each addl $5. Crib $5. Pet accepted. TV; cable (premium). Complimentary coffee in lobby. Restaurant adj 6 am-10 pm. Ck-out noon. Business servs avail. Some refrigerators. Cr cds: A, C, D, DS, MC, V.

Libertyville *(See also Gurnee)*

Motel

★ **BEST INNS OF AMERICA.** *1809 N Milwaukee Ave. 847/816-8006.* 90 rms, 3 story. Mid-June-mid-Sept: S $47.88-$51.88; D $53.88-$61.88; each addl $7; under 18 free; lower rates rest of yr. Crib free. Pet accepted. TV; cable (premium). Heated pool. Complimentary continental bkfst. Restaurant nearby. Ck-out 1 pm. Meeting rm. Some refrigerators. Cr cds: A, C, D, DS, MC, V.

Lincoln *(See also Bloomington, Decatur, Springfield)*

Motels

★ ★ **COMFORT INN.** *2811 Woodlawn Rd, I-55 exit 126. 217/735-3960; FAX 217/735-3960, ext. 304.* 52 rms, 2 story, 6 suites. S $46.95-$62.95; D $49.95-$62.95; each addl $5; suites $54.95-$64.95; under 18 free. Crib free. Pet accepted. TV; cable (premium), VCR avail. Indoor pool; whirlpool. Complimentary continental bkfst. Restaurant adj 5:30 am-11 pm. Ck-out 11 am. Meeting rms. Business servs avail. Game rm. Refrigerators, microwaves in suites. Cr cds: A, C, D, DS, MC, V.

★ **DAYS INN.** *2011 N Kickapoo St. 217/735-1202; FAX 217/735-1202, ext. 507.* 60 rms. S, D $39-$60; each addl $5; under 12 free. Crib free. Pet accepted, some restrictions; $10/day. TV; cable (premium). Indoor pool. Complimentary continental bkfst. Restaurant nearby. Ck-out noon. Meeting rms. Business servs avail. Sundries. Cr cds: A, C, D, DS, MC, V.

Macomb *(See also Galesburg, Monmouth)*

Motel

★ ★ **DAYS INN.** *1400 N Lafayette. 309/833-5511; FAX 309/836-2926.* 144 rms, 2 story. S $48-$55; D $53-$63; each addl $6; suites $95-$125; higher rates: Labor Day, special events. Crib free. Pet accepted. TV; cable (premium); VCR avail. Pool; wading pool, poolside serv. Playground. Restaurant 6 am-2 pm, 5-10 pm. Bar 4 pm-1 am; entertainment Fri, Sat. Ck-out noon. Coin lndry. Meeting rms. Business servs avail. In-rm modem link. Some refrigerators, microwaves. Cr cds: A, C, D, DS, JCB, MC, V. ▯ ⬚ ⬚ ⬚ ⬚ ⬚

Marion *(See also Benton, Carbondale)*

Motel

★ **BEST WESTERN AIRPORT INN.** *RR 8, Box 348-1, IL 13, adj to Williamson County Airport. 618/993-3222; FAX 618/993-8868.* 34 rms, 2 story, 10 suites. S $39-$49; D $44-$54; each addl $5; suites $52-$72; under 12 free; higher rates SIU special events. Crib free. Pet accepted. TV. Pool. Complimentary continental bkfst. Restaurant nearby. Ck-out 11 am. Meeting rms. Business servs avail. Free airport transportation. Refrigerator, wet bar in suites. Cr cds: A, C, D, DS, MC, V. ▯ ⬚ ⬚ ⬚ ⬚ ⬚ ⬚

Mattoon *(See also Arcola, Charleston, Effingham)*

Motel

★ ★ **RAMADA INN & CONFERENCE CENTER.** *300 Broadway Ave E, just off IL 16 on access road, 1 mi E of US 45, 1 mi W of I-57 exit IL 16 (W). 217/235-0313; FAX 217/235-6005.* 124 rms, 2 story. S $51-$90; D $59-$90; each addl $5; suites $76-$95; under 20 free. Crib free. Pet accepted. TV; cable (premium). 2 pools, 1 indoor; whirlpool, sauna. Complimentary coffee. Restaurant 6 am-10 pm. Bar 11:30-1 am. Ck-out noon. Coin lndry. Meeting rms. Business servs avail. Atrium. Game rm. Rec rm. Cr cds: A, C, D, DS, ER, JCB, MC, V. ▯ ⬚ ⬚ ⬚ ⬚ ⬚

McHenry *(See also Gurnee)*

Motel

★ **DAYS INN.** *(11200 US 12, Richmond 60071) 11 mi N on US 12/IL 31. 815/678-4711; FAX 815/678-4623.* 60 rms, 2 story. May-Sept: S $59-$69; D $65-$74; family, wkly, wkend, hol rates; higher rates special events; lower rates rest of yr. Crib free. Pet accepted, some restrictions. TV. Pool. Complimentary continental bkfst. Restaurant adj. Ck-out 11 am. Downhill/x-country ski 12 mi. Cr cds: A, C, D, DS, JCB, MC, V. ▯ ⬚ ⬚ ⬚ ⬚ ⬚ ⬚

Motor Hotel

★ ★ **HOLIDAY INN.** *(800 S IL 31, Crystal Lake 60014) 10 mi S on IL 31. 815/477-7000; FAX 815/477-7027.* 196 rms, 6 story. S $78-$99; D $78-$109; each addl $10; suites $159; under 18 free. Crib free. Pet accepted. TV; cable (premium). Indoor pool; whirlpool. Complimentary coffee in lobby. Restaurant 6:30 am-10 pm; Fri, Sat to 11 pm. Rm serv. Bar from 11 am. Ck-out noon. Meeting rms. Bellhops. Gift shop. Free RR station, bus depot transportation. Exercise equipt; weight machine, stair machine, sauna. Cr cds: A, C, D, DS, JCB, MC, V. ▯ ⬚ ⬚ ⬚ ⬚ ⬚ ⬚

Moline

Motels

★ ★ **HAMPTON INN.** *6920 27th St, near jct I-74 & I-280, adj to Quad City Airport. 309/762-1711; FAX 309/762-1788.* 138 rms, 2 story. S, D $51-$66; suites $99-$150; under 18 free. Pet accepted. TV; cable (premium). Heated pool. Complimentary continental bkfst. Restaurant adj 7 am-10:30 pm. Ck-out noon. Meeting rm. Business servs avail. Valet serv. Free airport transportation. Health club privileges. Cr cds: A, C, D, DS, MC, V. ▯ ⬚ ⬚ ⬚ ⬚ ⬚ ⬚

★ ★ **LA QUINTA INN.** *5450 27th St, near Quad City Airport. 309/762-9008; FAX 309/762-2455.* 126 rms, 2 story. May-Sept: S $47-$54; D $52-$55; each addl $5; under 18 free; lower rates rest of yr. Crib $5. Pet accepted. TV; cable (premium). Heated pool. Complimentary continental bkfst. Restaurant nearby. Ck-out noon. Coin lndry. Meeting rm. Business servs avail. In-rm modem link. Airport transportation. Downhill ski 15 mi. Some refrigerators. Cr cds: A, C, D, DS, MC, V. ▯ ⬚ ⬚ ⬚ ⬚ ⬚ ⬚ ⬚

Monmouth *(See also Galesburg)*

Motel

✔★★ **MELING'S.** *1129 N Main St, at jct US 34, 67. 309/734-2196; FAX 309/734-2127.* 55 rms, 1-2 story. S $33.95; D $39.30-$43.35; each addl $5. Crib free. Pet accepted. TV; cable. Restaurant 5:30 am-9:30 pm; dining rm 11 am-1:30 pm, 5-8 pm; Sun 7 am-8 pm. Bar, closed Sun. Ck-out 11 am. Lndry facilities. Meeting rm. Business servs avail. Sundries. Free RR station, bus depot transportation. Cr cds: A, C, D, DS, MC, V. 🐾 🖼 🖼

Morris *(See also Joliet)*

Motel

★★ **HOLIDAY INN.** *200 Gore Rd (IL 47), just N of I-80. 815/942-6600; FAX 815/942-8255.* 120 rms, 2 story. S $55-62; D $61-$68; each addl $6; under 18 free. Crib free. Pet accepted, some restrictions. TV; cable. Heated pool; wading pool. Restaurant 6 am-2 pm, 5-10 pm. Rm serv. Bar 4 pm-midnight; closed Sun. Ck-out noon. Meeting rms. Business servs avail. In-rm modem link. Valet serv. Sundries. Cr cds: A, C, D, DS, JCB, MC, V.
D 🐾 🖼 🖼 🖼 SC

Mt Vernon *(See also Benton)*

Motels

✔★ **BEST INNS OF AMERICA.** *222 S 44th St, jct I-57/64 & IL 15 (Broadway) exit 95. 618/244-4343.* 153 rms, 2 story. Mid-May-Oct: S $37.88; D $45.88; each addl $7; under 18 free; golf plan; lower rates rest of yr. Crib free. Pet accepted, some restrictions. TV; cable (premium). Pool. Complimentary continental bkfst. Restaurant adj open 24 hrs. Ck-out 1 pm. Cr cds: A, C, D, DS, MC, V. D 🐾 🖼 🖼 🖼 SC

★★ **DRURY INN.** *Box 805, 2 mi W, just off IL 15, 1/2 blk E of jct I-57, I-64. 618/244-4550.* 82 rms, 3 story. S $57; D $64-$70; each addl $7; under 18 free. Crib free. Pet accepted. TV; cable. Pool. Complimentary continental bkfst. Restaurant adj open 24 hrs. Ck-out noon. Meeting rms. Sundries. Some refrigerators, microwaves. Cr cds: A, C, D, DS, MC, V. D 🐾 🖼 🖼 🖼 SC

✔★ **RAMADA.** *I-57 & IL 15. 618/244-3670; FAX 618/244-6904.* 188 rms, 4 story. S $55-$61; D $61-$67; each addl $6; under 18 free; wkend rates. Crib free. Pet accepted. TV, cable (premium). Indoor pool; whirlpool. Complimentary continental bkfst. Restaurant 6 am-2 pm, 5-10 pm. Rm serv. Bar 11-1 am; Fri, Sat to 2 am; Sun to 10 pm; entertainment Tues-Sun. Ck-out noon. Meeting rms. Business center. In-rm modem link. Bellhops. Valet serv. Free airport, bus depot transportation. Exercise equipt; bicycles, rowers, sauna. Game rm. Rec rm. Cr cds: A, C, D, DS, JCB, MC, V. D 🐾 🖼 🏃 🖼 🖼 SC 🏃

Motor Hotel

★★ **HOLIDAY INN.** *222 Potomac, I-57/64 & IL 15 exit 95. 618/244-7100; FAX 618/242-8876.* 236 rms, 5 story. S $52-$74; D $56-$74; suites $156-$232; under 18 free; golf plan. Crib free. Pet accepted, some restrictions. TV; cable. Indoor pool; whirlpool. Restaurants 6 am-10 pm. Rm serv. Bar 11-2 am. Ck-out 1 pm. Meeting rms. Valet serv. Sundries. Free airport transportation. Saunas. Cr cds: A, C, D, DS, JCB, MC, V.
D 🐾 🖼 🖼 SC

Naperville *(See also Downers Grove)*

Motel

✔★ **RED ROOF INN.** *1698 W Diehl Rd (60563). 630/369-2500; FAX 630/369-9987.* 119 rms, 3 story. May-Sept: S $54.99-$68.99; D $62.99-$76.99; under 18 free; lower rates rest of yr. Crib free. Pet accepted. TV; cable (premium). Complimentary coffee in lobby. Restaurant opp. Ck-out noon. Business servs avail. In-rm modem link. Cr cds: A, C, D, DS, MC, V. D 🐾 🖼 🖼

Nauvoo *(See also Macomb)*

Motel

★★ **NAUVOO FAMILY.** *1875 Mulholland. 217/453-6527; res: 800/416-4470; FAX 217/453-6601.* Web www.nauvoonet.com. 71 rms, 2 story, 19 suites. Apr-Nov: S $44-$51; D $49-$56; suites $75-$90; under 12 free; lower rates rest of yr. Crib free. Pet accepted, some restrictions. TV; cable (premium). Restaurant nearby. Ck-out 11 am. Meeting rms. Indoor pool. Cr cds: A, D, MC, V. 🄳 📞 🏊 🔥 SC

Northbrook *(See also Glenview, Wheeling)*

Motor Hotel

★★ **RESIDENCE INN BY MARRIOTT.** *(530 Lake Cook Rd, Deerfield 60015) approx 1/2 mi W of Waukegan Rd.* 847/940-4644; FAX 847/940-7639. 128 kit. suites, 2 story. Kit. suites $129-$169; wknd rates. Crib free. Pet accepted. TV; cable (premium). Heated pool; whirlpool. Complimentary continental bkfst. Complimentary coffee in rms. Restaurant nearby. Ck-out noon. Coin lndry. Meeting rm. Business servs avail. In-rm modem link. Valet serv Mon-Fri. Sundries. Exercise equipt; bicycles, treadmill. Microwaves; many fireplaces. Balconies. Picnic tables, grills. Cr cds: A, D, DS, JCB, MC, V. 🄳 📞 🏊 🏃 ⛷ 🔥 SC

Hotels

★★ **MARRIOTT SUITES.** *(2 Parkway N, Deerfield 60015) I-94 exit Deerfield Rd then 1/3 mi W to Parkway N.* 847/405-9666; FAX 847/405-0354. 251 suites, 7 story. S, D $109-$140; under 18 free; family, wkly, wknd rates. Crib free. Pet accepted, some restrictions. TV; cable (premium), VCR avail. 2 pools, 1 indoor; whirlpool, poolside serv. Complimentary coffee in rms. Restaurant 6:30 am-11 pm. Bar. Ck-out 1 pm. Coin lndry. Convention facilities. Business center. In-rm modem link. Gift shop. Exercise equipt; weight machine, bicycles, sauna. Health club privileges. Refrigerators, wet bars; microwaves avail. Picnic tables. Cr cds: A, C, D, DS, ER, JCB, MC, V. 🄳 📞 🏊 🏃 ⛷ 🔥 SC 🛥

★★ **RADISSON.** *2875 N Milwaukee.* 847/298-2525; FAX 847/298-4615. 310 rms, 4 story, 30 suites. Mar-Nov: S $89-$149; D $99-$159; each addl $10; suites $175-$195; under 18 free; lower rates rest of yr. Crib free. Pet accepted, some restrictions; deposit. TV; cable (premium), VCR avail (movies). Complimentary coffee in lobby. Restaurant 8 am-10 pm. Bar 4 pm-midnight. Ck-out noon. Convention facilities. Business center. Concierge. Gift shop. Free airport transportation. Exercise equipt; treadmill, stair machine. Heated pool; whirlpool. Many balconies. Cr cds: A, C, D, DS, MC, V. 🄳 📞 🏊 🏃 ⛷ 🔥 SC 🛥

Oak Brook *(See also Downers Grove, Elmhurst, Hinsdale)*

Motel

★★ **LA QUINTA.** *(1 S 666 Midwest Rd, Oakbrook Terrace 60181) 2 mi W on 22nd St.* 630/495-4600; FAX 630/495-2558. 150 rms, 3 story. S $75-$82; D $82-$89; each addl $7; under 18 free. Crib free. Pet accepted, some restrictions. TV; cable (premium). Heated pool. Complimentary continental bkfst. Coffee in rms. Restaurant adj open 24 hrs. Ck-out noon. Meeting rms. Business servs avail. In-rm modem link. Free local transportation. Cr cds: A, C, D, DS, MC, V. 🄳 📞 🏊 ⛷ 🔥 SC

Motor Hotel

★★ **RESIDENCE INN BY MARRIOTT.** *(2001 S Highland Ave, Lombard 60148) 2 mi S, off I-88 Highland Ave exit.* 630/629-7800; FAX 630/629-6987. 144 rms, 2 story. S $89-$129; D $109-$159; under 18 free; wkly, wknd, hol rates. Crib free. Pet accepted; $50. TV; cable, VCR avail (movies). Heated pool; whirlpool. Complimentary continental bkfst. Restaurant nearby. Ck-out noon. Coin lndry. Sundries. Exercise equipt; weight machine, treadmill. Lawn games. Microwaves. Picnic tables. Cr cds: A, C, D, DS, MC, V. 🄳 📞 🏊 🏃 ⛷ 🔥 SC

Hotels

★★★ **HILTON SUITES.** *(10 Drury Lane, Oakbrook Terrace 60181) N of I-88, Cermak Rd exit.* 630/941-0100; FAX 630/941-0299. 212 suites, 10 story. S, D $155; under 18 free. Crib free. Pet accepted, some restrictions. TV; cable (premium), VCR (movies). Indoor pool; whirlpool. Complimentary full bkfst. Complimentary coffee in rms. Restaurant 11:30 am-1:30 pm, 5-10 pm. Rm serv from 5 pm. Bar 4 pm- midnight. Ck-out noon. Meeting rms. Business center. In-rm modem link. Gift shop. Exercise equipt; weight machine, stair machine, sauna. Health club privileges. Microwaves. Drury Lane Theater adj. Cr cds: A, C, D, DS, MC, V. 🄳 📞 🏊 🏃 ⛷ 🔥 SC 🛥

★★★ **MARRIOTT.** *1401 W 22nd St.* 630/573-8555; FAX 630/573-1026. 347 rms, 12 story. S $139; D $149; each addl $10; suites $149-$250; under 18 free; wkend rates. Crib free. Pet accepted. TV; cable (premium), VCR avail. Heated pool; whirlpool, poolside serv. Complimentary coffee in lobby. Restaurant 6:30 am-11 pm. Rm serv. Bar 11-1 am; Sun to midnight. Ck-out 1 pm. Coin lndry. Meeting rms. Business center. In-rm modem link. Gift shop. Valet. Exercise equipt; weights, stair machine, sauna. Some bathrm phones; microwaves avail. Luxury levels. Cr cds: A, C, D, DS, JCB, MC, V.

🄳 📞 🏊 🏃 ⛷ 🔥 SC 🛥

Oak Lawn

Motels

✔★★ **BUDGETEL INN.** *(12801 S Cicero, Alsip 60658) I-294 exit Cicero Ave. 708/597-3900; FAX 708/597-3979.* Web www.budgetel.com. 102 rms, 3 story. S, D $59.95-$105.95; suites $69.95-$109.95. Crib free. Pet accepted. TV; cable (premium), VCR avail (movies). Complimentary continental bkfst. Coffee in rms. Restaurant nearby. Ck-out noon. Meeting rm. Business servs avail. Some refrigerators. Cr cds: A, C, D, DS, MC, V.
🄳 ⌨ ⊠ 🛥 SC

★★ **EXEL INN.** *(9625 S 76th Ave, Bridgeview 60455) 4 mi W on 95th St (US 12/20), then N on IL 43. 708/430-1818; FAX 708/430-1894.* 113 rms, 3 story. S $46-$90; D $53-$130; under 18 free. Crib free. Pet accepted, some restrictions. TV; cable (premium). Complimentary continental bkfst. Coffee in rms. Restaurant nearby. Ck-out noon. Coin lndry. Business servs avail. Game rm. Exercise equipt; bicycle, treadmill. Microwaves avail. Cr cds: A, C, D, DS, MC, V. 🄳 ⌨ 🏋 ⊠ 🛥 SC

★★ **HAMPTON INN.** *(13330 S Cicero Ave, Crestwood 60445) 3 mi S on Cicero Ave. 708/597-3330; FAX 708/597-3691.* Web www.hamptoninn.com. 123 rms, 4 story. S $72-$92; D $78-$92; under 18 free; higher rates New Years Eve. Crib free. Pet accepted, some restrictions. TV; cable (premium), VCR avail. Indoor pool. Complimentary continental bkfst. Restaurant nearby. Ck-out noon. Meeting rms. Business servs avail. In-rm modem link. Free airport transportation. Exercise equipt; weight machine, bicycle. Cr cds: A, C, D, DS, JCB, MC, V. 🄳 ⌨ ≋ 🏋 ⊠ 🛥 SC

Peoria *(See also Bloomington)*

Motels

★ **BEST WESTERN EASTLIGHT INN.** *(401 N Main St, East Peoria 61611) 1 blk S of I-74 exit 95A. 309/699-7231.* 199 rms, 2 story. Apr-Sept: S $56; D $64; each addl $8; under 12 free; lower rates rest of yr. Crib free. Pet accepted, some restrictions. TV; cable (premium), VCR avail. Indoor pool; whirlpool. Complimentary continental bkfst. Restaurant adj 6 am-10 pm. Bar 4 pm-1 am. Ck-out noon. Coin lndry. Meeting rms. Business servs avail. Free airport, bus depot transportation. Exercise equipt; weight machine, stair machine, sauna. Cr cds: A, C, D, DS, MC, V. 🄳 ⌨ ≋ 🏋 ⊠ 🛥 SC

★★ **COMFORT SUITES.** *4021 N War Memorial Dr (61614), I-74 exit 89. 309/688-3800.* 66 suites, 2 story. S $54.95-$64.95; D $63.45-$69.95; each addl $5; under 18 free. Crib free. Pet accepted. TV, cable (premium). Indoor pool; whirlpool. Complimentary continental bkfst. Restaurant nearby. Ck-out 11 am. Meeting rm. Business servs avail. In-rm modem link. Health club privileges. Game rm. Cr cds: A, C, D, DS, ER, JCB, MC, V.
🄳 ⌨ ≋ ⊠ 🛥 SC

✔★ **RED ROOF INN.** *4031 N War Memorial Dr (61614). 309/685-3911; FAX 309/685-3941.* 108 rms, 2 story. S $35.99-$49.99; D $38.99-$59.99; under 18 free. Crib free. Pet accepted. TV; VCR avail. Complimentary coffee in lobby. Ck-out noon. Business servs avail. Cr cds: A, C, D, DS, MC, V. 🄳 ⌨ ⊠ 🛥

Hotels

★★ **HOLIDAY INN CITY CENTER.** *500 Hamilton Blvd (61602). 309/674-2500; FAX 309/674-1205.* 286 rms, 9 story. S $79-$89; D $89-$99; each addl $10; suites $105-$350; under 12 free. Crib free. Pet accepted. TV; cable. Pool. Coffee in rms. Restaurant 6 am-10 pm. Bar 11-2 am. Ck-out noon. Convention facilities. Business center. In-rm modem link. Gift shop. Barber. Free airport, bus depot transportation. Exercise equipt; weight machine, stair machine. Luxury level. Cr cds: A, C, D, DS, JCB, MC, V.
🄳 ⌨ ≋ 🏋 ⊠ 🛥 SC 🛶

★★ **JUMER'S CASTLE LODGE.** *117 N Western Ave (61604), at Moss Ave. 309/673-8040; FAX 309/673-9782; res: 800/285-8627.* 175 rms, 4 story. S $79-$128; D $88-$135; each addl $10; studio rms $89; under 18 free. Crib free. Pet accepted. TV; cable (premium), VCR avail. Pool; whirlpool. Complimentary coffee in lobby. Restaurant 6:30 am-10 pm. Bar 11-1 am; entertainment exc Sun. Ck-out noon. Meeting rms. Business servs avail. In-rm modem link. Valet parking. Free airport transportation. Sauna. Health club privileges. Game rm. Some fireplaces. Bavarian decor. Cr cds: A, C, D, DS, MC, V.
🄳 ⌨ ≋ ⊠ 🛥 SC

★★ **PERE MARQUETTE.** *501 Main St (61602). 309/637-6500; FAX 309/637-6500; res: 800/447-1676.* 288 rms, 12 story. S $89; D $99; each addl $15; suites, kit. units $175-$500; studio rms $175; under 18 free; wkly, wkend rates. Crib free. Pet accepted. TV;

cable (premium). Restaurants 6 am-10 pm. Bar. Ck-out noon. Convention facilities. Business servs avail. In-rm modem link. Gift shop. Free covered parking. Free airport transportation. Tennis privileges. Golf privileges. Exercise equipt; weights, bicycles, treadmill, stair machine. Health club privileges. Refrigerator in suites. Restored 1920s hotel. Cr cds: A, C, D, DS, MC, V. 🄳 ⬆ 🏋 🏌 🏃 ⬜ 🐾

Peru

Motels

✔ ★ **LASALLE PERU INN.** *(I-80 & IL 251 (May Rd), LaSalle 61301) ¼ mi N on IL 251 at I-80 exit 75. 815/224-2500; FAX 815/224-3693.* 104 rms, 2 story. S $32-$59; D $39-$65; each addl $8; under 18 free. Crib free. Pet accepted. TV; VCR avail (movies). Pool. Complimentary coffee in lobby. Restaurant 11 am-8 pm. Ck-out noon. Coin lndry. Meeting rms. Business servs avail. Valet serv. Cr cds: A, C, D, DS, ER, JCB, MC, V. 🄳 ⬆ ≋ ⬜ 🐾 SC

★ **SUPER 8.** *1851 May Rd, I-80 & US 251. 815/223-1848.* 62 rms, 3 story. June-Sept: S $36.88; D $47.88; each addl $5; under 12 free; higher rates special events; lower rates rest of yr. Crib free. Pet accepted, some restrictions. TV; cable (premium), VCR avail (movies). Complimentary coffee in lobby. Restaurant opp 11 am-9 pm. Ck-out 11 am. Cr cds: A, C, D, DS, JCB, MC, V. 🄳 ⬆ ⬜ 🐾 SC

Quincy

Motel

✔ ★ ★ **TRAVELODGE.** *200 S 300 St. 217/222-5620; FAX 217/224-2582.* 63 rms, 2 story. S $44; D $50-$56; each addl $5; under 12 free. Crib free. Pet accepted, some restrictions; $10. TV; cable (premium). Complimentary continental bkfst. Complimentary coffee in rms. Restaurant 11 am-11 pm. Rm serv. Bar. Ck-out noon. Business servs avail. Coin lndry. Pool. Some refrigerators, microwaves. Some balconies. Picnic table. Cr cds: A, C, D, DS, MC, V. 🄳 ⬆ ≋ 🐾 SC

Rockford *(See also De Kalb, Freeport)*

Motels

★ ★ **BEST WESTERN COLONIAL INN.** *4850 E State St (US 20) (61108). 815/398-5050; FAX 815/398-5050, ext. 404.* 84 rms, 2-3 story. S $60-$80; D $67-$88; suites $90-$154; under 12 free. Crib $3. Pet accepted. TV; cable, VCR avail (movies). Indoor pool; whirlpool. Complimentary coffee in lobby. Restaurant adj 11 am-11:30 pm. Bar noon-2 am. Ck-out noon. Meeting rm. Business servs avail. Exercise equipt; weight machine, bicycle. Refrigerator in suites. Rockford College adj. Cr cds: A, C, D, DS, ER, JCB, MC, V. 🄳 ⬆ ≋ 🏃 ⬜ 🐾 SC

★ ★ **COMFORT INN.** *7392 Argus Dr (61107). 815/398-7061.* 64 rms, 3 story. May-Oct: S $59.95; D $64.95; each addl $5; under 18 free; lower rates rest of yr. Crib free. Pet accepted, some restrictions. TV; cable (premium). Indoor pool. Complimentary continental bkfst. Restaurant nearby. Ck-out 11 am. Business servs avail. X-country ski 10 mi. Game rm. Some refrigerators. Cr cds: A, C, D, DS, MC, V. 🄳 ⬆ ≋ 🐾 SC

✔ ★ **EXEL INN.** *220 S Lyford Rd (61108), at I-90 & US 20 Business. 815/332-4915; FAX 815/332-4843.* 101 rms, 2 story. S $39.99-$47.99; D $45.99-$52.99; each addl $5; under 18 free. Crib free. Pet accepted; some restrictions. TV; cable (premium). Complimentary continental bkfst. Restaurant opp. Ck-out noon. Coin lndry. In-rm modem link. Cr cds: A, C, D, DS, MC, V. 🄳 ⬆ ⬜ 🐾 SC

✔ ★ ★ **SWEDEN HOUSE LODGE.** *4605 E State St (61108). 815/398-4130; FAX 815/398-9203; res: 800/886-4138.* 107 rms, 2-3 story. S $38.75-$48.75; D $40.75-$52.75; suites $49.75-$64.75; each addl $2; under 18 free. Crib free. Pet accepted, some restrictions. TV; cable (premium), VCR avail (movies). Indoor pool; whirlpool. Ck-out noon. Meeting rms. Business servs avail. Valet serv. Sundries. Exercise equipt; stair machine, rower. Game rm. Cr cds: A, C, D, DS, MC, V. ⬆ ≋ 🏃 ⬜ 🐾 SC

Motor Hotel

★ ★ **RESIDENCE INN BY MARRIOTT.** *7542 Colosseum Dr (61107), I-90 & US 20 Bus. 815/227-0013; FAX 815/227-0013, ext. 405.* 94 kit. units, 3 story. S, D $99-$144. Crib free. Pet accepted; $100 & $5/day. TV; cable (premium). Indoor pool; whirlpool. Complimentary coffee in rms. Complimentary continental bkfst. Restaurant nearby. Ck-out noon. Coin lndry. Meeting rm. Business servs avail. In-rm modem link. Exercise equipt; weight machine, stair machine. Cr cds: A, C, D, DS, JCB, MC, V. 🄳 ⬆ ≋ 🏃 ⬜ 🐾 SC

Schaumburg *(See also Arlington Heights, Chicago O'Hare Airport Area)*

Motels

★ ★ **HOMEWOOD SUITES.** *815 E American Lane (60173). 847/605-0400; FAX 847/619-0990.* 108 kit. suites, 3 story. S, D $99-$139; extended stay rates. Crib free. Pet accepted, some restrictions; $75 refundable. TV; cable (premium), VCR (movies $4). Pool; whirlpool. Complimentary continental bkfst. Complimentary coffee in rms. Restaurant nearby. Ck-out noon. Coin lndry. Meeting rms. Business center. In-rm modem link. Valet serv. Gift shop. Exercise equipt; weight machine, stair machine. Health club privileges. Microwaves. Picnic tables, grills. Cr cds: A, C, D, DS, MC, V.

D ⊡ ⌷ ⌷ ⌷ ⌷ SC ⌷

★ ★ **LA QUINTA MOTOR INN.** *1730 E Higgins Rd (IL 72) (60173), I-290 exit Higgins Rd, adj to Woodfield Mall. 847/517-8484; FAX 847/517-4477.* 127 rms, 3 story. S $74-$81; D $81-$88; under 18 free; wkend rates. Crib free. Pet accepted. TV; cable (premium). Heated pool. Complimentary continental bkfst. Restaurant adj open 24 hrs. Ck-out noon. Meeting rms. Business servs avail. In-rm modem link. Valet serv. Health club privileges. Some refrigerators; microwaves avail. Cr cds: A, C, D, DS, MC, V.

D ⊡ ⌷ ⌷ ⌷ SC

✔ ★ **RED ROOF INN.** *(2500 Hassell Rd, Hoffman Estates 60195) S of I-90 Barrington Rd exit. 847/885-7877; FAX 847/885-8616.* 118 rms, 3 story. S $46-$64; D $50-$70; each addl $7. Crib avail. Pet accepted. TV; cable (premium). Complimentary coffee in lobby. Restaurant opp 6 am-11 pm. Ck-out noon. Meeting rm. Business servs avail. In-rm modem link. Cr cds: A, C, D, DS, MC, V. D ⊡ ⌷ ⌷

Hotel

★ ★ ★ **MARRIOTT.** *50 N Martingale Rd (60173). 847/240-0100; FAX 847/240-2388.* 394 rms, 14 story. S $149-$169; D $159-$179; suites $250; family, wkend rates. Crib free. Pet accepted, some restrictions. TV; cable (premium). Indoor/outdoor pool; whirlpool, poolside serv. Complimentary coffee in rms. Restaurant 6:30 am-11 pm. Bar 11-2 am. Ck-out 1 pm. Coin lndry. Convention facilities. Business center. In-rm modem link. Gift shop. Exercise equipt; weights, bicycles, sauna. Some private patios. Luxury level. Cr cds: A, C, D, DS, ER, JCB, MC, V. D ⊡ ⌷ ⌷ ⌷ ⌷ SC ⌷

Skokie

Motel

★ ★ **HOWARD JOHNSON.** *9333 Skokie Blvd (60077). 847/679-4200; FAX 847/679-4218.* 132 rms, 2-5 story. S $92-$102; D $107-$116; each addl $10; under 18 free. Crib free. Pet accepted. TV; cable (premium), VCR avail. Indoor pool; whirlpool. Complimentary bkfst buffet. Restaurant adj 11:30 am-11 pm. Bar 11:30 am-midnight. Ck-out 1 pm. Meeting rms. Businss servs avail. In-rm modem link. Valet serv. Exercise equipt; bicycles, stair machine, sauna. Microwave avail. Private patios, balconies. Cr cds: A, C, D, DS, JCB, MC, V. D ⊡ ⌷ ⌷ ⌷ ⌷ SC

Motor Hotel

★ ★ **HOLIDAY INN NORTHSHORE.** *5300 W Touhy Ave (60077). 847/679-8900; FAX 847/679-7447.* 244 rms, 2-4 story. S, D $113-$130; each addl $10; under 19 free; higher rates: Dec 31, Northwestern Univ graduation. Crib free. Pet accepted. TV; cable (premium). Indoor pool; whirlpool. Restaurant 6:30 am-2 pm, 5-10 pm; Fri, Sat to 11 pm. Rm serv. Bar 11-1 am. Ck-out noon. Coin lndry. Meeting rms. In-rm modem link. Valet serv. Gift shop. Exercise equipt; bicycle, treadmill, sauna. Holidome. Game rm. Microwaves avail. Cr cds: A, C, D, DS, JCB, MC, V. D ⊡ ⌷ ⌷ ⌷ ⌷ SC

Hotel

★ ★ **DOUBLETREE.** *9599 Skokie Blvd (60077), at Golf Rd (IL 58). 847/679-7000; FAX 847/674-5204.* 366 rms, 11 story. S, D $124-$185; each addl $15; suites $225-$400; under 17 free; wkend rates. Crib free. Pet accepted, some restrictions; $250 deposit. TV; cable (premium). Indoor/outdoor pool; poolside serv. Restaurant 6 am-11 pm. Rm serv 24 hrs. Bar 4 pm-1 am. Ck-out noon. Convention facilities. Business center. In-rm modem link. Concierge. Gift shop. Airport transportation. Exercise equipt; weight machine, bicycles. Health club privileges. Luxury level. Cr cds: A, C, D, DS, ER, MC, V.

D ⊡ ⌷ ⌷ ⌷ ⌷ SC ⌷

Springfield *(See also Jacksonville, Lincoln)*

Motels

(Rates are generally higher during state fair)

★ ★ **BEST INNS OF AMERICA.** *500 N 1st St (62702), at Carpenter Ave.* 217/522-1100; FAX 217/753-8589; res: 800/237-8466. 91 rms, 2 story. S $48-$54; D $53-$61; each addl $7; under 18 free. Crib free. Pet accepted, some restrictions. TV; cable (premium), VCR avail. Pool. Complimentary continental bkfst. Restaurant adj 7 am-10 pm. Ck-out 1 pm. Coin lndry. In-rm modem link. Cr cds: A, C, D, DS, MC, V. D 🐾 🏊 🖎 🐾 SC

★ ★ **COMFORT INN.** *3442 Freedom Dr (62704), IL 36 exit 93.* 217/787-2250. 67 rms, 2 story. S, D $52.95-$62.95; each addl $5; under 18 free; wkend rates. Crib free. Pet accepted. TV; cable (premium). Indoor pool; whirlpool. Complimentary continental bkfst. Restaurant adj 6 am-midnight. Ck-out 11 am. Meeting rm. In-rm modem link. Some refrigerators, microwaves. Cr cds: A, C, D, DS, MC, V. D 🐾 🏊 🖎 🐾 SC

✔ ★ **DAYS INN.** *3000 Stevenson Dr (62703).* 217/529-0171; FAX 217/529-9431; res: 800/329-7466. 155 rms, 2 story. S $49-$56; D $56-$63; each addl $5; under 12 free; higher rates special events. Crib free. Pet accepted. TV; cable (premium). Pool. Complimentary continental bkfst. Ck-out noon. Meeting rms. Business servs avail. Free airport transportation. Microwaves avail. Picnic tables. Cr cds: A, C, D, DS, JCB, MC, V.
D 🐾 🏊 🖎 🐾 SC

★ ★ **HAMPTON INN.** *3185 S Dirksen Pkwy (62703).* 217/529-1100; FAX 217/529-1105. 123 rms, 4 story. S $55-$62; D $60-$67; suite $90; under 18 free. Crib free. Pet accepted, some restrictions. TV; cable (premium). Indoor pool; whirlpool. Complimentary continental bkfst. Restaurants nearby. Ck-out noon. Meeting rms. Business servs avail. Valet serv, wkdays. Exercise equipt; weight machine, bicycle. Refrigerator in suite. Cr cds: A, C, D, DS, MC, V. D 🐾 🏊 🏋 🖎 SC

★ ★ **RAMADA INN-SOUTH PLAZA.** *625 E St Joseph St (62703).* 217/529-7131; FAX 217/529-7160. 116 rms, 2 story. S $61, D $67; each addl $6; suites $100-$150; under 18 free. Crib free. Pet accepted, some restrictions. TV; cable (premium), VCR avail. Heated pool. Complimentary coffee in lobby. Restaurant 6:30 am-2 pm, 5-9 pm. Rm serv. Ck-out noon. Coin lndry. Meeting rms. Business servs avail. In-rm modem link. Valet serv. Airport transportation. Health club privileges. Some refrigerators, microwaves. Cr cds: A, C, D, DS, MC, V. D 🐾 🏊 🖎 🐾 SC

✔ ★ **RED ROOF INN.** *3200 Singer Ave (62703), off I-55S exit 96B.* 217/753-4302; FAX 217/753-4319. 108 rms, 2 story. S $29-$57; D $40-$55; under 18 free. Crib free. Pet accepted. TV; cable (premium). Complimentary coffee in lobby. Restaurants nearby. Ck-out noon. Business servs avail. In-rm modem link. Cr cds: A, C, D, DS, MC, V.
D 🐾 🖎 🐾 SC

★ ★ **SUPER 8-SOUTH.** *3675 S Sixth St (62703), off I-55 exit 92A.* 217/529-8898; FAX 217/529-4354. 122 rms, 3 story. S $32.99-$60.88; D $32.99-$85.88; each addl $5; suites $45.88-$99.88; under 12 free; higher rates special events; lower rates winter months. Crib free. Pet accepted, some restrictions. TV; cable. Complimentary coffee. Restaurants nearby. Ck-out 11 am. Coin lndry. Meeting rms. Business servs avail. Some refrigerators, microwaves. Some balconies. Cr cds: A, C, D, DS, ER, MC, V. D 🐾 🖎 🐾 SC

Hotel

★ ★ ★ **HILTON.** *700 E Adams St (62701).* 217/789-1530; FAX 217/789-0709. 367 rms, 30 story. S, D $99-$129; each addl $10; suites $119-$600; under 18 free; wkend rates. Crib free. Pet accepted, some restrictions. TV; cable (premium). Indoor pool. Restaurants 6:30 am-10 pm. Bar 2 pm-2 am; entertainment. Ck-out noon. Convention facilities. Business servs avail. Shopping arcade. Barber, beauty shop. Free airport, RR station transportation. Exercise rm; instructor, weight machines, bicycles, sauna. Luxury level. Cr cds: A, C, D, DS, ER, JCB, MC, V. D 🐾 🏊 🏋 🖎 🐾 SC

Vandalia *(See also Altamont, Greenville)*

Motels

✔ ★ **DAYS INN.** *1920 Kennedy Blvd.* 618/283-4400; FAX 618/283-4240. 95 rms, 2 story. Late May-early Sept: S $44; D $50; each addl $6; under 13 free; wkly rates; higher rates special events; lower rates rest of yr. Crib free. Pet accepted; $10 deposit. TV; cable (premium), VCR avail (movies). Complimentary continental bkfst. Restaurant 6 am-9 pm. Rm serv. Ck-out noon. Bellhops. Heated pool. Playground. Game rm. Cr cds: A, D, DS, MC, V. 🐾 🏊 🖎 🐾 SC

✔★ **JAY'S.** *1 mi N on US 40 (IL 185), 1 blk SW of jct I-70 & US 51. 618/283-1200; FAX 618/283-2363.* 21 rms, 2 story. S $35; D $45-$47. Crib free. Pet accepted. TV; cable (premium). Pool privileges adj. Coffee in rms. Restaurant 6 am-10 pm. Bar 4 pm-midnight. Ck-out noon. Sundries. Cr cds: A, D, DS, MC, V. 🐾 🐾 SC

★★ **RAMADA LIMITED.** *US 40W, I-70 exit 61. 618/283-1400; FAX 618/283-3465.* 61 rms, 2 story. May-Oct: S, D $49-$57; each addl $8; suites $69-$77; under 12 free; lower rates rest of yr. Crib free. Pet accepted; $10 deposit. TV; cable (premium), VCR avail. Pool. Complimentary full bkfst. Restaurant adj 7 am-9 pm; Fri, Sat to 10 pm. Ck-out noon. Meeting rms. Business servs avail. Exercise equipt; weight machine, bicycle. Refrigerator, microwaves in suites. Cr cds: A, C, D, DS, MC, V. D 🐾 ≈ ✗ ⊠ 🐾 SC

★ **TRAVELODGE.** *1500 N 6th St, 1 blk SW of jct I-70 & US 51, exit 63. 618/283-2363; FAX 618/283-2363, ext. 131.* 48 rms, 2 story. S $40; D $46-$48; each addl $5. Crib free. Pet accepted. TV; cable (premium). Pool. Playground. Complimentary coffee in rms. Restaurant adj 6 am-10 pm. Bar 4 pm-midnight. Ck-out noon. Sun deck. Cr cds: A, C, D, DS, ER, JCB, MC, V. D 🐾 ≈ ⊠ 🐾 SC

Waukegan *(See also Gurnee)*

Motel

★ **SUPER 8.** *630 N Green Bay Rd (60085). 847/249-2388.* 61 rms, 3 story. Apr-Sept: S $51.88-$71.88; D $51.88-$78.88; each addl $5; under 12 free; lower rates rest of yr. Crib free. Pet accepted; $25. TV; cable (premium). Complimentary coffee in lobby. Restaurant nearby. Ck-out 11 am. Business servs avail. Cr cds: A, C, D, DS, JCB, MC, V.
D 🐾 ⊠ 🐾 SC

Wheeling *(See also Arlington Heights, Glenview, Northbrook)*

Motel

★★ **EXEL INN.** *(540 N Milwaukee Ave, Prospect Heights 60070) S on Milwaukee Ave. 847/459-0545; FAX 847/459-8639.* 123 rms, 3 story. S $37.99-$59.99; D $46.99-$59.99; suites $90-$130; under 18 free; wkly rates. Crib free. Pet accepted, some restrictions. TV. Complimentary continental bkfst. Complimentary coffee in rms. Restaurant nearby. Ck-out noon. Coin lndry. Business servs avail. In-rm modem link. Health club privileges. Game rm. Some refrigerators; microwaves avail. Cr cds: A, C, D, DS, MC, V.
D 🐾 ⊠ 🐾 SC

Resort

★★★ **MARRIOTT'S LINCOLNSHIRE RESORT.** *(10 Marriott Dr, Lincolnshire 60069) off Milwaukee Ave (IL 21), 1/2 mi S of Half Day Rd (IL 22). 847/634-0100; FAX 847/634-1278.* 390 rms, 3 story. S, D $99-$159; suites from $250-$290; under 18 free; wkend rates; theater packages; golf plans. Crib free. Pet accepted, some restrictions. TV; cable (premium), VCR avail. 2 pools, 1 indoor; wading pool, whirlpool, poolside serv, lifeguard. Playground. Supervised child's activities (May-Oct). Complimentary coffee in lobby. Restaurants 6:30 am-11 pm. Rm serv. Bars 11-1 am. Ck-out noon, ck-in 4 pm. Coin lndry. Convention facilities. Business center. Valet serv. Concierge. Gift shop. Airport transportation. Sports dir. Indoor tennis, pro. 18-hole golf, greens fee $50-$60, pro, putting green. Canoeing, paddleboating. Lawn games. Entertainment Thurs-Sat. 900-seat theater-in-the-round featuring musical comedies. Game rm. Exercise rm; instructor (by appt), weights, bicycles, sauna, steam rm. Massage. Minibars; some refrigerators. Some private patios. Picnic tables. Luxury level. Cr cds: A, C, D, DS, ER, JCB, MC, V.
D 🐾 ✗ ⊠ ≈ ✗ ⊠ 🐾 SC ⋀

Indiana

Anderson (See also Indianapolis, Muncie)

Motels

(Rates may be higher during Indianapolis "500")

✔★ **BEST INNS OF AMERICA.** *5706 Scatterfield Rd (46013). 765/644-2000; res: 800/237-8466.* 93 rms, 2 story. S $43.88-$50.88; D $46.88-$53.88; each addl $7; under 18 free. Crib free. Pet accepted. TV; cable. Complimentary continental bkfst. Restaurant adj 6 am-10 pm. Ck-out 1 pm. Cr cds: A, C, D, DS, MC, V. 🄳 👫 🏊 🏋 🐾 SC

★ **COMFORT INN.** *2205 E 59th St (46013). 765/644-4422.* 56 rms, 2 story, 14 suites. Mar-July: S $38-$44; D $42-$59; each addl $5; suites $45-$61; under 19 free; wkend rates; lower rates rest of yr. Crib free. Pet accepted, some restrictions. TV; cable. Indoor pool; whirlpool. Complimentary continental bkfst. Ck-out 11 am. Game rm. Refrigerator, microwave in suites. Cr cds: A, C, D, DS, ER, JCB, MC, V. 🄳 👫 🏊 🏋 🐾 SC

★★ **HOLIDAY INN.** *5920 Scatterfield Rd (IN 109 Bypass) (46013), at jct I-69. 765/644-2581; FAX 765/642-8545.* 158 rms, 2 story. S, D $79-$94; each addl $7; under 18 free; 2-day min: Indianapolis "500." Crib free. Pet accepted. TV; cable (premium). 2 pools, 1 indoor; whirlpool, poolside serv. Coffee in rms. Restaurants 6-10 am, 11 am-midnight. Rm serv. Bar 11-2 am, Sun noon-midnight; entertainment. Ck-out 11 am. Coin lndry. Meeting rms. Business servs avail. In-rm modem link. Bellhops. Valet serv. Gift shop. Free Anderson airport transportation. Sauna. Cr cds: A, C, D, DS, JCB, MC, V. 🄳 👫 🏊 🏋 🐾 SC

★ **RAMADA INN.** *5901 Scatterfield Rd (IN 109 Bypass) (46013). 765/649-0451; FAX 765/649-5484.* 115 rms, 2 story. S $65-$75; D $71-$89; each addl $10; suites $139-$145; under 12 free. Pet accepted, some restrictions; $25. TV; cable. Indoor pool; whirlpool, poolside serv. Restaurant 6:30 am-10 pm. Rm serv. Bar noon-midnight; Fri, Sat to 2 am; entertainment. Ck-out noon. Coin lndry. Meeting rms. Sundries. Tennis. Sauna. Cr cds: A, C, D, DS, MC, V. 🄳 👫 🏌 🏊 🏋 🐾 SC

Auburn (See also Fort Wayne)

Motel

★ **HOLIDAY INN EXPRESS.** *404 Touring Dr. 219/925-1900; FAX 219/927-1138.* E-mail cndmgment@aol.com. 70 rms, 3 story. S $74-$80; D $80-$85; suites $90-$95; under 18 free; higher rates special events. Pet accepted. TV; cable (premium). Complimentary continental bkfst. Coffee in rms. Restaurant 6 am-10 pm. Ck-out noon. Meeting rm. Business servs avail. In-rm modem link. Coin lndry. Health club privileges. Indoor pool; whirlpool. Some refrigerators, microwaves. Cr cds: A, C, D, DS, JCB, MC, V. 🄳 👫 🏋 🐾 SC

Bedford (See also Bloomington, French Lick)

Motel

✔★ **MARK III.** *1711 M Street (US 50). 812/275-5935.* 21 rms, 2 story. S $35; D $38; each addl $3; under 12 free. Crib free. Pet accepted, some restrictions. TV; cable (premium). Complimentary coffee in rms. Restaurant adj 11 am-midnight. Ck-out 11 am. Grill. Cr cds: A, C, D, DS, MC, V. 👫 🏋 🐾 SC

Bloomington (See also Bedford, Nashville)

Motel

★★ **HAMPTON INN.** *2100 N Walnut (47401), IN 37 exit College to Walnut. 812/334-2100; FAX 812/334-8433.* 131 rms, 4 story. S $63; D $71; under 18 free. Crib free. Pet accepted, some restrictions. TV; cable (premium), VCR avail. Pool. Complimentary continental bkfst. Restaurant adj open 24 hrs. Ck-out noon. Meeting rms. Business servs avail. In-rm modem link. Valet serv. Downhill/x-country ski 12 mi. Some in-rm whirlpools. Cr cds: A, C, D, DS, MC, V. 🄳 👫 🏂 🏊 🏋 🐾 SC

Crawfordsville

Motel

★ ★ **HOLIDAY INN.** *2500 N Lafayette Rd, jct US 231 & I-74. 765/362-8700.* 150 rms, 2 story. S, D $65-$75; each addl $6; under 19 free; higher rates Indianapolis "500" (2-day min). Crib free. Pet accepted. TV; cable (premium), VCR avail. Heated pool. Restaurant 6 am-2 pm, 5-9 pm. Rm serv. Bar 11 am-midnight, Fri, Sat noon-2 am, Sun from 3 pm; entertainment. Ck-out noon. Coin lndry. Meeting rms. Business servs avail. In-rm modem link. Valet serv. Sundries. Game rm. Some microwaves. Cr cds: A, C, D, DS, JCB, MC, V.

D ⊷ ≋ ⊠ ⊠ SC

Elkhart (See also Goshen, South Bend)

Motels

(Rates may be higher during Mobile Home Show, football wkends)

★ ★ **COMFORT INN.** *3321 Plaza Ct (46514), Cassopolis & IN 19. 219/264-0404.* 54 rms, 2 story. S $53; D $61; each addl $8; suites $95; under 18 free. Crib free. Pet accepted, some restrictions. TV; cable (premium). Pool. Complimentary continental bkfst. Restaurant adj 4-10 pm. Ck-out 11 am. Business servs avail. Whirlpools in suites. Cr cds: A, C, D, DS, MC, V. D ⊷ ≋ ⊠ ⊠ SC

✔ ★ **ECONO LODGE.** *3440 Cassopolis (IN 19) (46514). 219/262-0540.* 35 rms, 2 story. May-Oct: S $36-$50; D $44-$60; each addl $6; suites $65-$85; under 16 free; family, wkend rates; higher rates special events; lower rates rest of yr. Crib $6. Pet accepted, some restrictions. TV; cable (premium), VCR avail. Complimentary continental bkfst. Restaurant opp 6 am-midnight. Ck-out 11 am. Coin lndry. Business servs avail. Golf privileges. Cr cds: A, C, D, DS, JCB, MC, V. D ⊷ ⊁ ⊠ ⊠ SC

★ ★ **KNIGHTS INN.** *3252 Cassopolis St (IN 19) (46514). 219/264-4262; res: 800/843-5644.* 118 rms, 10 kit. units. S $32.95-$70; D $35.95-$70; each addl $5; kit. units $39.95-$70; under 18 free. Crib free. Pet accepted; deposit. TV; cable (premium). Pool. Complimentary coffee in lobby. Restaurant opp open 24 hrs. Ck-out 11 am. Meeting rm. Business servs avail. In-rm modem link. Some refrigerators, microwaves. Cr cds: A, C, D, DS, MC, V. D ⊷ ≋ ⊠ ⊠ SC

★ ★ ★ **RAMADA INN.** *3011 Belvedere Rd (46514), I-80/90 exit 92, 2 blks S. 219/262-1581; FAX 219/262-1590.* 145 rms, 2 story. Apr-Sept: S $67-$79; D $75-$89; each addl $8; suites, kit. units $91-$98; under 18 free; lower rates rest of yr. Crib free. Pet accepted, some restrictions. TV; cable (premium), VCR avail. 2 pools, 1 indoor; whirlpool, poolside serv. Playground. Complimentary continental bkfst. Restaurant 6:30 am-2 pm, 5-9 pm. Rm serv. Bar 5-10 pm; Fri, Sat to 2 am; Sun 12:30-9 pm; entertainment. Ck-out noon. Meeting rms. Business center. In-rm modem link. Game rm. Putting green. Downhill ski 10 mi; x-country 5 mi. Sauna. Health club privileges. Some refrigerators. Cr cds: A, C, D, DS, MC, V.

D ⊷ ≋ ≋ ⊠ ⊠ SC ⊼

✔ ★ **RED ROOF INN.** *2902 Cassopolis St (IN 19) (46514). 219/262-3691; FAX 219/262-3695.* 80 rms, 2 story. S $40.99-$65.99; D $40.99-$79.99; under 19 free; 2-day min football wkends; higher rates special events. Crib free. Pet accepted. TV; cable (premium). Complimentary coffee in lobby. Restaurant adj open 24 hrs. Ck-out noon. Business servs avail. Downhill ski 20 mi. Cr cds: A, C, D, DS, MC, V. D ⊷ ⊁ ⊠ ⊠ SC

Evansville

Motels

★ **DRURY INN.** *3901 US 41N (47711), near airport. 812/423-5818.* 151 rms, 4 story. S $63-$79; D $73-$89; each addl $8; under 18 free. Crib free. Pet accepted. TV; cable. Indoor pool; whirlpool. Complimentary continental bkfst. Restaurant adj open 24 hrs. Ck-out noon. Coin lndry. Business servs avail. In-rm modem link. Valet serv. Exercise equipt; bicycle, treadmill. Cr cds: A, C, D, DS, MC, V. D ⊷ ≋ ⊁ ⊠ ⊠ SC

★ **STUDIO PLUS.** *301 Eagle Crest Dr (47715), 8 mi E on Lloyd Expy. 812/479-0103; FAX 812/469-7172.* Web www.studioplus.com. 71 kit. units, 3 story. S $59-$69; D $89; wkend, wkly, monthly rates. Crib free. Pet accepted; $200. TV; cable (premium). Complimentary coffee in rms. Restaurant nearby. Ck-out noon. Business servs avail. In-rm modem link. Valet serv. Coin lndry. Exercise equipt; bicycle, stair machine. Pool. Microwaves. Cr cds: A, C, D, DS, MC, V. D ⊷ ≋ ⊁ ⊠ ⊠ SC

Fort Wayne *(See also Auburn)*

Motels

✔★ **DAYS INN.** *3730 E Washington Blvd (46803). 219/424-1980; FAX 219/422-6525.* 120 rms, 2 story. S $28-$34; D $36-$41; each addl $4; under 12 free; wkly, monthly rates. Crib free. Pet accepted. TV; cable (premium). Pool. Restaurant 6 am-1:30 pm, 4:30-10 pm. Bar. Ck-out 11 am. Coin lndry. Meeting rms. Business servs avail. X-country ski 18 mi. Some refrigerators. Cr cds: A, C, D, DS, JCB, MC, V. 🐾 🎿 🏊 📶 🏋 SC

✔★ **RED ROOF INN.** *2920 Goshen Rd (US 33/30) (46808). 219/484-8641; FAX 219/484-3441.* 79 rms, 2 story. S, D $43.99-$71.99; under 18 free. Crib free. Pet accepted. TV. Complimentary coffee in lobby. Ck-out noon. Cr cds: A, C, D, DS, MC, V. 🐾 📶 🏋

★★ **RESIDENCE INN BY MARRIOTT.** *4919 Lima Rd (46808). 219/484-4700; FAX 219/484-9772.* 80 kit. units, 2 story. S, D $109-$129; higher rates special events. Crib free. Pet accepted; $50-$100. TV; cable (premium), VCR avail (movies). Complimentary continental bkfst. Coffee in rms. Restaurant nearby. Ck-out noon. Health club privileges. Heated pool. Playground. Microwaves; many fireplaces. Cr cds: A, C, D, DS, JCB, MC, V. D 🐾 🏊 📶 🏋 SC

Motor Hotel

★★★ **MARRIOTT.** *305 E Washington Center Rd (46825). 219/484-0411; FAX 219/483-2892.* 223 rms, 2-6 story. S $130; D $140; each addl $10; suites $235-$350; under 18 free; wkend package. Crib free. Pet accepted. TV; cable (premium). Indoor/outdoor pool; whirlpool, poolside serv. Restaurant 6 am-10 pm; Fri, Sat to 11 pm. Rm serv. Bar 11-2:30 am. Ck-out noon. Coin lndry. Meeting rms. Business servs avail. In-rm modem link. Bellhops. Valet serv. Sundries. Gift shop. Free airport transportation. Putting green. Exercise equipt; weights, bicycles. Game rm. Lawn games. Some refrigerators. Picnic tables. Cr cds: A, C, D, DS, ER, JCB, MC, V. D 🐾 🏊 🏃 📶 🏋 SC

French Lick *(See also Bedford)*

Motel

★ **LANE.** *IN 56, 1/2 mi N on IN 56, 1 1/2 mi S of US 150. 812/936-9919.* 43 rms. S, D $40; each addl $6. Crib $6. Pet accepted. TV; cable (premium). Pool. Restaurant nearby. Ck-out 11 am. Picnic tables. Grill. Cr cds: MC, V. D 🐾 🏊 🏋

★ **PATOKA LAKE VILLAGE-THE PINES.** *Rte 2, Box 255E, 10 mi S on IN 145, at jct Lake Village Dr. 812/936-9854.* 12 log cabins. No rm phones. S, D $89; each addl (after 2nd person) $10; 6-12, $5; under 6 free; wkly rates. Crib free. Pet accepted. TV. Playground. Ck-out 11 am. Coin lndry. Meeting rms. Microwaves. Picnic tables, grills. Surrounded by woods; near lake. Cr cds: A, DS, MC, V. 🐾 🏋

Goshen *(See also Elkhart)*

Motel

✔★★ **BEST WESTERN INN.** *900 Lincolnway East (US 33). 219/533-0408.* 77 rms, 2 story. S $53-$59; D $58-$61; each addl $3; under 12 free. Crib free. Pet accepted. TV; cable (premium), VCR avail. Complimentary continental bkfst. Restaurant opp 7 am-10 pm. Ck-out 11 am. Business servs avail. In-rm modem link. Valet serv Mon-Fri. Exercise equipt; weight machine, bicycle. Cr cds: A, C, D, DS, JCB, MC, V. D 🐾 🏃 📶 🏋 SC

Greenfield *(See also Indianapolis)*

Motel

★ **LEE'S INN.** *2270 N State St. 317/462-7112; FAX 317/462-9801.* 100 rms, 2 story. S, D $59-$67; each addl $7; suites $89-$119; under 15 free; higher rates Indianapolis 500. Crib avail. Pet accepted. TV; cable. Complimentary continental bkfst. Ck-out noon. Meeting rms. Valet serv. Cr cds: A, C, D, DS, JCB, MC, V. D 🐾 📶 🏋 SC

Hammond *(See also Chicago, IL)*

Motor Hotel

★★ **HOLIDAY INN.** *3830 179th St (46323), I-80/94 exit Cline Ave S. 219/844-2140; FAX 219/845-7760.* 154 rms, 4 story. S, D $76.50-$116.50; under 18 free. Crib free.

Pet accepted, some restrictions. TV; cable (premium). Heated pool; poolside serv. Restaurant 6:30-9:30 am, 6-9 pm. Rm serv. Bar 4 pm-1 am; Sat to 2 am. Ck-out noon. Coin lndry. Meeting rms. Business servs avail. In-rm modem link. Bellhops. Valet serv. Sundries. Exercise equipt; weight machine, bicycle. Luxury level. Cr cds: A, C, D, DS, JCB, MC, V.
D 📠 🏊 🏋 📶 🦺 SC

Indianapolis *(See also Anderson, Greenfield)*

Motels

(Rates are usually higher during Indianapolis "500" and state fair; may be 3-day min.)

★ **COMFORT INN.** *5040 S East St (US 31S) (46227), south of downtown.* 317/783-6711; FAX 317/787-3065. 104 rms, 3 story. S $49-$65; D $55-$90; each addl $5; under 18 free. Crib free. Pet accepted, some restrictions. TV; cable (premium). Pool. Complimentary continental bkfst. Restaurant nearby. Ck-out noon. Business servs avail. Refrigerator in suites. Cr cds: A, C, D, DS, JCB, MC, V. D 📠 🏊 📶 🦺 SC

★ **DRURY INN.** *9320 N Michigan Rd (46268), in College Park.* 317/876-9777; FAX 317/876-9777, ext. 473. 110 rms, 4 story. S $63-$73; D $73-$83; each addl $10; under 18 free; some wkend rates. Crib free. Pet accepted, some restrictions. TV; cable (premium). Pool. Complimentary bkfst. Restaurant nearby. Ck-out noon. Meeting rms. Business servs avail. In-rm modem link. Sundries. Cr cds: A, C, D, DS, MC, V. D 📠 🏊 📶 🦺 SC

★ ★ **HAMPTON INN.** *7220 Woodland Dr (46278), I-465 & 71st St, north of downtown.* 317/290-1212; FAX 317/291-1579. 124 rms, 4 story. S, D $69-$74; under 18 free. Crib free. Pet accepted, some restrictions. TV; cable (premium). Indoor pool; whirlpool. Complimentary continental bkfst. Restaurant adj 24 hrs. Ck-out noon. Meeting rms. Business servs avail. In-rm modem link. Valet serv. Exercise equipt; weight machine, bicycles. Cr cds: A, C, D, DS, MC, V. D 📠 🏊 🏋 📶 🦺 SC

★ ★ **HAMPTON INN-EAST.** *2311 N Shadeland Ave (46219), east of downtown.* 317/359-9900; FAX 317/359-1376. 125 rms, 4 story. S $64-$68; D $68-$76; under 18 free. Crib free. Pet accepted, some restrictions. TV; cable (premium). Indoor pool; whirlpool. Complimentary continental bkfst. Restaurant nearby. Ck-out noon. Meeting rm. Business servs avail. In-rm modem link. Cr cds: A, C, D, DS, MC, V. D 📠 🏊 📶 🦺 SC

★ ★ **HOMEWOOD SUITES.** *2501 E 86th St (46240), north of downtown.* 317/253-1919; FAX 317/255-8223. 116 suites, 3 story. No elvtr. S, D $94-$104; higher rates special events. Crib free. Pet accepted; $50. TV; cable (premium), VCR. Complimentary continental bkfst. Coffee in rms. Ck-out noon. Meeting rms. Business center. In-rm modem link. Valet serv. Coin lndry. Exercise equipt; weight machine, stair machine, sauna. Heated pool; whirlpool. Refrigerators, microwaves. Cr cds: A, C, D, DS, MC, V. D 📠 🏊 🏋 📶 🦺 SC 🛗

Motor Hotels

★ ★ **HOLIDAY INN-EAST.** *6990 E 21st St (46219), east of downtown.* 317/359-5341; FAX 317/351-1666. 184 rms, 6 story. S, D $89; higher rates special events. Crib free. Pet accepted. TV; cable (premium). Complimentary full bkfst (Mon-Fri). Coffee in rms. Restaurant 6 am-11 pm; Fri-Sun to midnight. Rm serv. Bar. Ck-out noon. Meeting rms. Business center. In-rm modem link. Bellhops. Valet serv. Sundries. Coin lndry. Exercise equipt; treadmill, stair machine. Indoor pool; whirlpool. Game rm. Cr cds: A, C, D, DS, JCB, MC, V. D 📠 🏊 🏋 📶 🦺 SC 🛗

★ ★ ★ **MARRIOTT.** *7202 E 21st St (46219), I-70E & I-465, east of downtown.* 317/352-1231; FAX 317/352-9775. 252 rms, 3-5 story. S, D, studio rms $119; each addl $10; suites $300; under 18 free; wkend rates; higher rates Memorial Day wkend. Crib free. Pet accepted, some restrictions. TV; cable, VCR avail. Indoor/outdoor pool; wading pool, whirlpool, poolside serv. Complimentary coffee in lobby. Restaurant 6:30 am-10 pm. Rm serv. Bar 11-1 am, Sun to midnight. Ck-out noon. Coin lndry. Meeting rms. Business center. In-rm modem link. Bellhops. Valet serv. Sundries. Gift shop. Tennis privileges. Putting green. Exercise equipt; weight machine, bicycles. Rec rm. Some private patios. Luxury level. Cr cds: A, C, D, DS, JCB, MC, V. D 📠 🏊 🏋 📶 🦺 SC 🛗

Jasper

Motel

✔ ★ **DAYS INN.** *Jct IN 162 & IN 164.* 812/482-6000; FAX 812/482-7207. 84 rms, 2 story. S $52-$60; D $66-$72; each addl $6; under 18 free. Crib free. Pet accepted, some restrictions; $5. TV; cable (premium), VCR avail. Pool. Complimentary continental bkfst. Restaurant adj. Ck-out noon. Meeting rms. Business servs avail. Valet serv. Sundries. Some refrigerators. Cr cds: A, C, D, DS, MC, V. D 📠 🏊 📶 🦺 SC

Jeffersonville

Motel

(Rates are generally much higher during Kentucky Derby)

✔ ★ **BEST WESTERN GREENTREE INN.** *(1425 Broadway St, Clarksville 47129) N of Louisville, KY on I-65 at IN 131 exit. 812/288-9281.* 107 rms. S $49; D $60-$65; each addl $5. Crib free. Pet accepted, some restrictions. TV; cable (premium). Pool. Restaurant adj open 24 hrs. Ck-out noon. Business servs avail. In-rm modem link. Health club privileges. Bathrm phones. Cr cds: A, C, D, DS, ER, JCB, MC, V. [D] ⬚ ⬚ ⬚ ⬚ SC

Hotel

★ **RAMADA.** *700 W Riverside Dr. 812/284-6711; FAX 812/283-3686.* 186 units, 10 story, 20 suites. S $72; D $82; each addl $10; suites $95-$145; under 18 free. Crib free. Pet accepted, some restrictions. TV; cable (premium). Pool. Restaurant 6:30 am-2 pm, 5-10 pm. Bar 5 pm-2 am. Ck-out noon. Meeting rms. Business servs avail. Free airport transportation. Game rm. On Ohio River. Cr cds: A, C, D, DS, MC, V. [D] ⬚ ⬚ ⬚ ⬚ SC

Lafayette

Motel

★ ★ **HOMEWOOD SUITES.** *3939 IN 26E (47905). 765/448-9700; FAX 765/449-1297.* 84 kit. suites, 3 story. S, D $89-$152; under 18 free; higher rates: university events, Indy "500". Crib free. Pet accepted, some restrictions. TV; cable, VCR (movies). Heated pool; whirlpool. Complimentary continental bkfst. Complimentary coffee in rms. Restaurant nearby. Ck-out noon. Coin lndry. Meeting rms. Business center. In-rm modem link. Sundries. Gift shop. Free airport, RR station, bus depot transportation. Exercise equipt; weight machine, treadmill, sauna. Lawn games. Microwaves. Cr cds: A, C, D, DS, JCB, MC, V. [D] ⬚ ⬚ ⬚ ⬚ ⬚ ⬚

Motor Hotels

★ ★ **HOLIDAY INN.** *5600 IN 43N (47906), at jct I-65 & IN 43 exit 178. 765/567-2131; FAX 765/567-2511.* Web www.nlci.com/holiday. 150 rms, 4 story. S $55-$74; D $60-$76; each addl $6; under 18 free; higher rates: football games, Indianapolis "500," other special events. Crib free. Pet accepted. TV. Indoor pool. Restaurant 6 am-10 pm. Rm serv. Bar 4 pm-1 am. Ck-out 11 am. Free guest lndry. Meeting rms. Valet serv. Golf privileges. Sauna. Game rm. Cr cds: A, C, D, DS, JCB, MC, V. [D] ⬚ ⬚ ⬚ ⬚ ⬚ SC

★ ★ **RADISSON INN.** *4343 IN 26E (47905). 765/447-0575; FAX 765/447-0901.* 124 rms, 6 story. S, D $89-$99; each addl $10; suites $145; under 18 free; higher rates: Indianapolis "500," university events (2-day min). Crib free. Pet accepted, some restrictions. TV; cable (premium). Indoor pool; whirlpool. Complimentary coffee in rm. Restaurant 6:30 am-2 pm, 5-10 pm. Rm serv. Bar 4 pm-midnight; pianist exc Mon, Thurs. Ck-out noon. Coin lndry. Meeting rms. In-rm modem link. Valet serv. Sauna. Refrigerators. Cr cds: A, C, D, DS, JCB, MC, V. [D] ⬚ ⬚ ⬚ ⬚ SC

La Porte *(See also Michigan City, South Bend)*

Motor Hotel

★ ★ **PINE LAKE HOTEL & CONFERENCE CENTER.** *444 Pine Lake Ave (IN 35). 219/362-4585; FAX 219/324-6993; res: 800/374-6338.* 146 rms, 2-4 story. S $69-$99; D $79-$99; each addl $10; under 18 free; higher rates special events. Crib free. Pet accepted. TV; cable (premium). Indoor/outdoor pool; whirlpool; poolside serv. Restaurant 6 am-2 pm, 5-10 pm. Rm serv. Bar 11 am-midnight; wkend hrs vary. Ck-out 11 am. Meeting rms. Business servs avail. In-rm modem link. Shopping arcade. Barber, beauty shop. Downhill ski 12 mi; x-country ski 10 mi. Exercise equipt; weights, weight machine, sauna. Rec rm. Game rm. Cr cds: A, C, D, DS, JCB, MC, V. [D] ⬚ ⬚ ⬚ ⬚ ⬚ ⬚ SC

Logansport

Motel

✔ ★ ★ **HOLIDAY INN.** *3550 Market St. 219/753-6351; FAX 219/722-1568.* 95 rms, 2 story. S $60-$86; D $66-$92; each addl $6; suites $125; under 19 free; higher rates Indianapolis "500." Crib free. Pet accepted. TV; cable. Heated pool. Restaurant 6 am-10 pm. Rm serv. Bar 4 pm-midnight. Ck-out noon. Meeting rms. Sundries. Free local airport transportation. Cr cds: A, C, D, DS, JCB, MC, V. [D] ⬚ ⬚ ⬚ ⬚ SC

Merrillville

Hotel

★ ★ ★ **RADISSON HOTEL AT STAR PLAZA.** *800 E 81st Ave, I-65 & US 30, at Star Plaza Theater Complex. 219/769-6311; FAX 219/769-1462.* 347 rms, 4 story. S $89-$135; D $99-$145; each addl $10; suites $225-$800; under 18 free; wkday, wkend packages. Crib free. Pet accepted. TV; cable (premium), VCR avail (movies). 2 pools, 1 indoor; poolside serv. Playground. Complimentary coffee in rms. Restaurant 6:30 am-10 pm. Bar 11:30-2 am, Sun 5 pm-midnight; entertainment. Ck-out 11 am. Coin lndry. Convention facilities. Business servs avail. In-rm modem link. Shopping arcade. Barber, beauty shop. Valet parking. Exercise equipt; weights, bicycles. Game rm. Bathrm phones; some refrigerators, in-rm whirlpools, saunas; microwaves avail. Health club privileges. Private patios, balconies. Cr cds: A, C, D, DS, ER, MC, V.

Michigan City (See also La Porte)

Motels

★ **BLACKHAWK.** *3651 W Dunes Hwy (US 12). 219/872-8656; FAX 219/872-5427.* 20 rms, showers only. May-Sept: S, D $35-$55; family, wkly, wkend rates; ski plans; lower rates rest of yr. Pet accepted; $20 deposit. TV; cable (premium). Heated pool. Complimentary coffee in lobby. Ck-out 11 am. Downhill/x-country ski 8 mi. Refrigerators. Picnic tables. Cr cds: A, MC, V.

★ **KNIGHTS INN.** *201 W Kieffer Rd, US 421 exit 34B. 219/874-9500; FAX 219/874-5122; res: 800/219-9555.* 103 rms. Mid-June-mid-Sept: S, kit. units $58-$99; D $68-$99; under 16 free; higher rates special events; lower rates rest of yr. Crib free. Pet accepted, some restrictions. TV; cable (premium). Pool. Complimentary coffee in lobby. Ck-out 11 am. Meeting rm. Some refrigerators. Cr cds: A, C, D, DS, ER, MC, V.

★ **RED ROOF INN.** *110 W Kieffer Rd. 219/874-5251; FAX 219/874-5287.* 79 rms, 2 story. S $35-$42; D $41-$48; under 18 free. Crib free. Pet accepted. TV; cable (premium). Complimentary coffee in lobby. Restaurant opp 6 am-10 pm. Ck-out noon. Business servs avail. In-rm modem link. Sundries. Cr cds: A, C, D, DS, MC, V.

Muncie (See also Anderson)

Motels

✔ ★ **DAYS INN.** *3509 Everbrook Lane (47304). 765/288-2311.* 62 rms, 2 story. S $45-$50; D $50-$65; each addl $5; under 12 free; higher rates: Indianapolis "500", university events. Crib free. Pet accepted; $20 deposit. TV. Complimentary continental bkfst. Restaurant nearby. Ck-out 11 am. Health club privileges. Cr cds: A, C, D, DS, MC, V.

★ **LEE'S INN.** *3302 N Everbrook Lane (47304). 765/282-7557; FAX 765/282-0345; res: 800/733-5337.* 92 rms, 2 story. S $64; D $74; each addl $7; suites $81-$157; under 15 free; higher rates Indianapolis "500". Crib avail. Pet accepted. Complimentary continental bkfst. Restaurant nearby. Ck-out noon. Meeting rms. Valet serv. Health club privileges. Minibars. Cr cds: A, DS, MC, V.

★ **RAMADA INN.** *3400 S Madison St (47302). 765/288-1911; FAX 765/282-9458.* 148 rms, 2 story. S, D $52-$109; under 18 free. Crib avail. Pet accepted, some restrictions. TV; cable (premium), VCR avail. Pool. Complimentary continental bkfst. Restaurant 6:30 am-2 pm, 5-10 pm; Sun 7 am-2 pm. Rm serv. Bar 2 pm-1 am; entertainment. Ck-out noon. Coin lndry. Meeting rms. Business servs avail. Valet serv. Cr cds: A, C, D, DS, JCB, MC, V.

Hotel

★ ★ **RADISSON.** *420 S High St (47305). 765/741-7777; FAX 765/747-0067.* 130 rms, 7 story, 28 suites. S, D $75-$86; suites $86-$225; under 17 free; wkend rates. Crib free. Pet accepted. TV; cable (premium). Indoor pool; whirlpool. Restaurant 6:30 am-10 pm. Rm serv 24 hrs. Bar noon-midnight; wkends to 1 am; entertainment. Ck-out noon. Meeting rms. Business servs avail. Free airport transportation. Health club privileges. Microwaves avail. Cr cds: A, C, D, DS, MC, V.

Nashville (See also Bloomington)

Motel

★ **SALT CREEK INN.** *551 E State Rd 46, 1/2 mi E on IN 46, at Salt Creek Rd. 812/988-1149.* 66 rms, 2 story, 20 kit. units (no equipt). S $40-$75; D $48-$83; each addl $5; suites $85-$110; kit. units $53-$85; under 16 free. Pet accepted, some restrictions; $5. TV; cable. Complimentary coffee in lobby. Restaurant nearby. Ck-out 11 am. Downhill ski 5 mi. Cr cds: A, DS, MC, V. 🅳 ⭐ 🐾 ⊠ 🐾 SC

Plymouth (See also South Bend)

Motel

★ ★ **HOLIDAY INN.** *2550 N Michigan St. 219/936-4013; FAX 219/936-4553.* 108 rms, 2 story. S, D $59-$64; each addl $5; under 19 free; higher rates special events. Crib free. Pet accepted. TV; cable (premium). Pool. Restaurant 6:30 am-9 pm; Fri, Sat 10 to 10 pm; Sun 7 am-9 pm. Rm serv. Bar 11-1 am; wkend hrs vary. Ck-out noon. Coin lndry. Meeting rms. Business servs avail. In-rm modem link. Sundries. 18-hole golf course adj. Health club privileges. Cr cds: A, C, D, DS, JCB, MC, V. 🅳 ⭐ ⊠ ⊠ 🐾 SC

Richmond

Motels

(Rates may be higher during the Indianapolis "500")

★ ★ **COMFORT INN.** *912 Mendelson Dr, I-70 exit 151. 765/935-4766.* 52 rms, 2 story. S, D $54.95-$59.95; each addl $5; suites $61.95-$69.95; under 18 free. Crib free. Pet accepted. Indoor pool; whirlpool. Restaurant adj 6 am-8 pm. Ck-out 11 am. Game rm. Refrigerators, microwaves in suites. Cr cds: A, C, D, DS, MC, V. 🅳 ⭐ ⊠ ⊠ 🐾 SC

✔ ★ **KNIGHTS INN.** *419 Commerce Dr, I-70 at US 40 exit 156 A. 765/966-6682.* 103 rms, 10 kits. S, D $37.95-$49.95; each addl $5; kit. units $41.95-$49.95; under 18 free; higher rates special events. Crib free. Pet accepted. TV; cable (premium). Pool. Complimentary coffee in lobby. Restaurant adj 6 am-10 pm; Fri, Sat open 24 hrs. Ck-out noon. Meeting rm. Some refrigerators. Cr cds: A, C, D, DS, MC, V. ⭐ ⊠ ⊠ 🐾 SC

★ ★ **LEE'S INN.** *6030 National Rd E, I-70 exit 156A. 765/966-6559; FAX 765/966-7732; res: 800/733-5337.* 91 rms, 2 story, 12 suites. S $65-$85; D $75-$95; each addl $10; suites $73-$162; under 16 free. Crib free. Pet accepted. TV; cable (premium), VCR avail. Complimentary continental bkfst. Restaurant adj 6 am-10 pm. Ck-out noon. Meeting rms. Business servs avail. Health club privileges. Some in-rm whirlpools, microwaves. Cr cds: A, C, D, DS, MC, V. 🅳 ⭐ ⊠ ⊠ 🐾 SC

★ **RAMADA INN.** *4700 National Rd E (Main St), 1 mi W of I-70 exit 156 A. 765/962-5551; FAX 765/966-6250.* 158 rms, 2 story. S, D $68-$98; each addl $10; under 18 free. Crib free. Pet accepted, some restrictions. TV; cable. Heated pool. Restaurant 11 am-11 pm. Rm serv. Bar. Ck-out noon. Meeting rms. Business servs avail. Valet serv. Sundries. Game rm. Health club privileges. Cr cds: A, C, D, DS, MC, V. 🅳 ⭐ ⊠ ⊠ 🐾 SC

Hotel

★ ★ **CLARION LELAND.** *900 South A St, I-70 exit 151. 765/966-5000; FAX 765/962-0887; res: 800/535-2630.* 112 rms, 7 story. S, D $70-$110; each addl $10; under 18 free; wkend rates. Crib free. Pet accepted, some restrictions. TV; cable (premium), VCR avail. Indoor pool. Restaurant 6 am-10 pm. Bar; entertainment Sat. Ck-out noon. Meeting rms. Business servs avail. Concierge. Health club privileges. In-rm whirlpools, microwaves avail. Restored hotel (1928); Queen Anne furnishings. Cr cds: A, C, D, DS, ER, JCB, MC, V. 🅳 ⭐ ⊠ ⊠ 🐾 SC

South Bend (See also Elkhart, La Porte)

Motels

(Rates may be higher football wkends)

★ ★ **BEST INNS OF AMERICA.** *425 Dixie Hwy (46637). 219/277-7700; FAX 219/277-7700, ext. 113; res: 800/237-8466.* 93 rms, 2 story. May-Nov: S, D $45.88-$56.88; each addl $6; under 18 free; lower rates rest of yr. Crib free. Pet accepted, some restrictions. TV; cable. Complimentary continental bkfst. Restaurant nearby. Ck-out 1 pm. Meeting rm. Cr cds: A, C, D, DS, MC, V. 🅳 ⭐ ⊠ 🐾 SC

★ **DAYS INN.** *52757 US 31N (46637). 219/277-0510; FAX 219/277-9316.* 180 rms, 3 story. S $39-$60; D $49-$70; each addl $5; under 8 free; higher rates special events. Crib free. Pet accepted. TV; cable (premium). Pool. Playground. Complimentary continental bkfst. Ck-out noon. Meeting rm. Business servs avail. In-rm modem link. Cr cds: A, C, D, DS, ER, JCB, MC, V. [D] [✦] [≋] [⟋] [✖] [SC]

★ ★ **HOLIDAY INN-UNIVERSITY AREA.** *515 Dixie Hwy (46637). 219/272-6600; FAX 219/272-5553.* 220 rms, 2 story. S $89-$99; D $99-$110; each addl $10; under 18 free; wkend, hol rates. Crib free. Pet accepted, some restrictions. TV; cable (premium). 2 pools, 1 indoor; wading pool, whirlpool. Complimentary continental bkfst. Coffee in rms. Restaurant 7-10 am, 11 am-1 pm, 5:30-9:30 pm. Rm serv. Bar 11 am-midnight; Fri, Sat to 1 am. Ck-out noon. Coin lndry. Meeting rms. Business servs avail. Bellhops. Free airport transportation. Exercise equipt; weight machine, bicycle, sauna. Game rm. Rec rm. Balconies. Picnic tables. Cr cds: A, C, D, DS, JCB, MC, V. [D] [✦] [≋] [⟋] [✖] [SC]

Motor Hotel

★ ★ **RESIDENCE INN BY MARRIOTT.** *716 N Niles Ave (46617). 219/289-5555.* 80 kit. suites, 2 story. July-Nov: S, D $99-$129; higher rates graduation; lower rates rest of yr. Crib free. Pet accepted; $100. TV; cable (premium), VCR avail (movies). Heated pool; whirlpool. Playground. Complimentary continental bkfst. Complimentary coffee in rms. Restaurant nearby. Ck-out noon. Coin lndry. Meeting rms. Business servs avail. Exercise equipt; weights, bicycle. Microwaves. Balconies. Cr cds: A, C, D, DS, JCB, MC, V. [D] [✦] [≋] [⟋]

Inn

★ ★ **OLIVER INN.** *630 W Washington St (46601). 219/232-4545; res: 888/697-4466; FAX 219/288-9788.* E-mail oliver@michiana.org; web michiana.org/users/oliver. 9 rms, 2 share bath, 3 story. S, D $75-$125; higher rates special events. Pet accepted, some restrictions. TV; cable (premium). Complimentary continental bkfst; afternoon refreshments. Restaurant adj 11:30 am-2 pm, 5-10 pm; Fri to 11 pm; Sat 4:30-11 pm; Sun 4-9 pm; Sun brunch 9 am-2 pm. Ck-out 11 am, ck-in 4-6 pm. Business servs avail. Luggage handling. 18-hole golf privileges, pro, putting green. Downhill/x-country ski 20 mi. Lawn games. Some fireplaces. Picnic tables. Built in 1886; Victorian decor. Totally nonsmoking. Cr cds: A, DS, MC, V. [✦] [≋] [⟋] [⟋] [≋] [SC]

Terre Haute

Motor Hotel

★ ★ **HOLIDAY INN.** *3300 US 41 S (47802), at I-70. 812/232-6081; FAX 812/238-9934.* 230 rms, 2-5 story. S, D $84-$97; suites $115-$175; under 20 free; higher rates special events. Crib free. Pet accepted. TV; cable (premium). Indoor pool; whirlpool. Complimentary coffee in rms. Restaurant 6:30 am-2 pm, 5-10:30 pm. Rm serv. Bar 11-1 am. Ck-out noon. Guest lndry. Meeting rms. Business servs avail. In-rm modem link. Bellhops. Valet serv. Exercise equipt; weights, bicycle. Cr cds: A, C, D, DS, ER, JCB, MC, V. [D] [✦] [≋] [⟋] [⟋] [✖] [SC]

Warsaw

Motel

★ ★ **COMFORT INN.** *2605 E Center St. 219/267-7337.* 60 rms, 2 story, 8 suites. S, D $65-$79; suites $79-$129; higher rates special events. Crib free. Pet accepted; $50 deposit. TV; cable (premium). Complimentary continental bkfst. Restaurant nearby. Ck-out noon. Business servs avail. In-rm modem link. Valet serv. Health club privileges. Heated pool. In-rm whirlpool, refrigerator, microwave in suites. Picnic tables, grills. Cr cds: A, C, D, DS, MC, V. [D] [✦] [≋] [⟋] [✖] [SC]

Motor Hotel

★ ★ **RAMADA INN.** *2519 E Center St. 219/269-2323; FAX 219/269-2432.* 156 rms, 4 story. S, D $76-$88; each addl $10; suites $95-$115; under 12 free; higher rates summer wkends. Crib free. Pet accepted. TV; cable, VCR avail. Complimentary coffee in rms. Restaurant 7-10:30 am, 11 am-2 pm, 5-10 pm. Rm serv. Bar. Ck-out noon. Meeting rms. Business servs avail. In-rm modem link. Valet serv. Sundries. Coin lndry. 18-hole golf privileges, pro. Exercise equipt; weights, stair machine, sauna. Indoor/outdoor pool; whirlpool, poolside serv. Game rm. Rec rm. Microwaves avail. Cr cds: A, C, D, DS, MC, V. [D] [✦] [⟋] [≋] [⟋] [✖]

Inn

★ ★ **WHITE HILL MANOR.** *2513 E Center St. 219/269-6933; FAX 219/268-1936.* 8 rms, 2 with shower only, 2 story. S $70-$99; D $80-$120; each addl $15. Children over 12 yrs only. Pet accepted. TV; VCR avail (movies). Complimentary full bkfst. Complimentary coffee in rms. Restaurant nearby. Ck-out 11 am, ck-in 3 pm. Business servs avail. In-rm modem link. X-country ski 5 mi. Lawn games. Microwaves avail. Picnic tables, grills. Built in 1934; restored English Tudor manor. Totally nonsmoking. Cr cds: A, C, D, DS, MC, V.

D ⬅ ⬆ ⬇ 🐾

Iowa

Amana Colonies *(See also Cedar Rapids, Iowa City)*

Motels

★ ★ **BEST WESTERN QUIET HOUSE SUITES.** *(1708 N Highland, Williamsburg 52361) 15 mi SW on I-80, exit 220 N. 319/668-9770; FAX 319/668-9777.* 33 rms, 2 story, 7 suites. S $63-$125; D $73-$135; suites $89-$99; under 12 free; higher rates: wkends, hols. Crib free. Pet accepted; $15. TV; cable (premium). Complimentary continental bkfst. Complimentary coffee in rms. Meeting rms. Business servs avail. Exercise equipt; bicycle, treadmill. Indoor/outdoor pool; whirlpool. Cr cds: A, D, DS, MC, V.
D ⊬ ≈ ⊁ ⊠ ⋈ SC

★ ★ ★ **HOLIDAY INN.** *(Amana) At I-80 exit 225. 319/668-1175; FAX 319/668-2853.* 155 rms, 2 story. S, D $84; under 19 free. Crib free. Pet accepted. TV; cable (premium). Indoor pool; wading pool, whirlpool, poolside serv. Playground. Complimentary coffee in rms. Restaurant 6 am-10 pm. Rm serv. Bar noon-11 pm. Ck-out 11 am. Coin lndry. Meeting rms. Business servs avail. Exercise equipt; bicycles, treadmills, sauna. Game rm. Little Amana complex adj; old-time general store & winery. Cr cds: A, C, D, DS, JCB, MC, V.
D ⊬ ≈ ⊁ ⊠ ⋈ SC

★ **SUPER 8.** *(2228 U Ave, Williamsburg 52361) I-80 exit 225. 319/668-2800.* 63 rms, 2 story. May-Oct: S, D $49.88; each addl $6; under 12 free; lower rates rest of yr. Crib $3. Pet accepted, some restrictions; $6. TV; cable (premium). Complimentary continental bkfst. Restaurant adj 6 am-10 pm. Ck-out 11 am. Business servs avail. Cr cds: A, C, D, DS, ER, JCB, MC, V. D ⊬ ⊠ ⋈ SC

Inn

✔ ★ **DIE HEIMAT COUNTRY INN.** *Homestead (52236), at jct US 6, 151. 319/622-3937.* 19 rms, 2 story. S, D $45.95-$76.95; each addl $5; under 6, $3. Crib $3. Pet accepted, some restrictions; $10. TV, some B/W. Complimentary full bkfst. Ck-out 10:30 am. Some refrigerators. Restored inn (1858). Cr cds: DS, MC, V. ⊬ ⊠ ⋈

Ames

Motels

★ ★ **BEST WESTERN STARLITE VILLAGE.** *I-35 & 13th St. 515/232-9260.* 131 rms, 3 story. S $45-$50; D $55-$60; each addl $6; higher rates special events. Crib $6. Pet accepted. TV; cable (premium), VCR avail. Indoor pool; whirlpool, sauna. Restaurant 6 am-10 pm. Rm serv to 9 pm. Bar noon-2 am. Ck-out noon. Meeting rms. Valet serv. Game rm. Cr cds: A, C, D, DS, MC, V. D ⊬ ≈ ⊠ ⋈ SC

★ **COMFORT INN.** *1605 S Dayton. 515/232-0689.* 52 rms, 2 story, 6 suites. Sept-Nov: S $43.95; D $49.95; each addl $5; suites $50.95-$60.95; under 18 free; higher rates football season; lower rates rest of yr. Crib free. Pet accepted. TV; cable. Indoor pool; whirlpool. Complimentary continental bkfst. Restaurant adj open 24 hrs. Ck-out 11 am. Meeting rms. Business servs avail. Some refrigerators. Cr cds: A, C, D, DS, MC, V.
D ⊬ ≈ ⊠ ⋈ SC

✔ ★ **HEARTLAND INN.** *I-35 & US 30, exit 111B. 515/233-6060; FAX 515/233-1911; res: 800/334-3277.* 91 rms, 2 story. S $45; D $62; each addl $7; under 16 free. Crib free. Pet accepted. TV; cable. Complimentary continental bkfst. Restaurant nearby. Ck-out noon. Whirlpool, sauna. Cr cds: A, C, D, DS, JCB, MC, V. D ⊬ ⊠ ⋈ SC

Motor Hotel

★ ★ **BUDGETEL.** *2500 Elwood Dr. 515/296-2500; FAX 515/296-2500.* 89 rms, 2 story. S $50; D $56; under 18 free. Crib free. Pet accepted. TV; cable (premium). Indoor pool; whirlpool. Complimentary continental bkfst. Restaurant nearby. Ck-out noon. Meeting rms. Some refrigerators. Cr cds: A, D, DS, MC, V. D ⊬ ≈ ⊠ ⋈ SC

Atlantic *(See also Avoca)*

Motel

✔ ★ **ECONO LODGE.** *US 71, 1/2 mi S of I-80 exit 60. 712/243-4067; FAX 712/243-1713.* 51 rms, 1-2 story. S $35-$37; D $39-$45; each addl $2. Crib $2. Pet accepted. TV;

cable. Pool. Coffee in rms. Restaurant nearby. Ck-out 11 am. Meeting rm. Sundries. Cr cds: A, C, D, DS, MC, V. [D] 🐾 ≋ 🚫 🐾 [SC]

Avoca *(See also Atlantic)*

Motel

✔ ★ **CAPRI.** *US 59, ¹/₂ mi S of I-80.* 712/343-6301. 26 rms. S $35; D $41; each addl $5. Crib $5. Pet accepted. TV; cable. Complimentary coffee in lobby. Restaurant nearby. Ck-out 10:30 am. Cr cds: A, DS, MC, V. 🐾 🚫 🐾

Bettendorf *(See also Clinton, Davenport)*

Motel

✔ ★ **ECONO LODGE-QUAD CITIES.** *2205 Kimberly Rd.* 319/355-6471; *FAX* 319/359-0559. 67 rms. S, D $40-$58; each addl $4; under 18 free. Crib free. Pet accepted, some restrictions. TV; cable (premium), VCR avail. Pool. Playground. Complimentary continental bkfst. Restaurant 10 am-10 pm. Bar from 11 am. Ck-out noon. Meeting rm. Business servs avail. Cr cds: A, C, D, DS, MC, V. [D] 🐾 ≋ 🚫 🐾 [SC]

Hotel

★ ★ ★ **JUMER'S CASTLE LODGE.** *900 Spruce Hills Dr.* 319/359-7141; *FAX* 319/359-7141; *res: 800/285-8637.* 210 rms. S $78; D $87; each addl $9; suites $88-$142; under 18 free. Crib free. Pet accepted, some restrictions; $25 refundable. TV; cable (premium). 2 pools, 1 indoor; whirlpool. Restaurant 6 am-10 pm. Bars 11-1 am; entertainment. Ck-out noon. Convention facilities. Business servs avail. Free airport, bus depot transportation. Putting green. Exercise equipt; weight machine, bicycles, sauna. Health club privileges. Rec rm. Lawn games. Bavarian architecture & decor; antiques, tapestries. Cr cds: A, D, DS, MC, V. [D] 🐾 ≋ 🏃 🚫 🐾 [SC]

Burlington *(See also Fort Madison)*

Motels

✔ ★ **COMFORT INN.** *3051 Kirkwood.* 319/753-0000; *FAX* 319/753-0000, ext. 301. 52 rms, 2 story. S $35-$50; D $45-$60; each addl $5; suites $99; under 18 free; higher rates: hol wkends, special events. Crib avail. Pet accepted. TV; cable (premium). Pool. Complimentary continental bkfst. Restaurant nearby. Ck-out 11 am. Business servs avail. In-rm modem link. Cr cds: A, C, D, DS, ER, JCB, MC, V. [D] 🐾 ≋ 🚫 🐾 [SC]

★ **DAYS INN.** *1601 N Roosevelt Ave, at jct US 34, 61.* 319/752-0000; *FAX* 319/754-1111. 43 rms. S $35-$45; D $45-$55; each addl $5; under 12 free. Crib free. Pet accepted. TV; cable (premium). Restaurant nearby. Ck-out 11 am. Meeting rm. Microwaves avail. Cr cds: A, C, D, DS, MC, V. 🐾 🚫 🐾 [SC]

Motor Hotel

★ ★ **BEST WESTERN PZAZZ MOTOR INN.** *3001 Winegard Dr, just N of jct US 34, 61.* 319/753-2223; *FAX* 319/753-2224. 151 rms, 3 story. S $59.75; D $67.75; each addl $4; suites $105; studio rms $55-$85; under 18 free. Crib free. Pet accepted. TV; cable (premium), VCR (movies). Indoor pool; whirlpool. Restaurant 6:30 am-10 pm. Rm serv. Bar 11:30-2 am; entertainment. Balconies. Coin lndry. Meeting rms. Business servs avail. In-rm modem link. Gift shop. Barber, beauty shop. Airport transportation. Game rm. Exercise equipt; rower, weight machine, sauna. Cr cds: A, C, D, DS, ER, MC, V. [D] 🐾 ≋ 🏃 🚫 🐾 [SC]

Cedar Falls *(See also Waterloo)*

Motel

★ ★ **HOLIDAY INN.** *5826 University Ave.* 319/277-2230; *FAX* 319/277-0364. 182 rms, 2 story. S $59; D $74; each addl $10; suites $125-$150. Crib free. Pet accepted. TV; cable (premium). Heated pool; poolside serv. Complimentary coffee in rm. Restaurant 6 am-10 pm. Rm serv. Bar 4 pm-midnight. Ck-out noon. Coin lndry. Meeting rms. Business servs avail. In-rm modem link. Bellhops. Valet serv. Free airport transportation. Exercise equipt; bicycle, stair machine. Game rm. Cr cds: A, C, D, DS, JCB, MC, V. [D] 🐾 ≋ 🏃 🚫 🐾 [SC]

Cedar Rapids *(See also Amana Colonies)*

Motels

★ **COMFORT INN-NORTH.** *5055 Rockwell Dr (52402), I-380 exit 24A. 319/393-8247.* 59 rms, 2 story. May-Aug: S, D $50.95-$65.95; under 18 free; lower rates rest of yr. Crib free. Pet accepted, some restrictions. TV; cable (premium), VCR avail. Complimentary continental bkfst. Ck-out 11 am. Business servs avail. In-rm modem link. Whirlpool. Some refrigerators. Cr cds: A, C, D, DS, ER, JCB, MC, V. [D] 🐕 ⛱ 🏊 🐾 SC

★ ★ **COMFORT INN-SOUTH.** *390 33rd Ave SW (52404). 319/363-7934.* 60 rms, 3 story. S $43-$60; D $45-$65; each addl $5; suites $53-$65; under 18 free. Crib free. Pet accepted. TV; cable (premium). Complimentary continental bkfst. Restaurant nearby. Ck-out 11 am. Meeting rms. Cr cds: A, C, D, DS, ER, JCB, MC, V. [D] 🐕 ⛱ 🏊 SC

★ **DAYS INN-SOUTH.** *3245 Southgate Place SW (52404), SW off I-380 exit 17. 319/365-4339.* 40 rms, 2 story, 4 suites. S $42-$50; D $44-$52; each addl $5; suites $55-$65; under 18 free. Crib free. Pet accepted. TV; cable. Indoor pool; whirlpool. Complimentary continental bkfst. Restaurant nearby. Ck-out 11 am. Business servs avail. In-rm modem link. Some refrigerators. Cr cds: A, D, DS, ER, MC, V. [D] 🐕 ⛱ 🏊 SC

✔ ★ **ECONO LODGE.** *622 33rd Ave SW (52404), 2 blks W of I-380, 33rd St exit. 319/363-8888.* 50 rms, 2 story. S $38.95-$58.95; D $42.95-$58.95; each addl $5; suites $70-$125; under 18 free; higher rates: farm show, conventions. Crib free. Pet accepted. TV; cable. Indoor pool; whirlpool. Complimentary continental bkfst. Restaurant nearby. Ck-out 11 am. Coin lndry. Cr cds: A, C, D, DS, MC, V. [D] 🐕 ⛱ 🏊 SC

✔ ★ **EXEL INN.** *616 33rd Ave SW (52404). 319/366-2475; FAX 319/366-5712.* 103 rms, 2 story. S $32.99-$41.99; D $37.99-$47.99; each addl $4; under 18 free. Crib free. Pet accepted. TV; cable. Complimentary continental bkfst. Restaurant nearby. Ck-out noon. Guest lndry. Business servs avail. In-rm modem link. Cr cds: A, C, D, DS, MC, V. [D] 🐕 ⛱ 🏊 SC

Motor Hotels

★ ★ **DAYS INN.** *2501 Williams Blvd SW (52404), at IA 151, 16th Ave. 319/365-9441; FAX 319/365-0255.* 184 rms, 2 story. S $62-$68; D $68-$74; each addl $6; under 19 free. Crib free. Pet accepted. TV; cable. Indoor pool; whirlpool, sauna. Restaurant 6 am-2 pm, 5-10 pm. Rm serv. Bar 4 pm-midnight; Sun to 10 pm. Ck-out noon. Coin lndry. Meeting rms. Business servs avail. In-rm modem link. Free airport transportation. Cr cds: A, C, D, DS, JCB, MC, V. [D] 🐕 ⛱ 🏊 SC

★ ★ ★ **FOUR POINTS BY SHERATON.** *525 33rd Ave SW (52404). 319/366-8671; FAX 319/362-1420.* 157 rms, 6 story. S $78-$88; D $88-$98; each addl $10; suites $185; under 18 free; wkend rates. Crib free. Pet accepted. TV; cable (premium). Indoor pool; whirlpool, poolside serv. Restaurant 6:30 am-10 pm; Sat 7 am-11 pm. Rm serv. Bar 11-2 am; Sun noon-10 pm; entertainment. Ck-out noon. Meeting rms. Business servs avail. In-rm modem link. Bellhops. Valet serv. Sundries. Free airport transportation. Exercise equipt; bicycles, treadmill, sauna. Game rm. Rec rm. Cr cds: A, C, D, DS, JCB, MC, V. [D] 🐕 ⛱ 🏋 🏊 SC

✔ ★ **VILLAGE INN.** *100 F Avenue NW (52405). 319/366-5323; res: 800/858-5511.* 86 rms, 4 story. S $42-$44; D $48-$50; each addl $2; under 12 free. Crib $5. Pet accepted, $5/day. TV; cable (premium). Restaurant 6-3 am; Sun to midnight. Rm serv. Bar 11-2 am; closed Sun. Ck-out noon. Meeting rms. Business servs avail. In-rm modem link. Valet serv. Cr cds: A, C, D, DS, JCB, MC, V. 🐕 🐾 SC

Hotel

★ ★ **FIVE SEASONS.** *350 1st Ave NE (52401). 319/363-8161; FAX 319/363-3804.* 275 rms, 16 story. S $79-$105; D $89-$115; each addl $10; suites $175-$325; under 18 free; wkend rates. Crib free. Pet accepted. Parking $3. TV; cable. Indoor pool; whirlpool. Complimentary coffee in rms. Restaurant 6:30 am-11 pm. Rm serv 24 hrs. Bar. Ck-out noon. Convention facilities. Business center. In-rm modem link. Concierge. Free airport transportation. Exercise equipt; weights, bicycles, sauna. Game rm. Cr cds: A, C, D, DS, MC, V. [D] 🐕 ⛱ 🏋 🏊 🐾 SC 🚶

Charles City *(See also Mason City)*

Motel

★ **HARTWOOD INN.** *1312 Gilbert St. 515/228-4352; FAX 515/228-2672; res: 800/972-2335.* 35 rms, 1 & 2 story. S $33-$45; D $45-$65; each addl $5; under 16 free. Crib free. Pet accepted, some restrictions. TV; cable (premium). Complimentary coffee in rms. Restaurant nearby. Ck-out 11 am. Coin lndry. Cr cds: A, C, D, DS, MC, V.

D 💺 🏊 📶 🐾 SC

Clear Lake (See also Mason City)

Motel

✔★ BUDGET INN. *1306 N 25th St, 1 blk W of I-35 on US 18 exit 194.* 515/357-8700; FAX 515/357-8811. 60 rms, 2 story. S $36.95; D $42.95; each addl $4; under 16 free. Crib free. Pet accepted. TV; cable (premium). Pool. Playground. Restaurant adj open 24 hrs. Ck-out noon. Meeting rms. Sundries. Cr cds: A, C, D, DS, MC, V. D 💺 🏊 📶 🐾 SC

Motor Hotel

★★ BEST WESTERN HOLIDAY MOTOR LODGE. *1 mi E on US 18, 1 blk W of I-35, near Mason City Municipal Airport.* 515/357-5253; FAX 515/357-8153. 144 rms, 5 story. S $47.95-$57.95; D $55.95-$59.95; each addl $8; suites $66.95-$116.90; under 12 free. Crib free. Pet accepted. TV; cable. Indoor pool; whirlpool, sauna, poolside serv. Complimentary bkfst. Restaurant 6 am-10 pm; dining rm from 5 pm. Rm serv. Bar 4 pm-2 am. Ck-out 11 am. Valet serv. Meeting rm. Sundries. Free airport transportation. Cr cds: A, C, D, DS, MC, V. 💺 🏊 ✈ 📶 🐾 SC

Clinton

Motels

★★★ BEST WESTERN FRONTIER MOTOR INN. *2300 Lincolnway, at jct US 30, 67W.* 319/242-7112; FAX 319/242-7117. 117 rms, 1-2 story. S $46-$66; D $54-$72; each addl $6; suites $89-$135; under 12 free. Crib $6. Pet accepted, some restrictions. TV; cable (premium). Indoor pool; whirlpool. Restaurant 6 am-9 pm. Rm serv. Bar 11:30-2 am; closed Sun. Ck-out noon. Meeting rms. Business servs avail. Valet serv. Sundries. Exercise equipt; bicycle, treadmill. X-country ski 5 mi. Some refrigerators. Cr cds: A, C, D, DS, MC, V.

D 💺 🏊 ✈ 📶 🐾 SC

★★ RAMADA INN. *1522 Lincoln Way.* 319/243-8841; FAX 319/242-6202. 103 rms, 2 story, 10 suites. S $54; D $60; each addl $6; suites $80-$90; under 18 free; package plans. Crib free. Pet accepted, some restrictions. TV; cable (premium), VCR avail. Complimentary coffee in lobby. Indoor pool. Rm serv. Bar 11-2 am. Ck-out noon. Meeting rms. Business servs avail. Game rm. Some refrigerators, microwaves. Cr cds: A, C, D, DS, MC, V. D 💺 🏊 🐾 SC

★ TRAVELODGE. *302 Sixth Ave S, at 3rd St.* 319/243-4730; FAX 319/243-4732. 51 rms, 2 story. S $38; D $48; each addl $5; under 17 free. Crib $5. Pet accepted. TV; cable (premium). Pool. Complimentary coffee. Restaurant adj 11 am-8 pm. Ck-out 11 am. Some refrigerators. Some private patios. Cr cds: A, C, D, DS, ER, JCB, MC, V.

D 💺 🏊 📶 🐾 SC

Council Bluffs (See also Omaha, NE)

Motel

★ BEST WESTERN-METRO. *3537 W Broadway (51501).* 712/328-3171. 89 rms, 2 story, 43 suites. Feb-Nov: S $59-$99; D $69-$109; each addl $6; under 18 free; lower rates rest of yr. Crib avail. Pet accepted. TV; cable (premium). Complimentary continental bkfst. Complimentary coffee in rms. Restaurant 6 am-10 pm. Ck-out noon. Meeting rms. Business servs avail. In-rm modem link. Free airport transportation. Indoor pool. Game rm. Refrigerators; microwave in suites. Cr cds: A, C, D, DS, MC, V. D 💺 🏊 📶 🐾 SC

Davenport

Motels

★★★ BEST WESTERN STEEPLEGATE INN. *100 W 76th St (52806).* 319/386-6900; FAX 319/388-9955. 121 rms, 2 story. S $67-$72; D $74-$80; each addl $6; suites $125-$150; under 12 free. Crib $4. Pet accepted; $3. TV; cable (premium). Indoor pool; whirlpool. Restaurant 6 am-9 pm; Fri, Sat to 10 pm. Rm serv. Bar 11-2 am; entertainment. Ck-out noon. Business servs avail. Valet serv. Free airport, bus depot transportation. Exercise equipt; bicycle, treadmill. Game rm. Some refrigerators, microwaves. Cr cds: A, C, D, DS, MC, V. D 💺 🏊 ✈ 📶 🐾 SC

★ COMFORT INN. *7222 Northwest Blvd (52806), just S of I-80 at exit 292.* 319/391-8222; FAX 319/391-1595. 89 rms, 2 story. S $45.50; D $54.50; each addl $4. Pet accepted, some restrictions; $20 refundable & $2/day. TV; cable (premium), VCR avail. Complimentary continental bkfst. Restaurant adj 6 am-10 pm. Ck-out 11 am. Business servs avail. Exercise equipt; weight machine, stair machine. Microwaves avail. Cr cds: A, C, D, DS, ER, JCB, MC, V. [D] [✦] [🏄] [⊠] [🐾] [SC]

★ **DAYS INN.** 3202 E Kimberley Rd (52807), I-74 exit Spruce Hills Dr. 319/355-1190. 65 rms, 2 story. Apr-Sept: S $40-$85; D $44-$85; under 13 free; lower rates rest of yr. Crib free. Pet accepted, some restrictions. TV; cable (premium). Indoor pool; whirlpool. Complimentary continental bkfst. Restaurant nearby. Ck-out 11 am. Meeting rms. Business servs avail. Valet serv. Game rm. Cr cds: A, D, DS, MC, V. [D] [✦] [≈] [⊠] [🐾] [SC]

✔ ★ **EXEL INN.** 6310 Brady St N (52806). 319/386-6350; FAX 319/388-1548. 103 rms, 2 story. S $37.99; D $44.99; each addl $5; under 18 free. Crib free. Pet accepted. TV; cable. Complimentary continental bkfst. Ck-out noon. In-rm modem link. Valet serv. Cr cds: A, C, D, DS, MC, V. [D] [✦] [⊠] [🐾] [SC]

★ ★ **HAMPTON INN.** 3330 E Kimberly Rd (52807). 319/359-3921; FAX 319/359-1912. 132 rms, 2 story. S $52-$59; D $54-$64; under 18 free. Crib free. Pet accepted, some restrictions. TV; cable (premium). Indoor pool. Complimentary continental bkfst. Ck-out noon. Business servs avail. In-rm modem link. Bellhops. Free airport transportation. Exercise equipt; bicycle, treadmill. Cr cds: A, C, D, DS, MC, V. [D] [✦] [≈] [🏄] [⊠] [🐾] [SC]

✔ ★ **HEARTLAND INN.** 6605 N Brady (52806). 319/386-8336; FAX 319/386-6005; res: 800/334-3277. 86 rms, 3 story. S, D $47-$66; each addl $9; suites $110-$140. Crib free. Pet accepted. TV; cable (premium). Indoor pool. Complimentary continental bkfst. Restaurant adj 6 am-11 pm. Ck-out 11 am. Meeting rm. Business servs avail. Sundries. Rec rm. Cr cds: A, C, D, DS, MC, V. [D] [✦] [≈] [⊠] [🐾] [SC]

★ **SUPER 8.** 410 E 65th St (52807). 319/388-9810; FAX 319/388-9810, ext. 198. 61 rms, 2 story. Apr-Sept: S $39.88; D $46.88-$58.88; each addl $5; suites $50.88-$52.88; under 12 free; higher rates: jazz festival, special events; lower rates rest of yr. Crib free. Pet accepted. TV; cable (premium). Complimentary continental bkfst. Restaurant adj 11 am-10 pm; Sat, Sun from 8 am. Ck-out 11 am. Business servs avail. Microwaves avail. Cr cds: A, C, D, DS, MC, V. [D] [✦] [⊠] [🐾] [SC]

Decorah

Motel

✔ ★ **SUPER 8.** 810 IA 9 East, 1¹/₂ mi E on IA 9 at jct US 52. 319/382-8771. 60 rms, 2 story. S $36.88-$38.88; D $45.88-$47.88; each addl $4; suites $52.88-$70.88. Crib $2. Pet accepted. TV; cable (premium), VCR avail. Complimentary continental bkfst. Restaurant nearby. Ck-out 11 am. Coin lndry. Meeting rm. Business servs avail. In-rm modem link. Cr cds: A, C, D, DS, MC, V. [D] [✦] [⊠] [🐾] [SC]

Des Moines

Motels

(Rates may be higher during state fair)

✔ ★ ★ **BEST INNS OF AMERICA.** (5050 Merle Hay Rd, Johnston 50131) Just N of I-35, I-80 exit 131. 515/270-1111; res: 800/BEST-INN. 92 rms, 2 story, 14 suites. S $49.88; D $52.88-$62.88; each addl $10; suites $67-$77; under 18 free. Crib free. Pet accepted. TV; cable (premium), VCR avail (movies $3). Indoor pool; whirlpool. Complimentary continental bkfst. Restaurant opp 6 am-midnight. Ck-out 1 pm. Meeting rms. Business servs avail. Health club privileges. Microwaves avail. Cr cds: A, C, D, DS, MC, V. [D] [✦] [≈] [⊠] [🐾] [SC]

★ ★ **BEST WESTERN AIRPORT INN.** 1810 Army Post Rd (50315), near Intl Airport, south of downtown. 515/287-6464; FAX 515/287-5818. 145 rms. S $62; D $72; each addl $5; suites $99; under 17 free. Crib free. Pet accepted. TV; cable, VCR avail (movies). Indoor pool; poolside serv. Complimentary continental bkfst. Restaurant 11 am-2 pm, 5-9 pm. Rm serv. Bar 4 pm-1 am. Ck-out noon. Coin lndry. Meeting rms. Business servs avail. Bellhops. Valet serv. Free airport transportation. Cr cds: A, D, DS, MC, V. [D] [✦] [≈] [🏄] [⊠] [🐾] [SC]

★ ★ **BEST WESTERN STARLITE VILLAGE.** (133 SE Delaware, Ankeny 50021) 14 mi N on I-35, exit 92. 515/964-1717; FAX 515/964-8781. 116 rms, 2 story. June-Aug: S $48-$53; D $53-$62; each addl $5; kits. $120; under 12 free; wkly rates; lower rates rest of yr. Crib $3. Pet accepted, some restrictions. TV; cable. Indoor pool; whirlpool. Restaurant 6 am-10 pm. Rm serv. Bar 1 pm-2 am; Sun to 10 pm. Meeting rms. Business servs avail. Sundries. Microwaves avail. Cr cds: A, D, DS, MC, V. [D] [✦] [≈] [⊠] [🐾] [SC]

✔★ **COMFORT INN.** *5231 Fleur Dr (50321), near Intl Airport, south of downtown.*
515/287-3434. 55 rms, 3 story, 16 suites. No elvtr. May-Aug: S $49-$64; D $59-$79; each
addl $5; suites $59-$95; under 18 free; higher rates special events; lower rates rest of yr.
Pet accepted, some restrictions. TV; cable (premium). Indoor pool; whirlpool. Complimentary continental bkfst. Restaurant nearby. Ck-out 11 am. Meeting rm. Business servs avail.
In-rm modem link. Sundries. Free airport transportation. Refrigerator in suites. Cr cds: A, D,
DS, MC, V. [D] [✆] [≈] [✕] [⊠] [⚲] [SC]

✔★ **COUNTRY INN.** *(3225 Adventureland Dr, Altoona 50009) Exit 142 off I-80.*
515/967-5252; res: 800/383-6545. 110 rms, 2 story. S $45.50-$57.50; D $62.50-$66.50;
suites $80.50; under 14 free. Crib $3. Pet accepted; $6. TV; cable (premium). Indoor pool;
whirlpool. Complimentary coffee in lobby. Restaurant adj open 24 hrs. Ck-out 11 am.
Meeting rm. Business servs avail. Cr cds: A, D, DS, MC, V. [D] [✆] [≈] [⊠] [⚲] [SC]

✔★ **HEARTLAND INN.** *11414 Forest Ave (50325), I-80/35 exit 124, west of*
downtown. 515/226-0414; FAX 515/226-9769. 87 rms, 2 story. S $48-$58; D $56-$66; each
addl $5; under 16 free. Crib free. Pet accepted, some restrictions; $10. TV; cable (premium).
Complimentary continental bkfst. Restaurant nearby. Ck-out 11 am. Business servs avail.
Sauna. Health club privileges. Whirlpool. Microwaves avail. Cr cds: A, D, DS, MC, V.
[D] [✆] [⊠] [⚲] [SC]

★★ **INN AT MERLE HAY.** *(5055 Merle Hay Rd, Johnston 50131) 2 mi W on*
I-35/80 exit 131. 515/276-5411; FAX 515/276-0696; res: 800/643-1197. 146 rms. S $50-$80;
D $55-$90; suites $119-$149; under 16 free. Crib $5. Pet accepted; $40 ($30 refundable).
TV; cable (premium). Indoor pool; whirlpool. Complimentary coffee in rms. Restaurant 6:30
am-11 pm. Bar. Ck-out noon. Meeting rms. Business servs avail. Bellhops. Free airport, bus
depot transportation. Microwaves avail. Cr cds: A, D, DS, ER, MC, V.
[D] [✆] [≈] [⊠] [⚲] [SC]

★★ **INN AT UNIVERSITY.** *(11001 University Ave, Clive 50325) 515/225-2222;*
FAX 515/224-9816; res: 800/369-7476. 104 rms, 2 story. S $49.50-$65; D $68-$78; each
addl $5; under 17 free. Pet accepted; $50 refundable. TV; cable. Heated pool; whirlpool.
Restaurant nearby. Bar 4:30 pm-2 am. Ck-out noon. Meeting rms. Business servs avail.
Sundries. Free airport transportation. Exercise equipt; weight machine, stair machine.
Microwaves avail. Cr cds: A, C, D, DS, MC, V. [D] [✆] [≈] [✕] [⊠] [⚲] [SC]

★★ **RESIDENCE INN BY MARRIOTT.** *(11428 Forest Ave, Clive 50325) I-35/80*
exit University Ave, N on 114th St, then W on Forest Ave. 515/223-7700; FAX 515/223-
7222. 112 kit. suites, 2 story. S $74-$99; D $84-$110; wkly, monthly rates. Crib free. Pet
accepted; $50. TV; cable (premium). Pool; whirlpool. Complimentary continental bkfst.
Complimentary coffee in rms. Restaurant nearby. Ck-out noon. Coin lndry. Meeting rms.
Business servs avail. In-rm modem link. Valet serv. Sundries. Exercise equipt; stair machine, bicycles. Health club privileges. Microwaves. Balconies. Picnic tables, grills. Cr cds:
A, C, D, DS, JCB, MC, V. [D] [✆] [≈] [✕] [⊠] [⚲] [SC]

Motor Hotel

★★ **BEST WESTERN EXECUTIVE CENTER.** *11040 Hickman Rd (50325), at jct*
US 6, I-35, I-80 exit 125, north of downtown. 515/278-5575; FAX 515/278-4078. 161 rms, 6
story. S $84; D $89; each addl $5; under 17 free. Crib free. Pet accepted. TV; cable
(premium). Indoor pool; wading pool, whirlpool. Restaurant 6:30 am-2 pm, 5-10:30 pm. Rm
serv. Bar 4 pm-midnight. Ck-out noon. Coin lndry. Meeting rms. Business servs avail. In-rm
modem link. Valet serv. Free airport transportation. Sauna. Health club privileges. Cr cds: A,
C, D, DS, JCB, MC, V. [D] [✆] [≈] [⊠] [⚲] [SC]

Hotels

★★★ **FORT DES MOINES.** *1000 Walnut St (50309), downtown. 515/243-1161; FAX*
515/243-4317; res: 800/532-1466. E-mail hotelfdm@radiks.net; web www.hotelfortdm.com.
242 rms, 11 story, 56 suites. S, D $59-$119; suites $75-$250; under 18 free; wkend rates.
Pet accepted. TV; cable. Pool; whirlpool. Restaurant 6:30 am-10:30 pm. Bar 11-2 am.
Ck-out noon. Meeting rms. In-rm modem link. Gift shop. Free airport transportation. Exercise
equipt; weight machines, bicycles. Refrigerator in some suites. Cr cds: A, C, D, DS, MC, V.
[D] [✆] [≈] [✕] [⊠] [⚲] [SC]

★★★ **MARRIOTT.** *700 Grand (50309), downtown. 515/245-5500; FAX 515/245-*
5567. 415 rms, 33 story. S, D $70-$140; suites $125-$600; under 18 free; wkend rates. Crib
free. Pet accepted, some restrictions. Covered parking $10/day, valet $10/day. TV; cable
(premium), VCR avail. Indoor pool; whirlpool, poolside serv. Restaurants 6:30 am-11 pm.
Bar. Ck-out noon. Convention facilities. Business servs avail. Free airport transportation.
Barber, beauty shop. Exercise equipt; weights, bicycles, sauna. Some bathrm phones.
Luxury level. Cr cds: A, C, D, DS, ER, JCB, MC, V. [D] [✆] [≈] [✕] [⊠] [⚲] [SC]

★ ★ **SAVERY.** *401 Locust St (50309), downtown. 515/244-2151; FAX 515/244-1408; res: 800/798-2151.* 221 units, 12 story, 20 kits. S, D $95-$125; each addl $10; suites $225-$500. Crib $10. Pet accepted, some restrictions. TV; cable. Indoor pool; whirlpool. Restaurants 6:30 am-2 pm, 5-8 pm. Rm serv 6:30 am-10 pm. Bar 11-1 am; entertainment. Ck-out noon. Meeting rms. Beauty shop. Free airport, bus depot transportation. Valet parking. Exercise equipt; weight machines, bicycles, sauna. Built 1919. Cr cds: A, C, D, DS, ER, MC, V. ⒟ 🐾 ≈ 🏋 🚶 ⊠ 🔥 SC

Dubuque

Motels

★ ★ **BEST WESTERN MIDWAY.** *3100 Dodge (52003), 2¹/₂ mi W on US 20. 319/557-8000; FAX 319/557-7692.* 151 rms, 4 story. June-Oct: S $63-$67; D $74-$82; each addl $5; suites $125-$150; under 18 free; wknd rates; lower rates rest of yr. Crib $3. Pet accepted, some restrictions. TV; cable, VCR (movies). Complimentary bkfst buffet Mon-Fri. Complimentary coffee in rms. Restaurant 6:30 am-10 pm; Sat from 7 am; Sun 7 am-1 pm, 5-9 pm. Rm serv. Bar 11 am-midnight; wkends to 2 am. Ck-out 11 am. Meeting rms. Business servs avail. In-rm modem link. Bellhops. Free airport transportation. Exercise equipt; bicycle, treadmill, sauna. Indoor pool; whirlpool. Game rm. Refrigerator, wet bar in suites. Picnic tables. Cr cds: A, C, D, DS, MC, V. ⒟ 🐾 ≈ 🏋 ⊠ SC

★ ★ **COMFORT INN.** *4055 Dodge St. 319/556-3006.* 52 rms, 3 story, 14 suites. May-Oct: S, D $59-$79; each addl $5; suites $69-$89; under 18 free; lower rates rest of yr. Crib free. Pet accepted. TV; cable (premium). Indoor pool; whirlpool. Complimentary continental bkfst. Ck-out 11 am. Meeting rms. Business servs avail. In-rm modem link. Sundries. Downhill ski 6 mi; x-country ski 5 mi. Refrigerator, microwave in suites. Cr cds: A, C, D, DS, ER, JCB, MC, V. ⒟ 🐾 ≈ 🐾 ≈ ⊠ 🔥 SC

★ ★ **DAYS INN.** *1111 Dodge St. 319/583-3297; FAX 319/583-5900.* 154 rms, 2 story. S $45-$69; D $55-$69; under 18 free. Crib free. Pet accepted. TV; cable (premium), VCR avail. Pool. Complimentary continental bkfst. Restaurant 11 am-10 pm. Bar to midnight. Ck-out 11 am. Meeting rms. Business servs avail. Bellhops. Valet serv. Sundries. Free airport transportation. Exercise equipt; bicycles, weight machine. Refrigerators, microwaves in suites. Picnic tables. Cr cds: A, C, D, DS, JCB, MC, V. ⒟ 🐾 ≈ 🏋 ⊠ 🔥 SC

🚶 ★ ★ **HEARTLAND INN.** *4025 McDonald Dr (52003), off US 20 (Dodge St). 319/582-3752; FAX 319/582-0113; res: 800/334-3277, ext. 12.* 88 rms, 2 story. S $51-$57; D $57-$63; each addl $6; under 16 free; ski plans. Crib free. Pet accepted, some restrictions. TV; cable (premium). Indoor pool; whirlpool. Complimentary continental bkfst. Ck-out 11 am. Meeting rm. Business servs avail. Downhill/x-country ski 5 mi. Sauna. Health club privileges. Cr cds: A, C, D, DS, MC, V. ⒟ 🐾 ≈ 🐾 ⊠ 🔥 SC

★ ★ **HEARTLAND INN.** *2090 Southpark Court (52003), US 61/151 S to Twin Valley Dr, then W. 319/556-6555; FAX 319/556-0542; res: 800/334-3277, ext. 13.* 59 rms, 2 story, 6 suites. S $44-$58; D $52-$66; each addl $5; suites $75-$115; under 16 free. Crib free. Pet accepted, some restrictions. TV; cable (premium). Indoor pool. Complimentary continental bkfst. Restaurant nearby. Ck-out 11 am. Business servs avail. In-rm modem link. Downhill ski/x-country ski 12 mi. Exercise equipt; weight machine, bicycle. Some microwaves. Cr cds: A, C, D, DS, MC, V. ⒟ 🐾 ≈ ≈ 🏋 ⊠ 🔥 SC

★ ★ **TIMMERMAN'S LODGE.** *(7777 Timmerman Dr, East Dubuque IL 61025) 1 mi E on US 20. 815/747-3181; FAX 815/747-6556; res: 800/336-3181.* 74 rms, 3 story. S $49-$85; D $64-$85; each addl $5; suites $149; under 18 free. Crib $4. Pet accepted. TV; cable, VCR (movies). Indoor pool; whirlpool. Restaurant 7 am-2 pm. Rm serv. Bar. Ck-out noon. Coin lndry. Meeting rm. Business servs avail. In-rm modem link. Sundries. Downhill ski 10 mi; x-country ski ¹/₄ mi. Sauna. Game rm. Rec rm. Private patios, balconies. Cr cds: A, DS, MC, V. ⒟ 🐾 ≈ ≈ ⊠ 🔥 SC

Motor Hotel

★ ★ **HOLIDAY INN.** *450 Main St. 319/556-2000; FAX 319/556-2303.* 193 rms, 5 story. May-Oct: S, D $59-$117; suites $120-$148; under 18 free; lower rates rest of yr. Crib free. Pet accepted, some restrictions. $75. TV; cable (premium), VCR avail. Indoor pool. Restaurant 6:30 am-10 pm. Rm serv. Bar. Ck-out noon. Meeting rms. Business center. Free airport transportation. Exercise equipt; weight machine, stair machine. Some refrigerators, microwaves. Cr cds: A, C, D, DS, MC, V. ⒟ 🐾 ≈ 🏋 ⊠ SC 🏃

Fairfield *(See also Mount Pleasant, Ottumwa)*

Motels

★★ **BEST WESTERN.** *2220 W Burlington, on US 34. 515/472-2200; FAX 515/472-7642.* 52 rms, 2 story. S $55-$64; D $62-$71; each addl $8; under 18 free. Crib free. Pet accepted, some restrictions. TV. Indoor pool; whirlpool. Complimentary continental bkfst. Restaurant 11 am-2 pm, 5-9 pm. Ck-out noon. Meeting rms. Cr cds: A, C, D, DS, ER, JCB, MC, V. 🅳 🖭 ⊠ 🏊 🐾 SC

✔★ **ECONOMY INN.** *2701 W Burlington, 1¹/₂ mi W on US 34. 515/472-4161.* 42 rms, 1-2 story. S $35; D $36-$45; each addl $5; Crib $3. Pet accepted, some restrictions. TV; cable. Restaurant opp 6 am-11 pm. Ck-out 11 am. Meeting rm. Cr cds: A, DS, MC, V. 🖭 ⊠ 🐾 SC

Fort Madison *(See also Burlington)*

Motel

✔★ **MADISON INN.** *3440 Avenue L. 319/372-7740; res: 800/728-7316.* 20 rms. S, D $38-$47; each addl $5; higher rates Tri-State Rodeo. Pet accepted, some restrictions; $2. TV; cable (premium). Complimentary coffee in rms. Restaurant adj 6 pm-midnight. Ck-out 11 am. Business servs avail. In-rm modem link. Cr cds: A, C, D, DS, MC, V. 🅳 🖭 ⊠ 🐾 SC

Grinnell *(See also Marshalltown, Newton)*

Motels

★ **DAYS INN.** *IA 146, I-80 exit 182. 515/236-6710; FAX 515/236-5783.* 41 rms, 2 story. S $49; D $65; under 12 free. Pet accepted; $5. TV; cable. Indoor pool. Complimentary continental bkfst. Ck-out 11 am. Cr cds: A, C, D, DS, MC, V. 🅳 🖭 ⊠ ⊠ 🐾 SC

✔★ **SUPER 8.** *exit 182, I-80 & IA 146. 515/236-7888.* 53 rms, 2 story. S $42.88; D $52.88; each addl $3; under 12 free; higher rates: special events, wkends. Crib $4. Pet accepted, some restrictions. TV; cable (premium). Complimentary continental bkfst. Restaurant opp 6:30 am-9 pm. Ck-out 11 am. Cr cds: A, C, D, DS, MC, V. 🅳 🖭 ⊠ 🐾 SC

Hampton

Motel

✔★ **GOLD KEY.** *US 65, Rte 2, 2 mi N on US 65. 515/456-2566.* 20 rms. S $26-$30; D $31-$40; each addl $3-$5. Crib free. Pet accepted. TV; cable. Restaurant adj 6:30 am-10:30 pm. Sundries. Ck-out 11 am. Cr cds: A, D, DS, MC, V. 🖭 🐾

Humboldt

Motel

★ **CORNER INN.** *US 169 & IA 3. 515/332-1672.* 22 rms, 1 story. S $29-$30; D $35-$39; each addl $6. Pet accepted. TV; cable. Restaurant opp 6 am-midnight. Ck-out 11 am. Cr cds: MC, V. 🅳 🖭 ⊠ 🐾

Iowa City *(See also Amana Colonies, Cedar Rapids)*

Motels

(Rates may be higher football wkends)

★★ **BEST WESTERN WESTFIELD INN.** *(1895 27th Ave, Coralville 52241) I-80 & IA 965 exit 240. 319/354-7770.* 155 rms, 2 story. S $57-$65; D $65-$73; each addl $8; under 17 free; wkly, monthly rates. Pet accepted. TV; cable (premium). Indoor pool; whirlpool. Complimentary continental bkfst. Restaurant 6:30 am-2 pm, 5-10 pm. Rm serv. Bar 4 pm-midnight. Ck-out 11 am. Meeting rms. Business servs avail. Airport transportation. Exercise equipt; treadmill, stair machine, sauna. Putting green. Game rm. Rec rm. Microwaves avail. Cr cds: A, C, D, DS, MC, V. 🅳 🖭 ⊠ 🏃 ⊠ 🐾 SC

★ **PRESIDENTIAL MOTOR INN.** *(711 S Downey Rd, West Branch 52358) I-80 exit 254. 319/643-2526.* 38 rms, 2 story. S $36-$44; D $55-$65; each addl $12; wkly rates. Crib $3. Pet accepted, some restrictions. TV; cable (premium). Complimentary coffee in lobby. Ck-out 11 am. Coin lndry. Refrigerators; microwaves avail. Cr cds: A, D, DS, MC, V. 🅳 🖭 ⊠ 🐾

Motor Hotel

★ ★ ★ **HOLIDAY INN.** *210 S Dubuque St (52240). 319/337-4058; FAX 319/337-9045.* E-mail holiday@ia.net. 236 rms, 9 story. S $79; D $89; each addl $10; suites $145-$160; under 19 free. Pet accepted, some restrictions. TV; cable (premium). Indoor pool; whirlpool. Restaurant 6 am-2 pm, 5-10 pm. Rm serv. Bar 4 pm-1 am. Ck-out noon. Meeting rms. Business servs avail. Bellhops. Beauty shop. Airport transportation. Exercise equipt; bicycles, treadmills, sauna. Game rm. Refrigerators. Cr cds: A, C, D, DS, MC, V.

[D] [✦] [≋] [✕] [⊠] [※] [SC]

Le Mars *(See also Sioux City)*

Motel

✔ ★ **AMBER INN.** *1 mi S on US 75. 712/546-7066; FAX 712/548-4058; res: 800/338-0298.* 73 rms. S $28-$32; D $30-$35; each addl $2. Crib $2. Pet accepted. TV; cable. Continental breakfast. Restaurant nearby. Ck-out 11 am. Meeting rm. Business servs avail. Cr cds: A, C, DS, MC, V. [D] [✦] [⊠] [※]

Maquoketa

Motel

✔ ★ **KEY.** *119 McKinsey Ave, 1 blk E of US 64/61 Bypass on McKinsey Dr. 319/652-5131; res: 800/622-3285.* 30 rms, 2 story. S, D $30-$40; each addl $5. Crib free. Pet accepted. TV; cable. Restaurant adj 6 am-10 pm. Ck-out 11 am. Cr cds: A, C, D, DS, MC, V. [D] [✦] [⊠] [※]

Marshalltown *(See also Grinnell)*

Motel

★ **COMFORT INN.** *2613 S Center St. 515/752-6000; FAX 515/752-8762.* 62 rms, 2 story. June-Aug: S, D $45.95-$75.95; suites $139.95; under 18 free; lower rates rest of yr. Crib free. Pet accepted; $10. TV; cable (premium). Indoor pool; whirlpool. Complimentary continental bkfst. Restaurant nearby. Ck-out noon. Business servs avail. Cr cds: A, D, DS, MC, V. [D] [✦] [≋] [⊠] [※] [SC]

Mason City *(See also Clear Lake)*

Motel

★ **DAYS INN.** *2301 4th St SW. 515/424-0210; FAX 515/424-0210, ext. 133.* 58 rms, 2 story. S $32-$44; D $42-$59; each addl $6; under 18 free. Crib free. Pet accepted. TV; cable. Complimentary continental bkfst. Ck-out noon. Business servs avail. Cr cds: A, C, D, DS, MC, V. [D] [✦] [⊠] [※] [SC]

Mount Pleasant *(See also Fairfield)*

Motel

★ **HEARTLAND INN.** *US 218 N, on Frontage Rd. 319/385-2102; FAX 319/385-3223.* 59 rms, 2 story. S $42-$51; D $56-$61; each addl $8; under 16 free. Crib free. Pet accepted. TV; cable (premium). Complimentary continental bkfst. Restaurant adj 11 am-9 pm. Ck-out 11 am. Business servs avail. Sauna. Whirlpool. Cr cds: A, C, D, DS, MC, V.

[D] [✦] [⊠] [※] [SC]

Newton *(See also Grinnell)*

Motels

★ **BEST WESTERN NEWTON INN.** *IA 14 at I-80 exit 164. 515/792-4200; FAX 515/792-0108.* 118 rms, 2 story. S $39-$53; D $45-$75; each addl $6; under 12 free; higher rates Knoxville racing season. Crib $3. Pet accepted. TV; cable (premium), VCR avail. Indoor pool; whirlpool. Complimentary full bkfst. Restaurant 6 am-1 pm, 5:30-10 pm. Bar 5:30 pm-1 am. Ck-out noon. Meeting rms. Business servs avail. Putting green. Exercise equipt; bicycles, treadmill, sauna. Game rm. Cr cds: A, C, D, DS, MC, V.

[D] [✦] [≋] [✕] [⊠] [※] [SC]

✔ **DAYS INN.** *1065 W 19th St S, 2 mi S on IA 14 at I-80 exit 164. 515/792-2330; FAX 515/792-1045.* 59 rms, 2 story. S $43-$48; D $49-$54; each addl $5. Crib free. Pet accepted. TV; cable (premium), VCR avail. Complimentary continental bkfst. Restaurant adj open 24 hrs. Ck-out 11 am. Business servs avail. Cr cds: A, C, D, DS, JCB, MC, V.

[D] [✦] [≈] [🐾] [SC]

Okoboji

Motels

★ **COUNTRY CLUB.** *Airport Rd, 1 blk W on US 71. 712/332-5617; FAX 712/332-7705; res: 800/831-5615.* 53 rms. Memorial Day-late Sept: S, D $80-$150; lower rates rest of yr. Crib $5. Pet accepted. TV; cable (premium). Heated pool. Restaurant nearby. Ck-out 10 am. Business servs avail. Picnic tables, grills. Cr cds: A, D, DS, MC, V.

[✦] [≈] [≈] [🐾] [SC]

★ ★ **FILLENWARTH BEACH.** *Arnolds Park (51331), 1 blk W on US 71. 712/332-5646.* 93 kit. units in motel, cottages, 1-3 story. No elvtr. Late June-late Aug: apts for 2-8, $500-$1,380/wk; daily rates; lower rates Apr-mid-June, Sept. Closed rest of yr. Crib free. Pet accepted. TV; cable, VCR. Indoor/outdoor pool. Playground. Supervised child's activities (late May-early Sept). Restaurant opp 6 am-midnight. Ck-out noon. Business servs avail. Free airport, bus depot transportation. Sports dir in season. Tennis. Rec rm. Private beach. Waterskiing, instruction. Boat dock, canoes, boats. Free sail and cruiser boat rides. Balconies. Picnic tables, grills. On West Okoboji Lake. No cr cds accepted.

[D] [✦] [🏊] [🎿] [≈] [🐾] [🔥]

✔★ **FOUR SEASONS RESORT.** *(US 71, Arnolds Park 51331) 1/2 mi S on US 71. 712/332-2103; res: 800/876-2103.* 32 units, 1-2 story. S, D, suites $45-$145. Pet accepted. Restaurant 9 am-11 pm. Bar to 2 am. Ck-out 11 am. Many private patios, balconies. Picnic tables, grills. On West Okoboji Lake. Cr cds: A, MC, V. [✦] [🏊] [≈] [🐾]

★ ★ ★ **VILLAGE EAST.** *1/2 mi N on US 71. 712/332-2161; FAX 712/332-7727; res: 800/727-4561.* 99 rms, 2 story. Late May-Sept: S $139; each addl $10; lower rates rest of yr. Pet accepted. TV; cable. 2 pools; whirlpool. Restaurant 6 am-10 pm. Rm serv. Bar. Ck-out 11 am. Meeting rms. Business servs avail. Beauty shop. Indoor & outdoor tennis. 18-hole golf, greens fee $39. X-country ski on site. Exercise rm; instructor, weight machines, bicycles, sauna. Rec rm. Private patios, balconies. Lake opp. Cr cds: A, C, D, DS, ER, MC, V. [D] [✦] [🎿] [🏃] [🎿] [≈] [🏃] [🔥] [🐾] [🏊]

Onawa

Motel

✔★ **SUPER 8.** *2 mi W at jct IA 175, I-29. 712/423-2101; FAX 712/423-3480.* 80 rms. S $40-$65; D $45-$65; each addl $3. Pet accepted. TV; cable. Restaurant nearby. Ck-out 11 am. Picnic table. Cr cds: A, D, DS, MC, V. [D] [✦] [≈] [🐾] [SC]

Osceola

Motel

✔★ **BLUE HAVEN.** *325 S Main St. 515/342-2115; res: 800/333-3180.* 24 rms, 1-2 story. S $33-$43; D $41-$49; each addl $4; higher rates hunting seasons. Crib free. Pet accepted. TV; cable (premium). Restaurant nearby. Ck-out 11 am. Cr cds: A, DS, MC, V.

[✦] [≈] [🐾] [SC]

Oskaloosa *(See also Ottumwa)*

Motel

★ **RED CARPET INN.** *2278 US 63N, 2 mi N on US 63. 515/673-8641; FAX 515/673-4111.* 41 rms, 2 story. S $30-$35; D $38-$45; each addl $5. Pet accepted. TV; cable (premium). Complimentary continental bkfst. Coffee in rms. Cr cds: A, DS, MC, V.

[✦] [≈] [🐾]

Ottumwa *(See also Oskaloosa)*

Motel

✔★ **HEARTLAND INN.** *125 W Joseph (US 63 N). 515/682-8526; FAX 515/682-7124.* 89 units. S $42; D $50-$57; each addl $8; under 17 free. Crib free. Pet accepted. TV; cable (premium). Pool; whirlpool. Complimentary continental bkfst. Restaurant nearby. Ck-out noon. Coin lndry. Meeting rm. Business servs avail. Sauna. Cr cds: A, C, D, DS, MC, V. [D] [✦] [≈] [≈] [🐾] [SC]

Shenandoah

Motel

✔★ **TALL CORN.** *1503 Sheridan Ave, at US 59.* *712/246-1550; FAX 712/246-4773.* 65 rms, 1-2 story. S $37; D $47; each addl $3; family rates. Crib $5. Pet accepted. TV; cable (premium). Indoor pool. Restaurant 6 am-9 pm. Rm serv. Bar 5 pm-1 am. Ck-out 11 am. Meeting rms. Business servs avail. Airport transportation. Cr cds: A, C, D, DS, MC, V.
D 🖚 ⚖ 🖹 📷 **SC**

Sioux City

Motels

★★ **BEST WESTERN REGENCY EXECUTIVE.** *2nd & Nebraska (51101), business exit 147B.* *712/277-1550; FAX 712/277-1120.* 114 rms, 2 story. S $50-$63; D $58-$69; each addl $10; suites $113-$173; under 18 free. Crib $6. Pet accepted, some restrictions. TV; cable. Heated pool. Bar 5-8 pm. Ck-out noon. Coin lndry. Meeting rms. Business servs avail. Free airport transportation. Cr cds: A, C, D, DS, JCB, MC, V. **D** 🖚 ⚖ 🖹 📷 **SC**

✔★ **PALMER HOUSE.** *3440 E Gordon Dr (51106).* *712/276-4221; FAX 712/276-9535; res: 800/833-4221.* 63 rms, 1-2 story. S $37; D $47.75; Pet accepted. TV; cable. Complimentary continental bkfst. Restaurant adj open 24 hrs. Ck-out 11 am. Business servs avail. Cr cds: A, D, DS, MC, V. **D** 🖚 🖹 📷 **SC**

★ **SUPER 8.** *4307 Stone Ave (51106).* *712/274-1520.* 60 rms, 2 story. Mid-May-mid-Oct: S $37.98; D $46.98; each addl $5. Crib. Pet accepted. TV; cable. Continental bkfst. Restaurant 5-10 pm. Ck-out 11 am. Cr cds: A, C, D, DS, MC, V. **D** 🖚 🖹 📷 **SC**

Waterloo *(See also Cedar Falls)*

Motels

✔★ **EXEL INN.** *3350 University Ave (50701).* *319/235-2165; FAX 319/235-7175.* 104 rms, 2 story. S $29.99; D $39.99; each addl $4; under 17 free. Pet accepted. TV; cable. Complimentary continental bkfst. Restaurant nearby. Ck-out noon. Coin lndry. In-rm modem link. Game rm. Cr cds: A, C, D, DS, MC, V. 🖚 🖹 📷 **SC**

★ **FAIRFIELD INN BY MARRIOTT.** *2011 La Porte Rd (50702), Crossroads Shopping Center.* *319/234-5452.* 57 rms, 3 story. S $48.95; D $48.95-$53.95; under 18 free. Crib free. Pet accepted, some restrictions. TV; cable. Indoor pool; whirlpool. Complimentary continental bkfst. Restaurant opp open 24 hrs. Ck-out 11 am. Cr cds: A, D, DS, MC, V.
D 🖚 ⚖ 🖹 📷 **SC**

★★ **HEARTLAND INN.** *1809 LaPorte Rd (50702).* *319/235-4461; FAX 319/235-0907; res: 800/334-3277.* 118 rms, 2 story. S $45-$57; D $53-$65; each addl $5; suites $120-$150; under 17 free. Crib free. Pet accepted; $10. TV; cable. Complimentary bkfst. Restaurant nearby. Ck-out noon. Meeting rm. Business servs avail. In-rm modem link. Exercise equipt; bicycle, stair machine, sauna. Cr cds: A, C, D, DS, MC, V.
D 🖚 🏃 🖹 📷 **SC**

★★ **HEARTLAND INN.** *3052 Marnie Ave (50701).* *319/232-7467; FAX 319/232-0403; res: 800/334-3277, ext. 11.* 56 rms, 2 story. S $42-$51; D $49-$58; suites $115-$130; under 17 free. Crib free. Pet accepted; $10. TV; cable. Complimentary bkfst. Restaurant adj 6 am-10 pm. Ck-out noon. Meeting rms. Business servs avail. Cr cds: A, C, D, DS, MC, V.
D 🖚 🖹 📷 **SC**

✔★ **SUPER 8.** *1825 Laporte Rd (50702), in Crossroads Shopping Center.* *319/233-1800.* 62 rms, 3 story. S $42.95; D $47.95; under 16 free. Crib free. Pet accepted, some restrictions. TV; cable. Complimentary continental bkfst. Restaurant opp open 24 hrs. Ck-out 11 am. Sundries. Cr cds: A, D, DS, MC, V. **D** 🖚 🖹 📷 **SC**

Hotels

★★ **BEST WESTERN STARLITE VILLAGE.** *214 Washington St (50701).* *319/235-0321; FAX 319/235-6343.* 219 rms, 11 story. S, D $52-$59; each addl $7; suites $95-$150; under 12 free. Crib free. Pet accepted. TV; cable. Indoor pool. Restaurant 6:30 am-2 pm, 5-9 pm; Sun 7 am-2 pm. Bar 4 pm-2 am. Ck-out noon. Meeting rms. Business servs avail. In-rm modem link. Airport, RR station, bus depot transportation. Cr cds: A, C, D, DS, MC, V. **D** 🖚 ⚖ 🖹 📷 **SC**

★★ **HOLIDAY INN-CONVENTION CENTER.** *4th & Commercial (50704).* *319/233-7560; FAX 319/236-9590.* 229 rms, 10 story. S $58-$66; D $60-$67; suites $85-

$190; under 18 free. Crib free. Pet accepted. TV; cable. Indoor pool; whirlpool, poolside serv. Restaurant 6 am-2 pm; dining rm 5-10 pm. Bar 11-2 am; entertainment. Ck-out noon. Meeting rms. In-rm modem link. Airport transportation. Some refrigerators. Atrium lobby. Cr cds: A, C, D, DS, JCB, MC, V. ☐ ☐ ☒ ☒ ☒ SC

Webster City

Motel

★ **BEST WESTERN NORSEMAN INN.** *(I-35 exit 144, Williams 50271) 15 mi E on Old US 20 to I-35.* 515/854-2281; FAX 515/854-2447. 33 rms. S $36; D $48; each addl $6. Crib $6. Pet accepted. TV; cable. Complimentary continental bkfst. Restaurant nearby. Bar. Ck-out noon. Cr cds: A, C, D, DS, MC, V. ☐ ☐ ☒ ☒ SC

Winterset

Motel

✓★ **VILLAGE VIEW MOTEL.** *711 E IA 92.* 515/462-1218; FAX 515/462-1231; res: 800/862-1218. 16 rms, 1 story. S $31.95-$41.95; D $41.95-$51.95; under 12 free. Crib free. Pet accepted. TV; cable (premium), VCR avail. Complimentary coffee in lobby. Restaurant nearby. Ck-out 11 am. Rec rm. Cr cds: A, C, D, DS, MC, V. ☐ ☐ ☒ ☒ SC

Kansas

Abilene (See also Junction City, Salina)

Motels

✔ ★ **DIAMOND.** *1407 NW 3rd St, I-70 exit 275. 785/263-2360.* 30 rms. S $20-$28; D $26-$40; each addl $4. Pet accepted, some restrictions. TV; cable (premium). Complimentary coffee in lobby. Ck-out 11 am. Refrigerators. Cr cds: DS, MC, V. 🐾 🖭 🐾

★ **SUPER 8.** *2207 N Buckeye, I-70 exit 275. 785/263-4545; FAX 785/263-7448.* 62 rms, 3 story. No elvtr. S $34.88-$39.88; D $42.88-$50.88; each addl $4; suites $47.88-$59.88; under 12 free. Crib free. Pet accepted, some restrictions; $10. TV; cable (premium). Complimentary coffee in lobby. Restaurant adj 6:30 am-midnight. Ck-out 11 am. Meeting rms. Business servs avail. Cr cds: A, C, D, DS, JCB, MC, V. 🆔 🐾 🖭 🐾 SC

Arkansas City (See also Ponca City, OK)

Motels

★ **BEST WESTERN HALLMARK MOTOR INN.** *1617 N Summit (US 77). 316/442-1400; FAX 316/442-4729.* 47 rms. S $44; D $49; each addl $6; under 12 free. Crib free. Pet accepted. TV; cable (premium). Pool. Complimentary continental bkfst. Complimentary coffee in rms. Ck-out 11 am. Business servs avail. Microwaves avail. Cr cds: A, C, D, DS, MC, V. 🐾 🖭 🖭 🐾 🐾

★ ★ **REGENCY COURT INN.** *3232 N Summit (US 77). 316/442-7700; FAX 316/442-1218; res: 800/325-9151.* 86 rms. S, D, studio rms $45-$65; each addl $6; suites $98.80; under 12 free. Crib free. Pet accepted; $5. TV; cable. Indoor pool; whirlpool. Restaurant 7 am-1:30 pm, 5-8:30 pm; Fri, Sat to 9 pm; Sun 7 am-1:30 pm. Private club 4:30-midnight, closed Sun. Ck-out 11 am. Meeting rms. Business servs avail. Game rm. Cr cds: A, D, DS, MC, V. 🆔 🐾 🖭 🖭 🐾 SC

Atchison (See also Leavenworth; also see St Joseph, MO)

Motel

★ **COMFORT INN.** *509 S 9th St. 913/367-7666; FAX 913/367-7566.* 45 rms, 3 story, 10 suites. No elvtr. S $42; D $46; each addl $4; suites $54; under 18 free. Crib $4. Pet accepted. TV; cable. Complimentary continental bkfst. Restaurant nearby. Bar 5 pm-2 am, closed Sun. Ck-out 11 am. Meeting rms. Picnic tables. Cr cds: A, C, D, DS, MC, V. 🆔 🐾 🖭 🐾 SC

Belleville (See also Concordia, Mankato)

Motel

✔ ★ ★ **BEST WESTERN BEL VILLA.** *215 US 36, at jct US 81. 785/527-2231; FAX 785/527-2572.* 40 rms. S $36; D $38-$54; each addl $4; higher rates: Memorial Day wkend, racing events, hunting season. Crib free. Pet accepted, some restrictions. TV; cable (premium). Pool. Playground. Restaurant 6 am-10 pm. Bar. Ck-out 11 am. Meeting rms. Business servs avail. In-rm modem link. Sundries. Free airport transportation. Cr cds: A, C, D, DS, MC, V. 🐾 🖭 🖭 🐾 SC

Beloit (See also Concordia, Mankato)

Motel

✔ ★ **MAINLINER INN.** *RFD 1, Box 47 A, at jct US 24 & KS 9. 785/738-3531; res: 800/794-8514.* 26 rms, 2 story. S $28-$43; D $40-$60; each addl $5; higher rates pheasant hunting season. Crib $5. Pet accepted. TV; cable (premium). Complimentary coffee in lobby 7-11 am. Restaurant adj 11:30 am-2 pm, 5-9 pm; closed Mon. Ck-out 11 am. In-rm modem link. Cr cds: A, C, D, DS, MC, V. 🆔 🐾 🖭 🐾

Coffeyville *(See also Independence, Parsons)*

Motel

✔ ★ ★ **APPLE TREE INN.** *820 E 11th St. 316/251-0002; FAX 316/251-1615.* 43 rms, 2 story. S $46; D $54; charge for each addl. Crib $2. Pet accepted; $3. TV; cable (premium). Indoor pool; whirlpool. Complimentary continental bkfst. Restaurant nearby. Ck-out noon. Business servs avail. In-rm modem link. Some refrigerators; microwaves avail. Cr cds: A, C, D, DS, MC, V. 🄳 🏋 ≈ 🔀 🔀

Colby *(See also Goodland, Oakley)*

Motel

★ **BEST WESTERN CROWN.** *2320 S Range (KS 25) at jct I-70. 785/462-3943.* 29 rms. June-Sept: S, D $50-$80; each addl $6; lower rates rest of yr. Crib free. Pet accepted. TV; cable (premium). Heated pool. Complimentary coffee in rms. Restaurant nearby. Ck-out 11 am. Business servs avail. In-rm modem link. Airport transportation. Cr cds: A, C, D, DS, MC, V. 🏋 ≈ 🔀 🔀 SC

Concordia *(See also Belleville, Beloit)*

Motel

✔ ★ **BEST WESTERN THUNDERBIRD MOTOR INN.** *US 81, 785/243-4545; FAX 785/243-5058.* 50 rms. S $39; D $46; each addl $5; under 12 free. Crib $5. Pet accepted, some restrictions. TV; cable (premium). Pool; whirlpool. Restaurant 6 am-9 pm; wkend hrs vary. Private club 5 pm-midnight; closed Sun. Ck-out 11 am. Coin lndry. Meeting rms. Business servs avail. Sundries. Cr cds: A, C, D, DS, MC, V. 🏋 ≈ 🔀 🔀 SC

Council Grove *(See also Emporia, Junction City)*

Motel

✔ ★ ★ **COTTAGE HOUSE.** *25 N Neosho, 1/2 blk N of US 56. 316/767-6828; res: 800/727-7903.* 36 rms, 1-2 story. S $30-$52; D $38-$68; each addl $8; suites $85-$90; under 12 free. Crib $8. Pet accepted, some restrictions; $8. TV; cable, VCR avail. Continental bkfst. Restaurant nearby. Ck-out 11 am. Meeting rm. Business servs avail. In-rm modem link. Gift shop. Whirlpool, sauna. Some refrigerators, in-rm whirlpools. Built in 1867 as a cottage and blacksmith shop; some antiques; gazebo. Cr cds: A, C, D, MC, V.
🏋 🔀 🔀 SC

Dodge City

Motels

(Rates may be higher during hunting season, special events)

★ ★ **BEST WESTERN SILVER SPUR LODGE.** *Box 119, 1510 W Wyatt Earp Blvd (US 50). 316/227-2125; FAX 316/227-2030.* 121 rms, 1-2 story. S $44-$54; D $52-$62; each addl $5; suites $60-$70. Crib $2. Pet accepted, some restrictions; $5. TV; cable (premium), VCR avail. Heated pool. Restaurant 6 am-9 pm. Rm serv. Bar 4 pm-midnight; entertainment, dancing. Ck-out noon. Meeting rms. Business servs avail. Valet serv exc Sun. Free airport transportation. Cr cds: A, C, D, DS, MC, V. 🄳 🏋 ≈ 🔀 🔀 SC

✔ ★ ★ **DAYS INN-DODGE HOUSE.** *2408 W Wyatt Earp Blvd (US 50). 316/225-9900.* 111 rms, 2 story. S, D $44-$60; each addl $6; suites $75-$120; under 12 free. Crib free. Pet accepted, some restrictions. TV; cable (premium), VCR avail (movies). 2 pools, 1 indoor; sauna. Restaurant 6 am-9 pm; Fri & Sat to 10 pm; Sun from 6:30 am. Bar 11 am-midnight; closed Sun. Ck-out 11 am. Meeting rms. Business servs avail. Free airport transportation. Game rm. Cr cds: A, C, D, DS, JCB, MC, V. 🄳 🏋 ≈ 🔀 🔀 SC

★ **SUPER 8.** *1708 W Wyatt Earp Blvd (US 50). 316/225-3924; FAX 316/225-5793.* 64 rms, 3 story. S $34.88-$40.88; D $42.88-$54.88; under 12 free; higher rates special events. Crib free. Pet accepted. TV; cable (premium), VCR avail. Pool. Complimentary continental bkfst. Complimentary coffee in rms. Restaurant adj 6 am-10 pm. Ck-out noon. Cr cds: A, C, D, DS, MC, V. 🄳 🏋 ≈ 🔀 🔀 SC

El Dorado *(See also Eureka, Newton, Wichita)*

Motel

✔★★ **BEST WESTERN RED COACH INN.** *2525 W Central St (US 254). 316/321-6900; FAX 316/321-6900, ext. 208.* 73 rms, 2 story, 1 kit. unit. S $38-$58; D $42-$62; each addl $5. Crib $4. Pet accepted, some restrictions. TV; cable (premium). Indoor pool; whirlpool, sauna. Restaurant 6 am-11 pm. Rm serv. Ck-out 11 am. Business servs avail. Exercise equipt; treadmill, bicycle. Game rm. Some in-rm whirlpools. Cr cds: A, C, D, DS, JCB, MC, V. 🔲 ⚊ 🍴 ≋ 🔥 SC

Emporia *(See also Council Grove)*

Motels

★★ **BEST WESTERN.** *3021 W US 50. 316/342-3770.* 56 rms. S $36-$50; D $44-$60; each addl $7; suites $75; under 18 free. Crib free. Pet accepted. TV; cable (premium). Indoor pool; whirlpool. Restaurant 6 am-9 pm. Rm serv. Ck-out 11 am. Meeting rm. Business servs avail. In-rm modem link. Exercise equipt; weights, bicycle. Game rm. Cr cds: A, C, D, DS, ER, JCB, MC, V. D ⚊ ≋ 🍴 ≋ 🔥 SC

✔★ **DAYS INN.** *3032 W US 50 Business. 316/342-1787; FAX 316/342-2292.* 39 rms, 1-2 story. S $36-$48; D $48-$58; each addl $6. Crib free. Pet accepted, some restrictions. TV; cable (premium). Indoor pool; whirlpool. Complimentary continental bkfst. Restaurant opp 6 am-9 pm. Ck-out 11 am. Business servs avail. In-rm modem link. Bus depot transportation. Game rm. Cr cds: A, C, D, DS, MC, V. D ⚊ ≋ ≋ 🔥 SC

Eureka *(See also El Dorado)*

Motel

✔★ **BLUE STEM LODGE.** *1314 E River St (US 54). 316/583-5531.* 27 rms. S $28-$32; D $32-$38; each addl $4. Pet accepted, some restrictions. Crib $2. Pool. Complimentary coffee in lobby. Restaurant nearby. Ck-out 11 am. Business servs avail. In-rm modem link. Golf privileges. Cr cds: A, C, D, DS, MC, V. D ⚊ 🍴 ≋ ≋ 🔥

Fort Scott *(See also Nevada, MO)*

Motel

✔★★ **BEST WESTERN FORT SCOTT INN.** *101 State St, at 1st St. 316/223-0100; FAX 316/223-1746.* 78 rms, 1-2 story. S $42-$45; D $44-$50; under 12 free. Crib free. Pet accepted; $5. TV; cable (premium), VCR avail. Pool; whirlpool. Complimentary continental bkfst. Restaurant open 24 hrs. Ck-out noon. Coin lndry. Meeting rms. Business servs avail. Exercise equipt; weight machine, bicycle, sauna. Picnic tables. Cr cds: A, C, D, DS, MC, V. ⚊ ≋ 🍴 ≋ 🔥 SC

Garden City

Motels

✔★★ **BEST WESTERN WHEAT LANDS MOTOR INN.** *1311 E Fulton. 316/276-2387; FAX 316/276-4252.* 86 units, 1-2 story. S $39-$47; D $47-$56; each addl $4; suites $58-$68; under 12 free; wkly rates. Crib $3. Pet accepted. TV; cable (premium), VCR avail. Heated pool. Complimentary coffee in lobby. Restaurant adj 6 am-9 pm. Bar 4 pm-2 am, closed Sun; entertainment. Ck-out 1 pm. Coin lndry. Meeting rms. Business servs avail. In-rm modem link. Valet serv. Gift shop. Barber, beauty shop. Airport, RR station, bus depot transportation. Golf privileges. Some bathrm phones; refrigerator in suites. Cr cds: A, C, D, DS, JCB, MC, V. ⚊ 🍴 ≋ ≋ 🔥 SC

★★ **PLAZA INN.** *1911 E Kansas Ave (US 156). 316/275-7471; FAX 316/275-4028; res: 800/875-5201.* 109 rms, 2 story. S $52-$58; D $62-$68; each addl $10; suites $84-$94. Crib free. Pet accepted. TV; cable (premium), VCR avail (movies). Indoor pool; whirlpool, sauna. Restaurant 6 am-10 pm; Sun 7 am-8 pm. Rm serv. Bar 4 pm-1 am; entertainment. Ck-out noon. Meeting rms. Business servs avail. Bellhops. Free airport transportation. Golf privileges. Game rm. Cr cds: A, C, D, DS, MC, V.
D ⚊ 🍴 ≋ ≋ 🔥

Goodland (See also Colby)

Motels

✔★★ **BEST WESTERN BUFFALO INN.** *830 W US 24, I-70 exit 19, near Municipal Airport. 785/899-3621; FAX 785/899-5072; res: 800/436-3621.* 93 rms, 2 story. June-Sept: S $40; D $55-$65; each addl $5-$8; lower rates rest of yr. Crib $5. Pet accepted; some restrictions. TV; cable (premium), VCR avail. Indoor pool; wading pool, whirlpool. Playground. Restaurant 6 am-9 pm; summer to 10 pm. Bar 5-10 pm. Ck-out 11 am. Guest lndry. Meeting rm. Business servs avail. Airport transportation. Cr cds: A, C, D, DS, MC, V.
[D] [🖊] [≋] [✈] [🔌] [🐾] [SC]

★★ **HOWARD JOHNSON.** *2218 Commerce Rd, I-70 exit 17. 785/899-3644; FAX 785/899-3646.* 79 rms, 2 story. S $49-$70; D $54-$75. Crib free. Pet accepted. TV; cable (premium), VCR avail. Indoor pool; whirlpool. Playground. Restaurant 6 am-2 pm, 5-10 pm. Rm serv. Bar 5 pm-midnight. Ck-out noon. Guest lndry. Meeting rms. Business servs avail. Airport, bus depot transportation. Miniature golf. Sauna. Game rm. Cr cds: A, C, D, DS, JCB, MC, V. [D] [🖊] [≋] [🔌] [🐾] [SC]

Great Bend (See also Larned)

Motel

★★ **BEST WESTERN ANGUS INN.** *2920 10th St (US 56, KS 96). 316/792-3541; FAX 316/792-8621.* 90 units, 2 story. S $44-$54; D $51-$71; studio rm $49-$59; each addl $4; under 18 free. Crib $3. Pet accepted; some restrictions. TV; cable (premium), VCR avail (movies $4). Indoor pool; whirlpool, sauna. Restaurant 6 am-11 pm. Rm serv from 5 pm. Ck-out 11 am. Meeting rms. Business servs avail. Airport transportation. Exercise equipt; bicycles, stair machine. Game rm. Rec rm. Cr cds: A, C, D, DS, MC, V.
[D] [🖊] [≋] [✈] [🔌] [🐾] [SC]

Motor Hotel

✔★★ **HOLIDAY INN.** *3017 W 10th St (US 56). 316/792-2431; FAX 316/792-5561.* 173 rms, 2 story. S, D $50-$55; under 18 free. Crib free. Pet accepted. TV; cable (premium). Indoor pool; whirlpool, sauna. Restaurant 6 am-10:30 pm. Rm serv. Bar 5 pm-1 am. Ck-out noon. Coin lndry. Meeting rms. Business servs avail. Airport transportation. Holidome. Cr cds: A, C, D, DS, JCB, MC, V. [D] [🖊] [≋] [🔌] [🐾] [SC]

Hays (See also WaKeeney)

Motels

(Rates may be higher during hunting season, special events)

★★ **BEST WESTERN VAGABOND.** *2524 Vine St (US 183). 785/625-2511; FAX 785/625-8879.* 92 rms, 1-2 story. S $46-$56; D $56-$75; each addl $4; suites $75-$135; under 12 free. Crib $4. Pet accepted. TV; cable (premium). Pool; whirlpool. Complimentary coffee in rms. Restaurant 7 am-9 pm. Bar 5 pm-midnight. Ck-out noon. Meeting rms. Business servs avail. In-rm modem link. Valet serv. Free airport transportation. Cr cds: A, C, D, DS, MC, V. [🖊] [≋] [🔌] [🐾] [SC]

✔★ **BUDGET HOST VILLA INN.** *810 E 8th St. 785/625-2563; FAX 785/625-3967.* 49 rms, 1-2 story. S $25-$40; D $30-$50; each addl $3; suites $49-$65. Crib $5. Pet accepted; some restrictions. TV; cable. Pool. Coffee in rms. Restaurant nearby. Ck-out noon. Business servs avail. Free airport transportation. Picnic tables. Cr cds: A, C, D, DS, MC, V. [D] [🖊] [≋] [🔌] [🐾] [SC]

✔★★ **HAMPTON INN.** *3801 Vine St (US 183), at jct I-70. 785/625-8103; FAX 785/625-3006.* 116 rms, 2 story. S, D $47-$60; suites $90. Crib free. Pet accepted. TV; cable (premium). Pool privileges adj. Complimentary continental bkfst. Restaurant adj. Ck-out noon. Business servs avail. In-rm modem link. Free airport transportation. Cr cds: A, C, D, DS, MC, V. [D] [🖊] [🔌] [🐾] [SC]

★★ **HOLIDAY INN.** *3603 Vine St (US 183), at jct I-70. 785/625-7371; FAX 785/625-7250.* 190 rms, 2 story. S, D $60-$75; suites $75-$100; under 19 free. Crib free. Pet accepted. TV; cable (premium). Indoor pool; whirlpool, sauna, steam rm. Restaurant 6:30 am-2 pm, 5-10 pm. Rm serv. Ck-out noon. Business servs avail. In-rm modem link. Valet serv. Gift shop. Airport transportation. Holidome. Rec rm. Cr cds: A, C, D, DS, JCB, MC, V.
[D] [🖊] [≋] [🔌] [🐾] [SC]

Hutchinson (See also McPherson, Newton, Wichita)

Motels

✔★★ **COMFORT INN.** *KS 61 & 17th St (67501). 316/663-7822; FAX 316/663-1055.* 64 rms, 3 story. S $45.95-$58.95; D $47.95-$60.95; under 18 free. Crib free. Pet accepted. TV; cable (premium), VCR avail (movies). Outdoor pool; whirlpool, sauna. Complimentary continental bkfst. Restaurant nearby. Ck-out noon. Business servs avail. In-rm modem link. Valet serv. Cr cds: A, C, D, DS, ER, JCB, MC, V. 🅓 📠 ≋ ⚲ 🐾 SC

★ **QUALITY INN CITY CENTER.** *15 W 4th St (67501), at Main St. 316/663-1211; FAX 316/663-6636.* 98 rms, 2 story. S $40.95-$48.95; D $48.95-$58.95; suites $48.95-$130; under 18 free; wkly rates; higher rates: state fair, college basketball tournament. Crib free. Pet accepted. TV; cable (premium), VCR avail. Pool. Restaurant 6:30 am-9 pm; Sun 7 am-2 pm. Rm serv. Bar 4 pm-midnight. Ck-out noon. Meeting rms. Business servs avail. In-rm modem link. Sundries. Golf privileges. Balconies. Cr cds: A, C, D, DS, ER, JCB, MC, V. 🅓 📠 🏌 ≋ ⚲ 🐾 SC

Independence (See also Coffeyville, Parsons)

Motels

★★ **APPLE TREE INN.** *201 N 8th St. 316/331-5500; FAX 316/331-0641.* 64 rms, 2 story. S $47-$49; D $53-$56; each addl $4; suites $58-$100; higher rates "Neewollah". Crib avail. Pet accepted. TV, cable (premium). Indoor pool; whirlpool. Complimentary continental bkfst. Restaurant opp 11 am-10 pm. Ck-out noon. Business servs avail. In-rm modem link. Health club privileges. Some refrigerators. Cr cds: A, C, D, DS, MC, V.
🅓 📠 ≋ ⚲ 🐾 SC

✔★ **BEST WESTERN PRAIRIE INN.** *3222 W Main, Jct US 160W & US 75. 316/331-7300; FAX 316/331-8740.* 40 rms. S $36-$44; D $44-$55; each addl $4. Crib $3. Pet accepted, some restrictions. TV; cable (premium). Pool. Complimentary continental bkfst. Ck-out 11 am. Business servs avail. Cr cds: A, C, D, DS, MC, V. 📠 ≋ ⚲ 🐾 SC

Junction City (See also Abilene, Council Grove, Manhattan)

Motels

✔★ **BEST WESTERN JAYHAWK.** *110 Flint Hills Blvd, in Grandview Plaza, I-70 exit 299. 785/238-5188; FAX 785/238-7585.* 48 rms, 1-2 story, 20 kits. S $35-$45; D $45-$55; each addl $4; kit. units $38-$56; under 12 free. Crib $4. Pet accepted. TV; cable (premium), VCR avail. Pool. Complimentary coffee in rms. Restaurant nearby. Ck-out noon. Some refrigerators. Picnic tables. Cr cds: A, C, D, DS, JCB, MC, V. 🅓 📠 ≋ ⚲ 🐾 SC

★ **DAYS INN.** *1024 S Washington, 1 blk NE of I-70 exit 296. 785/762-2727; FAX 785/762-2751.* 108 rms, 2 story. S $40-$58; D $47-$60; each addl $5; under 17 free. Crib free. Pet accepted, some restrictions. TV; cable (premium). 2 pools, 1 indoor; whirlpool, sauna. Complimentary continental bkfst. Coffee in rms. Restaurant adj open 24 hrs. Bar 4 pm-midnight, closed Sun. Ck-out noon. Coin lndry. Meeting rms. Business servs avail. Valet serv. Game rm. Rec rm. Cr cds: A, C, D, DS, ER, MC, V. 🅓 📠 ≋ ⚲ 🐾 SC

★ **SUPER 8.** *1001 E 6th St, ¼ mi NW of I-70 exit 299. 785/238-8101; FAX 785/238-7470; res: 800/762-0270.* 99 rms, 2 story. May-Sept: S $40; D $47; suites $65; under 12 free; wkly rates; lower rates rest of yr. Crib free. Pet accepted, some restrictions. TV; cable (premium). Pool. Restaurant 7 am-2 pm, 5-9 pm. Rm serv. Bar 5-10 pm. Ck-out noon. Coin lndry. Meeting rm. Business servs avail. In-rm modem link. Some refrigerators. Picnic tables. Cr cds: A, C, D, DS, MC, V. 🅓 📠 ≋ ⚲ 🐾 SC

Larned (See also Great Bend)

Motel

★★ **BEST WESTERN TOWNSMAN.** *123 E 14th St, at jct US 56 & US 156. 316/285-3114; FAX 316/285-7139.* 44 rms. S $36-$46; D $40-$50; each addl $3; under 17 free. Crib $2. Pet accepted. TV; cable (premium), VCR avail. Pool. Coffee in rms. Restaurant opp 6 am-10 pm. Ck-out noon. Business servs avail. In-rm modem link. Sundries. Tennis privileges. Golf privileges. Cr cds: A, C, D, DS, MC, V. 🅓 📠 🏌 🏃 ≋ ⚲ 🐾 SC

Lawrence (See also Leavenworth, Ottawa, Topeka)

Motels

★ ★ **BEST WESTERN HALLMARK INN.** *730 Iowa St (66044), 1 mi W on US 59.785/841-6500; FAX 785/841-6612.* 59 rms, 2 story. S $42.95-$55.95; D $46.95-$55.95; each addl $4; under 12 free; higher rates U of K events. Crib free. Pet accepted, some restrictions. TV; cable (premium). Pool. Complimentary continental bkfst. Complimentary coffee in rms. Restaurant nearby. Ck-out noon. Coin lndry. Business servs avail. In-rm modem link. Cr cds: A, C, D, DS, MC, V. 🅳 🐾 ≊ ⬚ 🔥 SC

★ **DAYS INN.** *2309 Iowa St (66046). 785/843-9100; FAX 785/843-0486.* 101 rms, 3 story. S, D $42-$75; each addl $4; suite $95; under 18 free; monthly rates. Crib free. Pet accepted, some restrictions. TV; cable (premium). Pool. Complimentary continental bkfst. Coffee in rms. Ck-out noon. Restaurants adj 11:30 am-10:30 pm. Coin lndry. Business servs avail. In-rm modem link. Sundries. 18-hole golf privileges, greens fee $35-$45. Some refrigerators. Cr cds: A, C, D, DS, JCB, MC, V. 🅳 🐾 🏌 ≊ ⬚ 🐾 SC

✔ ★ **WESTMINSTER INN.** *2525 W 6th St (US 40) (66049). 785/841-8410; FAX 785/841-1901.* 60 rms, 2 story. S $40; D $50-$58; each addl $4. Crib free. Pet accepted. TV; cable (premium). Pool. Complimentary coffee in lobby. Restaurant nearby. Ck-out noon. Meeting rm. Cr cds: A, C, D, DS, MC, V. 🅳 🐾 ≊ ⬚ 🔥 SC

Motor Hotel

★ ★ ★ **HOLIDAY INN.** *200 McDonald Dr (66044). 785/841-7077; FAX 785/841-2799.* 192 rms, 4 story. S, D $69-$99; suites $125-$185; under 17 free; higher rates major college activities. Crib free. Pet accepted. TV; cable, VCR avail. Indoor pool; whirlpool, poolside serv. Restaurant 6 am-2 pm, 5-10 pm. Rm serv. Bar 2 pm-1 am. Ck-out noon. Business servs avail. Coin lndry. Exercise equipt; bicycle, stair machine, sauna. Game rm. Rec rm. Cr cds: A, C, D, DS, JCB, MC, V. 🅳 🐾 ≊ 🏃 ⬚ 🐾 SC

Leavenworth
(See also Atchison, Lawrence; also see Kansas City, MO, St Joseph, MO)

Motel

★ **RAMADA INN.** *101 S 3rd St, 1 blk E of US 73. 913/651-5500; FAX 913/651-6981.* 97 rms, 2 story. S $40-$70; D $46-$70; each addl $6; suites $60-$70; under 18 free. Crib free. Pet accepted, some restrictions. TV; cable (premium). Pool. Restaurant 6 am-2 pm, 5-9pm. Rm serv. Bar 5-11 pm. Ck-out 1 pm. Meeting rms. Business servs avail. Valet serv. Sundries. Cr cds: A, C, D, DS, JCB, MC, V. 🅳 🐾 ≊ ⬚ 🐾 SC

Liberal

Motels

✔ ★ ★ **GATEWAY INN.** *720 E Hwy 54, 2 mi E on US 54, near Municipal Airport. 316/624-0242; res: 800/833-3391.* 101 rms, 2 story. S $36-$39; D $44-$47; each addl $3; under 12 free. Crib free. Pet accepted, some restrictions. TV; cable (premium). Pool. Restaurant 6 am-2 pm, 5-9 pm. Bar 4 pm-2 am. Ck-out noon. Coin lndry. Meeting rms. Business servs avail. In-rm modem link. Valet serv (wkdays only). Gift shop. Free airport transportation. Tennis. Picnic tables, grill. Cr cds: A, C, D, DS, MC, V.
🅳 🐾 🏃 ≊ 🏌 ⬚ 🐾 SC

★ **LIBERAL INN.** *603 E Pancake Blvd (US 54). 316/624-7254; res: 800/458-4667.* 123 rms, 2 story. S $35-$47; D $37-$54; each addl $5; suites $65-$100; under 12 free; higher rates: pheasant season, Compressor Institute. Crib free. Pet accepted. TV; cable (premium). Indoor pool; whirlpool. Restaurant 6 am-10:30 pm; Sun from 7 am. Rm serv. Private club 5 pm-1 am. Ck-out noon. Coin lndry. Meeting rms. In-rm modem link. Bellhops. Valet serv Mon-Fri. Sundries. Free airport transportation. Picnic tables. Cr cds: A, C, D, DS, MC, V. 🅳 🐾 ≊ ⬚ 🐾 SC

Manhattan (See also Junction City)

Motel

✔ ★ **DAYS INN.** *1501 Tuttle Creek Blvd, at US 24 Bypass. 785/539-5391; FAX 785/539-0847.* 119 rms, 2 story. S $45-$65; D $50-$65; each addl $4; under 18 free. Crib free. Pet accepted. TV; cable (premium), VCR avail. Heated pool. Playground. Complimentary coffee in rms. Complimentary continental bkfst. Ck-out noon. Coin lndry. Meeting rms.

Business servs avail. In-rm modem link. Valet serv. Sundries. Lawn games. Some refrigerators. Picnic tables, grills. Cr cds: A, C, D, DS, JCB, MC, V. [D] ⟨icons⟩

Motor Hotels

★ ★ ★ **HOLIDAY INN.** *530 Richards Dr (Ft Riley Blvd). 785/539-5311; FAX 785/539-8368.* 197 rms, 3 story. S, D $76-$89; each addl $5; suites $165-$260; under 19 free; higher rates special events. Crib free. Pet accepted. TV; cable (premium). Indoor pool; wading pool; whirlpool, sauna. Coffee in rms. Restaurant 6 am-10 pm. Rm serv. Bar 4 pm-midnight. Ck-out noon. Coin lndry. Meeting rms. Business servs avail. In-rm modem link. Gift shop. Local airport transportation. Holidome. Health club privileges. Game rm. Balconies. Cr cds: A, D, DS, MC, V. [D] ⟨icons⟩

★ ★ ★ **RAMADA INN.** *17th & Anderson, adj to Kansas State University. 785/539-7531; FAX 785/751-3909.* 116 rms, 6 story. S, D $67-$88; each addl $6; under 18 free. Crib free. Pet accepted. TV; cable (premium), VCR avail. Heated pool. Restaurant 6:30 am-2 pm, 5-10 pm; Sun 6 am-2 pm, 5-10 pm. Rm serv. Bar 2-10 pm; Fri & Sat to 11 pm. Ck-out noon. Meeting rms. Business servs avail. In-rm modem link. Valet serv. Sundries. Free airport transportation. Health club privileges. Some refrigerators. Cr cds: A, C, D, DS, JCB, MC, V. [D] ⟨icons⟩

Mankato (See also Belleville, Beloit)

Motel

★ **CREST-VUE.** *US 36 E. 785/378-3515.* 12 rms. S $25; D $32; each addl $2; under 5 free; higher rates hunting season. Crib free. Pet accepted. TV; cable. Complimentary coffee in lobby. Restaurant adj 11 am-1:30 pm, 5-9 pm. Ck-out 11 am. Picnic tables. Cr cds: A, MC, V. [D] ⟨icons⟩

Marysville (See also Seneca)

Motels

★ **BEST WESTERN SURF.** *2005 Center St, US 36E. 785/562-2354.* 52 rms. S $30-$40; D $38-$48; each addl $4-$6. Crib free. Pet accepted, some restrictions. TV; cable (premium), VCR avail. Playground. Complimentary coffee in lobby. Restaurant nearby. Ck-out 11 am. Coin lndry. Business servs avail. Exercise equipt; bicycle, stair machine, sauna. Refrigerators. Cr cds: A, C, D, DS, ER, MC, V. [D] ⟨icons⟩

✔★ **THUNDERBIRD.** *Rte 1, US 36 W, 1 mi W of jct US 77. 785/562-2373; res: 800/662-2373.* 21 rms. S $28.75-$34.75; D $37.75-$42.75; each addl $4. Crib $4. Pet accepted, some restrictions. TV; cable (premium). Continental bkfst. Complimentary coffee in rms. Ck-out 11 am. In-rm modem link. Golf privileges. Refrigerators. Cr cds: A, C, D, DS, MC, V. ⟨icons⟩

McPherson (See also Hutchinson, Newton, Salina)

Motels

★ ★ **BEST WESTERN HOLIDAY MANOR.** *(2211 E Kansas (US 56), McPherson) at jct I-135. 316/241-5343; FAX 316/241-8086.* 110 rms, 2 story. S $37-$47; D $43-$53; suites $85-$100; each addl $2; under 12 free. Crib $2. Pet accepted, some restrictions. TV; cable (premium). 2 pools, 1 indoor; whirlpool, sauna. Restaurant 6 am-10 pm. Rm serv. Private club 5 pm-midnight. Ck-out noon. Meeting rms. Business servs avail. Valet serv. Cr cds: A, C, D, DS, MC, V. [D] ⟨icons⟩

✔★ ★ **RED COACH INN.** *(2111 E Kansas (US 56), McPherson) at jct I-135. 316/241-6960; FAX 316/241-4340; res: 800/362-0072 (exc KS), 800/362-0072 (KS).* 88 rms, 1-2 story. S $38-$48; D $43-$55; each addl $5; suites $60-$85. Crib $5. Pet accepted, some restrictions. TV; cable (premium), VCR avail (movies $3). Indoor pool; whirlpool, sauna. Playground. Restaurant 6 am-11 pm. Rm serv. Ck-out noon. Meeting rms. Business servs avail. In-rm modem link. Sundries. Rec rm. Cr cds: A, C, D, DS, MC, V. [D] ⟨icons⟩

Medicine Lodge

Motel

✔★ **COPA.** *401 W Fowler, ¼ mi E of jct US 160, 281. 316/886-5673; FAX 316/886-5241; res: 800/886-2672.* 54 rms, 2 story. S $31-$37; D $35-$40; each addl $3. Crib

$3. Pet accepted. TV; cable (premium). Pool. Complimentary continental bkfst. Restaurant adj 6 am-10 pm. Ck-out 11 am. Picnic tables. Lake 1 mi. Cr cds: A, C, D, DS, MC, V.

★ ☒ ☒ ☒ SC

Newton *(See also El Dorado, Hutchinson, McPherson, Wichita)*

Motel

★ ★ **BEST WESTERN RED COACH INN.** *1301 E 1st St, I-135 exit 31. 316/283-9120; FAX 316/283-4105; res: 800/777-9120.* 81 rms, 1-2 story. S $40-$64; D $46-$64; each addl $6; suites $70; under 18 free. Crib $4. Pet accepted, some restrictions. TV; cable (premium), VCR avail. Indoor pool; whirlpool. Restaurant 6 am-11 pm; closed Dec 25. Rm serv. Ck-out 11 am. Meeting rm. Valet serv. Free airport transportation. Exercise equipt; bicycle, stair machine, sauna. Game rm. Rec rm. Cr cds: A, C, D, DS, ER, JCB, MC, V.

D ★ ☒ ✗ ☒ ☒ SC

Oakley *(See also Colby)*

Motel

★ **FIRST INTERSTATE INN.** *I-70 & US 40, E Oakley exit 76. 785/672-3203; res: 800/462-4667.* 29 rms, 1-2 story. S $33.95; D $39.95; each addl $5; under 12 free. Pet accepted. Crib free. TV; cable (premium). Restaurant opp open 24 hrs. Ck-out 11 am. Business servs avail. Cr cds: A, C, D, DS, MC, V. ★ ☒ ☒ SC

Ottawa *(See also Lawrence)*

Motel

✔ ★ **BEST WESTERN HALLMARK INN.** *2209 S Princeton Rd (US 59). 785/242-7000; FAX 785/242-8572.* 60 rms, 2 story. S $42-$52; D $46-$56; each addl $4; under 13 free. Crib free. Pet accepted, some restrictions. TV; cable (premium). Pool. Complimentary continental bkfst. Complimentary coffee in rms. Restaurant adj 6 am-11 pm; wkends open 24 hrs. Ck-out noon. Coin lndry. Meeting rm. Business servs avail. Cr cds: A, C, D, DS, MC, V. D ★ ☒ ☒ ☒ SC

Overland Park *(See also Kansas City, MO)*

Motels

★ ★ **DRURY INN.** *10951 Metcalf Ave (66210). 913/345-1500.* Web www.Drury-Inn.com. 155 rms, 4 story. S $75-$81; D $85-$91; each addl $10; under 18 free. Crib free. Pet accepted, some restrictions. TV; cable (premium). Pool. Complimentary continental bkfst. Restaurant nearby. Ck-out noon. Meeting rms. Business servs avail. In-rm modem link. Valet serv. Health club privileges. Microwaves avail. Cr cds: A, C, D, DS, MC, V.

D ★ ☒ ☒ ☒ SC

★ ★ **RESIDENCE INN BY MARRIOTT.** *6300 W 110th St (66211), I-435, S on Metcalf, E on College, N on Lamar. 913/491-3333; FAX 913/491-1377.* 112 suites, 2 story. S, D $79-$199; under 12 free; wkly, monthly rates. Crib free. Pet accepted, some restrictions. TV; cable (premium). Pool; whirlpool. Complimentary continental bkfst. Ck-out noon. Coin lndry. Meeting rm. Business servs avail. In-rm modem link. Valet serv. Exercise equipt; weights, bicycles, sauna. Sports court. Microwaves; some fireplaces. Private patios, balconies. Picnic tables, grills. Cr cds: A, C, D, DS, JCB, MC, V. D ★ ☒ ✗ ☒ ☒ SC

✔ ★ ★ **WHITE HAVEN.** *8039 Metcalf Ave (66204). 913/649-8200; res: 800/752-2892.* 79 rms, 1-2 story, 10 kit. units. S $39-$44; D $46-$50; suites, kit. units $70. Crib $2. Pet accepted, some restrictions. TV; cable (premium). Pool. Complimentary coffee. Restaurant nearby. Ck-out noon. Business servs avail. Refrigerators. Microwaves avail. Cr cds: A, C, D, DS, MC, V. D ★ ☒ ☒ ☒

Motor Hotel

★ **AMERISUITES.** *6801 W 112th St (66211). 913/451-2553; FAX 913/451-3098.* 126 suites, 6 story. May-Nov: suites $97-$107; under 18 free; wkend rates; lower rates rest of yr. Crib free. Pet accepted, some restrictions. TV; cable (premium), VCR (movies). Complimentary continental bkfst. Complimentary coffee in rms. Restaurant nearby. Ck-out 11 am. Meeting rms. Business center. In-rm modem link. Sundries. Coin lndry. Exercise equipt; weight machine, bicycle. Health club privileges. Pool. Refrigerators, microwaves. Cr cds: A, C, D, DS, MC, V. D ★ ☒ ✗ ☒ ☒ SC ✗

Hotel

★ ★ ★ **DOUBLETREE.** *10100 College Blvd (66210).* 913/451-6100; FAX 913/451-3873. E-mail mcidt@aol.com; web www.doubletree hotels.com. 357 rms, 18 story. S, D $119-$149; suites $175-$450; under 18 free; wkend rates. Crib free. Pet accepted, some restrictions. TV; cable (premium). Indoor pool; whirlpool, sauna, poolside serv. Coffee in rms. Restaurants 6 am-11 pm. Bar 4-1 am, Sun 4 pm-midnight. Ck-out noon. Convention facilities. Business center. In-rm modem link. Gift shop. Airport transportation. Exercise equipt; treadmill, bicycles. Some refrigerators. Cr cds: A, C, D, DS, ER, JCB, MC, V.

D ⇆ ≋ 🏋 🏃 ✈ 🏳 🏊 SC 🚣

Parsons *(See also Coffeyville, Independence)*

Motel

★ **TOWNSMAN.** *US 59 S.* 316/421-6990; FAX 316/421-4767; res: 800/552-4408. 38 rms. S $28-$30; D $35-$37; each addl $2; under 4 free. Crib free. Pet accepted, some restrictions. TV; cable (premium). Pool. Restaurant 6 am-9 pm. Ck-out 11 am. Business servs avail. Refrigerators avail. Cr cds: A, C, D, DS, MC, V.

D ⇆ ≋ 🏳 🏊 SC

Pratt *(See also Medicine Lodge)*

Motel

↙ ★ ★ **BEST WESTERN HILLCREST.** *1336 E 1st St.* 316/672-6407; FAX 316/672-6707. 42 rms. S $32-$38; D $38-$43; each addl $4; under 12 free. Crib $4. Pet accepted. TV; cable (premium), VCR avail. Pool. Complimentary continental bkfst. Restaurant nearby. Ck-out noon. Meeting rm. Business servs avail. In-rm modem link. Refrigerators. Cr cds: A, D, DS, MC, V. D ⇆ ≋ 🏳 🏊 SC

Salina *(See also Abilene, McPherson)*

Motels

★ **BEST WESTERN MID-AMERICA.** *1846 N 9th, I-70 exit 252.* 785/827-0356; FAX 785/827-7688. 108 rms, 2 story. Mid-May-mid-Oct: S $39-$46; D $46-$54; each addl $3; suites $70-$75; under 12 free; lower rates rest of yr. Crib $1. Pet accepted, some restrictions. TV; cable (premium), VCR avail. Indoor/outdoor pool; whirlpool, sauna, poolside serv. Restaurant 6 am-10 pm. Rm serv. Bar 5 pm-1 am. Ck-out noon. Meeting rms. Business servs avail. In-rm modem link. Sundries. Cr cds: A, C, D, DS, MC, V.

D ⇆ ≋ 🏳 🏊 SC

↙ ★ **BUDGET HOST VAGABOND II.** *217 S Broadway (US 81 Business).* 785/825-7265; FAX 785/825-7003. 45 rms, 2 story. S $32-$40; D $34-$45; each addl $4; kit. $4/day addl. Crib $1. Pet accepted. TV; cable (premium). Pool. Complimentary coffee in rms. Restaurant adj 6 am-10 pm; Sun to 2 pm. Ck-out 11 am. Business servs avail. Cr cds: A, C, D, DS, MC, V. ⇆ ≋ 🏳 🏊 SC

★ **COMFORT INN.** *1820 W Crawford.* 785/826-1711. 60 rms. S $50-$57; D $52-$73; each addl $7; under 18 free. Crib free. Pet accepted, some restrictions. TV; cable (premium), VCR avail. Indoor pool; whirlpool. Complimentary continental bkfst. Restaurant nearby. Ck-out 11 am. Business servs avail. In-rm modem link. Some refrigerators. Cr cds: A, C, D, DS, ER, JCB, MC, V. D ⇆ ≋ 🏳 🏊 SC

★ ★ **RAMADA INN.** *1949 N 9th St, I-70, exit 252.* 785/825-8211; FAX 785/823-1048. 103 rms, 2 story. May-Nov: S $50; D $58; each addl $6; under 18 free. Crib free. Pet accepted; $10 deposit. TV; cable (premium). Heated pool. Restaurant 6 am-9 pm. Rm serv. Bar 5 pm-midnight. Ck-out noon. Meeting rms. Business servs avail. Cr cds: A, C, D, DS, MC, V. D ⇆ ≋ 🏳 🏊 SC

★ ★ **RED COACH INN.** *2020 W Crawford, I-135, exit 92.* 785/825-2111; FAX 785/825-6973. 114 rms, 2 story. S $42-$47; D $50-$54; each addl $5; suites $72-$99; under 12 free. Crib $3. Pet accepted, some restrictions. TV; cable (premium), VCR (movies). Indoor pool; whirlpool, sauna. Playground. Restaurant 6 am-10 pm; wkends to 11 pm. Rm serv. Ck-out noon. Meeting rms. Business servs avail. In-rm modem link. Sundries. Coin lndry. Lighted tennis. Miniature golf. Game rm. Refrigerator in suites. Cr cds: A, C, D, DS, MC, V. D ⇆ 🏃 ≋ 🏳 🏊 SC

Seneca (See also Marysville)

Motels

★ **SENECA.** *1106 North St, on US 36W. 913/336-6127.* 12 rms. S $24; D $30; each addl $2. Crib avail. Pet accepted, some restrictions. TV; cable. Complimentary coffee in lobby. Restaurant nearby. Ck-out 11 am. Many refrigerators. Cr cds: A, D, DS, MC, V. 🖋 🖼

★ **STARLITE.** *410 North St, on US 36. 913/336-2191.* 16 rms. S $27; D $30-$34; each addl $3; under 12 free. Crib $3. Pet accepted, some restrictions. TV; cable (premium). Complimentary coffee in lobby. Restaurant opp 11 am-9 pm. Ck-out 11 am. Cr cds: A, C, D, DS, MC, V. 🖋 🖼 🖼

Topeka (See also Lawrence; also see Kansas City, MO)

Motels

★ ★ **DAYS INN.** *1510 SW Wanamaker Rd (66604). 785/272-8538.* 62 rms, 2 story, 6 suites. S $42.95-$59.95; D $47.95-$69.95; each addl $5; suites $49.95-$69.95; under 12 free; higher rates Heartland auto races. Crib $5. Pet accepted. TV; cable (premium). Indoor pool; whirlpool. Complimentary continental bkfst. Restaurant nearby. Ck-out 11 am. Business servs avail. Game rm. Refrigerator in suites. Cr cds: A, D, DS, MC, V.
D 🖋 ≈ 🖼 🖼 SC

✔ ★ **LIBERTY INN.** *3839 S Topeka Blvd (US 75) (66609). 785/266-4700; FAX 785/267-3311.* 132 rms, 2 story. S $37-$48; D $41-$55; each addl $6; suites $95. Crib free. Pet accepted, some restrictions. TV; cable. Pool. Playground. Restaurant 6:30 am-2 pm. Rm serv. Bar 5 pm-2 am, closed Sun. Ck-out noon. Meeting rms. Business servs avail. Valet serv. Airport transportation. Many refrigerators. Private patios, balconies. Cr cds: A, C, D, DS, ER, JCB, MC, V. D 🖋 ≈ 🖼 🖼 SC

Motor Hotels

★ ★ ★ **HOLIDAY INN-CITY CENTRE.** *914 Madison (66607), I-70 10th St exit. 785/232-7721.* 196 rms, 9 story. S, D $65; each addl $6; under 18 free. Crib free. Pet accepted, some restrictions. TV; cable (premium). Pool. Restaurant 6 am-2 pm, 5-10 pm. Rm serv. Bar 11 am-midnight; closed Sun. Ck-out noon. Coin lndry. Meeting rms. Business servs avail. In-rm modem link. Bellhops. Valet serv. Airport transportation. Health club privileges. Luxury level. Cr cds: A, C, D, DS, ER, JCB, MC, V. D 🖋 ≈ 🖼 🖼 SC

★ ★ **RAMADA INN.** *Box 1598 (66601), 420 E 6th St, at downtown jct US 40 & I-70. 785/234-5400; FAX 785/232-0011.* 422 rms, 3-11 story. S, D $48-$76; each addl $7; suites $80-$250; wknd rates. Crib free. Pet accepted, some restrictions; $20. TV; cable (premium), VCR avail. Pool; whirlpool. Restaurants 6 am-9 pm. Rm serv. Bar 4 pm-midnight; entertainment. Ck-out noon. Coin lndry. Convention facilities. Business servs avail. Bellhops. Valet serv. Sundries. Gift shop. Barber, beauty shop. Free airport transportation. Exercise equipt; bicycles, stair machine, sauna. Some bathrm phones, refrigerators. Cr cds: A, C, D, DS, MC, V. D 🖋 ≈ 🏋 🖼 🖼 SC

WaKeeney (See also Hays)

Motel

✔ ★ **BUDGET HOST TRAVEL INN.** *RR 2, Box 2B, at I-70 exit 128 & US 283. 785/743-2121; FAX 785/743-6704.* 27 rms. S $25-$30; D $35-$45; each addl $3; under 18 free. Crib free. Pet accepted. TV; cable (premium). Pool. Restaurant adj 6 am-10 pm. Ck-out 11 am. Cr cds: A, D, DS, MC, V. 🖋 ≈ 🖼 🖼 SC

Wichita (See also El Dorado, Hutchinson, Newton)

Motels

★ ★ **CAMBRIDGE SUITES.** *120 W Orme St (67213), 1 blk S of Kellogg St (US 54). 316/263-1061; FAX 316/263-3817.* 64 kit. suites, 2 story. 1-bedrm suites $94; 2 bedrm suites $114; wkend, wkly, monthly rates. Crib free. Pet accepted; $5/day. TV; cable (premium), VCR avail. Pool; whirlpool. Complimentary continental bkfst. Ck-out noon. Coin lndry. Business servs avail. In-rm modem link. Health club privileges. Many fireplaces. Private patios, balconies. Grill. Cr cds: A, C, D, DS, JCB, MC, V. D 🖋 ≈ 🖼 🖼 SC

★ ★ **LA QUINTA INN.** *7700 E Kellogg St (US 54, KS 96) (62707). 316/681-2881; FAX 316/681-0568.* 122 rms, 2 story. S $55-$65; D $63-$73; each addl $7; under 18 free.

Crib free. Pet accepted, some restrictions. TV; cable (premium), VCR avail. Pool. Complimentary continental bkfst. Restaurant adj 11:30 am-11 pm; Fri, Sat to midnight; Sun to 10 pm. Ck-out noon. Meeting rms. Business servs avail. In-rm modem link. Cr cds: A, C, D, DS, MC, V. ⓓ 👷 ⌦ 🆉 🐾 **SC**

★ ★ **RESIDENCE INN BY MARRIOTT-EAST.** *411 S Webb Rd (67207). 316/686-7331; FAX 316/686-2345.* 64 kit. suites, 2 story. S $99; D $124; wknd rates. Crib free. Pet accepted; $50 refundable and $7/day. TV; cable (premium), VCR avail. Pool; whirlpool. Complimentary continental bkfst. Ck-out noon. Coin lndry. Business servs avail. In-rm modem link. Health club privileges. Lawn games. Refrigerators. Many fireplaces. Grills. Cr cds: A, C, D, DS, MC, V. ⓓ 👷 ⌦ 🆉 🐾 **SC**

✔ ★ **STRATFORD HOUSE INN.** *5505 W Kellogg St (US 54) (67209), W of I-235. 316/942-0900.* 40 rms, 2 story. S $35.95; D $39.95-$43.95; under 12 free. Crib free. Pet accepted. TV; cable (premium). Complimentary continental bkfst. Restaurant nearby. Ck-out 11 am. Business servs avail. Cr cds: A, C, D, DS, MC, V. ⓓ 👷 🆉 🐾

Motor Hotels

★ **FAMILY INN.** *221 E Kellogg (67202), on US 54. 316/267-9281; FAX 316/267-3665; res: 800/435-8282.* 150 rms, 7 story. Apr-Sept: S $44.77; D $49.77; suites $69.77; under 18 free; wkly rates; lower rates rest of yr. Crib free. Pet accepted, some restrictions. $15. TV; cable. Pool. Restaurant 6 am-10 pm. Rm serv. Bar 10:30-2 am. Ck-out 11 am. Coin lndry. Meeting rms. Business servs avail. Game rm. Refrigerator avail. Minibars. Cr cds: A, D, DS, MC, V. 👷 ⌦ 🐾 **SC**

★ ★ ★ **HOLIDAY INN AIRPORT.** *5500 W Kellogg (67209), near Mid-Continent Airport. 316/943-2181; FAX 316/943-6587.* 152 rms, 5 story. S $79-$84; D $87-$92; each addl $8; under 12 free; wkend rates. Crib free. Pet accepted. TV; cable, VCR avail. Indoor pool; whirlpool, sauna, poolside serv. Complimentary coffee in rms. Restaurant 6 am-10 pm. Rm serv. Bar 5 pm-1 am. Ck-out noon. Coin lndry. Meeting rms. Business servs avail. Bellhops. Valet serv. Free airport transportation. Cr cds: A, C, D, DS, JCB, MC, V.
ⓓ 👷 ⌦ ✈ 🆉 🐾 **SC**

★ ★ ★ **HOLIDAY INN-EAST.** *7335 E Kellogg St (US 54) (67207), ¹/₂ mi W of KS Tpke, W Kellogg St exit. 316/685-1281; FAX 316/685-8621.* 192 rms, 6 story. S, D $69-$82; suites $82-$150; under 18 free. Crib free. Pet accepted. TV; cable (premium), VCR avail. Indoor pool; whirlpool. Coffee in rms. Restaurant 6-10 am, 6-10 pm; wknds 7-11 am, 6-10 pm. Rm serv. Bar 5 pm-midnight. Ck-out noon. Coin lndry. Meeting rms. Business servs avail. In-rm modem link. Bellhops. Valet serv. Free airport transportation. Exercise equipt; treadmill, bicycle. Game rm. Cr cds: A, C, D, DS, JCB, MC, V. ⓓ 👷 ⌦ 🏋 🆉 🐾 **SC**

Hotels

★ ★ ★ **HARVEY.** *549 S Rock Rd at E Kellogg St (US 54) (67207). 316/686-7131; FAX 316/686-0018.* 260 rms, 9 story. S, D $89-$99; suites $125-$375; wknd, family rates. Crib free. Pet accepted; $125 ($100 refundable). TV; cable (premium), VCR avail. Pool. Coffee in rms. Restaurant 6:30 am-10 pm; Sun from 7 am. Bar 2 pm-midnight. Ck-out 1 pm. Meeting rms. Business servs avail. In-rm modem link. Gift shop. Free airport transportation. Cr cds: A, C, D, DS, MC, V. ⓓ 👷 ⌦ 🆉

★ ★ ★ **MARRIOTT.** *9100 Corporate Hills Dr (67207). 316/651-0333; FAX 316/651-0990.* 294 units, 11 story. S $115-$136; D $125-$146; suites $175-$275; under 18 free; wkly, wknd rates. Crib free. Pet accepted. TV; cable (premium), VCR avail. Indoor/outdoor pool; whirlpool, poolside serv. Coffee in rms. Restaurant 6:30 am-11 pm. Bar noon-2 am. Ck-out noon. Business center. Concierge. Gift shop. Free airport transportation. Exercise equipt; weight machine, bicycles, sauna. Luxury level. Cr cds: A, C, D, DS, ER, JCB, MC, V. ⓓ 👷 ⌦ 🏋 🎿 🆉 🐾 **SC** 🚶

Kentucky

Ashland

Motels

★ ★ **DAYS INN.** *12700 KY 180 (41102). 606/928-3600; FAX 606/928-6515.* E-mail CJones@ramlink.net; web www.daysinn.com/kentucky/ashland. 63 rms, 2 story. S $46-$59; D $52-$64; each addl $5; under 18 free. Crib free. Pet accepted; $5. TV; cable (premium), VCR avail (movies). Pool. Complimentary continental bkfst. Complimentary coffee in rms. Restaurant nearby. Ck-out noon. Coin lndry. Meeting rms. Business center. In-rm modem link. Some refrigerators, microwaves. Picnic tables. Cr cds: A, C, D, DS, MC, V.

🄳 💶 ≋ 🈁 🈁 SC ⚓

✔ ★ ★ **KNIGHTS INN.** *7216 US 60 (41102). 606/928-9501; FAX 606/928-4436.* 124 rms. S $38; D $43; kit. units $42-$47; each addl $5; under 18 free. Crib free. Pet accepted; $5. TV; cable (premium). Pool. Complimentary continental bkfst. Restaurant nearby. Ck-out noon. Meeting rms. Business servs avail. Refrigerators. Cr cds: A, C, D, DS, ER, MC, V.

🄳 💶 ≋ 🈁 🈁 SC

Bardstown *(See also Elizabethtown)*

Motels

(Most motels increase their rates for Derby wkend; reservations should be made as far ahead as possible and confirmed)

★ ★ **HOLIDAY INN.** *1875 New Haven Rd, 2 mi S on US 31E exit 21 at Bluegrass Pkwy. 502/348-9253; FAX 502/348-5478.* 102 rms, 2 story. May-Sept: S, D $59-$70; each addl $5; under 19 free. Crib free. Pet accepted, some restrictions. TV; cable (premium), VCR avail (movies). Pool; wading pool. Playground. Restaurant 6 am-2 pm, 5-9 pm; Fri & Sat to 10 pm. Bar. Ck-out 11 am. Meeting rms. Business servs avail. In-rm modem link. 9-hole par 3 golf; driving range. Exercise equipt; weights, bicycle. Cr cds: A, C, D, DS, JCB, MC, V. 🄳 💶 🏋 ≋ 🏃 🈁 🈁 SC

★ ★ **PARKVIEW.** *418 E Stephen Foster Ave (US 62), at jct US 150. 502/348-5983; FAX 502/349-6973; res: 800/732-2384.* 38 rms, 1-2 story, 10 kit. units. June-Labor Day: S $45; D $50; each addl $5; suites $60-$80; kit. units $60-$70; lower rates rest of yr. Pet accepted. TV; cable. Pool. Complimentary continental bkfst. Restaurant 11 am-9 pm; Sun 8 am-9 pm. Bar. Ck-out 11 am. Coin lndry. My Old Kentucky Home State Park opp. Cr cds: A, DS, MC, V. 💶 ≋ 🈁 SC

Berea *(See also Mount Vernon, Richmond)*

Motel

★ ★ **DAYS INN.** *I-75 exit 77, at jct KY 595. 606/986-7373; FAX 606/986-3144.* 60 rms, 2 story. S $43-$45; D $49-$51; each addl $5; family rates. Crib free. Pet accepted; $5. TV. Pool. Complimentary coffee in lobby. Restaurant adj. Ck-out 11 am. Meeting rm. Business servs avail. Miniature golf. Cr cds: A, C, D, DS, MC, V. 🄳 💶 ≋ 🈁 🈁 SC

Bowling Green

Motel

★ ★ **HOLIDAY INN I-65.** *3240 Scottsville Rd (42104), 2³/₄ mi SE on US 231, 1 blk W of I-65 exit 22. 502/781-1500; FAX 502/842-0030.* 107 rms, 2 story. S $39-$80; D $90; each addl $10; under 19 free. Crib free. Pet accepted. TV; cable. Pool; wading pool. Playground. Restaurant 6:30 am-10 am, 5-9 pm. Rm serv. Bar 5 pm-11 pm. Ck-out noon. Business servs avail. In-rm modem link. Sundries. Exercise equipt; bicycle, treadmill. Game rm. Picnic tables. Cr cds: A, C, D, DS, JCB, MC, V. 🄳 💶 ≋ 🏃 🈁 🈁 SC

Cadiz

Motel

★ ★ **COUNTRY INN BY CARLSON.** *5909 Hopkinsville Rd, I-24 exit 65. 502/522-7007; FAX 502/522-3893; res: 800/456-4000.* 48 rms, 2 story. S $52; D $55; each addl $4; under 18 free. Crib free. Pet accepted. TV; cable (premium), VCR avail (movies). Pool.

Complimentary continental bkfst. Coffee in rms. Restaurant adj. Ck-out noon. Business servs avail. Cr cds: A, C, D, DS, MC, V. [D] 🐾 ≈ ⚔ 🐾 SC

Carrollton

Motel

★ ★ **HOLIDAY INN EXPRESS.** *141 Inn Rd, at I-71 exit 44. 502/732-6661; FAX 502/732-6661.* 62 rms, 2 story. S, D $59; each addl $6; under 19 free; some wkend rates; higher rates special events. Crib free. Pet accepted, some restrictions. TV; cable (premium). Complimentary continental bkfst. Restaurant adj. Ck-out noon. Meeting rm. Business servs avail. In-rm modem link. Downhill ski 2 mi. Microwaves avail. Cr cds: A, C, D, DS, JCB, MC, V. [D] 🐾 ≈ ⚔ 🐾 SC

Cave City *(See also Glasgow)*

Motels

★ **DAYS INN.** *3/4 mi W on KY 70; 2 blks NE of I-65 exit 53. 502/773-2151.* 110 rms, 2 story. Late May-early Sept: S $56; D $66; each addl $5; under 12 free; lower rates rest of yr. Crib free. Pet accepted. TV; cable (premium); VCR avail (movies). Heated pool; wading pool. Restaurant 5:30 am-8:30 pm. Ck-out noon. Coin lndry. Meeting rms. Business servs avail. Game rm. Private patios, balconies. Cr cds: A, C, D, DS, JCB, MC, V. 🐾 ≈ ⚔ 🐾 SC

✔ ★ ★ **QUALITY INN.** *Mammoth Cave Rd, W on KY 70, 90. 502/773-2181; FAX 502/773-2182.* 100 rms, 2 story. Memorial Day-Labor Day: S $36-$56; D $42-$62; each addl $6; suites $68; under 18 free; higher rates special events; lower rates rest of yr. Crib $6. Pet accepted. TV; cable (premium), VCR avail (movies). Pool. Playground. Restaurant to 11 pm. Rm serv 6 am-10 pm. Ck-out 11 am. Business servs avail. Gift shop. Picnic tables. Cr cds: A, C, D, DS, ER, MC, V. [D] 🐾 ≈ ⚔ 🐾 SC

Covington (Cincinnati Airport Area) *(See also Walton)*

Motels

★ ★ **HOLIDAY INN-SOUTH.** *(2100 Dixie Hwy, Ft Mitchell 41011) 8 mi SW on I-75/71, exit 188B. 606/331-1500; FAX 606/331-2259.* 214 rms, 2 story. S, D $109-$129; under 18 free; family, wkend rates; higher rates: special events, Jazz Festival. Crib free. Pet accepted, some restrictions. TV; cable (premium). Indoor pool; whirlpool. Playground. Complimentary coffee in rms. Restaurant 6:30-11 am, 5:30-10 pm. Rm serv. Ck-out 11 am. Coin lndry. Meeting rms. Business servs avail. Bellhops. Valet serv. Sundries. Free airport transportation. Exercise equipt; weight machine, bicycle, sauna. Health club privileges. Holidome. Game rm. Cr cds: A, C, D, DS, JCB, MC, V.. [D] 🐾 ≈ 🏋 ⚔ 🐾 SC

✔ ★ **KNIGHTS INN.** *(8049 Dream St, Florence 41042) Jct I-75/71 and US 42/127. 606/371-9711; FAX 606/371-4325.* 116 rms, 10 kits. S, D $37-$62; each addl $6; kit. units $48-$58; under 18 free. Crib free. Pet accepted, some restrictions. TV; cable (premium). Pool. Restaurant nearby. Ck-out noon. Meeting rm. Business servs avail. Some microwaves. Cr cds: A, C, D, DS, MC, V. [D] 🐾 ≈ ⚔ 🐾 SC

Hotel

★ ★ ★ **QUALITY HOTEL-RIVERVIEW.** *666 5th St (41011), at I-71/75 exit 192. 606/491-1200; FAX 606/491-0326.* 236 rms, 18 story. S, D $70-$98; suites $189; under 18 free. Crib free. Pet accepted. TV; cable (premium), VCR avail. Indoor/outdoor pool; whirlpool, poolside serv. Coffee in rms. Restaurants 7-1 am. Rm serv to 11 pm. Bars from 11 am. Ck-out 11 am. Meeting rms. Business servs avail. In-rm modem link. Gift shop. Barber. Free airport transportation. Exercise equipt; weights, bicycles. Rec rm. Cr cds: A, C, D, DS, ER, JCB, MC, V. [D] 🐾 ≈ 🏋 ⚔ 🐾 SC

Danville

Motels

★ **DAYS INN.** *4th St, at jct US 127S, 127 Bypass, 150 Bypass. 606/236-8601; FAX 606/236-0314.* 81 rms, 2 story. S, D $55-$65; each addl $6; under 19 free. Crib free. Pet accepted. TV; cable (premium). Pool. Coffee in rms. Restaurant open 24 hrs. Ck-out noon. Meeting rms. Business servs avail. In-rm modem link. Refrigerators, microwaves avail. Cr cds: A, D, DS, JCB, MC, V. [D] 🐾 ≈ ⚔ 🐾 SC

★ **HOLIDAY INN EXPRESS.** *96 Daniel Dr. 606/236-8600; FAX 606/236-4299.* 63 rms. S, D $55-69; under 19 free. Crib free. Pet accepted, some restrictions. TV; cable (premium). Indoor pool; whirlpool, sauna. Complimentary continental bkfst. Restaurant adj 11 am-9 pm. Ck-out noon. Meeting rm. Business servs avail. Coin lndry. Microwaves avail. Cr cds: A, D, DS, JCB, MC, V.

✔ ★ **SUPER 8.** *3663 US 150, at US 127 Bypass. 606/236-8881.* 49 units, 2 story. S $41.88; D $51.88-$56.88; each addl $5; under 12 free. Crib free. Pet accepted, some restrictions. TV; cable (premium). Complimentary coffee. Restaurant nearby. Ck-out 11 am. Meeting rms. Business servs avail. Valet serv. Some refrigerators; microwaves avail. Cr cds: A, C, D, DS, MC, V.

Elizabethtown *(See also Bardstown)*

Motels

✔ ★ **BEST WESTERN CARDINAL INN.** *642 E Dixie. 502/765-6139.* 67 rms, 2 story. S $28-$40; D $36-$48; each addl $4; under 12 free; higher rates Kentucky Derby. Crib $4. Pet accepted, some restrictions; $25 deposit. TV; cable. Pool. Playground. Ck-out 11 am. Coin lndry. Cr cds: A, C, D, DS, MC, V.

★ **TRAVELODGE.** *2009 N Mulberry, I-65 exit 94, at US 62. 502/765-4166; FAX 502/769-9396.* 106 rms, 2 story. S, D $31-$44; under 17 free; higher rates Derby wkend. Crib free. Pet accepted; fee. TV; cable. Pool. Ck-out noon. Meeting rms. Business servs avail. Valet serv. Sundries. Health club privileges. Balconies. Cr cds: A, C, D, DS, MC, V.

Frankfort *(See also Lexington)*

Motel

★ **BLUEGRASS INN.** *635 Versailles Rd. 502/695-1800; FAX 502/695-3628; res: 800/322-1802.* 62 rms, 2 story. S $36-$42; D $42-$48; each addl $6; under 14 free; higher rates Kentucky Derby. Crib free. Pet accepted. TV; cable. Pool. Complimentary coffee in lobby. Restaurant adj 9 am-10 pm. Ck-out noon. Business servs avail. Some refrigerators. Cr cds: A, C, D, DS, ER, MC, V.

Glasgow *(See also Cave City)*

Motel

✔ ★ ★ **FAMILY BUDGET INN.** *1003 W Main, 1/2 mi W on US 68; 1/2 blk W of US 31E Bypass. 502/651-5191.* 80 rms, 2 story. S $34-$50; D $40-$55; each addl $8; under 19 free. Crib free. Pet accepted; $5. TV; cable. Heated pool. Complimentary continental bkfst. Restaurant nearby. Ck-out 11 am. Meeting rms. Business servs avail. Exercise equipt; bicycle, treadmill. Cr cds: A, C, D, DS, ER, MC, V.

Henderson *(See also Owensboro)*

Motel

✔ ★ **SCOTTISH INN.** *2820 US 41N. 502/827-1806; FAX 502/827-8192; res: 800/251-1962.* 60 rms, 1-2 story. S $30-$35; D $35-$45; each addl $3; under 10 free. Crib $5. Pet accepted; $5. TV; cable (premium), VCR avail (movies). Pool; wading pool. Complimentary coffee in lobby. Restaurant nearby. Ck-out 11 am. Business servs avail. Cr cds: A, C, D, DS, MC, V.

Hopkinsville *(See also Cadiz; also see Clarksville, TN)*

Motel

✔ ★ ★ **HOLIDAY INN.** *2910 Ft Campbell Blvd. 502/886-4413.* 101 rms, 5 story. S, D $49-$72; each addl $6; under 19 free. Crib free. Pet accepted. TV; cable. Indoor pool; sauna. Restaurant 6 am-2 pm, 5-9 pm. Rm serv. Bar 4 pm-1 am. Ck-out noon. Meeting rms. Business servs avail. In-rm modem link. Valet serv. Sundries. Exercise equipt; bicycle, treadmill. Cr cds: A, C, D, DS, JCB, MC, V.

Kenlake State Resort Park *(See also Cadiz)*

(16 mi NE of Murray on KY 94)

Motel

✔ ★ **EARLY AMERICAN.** *(16749 US Hwy 68, Aurora 42048) At jct US 68, KY 80 & jct KY 94. 502/474-2241.* 18 rms, 7 kits. Late May-early Sept: S $37.95; D $41.95-$63.95;

each addl $5; kit. units $48.95-$68.95; under 12 free; wkly rates; lower rates rest of yr. Crib free. Pet accepted. TV; cable. Pool. Playground. Complimentary coffee in rms. Restaurant adj 6 am-9 pm. Ck-out 10 am. Rec rm. Lawn games. Picnic tables, grills. Cr cds: A, DS, MC, V. 🛏️ 🏊 🐾 SC

Lexington (See also Frankfort, Richmond)

Motels

✔ ★ ★ **BEST WESTERN REGENCY.** *2241 Elkhorn (40505), I-75 exit 110. 606/293-2202; FAX 606/293-1821.* 112 rms, 2 story. S $49-$79; D $59-$99; each addl $10; suite $139; under 18 free. Crib free. Pet accepted; $10. TV; cable (premium). Pool; whirlpool, sauna. Complimentary continental bkfst. Restaurant nearby. Ck-out 11 am. Coin lndry. Meeting rms. Business servs avail. In-rm modem link. Cr cds: A, C, D, DS, MC, V. D 🛏️ 🏊 🐾 SC

✔ ★ **DAYS INN.** *5575 Athens Boonesboro Rd (40509), I-75 exit 104. 606/263-3100; FAX 606/263-3120.* 56 rms, 2 story. S $40-$50; D $45-$65; each addl $5; family rates; higher rates special events. Crib free. Pet accepted. TV. Complimentary continental bkfst. Restaurant nearby. Ck-out 11 am. Business servs avail. In-rm modem link. Some microwaves. Cr cds: A, C, D, DS, MC, V. D 🛏️ 🏊 🐾 SC

★ ★ **HOLIDAY INN-NORTH.** *1950 Newtown Pike (40511), 1/2 blk S of I-75 exit 115. 606/233-0512; FAX 606/231-9285.* 303 rms, 2 story. S $104.95; D $109.95; suites $250; under 18 free. Crib free. Pet accepted, some restrictions. TV; cable (premium). Indoor pool; whirlpool. Supervised child's activities (Memorial Day-Labor Day). Coffee in rms. Restaurant 6 am-2 pm, 5-10 pm. Rm serv. Bar 2 pm-1 am; entertainment. Ck-out noon. Coin lndry. Convention facilities. Business center. In-rm modem link. Bellhops. Valet serv. Concierge. Sundries. Gift shop. Putting green. Exercise equipt; weight machine, bicycle, sauna. Holidome. Game rm. Some refrigerators, microwaves. Cr cds: A, C, D, DS, ER, MC, V. D 🛏️ 🏊 🏋️ 🐾 SC ⛷️

★ ★ **HOLIDAY INN-SOUTH.** *5532 Athens Boonesboro Rd (40509), I-75 exit 104. 606/263-5241; FAX 606/263-4333.* 149 rms, 2 story. S, D $60-$75; each addl $6; under 18 free; higher rates horse racing and special events. Crib free. Pet accepted, some restrictions. TV; cable (premium). Pool. Restaurant 6 am-2 pm, 5-10 pm. Rm serv. Bar; entertainment Tues-Sat. Coin lndry. Meeting rms. Business servs avail. In-rm modem link. Valet serv. Exercise equipt; weight machine, stair machine, whirlpool, sauna. Sundries. Holidome. Cr cds: A, C, D, DS, JCB, MC, V. D 🛏️ 🏊 🏋️ 🐾 SC

★ ★ **LA QUINTA INN.** *1919 Stanton Way (40511), I-64/75 exit 115. 606/231-7551; FAX 606/281-6002.* Web www.laquinta.com. 130 rms, 2 story. S $64; D $68; each addl $8; under 18 free; some wkends higher. Crib free. Pet accepted, some restrictions. TV; cable. Pool. Complimentary continental bkfst. Restaurant adj 6 am-10 pm; wkends to 11 pm. Ck-out noon. Business servs avail. In-rm modem link. Valet serv. Cr cds: A, C, D, DS, MC, V. D 🛏️ 🏊 🐾 SC

★ ★ **QUALITY INN-NORTHWEST.** *1050 Newtown Pike (KY 922) (40511). 606/233-0561; FAX 606/231-6125.* 109 rms, 2 story. S, D $40.50-$75.95; each addl $5; suite $131; under 19 free. Crib $1. Pet accepted. TV; cable. Heated pool; lifeguard (in season). Playground. Complimentary continental bkfst. Ck-out noon. Meeting rms. Business servs avail. Valet serv. Sundries. Gift shop. Some microwaves. Cr cds: A, C, D, DS, JCB, MC, V. D 🛏️ 🏊 🐾 SC

✔ ★ **RED ROOF INN.** *483 Haggard Lane (40505), US 27, 68 at jct I-64, I-75 exit 113. 606/293-2626; FAX 606/299-8353.* 107 rms, 2 story. S $35.99-$45.99; D $41.99-$61.99; each addl $7; under 18 free. Crib free. Pet accepted, some restrictions. TV; cable (premium). Complimentary coffee in lobby. Restaurant nearby. Ck-out noon. Business servs avail. Cr cds: A, C, D, DS, MC, V. D 🛏️ 🏊 🐾

Inn

★ ★ **TYRONE PIKE BED & BREAKFAST.** *(3820 Tyrone Pike, Versailles 40383) approx 15 mi W on US 62. 606/873-2408; res: 800/736-7722.* E-mail tyronebb@uky.campus.mci.net; web www.bbonline.com/ ky/tyrone. 4 rms, 1 with shower only, 2 share bath, 2 story, 1 suite, 1 kit. unit. S $89-$125; D $98-$125; suite, kit. unit $125; family, wkly rates. Pet accepted. TV; VCR avail (movies). Complimentary full bkfst. Ck-out noon, ck-in 4 pm. Luggage handling. Game rm. Some refrigerators; microwaves avail. Picnic tables. Cr cds: MC, V. 🛏️ 🐾 SC

Resort

★ ★ ★ **MARRIOTT'S GRIFFIN GATE RESORT.** *1800 Newtown Pike (KY 922) (40511), I-64 & I-75 exit 115. 606/231-5100; FAX 606/255-9944.* Web www.marriott .com/lex. This gleaming, contemporary resort caters to those who like a mix of activities and comfort. The lobby has an atrium with waterfalls, mahogany tables and leather chairs. 409 rms, 7 story. S $129-$149; D $139-$159; suite $250-$850; under 18 free; golf plans. Crib free. Pet accepted, some restrictions; $40. TV; cable (premium). 2 pools, 1 indoor; whirlpool, poolside serv, lifeguard. Playground. Supervised child's activities (summer). Dining rm 6 am-11 pm. Rm serv. Bar 11-1 am. Ck-out noon. Coin lndry. Convention facilities. Business center. In-rm modem link. Valet serv. Gift shop. Barber, beauty shop. Package store 1 mi. Airport transportation. Sports dir. Lighted tennis, pro. 18-hole golf, greens fee $28-$62, pro, putting green. Seasonal activities incl walking tours, pool activities. Game rm. Exercise rm; instructor, weights, bicycles, sauna. Refrigerator in suites. Private patios, balconies. Picnic tables. Luxury level. Cr cds: A, C, D, DS, JCB, MC, V.

D 🐾 🏋 🏃 ≈ ✈ 🔾 🐾 **SC** 🎣

London

Motels

✔ ★ **BUDGET HOSET-WESTGATE INN.** *254 W Daniel Boone Pkwy, exit 41 on KY 80. 606/878-7330.* 46 rms, 2 story. Memorial Day-Oct: S $39.30; D $46.95; each addl $4; under 12 free; wkly rates; lower rates rest of yr. Crib free. Pet accepted, some restrictions. TV; cable. Complimentary coffee in lobby. Restaurant adj 6 am-11 pm. Ck-out noon. Pool. Cr cds: A, D, DS, MC, V. **D** 🐾 ≈ 🔾 🐾 **SC**

★ ★ **HOLIDAY INN EXPRESS.** *400 GOP Dr, jct I-75 & KY 80. 606/878-7678; FAX 606/878-7654.* 60 rms, 2 story. S, D $58-$68. Crib avail. Pet accepted. TV; cable (premium). Indoor/outdoor pool. Complimentary continental bkfst. Restaurant opp 6 am-11 pm. Ck-out 11 am. Business servs avail. Game rm. Cr cds: A, C, D, DS, JCB, MC, V.

D 🐾 ≈ 🔾 🐾 **SC**

Louisville *(See also Shepherdsville)*

Motel

(Rates are generally much higher during Kentucky Derby; may be 3-day min)

✔ ★ **RED ROOF INN.** *9330 Blairwood Rd (40222), 1 blk N of I-64 exit 15, east of downtown. 502/426-7621; FAX 502/426-7933.* 108 rms, 2 story. S $35.99-$69.99; D $43.99-$79.99; each addl $8-$10; under 18 free. Crib free. Pet accepted. TV; cable. Complimentary coffee. Restaurant adj 6 am-11 pm. Ck-out noon. Business servs avail. In-rm modem link. Cr cds: A, C, D, DS, MC, V. **D** 🐾 🔾 🐾 **SC**

Motor Hotels

★ ★ **BRECKINRIDGE INN.** *2800 Breckinridge Lane (40220), I-264 exit 18A, south of downtown. 502/456-5050; FAX 502/451-1577.* 123 rms, 2 story. S, D $65-$95; each addl $7; under 12 free. Crib $7. Pet accepted; $50. TV; cable. 2 pools, 1 indoor; lifeguard. Restaurant 7 am-1:30 pm, 5-9 pm. Rm serv. Bar. Ck-out noon. Meeting rms. Business servs avail. Valet serv. Sundries. Gift shop. Barber shop. Free airport transportation. Lighted tennis. Exercise equipt; weights, bicycle, sauna. Cr cds: A, C, D, DS, MC, V.

🐾 🏋 ≈ ✈ 🔾 🐾 **SC**

★ ★ **EXECUTIVE WEST.** *830 Phillips Lane (40209), Freedom Way at Fairgrounds, near Standiford Field Airport, south of downtown. 502/367-2251; FAX 502/363-2087; res: 800/626-2708 (exc KY).* E-mail exwest@iglou.com; web wl.iglou.com/exwest. 611 rms, 8 story. S, D $84-$124; suites $105-$240; under 17 free; wkend rates. Crib free. Pet accepted; $100. TV; cable. Indoor/outdoor pool; poolside serv, lifeguard. Restaurant 6:30 am-11 pm. Rm serv. Bar; entertainment. Ck-out noon. Convention facilities. Business servs avail. In-rm modem link. Bellhops. Gift shop. Barber, beauty shop. Free airport transportation. Health club privileges. Refrigerator in suites. Kentucky Kingdom Amusement Park opp. Cr cds: A, C, D, DS, MC, V. **D** 🐾 ≈ ✈ 🔾 🐾 **SC**

★ ★ **HOLIDAY INN AIRPORT.** *1465 Gardiner Lane (40213). 502/452-6361; FAX 502/451-1541.* 200 rms, 3 story. S, D $92; each addl $7; under 18 free; wkend rates. Crib free. Pet accepted. TV; cable (premium). Pool; poolside serv, lifeguard. Complimentary coffee in rms. Restaurant 11 am-11 pm. Rm serv. Bar to midnight. Ck-out noon. Coin lndry. Meeting rms. Business servs avail. In-rm modem link. Bellhops. Sundries. Valet serv. Free airport transportation. Tennis. Exercise equipt; weight machine, rowers. Game rm. Cr cds: A, C, D, DS, JCB, MC, V. **D** 🐾 🏋 ≈ 🏃 ✈ 🔾 🐾 **SC**

✔ ★ **WILSON INN.** *9802 Bunsen Pkwy (40299), I-64 exit 15, east of downtown. 502/499-0000; res: 800/945-7667.* 108 rms, 5 story, 30 suites, 38 kit. units. S, D $44.95; each addl $5; suites $54.95; kit. units $44.95; under 19 free. Crib free. Pet accepted, some restrictions. TV; cable (premium). Complimentary continental bkfst 6-10 am. Restaurant nearby. Ck-out noon. Meeting rms. Business servs avail. In-rm modem link. Free airport transportation. Refrigerators; microwaves avail. Cr cds: A, D, DS, JCB, MC, V.

[D] [✦] [≋] [⊠] [▨] [SC]

Hotels

★ ★ **HOLIDAY INN-DOWNTOWN.** *120 W Broadway (40202), downtown. 502/582-2241; FAX 502/584-8591.* 287 rms, 12 story. S $93-$110; D $103-$125; each addl $10; suites $350; under 19 free. Crib free. Pet accepted. TV; cable VCR avail (movies). Indoor pool; lifeguard. Coffee in rms. Restaurant 6 am-11 pm. Bar 11-2 am. Ck-out noon. Convention facilities. Business servs avail. In-rm modem link. Gift shop. Barber. Free airport transportation. Health club privileges. Some refrigerators, minibars. Some balconies. Luxury level. Cr cds: A, C, D, DS, JCB, MC, V. [D] [✦] [≋] [⊠] [▨] [SC]

★ ★ ★ **SEELBACH.** *500 Fourth Ave (40202), downtown. 502/585-3200; FAX 502/585-9239; res: 800/333-3399.* The lobby in this restored hotel, originally opened in 1905, has eight murals by Arthur Thomas depicting Kentucky pioneers and Native Americans. Rooms have four-poster beds, armoires and marble baths. 321 rms, 11 story. S $170-$230; D $180-$230; each addl $10; suites $210-$510; under 18 free; wknd rates. Crib free. Pet accepted; $50 deposit. Parking $10; valet $14. TV; cable, VCR avail. Pool privileges. Restaurants 6:30 am-midnight. Bar 4 pm-2 am; entertainment. Ck-out 1 pm. Convention facilities. Business center. In-rm modem link. Concierge. Shopping arcade. Free airport transportation. Health club privileges. Luxury level. Cr cds: A, C, D, DS, MC, V.

[D] [✦] [⚹] [≋] [⊠] [▨] [SC] [⚐]

Inn

★ ★ **WOODHAVEN.** *401 S Hubbards Lane (40207), east of downtown. 502/895-1011; res: 888/895-1011.* 7 rms, 2 story. S, D $65-$85. Crib free. Pet accepted. TV; cable (premium), VCR avail. Complimentary full bkfst. Complimentary coffee in rms. Ck-out 11 am, ck-in 3 pm. Gothic Revival house built in 1853. Totally nonsmoking. Cr cds: MC, V.

[✦] [⊠] [▨]

Madisonville

Motel

★ ★ **DAYS INN.** *1900 Lantaff Blvd, US 41 Bypass exit 44. 502/821-8620; FAX 502/825-9282.* 143 rms, 2 story. S $49-$54; D $54-$59; each addl $5; suites $70-$100. Crib free. Pet accepted. TV; cable (premium). Indoor pool; sauna. Complimentary continental bkfst. Restaurant 6 am-10 am, 11 am-2 pm, 5-10 pm. Rm serv 11 am-2 pm, 5-9 pm. Ck-out noon. Meeting rms. Business center. Sundries. Health club privileges. Cr cds: A, C, D, DS, MC, V. [D] [✦] [≋] [⊠] [▨] [SC] [⚐]

Mammoth Cave National Park *(See also Cave City)*

(On KY 70, 10 mi W of Cave City or 8 mi NW of Park City on KY 255)

Motel

★ **MAMMOTH CAVE.** *10 mi W of US 31W (42259), I-65 exit 53 on KY 70 to park entrance, or exit 48 on KY 255 to entrance, then 3 mi inside park. 502/758-2225; FAX 502/758-2301.* 42 rms, 2 story. 20-rm motor lodge. Memorial Day-Labor Day: S, D $61-$67; each addl $6; cottages: S, D $45-$51; family rates; lower rates rest of yr. Crib $5. Pet accepted. TV. Restaurants 7 am-7:30 pm. Ck-out noon. Coin lndry (summer). Meeting rms (winter). Business servs avail. Gift shop. Tennis. Lawn games. Private patios, balconies. Cr cds: A, C, D, MC, V. [✦] [⚹] [▨]

Mount Vernon *(See also Berea)*

Motels

★ **ECONO LODGE.** *1630 Richmond St, US 25 & I-75 exit 62. 606/256-4621.* 35 rms, 2-3 story. S $29.50-$32, D $36-$40.50; family rates; higher rates: hol wkends, special events. Crib $5. Pet accepted, some restrictions. TV; cable. Pool. Complimentary coffee in lobby. Restaurant nearby. Ck-out 11 am. Cr cds: A, C, D, DS, ER, JCB, MC, V.

[D] [✦] [≋] [⊠] [▨] [SC]

✔ ★ ★ **KASTLE INN.** *E of I-75 exit 59. 606/256-5156.* 50 rms, 2 story. S $36-$40; D $44-$50; each addl $8; under 12 free. Pet accepted, some restrictions. TV; cable (premium), VCR avail (movies). Pool. Restaurant 6 am-10 pm. Ck-out 11 am. Sundries. Cr cds: A, C, D, DS, ER, JCB, MC, V. 🔲 🔲 🔲 🔲 🔲

Murray

Motels

★ **DAYS INN.** *517 S 12th St, US 641 S. 502/753-6706.* S $47.50-$60; D $52.50-$65; each addl $5; under 13 free; higher rates special events. Crib free. Pet accepted; $5. TV; cable (premium). Complimentary continental bkfst, coffee in rms. Restaurant nearby. Ck-out 11 am. Business servs avail. Pool. Some in-rm whirlpool, refrigerators, microwaves. Cr cds: A, C, D, DS, JCB, MC, V. 🔲 🔲 🔲 🔲 🔲 🔲

✔ ★ **PLAZA COURT.** *US 641 S. 502/753-2682.* 40 rms, 2 story. S $33; D $36.30; each addl $5; wkly plans; higher rates special events. Crib $6. Pet accepted, some restrictions. TV; cable (premium). Complimentary coffee in lobby. Restaurant opp 6 am-10 pm. Ck-out noon. Cr cds: A, DS, MC, V. 🔲 🔲 🔲

✔ ★ **SHONEY'S INN.** *1503 N 12th St. 502/753-5353.* 67 rms, 2 story. S $44-$48; D $49-$53; each addl $5; higher rates special events; crib free. Pet accepted; $5; TV; cable (premium). Complimentary coffee in lobby. Restaurant adj 6 am-10 pm. Ck-out noon. Meeting rms. Business servs avail. In-rm modem link. Pool. Cr cds: A, C, D, DS, MC, V. 🔲 🔲 🔲 🔲 🔲 🔲

Owensboro

Motels

✔ ★ **DAYS INN.** *3720 New Hartford Rd, jct US 60 Bypass & US 231. 502/684-9621; FAX 502/684-9626.* 122 rms, 2 story. S $42; D $46; each addl $4; under 12 free. Crib free. Pet accepted. TV. Pool. Complimentary coffee in rms. Restaurant 6 am-9 pm. Rm serv 5-9 pm. Ck-out noon. Business servs avail. In-rm modem link. Cr cds: A, D, DS, MC, V. 🔲 🔲 🔲 🔲 🔲 🔲

★ ★ **HOLIDAY INN.** *3136 W 2nd St. 502/685-3941; FAX 502/926-2917.* 145 rms, 2 story. S $59-$69; each addl $10; suites $95-$110; under 19 free. Crib free. Pet accepted. TV; cable. Indoor pool. Playground. Coffee in rms. Restaurant 6 am-2 pm, 5-9 pm; Sun 6 am-2 pm. Rm serv. Bar 11-2 am; closed Sun. Ck-out noon. Meeting rms. Business center. In-rm modem link. Exercise equipt; bicycles, treadmill, whirlpool, sauna. Cr cds: A, C, D, DS, JCB, MC, V. 🔲 🔲 🔲 🔲 🔲 🔲 🔲

Paducah

Motels

★ **DRURY INN.** *3975 Hinkleville Rd (42001). 502/443-3313.* 118 rms, 5 story. S $59-$70; D $65-$80 each addl $8; suites $70-$80; under 18 free. Crib free. Pet accepted. TV; cable. Indoor pool; whirlpool. Complimentary full bkfst. Ck-out noon. Cr cds: A, C, D, DS, MC, V. 🔲 🔲 🔲 🔲 🔲 🔲

★ ★ **HOLIDAY INN EXPRESS.** *3994 Hinkleville Rd (42001), I-24 and US 60, exit 4. 502/442-8874.* 76 rms, 3 story. S $80.50; D $90.50; each addl $10; under 18 free; higher rates special events. Crib avail. Pet accepted, some restrictions. TV; cable (premium), VCR avail. Complimentary continental bkfst. Restaurant 10 am-midnight. Ck-out 11 am. Meeting rms. Business servs avail. Coin lndry. Indoor pool; whirlpool. Game rm. Bathm phones, refrigerators, microwaves, minibars. Picnic tables. Cr cds: A, C, D, DS, JCB, MC, V. 🔲 🔲 🔲 🔲 🔲 🔲

✔ ★ **QUALITY INN.** *1380 Irvin Cobb Dr (42003), W on I-24, exit 7. 502/443-8751; FAX 502/442-0133.* 101 rms, 2 story. Mar-Nov: S $39.99-$48.99; D $48.99-$58.99; each addl $7; family, wkly rates; higher rates special events; lower rates rest of yr. Crib avail. Pet accepted, some restrictions. TV; cable (premium). Complimentary continental bkfst. Restaurant nearby. Ck-out 11 am. Meeting rms. Business servs avail. Coin lndry. Pool. Cr cds: A, C, D, DS, MC, V. 🔲 🔲 🔲 🔲 🔲 🔲

Pikeville (See also Prestonsburg)

Motor Hotel

★ ★ **LANDMARK INN.** *146 S Mayo Trail. 606/432-2545; res: 800/831-1469.* 103 rms, 4 story. S $55; D $65; each addl $10; under 12 free. Crib free. Pet accepted, some restrictions. TV; cable (premium), VCR avail (movies). Pool. Rooftop restaurant 6 am-10 pm; Sun to 3 pm. Rm serv. Bar; entertainment. Ck-out noon. Coin lndry. Sundries. Meeting rms. Valet serv. Some balconies. Cr cds: A, C, D, DS, MC, V. 🄳 ✦ ≈ ⊠ ⚭ SC

Prestonsburg (See also Pikeville)

Motel

✔ ★ **DAYS INN.** *(512 South Mayo Trail, Paintsville 41240) 12 mi N on US 23/460. 606/789-3551; FAX 606/789-9299.* 72 rms, 2 story. S $45-$70; D $55-$70; each addl $5; under 12 free; higher rates Apple Festival. Crib free. Pet accepted. TV; cable (premium). Pool. Complimentary continental bkfst. Restaurant opp 6 am-9:30 pm. Ck-out 11 am. Business servs avail. Exercise equipt; bicycle, treadmill. Cr cds: A, C, D, DS, MC, V. 🄳 ✦ ≈ ⚔ ⊠ ⚭ SC

Motor Hotels

★ ★ **CARRIAGE HOUSE.** *(624 2nd St, Paintsville 41240) Off US 23. 606/789-4242; FAX 606/789-6788; res: 800/951-4242.* 125 rms, 3 story. S $52; D $60; each addl $3; suites $120-$130; under 12 free. Crib free. Pet accepted. TV; cable. Indoor/outdoor pool; whirlpool, poolside serv. Restaurant 11 am-8 pm; Sun to 4 pm. Rm serv. Ck-out 11 am. Coin lndry. Meeting rms. Business servs avail. Gift shop. Balconies. Cr cds: A, C, D, DS, MC, V. 🄳 ✦ ≈ ⊠ ⚭

★ ★ **HOLIDAY INN.** *575 US 23S. 606/886-0001; FAX 606/886-9850.* 117 rms, 3 story. S, D $66; each addl $6; under 19 free. Crib free. Pet accepted, some restrictions. TV; cable. Heated pool; poolside serv. Restaurant 6 am-10 pm. Rm serv from 7 am. Bar; entertainment Thurs, Fri. Ck-out noon. Coin lndry. Meeting rms. Business servs avail. In-rm modem link. Exercise equipt; weight machine, treadmill, whirlpool. Refrigerators avail. Cr cds: A, C, D, DS, JCB, MC, V. 🄳 ✦ ≈ ⚔ ⊠ ⚭ SC

Richmond (See also Berea, Lexington)

Motels

✔ ★ **DAYS INN.** *2109 Belmont Dr, I-75 exit 90B. 606/624-5769; FAX 606/624-1406.* 70 rms, 2 story. S $42; D $47; each addl $5; under 18 free. Pet accepted, some restrictions; $5. TV; cable (premium). Pool. Restaurant adj open 24 hrs. Ck-out 11 am. Meeting rm. Business servs avail. Cr cds: A, C, D, DS, JCB, MC, V. 🄳 ✦ ≈ ⊠ ⚭ SC

★ **SUPER 8.** *107 N Keeneland, I-75, exit 90B. 606/624-1550; FAX 606/624-1553.* 63 rms, 2 story. S $39.88; D $49.88; each addl $5; under 18 free; weekly rates; higher rates college events, races. Crib free. Pet accepted; $5. TV; cable (premium). Complimentary continental bkfst. Restaurant adj open 24 hrs. Ck-out 11 am. Cr cds: A, C, D, DS, MC, V. 🄳 ✦ ⊠ ⚭ SC

Shepherdsville (See also Elizabethtown, Louisville)

Motel

✔ ★ **DAYS INN.** *KY 44E, I-65 exit 117. 502/543-3011.* 120 rms, 2 story. S $38; D $44; each addl $6; under 12 free; higher rates Kentucky Derby, special events. Crib free. Pet accepted. TV; cable. Pool. Restaurant adj open 24 hrs. Ck-out 11 am. Cr cds: A, C, D, DS, MC, V. ✦ ≈ ⊠ ⚭ SC

Somerset (See also London)

Motel

✔ ★ **SOMERSET LODGE.** *725 S US 27. 606/678-4195; FAX 606/679-3299.* 100 rms, 1-2 story. S $42; D $50; each addl $5; under 12 free. Pet accepted; $85. TV; cable (premium). Pool; wading pool. Playground. Restaurant 6 am-9 pm. Rm serv. Ck-out noon. Meeting rms. Business servs avail. Lawn games. Cr cds: A, C, D, DS, MC, V. 🄳 ✦ ≈ ⊠ ⚭ SC

Walton *(See also Covington)*

Motel

✔★ **DAYS INN RICHWOOD.** *11177 Frontage Rd, Jct I-75, KY 338 exit 175.* 606/485-4151. 137 rms, 2 story. S, D $38-$55; each addl $7. Crib free. Pet accepted. TV; cable. Pool. Playground. Restaurant adj open 24 hrs. Ck-out 11 am. Sundries. Cr cds: A, C, D, DS, MC, V. 🐾 🏊 ⊠ 🐾 **SC**

Williamsburg

Motel

★★ **HOLIDAY INN EXPRESS.** *30 KY 92W, I-75 exit 11. 606/549-3450; FAX 606/549-8161.* 100 rms, 2-3 story. No elvtr. S, D $65; under 18 free. Crib free. Pet accepted. TV; cable (premium). Pool. Complimentary continental bkfst. Rm serv. Ck-out noon. Meeting rms. Business servs avail. In-rm modem link. Cr cds: A, C, D, DS, JCB, MC, V. **D** 🐾 🏊 ⊠ 🐾 **SC**

Williamstown *(See also Covington)*

Motel

★ **DAYS INN.** *211 W KY 36, 1-75 exit 154. 606/824-5025; FAX 606/824-5028.* 50 rms, 1-2 story. S $36-$40; D $45-$51; each addl $5; under 12 free. Crib free. Pet accepted, some restrictions. TV; cable. Pool. Coffee in lobby. Restaurant adj. Ck-out 11 am. Cr cds: A, C, D, DS, MC, V. 🐾 🏊 ⊠ 🐾 **SC**

Louisiana

Alexandria

Motels

★ ★ **BEST WESTERN OF ALEXANDRIA.** *2720 W MacArthur Dr (71303). 318/445-5530; FAX 318/445-8496.* 150 rms, 2 story. S $49; D $56; each addl $6; suites $81-$125; under 18 free. Crib free. Pet accepted. TV; cable (premium). Pool; wading pool, poolside serv. Restaurant adj 5-10 pm. Bar 4-10 pm. Ck-out noon. Meeting rms. Business servs avail. Bellhops. Valet serv. Airport transportation. Microwaves avail. Picnic tables. Cr cds: A, C, D, DS, MC, V. 🐾 🏊 ⛦ 🔥 **SC**

↙ ★ ★ **RAMADA INN.** *2211 N MacArthur Dr (71301). 318/443-2561; FAX 318/473-0142.* 167 rms, 2 story. S $46; D $51; each addl $5; suites $95-$125; under 18 free. Pet accepted, some restrictions. TV; cable (premium). Pool. Restaurant 6 am-2 pm, 5-9 pm. Bar 9-2 am. Coin lndry. Meeting rms. Business servs avail. Valet serv. Airport transportation. Cr cds: A, D, MC, V. **D** 🐾 🏊 ⛦ **SC**

↙ ★ **RODEWAY INN.** *742 MacArthur Dr (71301). 318/448-1611; FAX 318/473-2984.* 121 rms, 2 story. S $36-$40; D $40-$50; each addl $10; suites $57-$62; studio rms $38-$50; under 17 free. Crib free. Pet accepted; $25 deposit. TV; cable (premium), VCR avail. Pool; wading pool. Restaurant adj open 24 hrs. Ck-out noon. Business servs avail. Airport transportation. Microwaves avail. Cr cds: A, C, D, DS, MC, V. 🐾 🏊 🔥 **SC**

Baton Rouge

Motels

(Rates may be higher during Mardi Gras Festival & football wkends)

↙ ★ ★ **LA QUINTA.** *2333 S Acadian Thrwy (70808), off I-10 exit 157B. 504/924-9600; FAX 504/924-2609.* 142 rms, 2 story. S, D $67-$74; each addl $7; under 18 free. Crib free. Pet accepted, some restrictions. TV; cable (premium). Pool. Complimentary continental bkfst. Coffee in rms. Restaurant adj open 24 hrs. Ck-out noon. Coin lndry. Meeting rms. Business servs avail. In-rm modem link. Valet serv. Airport transportation. Health club privileges. Cr cds: A, C, D, DS, MC, V. **D** 🐾 🏊 ⛦ 🔥 **SC**

↙ ★ ★ **SHONEY'S INN.** *9919 Gwenadele Dr (70816), at jct I-12, US 61; Airline Hwy exit 2B. 504/925-8399; FAX 504/927-1731; res: 800/222-2222.* 196 rms, 2 story. S $70; D $78; suites $100; under 18 free; wkend rates. Crib free. Pet accepted, some restrictions. TV; cable. Pool. Complimentary coffee. Complimentary continental bkfst. Restaurant 6 am-midnight; Fri-Sat to 3 am. Ck-out noon. Meeting rms. Business servs avail. Microwaves avail. Cr cds: A, C, D, DS, ER, MC, V. **D** 🐾 🏊 ⛦ 🔥 **SC**

Bossier City <small>(See also Shreveport)</small>

Motel

★ ★ **RESIDENCE INN BY MARRIOTT.** *1001 Gould Dr (71111), at I-20 Old Minden Rd exit. 318/747-6220; FAX 318/747-3424.* 72 kit. units, 2 story. S, D $94-$134. Pet accepted, some restrictions; $90-$150. TV; cable (premium). Pool; whirlpool. Complimentary continental bkfst. Ck-out noon. Business servs avail. In-rm modem link. Valet serv. Sundries. Health club privileges. Refrigerators. Private patios, balconies. Picnic tables, grills. Cr cds: A, C, D, DS, JCB, MC, V. **D** 🐾 🏊 ⛦ 🔥 **SC**

Hammond <small>(See also Baton Rouge)</small>

Motel

↙ ★ **BEST WESTERN.** *3020 US 190 W (70401). 504/542-8555.* 62 rms, 2 story. S $43; D $48; each addl $5; under 12 free; higher rates special events. Pet accepted, some restrictions. TV; cable (premium). Restaurant 6 am-10 pm. Bar. Ck-out 11 am. Meeting rm. Valet serv. Cr cds: A, C, D, DS, MC, V. **D** 🐾 🏊 ⛦ 🔥 **SC**

Lafayette *(See also New Iberia)*

Motels

★ ★ **HOLIDAY INN NORTH.** *2716 NE Evangeline Thrwy (70507), at I-10.* 318/233-0003; FAX 318/233-0360. 196 rms, 2 story. S, D $65-$77; each addl $4; under 18 free. Crib free. Pet accepted, some restrictions. TV; cable (premium). Pool; wading pool. Complimentary continental bkfst. Complimentary coffee in rms. Restaurant 6:30 am-10 pm. Rm serv. Bar 4:30 pm-2 am. Ck-out noon. Coin lndry. Meeting rms. In-rm modem link. Bellhops. Valet serv. Free airport transportation. Game rm. Cr cds: A, C, D, DS, JCB, MC, V.
D 🐾 🖎 🖎 SC

★ ★ **LA QUINTA.** *2100 NE Evangeline Thrwy (70501), at I-10.* 318/233-5610; FAX 318/235-2104. 140 rms, 2 story. S $59-$73; D $66-$73; each addl $7; under 18 free. Crib free. Pet accepted, some restrictions. TV; cable (premium). Pool. Complimentary continental bkfst. Restaurant adj open 24 hrs. Ck-out noon. Business servs avail. In-rm modem link. Microwaves avail. Cr cds: A, C, D, DS, MC, V. D 🐾 🖎 🖎 SC

✔ ★ **RED ROOF INN.** *1718 N University Ave (70507), I-10 exit 101.* 318/233-3339; FAX 318/233-7206. 108 rms, 2 story. S $33; D $41-$49; each addl $8; under 18 free; higher rates special events. Crib free. Pet accepted, some restrictions. TV. Complimentary coffee in lobby. Restaurant nearby. Ck-out noon. Business servs avail. Valet serv. Cr cds: A, C, D, DS, MC, V. D 🐾 🖎 🖎 🖎 SC

Metairie *(See also New Orleans)*

Motor Hotel

(Rates may be higher during Mardi Gras Festival & football wkends)

★ ★ **QUALITY HOTEL.** *2261 N Causeway Blvd (70001), I-10 and Causeway, exit 228.* 504/833-8211; FAX 504/833-8213. 204 rms, 10 story. S, D $69-$119; under 18 free; wkend rates; higher rates special events. Crib free. Pet accepted; $25 deposit. TV; cable (premium), VCR avail. Heated pool. Complimentary coffee in rms. Restaurant 6:30 am- 2 pm, 5-10 pm. Rm serv. Ck-out noon. Coin lndry. Meeting rms. Business servs avail. In-rm modem link. Bellhops. Valet serv. Gift shop. Free airport, French Quarter transportation. Exercise equipt; weights, treadmill, sauna. Microwaves avail. Cr cds: A, D, DS, MC, V.
D 🐾 ≈ 🏋 🖎 🖎 SC

Hotel

★ ★ ★ **DOUBLETREE-LAKESIDE.** *3838 N Causeway Blvd (70002).* 504/836-5253; FAX 504/846-4562. 210 rms, 16 story. S, D $79-$165; suites $180; under 17 free; wkend rates. Crib free. Pet accepted; fee. TV; cable (premium). Indoor pool; whirlpool. Coffee in rms. Restaurant 6 am-2 pm, 5-10 pm. Bar noon-midnight. Ck-out noon. Meeting rms. Business servs avail. In-rm modem link. Gift shop. Barber. Garage parking $4. Free airport transportation. Lighted tennis. Exercise rm; instructor, weights, bicycles, sauna. Some refrigerators; microwaves avail. View of Lake Pontchartrain. Luxury level. Cr cds: A, C, D, DS, JCB, MC, V. D 🐾 🏋 ≈ 🏋 🖎 🖎 🖎 SC

Monroe and West Monroe

Motels

★ ★ **LA QUINTA.** *(1035 US 165 Bypass, Monroe 71203)* 318/322-3900; FAX 318/323-5537. 130 units, 2 story. S $55; D $61; each addl $5; suites $75; under 18 free. Crib free. Pet accepted. TV; cable. Pool. Complimentary continental bkfst. Restaurant nearby. Meeting rms. Business servs avail. In-rm modem link. Free airport, bus depot transportation. Cr cds: A, C, D, DS, MC, V. D 🐾 ≈ 🖎 🖎 SC

★ **RED ROOF INN.** *(102 Constitution Dr, West Monroe 71292)* 318/388-2420; FAX 318/388-2499. 97 rms, 3 story. S $36.99-$47.99; D $41.99-$52.99; each addl $6; under 18 free. Crib free. Pet accepted. TV; cable (premium). Complimentary coffee in lobby. Restaurant adj open 24 hrs. Ck-out noon. Business servs avail. Cr cds: A, D, DS, MC, V.
D 🐾 🖎 🖎

✔ ★ **TRAVELODGE.** *(2102 Louisville Ave, Monroe 71201)* 318/325-5851; FAX 318/323-3808. 130 rms. S $37; D $43; suites $51-$53. Pet accepted. TV; cable. Pool. Playground. Complimentary continental bkfst. Restaurant 6:30-10:30 am. Bar 4 pm-2 am. Ck-out noon. Coin lndry. Meeting rms. Business servs avail. Valet serv. Cr cds: A, C, D, DS, MC, V. D 🐾 ≈ 🖎 🖎 SC

New Iberia (See also Lafayette)

Motel

✔ ★ ★ **HOLIDAY INN.** 2915 LA 14, 1 mi W at jct US 90, LA 14. 318/367-1201; FAX 318/367-7877. 177 rms, 2 story. S $51-$61; D $57-$67; each addl $6; under 18 free. Crib free. Pet accepted, some restrictions. TV; cable (premium), VCR avail. Pool. Playground. Restaurant 6 am-2 pm, 6-10 pm. Rm serv. Bar 5 pm-midnight. Ck-out 11 am. Coin lndry. Meeting rms. Business servs avail. In-rm modem link. Valet serv. Sundries. Cr cds: A, C, D, DS, JCB, MC, V. 🅳 ⭐ 🏊 📶 🐾 SC

New Orleans

Motels

(Most accommodations increase their rates greatly for the Mardi Gras Festival and the Sugar Bowl Game wkend. Reservations should be made as far ahead as possible and confirmed.)

★ ★ **AMBASSADOR HOTEL.** 535 Tchoupitoulas St (70130), in central business district. 504/527-5271; res: 888/527-5271; FAX 504/527-5270. E-mail amb@neworleans .com; web www.neworleans.com/ambas sador. 71 rms, 4 story. S, D $59-$179; under 16 free; higher rates special events (3, 4-day min). Crib free. Pet accepted; $50 deposit. Valet parking $12. TV; cable. Complimentary coffee in rms. Restaurant 7 am-10 pm. Rm serv noon-2 pm, 7-9 pm. Bar. Ck-out noon. Business servs avail. In-rm modem link. Bellhops. Concierge. Airport transportation. Cr cds: A, C, D, DS, MC, V. 🅳 ⭐ 📶 🐾 SC

★ **FRENCH QUARTER COURTYARD.** 1101 N Rampart (70116), in French Quarter. 504/522-7333; FAX 504/522-3908; res: 800/290-4233. E-mail amb@neworleans .com; web www.neworleans.com /ambassador. 51 rms, 2-3 story. S, D $69-$250; under 17 free; higher rates special events. Pet accepted. Valet parking $10. TV; cable. Pool; poolside serv. Complimentary continental bkfst. Restaurant nearby. Bar open 24 hrs. Ck-out noon. Business servs avail. Bellhops. Valet serv. Some balconies. Cr cds: A, C, D, DS, MC, V. ⭐ 📶 🐾 SC

Inns

★ ★ **CHIMES.** Constantinople St & Coliseum St (70115), west of central business district. 504/899-2621; res: 800/729-4640. 5 rms, 3 with full bathrm. Oct-May: S, D $79-$129; wkends (3-day min); higher rates Jazz Fest; lower rates rest of yr. Crib free. Pet accepted, some restrictions. TV; cable (premium). Complimentary continental bkfst. Complimentary coffee in rm. Ck-out, Ck-in hrs vary. Luggage handling. Picnic tables. Totally nonsmoking. Antiques. No cr cds accepted. 🅳 ⭐ 📶 🐾

★ ★ **RATHBONE INN.** 1227 Esplanade Ave (70116), near French Quarter. 504/947-2101; res: 800/947-2101. 9 kit. units, shower only, 3 story, 3 suites. S, D $90-$145; each addl $10; under 12 free; higher rates jazz fest. Pet accepted. TV; cable. Complimentary continental bkfst. Complimentary coffee in rms. Ck-out noon, ck-in 1-2 pm. Business servs avail. Luggage handling. Coin lndry. Street parking. Whirlpool. Refrigerators, microwaves. Built in 1850 as mansion for private family. Antebellum period decor; ornamental cast-iron fence. Cr cds: A, C, D, DS, MC, V. ⭐ 🐾 SC

✔ ★ **RUE ROYAL INN.** 1006 Rue Royal (70116), in French Quarter. 504/524-3900; res: 800/776-3901; FAX 504/558-0566. 17 kit. units, 4 story. Sept-May: S, D $75-$120; each addl $15; suites $145; under 12 free; hols, special events (3-4-day min); higher rates jazz fest; lower rates rest of yr. Pet accepted, some restrictions. TV; cable, VCR avail. Complimentary continental bkfst. Coffee in rms. Ck-out noon, ck-in varies. Luggage handling. Parking $8. Airport, RR station transportation. Refrigerators, microwaves. Built in 1830 as Creole townhouse. Cr cds: A, C, D, DS, JCB, MC, V. 🅳 ⭐ 🐾 SC

Ruston

Motel

★ ★ **HOLIDAY INN.** 3/4 mi E at jct US 167, I-20. 318/255-5901; FAX 318/255-3729. 231 rms, 1-2 story. S, D $69-$79; each addl $10; suites $129; under 19 free. Crib free. Pet accepted. TV; cable. 2 pools; wading pool. Playground. Restaurant 6 am-10 pm. Rm serv. Ck-out noon. Coin lndry. Meeting rms. Business servs avail. In-rm modem link. Valet serv. Cr cds: A, C, D, DS, JCB, MC, V. 🅳 ⭐ 🏊 📶 🐾 SC

Shreveport *(See also Bossier City)*

Motor Hotel

★ ★ **RAMADA INN.** *5116 Monkhouse Dr (71109). 318/635-7531; FAX 318/635-1600.* 255 rms, 2-4 story. S $59-$69; D $64-$74; each addl $10; suites $125-$150; under 18 free. Crib avail. Pet accepted. TV; cable (premium). Pool; whirlpool. Restaurant 6 am-10 pm. Rm serv. Bar 11-2 am; entertainment. Ck-out noon. Convention facilities. Business servs avail. Bellhops. Gift shop. Free airport, bus depot transportation. Exercise equipt; weight machine, bicycles. Game rm. Cr cds: A, C, D, DS, JCB, MC, V. [D] 🐾 🏊 ✗ 🏋 🔥 SC

Slidell *(See also New Orleans)*

Motel

★ ★ **LA QUINTA.** *794 E I-10 Service Rd (70461), exit 266. 504/643-9770; FAX 504/641-4476.* Web www.laquinta.com. 177 rms, 2 story. S $59-$69; D $69-$79; each addl $6; under 18 free; higher rates special events. Crib free. Pet accepted. TV; cable (premium), VCR avail. Pool. Complimentary continental bkfst. Restaurant adj 6 am-10 pm. Bar. Ck-out noon. Coin lndry. Meeting rms. Business servs avail. In-rm modem link. Health club privileges. Game rm. Microwaves avail. Cr cds: A, C, D, DS, MC, V. [D] 🐾 🏊 🏋 🔥 SC

Thibodaux

Motel

★ ★ **HOWARD JOHNSON.** *201 N Canal Blvd. 504/447-9071; res: 800/952-2968; FAX 504/447-5752.* 118 rms, 2 story. S $48-$150; D $53-$150; each addl $5; suites $75-$150; under 18 free; higher rates special events. Crib free. Pet accepted, some restrictions; $10. TV; cable (premium), VCR avail (movies). Complimentary full bkfst. Restaurant open 24 hrs. Rm serv 6 am-midnight. Bar noon-2 am; entertainment Sat. Ck-out noon. Meeting rms. Business servs avail. Valet serv. Lighted tennis, pro. Exercise equipt; weight machine, treadmill, sauna. Pool; poolside serv. Game rm. Rec rm. Refrigerators, microwaves avail. Cr cds: A, C, D, DS, JCB, MC, V. [D] 🐾 🏌 🏊 ✗ 🏋 🔥

Maine

Augusta *(See also Waterville)*

Motels

★ ★ **AUGUSTA.** *390 Western Ave. 207/622-6371; FAX 207/621-0349.* 98 rms, 30 kit. suites, 2 story. Mid-June-late Oct: S, D $89-$169; each addl $10; under 18 free; lower rates rest of yr. Pet accepted. TV; cable (premium). Pool; wading pool. Complimentary continental bkfst. Coffee in rms. Restaurant 6 am-2 pm, 4 pm-1 am. Bar. Ck-out 11 am. Coin lndry. Meeting rms. Business servs avail. Valet serv. Microwaves avail. Cr cds: A, C, D, DS, MC, V. Ⓓⓟ🏊⚐🐾 SC

★ ★ ★ **BEST WESTERN SENATOR INN.** *284 Western Ave, at I-95 exit 30. 207/622-5804.* 103 rms, 1-2 story. July-Aug: S $79-$99; D $89-$109; each addl $9; suites $149-$189; under 18 free; varied lower rates rest of yr. Crib free. Pet accepted, some restrictions; $50. TV; cable (premium), VCR avail (movies). 2 heated pools, 1 indoor. Playground. Complimentary full bkfst. Complimentary coffee in rms. Restaurant 6:30 am-10 pm. Rm serv. Bar to 1 am. Ck-out noon. Coin lndry. Meeting rms. Business servs avail. In-rm modem link. Sundries. Exercise rm; instructor, stair machine, treadmill, sauna. Indoor putting green. Massage. Game rm. Some refrigerators, fireplaces. Picnic tables. Cr cds: A, C, D, DS, MC, V. Ⓓⓟ🏊🏃🐾⚐🔥 SC

★ **MOTEL 6.** *18 Edison Dr. 207/622-0000; FAX 207/622-1048.* 68 rms, 2 story. Late June-Sept: S $32.99; D $38.99; each addl $3; under 18 free. Crib free. Pet accepted, some restrictions. TV; cable (premium). Complimentary coffee in lobby. Restaurant nearby. Ck-out noon. Coin lndry. Cr cds: A, D, DS, MC, V. Ⓓⓟ⚐🔥

Bailey Island *(See also Brunswick)*

Motel

★ **COOK'S ISLAND VIEW.** *on ME 24. 207/833-7780.* 18 rms, 3 kits. No A/C. July-Labor Day, hol wkends: D $68-$78; kit. units $12 addl; under 18 free; lower rates after Memorial Day-June, after Labor Day-Oct. Closed rest of yr. Pet accepted, some restrictions. TV; cable. Pool. Restaurant nearby. Ck-out noon. Cr cds: A, MC, V. Ⓓⓟ🏊🔥

Bangor

Motels

★ ★ ★ **BEST WESTERN WHITE HOUSE.** *155 Littlefield Ave, W at I95 exit 44. 207/862-3737; FAX 207/862-6465.* 64 rms, 3 story. May-Oct: S $59-$72; D $64-$78; each addl $5; family rm $79-$94; under 12 free; lower rates rest of yr. Crib $3. Pet accepted. TV; cable, VCR avail (movies). Heated pool. Complimentary continental bkfst. Complimentary coffee in rms. Restaurant adj open 24 hrs. Bar 4 pm-1 am. Ck-out 11 am. Coin lndry. Business servs avail. In-rm modem link. Sundries. Downhill/x-country ski 4 mi. Sauna. Lawn games. Refrigerators avail. Picnic tables. Cr cds: A, C, D, DS, ER, MC, V. ⓟ➤🏊⚐🔥 SC

★ ★ **COMFORT INN.** *750 Hogan Rd. 207/942-7899; FAX 207/942-6463.* 95 rms, 2 story. Mid-June-Oct: S $59-$69; D $69-$79; each addl $5; under 19 free; lower rates rest of yr. Crib free. Pet accepted; $6. TV; cable (premium). Pool; poolside serv. Complimentary continental bkfst. Complimentary coffee in rms. Restaurant 7 am-9 pm. Ck-out noon. Meeting rms. Business servs avail. Sundries. Free airport transportation. X-country ski 10 mi. Shopping mall adj. Cr cds: A, C, D, DS, ER, MC, V. Ⓓⓟ➤🏊⚐🔥 SC

★ ★ **DAYS INN.** *250 Odlin Rd. 207/942-8272; FAX 207/942-1382.* 101 rms, 2 story. July-Oct: S $50-$65; D $55-$80; each addl $6; under 12 free; lower rates rest of yr. Crib free. Pet accepted; $16. TV; cable (premium), VCR avail. Indoor pool; whirlpool. Complimentary continental bkfst. Restaurant adj 11-1 am. Ck-out 11 am. Business servs avail. Sundries. Free airport transportation. Downhill/x-country ski 12 mi. Game rm. Cr cds: A, C, D, DS, ER, JCB, MC, V. Ⓓⓟ➤🏊⚐🔥 SC

✔ ★ **ECONO LODGE.** *327 Odlin Rd. 207/945-0111; FAX 207/942-8856; res: 800/393-0111.* 128 rms, 4 story. S $28.95-$47.95; D $29.95-$55.95; under 19 free. Crib $6. Pet accepted. TV; cable (premium). Complimentary coffee in lobby. Ck-out 11 am. Coin

Indry. Business servs avail. In-rm modem link. Downhill/x-country ski 7 mi. Cr cds: A, D, DS, MC, V. [D] [⟲] [⟰] [⟲] [⟲] [SC]

★ ★ ★ **HOLIDAY INN-CIVIC CENTER.** *500 Main St. 207/947-8651; FAX 207/942-2848.* 122 rms, 2-4 story. May-Oct: S, D $75; each addl $10; suites $100-$150; under 19 free; varied lower rates rest of yr. Crib free. Pet accepted. TV; cable (premium). Pool. Complimentary coffee in rms. Restaurant 6:30 am-2 pm, 5-10 pm. Rm serv. Bar 3:30 pm-1 am; entertainment Tues-Sat. Ck-out noon. Coin lndry. Meeting rms. Business servs avail. In-rm modem link. Valet serv. Sundries. Free airport transportation. Health club privileges. Opp Civic Center. Cr cds: A, C, D, DS, JCB, MC, V. [D] [⟲] [⟰] [⟲] [⟲] [SC]

✔ ★ **MAIN STREET INN.** *480 Main St. 207/942-5281; FAX 207/947-8733.* 64 rms, 2 story. July-Oct: S, D $36-$59; each addl (after 4) $5; under 18 free; lower rates rest of yr. Crib free. Pet accepted. TV; cable. Complimentary continental bkfst. Ck-out 11 am. Business servs avail. Cr cds: A, D, DS, MC, V. [⟲] [⟲] [⟲] [SC]

★ **PENOBSCOT INN.** *570 Main St. 207/947-0566; res: 800/468-2878 (New England States & CN).* 50 rms, 2 story. June-Oct: S $59-$69; D $64-$74; each addl $5; under 12 free; lower rates rest of yr. Crib free. Pet accepted. TV; cable, VCR avail. Restaurant 7 am-10 pm; Sun to 9 pm. Bar 11-1 am. Ck-out 11 am. Business servs avail. Sundries. Cr cds: A, D, DS, MC, V. [⟲] [⟲] [⟲] [SC]

✔ ★ **RODEWAY INN.** *482 Odlin Rd, near Intl Airport. 207/942-6301; FAX 207/941-0949.* 98 rms, 2 story. July-mid-Oct: S $39.95-$49.95; D $44.95-$59.95; each addl $5; under 18 free; lower rates rest of yr. Crib free. Pet accepted; $5. TV; cable (premium). Restaurant 11 am-9 pm. Bar from noon. Ck-out 11 am. Meeting rms. Business servs avail. Sundries. Airport, bus depot transportation. Downhill ski 12 mi; x-country ski 5 mi. Picnic tables. Cr cds: A, D, DS, ER, MC, V. [⟲] [⟲] [✈] [⟲] [⟲] [SC]

✔ ★ **SCOTTISH INNS.** *1476 Hammond St. 207/945-2934; FAX 207/945-3456.* 89 rms, 36 A/C, 30 kits. July-Aug: S $49.95; D, kit. units $59.95; each addl $5; under 18 free; wkly rates (off season); higher rates: Univ of Maine graduation, hols; lower rates rest of yr. Crib $5. Pet accepted; $5. TV; cable (premium). Complimentary coffee in lobby. Restaurant nearby. Bar 4 pm-midnight. Ck-out 11 am. Coin lndry. Business servs avail. Downhill ski 4 mi. Cr cds: A, C, D, DS, MC, V. [⟲] [⟲] [⟲] [⟲] [SC]

Motor Hotel

★ ★ ★ **HOLIDAY INN.** *404 Odlin Rd, 3 mi W on I-395, near Intl Airport. 207/947-0101; FAX 207/947-7619.* 207 rms, 3 story. July-Oct: S $65-$80; D $75-$90; each addl $10; under 19 free; lower rates rest of yr. Crib free. Pet accepted. TV; cable (premium), VCR avail. 2 pools; 1 indoor, whirlpool. Complimentary coffee in rms. Restaurant 6:30 am-1:30 pm, 5-10 pm. Rm serv. Bar noon-1 am; entertainment. Ck-out noon. Coin lndry. Meeting rms. Business servs avail. In-rm modem link. Sundries. Valet serv. Free airport transportation. Downhill ski 15 mi; x-country ski 10 mi. Health club privileges. Some refrigerators. Cr cds: A, C, D, DS, JCB, MC, V. [D] [⟲] [⟰] [⟲] [✈] [✈] [⟲] [⟲] [SC]

Hotel

★ ★ ★ **MARRIOTT-BANGOR AIRPORT.** *308 Godfrey Blvd, at Intl Airport. 207/947-6721; FAX 207/941-9761.* 101 rms, 9 story. S, D $98-$155; each addl $15; under 18 free. Crib free. Pet accepted. TV; cable (premium). Pool. Restaurant 6 am-2:30 pm, 5-11 pm. Bar 2 pm-midnight. Ck-out noon. Meeting rms. Business servs avail. In-rm modem link. Gift shop. Validated parking. Airport transportation. Downhill/x-country ski 7 mi. Exercise equipt; stair machine, treadmill. Enclosed walkway to airport. Cr cds: A, C, D, DS, ER, MC, V. [⟲] [⟲] [⟰] [✈] [✈] [⟲] [⟲] [SC]

Inns

✔ ★ ★ **PHENIX INN AT WEST MARKET SQUARE.** *20 Broad St, in West Market Square. 207/947-0411; FAX 207/947-0255.* 32 rms, 4 story. Mid-July-mid-Oct: S, D $64.95-$89.95; under 13 free; lower rates rest of yr. Crib free. Pet accepted. TV; cable, VCR avail (movies $3). Complimentary continental bkfst. Restaurant adj 11 am-midnight. Ck-out noon, ck-in 1 pm. Coin lndry. Meeting rm. Business servs avail. Refrigerator avail. Restored commercial building (1873) located in West Market Square; furnished with antique reproductions. Near river. Cr cds: A, C, D, DS, MC, V. [D] [⟲] [⟲] [⟲] [⟲] [SC]

Bar Harbor

Motel

★ ★ **WONDER VIEW INN.** *50 Eden St. 207/288-3358; res: 888/439-8439; FAX 207/288-2005; 800 888/439-8439.* E-mail wonderview@acadia.net; web www.maineguide .com/barharbor/wonderview/. 79 rms, 10 with shower only, 14 A/C, 1-2 story. July-Labor

Day: S $80; D $85-$130; each addl $10; under 12 free; lower rates early May-June, Labor Day-Oct. Closed rest of yr. Crib $10. Pet accepted, some restrictions; $10. TV; cable. Pool. Complimentary coffee in lobby. Restaurant 7-10 am, 5-9 pm. Bar from 5 pm. Ck-out 11 am. Business servs avail. Refrigerator avail. Balconies. Picnic tables. Cr cds: A, DS, MC, V.

Bath (See also Boothbay Harbor, Brunswick, Freeport)

Motel

★ ★ ★ **HOLIDAY INN.** *139 Western Ave. 207/443-9741; FAX 207/442-8281.* 141 rms, 3 story. Late June-early Oct: S $79-$89; D $89-$99; each addl $10; under 19 free; lower rates rest of yr. Crib free. Pet accepted. TV; cable, premium. Heated pool; whirlpool. Complimentary coffee in rms. Restaurant 6 am-2 pm, 5-9 pm; wkends 7-11 am, 5-9 pm. Bar 11-1 am, Sun from noon; entertainment Wed-Sat. Ck-out noon. Meeting rm. Business servs avail. In-rm modem link. Valet serv. Sundries. Exercise equipt; treadmill, stair machine, sauna. Many refrigerators. Cr cds: A, C, D, DS, ER, JCB, MC, V.

Belfast (See also Bucksport)

Motels

★ ★ **BELFAST HARBOR INN.** *1/2 mi N on US 1. 207/338-2740; FAX 207/338-5205; res: 800/545-8576.* 61 rms, 2 story. July-Sept: S, D $85-$95; under 12 free; wkly rates; lower rates rest of yr. Crib free. Pet accepted. TV; cable (premium). Pool. Restaurant 6 am-9 pm. Ck-out 11 am. Meeting rm. Business servs avail. Downhill/x-country ski 15 mi. Balconies. Picnic tables. Overlooks Penobscot Bay. Cr cds: A, C, D, DS, MC, V.

★ **WONDERVIEW COTTAGES.** *Searsport Ave, 3 mi NE on US 1, ME 3. 207/338-1455.* 20 kit. cottages. No A/C. July-Labor Day, wkly: kit. cottages for 2-6, $440-$760; lower rates Apr-June, Sept-late Oct. Closed rest of yr. Crib free. Pet accepted. TV; cable. Playground. Restaurant nearby. Ck-out 10:30 am. Lawn games. Fireplaces. Screened porches. Picnic tables, grills. Private beach on Penobscot Bay. Cr cds: DS, MC, V.

Inn

★ ★ **BELFAST BAY MEADOWS.** *192 Northport Ave, S on US 1. 207/338-5320; FAX 207/338-5715; res: 800/335-2370.* 19 rms, 1-3 story. July-Aug: S, D $75-$145; each addl $10; lower rates rest of yr. Crib free. Pet accepted. TV in sitting rm, some rooms; cable, VCR avail (free movies). Complimentary full bkfst. Restaurant 6-9 pm. Ck-out 11 am, ck-in 2:30 pm. Meeting rm. Business servs avail. Refrigerators avail. Turn-of-the-century country inn; antiques. Overlooks bay. Totally nonsmoking. Cr cds: A, DS, MC, V.

Bethel

Inn

★ ★ **BRIAR LEA B & B.** *150 Mayville Rd, 1 mi N on US 2 at jct ME 26. 207/824-4717; res: 888/479-5735.* E-mail briarlea@megalink.com. 6 rms, 3 with shower only. No A/C. No rm phones. Jan-Apr, mid-Sept-mid-Oct: S $71; D $81-$91; each addl $15; ski plans; wkends, hols (2-day min); higher rates major hols; lower rates rest of yr. Crib $15. Pet accepted, some restrictions. TV in common rm; cable, VCR avail. Complimentary full bkfst. Restaurant 6:30-11 am, 5-9:30 pm; Sun to noon. Ck-out 11 am, ck-in 4 pm. Downhill ski 5 mi; x-country ski on site. Built in 1850s; farmhouse atmosphere; antiques. Cr cds: A, MC, V.

Resort

★ ★ **BETHEL INN & COUNTRY CLUB.** *On the town common, at jct US 2, ME 5, 26, 35. 207/824-2175; FAX 207/824-2233; res: 800/654-0125.* E-mail connorsa@nxi.com; web www.bethelinn.com. 60 rms in 5-bldg complex, 40 2-bedrm townhouses. No A/C. May-Oct, Dec-Mar: S $79-$129/person; each addl $55; MAP: suites $90-$175; EP: townhouses $79-$129/person; lower rates rest of yr. Pet accepted. TV; cable, VCR avail. Heated pool; whirlpool; poolside serv. Supervised child's activities (July 7-Labor Day); ages 5-12. Dining rm 7:30-9:30 am, 11:30 am-3 pm, 5:30-9 pm. Bars; entertainment. Ck-out 11 am, ck-in 2 pm. Meeting rms. Business servs avail. Gift shop. Tennis. 18-hole golf, greens fee $35-$40, pro, putting green, driving range. Canoes, sailboats. Downhill ski 7 mi; x-country ski on site. Exercise equipt; weights, bicycles, saunas. Massage. Lawn games. Cr cds: A, C, D, DS, MC, V.

Bingham (See also Skowhegan)

Motel

✔ ★ **BINGHAM MOTOR INN.** US 201, Solon Rd, 1 mi S on US 201. 207/672-4135. 20 rms, 4 kits. July-Labor Day, hunting season: S $45.95; D $57.95; each addl $5; kit. units $5 addl; wkly; lower rates rest of yr. Crib $3. Pet accepted, some restrictions. TV; cable. Pool. Restaurant nearby. Ck-out 10 am. Downhill ski 3 mi. Lawn games. Some refrigerators. Picnic tables. Cr cds: A, MC, V.

Boothbay Harbor

Motels

✔ ★ **HILLSIDE ACRES.** (Adams Pond Rd, Boothbay 04537) 1¹/₂ mi N on Adams Rd, off ME 27. 207/633-3411. 10 units, 2 share bath, 1-2 story, 4 kit. units, 7 cottages. No A/C. No rm phones. July-Aug: S, D $40-$68; kit. cottages $63-$71; cottages $57; wkly rates; lower rates mid-May-June, Sept-mid-Oct. Closed rest of yr. Crib free. Pet accepted. TV; cable. Pool. Complimentary continental bkfst (mid-June-Labor Day). Ck-out 10:30 am. Picnic tables, grills. Cr cds: MC, V.

★ ★ **LAWNMEER INN.** (Box 505, West Boothbay Harbor 04575) 2¹/₂ mi S on ME 27. 207/633-2544; FAX 207/633-7708; res: 800/633-7645. Web www.lawnmeerinn.com. 35 rms, 1-2 story. No A/C. July-Labor Day: D $78-$138; each addl $25; lower rates: mid-May-June, wkdays after Labor Day-mid-Oct. Closed rest of yr. Pet accepted; $25. TV; cable. Restaurant 7:30-10 am, 6-9 pm. Bar 5:30-9 pm. Ck-out 11 am. Lawn games. Balconies. Built 1898. On inlet; dock. Cr cds: MC, V.

★ **THE PINES.** Box 693, Sunset Rd, 1¹/₄ mi SE, off Atlantic Ave. 207/633-4555. 29 rms. No A/C. July-Aug: S $70; D $80; each addl $6; lower rates May-June, after Sept-mid-Oct. Closed rest of yr. Crib free. Pet accepted. TV; cable. Heated pool. Playground. Ck-out 11 am. Tennis. Lawn games. Refrigerators. Balconies, decks. In wooded area; view of harbor. Cr cds: DS, MC, V.

★ ★ **SMUGGLERS COVE INN.** East Boothbay (04544), 4¹/₄ mi E on ME 96. 207/633-2800; FAX 207/633-5926; res: 800/633-3008. 60 units, 2 story, 6 kit. units (most without ovens). No A/C. Late June-Labor Day: S, D $60-$140; each addl $10; kit. units $85-$140; under 12 free; wkly rates; lower rates after Labor Day-mid-Oct. Closed rest of yr. Crib $10. Pet accepted, some restrictions; $50 deposit. TV; cable. Heated pool. Restaurant 8-10:30 am, 6-9:30 pm. Bar from 5:30 pm. Ck-out 11 am. Business servs avail. Balconies. On ocean; swimming beach. Cr cds: A, DS, MC, V.

Brunswick (See also Bailey Island)

Motels

★ **ATRIUM INN & CONVENTION CENTER.** 21 Gurnet Rd (ME 24). 207/729-5555; FAX 207/729-5149. 186 rms, 3 story. July-Aug: S, D $74-$86; each addl $5; suites $125; under 19 free; lower rates rest of yr. Crib free. Pet accepted. TV; cable, VCR (movies). Indoor pool; wading pool, whirlpool, poolside serv. Complimentary coffee in lobby. Restaurant 6 am-10 pm. Rm serv. Bar to midnight. Ck-out noon. Meeting rms. Business servs avail. Sundries. Valet serv. Coin lndry. Exercise equipt; bicycles, weight machine, sauna. Game rm. Lawn games. Refrigerators. Cr cds: A, C, D, DS, MC, V.

✔ ★ **VIKING MOTOR INN.** 287 Bath Rd. 207/729-6661; res: 800/429-6661. 26 rms, 9 kit. units. July-Oct: S, D $59-$84; each addl $5; under 12 free; wkly rates; lower rates rest of yr. Pet accepted. TV; cable. Pool. Playground. Ck-out 10 am. Lawn games. Refrigerators avail. Picnic tables, grill. Cr cds: A, D, DS, MC, V.

Bucksport (See also Bangor, Belfast, Ellsworth)

Motels

★ ★ **BEST WESTERN JED PROUTY.** 53 Maim St. 207/469-3113; FAX 207/469-3113. 40 rms, 2-4 story. July-Oct: S $79; D $89; each addl $10; suites $125; under 12 free; lower rates rest of yr. Pet accepted; some restrictions. TV; cable. Restaurant opp 5:30-9:30 pm. Ck-out 11 am. Business servs avail. In-rm modem link. On Penobscot River. Cr cds: A, C, D, DS, MC, V.

✔ ★ **BUCKSPORT MOTOR INN.** 151 Main St, ¹/₂ mi NE on US 1 (ME 3). 207/469-3111; res: 800/626-9734. 24 rms. No A/C. Aug: S $55; D $60; each addl $5; lower rates rest of yr. Pet accepted. TV; cable. Complimentary coffee in rms. Restaurant nearby. Ck-out 11 am. Cr cds: A, DS, MC, V.

Eastport *(See also Lubec)*

Inn

★ ★ **TODD HOUSE.** *1 Capen Ave. 207/853-2328.* 8 rms, 6 share bath, 2 story, 2 kits. No A/C. No rm phones. D $45-$80; each addl $5-$10; under 5 free; wkly rates. Pet accepted. TV in most rms; cable. Complimentary continental bkfst. Restaurant nearby. Ck-out 11 am, ck-in 2 pm. Picnic tables, grill. This authentic New England Cape once housed soldiers during the War of 1812. Period antiques; original chimney. Near ocean; view of bay. Cr cds: MC, V.

Ellsworth *(See also Bar Harbor)*

Motels

★ ★ **COLONIAL MOTOR LODGE.** *Bar Harbor Rd. 207/667-5548; FAX 207/667-5549.* 69 rms, 2 story, 18 kit. units. July-Aug: S $68; D $78-$88; each addl $6; suites $125; kit. units $78-$88; under 13 free; wkly rates; lower rates rest of yr. Crib $4. Pet accepted. TV; cable (premium). Indoor pool; whirlpool. Complimentary continental bkfst (June-Sept). Restaurant 11 am-9 pm. Ck-out 11 am. Business servs avail. X-country ski 15 mi. Refrigerator avail. Balconies. Picnic tables. Cr cds: A, MC, V.

★ **TWILITE.** *1 mi W on US 1 (ME 3). 207/667-8165; res: 800/395-5097.* 23 rms, some A/C. July-Labor Day: S, D $48-$75; each addl $5; lower rates Apr-June & Labor Day-mid-Dec. Closed rest of yr. Pet accepted; $25 deposit. TV; cable. Complimentary continental bkfst. Ck-out 10 am. Some refrigerators. Picnic table, grill. Cr cds: A, DS, MC, V.

Freeport *(See also Bath, Brunswick)*

Motel

★ ★ **FREEPORT INN AND CAFE.** *335 US 1S, exit 17 off I-95. 207/865-3106; FAX 207/865-6364; res: 800/998-2583.* 89 rms, 3 story. No elvtr. May-Oct: S, D $70-$120; each addl $10; lower rates rest of yr. Crib $10. Pet accepted, some restrictions. TV; cable (premium), VCR avail (movies). Pool. Restaurant 6 am-9 pm; to 8 pm off season. Ck-out 11 am. Meeting rms. Business servs avail. Valet Serv. Game rm. Lawn games. Balconies. Picnic tables. On 25 acres; river, pond; canoe. Some refrigerators. Cr cds: A, C, D, DS, MC, V.

Greenville

Motels

★ **CHALET MOOSEHEAD.** *(Greenville Junction 04442) 1 mi W, just off ME 6/15. 207/695-2950; res: 800/290-3645.* 15 rms, 8 kit. units (no ovens); 2-story motel unit, 2 kit. cottages. No A/C. Late June-early Sept, also Memorial Day, Columbus Day wkends: S, D $65; each addl $6; cottages $80-$100; kit. units $72; under 5 free; lower rates rest of yr. Pet accepted; $5. TV; cable (premium). Complimentary coffee in lobby. Restaurant nearby. Ck-out 10 am. Boat rentals. Seaplane rides nearby. Lawn games. Picnic tables, grills. On Moosehead Lake; dockage, canoes, paddleboats. Cr cds: A, DS, MC, V.

★ **GREENWOOD.** *(Greenville Junction 04442) 3 mi NW on ME 6/15. 207/695-3321; FAX 207/695-2122; res: 800/477-4386 (US & CAN).* 16 rms, 2 story. Mid-May-mid-Sept: S $55; D $55-70; each addl $5; hunting plans; lower rates rest of yr. Crib free. Pet accepted; $5. TV; cable (premium). Complimentary continental bkfst. Complimentary coffee in rms. Restaurant nearby. Ck-out 10:30 am. Meeting rm. Business servs avail. 9-hole golf privileges. Downhill/x-country ski 3 mi. Hiking trails. Lawn games. Refrigerators. Picnic tables, grills. Cr cds: A, C, D, DS, MC, V.

★ **KINEO VIEW MOTOR LODGE.** *2 mi S on ME 15/6. 207/695-4470; FAX 207/695-4656; res: 800/659-8439.* Web www.maineguide.com/moosehead/kineo.html. 12 rms, 2 story. No A/C. Memorial Day-mid-Oct: D $65-$75; each addl $5; under 13 free; wkly rates; lower rates rest of yr. Pet accepted; $5. TV. Whirlpool. Complimentary continental bkfst in season. Ck-out 10:30 am. Downhill ski 9 mi; x-country ski on site. Game rm. Lawn games. Balconies. Picnic tables. Lake views. Cr cds: A, DS, MC, V.

Houlton

Motel

★ **SCOTTISH INNS.** *RFD #4 Box 450 (Bangor Rd), 1 mi S on US 2A.* 207/532-2236; FAX 207/532-9893. 43 rms. May-mid-Nov: S, D $44-$48; each addl $6; lower rates rest of yr. Crib $6. Pet accepted; $6. TV; cable (premium). Complimentary coffee in lobby. Restaurant nearby. Ck-out 11 am. Business servs avail. Refrigerators. Cr cds: A, DS, MC, V. 🐾 ⬧ ⬧ ⬧ SC

Kennebunk *(See also Kennebunkport, Old Orchard Beach, Portland, Saco)*

Inn

★ ★ **KENNEBUNK INN 1799.** *45 Main St (US 1).* 207/985-3351; FAX 207/985-8865. 28 rms, 3 story, 4 suites. Some rm phones. Mid-June-late Oct: D $95-$105; each addl $10; suites $155; under 13 free; lower rates rest of yr. Crib $10. Pet accepted. TV in some rms, sitting rm; cable. Complimentary continental bkfst. Dining rm 5-9:30 pm. Ck-out 11 am, ck-in 3 pm. Business servs avail. Built 1799; turn-of-the-century decor, antiques, library. Cr cds: A, DS, MC, V. 🐾 ⬧ ⬧

Kennebunkport *(See also Kennebunk, Old Orchard Beach, Portland, Saco)*

Motel

★ ★ **SEASIDE.** *Gooch's Beach, ³/₄ mi S on ME 35.* 207/967-4461; FAX 207/967-1135. Web www.kennebunkbeach.com. 22 rms, 1-2 story, 10 kit. cottages. No A/C. July-late Aug: S, D $109-$178; wkly rates; varied lower rates rest of yr. Cottages closed Nov-Apr. Crib avail. Pet accepted, some restrictions; $50 refundable. TV; cable. Playground. Ck-out 11 am. Coin lndry. Lawn games. Refrigerators. Private patios, balconies. Private beach; boat ramps. Cr cds: A, MC, V. D 🐾 ⬧ ⬧ ⬧ ⬧

Inn

★ ★ ★ **CAPTAIN JEFFERDS.** *5 blks S on Ocean Ave, left at River Green, then left at next corner.* 207/967-2311; res: 800/839-6844; FAX 207/967-0721. E-mail captjeff@captainjefferdsinn.com; web www.captainjefferdsinn.com. 16 rms, 3 story, 1 kit. suite in attached carriage house. Some A/C. No rm phones. Memorial Day-Oct: S, D $90-$220; each addl $20; lower rates Feb-Memorial Day, Nov-Dec. Closed Jan. Pet accepted; $20. TV in sitting rm; VCR avail. Complimentary full bkfst. Restaurant nearby. Ck-out 11 am, ck-in 3 pm. Some fireplaces. Federal-style house (1804) built by a merchant sea captain. Solarium; antique furnishings. Near harbor. Totally nonsmoking. Cr cds: MC, V. 🐾 ⬧ ⬧

Resort

★ ★ ★ **THE COLONY HOTEL.** *Ocean Ave & King's Hwy.* 207/967-3331; FAX 207/967-8738; res: 800/552-2363. E-mail infome@thecolonyhotel.com; web www.thecolonyhotel.com/maine. 121 rms in hotel, annex and motel, 2-4 story. No A/C. July-Labor Day (hol wkends 2-day min), MAP: D $200-$300; each addl $40; EP, $15 less each; lower rates mid-May-June, after Labor Day-mid-Oct. Closed rest of yr. Crib free. Pet accepted; $22. TV in motel rms, annex. Heated saltwater pool. Dining rm 8-9:30 am, 6:30-8 pm; Sat to 8:30 pm; Sun brunch 11 am-2 pm; poolside lunches in season. Rm serv. Bar. Ck-out 11 am, ck-in 3 pm. Meeting rms. Business servs avail. Bellhops. Gift shop. Tennis privileges. Golf privileges. Putting green. Private beach. Bicycles. Lawn games. Soc dir in summer; entertainment; movies. On trolley route. Spacious grounds; on ocean peninsula. Family-operated since 1948. Totally nonsmoking. Cr cds: A, MC, V. D 🐾 ⬧ ⬧ ⬧ ⬧ ⬧

Kingfield

Inn

✔ ★ ★ **HERBERT.** *Main St.* 207/265-2000; FAX 207/265-4594; res: 800/843-4372. E-mail herbert@somtel.com; web www.byme.com/theherbert. 33 rms, 3 story, 4 suites. No A/C. No rm phones. Dec 25-Mar: S $38-$65; D $60-$95; each addl $10; suites $90-$150; under 12 free; MAP avail; wkly rates; package plans; lower rates rest of yr. Crib free. Pet accepted. TV in sitting rm. Complimentary continental bkfst. Dining rm (public by res) 5:30-9 pm. Rm serv. Ck-out 11 am, ck-in noon. Gift shop. Downhill/x-country ski 14 mi. Massage. In-rm whirlpools. Built 1917; antiques, elaborate fumed oak woodwork. On river. Cr cds: A, D, DS, MC, V. 🐾 ⬧ ⬧ ⬧ SC

Lincoln

Motels

★ **BRIARWOOD MOTOR INN.** *outer W Broadway, 1 mi S. 207/794-6731; res: 800/734-6731 (ME only).* 24 rms, 2 story. July-Aug: S $55; D $60; each addl $5; lower rates rest of yr. Crib $5. Pet accepted. TV; cable (premium). Complimentary coffee in lobby. Restaurant nearby. Ck-out 11 am. Downhill ski 11 mi; x-country ski 2 mi. Refrigerators avail. Cr cds: A, DS, MC, V.

✔★ **LINCOLN HOUSE.** *85 Main St. 207/794-3096; FAX 207/794-9059.* 19 rms. June-mid-Sept: S $40; D $44-$52; each addl $5; under 13 free; lower rates rest of yr. Pet accepted, some restrictions; $5. TV; cable. Ck-out 11 am. Business servs avail. Valet serv. Restaurant nearby. Downhill ski 12 mi. Refrigerators, microwaves avail. Cr cds: A, DS, MC, V.

Lubec *(See also Eastport)*

Motel

✔★ **EASTLAND.** *ME 189, 4 mi W. 207/733-5501; FAX 207/733-2932.* E-mail eastland@nemaine.com. 20 rms. No A/C. Mid-June-Oct: S $38-$45; D $52-$62; each addl $4; under 17, $2; lower rates rest of yr. Crib free. Pet accepted; $3. TV; cable (premium). Ck-out 10 am. Complimentary coffee in lobby. Airport for small planes adj. Cr cds: DS, MC, V.

Machias *(See also Lubec)*

Motels

★ **BLUEBIRD.** *Rte 1, Box 45, 1 mi W on US 1. 207/255-3332.* 40 rms. Mid-June-mid-Sept: S $50; D $56; each addl $4; some lower rates rest of yr. Crib free. Pet accepted. TV; cable. Ck-out 11 am. Cr cds: A, C, MC, V.

✔★ **MAINELAND.** *(Rte 1, Box 177, East Machias 04630) 1 mi E on US 1. 207/255-3334.* 30 rms, 18 A/C. June-mid-Sept: S $40-$45; D $45-$55; each addl $5; lower rates rest of yr. Pet accepted, some restrictions. TV; cable. Complimentary coffee in rms. Restaurant adj 11 am-8 pm. Ck-out 11 am. Some refrigerators; microwaves avail. Picnic tables. Cr cds: A, C, D, DS, MC, V.

Millinocket

Motels

★★ **ATRIUM.** *740 Central St. 207/723-4555.* 82 rms, 3 story, 10 suites. June-Oct: S $65-$75; D $70-$80; each addl $5; suites $90; under 18 free; ski plans; lower rates rest of yr. Crib free. Pet accepted. TV; cable, VCR avail. Indoor pool; wading pool, whirlpool. Playground. Complimentary bkfst buffet. Restaurant nearby. Bar 4 pm-midnight. Ck-out noon. Coin lndry. Meeting rms. Sundries. X-country ski 10 mi. Exercise equipt; weight machines, bicycles. Rec rm. Some refrigerators; microwaves avail; bathrm phone, wet bar in suites. Cr cds: A, D, DS, MC, V.

★★ **BEST WESTERN HERITAGE.** *935 Central St. 207/723-9777; FAX 207/723-9777, ext. 284.* 49 rms, 2 story. June-Aug: S $69; D$79; each addl $10; under 12 free; lower rates rest of yr. Crib free. Pet accepted, some restrictions. TV; cable. Complimentary continental bkfst. Restaurant 4-10 pm. Bar. Ck-out 11 am. Meeting rm. Business servs avail. Sundries. Exercise equipt; bicycle, treadmill. Whirlpools. Refrigerators avail. Cr cds: A, D, DS, MC, V.

Newport *(See also Skowhegan)*

Motel

✔★★ **LOVLEY'S.** *RFD 2, 1/2 mi W at jct US 2, ME 11/100, just N of I-95 Newport-Detroit exit 39. 207/368-4311; res: 800/666-6760.* 63 rms, 1-2 story, 3 kits. (no ovens, equipt). June-Nov: S $29.70-$49.90; D $39.90-$89.90; each addl $5; kit. units $8 addl; lower rates rest of yr. Crib $8. Pet accepted. TV; cable (premium). Heated pool; whirlpool. Complimentary coffee in rms. Restaurant nearby. Ck-out 11 am. Coin lndry. Business servs avail. Lawn games, gliders. Picnic tables. Cr cds: A, DS, MC, V.

Norway

Motel

★ **GOODWIN'S.** *(191 Main St, South Paris 04281) ¹/₂ mi W on ME 26. 207/743-5121; res: 800/424-8803 (exc ME).* 24 rms. S $40; D $48; under 12 free; higher rates special events. Pet accepted. TV; cable. Restaurant nearby. Ck-out 11 am. Downhill/x-country ski 6 mi. Some refrigerators. Two family units. Cr cds: A, C, D, DS, MC, V.

Inn

★ ★ ★ **WATERFORD.** *(Box 149, Waterford 04088) 8 mi W via ME 118, then S on ME 37 to Chadbourne Rd. 207/583-4037.* 9 rms, 2 share bath, 2 story. No rm phones. S, D $75-$100; each addl $29. Closed Apr. Pet accepted; $10. Dining rm 8-9:30 am, 5-9 pm. Ck-out 11 am, ck-in 2 pm. Downhill ski 20 mi, x-country ski on site. Lawn games. Private patios, balconies. Built 1825; antiques. Parlor, library. Extensive grounds; flower gardens. Cr cds: A.

Old Orchard Beach *(See also Portland, Saco)*

Motels

✔ ★ **FLAGSHIP.** *54 W Grand Ave (ME 9), 54 W Grand Ave (ME 9). 207/934-4866; res: 800/486-1681.* 27 rms, 24 A/C, 2 story, 8 suites, 1 cottage. July-Labor Day: D, suites $74-$105; each addl $10; under 12 free; lower rates mid-May-June, after Labor Day-mid-Oct. Closed rest of yr. Crib free. Pet accepted, some restrictions. TV; cable. Pool. Complimentary coffee in lobby. Restaurant opp 7-11 am, 5-10 pm. Ck-out 11 am. Refrigerators. Balconies. Picnic tables. Opp ocean; beach. Cr cds: A, DS, MC, V.

✔ ★ **GRAND BEACH INN.** *198 E Grand Ave (ME 9). 207/934-3435; res: 800/926-3242.* 87 units, 2-3 story, 37 kits. No elvtr. July-early Sept: S, D $85-$115; suites, kit. units $140-$175; under 13 free; lower rates May-June & Sept-Oct. Closed rest of yr. Crib $10. Pet accepted, some restrictions. TV; cable. Heated pool. Playground. Cafe 6 am-2 pm, 4:30-10 pm; closed Oct-May. Ck-out 10 am. Coin lndry. Balconies. Picnic tables, grills. Cr cds: DS, MC, V.

Orono

Motels

★ ★ **BEST WESTERN BLACK BEAR INN.** *4 Godfrey Dr, I-95 exit 51. 207/866-7120; FAX 207/866-7433.* 68 rms, 3 story. July-Oct: S $75; D $80; each addl $5; suites $109-$119; under 12 free; lower rates rest of yr. Pet accepted. TV; cable (premium), VCR avail. Complimentary continental bkfst. Complimentary coffee in rms. Restaurant 5-8 pm; closed Sun. Ck-out 11 am. Meeting rms. Business center. Exercise equipt: bicycles, ski machine, sauna. Microwaves avail. Cr cds: A, C, D, DS, MC, V.

✔ ★ **MILFORD.** *(154 US 2, Milford 04461) US 95 exit 51, US 2A to US 2. 207/827-3200; res: 800/282-3330.* E-mail milford@mint.net; web www.mint.net/milford .motel. 22 rms, 2 with shower only, 2 story, 8 suites. Mid-June-Aug: S $49; D $59-$69; suites $84; under 18 free; wkly rates; lower rates rest of yr. Crib free. Pet accepted. TV; cable (premium). Complimentary coffee in rms. Restaurant nearby. Ck-out 10 am. Coin lndry. Refrigerators. Some balconies. Picnic tables. On river. Cr cds: A, DS, MC, V.

✔ ★ ★ **UNIVERSITY MOTOR INN.** *5 College Ave. 207/866-4921; FAX 207/866-4550; res: 800/321-4921.* 48 rms, 2 story. June-Sept: S $48; D $58; each addl $4-$6; under 13 free; higher rates; Univ ME graduation, homecoming; lower rates rest of yr. Crib free. Pet accepted. TV; cable. Pool. Complimentary continental bkfst. Restaurant 3-11 pm Wed-Sat. Bar. Ck-out 11 am. Business servs avail. Sundries. Private patios, balconies. Cr cds: A, C, D, DS, MC, V.

Portland *(See also Old Orchard Beach)*

Motels

✔ ★ ★ **BEST WESTERN MERRY MANOR INN.** *(700 Main St, South Portland 04106) 3¹/₂ mi S on US 1, 2 mi off ME Tpke exit 7. 207/774-6151; FAX 207/871-0537.* 151 rms, 1-3 story. No elvtr. June-late Oct: S $89.95; D $99.95; each addl $5; under 12 free; lower rates rest of yr. Crib $3. Pet accepted. TV; cable (premium), VCR avail (movies). Heated pool. Coffee in rms. Restaurant 6 am-10 pm. Ck-out 11 am. Coin lndry. Meeting rms. Business servs avail. In-rm modem link. Valet serv. Health club privileges. Some refrigerators; microwaves avail. Cr cds: A, C, D, DS, MC, V. 🄳 ⌨ ≈ ⊠ 🔥 SC

★ ★ **HOWARD JOHNSON.** *155 Riverside St (04103), ME Tpke exit 8. 207/774-5861.* 119 rms, 3 story. July-mid-Oct: S, D $84.95-$109.95; each addl $10; under 18 free; lower rates rest of yr. Crib free. Pet accepted; $50 deposit. TV; cable (premium). Indoor pool; whirlpool. Coffee in rms. Restaurant 7 am-10 pm. Rm serv. Bar noon-1 am; entertainment Fri, Sat. Ck-out noon. Coin lndry. Meeting rms. Business servs avail. Bellhops. Valet serv. Sundries. Free airport transportation. Exercise equipt; weight machine, bicycles. Some in-rm whirlpools, microwaves. Some private patios, balconies. Cr cds: A, C, D, DS, ER, JCB, MC, V. ⌨ ≈ 🏋 ⊠ 🔥 SC

Motor Hotels

★ ★ ★ **INN BY THE SEA.** *(40 Bowery Beach Rd, Cape Elizabeth 04107) 6 mi SE on ME 77. 207/799-3134; FAX 207/799-4779; res: 800/888-4287.* E-mail innmaine@aol.com; web www.innbythesea.com. 43 kit. suites, 3 story. No A/C. July-Aug: S, D $180-$420; package plans off-season; lower rates rest of yr. Crib free. TV; cable (premium), VCR (movies). Heated pool; poolside serv. Coffee in rms. Restaurant 7:30 am-9:30 pm. Rm serv. Ck-out noon. Meeting rms. Business servs avail. In-rm modem link. Bellhops. Concierge. Lighted tennis. Lawn games. Bicycles. Health club privileges. Bathrm phones. Balconies, decks. Picnic tables. On ocean; access to swimming beach. Totally nonsmoking. Cr cds: A, DS, MC, V. 🄳 ⌨ 🎿 ≈ 🚶 ⊠ 🔥 SC

★ ★ **MARRIOTT AT SABLE OAKS.** *(200 Sable Oaks Dr, South Portland 04106) 4 mi S on I-295 exit 1, W to Maine Mall Rd, N to Running Hill Rd, then W. 207/871-8000; FAX 207/871-7971.* 227 rms, 6 story. Late May-early Nov: S, D $129-$159; suites $125-$300; lower rates rest of yr. Crib free. Pet accepted, some restrictions. TV; cable (premium), VCR avail. Indoor pool; whirlpool, poolside serv. Complimentary coffee in rms. Restaurant 6:30 am-11 pm. Rm serv. Bar noon-1 am. Ck-out noon. Meeting rms. Business servs avail. In-rm modem link. Bellhops. Valet serv. Gift shop. Exercise equipt; weights, bicycles, sauna. Cr cds: A, C, D, DS, ER, JCB, MC, V. 🄳 ⌨ ≈ 🚶 ⊠ 🔥 SC

Hotel

★ ★ **RADISSON EASTLAND.** *157 High St (04101). 207/775-5411; FAX 207/775-2872.* Web www.radisson.com. 204 rms, 12 story. June-Oct: S, D $119-$139; each addl $15; suites $275-$350; under 18 free; lower rates rest of yr. Crib free. Pet accepted; $100 deposit. Garage parking, fee. TV; cable (premium). Restaurant 6:30 am-2 pm, 5:30-9 pm; Fri, Sat to 10 pm. Bar 4:30 pm-1 am; entertainment wkends. Ck-out noon. Meeting rms. Business servs avail. Concierge. Gift shop. Free airport transportation. Exercise equipt; weight machine, treadmill, sauna. Cr cds: A, C, D, DS, ER, MC, V. 🄳 ⌨ 🚶 ⊠ 🔥 SC

Inn

★ ★ **INN AT ST JOHN.** *939 Congress St (04102), near Intl Airport. 207/773-6481; res: 800/636-9127; FAX 207/756-7629.* 31 rms, 4 share bath, 4 with shower only, 4 story. Some A/C. No elvtr. July-Oct: S, D $39.70-$124.70; each addl $6; under 13 free; lower rates rest of yr. Crib free. Pet accepted. TV; cable (premium). Complimentary continental bkfst. Complimentary coffee in rms. Restaurant adj open 24 hrs. Ck-out 11 am; ck-in varies. Business servs avail. Coin lndry. Free airport, bus depot transportation. Refrigerators, microwaves avail. Built in 1896; European motif, antiques. Cr cds: A, C, D, DS, MC, V. ⌨ ⊠ 🔥

Presque Isle

Motel

★ **NORTHERN LIGHTS.** *72 Houlton Rd. 207/764-4441.* 14 rms. S $24.95; D $39.95; each addl $5; under 12 free. Crib $5. Pet accepted; $10. TV; cable. Morning coffee. Ck-out 11 am. Cr cds: A, DS, MC, V. ⌨ 🔥

Rockland

Motel

(Rates may be higher during Seafood Festivals)

★ ★ **NAVIGATOR MOTOR INN.** *520 Main St, across from State Ferry terminal. 207/594-2131; FAX 207/594-7763; res: 800/545-8026.* 81 rms, 4-5 story, 6 kits. Mid-June-Aug: D $70-$95; each addl $5; under 16 free; lower rates rest of yr. Pet accepted. TV; cable. Restaurant 6:30 am-2 pm, 5:30-9:30 pm. Rm serv. Bar 11-1 am. Ck-out 11 am. Coin lndry. Meeting rms. Business servs avail. Downhill ski 10 mi; x-country ski 2 mi. Refrigerators. Balconies. Near ocean. Cr cds: A, D, DS, MC, V. ⌨ ⊠ 🔥

Rockwood

Resort

★ **THE BIRCHES.** *2 mi NE of ME 6/15. 207/534-7305; FAX 207/534-8835; res: 800/825-9453.* E-mail wwld@aol.com; web www.webcom.com/birches/. 3 rms in main lodge, shared baths; 17 kit. cottages, shower only. No A/C. AP, May-Nov: S $105; D $65/person; wkly rates; housekeeping plan (no maid serv) $550-$750/wk (4 people); lower rates rest of yr. Pet accepted; $5. Dining rm (res accepted) 7-10 am, 6-9 pm; also 11 am-3 pm in season. Box lunches. Bar. Ck-out 10 am, ck-in 3 pm. Business servs avail. Gift shop. Grocery, package store 2 mi. Private beach. Marina, dockage. Boats, motors; canoes, sailboats. Canoe, rafting trips. Moose watching cruises. Downhill ski 15 mi; x-country ski on site. Ski, kayak, snowmobile rentals. Bicycles. Sauna. Whirlpool. Fishing guides; clean/store area. Rustic log cabins. On Moosehead Lake. Cr cds: A, DS, MC, V.

Rumford (See also Bethel)

Motel

★ **LINNELL.** *Rte 2, 2 mi W just off US 2. 207/364-4511; FAX 207/369-0800; res: 800/446-9038.* 50 rms, 1-2 story. S $44-$55; D $49-$60; each addl $5; kit. units $55-$60; under 12 free. Crib free. Pet accepted; $5. TV; cable. Complimentary continental bkfst. Restaurant adj 6 am-11 pm. Ck-out 11 am. Coin lndry. Meeting rms. Business servs avail. Downhill/x-country ski 3 mi. Many refrigerators. Some balconies. Picnic tables. Cr cds: A, D, DS, MC, V.

Saco (See also Old Orchard Beach, Portland)

Motel

★ **CLASSIC.** *21 Ocean Park Rd (ME 5). 207/282-5569; res: 800/290-3909.* 17 rms, 2 story, 15 kits. (no ovens). Mid-June-Labor Day: S $75; D $78; each addl $10; under 13 $5; lower rates rest of yr. Pet accepted, some restrictions. TV; cable. Indoor pool. Complimentary coffee. Restaurant nearby. Ck-out 11 am. In-rm modem link. Many refrigerators. Balconies. Picnic tables. Cr cds: A, DS, MC, V.

Sebago Lake

Motel

✔ ★ **SUBURBAN PINES.** *(322 Roosevelt Trail, Windham 04062) Approx 5 mi S on US 302. 207/892-4834.* 24 rms, 10 kits, 1-2 story. June-Sept: S, D $50-$60; suites $75; under 12 free; lower rates rest of yr. Pet accepted; $50 deposit. TV; cable. Complimentary coffee. Ck-out 11 am. Coin lndry. Picnic table, grill. Maine state picnic area opp. Cr cds: DS, MC, V. D ✔ ☒ ☒

Skowhegan (See also Newport, Waterville)

Motel

✔ ★ ★ **BELMONT.** *425 Madison Ave. 207/474-8315; res: 800/235-6669.* 36 rms. July-Oct: S $50; D $60; each addl $5; suites $90-$100; higher rates: State Fair, special events; lower rates rest of yr. Pet accepted. TV; cable (premium), VCR avail. Pool. Restaurant nearby. Ck-out 11 am. Sundries. Downhill ski 5 mi; x-country ski 1 mi. Lawn games. Refrigerators avail. Picnic tables. Cr cds: A, D, DS, MC, V. D ✔ ☒ ☒ ☒ ☒

Waterville (See also Augusta)

Motels

(Rates may be higher last two wkends in July, also special college wkends)

✔ ★ **ATRIUM.** *332 Main St. 207/873-2777; FAX 207/872-2838.* 102 rms, 4 story. July-Sept: S $51-$60; D $61-$86; each addl $10; under 18 free; lower rates rest of yr. Crib free. Pet accepted. TV; cable. Indoor pool; wading pool. Complimentary continental bkfst. Ck-out noon. Coin lndry. Meeting rm. Business servs avail. Valet serv. Sundries. Exercise equipt; weight machines, bicycle, sauna. Rec rm. Some refrigerators. Microwaves avail. Cr cds: A, D, DS, MC, V. D ✔ ☒ ☒ ☒ ☒ SC

★ ★ **BEST WESTERN.** *356 Main St, at I-95 exit 34 (Main St). 207/873-3335; FAX 207/873-3335.* E-mail pdaigle@uninet.net; web www.bestwestern.com/thisco/bw/20018 /20018_b.html. 86 rms, 2 story. July-Oct: S, D $70-$80; each addl $10; under 18 free; higher rates Colby graduation wkend; lower rates rest of yr. Crib $3. Pet accepted. TV; cable, VCR avail (movies). Pool. Coffee in rms. Restaurant 6 am-10 pm. Bar. Ck-out noon. Meeting rms. Business servs avail. Valet serv. Health club privileges. Sundries. Refrigerators, microwaves avail. Cr cds: A, C, D, DS, JCB, MC, V. 🐾 🏊 🏋 🎿 SC

★ ★ ★ **HOLIDAY INN.** *375 Main St. 207/873-0111; FAX 207/872-2310.* E-mail hiw lume@mint.net; web www.acadia.net/hiwat-cm. 138 rms, 3 story. May-Oct: S $85; D $95; each addl $10; suite $150; under 19 free; lower rates rest of yr. Crib free. Pet accepted. TV; cable (premium), VCR avail. Indoor pool; whirlpool. Complimentary coffee in rms. Restaurant 6 am-2 pm, 5-10 pm. Rm serv. Bar 11-1 am. Ck-out noon. Coin lndry. Meeting rms. Business servs avail. In-rm modem link. Sundries. Exercise equipt; weight machine, bicycle, sauna. Refrigerators, microwaves avail. Cr cds: A, C, D, DS, JCB, MC, V.

D 🐾 🏊 🏃 🎿 🏋 SC

Wells *(See also Kennebunk, York)*

Motels

✔ ★ **NE'R BEACH.** *(US 1, Moody 04054) 2 mi S on US 1. 207/646-2636.* 47 rms, 1-2 story, 21 kits. (some ovens). Late June-Aug: S, D $49-$99; kit. units $89-$139; wkly rates for kit. units; lower rates Apr-late June, after Labor Day-mid-Nov. Closed rest of yr. Crib $7. Pet accepted. TV; cable. Heated pool. Playground. Restaurant nearby. Ck-out 11 am. Lawn games. Refrigerators avail. Picnic tables. Cr cds: A, DS, MC, V. 🐾 🏊 🎿 🏋

✔ ★ **WATERCREST COTTAGES & MOTEL.** *1277 Post Rd (US 1), 1/2 mi S on US 1, 1 1/2 mi SE of ME Tpke exit 2. 207/646-2202; FAX 207/646-7067; res: 800/847-4693.* E-mail wcrest@cybertours.com. 9 motel rms, 4 kits., 50 kit. cottages. July-late Aug, hol wkends: S, D $64-$70; each addl $10; cottages for 2-8 (late June-Labor Day, 1-wk min) $435-$735/wk; lower rates May-June, late Aug-mid-Oct. Closed rest of yr. Crib free. Pet accepted, some restrictions. TV; cable, VCR avail (free movies). Pool; whirlpool. Playground. Restaurant nearby. Ck-out 11 am; cottages 10 am. Coin lndry. Lawn games. Microwaves in cottages. Picnic tables, grills. Screened porch on cottages. Cr cds: DS, MC, V. D 🐾 🏊 🎿 🏋

York *(See also Wells)*

Motel

★ ★ **YORK COMMONS INN.** *362 US 1. 207/363-8903; FAX 207/363-1130; res: 800/537-5515 (NY, NE only).* 90 rms. Mid-June-mid-Oct: S, D $89-$99; each addl $5; under 18 free; lower rates rest of yr. Crib free. Pet accepted, some restrictions. TV; cable. Indoor pool. Complimentary continental bkfst. Restaurant opp 11 am-8 pm. Business servs avail. Sundries. Refrigerators, microwaves avail. Cr cds: A, D, DS, MC, V.

D 🐾 🏊 🎿 🏋 SC

Maryland

Aberdeen

Motels

✔ ★ **DAYS INN.** *783 W Bel Air Ave, I-95 exit 85.* 410/272-8500; FAX 410/272-5782. 49 rms, 2 story. S $43; D $47; each addl $4; under 16 free. Crib free. Pet accepted; $5. TV; cable (premium). Pool. Complimentary continental bkfst. Restaurant nearby. Ck-out 11 am. Business servs avail. Refrigerators avail. Cr cds: A, C, D, DS, JCB, MC, V.

D ✦ ≈ ☒ ☒ SC

★ ★ **HOLIDAY INN-CHESAPEAKE HOUSE.** *1007 Beards Hill Rd.* 410/272-8100; FAX 410/272-1714. 122 rms, 5 story. S, D $93-$99; each addl $10; suites $125; kit. units $99-$109; under 18 free; wkend rates. Pet accepted. TV; cable (premium), VCR avail. Indoor pool. Restaurant 6 am-2 pm, 5-10 pm; Sat, Sun from 7 am. Bar. Ck-out noon. Meeting rms. Sundries. Exercise equipt; stair machine, bicycle. Some refrigerators. Balconies. Cr cds: A, C, D, DS, JCB, MC, V. D ✦ ≈ 🛠 ☒ ☒ SC

Annapolis *(See also Baltimore, Baltimore/Washington Intl Airport Area)*

Motor Hotel

★ ★ ★ **HOLIDAY INN.** *210 Holiday Ct at Riva Rd (21401).* 410/224-3150; FAX 410/224-3413. 220 rms, 6 story. S $79-$119; D $89-$129; suites $139; under 18 free. Crib free. Pet accepted. TV; cable (premium). Pool; lifeguard. Restaurant 6:30 am-2 pm, 5-10 pm. Rm serv. Bar 4 pm-midnight. Ck-out noon. Meeting rms. Business servs avail. In-rm modem link. Bellhops. Valet serv. Sundries. Health club privileges. Microwaves avail. Cr cds: A, C, D, DS, JCB, MC, V. D ✦ ≈ ☒ ☒ SC

Hotel

★ ★ ★ **LOEWS.** *126 West St (21401).* 410/263-7777; FAX 410/263-0084. Web www.loewsannapolis.com. 217 rms, 6 story, 11 suites. S, D $119-$185; each addl $15; suites $185-$350; under 17 free. Crib free. Pet accepted. Valet parking $10. TV; cable (premium). Pool privileges. Restaurant 6:30 am-2 pm, 5-10 pm. Bar 11-2 am. Ck-out noon. Meeting rms. Business center. In-rm modem link. Concierge. Gift shop. Barber, beauty shop. Exercise equipt; weight machine, bicycles. Health club privileges. Minibars, refrigerators. Private patios, balconies. Luxury level. Cr cds: A, C, D, DS, MC, V.

D ✦ 🛠 ☒ ☒ SC 🏃

Baltimore

Motel

(In this area I-95 is Kennedy Memorial Hwy; I-695 is the Beltway)

(Rates may be much higher Preakness wkend, mid-May)

★ ★ **HOLIDAY INN SECURITY/BELMONT.** *1800 Belmont Ave (21224), I-695 exit 17, north of Central Area.* 410/265-1400; FAX 410/281-9569. 135 units, 2 story. S, D $59-$83. Crib free. Pet accepted. TV; cable (premium). Pool; lifeguard. Restaurant 6 am-2 pm, 5-10 pm; Sat, Sun from 7 am. Rm serv. Bar 5 pm-midnight. Ck-out noon. Meeting rms. Business servs avail. In-rm modem link. Valet serv. Sundries. Health club privileges. Some refrigerators; microwaves avail. Cr cds: A, C, D, DS, ER, JCB, MC, V.

D ✦ ≈ ☒ ☒ SC

Hotels

★ ★ ★ **DOUBLETREE INN AT THE COLONNADE.** *4 West University Pkwy (21218), Charles St N to University Pkwy, north of Central area.* 410/235-5400; FAX 410/235-5572. Web www.doubletreehotel.com. 125 units, 3 story, 31 suites. S, D $124-$169; each addl $15; suites $149-$475; family rates; wkend plans. Crib free. Pet accepted. TV; cable (premium). Indoor pool; whirlpool, poolside serv, lifeguard. Coffee in rms. Restaurant 6 am-11 pm. Rm serv to 10 pm. Ck-out noon. Meeting rm. Business center. In-rm modem link. Gift shop. Barber, beauty shop. Exercise equipt; bicycles, treadmill. Some wet bars; microwaves avail. Balconies. Biedermeier-inspired furnishings; extensive collection of 18th-century European masters. Adj to Johns Hopkins University. Cr cds: A, C, D, DS, ER, JCB, MC, V. D ✦ ≈ 🛠 ☒ ☒ SC 🏃

★ ★ **HOLIDAY INN BALTIMORE-INNER HARBOR.** *301 W Lombard St (21201), in Central Area. 410/685-3500; FAX 410/727-6169.* 375 rms; 10, 13 story. Apr-Sept: S $139; D $149; each addl $10; suites $275; under 13 free; lower rates rest of yr. Crib free. Pet accepted, some restrictions. Garage parking $6. TV; cable (premium). Indoor pool; lifeguard. Complimentary coffee in rms. Restaurant 6:30 am-11 pm. Bar 11-1 am. Ck-out noon. Convention facilities. Business center. Gift shop. Exercise equipt; weight machine, bicycles, sauna. Some balconies. Cr cds: A, C, D, DS, ER, JCB, MC, V.

D 🖊 🏊 🎿 ⛷ 🏂 SC 🏃

✔ ★ ★ **TREMONT.** *8 E Pleasant St (21202), in Central Area. 410/576-1200; FAX 410/244-1154; res: 800/873-6668.* 58 kit. suites, 13 story. S $89-$119; D $109-$139; each addl $20; under 16 free; wkend rates. Crib free. Pet accepted; $5. Valet parking $11. Pool privileges. TV; cable, VCR avail (free movies). Complimentary continental bkfst. Restaurant 5-9 pm. Bar to 10 pm. Ck-out noon. Meeting rms. Business servs avail. Health club privileges. Microwaves. Cr cds: A, C, D, DS, MC, V. D 🖊 ⛷ 🏂 SC

Baltimore/Washington Intl Airport Area

(See also Baltimore; also see District of Columbia)

Motel

✔ ★ **HOLIDAY INN-GLEN BURNIE SOUTH.** *(6600 Ritchie Hwy, Glen Burnie 21061) I-195 to I-695, E to MD 2 (Ritchie Hwy). 410/761-8300; FAX 410/760-4966.* 100 rms, 3 story. S, D $75; each addl $10; under 18 free. Crib free. Pet accepted, some restrictions. TV; cable (premium). Pool; lifeguard. Restaurant 6 am-2 pm, 5-10 pm; Sat, Sun from 7 am. Rm serv. Bar 4 pm-midnight. Ck-out noon. Meeting rms. In-rm modem link. Valet serv. Health club privileges. Microwaves avail. Mall opp. Cr cds: A, C, D, DS, ER, JCB, MC, V.

D 🖊 🏊 🎿 ⛷ 🏂 SC

Motor Hotels

★ ★ **COMFORT INN-AIRPORT.** *(6921 Baltimore Annapolis Blvd (MD 648), Baltimore 21225) N on MD 170 to Baltimore Annapolis Blvd. 410/789-9100; FAX 410/355-2854.* 188 rms, 6 story. S $79; D $89; each addl $8; suites $125-$225; studio rms $79-$89; under 12 free; wkend rates. Crib free. Pet accepted. TV; cable (premium), VCR avail. Complimentary bkfst buffet. Restaurant 7 am-11 pm. Bar 11 am-midnight. Ck-out 11 am. Meeting rms. Business servs avail. In-rm modem link. Bellhops. Valet serv. Airport transportation. Exercise equipt; weights, bicycles, whirlpool, sauna. Game rm. Microwaves avail. Cr cds: A, C, D, DS, ER, JCB, MC, V. D 🖊 🎿 ⛷ 🏂 SC

✔ ★ **HAMPTON INN.** *(829 Elkridge Landing Rd, Linthicum 21090) From I-95 or I-295 take I-195E to exit 1A (MD 170N). 410/850-0600; FAX 410/691-2119.* 139 rms, 5 story. S $79; D $85; under 18 free. Crib free. Pet accepted. TV; cable (premium). Complimentary continental bkfst. Restaurant nearby. Ck-out noon. Meeting rms. In-rm modem link. Valet serv. Free airport transportation. Microwaves avail. Cr cds: A, C, D, DS, ER, JCB, MC, V.

D 🖊 🎿 ⛷ 🏂 SC

Bethesda *(See also District of Columbia)*

Hotels

✔ ★ ★ **HOLIDAY INN-CHEVY CHASE.** *(5520 Wisconsin Ave, Chevy Chase 20815) S on Wisconsin Ave. 301/656-1500; FAX 301/656-5045.* E-mail cornel@pop.net; web www.holidayinn.com. 215 rms, 12 story. S, D $79-$139; each addl $10; suites $115-$169; under 18 free. Crib free. Pet accepted, some restrictions; $50 deposit. TV; cable (premium), VCR avail. Pool. Complimentary coffee in rms. Restaurant 6:30 am-11 pm. Bar. Ck-out noon. Free lndry facilities. Meeting rms. Business center. In-rm modem link. Gift shop. Health club privileges. Bathrm phones; microwaves avail. Cr cds: A, C, D, DS, ER, JCB, MC, V. D 🖊 🏊 ⛷ 🏂 SC 🏃

★ ★ ★ **RESIDENCE INN BY MARRIOTT.** *7335 Wisconsin Ave (20814). 301/718-0200; FAX 301/718-0679.* 187 kit suites, 13 story. S, D $179-$275; under 16 free; wkend, wkly, monthly rates. Crib free. Pet accepted; $100 and $5/day. Valet parking $12. TV; cable (premium), VCR avail (movies). Pool; lifeguard. Complimentary continental bkfst. Complimentary coffee in rms. Restaurant adj 6:30 am-midnight. Ck-out noon. Coin lndry. Meeting rms. Business servs avail. Exercise equipt; weight machine, bicycles, sauna. Rec rm. Microwaves. Cr cds: A, C, D, DS, JCB, MC, V. D 🖊 🏊 🎿 ⛷ 🏂 SC

Bowie (See also District of Columbia)

Motel

★ **FOREST HILLS.** *(2901 Crain Hwy (US 301), Upper Marlboro 20772) 8 mi S on US 301. 301/627-3969; res: 800/7932828; FAX 301/627-4058.* 13 rms, shower only. Apr-Oct: S $42-$44; D $46-$49; under 13 free; lower rates rest of yr. Crib free. Pet accepted. TV. Complimentary coffee in rms. Ck-out 11 am. Some refrigerators. Picnic tables. Cr cds: A, C, D, DS, MC, V. [D] [✦] [☜] [SC]

Cockeysville (See also Baltimore)

Motor Hotel

★ ★ ★ **MARRIOTT'S HUNT VALLEY INN.** *(245 Shawan Rd, Hunt Valley 21031) I-83 exit 20-A. 410/785-7000; FAX 410/785-0341.* 390 rms, 4 story. Mar-Nov: S $129; D $149; suites $179-$350; under 18 free; wkend rates; higher rates Preakness; lower rates rest of yr. Pet accepted, some restrictions. TV; cable (premium). Complimentary coffee in lobby. Restaurant 6:30 am-10 pm; Fri to 11 pm; Sat 7 am-11 pm; Sun from 7 am. Rm serv. Bar 3 pm-1 am. Ck-out noon. Convention facilities. Business center. In-rm modem link. Bellhops. Valet serv. Concierge. Sundries. Gift shop. Coin lndry. Tennis. 4-hole golf privileges, pro, putting green, driving range. Exercise rm; instructor, weights, stair machine, sauna. Heated indoor/outdoor pool; wading pool, whirlpool, poolside serv, lifeguard. Refrigerator in suites. Luxury level. Cr cds: A, C, D, DS, JCB, MC, V. [D] [✦] [🏋] [🏃] [≈] [🎿] [⛷] [☜] [SC] [⛷]

Columbia (See also Baltimore)

Hotel

★ ★ **COLUMBIA INN HOTEL AND CONFERENCE CENTER.** *10207 Wincopin Circle (21044), opp Columbia Mall. 410/730-3900; FAX 410/730-1290; res: 800/638-2817.* E-mail sales@columbiainn; web www.columbiainn.com. 289 rms, 3-10 story. S $115-$130; D $130-$145; each addl $10; suites $250-$375; under 12 free; wkend plan. Crib free. Pet accepted, some restrictions; $75 refundable. TV; cable (premium). Pool; poolside serv (in season), lifeguard. Coffee in rms. Restaurant 7 am-2:30 pm, 5:30-10:30 pm. Bar 4 pm-2 am. Ck-out noon. Lndry facilities. Meeting rms. Business servs avail. In-rm modem link. Gift shop. Tennis privileges. 18-hole golf privileges, greens fee $35-$44. Health club privileges. Some bathrm phones; microwaves avail. Overlooks Lake Kittamaqundi; boat rides, entertainment on lake (summer). Cr cds: A, C, D, DS, MC, V. [D] [✦] [🏋] [🏃] [≈] [⛷] [☜] [☜] [SC]

Cumberland

Motor Hotel

★ ★ **HOLIDAY INN.** *100 S George St, I-68 exit 43C. 301/724-8800; FAX 301/724-4001.* 130 rms, 6 story. S, D $79; under 18 free. Crib free. Pet accepted. TV; cable (premium), VCR avail. Pool; lifeguard. Restaurant 6:30 am-2 pm, 5-10 pm; Sun from 7 am. Rm serv. Bar noon-2 am; Sun from 1 pm; entertainment. Ck-out noon. Meeting rms. Business center. In-rm modem link. Sundries. Airport transportation. Cr cds: A, C, D, DS, JCB, MC, V. [D] [✦] [≈] [☜] [☜] [SC] [⛷]

Easton

Motel

★ **DAYS INN.** *7018 Ocean Gateway. 410/822-4600; FAX 410/820-9723.* E-mail bsdiggs@ix.netcom.com. 80 rms, 2 story. Apr-Nov: S $69-$89; D, suites $79-$99; under 18 free; higher rates Waterfowl Festival; lower rates rest of yr. Crib free. Pet accepted, some restrictions; $8. TV; cable. Complimentary continental bkfst. Ck-out 11 am. Pool; wading pool. Some refrigerators. Cr cds: A, C, D, DS, ER, JCB, MC, V. [D] [✦] [≈] [☜] [☜] [SC]

Elkton

Motel

★ **SUTTON.** *405 E Pulaski Hwy. 410/398-3830.* 11 rms, shower only. No rm phones. S $30; D $33-$35; each addl $2. Crib $1. Pet accepted, some restrictions. TV. Restaurant nearby. Ck-out 11 am. No cr cds accepted. [✦] [☜]

Emmitsburg (See also Frederick, Hagerstown)

Inn

★ ★ ★ **ANTRIM 1844.** (30 Trevanion Rd, Taneytown 21787) Approx 10 mi E on MD 140. 410/756-6812; FAX 410/756-2744; res: 800/858-1844. 14 rms, 2 with shower only, 3 story, 2 suites. No rm phones. S $125-$225; D $150-$250; each addl $50; suites $300; under 3 free; ski, golf plans; 2-day min wkends, hols; higher rates Dec 31. Pet accepted, some restrictions. TV in main rm; cable, VCR. Heated pool; whirlpools. Complimentary full bkfst. Complimentary coffee in rms. Restaurant. Ck-out noon, ck-in 3 pm. Luggage handling. Business servs avail. Airport transportation. Tennis. Putting green. Croquet. Downhill ski 14 mi, x-country 15 mi. Health club privileges. Lawn games. Some balconies. Antebellum plantation (1844) built on 25 acres. Elegant antique furnishings, 3-story spiral staircase, 23 fireplaces. Formal gardens and gazebo. Totally nonsmoking. Cr cds: A, C, D, DS, MC, V.

D ◆ ≈ ♣ ≈ ⋈ 🐾

Frequency Frederick (See also Hagerstown)

Motor Hotel

★ ★ **HAMPTON INN.** 5311 Buckeystown Pike (MD 85). 301/698-2500; FAX 301/695-8735. 160 rms, 6 story. S, D $69-$100; suites $150; under 18 free. Crib free. Pet accepted, some restrictions. TV; cable (premium). Pool; lifeguard. Complimentary continental bkfst. Restaurant 11:30 am-9 pm. Bar; entertainment. Ck-out noon. Coin Indry. Meeting rms. Business servs avail. In-rm modem link. Sundries. Valet serv. Exercise equipt; bicycles, rowers. Health club privileges. Some refrigerators; microwaves avail. Cr cds: A, C, D, DS, MC, V. D ◆ ≈ ⊀ ⋈ 🐾 SC

Gaithersburg (See also Rockville)

Motel

✔ ★ ★ **COMFORT INN-SHADY GROVE.** 16216 Frederick Rd (20877). 301/330-0023; FAX 301/258-1950. 127 rms, 7 story. Apr-Oct: S, D $49-$109; each addl $10; under 18 free; monthly rates; lower rates rest of yr. Crib free. Pet accepted, some restrictions. TV; cable (premium). Pool; lifeguard. Complimentary continental bkfst. Restaurant adj 11 am-9 pm. Ck-out 11 am. Coin Indry. Meeting rms. Business center. In-rm modem link. Valet serv. Gift shop. Exercise equipt; weight machine, bicycles. Some refrigerators; microwaves. Picnic tables. Cr cds: A, C, D, DS, ER, JCB, MC, V. D ◆ ≈ ⊀ ⋈ 🐾 SC 🏃

Motor Hotel

★ ★ **HOLIDAY INN.** 2 Montgomery Village Ave (20879). 301/948-8900; FAX 301/258-1940. 301 rms, 1-8 story. S $109-$124; D $119-$144; suites $300-$350; kit. units $115-$125; under 18 free. Crib free. Pet accepted, some restrictions. TV; cable (premium). Indoor pool; whirlpool, poolside serv, lifeguard. Coffee in rms. Restaurant 6:30 am-10 pm. Rm serv 6:30 am-midnight. Bar noon-midnight. Ck-out noon. Coin Indry. Convention facilities. Business servs avail. In-rm modem link. Bellhops. Gift shop. Exercise equipt; weights, bicycles. Game rm. Some refrigerators; microwaves avail. Balconies. Cr cds: A, C, D, DS, JCB, MC, V. D ◆ ≈ ⊀ ⋈ 🐾 SC

Hotel

★ ★ **HILTON.** 620 Perry Pkwy (20877), 1 blk E of I-270 exit 11. 301/977-8900; FAX 301/869-8597. Web www.hilton.com. 301 rms, 12 story. S, D $115-$155; suites $325; under 18 free; wkend rates. Crib free. Pet accepted. TV; cable (premium). Indoor/outdoor pool. Restaurant 6:30 am-11 pm; wkends from 7 am. Bars 11-1 am. Convention facilities. Business servs avail. In-rm modem link. Exercise equipt; weights, bicycles. Health club privileges. Refrigerators avail. Some private patios, balconies. Adj to Lake Forest shopping center. Cr cds: A, C, D, DS, ER, JCB, MC, V. D ◆ ≈ ⊀ ⋈ 🐾 SC

Hagerstown (See also Frederick)

Motor Hotels

✔ ★ ★ **BEST WESTERN VENICE INN.** 431 Dual Hwy (US 40), I-70 exit 32B, I-81 exit 6A. 301/733-0830; FAX 301/733-4978. 220 rms, 2-5 story. Apr-Oct: S $58-$68; D $63-$73; each addl $6; suites $125-$250; under 18 free; lower rates rest of yr. Crib $6. Pet accepted, some restrictions. TV; cable (premium), VCR (movies). Pool. Complimentary coffee in lobby. Restaurant 6 am-10:30 pm. Rm serv. Bar; entertainment Tues-Sat. Ck-out noon. Meeting rms. Bellhops. Valet serv. Beauty shop. Airport transportation. Game rm. Golf adj. Exercise equipt; bicycles, treadmill. Refrigerators, microwaves avail. Whirlpool in suites. Cr cds: A, C, D, DS, MC, V. [D] 🐾 ≈ 🏋 🎿 ⛷ 🐾 SC

★ ★ ★ **FOUR POINTS BY SHERATON.** *1910 Dual Hwy (US 40), I-70 exit 32B.* *301/790-3010; FAX 301/733-4559.* 108 rms, 2 story. S $60-$75; D $64-$79; each addl $6; suites $150; under 18 free. Crib $6. Pet accepted; $50 deposit. TV; cable (premium). Pool; whirlpool. Complimentary continental bkfst. Restaurant 6:30 am-10 pm; Sat, Sun 7 am-9 pm. Rm serv. Bar 11-2 am. Ck-out noon. Meeting rms. Business servs avail. Bellhops. Valet serv. Sundries. Free airport transportation. Exercise equipt; weights, bicycles, sauna. Microwaves avail. Cr cds: A, C, D, DS, MC, V. [D] 🐾 ≈ 🏋 🎿 ⛷ 🐾 SC

Laurel *(See also Bowie; also see District of Columbia)*

Motor Hotel

★ ★ **COMFORT SUITES.** *14402 Laurel Place (20707), US 1 at Laurel Lakes Center.* *301/206-2600; FAX 301/725-0056.* Web www.mu pages.com/washdc/comfort suites. 119 rms, 5 story. S, D $80-$100; each addl $10; suites $95-$125; under 18 free; wkly, wkend rates; higher rates: cherry blossom, Memorial Day wkend. Crib free. Pet accepted; $50 refundable. TV; cable (premium). Indoor pool; whirlpool, lifeguard. Complimentary continental bkfst. Complimentary coffee in rms. Restaurant nearby. Ck-out noon. Coin lndry. Meeting rms. Business servs avail. Sundries. Valet serv. Airport transportation. Exercise equipt; treadmill, bicycles. Refrigerators, microwaves. Cr cds: A, C, D, DS, ER, JCB, MC, V. [D] 🐾 ≈ 🏋 🎿 ⛷ 🐾 SC

Ocean City

Motel

★ **SAFARI.** *Boardwalk at 13th St.* *410/289-6411; res: 800/787-2183.* 46 rms in 2 bldgs, 3 & 4 story. July-Aug (3-day min wkends): S, D $98; under 12 free; lower rates Apr-June & Sept-Oct. Closed rest of yr. Crib free. Pet accepted, some restrictions; $7. TV; cable (premium). Restaurant opp from 8 am. Ck-out 11 am. Bellhops. Balconies. On ocean. Cr cds: A, C, D, DS, MC, V. [D] 🐾 🔥 🐾 SC

Hotel

★ ★ ★ **SHERATON FONTAINEBLEAU.** *10100 Ocean Hwy (MD 528).* *410/524-3535; FAX 410/524-3834.* 250 rms, 16 story, 8 kits. June-Aug: S, D $150-$245; each addl $15; suites, kit. units $285-$315; studio rms $220-$270; condos $1,600-$2,000/wkly; under 17 free; higher rates hol wkends (3-day min); lower rates rest of yr. Crib $15. Pet accepted; $15. TV; cable (premium), VCR avail. Heated pool; whirlpool, poolside serv in season, lifeguard. Coffee in rms. Restaurant 6:30 am-11 pm. Bar to 2 am; entertainment. Ck-out 11 am. Meeting rms. Business center. In-rm modem link. Beauty shop. Airport, bus depot transportation. Exercise rm; instructor, weights, bicycles, steam rm, sauna. Tennis privileges. Golf privileges. Game rm. Refrigerators. Balconies. On ocean, beach. Cr cds: A, C, D, DS, ER, JCB, MC, V. [D] 🐾 🏊 🏋 🎿 ≈ 🏋 🎿 ⛷ 🐾 🏄

Pikesville *(See also Baltimore)*

Motel

★ **HOLIDAY INN.** *1721 Reisterstown Rd, at I-695 exit 20S.* *410/486-5600; FAX 410/484-9377.* Web www.holiday-inn.com. 108 rms, 2 story. S, D $69; under 18 free; higher rates Preakness. Crib free. Pet accepted. TV; cable (premium). Pool; poolside serv, lifeguard. Restaurant 6 am-1 pm, 5-10 pm; Sat, Sun from 7 am. Rm serv. Bar 5 pm-midnight. Ck-out noon. Meeting rms. Business servs avail. Valet serv. Health club privileges. Some refrigerators; microwaves avail. Cr cds: A, C, D, DS, ER, JCB, MC, V. [D] ≈ 🎿 ⛷ 🐾 SC

Pocomoke City *(See also Crisfield)*

Motels

★ **DAYS INN.** *1540 Ocean Hwy, on US 13S.* *410/957-3000; FAX 410/957-3147.* 87 rms, 2 story. Mid-June-mid-Sept: S, D $63-$68; each addl $6; under 18 free; higher rates Pony Penning; lower rates rest of yr. Crib free. Pet accepted. TV; cable (premium). Pool. Restaurant 6:30 am-2 pm, 5-9 pm; Sun 7 am-9 pm. Rm serv. Bar 5-11 pm. Ck-out 11 am. Meeting rms. Refrigerators. Cr cds: A, C, D, DS, JCB, MC, V. [D] 🐾 ≈ 🎿 🐾 SC

✔ ★ **QUALITY INN.** *825 Ocean Hwy, 2½ mi S on US 13.* *410/957-1300; FAX 410/957-9329.* 64 rms. S $42-$56; D $46-$70; each addl $5; under 18 free; higher rates

Pony Penning. Crib free. Pet accepted. TV; cable (premium). Pool; wading pool. Restaurant 6 am-10 pm. Bar 11-1 am. Ck-out 11 am. Business servs avail. In-rm modem link. Some in-rm whirlpools, refrigerators. Picnic tables, grills. Cr cds: A, C, D, DS, ER, JCB, MC, V. Ⓓ 🐾 🏊 🏋 🐾 SC

Rockville (See also Gaithersburg)

Motel

✔★ **DAYS INN.** 16001 Shady Grove Rd (20850). 301/948-4300; FAX 301/947-3235. 189 rms, 2 story. S, D $45-$70; each addl $5; under 18 free; wkend rates. Crib free. Pet accepted. TV; cable (premium). Pool. Playground. Restaurant 6:30 am-10 pm. Bar 10-12:30 am, Sun from 11 am. Ck-out 11 am. Business servs avail. Cr cds: A, C, D, DS, MC, V. Ⓓ 🐾 🏊 🏋 🐾 SC

St Mary's City (See also Waldorf; also see District of Columbia)

Motel

✔★★ **DAYS INN.** (60 Main St, Lexington Park 20653) 11 mi N on MD 235. 301/863-6666. 165 rms, 2 story. S $54-$62; D $58-$70; each addl $4; kit. units $57-$78; under 17 free. Crib free. Pet accepted. TV; cable (premium). Pool. Complimentary continental bkfst. Restaurant 11 am-2 pm, 4:30-9 pm. Bar 11-1:30 am. Ck-out noon. Coin lndry. Some refrigerators. Cr cds: A, C, D, DS, MC, V. Ⓓ 🐾 🏊 🏋 🐾 SC

Salisbury (See also Ocean City)

Motels

✔★★ **COMFORT INN.** 2701 N Salisbury Blvd, 4¹/₂ mi N on US 13. 410/543-4666; FAX 410/749-2639. 96 units, 2 story, 24 suites. Mid-May-mid-Sept: S $45.95; D $55.95; each addl $8; suites $55.95-$79.95; under 18 free; higher rates wkends; lower rates rest of yr. Crib avail. Pet accepted. TV; cable (premium). Pool privileges. Complimentary continental bkfst. Restaurant nearby. Ck-out 11 am. Meeting rm. Business servs avail. Refrigerator, wet bar in suites. Cr cds: A, C, D, DS, ER, JCB, MC, V. Ⓓ 🐾 🏋 🐾 SC

★★ **HOLIDAY INN.** 2625 N Salisbury Blvd, 3 mi N on US 13. 410/742-7194; FAX 410/742-5194. 123 rms, 2 story. Mid-June-mid-Sept: S $49-$99; D $49-$107; each addl $8; under 18 free; lower rates rest of yr. Crib free. Pet accepted, some restrictions. TV; cable (premium). Pool. Complimentary bkfst buffet. Restaurant 5-10 pm. Rm serv. Bar 4:30 pm-midnight. Ck-out 11 am. Coin lndry. Meeting rms. Business servs avail. Valet serv. Cr cds: A, C, D, DS, MC, V. Ⓓ 🐾 🏊 🏋 🐾 SC

Waldorf (See also District of Columbia)

Motels

★ **DAYS INN.** 5043 US 301 (20603). 301/932-9200; FAX 301/843-9816. 101 rms, 3 story. S $43.95-$50; D $48.95-$80; suite $125-$150. each addl $5; under 18 free; wkly, monthly rates. Crib free. Pet accepted; $10. TV; cable (premium), VCR avail. Complimentary continental bkfst. Restaurant adj 11 am-10 pm. Ck-out 11 am. Coin lndry. Business servs avail. Game rm. Some refrigerators, in-rm whirlpools. Cr cds: A, C, D, DS, ER, JCB, MC, V. Ⓓ 🐾 🏋 🐾 SC

★★ **HOLIDAY INN.** 1 St Patrick's Dr (20603). 301/645-8200; FAX 301/843-7945. 192 rms, 3 story, 8 kit. units. S, D $62-$68; each addl $6; suites, kit. units $70-$90; under 19 free. Crib free. Pet accepted; $50. TV; cable (premium). Pool; lifeguard. Complimentary coffee in rms. Restaurant 6:30 am-10 pm. Rm serv. Bar noon-11 pm. Ck-out 11 am. Coin lndry. Meeting rms. Business servs avail. In-rm modem link. Bellhops. Valet serv. Beauty shop. Health club privileges. Refrigerators avail. Cr cds: A, C, D, DS, JCB, MC, V. Ⓓ 🐾 🏊 🏋 🐾 SC

✔★ **HOWARD JOHNSON.** 3125 S Crain Hwy (US 301) (20602). 301/932-5090; res: 800/826-4504. 109 rms. S $30-$45; D $30-$50; suites, kit. units $45-$60; under 18 free. Crib free. Pet accepted; $10. TV; cable (premium), VCR (movies). Pool. Complimentary continental bkfst. Restaurant adj 11 am-10 pm. Ck-out noon. Meeting rms. Business servs avail. Picnic tables, grills. Refrigerators avail. Cr cds: A, C, D, DS, JCB, MC, V. Ⓓ 🐾 🏊 🏋 🐾 SC

Westminster (See also Baltimore, Frederick)

Motel

★ ★ **COMFORT INN.** *451 WMC Dr (MD 140) (21158), adj to Western Maryland College. 410/857-1900; FAX 410/857-9584.* 101 rms, 1-2 story. May-June: S $69-$89; D $69-$159; each addl $10; under 18 free; wkly rates; monthly rates; higher rates: WMC parents wkend, graduation, Dec 31; lower rates rest of yr. Crib free. Pet accepted, some restrictions; $25 refundable. TV; cable. Pool; whirlpool. Complimentary continental bkfst. Ck-out 11 am. Meeting rms. Business servs avail. Valet serv. Tennis privileges. Golf privileges. Exercise equipt; bicycle, rower. Some in-rm whirlpools; microwaves avail. Cr cds: A, C, D, DS, ER, JCB, MC, V. 🅳 ⬅ 👬 🏌 ≈ ✕ 🐾 SC

Massachusetts

Amherst

Motel

✔★★ **HOWARD JOHNSON.** *(401 Russell St, Hadley 01035) MA 9 at jct MA 116.* 413/586-0114; FAX 413/584-7163. 100 rms, 3 story. S $49-$109; D $59-$109; each addl $10; suites $79-$152; under 18 free; higher rates special events. Crib free. Pet accepted. TV; cable (premium). Pool. Complimentary bkfst. Ck-out noon. Meeting rm. Business servs avail. In-rm modem link. Downhill ski 16 mi; x-country ski 12 mi. Private patios, balconies. Cr cds: A, C, D, DS, JCB, MC, V. 🇩 📶 📺 ≈ 📵 📵 SC

Andover & North Andover

Motor Hotel

★★ **RAMADA HOTEL/ROLLING GREEN.** *(311 Lowell St, Andover 01810) 2¹/₂ mi W on MA 133, 1 blk E of I-93 exit 43A.* 978/475-5400; FAX 978/470-1108. 182 rms, 2 story. S $79-$109; D $89-$119; each addl $12; suites $125-$250; under 18 free; group, wkend rates. Crib free. Pet accepted. TV; cable. 2 pools, 1 indoor; whirlpool. Restaurant 6:30 am-2 pm, 5-10 pm. Rm serv. Bar 11:30-1 am. Ck-out noon. Meeting rms. Business servs avail. Valet serv. Airport transportation. Indoor tennis, pro. 9-hole par 3 golf, greens fee $10-$12. Exercise equipt; weights, stair machine, sauna. Microwaves avail. Cr cds: A, C, D, DS, JCB, MC, V. 🇩 📶 🎿 📵 ≈ 🏃 📵 📵 SC

Inn

★★★ **ANDOVER.** *(Chapel Ave, Andover 01810) ³/₄ mi S on MA 28.* 978/475-5903; FAX 978/475-1053; res: 800/242-5903. 23 rms, 3 story. S $89; D $99; each addl $10; suites $140; under 12 free. Pet accepted, some restrictions. TV; VCR avail. Dining rm 7:30 am-9:45 pm. Rm serv. Bar 11:30 am-midnight. Ck-out noon. Meeting rms. Business center. In-rm modem link. Valet serv. Beauty shop. On campus of Phillips Academy. Cr cds: A, C, D, DS, MC, V. 📶 📵 📵 📵

Bedford

Hotel

★★★ **RENAISSANCE BEDFORD.** *44 Middlesex Tpke, MA 3 exit 26 to MA 62.* 781/275-5500; FAX 781/275-8956. 285 rms, 2-3 story. S, D $170-$210; suites $200-$225; wkend rates; under 18 free. Crib free. Pet accepted, some restrictions. TV; cable (premium), VCR avail. Indoor pool; whirlpool, poolside serv. Restaurant 6:30 am-11 pm; Sat, Sun from 7:30 am. Rm serv 24 hrs. Complimentary coffee delivered to rms. Bar 11:30-1 am; entertainment. Ck-out 1 pm. Convention facilities. Business center. In-rm modem link. Concierge. Indoor & outdoor tennis, pro. Exercise rm; instructor, weight machine, bicycles, sauna. Health club privileges. Refrigerators, minibars. On 24 wooded acres. Cr cds: A, C, D, DS, ER, JCB, MC, V. 🇩 📶 🏃 ≈ 🏃 🏃 📵 📵 SC 🏃

Boston

Hotels

★★★★ **BOSTON HARBOR.** *70 Rowes Wharf (02110), on the waterfront, in Financial District.* 617/439-7000; FAX 617/330-9450; res: 800/752-7077. Located on Boston's waterfront within walking distance of major sights, this property has a copper-domed observatory with views of Boston. Numerous objets d'art embellish the public areas. 230 rms, 16 story, 26 suites. S $195-$450; D $225-$485; each addl $50; suites $435; under 18 free; wkend rates. Crib free. Pet accepted, some restrictions. Garage parking, valet $26; self-park. TV; cable (premium), VCR avail. Indoor pool; whirlpool, poolside serv. Restaurant 6 am-11 pm. Rm serv 24 hrs. Bar 11:30-1 am; entertainment. Ck-out 1 pm. Meeting rms. Business center. In-rm modem link. Concierge. Airport transportation. Exercise rm; instructor, weight machines, bicycles, sauna, steam rm. Extensive spa. Bathrm phones, minibars; microwaves avail. Balconies. Cr cds: A, C, D, DS, JCB, MC, V. 🇩 📶 ≈ 🏃 📵 📵

★★★ **THE COLONNADE.** *120 Huntington Ave (02116), in Back Bay, opp Hynes Convention Ctr, adj to Copley Plaza Shopping Ctr.* 617/424-7000; FAX 617/424-1717; res: 800/962-3030. 288 rms, 11 story. Apr-June, Sept-Nov: S $205-$265; D $230-$290; suites $435-$1,400; under 12 free; wkly, wkend & hol rates; higher rates: marathon, graduation;

lower rates rest of yr. Crib free. Pet accepted, some restrictions. Parking $20. TV; cable (premium), VCR avail. Pool (in season); poolside serv. Supervised child's activities (May-Sept); ages 8-13. Restaurant 7 am-11 pm. Rm serv 24 hrs. Bar; entertainment Fri, Sat. Ck-out noon. Meeting rms. Business center. In-rm modem link. Concierge. Exercise equipt; weights, bicycles. Minibars; refrigerators avail. Cr cds: A, C, D, DS, ER, JCB, MC, V.

D 🐾 ≋ 🏋 ⛷ 🏃 SC 🏄

★ ★ ★ ★ **THE ELIOT.** *370 Commonwealth Ave (02215), at Massachusetts Ave, in Back Bay. 617/267-1607; FAX 617/536-9114; res: 800/44-ELIOT.* E-mail bostbest@aol.com; web www.hoteleliot.com. The Eliot exudes the atmosphere of an elegant European hotel. Suites have marble baths and period furnishings. 95 kit. suites, 9 story. S $205-$245; D $245-$265. Crib free. Pet accepted, some restrictions. Valet parking $20. TV; cable (premium), VCR avail (movies). Restaurant 6:30-10:30 am, 5:30-10 pm; Sat, Sun 7-11 am, 5:30-10 pm. Ck-out noon. Meeting rms. Business center. In-rm modem link. Concierge. Health club privileges. Minibars; microwaves avail. Some balconies. Cr cds: A, D, MC, V.

D 🐾 ≋ 🏃 🏄

★ ★ ★ **FAIRMONT COPLEY PLAZA.** *138 St James Ave (02116), in Copley Square. 617/267-5300; FAX 617/247-6681.* 373 rms, 7 story. S $159-$349; D $179-$379; each addl $30; suites $379-$1,500; under 17 free; special wknd rates. Crib free. Pet accepted, some restrictions. Valet parking $24. TV; cable (premium), VCR avail. Pool privileges. Restaurants. Rm serv 24 hrs. Bars 11:30-2 am; pianist. Ck-out 1 pm. Meeting rms. Business center. In-rm modem link. Concierge. Shopping arcade. Barber, beauty shop. Exercise equipt; bicycles, weights. Cr cds: A, C, D, DS, ER, JCB, MC, V. D 🐾 🏋 ≋ 🏃 SC 🏄

★ ★ ★ ★ **FOUR SEASONS.** *200 Boylston St (02116), in Boston Common, in Downtown Crossing Area. 617/338-4400; FAX 617/423-0154.* Web www.fshr.com. The Four Seasons hotel is elegant, has a highly attentive staff and is eminently comfortable for leisure or work. Rooms are large and tastefully furnished, and most face the Boston Public Garden or an attactively landscaped business area behind it. 288 rms, 15 story. S $295-$455; D $350-$490; each addl $40; suites $455-$3,000; under 18 free; wknd rates. Crib free. Pet accepted, some restrictions. Valet, garage parking $28. TV; cable (premium), VCR avail (movies). Indoor pool; whirlpool, poolside serv. Complimentary continental bkfst. Restaurants 7-12:30 am. Rm serv 24 hrs. Bar 11-2 am; entertainment. Ck-out 1 pm. Convention facilities. Business center. In-rm modem link. Concierge. Gift shop. Exercise rm; instructor, weights, bicycles, sauna. Massage. Bathrm phones, refrigerators. Cr cds: A, C, D, ER, JCB, MC, V. D 🐾 ≋ 🏋 🏃 🏄

★ ★ **HILTON-BACK BAY.** *40 Dalton St (02115), in Back Bay adj to Hynes Convention Ctr. 617/236-1100; FAX 617/267-8893.* 335 rms, 26 story. S $170-$250; D $190-$270; each addl $20; suites $400-$900; family, wknd rates. Pet accepted, some restrictions. Garage $15. TV; cable (premium), VCR avail (movies). Indoor pool. Restaurant 7 am-midnight. Bar 5:30 pm-12:30 am. Ck-out noon. Convention facilities. Business center. In-rm modem link. Concierge. Gift shop. Exercise equipt; weight machine, bicycles. Some balconies, sundeck. Cr cds: A, C, D, DS, ER, JCB, MC, V. D 🐾 ≋ 🏋 ⛷ 🏃 SC 🏄

★ ★ ★ **LE MERIDIEN.** *250 Franklin St (02110), in Financial District. 617/451-1900; FAX 617/423-2844.* Web www.lemeridien.com. 326 rms, 9 story. S, D $275-$295; each addl $25; suites $400-$790; under 12 free; wknd rates. Crib free. Pet accepted, some restrictions. Valet parking $29. TV; cable (premium), VCR avail. Pool. Restaurants 7 am-10 pm. Rm serv 24 hrs. Bar 5 pm-1 am; pianist. Ck-out 1 pm. Meeting rms. Business center. In-rm modem link. Concierge. Exercise rm; instructor, weights, treadmill, sauna. Massage. Bathrm phones, minibars, refrigerators; microwaves avail. Renaissance Revival bldg. Cr cds: A, C, D, DS, ER, JCB, MC, V. D 🐾 ≋ 🏋 ⛷ 🏃 🏄

★ ★ **RAMADA-LOGAN AIRPORT.** *Logan Intl Airport (02128), on grounds of Logan Intl Airport. 617/569-9300; FAX 617/569-3981.* 516 rms, 14 story. S $129-$195; D $149-$245; each addl $20; suites $400; family, wknd rates. Crib free. Pet accepted, some restrictions. TV; cable (premium). Pool; poolside serv, lifeguard. Coffee in rms avail. Restaurant 5:30 am-10:30 pm. Bar 11-2 am. Ck-out 11 am. Convention facilities. Business center. In-rm modem link. Concierge. Free airport transportation. Exercise equipt; treadmill, stair machine. Many minibars. Cr cds: A, C, D, DS, ER, JCB, MC, V.

D 🐾 ≋ 🏋 ⛷ 🏃 SC 🏄

★ ★ ★ **THE RITZ-CARLTON, BOSTON.** *15 Arlington St (02117), at Newbury St, in Back Bay. 617/536-5700; FAX 617/536-1335.* 278 rms, 17 story. S $260-$375; D $300-$415; each addl $20; 1-2 bedrm suites $345-$1,495; under 12 free; wknd rates. Crib free. Pet accepted, some restrictions. Garage $22. TV; cable (premium), VCR avail (movies). Restaurants 6:30 am-midnight. Rm serv 24 hrs. Bar 11:30-1 am. Ck-out noon. Convention facilities. Business servs avail. In-rm modem link. Concierge. Barber. Airport transportation. Exercise equipt; weights, bicycles, sauna. Massage. Health club privileges. Bathrm phones, refrigerators. Fireplace in suites. Overlooks Public Garden. Luxury level. Cr cds: A, C, D, DS, ER, JCB, MC, V.

★ ★ ★ **SHERATON BOSTON HOTEL & TOWERS.** *39 Dalton St (02199), at Pruden-tial Ctr, in Back Bay.* 617/236-2000; FAX 617/236-6061. 1,181 rms, 29 story. S $189-$240; D $209-$260; each addl $20; suites from $260; under 18 free; wkend rates. Crib free. Pet accepted. Garage $23. TV; cable (premium). Indoor/outdoor pool; whirlpool; poolside serv. Coffee in rms. Restaurant 6:30-1:30 am. Bars 11:30-2 am; entertainment. Ck-out noon. Convention facilities. Business center. In-rm modem link. Gift shop. Exercise equipt; weights, bicycles. Luxury level. Cr cds: A, C, D, DS, ER, JCB, MC, V.

★ ★ ★ **SWISSÔTEL.** *1 Avenue de Lafayette (02111), in Financial District.* 617/451-2600; FAX 617/451-2198; res: 800/621-9200. 500 rms, 22 story. S, D $235-$260; each addl $25; under 16 free; wkend rates. Crib free. Pet accepted, some restrictions. Garage $22, valet parking $26. TV; cable (premium), VCR avail (movies). Indoor pool. Restaurant 7 am-11 pm. Rm serv 24 hrs. Bar 4 pm-1 am; entertainment. Ck-out noon. Convention facilities. Business center. In-rm modem link. Concierge. Gift shop. Exercise equipt; bicy-cles, rowers, sauna. Luxury level. Cr cds: A, C, D, DS, ER, JCB, MC, V.

Braintree

Motels

✔ ★ ★ **DAYS INN.** *190 Wood Rd, MA 128 exit 6.* 781/848-1260; FAX 781/848-9799. 103 rms, 3 story. S $55-$80; D $60-$85; each addl $5; suites $75-$125; under 18 free. Crib free. Pet accepted, some restrictions. TV; cable (premium). Complimentary continental bkfst. Restaurant nearby. Ck-out 11 am. Meeting rm. Business servs avail. Valet serv. Microwaves avail. Boston tours. Cr cds: A, C, D, DS, MC, V.

★ ★ **HOLIDAY INN EXPRESS.** *(909 Hingham St, Rockland 02370) Approx 10 mi S of MA 93 on MA 3, exit 14.* 781/871-5660; FAX 781/871-7255. 76 rms, 2 story. S $63-$72; D $70-$84; each addl $5; under 18 free. Pet accepted. TV. Continental bkfst. Coffee in rms. Ck-out 11 am. Free guest lndry. Meeting rm. Business servs avail. Health club privileges. Microwaves avail. Cr cds: A, C, D, DS, ER, JCB, MC, V.

Brewster (Cape Cod)

Inn

★ ★ ★ **HIGH BREWSTER INN.** *964 Satucket Rd, W on Main St, left on Stony Brook Rd, left on Satucket Rd.* 508/896-3636; FAX 508/896-3734; res: 800/203-2634. 3 rms in main house, 2 story, 4 air-cooled kit. cottages. No rm phones in main house. Memorial Day-Labor Day: D $90-$110; kit. cottages $150-$210; under 16 free; wkly rates. Closed Jan-Mar. Crib free. Pet accepted, some restrictions; $25-$50. Complimentary continental bkfst. Restaurant 5:30-9 pm. Rm serv. Ck-out 11 am, ck-in 3 pm. Lawn games. Antiques; library. Situated on 3 acres, house (1738) overlooks Lower Mill Pond. Adj is historic gristmill and herring run. Cr cds: A, MC, V.

Burlington

Motor Hotel

★ ★ **HAMPTON INN.** *(315 Mishawum Rd, Woburn 01801) 5 mi E on I-95, S on MA 38.* 617/935-7666; FAX 617/933-6899. 99 rms, 5 story. S, D $79-$125; wkend rates. Pet accepted. TV; cable (premium). Complimentary continental bkfst. Restaurant 10 am-11 pm. Rm serv noon-10 pm. Bar. Ck-out noon. Business servs avail. In-rm modem link. Valet serv. Sundries. Health club privileges. Some refrigerators. Cr cds: A, C, D, DS, MC, V.

Buzzards Bay (Cape Cod)

Motel

✔ ★ **BAY MOTOR INN.** *223 Main St.* 508/759-3989. 17 rms, 1-2 story, 3 kits. Late June-Labor Day: D $49-$74; each addl $10; kit. units $69-$85; wkly rates; lower rates Apr-late June, Labor Day-Oct. Closed rest of yr. Crib $7. Pet accepted. TV; cable (premium). Pool. Complimentary coffee in lobby. Restaurant adj. Ck-out 11 am. Free bus depot transportation. Picnic tables, grills. Cr cds: A, DS, MC, V.

Cambridge (See also Boston)

Hotels

★ ★ ★ **CHARLES HOTEL IN HARVARD SQUARE.** *One Bennett St (02138), 1 blk S of Harvard Square. 617/864-1200; FAX 617/864-5715; res: 800/882-1818.* 296 rms, 10 story. S $245-$275; D $275-$295; each addl $20; suites $389-$1,500; under 18 free; wknd rates. Pet accepted, some restrictions. TV; cable (premium), VCR avail (free movies). Indoor pool; whirlpool. Restaurants. Rm serv 24 hrs. Bar 11-2 am; entertainment. Ck-out 1 pm. Meeting rms. Business servs avail. In-rm modem link. Concierge. Shopping arcade. Barber, beauty shop. Exercise rm; instructor, weights, bicycles, steam rm. Massage. Spa. Bathrm phones, minibars; microwaves avail. On Charles River. Cr cds: A, C, D, JCB, MC, V.

★ **HOWARD JOHNSON.** *777 Memorial Dr (02139). 617/492-7777; FAX 617/492-6038.* 201 rms, 16 story. S $90-$185; D $110-$225; each addl $10; under 18 free. Crib free. Pet accepted. TV; cable (premium). 5th-floor indoor pool. Restaurant 7-11 am, 5-10 pm. Bar 4 pm-2 am. Ck-out noon. Meeting rms. Business servs avail. In-rm modem link. Some refrigerators; microwaves avail. Some balconies. On river. Cr cds: A, C, D, DS, ER, JCB, MC, V.

Centerville (Cape Cod) (See also Hyannis)

Motel

★ **CENTERVILLE CORNERS MOTOR LODGE.** *1338 Craigville Rd. 508/775-7223; FAX 508/775-4147; res: 800/242-1137.* E-mail komenda@capecod.com. 48 rms, 2 story. July-Labor Day: D $92-$125; each addl $7; kit. unit $95-$125; under 14 free; wkly rates; golf plan; lower rates rest of yr. Closed Dec-Apr. Crib $5. Pet accepted; $5. TV; cable. Indoor pool; sauna. Complimentary continental bkfst (in season). Complimentary coffee in rms. Ck-out 11 am. Lawn games. Picnic tables, grills. Cr cds: A, DS, MC, V.

Concord (See also Sudbury Center)

Motel

✔ ★ ★ **BEST WESTERN.** *740 Elm St, I-495 exit 29, 7 mi E on MA 2. 978/369-6100; FAX 978/371-1656.* 106 rms, 2 story. S $74-$85; D $79-$95; each addl $8; under 18 free. Crib free. Pet accepted. TV; cable (premium). Pool; whirlpool. Complimentary continental bkfst. Ck-out noon. Coin lndry. Meeting rms. Business servs avail. Valet serv. Downhill/x-country ski 3 1/2 mi. Exercise equipt; weight machine, stair machine. Balconies. Cr cds: A, C, D, DS, ER, JCB, MC, V.

Danvers

Motels

★ ★ **RESIDENCE INN BY MARRIOTT.** *51 Newbury St (US 1N). 508/777-7171; FAX 508/774-7195.* Web www.residenceinn.com. 96 suites, 2 story. Suites $89-$189; wkly, wknd rates. Pet accepted, some restrictions. TV; cable. Pool. Complimentary continental bkst. Restaurant nearby. Ck-out noon. Coin lndry. Business servs avail. In-rm modem link. Valet serv. Lighted tennis. Exercise equipt; weights, bicycles. Refrigerators, microwaves. Balconies. Picnic tables. Cr cds: A, C, D, DS, JCB, MC, V.

✔ ★ **SUPER 8.** *225 Newbury St (US 1N). 508/774-6500; FAX 508/762-6491.* 78 rms, 2 story, 11 kit. units. Mid-June-mid-Oct: S, D $51-$61; each addl $10; kit. units $79; under 18 free; lower rates rest of yr. Crib free. Pet accepted. TV. Pool. Complimentary continental bkfst. Restaurant 11:30 am-10 pm. Bar to 12:30 am; entertainment Thurs-Sat. Ck-out 11 am. Meeting rms. Business servs avail. Microwaves avail. Cr cds: A, C, D, DS, MC, V.

Dedham

Hotel

★ ★ ★ **HILTON AT DEDHAM PLACE.** *25 Allied Dr, off I-95 exit 14. 781/329-7900; FAX 781/329-5552.* 248 rms, 4 story. S $149-$205; D $164-$220; each addl $15; suites $375-$650; under 18 free; wknd packages. Crib free. Pet accepted. TV; cable (premium), VCR avail (movies). Indoor pool; whirlpool, poolside serv (in season). Supervised child's activities (in season). Coffee in rms. Restaurant 6:30 am-11 pm. Bar 11-12:30 am; pianist.

Ck-out noon. Meeting rms. Business center. In-rm modem link. Garage, valet parking. Lighted tennis. Exercise rm; instructor, weights, bicycles, sauna. Bathrm phones; refrigerators avail. Cr cds: A, C, D, DS, ER, JCB, MC, V. 🄳

Eastham (Cape Cod) *(See also Orleans)*

Motels

★ **BLUE DOLPHIN INN.** *(US 6, North Eastham 02651) 3 mi N of Natl Seashore entrance.* 508/255-1159; FAX 508/240-3676; res: 800/654-0504. E-mail bluedolphin@cape cod.net; web www.capecod.net/bluedolphin.com. 49 rms. Mid-June-early Sept: S, D $75-$115; each addl $10; under 16 free; lower rates Apr-mid-June, early Sept-late Oct. Closed rest of yr. Crib $10. Pet accepted. TV; cable (premium). Pool; poolside serv. Restaurant 6:30 am-1 pm. Ck-out 11 am. Lawn games. Refrigerators. Private patios. On 7 wooded acres. Cr cds: A, MC, V. 🄳

★ **TOWN CRIER.** *US 6, 1/2 mi N of Eastham visitor center.* 508/255-4000; FAX 508/255-7491; res: 800/932-1434 (exc MA), 800/872-8780 (MA). E-mail joe111@msn.com; web www.capecod.com/towncrier. 36 rms, 2 story. July-Labor Day: S, D $75-$95; each addl $8; lower rates rest of yr. Pet accepted; $10. TV; cable (premium). Indoor pool. Restaurant 7-11 am. Ck-out 11 am. Free beach transportation. Rec rm. Refrigerators. Cr cds: A, C, D, DS, MC, V.

Fall River *(See also New Bedford; also see Providence, RI)*

Motels

★ **DAYS INN.** *332 Milliken Blvd (02721).* 508/676-1991; FAX 508/676-1991. 102 rms, 3 story. July-mid-Oct: D $69-$94.90; each addl $6; under 14 free; lower rates rest of yr. Crib free. Pet accepted, some restrictions. TV; cable, VCR avail (movies). Pool. Restaurant 7 am-10 pm. Bar noon-1 am. Ck-out noon. Meeting rms. Business servs avail. Cr cds: A, C, D, DS, JCB, MC, V. 🄳

★ ★ **QUALITY INN.** *(1878 Wilbur Ave, Somerset 02725) I-195 W, MA exit 4B; I-195E, MA exit 4.* 508/678-4545; FAX 508/678-9352. 107 rms, 2 story. Late May-Aug: S, D $60-$95; each addl $10; lower rates rest of yr; under 18 free. Crib free. Pet accepted, some restrictions. TV; cable (premium), VCR avail. Indoor/outdoor pool. Continental bkfst. Restaurant adj 6 am-10 pm. Ck-out noon. Coin lndry. Meeting rm. Business servs avail. In-rm modem link. Private patios, balconies. Cr cds: A, C, D, DS, JCB, MC, V.
🄳

Foxboro

Motor Hotel

★ ★ **HOLIDAY INN.** *(31 Hampshire St, Mansfield 02048) 3 mi S on MA 140, off I-95 exit 7A, in Cabot Industrial Park.* 508/339-2200; FAX 508/339-1040. 202 rms, 2-3 story. S $99-$159; D $109-$169; each addl $10; suites $300; under 18 free; wknd rates. Crib free. Pet accepted, some restrictions. TV; cable (premium), VCR avail. Indoor pool. Supervised child's activities (May-Aug); ages 4 yrs and up. Complimentary coffee in rms. Restaurant 6:30 am-10 pm. Rm serv. Bars 11:30-1 am; entertainment. Ck-out noon. Coin lndry. Meeting rms. Business servs avail. In-rm modem link. Bellhops. Lighted tennis. Exercise rm; instructor, bicycles, weights. Some in-rm whirlpools. Private patios, balconies. Cr cds: A, C, D, DS, ER, JCB, MC, V. 🄳

Gloucester

Inns

✔ ★ **THE MANOR.** *141 Essex Ave (MA 133).* 978/283-0614. 11 rms in 3 story manor, 4 share bath; 16 motel rms. Late June-early Sept: D $59-$100; lower rates Apr-late June, early Sept-Oct. Closed rest of yr. Crib $5. Pet accepted; $5. TV. Complimentary continental bkfst (in season). Restaurant nearby. Ck-out 11 am, ck-in 1 pm. Victorian manor house; sitting rm. Some rms overlook river. Cr cds: A, DS, MC, V.

★ ★ **OCEAN VIEW INN.** *171 Atlantic Rd.* 978/283-6200; FAX 978/283-1852; res: 800/315-7557 (exc MA), 800/283-6200 (MA). 72 rms, 3 story. May-Oct: S, D $69-$160; lower rates rest of yr. Crib $10. Pet accepted. TV; cable, VCR avail. 2 heated pools. Restaurants 7 am-9:30 pm. Ck-out 11 am, ck-in 2 pm. Meeting rms. Business servs avail. In-rm modem link. Luggage handling. Rec rm. Lawn games. Some balconies. On ocean. Several buildings have accomodations, including turn-of-the-century English manor house. Cr cds: A, C, D, DS, MC, V. 🄳

Great Barrington

Inn

★ ★ RACE BROOK LODGE. *(864 S Under Mountain Rd, Sheffield 01257) Approx 9 mi S on MA 41.* 413/229-2916; FAX 413/229-6629; res: 888/725-6343. 20 rms, some with shower only, 3 story. No rm phones. S $79-$99; D $89-$129; each addl $10-$15; under 5 free; min stay wkends (summer). Pet accepted, some restrictions. TV; cable in common rm. Complimentary continental bkfst. Restaurant adj 5:30-9:30 pm. Ck-out 11 am. Meeting rm. Downhill/x-country ski 9 mi. Lawn games. Barn built in 1790s. Rustic decor. Totally non-smoking. Cr cds: A, MC, V.

Haverhill

Motel

✓ ★ ★ BEST WESTERN-MERRIMACK VALLEY LODGE. *401 Lowell Ave (08132), at jct MA 110, 113, off I-495 exit 49.* 508/373-1511. 127 rms, 3 story. Apr-Oct: S $48-$52; D $70-$90; under 18 free; higher rates special events; lower rates rest of yr. Crib free. Pet accepted, some restrictions. TV; cable (premium). Pool; lifeguard. Coffee in rms. Restaurant adj. Ck-out 11 am. Meeting rms. Business center. In-rm modem link. Valet serv. Airport transportation. Exercise equipt; weight machine, treadmill; Some refrigerators. Microwaves avail. Some private patios. Cr cds: A, C, D, DS, MC, V.

Holyoke *(See also Springfield)*

Motor Hotel

★ ★ HOLIDAY INN HOLYOKE HOLIDOME AND CONFERENCE CENTER. *245 Whiting Farms Rd, off I-91 exit 15.* 413/534-3311; FAX 413/533-8443. 219 rms, 4 story. S $76-$80; D $86-$90; each addl $10; family rates; higher rates some college events. Crib free. Pet accepted; $25. TV; cable. Indoor pool; whirlpool, poolside serv. Restaurant 6:30 am-10 pm. Rm serv. Bar 11:30-2 am; entertainment Tues-Sat. Ck-out 11 am. Meeting rms. Bellhops. Concierge. Downhill ski 3 mi. Exercise equipt; weight machine, bicycles, sauna. Game rm. Luxury level. Cr cds: A, C, D, DS, JCB, MC, V.

Hyannis (Cape Cod) *(See also South Yarmouth)*

Inn

★ ★ SIMMONS HOMESTEAD. *(288 Scudder Ave, Hyannis Port 02647) ¹/₂ mi W on Main St to Scudder Ave.* 508/778-4999; FAX 508/790-1342; res: 800/637-1649. E-mail simmonsinn@aol.com; web www.capecod.com/simmonsinn. 10 rms, 2 story. No rm phones. Mid-May-Oct: D $140-$180; each addl $20; suite $260; wkly rates; lower rates rest of yr. Crib free. Pet accepted. TV in sitting rm; cable. Complimentary full bkfst. Restaurant nearby. Ck-out 11 am, ck-in 1 pm. Business servs avail. Concierge. Lawn games. Balconies. Restored sea captain's home built in 1820; some canopied beds, fireplaces. Unique decor; all rms have different animal themes. Library; antiques. Cr cds: A, DS, MC, V.

Lenox

Inn

✓ ★ ★ WALKER HOUSE. *64 Walker St.* 413/637-1271; FAX 413/637-2387; res: 800/235-3098. E-mail phoudek@vgernet.net; web www.regionnet.com/colberk/walker house.html. 8 rms, 2 story. No rm phones. Late June-early Sept: S, D $80-$190; each addl $5-$15; ski plans; lower rates rest of yr. Children over 12 yrs only. Pet accepted, some restrictions. TV in sitting rm; VCR avail. Complimentary continental bkfst. Restaurant opp 11 am-10 pm. Ck-out noon, ck-in 2 pm. Business servs avail. Downhill ski 6 mi; x-country ski ¹/₂ mi. Antiques. Library. Rms named after composers. Built 1804. Totally nonsmoking. No cr cds accepted.

Leominster

Motel

✓ ★ INN ON THE HILL. *450 N Main St.* 978/537-1661; FAX 978/840-3341; res: 800/357-0052. 100 rms, 2 story. S, D $39-$49; each addl $7; under 18 free; wkly rates. Crib free. Pet accepted, some restrictions; $20. TV; cable. Pool. Restaurant 6:30 am-11 pm. Rm serv. Bar 5:30-10 pm. Ck-out noon. Meeting rms. Sundries. Downhill/x-country ski 20 mi. Cr cds: A, C, D, DS, ER, JCB, MC, V.

Lowell

Motor Hotel

✔ ★ ★ **BEST WESTERN.** *(187 Chelmsford St, Chelmsford 01824) I-495 exit 34. 978/256-7511; FAX 978/250-1401.* 120 rms, 5 story. S $70-$85; D $75-$90; each addl $5; suites $85; under 18 free; wkend rates. Crib free. Pet accepted. TV; cable (premium), VCR avail (movies). Pool; whirlpool; poolside serv. Complimentary coffee in rms. Restaurant adj 6-1 am. Ck-out noon. Meeting rms. Business sevs avail. In-rm modem link. Valet serv. Exercise equipt; weights, bicycles, sauna. Some refrigerators, microwaves avail, minibars. Some balconies. Cr cds: A, C, D, DS, JCB, MC, V.

Hotels

★ ★ ★ **SHERATON INN.** *50 Warren St (01852). 978/452-1200; FAX 978/453-4674.* 251 rms, 9 story. S, D $79-$109; suites $125-$250; under 18 free. Crib free. Pet accepted. TV; cable (premium), VCR avail. Indoor pool; whirlpool, wading pool, poolside serv. Restaurant 6:30 am-10 pm. Bar. Ck-out 11 am. Coin lndry. Convention facilities. Business servs avail. In-rm modem link. Free garage parking. Exercise equipt; weights, bicycles, sauna. Cr cds: A, C, D, DS, MC, V.

★ ★ ★ **WESTFORD REGENCY.** *(219 Littleton Rd (MA 110), Westford 01886) 10 mi S on MA 110; 1/4 mi E of I-495 exit 32. 978/692-8200; FAX 978/692-7403; res: 800/543-7801 (exc MA), 800/543-7802 (MA).* 193 units, 4 story, 15 suites. S $114; D $140; each addl $8; suites $125-$235; under 18 free; wkend rates. Crib free. Pet accepted, some restrictions. TV; cable, VCR avail (movies). Indoor pool; whirlpool, poolside serv. Restaurant 6:30 am-10 pm. Bar 11-11 pm; entertainment. Ck-out noon. Convention facilities. Business servs avail. In-rm modem link. Exercise rm; instructor, weights, bicycles, sauna. Bathrm phones; some refrigerators. Atrium in lobby. Cr cds: A, C, D, MC, V.

Lynn *(See also Boston, Salem)*

Inn

★ ★ ★ **DIAMOND DISTRICT.** *142 Ocean St (01902), Off Lynn Shore Drive at Wolcott. 781/599-4470; FAX 781/595-2200; res: 800/666-3076.* 9 rms, 1 with shower only, 3 story. June-Oct: S, D $80-$195; each addl $20; under 2 free; lower rates rest of yr. Crib free. Pet accepted, some restrictions; $10. TV. Complimentary full bkfst. Restaurant nearby. Ck-out 11 am. Business servs avail. In-rm modem link. Gift shop. Microwaves avail. Georgian-style residence built in 1911. Totally nonsmoking. Cr cds: A, C, D, DS, MC, V.

Nantucket Island *(See also Hyannis)*

Motel

★ ★ **NANTUCKET INN.** *27 Macy's Lane, near Memorial Airport. 508/228-6900; FAX 508/228-9861; res: 800/321-8484.* 100 rms, 1-2 story. June-Sept: S, D $130-$190; each addl $12; under 18 free; lower rates rest of yr. Pet accepted; $25. TV; cable. 2 pools, 1 indoor; whirlpool, lifeguard. Restaurant 7:30-10:30 am, noon-2 pm, 5:30-9 pm. Rm serv. 2 bars. Ck-out 11 am. Coin lndry. Meeting rms. Business servs avail. Bellhops. Sundries. Free airport transportation. Lighted tennis. Exercise equipt; treadmill, weight machine. Refrigerators. Cr cds: A, C, D, DS, MC, V.

Inn

✔ ★ ★ ★ **JARED COFFIN HOUSE.** *29 Broad St, in Historic District. 508/228-2400; FAX 508/325-7752; res: 800/248-2405.* 60 rms in 6 bldgs. Some A/C. Elvtr in main bldg. July-Sept: S $75; D $135-$200; each addl $15; lower rates rest of yr. Crib $5. Pet accepted; $10. TV. Complimentary full bkfst. Restaurant 7:30-11 am, 6-9 pm. Limited rm serv. Bar 11:30 am-11 pm. Ck-out 11 am, ck-in after 3 pm. Meeting rms. Business servs avail. In-rm modem link. Bellhops. Concierge. Some refrigerators. Restored 1845 mansion; historical objets d'art. Cr cds: A, C, D, DS, MC, V.

New Bedford

Motel

✔ ★ ★ **DAYS INN.** *500 Hathaway Rd (02740), off I-195 at exit 13B, near Municipal Airport. 508/997-1231; FAX 508/984-7977.* 153 rms, 3 story. S $64-$75; D $69-$82; each addl $5; under 12 free. Crib free. Pet accepted, some restrictions. TV; cable (premium). Indoor pool. Coffee in rms. Restaurant 7 am-11 pm. Rm serv. Bar 4 pm-midnight. Ck-out 11 am. Meeting rm. Business servs avail. In-rm modem link. Coin lndry. Free airport transportation. Golf course opp. Cr cds: A, C, D, DS, ER, JCB, MC, V. D ☜ ⩳ ✕ ⬚ ⬚ SC

Newburyport

Inns

　　✔ ★ ★ **MORRILL PLACE.** *209 High St (MA 113). 508/462-2808; res: 888/594-4667; FAX 508/462-9966.* E-mail morrill@aol.com. 9 rms, 4 share bath, 3 story. No A/C. S, D $72-$95; each addl $10; EP avail; wkly rates. Pet accepted. TV rm; cable, VCR avail. Complimentary continental bkfst. Restaurant nearby. Ck-out noon, ck-in 4 pm. Tennis privileges. 18-hole golf privileges, pro. Built in 1806. Once owned by law partner of Daniel Webster; Webster was frequent visitor. Formal front parlor and library. No cr cds accepted. D ☜ ⬚ ⬚ ⬚

　　★ ★ **WINDSOR HOUSE.** *38 Federal St. 508/462-3778; FAX 508/465-3443.* E-mail tintagel@greennet.net. 5 rms, 3 story. S $80-$90; D $95-$135; each addl $25; under 3 free. Crib free. Pet accepted. TV in sitting rm; VCR. Complimentary full bkfst. Restaurant nearby. Ck-out 11 am, ck-in 4 pm. Meeting rm. Business servs avail. In-rm modem link. Microwaves avail. Federal mansion (1786) built by a lieutenant of the Continental Army for his wedding. Antiques. Totally nonsmoking. Cr cds: A, DS, MC, V. ☜ ⬚ ⬚

Newton *(See also Boston)*

Motor Hotel

　　★ ★ ★ **MARRIOTT.** *2345 Commonwealth Ave (02166), I-95 Exit 24. 617/969-1000; FAX 617/527-6914.* 430 rms, 7 story. Sept-Nov: S, D $165; suites $300-$500; under 18 free; wkend rates; lower rates rest of yr. Crib free. Pet accepted, some restrictions. TV; cable (premium). 2 pools, 1 indoor; whirlpool; poolside serv, lifeguard. Playground. Restaurant 6:30 am-midnight. Rm serv. Bar; entertainment. Ck-out 1 pm. Coin lndry. Convention facilities. Business servs avail. In-rm modem link. Bellhops. Sundries. Barber. X-country ski 1 mi. Exercise equipt; treadmill, stair machine, sauna. Canoes. Game rm. Lawn games. Some private patios, balconies. Picnic tables. On Charles River. Luxury level. Cr cds: A, C, D, DS, ER, JCB, MC, V. D ☜ ⬚ ✕ ⩳ ⬚ ✕ ⬚ ⬚ SC

Orleans (Cape Cod) *(See also Eastham)*

Motel

　　★ ★ **SKAKET BEACH.** *203 Cranberry Hwy. 508/255-1020; FAX 508/255-6487; res: 800/835-0298.* 46 rms, 1-2 story, 6 kits. 3rd wk June-early Sept: S, D $79-$156; each addl $9; lower rates Apr-mid-June, mid-Sept-Oct. Closed rest of yr. Crib free. Pet accepted, some restrictions; $9 (off season). TV; cable (premium). Heated pool. Complimentary continental bkfst. Restaurant nearby. Ck-out 11 am. Coin lndry. Lawn games. Refrigerators. Microwaves avail. Picnic tables, grills. Cr cds: A, D, DS, MC, V. ☜ ⩳ ⬚ ⬚

Provincetown (Cape Cod)

Inn

　　★ ★ **WHITE WIND INN.** *174 Commercial St, near Municipal Airport. 508/487-1526; FAX 508/487-3985.* E-mail wwinn@capecod.net; web www.nj-marketplace.com/winn. 11 rms, 7 A/C, 4 air-cooled, 8 with shower only, 3 story. No elvtr. No rm phones. Late May-mid-Sept: S, D $105-$130; wkend, wkly rates; wkends, hols (2-day min); higher rates hols; lower rates rest of yr. Pet accepted. TV; cable, VCR avail (movies). Complimentary continental bkfst. Restaurant nearby. Ck-out 11 am, ck-in 2 pm. Luggage handling. Concierge serv. Refrigerators; some fireplaces. Some balconies. Picnic tables. Opp harbor. Built in 1845; former shipbuilder's home. Totally nonsmoking. Cr cds: A, MC, V. ☜ ⬚ ⬚

Rockport

Motel

　　★ ★ ★ **SANDY BAY MOTOR INN.** *173 Main St. 508/546-7155; FAX 508/546-9131; res: 800/437-7155.* 80 rms, 2 story, 23 kits. Late June-Labor Day: S, D $92-$140; each addl $6; family rates; lower rates rest of yr. Crib free. Pet accepted, some restrictions; deposit. TV; cable (premium), VCR avail. Indoor pool; whirlpool, sauna. Restaurant 7-11 am, wkends, hols to noon. Ck-out 11 am. Coin lndry. Meeting rms. Business servs avail. In-rm modem links. Free RR station transportation. Tennis. Putting green. Refrigerators avail. Cr cds: A, MC, V.

Salem *(See also Danvers, Lynn)*

Hotel

★ ★ **HAWTHORNE.** *18 Washington Sq W, Rte 1A N, on the Common. 978/744-4080; FAX 978/745-9842; res: 800/729-7829.* E-mail info@hawthornehotel.com; web www.hawthornehotel.com. 89 rms, 6 story. July-Oct: S $99-$149; D $99-$161; each addl $12; suites $240-$285; under 18 free; lower rates rest of yr. Crib free. Pet accepted; $15. TV; cable (premium). Restaurant 6:30-11 pm; Sat, Sun from 7 am. Ck-out 11 am. Meeting rms. Business servs avail. In-rm modem link. Lndry serv. Exercise equipt; weights, bicycles. Health club privileges. Cr cds: A, C, D, DS, MC, V.

Inn

★ ★ **SALEM INN.** *7 Summer St, Rte 114 East. 978/741-0680; FAX 978/744-8924; res: 800/446-2995.* 33 units, 4 story, 5 suites, 6 kits. No elvtr. S, D $99-$175; each addl $15; suites $119-$150. Pet accepted. TV; cable (premium). Complimentary continental bkfst. Ck-out 11 am, ck-in 3 pm. Meeting rm. Business servs avail. In-rm modem link. Many fireplaces; some in-rm whirlpools. Brick patio, rose garden. Sea captain's house (1834); on Salem's Heritage trail; many antiques. Cr cds: A, C, D, DS, JCB, MC, V.

Sandwich (Cape Cod)

Motels

✔ ★ ★ **EARL OF SANDWICH MOTOR MANOR.** *(378 MA 6A, East Sandwich 02537)* 2¹/₂ mi E on MA 6A. *508/888-1415; res: 800/442-3275.* 24 rms. Late June-early Sept: S, D $65-$89; each addl $10; lower rates rest of yr. Crib $5. Pet accepted. TV. Complimentary continental bkfst. Restaurant nearby. Ck-out 11 am. Tudor motif. Cr cds: A, C, D, DS, MC, V.

★ **SANDWICH MOTOR LODGE.** *(54 Rte 6A, East Sandwich)* Go over the Sagamore Bridge, exit 1, at the light turn right onto MA 6A, continue on MA 6A for approx 2 mi. *508/888-2275; FAX 508/888-8102; res: 800/282-5353.* 68 rms, 2 story, 33 suites, 4 kit. units. July-Aug: D $79; each addl $10; suites $95-$110; kit. units $450/wk; lower rates rest of yr. Crib $5. Pet accepted; $15. TV; cable (premium), VCR avail. 2 pools, 1 indoor; whirlpool. Complimentary continental bkfst. Restaurant adj 11:30 am-9 pm. Ck-out 11 am. Coin lndry. Meeting rms. Exercise equipt; weight machine, bicycles. Game rm. Refrigerators. Wet bars. Cr cds: A, D, DS, MC, V.

SouthYarmouth (Cape Cod) *(See also Hyannis)*

Inn

★ ★ **COLONIAL HOUSE.** *(Old Kings Hwy (MA 6A), Yarmouth Port 02675)* 508/362-4348; FAX 508/362-8034; res: 800/999-3416. 21 rms, 3 story. July-mid-Oct: S, D $85-$95; each addl $10; higher rates hol wkends; lower rates rest of yr. Crib $5. Pet accepted, some restrictions. TV; VCR avail. Indoor pool; whirlpool. Complimentary bkfst. Dining rm 11:30 am-2:30 pm, 4-9 pm. Bar to 1 am. Ck-out noon, ck-in 2 pm. Meeting rm. Business center. In-rm modem link. Massage. Lawn games. Old mansion (1730s); many antiques, handmade afghans. Cr cds: A, C, DS, ER, MC, V.

Springfield *(See also Holyoke)*

Hotel

★ ★ **HOLIDAY INN.** *711 Dwight St (01104). 413/781-0900; FAX 413/785-1410.* 245 rms, 12 story. S $85-$110; D $95-$120; suites $130-$210; under 19 free; wkend, family rates. Pet accepted; $25. TV; cable. Indoor pool; whirlpool. Restaurant 6:30 am-2 pm, 5-10 pm. Bar from 4:30 pm; Sat, Sun from noon. Ck-out noon. Meeting rm. Downhill/x-country ski 10 mi. Exercise equipt; weights, bicycle. Game rm. Some refrigerators. Cr cds: A, C, D, DS, ER, JCB, MC, V.

Sturbridge

Motel

✔ ★ **ECONO LODGE.** *682 Main St (US 20W), I-90 exit 9, I-84 exit 20W. 508/347-2324.* 47 rms, 7 suites. June-Oct: S, D $50-$80; each addl $5; suites $65-$80; wkly rates;

lower rates rest of yr. Crib avail. Pet accepted. TV; cable. Pool. Ck-out 11 am. Coin lndry. Some refrigerators. Cr cds: A, DS, MC, V. 🐾 🖼 🐾

Sudbury Center *(See also Boston)*

Inn

★ ★ **ARABIAN HOUSE.** *(277 Old Sudbury Rd, Sudbury) 978/443-7400; res: 800/272-2426; FAX 978/443-0234.* 4 rms, 2 with shower only, 3 story, 1 suite. June-Nov: S, D $100-$175; lower rates rest of yr. Crib free. Pet accepted. TV; cable (premium). Complimentary full bkfst. Complimentary coffee in rms. Restaurant nearby. Ck-out 11 am, ck-in 2 pm. In-rm modem link. X-country ski on site. Some balconies. Built in 1879. Arabian horses, antique cars on site. Totally nonsmoking. No cr cds accepted. 🐾 🐾 🐾 🐾

Williamstown

Motel

★ ★ ★ **WILLIAMS INN.** *1090 Main St, at Williams College, jct US 7 & MA 2. 413/458-9371; FAX 413/458-2767; res: 800/828-0133.* 100 rms, 3 story. May-Oct: S $100-$120; D $120-$175; each addl $15; under 14 free; package plan; lower rates rest of yr. Crib free. Pet accepted, some restrictions; $10. TV; cable. Indoor pool; whirlpool. Restaurant 7 am-10 pm. Rm serv. Bar 11-1 am; entertainment Fri, Sat. Ck-out 11 am. Meeting rms. Business servs avail. Valet serv. Sundries. Downhill/x-country ski 6 mi. Sauna. Refrigerators avail. Picnic tables. Cr cds: A, C, D, DS, MC, V. [D] 🐾 🐾 🖼 🐾 🐾

Worcester

Motor Hotel

✔ ★ **HAMPTON INN.** *110 Summer St (01608). 508/757-0400; FAX 508/831-9839.* 99 rms, 5 story, 10 kits. (no equipt). S, D $55-$85; suites $125. Crib free. Pet accepted. TV; cable (premium), VCR avail. Complimentary bkfst buffet. Restaurant nearby. Ck-out 11 am. Meeting rms. Business servs avail. In-rm modem link. Sundries. Downhill ski 20 mi. Some refrigerators. Cr cds: A, C, D, DS, MC, V. [D] 🐾 🐾 🐾 🐾 [SC]

Michigan

Alma *(See also Mount Pleasant)*

Motel

★ **PETTICOAT INN.** *2454 W Monroe Rd.* *517/681-5728.* 11 rms. S $32-$36; D $36-$40; each addl $3; higher rates special events. Pet accepted. TV; cable (premium). Restaurant adj open 24 hrs. Ck-out 11 am. Country setting. Cr cds: A, DS, MC, V.
⊌ ⊠ **SC**

Alpena

Motel

★ **FLETCHER'S.** *1001 US 23N.* *517/354-4191; FAX 517/354-4056; res: 800/334-5920.* 96 rms, 2 story. June-Oct: S $55; D $61; each addl $6; suites $100; kit. units $75; under 16 free; wkly rates; lower rates rest of yr. Crib $6. Pet accepted. TV; cable, VCR avail. Indoor pool; whirlpool, sauna. Restaurant 7 am-10 pm. Rm serv. Bar 11-2 am; Sun from noon. Ck-out 11 am. Meeting rms. Bellhops. Free airport, bus depot transportation. Tennis. Nature trail. Refrigerators; some in-rm whirlpools. Some balconies. Grills. Overlooks wooded acres. Cr cds: A, C, D, DS, ER, MC, V. D ⊌ ⊀ ≋ ⊠ ⊠ **SC**

Motor Hotel

★ ★ **HOLIDAY INN.** *1000 Chisholm (US 23N).* *517/356-2151; FAX 517/356-2151, ext. 201.* 148 rms, 2 story. S $65-$95; D $75-$105; each addl $10; studio rms $95; under 19 free. Crib free. Pet accepted. TV; cable. Indoor pool; whirlpool, poolside serv. Restaurant 6:30 am-2 pm, 5-10 pm. Rm serv. Bar 4 pm-2 am; entertainment. Ck-out noon. Coin lndry. Meeting rms. Business servs avail. Bellhops. Valet serv. Sundries. Gift shop. Free airport, bus depot transportation. Putting green. X-country ski 8 mi. Exercise equipt; bicycle, stair machine, sauna. Game rm. Cr cds: A, C, D, DS, ER, JCB, MC, V.
D ⊌ ⊱ ≋ ⊀ ⊠ ⊠ **SC**

Ann Arbor *(See also Dearborn, Detroit, Jackson)*

Motels

★ ★ **HAMPTON INN-NORTH.** *2300 Green Rd (48105).* *734/996-4444; FAX 734/996-0196.* 130 rms, 4 story. S $59-$85; D $66-$95; under 18 free. Crib free. Pet accepted, some restrictions. TV; cable (premium). Indoor pool; whirlpool. Complimentary continental bkfst. Restaurant nearby. Ck-out noon. Meeting rms. Business servs avail. Valet serv. X-country ski 3 mi. Cr cds: A, C, D, DS, JCB, MC, V. D ⊌ ⊱ ≋ ⊠ ⊠ **SC**

★ **LAMP POST INN.** *2424 E Stadium Blvd (48104).* *734/971-8000; FAX 734/971-7483.* 54 rms, 27 with shower only, 2 story. S, D $39-$64; family, wkly rates; higher rates special events. Crib free. Pet accepted, some restrictions. TV; cable, VCR avail. Pool. Complimentary continental bkfst. Ck-out 11 am. Downhill ski 20 mi; x-country ski 1¹/₂ mi. Health club privileges. Cr cds: A, D, DS, MC, V. D ⊌ ⊱ ≋ ⊠ ⊠ **SC**

✔ ★ **RED ROOF INN.** *3621 Plymouth Rd (48105).* *734/996-5800; FAX 734/996-5707.* 108 rms, 2 story. S $39.99-$54.99; D $48.99-$61.99; 3 or more persons $51.99-$64.99; under 18 free; higher rates special events. Crib free. Pet accepted. TV; cable (premium). Restaurant adj 6 am-midnight. Ck-out noon. X-country ski 2¹/₂ mi. Cr cds: A, C, D, DS, MC, V.
D ⊌ ⊱ ⊠ ⊠

★ ★ **RESIDENCE INN BY MARRIOTT.** *800 Victors Way (48108).* *734/996-5666.* 112 kit. suites, 2-3 story. S, D $110-$160. Crib free. Pet accepted; fee. TV; cable (premium). Heated pool; whirlpool. Complimentary continental bkfst. Restaurant opp 6 am-11 pm. Ck-out noon. Coin lndry. Meeting rm. Valet serv. Balconies. Picnic tables; grills. Cr cds: A, C, D, DS, JCB, MC, V. D ⊌ ≋ ⊠ ⊠ **SC**

Motor Hotel

★ ★ ★ **HOLIDAY INN-NORTH CAMPUS.** *3600 Plymouth Rd (48105).* *734/769-9800; FAX 734/761-1290.* 222 rms, 2-5 story. S $85; D $95; under 18 free; wkend rates. Crib free. Pet accepted, some restrictions; $50 refundable. TV; cable. Indoor/outdoor pool. Restaurant 6:30 am-10 pm; Fri, Sat to 11 pm; Sun 7:30 am-9 pm. Rm serv. Bar. Ck-out 11 am. Meeting rms. Business servs avail. Valet serv. Tennis. X-country ski 2½ mi. Exercise equipt; weight machine, bicycles. Game rm. Picnic tables. Cr cds: A, C, D, DS, ER, JCB, MC, V.

Battle Creek *(See also Kalamazoo)*

Motels

✔★ **APPLETREE INN.** *4786 Beckley Rd (49017). 616/979-3561; FAX 616/979-1400; res: 800/388-7829.* 86 rms, 9 kit. units. S $40.75-$44.75; D $42.75-$54.75; each addl $4; kit. units $51.25-$63.75; under 18 free; wkly rates; golf plans; higher rates Balloon Festival. Crib free. Pet accepted. TV; cable (premium). Coffee in rms. Complimentary continental bkfst. Restaurant opp open 24 hrs. Ck-out noon. Meeting rm. Business servs avail. Tennis privileges. X-country ski 4 mi. Health club privileges. Some in-rm whirlpools. Cr cds: A, C, D, DS, ER, MC, V.

★★ **BATTLE CREEK INN.** *5050 Beckley Rd (49015), I-94 at Capital Ave (exit 97). 616/979-1100; FAX 616/979-1899; res: 800/232-3405.* 211 rms, 2 story. S $60-$70; D $73-$77; each addl $8; family rates, golf plans. Crib free. Pet accepted. TV; cable (premium). Indoor heated pool; poolside serv. Coffee in rms. Complimentary continental bkfst. Restaurant 6:30 am-2 pm, 5-10 pm. Rm serv. Bar 4 pm-midnight. Ck-out noon. Coin lndry. Meeting rms. Business servs avail. Valet serv. Putting green. Exercise equipt; stair machine, bicycle. Health club privileges. Game rm. Refrigerators avail. Cr cds: A, C, D, DS, JCB, MC, V.

Bay City *(See also Midland, Saginaw)*

Motor Hotel

★★ **HOLIDAY INN.** *501 Saginaw St (48708). 517/892-3501; FAX 517/892-9342.* 100 rms, 4 story. S $70-$89; D $75-$96; each addl $7; under 18 free. Crib free. Pet accepted. TV; cable. Indoor pool; whirlpool, sauna. Restaurant 6:30 am-10 pm; Sat, Sun from 7 am. Rm serv. Bar from noon. Ck-out noon. Coin lndry. Meeting rms. Business servs avail. Valet serv. Sundries. Cr cds: A, C, D, DS, ER, JCB, MC, V.

Cadillac

Motels

★★ **CADILLAC SANDS RESORT.** *6319 E MI 115. 616/775-2407; FAX 616/775-6422; res: 800/647-2637.* 55 rms, 2 story. June-Sept: S, D $69.95-$125; each addl $5; under 12 free. Crib $2. Pet accepted. TV; cable (premium). Indoor pool. Complimentary continental bkfst. Restaurant 5-10:30 pm; also Sat, Sun 8-11 am (in season). Bar 4 pm-2:30 am; entertainment. Ck-out 11 am. Meeting rm. Business servs avail. Free airport transportation. Golf privileges, putting green. Downhill ski 13 mi; x-country ski 3½ mi. Lawn games. Some private patios, balconies. Boat rentals, paddleboats. Private beach; dockage. Cr cds: A, C, D, DS, MC, V.

★★ **DAYS INN.** *6001 E MI 115, ¼ mi N of jct MI 55. 616/775-4414; FAX 616/779-0370.* 60 rms, 2 story. June-Sept & Dec-Feb: S $63-$111; D $68-$121; family, mid-wk rates; lower rates rest of yr. Crib free. Pet accepted. TV; cable (premium), VCR avail (movies). Indoor pool; whirlpool. Complimentary continental bkfst. Restaurant nearby. Ck-out 11 am. Meeting rm. Business servs avail. Valet serv. Downhill ski 12 mi; x-country ski 2 mi. Volleyball. Some refrigerators. Lake ¼ mi; swimming beach. Cr cds: A, C, D, DS, JCB, MC, V.

✔★ **SOUTH SHORE RESORT.** *1246 Sunnyside Dr (MI 55). 616/775-7641; FAX 616/775-1185; res: 800/569-8651.* 16 rms, 6 kits. May-mid-Sept, Oct, hunting season, Christmas wk: S $49; D $59; each addl $5; kit. units $64-$99; lower rates rest of yr. Crib free. Pet accepted. TV; cable. Complimentary coffee. Restaurant nearby. Ck-out 11 am. Business servs avail. Downhill ski 15 mi; x-country ski 3 mi. Lawn games. Private beach. Boats; launch, dock. Refrigerators. Picnic tables. Cr cds: DS, MC, V.

✔★ **SUN 'N SNOW.** *301 S Lake Mitchell, at jct MI 55 & MI 115. 616/775-9961; res: 616/477-9961; FAX 616/775-3846.* 29 rms. June-Labor Day, winter wkends, Christmas wk: S $45-$54; D $59-$69; suites $90-$115; lower rates rest of yr. Crib free. Pet accepted. TV; cable. Restaurant nearby. Ck-out 11 am. Business servs avail. Downhill ski 15 mi; x-country ski ¼ mi. Golf privileges. Lawn games. Private beach. On Lake Mitchell. Park opp. Cr cds: DS, MC, V.

Cheboygan *(See also Mackinaw City)*

Motel

★ ★ **DAYS INN.** *889 S Main St (US 27). 616/627-3126; FAX 616/627-2889.* 28 rms, 2 story. Mid-June-mid-Sept: S $58-$98; D $62-$110; suites $75-$150; under 16 free; higher rates Labor Day wkend; lower rates rest of yr. Crib $5. Pet accepted. TV; cable (premium). Complimentary continental bkfst. Restaurant adj 6 am-11 pm. Ck-out 11 am. Free airport, bus depot transportation. X-country ski 3 mi. Refrigerators. Balconies. On river; dockage. Cr cds: A, C, D, DS, MC, V. 🄳 ⊷ ☞ ⊁ ⊠ ⊠ SC

Clare *(See also Midland, Mount Pleasant)*

Motor Hotel

★ **DOHERTY.** *604 McEwan St (Old US 27 Business). 517/386-3441; FAX 517/386-4231; res: 800/525-4115.* 92 rms, 3 story. S $36-$65; D $46-$70; each addl $5; suites $102-$115; wkly rates; golf plans. Crib $5. Pet accepted. Indoor pool; whirlpool, poolside serv. Complimentary full bkfst Mon-Fri. Restaurant 6 am-2 pm, 5-10 pm. Bar 11-2 am; entertainment Wed-Sat. Ck-out noon. Meeting rms. Business servs avail. Bellhops. Valet serv. Free airport transportation. Golf privileges. Downhill ski 5 mi; x-country ski 7 mi. Game rm. Balconies. Cr cds: A, D, DS, MC, V. 🄳 ⊷ ⊁ 🏌 ≃ ⊠ ⊠

Coldwater

Motel

★ ★ **QUALITY INN.** *1000 Orleans Blvd. 517/278-2017; FAX 517/279-7214.* 122 rms, 2 story, 24 kits. May-Oct: S $60-$65; D $67-$72; each addl $7; suites, kit. units $72-$77; under 18 free; higher rates race wkends; lower rates rest of yr. Crib free. Pet accepted. TV; cable (premium). Indoor pool; whirlpool. Complimentary continental bkfst. Restaurant 11 am-2 pm, 5-8 pm; wkend hrs vary. Rm serv. Bar 5 pm-midnight; Fri, Sat to 2 am; closed Sun; entertainment Thurs-Sat. Ck-out 11 am. Meeting rms. Business servs avail. Valet serv. X-country ski 2 mi. Game rm. Cr cds: A, C, D, DS, ER, JCB, MC, V.
🄳 ⊷ ⊁ ≃ ⊠ ⊠ SC

Copper Harbor

Motel

✔ ★ **MINNETONKA RESORT.** *560 Gratiot St, jct US 41 & MI 26. 906/289-4449; res: 800/433-2770.* 13 motel rms, 12 cottages, 8 kits. No A/C. Early May-late Oct: S $46; D $46-$58; cottages for 2-10, $46-$95; $285-$500/wk. Closed rest of yr. Crib $5. Pet accepted; $5. TV; cable (premium). Restaurant opp 8 am-10 pm. Ck-out 10:30 am. Gift shop. Saunas. Picnic tables, grill. Pine-paneled cottages, many overlooking harbor, lake. Astor House Museum on premises. 8 rms across street. Cr cds: DS, MC, V. 🄳 ⊷ ⊠

Dearborn *(See also Detroit)*

Motel

✔ ★ **RED ROOF INN.** *24130 Michigan Ave (US 12) (48124). 313/278-9732; FAX 313/278-9741.* 112 rms, 2 story. June-Aug: S $39.99-$59.99; D $49.99-$69.99; 1-2 addl, $59.99-$69.99; under 18 free; lower rates rest of yr. Crib free. Pet accepted, some restrictions. TV; cable (premium). Complimentary coffee in lobby. Restaurant adj 6:30 am-5:30 pm; cafe opp to 11 pm. Ck-out noon. Business servs avail. Cr cds: A, C, D, DS, MC, V.
🄳 ⊷ ⊠ ⊠

Hotel

★ ★ ★ **DEARBORN INN, A MARRIOTT HOTEL.** *20301 Oakwood Blvd (48124). 313/271-2700; FAX 313/271-7464.* 222 rms, 2-4 story, 22 suites. S $119-$139; D $129-$149; suites $200-$275; under 18 free; wkend rates; package plans. Crib free. Pet accepted, some restrictions. TV; cable (premium), VCR avail. Heated pool; wading pool, poolside serv. Coffee in rms. Restaurant 6:30 am-11 pm. Bar 11-1 am; entertainment. Ck-out noon. Meeting rms. Business servs avail. In-rm modem link. Concierge. Gift shop. Tennis. Exercise equipt; treadmill, stair machine. Lawn games. Some refrigerators. Consists of Georgian-style inn built by Henry Ford (1931), two Colonial-style lodges and five Colonial-style houses; early Amer decor and furnishings. On 23 acres; gardens. Luxury level. Cr cds: A, C, D, DS, ER, JCB, MC, V. 🄳 ⊷ 🏌 ≃ 🏋 ⚏ ⊠ ⊠ SC

Detroit

Motels

★★ **PARKCREST INN.** *(20000 Harper Ave, Harper Woods 48225) NE on I-94, exit 224B. 313/884-8800; FAX 313/884-7087.* 49 rms, 2 story. S $59; D $67-$72; kit. units $84; family rates. Crib free. Pet accepted. TV; cable (premium). Heated pool. Restaurant 6:30-2:30 am; Sun 7:30 am-10 pm. Rm serv. Bar to 2 am. Ck-out 11 am. Valet serv. X-country ski 15 mi. Cr cds: A, C, D, DS, MC, V. 🛏️ 🏊 ⛱️ 🎿 🏄 SC

↙★ **SHORECREST MOTOR INN.** *1316 E Jefferson Ave (48207), downtown. 313/568-3000; FAX 313/568-3002; res: 800/992-9616.* 54 rms, 2 story. S $49-$63; D $55-$79; family, wkly, wkend rates. Crib free. Pet accepted, some restrictions. TV; cable (premium). Restaurant 6 am-10 pm; wkends from 7 am. Rm serv. Ck-out noon. Business servs avail. Valet serv. Refrigerators. Cr cds: A, C, D, DS, MC, V. D 🛏️ 🏄 SC

Hotels

★★ **THE RIVER PLACE.** *1000 River Place (48207), in Rivertown. 313/259-9500; FAX 313/259-3744; res: 800/890-9505.* 108 rms, 5 story, 18 suites. S $115-$185; D $135-$205; each addl $20; suites $165-$500; under 12 free; hol rates; higher rates some special events. Crib free. Valet parking $6. Pet accepted. TV; cable (premium), VCR avail. Indoor pool; whirlpool. Restaurant 7 am-10 pm. Bar 11 am-11 pm; Fri, Sat to 1 am. Ck-out noon. Meeting rms. Business servs avail. In-rm modem link. Tennis privileges. Exercise rm; instructor, weight machine, treadmill, sauna. Massage. Croquet court. On Detroit River. Cr cds: A, C, D, DS, JCB, MC, V. D 🛏️ ⛱️ 🎿 🏄 SC

★★★ **WESTIN-RENAISSANCE CENTER.** *Renaissance Center (48243), Jefferson Ave at Brush, downtown. 313/568-8000; FAX 313/568-8146.* 1,400 rms, 73 story. S $105-$165; D $130-$180; each addl $20; suites $330-$1,200; under 18 free; wkend rates. Crib free. Pet accepted. TV; cable, VCR avail (movies). Indoor pool. Restaurants 6 am-11 pm. Rm serv 24 hrs. Bar 11:30-1:30 am. Ck-out 1 pm. Convention facilities. Business center. In-rm modem link. Shopping arcade. Barber, beauty shop. Exercise rm; instructor, weights, bicycles, sauna. Many minibars. Luxury level. Cr cds: A, C, D, DS, ER, JCB, MC, V.

D 🛏️ ⛱️ 🏋️ 🏃 🎿 🏄 SC 🚶

Detroit Wayne County Airport Area

(See also Dearborn, Detroit)

Hotel

★★★ **CROWNE PLAZA.** *(8000 Merriman Rd, Romulus 48174) 1 mi N on Merriman Rd. 313/729-2600; FAX 313/729-9414.* 365 rms, 11 story. S, D $104-$132; each addl $10; suites $179-$229; family, wkend rates. Crib free. Pet accepted, some restrictions. TV; cable (premium), VCR avail. Indoor pool; whirlpool. Coffee in rms. Restaurant 6 am-10 pm. Bar noon-1 am. Ck-out noon. Convention facilities. Business center. In-rm modem link. Gift shop. Free airport transportation. Exercise equipt; weights, bicycles. Game rm. Some balconies. Luxury level. Cr cds: A, C, D, DS, JCB, MC, V.

D 🛏️ ⛱️ 🏋️ ✈️ 🎿 🏄 SC 🚶

Escanaba

Motel

↙★ **BAY VIEW.** *(7110 US 2/41/MI 35, Gladstone 49837) 4 mi N on US 2/41 (MI 35). 906/786-2843; FAX 906/786-6218; res: 800/547-1201.* 23 rms, 1-2 story. Mid-June-mid-Sept: S $40-$55; D $45-$60; family rates; some lower rates rest of yr. Crib free. Pet accepted. TV; cable (premium). Sauna. Indoor pool. Playground. Complimentary coffee in rms. Restaurant adj 7 am-8 pm. Ck-out 11 am. Business servs avail. Some refrigerators. Picnic tables, barbecue area. Cr cds: A, DS, MC, V. D 🛏️ ⛱️ 🎿 🏄 SC

Farmington *(See also Detroit, Southfield)*

Motel

↙★ **RED ROOF INN.** *(24300 Sinacola Court, Farmington Hills 48335) 3 mi W. 810/478-8640; FAX 810/478-4842.* 108 rms. S $31.99-$33.99; D $37.99-$39.99; 3 or more $47.99; under 18 free. Crib free. Pet accepted. TV; cable. Restaurant adj open 24 hrs. Ck-out noon. Cr cds: A, C, D, DS, MC, V. D 🛏️ 🎿 🏄

Hotel

★ ★ ★ **HILTON.** *(21111 Haggerty Rd, Novi 48375) NW on Grand River Ave, then S on Haggerty Rd to jct Eight Mile Rd. 810/349-4000; FAX 810/349-4066.* 239 rms, 7 story. S $105-$145; D $110-$160; each addl $15; suites $275-$525; family, wknd rates. Crib free. Pet accepted, some restrictions. TV; cable (premium). Pool; whirlpool. Restaurant 6:30 am-11 pm. Rm serv 24 hrs. Bar 11-2 am. Ck-out noon. Meeting rms. Business servs avail. In-rm modem link. Downhill ski 10 mi; x-country ski 2 mi. Exercise equipt; weights, bicycles, sauna. Refrigerator in suites. Cr cds: A, C, D, DS, ER, JCB, MC, V.

D ✔ ⊠ ⬚ ✗ ⬚ ⬚ SC

Flint *(See also Saginaw)*

Motel

✔ ★ **SUPER 8.** *3033 Claude Ave (48507), at I-75 exit 117. 810/230-7888.* 62 rms, 3 story. No elvtr. S $38.98; D $44.98; each addl $6; under 12 free; higher rates Buick Open. Pet accepted. TV; cable. Complimentary coffee in lobby. Restaurant nearby. Ck-out 11 am. Cr cds: A, C, D, DS, JCB, MC, V. D ✔ ⬚ ⬚ SC

Frankfort

Motel

★ **BAY VALLEY INN.** *1561 Scenic Hwy (MI 22), 1¹/₂ mi S. 616/352-7113; FAX 616/352-7114; res: 800/352-7113.* 20 rms. Memorial Day-Labor Day: S $45-$55; D $65-$75; suite $90; family, wkly rates; lower rates rest of yr. Crib free. Pet accepted. TV; cable, VCR avail (free movies). Playground. Complimentary continental bkfst. Ck-out 11 am. Free lndry. Meeting rms. Business servs avail. Downhill/x-country ski 18 mi. Rec rm. Refrigerators. Picnic tables, grills. Cr cds: A, DS, MC, V. D ✔ ⬚ ⬚ ⬚ SC

Resort

★ ★ **CHIMNEY CORNERS.** *1602 Crystal Dr (MI 22). 616/352-7522.* 8 rms in lodge, all share bath, 1-2 story, 7 kit. apts (1-2 bedrm), 13 kit. cottages for 1-20. No A/C. Mid-June-Labor Day: lodge rms for 2, $40-$45 (maid serv avail); kit. apts for 2-6, $760-$795/wk; kit. cottages $1,100-$1,300/wk; lower rates May-mid-June, after Labor Day-Oct. Closed rest of yr. Crib free. Pet accepted, some restrictions. TV in lobby; cable. Playground. Dining rm in season 8-10:30 am, noon-2 pm. Ck-out 10 am, ck-in 3 pm. Grocery, coin lndry, package store 7 mi. Tennis. Private beach; rowboats, hoists; paddle boats. Sailboats. Fireplaces. Many private patios. Picnic tables, grills. 1,000-ft beach on Crystal Lake, 300 acres of wooded hills. Cr cds: V. ✔ ⬚ ✗ ⬚ ⬚

Gaylord *(See also Grayling)*

Motels

✔ ★ **BEST WESTERN ROYAL CREST.** *803 S Otsego Ave (Old US 27). 517/732-6451; FAX 517/732-7634; res: 800/876-9252.* 44 rms, 1-2 story. Mid-May-Oct, Christmas wk, ski wkends: S $59-$79; D $69-$89; each addl $6; under 16 free; lower rates rest of yr. Crib free. Pet accepted. TV; cable. Complimentary continental bkfst. Complimentary coffee in rms. Ck-out 11 am. Exercise equipt; treadmill, stair machine, whirlpool, sauna. Downhill/x-country ski 3 mi. Cr cds: A, C, D, DS, ER, MC, V. D ✔ ⬚ ✗ ⬚ ⬚ SC

★ ★ ★ **HOLIDAY INN.** *833 W Main St (MI 32). 517/732-2431; FAX 517/732-9640.* 140 rms, 2 story. Mid-June-Sept, ski wkends, Christmas wk: S, D $85-$91; each addl $6; under 19 free; golf plans; lower rates rest of yr. Crib free. Pet accepted. TV; cable, VCR avail (movies). Indoor pool; whirlpool. Restaurant 6 am-10 pm. Rm serv. Bar 3 pm-midnight. Ck-out 11 am. Coin lndry. Meeting rms. Business servs avail. Valet serv. Sundries. Downhill/x-country ski 4 mi. Exercise equipt; bicycle, stair machine, sauna. Game rm. Cr cds: A, C, D, DS, JCB, MC, V. D ✔ ⬚ ⬚ ✗ ⬚ ⬚ SC

Grand Marais

Motel

★ ★ **BUDGET HOST-WELKER'S RESORT.** *Box 277, on Canal St, 1 mi E of MI 77. 906/494-2361; FAX 906/494-2371.* 41 rms, 1-2 story, 9 kit. cottages. Some A/C. Some rm phones. S $34-$47; D $40-$52; each addl $5; kit. cottages $227-$297/wk. Crib $5. Pet accepted. TV; cable (premium), VCR avail (movies $5). Indoor pool; whirlpool, sauna. Playground. Restaurant 7:30 am-8:30 pm. Bar. Ck-out 11 am, cottages 10 am. Coin lndry. Meeting rm. Business servs avail. Tennis. Lawn games. On Lake Superior; private beach. Cr cds: A, DS, MC, V. D ✔ ⬚ ✗ ⬚ ⬚

Grand Rapids

Motels

(Rates may be higher during Tulip Time Festival, mid-May)

✔ ★ **EXEL INN.** *(4855 28th St SE, Kentwood 49512) 11 mi SE, 1/2 mi W of I-96 exit 43A.* 616/957-3000; FAX 616/957-0194. 110 rms, 2 story. S $36.99-$38.99; D $41.99-$47.99; each addl $4; under 18 free. Crib free. Pet accepted. TV. Complimentary continental bkfst. Ck-out noon. Downhill ski 15 mi; x-country ski 4 mi. Cr cds: A, C, D, DS, MC, V.
🄳 🐾 ⌖ ⊠ ➤ 🔥 SC

✔ ★ **RED ROOF INN.** *5131 28th St SE (49512), just W of I-96 exit 43A.* 616/942-0800; FAX 616/942-8341. 107 rms, 2 story. S $40.99-$47.99; D $46.99-$54.99; 1st addl $6; under 18 free. Crib free. Pet accepted. TV; cable (premium). Complimentary coffee in lobby. Restaurant adj 6 am-11 pm; Fri, Sat 24 hrs; Sun to 10 pm. Ck-out noon. Business servs avail. Downhill ski 15 mi; x-country ski 5 mi. Cr cds: A, C, D, DS, MC, V.
🄳 🐾 ⌖ ⊠ ➤ 🔥

★ ★ **RESIDENCE INN BY MARRIOTT.** *2701 E Beltline SE (49546).* 616/957-8111; FAX 616/957-3699. 96 kit. suites, 2 story. Suites $102-$135; under 12 free. Crib free. Pet accepted, some restrictions; $60 & $6/day. TV; cable (premium), VCR avail. Heated pool; whirlpool. Complimentary continental bkfst. Restaurant adj 11-2 am. Ck-out noon. Coin lndry. Meeting rm. Business servs avail. Valet serv. Free airport transportation. Downhill ski 15 mi; x-country ski 5 mi. Exercise equipt; stair machine, bicycle. Health club privileges. Private patios; some balconies. Picnic tables, grills. Cr cds: A, C, D, DS, JCB, MC, V.
🄳 🐾 ⌖ ⊠ 🍽 ➤ 🔥 SC

Motor Hotel

★ ★ **NEW ENGLAND SUITES HOTEL.** *2985 Kraft Ave SE (49512).* 616/940-1777; FAX 616/940-9809; res: 800/784-8371. 40 suites, 2 story. S $75, D $80. Crib free. Pet accepted. TV; cable (premium), VCR avail (movies free). Complimentary continental bkfst. Complimentary coffee in rms. Restaurant nearby. Ck-out noon. Business servs avail. Valet serv. Refrigerators. Cr cds: A, C, D, DS, MC, V. 🄳 🐾 ➤ 🔥 SC

Hotel

★ ★ **HOLIDAY INN NORTH.** *270 Ann St NW (49504), US 131 exit 88.* 616/363-9001; FAX 616/363-0670. 164 rms, 7 story. S $74, D $82; each addl $8; under 20 free; ski plan; wkend, hol rates. Crib free. Pet accepted, some restrictions. TV; cable (premium), VCR avail. Indoor pool; whirlpool, sauna, poolside serv. Restaurant 6:30 am-10 pm; Fri, Sat 7 am-11 pm. Bar 11-1 am; entertainment. Ck-out noon. Coin lndry. Meeting rms. Business servs avail. Downhill/x-country ski 14 mi. Game rm. Picnic tables. On Grand River. Cr cds: A, C, D, DS, JCB, MC, V. 🄳 🐾 ⌖ ⊠ ➤ 🔥 SC

Grayling *(See also Gaylord, Houghton Lake)*

Motels

★ ★ ★ **HOLIDAY INN.** *2650 I-75 S Business, at exit 254.* 517/348-7611; FAX 517/348-7984. 151 rms, 2 story. July-Aug: S, D $89-$109; each addl $6; suites $150-$175; under 19 free; lower rates rest of yr. Pet accepted. TV; cable (premium), VCR avail. Indoor pool; wading pool, whirlpool, poolside serv. Playground. Restaurant 6 am-2 pm, 5-10 pm; Sun 6 am-9 pm. Rm serv. Bar 11-2 am; entertainment. Ck-out 11 am. Meeting rms. Business servs avail. Bellhops. Valet serv. Sundries. Airport, bus depot transportation. Downhill ski 5 mi; x-country ski on site. Game rm. Lawn games. Exercise equipt; weight machine, bicycle, sauna. Picnic tables. On wooded property. Some refrigerators. Cr cds: A, C, D, DS, ER, JCB, MC, V. 🄳 🐾 ⌖ ⊠ 🍽 ➤ 🔥 SC

✔ ★ **NORTH COUNTRY LODGE.** *Box 290, 3/4 mi N on Old US 27, I-75 Business.* 517/348-8471; FAX 517/348-6114; res: 800/475-6300. 24 rms, 8 kits. Mid-June-Labor Day, winter wkends, Christmas wk: S, D $40-$90; each addl $2; kit. units $45-$65; suite $125-$150; family, wkly rates; lower rates rest of yr. Crib free. Pet accepted. TV; cable. Restaurant nearby. Ck-out 11 am. Free airport, bus depot transportation. Downhill/x-country ski 3 mi. Cr cds: A, C, D, DS, MC, V. 🄳 🐾 ⌖ ➤ 🔥

✔ ★ **SUPER 8.** *5828 Nelson A Miles Pkwy.* 517/348-8888; FAX 517/348-2030. 61 rms, 2 story. Apr-Sept: S $46.69; D $55.88-$67.88; each addl $4; under 12 free; lower rates rest of yr. TV; cable (premuim). Pet accepted. Complimentary continental bkfst. Restaurant adj open 24 hrs. Ck-out 11 am. Meeting rm. Coin lndry. Downhill ski 1 mi; x-country ski 6 mi. Lawn games. Cr cds: A, C, D, DS, MC, V. 🄳 🐾 ⌖ ➤ 🔥 SC

Houghton

Motels

✔★ **L'ANSE.** *(Rt 2 Box 506, L'Anse 49946) 33 mi SW on US 41. 906/524-7820; FAX 906/524-7247; res: 800/800-6198.* 21 rms, 2 with shower only, 1 story. S $26-$34; D $36; each addl $2; higher rates special events. Crib $2. Pet accepted, some restrictions. TV; cable (premium). Complimentary coffee in lobby. Ck-out 11 am. X-country ski 2 mi. Cr cds: C, D, DS, MC, V. 🐾 🎿 ⛷ 🏊

★ **SUPER 8.** *(790 Michigan Ave, Baraga 49908) 30 mi SW on MI 38, 1 mi W of US 41. 906/353-6680; FAX 906/353-7246.* 40 rms, 2 story. S $41.88; D $49.88; each addl $4; under 12 free. Crib $2. Pet accepted. TV; cable. Complimentary continental bkfst. Restaurant opp. Ck-out 11 am. Meeting rm. Business servs avail. X-country ski 8 mi. Cr cds: A, C, D, DS, MC, V. D 🐾 🎿 ⛷ 🏊 SC

Motor Hotel

★ **BEST WESTERN KING'S INN.** *215 Sheldon Ave. 906/482-5000; FAX 906/482-9795.* 68 rms, 4 story. July-Sept: S $61-$82; D $67-$88; each addl $6; under 17 free; lower rates rest of yr. Crib free. Pet accepted. TV; cable (premium), VCR avail (movies). Indoor pool; whirlpool, sauna. Complimentary continental bkfst. Restaurant adj 11 am-midnight. Ck-out 11 am. Meeting rm. Valet serv. Downhill ski 2 mi; x-country ski 3 mi. Cr cds: A, C, D, DS, MC, V. D 🐾 🎿 ⛷ 🏊 🏊 SC

Houghton Lake *(See also Grayling)*

Motel

(Rates may be higher during Tip-Up-Town USA Ice Festival)

★ ★ **VAL HALLA.** *9869 Old US 27. 517/422-5137.* 12 rms, 2 kits. Memorial Day wkend-Labor Day: S, D $45-$62; each addl $5; 2-bedrm kit. apts $525/wk; some lower rates rest of yr. Crib $1. Pet accepted. TV. Heated pool. Restaurant nearby. Ck-out 11 am. Free airport transportation. Putting green. Downhill ski 17 mi; x-country ski 2 mi. Lawn games. Private patios. Picnic table, grills. Cr cds: MC, V. 🐾 🎿 ⛷ 🏊 🏊 SC

Iron Mountain

Motel

★ ★ **BEST WESTERN EXECUTIVE INN.** *1518 S Stephenson Ave (US 2). 906/774-2040; FAX 906/774-0238.* 57 rms, 2 story. June-Sept: S $56; D $63; each addl $6; lower rates rest of yr. Crib free. Pet accepted. TV; cable (premium), VCR avail (movies $2.50). Indoor pool. Complimentary continental bkfst. Ck-out 11 am. Downhill/x-country ski 3 mi. Cr cds: A, C, D, DS, MC, V. D 🐾 🎿 ⛷ 🏊 SC

Jackson *(See also Ann Arbor, Battle Creek, Lansing)*

Motels

✔★ **BUDGETEL INN.** *2035 Service Dr (49201). 517/789-6000; FAX 517/782-6836.* 67 rms, 2 story. S $39.95-$52.95; D $46.95-$59.95; family rates. Crib free. Pet accepted. TV, cable (premium). Complimentary continental bkfst. Complimentary coffee in rms. Restaurant adj 6:30 am-10 pm. Ck-out noon. Meeting rm. Business servs avail. Valet serv. Some refrigerators. Cr cds: A, C, D, DS, MC, V. D 🐾 ⛷ 🏊 SC

★ ★ **HOLIDAY INN.** *2000 Holiday Inn Dr (49202), jct US 127 & I-94 exit 138. 517/783-2681; FAX 517/783-5744.* 184 rms, 2 story. S, D $65-$85; under 19 free; wkend, special events rates. Crib free. Pet accepted. TV; cable (premium), VCR avail. Heated pool; whirlpool, sauna. Restaurant 6:30 am-2 pm, 5-10 pm. Rm serv. Bar 4 pm-midnight, Sun 5-10 pm. Ck-out 11 am. Coin lndry. Meeting rms. Business servs avail. Bellhops. Putting green; miniature golf. X-country ski 10 mi. Game rm. Cr cds: A, C, D, DS, JCB, MC, V.

D 🐾 🎿 ⛷ 🏊 🏊 SC

Kalamazoo *(See also Battle Creek)*

Motels

★ ★ **HOLIDAY INN-AIRPORT.** *3522 Sprinkle Rd (49002). 616/381-7070; FAX 616/381-4341.* 146 rms, 2 story. S, studio rms $75; D $83; under 18 free. Crib free. Pet accepted. TV; cable (premium), VCR avail. 2 pools, 1 indoor; whirlpool, sauna, poolside serv. Restaurant 6:30 am-10 pm; Fri, Sat to 11 pm. Rm serv. Bar 11:30 am-midnight; closed

Sun. Ck-out noon. Coin lndry. Meeting rms. Business servs avail. Bellhops. Valet serv. Sundries. Free airport transportation. Downhill/x-country ski 15 mi. Adj to stadium. Cr cds: A, C, D, DS, ER, JCB, MC, V. 🇩 ▨ ▨ ▨ ▨ ▨ SC

★ ★ **LA QUINTA.** *3750 Easy St (49002), near Municipal Airport. 616/388-3551; FAX 616/342-9132.* 122 rms, 2 story. S $48; D $54; each addl $6; under 18 free. Crib free. Pet accepted. TV; cable (premium). Heated pool. Complimentary continental bkfst. Restaurant adj 6 am-11 pm. Ck-out noon. Meeting rms. Business servs avail. Valet serv. Free airport, RR station, bus depot transportation. Downhill/x-country ski 15 mi. Cr cds: A, C, D, DS, MC, V. 🇩 ▨ ▨ ▨ ✈ ▨ ▨ ▨ SC

✔ ★ **RED ROOF INN-WEST.** *5425 W Michigan Ave (49009). 616/375-7400; FAX 616/375-7533.* 108 rms, 2 story. S $36-$45; D $40-$52; 3 or more $50; under 18 free; higher rates special events. Crib free. Pet accepted. TV. Complimentary coffee. Restaurant nearby. Ck-out noon. Business servs avail. Downhill ski 8 mi; x-country ski 3 mi. Picnic tables, grill. Cr cds: A, C, D, DS, MC, V. 🇩 ▨ ▨ ▨ ▨

★ ★ **RESIDENCE INN BY MARRIOTT.** *1500 E Kilgore Rd (49001), near Municipal Airport. 616/349-0855; FAX 616/349-0855, ext. 211.* 83 kit. suites, 2 story. S, D $105-$130; under 12 free; wkly rates; ski, golf plans. Crib free. Pet accepted. TV; cable, VCR avail (movies). Heated pool; whirlpool. Complimentary full bkfst. Complimentary coffee in rms. Restaurant nearby. Ck-out noon. Coin lndry. Meeting rms. Business servs avail. In-rm modem link. Bellhops. Valet serv. Free airport, RR station, bus depot transportation. 9-hole golf privileges. Downhill/x-country ski 20 mi. Health club privileges. Some fireplaces. Picnic tables, grills. Cr cds: A, C, D, DS, JCB, MC, V. 🇩 ▨ ▨ ▨ ▨ ✈ ▨ ▨ SC

✔ ★ **SUPER 8.** *618 Maple Hill Dr (49009). 616/345-0146.* 62 rms, 3 story. No elvtr. Apr-Oct: S $41.88; D $48.88-$52.88; under 12 free; lower rates rest of yr. Crib free. Pet accepted. TV; cable (premium). Complimentary coffee in lobby. Restaurant adj 7 am-10 pm. Ck-out 11 am. Downhill ski 11 mi. Some refrigerators. Cr cds: A, C, D, DS, MC, V. 🇩 ▨ ▨ ▨ ▨

Motor Hotel

★ ★ **HOLIDAY INN-WEST.** *2747 S 11th St (49009). 616/375-6000; FAX 616/375-1220.* 186 rms, 4 story. S, D $79-$89; studio rms $79; under 19 free. Crib free. Pet accepted. TV. Indoor pool; whirlpool, poolside serv. Restaurant 6:30 am-10:30 pm; Fri, Sat to 11 pm. Rm serv. Bar 11:30 am-midnight; Fri, Sat to 1 am. Ck-out 11 am. Coin lndry. Meeting rm. Business servs avail. Bellhops. Valet serv. Putting green. Downhill ski 8 mi; x-country ski 3 mi. Exercise rm; stair machine, bicycles, sauna. Game rm. Cr cds: A, C, D, DS, ER, JCB, MC, V. 🇩 ▨ ▨ ▨ ✈ ▨ ▨ SC

Lansing & East Lansing

Motels

★ ★ ★ **BEST WESTERN MIDWAY.** *(7711 W Saginaw Hwy, Lansing 48917) 517/627-8471; FAX 517/627-8597.* 149 rms, 2-3 story. Sept-May: S $65-$82; D $70-$87; each addl $5; under 12 free; lower rates rest of yr. Crib free. Pet accepted. TV; cable (premium). Indoor pool; whirlpool. Coffee in rms. Restaurant 6:30 am-10 pm; wknd hrs vary. Rm serv. Bar 11-2 am. Ck-out noon. Meeting rms. Business servs avail. Bellhops. Valet serv. Sundries. Free airport transportation. Exercise equipt; rower, stair machine, sauna. Game rm. Refrigerators avail. Cr cds: A, C, D, DS, JCB, MC, V. 🇩 ▨ ▨ ✈ ▨ ▨ SC

✔ ★ **RED ROOF INN-EAST.** *(3615 Dunckel Rd, Lansing 48910) 517/332-2575; FAX 517/332-1459.* 80 rms, 2 story. S $41-$51; D $42-$54; each addl $6; under 18 free. Crib free. Pet accepted. TV. Restaurant opp 7 am-11 pm. Ck-out noon. Business servs avail. X-country ski 7 mi. Cr cds: A, C, D, DS, MC, V. 🇩 ▨ ▨ ▨ ▨

Ludington

Motel

★ **NADER'S LAKE SHORE MOTOR LODGE.** *612 N Lakeshore Dr. 616/843-8757; res: 800/968-0109.* 26 rms, 2 kits. Mid-June-early Sept: S, D $64; kit. units $50-$58; lower rates May-mid-June, early Sept-Oct. Closed rest of yr. Crib free. Pet accepted. TV; cable. Heated pool. Restaurant nearby. Ck-out 11 am. Lawn games. Refrigerators. Private patios. Picnic tables. Beach 1 blk. Cr cds: A, D, DS, MC, V. ▨ ▨ ▨ SC

Mackinaw City *(See also Cheboygan, St Ignace)*

Motels

★ **BEACHCOMBER.** *1011 S Huron Ave (US 23). 616/436-8451.* 22 rms. July-early Aug: S, D $65-$115; each addl $3; cottage $550/wk; higher rates: July 4, antique car show, Labor Day wkend (2-day min); lower rates mid-Apr-June, early Sept-Oct. Closed rest of yr. Crib free. Pet accepted, some restrictions. TV; cable (premium). Restaurant nearby. Ck-out 10 am. Refrigerators avail. Picnic tables. On lake; private beach. Cr cds: A, DS, MC, V. [D] 🛇 🛇 🛇 🛇 SC

★ **KEWADIN.** *619 S Nicolet St (MI 108). 616/436-5332.* 76 rms, 2 story. Mid-June-early Sept: S $64.50-$84.50; D $69.50-$84.50; each addl $5; family rates; higher rates special events; lower rates May-mid-June, early Sept-mid-Oct. Closed rest of yr. Crib free. Pet accepted. TV; cable. Heated pool. Playground. Restaurant nearby. Ck-out 11 am. Refrigerators. Cr cds: A, C, D, DS, MC, V. 🛇 🛇 🛇 🛇 SC

★ ★ **LA MIRAGÉ.** *699 N Huron Ave. 616/436-5304.* 25 rms, 2 story. July-early Sept: S, D $45-$95; each addl $5; family, wkly rates; higher rates: antique auto show, hol wkends, Labor Day wkend (2-day min); lower rates May-June, early Sept-Oct. Closed rest of yr. Crib $4. Pet accepted, some restrictions. TV; cable. Indoor pool; whirlpool, sauna. Restaurant nearby. Ck-out 11 am. Some in-rm whirlpools, saunas, refrigerators. Beach opp. Cr cds: A, D, DS, MC, V. [D] 🛇 🛇 🛇 🛇

🛇 ★ ★ **MOTEL 6.** *206 Nicolet St. 616/436-8961; FAX 616/436-7317; res: 800/388-9508.* 53 rms, 2 story. Mid-June-Labor Day: S, D $38.95-$88.95; each addl $6; higher rates: hol wkends, special events; Labor Day wkend (2-day min); lower rates rest of yr. Crib free. Pet accepted; $3. TV; cable (premium). Indoor pool; whirlpool. Restaurant adj 7 am-10 pm. Ck-out 11 am. X-country ski on site. Some refrigerators. Cr cds: A, C, D, DS, MC, V. [D] 🛇 🛇 🛇 🛇 🛇

★ ★ **PARKSIDE INN-BRIDGESIDE.** *102 Nicolet St. 616/436-8301; res: 800/827-8301.* 44 rms, 1-2 story. Late June-early Sept: S, D $48-$88; family rates; higher rates: antique auto show, hol wkends; lower rates May-late June, early Sept-late Oct. Closed rest of yr. Crib $3. Pet accepted, some restrictions. TV; cable (premium). Indoor pool; whirlpool. Restaurant adj 6 am-10 pm. Ck-out 10 am. Game rm. Refrigerators avail. Picnic tables, sun deck. Some rms overlook lake, bridge. Colonial Michilimackinac State Park opp. Cr cds: A, DS, MC, V. [D] 🛇 🛇 🛇 🛇 🛇 SC

★ ★ **QUALITY INN.** *917 S Huron Ave (US 23). 616/436-5051; FAX 616/436-7221.* 60 rms, 1-2 story. Late June-early Sept: S $65.50; D $85-$109.50; each addl $5; family rates; higher rates: hol wkends, antique auto show, Labor Day wkend (2-day min); lower rates mid-Apr-late June, early Sept-Oct. Closed rest of yr. Pet accepted, some restrictions. TV; cable (premium), VCR avail. Indoor pool; whirlpool, sauna. Playground. Restaurant nearby. Ck-out 10 am. Business servs avail. Lawn games. Many refrigerators. Many balconies. Picnic area, grills. Private beach on Lake Huron. Near ferry dock. Cr cds: A, C, D, DS, ER, JCB, MC, V. [D] 🛇 🛇 🛇 🛇 🛇 SC

★ **STARLITE BUDGET INNS.** *116 Old US 31. 616/436-5959; FAX 616/436-5101; res: 800/288-8190.* 33 rms. Mid-July-late Aug: S $49-$59; D $52-$60; family, wkly rates; higher rates: July 4, Labor Day, auto show; lower rates May-mid-July & late Aug-Oct. Closed rest of yr. Crib free. Pet accepted, some restrictions; $5. TV; cable (premium). Heated pool. Playground. Complimentary coffee in rms. Restaurant nearby. Ck-out 10 am. Refrigerators. Cr cds: A, D, DS, MC, V. [D] 🛇 🛇 🛇 🛇 🛇 SC

★ **SUPER 8.** *601 N Huron Ave. 616/436-5252; FAX 616/436-7004.* 50 rms, 2 story. July-mid-Oct: S $74-$135; D $79-$145; each addl $6; higher rates special events (2-day min); lower rates rest of yr. Crib $6. Pet accepted, some restrictions. TV; cable, VCR avail. Indoor pool; whirlpool, sauna. Complimentary coffee in lobby. Restaurant nearby. Ck-out 11 am. Coin lndry. Game rm. Refrigerators avail. Some balconies. Cr cds: A, C, D, DS, MC, V. [D] 🛇 🛇 🛇 🛇 🛇 SC

★ ★ **SURF.** *907 S Huron Ave (US 23). 616/436-8831; res: 800/822-8314.* 40 rms, 1-2 story. Late June-early Sept: S, D $65-$95; each addl $5; family, wkly rates off-season; lower rates May-late June, early Sept-Oct. Closed rest of yr. Crib $5. Pet accepted, some restrictions; $5-$10. TV; cable (premium). Indoor pool; whirlpool. Playground. Complimentary coffee. Restaurant nearby. Ck-out 11 am. Business servs avail. Lawn games. Refrigerators. Balconies, patios. Grills. Private sand beach; overlooks Lake Huron. Cr cds: A, DS, MC, V. [D] 🛇 🛇 🛇 🛇 🛇 SC

✔★★ **WATERFRONT INN.** *1009 S Huron Ave (US 23). 616/436-5527; res: 800/962-9832.* 69 rms. July-early Sept: S $63-$71.95; D $49-$96.95; each addl $5; kit. units (up to 6) $435/wk; higher rates: Labor Day wknd, antique auto show (3-day min); lower rates rest of yr. Pet accepted, some restrictions. TV; cable (premium). Pool; whirlpool. Playground. Coffee in rms. Restaurant nearby. Ck-out 11 am. Picnic table. Private beach on Lake Huron. Cr cds: A, DS, MC, V. 🅳 💶 💷 ≋ ⊠ ⊠ SC

Manistique

Motels

★ **ECONO LODGE.** *Box 184, 1¹/₄ mi E on US 2. 906/341-6014.* 31 rms. July-Labor Day: S, D $58-$66; each addl $5; under 18 free; lower rates rest of yr. Pet accepted; $5. TV; cable (premium). Complimentary continental bkfst. Restaurant nearby. Ck-out 11 am. X-country ski 10 mi. Lake Michigan boardwalk opp. Cr cds: A, C, D, DS, JCB, MC, V. 🅳 💶 ≋ ⊠ ⊠ SC

✔★ **HOLIDAY.** *Rte 1, 4 mi E on US 2. 906/341-2710.* 20 rms. No A/C. June-Labor Day: D $46;lower rates rest of yr. Crib $5. Pet accepted. TV; cable (premium). Heated pool. Playground. Complimentary continental bkfst. Restaurant nearby. Ck-out 11 am. Lawn games. Picnic tables. Cr cds: A, DS, MC, V. 💶 ≋ ⊠ ⊠ SC

Marquette

Motor Hotels

★★ **HOLIDAY INN.** *1951 US 41W. 906/225-1351; FAX 906/228-4329.* 203 rms, 5 story. S, D $75-$79; each addl $4; family; ski plans. Crib free. Pet accepted. TV; cable (premium). Indoor pool; whirlpool, sauna. Restaurant 6 am-2 pm, 5-10 pm. Rm serv. Bar 3 pm-2 am; Sun to midnight. Ck-out noon. Meeting rm. Business servs avail. Bellhops. Valet serv. Sundries. Free airport transportation. Downhill ski 7 mi; x-country ski 3 mi. Health club privileges. Nature trails. Picnic tables. Cr cds: A, C, D, DS, ER, JCB, MC, V. 🅳 💶 ≋ ⊠ ⊠ SC

★★ **RAMADA INN.** *412 W Washington St (US 41 Business). 906/228-6000; FAX 906/228-2963.* 113 rms, 2-7 story. S $70-$120; D $80-$150; each addl $5; under 18 free. Crib free. Pet accepted. TV; cable (premium). Indoor pool; whirlpool, sauna. Restaurant 6 am-10 pm; Fri, Sat to 11 pm. Rm serv. Bar 11-2 am. Ck-out noon. Coin lndry. Meeting rms. Business servs avail. Airport transportation. Downhill ski 5 mi; x-country ski ¹/₂ mi. Many poolside rms. Cr cds: A, C, D, DS, MC, V. 🅳 💶 ≋ ⊠ ⊠ SC

Midland (See also Bay City, Mount Pleasant, Saginaw)

Motels

★★★ **BEST WESTERN VALLEY PLAZA.** *5221 Bay City Rd (48642). 517/496-2700; FAX 517/496-9233.* 161 rms, 2 story. S $59-$69; D $69-$79; suites $110-$155; under 18 free; higher rates wknds. Crib free. Pet accepted, some restrictions. TV; cable. Indoor pool; wading pool. Restaurant 6 am-10 pm; Sat from 7 am; Sun to noon. Rm serv. Bar noon-1 am. Ck-out noon. Meeting rms. In-rm modem link. Bellhops. Valet serv. Gift shop. Free airport transportation. Health club privileges. Game rm. Lawn games. Small lake with beach. Cr cds: A, C, D, DS, MC, V. 🅳 💶 ≋ ⊠ ⊠ SC

★★ **HOLIDAY INN.** *1500 W Wackerly St (48640). 517/631-4220; FAX 517/631-3776.* 236 rms, 2 story. S $74-$139; D $84-$147; each addl $10; under 18 free; wknd rates. Crib free. Pet accepted, some restrictions. TV; cable (premium). Indoor pool; whirlpool, poolside serv. Restaurant 6 am-3 pm, 5:30-10 pm. Rm serv. Bar 11:30-2 am; entertainment. Ck-out noon. Meeting rms. Business center. In-rm modem link. Bellhops. Valet serv. Sundries. Gift shop. Free airport transportation. Tennis privileges. X-country ski 2 mi. Exercise equipt; weights, bicycles, sauna. Game rm. Minibars. Cr cds: A, C, D, DS, JCB, MC, V. 🅳 💶 ≋ 🏂 ≋ 🍴 ⊠ ⊠ SC 🚶

Monroe (See also Detroit; also see Toledo, OH)

Motel

★ **ECONO LODGE.** *1440 N Dixie Hwy (MI 50). 734/289-4000; FAX 734/289-4262.* 115 rms, 2 story. S $40-$51; D $54-$72; each addl $6; under 12 free. Crib free. Pet accepted. TV; cable (premium); VCR avail. Indoor pool; whirlpool, sauna. Restaurant 5 am-10 pm. Rm serv. Bar 11-2 am. Ck-out noon. Meeting rms. Business servs avail. In-rm modem link. Game rm. Private patios, balconies. Cr cds: A, D, DS, MC, V. 💶 ≋ ⊠ ⊠ SC

Motor Hotel

★ **HOLIDAY INN.** *1225 N Dixie Hwy (MI 50). 734/242-6000; FAX 734/242-0555.* 127 rms, 4 story. S $60; D $68; each addl $8; under 18 free; wkend rates off-season; golf plans. Crib free. Pet accepted. TV; cable (premium), VCR avail. Indoor pool; whirlpool, sauna, poolside serv. Restaurant 6 am-10 pm. Rm serv. Bar 11-2 am; Sun noon-midnight; entertainment exc Sun. Ck-out noon. Meeting rms. In-rm modem link. Bellhops. Valet serv. Sundries. Golf privileges. Game rm. Cr cds: A, C, D, DS, JCB, MC, V.

D 🕸 👫 ≈ 🏊 🐾 SC

Mount Pleasant *(See also Alma, Clare, Midland)*

Motels

★ ★ **COMFORT INN UNIVERSITY PARK.** *2424 S Mission St, adj to Central Michigan Univ. 517/772-4000; FAX 517/773-6052.* 138 rms, 2 story, 12 suites. S, D $48.50-$119.50; each addl $5; suites $135; under 18 free; wkly, wkday rates; golf plans; higher rates: CMU football wkends, festivals. Crib free. Pet accepted. TV; cable (premium), VCR (movies). Indoor pool. Complimentary continental bkfst. Restaurant nearby. Ck-out noon. Coin lndry. Meeting rms. Business servs avail. In-rm modem link. Game rm. Cr cds: A, D, DS, ER, JCB, MC, V. D 🕸 ≈ 🐾 SC

★ ★ **HOLIDAY INN.** *5665 E Pickard Rd. 517/772-2905; FAX 517/772-4952.* 184 rms, 2-3 story. S, D $58-$145; each addl $10; under 12 free; golf plan. Crib free. Pet accepted. TV; cable (premium). 2 pools, 1 indoor; whirlpool. Playground. Coffee in rms. Restaurants 6:30 am-10 pm; Sun to 8 pm. Rm serv. Bar noon-2 am; Sun to 8 pm; entertainment exc Sun. Ck-out 11 am. Coin lndry. Meeting rms. Business servs avail. In-rm modem link. Bellhops. Valet serv. Sundries. Free airport, bus depot transportation. Lighted tennis. 36-hole golf, greens fee $35-$65, putting green, driving range. Exercise equipt; weights, stair machine, sauna. Rec rm. Lawn games. In-rm whirlpools, refrigerators; some minibars. Balconies. Cr cds: A, C, D, DS, JCB, MC, V. D 🕸 👫 💺 ≈ 🏃 🐾 SC

★ **SUPER 8.** *2323 S Mission. 517/773-8888; FAX 517/772-5371.* 143 rms, 3 story. Apr-Sept: S $54.88-$84.88; D $59.88-$89.88; each addl $5; under 16 free; lower rates rest of yr. Crib free. Pet accepted. TV; cable (premium), VCR avail (movies). Complimentary continental bkfst. Restaurant nearby. Ck-out noon. Meeting rm. Business servs avail. Valet serv. Tennis privileges. X-country ski 3 mi. Some refrigerators. Cr cds: A, C, D, DS, JCB, MC, V. D 🕸 ≈ 👫 🐾 SC

Munising

Motels

✔ ★ **ALGER FALLS.** *Rte 1, Box 967, 2 mi E on MI 28/94. 906/387-3536.* 17 rms. July-Labor Day: S $39-$45; D $45-$50; kit. cottages $55-$65; lower rates rest of yr. Crib $4. Pet accepted. TV; cable. Restaurant nearby. Ck-out 11 am. X-country ski 3 mi. Rec rm. Picnic tables. Wooded area with trails. Cr cds: DS, MC, V. 🕸 ≈ 🐾 🐾

★ ★ **BEST WESTERN.** *Box 310, 3 mi E on MI 28. 906/387-4864; FAX 906/387-2038.* 80 rms, 2 story. Late June-Aug: S, D $59-$64; each addl $5; suites $80-$95; lower rates rest of yr. Crib $5. Pet accepted. TV. Indoor pool; whirlpool, sauna. Restaurant 7 am-10 pm. Bar 11-1 am; Sun from noon. Ck-out 11 am. Meeting rm. Business servs avail. Picnic tables. Some refrigerators. Cr cds: A, D, DS, MC, V. D 🕸 ≈ 🐾 SC

★ ★ **COMFORT INN.** *PO Box 276, on MI 28E. 906/387-5292; FAX 906/387-3753.* 61 rms, 2 story. S, D $63-$95. Crib free. Pet accepted. TV; cable (premium), VCR (movies). Indoor pool; whirlpool. Complimentary continental bkfst. Ck-out 11 am. Coin lndry. Meeting rms. Business servs avail. X-country ski 6 mi. Exercise equipt; bicycle, stair machine. Game rm. Cr cds: A, C, D, DS, ER, JCB, MC, V. D 🕸 ≈ 🏃 🐾 SC

✔ ★ **SUNSET RESORT.** *1315 Bay St, 1315 Bay St. 906/387-4574.* 16 units (1-3-rm), 6 kits. No A/C. June-Labor Day: S, D $49-$55; kit. units $54-$60; lower rates rest of yr. Closed 3rd wk Oct-Apr 30. Crib $1. Pet accepted. TV; cable. Playground. Complimentary coffee. Restaurant nearby. Ck-out 11 am. Lawn games. Picnic tables, grills. On Lake Superior; dockage. Cr cds: MC, V. 🕸 ≈ 🐾 🐾

Newberry

Motels

★ **MANOR.** *Rte 04, Box 979, S Newberry Ave (MI 123), 3 mi N of jct MI 28. 906/293-5000.* 12 rms. Mid-June-mid-Oct, Christmas wk: S, D $38-$58; each addl $4; suites

$54-$72; family rates; lower rates rest of yr. Crib free. Pet accepted. TV; cable (premium). Restaurant nearby. Ck-out 10 am. Lawn games. Cr cds: DS, MC, V.

✔★ **ZELLAR'S VILLAGE INN.** *S Newberry Ave (MI 123), 2¹/₂ mi N of jct MI 28. 906/293-5114; FAX 906/293-5116.* 20 rms. S $40; D $50-$60; each addl $4. Crib $5. Pet accepted. TV; cable (premium). Restaurant 6 am-10 pm. Rm serv. Bar. Ck-out 11 am. Meeting rms. Business servs avail. In-rm modem link. Sundries. Game rm. Cr cds: A, C, D, DS, MC, V.

Petoskey

Motel

✔★ **ECONO LODGE.** *1858 US 131S. 616/348-3324; FAX 616/348-3521.* 60 rms, 2 story. Mid-June-early Sept: S $46-$85; D $51-$95; family rates; ski, package plans; lower rates rest of yr. Crib avail. Pet accepted. TV; cable. Indoor pool; whirlpool. Complimentary continental bkfst. Restaurant nearby. Ck-out 11 am. Business servs avail. Downhill ski 15 mi; x-country ski 10 mi. Cr cds: A, D, DS, MC, V.

Plymouth

Motel

✔★ **RED ROOF INN.** *39700 Ann Arbor Rd, at I-275 exit 28. 313/459-3300; FAX 313/459-3072.* 109 rms, 2 story. S $33.99-$48.99; D $41.99-$50.99; under 18 free. Crib free. Pet accepted. TV; cable (premium). Restaurant opp open 24 hrs. Ck-out noon. In-rm modem link. Cr cds: A, C, D, DS, MC, V.

Pontiac (See also Detroit, Southfield)

Motor Hotel

★ ★ ★ **HILTON SUITES.** *(2300 Featherstone Rd, Auburn Hills 48326) Just W of I-75, opp Silverdome. 248/334-2222; FAX 248/334-2922.* 224 suites, 5 story. S, D $89-$149; each addl $15; family, wkend rates; package plans. Crib free. Pet accepted, some restrictions. TV; cable (premium), VCR (movies $3). Indoor pool; whirlpool. Complimentary full bkfst. Complimentary coffee in rms. Restaurant 6-9:30 am, 11:30 am-1:30 pm, 5:30-10 pm; wkend hrs vary. Rm serv. Bar. Ck-out noon. Coin lndry. Meeting rms. Business center. In-rm modem link. Bellhops. Sundries. Valet serv. Gift shop. Golf privileges. Downhill/x-country ski 12 mi. Exercise equipt; weights, treadmill, sauna. Game rm. Refrigerators. Some balconies. Cr cds: A, C, D, DS, ER, JCB, MC, V.

Port Huron

Motel

★ **KNIGHTS INN.** *2160 Water St. 810/982-1022; FAX 810/982-0927; res: 800/843-5644.* 104 units. Apr-Oct: S $51.95-$62.95; D $57.99-$67.95; each addl $5; kit. units $61.95-$77.95; under 18 free; lower rates rest of yr. Crib free. Pet accepted. TV; cable (premium), VCR avail. Pool. Coffee in rms. Restaurant nearby. Ck-out noon. Cr cds: A, C, D, DS, MC, V.

Saginaw (See also Bay City, Midland)

Motel

✔★ **SUPER 8.** *4848 Town Centre Rd (48603). 517/791-3003.* 62 rms, 3 story. Apr-Sept: S $37.88; D $43.88-$47.88; each addl $5; suite $53.88; under 12 free; lower rates rest of yr. Crib free. Pet accepted, some restrictions. TV; cable (premium). Restaurant nearby. Ck-out 11 am. Cr cds: A, C, D, DS, MC, V.

Motor Hotel

★ ★ **FOUR POINTS BY SHERATON.** *4960 Towne Centre Rd (48604). 517/790-5050; FAX 517/790-1466.* 156 rms, 6 story. S $68-$98; D $78-$108; each addl $10; under 18 free; wkend plan. Crib free. Pet accepted, some restrictions; $20 refundable. TV; cable (premium), VCR avail. Indoor/outdoor pool; whirlpool. Restaurant 6:30 am-10 pm. Rm serv. Bar 11-2 am; entertainment. Ck-out noon. Meeting rms. Business servs avail. Bellhops. Valet serv. Free airport transportation. Sauna. Health club privileges. Game rm. Country French decor. Cr cds: A, C, D, DS, ER, JCB, MC, V.

St Ignace *(See also Mackinaw City)*

Motels

★★**BUDGET HOST GOLDEN ANCHOR.** *700 N State St (I-75 Business).* *906/643-9666; FAX 906/643-9126.* 56 rms, 2 story. Mid-June-Labor Day: S, D $54-$92; each addl $4; higher rates special events, holidays, Auto Show (3-day min); Labor day (2-day min); lower rates rest of yr. Crib free. Pet accepted; $20 refundable. TV; cable (premium). Indoor pool; whirlpool. Guest lndry. Playground. Ck-out 11 am. Business servs avail. In-rm modem link. Downhill/x-country ski 5 mi. Some refrigerators, in-rm whirlpools. Sun deck. Overlooks Moran Bay. Ferry 1 blk. Cr cds: A, C, D, DS, MC, V.

★★**HOWARD JOHNSON-LODGE DUPONT.** *913 Boulevard Dr. 906/643-9700; FAX 906/643-6762.* 57 rms, 2 story. Mid-June-mid-Sept: S $68-$76; D $73-$87; each addl $6; under 18 free; higher rates: Labor Day (2-day min), auto show (3-day min); lower rates rest of yr. Crib free. Pet accepted; $6. Indoor pool; whirlpool. TV; cable, VCR avail. Complimentary coffee in lobby. Restaurant nearby. Ck-out noon. Coin lndry. Meeting rms. Sundries. X-country ski 7 mi. Game rm. Cr cds: A, C, D, DS, ER, JCB, MC, V.

St Joseph

Motels

★★**COMFORT INN.** *(1598 Mall Dr, Benton Harbor 49022) I-94 exit 29. 616/925-1880.* 52 rms, 2 story. Mid-May-mid-Sept: S $59.95; D $64.95; family rates; lower rates rest of yr. Crib free. Pet accepted. TV; cable (premium). Indoor pool; whirlpool. Complimentary continental bkfst. Restaurant nearby. Ck-out 11 am. Business servs avail. Game rm. Some refrigerators. Cr cds: A, D, DS, MC, V.

✔★**SUPER 8.** *(1950 E Napier Ave, Benton Harbor 49022) I-94 exit 30. 616/926-1371; FAX 616/926-1371, ext. 169.* 62 rms, 3 story. S $35.88-$47.88; D $46.88-$60.88; under 12 free; higher rates wkends, special events. Crib free. Pet accepted. TV; cable (premium). Complimentary coffee in lobby. Restaurant nearby. Ck-out 11 am. Business servs avail. Cr cds: A, C, D, DS, MC, V.

Sault Ste Marie *(See also Sault Ste Marie, ON, Canada)*

Motels

★**CRESTVIEW THRIFTY INNS.** *1200 Ashmun St (I-75 Business). 906/635-5213; FAX 906/635-9672; res: 800/955-5213.* 44 rms. July-mid-Oct: S $54; D $64-$74; package plans; lower rates rest of yr. Crib free. Pet accepted. TV; cable (premium). Complimentary coffee in lobby. Restaurant nearby. Ck-out 11 am. In-rm modem link. Some refrigerators. Locks 1 mi. Cr cds: A, D, DS, MC, V.

★**SEAWAY.** *1800 Ashmun St (I-75 Business). 906/632-8201; FAX 906/632-8210; res: 800/782-0466.* 18 rms. June-mid-Sept: S $63.70; D $68.25; each addl $5; lower rates rest of yr. Crib free. Pet accepted, some restrictions. TV; cable. Complimentary coffee in lobby. Restaurant opp 5 am-midnight. Ck-out 10 am. Free airport transportation. Downhill ski 18 mi; x-country ski 1/4 mi. Cr cds: A, C, D, DS, MC, V.

★**SUPER 8.** *3826 I-75 Business Spur. 906/632-8882; FAX 906/632-3766.* 61 rms, 2 story. July-Aug: S $54.88-$70.88; D $60.88-$72.88; under 12 free; lower rates rest of yr. Crib free. Pet accepted, some restrictions; $50 deposit. TV; cable (premium). Complimentary continental bkfst. Restaurant nearby. Ck-out 11 am. Coin lndry. Cr cds: A, C, D, DS, MC, V.

Southfield *(See also Birmingham, Bloomfield Hills, Detroit, Farmington, Pontiac)*

Motor Hotel

★★★**HOLIDAY INN.** *26555 Telegraph Rd (48034). 810/353-7700; FAX 810/353-8377.* 417 rms, 2-16 story. S, D $75-$81; each addl $8; suites $175-$249; under 19 free; wkend rates. Crib free. Pet accepted, some restrictions. TV; cable (premium). Indoor pool; whirlpool. Restaurant 6:30 am-2 pm, 5-10 pm; Sat, Sun from 7 am. Rm serv. Bar 11-1 am. Ck-out noon. Coin lndry. Convention facilities. Bellhops. Sundries. Gift shop. Barber, beauty shop. Downhill/x-country ski 20 mi. Game rm. Rec rm. Many rms in circular tower. Cr cds: A, C, D, DS, JCB, MC, V.

Hotel

★ ★ **HILTON GARDEN INN.** 26000 American Dr (48034). 810/357-1100; FAX 810/799-7030. 195 rms, 7 story. S, D $89; each addl $10; suites $175; under 12 free; wkend rates. Crib free. Pet accepted, some restrictions. TV; cable (premium). Indoor pool; whirlpool. Restaurant 6-10 am, 11 am-2 pm, 5-10 pm; wkend hrs vary. Bar 5 pm-midnight. Ck-out 1 pm. Meeting rms. Business center. In-rm modem link. Exercise equipt; weight machine, stair machine, sauna. Cr cds: A, C, D, DS, ER, JCB, MC, V.

South Haven

Motel

✔ ★ ★ **ECONO LODGE.** 09817 MI 140, I-196 exit 18. 616/637-5141; FAX 616/637-1109. 60 rms. May-Sept: S $70-$82; D $80-$90; each addl $5; suites $100-$120; under 18 free; higher rates: Tulip Festival, some hols; lower rates rest of yr. Crib $5. Pet accepted. TV; cable (premium), VCR avail (movies). Playground. Indoor pool. Complimentary coffee in rms. Restaurant adj 6:30 am-8 pm; Fri, Sat to 10 pm. Bar. Ck-out 11 am. Coin lndry. Valet serv. Downhill ski 20 mi; x-country ski 5 mi. Exercise rm; instructor, weights, bicycles, sauna. Cr cds: A, C, D, DS, JCB, MC, V.

Traverse City

Motels

★ **MAIN STREET INN.** 618 E Front St (49686). 616/929-0410; FAX 616/929-0489; res: 800/255-7180. 95 rms, 21 kit. units. June-Aug: S, D $89.95-$125; each addl $6; kit. units $99.95; under 18 free; lower rates rest of yr. Crib free. Pet accepted. TV; cable (premium), VCR avail (movies). Heated pool. Ck-out 11 am. Coin lndry. Meeting rm. Business servs avail. Downhill ski 5 mi; x-country ski 8 mi. Putting green. Opp beach. Cr cds: A, C, D, DS, ER, MC, V.

★ ★ **TRAVERSE BAY INN.** 2300 US 31N (49686). 616/938-2646; FAX 616/938-5845; res: 800/968-2646. 24 rms, 2 story. July-late Aug: S $55; D $65; suites $95-$165; under 12 free; lower rates rest of yr. Crib free. Pet accepted. TV; cable (premium), VCR avail (movies). Pool; whirlpool. Playground. Restaurant nearby. Ck-out 11 am. Business servs avail. Gift shop. Valet serv. Coin lndry. Downhill/x-country ski 1 mi. Game rm. Some refrigerators. Cr cds: A, DS, MC, V.

Motor Hotel

★ ★ ★ **HOLIDAY INN.** 615 E Front St (49686). 616/947-3700; FAX 616/947-0361. 179 rms, 4 story. June-Labor Day: S, D $140-$170; each addl $8; under 19 free; lower rates rest of yr. Crib free. Pet accepted. TV; cable (premium). Indoor pool; whirlpool. Restaurant 7-1 am. Rm serv. Ck-out 11 am. Meeting rm. Business servs avail. Bellhops. Sundries. Gift shop. Valet serv. Free airport, bus depot transportation. Downhill ski 5 mi; x-country ski 8 mi. Exercise equipt; bicycle, weight machine, sauna. Game rm. Lawn games. Some refrigerators. Cr cds: A, C, D, DS, JCB, MC, V.

Troy (See also Detroit, Pontiac, Warren)

Motels

★ ★ **HAMPTON INN.** (32420 Stephenson Hwy, Madison Heights 48071) Approx 2 mi S via I-75 exit 65B. 810/585-8881; FAX 810/585-9446. 124 rms, 4 story. S $53-$65; D $57-$70; under 18 free. Crib free. Pet accepted, some restrictions. TV; cable (premium). Complimentary continental bkfst, coffee. Restaurant nearby. Ck-out noon. Meeting rm. In-rm modem link. Valet serv. Exercise equipt; weights, bicycles, sauna. Cr cds: A, C, D, DS, MC, V.

✔ ★ **RED ROOF INN.** 2350 Rochester Court (48083). 810/689-4391; FAX 810/689-4397. 109 rms, 2 story. S $36.99-$44.99; D $42.99-$50.99; 3 or more $58.99; under 18 free. Crib free. Pet accepted. TV; cable (premium). Restaurant nearby. Ck-out noon. In-rm modem link. X-country ski 10 mi. Cr cds: A, C, D, DS, MC, V.

★ ★ **RESIDENCE INN BY MARRIOTT.** 2600 Livernois Rd (48083). 810/689-6856; FAX 810/689-3788. 152 kit. suites, 2 story. May-Sept: S $109-$129; D $119-$179; family, wkly, wkend, hol rates; 2-day min hols; lower rates rest of yr. Crib free. Pet accepted, some restrictions; $6/day. TV; cable (premium), VCR avail. Whirlpool. Complimentary coffee in rms. Complimentary continental bkfst. Restaurant opp 7 am-8 pm. Ck-out noon. Coin lndry. In-rm modem link. Valet serv. Downhill/x-country ski 20 mi. Health club privileges. Balconies. Picnic tables. Cr cds: A, C, D, DS, MC, V.

Motor Hotels

★ ★ **DRURY INN.** *575 W Big Beaver Rd (48084). 810/528-3330.* 153 rms, 4 story. S, D $66-$76; each addl $6; under 18 free; wkend rates. Crib free. Pet accepted, some restrictions. TV; cable (premium), VCR avail. Pool. Complimentary continental bkfst. Restaurant adj 6 am-midnight; Thurs-Sat open 24 hrs. Ck-out noon. Meeting rms. In-rm modem link. Valet serv. X-country ski 4 mi. Health club privileges. Cr cds: A, C, D, DS, MC, V.

★ ★ ★ **HILTON INN NORTHFIELD.** *5500 Crooks Rd (48098), at I-75. 810/879-2100; FAX 810/879-6054.* 191 rms, 3 story. S $114-$134; D $124-$144; each addl $10; suites $250-$350; family, wkend rates; package plans. Crib free. Pet accepted, some restrictions. TV; cable (premium). Sauna. Indoor pool. Coffee in rms. Restaurant 6:30 am-11 pm; Sat, Sun from 7 am. Rm serv. Bar 10:30-2 am; entertainment. Ck-out noon. Meeting rms. Business center. In-rm modem link. Bellhops. Valet serv. Sundries. X-country ski 3 mi. Game rm. Some refrigerators. Private patios, balconies. Cr cds: A, C, D, DS, ER, MC, V.

★ ★ **HOLIDAY INN.** *2537 Rochester Ct (48083). 810/689-7500; FAX 810/689-9015.* 153 rms, 4 story. S $78-$88; D $85-$95; suites $92-$109; under 18 free; wkend rates. Crib free. Pet accepted, some restrictions. TV; cable, VCR avail. Heated pool; poolside serv. Restaurant 6:30 am-1 pm, 5:30-10 pm; Sat & Sun from 7 am. Rm serv. Bar. Ck-out noon. Coin lndry. Meeting rms. In-rm modem link. Bellhops. Valet serv. X-country ski 5 mi. Exercise equipt; weights, bicycles, sauna. Cr cds: A, C, D, DS, JCB, MC, V.

Hotel

★ ★ ★ **MARRIOTT.** *200 W Big Beaver Rd (48084). 810/680-9797; FAX 810/680-9774.* 350 rms, 17 story. S $139-$144; D $169-$174; each addl $30; suites $600; under 18 free; wkend rates. Crib free. Pet accepted. Valet parking $4/day, $8/overnight; free garage. TV; cable (premium), VCR avail. Indoor pool; whirlpool, poolside serv. Restaurant 7 am-11 pm. Bar 4 pm-1 am; entertainment Tues-Sat. Ck-out noon. Convention facilities. Business servs avail. In-rm modem link. Concierge. Gift shop. X-country ski 5 mi. Exercise equipt; stair machine, treadmill, sauna. Refrigerators avail. Luxury level. Cr cds: A, C, D, DS, ER, MC, V.

Wakefield

Resort

★ ★ **INDIANHEAD MOUNTAIN.** *500 Indianhead Rd, 1 mi W on US 2, then 1 mi N. 906/229-5181; FAX 906/229-5920; res: 800/346-3426.* 62 rms, 2-3 story, 51 chalets, 32 condo units. S, D $58-$160; mid-wk rates; ski plan. Closed mid-Apr-June & Oct-mid-Nov. Pet accepted. TV; cable, VCR avail (movies). Indoor pool; whirlpool. Playground. Supervised child's activities (Nov-mid-Apr). Dining rm 7:30 am-9 pm. Bar 8-2 am, Sun from noon, summer from 4 pm. Ck-out 11 am, ck-in 4 pm. Meeting rms. Business servs avail. Free bus depot transportation. Tennis. 9-hole, par 3 golf, greens fee $6-$10. Downhill ski on site. Hiking, mountain biking, nature trails. Game rm. Exercise rm; instructor, weights, bicycles, sauna. Cr cds: A, DS, MC, V.

Warren *(See also Detroit, Troy)*

Motels

★ ★ **GEORGIAN INN.** *(31327 Gratiot Ave, Roseville 48066) 13 Mile Rd at I-94. 810/294-0400; FAX 810/294-1020; res: 800/477-1466.* 111 rms, 2 story. Mid-May-mid-Sept: S, D $60-$73; each addl $5; suites $135; kit. units $81; under 12 free; lower rates rest of yr. Crib free. Pet accepted, some restrictions. TV; cable. Heated pool; poolside serv. Restaurant 6 am-11 pm. Rm serv. Bar. Ck-out noon. Coin lndry. Meeting rms. Business servs avail. In-rm modem link. Valet serv. Exercise equipt; weights, bicycle. Game rm. Cr cds: A, C, D, DS, MC, V.

★ ★ **HOMEWOOD SUITES.** *30180 N Civic Center Dr (48093). 810/558-7870; FAX 810/558-8072; res: 800/225-5466.* 76 kit. suites, 3 story. Suites $64-$139. Crib avail. Pet accepted, some restrictions; $100 refundable. TV; cable (premium), VCR. Pool; whirlpool. Complimentary continental bkfst. Complimentary coffee in rms. Restaurant nearby. Ck-out noon. Coin lndry. Meeting rms. Business center. In-rm modem link. Valet serv. Sundries. Gift shop. Downhill/x-country ski 20 mi. Exercise equipt; weight machine, bicycles. Grills. Cr cds: A, C, D, DS, MC, V.

✔ ★ **RED ROOF INN.** *26300 Dequindre Rd (48091). 810/573-4300; FAX 810/573-6157.* 136 rms, 2 story. S $32.99-$42.99; D $46.99-$53.99; 3 or more $44.99-$60.99; under

18 free; higher rates special events. Crib free. Pet accepted, some restrictions. TV; cable (premium). Complimentary coffee. Restaurant nearby. Ck-out noon. Business servs avail. In-rm modem link. Cr cds: A, C, D, DS, MC, V. [D] [✦] [⬦] [⬦] [SC]

★ ★ RESIDENCE INN BY MARRIOTT. *30120 Civic Center Dr (48093). 810/558-8050; FAX 810/558-8214.* 133 kit. suites, 3 story. Mid-May-mid-Sept: S, D $104; under 18 free; wkly, wkend rates; lower rates rest of yr. Crib free. Pet accepted; $50 deposit & $8/day. TV; cable (premium), VCR. Pool; whirlpool. Complimentary coffee in rms. Complimentary continental bkfst. Restaurant nearby. Ck-out noon. Coin lndry. In-rm modem link. Valet serv. Exercise equipt; weight machine, bicycle. Health club privileges. Some balconies. Picnic tables. Cr cds: A, C, D, DS, ER, JCB, MC, V. [D] [✦] [≈] [✗] [⬦] [⬦] [SC]

Minnesota

Aitkin (See also Brainerd, Deerwood)

Motel

✔★ **RIPPLE RIVER.** 701 S Minnesota Ave, ½ mi S on US 169. 218/927-3734; FAX 218/927-3540; res: 800/258-3734. 28 rms. S $35-$75; D $42-$85; each addl $6. Pet accepted. TV; cable. Complimentary coffee in lobby. Restaurant nearby. Ck-out 11 am. Business servs avail. X-country ski ¼ mi. Some refrigerators, microwaves. On 7 acres. Cr cds: DS, MC, V. 🐾 🖼 🏊 🎿 🐟 SC

Albert Lea (See also Austin)

Motels

✔★ **BEL AIRE.** 700 US 69S, 1 blk S of jct 16 & MN 13. 507/373-3983; FAX 507/373-5161; res: 800/373-4073. 46 rms, 1 story. S $28-$34; D $34-$45; each addl $4; under 14 free. Crib free. Pet accepted. TV; cable. Pool. Playground. Complimentary continental bkfst. Restaurant nearby. Ck-out 11 am. Cr cds: DS, MC, V. 🐾 🏊 🎿 🐟 SC

★★ **BEST WESTERN ALBERT LEA INN.** 2301 E Main St. 507/373-8291; FAX 507/373-4043. 124 rms, 3 story. S $46-$56; D $59-$69; each addl $5; under 18 free. Crib free. Pet accepted. TV. Indoor pool; wading pool, whirlpool. Restaurant 6:30 am-9:30 pm. Bar 5 pm-midnight, closed Sun; entertainment wkends. Ck-out 11 am. Coin lndry. Meeting rms. Business servs avail. Sundries. X-country ski 1 mi. Exercise equipt; bicycle, stair machine, sauna. Game rm. Cr cds: A, C, D, DS, MC, V. D 🐾 🏊 🚴 🎿 🐟 SC

★★ **DAYS INN.** 2306 E Main St. 507/373-6471; FAX 507/373-7517. 129 rms, 2 story. S, D $59-$75; each addl $5; under 18 free. Crib free. Pet accepted. TV. Indoor pool. Restaurant 6:30 am-9 pm. Bar 4 pm-12:30 am. Ck-out 11 am. Coin lndry. Meeting rms. Business servs avail. In-rm modem link. Sundries. X-country ski 1 mi. Cr cds: A, C, D, DS, ER, JCB, MC, V. D 🐾 🏊 🎿 🐟 SC

✔★ **SUPER 8.** 2019 E Main St. 507/377-0591. 60 rms, 3 story. No elvtr. S $36.88; D $47.88; each addl $4. Crib $2. Pet accepted. TV; cable, VCR avail (movies $5). Complimentary coffee Mon-Fri. Restaurants adj. Ck-out 11 am. Business servs avail. Sundries. X-country ski 1 mi. Snowmobile trail adj. Cr cds: A, C, D, DS, MC, V. D 🐾 🏊 🎿 🐟 SC

Alexandria (See also Glenwood, Sauk Centre)

Motel

✔★ **AMERICINN.** 4520 S MN 29. 320/763-6808. 53 rms, 2 story. Memorial Day-Labor Day: S $46.90; D $60.90; each addl $6; under 12 free; lower rates rest of yr. Crib free. Pet accepted. TV; cable (premium). Complimentary continental bkfst. Restaurant adj 6 am-11 pm. Ck-out 11 am. Business servs avail. Indoor pool; whirlpool. Cr cds: A, C, D, DS, MC, V. D 🐾 🏊 🎿 🐟 SC

Austin

Motor Hotel

★★ **HOLIDAY INN.** 1701 4th St NW. 507/433-1000; FAX 507/433-8749. 121 rms, 2 story. S $59-$79; D $69-$89; each addl $10; suites $88-$150; under 19 free. Crib avail. Pet accepted. TV; cable (premium). Indoor pool; wading pool; poolside serv. Complimentary coffee in lobby. Restaurant 6 am-10 pm. Rm serv. Bar 11-1 am; entertainment Mon-Sat. Ck-out 11 am. Coin lndry. Meeting rms. Business servs avail. In-rm modem link. Airport, RR station transportation. Exercise equipt; weights, bicycles, whirlpool, sauna. Game rm. Refrigerator in suites. Cr cds: A, C, D, DS, JCB, MC, V. D 🐾 🏊 🚴 🎿 🐟 SC

Bemidji

Motel

★★★ **NORTHERN INN.** US 2W (56601), near Municipal Airport. 218/751-9500. 123 rms, 2 story. Mid-May-Oct: S $59-$69; D $69-$79; each addl $10; suites $130; family rates; lower rates rest of yr. Crib free. Pet accepted. TV; cable, VCR avail (movies). Indoor pool;

whirlpool, poolside serv. Restaurant 6 am-10 pm; Fri, Sat to 11 pm. Rm serv. Bar 3 pm-1 am; Sat, Sun from noon. Ck-out noon. Coin Indry. Meeting rms. Business servs avail. In-rm modem link. Valet serv. Sundries. Beauty shop. Free airport, bus depot transportation. Indoor putting green. Downhill ski 10 mi; x-country ski 4 mi. Exercise equipt; weight machine, stair machine, sauna. Game rm. Rec rm. Cr cds: A, C, D, DS, JCB, MC, V.

Resort

★ ★ ★ **RUTTGER'S BIRCHMONT LODGE.** *530 Birchmont Beach Rd NE (56601), 4 mi N on Bemidji Ave (County 21).* 218/751-1630; 800 888/788-8437. 28 rms in 3-story lodge, 29 cottages (1-4 bedrm), 11 kits. Some A/C. No elvtr. Late June-mid-Aug: S $66-$69; D $78-$148; MAP avail; family rates; package plans; lower rates rest of yr. Fewer units late Sept-early May. Crib $4. Pet accepted. TV; cable. 2 pools, 1 indoor; whirlpool, poolside serv. Free supervised child's activities (June-Labor Day). Dining rm (seasonal) 7:30-10:30 am, 11:30-2 pm, 5:30-8:30 pm. Bar (seasonal) noon-1 am. Ck-out 11:30 am, ck-in after 4:30 pm. Coin Indry. Grocery, package store 4 mi. Meeting rms. Business servs avail. In-rm modem link. Airport, bus depot transportation. Sports dir. Tennis. 18-hole golf privileges, greens fee $28. Private beach. Waterskiing instruction. Boats, motors, sailboats, boat launch, dockage. Downhill ski 15 mi; x-country ski on site. Indoor, outdoor games. Soc dir. Movies. Exercise rm; instructor, weights, bicycles, sauna. Some refrigerators; fireplace in most cabins. Screened porches. Cr cds: A, DS, MC, V.

Bloomington *(See also Minneapolis)*

Motels

★ ★ **BEST WESTERN THUNDERBIRD.** *2201 E 78th St (55425).* 612/854-3411; FAX 612/854-1183. 263 rms, 2 story. S $85-$110; D $91-$110; each addl $6; suites $135-$370; under 13 free. Crib free. Pet accepted. TV; cable. 2 pools, 1 indoor; whirlpool. Restaurant 6:30 am-10:30 pm. Rm serv to 11 am. Bar 4-11:30 pm; entertainment. Ck-out 11 am. Meeting rms. Business servs avail. Valet serv. Sundries. Gift shop. Free airport transportation. Downhill ski 10 mi; x-country ski 1 mi. Exercise equipt; weights, bicycles, sauna. Game rm. Refrigerators, microwaves avail. Cr cds: A, C, D, DS, ER, JCB, MC, V.

✔ ★ **BUDGETEL INN.** *7815 Nicollet Ave S (55420).* 612/881-7311; FAX 612/881-0604. 190 rms, 2 story. S $55.95; D $63.95; under 18 free. Crib free. Pet accepted, some restrictions. TV; cable (premium). Complimentary continental bkfst. Restaurant nearby. Ck-out noon. Meeting rms. Business servs avail. In-rm modem link. Downhill ski 10 mi; x-country ski 1/2 mi. Cr cds: A, C, D, DS, MC, V.

★ ★ **RESIDENCE INN BY MARRIOTT.** *(7780 Flying Cloud Dr, Eden Prairie 55344)* W on I-494. 612/829-0033; FAX 612/829-1935. 126 kit. suites, 1-2 story. S, D $129-$195; under 18 free. Pet accepted, some restrictions; $50. TV; cable (premium), VCR (movies $3.50). Heated pool; whirlpool. Complimentary bkfst buffet. Ck-out noon. Coin Indry. Meeting rms. Business servs avail. In-rm modem link. Valet serv. Airport transportation avail. Downhill ski 10 mi; x-country ski 1 mi. Exercise equipt; stair machine, weights. Refrigerators. Private patios, balconies. Cr cds: A, C, D, DS, JCB, MC, V.

✔ ★ **SELECT INN.** *7851 Normandale Blvd (55435).* 612/835-7400; FAX 612/835-4124; res: 800/641-1000. 148 rms, 2 story. S $46.90; D $55.90; each addl $4; under 13 free. Crib $3. Pet accepted; $25. TV; cable. Indoor pool. Complimentary continental bkfst. Restaurant nearby. Ck-out 11 am. Coin Indry. Meeting rms. Business servs avail. Free airport transportation. Downhill ski 5 mi. Exercise equipt; weights, treadmill. Cr cds: A, C, D, DS, MC, V.

Motor Hotel

★ ★ **FAIRFIELD INN BY MARRIOTT.** *2401 E 80th St (55425).* 612/858-8475; FAX 612/858-8475. 134 rms, 4 story. May-Oct: S, D $79-$140; under 18 free; lower rates rest of yr. Crib avail. Pet accepted. TV; cable (premium). Indoor pool; whirlpool. Complimentary continental bkfst. Restaurant adj 6 am-11 pm. Ck-out noon. Meeting rms. Business servs avail. Downhill ski 15 mi; x-country ski 1 mi. Rec rm. Some refrigerators. Cr cds: A, C, D, DS, JCB, MC, V.

Brainerd *(See also Aitkin, Deerwood, Little Falls)*

Motels

★ ★ **COUNTRY INN.** *(1220 Dellwood Dr N, Baxter 56425)* 1 mi N on MN 371. 218/828-2161; FAX 218/825-8419. 68 rms, 2 story. Mid-May-Sept: S, D $68-$78; suites

$99-$107; under 18 free; higher rates auto races; lower rates rest of yr. Crib free. Pet accepted. TV; cable (premium), VCR avail (movies). Complimentary continental bkfst. Complimentary coffee in rms. Ck-out noon. Meeting rms. Business servs avail. In-rm modem link. Valet serv. Coin lndry. X-country ski 1½ mi. Health club privileges. Indoor pool; whirlpool, sauna. Refrigerators, microwaves; many wet bars; some in-rm whirlpools. Cr cds: A, D, DS, MC, V. ⊡ 🖘 🏊 ⚓ 🎿 🐾 SC

★ **DAYS INN.** *1630 Fairview Rd, 2 mi W of town at jct MN 210, MN 371. 218/829-0391; FAX 218/828-0749.* 59 rms, 2 story. May-Sept: S $48-$57; D $54-$66; each addl $6; higher rates special events; lower rates rest of yr. Crib free. Pet accepted, some restrictions. TV; cable (premium). Complimentary continental bkfst. Restaurant adj open 24 hrs. Ck-out 11 am. Business servs avail. Downhill ski 15 mi; x-country ski 1 mi. Cr cds: A, C, D, DS, MC, V. ⊡ 🖘 🏊 ⚓ 🎿 🐾 SC

★ ★ **DAYS INN-NISSWA.** *(45 N Smiley Rd, Nisswa 56468) 13 mi N on MN 371. 218/963-3500; FAX 218/963-4936.* 46 rms, 2 story. Mid-May-Sept: S $51.90-$61.90; D $54.90-$71.90; each addl $5; under 12 free; higher rates special events; lower rates rest of yr. Crib free. Pet accepted; $25 deposit. TV; cable, VCR avail (movies). Indoor pool; whirlpool. Complimentary continental bkfst. Restaurant nearby. Ck-out 11 am. Coin lndry. Downhill ski 15 mi; x-country ski 3 blks. Cr cds: A, C, D, DS, MC, V.
⊡ 🖘 🏊 ⚓ 🎿 🐾 SC

★ ★ **HOLIDAY INN.** *MN 371S, 1 mi S on MN 371. 218/829-1441; FAX 218/829-1444.* 150 rms, 2 story. Mid-May-early Sept: S, D $65-$89; under 18 free; lower rates rest of yr. Crib free. Pet accepted. TV; cable. Indoor pool; whirlpool, poolside serv. Restaurant 6 am-2 pm, 5-10 pm. Rm serv. Bar 3 pm-1 am. Ck-out noon. Coin lndry. Meeting rms. Business servs avail. In-rm modem link. Bellhops. Valet serv. Free airport, bus depot transportation. Tennis. Downhill ski 7 mi; x-country ski 3 mi. Sauna. Rec rm. Cr cds: A, C, D, DS, JCB, MC, V. ⊡ 🖘 🏊 🎾 ⛷ 🎿 ⚓ 🐾 SC

Cloquet *(See also Duluth)*

Motel

✔ ★ **AMERICINN.** *MN 33 & Big Lake Rd, N of I-35 Cloquet exit. 218/879-1231; FAX 218/879-2237; res: 800/634-3444.* 51 rms, 2 story. S $41.90-$80.90; D $46.90-$80.90; each addl $4. Crib free. Pet accepted. TV; cable (premium). Indoor pool; whirlpool. Complimentary continental bkfst. Restaurant adj open 24 hrs. Ck-out 11 am. Meeting rm. Business servs avail. Sauna. Many refrigerators. Cr cds: A, D, DS, MC, V. ⊡ 🖘 ⚓ 🎿 🐾 SC

Cook

Motel

✔ ★ **NORTH COUNTRY INN.** *(4483 US 53, Orr 55771) N on US 53. 218/757-3778.* 12 rms. May-Sept: S $38.90; D $43.90-$45.90; each addl $6; under 12 free; lower rates rest of yr. Crib free. Pet accepted. TV; cable (premium), VCR avail. Complimentary coffee in lobby. Restaurant nearby. Ck-out 11 am. Picnic tables. Cr cds: A, DS, MC, V.
⊡ 🖘 🎿 🐾

Deerwood *(See also Aitkin, Brainerd)*

Motel

★ ★ **COUNTRY INN BY CARLSON.** *115 E Front St. 218/534-3101; FAX 218/534-3685; res: 800/456-4000.* 38 rms, 2 story. Late May-Aug: S, D $65-$85; each addl $6; under 18 free; lower rates rest of yr. Crib free. Pet accepted, some restrictions. TV; cable (premium), VCR avail (movies). Indoor pool; whirlpool. Complimentary continental bkfst. Complimentary coffee in rms. Restaurant nearby. Ck-out 11 am. Coin lndry. X-country ski 1 mi. Sauna. Game rm. Some refrigerators, wet bars. Cr cds: A, D, DS, MC, V.
⊡ 🖘 🏊 ⚓ 🎿 🐾 SC

Duluth

Motels

✔ ★ **ALLYNDALE.** *510 N 66th Ave W (55807), I-35N exit 251A or I-35S exit 252, near Spirit Mountain Recreation Area. 218/628-1061; res: 800/806-1061.* 21 rms. Mid-Apr-mid-Oct: S $38; D $43-$48; each addl $5; lower rates rest of yr. Crib $5. Pet accepted, some restrictions; $5. TV; cable. Playground. Complimentary coffee. Restaurant nearby. Ck-out 11 am. Downhill/x-country ski 1½ mi. Refrigerators, microwaves. Picnic tables. Cr cds: A, C, D, DS, MC, V. 🖘 🎿 ⚓ 🐾

★ ★ **BEST WESTERN EDGEWATER EAST & WEST.** *2400 London Rd (55812). 218/728-3601; FAX 218/728-3727; res: 800/777-7925.* 283 rms, 2-5 story. June-mid-Oct: D $64-$115; each addl $6; suites $98-$169; under 18 free; ski plans; lower rates rest of yr. Crib $2. Pet accepted, some restrictions. TV; cable (premium). Indoor pool; whirlpool. Playground. Complimentary continental bkfst. Restaurant adj. Ck-out noon. Meeting rm. Business servs avail. Valet serv. Miniature golf. Downhill ski 7 mi; x-country ski 1 mi. Sauna. Game rm. Lawn games. Refrigerators. Many rms with balcony, view of Lake Superior. Cr cds: A, C, D, DS, ER, JCB, MC, V. ⬜ 🐾 🏊 ≋ ⛷ 🐾 **SC**

★ **DAYS INN.** *909 Cottonwood Ave (55811), opp Hill Mall. 218/727-3110; FAX 218/727-3110, ext. 301.* 86 rms, 2-3 story. No elvtr. June-mid-Oct: S $59-$82; D $68-$82; each addl $6; higher rates special events; lower rates rest of yr. Crib free. Pet accepted. TV; cable (premium), VCR avail. Complimentary continental bkfst. Restaurant opp open 24 hrs. Ck-out noon. Business servs avail. Cr cds: A, C, D, DS, JCB, MC, V. ⬜ 🐾 ⛷ 🐾 **SC**

Hotels

★ ★ ★ **FITGER'S INN.** *600 E Superior St (55802). 218/722-8826; res: 800/726-2982.* E-mail fitgers@fitgers.com; web www.fitgers.com. 60 rms, 5 story, 18 suites. May-Oct: S, D $90-$120; suites $145-$245; under 17 free; lower rates rest of yr. Pet accepted, some restrictions. TV; cable (premium), VCR avail. Restaurant 7 am-10 pm. Rm serv. Bar 11 am-11 pm; entertainment wkends. Ck-out noon. Meeting rms. Business servs avail. In-rm modem link. Shopping arcade. Exercise equipt; stair machine, ski machine. Some in-rm whirlpools, fireplaces. Most rms overlook Lake Superior. Part of renovated 1858 brewery; shops, theater adj. Cr cds: A, C, D, DS, MC, V. ⬜ 🐾 🏋 ⛷ 🐾

★ ★ ★ **RADISSON.** *505 W Superior St (55802), NE of I-35 Superior St exit. 218/727-8981; FAX 218/727-0162.* Web www.radisson.com. 268 rms, 15 story. June-mid-Oct: S $80-$110; D $80-$110; each addl $10; suites $135-$250; under 18 free; seasonal package plans; lower rates rest of yr. Crib free. Pet accepted. TV; cable, VCR avail. Indoor pool; whirlpool, poolside serv. Restaurant 6:30 am-2 pm, 4:30-10 pm. Bar 11:30-1 am; closed Sun. Ck-out noon. Meeting rms. Business servs avail. Downhill/x-country ski 10 mi. Sauna. Health club privileges. Cr cds: A, C, D, DS, ER, JCB, MC, V. ⬜ 🐾 🏊 ≋ ⛷ 🐾 **SC**

Elk River (See also Minneapolis, St Cloud, St Paul)

Motel

★ ★ **AMERICINN.** *17432 US 10. 612/441-8554; res: 800/634-3444.* 42 rms, 2 story. S $49.90-$56.90; D $56.90-$92.90; under 12 free. Crib free. Pet accepted, some restrictions; $5. TV; cable, VCR (movies). Indoor pool; whirlpool. Complimentary continental bkfst. Restaurant opp 6 am-11 pm. Ck-out 11 am. Meeting rms. X-country ski 3 blks. Sauna. Mississippi River 1 blk. Cr cds: A, C, D, DS, MC, V. ⬜ 🐾 ⛷ ≋ ⛷ 🐾 **SC**

Ely

Motel

✔ ★ **BUDGET HOST.** *1047 E Sheridan St. 218/365-3237; FAX 218/365-3099.* E-mail pat@ely-motels.com; web www.ely-motels.com. 17 rms. S $44.95; D $54.95-$59.95; each addl $5-$8; family rates. Crib free. Pet accepted; $10/day. TV; cable (premium). Complimentary coffee in rms. Restaurant nearby. Ck-out 10 am. Business servs avail. Free airport transportation. X-country ski ½ mi. Sauna. Cr cds: A, C, D, DS, MC, V. 🐾 ⛷ 🐾 **SC**

Cottage Colony

★ ★ **TIMBER BAY LODGE & HOUSEBOATS.** *(Babbitt 55706) 15 mi S on County 21, then 3 mi E on County 70; 2 mi NE of Babbitt, in Superior Natl Forest. 218/827-3682; res: 800/846-6821.* E-mail timber @uslink.net; web www.timberbay.com. 12 kit. cabins (1-3-bedrm), 12 houseboats. No A/C. Mid-June-mid-Aug: houseboats for 2-10, $150-$300/day (3-day min); cabins: $650-$1,075/wk; daily rates; lower rates mid-May-mid-June, mid-Aug-Sept. Closed rest of yr. Pet accepted; $6/day, $30/wk. No maid serv. TV in cabins. Free supervised child's activities (mid-June-mid-Aug). Ck-out 10 am, ck-in 3 pm. Grocery, coin lndry, package store 2 mi. Golf privileges. Private beach. Boats, motors, canoes, kayaks, marina. Naturalist program. Lawn games. Rec rm. Game rm. Microwaves in cabins. Cabins with fireplaces & decks. On Birch Lake, among tall pines. Cr cds: DS, MC, V. 🐾 ⛷ 🏋 ≋ 🐾

Eveleth *(See also Cook, Hibbing, Virginia)*

Motel

★ ★ ★ **HOLIDAY INN.** *On Hat Trick Ave (US 53), adj to US Hockey Hall of Fame.* 218/744-2703; FAX 218/744-5865. 145 rms, 2 story. S, D $59-$92; under 19 free. Crib free. Pet accepted. TV; cable (premium). Indoor pool. Restaurant 6 am-10 pm. Rm serv. Bar 4 pm-1 am. Ck-out noon. Coin lndry. Meeting rms. Business servs avail. Sundries. Gift shop. Sauna. Rec rm. Some refrigerators, microwaves. Cr cds: A, C, D, DS, JCB, MC, V.
D ❖ ≋ ⊠ 🔥 SC

Fairmont

Motel

★ **SUPER 8.** *MN 15 & I-90, exit 102.* 507/238-9444; FAX 507/238-9371. 47 rms, 2 story. S, D $44.98-$53.98; each addl $5; under 12 free. Crib $5. Pet accepted. TV; cable. Continental bkfst. Restaurant opp 6 am-10 pm. Ck-out noon. Business servs avail. Free airport transportation. Cr cds: A, C, D, DS, MC, V. D ❖ ≋ ⊠ 🔥 SC

Glenwood *(See also Alexandria, Morris, Sauk Centre)*

Motel

✔ ★ **HI-VIEW.** *MN 55, 1 mi NE, between MN 28 & 29.* 320/634-4541. 12 rms. S $26; D $40; each addl $3. Crib free. Pet accepted. TV; cable (premium). Playground. Restaurant nearby. Ck-out 11 am. Sundries. Picnic tables, grill. Overlooks city, Lake Minnewaska. Cr cds: DS, MC, V. ❖ 🔥

Grand Marais *(See also Lutsen)*

Motels

★ ★ **BEST WESTERN SUPERIOR INN & SUITES.** *1st Ave E, 1 blk E, just off US 61.* 218/387-2240; FAX 218/387-2244; res: 800/842-8439. Web www.bestwestern.com. 50 rms, 2-3 story. June-Oct: D $79-$109; suites $89-$149; lower rates rest of yr. Crib free. Pet accepted. TV; cable (premium), VCR avail (movies). Complimentary continental bkfst. Coffee in rms. Restaurant nearby. Ck-out 11 am. Coin lndry. Business servs avail. Downhill ski 18 mi; x-country ski ½ mi. Snowmobiling. Whirlpool. Refrigerators; some bathrm phones, whirlpools, fireplaces. Balconies. Private beach on lake. View of Lake Superior. Cr cds: A, C, D, DS, ER, MC, V. D ❖ ⤇ ≋ ⊠ 🔥 SC

★ ★ **EAST BAY.** 218/387-2800; res: 800/414-2807; FAX 218/387-2801. 36 rms, 2-3 story, 4 suites. No A/C. Mid-May-Oct: S, D $51-$92.50; suites $125-$150; under 12 free; lower rates rest of yr. Crib free. Pet accepted. TV; cable. Restaurant 7 am-2 pm, 5-9 pm. Rm serv. Bar 11 am-9 pm; entertainment. Ck-out 11 am. Downhill ski 18 mi; x-country ski 5 mi. Massage. Whirlpool. Many refrigerators. Some in-rm whirlpools, refrigerators. Microwave, wet bar, fireplace in suites. On lake. Cr cds: A, DS, MC, V. D ❖ ⤇ ≋ ⊠ 🔥

★ ★ **ECONO LODGE.** *US 61E (55604-0667), 2 blks E on US 61.* 218/387-2500; FAX 218/387-2647. E-mail gmhotel@worldnet.att.net. 52 rms. Mid-June-mid-Oct, mid-Dec-mid-Mar: S $46-$79; D $49-$89; suites $65-$136; package plans avail; lower rates rest of yr. Pet accepted, some restrictions. TV; cable (premium). Indoor pool; whirlpool. Complimentary continental bkfst. Restaurant nearby. Ck-out 11 am. Guest lndry. Meeting rm. Business servs avail. In-rm modem link. Downhill ski 18 mi; x-country ski 1 mi. Snowmobiling. Refrigerators; some in-rm whirlpools. Cr cds: A, C, D, DS, MC, V.
D ❖ ≋ ⤇ ⊠ 🔥 SC

✔ ★ **SUPER 8.** *US 61W (55604-0667), 1 mi SW on US 61.* 218/387-2448; FAX 218/387-9859; res: 800/247-6020 (MN). E-mail gmhotel@worldnet.att.com. 35 rms. Mid-June-mid-Oct & mid-Dec-mid-Mar: S $45-$72; D $69-$79; each addl $8; package plans; lower rates rest of yr. Crib free. Pet accepted, some restrictions. TV; cable (premium). Complimentary continental bkfst. Restaurant nearby. Ck-out 11 am. Guest lndry. Business servs avail. In-rm modem link. Downhill ski 18 mi; x-country ski 2 mi. Snowmobiling. Sauna. Whirlpool. Refrigerators. Cr cds: A, C, D, DS, MC, V. D ❖ ≋ ⊠ 🔥 SC

Resorts

★ **CLEARWATER LODGE.** *5 Old Rail Ln, 28 mi NW on Gunflint Trail, 4 mi NE on Clearwater Lake Rd.* 218/388-2254; res: 800/527-0554. E-mail clearwater@canoe-bwca.com; web www.canoe-bwca.com. 6 kit. log cabins (2-3 bedrm); 5 rms in lodge, 2 story. No A/C. Mid-May-mid-Oct, cabins: D $715-$750/wk; each addl $60-$100; lodge rms: D

$65-$95; family rates; lower rates. Closed rest of yr. Pet accepted. Playground. Box lunches avail. Ck-out 10 am, ck-in 2 pm. Grocery 6 mi. Coin lndry 8 mi. Sand beach. Private docks; boats, motors, kayaks, canoe outfitting (with bunkhouses). Hiking trails. Nature program. Mountain bikes. Sauna. Microwaves, fireplaces. Some porches. Picnic tables, grills. Cr cds: DS, MC, V. ⬅ ⬅ 🐾

★ **NOR'WESTER LODGE.** *7778 Gunflint Trail, 30 mi NW. 218/388-2252; res: 800/992-4386.* 10 kit. cottages (1-4 bedrm), 1-2 levels. No A/C. EP, wkly: D $774-$1,134; each addl $120-$180; under 3 free; spring, fall rates. Crib avail. Pet accepted; $40/wk. TV; cable in lodge, VCR avail (movies). Playground. Ck-out 10 am, ck-in 3 pm. Grocery. Coin lndry. Package store 1 mi. Gift shop. Private sand beach. Waterskiing. Pontoon boat, motors, canoes & outfitting serv; boat launch. X-country ski 4 mi. Snowmobile trails. Hunting. Lawn games. Sauna. Fishing guide. Trophy display in lodge. Fireplaces, microwaves. Picnic tables, grills. Private docks. Cr cds: DS, MC, V. ⬅ ⬅ ⬄ ⬄ 🐾

Grand Rapids (See also Hibbing)

Motels

★★ **COUNTRY INN.** *2601 US 169S. 218/327-4960; FAX 218/327-4964.* 46 rms, 2 story. June-Aug: S $55-$65; D $63-$73; each addl $5; under 18 free; lower rates rest of yr. Crib free. Pet accepted, some restrictions. TV; cable (premium). Indoor pool; whirlpool. Complimentary continental bkfst. Restaurant adj 6:30 am-10 pm. Ck-out noon. Downhill ski 10 mi; x-country 2 mi. Some refrigerators. Cr cds: A, C, D, DS, MC, V.
D ⬅ ⬄ ⬄ ⬄ 🐾 SC

★ **DAYS INN.** *311 E US 2, at US 169. 218/326-3457; FAX 218/326-3795.* 34 rms, 2 story. Mid-Apr-late Sept: S, D $50-$69; each addl $4; under 12 free; lower rates rest of yr. Crib free. Pet accepted. TV; cable, VCR avail (movies $1). Playground. Complimentary coffee in lobby. Restaurant adj open 24 hrs. Ck-out 11 am. Business servs avail. Free airport, bus depot transportation. Grill. Cr cds: A, D, DS, MC, V. ⬅ ⬄ 🐾 SC

★★★ **SAWMILL INN.** *2301 S Pokegama Ave, 1¹/₂ mi S on US 169, near Itasca County Airport. 218/326-8501; FAX 218/326-1039; res: 800/235-6455 (MN).* 124 rms, 2 story. S $51-$72; D $61-$72; each addl $4; suites $84-$105; under 12 free. Crib free. Pet accepted. TV; cable. Indoor pool; whirlpool, sauna, poolside serv. Restaurant 6:30 am-10 pm; Fri, Sat to 11 pm. Rm serv. Bar 11-1 am. Ck-out noon. Coin lndry. Meeting rms. Business servs avail. Sundries. Free airport, bus depot transportation. Downhill/x-country ski 18 mi. Game rm. Cr cds: A, C, D, DS, MC, V. D ⬅ ⬄ ⬄ ✈ ⬄ 🐾 SC

Granite Falls (See also Marshall)

Motel

★ **VIKING SUNDANCE INN.** *US 212W, at jct MN 67 & MN 23. 320/564-2411.* 20 rms. S $28; D $31-$42; each addl $3. Crib $3. Pet accepted. TV; cable, VCR avail (movies). Ck-out 11 am. Cr cds: A, DS, MC, V. ⬅ ⬄ 🐾 SC

Hibbing (See also Cook, Eveleth, Grand Rapids, Virginia)

Motels

★ **DAYS INN.** *1520 E MN 37, Jct US 169 & MN 37. 218/263-8306.* 60 rms, 2 story. S $40.95-$45.95; D $43.95-$50; each addl $3. Crib free. Pet accepted, some restrictions. TV; cable (premium), VCR avail (movies). Complimentary continental bkfst. Ck-out 11 am. Business servs avail. Cr cds: A, C, D, DS, MC, V. D ⬅ ⬄ 🐾 SC

★ **SUPER 8.** *1411 E 40th St, jct US 169 & MN 37. 218/263-8982.* 49 rms, 2 story. Apr-Sept: S $36.79-$40.88; D $47.59-$52.88; each addl $3; under 13 free; wkly rates; higher rates special events; lower rates rest of yr. Crib free. Pet accepted, some restrictions; $25 deposit. TV; cable (premium), VCR avail. Complimentary coffee in lobby. Restaurant opp 6 am-11 pm. Ck-out 11 am. Meeting rms. Business servs avail. X-country ski 2 mi. Cr cds: A, C, D, DS, MC, V. D ⬅ ⬄ ⬄ 🐾 SC

Hinckley (See also Mora)

Motels

★★ **DAYS INN.** *104 Grindstone Court, I-35 exit 183, at MN 48. 612/384-7751.* 69 rms, 2 story. S $44-$75; D $49-$85; each addl $5; suites $90-$135; under 18 free. Crib free. Pet accepted; $5. TV; cable, VCR avail. Indoor pool; whirlpool. Complimentary continental bkfst. Complimentary coffee in rms. Restaurant adj open 24 hrs. Ck-out 11 am. Coin lndry.

Business servs avail. X-country ski 10 mi. Sauna. Some refrigerators; microwaves avail. Cr cds: A, C, D, DS, MC, V. [D] [♦] [≥] [≈] [⋈] [⋈] [SC]

★ ★ **HOLIDAY INN EXPRESS.** *604 Weber Ave, I-35 exit 183.* 320/384-7171; FAX 320/384-7735. 101 rms, 2 story. May-Sept: D $69-$89; each addl $10; whirlpool rms $85-$129; under 19 free; lower rates rest of yr. Crib free. Pet accepted. TV; cable. Indoor pool; whirlpool. Complimentary continental bkfst. Coffee in rms. Ck-out noon. X-country ski 10 mi. Sauna. Microwaves avail. Cr cds: A, C, D, DS, MC, V. [D] [♦] [≥] [≈] [⋈] [⋈] [SC]

★ **SUPER 8.** *(2811 MN 23, Finlayson 55735) 10 mi N on I-35 exit 195.* 320/245-5284; FAX 320/245-2233. 30 rms, 2 story. S $44.88-$56.88; D $48.88-$56.88; each $4; under 12 free. Crib free. Pet accepted. TV; cable (premium). Complimentary continental bkfst. Restaurant opp 6 am-10 pm. Ck-out 11 am. Coin lndry. Business servs avail. X-country ski opp. Whirlpool. Game rm. Cr cds: A, C, D, DS, MC, V. [D] [♦] [≥] [⋈] [⋈]

International Falls

Motels

★ **DAYS INN.** *2331 US 53S.* 218/283-9441. 58 rms, 2 story. S $46-$58; D $60-$70; under 18 free. Crib free. Pet accepted, some restrictions. TV; cable (premium). Complimentary continental bkfst. Restaurant adj open 24 hrs. Ck-out noon. Business servs avail. Exercise equipt; bicycle, treadmill, sauna. Whirlpool. Cr cds: A, C, D, DS, JCB, MC, V. [♦] [乂] [⋈] [⋈] [SC]

★ ★ **HOLIDAY INN.** *1500 Hwy 71.* 218/283-4451; FAX 218/283-3774. 126 rms, 2 story. S, D $69-$109; suites $85-$135; family rates. Crib free. Pet accepted. TV; cable (premium). Indoor pool; wading pool, whirlpool. Restaurant 6 am-10 pm. Rm serv. Bar. Ck-out noon. Coin lndry. Meeting rms. Business servs avail. In-rm modem link. Bellhops. Sundries. Free airport transportation. Sauna. Health club privileges. Some refrigerators; microwaves avail. View of Rainy River. Cr cds: A, C, D, DS, JCB, MC, V. [D] [♦] [≈] [⋈] [⋈] [SC]

Cottage Colonies

★ **ISLAND VIEW LODGE & MOTEL.** *1817 MN 11E, 12 mi E on MN 11, on Rainy Lake.* 218/286-3511; res: 800/777-7856. E-mail jbischol@northernnet.com; web www.north ernnet.com/islandview/. 9 A/C rms in 2-story lodge, 12 kit. cottages (1-6 bedrm), 5 A/C. S, D $65-$70; each addl $11; cottages (3-day min) 1-6 bedrm, $115-$250/day. Pet accepted, some restrictions. TV in lodge rms, some cabins. Dining rm 6:30 am-2 pm, 5-10 pm. Box lunches, snack bar. Bar noon-1 am. Ck-out 10 am, ck-in 3 pm. Grocery, coin lndry 12 mi. Package store. Free airport transportation. Private beach; dockage, boats, motors, guides. Snowmobiling. National park tours. Jukebox dancing. Rec rm. Picnic table, grills. Cr cds: DS, MC, V. [D] [♦] [⊒] [≈] [⋈]

★ **NORTHERNAIRE FLOATING LODGES.** *2690 County Rd 94, at Jackfish Bay, 7 mi E on MN 11, then 2 mi N on County 94, on Rainy Lake.* 218/286-5221. E-mail nflhboat@northernnet.com; web www.northern net.com/nflhboat. 15 power-driven floating kit. lodges on pontoon boats. No A/C. Mid-May-mid-Oct (3-day min): for 2-10, $795-$2,100/wk; package plans avail; daily rates. Res, deposit required. Closed rest of yr. Pet accepted, some restrictions. Ck-out noon. Grocery. Waterskiing, motors. Hunting; guides, cooks. Unique houseboat living. Cr cds: MC, V. [♦] [⊒]

Lakeville (See also Minneapolis, Red Wing, St Paul)

Motel

✔ ★ **MOTEL 6.** *11274 210th St (11274).* 612/469-1900; FAX 612/469-5359. 84 rms, 2 story. S $30-$34; D $36-$42; under 17 free. Crib free. Pet accepted. Complimentary coffee in lobby. Restaurant opp 7 am-11 pm. Ck-out noon. Downhill ski 5 mi; x-country ski 2 mi. Cr cds: A, C, D, DS, MC, V. [D] [♦] [≥] [⋈] [⋈] [SC]

Litchfield (See also Minneapolis, Willmar)

Motel

★ **SCOTWOOD.** *1017 E Frontage Rd.* 612/693-2496; res: 800/225-5489. 35 rms, 2 story. S $38.95-$41.50; D $42.95-$45.75; each addl $5. Crib free. Pet accepted, some restrictions. TV; cable (premium). Complimentary continental bkfst. Restaurant nearby. Ck-out 11 am. Sundries. Cr cds: A, C, D, DS, MC, V. [D] [♦] [⋈] [SC]

Little Falls *(See also Brainerd, St Cloud)*

Motel

✔★ **PINE EDGE.** *308 First St SE. 320/632-6681; res: 800/344-6681; FAX 320/632-4332.* 56 rms, 1-2 story. S $35-$40; D $40-$50; each addl $5; suites $60-$95; under 12 free. Crib $5. Pet accepted. TV; cable (premium). Heated pool. Playground. Restaurant 7 am-9 pm. Rm serv. Bar 11:30 am-midnight. Ck-out 11 am. Business servs avail. On river; built in 1923; hosted Charles Lindbergh after historic trans-Atlantic flight. Cr cds: A, C, D, DS, MC, V. ⊕ ⊕ ⊠ ⊠ ⊠ SC

Lutsen *(See also Grand Marais)*

Motels

★★ **BEST WESTERN CLIFF DWELLER.** *6452 US 61 (55615), 3¹/₂ mi SW. 218/663-7273.* E-mail gmhotel@worldnet.att.com. 22 rms, 2 story. Mid-June-mid-Oct, mid-Dec-mid-Mar: S $49-$69; D $59-$79; each addl $8; package plans; lower rates rest of yr. Crib free. Pet accepted, some restrictions. TV; cable (premium). Restaurant (late June-Sept) 7 am-9 pm. Ck-out 11 am. Business servs avail. In-rm modem link. Downhill ski 3 mi; x-country ski adj. 18-hole golf privileges. Balconies. On lake; scenic view. Cr cds: A, C, D, DS, MC, V. D ⊕ ⊠ ⊠ ⊠ ⊠ SC

★★★ **BLUEFIN BAY.** *(US 61S, Tofte 55615) 218/663-7296; FAX 218/663-7130; res: 800/258-3346.* E-mail bluefin@boreal.org; web www .bluefinbay.com. 72 units, 2 story, 56 kits. No A/C. Late Dec-Mar, June-Oct: S, D, kit. units $69-$345; each addl $10; under 12 free; ski plans; higher rates; ski wkends, hols; lower rates rest of yr. Crib free. Pet accepted. TV; cable, VCR avail (movies). 2 pools, 1 indoor; whirlpool. Supervised child's activities. Complimentary coffee in rms. Restaurant 7:30 am-10 pm. Bar 3 pm-1 am. Ck-out noon. Coin lndry. Meeting rms. Business servs avail. Gift shop. Tennis. 18-hole golf privileges. Downhill ski 9 mi; x-country ski opp. Exercise equipt; weight machine, bicycles, sauna. Massage. Game rm. Lawn games. Many in-rm whirlpools, fireplaces; microwaves avail. Balconies. Grills. On Lake Superior. Cr cds: DS, JCB, MC, V. ⊕ ⊕ ⊠ ⊠ ⊠ ⊠ ⊠ ⊠

★★ **HOLIDAY INN EXPRESS.** *(Tofte 55615) S on US 61. 218/663-7899; FAX 218/663-7387.* 52 rms, 2 story. Late Dec-Mar, mid-June-mid-Oct: S, D $75-$130; suite, kit. unit $170-$230; under 19 free; ski, golf plans; wkends (2-day min); lower rates rest of yr. Crib free. Pet accepted. TV; cable. Complimentary continental bkfst. Restaurant nearby. Ck-out noon. Meeting rms. Business servs avail. Downhill ski 7 mi; x-country ski on site. Indoor pool; whirlpool, sauna. Many refrigerators, microwaves; some in-rm whirlpools. Picnic tables. Opp lake. Cr cds: A, D, DS, MC, V. D ⊕ ⊠ ⊠ ⊠ ⊠ SC

★ **THE MOUNTAIN INN.** *Ski Hill Rd, 1¹/₂ mi W off US 61. 218/663-7244; res: 800/686-4669; FAX 218/387-2446.* 30 rms, 2 story. Jan-Mar, July-mid-Oct: S, D $99-$119; each addl $8; under 18 free; wkend rates; ski, golf plans; hols (2-day min); lower rates rest of yr. Crib free. Pet accepted, some restrictions. TV; cable (premium), VCR avail. Complimentary continental bkfst. Restaurant opp 7 am-11 pm. Ck-out noon. Business servs avail. 18-hole golf privileges, greens fee $23, pro, putting green, driving range. Downhill ski 1 blk; x-country ski on site. Sauna, whirlpool. Many refrigerators, microwaves, wet bars. Picnic tables. Opp lake. Cr cds: A, D, DS, MC, V. D ⊕ ⊠ ⊠ ⊠ ⊠ SC

Resort

★★ **LUTSEN.** *1¹/₂ mi SW on US 61. 218/663-7212; res: 800/258-8736.* E-mail lutsen@lutsenresort.com; web www.lutsenresort .com. 49 rms in 2 lodges; 6 cabins; 51 kit. units in townhome villas (2¹/₂ mi S of lodge on lake). No A/C. Lodge: S $33-$125; D $38-$135; cabins: S, D $125-$249; villas for 2-8 (2-day min): S $80-$159; D $95-$219; each addl $10; under 12 free; honeymoon rates. Crib avail. Pet accepted, some restrictions. TV; cable, VCR avail. Indoor pool; whirlpool. Playground. Dining rm 7:30 am-2 pm, 5:30-9 pm. Box lunches. Bar 4 pm-1 am, wkends from noon. Ck-out 11 am; ck-in after 4 pm. Grocery 1¹/₂ mi. Meeting rms. Coin lndry 20 mi. Tennis. 9-hole golf course. Downhill ski 1¹/₂ mi; x-country ski adj. Sauna. Lawn games. Rec rm; indoor games. Fireplace, balcony in villas. Sun deck. On Lake Superior. Cr cds: A, D, DS, MC, V. ⊕ ⊕ ⊠ ⊠ ⊠ ⊠ ⊠

Luverne *(See also Sioux Falls, SD)*

Motel

✔★ **SUPER 8.** *I-90 & US 75. 507/283-9541.* 36 rms, 2 story. S $40.88-$54.88; D $45.88-$64.88; each addl $5. Crib free. Pet accepted. TV; cable (premium). Ck-out 11 am. Cr cds: A, C, D, DS, MC, V. D ⊕ ⊠ ⊠ SC

Mankato *(See also New Ulm)*

Motels

✔★ **BUDGETEL INN.** *111 W Lind Court (56001). 507/345-8800; FAX 507/345-8921.* 66 rms, 2 story. S $35.95-$39.95; D $44.95-$49.95; under 18 free. Crib free. Pet accepted, some restrictions. TV; cable. Continental bkfst. Coffee in rms. Restaurant adj 7 am-11 pm. Ck-out noon. Business servs avail. Valet serv. Sundries. Downhill ski 6 mi; x-country ski 2 mi. Whirlpool, sauna. Cr cds: A, C, D, DS, MC, V. 🄳 💳 🏊 🔍 🐾 SC

★ **DAYS INN.** *1285 Range St (56001). 507/387-3332.* 50 rms, 2 story. S $37.95-$59.95; D $42.95-$69.95; suites $65-$125; under 18 free. Crib free. Pet accepted. TV; cable. Indoor pool; whirlpool. Complimentary continental bkfst. Restaurant nearby. Ck-out 11 am. Business servs avail. In-rm modem link. Downhill/x-country ski 5 mi. Cr cds: A, C, D, DS, MC, V. 🄳 💳 🏊 🏊 🔍 🐾 SC

✔★ **RIVERFRONT INN.** *1727 N Riverfront Dr (56001). 507/388-1638; FAX 507/388-6111.* 19 rms. S $30-$59; D $39-$79; each addl $7. Crib free. Pet accepted, some restrictions. TV; cable, VCR avail (movies). Complimentary coffee in rms. Restaurant nearby. Ck-out 11 am. Business servs avail. In-rm modem link. Downhill ski 5 mi; x-country ski 1 mi. Refrigerators. Cr cds: A, C, D, DS, MC, V. 🄳 💳 🏊 🔍 🐾 SC

Marshall *(See also Granite Falls)*

Motels

★ **COMFORT INN.** *1511 E College Dr, at jct MN 23 & MN 19. 507/532-3070.* 49 rms, 2 story. S $48-$100; D $54-$100; each addl $6; under 18 free. Crib $2. Pet accepted. TV; cable (premium), VCR avail (movies). Complimentary continental bkfst. Restaurant nearby. Ck-out 11 am. Meeting rm. Business servs avail. In-rm modem link. Whirlpool. Cr cds: A, C, D, DS, ER, JCB, MC, V. 🄳 💳 🔍 🐾 SC

★ **SUPER 8.** *1106 E Main St, ³/₄ mi S on US 59, 2 blks S of US 23. 507/537-1461.* 50 rms, 2 story. S $42.88-$45.88; D $50.88; each addl $5. Crib free. Pet accepted. TV; cable (premium). Restaurant adj 6 am-10 pm. Ck-out 11 am. Coin lndry. Meeting rm. Business servs avail. X-country ski 1 mi. Cr cds: A, C, D, DS, MC, V. 🄳 💳 🏊 🔍 🐾 SC

✔★★ **TRAVELER'S LODGE.** *1425 E College Dr (MN 19), SW State University adj. 507/532-5721; FAX 507/532-4911; res: 800/532-5721.* 90 rms, 1-2 story. S, D $34-$42; each addl $4; under 12 free. Crib free. Pet accepted. TV; cable (premium), VCR avail (movies $3.50). Complimentary continental bkfst. Restaurant adj open 24 hrs. Ck-out noon. Meeting rm. Business servs avail. Sundries. Free airport transportation. X-country ski 1 mi. Cr cds: A, C, D, DS, MC, V. 💳 🏊 🔍 🐾 SC

Motor Hotel

★★★ **BEST WESTERN MARSHALL INN.** *E College Dr, SW State University opp. 507/532-3221; FAX 507/532-4089.* 100 rms, 2 story. S $43.95-$60.95; D $53.95-$60.95; suites $79.95-$84.95; under 17 free. Crib free. Pet accepted. TV; cable. Indoor pool; whirlpool, sauna, poolside serv. Restaurant 6:30 am-2 pm, 5-9:30 pm; wkend hrs vary. Rm serv. Bar noon-11:30 pm. Ck-out noon. Meeting rms. Business servs avail. In-rm modem link. Sundries. Free airport, bus depot transportation. X-country ski 1 mi. Cr cds: A, C, D, DS, MC, V. 🄳 💳 🏊 🏊 🔍 🐾 SC

Minneapolis *(See also Bloomington, St Paul)*

Motels

★ **AMERICINN OF ROGERS.** *(Jct 1-94 & MN 101, Rogers 55374) 612/428-4346; res: 800/634-3444.* 35 rms, 2 story. S $39.90-$48.90; D $46.90-$57.90; each addl $5; whirlpool rms $89.90-$109.90; under 12 free. Crib free. Pet accepted. TV; cable (premium), VCR. Complimentary continental bkfst. Restaurant adj open 24 hrs. Ck-out 11 am. Business servs avail. Cr cds: A, C, D, DS, MC, V. 🄳 💳 🔍 🐾 SC

✔★ **METRO INN.** *5637 Lyndale Ave S (55419), south of downtown. 612/861-6011; FAX 612/869-1041.* 35 rms. Apr-Oct: S $35-$44; D $42-$52; each addl $6; lower rates rest of yr. Crib $4-$5. Pet accepted, some restrictions; $3. TV; cable (premium). Ck-out 11 am. X-country ski ¹/₂ mi. Cr cds: A, C, D, DS, MC, V. 💳 🔍 🐾 SC

Motor Hotel

★★**BEST WESTERN KELLY INN.** *(5201 Central Ave NE, Fridley 55421) 612/571-9440; FAX 612/571-1720.* 95 rms, 2 story. S, D $64-$72; each addl $8; suites $105-$185; under 18 free. Crib free. Pet accepted. TV; cable (premium). Indoor pool; whirlpool. Restaurant 6 am-9 pm. Rm serv. Ck-out 11 am. Meeting rms. Business servs avail. Exercise equipt; weight machine, bicycles, sauna. Game rm. Some refrigerators. Cr cds: A, D, DS, MC, V. [D] [🏊] [➰] [🏋] [🚫] [🐾] [SC]

Hotels

★★★**RADISSON-METRODOME.** *615 Washington Ave SE (55414). 612/379-8888; FAX 612/379-8436.* 304 rms, 8 story. S $102; D $112; each addl $10; suites $135-$325; under 18 free. Crib avail. Pet accepted. Valet parking $9.50; garage $6.50. TV; cable, VCR avail. Pool privileges. Complimentary coffee in rms. Restaurants 6:30 am-10:30 pm. Bar to 1 am. Ck-out noon. Meeting rms. Business servs avail. In-rm modem link. Gift shop. Downhill ski 20 mi; x-country ski 1 mi. Exercise equipt; bicycle, weights. Health club privileges. Some refrigerators. Cr cds: A, C, D, DS, ER, JCB, MC, V.
[D] [🏊] [➰] [🏋] [🚫] [🐾]

★★★**REGAL MINNEAPOLIS.** *1313 Nicollet Mall (55403), in Nicollet Ave Mall Area. 612/332-6000; FAX 612/359-2160; res: 800/522-8856.* 325 rms, 14 story. S $175; D $195; suites $190-$250. Crib free. Pet accepted. TV; cable (premium). Indoor pool. Restaurant 6:30 am-2 pm, 5-10 pm. Bars 11-1 am. Ck-out noon. Coin Indry. Convention facilities. Business servs avail. In-rm modem link. Gift shop. Airport transportation avail. X-country ski 1 mi. Exercise equipt; weight machine, bicycle, sauna. Cr cds: A, C, D, DS, ER, JCB, MC, V. [D] [🏊] [➰] [🏋] [🚫] [🐾] [SC]

Mora *(See also Hinckley)*

Motel

✔★**MOTEL MORA.** *301 S MN 65, on MN 23/65. 320/679-3262; FAX 320/679-5135; res: 800/657-0167.* 23 rms. S $29-$42; D $36-$42; each addl $5; kit. units $29-$42. Crib $5. Pet accepted, some restrictions; $5. TV; cable (premium). Complimentary coffee in rms. Restaurant nearby. Ck-out 11 am. Business servs avail. In-rm modem link. X-country ski 1 mi. Picnic tables. Sun deck. Many refrigerators; microwaves avail. Cr cds: A, C, D, DS, MC, V. [🏊] [➰] [🚫] [🐾]

Morris *(See also Glenwood)*

Motel

★★**PRAIRIE INN.** *200 MN 28E, 2 mi N on MN 28. 320/589-3030; res: 800/535-3035.* 90 rms, 2 story. S, D $34-$84; under 17 free. Crib free. Pet accepted, some restrictions. TV; cable (premium). Indoor pool; wading pool, whirlpool, poolside serv. Complimentary continental bkfst. Restaurant 6:30 am-10 pm. Bar 4 pm-1 am. Ck-out 11 am, Sun noon. Meeting rms. Business servs avail. Sauna. Game rm. Cr cds: A, C, D, DS, MC, V. [D] [🏊] [➰] [🚫] [🐾] [SC]

New Ulm *(See also Mankato)*

Motel

★**BUDGET HOLIDAY.** *1316 N Broadway. 507/354-4145; FAX 507/354-4146.* 45 rms. S $26.95-$32.95; D $29.95-$34.95; each addl $5. Crib $5. Pet accepted. TV; cable (premium). Restaurant nearby. Ck-out 11 am. Business servs avail. X-country ski 2 mi. Cr cds: A, C, D, DS, MC, V. [🏊] [➰] [🚫] [🐾]

Red Wing *(See also Lakeville, St Paul)*

Motels

★★**BEST WESTERN QUIET HOUSE SUITES.** *752 Withers Harbor Dr. 612/388-1577; FAX 612/388-1150.* 51 rms, 2 story. S $69-$152; D $79-$162; under 5 free. Pet accepted. TV; cable. Indoor/outdoor pool; whirlpool. Complimentary coffee. Restaurant nearby. Ck-out 11 am. In-rm modem link. Exercise equipt; weights, stair machine. Some refrigerators. Balconies. Cr cds: A, C, D, DS, ER, MC, V. [D] [🏊] [➰] [🏋] [🚫] [🐾] [SC]

★★**DAYS INN.** *955 E 7th St, US 61 & 63 S. 612/388-3568; FAX 612/385-1901.* 48 rms. S, D $40.50-$80.50; each addl $5; under 13 free. Pet accepted. TV; cable. Indoor pool; whirlpool. Complimentary coffee in rms. Complimentary continental bkfst. Restaurant nearby. Ck-out 11 am. Business servs avail. Downhill ski 7 mi; x-country ski 1 mi. Municipal park, marinas opp. Cr cds: A, C, D, DS, JCB, MC, V. [D] 💳 ⛷ 🏊 🚫 🐾 [SC]

Rochester

Motels

✔ ★ **AMERICINN OF STEWARTVILLE.** *(1700 2nd Ave NW, Stewartville 55976) 1 mi S of I-90 on MN 63.* 507/533-4747. 29 rms. S $40-$45; D $45-$50; each addl $6; under 12 free. Crib free. Pet accepted. TV; cable. Complimentary continental bkfst. Restaurant nearby. Ck-out 11 am. Business servs avail. Cr cds: A, C, D, DS, MC, V.
[D] 💳 🚫 🐾 [SC]

★ **BEST WESTERN.** *20 5th Ave NW (55901).* 507/289-3987; FAX 507/289-3987, ext. 130. 91 rms, 3 story. S, D $56; each addl $5; under 18 free. Crib free. Pet accepted. TV; cable (premium). Indoor pool. Complimentary coffee in lobby. Restaurant nearby. Ck-out noon. X-country ski 1 mi. Cr cds: A, C, D, DS, MC, V.
[D] 💳 ⛷ 🏊 🚫 🐾 [SC]

★ ★ **BEST WESTERN-APACHE.** *1517 16th St SW (55902).* 507/289-8866; FAX 507/289-8866, ext. 312. 151 rms, 3 story. S $51.95-$99.95; D $61.95-$109.95; each addl $5; suites $85-$159; under 18 free; wkend rates. Pet accepted. TV; cable (premium), VCR avail. Indoor pool; whirlpool. Complimentary bkfst. Restaurant 6:30 am-10 pm. Rm serv. Bar 5 pm-1 am. Ck-out noon. Meeting rms. Business servs avail. In-rm modem link. Valet serv. Sundries. Free airport transportation. X-country ski 2 mi. Game rm. Tropical atrium. Cr cds: A, C, D, DS, MC, V. [D] 💳 ⛷ 🏊 🚫 🐾 [SC]

★ **BLONDELL'S CROWN SQUARE.** *1406 2nd St SW (55902).* 507/282-9444; FAX 507/282-8683; res: 800/441-5209. 60 rms, 3 story, 7 suites. S $42-$50; D $47-$55; each addl $5; suites $85-$94; kit. units $42-$50; under 12 free. Crib free. Pet accepted. TV; cable (premium). Restaurant 6 am-10 pm. Rm serv. Bar 11-1:30 am. Ck-out 1 pm. Meeting rms. Business servs avail. Gift shop. X-country ski 1 mi. Cr cds: A, MC, V.
[D] 💳 ⛷ 🏊 🚫 🐾 [SC]

★ **DAYS INN.** *6 First Ave NW (55901).* 507/282-3801. 71 rms, 5 story. S $43-$75; D $49-$75; each addl $6; under 17 free. Crib free. Pet accepted. TV; cable. Restaurant 6 am-8 pm. Ck-out noon. Coin lndry. Some refrigerators. Cr cds: A, C, D, DS, MC, V. 💳 🚫 🐾 [SC]

★ **DAYS INN-SOUTH.** *111 28th St (55901).* 507/286-1001. 130 rms. S $46-$62; D $52-$62; each addl $5; under 18 free. Crib free. Pet accepted. TV; cable (premium). Complimentary continental bkfst. Restaurant nearby. Ck-out noon. Business servs avail. Free airport transportation. X-country ski 2 mi. Cr cds: A, C, D, DS, ER, JCB, MC, V.
[D] 💳 🚫 🐾 [SC]

★ ★ **DAYS INN-WEST.** *435 16th Ave NW (55901), US 52 exit 5th St.* 507/288-9090; FAX 507/288-9090, ext. 502. 120 rms, 3 story, 20 kit. units. S $45-$66; D $50-$70; each addl $6; under 18 free. Crib free. Pet accepted. TV; cable (premium). Heated pool. Restaurant 6:30 am-8 pm. Ck-out noon. Coin lndry. Meeting rms. Valet serv. Sundries. X-country ski 1 mi. Cr cds: A, C, D, DS, MC, V. [D] 💳 ⛷ 🏊 🚫 🐾 [SC]

★ ★ **HOLIDAY INN-SOUTH.** *1630 S Broadway (55904).* 507/288-1844; FAX 507/288-1844, ext. 440. 200 rms, 2 story, 7 kits. S, D $59-$69; each addl $7; kit. units $79-$119. Crib free. Pet accepted. TV; cable. Indoor pool. Restaurant 6 am-10 pm; Fri, Sat to 11 pm. Rm serv. Bar 11:30-1 am. Ck-out 2 pm. Sat noon. Coin lndry. Meeting rms. Business servs avail. Valet serv. Sundries. Free airport, bus depot transportation. Rec rm. Cr cds: A, C, D, DS, JCB, MC, V. [D] 💳 🏊 🚫 🐾 [SC]

★ **RED CARPET INN.** *2214 S Broadway (55904).* 507/282-7448. 47 rms, 2 story, 6 kits. S $36.45; D $40.45-$42.45; each addl $5; kit. units $28.95-$31.95; under 12 free; wkend rates. Crib free. Pet accepted. TV; cable. Indoor pool. Complimentary coffee in lobby. Restaurant nearby. Ck-out noon. Coin lndry. Meeting rm. Business servs avail. Sundries. X-country ski 1 mi. Cr cds: A, DS, MC, V. [D] 💳 ⛷ 🏊 🚫 🐾 [SC]

★ **SUPER 8.** *1230 S Broadway (55904).* 507/288-8288; FAX 507/288-8288, ext. 350. 89 rms. S $49.88-$52.88; D $54.88-$60; each addl $5; under 18 free. Crib free. Pet accepted. TV; cable. Restaurant adj open 24 hrs. Ck-out noon. In-rm modem link. X-country ski adj. Cr cds: A, DS, MC, V. [D] 💳 ⛷ 🚫 🐾 [SC]

★ **THRIFTLODGE.** *1837 S Broadway (55904). 507/288-2031.* 27 rms. S, D $33-$50; each addl $5. Crib free. Pet accepted. TV; cable. Complimentary coffee in lobby. Restaurant nearby. Ck-out noon. X-country ski 1 mi. Cr cds: A, C, D, DS, MC, V.

⟡ ⊵ ⊠ ⋈ sc

Motor Hotels

★★ **KAHLER INN AND SUITES.** *9 NW 3rd Ave (55901). 507/289-8646; FAX 507/282-4478.* 266 rms, 9 story. S $71.95-$102.95; D $81.95-$112.95; each addl $10; under 18 free. Crib free. Pet accepted. TV; cable (premium). Indoor pool; whirlpool. Complimentary continental bkfst. Restaurant 6 am-9 pm. Bar 3-9 pm. Ck-out 2 pm. Meeting rm. Business servs avail. In-rm modem link. Sundries. Grocery store. Valet serv. Coin lndry. X-country ski 1 mi. Exercise equipt; bicycle, treadmil, sauna. Rec rm. Some refrigerators. Cr cds: A, C, D, DS, MC, V. ⒹⒹ ⟡ ⊵ ⋈ 𝔛 ⊠ ⋈ sc

★ **QUALITY INN & SUITES.** *1620 1st Ave SE (55904). 507/282-8091.* 40 suites, 2 story. S, D $69-$74; each addl $7; under 18 free. Crib free. Pet accepted. TV; cable (premium). Complimentary continental bkfst. Complimentary coffee in rms. Restaurant nearby. Ck-out noon. Coin lndry. Business servs avail. In-rm modem link. Airport transportation. Cr cds: A, C, D, DS, MC, V. Ⓓ ⟡ ⊠ ⋈ sc

Hotel

★★★ **KAHLER.** *20 2nd Ave SW (55902). 507/282-2581; FAX 507/285-2775; res: 800/533-1655.* 700 rms, 11 story. S $55-$140; D $65-$150; each addl $10; suites $350-$1,500; under 18 free. Crib free. Pet accepted. TV; cable. Indoor pool; whirlpool, poolside serv. Restaurant 6:30 am-11 pm, 5:30-9 pm. Bars 11-12:45 am; entertainment exc Sun. Ck-out 2 pm. Meeting rms. Business servs avail. In-rm modem link. Concierge. Drugstore. Barber, beauty shop. Airport transportation. X-country ski 2 mi. Exercise equipt; weights, bicycles, sauna. Game rm. Refrigerators. Original section English Tudor; vaulted ceilings, paneling. Walkway to clinic. Cr cds: A, C, D, DS, MC, V. Ⓓ ⟡ ⊵ ⋈ 𝔛 ⊠ ⋈ sc

St Cloud *(See also Elk River, Little Falls)*

Motels

✔★ **BUDGETEL INN.** *70 S 37th Ave (56301). 320/253-4444; FAX 320/259-7809.* 91 units, 2 story. Mid-June-early Sept: S $39.95-$42.95; D $44.95-$49.95; each addl $7; under 18 free; lower rates rest of yr. Crib free. Pet accepted, some restrictions. TV; cable (premium). Restaurant nearby. Ck-out noon. Sauna. Whirlpool. Cr cds: A, C, D, DS, MC, V. Ⓓ ⟡ ⊠ ⋈ sc

★ **DAYS INN-EAST.** *420 SE US 10, jct MN 23. 320/253-0500.* 78 rms, 2 story. S $38.95-$56.95; D $45.95-$59.95; each addl $7; under 18 free. Crib free. Pet accepted. TV; cable (premium). Indoor pool; whirlpool. Complimentary continental bkfst. Ck-out 11 am. Business servs avail. Sundries. Downhill ski 10 mi; x-country ski 1 mi. Cr cds: A, C, D, DS, MC, V. Ⓓ ⟡ ⊵ ⊠ ⋈ sc

★ **SUPER 8.** *50 Park Ave S (56301). 320/253-5530; FAX 320/253-5292.* 68 rms, 2 story. S $34.88-$45.88; D $42.88-$58.88; each addl $5; under 13 free. Crib free. Pet accepted. TV; cable (premium). Complimentary continental bkfst. Restaurant adj open 24 hrs. Ck-out 11 am. Meeting rms. Business servs avail. Downhill ski 8 mi; x-country ski 1 mi. Cr cds: A, C, D, DS, MC, V. Ⓓ ⟡ ⊵ ⊠ ⋈ sc

Motor Hotels

★★ **BEST WESTERN AMERICANNA INN.** *520 S US 10 (56304), S of jct US 10 & MN 23. 320/252-8700.* 64 rms, 2 story. S $42.95-$60.95; D $59.95-$68.95; each addl $5; suites for 2-6, $74.95-$99.95; under 19 free. Crib $2. Pet accepted, some restrictions. TV; cable (premium). Indoor pool; whirlpool. Complimentary coffee in rms. Restaurant 11 am-10 pm; Sun to 9 pm. Rm serv. Bar 10:30-1 am; entertainment. Ck-out 11 am. Meeting rms. Business servs avail. In-rm modem link. Valet serv. Sundries. Sauna. Game rm. Cr cds: A, C, D, DS, ER, JCB, MC, V. Ⓓ ⟡ ⊠ ⋈ sc

★★ **BEST WESTERN KELLY INN.** *1 Sunwood Dr (56301). 320/253-0606; FAX 320/202-0505.* 230 rms, 6 story. S $58-$81; D $65-$79; each addl $6; suites $95-$175; under 18 free. Crib free. Pet accepted, some restrictions. TV; cable (premium), VCR avail (movies). Indoor pool; wading pool, whirlpool. Restaurant 6:30 am-10 pm. Bar 11-1 am; Sun to midnight. Ck-out 11 am. Coin lndry. Meeting rms. Business servs avail. In-rm modem link. Valet serv. Sundries. Gift shop. Sauna. Game rm. Poolside rms. Cr cds: A, C, D, DS, ER, MC, V. Ⓓ ⟡ ⊠ ⋈ sc

St Paul *(See also Minneapolis, Stillwater)*

Motels

★ ★ **BEST WESTERN MAPLEWOOD INN.** *1780 E County Road D (55109), adj to Maplewood Mall, north of downtown.* 612/770-2811; FAX 612/770-2811, ext. 184. 118 rms, 2 story. S $58-$108; D $62-$108; each addl $4; under 18 free. Crib free. Pet accepted; $5 deposit. TV; cable (premium). Indoor pool; whirlpool. Coffee in rms. Restaurant 6:30 am-2 pm, 5-10 pm. Rm serv. Bar 4 pm-1 am; entertainment Fri, Sat. Ck-out noon. Coin lndry. Meeting rms. Business servs avail. In-rm modem link. Valet serv. Sundries. Sauna. Health club privileges. Game rm. Microwaves avail. Cr cds: A, C, D, DS, ER, JCB, MC, V.
[D] [≈] [≈] [⊠] [⊠] [SC]

✓ ★ **EXEL INN.** *1739 Old Hudson Rd (55106).* 612/771-5566; FAX 612/771-1262. 100 rms, 3 story. S $38.99-$53.99; D $43.99-$58.99; each addl $5; under 18 free; ski, wkly plans; higher rates special events. Crib free. Pet accepted. TV; cable (premium). Complimentary continental bkfst. Restaurant adj open 24 hrs. Ck-out noon. Coin lndry. Business servs avail. In-rm modem link. Downhill ski 15 mi; x-country ski 2 mi. Game rm. Refrigerators; microwaves avail. Cr cds: A, C, D, DS, MC, V. [D] [≈] [≈] [⊠] [⊠] [SC]

✓ ★ **RED ROOF INN.** *(1806 Wooddale Dr, Woodbury 55125)* I-494 at Valley Creek Rd. 612/738-7160; FAX 612/738-1869. 108 rms, 2 story. S $33.99-$58.99; D $46.99-$68.99; each addl $8; under 18 free. Crib free. Pet accepted. TV; cable (premium). Complimentary coffee. Restaurant nearby. Ck-out noon. Business servs avail. In-rm modem link. Downhill ski 15 mi; x-country ski 3 mi. Cr cds: A, C, D, DS, MC, V. [D] [≈] [≈] [⊠] [⊠]

★ **SUPER 8.** *(285 N Century Ave, Maplewood 55119)* 612/738-1600; FAX 612/738-9405. 112 rms, 4 story. Late May-early Sept: S $48.88-$55.88; D $55.88-$60.88; each addl $5; under 12 free; lower rates rest of yr. Crib free. Pet accepted; $50. TV; cable (premium). Complimentary continental bkfst. Restaurant adj. Ck-out 11 am. Coin lndry. Business servs avail. In-rm modem link. Sundries. Airport transportation. Downhill ski 15 mi; x-country ski 2 mi. Health club privileges. Microwaves avail. Picnic tables. On lake. Cr cds: A, C, D, DS, MC, V. [D] [≈] [≈] [≈] [⊠] [⊠] [SC]

Motor Hotels

★ **BEST WESTERN KELLY INN.** *161 St Anthony Blvd (55103),* I-94 exit Marion St, west of downtown. 612/227-8711; FAX 612/227-1698. 126 rms, 7 story. S $74-$89; D $79-$99; each addl $8; suites $115-$185; under 18 free; higher rates special events. Crib free. Pet accepted. TV; cable. Indoor pool; wading pool, whirlpool. Restaurant 6:30 am-9 pm. Rm serv. Bar 11-1 am; Sat 4 pm-midnight; Sun 4-10 pm. Meeting rms. Business servs avail. In-rm modem link. Sundries. Valet serv. Downhill ski 20 mi; x-country ski 4 mi. Sauna. Game rm. Microwaves in suites. Cr cds: A, C, D, DS, MC, V. [D] [≈] [≈] [≈] [⊠] [⊠] [SC]

★ **DAYS INN-CIVIC CENTER.** *175 W Seventh St (55102),* at Kellogg, opp St Paul Civic Center, downtown. 612/292-8929; FAX 612/292-1749. E-mail daysinnmn @aol.com. 203 rms, 8 story. S $60-$75; D $68-$83; each addl $8; suites $115-$155; under 18 free; wknd rates; higher rates state tournament wknds. Crib free. Pet accepted. TV; cable (premium). Restaurant 6 am-midnight. Bar 4 pm-1 am. Ck-out 11 am. Meeting rms. Business servs avail. In-rm modem link. Valet serv. Downhill ski 20 mi; x-country ski 4 mi. Health club privileges. Some refrigerators; microwaves avail. Cr cds: A, C, D, DS, ER, JCB, MC, V. [D] [≈] [≈] [⊠] [⊠] [SC]

Hotel

★ ★ ★ **RADISSON.** *11 E Kellogg Blvd (55101), downtown.* 612/292-1900; FAX 612/224-8999. Web www.radisson.com. 475 rms, 22 story. S $110; D $140; each addl $10; under 18 free; package plans. Crib free. Pet accepted, some restrictions. Garage parking $11. TV; cable (premium), VCR avail. Indoor pool. Restaurant 6:30 am-10:30 pm; Fri, Sat to 11:30 pm. Bars 11:30-1 am. Ck-out noon. Convention facilities. Business servs avail. In-rm modem link. Concierge. Downhill ski 15 mi; x-country ski 4 mi. Exercise equipt; weight machine, stair machine. Health club privileges. Some refrigerators, microwaves. Indoor skyway to major stores, businesses. Luxury level. Cr cds: A, C, D, DS, ER, MC, V.
[D] [≈] [≈] [⊠] [✗] [⊠] [SC]

Sauk Centre *(See also Alexandria, Glenwood)*

Motel

✓ ★ **ECONO LODGE.** I-94 & US 71. 320/352-6581; FAX 320/352-6584. 38 rms, 2 story. S $40-$50; D $50-$65; each addl $5; under 12 free. Crib $2.50. Pet accepted, some restrictions. TV; cable (premium). Indoor pool. Ck-out 11 am. Business servs avail. Cr cds: A, C, D, DS, JCB, MC, V. [≈] [≈] [⊠] [⊠] [SC]

Stillwater *(See also St Paul)*

Motel

★ ★ **BEST WESTERN STILLWATER INN.** *1750 Frontage Rd W, near St Croix Mall. 612/430-1300; FAX 612/430-0596.* 60 rms, 2 story. Mid-May-mid-Oct:S $55-$69; D $61-$75; each addl $4; under 18 free; lower rates rest of yr. Crib free. Pet accepted. TV; cable (premium). Complimentary continental bkfst. Restaurant nearby. Ck-out 11 am. Business servs avail. In-rm modem link. Downhill ski 20 mi; x-country ski 2 mi. Exercise equipt; bicycles, treadmill. Whirlpool. Picnic table. Cr cds: A, D, DS, MC, V.

[D] [image] [image] [image] [image] [image] [SC]

Thief River Falls

Motel

★ **C'MON INN.** *1586 US 59S. 218/681-3000; FAX 218/681-3060; res: 800/950-8111.* 44 rms, 2 story. S $42.90-$48.90; D $49.90-$65.90; each addl $7; suites $74.90-$79.90; under 13 free. Crib free. Pet accepted, some restrictions. TV; cable. Indoor pool; whirlpool. Complimentary continental bkfst. Restaurant nearby. Ck-out noon. Meeting rms. Business servs avail. In-rm modem link. Game rm. Balconies. Cr cds: A, DS, MC, V.

[D] [image] [image] [image] [image] [SC]

Two Harbors *(See also Duluth)*

Motel

★ ★ **COUNTRY INN BY CARLSON.** *1204 Seventh Ave, on US 61. 218/834-5557; FAX 218/834-3777; res: 800/456-4000.* 46 rms, 2 story. Mid-May-mid-Oct: S, D $59-$109; each addl $5; under 18 free; higher rates special events; lower rates rest of yr. Crib free. Pet accepted, some restrictions; $5/day. TV; cable (premium), VCR avail (movies). Indoor pool; whirlpool. Complimentary continental bkfst. Complimentary coffee in rms. Restaurant adj 6 am-11 pm. Ck-out 11 am. Coin lndry. Business servs avail. X-country ski 1 mi. Sauna. Some refrigerators, microwaves, wet bars. Near Lake Superior. Cr cds: A, C, D, DS, MC, V.

[D] [image] [image] [image] [image] [image] [SC]

Resort

★ ★ ★ **SUPERIOR SHORES.** *10 Superior Shores Dr, just off US 61. 218/834-5671; FAX 218/834-5677; res: 800/242-1988.* E-mail sup shores@norshor.dst.mn.us.; web www.superiorshores.com. 104 rms in 3-story lodge, 42 kit. units in 3-story townhouses. Mid-June-mid Oct: S, D $69-$269; under 18 free; wkly rates; 2-day min wkends, 3-day min hols; lower rates rest of yr. Pet accepted. TV; cable, VCR (movies). 3 pools, 1 indoor; whirlpool. Restaurant 7 am-9 pm. Bar 11-1 am. Ck-out 11 am, ck-in by arrangement. Gift shop. Meeting rms. Business servs avail. Tennis. X-country ski opp. Sauna. Snowmobiles. Hiking trails. Game rm. Many refrigerators, microwaves. Balconies. Picnic tables, grills. On Lake Superior. Cr cds: A, DS, MC, V. [D] [image] [image] [image] [image] [image] [image] [image] [SC]

Virginia *(See also Cook, Eveleth, Hibbing)*

Motels

★ **LAKESHORE MOTOR INN.** *404 N 6th Ave. 218/741-3360; res: 800/569-8131.* 16 rms, 2 story. Mid-May-Aug: S $34; D $42-$46; each addl $4; family rates; lower rates rest of yr. Crib avail. Pet accepted. TV; cable. Complimentary coffee in rms. Restaurant nearby. Ck-out 11 am. Gift shop. Downhill ski 18 mi; x-country ski 4 mi. Cr cds: A, C, D, DS, MC, V. [image] [image] [image] [image] [image] [image] [SC]

★ **SKI VIEW.** *903 N 17th St. 218/741-8918.* 59 rms, 2 story. S $28-$30; D $38-$40; each addl $4. Crib $5. Pet accepted. TV; cable (premium). Complimentary continental bkfst. Complimentary coffee in rms. Restaurant nearby. Ck-out 11 am. Downhill/x-country ski 20 mi. Snowmobile trails adj. Sauna. Microwaves avail. Cr cds: A, C, D, DS, MC, V. [image] [image] [image] [image]

Willmar *(See also Granite Falls, Litchfield)*

Motels

★ ★ **DAYS INN.** *1200 E US 12. 320/231-1275.* 59 rms, 2 story. S $38.99-$51.99; D $44.99-$57.99; each addl $6; under 18 free. Crib free. Pet accepted. TV; cable (premium). Complimentary continental bkfst. Restaurant nearby. Ck-out 11 am. Exercise equipt; bicycle, treadmill, sauna. Whirlpool. Cr cds: A, C, D, DS, MC, V. [D] [image] [image] [image] [image] [SC]

✔ ★ **SUPER 8.** *2655 1st St S. 320/235-7260; FAX 320/235-5580.* 60 rms, 3 story. No elvtr. S $37.88-$40.38; D $42.58-$45.88; each addl $5; under 12 free. Crib free. Pet accepted. TV; cable (premium). Complimentary coffee in lobby. Restaurant nearby. Ck-out 11 am. Business servs avail. Cr cds: A, DS, MC, V. [D] [✔] [≋] [🐾] [SC]

Motor Hotel

★ ★ ★ **HOLIDAY INN.** *2100 E US 12. 320/235-6060; FAX 320/235-4731.* 98 rms, 2 story. S $63-$69; D $73-$79; each addl $10; under 18 free. Crib free. Pet accepted. TV; cable (premium). Complimentary coffee in lobby. Restaurant 6 am-10 pm. Rm serv. Bar 4 pm-1 am. Ck-out noon. Business servs avail. In-rm modem link. Indoor pool; wading pool, whirlpool, poolside serv. Some balconies. Cr cds: A, C, D, DS, JCB, MC, V. [D] [✔] [≋] [≋] [🐾] [SC]

Winona *(See also Rochester)*

Motel

★ ★ **BEST WESTERN RIVERPORT INN.** *900 Bruski Dr. 507/452-0606; FAX 507/457-6489.* 106 rms, 3 story. May-Oct: S $52-$89; D $62-$89; each addl $10; suites $52-$89; under 13 free; lower rates rest of yr. Crib free. Pet accepted; $10. TV; cable (premium), VCR avail. Indoor pool; whirlpool. Complimentary continental bkfst. Restaurant 11 am-10 pm. Rm serv. Bar 11-1 am. Ck-out noon. Meeting rms. Gift shop. Downhill ski 8 mi; x-country ski 1 mi. Game rm. Some refrigerators. Cr cds: A, C, D, DS, MC, V. [D] [✔] [🐾] [≋] [≋] [🐾] [SC]

Mississippi

Biloxi *(See also Gulfport, Ocean Springs, Pascagoula, Pass Christian)*

Motel

(Rates may be higher during Mardi Gras)

★ **BREAKERS INN.** *2506 Beach Blvd (US 90) (39531).* 228/388-6320; res: 800/624-5031. 28 kit. suites, 1-2 story. May-Sept: S, D $121-$171; higher rates: Memorial Day wknd, July 4, Labor Day; lower rates rest of yr. Pet accepted. TV; cable. Pool; wading pool. Playground. Restaurant nearby. Ck-out 11 am. Lndry facilities in rms. Business servs avail. In-rm modem link. Tennis. Lawn games. Opp gulf. Cr cds: A, C, D, DS, MC, V.
🐾 📶 🏊 🐾 SC

Grenada

Motel

★ ★ **BEST WESTERN MOTOR INN.** *1750 Sunset Dr, I-55 exit 206.* 601/226-7816; FAX 601/226-5623. 61 rms, 2 story. S $42-$49; D $54-$66. Crib $5. Pet accepted,some restrictions. TV; cable. Pool. Complimentary full bkfst. Restaurant 6 am-10 pm. Rm serv. Ck-out noon. Meeting rms. Business servs avail. In-rm modem link. Lawn games. Cr cds: A, C, D, DS, MC, V. 🐾 🏊 🐾 🐾 SC

Hattiesburg

Motel

✔ ★ **COMFORT INN.** *6595 US 49 (39401).* 601/268-2170. 119 rms, 2 story. S, D $56-$60; each addl $6; suites $90-$100; under 18 free. Crib free. Pet accepted, some restrictions. TV; cable (premium). Pool. Complimentary full bkfst. Restaurant 6 am-9:30 pm. Rm serv. Bar 5 pm-midnight; entertainment Fri, Sat. Ck-out noon. Coin lndry. Meeting rms. Business servs avail. Valet serv. Golf privileges. Cr cds: A, C, D, DS, MC, V.
D 🐾 🍴 🏊 🐾 🐾 SC

Jackson

Motels

✔ ★ **BEST WESTERN-NORTHEAST.** *Box 16275 (39236), 5035 I-55N.* 601/982-1011; FAX 601/982-1011, ext. 199. 133 rms, 2 story. S $46-$50; D $48-$54; each addl $5; suites $70-$100; under 17 free. Crib free. Pet accepted. TV; cable (premium). Pool. Restaurant 6 am-9 pm; closed Sat, Sun. Rm serv. Bar 5 pm-midnight. Ck-out noon. Coin lndry. Meeting rms. Business servs avail. In-rm modem link. Valet serv. Cr cds: A, C, D, DS, MC, V. D 🐾 🏊 🐾 🐾 SC

★ ★ **LA QUINTA MOTOR INN.** *150 Angle St (39204), I-20W, exit 43S.* 601/373-6110; FAX 601/373-6115. 101 rms, 2-3 story. S $51; D $57; suites $69-$81; each addl $6; under 18 free. Crib free. Pet accepted. TV; cable. Pool. Ck-out noon. Business servs avail. In-rm modem link. Valet serv. Airport transportation. Cr cds: A, C, D, DS, MC, V. D 🐾 🏊 🐾 🐾 SC

★ ★ **LA QUINTA-NORTH.** *616 Briarwood Dr (39236), just E off I-55N.* 601/957-1741; FAX 601/956-5746. 145 rms, 2 story. S, D $56-64; each addl $8; under 17 free. Crib free. Pet accepted. TV; cable (premium). Pool. Restaurant adj. Ck-out noon. Business servs avail. In-rm modem link. Cr cds: A, C, D, DS, MC, V. D 🐾 🏊 🐾 🐾 SC

Meridian

Motel

★ ★ **HOLIDAY INN EXPRESS.** *1401 Roebuck Dr (39302), US 45 at jct I-20, I-59.* 601/693-4421; FAX 601/693-4521, ext. 7625. 172 rms, 1-2 story. S, D $49-$54; under 12 free. Crib free. Pet accepted. TV; cable (premium). Pool. Playground. Coffee in rms. Ck-out noon. Coin lndry. Meeting rms. Business servs avail. In-rm modem link. Valet serv. Cr cds: A, C, D, DS, JCB, MC, V. D 🐾 🏊 🐾 🐾 SC

Natchez

Hotels

✔ ★ ★ **LADY LUCK.** *645 S Canal St. 601/445-0605; FAX 601/442-9823.* 147 units, 6 story. S $59-$69; D $69; each addl $5; suites $155; under 18 free. Crib free. Pet accepted. TV; cable, VCR avail. Pool; whirlpool, poolside serv. Restaurant 6:30 am-2 pm, 5:30-9:30 pm. Bar 4:30 pm-midnight. Ck-out 1 pm. Meeting rms. Business servs avail. Gift shop. Cr cds: A, C, D, DS, MC, V. D

★ ★ **NATCHEZ EOLA.** *110 N Pearl St. 601/445-6000; FAX 601/446-5310; res: 800/888-9140.* 125 rms, 7 story. S, D $55-$175; suites $100-$160. Crib free. Pet accepted. TV; cable. Restaurant 7 am-2 pm, 5-9 pm. Bar 11:30 am-midnight; Fri, Sat to 1 am. Ck-out noon. Meeting rms. Business servs avail. Balconies; many with view of river. Classic architecture; antique furniture. Cr cds: A, C, D, MC, V. D

Oxford

Inn

✔ ★ ★ **OLIVER-BRITT HOUSE.** *512 Van Buren Ave. 601/234-8043; FAX 601/281-8065.* 5 rms, 2 story. No rm phones. S, D $45-$55; higher rates football games. Pet accepted, some restrictions. TV; cable. Complimentary full bkfst. Restaurant nearby. Ck-out 11 am, ck-in 2 pm. Business servs avail. Restored manor house built 1905; some period furnishings. Cr cds: A, DS, MC, V.

Pascagoula *(See also Biloxi; also see Mobile, AL)*

Motel

✔ ★ ★ ★ **LA FONT INN.** *2703 Denny Ave, 2703 Denny Ave. 228/762-7111; FAX 228/934-4324; res: 800/647-6077 (exc MS), 800/821-3668 (MS).* 192 rms, 2 story, 13 kits. S $61-$78; D $66-$78; each addl $5; suites $121-$148; under 14 free. Crib free. Pet accepted. TV; cable (premium). Pool; wading pool, whirlpool, poolside serv. Playground. Complimentary coffee in rms. Restaurant 6 am-10 pm. Rm serv. Bar 11 am-midnight. Ck-out 1 pm. Coin lndry. Meeting rms. Business servs avail. In-rm modem link. Bellhops. Valet serv. Sundries. Lighted tennis. 18-hole golf privileges. Exercise equipt; weights, bicycles, steam rm, sauna. Lawn games. Refrigerators. Cr cds: A, C, D, DS, MC, V.

Starkville

Motel

✔ ★ ★ **HOLIDAY INN.** *Box 751, MS 12 & Montgomery St, opp MSU. 601/323-6161; FAX 601/323-8073.* 173 rms, 2 story. S, D $55; each addl $6; under 18 free; higher rates football wkends. Crib free. Pet accepted. TV; cable (premium). Pool. Restaurant 6 am-2 pm, 5-10 pm. Rm serv. Bar 5 pm-midnight; closed Sun. Ck-out noon. Meeting rms. Business servs avail. Cr cds: A, C, D, DS, JCB, MC, V. D

Tupelo

Inn

★ ★ **MOCKINGBIRD INN.** *305 N Gloster. 601/841-0286; FAX 601/840-4158.* 7 rms, 2 story. S, D $65-$125; each addl $10; wkend rates. Children over 13 yrs only. Pet accepted, some restrictions; $5. TV; cable. Complimentary full bkfst; afternoon refreshments. Restaurant opp 11 am-10 pm. Ck-out noon, ck-in 3-9 pm. Business servs avail. Built in 1925; sun porch, gazebo. Cr cds: A, DS, MC, V. D

Vicksburg

Motel

★ ★ **PARK INN INTERNATIONAL.** *4137 I-20 Frontage Rd, exit 4B. 601/638-5811; FAX 601/638-9249.* 117 rms, 2 story. S $35-$57; D $45-$67; each addl $7; under 16 free. Crib free. Pet accepted. TV; cable (premium). Pool. Complimentary bkfst buffet. Restaurant 6-10 am, 5-9 pm. Rm serv 5-9 pm. Bar 5-11 pm; entertainment. Ck-out 12:30 pm. Meeting rms. Business servs avail. In-rm modem link. Bellhops. Airport transportation. Some refrigerators. Cr cds: A, C, D, DS, ER, MC, V.

Motor Hotel

★ ★ **HOLIDAY INN.** *3330 Clay St. 601/636-4551; FAX 601/636-4552.* 173 rms, 2 story. S, D $65-$72; each addl $7; under 18 free. Crib free. Pet accepted. TV; cable (premium). Indoor pool; sauna. Restaurant 6 am-10 pm. Rm serv. Bar 3 pm-midnight. Ck-out noon. Coin lndry. Meeting rms. Business servs avail. In-rm modem link. Bellhops. Game rm. Cr cds: A, C, D, DS, JCB, MC, V. [D] 🐾 ≈ ⊠ 🐾 SC

Inn

★ ★ ★ **DUFF GREEN MANSION.** *1114 First East St. 601/638-6662; FAX 601/634-1061; res: 800/992-0037.* 7 units, 3 story. Mar-Nov: S, D $65-$160; each addl $10; suites $120-$160; under 5 free; wkly plan; lower rates rest of yr. Pet accepted. TV; cable, VCR avail. Pool; whirlpool. Complimentary full bkfst. Restaurant nearby. Ck-out 11 am, ck-in 3 pm. Business center. Paladian mansion (1856), used as both Confederate and Union hospital during Civil war, was shelled during siege; completely restored, many antiques. Cr cds: A, MC, V. [D] 🐾 ≈ ⊠ 🐾 🏃

Missouri

Bethany (See also Cameron)

Motel

✔★★ **BEST WESTERN I-35 INN.** *I-35, Jct I-35 & US 136 exit 92. 816/425-7915; FAX 816/425-3697.* 78 rms. S $45-$51; D $51-$61; each addl $5. Crib free. Pet accepted. TV; cable. Complimentary continental bkfst. Restaurant adj 6 am-11 pm. Ck-out 11 am. Coin lndry. Business servs avail. Whirlpool. Picnic tables. Cr cds: A, C, D, DS, MC, V.

Branson/Table Rock Lake Area
(See also Springfield; also see Bull Shoals Lake Area, AR)

Motels

✔★ **DAYS INN.** *3524 Keeter St. 417/334-5544; FAX 417/334-2935.* 425 rms, 4 story. Mid-Apr-Oct: S, D $42-$92; each addl $6; under 12 free; lower rates rest of yr. Pet accepted; $8.50/day. TV. Pool; wading pool, whirlpool. Playground. Complimentary continental bkfst. Restaurant 7 am-8 pm. Ck-out 11 am. Business servs avail. Sundries. Cr cds: A, D, DS, MC, V.

★★ **SETTLE INN.** *3050 Green Mt Dr. 417/335-4700; FAX 417/335-3906; res: 800/677-6906.* 300 rms, 3-4 story. Sept-Oct: S, D $45-$72; suites $99-$129; under 5 free; lower rates rest of yr. Crib free. Pet accepted; $5. TV; cable (premium). 2 indoor pools; whirlpool, sauna. Complimentary full bkfst. Restaurant 11 am-midnight. Rm serv. Bar; entertainment. Ck-out 2 pm. Coin lndry. Meeting rms. Business center. Concierge. Gift shop. Valet serv. Game rm. Balconies. Cr cds: A, DS, MC, V.

Cameron (See also St Joseph)

Motel

✔★ **RAMBLER.** *1/2 mi N on US 69, I-35 Business Loop at jct US 36. 816/632-6571.* 36 rms, 1-2 story. S $33-$41; D $36-$47; each addl $5. Pet accepted. TV; cable. Pool. Complimentary continental bkfst. Restaurants nearby. Ck-out 11 am. Cr cds: A, C, D, DS, ER, MC, V.

Cape Girardeau (See also Sikeston)

Motels

★★ **DRURY LODGE.** *PO Box 910, at jct I-55 & County K exit 96. 573/334-7151.* 139 rms, 2 story. S $56.95-$66.95; D $60-$73; each addl $8; under 18 free. Crib free. Pet accepted, some restrictions. TV; cable (premium), VCR avail. Pool; wading pool. Playground. Complimentary bkfst buffet. Restaurant 6 am-10 pm. Rm serv. Bars 4 pm-1:30 am. Ck-out noon. Meeting rms. Business servs avail. Valet serv. Exercise equipt; bicycle, treadmill. Health club privileges. Sundries. Game rm. Microwaves avail. Cr cds: A, C, D, DS, MC, V.

★ **HAMPTON INN.** *103 Cape West Pkwy. 573/651-3000; FAX 573/651-0882.* 80 rms, 3 story. S $64.95-$69.95; D $74.95-$79.95; under 18 free. Crib free. Pet accepted, some restrictions. TV; cable (premium). Complimentary continental bkfst. Restaurant nearby. Ck-out noon. Meeting rms. Business servs avail. Valet serv. Cr cds: A, C, D, DS, MC, V.

★★ **HOLIDAY INN WEST PARK.** *I-55 & William St (Rte K). 573/334-4491; FAX 573/334-7459.* 186 rms, 2 story. S, D $79-$89; each addl after 1, $10; under 18 free. Crib free. Pet accepted. TV; cable (premium). Indoor/outdoor pool; wading pool. Restaurant 6 am-2 pm, 5-9 pm. Rm serv. Bar 4 pm-midnight. Ck-out 11 am. Coin lndry. Meeting rms. Business servs avail. In-rm modem link. Valet serv. Free airport transportation. Exercise equipt; bicycles, rower. Health club privileges. Rec rm. Holidome. Bathrm phones. Cr cds: A, C, D, DS, JCB, MC, V.

✔★ **PEAR TREE INN.** *3248 William (63702). 573/334-3000.* 78 rms, 3 story. No elvtr. S $48-$54; D $58-$64; each addl $8; under 18 free. Crib free. Pet accepted, some

restrictions. TV; cable (premium). Complimentary continental bkfst. Restaurant adj 6 am-10 pm. Ck-out noon. Business servs avail. Pool; wading pool. Cr cds: A, C, D, DS, MC, V.
[D] [symbols]

Motor Hotel

★ **DRURY SUITES.** *3303 Campster Dr. 573/339-9500.* 87 suites, 5 story. S $78.95; D $88.95; each addl $10; under 18 free; golf plans. Crib free. Pet accepted, some restrictions. TV; cable (premium). Complimentary continental bkfst. Complimentary coffee in rms. Restaurant adj 4-10 pm. Rm serv. Bar. Ck-out noon. Meeting rms. Business servs avail. Health club privileges. Indoor pool; whirlpool. Refrigerators, microwaves. Cr cds: A, C, D, DS, MC, V. [D] [symbols]

Chillicothe

Motels

✔ ★ ★ **BEST WESTERN INN.** *1020 S Washington, at jct US 36 & 65. 816/646-0572; FAX 816/646-1274.* 60 rms, 1-2 story. S $39-$49; D $42-$52; each addl $5. Crib $5. Pet accepted; $5. TV; cable. Pool. Continental bkfst. Restaurants nearby. Ck-out noon. Meeting rm. Business servs avail. In-rm modem link. Refrigerators. Cr cds: A, C, D, DS, MC, V. [D] [symbols]

★ ★ **GRAND RIVER INN.** *606 W Business 36. 816/646-6590.* 60 rms, 2 story, 5 suites. S $54-$58; D $63-$67; each addl $9; suites $63-$83. Family rates; wknd, wkly rates; golf plans. Crib free. Pet accepted, some restrictions. TV; cable (premium), VCR avail (movies). Heated pool; whirlpool, sauna. Complimentary continental bkfst. Restaurant 6:30 am-9 pm; Fri to 10 pm; Sat 7 am-10 pm; Sun 7 am-2 pm. Rm serv. Bar 5 pm-1:30 am; closed Sun. Ck-out noon. Meeting rms. Business servs avail. In-rm modem link. Valet serv. Health club privileges. Some refrigerators. Cr cds: A, C, D, DS, MC, V. [D] [symbols]

Clayton *(See also St Louis)*

Hotel

★ ★ ★ **DANIELE.** *216 N Meramac, I-64 W to I-170 N, to Ladue Rd, E to Meramac. 314/721-0101; res: 800/325-8302; FAX 314/721-0609.* 82 rms, 4 story. S, D $129; suites $200-$500; under 18 free; wknd rates. Pet accepted. TV; cable (premium), VCR avail. Pool. Restaurant 6 am-10 pm. Bar. Ck-out noon. Meeting rms. Business servs avail. In-rm modem link. Free covered parking. Free airport transportation. Health club privileges. Some refrigerators, wet bars. Cr cds: A, C, D, DS, MC, V. [symbols]

Columbia *(See also Jefferson City)*

Motels

(Rates may be higher during special college events)

✔ ★ **BUDGET HOST.** *900 Vandiver Dr (65202), I-70 exit 127. 573/449-1065; FAX 573/442-6266.* 156 rms, 2 story. S $25.95-$34.95; D $39.95-$49.95; each addl $5; under 12 $1; wkly rates; higher rates special events. Crib $5. Pet accepted, some restrictions; $3. TV; cable. Heated pool. Complimentary continental bkfst. Restaurant nearby. Ck-out 11 am. Coin lndry. Business servs avail. Sundries. Some refrigerators. Picnic tables. Cr cds: A, C, D, DS, MC, V. [D] [symbols]

★ ★ **HOLIDAY INN-EAST.** *1412 N Providence Rd (65202), I-70 exit 126. 573/449-2491; FAX 573/874-6720.* 142 rms, 2 story. S $59-$79; D $60-$79; suites $175; under 18 free. Crib free. Pet accepted, some restrictions. TV; cable. Heated pool; whirlpool. Restaurant 6 am-2 pm, 5-10 pm. Rm serv. Bar 5 pm-midnight. Ck-out noon. Meeting rms. Sundries. Exercise equipt; bicycle, treadmill, sauna. Holidome. Cr cds: A, C, D, DS, JCB, MC, V. [D] [symbols]

Motor Hotel

★ ★ ★ **HOLIDAY INN EXECUTIVE CENTER.** *2200 I-70 Dr SW (65203), I-70 exit 124. 573/445-8531; FAX 573/445-7607.* 311 rms, 6 story. S $78-$95; D $78-$98; mini-suites $135-$250, suites $175-$250. Crib free. Pet accepted. TV; cable, VCR avail. 2 pools, 1 indoor; whirlpool, poolside serv. Restaurant open 24 hrs. Rm serv. Bar 11-1:30 am, Sun noon-midnight. Ck-out 11 am. Meeting rms. Business servs avail. In-rm modem link. Bellhops. Concierge. Gift shop. Beauty shop. Exercise equipt; weights, bicycles, sauna. Microwave avail. Adj Exposition Center. Luxury level. Cr cds: A, C, D, DS, MC, V. [D] [symbols]

Hannibal (See also Monroe City)

Motels

★ ★ ★ **RAMADA INN.** *4141 Market St, at jct US 61. 573/221-6610; FAX 573/221-3840.* 241 rms, 2 story. Memorial Day-Labor Day: S $70-$95; D $80-$95; each addl $7; under 19 free; lower rates rest of year. Crib free. Pet accepted. TV; cable (premium). Indoor pool; whirlpool, sauna, poolside serv. Restaurant 6 am-10 pm. Rm serv 7 am-2 pm, 5-9 pm. Bar 11-1 am. Ck-out 11 am. Coin lndry. Meeting rms. Business servs avail. In-rm modem link. Bellhops. Gift shop. Beauty shop. Cr cds: A, C, D, DS, JCB, MC, V.

D ⚿ ≈ ⌕ ⚑ SC

Motor Hotel

✔ ★ ★ **BEST WESTERN HOTEL CLEMENS.** *401 N 3rd St, opp Mark Twain Home & Museum. 573/248-1150; FAX 573/248-1155.* 78 rms, 3 story. Mid-May-mid-Sept: S $55-$75; D $68-$95; each addl $6; higher rates: Memorial Day, July 4, Labor Day; lower rates rest of yr. Crib $5. Pet accepted. TV; cable (premium), VCR avail. Indoor pool; whirlpool. Complimentary continental bkfst. Restaurant opp 6 am-10 pm. Ck-out 11 am. Coin lndry. Meeting rms. Business servs avail. Free airport, bus depot transportation. Game rm. In historic district near the Mississippi River. Cr cds: A, C, D, DS, ER, JCB, MC, V.

D ⚿ ≈ ⌕ ⚑ SC

Independence (See also Kansas City)

Motels

★ ★ **HOWARD JOHNSON EAST.** *4200 S Noland Rd (64055), I-70, exit Noland Rd. 816/373-8856; FAX 816/373-3312.* 171 rms, 2 story. S $59-$89; D $69-$89; suites $89; under 18 free. Crib free. Pet accepted. TV; cable (premium), VCR avail. 2 pools, 1 indoor; whirlpool, saunas. Restaurant adj open 24 hrs. Bar 4 pm-1 am. Ck-out noon. Meeting rms. Business servs avail. Valet serv. Some refrigerators. Private patios, balconies. Cr cds: A, C, D, DS, ER, JCB, MC, V. D ⚿ ≈ ⌕ ⚑ SC

✔ ★ **RED ROOF INN.** *13712 E 42nd Terrace (64055), I-70, exit 12. 816/373-2800; FAX 816/373-0067.* Web www.redroof.com. 108 rms, 2 story. S, D $38-$63; each addl $8; under 18 free. Crib free. Pet accepted. TV; cable. Complimentary coffee. Restaurant nearby. Ck-out noon. Business servs avail. Health club privileges. Cr cds: A, C, D, DS, MC, V.

D ⚿ ⌕ ≈

Jefferson City (See also Columbia)

Motor Hotels

✔ ★ ★ **HOTEL DE VILLE.** *319 W Miller St (65101), 2 blks S of Capitol Building. 573/636-5231; FAX 573/636-5260.* 98 rms, 3 story. S, D $60.90; each addl $10; suites $81.90; under 17 free. Crib free. Pet accepted. TV; cable (premium), VCR avail (movies). Pool. Restaurant 6 am-10 pm. Rm serv. Bar 11-1 am, closed Sun. Ck-out noon. Meeting rms. Business servs avail. Valet serv. Health club privileges. Cr cds: A, C, D, DS, ER, JCB, MC, V. D ⚿ ≈ ⌕ ⚑ SC

★ ★ **RAMADA INN.** *1510 Jefferson St (65109). 573/635-7171; FAX 573/635-8006.* 234 rms, 2 story S $62; D $67; each addl $5; suites $140; under 18 free. Crib free. Pet accepted. TV; cable (premium). Pool. Coffee in rms. Restaurant 6:30 am-2 pm, 5-10 pm; Sun from 7 am. Rm serv. Bar 5 pm-1:30 am, Sun noon-8 pm; entertainment exc Sun. Ck-out 11 am. Meeting rms. Business center. Sundries. Free RR station, bus depot transportation. Airport transportation. Exercise equipt; weights, bicycles. Game rm. Refrigerator in suites. Cr cds: A, C, D, DS, MC, V. D ⚿ ≈ 🏋 ⌕ ⚑ SC 🚶

Joplin (See also Mount Vernon)

Motels

★ ★ **DRURY INN.** *3601 Range Line (64804), I-44 exit 8B. 417/781-8000.* 109 rms, 4 story. Memorial Day-Labor Day: S $58; D $64-$80; each addl $5; under 18 free; lower rates rest of yr. Crib free. Pet accepted, some restrictions. TV; cable (premium), VCR avail. Indoor pool; whirlpool. Complimentary continental bkfst. Restaurant adj 6 am-10 pm. Ck-out noon. Meeting rms. Business servs avail. In-rm modem link. Health club privileges. Some refrigerators. Cr cds: A, C, D, DS, MC, V. D ⚿ ≈ ⌕ ⚑ SC

★ **WESTWOOD.** *1700 W 30th St (64804), I-44 exit 6. 417/782-7212; FAX 417/624-0265.* 33 rms, 2 story. S $32; D $39; each addl $4; kits. $44; under 12 free; wkly rates. Crib $5. Pet accepted; $25. TV; cable (premium). Pool. Complimentary coffee in lobby. Ck-out 11 am. Coin lndry. Cr cds: A, DS, MC, V. 🅳 ✉ ≈ ⬚ ⬚ SC

Motor Hotels

★ ★ ★ **HOLIDAY INN HOTEL & CONVENTION CENTER.** *3615 Range Line Rd (64804). 417/782-1000; FAX 417/623-4093.* 264 rms, 2-5 story. S, D $67-$74.50; each addl $10; suites $89.50-$175.50; under 18 free. Crib free. Pet accepted, some restrictions. TV; cable (premium), VCR avail. 2 pools, 1 indoor; whirlpool. Restaurant 6 am-10 pm. Rm serv. Bar; entertainment. Ck-out noon. Meeting rms. Business servs avail. In-rm modem link. Bellhops. Valet serv. Free airport, bus depot transportation. Exercise equipt; weights, bicycles, sauna, steam rm. Atrium. Cr cds: A, C, D, DS, JCB, MC, V.
🅳 ✉ ≈ ✗ ⬚ ⬚ SC

★ **RAMADA INN.** *3320 Range Line Rd (64804), jct I-44 & US 71. 417/781-0500; FAX 417/781-9388.* 171 rms, 2-3 story. S $50-$62; D $58-$72; each addl $8; suites $95-$130; under 18 free. Crib free. Pet accepted. TV; cable (premium). 2 pools, 1 indoor; whirlpool, sauna. Playground. Restaurant 6:30 am-10 pm. Rm serv. Bar. Ck-out noon. Meeting rms. Business servs avail. In-rm modem link. Bellhops. Valet serv. Free airport transportation. Lighted tennis. Cr cds: A, C, D, DS, ER, MC, V. 🅳 ✉ 🎾 ≈ ⬚ ⬚ SC

Kansas City

Motels

✔ ★ **BUDGETEL INN.** *2214 Taney (64116), I-435 exit 55A (US 210 W). 816/221-1200; FAX 816/471-6207.* Web www.budgetel.com. 100 rms, 3 story. S $43.95-$58.95; D $50.95-$70.95; each addl $7; under 18 free. Pet accepted, some restrictions. TV; cable (premium). Complimentary continental bkfst. Restaurant adj 7 am-midnight. Ck-out noon. Business servs avail. In-rm modem link. Sundries. Microwaves avail. Cr cds: A, C, D, DS, MC, V. 🅳 ✉ ⬚ ⬚ SC

★ ★ **RESIDENCE INN BY MARRIOTT.** *9900 NW Prairie View Rd (64153), north of downtown. 816/891-9009; FAX 816/891-8623.* Web www.marriott.com. 110 kit. suites, 2 story. S, D $69-$159; wkly, monthly rates. Crib free. Pet accepted, some restrictions; $100. TV; cable (premium), VCR avail (movies). Heated pool; wading pool, whirlpool. Complimentary continental bkfst. Ck-out noon. Coin lndry. Meeting rms. Business servs avail. In-rm modem link. Valet serv. Sundries. Free airport transportation. Lawn games. Exercise equipt; stair machine, bicycles. Microwaves. Private patios, balconies. Gazebo area with grills. Cr cds: A, C, D, DS, JCB, MC, V. 🅳 ✉ ≈ ✗ ✗ ⬚ ⬚ SC

Motor Hotel

★ ★ **MARRIOTT-AIRPORT.** *775 Brasilia (64153), 15 mi NW on I-29, at Intl Airport, north of downtown. 816/464-2200; FAX 816/464-5915.* Web www.marriott.com. 382 rms, 9 story. S, D, studio rms $69-$150; suites $250-$450; under 18 free; wkend plan. Crib free. Pet accepted. TV; cable (premium). Indoor pool; whirlpool. Restaurant 6 am-11 pm. Rm serv. Bar 11:30-1 am, Sun 12:30 pm-midnight. Ck-out noon. Coin lndry. Meeting rms. Business servs avail. In-rm modem link. Bellhops. Valet serv. Gift shop. Free airport transportation. Downhill ski 15 mi. Excercise equipt; weights, bicycles, sauna. Rec rm. Lawn games. Private patios, picnic tables. On lake. Luxury level. Cr cds: A, C, D, DS, JCB, MC, V. 🅳 ✉ ≈ ✗ ✗ ⬚ ⬚ SC

Hotels

★ ★ **HISTORIC SUITES.** *612 Central (64105), downtown. 816/842-6544; FAX 816/842-0656; res: 800/733-0612.* 100 suites, 5 story. S, D $140-$215; under 18 free; wkly rates; lower rates hol wkends. Crib free. Pet accepted, some restrictions. TV; cable (premium). Pool; whirlpool. Complimentary continental bkfst. Complimentary coffee in rms. Restaurant nearby. No rm serv. Coin lndry. Meeting rms. Business servs avail. In-rm modem link. No bellhops. Garage parking. Exercise equipt; weight machine, bicycles, sauna. Microwaves. Turn-of-the-century design. Cr cds: A, C, D, DS, MC, V. 🅳 ✉ ≈ ✗ ✗ ⬚ ⬚ SC

✔ ★ **PARK PLACE.** *1601 N Universal Ave (64120), I-435 Front St exit, north of downtown. 816/483-9900; FAX 816/231-1418; res: 800/821-8532.* 330 rms, 9 story. S, D $65-$90; each addl $10; suites $89-$129; under 18 free; wkend rates; package plans. Crib free. Pet accepted, some restrictions; $25 deposit. TV; cable (premium). Indoor/outdoor pool. Complimentary coffee in rms. Restaurant 6:30 am-10 pm; Fri, Sat to 11 pm. Bar 11-1:30 am; entertainment exc Sun. Ck-out noon. Meeting rms. Business servs avail. Gift shop. Exercise equipt; weights, bicycles, sauna. Some bathrm phones, refrigerators. Private patios; some balconies. Cr cds: A, C, D, DS, ER, MC, V. 🅳 ✉ ≈ ✗ ✗ ⬚ ⬚

★ ★ ★ **THE WESTIN CROWN CENTER.** *1 Pershing Rd (64108), at Main St, in Crown Center. 816/474-4400; FAX 816/391-4438; res: 800/228-3000.* Web www.westin

.com. 725 rms, 18 story. S $99-$205; D $99-$230; each addl $25; suites $300-$1,000; under 18 free; wkend package. Crib free. Pet accepted. TV; cable, VCR avail. Heated pool; whirlpool, poolside serv. Supervised childs activities (ages 6-12). Restaurants 6 am-midnight. Bars 11:30-1 am; entertainment. Ck-out noon. Convention facilities. Business center. In-rm modem link. Barber. Airport transportation. Lighted tennis. Exercise rm; instructor, weights, bicycles, sauna, steam rm. Rec rm. Lawn games. Refrigerators, wet bars. Private patios, balconies. Indoor tropical waterfall and garden. Luxury level. Cr cds: A, C, D, DS, ER, JCB, MC, V. 🄳 ✦ 🏊 🏋 🚶 🏃 ✕ 🔌 📵 SC 🛠

Kirksville (See also Macon)

Motels

✔★ ★ **BEST WESTERN SHAMROCK INN.** 2 mi S on US 63 Business. 816/665-8352; res: 816/665-6700; FAX 816/665-0072. 45 rms. S $48; D $56; each addl $6; under 12 free. Crib free. Pet accepted, some restrictions. TV; cable (premium), VCR avail (movies). Pool. Playground. Restaurant 6 am-10 pm. Ck-out 11 am. Meeting rms. Sundries. Cr cds: A, C, D, DS, MC, V. 🔌 🏊 📵 🛠 SC

✔★ **BUDGET HOST VILLAGE INN.** 1304 S Baltimore. 816/665-3722; FAX 816/665-6334. 30 rms, 1-2 story. S $40-$42; D $44-$49; each addl $5; under 10 free. Crib free. Pet accepted, some restrictions. TV; cable (premium). Complimentary coffee in office. Restaurant nearby. Ck-out noon. Business servs avail. In-rm modem link. In-rm steam baths. Cr cds: A, C, D, DS, ER, MC, V. 🔌 📵 🛠 SC

Lake Ozark (See also Osage Beach)

Motor Hotel

★ ★ **HOLIDAY INN.** MO 54 Business, 2 mi S of Bagnell Dam. 573/365-2334; FAX 573/365-6887. Web www.funlake.com. 213 rms, 2 story. Late May-early Sept: S, D $89.50-$149; suites $169-$299; under 20 free; lower rates rest of yr. Crib free. Pet accepted. TV; cable (premium). 3 pools, 1 indoor; whirlpool. Playground. Restaurant 6:30 am-10 pm, under 12 free. Rm serv. Bar noon-midnight. Ck-out noon. Coin lndry. Meeting rms. Business servs avail. In-rm modem link. Bellhops. Gift shop. Exercise equipt; bicycle, treadmill, sauna, steam rm. Miniature golf. Game rm. Rec rm. Lawn games. Microwaves avail. On lake. Cr cds: A, C, D, DS, JCB, MC, V. 🄳 ✦ 🔌 🏊 🏋 ✕ 📵 🛠 SC

Lebanon (See also Waynesville)

Motels

✔★ **BEST WESTERN WYOTA INN.** E I-44 Business Loop & I-44 exit 130. 417/532-6171; FAX 417/532-6174. 52 rms, 1-2 story. May-Oct: S $36-$40; D $42-$52; each addl $5; under 12 free; lower rates rest of yr. Crib $5. Pet accepted, some restrictions. TV; cable (premium). Pool. Restaurant 6 am-9 pm. Ck-out 11 am. Coin lndry. Cr cds: A, C, D, DS, MC, V. 🔌 🏊 📵 🛠 SC

★ **QUALITY INN.** I-44 Business Loop W exit 127. 417/532-7111; FAX 417/532-7005. 82 rms, 2 story. S, D $40-$56; each addl $5; under 19 free. Crib free. Pet accepted. TV; cable, VCR avail. Pool; poolside serv. Restaurant 6:30 am-2 pm, 5-10 pm. Rm serv. Bar 3 pm-midnight. Ck-out noon. Coin lndry. Meeting rm. Business servs avail. Cr cds: A, C, D, DS, JCB, MC, V. 🄳 ✦ 🏊 📵 🛠 SC

Lexington (See also Independence, Kansas City)

Motel

✔★ **LEXINGTON INN.** MO 13, Jct US 24 & MO 13. 816/259-4641; res: 800/289-4641. 60 rms, 2 story. S $37; D $43; under 5 free. Crib $3. Pet accepted; $100 deposit. TV; cable. Pool. Restaurant 6 am-10 am; closed Sun. Bar 4 pm-1:30 am; entertainment, dancing Fri, Sat. Ck-out 11 am. Coin lndry. Meeting rms. Business servs avail. Cr cds: A, C, D, DS, MC, V. 🄳 🔌 🏊 📵 🛠 SC

Macon (See also Kirksville)

Motel

✔★ **BEST WESTERN INN.** 28933 Sunset Dr, 1¹/₂ mi W of US 63, Long Branch Lake exit. 816/385-2125. 46 rms, 2 story. S $39-$43; D $47; each addl $4. Crib $4. Pet accepted, some restrictions. TV; cable. Pool. Coffee in rms. Restaurant adj 6 am-9 pm; Sun

7 am-8 pm. Ck-out 11 am. Meeting rm. Business servs avail. In-rm modem link. Cr cds: A, C, D, DS, MC, V. 🐾 📶 🎿 🏊 SC

Mexico *(See also Columbia)*

Motel

✔ ★ **BEST WESTERN INN.** *1010 E Liberty. 573/581-1440; FAX 573/581-1487.* 63 rms, 2 story. S $36-$40; D $43-$48; each addl $4; under 12 free. Crib $4. Pet accepted; $5/day. TV; cable (premium). Pool. Complimentary continental bkfst. Complimentary coffee in rms. Restaurant 11 am-2 pm, 5-9 pm; closed Sun. Rm serv. Bar 11-1:30 am; closed Sun. Ck-out noon. Coin lndry. Meeting rm. Business servs avail. Sundries. Refrigerators. Cr cds: A, C, D, DS, ER, MC, V. D 🐾 📶 🎿 🏊 SC

Monroe City *(See also Hannibal)*

Motel

★ **ECONO LODGE.** *#3 Gateway Square, US 36 Business & US 24. 573/735-4200; FAX 573/735-3493.* 47 rms, 2 story. Mar-Oct: S $40-$50; D $45-$50; under 12 free; lower rates rest of yr. Crib free. Pet accepted, some restrictions; $5. TV; cable. Indoor pool; whirlpool. Ck-out 11 am. Meeting rm. Cr cds: A, D, DS, MC, V. D 🐾 📶 🎿 🏊 SC

Mount Vernon *(See also Joplin, Springfield)*

Motel

✔ ★ **BUDGET HOST RANCH.** *Rte 1, Box 6B, on MO 39 at jct I-44, exit 46. 417/466-2125; FAX 417/466-4440.* 21 rms. S $38-$40; D $38-$46; each addl $3; wkly rates winter, extended stay rates. Crib $3. Pet accepted, some restrictions. TV; cable (premium), VCR avail. Pool. Restaurant nearby. Ck-out 11 am. Picnic tables. Cr cds: A, DS, MC, V. 🐾 📶 🎿 🏊 SC

Nevada *(See also Fort Scott, KS)*

Motels

★ ★ **COMFORT INN.** *2345 Marvel Dr, US 71 exit Camp Clark W. 417/667-6777; FAX 417/667-6135.* 46 rms, 2 story. S $44.95; D $49.95; each addl $2; suites $51.95-$71.95; under 12 free; higher rates special events. Pet accepted, some restrictions; $25. TV; cable (premium). Indoor pool; whirlpool. Complimentary continental bkfst. Restaurant nearby. Ck-out 11 am. Coin lndry. Meeting rms. Some minibars. Cr cds: A, C, D, DS, MC, V. D 🐾 📶 🎿 🏊 SC

★ **SUPER 8.** *2301 E Austin. 417/667-8888; FAX 417/667-8883.* 60 rms, 2 story. S $36.88-$46.88; D $42.88-$50.88; each addl $2. Crib avail. Pet accepted. TV; cable (premium), VCR avail. Indoor pool; whirlpool. Complimentary continental bkfst. Restaurant nearby. Ck-out 11 am. Business servs avail. Coin lndry. Cr cds: A, C, D, DS, MC, V. D 🐾 📶 🎿 SC

Osage Beach *(See also Lake Ozark)*

Motel

✔ ★ ★ **BEST WESTERN DOGWOOD HILLS RESORT INN.** *Rte 4, Box 1300, off US 54, 1 mi on MO KK. 573/348-1735; FAX 573/348-0014.* Web www.bestwestern.com/best.html. 47 rms, 4 fairway villas, 2-3 story. S, D $45-$92; each addl $8; villas $99-$336; under 19 free; wkend rates. Crib $5. Pet accepted, some restrictions. TV; cable. Pool; whirlpool. Dining rm 7 am-2 pm; closed Nov-Feb. Bar. Ck-out 11 am, ck-in 4 pm. Package store 1 mi. Meeting rm. Business servs avail. 18-hole golf, pro, putting green, driving range. Some refrigerators. Some private patios, balconies. Extensive grounds. Cr cds: A, C, D, DS, MC, V. D 🐾 🎿 🏊 SC

Poplar Bluff *(See also Sikeston)*

Motels

✔ ★ ★ **DRURY INN.** *2220 Westwood Blvd N. 573/686-2451.* 78 rms, 3 story. S $55-$59; D $63-$68; each addl $8; under 18 free. Crib free. Pet accepted, some restrictions. TV; cable. Pool. Complimentary bkfst. Restaurant adj 6 am-11 pm. Ck-out noon. Business servs avail. In-rm modem link. Valet serv. Cr cds: A, C, D, DS, MC, V. D 🐾 📶 🎿 🏊 SC

★ **HOLIDAY INN.** *2115 N Westwood Blvd (US 67N). 573/785-7711; FAX 573/785-5215.* 143 rms, 1-2 story. S $55; D $63; each addl $8; suites $150; under 18 free. Crib free. Pet accepted. TV; cable (premium). Pool. Restaurant 6 am-10 pm. Rm serv. Bar 11-1:30 am, Sun 1-10 pm; entertainment exc Sun. Ck-out noon. Meeting rms. Cr cds: A, C, D, DS, JCB, MC, V. ⒹⓌ≋⛵🐾SC

Rolla *(See also Sullivan, Waynesville)*

Motels

✔★ **BEST WESTERN COACHLIGHT.** *1403 Martin Spring Dr, I-44 at exit 184. 573/341-2511.* 88 rms, 2 story. May-Oct: S, D $48; each addl $4; under 12 free; higher rates special events; lower rates rest of yr. Crib $8. Pet accepted. TV; cable (premium). Pool. Playground. Continental bkfst. Restaurant adj 11 am-10 pm. Ck-out noon. Meeting rms. In-rm modem link. Some refrigerators. Cr cds: A, C, D, DS, MC, V. Ⓦ≋⛵🐾SC

★ ★ **DRURY INN.** *2006 N Bishop Ave, I-44 exit 186. 573/364-4000; FAX 573/364-4000, ext. 475.* Web www.drury-inn.com. 86 rms, 2 story. S, D $64-$78; each addl $10; under 18 free. Crib free. Pet accepted. TV; cable. Complimentary continental bkfst. Pool. Ck-out noon. Meeting rms. Business servs avail. Valet serv. Health club privileges. Cr cds: A, C, D, DS, MC, V. ⒹⓌ≋⛵🐾SC

St Charles *(See also St Louis, Wentzville)*

Motel

✔★ **KNIGHTS INN.** *3800 Harry S Truman Blvd (63301). 314/925-2020; res: 800/843-5644.* 110 rms. S $49.95-$55; D $55-$65; kits. $55-$65; under 18 free. Crib free. Pet accepted. TV; cable. Pool. Complimentary coffee in lobby. Restaurant opp 6 am-10:30 pm. Ck-out noon. Some refrigerators. Cr cds: A, C, D, DS, MC, V. ⒹⓌ≋⛵🐾SC

St Joseph *(See also Cameron, Kansas City; also see Atchison, KS)*

Motels

★ ★ **DRURY INN.** *4213 Frederick Blvd (64506). 816/364-4700.* 133 rms, 4 story. S $56-$66; D $66-$76; each addl $10; under 18 free. Crib free. Pet accepted. TV; cable (premium). Pool. Complimentary bkfst. Restaurant adj 6 am-11 pm. Ck-out noon. Meeting rms. Business servs avail. In-rm modem link. Valet serv. Sundries. Exercise equipt; treadmill, weight machine. Cr cds: A, C, D, DS, MC, V. ⒹⓌ≋🏃⛵🐾SC

★ **RAMADA INN.** *4016 Frederick Blvd (64506), I-29, Exit 47. 816/233-6192; FAX 816/233-6001.* 161 rms, 2 story. S, D $65-$85; suites $85; under 18 free. Crib free. Pet accepted. TV; cable (premium). Indoor pool; whirlpool. Restaurants 6 am-2 pm, 5-10 pm. Rm serv. Bar 4 pm-midnight. Ck-out noon. Coin lndry. Meeting rms. Business servs avail. Valet serv. Rec rm. Picnic tables. Cr cds: A, C, D, DS, ER, JCB, MC, V. ⒹⓌ≋⛵🐾SC

Motor Hotel

★ ★ **HOLIDAY INN-DOWNTOWN.** *102 S 3rd St (64501). 816/279-8000; FAX 816/279-8000, ext. 698.* 170 rms, 6 story. S, D $74-$94; suites $95-$135; under 18 free; wkend rates. Crib free. Pet accepted. TV; cable. Indoor pool; whirlpool, sauna. Restaurant 6:30 am-2 pm, 5:30-10:30 pm. Rm serv. Bar 4 pm-1 am, Sun to 9 pm. Ck-out noon. Meeting rms. Business servs avail. Bellhops. Sundries. Gift shop. Game rm. Refrigerator, wet bar in suites. Opp river. Cr cds: A, C, D, DS, JCB, MC, V. ⒹⓌ≋⛵🐾SC

St Louis

Motels

★ ★ **RESIDENCE INN BY MARRIOTT.** *1881 Craigshire Rd (63146), I-270, Page Ave E exit, west of downtown. 314/469-0060; FAX 314/469-3751.* 128 kit. suites, 2 story. Suites $79-$139; wkly, monthly rates; wkend plans. Crib free. Pet accepted, some restrictions; $25. TV; cable (premium), VCR (movies). Heated pool; whirlpool. Complimentary continental bkfst. Restaurant nearby. Ck-out noon. Coin lndry. Meeting rm. Business servs avail. In-rm modem link. Airport transportation. Health club privileges. Refrigerators, microwaves; many fireplaces. Private patios, balconies. Picnic tables, grills. Cr cds: A, C, D, DS, MC, V. ⒹⓌ≋⛵🐾SC

★ ★ **SUMMERFIELD SUITES.** *1855 Craigshire Rd (63146), I-270, Page Ave exit E to Craigshire Rd, north of downtown. 314/878-1555; FAX 314/878-9203; res: 800/833-4353.* 106 kit. suites, 2 story. 1-bedrm $139; 2-bedrm $159; wkend rates. Crib free. Pet accepted, some restrictions; $75. TV; cable (premium), VCR (movies). Heated pool; whirl-pool. Complimentary continental bkfst. Complimentary coffee in rms. Restaurant nearby. Ck-out noon. Coin lndry. Meeting rms. Business servs avail. In-rm modem link. Valet serv. Sundries. Free airport transportation. Exercise equipt; weight machine, bicycles. Micro-waves. Picnic tables, grills. Cr cds: A, C, D, DS, MC, V. 🄳 👄 ≈ 🕇 📐 🐾 SC

Motor Hotel

★ **HOLIDAY INN-FOREST PARK.** *5915 Wilson Ave (63110), I-44 W, exit Hampton Ave, S 1 mi.* 314/645-0700. 120 rms, 7 story. S $69-$99; D $69-$115; each addl $10; under 12 free; family rates. Crib free. Pet accepted. TV; VCR avail. Complimentary coffee in rms. Restaurant 5:30 am-10 pm. Rm serv. Bar 4 pm-midnight; Sun to 10 pm. Ck-out noon. Meeting rms. Business center. In-rm modem link. Heated pool. Refrigerators, microwaves avail. Balconies. Cr cds: A, C, D, DS, JCB, MC, V. 🄳 👄 ≈ 📐 🐾 SC 🏃

Hotels

★ ★ **DRURY INN UNION STATION.** *201 S 20th St (63103), west of downtown.* 314/231-3900; FAX 314/231-3900. 176 rms, 7 story. Apr-Oct: S $98-$113; D $108-$123; each addl $10; suites $150; under 18 free; hol rates; lower rates rest of yr. Crib avail. Pet accepted, some restrictions. TV; cable (premium), VCR avail. Indoor pool; whirlpool, lifeguard. Complimentary continental bkfst. Restaurant 11 am-10 pm. Bar. Ck-out noon. Coin lndry. Meeting rms. In-rm modem link. No bellhops. Exercise equipt; bicycle, treadmill. Health club privileges. Some refrigerators. Restored 1907 railroad hotel. Cr cds: A, C, D, DS, JCB, MC, V.
🄳 👄 ≈ 🕇 🐾 SC

★ ★ **DRURY INN-CONVENTION CENTER.** *711 N Broadway (63102), in Union Market Building, downtown.* 314/231-8100; FAX 314/621-6568. Web www.drury-inn.com. 178 rms, 2 flrs in 6 story bldg. May-Sept: S $96-$112; D $106-$122; each addl $10; under 18 free; wkend rates; higher rates July 4th; lower rates rest of yr. Crib free. Pet accepted, some restrictions. TV; cable (premium). Indoor pool; whirlpool, poolside serv, lifeguard. Complimentary continental bkfst. Restaurant adj 11 am-2 pm, 4:30-11 pm; wkend hrs vary. Ck-out noon. Meeting rms. Business servs avail. In-rm modem link. No bellhops. Some refrigerators. Microwaves avail. Cr cds: A, C, D, DS, MC, V. 🄳 👄 ≈ 📐 🐾 SC

★ ★ **HAMPTON INN.** *2211 Market St (63103), opp Union Station, west of downtown.* 314/241-3200; FAX 314/241-9351. 239 rms, 11 story, 14 suites. S $84-$125; D $95-$125; suites $110-$135; under 18 free; wkend rates. Crib free. Pet accepted, some restrictions. TV; cable (premium). Indoor pool; whirlpool. Complimentary continental bkfst. Restaurant 11-3 am. Bar. Ck-out noon. Coin lndry. Business servs avail. In-rm modem link. No bellhops. Free garage parking. Exercise equipt; treadmills, bicycles. Refrigerators avail. Cr cds: A, C, D, DS, MC, V. 🄳 👄 ≈ 🕇 📐 🐾 SC

★ ★ **MAYFAIR.** *806 St Charles St (63101), downtown.* 314/421-2500; res: 800/757-8483; FAX 314/421-0770. Web www.grandheri tage.com. 167 rms, 18 story. S, D $95-$175; each addl $10; under 12 free. Crib free. Pet accepted; $50 deposit. TV; cable (premium). Complimentary coffee in rms. Restaurant 6:30 am-2 pm, 5-10:30 pm. Bar 11:30 am-midnight. Ck-out noon. Meeting rms. Business center. In-rm modem link. Concierge. Exercise equipt; weights, stair machine. Bathrm phones, refrigerators, minibars. Luxury level. Cr cds: A, C, D, DS, MC, V. 🄳 👄 🕇 📐 🐾 SC 🏃

St Louis Lambert Airport Area *(See also St Charles, St Louis)*

Motels

★ ★ **DRURY INN.** *(10490 Natural Bridge Rd, St Louis 63134) W via I-70, 1 blk N of exit 236.* 314/423-7700. Web www.drury-inn.com. 172 rms, 6 story. S $79.95-$85.95; D $89.95-$99.95; suites $103-$123; under 18 free; some wkend rates. Crib free. Pet accepted, some restrictions. TV; cable (premium), VCR avail. Heated pool. Complimentary continental bkfst. Restaurant adj noon-10 pm. Ck-out noon. Meeting rms. Business servs avail. In-rm modem link. Free airport transportation. Cr cds: A, C, D, DS, MC, V.
🄳 👄 ≈ 🕇 🐾 SC

★ ★ **HOLIDAY INN-AIRPORT WEST.** *(3551 Pennridge Dr, Bridgeton 63044) 1-270 to St Charles Rock Rd, W to Boenker.* 314/291-5100. 327 rms, 4 story. S, D $92-$97; each addl $10; under 18 free. Crib free. Pet accepted. TV; cable (premium), VCR avail. Complimentary coffee in rms. Restaurant 6-10 am. Rm serv. Bar 4 pm-1 am. Ck-out noon. Convention facilities. Business center. In-rm modem link. Bellhops. Valet serv. Coin lndry. Free airport transportation. Exercise equipt; weights, treadmill, sauna. Indoor pool; whirlpool. Game rm. Rec rm. Some refrigerators. Luxury level. Cr cds: A, C, D, DS, MC, V.
🄳 👄 ≈ 📐 🐾 SC 🏃

Hotels

★ ★ ★ **MARRIOTT.** *(I-70 at Lambert St Louis Intl Airport, St Louis 63134) I-70 exit 236.* 314/423-9700; FAX 314/423-0213. Web www.marriott.com. 601 rms, 9 story. S, D $99-$134; suites $200-$375. Crib free. Pet accepted. TV; cable (premium), VCR avail. 2 pools, 1 indoor/outdoor; poolside serv, whirlpool. Restaurant 6 am-midnight. Bars 11:30-1 am. Ck-out 1 pm. Coin lndry. Convention facilities. Business center. In-rm modem link. Gift shop. Free airport transportation. 2 lighted tennis courts. Exercise equipt; weights, sauna. Luxury level. Cr cds: A, C, D, DS, ER, JCB, MC, V. 🅳 ⊷ ≅ 🛌 🏃 ✈ ⊠ 🐾 SC 🏌

✓ ★ **RAMADA.** *(9600 Natural Bridge Rd, Berkeley 63134) 2 mi E on Natural Bridge Rd.* 314/427-7600; FAX 314/427-1614. 197 rms, 7 story. S, D $79-$89; each addl $7; under 18 free; wkend rates. Crib free. Pet accepted, some restrictions; $50 deposit. TV; cable. Pool; whirlpool. Bar 5:30 pm-1:30 am. Ck-out noon. Meeting rms. Business servs avail. In-rm modem link. Free airport transportation. Exercise equipt; weight machine, stair machine, sauna. Some bathrm phones, refrigerators, minibars. Balconies. Cr cds: A, C, D, DS, MC, V. ⊷ ≅ 🏃 ✈ ⊠ 🐾 SC

Sedalia *(See also Jefferson City)*

Motel

(Rates usually higher State Fair)

✓ ★ **BEST WESTERN STATE FAIR MOTOR INN.** *3120 S Limit (US 65).* 660/826-6100; FAX 660/827-3850. 119 rms, 2 story. S $38-$49; D $49-$59; each addl $5; under 18 free. Crib free. Pet accepted. TV; cable (premium). Indoor pool; wading pool, whirlpool, poolside serv. Restaurant 5:45 am-2 pm, 5-9:30 pm. Rm serv. Bar. Ck-out noon. Coin lndry. Meeting rms. Business servs avail. Free airport transportation. Exercise equipt; weights, bicycles, sauna. Miniature golf. Game rm. Cr cds: A, C, D, DS, MC, V. ⊷ ≅ 🏃 ⊠ ⊠ 🐾 SC

Sikeston *(See also Cape Girardeau)*

Motels

★ ★ **BEST WESTERN COACH HOUSE INN.** *220 S Interstate Dr.* 573/471-9700. 65 suites, 2 story. S $47-$80; D $58-$100; each addl $8; under 18 free; higher rates rodeo. Crib free. Pet accepted, some restrictions. TV; cable. Complimentary coffee in rms. Restaurant 7-11 am, 5-9 pm. Bar 4-11 pm; entertainment. Ck-out noon. Meeting rms. Business servs avail. In-rm modem link. Free guest lndry. Pool; poolside serv. Game rm. Rec rm. Refrigerators; microwaves avail. Cr cds: A, C, D, DS, MC, V. 🅳 ⊷ ≅ ⊠ 🐾 SC

★ **DRURY INN.** *2602 E Malone.* 573/471-4100. 78 rms, 4 story. S $58-$72; D $68-$82; each addl $10; suites $72-$82; under 18 free. Crib free. Pet accepted, some restrictions. TV; cable (premium), VCR avail (movies). Complimentary continental bkfst. Restaurant nearby. Ck-out noon. Meeting rms. Business servs avail. Valet serv. Heated indoor/outdoor pool; whirlpool. Some refrigerators, microwaves. Cr cds: A, C, D, DS, MC, V. 🅳 ⊷ ≅ ⊠ 🐾 SC

★ ★ **HOLIDAY INN EXPRESS.** *2602 Rear E Malone.* 573/471-8660. 67 rms, 3 story. No elvtr. S $52-$57; D $60-$65; each addl $8; under 19 free. Crib free. Pet accepted, some restrictions. TV; cable (premium). Complimentary continental bkfst. Restaurant adj 6 am-10 pm. Meeting rms. Business servs avail. In-rm modem link. Valet serv. Pool. Microwaves avail. Cr cds: A, C, D, DS, MC, V. 🅳 ⊷ ≅ ⊠ 🐾 SC

Springfield *(See also Branson/Table Rock Lake Area)*

Motels

★ ★ **BEST WESTERN SYCAMORE.** *203 S Glenstone (65802), 1 blk S of I-44 exit 80A.* 417/866-1963. 93 rms. May-Oct: S, D $48-$53; each addl $5; suites $60-$65; under 18 free; lower rates rest of yr. Crib free. Pet accepted, some restrictions. TV; cable (premium), VCR avail (movies). Pool; whirlpool. Complimentary continental bkfst. Restaurant adj open 24 hrs. Ck-out noon. Business servs avail. In-rm modem link. Valet serv. Refrigerator in suites. Cr cds: A, C, D, DS, MC, V. ⊷ ≅ ⊠ 🐾 SC

★ ★ **CLARION.** *3333 S Glenstone (65804).* 417/883-6550; FAX 417/887-1823. 199 rms, 11 with shower only, 2 story. S, D $79-$89; each addl $5; suites $150; under 18 free. Crib free. Pet accepted, some restrictions; $10. TV; cable (premium). Pool. Restaurant 6 am-2 pm, 5-10 pm. Rm serv to 2 pm. Bar 11-1 am. Ck-out noon. Meeting rms. Business servs avail. In-rm modem link. Bellhops. Valet serv. Sundries. Free airport transportation. Health club privileges. Some refrigerators. Picnic tables. Cr cds: A, D, DS, MC, V.

D ⊱ ≋ ⊠ ⊼ SC

★ ★ **RAMADA INN.** *2820 N Glenstone (65803), I-44 exit 88.* 417/869-3900; FAX 417/865-5378; res: 800/707-0326. 130 rms, 3 story. May-Oct: S, D $55-$65; each addl $5; under 18 free; higher rates special events; lower rates rest of yr. Crib avail. Pet accepted. TV; cable (premium). Pool. Complimentary coffee in rms; continental bkfst. Restaurant 6:30 am-8 pm. Bar. Ck-out noon. Meeting rms. Business center. In-rm modem link. Valet serv. Free airport transportation. Some refrigerators. Cr cds: A, C, D, DS, MC, V.

D ⊱ ≋ ⊠ ⊼ SC ⊿

★ ★ **RESIDENCE INN BY MARRIOTT.** *1550 E Raynell Pl (65804).* 417/883-7300; FAX 417/883-5779. 80 kit. suites, 2 story. S, D $99-$139. Crib $5. Pet accepted, some restrictions; $100 deposit ($75 refundable). TV; cable (premium). Pool; whirlpool. Complimentary continental bkfst. Restaurant nearby. Ck-out noon. Coin lndry. Meeting rms. Business servs avail. Valet serv. Health club privileges. Picnic tables, grills. Gazebo. Cr cds: A, C, D, DS, MC, V. D ⊱ ≋ ⊠ ⊼ SC

Hotels

★ ★ ★ **HOLIDAY INN UNIVERSITY PLAZA & CONVENTION CENTER.** *333 John Q. Hammons Pkwy (65806).* 417/864-7333; FAX 417/831-5893. 271 rms. S, D $79.50-$98.50; each addl $10; suites $111.50; under 19 free. Crib free. Pet accepted, some restrictions. TV; cable (premium), VCR avail. 2 pools, 1 indoor; whirlpool, poolside serv. Restaurant 6 am-10 pm. Bar noon-1 am; entertainment. Ck-out noon. Coin lndry. Convention facilities. Business servs avail. In-rm modem link. Gift shop. Barber, beauty shop. Free airport, bus depot transportation. Lighted tennis. Exercise equipt; weights, bicycles, sauna. Game rm. Refrigerators. Some private patios. 9-story atrium tower with multi-tiered waterfall. Cr cds: A, C, D, DS, JCB, MC, V. D ⊱ ⚖ ≋ ⊼ ⊠ ⊼ SC

★ ★ ★ **SHERATON HAWTHORNE PARK.** *2431 N Glenstone (65803), I-44 exit 80A.* 417/831-3131; FAX 417/831-9786. 203 rms, 10 story. S $99; D $109; under 18 free. Crib free. Pet accepted, some restrictions; $25 deposit. TV; cable, (premium). Indoor/outdoor pool; whirlpool, sauna. Complimentary coffee in rms. Restaurant 6:30 am-1:30 pm, 5:30-10:30 pm. Bar 1 pm-1 am; Sun to midnight. Ck-out 11 am. Coin lndry. Meeting rms. Business servs avail. In-rm modem link. Concierge. Free airport, bus transportation. Game rm. Luxury level. Cr cds: A, C, D, DS, MC, V. D ⊱ ≋ ⊠ ⊼ SC

Sullivan

Motels

✔ ★ **BUDGET.** *(866 S I-44 Outer Rd, St Clair 63077) I-44 & MO 47.* 573/629-1000. 68 rms, 2 story. Mid-May-mid-Oct: S $48; D $53; each addl $15; under 12 free; higher rates hols; lower rates rest of yr. Crib $5. Pet accepted; $5. TV; cable, VCR avail (movies). Complimentary continental bkfst. Restaurant adj 10 am-11 pm. Ck-out 11 am. Meeting rms. Business servs avail. Valet serv. Coin lndry. Pool. Cr cds: A, C, D, DS, MC, V.

D ⊱ ≋ ⊠ ⊼ SC

✔ ★ **FAMILY MOTOR INN.** *209 N Service Rd.* 573/468-4119; FAX 573/468-3891. 63 rms, 14 kits. Late May-early Sept: S $36.95; D $43.95; each add $4; suites $45-$55; under 12 free; lower rates rest of yr. Crib $4. Pet accepted; $3. TV; VCR avail (movies $5). Pool; whirlpool. Complimentary coffee. Restaurant nearby. Ck-out 11 am. Meeting rm. Business servs avail. Coin lndry. Microwaves avail. Game rm. Antique shop adj. Cr cds: A, C, D, DS, MC, V. D ⊱ ≋ ⊠ ⊼ SC

★ **SUPER 8.** *601 N Service Rd.* 573/468-8076. 60 rms, 3 story. No elvtr. S $43.88; D $48.88-$58.88; each addl $3; suites $69.88; under 12 free. Crib. Pet accepted; $5. TV; cable. Complimentary coffee. Ck-out 11 am. Coin lndry. Whirlpool in suites. Cr cds: A, C, D, DS, MC, V. D ⊱ ⊠ ⊼ SC

Waynesville *(See also Lebanon, Rolla)*

Motels

✔ ★ **BEST WESTERN MONTIS INN.** *14086 Hwy Z, I-44 at jct MO 28 exit 163.* 573/336-4299; FAX 573/336-2872. 45 rms, 2 story, 4 kit. units. May-Oct: S, D $48-$58; each addl $5. Crib $5. Pet accepted, some restrictions. TV; cable, VCR avail (movies). Pool. Complimentary continental bkfst. Restaurant adj 6 am-9 pm. Ck-out noon. Coin lndry. Business servs avail. Some refrigerators, microwaves. Cr cds: A, C, D, DS, ER, JCB, MC, V. ⊱ ≋ ⊠ ⊼ SC

★ ★ **RAMADA INN.** *at I-44, Ft Leonard Wood exit 161. 573/336-3121; FAX 573/336-4752.* 82 rms, 2 story. S $53-$65; D $62-$74; each addl $9; suites $75-$115; under 18 free. Crib free. Pet accepted. TV; cable (premium), VCR avail. 2 pools, 1 indoor; whirlpool. Restaurant 6 am-2 pm, 5-10 pm. Bar 5 pm-1 am, Sun to midnight; entertainment. Ck-out noon. Meeting rms. Business center. In-rm modem link. Gift shop. Exercise rm; instructor, weights, bicycles, sauna. Game rm. Near Ft Leonard Wood. Cr cds: A, C, D, DS, JCB, MC, V. D 🐾 ≋ 🏃 🚶 🛏 🐾 SC 🏃

Wentzville *(See also St Charles, St Louis)*

Motor Hotel

★ ★ **HOLIDAY INN.** *900 Corporate Pkwy, I-70 exit 212. 314/327-7001; FAX 314/327-7019.* 138 rms, 4 story. S, D $66-$76; suites $115-$125; under 18 free. Crib free. Pet accepted, some restrictions. TV; cable (premium). Pool; poolside serv. Restaurant 6 am-10 pm. Rm serv. Bar 4-11 pm. Ck-out 1 pm. Meeting rms. Business servs avail. In-rm modem link. Bellhops. Valet serv. Sundries. Health club privileges. Some refrigerators. Cr cds: A, C, D, DS, ER, JCB, MC, V. D 🐾 ≋ 🛏 🐾 SC

West Plains

Motel

✔ ★ **DAYS INN.** *2105 Porter Wagoner Blvd, MO 63, at N end of town. 417/256-4135; FAX 417/256-1106.* 109 rms, 2 story. S $40-$50; D $46-$56; each addl $5; suite $95; under 12 free; wkly rates. Pet accepted, some restrictions. TV; cable (premium), VCR avail. Pool. Complimentary coffee in rms. Restaurant 6 am-8 pm. Rm serv. Bar 4 pm-1 am; closed Sun. Ck-out noon. Coin lndry. Meeting rms. Business servs avail. Cr cds: A, D, DS, MC, V. D 🐾 ≋ 🛏 🐾 SC

Motor Hotel

★ ★ **RAMADA INN.** *1301 Preacher Roe. 417/256-8191.* 80 rms, 2 story. S $38-$60; D $48-$60; each addl $7; suites $50-$60; under 18 free. Crib free. Pet accepted. TV; cable (premium), VCR avail. Pool. Restaurant 6 am-10 pm. Rm serv. Bar 4 pm-midnight. Ck-out noon. Meeting rms. Business servs avail. Coin lndry. Sundries. Cr cds: A, C, D, DS, MC, V. D 🐾 ≋ 🛏 🐾 SC

Montana

Bigfork *(See also Kalispell)*

Motel

★ **TIMBERS.** *8540 MT 35, at jct MT 35 & MT 209. 406/837-6200; FAX 406/837-6203; res: 800/821-4546.* 40 rms, 1-2 story. Mid-June-mid-Sept: S $58; D $58-$68; each addl $5; lower rates rest of yr. Crib $5. Pet accepted; $50 deposit & $5/day. TV; cable. Heated pool; whirlpool. Complimentary coffee in rms. Restaurant nearby. Ck-out 11 am. X-country ski 7 mi. Sauna. Cr cds: A, DS, MC, V. 🗇 🐾 🐎 🌊 🏂 🔥

Inn

★ ★ **O'DUACHAIN COUNTRY INN.** *675 Ferndale Dr, 3¹/₂ mi E off MT 209. 406/837-6851; res: 800/837-7460; FAX 406/837-0778.* E-mail knollmc@aol.com. 5 rms, all share bath, 3 story, 1 guest house. No A/C. No rm phones. June-Sept: S, D, guest house $95-$110; each addl $15; under 5 free; lower rates rest of yr. Crib free. Pet accepted, some restrictions. TV in common rm; cable (premium), VCR avail. Complimentary full bkfst. Ck-out 11 am, ck-in 2 pm. Luggage handling. Whirlpool. Authentic log home. Totally nonsmoking. Cr cds: A, DS, MC, V. 🐾 🌊 🔥

Big Timber *(See also Bozeman, Livingston)*

Motel

★ **SUPER 8.** *I-90 exit 367. 406/932-8888; FAX 406/932-4103.* 39 rms, 2 story. May-Sept: S $46.88; D $50.88-$55.88; each addl $4; lower rates rest of yr. Crib free. Pet accepted; $15 deposit. TV; cable. Complimentary continental bkfst. Restaurant adj 6 am-10 pm. Ck-out 11 am. Coin lndry. Cr cds: A, D, DS, JCB, MC, V. 🗇 🐾 🔥 SC

Billings *(See also Hardin)*

Motels

★ ★ **BEST WESTERN.** *5610 S Frontage Rd (59101), I-90 exit 446. 406/248-9800; FAX 406/248-2500.* 80 rms, 3 story, 12 suites. June-Aug: S $54-$58; D $66-$76; each addl $5; suites $78-$110; under 18 free; lower rates rest of yr. Crib free. Pet accepted, some restrictions. TV; cable (premium). Indoor pool; whirlpool. Complimentary continental bkfst. Restaurant adj open 24 hrs. Ck-out noon. Coin lndry. Meeting rms. Business servs avail. Valet serv. Sauna. Cr cds: A, C, D, DS, ER, MC, V. 🗇 🐾 🌊 🔥 SC

★ ★ **BEST WESTERN PONDEROSA INN.** *2511 First Ave N (59103), I-90 exit 27th St S, near Logan Field Airport. 406/259-5511; FAX 406/245-8004.* 130 rms, 2 story. S $50-$60; D $60-$70; each addl $5. Crib free. Pet accepted, some restrictions. TV; cable (premium). Pool. Complimentary coffee in rms. Restaurant open 24 hrs. Bar 3 pm-2 am; closed Sun. Ck-out 11 am. Coin lndry. Meeting rm. Business servs avail. Valet serv. Free airport transportation. Exercise equipt; rowing machine, bicycles, sauna. Cr cds: A, C, D, DS, ER, JCB, MC, V. 🐾 🌊 🏋 ✈ 🔥 SC

✔ ★ ★ **BILLINGS INN.** *880 N 29th St (59101), I-90 exit 27th St, then 2 mi N, near Logan Field Airport. 406/252-6800; FAX 406/252-6800; res: 800/231-7782.* E-mail tbi@wtp.net. 60 rms, 4 story. S $42.50; D $46.50-$52; each addl $5; under 12 free. Crib $5. Pet accepted, some restrictions; $5. TV; cable. Complimentary continental bkfst. Ck-out 11 am. Coin lndry. Valet serv. Sundries. Airport transportation. Some refrigerators, microwaves. Cr cds: A, C, D, DS, MC, V. 🗇 🐾 🏋 🔥 SC

★ ★ **COMFORT INN.** *2030 Overland Ave (59102). 406/652-5200.* 60 rms, 2 story. June-mid-Sept: S $64.95; D $76.95; each addl $5; suites $84-$90; under 18 free; lower rates rest of yr. Crib free. Pet accepted, some restrictions. TV; cable (premium). Indoor pool; whirlpool. Complimentary continental bkfst. Ck-out 11 am. Business servs avail. Game rm. Some refrigerators. Cr cds: A, C, D, DS, ER, JCB, MC, V. 🗇 🐾 🌊 🔥 SC

✔ ★ **DAYS INN.** *843 Parkway Lane (59101). 406/252-4007; FAX 406/252-4007, ext. 301.* 63 rms. S $65; D $55-$80; each addl $5; under 12 free. Crib free. Pet accepted, some restrictions. TV; cable, VCR avail (movies). Complimentary continental bkfst. Restaurant nearby. Ck-out noon. Coin lndry. Whirlpool. Cr cds: A, D, DS, JCB, MC, V. 🐾 🌊 🔥 SC

✔ ★ ★ **HILLTOP INN.** *1116 N 28th St (59101). 406/245-5000; FAX 406/245-7851; res: 800/878-9282.* E-mail hilltop@wtp.net. 45 rms, 3 story. S $42.50; D $46.50; each addl $5; under 12 free. Crib $5. Pet accepted. TV; cable. Complimentary continental bkfst. Restaurant nearby. Ck-out 11 am. Sundries. Valet serv. Coin lndry. Some refrigerators, microwaves. Cr cds: A, D, DS, MC, V. 🄳 ❄ ⛷ 🐾 SC

★ ★ **QUALITY INN HOMESTEAD.** *2036 Overland Ave (59102). 406/652-1320; FAX 406/652-1320.* 119 rms, 2 story. S, D $56-$75; each addl $5; suites $62-$80; under 18 free. Crib free. Pet accepted; $25 deposit. TV; cable (premium), VCR avail (movies). Indoor pool; whirlpool. Complimentary full bkfst; afternoon refreshments. Restaurant nearby. Ck-out noon. Coin lndry. Bellhops. Valet serv. Free airport transportation. Golf privileges. Sauna. Health club privileges. Some refrigerators. Cr cds: A, C, D, DS, ER, JCB, MC, V. 🄳 ❄ 🏋 ⛷ 🐾 SC

★ **RAMADA LIMITED.** *1345 Mullowney Lane (59101), at jct I-90 & King Ave exit. 406/252-2584; FAX 406/252-2584, ext. 308.* 116 rms, 2 story. S $58-$68; D $63-$68; each addl $5; under 18 free. Crib free. Pet accepted, some restrictions. TV; cable (premium). Pool. Playground. Complimentary continental bkfst. Restaurant nearby. Ck-out noon. Business servs avail. Exercise equipt; weight machine, treadmill. Cr cds: A, D, DS, MC, V. 🄳 ❄ ⛷ 🐾 SC

✔ ★ **SUPER 8 LODGE.** *5400 Southgate Dr (59102), at I-90 exit 446. 406/248-8842; FAX 406/248-8842.* 115 rms, 2 story. S $50.88; D $55.88-$59.88; each addl $5; suites $72.11; under 12 free. Crib free. Pet accepted, some restrictions; $20. TV; cable (premium), VCR avail (movies). Restaurant nearby. Ck-out 11 am. Cr cds: A, C, D, DS, MC, V. 🄳 ❄ 🐾 SC

Hotels

★ ★ ★ **RADISSON NORTHERN.** *Broadway & First Ave N (59101), downtown. 406/245-5121; FAX 406/259-9862.* Web www.radisson.com. 160 rms, 10 story. S, D $112; each addl $10; under 18 free. Crib free. Pet accepted, some restrictions. TV; cable (premium). Restaurant 6:30 am-10 pm. Bar 11-1 am. Ck-out noon, ck-in 3 pm. Meeting rms. Business servs avail. Gift shop. Free covered parking. Airport transportation. Exercise equipt; weight machine, bicycles. Some refrigerators. Cr cds: A, C, D, DS, ER, JCB, MC, V. 🄳 ❄ 🏋 🐾 SC

★ ★ ★ **SHERATON.** *27 N 27th St (59101), near Logan Field Airport. 406/252-7400; FAX 406/252-2401.* 282 rms, 23 story. S $90; D $100; each addl $10; suites $140-$190; under 18 free; wkend rates. Crib free. Pet accepted, some restrictions. TV; cable (premium). Indoor pool; wading pool, whirlpool. Coffee in rms. Restaurant 6:30 am-10 pm. Bar 11-2 am. Ck-out noon. Convention facilities. Business servs avail. Gift shop. Airport transportation. Exercise rm; instructor, weight machines, bicycles, sauna. Game rm. Some refrigerators. Cr cds: A, C, D, DS, ER, MC, V. 🄳 ❄ ⛷ ✈ 🐾 SC

Bozeman *(See also Livingston, Three Forks)*

Motels

✔ ★ **DAYS INN.** *1321 N 7th Ave (59715). 406/587-5251.* 79 rms, 2 story. S $56; D $72-$76; each addl $5; under 12 free. Crib free. Pet accepted; $25 deposit. TV; cable (premium), VCR avail (movies). Complimentary continental bkfst. Restaurant adj 6 am-10 pm. Ck-out noon. Business servs avail. Downhill/x-country ski 17 mi. Whirlpool, sauna. Cr cds: A, C, D, DS, MC, V. 🄳 ❄ ⛷ 🐾 SC

★ ★ ★ **HOLIDAY INN.** *5 Baxter Lane (59715), 1½ mi NW on N 7th St, S of I-90, N 7th Ave exit. 406/587-4561; FAX 406/587-4413.* 178 rms, 2 story. S, D $74-$95; under 18 free. Crib free. Pet accepted. TV; cable. Indoor pool; whirlpool. Restaurant 6 am-2 pm, 5-10 pm. Rm serv. Bar 2 pm-midnight. Ck-out noon. Coin lndry. Meeting rms. Business servs avail. Bellhops. Valet serv. Free airport, bus depot transportation. Downhill/x-country ski 16 mi. Lawn games. Exercise equipt; weights, bicycles. Rec rm. Some refrigerators. Picnic tables. Cr cds: A, C, D, DS, MC, V. 🄳 ❄ ⛷ ✈ 🐾 SC

★ **HOMESTEAD INN.** *(6261 Jackrabbit Ln, Belgrade 59714) 406/388-0800; FAX 406/388-0804; res: 800/542-6791.* 67 rms, 3 story. June-Aug: S, D $54.95-$64.95; under 12 free; lower rates rest of yr. Crib free. Pet accepted. TV; cable (premium). Complimentary coffee in lobby. Restaurant adj open 24 hrs. Ck-out 11 am. Totally nonsmoking. Cr cds: A, D, DS, MC, V. 🄳 ❄ 🐾 SC

✔ ★ **RAMADA LIMITED.** *2020 Wheat Dr (59715). 406/585-2626; FAX 585/-2727.* 50 rms, shower only, 2 story. June-Aug: S $49-$79; D $49-$109; suites $69-$119; lower rates rest of yr. Crib free. Pet accepted. TV; cable. Indoor pool. Complimentary continental bkfst. Restaurant nearby. Ck-out noon. Valet serv. Downhill/x-country ski 16 mi. Cr cds: A, C, D, DS, MC, V. 🖍 🖍 🖍 🖍 🖍 SC

✔★ **ROYAL 7.** *310 N 7th Ave (59715), on business loop from I-90, exit 306W. 406/587-3103; res: 800/587-3103.* 47 units. S $39.75-$42.75; D $48.75-$58.75; kit. unit $63.75. Crib $4. Pet accepted. TV; cable (premium). Playground. Restaurant adj 7 am-10 pm. Ck-out noon. Business servs avail. Downhill/x-country ski 16 mi. Whirlpool. Picnic tables. Cr cds: A, D, DS, MC, V. 🖍 🖍 🖍 🖍

★★ **WESTERN HERITAGE.** *1200 E Main (59715). 406/586-8534; FAX 406/587-8729; res: 800/877-1094.* 38 rms, 3 story. June-Sept: S $53-$73; D $58-$83; each addl $7; suites $95-$150; studio rms $95; under 13 free; ski plan; higher rates Sweet Pea Festival; lower rates rest of yr. Crib $7.50. Pet accepted. TV; cable (premium). Complimentary continental bkfst. Restaurant adj 6 am-10:30 pm. Ck-out 11 am. Coin lndry. Meeting rms. Business servs avail. Valet serv. Sundries. Downhill/x-country ski 16 mi. Exercise equipt; treadmill, bicycles, whirlpool, steam rm. Some in-rm whirlpools. Cr cds: A, C, D, DS, MC, V. 🖍 🖍 🖍 🖍 🖍 🖍 SC

Butte *(See also Three Forks)*

Motels

★★ **BEST WESTERN COPPER KING PARK HOTEL.** *4655 Harrison Ave S, S of I-90, Harrison Ave exit, near Bert Mooney Airport. 406/494-6666; FAX 406/494-3274.* 150 rms, 2 story. S, D $76-$92; each addl $8; under 18 free. Crib free. Pet accepted. TV; cable. Indoor pool. Coffee in rms. Restaurants 6 am-9 pm. Rm serv. Bar 11-2 am; entertainment Fri, Sat. Ck-out 11 am. Coin lndry. Meeting rms. Business servs avail. Bellhops. Free airport transportation. Indoor tennis. Exercise equipt; weight machine, bicycles, sauna. Private patios. Cr cds: A, C, D, DS, MC, V. 🖍 🖍 🖍 🖍 🖍 🖍 🖍 🖍 SC

★ **COMFORT INN.** *2777 Harrison Ave, near Bert Mooney Airport. 406/494-8850; FAX 406/494-2801.* 150 rms, 3 story. No elvtr. Mid-May-Sept: S $58.99; D $63.99; each addl $10; suites $80-$125; under 18 free; lower rates rest of yr. Pet accepted; $5. TV; cable (premium), VCR avail (movies). Complimentary continental bkfst. Restaurant nearby. Ck-out 11 am. Coin lndry. Meeting rms. Business servs avail. Airport transportation. Exercise equipt; weight machines, bicycles, whirlpool, sauna. Cr cds: A, C, D, DS, MC, V. 🖍 🖍 🖍 🖍 🖍 🖍 SC

Columbia Falls *(See also Kalispell, Whitefish)*

Resort

★★★ **MEADOW LAKE.** *100 St Andrews Dr. 406/892-7601; FAX 406/892-0330; res: 800/321-4653.* E-mail mdwlake@meadowlake.com; web www.meadowlake.com. 114 units, 24 inn rms, 1-3 story, 60 condos, 30 townhouses. June-Sept: D $134; each addl $15; condos $184-$273; townhouses $304-$443; lower rates rest of yr. Crib $5. Pet accepted, some restrictions. TV; cable (premium), VCR (movies). 2 pools, 1 indoor; wading pool, whirlpools. Playground. Supervised child's activities. Restaurant 7 am-10 pm. Ck-out 10 am, ck-in 4 pm. Meeting rms. Business servs avail. Free airport, RR station transportation. Tennis. 18-hole golf, greens fee $38, pro, putting green, driving range. Downhill ski 18 mi; x-country ski on site. Ice skating. Rec rm. Exercise equipt; weight machine, treadmill. Some woodburning fireplaces. Balconies. Cr cds: A, D, DS, MC, V. 🖍 🖍 🖍 🖍 🖍 🖍 🖍 🖍 🖍 🖍 SC

Cooke City *(See also Red Lodge; also see Cody, WY)*

Motel

✔★ **HIGH COUNTRY.** *US 212. 406/838-2272.* 15 rms, 1-2 story, 4 kits. No A/C. S $40; D $40-$58; each addl $5; kit. units $52-$65. Crib $2. Pet accepted. TV. Restaurant nearby. Ck-out 10 am. X-country ski 1 mi. Some refrigerators. Cabins avail. Cr cds: A, D, DS, MC, V. 🖍 🖍 🖍 🖍 SC

Deer Lodge *(See also Helena)*

Motel

✔★ **SUPER 8.** *1150 N Main St. 406/846-2370; FAX 406/846-2373.* 54 rms, 2 story. June-Aug: S $46.68; D $51.88-$55.88; each addl $5; suites $63.88; under 5 free; lower rates rest of yr. Crib free. Pet accepted. TV; cable, VCR avail (movies $3). Complimentary coffee in lobby. Restaurant adj open 24 hrs. Ck-out 11 am. Meeting rms. Cr cds: A, C, D, DS, MC, V. 🖍 🖍 SC

Dillon

Motels

★ **COMFORT INN-DILLON.** *Box 666, 450 N Interchange, $^1/_2$ blk from I-15 exit 63. 406/683-6831; FAX 406/683-2021.* 48 rms, 2 story. July-mid-Sept: S $47.99-$58.99; D $51.99-$62.99; each addl $4; under 12 free; lower rates rest of yr. Crib $3. Pet accepted. TV; cable (premium), VCR avail (movies $6). Indoor pool. Restaurant nearby. Bar. Ck-out 11 am. Coin lndry. Sundries. Cr cds: A, D, DS, MC, V. 🐾 ≈ 🖥 🐾 SC

★ **SUPER 8.** *550 N Montana St. 406/683-4288.* 46 rms, 3 story. No elvtr. May-Aug: S $45.88; D $53.88-$57.88; each addl $5; under 12 free; lower rates rest of yr. Crib free. Pet accepted. TV; cable. Restaurant opp open 24 hrs. Ck-out 11 am. Cr cds: A, C, D, DS, MC, V. D 🐾 🖥 🐾 SC

Ennis *(See also Three Forks)*

Motels

★ ★ **EL WESTERN.** *Box 487, $^1/_2$ mi S on US 287. 406/682-4217; FAX 406/682-5207; res: 800/831-2773.* 28 units, 18 kits. No A/C. May-mid-Oct: S, D $65-$90; each addl $5-$10; kit. units $85-$300. Closed rest of yr. Crib $5. Pet accepted. TV; cable (premium). Restaurant nearby. Ck-out 11 am. Patios. Some fireplaces. Western decor. Cr cds: DS, MC, V. 🐾 🐾

✔ ★ **FAN MOUNTAIN INN.** *204 N Main. 406/682-5200.* 28 rms, 2 story. S $37.50; D $48-$54; each addl $5; suite $75. Pet accepted; $5. TV; cable (premium), VCR avail (movies). Complimentary coffee in lobby. Restaurant nearby. Ck-out 11 am. Meeting rm. Cr cds: A, C, D, DS, MC, V. D 🐾 🖥 🐾

Gardiner

Motels

★ **ABSAROKA.** *US 89 at Yellowstone River Bridge. 406/848-7414; FAX 406/848-7560; res: 800/755-7414.* 41 rms, 2 story, 8 kit. units. June-mid-Sept: S, D $80-$90; each addl $5; kit. units $90-$100; under 12 free; lower rates rest of yr. Pet accepted; $5. TV; cable. Complimentary coffee in lobby. Restaurant nearby. Ck-out 11 am. Balconies overlooking Yellowstone River. Cr cds: A, C, D, DS, MC, V. D 🐾 🖥 🐾

★ ★ **BEST WESTERN BY MAMMOTH HOT SPRINGS.** *US 89, $^1/_2$ mi N on US 89, at N entrance to Yellowstone Park. 406/848-7311; FAX 406/848-7120.* 85 rms, 2 story, 4 kits. June-Sept: S, D $89-$104; each addl $5; kit. units $145-$165; under 13 free; lower rates rest of yr. Crib $5. Pet accepted. TV; cable, VCR avail (movies). Indoor pool; whirlpool. Restaurant adj. Meeting rm. Business servs avail. Sauna. Some in-rm whirlpools, microwaves, refrigerators. Some balconies. On the Yellowstone River. Cr cds: A, D, DS, MC, V. 🐾 🐾 ≈ 🖥 🐾 SC

★ **SUPER 8.** *Hwy 89 S, $^1/_4$ mi N on US 89. 406/848-7401; FAX 406/848-9401.* Web super8gomontana.com. 65 rms, 2 story. Mid-June-mid-Sept: S, D $85; suites $120-$150; each addl $5; lower rates rest of yr. Crib $5. Pet accepted, some restrictions; $5. TV; cable (premium). Indoor pool. Complimentary continental bkfst. Restaurant nearby. Ck-out 10 am. Opp river. Cr cds: A, C, D, DS, MC, V. 🐾 🐾 ≈ 🖥 SC

Glacier National Park

Motel

★ **JACOBSON'S COTTAGES.** *(MT 49, East Glacier 33950) $^1/_2$ mi N. 406/226-4422.* 12 cottages, 1 kit. No A/C. No rm phones. Mid-May-Oct: S $50; D $50-$56; each addl $3; kit. cottage $65; under 6 free. Closed rest of yr. Crib free. Pet accepted, some restrictions. TV; cable. Restaurant adj 6:30 am-10:30 pm. Ck-out 11 am. Picnic table. Cr cds: A, DS, MC, V. 🐾 🐾

Lodge

★ ★ **ST MARY LODGE & RESORT.** *(US 89, St Mary 59417) at Going To The Sun Rd. 406/732-4431; res: 800/368-3689; FAX 406/732-9265.* 76 rms, 62 with shower only, 34 with AC, 1-2 story. Mid-June-mid-Sept: S, D $89-$100; each addl $10; suites $160-$250; kits. $130-$150; under 12 free; lower rates May-mid-June & mid-Sept-early Oct. Closed rest of yr. Crib $3. Pet accepted; $50. Restaurant 7 am-10 pm. Bar noon-1 am; entertainment exc Sun. Ck-out 11 am, ck-in 4 pm. Coin lndry. Gift shop. Some balconies. Views of St Mary Lake & Glacier Park. Totally nonsmoking. Cr cds: A, DS, MC, V. 🄳 ⬤ ⬤ ⬤ ⬤

Glasgow

Motel

✔★ **COTTONWOOD INN.** *Hwy 2E, 1 mi E on US 2, near City-County Airport.* 406/228-8213; FAX 406/228-8248; res: 800/321-8213. 92 rms, 2 story. S $48; D $55-$60; each addl $5; studio rms $75-$80; under 12 free. Pet accepted, some restrictions. TV; cable (premium). Indoor pool; whirlpool. Restaurant 6 am-10 pm. Rm serv. Bar 11-2 am. Ck-out 11 am. Coin lndry. Business servs avail. Valet serv. Airport, RR station transportation. Exercise equipt; weight machine, bicycles, sauna. Some refrigerators. Cr cds: A, C, D, DS, MC, V. 🄳 ⬤ ⬤ ⬤ ⬤ ⬤ ⬤ SC

Glendive

Motel

✔★ **DAYS INN.** *2000 N Merrill.* 406/365-6011; FAX 406/365-2876. 59 rms, 2 story. S $37; D $44-$47; each addl $5; under 12 free; lower rates winter. Crib free. TV; cable (premium). Complimentary continental bkfst. Restaurant adj 6 am-10 pm. Ck-out 11 am. Cr cds: A, C, D, DS, MC, V. ⬤ ⬤ ⬤ SC

Great Falls

Motels

✔★ **BUDGET INN.** *2 Treasure State Dr (59404), W of I-15 10th Ave exit S, near Intl Airport.* 406/453-1602; res: 800/362-4842. 60 rms, 2 story. S $46; D $52; each addl $4; under 16 free; lower rates winter. Crib free. Pet accepted, some restrictions. TV; cable. Complimentary continental bkfst. Coffee in rms. Restaurant adj 6 am-11 pm. Ck-out noon. Airport transportation. Valet serv. Health club privileges. Cr cds: A, D, DS, MC, V. 🄳 ⬤ ⬤ ⬤ ⬤ SC

★★ **COMFORT INN.** *1120 Ninth St S (59403).* 406/454-2727. 64 rms, 3 story. S, D $69.95; each addl $5; suites $79.95; under 18 free. Crib free. Pet accepted; $5. TV; cable (premium). Indoor pool; whirlpool. Complimentary continental bkfst. Restaurant nearby. Ck-out 11 am. Business servs avail. Health club privileges. Cr cds: A, D, DS, MC, V. 🄳 ⬤ ⬤ ⬤ ⬤ SC

★ **TOWNHOUSE INN.** *1411 10th Ave S (59405).* 406/761-4600; FAX 406/761-7603; res: 800/442-4667. 109 rms, 2 story, May-Sept: S $65; D $70; each addl $5; under 13 free; lower rates rest of yr. Crib free. Pet accepted; $5. TV; cable (premium). Indoor pool; whirlpool. Restaurant 7 am-10 pm. Rm serv. Bar. Ck-out 11 am. Coin lndry. Meeting rms. Business servs avail. Bellhops. Sundries. Valet serv. Free airport transportation. Sauna. Game rm. Cr cds: A, D, DS, MC, V. ⬤ ⬤ ⬤ ⬤ SC

Motor Hotel

★★ **BEST WESTERN HERITAGE INN.** *1700 Fox Farm Rd (59404), I-15 exit 10th Ave S.* 406/761-1900; FAX 406/761-0136; res: 800/548-0361. 239 rms, 2 story. S $79; D $87; each addl $6; suites $85-$125; under 18 free. Crib free. Pet accepted, some restrictions. TV; cable. Indoor pool; whirlpool. Coffee in rms. Restaurant 6 am-10 pm. Rm serv. Bar 9-2 am. Ck-out noon. Business servs avail. Coin lndry. Bellhops. Valet serv. Gift shop. Free airport, bus depot transportation. Exercise equipt; treadmill, stair machine, sauna. Microwaves avail. Cr cds: A, D, DS, MC, V. 🄳 ⬤ ⬤ ⬤ ⬤ ⬤ SC

Hotel

★★★ **HOLIDAY INN.** *400 10th Ave S (59405).* 406/727-7200. 169 rms, 7 story. S, D $75; suites $145. Crib free. Pet accepted, some restrictions. TV; cable (premium). Indoor pool; whirlpool. Coffee in rms. Restaurant 6 am-11 pm. Bar noon-2 am. Ck-out noon. Meeting rms. Business servs avail. Free airport, bus depot transportation. Sauna. Health club privileges. Cr cds: A, C, D, DS, ER, JCB, MC, V. 🄳 ⬤ ⬤ ⬤ ⬤ SC

Hamilton *(See also Missoula)*

Motel

★ **COMFORT INN.** *1113 N 1st St, 1 mi N on US 93.* 406/363-6600; FAX 406/363-5644. 64 rms, 2 story. May-Sept: S $55; D $62-$64; each addl $5; under 18 free; lower rates rest of yr. Crib $4. Pet accepted. TV; cable (premium), VCR avail (movies).

Complimentary coffee in lobby. Restaurant adj 8 am-10 pm. Rm serv. Ck-out 11 am. Meeting rm. Business servs avail. Coin lndry. Whirlpool, sauna. Cr cds: A, D, DS, MC, V. ⌷D⌷ 🐾 📶 🐾 🆂🅲

Hardin *(See also Billings)*

Motel

★ **SUPER 8.** *201 14th St.* 406/665-1700. 53 rms, 2 story. May-Sept: S $44.88; D $46.88-$50.88; each addl $4; under 12 free; higher rates special events; lower rates rest of yr. Crib $2. Pet accepted. TV; cable. Complimentary continental bkfst. Ck-out 11 am. Coin lndry. Meeting rms. Cr cds: A, C, D, DS, MC, V. ⌷D⌷ 🐾 📶 🐾 🆂🅲

Havre

Motel

★ **TOWNHOUSE INN.** *629 W First St.* 406/265-6711; FAX 406/265-6213; res: 800/422-4667. 104 rms, 1-2 story. S $58; D $62-$66; each addl $4; suites $88-$170. Crib free. Pet accepted, some restrictions; $4. TV; cable (premium). Indoor pool; whirlpool. Restaurant opp open 24 hrs. Bar 8-12:30 am. Ck-out noon. Coin lndry. Meeting rm. Free airport, RR station, bus depot transportation. Cr cds: A, C, D, DS, MC, V. 🐾 📶 📶 🐾 🆂🅲

Helena *(See also Deer Lodge)*

Motels

✔ ★ ★ **COMFORT INN.** *750 Fee St.* 406/443-1000. 56 rms, 2 story, 14 suites. June-Aug: S $59.95; D $79.95; each addl $5; suites $69-$79; under 18 free; lower rates rest of yr. Crib free. Pet accepted. TV; cable (premium). Indoor pool; whirlpool. Complimentary continental bkfst. Restaurant opp open 24 hrs. Ck-out 11 am. Ck-in 2 pm. Business servs avail. Cr cds: A, C, D, DS, ER, JCB, MC, V. ⌷D⌷ 🐾 📶 📶 🐾 🆂🅲

★ ★ **SHILO INN.** *2020 Prospect Ave, W of I-15 on US 12, Capitol exit.* 406/442-0320; FAX 406/449-4426. 47 rms, 3 story, 3 kits. No elvtr. S,D $75; each addl $9; kit. units $85. Crib free. Pet accepted. TV; cable (premium); VCR (movies $5). Indoor pool; whirlpool, sauna, steam rm. Complimentary continental bkfst. Restaurant adj open 24 hrs. Ck-out noon. Coin lndry. Meeting rm. Valet serv. Free airport, bus depot transportation. Bathrm phones, refrigerators. Cr cds: A, C, D, DS, ER, JCB, MC, V. 🐾 📶 📶 🐾 🆂🅲

Hotel

✔ ★ ★ **PARK PLAZA.** *22 N Last Chance Gulch.* 406/443-2200; FAX 406/442-4030; res: 800/332-2290 (MT). 71 rms, 7 story. S $60; D $66; each addl $6; under 12 free. Crib $5. Pet accepted. TV; cable. Restaurant 6:30 am-9 pm. Bar 11-2 am. Ck-out 3 pm. Meeting rms. Business servs avail. Airport transportation. Cr cds: A, C, D, DS, ER, MC, V. 🐾 📶 🐾

Inn

★ ★ **BARRISTER.** *416 N Ewing St.* 406/443-7330; FAX 406/442-7964. 5 rms, 2 story. No rm phones. S $80; D $80-$100; each addl $15; under 10 free. Pet accepted. TV; cable, VCR avail. Complimentary full bkfst. Restaurant nearby. Ck-out 10:30 am, ck-in 4-7 pm. Luggage handling. Business servs avail. Free airport transportation. Built in 1880; furnished with antiques. Totally nonsmoking. Cr cds: A, MC, V. 🐾 📶

Kalispell *(See also Bigfork, Columbia Falls, Whitefish)*

Motel

★ ★ **HAMPTON INN.** *1140 US 2 W.* 406/755-7900; FAX 406/755-5056. 120 rms, 3 story. June-Sept: S $78; D $88; suites $155-$205; under 19 free; lower rates rest of yr. Crib free. Pet accepted. TV; cable (premium), VCR. Complimentary continental bkfst. Complimentary coffee in rms. Restaurant adj 7 am-10 pm. Ck-out noon. Meeting rms. Business center. Bellhops. Valet serv. Sundries. Gift shop. Coin lndry. Free airport transportation. Downhill/x-country ski 16 mi. Exercise equipt; bicycles, treadmill. Indoor pool; whirlpool. Rec rm. Refrigerators; in-rm whirlpool, microwave, wet bar, fireplace in suites. Cr cds: A, D, DS, MC, V. ⌷D⌷ 🐾 📶 📶 🏃 📶 🐾 🆂🅲 🏂

Motor Hotels

★ ★ **BEST WESTERN OUTLAW INN.** *1701 US 93S.* 406/755-6100; FAX 406/756-8994. 220 rms, 3 story. S $82-$135; D $92-$175; each addl $10; under 12 free; package plans. Crib $7. Pet accepted; $10. TV; cable (premium). 2 indoor pools; wading pool, whirlpool. Playground. Coffee in rms. Restaurant 6 am-10 pm. Rm serv. Bar 11-2 am. Ck-out 11 am. Coin Indry. Meeting rms. Business servs avail. Bellhops. Valet serv. Sundries. Gift shop. Barber, beauty shop. Tennis. Exercise equipt; weight machine, bicycle, sauna. Game rm. Microwaves avail. Some balconies. Casino. Western art gallery. Cr cds: A, C, D, DS, ER, JCB, MC, V. 🄳 👤 💱 🏊 🏋 🛇 🐾 SC

★ ★ ★ CAVANAUGH'S. *20 N Main St. 406/752-6660; FAX 406/752-6628; res: 800/843-4667.* Web www.cavanaughs.com. 132 rms, 3 story, 14 suites. Mid-May-Sept: S $98; D $105; each addl $12; suites $120-$190; kit. units $150, under 18 free; ski, golf plans; lower rates rest of yr. Crib free. Pet accepted, some restrictions. TV; cable. Indoor pool; whirlpools. Coffee in rms. Restaurant 6:30 am-10 pm. Rm serv. Bar 4 pm-2 am; entertainment Fri, Sat. Ck-out noon. Meeting rms. Business servs avail. Bellhops. Shopping arcade. Barber, beauty shop. Downhill ski 20 mi; x-country ski 15 mi. Exercise equipt; rower, stair machine, sauna. Casino. Adj to 50-store indoor shopping mall. Cr cds: A, C, D, DS, ER, MC, V. 🄳 👤 💱 🏊 🏋 🛇 🐾

Hotel

★ KALISPELL GRAND. *100 Main St. 406/755-8100; FAX 406/752-8012.* E-mail grand@vtown.com; web www.vtown.com/grand. 40 rms, 38 with shower only, 3 story. No elvtr. June-Aug: S $65; D $75; each addl $7; suites $79-$115; under 12 free; lower rates rest of yr. Crib free. Pet accepted, some restrictions. TV; cable. Complimentary continental bkfst. Bar 8-2 am; entertainment Thurs-Sat. Ck-out 11 am. Business servs avail. Exercise equipt; weight machine, treadmill. Casino. Cr cds: A, D, DS, MC, V. 👤 🏋 🛇 🐾 SC

Livingston *(See also Big Timber, Bozeman)*

Motels

★ BEST WESTERN YELLOWSTONE INN. *1515 W Park St. 406/222-6110; FAX 406/222-3976.* 99 rms, 3 story. Mid-May-mid-Sept: S, D $69-$89; each addl $5; kit. unit $139; under 13 free; wkly rates; lower rates rest of yr. Crib free. Pet accepted; $5. TV; cable. Complimentary coffee in lobby. Restaurant 6 am-10 pm. Bar noon-2 am. Ck-out noon. Meeting rms. Business servs avail. Bellhops. Sundries. Barber, beauty shop. Indoor pool. Game rm. Cr cds: A, C, D, DS, MC, V. 👤 🏊 🛇 🐾 SC

★ PARADISE INN. *I-90 & MT 89, exit 333. 406/222-6320; FAX 406/222-2481; res: 800/437-6291.* 43 rms. Mid-May-Sept: S, D $79-$89; each addl $5; suites $99-$129; lower rates rest of yr. Crib $5. Pet accepted. TV; cable (premium). Indoor pool. Restaurant 6 am-10:30 pm. Bar 12:30 pm-2 am. Ck-out 11 am. Cr cds: A, MC, V. 🄳 👤 🏊 🛇 🐾

Lodge

★ ★ CHICO HOT SPRINGS. *(Pray 59065) approx 25 mi S on US 89 to Emigrant, then E on MT 540. 406/333-4933; FAX 406/333-4694; res: 800/468-9232.* 49 lodge rms, 3 story, 29 motel units, 16 cottages. No A/C. Some rm phones. June-Sept: (lodge) S, D $85; (motel) S, D $105; cabins $75-$85; chalets (1-5 bedrm) $129-$300; under 7 free; lower rates rest of yr. Crib free. Pet accepted; $5. Heated pool. Supervised child's activities (summer only). Dining rm 7-11 am, 5:30-10 pm. Box lunches. Bar 11-2 am; entertainment Fri, Sat. Ck-out 11 am, ck-in 3 pm. Grocery. Coin Indry 5 mi. Meeting rms. Business servs avail. Gift shop. Exercise equipt; bicycles, treadmill. X-country ski 3 mi. Hiking. Bicycle rentals. Lawn games. Fishing/hunting guides. Massage. Some refrigerators. Picnic tables. Rustic surroundings; secluded in Paradise Valley. Cr cds: A, DS, MC, V. 👤 💱 🏊 🏋 🛇 🐾

Miles City

Motel

★ BEST WESTERN WAR BONNET INN. *1015 S Haynes, just off I-90 exit 138. 406/232-4560; FAX 406/232-0363.* 54 rms, 2 story. May-Sept: S $66; D $71; each addl $6; suites $100; under 12 free; higher rates Bucking Horse Sale; lower rates rest of yr. Crib $6. Pet accepted. TV; cable. Indoor pool; whirlpool, sauna. Complimentary continental bkfst. Ck-out noon. Meeting rms. Cr cds: A, C, D, DS, JCB, MC, V. 👤 🏊 🛇 🐾 SC

Missoula *(See also Hamilton)*

Motels

★ 4 B'S INN-NORTH. *4953 N Reserve St (59802), I-90 exit 101. 406/542-7550; FAX 406/721-5931; res: 800/272-9500 (exc MT).* 67 rms, 3 story. Mid-May-mid-Sept: S $50.95; D $61.50; suites $71.50; under 12 free. Crib $5. Pet accepted. TV; cable. Complimentary coffee in lobby. Restaurant adj open 24 hrs. Ck-out 11 am. Coin lndry. Whirlpool. Refrigerator in suites. Cr cds: A, C, D, DS, MC, V. [D] 🐾 ⚊ 🔥 [SC]

★ ★ **HAMPTON INN.** *4805 N Reserve St (59802). 406/549-1800; FAX 406/549-1737.* 60 rms, 4 story. S $66-$69; D $76-$79; under 18 free. Crib free. Pet accepted. TV; cable (premium). Indoor pool; whirlpool. Complimentary continental bkfst. Restaurant nearby. Ck-out noon. Meeting rms. Business servs avail. Bellhops. Valet serv. Free airport transportation. Exercise equipt; bicycles, treadmill. Cr cds: A, C, D, DS, MC, V.
[D] 🐾 ⚊ 🏋 🔥 🐾 [SC]

★ **ORANGE STREET BUDGET MOTOR INN.** *801 N Orange St (59802). 406/721-3610; FAX 406/721-8875; res: 800/328-0501.* 81 rms, 3 story. May-Sept: S $51; D $53-$58; each addl $5; lower rates rest of yr. Crib $3. Pet accepted. TV; cable (premium), VCR avail (movies). Complimentary continental bkfst. Restaurant nearby. Ck-out 11 am. Meeting rms. Business servs avail. Free airport transportation. Exercise equipt; bicycles, rower. Cr cds: A, C, D, DS, MC, V. 🐾 🏋 ⚊ 🐾 [SC]

★ **RED LION.** *700 W Broadway (59802), 1/2 mi S of I-90 Orange St exit. 406/728-3300; FAX 406/728-4441.* 76 rms, 2 story. S $69; D $79-$84; each addl $10; under 18 free. Crib free. Pet accepted; $5. TV; cable (premium). Heated pool. Complimentary coffee in rms. Restaurant adj 6:30 am-10 pm. Ck-out noon. Meeting rm. Business servs avail. In-rm modem link. Valet serv. Sundries. Free airport, bus depot transportation. Downhill/x-country ski 20 mi. Cr cds: A, C, D, DS, MC, V. 🐾 ⚊ ⚊ 🔥 🐾 [SC]

Motor Hotels

★ ★ ★ **HOLIDAY INN-PARKSIDE.** *200 S Pattee St (59802). 406/721-8550; FAX 406/721-7427.* 200 rms, 4 story. S, D $85-$95; suites $125-$150; under 18 free. Pet accepted. TV; cable. Indoor pool; whirlpool. Restaurant 6:30 am-2 pm, 5:30-10:30 pm. Rm serv. Bar 2 pm-2 am; entertainment Fri, Sat. Ck-out noon. Meeting rms. Business servs avail. Bellhops. Gift shop. Free airport transportation. Downhill ski 12 mi; x-country ski 5 mi. Exercise equipt; weights, bicycles, sauna. Balconies. Open atrium, outside patio dining. On Clark Fork River and park. Cr cds: A, C, D, DS, ER, JCB, MC, V.
[D] 🐾 ⚊ 🏋 🐾 [SC]

★ ★ **RED LION VILLAGE INN.** *100 Madison St (59802), 1/4 mi SW of I-90 Van Buren exit. 406/728-3100; FAX 406/728-2530.* 171 rms, 3 story. S $73-$85; D $83-$95; each addl $10; suites $125-$285; under 18 free. Crib free. Pet accepted. TV; cable, VCR avail. Heated pool; whirlpool. Coffee in rms. Restaurant 6 am-10 pm. Rm serv. Bar 11-2 am. Ck-out noon. Meeting rms. Business servs avail. In-rm modem link. Bellhops. Gift shop. Beauty shop. Free airport transportation. Downhill/x-country ski 12 mi. Exercise equipt; stair machine, treadmill. Some refrigerators. Balconies. On Clark Fork River. Cr cds: A, C, D, DS, ER, MC, V. [D] 🐾 🐾 ⚊ 🏋 🐾 [SC]

Red Lodge (See also Cooke City; also see Cody, WY)

Motels

★ ★ **BEST WESTERN LU PINE INN.** *702 S Hauser. 406/446-1321; FAX 406/446-1465.* 46 rms, 2 story. S $62; D $72; kit. unit $4 addl; under 12 free; higher rates special events; lower rates May & Labor Day-Thanksgiving. Crib free. Pet accepted, some restrictions. TV; cable (premium). Indoor pool; whirlpool. Playground. Restaurant nearby. Ck-out noon. Coin lndry. Meeting rms. Business servs avail. Sundries. Downhill/x-country ski 6 mi. Exercise equipt; bicycles, stair machine, sauna. Game rm. Some in-rm whirlpools. Some balconies. Cr cds: A, C, D, DS, MC, V. [D] 🐾 ⚊ ⚊ 🏋 🐾 [SC]

★ ★ **COMFORT INN.** *612 N Broadway. 406/446-4469.* 55 rms, 2 story. July-Aug: S, D $79; each addl $10; suites $89-$99; under 18 free; ski plans; lower rates rest of yr. Crib free. Pet accepted; $25 deposit. TV; cable, VCR avail. Complimentary continental bkfst. Ck-out 11 am. Meeting rms. Business servs avail. Downhill/x-country ski 6 mi. Indoor pool; whirlpool. Cr cds: A, D, DS, JCB, MC, V. [D] 🐾 ⚊ ⚊ 🐾 [SC]

✔ ★ **SUPER 8.** *1223 S Broadway. 406/446-2288; FAX 406/446-3162.* 50 rms, 2 story. S $59.88; D $59.88-$89.88. Crib free. Pet accepted, some restrictions. TV; cable (premium). Indoor pool; whirlpool. Complimentary continental bkfst. Ck-out 11 am. Coin lndry. Meeting rm. Downhill/x-country ski 5 mi. Game rm. Some refrigerators, in-rm whirlpools; microwaves avail. Some rms with view of mountains. Cr cds: A, C, D, DS, MC, V.
[D] 🐾 ⚊ ⚊ 🔥 🐾 [SC]

Three Forks *(See also Bozeman, Butte, Ennis)*

Motel

✔★ **FORT THREE FORKS.** *10776 US 287, I-90 exit 274. 406/285-3233; FAX 406/285-3787; res: 800/477-5690.* 24 rms, 2 story. June-Sept: S $38; D $48-$52; each addl $4; suites $75; under 12 free; lower rates rest of yr. Crib $5. Pet accepted; $5. TV; cable. Complimentary continental bkfst. Restaurant adj 6 am-8 pm. Ck-out 11 am. Coin lndry. Meeting rm. Business servs avail. Cr cds: A, C, D, DS, MC, V. 🐾 ⊠ 🐾

Inn

★★ **SACAJAWEA.** *5 N Main St, 5 N Main St. 406/285-6515; FAX 406/285-4210; res: 800/821-7326.* 33 rms, 3 story. June-Sept: S $69; D $69-$99; each addl $10; under 12 free; wkly rates; fishing plan; lower rates rest of yr. Crib free. Pet accepted; $5. TV; cable. Restaurant 5-9 pm. Rm serv. Ck-out 11 am, ck-in 3 pm. Meeting rm. Business servs avail. Restored grand old railroad hotel (1910). Cr cds: A, DS, MC, V. 🐾 ⊠ 🐾

West Yellowstone

Motel

★★ **KELLY INN.** *104 S Canyon St. 406/646-4544; res: 800/259-4672; FAX 406/646-9838.* 78 rms, 3 story. June-Sept: S, D $105-$120; each addl $8; under 12 free; lower rates rest of yr. Crib free. Pet accepted. TV; cable. Complimentary continental bkfst. Restaurant nearby. Ck-out 11 am. Business servs avail. Coin lndry. X-country ski 3 blks. Indoor pool; whirlpool. Many refrigerators, microwaves. Cr cds: A, D, DS, MC, V.
D 🐾 ⊠ ≈ ⊠ 🐾 SC

Whitefish *(See also Columbia Falls, Kalispell)*

Motels

★★ **QUALITY INN PINE LODGE.** *920 Spokane Ave. 406/862-7600; FAX 406/862-7616.* 76 rms, 4 story, 25 suites. June-Sept: S $80-$100; D $80-$110; suites $125-$195; under 18 free; ski plan; lower rates rest of yr. Crib $5. Pet accepted, some restrictions. TV; cable. Indoor pool; whirlpool. Complimentary continental bkfst. Ck-out 11 am. Coin lndry. Meeting rms. Business servs avail. Valet serv. Free airport transportation. Exercise equipt; weights, bicycles. Game rm. Refrigerators, microwaves in suites. Cr cds: A, C, D, DS, JCB, MC, V. D 🐾 ≈ 🏃 ⊠ 🐾 SC

★ **SUPER 8.** *800 Spokane Ave. 406/862-8255.* 40 rms, 3 story. No elvtr. July-Aug: S, D $74.88-$79.88; each addl $5; lower rates rest of yr. Crib free. Pet accepted, some restrictions; $5. TV; cable (premium). Complimentary coffee in lobby. Ck-out 11 am. Free RR transportation. Whirlpool. Grill. Cr cds: A, D, DS, MC, V. D 🐾 ⊠ 🐾 SC

Nebraska

Auburn

Motel

★ **AUBURN INN.** *517 J St, on US 75/73N. 402/274-3143; FAX 402/274-4404; res: 800/272-3143.* 36 rms. S $32; D $38-$45; each addl $5. Pet accepted, some restrictions. TV; cable (premium). Coffee in rms. Restaurant opp 6 am-10 pm. Ck-out 11 am. Refrigerators, microwaves. Cr cds: A, C, D, DS, MC, V. 🐾 🏊 📶 🔥

Beatrice (See also Lincoln)

Motels

★ ★ **BEATRICE INN.** *3500 N 6th St. 402/223-4074; FAX 402/223-4074, ext. 300; res: 800/232-8742.* 63 rms, 2 story. May-Dec: S $35.75-$42.75; D $41.75-$48.50; each addl $3; under 12 free; lower rates rest of yr. Crib $4. Pet accepted, some restrictions. TV; cable (premium). Heated pool. Restaurant 6 am-9 pm; Sun to 8 pm. Bar 5 pm-1 am. Ck-out 11 am. Coin lndry. Meeting rms. Sundries. Cr cds: A, C, D, DS, MC, V. 🐾 🏊 📶 🔥 SC

✔ ★ **HOLIDAY VILLA.** *1820 N 6th St. 402/223-4036; FAX 402/228-3875.* 46 rms, 1-2 story, 8 kits. S $26-$29; D $34-$40; each addl $4; kit. units $42; under 10 free. Crib free. Pet accepted, some restrictions. TV; cable. Playground. Complimentary coffee in lobby. Ck-out 11 am. Meeting rms. Cr cds: A, D, DS, MC, V. 🐾 📶 🔥 SC

★ **VICTORIAN INN.** *1903 N 6th. 402/228-5955.* 31 rms, 2 story. S $29.95; D $36.95-$39.95; each addl $3. Pet accepted. TV; cable (premium), VCR avail. Complimentary continental bkfst. Ck-out 11 am. Cr cds: A, C, D, DS, MC, V. D 🐾 🔥 SC

Blair (See also Fremont, Omaha)

Motel

✔ ★ **RATH INN.** *US 30W. 402/426-2340; FAX 402/426-8703.* 32 rms, 2 story. S $32.99; D $41.98; each addl $5; suites $43.96. Pet accepted. TV; cable (premium). Heated pool. Continental bkfst. Restaurant adj 6 am-11 pm. Ck-out 11 am. Refrigerator in suites. Cr cds: A, D, DS, MC, V. 🐾 🏊 📶 🔥

Broken Bow

Motels

★ **GATEWAY.** *1 mi E on NE 2, 70, 92. 308/872-2478.* 23 rms. S $25; D $34. Crib $1. Pet accepted, some restrictions. TV; cable (premium). Restaurant nearby. Ck-out 11 am. Sauna. Cr cds: A, C, D, DS, MC, V. 🐾 📶 🔥 SC

★ **WM PENN LODGE.** *853 E South St, E on NE 2. 308/872-2412.* 28 rms. S $24-$30; D $28-$40; each addl $3. Crib $5. Pet accepted. TV; cable (premium). Restaurant opp 6 am-11 pm. Ck-out 10 am. Refrigerators. Cr cds: A, DS, MC, V. 🐾 🔥

Chadron

Motels

★ ★ **BEST WESTERN WEST HILLS INN.** *Jct US 385 & 10th St, 1 mi SW, 6 blks S of US 20. 308/432-3305; FAX 308/432-5990.* 67 rms, 2 story. S $55; D $65; each addl $5; suites $65-$105. Crib free. Pet accepted. TV; cable (premium). Indoor pool (heated); whirlpool. Complimentary continental bkfst. Coffee in rms. Restaurant nearby. Ck-out 11 am. Coin lndry. Meeting rms. Exercise equipt; weights, treadmill. Game rm. Some refrigerators, in-rm whirlpools. Cr cds: A, C, D, DS, MC, V. D 🐾 🏊 🏋 📶 🔥 SC

★ **ECONOMY 9.** *1201 W US 20. 308/432-3119; FAX 308/432-3119.* 21 rms. Mid-May-Sept: S $45; D $52.99-$62.99; under 12 free; higher rates: rodeo, college graduation, fur trade days; lower rates rest of yr. Crib $2. Pet accepted. TV; cable (premium). Complimentary coffee in lobby. Restaurant opp 6 am-9 pm. Ck-out 10:30 am. Whirlpool. Cr cds: A, C, D, DS, MC, V. 🐾 📶 🔥 SC

Cozad (See also Lexington)

Motel

★ **BUDGET HOST CIRCLE "S".** *440 S Meridian, at I-80.* 308/784-2290; FAX 308/784-3917. 49 rms, 2 story. S $30; D $38; each addl $4. Crib $3. Pet accepted. TV; cable (premium). Heated pool. Restaurant 6 am-10 pm. Ck-out 11 am. Cr cds: A, DS, MC, V. 🐾 ≋ ⊠ 🅈

Fremont (See also Omaha)

Motels

★ ★ **COMFORT INN.** *1649 E 23rd St (68025).* 402/721-1109. 48 rms, 2 story. June-Sept: S $47.95-$52.95; D $50.95-$55.95; each addl $5; suites $59.95-$64.95; under 16 free; higher rates special events. Crib free. Pet accepted, some restrictions. TV; cable (premium). Indoor pool; whirlpool. Complimentary continental bkfst. Restaurant adj 6 am-midnight. Ck-out 11 am. Business servs avail. Refrigerators in suites; microwaves avail. Cr cds: A, D, DS, MC, V. D 🐾 ≋ ⊠ 🅈 SC

★ ★ **HOLIDAY LODGE.** *1220 E 23rd St (68025), at jct US 30 & Old US 275.* 402/727-1110; FAX 402/727-4579; res: 800/743-7666. 100 rms, 2 story. S $42-$45; D $49-$63. Crib free. Pet accepted. TV; cable (premium). Indoor pool; whirlpool. Restaurant 6 am-9:30 pm. Bar 3 pm-1 am. Ck-out noon. Meeting rms. Business servs avail. Exercise equipt; treadmill, rowers. Cr cds: A, C, D, DS, MC, V. D 🐾 ≋ 🏋 ⊠ 🅈 SC

Grand Island (See also Hastings)

Motor Hotels

★ ★ **BEST WESTERN RIVERSIDE INN.** *3333 Ramada Rd (68801), at S Locust St.* 308/384-5150; FAX 308/384-6551. 183 rms, 2 story. S $46; D $51; suites $78; under 18 free. Crib free. Pet accepted. TV; cable (premium). Heated pool; whirlpool, sauna. Complimentary continental bkfst. Restaurant 6 am-1:30 pm, 5-9 pm. Rm serv. Bar 4 pm-1 am. Ck-out noon. Coin lndry. Meeting rms. Business servs avail. Sundries. Cr cds: A, C, D, DS, MC, V. D 🐾 ≋ ⊠ 🅈 SC

★ ★ **HOLIDAY INN-MIDTOWN.** *2503 S Locust St (68801).* 308/384-1330; FAX 308/382-4615. 206 rms, 2 story. S $61-$69; D $66-$74; suites $95; under 18 free. Crib free. Pet accepted. TV; cable (premium). Heated pool; wading pool, whirlpool, poolside serv. Restaurant 6 am-10 pm. Rm serv. Bar 3 pm-1 am. Ck-out noon. Coin lndry. Meeting rms. Cr cds: A, C, D, DS, JCB, MC, V. D 🐾 ≋ ⊠ 🅈 SC

Hastings (See also Grand Island)

Motels

★ **SUPER 8.** *2200 N Kansas, US 281 N.* 402/463-8888; FAX 402/463-8899. 50 rms, 2 story. May-Sept: S $37.88-$42.88, D $44.88-$48.88; lower rates rest of yr. Crib free. Pet accepted. TV; cable (premium). Restaurant adj 6 am-10 pm. Ck-out 11 am. Cr cds: A, D, DS, MC. D 🐾 🅈

★ **USA INNS.** *2424 E Osborne Dr, US 281N & US 6 Bypass.* 402/463-1422; FAX 402/463-2956. 62 rms, 2 story. S $37.50; D $46.50; each addl $2. Crib free. Pet accepted, some restrictions. TV; cable (premium), VCR avail. Complimentary coffee. Ck-out 11 am. Some refrigerators. Cr cds: A, D, DS, MC, V. D 🐾 ⊠ 🅈 SC

Kearney (See also Grand Island, Lexington)

Motel

★ ★ ★ **BEST WESTERN TEL-STAR.** *1010 3rd Ave.* 308/237-5185; FAX 308/234-1002. 69 rms, 2 story. June-Aug: S $49; D $62; each addl $5; under 12 free; lower rates rest of yr. Crib free. Pet accepted. TV; cable (premium), VCR avail (movies). Heated pool; wading pool, whirlpool, sauna. Complimentary full bkfst. Restaurant 5-9 pm. Rm serv. Ck-out noon. Meeting rms. Business servs avail. Exercise equipt; weights, treadmill, rower. Cr cds: A, C, D, DS, MC, V. 🐾 ≋ 🏋 ⊠ 🅈 SC

Motor Hotels

★ ★ **HOLIDAY INN.** *301 S 2nd Ave.* 308/237-3141; FAX 308/234-4675. 210 rms, 2 story. S, D $69-$79; suites $80-$150; under 20 free. Crib free. Pet accepted. TV; cable (premium). Indoor pool; wading pool, whirlpool, sauna, poolside serv. Restaurant 6 am-10 pm. Rm serv. Bar 3 pm-1 am; entertainment exc Sun. Ck-out noon. Coin lndry. Meeting rms. Business servs avail. Sundries. Gift shop. Private patios, balconies. Cr cds: A, C, D, DS, JCB, MC, V. [D] [✦] [≊] [✕] [🐾] [SC]

★ ★ ★ **RAMADA INN.** *S 2nd Ave, 1 blk N of I-80 exit 272. 308/237-5971; FAX 308/236-7549.* 155 rms, 2 story. S $65; D $80; suites $110; under 18 free. Crib free. Pet accepted. TV; cable (premium). Indoor pool; whirlpool. Restaurant 6 am-9 pm. Rm serv. Bar 11-1 am; Sun 6-9 pm. Ck-out 11 am. Coin lndry. Meeting rms. Business servs avail. In-rm modem link. Gift shop. Game rm. Cr cds: A, C, D, DS, MC, V. [D] [✦] [≊] [✕] [🐾] [SC]

Lexington *(See also Cozad, Kearney)*

Motel

★ ★ **ECONO LODGE.** *1¹/₂ mi S on US 283 at I-80. 308/324-5601; FAX 308/324-4284.* 50 rms, 2 story. May-Nov: S $29.95-$31.95; D $33.95-$37.95; each addl $5; kit. units $5 addl; lower rates rest of yr. Crib free. Pet accepted. TV; cable (premium). Heated pool. Complimentary continental bkfst. Ck-out noon. Lndry facilities. Meeting rm. Cr cds: A, C, D, DS, ER, JCB, MC, V. [✦] [≊] [✕] [🐾] [SC]

Lincoln *(See also Omaha)*

Motels

(Rates may be higher state fair week)

★ ★ **BEST WESTERN VILLAGER MOTOR INN.** *5200 O St (68510). 402/464-9111; FAX 402/467-0505.* 186 rms, 2 story. S, D $60-$70; each addl $6; suites $150; under 18 free. Crib free. Pet accepted, some restrictions. TV; cable (premium), VCR avail. Pool; whirlpool. Restaurant 6 am-10 pm; Fri, Sat to 11 pm. Rm serv. Bar 3:30 pm-1 am. Ck-out noon. Coin lndry. Meeting rms. Bellhops. Valet serv. Cr cds: A, C, D, DS, MC, V. [✦] [≊] [✕] [🐾] [SC]

★ **COMFORT INN.** *2940 NW 12th St (68521), near Municipal Airport. 402/475-2200.* 67 rms, 2 story. May-Oct: S $45-$50; D $48-$55; each addl $5; under 18 free; higher rates university football season; lower rates rest of yr. Crib free. Pet accepted. TV; cable (premium). Complimentary continental bkfst. Restaurant adj open 24 hrs. Ck-out 11 am. Meeting rms. Business servs avail. Whirlpool. Game rm. Microwaves avail. Cr cds: A, C, D, DS, ER, JCB, MC, V. [D] [✦] [✕] [🐾] [SC]

★ ★ **RESIDENCE INN BY MARRIOTT.** *200 S 68th Place (68510). 402/483-4900; FAX 402/483-4464.* 120 kit. suites, 2 story. S, D $98-$150; under 16. Crib free. Pet accepted; $100 ($50 refundable). TV; cable (premium), VCR avail. Heated pool; whirlpool. Complimentary full bkfst. Complimentary coffee in rms. Ck-out noon. Coin lndry. Meeting rms. Business servs avail. Valet serv. Sundries. Lighted tennis. Exercise equipt; weights, bicycles. Health club privileges. Microwaves. Balconies. Picnic tables, grills. Cr cds: A, C, D, DS, JCB, MC, V. [D] [✦] [⛷] [≊] [🏃] [✕] [🐾] [SC]

McCook

Motels

★ ★ **BEST WESTERN CHIEF.** *612 West B St, Near Municipal Airport. 308/345-3700; FAX 308/345-7182.* 111 rms, 1-2 story. May-Dec: S $48; D $56; each addl $4; suites $72-$80; higher rates: pheasant season, first wk Nov; lower rates rest of yr. Crib $5. Pet accepted. TV; cable (premium). Indoor pool; whirlpool, poolside serv. Restaurant 6:30 am-10 pm. Ck-out 11 am. Meeting rm. Business servs avail. Cr cds: A, C, D, DS, MC, V. [D] [✦] [≊] [✕] [🐾] [SC]

✔ ★ **SUPER 8.** *1103 East B Street. 308/345-1141; FAX 308/345-1144.* 40 rms. S $33.88; D $40.88; each addl $2; under 12 free. Crib $3. Pet accepted. TV; cable (premium). Complimentary coffee in rms. Ck-out 11 am. Cr cds: A, C, D, DS, MC, V. [D] [✦] [✕] [🐾] [SC]

North Platte

Motels

★ **1ST INTERSTATE INN.** *on US 83 at jct I-80. 308/532-6980; res: 800/992-9026 (exc NE), 800/682-0021 (NE).* 29 rms. Mid-May-mid-Sept: S $34.95; D $40.95; each addl $2; under 12 free; lower rates rest of yr. Crib $3. Pet accepted. TV; cable (premium).

Coffee in lobby. Restaurant nearby. Ck-out 11 am. Some refrigerators. Cr cds: A, C, D, DS, JCB, MC, V. 🔊 ⊠ 🖊 SC

★ **BLUE SPRUCE.** *821 S Dewey St. 308/534-2600; res: 800/434-2602.* 14 rms. June-mid-Sept: S $24-$31; D $31-$39; each addl $2; lower rates rest of yr. Crib $2. Pet accepted, some restrictions. TV; cable (premium). Complimentary coffee. Restaurant nearby. Ck-out 11 am. Cr cds: A, DS, MC, V. 🔊 ⊠ 🖊 SC

Motor Hotel

★ ★ **STOCKMAN INN.** *1402 S Jeffers. 308/534-3630; FAX 308/534-0110; res: 800/624-4643 (exc NE), 800/237-2222 (NE).* 150 rms, 2 story. S $45-$50; D $50-$55; each addl $5; higher rates May-Sept. Crib free. Pet accepted, some restrictions. TV; cable (premium). Heated pool. Restaurant 6 am-10 pm. Rm serv. Bar 4 pm-1 am; entertainment exc Sun. Ck-out 11 am. Meeting rms. Business servs avail. Cr cds: A, C, D, DS, MC, V. D 🔊 ⊠ ⊠ 🖊 SC

Ogallala

Motor Hotels

✔★ **BEST WESTERN STAGECOACH INN.** *201 Stagecoach Trail, at jct NE 61 & I-80. 308/284-3656; FAX 308/284-6734.* 100 rms, 2 story. May-Sept: S $57-$67; D $62-$67; each addl $5; under 12 free; lower rates rest of yr. Crib free. Pet accepted. TV; cable, VCR (movies). Indoor/outdoor pool; wading pool, whirlpool. Playground. Restaurant 6 am-9 pm. Bar 5-10 pm. Ck-out 11 am. Coin lndry. Meeting rms. Business center. In-rm modem link. Free airport transportation. Cr cds: A, C, D, DS, MC, V. D 🔊 ⊠ ⊠ 🖊 SC 🏃

★ ★ **RAMADA LIMITED.** *201 Chuckwagon Rd, at jct NE 61, I-80. 308/284-3623; FAX 308/284-4949.* 152 rms, 2 story. S, D $66; each addl $7; under 18 free. Pet accepted. TV; cable. Heated pool; wading pool, poolside serv. Continental bkfst. Restaurant 6 am-10 pm. Rm serv. Bar 5 pm-1 am. Ck-out noon. Ck-in 3 pm. Coin lndry. Meeting rms. Business servs avail. Free airport transportation. Game rm. Cr cds: A, C, D, DS, MC, V. D 🔊 ⊠ ⊠ 🖊 SC

Omaha (See also Blair, Lincoln; also see Council Bluffs, IA)

Motels

★ ★ **BUDGETEL INN.** *10760 M Street (68127), south of downtown. 402/592-5200; FAX 402/592-1416.* 96 rms, 2 story. S $42.95; D $49.95; suites $49.95-$51.95; under 19 free; wkend, special events rates. Crib free. Pet accepted. TV; cable (premium). Complimentary continental bkfst. Complimentary coffee in rms. Restaurant nearby. Ck-out noon. Business servs avail. In-rm modem link. Cr cds: A, C, D, DS, MC, V. D 🔊 ⊠ 🖊 SC

★ ★ **HAMPTON INN.** *10728 L Street (68127), south of downtown. 402/593-2380; FAX 402/593-0859.* 133 rms, 4 story. S $56-$62; D $61-$68; under 18 free. Crib free. Pet accepted. TV; cable, VCR avail (movies). Pool. Complimentary continental bkfst. Restaurant nearby. Meeting rms. Business servs avail. In-rm modem link. Cr cds: A, C, D, DS, MC, V. D 🔊 ⊠ ⊠ 🖊 SC

★ ★ **LA QUINTA.** *3330 N 104th Ave (68134), north of downtown. 402/493-1900; FAX 402/496-0757.* 130 rms, 2 story. S $56; D $54-$61; 1st addl $5; suites $68-$80; under 18 free. Crib free. Pet accepted, some restrictions. TV; cable (premium). Heated pool. Continental bkfst in lobby. Restaurant adj open 24 hrs. Ck-out noon. Coin lndry. Meeting rms. In-rm modem link. Sundries. Cr cds: A, C, D, DS, MC, V. D 🔊 ⊠ ⊠ 🖊 SC

✔★ **PARK INN INTERNATIONAL.** *9305 S 145th St (68138), south of downtown. 402/895-2555; FAX 402/895-1565.* 56 rms, 3 story. No elvtr. S $41.50; D $46.50; each addl $5; suites $85; under 16 free. Crib free. Pet accepted; $25. TV; cable (premium), VCR avail (movies). Complimentary coffee in lobby. Bar 1 pm-1 am. Ck-out 11 am. Coin lndry. Whirlpool. Cr cds: A, C, D, DS, ER, JCB, MC, V. D 🔊 ⊠ 🖊 SC

★ ★ **RESIDENCE INN BY MARRIOTT.** *6990 Dodge St (68132), east of downtown. 402/553-8898.* 80 kit. suites. S $120; D $150. Crib free. Pet accepted, some restrictions; $25. TV; cable (premium), VCR avail (movies). Heated pool; whirlpool. Complimentary continental bkfst. Ck-out noon. Business servs avail. In-rm modem link. Tennis. Health club privileges. Fireplaces. Balconies. Cr cds: A, C, D, DS, JCB, MC, V. D 🔊 🏋 ⊠ ⊠ 🖊 SC

Motor Hotels

★ ★ ★ **BEST WESTERN-CENTRAL.** *3650 S 72nd St (68124), I-80 exit 449, west of downtown. 402/397-3700; FAX 402/397-8362.* 213 rms, 5 story. June-Aug: S $59-$69; D

$69-$89; each addl $6; suites $85-$150; under 18 free; wkend rates; lower rates rest of yr. Crib free. Pet accepted, some restrictions. TV; cable (premium). Indoor pool; whirlpool, sauna. Restaurant 6:30 am-10 pm. Rm serv. Bar 4 pm-1 am. Ck-out noon. Coin lndry. Meeting rms. Business servs avail. In-rm modem link. Bellhops. Airport transportation. Game rm. Refrigerator in suites. Cr cds: A, C, D, DS, ER, JCB, MC, V.

D ✦ ≋ ⋈ 🔥 SC

★ ★ ★ **CLARION CARLISLE HOTEL.** *10909 M Street (68137), west of downtown. 402/331-8220; FAX 402/331-8729.* 139 rms, 2-3 story. S, D $69-$99; suites $175; under 18 free. Crib free. Pet accepted, some restrictions; $30. TV; cable. Indoor pool; whirlpool. Complimentary continental bkfst. Coffee in rms. Restaurant 6:30-10:30 am, noon-2 pm, 5-10 pm. Rm serv. Bar 4:30 pm-midnight. Ck-out noon. Coin lndry. Meeting rms. Business center. In-rm modem link. Bellhops. Valet serv. Free airport transportation. Cr cds: A, C, D, DS, ER, JCB, MC, V. D ✦ ≋ ⋈ 🔥 SC 🚶

★ ★ **SHERATON INN.** *4888 S 118th St (68137), west of downtown. 402/895-1000; FAX 402/895-9247.* 168 rms, 6 story. S $74; D $84; under 17 free. Crib free. Pet accepted, some restrictions. TV; cable (premium). Indoor pool; wading pool, whirlpool, sauna. Restaurant 6:30 am-10 pm. Rm serv. Bar 11-1 am. Ck-out noon. Coin lndry. Meeting rm. Business servs avail. Valet serv. Sundries. Free airport transportation. Game rm. Sun deck. Cr cds: A, C, D, DS, JCB, MC, V. D ✦ ≋ ⋈ 🔥 SC

Hotels

★ ★ ★ **MARRIOTT.** *10220 Regency Circle (68114), west of downtown. 402/399-9000; FAX 402/399-0223.* 301 rms, 4-6 story. S, D $180; suites $250; under 18 free; long-wkend rates. Crib free. Pet accepted, some restrictions. TV; cable, VCR avail. Indoor/outdoor pool; whirlpool, poolside serv, lifeguard. Restaurants 6:30 am-11 pm. Bar 4 pm-1 am. Ck-out noon. Convention facilities. Business servs avail. In-rm modem link. Shopping arcade. Exercise equipt; weights, bicycles, sauna, steam rm. Private patios, balconies. Luxury level. Cr cds: A, C, D, DS, ER, JCB, MC, V. D ✦ ≋ 🏋 ⋈ 🔥 SC

✔ ★ ★ **RAMADA-CENTRAL.** *7007 Grover St (68106), south of downtown. 402/397-7030; FAX 402/397-8449.* 215 rms, 9 story. S, D $79-$89; each addl $10; suites $135-$145; under 18 free; wkend rates. Crib free. Pet accepted. TV; cable (premium). Indoor pool; whirlpool, sauna. Playground. Restaurant 6 am-10 pm; Sat, Sun from 7 am. Bar 5 pm-1 am. Ck-out noon. Meeting rms. Business servs avail. In-rm modem link. Gift shop. Free airport transportation. Cr cds: A, C, D, DS, MC, V. D ✦ ≋ ⋈ 🔥 SC

O'Neill

Motels

★ **CAPRI.** *1/2 mi E on US 20, 275. 402/336-2762; FAX 402/336-4365; res: 800/341-8000.* 26 rms. S $29-$38; D $38-$45; each addl $2. Crib free. Pet accepted. TV; cable (premium). Playground. Complimentary coffee in lobby. Restaurant nearby. Ck-out 11 am. Free airport transportation. Picnic tables, grill. Cr cds: A, C, D, DS, MC, V. ✦ ⋈ 🔥

✔ ★ **ELMS.** *1 mi E on US 20, 275. 402/336-3800; res: 800/526-9052.* 21 rms. S $25; D $30-$38; each addl $3. Crib $2. Pet accepted. TV; cable (premium). Playground. Restaurant opp 7 am-11 pm. Ck-out 11 am. Cr cds: A, DS, MC, V. ✦ ⋈ 🔥 SC

★ **GOLDEN HOTEL.** *406 E Douglas, jct US 20, 281. 402/336-4436; FAX 402/336-3549; res: 800/658-3148.* 27 rms, 3 story. S $27; D $32; each addl $5. Crib free. Pet accepted, some restrictions. TV; cable (premium), VCR (movies). Complimentary continental bkfst. Restaurant adj 6 am-10 pm. Ck-out 11 am. Valet serv. Restored hotel built 1913. Cr cds: A, DS, MC, V. D ✦ 🔥

South Sioux City *(See also Sioux City, IA)*

Motel

✔ ★ **TRAVELODGE.** *400 Dakota Ave. 402/494-3046; FAX 402/494-8299.* 61 rms, 2 story. S $40; D $48-$60; each addl $4. Pet accepted. TV; cable (premium). Complimentary continental bkfst. Restaurant nearby. Ck-out 11 am. Business servs avail. Airport transportation. Cr cds: A, D, DS, MC, V. D ✦ ⋈ 🔥 SC

Motor Hotel

★ ★ ★ **MARINA INN.** *4th & B Streets, I-29 exit 148. 402/494-4000; FAX 402/494-2550; res: 800/798-7980.* 182 rms, 5 story. S $65-$77; D $75-$87; each addl $10; under 18 free. Crib free. Pet accepted. TV; cable, VCR avail. Indoor pool; whirlpool. Restaurant 6:30

am-10 pm. Rm serv. Bars 11-1 am. Ck-out 11 am. Meeting rms. Free airport transportation. Some private patios. On Missouri River. Cr cds: A, D, DS, MC, V. 🄳 ⬮ ⬮ ⬮ 🆂🅲

Valentine

Motels

    ✔ ★ **RAINE.** *W US 20. 402/376-2030; res: 800/999-3066.* 34 rms. May-Oct: S $36; D $36-$42; each addl $2. Crib $2. Pet accepted. TV; cable. Coffee in rms. Restaurant nearby. Ck-out 11 am. Free airport transportation. Cr cds: A, C, D, DS, MC, V. ⬮ ⬮ ⬮

    ★ **TRADE WINDS LODGE.** *US 20E & 83. 402/376-1600; res: 800/341-8000.* 32 rms. May-Sept: S $27-$40; D $42-$50; each addl $2; lower rates rest of yr. Crib free. Pet accepted. TV; cable. Heated pool. Complimentary coffee. Ck-out 11 am. Free airport transportation. Cr cds: A, C, D, DS, MC, V. ⬮ ⬮ ⬮ ⬮ 🆂🅲

Nevada

Battle Mountain

Motel

★ ★ **MINORS INN.** *521 E Front St, on I-80 Business. 702/635-5880; FAX 702/635-5788.* 72 rms, 3 story. June-Aug: S,D $56-$61; each addl $5; under 6 free. Crib $5. Pet accepted; $20 deposit. TV; cable (premium). Heated pool; whirlpool. Complimentary continental bkfst. Restaurant adj 11 am-9 pm. Ck-out 11 am. Coin lndry. Meeting rms. Business servs avail. Refrigerators. Cr cds: A, C, D, DS, MC, V. 🐾 ⛱ ⊠ 🖐 SC

Elko

Motels

★ ★ **HOLIDAY INN.** *3015 E Idaho St. 702/738-8425; FAX 702/753-7906.* 170 rms, 4 story. Apr-Oct: S $64-$84, D $74-$94; each addl $10; higher rates: Cowboy Poetry Gathering, Mining Exposition; lower rates rest of yr. Crib free. Pet accepted. TV; cable. Indoor pool; whirlpool. Coffee in rms. Restaurant 6 am-10 pm. Rm serv. Bar 4 pm-midnight. Ck-out noon. Coin lndry. Meeting rms. Valet serv. Free airport, RR station, bus depot transportation. Exercise equipt; weight machine, bicycles. Cr cds: A, C, D, DS, JCB, MC, V. D 🐾 ⛱ 🏃 ✈ ⊠ 🖐 SC

★ ★ **RED LION INN & CASINO.** *2065 E Idaho St. 702/738-2111; FAX 702/753-9859.* 223 rms, 3 story. S $69-$79; D $79-$89; each addl $10; suites $259; under 18 free. Crib free. Pet accepted. TV; cable (premium). Heated pool. Coffee in rms. Restaurant open 24 hrs. Bar; entertainment. Ck-out noon. Business servs avail. Gift shop. Barber, beauty shop. Free airport transportation. Game rm. Casino. Cr cds: A, C, D, DS, ER, MC, V. D 🐾 ⛱ ⊠ 🖐 SC

★ ★ **SHILO INN.** *2401 Mountain City Hwy, near JC Harris Airport. 702/738-5522; FAX 702/738-6247.* 70 rms, 2 story, 16 kit. units. S, D $69-$89; kit. units $69-$119; under 12 free; wkly rates; higher rates special events. Crib free. Pet accepted; $7. TV; cable (premium), VCR avail. Indoor pool; whirlpool. Complimentary continental bkfst. Restaurant nearby. Ck-out noon. Coin lndry. Meeting rm. Business servs avail. In-rm modem link. Sundries. Free airport, RR station, bus depot transportation. Exercise equipt; weight machine, bicycles, sauna. Bathrm phones, refrigerators, wet bars. Cr cds: A, C, D, DS, ER, JCB, MC, V. D 🐾 ⛱ 🏃 ✈ ⊠ 🖐 SC

Fallon

Motels

★ **BONANZA INN & CASINO.** *855 W Williams Ave. 702/423-6031; FAX 702/423-6282.* 75 rms, 2 story. S $40; D $46; each addl $5; suite $59-$76; under 12 free. Crib $5. Pet accepted; $20. TV; cable (premium). Restaurant open 24 hrs. Bar. Ck-out 11 am. Business servs avail. Casino. RV park. Cr cds: A, C, D, DS, MC, V. D 🐾 ⊠ 🖐 SC

✔ ★ **WESTERN.** *125 S Carson St. 702/423-5118.* 22 rms, 2 story. S $35; D $39; each addl $5. Crib $4. Pet accepted, some restrictions. TV. Heated pool. Complimentary coffee in lobby. Restaurant nearby. Ck-out 11 am. Some refrigerators. Cr cds: A, C, D, MC, V. 🐾 ⛱ ⊠ 🖐 SC

Gardnerville *(See also Stateline)*

Inn

★ ★ **THE NENZEL MANSION.** *1431 Ezell St. 702/782-7644.* 4 air-cooled rms, 2 share bath, 3 story. No rm phones. S, D $80-$110; each addl $10; family & wkly rates. Crib free. Pet accepted. TV in sitting rm; cable. Complimentary full bkfst. Restaurant nearby. Ck-out 11 am, ck-in 3 pm. Downhill ski 18 mi; x-country ski 20 mi. Picnic tables, grills. Built 1910; period furnishings. Cr cds: MC, V. 🐾 ⛱ ⊠ 🖐 SC

Hawthorne

Motel

✔★ **SAND N SAGE LODGE.** *1301 E 5th St, 1 blk NE of US 95. 702/945-3352.* 37 rms, 2 story. S $29.95; D $34.95; each addl $5; kit. units $6 addl. Pet accepted, some restrictions. TV; cable. Complimentary coffee in lobby. Restaurant nearby. Ck-out 11 am. Some refrigerators. Balconies. Cr cds: A, DS, MC, V. 🐾 ⊠ 🔥

Las Vegas

Motels

(Note on accommodations: Rates are likely to vary upward in Las Vegas at peak occupancy and sometimes a minimum of three days occupancy is required. In addition, minimum rates quoted are generally available only from Sun through Tues, sometimes on Wed, rarely on holidays. This is not true of all accommodations but is true of many. We urge you to check the rate on any room you occupy and to make certain no other special conditions apply. Show reservations are available at most accommodations.)

✔★ **CENTER STRIP INN.** *3688 Las Vegas Blvd S (89109), on the Strip. 702/739-6066; FAX 702/736-2521; res: 800/777-7737.* 156 rms, 5 story, 44 suites. S, D $29.95-$89.95; each addl $10; suites $69-$189; under 18 free. Pet accepted. TV; cable (premium), VCR (movies $3). Pool. Complimentary continental bkfst. Restaurant adj open 24 hrs. Ck-out 11 am. Business servs avail. In-rm modem link. Refrigerators. Whirlpool in suites. Cr cds: A, C, D, DS, JCB, MC, V. Ⓓ 🐾 ⊠ ⊠ 🔥 SC

★★ **RESIDENCE INN BY MARRIOTT.** *3225 Paradise Rd (89109), near McCarran Intl Airport, east of the Strip. 702/796-9300; FAX 702/796-9562.* 192 kit. units, 1-2 story. S, D $95-$219. Crib free. Pet accepted, some restrictions; $7/day. TV; cable (premium), VCR (movies $3.50). Heated pool; whirlpool. Complimentary continental bkfst. Restaurant adj 6:30 am-9 pm. Ck-out noon. Coin lndry. Meeting rms. Business servs avail. Free airport transportation. Balconies. Picnic tables, grills. Cr cds: A, C, D, DS, JCB, MC, V. Ⓓ 🐾 ⊠ ✈ ⊠ 🔥 SC

Hotels

★★★ **ALEXIS PARK RESORT.** *375 E Harmon Ave (89109), near McCarran Intl Airport, 1 mi E of the Strip. 702/796-3300; FAX 702/796-4334; res: 800/582-2228 (exc NV).* 500 suites, 2 story. 1-bedrm $85-$500; 2-bedrm $475-$1,150; each addl $15; under 12 free. Crib free. Pet accepted, some restrictions; $60. TV; cable (premium), VCR avail. 3 pools, 1 heated; whirlpool; poolside serv. Restaurant 6 am-3 pm, 6-11 pm. Bar 10-1 am; entertainment. Ck-out noon. Convention facilities. Business center. In-rm modem link. Concierge. Gift shop. Barber, beauty shop. Golf privileges. Putting green. Exercise equipt; weights, bicycles, sauna, steam rm. Refrigerators, minibars; some bathrm phones, in-rm whirlpools. Cr cds: A, C, D, DS, JCB, MC, V. Ⓓ 🐾 🍴 ⊠ 🏃 ⊠ 🔥 🏃

★★ **HOLIDAY INN CROWNE PLAZA SUITES.** *4255 Paradise Rd (89109), near McCarran Intl Airport, east of the Strip. 702/369-4400; FAX 702/369-3770.* Web www.crowneplaza.com. 201 suites, 6 story. S, D $105-$250; each addl $20; under 18 free. Crib free. Pet accepted. TV; cable (premium), VCR avail. Heated pool; whirlpool, poolside serv. Complimentary coffee in rms. Restaurant 6 am-2 pm, 5-10 pm. Bar 11 am-midnight. Ck-out noon. Meeting rms. Business center. In-rm modem link. Concierge. Gift shop. Free airport transportation. Exercise equipt; weights, bicycles, sauna. Minibars. Cr cds: A, C, D, DS, ER, JCB, MC, V. Ⓓ 🐾 ⊠ 🏃 ✈ ⊠ 🔥 🏃

Reno

Motels

(Note on accommodations: Rates are likely to vary upward in Reno at peak occupancy and sometimes a minimum of three days occupancy is required. In addition, minimum rates quoted are generally available only from Mon through Thurs. We urge you to check the rate on any room you occupy and to make certain no other special conditions apply.)

★★ **LA QUINTA INN-AIRPORT.** *4001 Market St (89502), US 395 exit Villanova & Vassar Sts, near Reno Cannon Intl Airport. 702/348-6100; FAX 702/348-8794.* Web www.laquinta.com. 130 rms, 2 story. S $59-$69; D $67-$77; each addl $8; under 18 free. Crib free. Pet accepted. TV; cable. Pool. Complimentary continental bkfst. Coffee in rms. Restaurant adj open 24 hrs. Ck-out noon. Business servs avail. Free airport transportation. Health club privileges. Cr cds: A, C, D, DS, MC, V. 🐾 ⊠ 🏃 ⊠ 🔥 SC

★ **TRAVELODGE CENTRAL.** *2050 Market St (89502), US 395S exit Mill St W, near Reno-Tahoe Intl Airport. 702/786-2500; FAX 702/786-3884.* 211 units, 4 story, 70 kits. (no equipt). Late May-Oct: S $49, D $127; each addl $9; kit. suites $64-$127; under 18 free;

wkly rates; higher rates: wkends, hols, special events; lower rates rest of yr. Crib free. Pet accepted; $5 per day. TV; cable. Pool; whirlpool, sauna. Complimentary continental bkfst. Restaurant nearby. Ck-out noon. Coin lndry. Business servs avail. Airport, casino transportation. Microwaves in kit. units. Cr cds: A, C, D, DS, JCB, MC, V. 🖎 🛏 ✈ 🏄 🐾 SC

✔ ★ **VAGABOND INN.** 3131 S Virginia St (89502). 702/825-7134; FAX 702/825-3096. 129 rms, 2 story. May-Oct: S $45-$65; D $49-$69; each addl $5; under 18 free; higher rates special events, hols; lower rates rest of yr. Crib free. Pet accepted, some restrictions; $5 per day. TV; cable (premium). Pool. Complimentary continental bkfst. Restaurant adj 11-4 am. Ck-out 11 am. Meeting rm. Business servs avail. Airport, RR station, bus depot transportation. Some private patios, balconies. Cr cds: A, C, D, DS, MC, V. 🖎 🛏 ✈ 🏄 🐾 SC

Hotels

★ ★ **HAMPTON INN.** 175 E 2nd St (89504). 702/788-2300; FAX 702/788-2301. 408 rms, 26 story. May-Oct: S, D $69-$84; each addl $10; under 12 free; lower rates rest of yr. Crib free. Pet accepted. TV; cable (premium). Pool. Complimentary continental bkfst. Restaurant adj open 24 hrs. Bar. Ck-out noon. Meeting rms. Business servs avail. In-rm modem link. Sundries. Shopping arcade. Barber, beauty shop. Valet serv. Free airport transportation. Exercise equipt; bicycles, weights. Health club privileges. Cr cds: A, C, D, DS, JCB, MC, V. D 🖎 🛏 🏄 🏄 🐾 SC

★ ★ ★ **HARRAH'S.** 210 N Center St (89504), at 2nd St, downtown. 702/786-3232; FAX 702/788-3274; res: 800/427-7247. 565 rms, 24 story, no rms on 1st 5 floors. May-Oct: S, D $79-$89; each addl $10; suites $210-$425; under 15 free; higher rates wkends; lower rates rest of yr. Crib free. Pet accepted, some restrictions. TV; cable. Heated pool; whirlpool, lifeguard in season. Restaurant open 24 hrs. Bars; entertainment. Ck-out noon. Convention facilities. Business servs avail. In-rm modem link. Shopping arcade. Barber, beauty shop. Covered parking; valet. Free airport, bus depot transportation. Exercise rm; instructor, weight machines, bicycles, sauna, steam rm. Massage. Game rm. Rec rm. Casino. Some bathrm phones. Some private patios. Cr cds: A, C, D, DS, JCB, MC, V. D 🖎 🛏 🏄 🏄 🐾 SC

Stateline

Hotel

★ ★ ★ ★ **HARRAH'S HOTEL CASINO.** US 50, on US 50, downtown. 702/588-6611; FAX 702/586-6607; res: 800/648-3773. Web harrahstahoe.com. Top-name entertainment and extensive gaming opportunities are available at this property. The guest rooms offer lake and mountain views. 532 rms, 18 story. Mid-June-mid-Sept: S, D $149-$209; each addl $20; suites $199-$950; under 15 free; ski plans; higher rates wkends, hols; lower rates rest of yr. Crib free. Pet accepted. TV; cable, VCR avail. Indoor pool; whirlpool, poolside serv. 7 restaurants open 24 hrs. Bars; theater-restaurant; entertainment. Ck-out noon. Convention facilities. Business servs avail. Concierge. Shopping arcade. Barber, beauty shop. Free covered valet parking. Exercise equipt; weights, bicycles, sauna, steam rm. Massage. Game rm. Casino. Wedding chapel. Youth center. Each rm has 2 bathrms with phone & TV; microwaves avail. Butler serv in suites. Cr cds: A, C, D, DS, ER, JCB, MC, V. D 🖎 🛏 🏄 🏄 🐾 SC

Tonopah

Motels

★ **JIM BUTLER.** 100 S Main St (88049). 702/482-3577; FAX 702/482-5240; res: 800/635-9455. 24 rms, 2 story. S, D $29.50-$35.50. Crib $5. Pet accepted, some restrictions. TV; cable (premium). Restaurant adj 24 hrs. Ck-out 11 am. Cr cds: A, D, DS, MC, V. 🖎 🏄 SC

✔ ★ **SILVER QUEEN.** 255 S Main (US 95). 702/482-6291; FAX 702/482-3190. 85 rms, 1-2 story. No elvtr. S, D $28; kit. units $38. Crib $4. Pet accepted. TV; cable (premium), VCR avail (movies). Pool. Restaurant adj 6 am-10 pm. Bar 11 am-midnight. Ck-out 11 am. Cr cds: A, C, D, DS, MC, V. 🖎 🛏 🐾 SC

Winnemucca

Motels

★ ★ **BEST WESTERN GOLD COUNTRY INN.** 921 W Winnemucca Blvd. 702/623-6999; FAX 702/623-9190. 71 rms, 2 story. June- Labor Day: S, D $65-$75; each addl $10; under 12 free; lower rates rest of yr. Crib $5. Pet accepted, some restrictions. TV; cable (premium). Heated pool. Complimentary coffee in lobby. Restaurant adj open 24 hrs. Ck-out noon. Business servs avail. In-rm modem link. Airport transportation. Cr cds: A, C, D, DS, ER, MC, V. [D] 🐾 ⌘ 🍳 🏋 [SC]

★ **DAYS INN.** *511 W Winnemucca Blvd. 702/623-3661; FAX 702/623-4234.* 50 rms, 2 story. June-Labor Day: S $60; D $65; each addl $5; lower rates rest of yr. Crib $5. Pet accepted. TV; cable (premium). Heated pool. Coffee in lobby. Restaurant nearby. Ck-out noon. Cr cds: A, C, D, DS, MC, V. 🐾 ⌘ 🍳 🏋 [SC]

✔ ★ **LA VILLA.** *390 Lay St. 702/623-2334; FAX 702/623-0158.* 37 rms, 2 story. May-Labor Day: S $45; D $50-$65; each addl $5; suites $70; lower rates rest of yr. Pet accepted. TV; cable (premium). Continental bkfst in lobby. Restaurant nearby. Ck-out 11 am. Coin lndry. Cr cds: A, DS, MC, V. [D] 🐾 🍳 🏋 [SC]

★ ★ **RED LION INN & CASINO.** *741 W Winnemucca Blvd. 702/623-2565; FAX 702/623-2527.* 107 units, 2 story. June-Oct: S, D $79-$89; each addl $10; suites $99-$150; under 12 free; lower rates rest of yr. Crib $5. Pet accepted, some restrictions; $50 deposit. TV; cable (premium), VCR avail. Heated pool. Restaurant open 24 hrs. Bar. Ck-out noon. Business servs avail. Airport transportation. Game rm. Some balconies. Casino. Cr cds: A, C, D, DS, MC, V. [D] 🐾 ⌘ 🍳 🏋 [SC]

★ **VAL-U INN.** *125 E Winnemucca Blvd. 702/623-5248; FAX 702/623-4722; res: 800/443-7777.* 80 rms, 3 story. No elvtr. Mid-May-Sept: S $45-$50; D $48-$57; each addl $5; lower rates rest of yr. Crib $4. Pet accepted; $5. TV; cable (premium), VCR avail. Heated pool; sauna, steam rm. Continental bkfst in lobby. Restaurant nearby. Ck-out noon. Business servs avail. Cr cds: A, C, D, DS, MC, V. 🐾 ⌘ 🍳 🏋 [SC]

New Hampshire

Concord (See also Manchester)

Motel

✔★ **BRICK TOWER MOTOR INN.** *414 S Main St. 603/224-9565; FAX 603/224-6027.* 51 rms. May-Oct: S $52; D $59-$64; each addl $5; under 12 free; higher rates special events; lower rates rest of yr. Crib free. Pet accepted. TV; cable. Pool. Complimentary continental bkfst. Ck-out 11 am. Some in-rm saunas. Cr cds: A, DS, MC, V.

Motor Hotel

★★ **COMFORT INN.** *71 Hall St. 603/226-4100; FAX 603/228-2106.* 100 rms, 3 story. S, D $72-$130; each addl $10; suites $175; under 18 free. Crib free. Pet accepted. TV; cable. Indoor pool; whirlpool. Sauna. Complimentary continental bkfst. Restaurant nearby. Ck-out noon. Meeting rms. Business servs avail. In-rm modem link. Valet serv. Game rm. Some bathrm phones, in-rm whirlpools, refrigerators. Cr cds: A, C, D, DS, ER, JCB, MC, V.

Franconia (See also Littleton)

Inns

✔★ **HILLTOP.** *(Main St, Sugar Hill 03585) 2¼ mi W on NH 117. 603/823-5695; FAX 603/823-5518; res: 800/770-5695.* 6 rms, 2 story, 1 suite. No A/C. No rm phones. S $60-$70; D $70-$95; each addl $15-$25; suite $90-$130; wkly rates; higher rates fall foliage (2-day min). Pet accepted; $10/day. TV in sitting rm; cable. Complimentary full bkfst, afternoon tea. Rm serv. Ck-out 11 am, ck-in 2-6 pm. Downhill ski 8 mi; x-country ski on site. Built 1895; antiques, quilts. Cr cds: DS, MC, V.

★ **HORSE & HOUND.** *205 Wells Rd. 603/823-5501; res: 800/450-5501.* 10 rms, 2 share bath, 2 story. No A/C. S $67.65; D $79.95; under 6 free; ski plans; 2-day min hols. Closed Apr. Crib $10. Pet accepted; $8.50. TV; VCR in pub rm. Complimentary full bkfst. Restaurant 6-9 pm. Ck-out 11 am, ck-in 3 pm. Downhill ski 2 mi; x-country ski on site. Secluded country inn near Cannon Mt. Cr cds: A, C, D, DS, MC, V.

Gorham

Motels

✔★ **GORHAM MOTOR INN.** *324 Main St. 603/466-3381; res: 800/445-0913.* 39 rms. S $38-$60; D $42-$76; each addl $6; higher rates fall foliage. Crib free. Pet accepted, some restrictions; $6. TV; cable (premium). Heated pool. Restaurant nearby. Bar 11:30 am-midnight. Ck-out 11 am. Downhill/x-country ski 8 mi. Some refrigerators. Cr cds: A, DS, MC, V.

★★ **ROYALTY INN.** *130 Main St. 603/466-3312; FAX 603/466-5802; res: 800/437-3529.* 90 rms, 1-2 story. July-Labor Day, mid-Sept-Oct: S, D $56-$78; each addl $6; kit. units $82; lower rates rest of yr. Crib $5. Pet accepted. TV; cable. VCR avail. 2 pools; 1 indoor. Restaurant 6-10:30 am, 5-9 pm. Bar 5-11 pm; Fri, Sat to 1 am. Ck-out 11 am. Coin lndry. Meeting rm. Business servs avail. Downhill ski 9 mi; x-country ski 7 mi. Exercise equipt; weight machines, stair machine. Health club privileges. Game rm. Some refrigerators. Cr cds: A, C, D, DS, MC, V.

✔★★★ **TOWN & COUNTRY MOTOR INN.** *½ mi E on US 2. 603/466-3315; FAX 603/466-3315, ext. 207; res: 800/325-4386 (NH).* 160 rms, 2 story. June-Oct: S $48-$64; D $56-$70; each addl $6; suites $70-$82; golf & ski plans; lower rates rest of yr. Crib $6. Pet accepted. TV; cable, VCR avail. Indoor/outdoor pool; whirlpool. Restaurant 6-10:30 am, 5:30-10 pm. Bar 4:00 pm-12:30 am; entertainment Wed-Sat. Ck-out 11 am. Meeting rms. Business servs avail. Sundries. Golf privileges, putting green. Downhill/x-country ski 6 mi. Snowmobile trails. Exercise equipt; weights, bicycles, sauna. Game rm. Refrigerators avail. Some in-rm whirlpools. Private patios, balconies. Cr cds: A, C, D, DS, MC, V.

Hampton Beach *(See also Portsmouth)*

Motel

★ ★ ★ **HAMPTON FALLS MOTOR INN.** *(11 Lafayette Rd (US 1), Hampton Falls 03844) W on NH 101, S on US 1. 603/926-9545; FAX 603/926-4155; res: 800/356-1729.* 47 rms, 3 story. Mid-May-mid-Oct: S, D $88-$108; each addl $10; suites $128; under 12 free; wkly, wkend, hol rates (2-day min wkends, hols); lower rates rest of yr. Crib free. Pet accepted, some restrictions; $25 refundable. TV; cable, VCR avail. Indoor pool; whirlpool. Complimentary coffee in lobby. Restaurant 5:30 am-1:30 pm. Ck-out 11 am. Meeting rms. Business servs avail. Bellhops. Valet serv. Sundries. Health club privileges. Game rm. Refrigerators. Balconies. Picnic tables. Cr cds: A, C, D, DS, MC, V. [D] [icons]

Hanover

Motels

(Rates may be higher during Dartmouth events, foliage season)

✔ ★ **LOCH LYME LODGE.** *(70 Orford Rd, Lyme 03768) 11 mi N on NH 10. 603/795-2141; res: 800/423-2141.* Web www.dartbook.com. 24 cottages (12 kits.), 4 rms in 2-story inn (share bath). No A/C. No rm phones. Inn rms S, D $40-$70; cottages $420-$700/wk; under 4 free; MAP avail; wkly rates. Cottages closed Sept-May. Crib $6. Pet accepted. Playground. Complimentary full bkfst for rms without kits. Ck-out 10 am. Tennis privileges. Downhill ski 4 mi; x-country ski 10 mi. Lawn games. Some refrigerators. Fireplaces. On Post Pond; swimming beach. Picnic tables, grills. No cr cds accepted. [icons]

Motor Hotel

★ ★ **HANOVER INN AT DARTMOUTH COLLEGE.** *PO Box 151, at Main & Wheelock Sts. 603/643-4300; FAX 603/646-3744; res: 800/443-7024 (exc NH).* E-mail hartson@dartmouth.edu; web www.dart mouth.edu/inn. 92 rms, 5 story, 22 suites. S, D $207-$217; suites $217-$287; ski, golf plans. Crib free. Pet accepted. Covered parking $5; free valet parking. TV; cable, VCR avail. Indoor pool privileges; sauna. Restaurant 7 am-10 pm. Rm serv. Bar 11:30 am-midnight. Ck-out noon. Meeting rms. Business servs avail. Free airport transportation. Bellhops. Valet serv. Gift shop. Lighted tennis privileges, pro. 18-hole golf privileges, greens fee $33, pro, putting green, driving range. Downhill ski 7 mi. Exercise equipt; weight machines, bicycles. Health club privileges. Bathrm phones. Georgian-style brick structure owned by college; used as guest house since 1780. Cr cds: A, D, DS, MC, V. [icons]

Jackson *(See also North Conway)*

Inn

★ ★ **DANA PLACE.** *5 mi N on NH 16 in Pinkham Notch. 603/383-6822; FAX 603/383-6022; res: 800/537-9276.* 35 rms, 4 share baths, 3 story. S, D $75-$135; each addl $25; under 18 free; MAP avail; tennis, ski packages. Crib avail. Pet accepted, some restrictions. TV rm; VCR. Indoor pool; whirlpool. Complimentary bkfst; afternoon refreshments. Restaurant hrs vary. Bar 4-11 pm. Ck-out 11 am, ck-in 3 pm. Business servs avail. Tennis. Downhill ski 5 mi; x-country ski on site. Picnic tables. Historic farm house (1890) situated on 300 wooded acres, bordered by White Mtn National Forest & Ellis River. Cr cds: A, C, D, DS, MC, V. [icons]

Keene

Motel

★ ★ **BEST WESTERN SOVEREIGN HOTEL.** *401 Winchester St. 603/357-3038; FAX 603/357-4776.* 131 rms, 2 story. S, D $55-$115; each addl $10; studio rms $90; under 18 free. Crib free. Pet accepted. TV; cable. Indoor pool. Complimentary full bkfst. Coffee in rms. Restaurant 6:30 am-10 pm. Bar 3 pm-12:30 am; entertainment. Ck-out noon. Meeting rms. Business servs avail. In-rm modem link. Game rm. Balconies. Picnic tables. Cr cds: A, C, D, DS, ER, JCB, MC, V. [icons]

Littleton *(See also Franconia)*

Motel

✔ ★ ★ **EASTGATE MOTOR INN.** *Cottage St, I-93 exit 41. 603/444-3971.* 55 rms. S $41.70; D $47.70; each addl $5; under 6 free. Crib $5. Pet accepted. TV; cable (premium).

Heated pool; wading pool. Playground. Complimentary continental bkfst. Restaurant 5:30-9 pm; Fri, Sat to 10 pm. Bar. Ck-out 11 am. Meeting rms. Business servs avail. Downhill ski 7 mi; x-country ski 6 mi. Lawn games. Cr cds: A, C, D, DS, MC, V.

Manchester (See also Concord, Nashua)

Motor Hotels

★ ★ **COMFORT INN & CONFERENCE CENTER.** *298 Queen City Ave (03102), I-293 exit 4. 603/668-2600.* 100 rms, 5 story. S $62.90-$84.90; D $68.90-$89.90; each addl $6; suites $225-$270; under 18 free; higher rates some wkends. Crib free. Pet accepted. TV; cable (premium). Indoor pool. Complimentary continental bkfst. Ck-out noon. Coin lndry. Meeting rms. Business servs avail. In-rm modem link. Bellhops. Free airport, bus depot transportation. Exercise equipt; weights, bicycles, sauna. Some refrigerators. Cr cds: A, C, D, DS, JCB, MC, V.

✓ ★ **ECONO LODGE.** *75 W Hancock St (03102), I-293 exit 4. 603/624-0111; FAX 603/623-0268.* 120 rms, 5 story. S $40; D $45; each addl $5; under 18 free; wkly, monthly rates. Crib free. Pet accepted. TV; cable. Complimentary coffee in lobby. Restaurant opp 6:30 am-9 pm. Ck-out 11 am. Coin lndry. Business servs avail. Some refrigerators. Cr cds: A, C, D, DS, MC, V.

★ ★ **FOUR POINTS BY SHERATON.** *55 John Devine Dr (03103), I-293 exit 1. 603/668-6110; FAX 603/668-0408.* 124 rms, 4 story. S $66.95-$85; D $70.95-$94.95; each addl $6; under 18 free; higher rates fall foliage season. Crib free. Pet accepted. TV; cable (premium). Indoor pool; whirlpool. Restaurant 6-10 am, 5-10 pm. Rm serv. Bar. Ck-out noon. Meeting rms. Business servs avail. Valet serv. Sundries. Airport transportation. Health club privileges. Mall of New Hampshire opp. Refrigerator avail. Cr cds: A, C, D, DS, ER, JCB, MC, V.

Meredith (See also Plymouth)

Motel

✓ ★ **MEADOWS LAKESIDE.** *(Box 204, NH 25, Center Harbor 03226) 5 mi NE on NH 25. 603/253-4347.* 39 rms, 4 story. No rm phones. June-Sept: S $69-$110; D $79-$110; each addl $10; kit. units $110; under 4 free; wkly rates; lower rates May, Oct. Closed rest of yr. Crib $10. Pet accepted; $7/day. TV; VCR avail (movies). Complimentary coffee in lobby. Restaurant nearby. Ck-out 11 am. Private patios, balconies. Picnic tables. On lake; beach, dockage. Cr cds: A, DS, MC, V.

Nashua (See also Manchester, Salem)

Motels

★ ★ **HOLIDAY INN.** *9 Northeastern Blvd (03062), at US 3 exit 4. 603/888-1551; FAX 603/888-7193.* 215 rms, 3-4 story, 34 suites. May-Nov: S, D $89-$99; each addl $4; suites $99-$129; under 19 free; package plans; lower rates rest of yr. Crib free. Pet accepted. TV; cable (premium), VCR avail. Heated pool. Restaurant 6:30 am-10 pm. Rm serv. Bar 11:30-12:30 am; entertainment. Ck-out noon. Coin lndry. Meeting rms. Business servs avail. Valet serv. Exercise equipt; weights, treadmill. Some refrigerators. Private patios, balconies. Cr cds: A, C, D, DS, ER, JCB, MC, V.

✓ ★ **RED ROOF INN.** *77 Spit Brook Rd (03060), at US 3 exit 1. 603/888-1893; FAX 603/888-5889.* 115 rms, 3 story. S $35.99-$64.99; D $39.99-$69.99; under 19 free. Crib free. Pet accepted. TV; cable (premium), VCR avail. Complimentary coffee in lobby. Ck-out noon. Business servs avail. Picnic table. Cr cds: A, C, D, DS, MC, V.

★ ★ **RESIDENCE INN BY MARRIOTT.** *(246 Daniel Webster Hwy, Merrimack 03054) 5 mi N on US 3. 603/424-8100; FAX 603/424-3128.* 96 kit. suites, 2 story. Kit. suites $105-$155. Crib free. Pet accepted; $5/day. TV; cable (premium), VCR avail (movies). Pool; whirlpool. Complimentary continental bkfst. Ck-out noon. Coin lndry. Meeting rms. Business servs avail. In-rm modem link. Valet serv. Health club privileges. Lawn games. Many fireplaces. Grills. Cr cds: A, C, D, DS, MC, V.

New London

Motel

✓ ★ **LAMPLIGHTER MOTOR INN.** *6 Newport Rd. 603/526-6484.* 14 rms, 2 story. S, D $55-$65; kit. units $65-$70; each addl $5. Pet accepted, some restrictions. TV; cable,

VCR avail. Complimentary continental bkfst. Restaurant nearby. Ck-out 11 am. Business servs avail. Downhill/x-country ski 10 mi. Refrigerators avail. Cr cds: A, C, D, DS, MC, V.

North Conway (See also Jackson)

Motel

✔ ★ **SWISS CHALETS VILLAGE INN.** (NH 16A, Intervale 03845) 3 mi N on NH 16A. 603/356-2232; res: 800/831-2727. 38 rms, 1-3 story. No elvtr. S $69-$89; D $79-$129; each addl $10; suites $109-$139; under 12 free; ski plans; higher rates fall foliage. Crib free. Pet accepted; $10/day. TV; cable. Heated pool. Playground. Complimentary coffee in lobby. Ck-out 11 am. Downhill ski 4 mi; x-country ski on site. Game rm. Refrigerators. Some fireplaces, in-rm whirlpools. Some balconies. Picnic tables. Rms in Swiss chalet-style buildings; on 12 acres. Cr cds: A, DS, MC, V.

Plymouth (See also Meredith)

Motel

★ **SUSSE CHALET.** US 3, I-93 exit 26. 603/536-2330; FAX 603/536-2686. 38 rms, 2 story. S $49.95; D $59.95; each addl $5; suite $63; family rates; ski, golf, bicycle plans. Crib free. Pet accepted. TV; cable, VCR avail. Pool. Complimentary continental bkfst. Restaurant opp 6 am-11 pm. Ck-out 11 am. Coin lndry. Meeting rm. Business servs avail. In-rm modem link. Downhill/x-country ski 15 mi. Some refrigerators. Picnic tables. Cr cds: A, D, DS, MC, V.

Portsmouth (See also Hampton Beach)

Motel

✔ ★ ★ **PORT MOTOR INN.** 505 US 1 Bypass, at Portsmouth Circle, I-95 exit 5. 603/436-4378; FAX 603/436-4378, ext. 200; res: 800/282-7678. 56 rms, 1-2 story, 20 studios. July-early Sept: S $62.95-$99.95; D $68.95-$99.95; each addl $6; studios $79.95-$119.95; under 13 free; lower rates rest of yr. Crib free. Pet accepted. TV; cable (premium). Pool. Complimentary continental bkfst. Ck-out 11 am. Refrigerator in studios. Picnic tables. Cr cds: A, C, D, DS, MC, V.

Salem

Hotel

★ ★ **HOLIDAY INN.** 1 Keewaydin Dr. 603/893-5511; FAX 603/894-6728. 83 rms, 6 story. May-Oct: S, D $89-$95; lower rates rest of yr. Pet accepted. TV; cable (premium). Pool; poolside serv. Complimentary continental bkfst. Complimentary coffee in rms. Restaurant 6:30 am-10 pm. Ck-out 11 am. No bellhops. Meeting rms. Business servs avail. In-rm modem link. Health club privileges. Refrigerator avail. Cr cds: A, C, D, DS, ER, JCB, MC, V.

Wolfeboro

Motel

★ ★ **LAKE.** 280 S Main St (US 28), 1 mi S on NH 28, 3/4 mi S of jct NH 109. 603/569-1100; FAX 603/569-1620. 30 rms, 5 kit. units. July-Labor Day: S, D $87-$96; each addl $6; kit. units for 2, $610/wk; each addl $9; lower rates mid-May-June & after Labor Day-mid-Oct. Closed rest of yr. Pet accepted, some restrictions. TV; cable. Playground. Coffee in lobby. Restaurant adj 7:30 am-10 pm in summer. Ck-out 11 am. Business servs avail. Sundries. Tennis. Lawn games. On Crescent Lake; private beach, dockage. Cr cds: DS, MC, V.

New Jersey

Bernardsville

Hotel

★ ★ ★ **SOMERSET HILLS.** *(200 Liberty Corner Rd, Warren 07059) SW on I-287 to I-78E, exit 33 (Martinsville-Bernardsvile), left at top of ramp, right at 3rd light. 908/647-6700; FAX 908/647-8053; res: 800/688-0700.* E-mail shhotel@aol.com; web www.shh.com. 111 units, 4 story. S $99-$165; D $99-$170; each addl $10; suites $250-$310; kits. $145-$185. Crib free. Pet accepted. TV; cable (premium). Pool; poolside serv. Restaurant 6:30 am-11 pm. Bar 11:30-1 am. Ck-out noon. Meeting rms. Business servs avail. In-rm modem link. Concierge. Gift shop. Tennis privileges. 18-hole golf privileges, pro, putting green, driving range. Exercise equipt; weight machine, bicycles. Microwaves avail. Nestled in the Watchung Mountains near the crossroads of historical Liberty Corner. Cr cds: A, C, D, MC, V. D ✋ 🏋 🏃 ≈ 🍴 ⊠ 🐾 SC

Bordentown (See also Trenton)

Motel

★ **DAYS INN.** *1073 US 206, just N of NJ Tpke exit 7. 609/298-6100; FAX 609/298-7509.* 131 rms, 2 story. S, D $85-$95; each addl $10; under 12 free; lower rates winter months. Crib free. Pet accepted. TV; cable. Pool; lifeguard. Restaurant 6:30-10 am, 5-9 pm. Rm serv. Bar 5 pm-1:30 am; entertainment Fri, Sat. Ck-out 11 am. Coin lndry. Meeting rms. Business servs avail. Sundries. Cr cds: A, C, D, DS, JCB, MC, V.

D ✋ ≈ ⊠ 🐾 SC

Cape May

Motor Hotel

★ ★ **MARQUIS DE LAFAYETTE.** *501 Beach Dr. 609/884-3500; FAX 609/884-0669; res: 800/257-0432.* 73 units, 6 story, 43 kits. July-Labor Day: S, D $188-$260; each addl $18; kit. units $198-$274; 2 children under 8 free; package plans; wknd rates; varied lower rates rest of yr. Crib avail. Pet accepted, some restrictions; $20/day. TV. Pool; sauna, poolside serv. Complimentary full bkfst. Restaurant 5:30-10 pm. Bar; entertainment. Ck-out 1 pm. Coin lndry. Meeting rms. Business servs avail. Bellhops. Valet serv. Golf privileges. Balconies. On ocean. Cr cds: A, C, D, DS, MC, V. ✋ 🏋 ≈ ⊠ 🐾 SC

Cherry Hill

Motel

★ ★ **HAMPTON INN.** *(121 Laurel Oak Rd, Voorhees 08043) I-295, exit 32, 2 mi E NJ 561. 609/346-4500; FAX 609/346-2402.* 122 rms, 50 with shower only, 4 story. S, D $88-$95; under 18 free. Crib avail. Pet accepted. TV; cable (premium), VCR avail. Pool. Complimentary continental bkfst. Restaurant adj 11 am-11 pm. Ck-out noon. Business servs avail. In-rm modem link. Health club privileges. Microwaves avail. Cr cds: A, D, DS, MC, V.

D ✋ ≈ ⊠ 🐾

Motor Hotel

★ ★ **HOLIDAY INN.** *NJ 70 & Sayer Ave (08002), 3 mi W of I-295, 7 mi W of NJ Tpke exit 4, opp Garden State Racetrack. 609/663-5300; FAX 609/662-2913.* 186 rms, 6 story. S, D $89-$105; each addl $8; under 19 free; wknd rates. Crib free. Pet accepted. TV; cable (premium), VCR avail. 2 pools, 1 indoor; wading pool. Restaurant 11 am-10 pm. Rm serv. Bar 11 am-11 pm. Ck-out noon. Coin lndry. Meeting rms. Business servs avail. In-rm modem link. Valet serv. Exercise equipt; weights, bicycles, sauna. Microwaves avail. Cr cds: A, C, D, DS, ER, JCB, MC, V. D ✋ ≈ 🍴 ⊠ 🐾 SC

Hotel

★ ★ ★ **RADISSON AT MOUNT LAUREL.** *(NJ 73 & I-295, Mount Laurel 08054) 1/2 mi N of NJ Tpke exit 4 on NJ 73N. 609/234-7300; FAX 609/866-9401.* Web www.radisson.com. 283 rms, 10 story. S, D $99-$109; suites $250-$350; under 17 free. Crib free. Pet accepted. TV; cable (premium). Pool; poolside serv, lifeguard. Restaurant 6:30 am-10 pm; Sat, Sun from 7 am. Bar. Ck-out 11 am. Coin lndry. Convention facilities. Business servs avail. In-rm modem link. Gift shop. Lighted tennis. Golf privileges. Exercise equipt; bicycles, treadmill.

Health club privileges. Game rm. Some in-rm whirlpools, refrigerators; microwaves avail. Picnic tables. Some private patios, balconies. Luxury level. Cr cds: A, C, D, DS, JCB, MC, V. [D] [icons]

Clifton

Motel

★ ★ **HOWARD JOHNSON.** *680 NJ 3 W (07014), NJ Tpke exit 16W.* 973/471-3800; *FAX* 973/471-2125. E-mail www.hojo.com. 116 rms, 4 story. S $84-$114; D $94-$124; each addl $10; under 18 free; wkend rates. Crib free. Pet accepted, some restrictions. TV; cable (premium). Pool; lifeguard. Complimentary continental bkfst. Restaurant 7 am-midnight. Bar 4 pm-2 am. Ck-out noon. Meeting rm. Business servs avail. In-rm modem link. Sundries. Microwaves avail. Private patios, balconies. Cr cds: A, C, D, DS, ER, JCB, MC, V.

[D] [icons] [SC]

Eatontown

Motels

✔ ★ **RED ROOF INN.** *(11 Centre Plaza, Tinton Falls) Off Garden State Pkwy exit 105, turn right on Hope Rd.* 732/389-4646; *FAX* 732/389-4509. 119 rms, 3 story. May-Labor Day: S, D $75-$79; each addl $7; under 18 free; lower rates rest of yr. Crib free. Pet accepted, some restrictions. TV; cable (premium). Restaurant nearby. Ck-out noon. In-rm modem link. Cr cds: A, C, D, DS, MC, V. [D] [icons] [SC]

★ ★ **RESIDENCE INN BY MARRIOTT.** *(90 Park Rd, Tinton Falls) off Garden State Pkwy exit 105, on Hope Rd, then 1st left on Park Rd.* 732/389-8100; *FAX* 732/389-1573. 96 kit. suites. S, D $125-$152. Crib free. Pet accepted; $150. TV; cable (premium), VCR avail. Pool; whirlpool. Complimentary continental bkfst. Restaurant nearby. Ck-out noon. Coin lndry. Meeting rms. Business servs avail. In-rm modem link. Valet serv. Health club privileges. Microwaves. Balconies. Picnic tables, grills. Cr cds: A, C, D, DS, JCB, MC, V.

[D] [icons] [SC]

Edison

Hotel

★ ★ ★ **CROWNE PLAZA.** *125 Raritan Center Pkwy (08837).* 732/225-8300. 274 rms, 12 story. S, D $125-$140; suites $275; under 12 free; wkend rates. Crib free. Pet accepted. TV; cable (premium), VCR avail. Indoor pool; whirlpool, poolside serv. Complimentary coffee in rms. Restaurant 6 am-2 pm, 5-10 pm. Bar. Ck-out noon. Coin lndry. Convention facilities. Business servs avail. In-rm modem link. Concierge. Gift shop. Exercise equipt; weights, treadmill, sauna. Game rm. Cr cds: A, C, D, DS, ER, MC, V.

[D] [icons] [SC]

Fort Lee *(See also Hackensack)*

Hotel

★ ★ ★ **RADISSON.** *(401 S Van Brunt St, Englewood 07631) NJ 4W exit Van Brunt St.* 201/871-2020; *FAX* 201/871-7116. 192 rms, 9 story. Late Nov-mid Dec: S, D $145-$165; suites $185-$275; wkend rates; lower rates rest of yr. Crib free. Pet accepted, some restrictions; $25. TV; cable (premium), VCR avail. Complimentary coffee in rms. Restaurant 6:30 am-10 pm. Bar 11:30-1 am. Ck-out noon. Meeting rms. Business servs avail. Concierge. Coin lndry. Exercise equipt; treadmill, stair machine. Indoor pool. Some bathrm phones. Refrigerators, microwaves avail. Luxury level. Cr cds: A, C, D, DS, ER, JCB, MC, V. [D] [icons] [SC]

Freehold *(See also Eatontown, Hightstown, Lakewood)*

Motor Hotel

★ ★ **FREEHOLD GARDENS.** *NJ 537 & Gibson Place, 1 mi W on NJ 537.* 732/780-3870; *FAX* 732/780-8725. 114 rms, 5 story. S, D $69-$90; each addl $10; under 18 free; higher rates late May-early Sept. Crib free. Pet accepted, some restrictions; $100 deposit. TV; cable. Pool. Complimentary continental bkfst. Restaurant 5-11 pm. Rm serv. Entertainment. Ck-out noon. Meeting rms. Business servs avail. Health club privileges. Refrigerators avail. Cr cds: A, C, D, MC, V. [D] [icons] [SC]

Gibbstown

Motel

✔★★ **DUTCH INN.** *Harmony Rd, just off I-295 at exit 17. 609/423-6600; FAX 609/423-0757.* 124 rms, 2 story. S, D $40-$54; each addl $5; under 12 free. Crib $6. Pet accepted. TV. Pool; lifeguard. Restaurant open 24 hrs; dining rm 11:30 am-2 pm, 4:30-9:30 pm; wkend hrs vary. Bar 11-2 am; closed Sun; entertainment. Ck-out noon. Meeting rms. Business servs avail. Cr cds: A, C, D, DS, MC, V.

Hackensack *(See also Fort Lee)*

Hotel

★★★ **CROWN PLAZA HASBROUCK HEIGHTS.** *(650 Terrace Ave, Hasbrouck Heights 07604) At jct NJ 17N, I-80. 201/288-6100; FAX 201/288-4717.* E-mail jpear@ cybernex.net; web www.crownplaza.com. 355 rms, 12 story. S, D $159-$199; each addl $20; suites $220-$500; under 17 free; wkend rates. Crib free. Pet accepted. TV; cable (premium), VCR avail. Heated pool; poolside serv. Restaurant 6:30 am-11 pm; wkends from 7 am. Bars 12:30 pm-1:30 am, Sat to 2:30 am. Ck-out 1 pm. Convention facilities. Business center. In-rm modem link. Gift shop. Exercise equipt; weights, bicycles, sauna. Luxury level. Cr cds: A, C, D, DS, ER, MC, V.

Hightstown

Motel

★★ **TOWN HOUSE.** *NJ Tpke exit 8, on NJ 33. 609/448-2400; FAX 609/443-0395; res: 800/922-0622.* 104 rms, 1-2 story. S $55-$125; D $58-$125; each addl $10; suites, studio rms $95-$150; under 12 free; package plans. Crib free. Pet accepted. TV; VCR avail (movies $2). Pool; wading pool, lifeguard. Complimentary continental bkfst. Restaurant 10 am-midnight. Bar 11-1 am; entertainment. Ck-out 1 pm. Meeting rms. In-rm modem link. Sundries. Refrigerators; whirlpool in some suites. Cr cds: A, C, D, DS, MC, V.

Motor Hotel

★★ **RAMADA INN.** *(399 Monmouth St, East Windsor) NJ Turnpike, exit 8. 609/448-7000.* 200 rms, 4 story. Mid-June-Aug: S $79-$109; D $85-$115; each addl $10; suite $139-$199; under 12 free; lower rates rest of yr. Crib free. Pet accepted. TV; cable (premium). Pool; sauna. Restaurant opp 7:30 am-9 pm. Bar 5 pm-1 am. Ck-out noon. Meeting rms. Business servs avai. Coin lndry. Exercise equipt; stair machine, weight machine. Cr cds: A, C, D, DS, MC, V.

Lake Hopatcong

Motor Hotel

★★★ **FOUR POINTS BY SHERATON.** *(15 Howard Blvd, Mount Arlington 07856) I-80 exit 30. 973/770-2000; FAX 973/770-1287.* Web www.ITTsheraton.com. 124 rms, 5 story. S, D $120-$130; each addl $10; suites $140-$160; under 18 free; wkend rates. Crib free. Pet accepted. TV; cable (premium), VCR avail. Indoor pool. Coffee in rms. Restaurant 6:30 am-10 pm. Rm serv. Bar 11-1 am; entertainment Wed-Sat. Ck-out noon. Meeting rms. Business servs avail. Valet serv. Exercise equipt; weight machine, bicycles. Refrigerators; microwaves avail. Cr cds: A, C, D, DS, MC, V.

Lakewood *(See also Toms River)*

Motel

★★ **BEST WESTERN LEISURE INN.** *1600 NJ 70, Garden State Pkwy exit 88. 908/367-0900; FAX 908/370-4928.* 105 rms. Memorial Day-Sept: S, D $70-$104; each addl $10; lower rates rest of yr. Crib free. Pet accepted. TV; cable (premium), VCR (movies $3.50). Pool. Complimentary continental bkfst. Restaurant 7 am-10 pm. Bar 6-11 pm. Ck-out 11 am. Coin lndry. Meeting rm. Business servs avail. In-rm modem link. Refrigerators avail. Cr cds: A, C, D, DS, MC, V.

Long Beach Island

Motel

★ ★ ★ **ENGLESIDE INN.** *(30 Engleside Ave, Beach Haven 08008) 7 mi S of NJ 72. 609/492-1251; FAX 609/492-9175; res: 800/762-2214.* 72 units, 3 story, 37 kits. No elvtr. July-Labor Day: S, D $135-$190; each addl $12; suites $195-$254; kit. units for 2-4, $155-$200; lower rates rest of yr. Crib avail. Pet accepted, some restrictions. TV; cable, VCR (movies $2). Pool; poolside serv (in season), lifeguard. Restaurant 8 am-noon, 5-9 pm. Bar. Ck-out 11 am. Meeting rms. Business servs avail. Sundries. Refrigerators. Private patios, balconies. On beach. Cr cds: A, C, D, DS, MC, V.

Matawan *(See also Freehold)*

Motel

↙ ★ ★ **WELLESLEY INN.** *(3215 NJ 35, Hazlet 07730) 1 mi S of Garden State Pkwy, exit 117, S on NJ 35. 732/888-2800; FAX 732/888-2902.* 89 rms, 3 story. S $63-$109; D $65-$119; each addl $5; under 18 free; higher rates summer wkends. Crib free. Pet accepted, some restrictions; $5. TV; cable (premium). Complimentary continental bkfst. Restaurant nearby. Ck-out 11 am. Business servs avail. Health club privileges. Refrigerators, microwaves avail. Cr cds: A, D, DS, JCB, MC, V.

Montvale

Hotel

★ ★ ★ **MARRIOTT-PARK RIDGE.** *(300 Brae Blvd, Park Ridge 07656) Garden State Pkwy exit 172N (Grand Ave), then first 3 right turns. 201/307-0800; FAX 201/307-0859.* Web www.marriott.com. 289 units, 4 story. S, D $99-$165; suites $275; under 18 free; wkly, wkend rates. Crib avail. Pet accepted, some restrictions. TV; cable (premium), VCR avail. Indoor/outdoor pool; whirlpool, poolside serv. Restaurant 6:30 am-10 pm. Bars 4:30 pm-2 am; pianist. Ck-out noon. Meeting rms. Business center. In-rm modem link. Concierge. Gift shop. Exercise equipt; weights, bicycles, sauna. Refrigerators avail. Many private patios, balconies. Extensive grounds; small lake. Luxury level. Cr cds: A, C, D, DS, JCB, MC, V.

Mount Holly

Motel

★ ★ **HOWARD JOHNSON.** *NJ 541, on NJ 541 at NJ Tpke exit 5. 609/267-6550; FAX 609/267-2575.* 90 rms, 2 story. S $58-$90; D $60-$90; each addl $7; under 12 free. Crib free. Pet accepted. TV; cable (premium), VCR avail. Pool; lifeguard, sauna. Playground. Restaurant 6 am-midnight. Bar 5-11 pm. Ck-out noon. Meeting rms. Business center. Cr cds: A, C, D, DS, ER, MC, V.

Newark Intl Airport Area

Hotel

★ ★ **HOLIDAY INN.** *(1000 Spring St, Elizabeth 07201) 3 mi N on NJ Tpke, exit 13-A. 908/355-1700; FAX 908/355-1741.* 392 rms, 10 story. S $121-$145; D $131-$155; each addl $13; suites $175-$350; under 18 free; wkend, hol rates. Pet accepted, some restrictions. TV; cable (premium), VCR avail (movies). Complimentary coffee in lobby. Restaurant 6:30 am-10:30 pm. Bar; entertainment Tues, Fri, Sat. Ck-out noon. Convention facilities. Business servs avail. In-rm modem link. Gift shop. Coin lndry. Free airport, RR station transportation. Exercise equipt; bicycle, treadmill. Indoor pool; lifeguard. Some bathrm phones. Refrigerators avail. Cr cds: A, C, D, DS, JCB, MC, V.

Ocean City

Motel

★ ★ **RESIDENCE INN BY MARRIOTT.** *(900 Mays Landing Rd, Somers Point 08244) 3 mi NW on NJ 52, then W on Mays Landing Rd; E of Garden State Pkwy exits 29N, 30S. 609/927-6400; FAX 609/926-0145.* 120 kit. suites, 2 story. Memorial Day-Labor Day: S, D $160-$240; each addl $10; under 12 free; wkly rates; lower rates rest of yr. Pet accepted. TV; cable, VCR avail (movies). Heated pool; lifeguard. Complimentary continental bkfst. Ck-out 11 am. Coin lndry. Meeting rms. Business servs avail. In-rm modem link. Valet serv. Airport transportation. Golf. Health club privileges. Rec rm. Microwaves. Some private patios, balconies. Picnic tables, grills. Cr cds: A, C, D, DS, JCB, MC, V.

Paramus

Motor Hotel

★ ★ **RADISSON.** *601 From Rd, adj to Paramus Park Mall, Garden State Pkwy exit 165. 201/262-6900; FAX 201/262-4955.* Web www.radisson.com. 119 rms, 2 story. S, D $129; each addl $10; wkend rates. Crib free. Pet accepted, some restrictions. TV; cable (premium). Pool. Complimentary coffee in rms. Restaurant 6:30 am-10 pm; Sat, Sun from 7 am. Rm serv. Bar; entertainment Sat. Ck-out noon. Coin lndry. Meeting rms. Business servs avail. In-rm modem link. Bellhops. Sundries. Health club privileges. Refrigerators. Cr cds: A, C, D, DS, ER, JCB, MC, V.

Parsippany

Motel

★ ★ **HOWARD JOHNSON.** *(1255 NJ 10, Whippany 07981) I-80 to I-287S exit 39B (NJ 10). 973/539-8350; FAX 973/539-9338.* Web www.hojo.com. 108 rms, 2 story. S $79-$89; D $89-$99; each addl $10; under 18 free; family, wkend, wkly, hol rates. Crib free. Pet accepted, some restrictions. TV; cable (premium). Complimentary continental bkfst. Restaurant 6:30 am-10 pm. Ck-out noon. Meeting rms. Business servs avail. Valet serv. Coin lndry. Pool. Refrigerators, microwaves avail. Cr cds: A, C, D, DS, JCB, MC, V.

Hotel

★ ★ ★ **HILTON.** *1 Hilton Ct, jct NJ 10 & I-287. 973/267-7373; FAX 973/984-6853.* Web www.hilton.com. 508 rms, 6 story. S $135-$175; D $155-$185; each addl $20; suites $350-$675; family, wkend rates. Crib free. Pet accepted, some restrictions. TV; cable (premium), VCR avail. Indoor/outdoor pool; whirlpool. Playground. Restaurants 6:30 am-11 pm; wkends from 7 am. Rm serv Mon-Thurs 6:30-2 am. Bar 11-2 am; entertainment. Ck-out noon. Convention facilities. Business center. In-rm modem link. Airport transportation. Tennis. Exercise equipt; weights, bicycles. Some bathrm phones. Wet bar, refrigerator in suites. Cr cds: A, C, D, DS, ER, JCB, MC, V.

Plainfield

Motor Hotel

★ ★ **HOLIDAY INN.** *(4701 Stelton Rd, South Plainfield 07080) At jct NJ 529, I-287. 908/753-5500; FAX 908/753-5500, ext. 620.* 173 rms, 4 story. S, D $89-$109; under 19 free; wkend rates. Crib free. Pet accepted, some restrictions. TV; cable (premium). Indoor pool; whirlpool, lifeguard. Restaurant 6:30 am-10 pm. Rm serv. Ck-out 1 pm. Coin lndry. Meeting rms. Business servs avail. In-rm modem link. Valet serv. Exercise equipt; weights, bicycles, sauna. Refrigerators; microwaves avail. Cr cds: A, C, D, DS, MC, V.

Princeton *(See also Trenton)*

Motel

★ ★ **RESIDENCE INN BY MARRIOTT.** *4225 US 1 (08543), 4 mi NE, just S of Raymond Rd on US 1. 732/329-9600; FAX 732/329-8422.* Web www.pacpub.com/resi dence. 208 kit. suites, 2 story. S, D $139-$159; under 18 free; wkly, wkend rates. Crib free. Pet accepted, some restrictions; $10. TV; cable (premium). Heated pool; whirlpool. Complimentary continental bkfst. Ck-out noon. Coin lndry. Meeting rms. Business center. Valet serv. Health club privileges. Microwaves; many fireplaces. Balconies. Picnic tables, grills. Cr cds: A, C, D, DS, ER, JCB, MC, V.

Motor Hotel

★ ★ **NOVOTEL.** *100 Independence Way (08540), jct NJ 522, US 1. 609/520-1200; FAX 609/520-0594.* 180 rms, 4 story. S, D $135; suites $155; under 16 free; wkend rates. Crib free. Pet accepted, some restrictions. TV; cable (premium), VCR avail. Pool; whirlpool. Restaurant 6 am-10:30 pm. Rm serv. Bar. Ck-out 1 pm. Coin lndry. Meeting rms. Business servs avail. In-rm modem link. Valet serv. Free RR station transportation. Exercise equipt; weight machine, bicycles. Microwaves avail. Cr cds: A, C, D, DS, ER, MC, V.

Hotel

★ ★ ★ **NASSAU INN.** *10 Palmer Sq (08542). 609/921-7500; FAX 609/921-9385; res: 800/627-7286 (exc NJ).* E-mail lorginjam@aol.com; web www.nassauinn.com. 215 rms, 5 story. S $135-$175; D $155-$195; each addl $20; suites $310-$535; under 13 free. Crib free. Pet accepted. TV; cable (premium). Restaurant 7 am-10 pm. Bar 4 pm-1 am; entertainment Fri, Sat. Ck-out noon. Business center. In-rm modem link. Exercise equipt; weight machine, treadmills. Refrigerators avail. Colonial atmosphere, beamed ceilings, fireplaces in public rms. Cr cds: A, D, MC, V. 🄳 👇 ✗ ⚊ ⚊ 🖐

Inn

★ ★ **PEACOCK INN.** *20 Bayard Lane (08540). 609/924-1707; FAX 609/924-0788.* 17 rms, 7 share bath, 3 story. S $90-$125; D $100-$135; each addl $15; higher rates graduation. Crib free. Pet accepted; $20. TV in some rms, lobby; cable (premium). Complimentary bkfst buffet. Dining rm 11:45 am-2:30 pm, 5:30-9:30 pm. Ck-out noon, ck-in 2 pm. Business servs avail. Historic late Georgian colonial house, built in 1775 and relocated from Nassau St to its present site. Antique furnishings; rms individually decorated. 3 blks from Princeton Univ campus. Cr cds: A, MC, V. 👇 ⚊ **SC**

Ramsey

Motel

★ ★ **WELLESLEY INN.** *946 NJ 17 N. 201/934-9250; res: 800/444-8888.* 89 rms, 3 story. S $64-$85; D $69-$94; each addl $5; under 18 free; wkend, wkly rates; higher rates: Pathmark tennis tournament, West Point graduation. Crib free. Pet accepted, some restrictions; $3. TV; cable (premium). Complimentary continental bkfst. Complimentary coffee in rms. Restaurant adj open 24 hrs. Ck-out 11 am. Business servs avail. Health club privileges. Refrigerators, microwaves avail. Cr cds: A, C, D, DS, JCB, MC, V. 🄳 👇 ⚊ ⚊ **SC**

Hotel

★ ★ ★ **SHERATON CROSSROADS.** *(Crossroads Corporate Center, Mahwah 07495) jct I-87, I-287, NJ 17. 201/529-1660; FAX 201/529-4709.* 225 units, 14-22 story. S $139-$159; D $149-$169; each addl $10; suites $260-$750; under 18 free; wkend rates. Crib free. Pet accepted, some restrictions. TV; cable (premium). Indoor pool. Restaurant 6:30 am-11 pm. Bar noon-2 am; entertainment exc Sun. Ck-out noon. Convention facilities. Business center. Concierge. Shopping arcade. Covered parking. Tennis. Exercise equipt; weights, bicycles, sauna. Refrigerators, microwaves avail. Luxury level. Cr cds: A, C, D, DS, ER, JCB, MC, V. 🄳 👇 ⚷ ⚊ ✗ ⚊ ⚊ **SC** 🖐

Rutherford

Hotels

★ ★ **NOVOTEL.** *(1 Polito Ave, Lyndhurst 07071) NJ 17 S. 201/896-6666; res: 800/668-6735.* E-mail meadmail@aol.com. 219 rms, 5 story. S $139; D $149; each addl $10; under 16 free; family, wkend, hol rates. Crib free. Pet accepted, some restrictions. TV; cable (premium), VCR avail (movies). Complimentary coffee in lobby. Restaurant 6:30 am-midnight. Bar 5 pm-1 am; entertainment Tues-Thurs. Ck-out 1 pm. Meeting rms. Business center. In-rm modem link. Coin lndry. Exercise equipt; weight machine, bicycle, sauna. Massage. Health club privileges. Indoor pool; whirlpool. Refrigerators, microwaves avail. Cr cds: A, C, D, DS, ER, JCB, MC, V. 👇 ⚊ ✗ ⚊ ⚊ **SC** 🖐

★ ★ ★ **SHERATON MEADOWLANDS.** *(2 Meadowlands Plaza, East Rutherford 07073) 1/4 mi E of NJ Tpke exit 16W, opp Meadowlands Sports Complex. 201/896-0500; FAX 201/896-9696.* 425 units, 21 story. S, D $130-$160; each addl $20; suites $230-$550; under 18 free; wkend rates. Crib free. Pet accepted, some restrictions. TV; cable (premium), VCR avail. Indoor pool; whirlpool, poolside serv. Restaurant 6:30 am-11 pm. Bars noon-2 am. Ck-out 1 pm. Convention facilities. Business center. In-rm modem link. Concierge. Gift shop. Exercise equipt; weights, bicycles, sauna. Bathrm phone, wet bar in suites. Cr cds: A, C, D, DS, ER, JCB, MC, V. 🄳 👇 ⚊ ✗ ⚊ ⚊ **SC** 🖐

Secaucus

Hotels

★ ★ ★ **RADISSON SUITE.** *350 NJ 3 W (07094). 201/863-8700; FAX 201/863-6209.* 151 suites, 9 story. S $179-$239; D $189-$249; each addl $20; under 12 free; wkend, wkly rates; higher rates hockey and football season. Crib avail. Pet accepted, some restrictions. TV; cable (premium), VCR avail. Complimentary coffee in rms. Restaurant 7 am-10 pm. Bar noon-midnight. Ck-out noon. Meeting rms. Business servs avail. In-rm modem link. Coin lndry. Airport, RR station transportation. Exercise equipt; weights, treadmill. Indoor pool. Refrigerators, wet bars; microwaves avail. Cr cds: A, C, D, DS, JCB, MC, V.

★ ★ ★ **RAMADA.** (500 Harbor Blvd, Weehawken 07087) 201/617-5600; FAX 201/617-5627. 244 suites, 10 story. Mar-Dec: S $189-$229; D $209-$249; each addl $20; under 18 free; family, wkly, wkend, hol rates; lower rates rest of yr. Crib free. Pet accepted. TV; cable (premium), VCR avail. Complimentary continental bkfst. Complimentary coffee in rms. Restaurant 11:30 am-10 pm. Rm serv from 7 am. Bar from noon. Ck-out noon. Meeting rms. Business center. In-rm modem link. Concierge. Gift shop. Exercise equipt; weights, bicycle. Indoor pool. Refrigerators, microwaves, wet bars. On river. Cr cds: A, C, D, DS, ER, JCB, MC, V.

Toms River

Motels

★ ★ **HOLIDAY INN.** 290 NJ 37E (08753). 908/244-4000. 123 rms, 4 story. Memorial Day-Labor Day: S, D $104-$114; each addl $10; higher rates wkends; lower rates rest of yr. Crib free. Pet accepted. TV; cable (premium). Indoor pool; whirlpool, sauna, poolside serv. Restaurant 6:30 am-10 pm. Rm serv. Bar 11-2 am; entertainment. Ck-out noon. Coin lndry. Valet serv. Meeting rms. Business servs avail. Game rm. Refrigerators. Cr cds: A, C, D, DS, JCB, MC, V.

★ ★ **HOWARD JOHNSON.** 955 Hooper Ave (08753). 908/244-1000; FAX 908/505-3194. 96 rms, 2 story. S $75-$99, D $85-$120; each addl $6; under 18 free; higher rates some hols. Crib free. Pet accepted, some restrictions; $10. TV; cable, VCR avail (movies). Indoor/outdoor pool. Restaurant 11 am-9 pm. Bar. Ck-out noon. Meeting rms. Business servs avail. In-rm modem link. Cr cds: A, C, D, DS, MC, V.

Trenton (See also Princeton)

Motel

★ **HOWARD JOHNSON.** (2995 Brunswick Pike, Lawrenceville 08648) 5 mi N on US 1. 609/896-1100; FAX 609/895-1325. 104 rms, 2 story. S $62.50-$84.50; D $68.50-$84.50; each addl $10; under 18 free. Crib free. Pet accepted. TV; cable (premium). Pool. Complimentary continental bkfst. Restaurant open 24 hrs. Ck-out noon. Meeting rm. Business servs avail. In-rm modem link. Valet serv. Sundries. Private patios, balconies. Cr cds: A, C, D, DS, JCB, MC, V.

Wayne

Motel

✔ ★ ★ **HOWARD JOHNSON.** 1850 NJ 23 and Ratzer Rd. 973/696-8050; FAX 973/696-0682. 149 rms, 2 story. S $63-$73; D $65-$75; each addl $10; under 16 free. Crib free. Pet accepted, some restrictions. TV; cable (premium). Pool. Complimentary full bkfst. Ck-out noon. Coin lndry. Meeting rms. Business servs avail. In-rm modem link. Valet serv. Health club privileges. Airport, RR station transportation. Some refrigerators; microwaves avail. Private patios, balconies. Cr cds: A, C, D, DS, JCB, MC, V.

Motor Hotel

★ ★ **BEST WESTERN EXECUTIVE INN.** (216 NJ 46E, Fairfield 07004) NJ 23S, exit 53 to I-80W. 973/575-7700; FAX 973/575-4653. 170 rms, 4 story. S $83-$164; each addl $13; suites $112-$164; under 16 free; family, wkend, wkly, hol rates. Crib free. Pet accepted, some restrictions. TV; cable (premium), VCR avail (movies). Complimentary full bkfst. Complimentary coffee in rms. Restaurant 6 am-11 pm. Rm serv. Bar 11-1:30 am; entertainment Thurs-Sun. Ck-out noon. Meeting rms. Business center. In-rm modem link. Bellhops. Valet serv. Sundries. Coin lndry. Exercise equipt; bicycle, stair machine, sauna. Health club privileges. Indoor pool; whirlpool, poolside serv. Game rm. Rec rm. Refrigerators; some in-rm whirlpools; wet bar in suites; microwaves avail. Cr cds: A, C, D, MC, V.

New Mexico

Alamogordo (See also Ruidoso)

Motels

★ ★ **BEST WESTERN DESERT AIRE.** *1021 S White Sands Blvd (US 54, 70, 82). 505/437-2110; FAX 505/437-1898.* 100 rms, 2 story. S $47-$57; D $58; under 16 free. Crib free. Pet accepted; some restrictions. TV; cable. Heated pool; whirlpool, sauna. Complimentary continental bkfst. Ck-out noon. Coin lndry. Valet serv. Sundries. Game rm. Microwaves avail. Cr cds: A, C, D, DS, MC, V. D ⮞ ☒ ⊠ ☒ SC

✔ ★ **SATELLITE INN.** *2224 N White Sands Blvd (US 54, 70, 82), at 23rd St. 505/437-8454; FAX 505/434-6015; res: 800/221-7690.* 40 rms, 1-2 story. S $32-$34; D $34-$38; each addl $2; kit. unit $38-$46; family unit $32-$42. Crib free. Pet accepted. TV; cable (premium), VCR avail (movies). Pool. Restaurant adj 6 am-9 pm. Ck-out noon. Refrigerators, microwaves avail. Cr cds: A, C, DS, MC, V. ⮞ ☒ ⊠ ☒ SC

Albuquerque

Motels

(Rates may be higher during the Balloon Fiesta, the State Fair and other special events)

★ ★ ★ **BEST WESTERN INN AT RIO RANCHO.** *(1465 Rio Rancho Dr, Rio Rancho 87124) 3 mi W on I-40 exit 155, then 8 mi N on NM 45. 505/892-1700; FAX 505/892-4628.* 121 rms, 10 kits. S $55-$73; D $61-$73; each addl $6; kit. units $61-$67; under 12 free. Crib $6. Pet accepted, some restrictions; $3/day. TV; cable (premium). Pool; whirlpool, poolside serv. Coffee in rms. Restaurant 6:30 am-10 pm. Rm serv. Bar 11-2 am; entertainment Fri, Sat. Ck-out 11 am. Coin lndry. Meeting rms. Business servs avail. In-rm modem link. Valet serv. Sundries. Gift shop. Free airport, RR station, bus depot transportation. Golf privileges, greens fee, pro, putting green, driving range. Downhill/x-country ski 20 mi. Exercise equipt: weights, stair machine. Lawn games. Microwaves avail. Picnic tables, grills. Cr cds: A, C, D, DS, JCB, MC, V. D ⮞ ☒ ⟨ ⊠ ⟨ ⟨ ☒ ☒ SC

✔ ★ ★ **COMFORT INN EAST.** *13031 Central NE (87123), I-40 at Tramway exit 167. 505/294-1800; FAX 505/293-1088.* 122 rms, 2 story. May-mid-Sept: S $52-$55; D $58-$67; each addl $6; under 17 free; lower rates rest of yr. Crib free. Pet accepted; $6/day. TV; cable (premium). Pool; whirlpools. Complimentary full bkfst. Restaurant 6-10 am, 5-8:30 pm. Ck-out noon. Coin lndry. Meeting rms. Business servs avail. Downhill ski 9 mi. Cr cds: A, C, D, DS, JCB, MC, V. D ⮞ ☒ ⊠ ☒ ☒ SC

✔ ★ ★ **DAYS INN.** *6031 Iliff Rd NW (87121), I-40 exit 155. 505/836-3297; FAX 505/836-1214.* 81 rms, 2 story. June-Oct: S $55-$75; D $60-$80; each addl $5; under 12 free. Pet accepted; $5/day. TV; cable (premium). Indoor pool; whirlpool, sauna. Complimentary continental bkfst. Restaurant nearby. Ck-out 11 am. Guest lndry. Business servs avail. Downhill/x-country ski 10 mi. Cr cds: A, D, DS, JCB, MC, V. D ⮞ ☒ ⊠ ☒ ☒ SC

★ **HAMPTON INN.** *5101 Ellison NE (87109), I-25 exit 231. 505/344-1555; FAX 505/345-2216.* 125 rms, 3 story. May-Aug: S $57-62; D $63-$67; under 18 free; lower rates rest of yr. Crib free. Pet accepted, some restrictions. TV; cable (premium), VCR avail. Heated pool. Complimentary continental bkfst. Restaurant nearby. Ck-out noon. Health club privileges. Cr cds: A, C, D, DS, MC, V. D ⮞ ☒ ☒ ☒ SC

★ ★ **LA QUINTA-AIRPORT.** *2116 Yale Blvd SE (87106), 1 mi E of I-25 Gibson Airport exit, near Intl Airport. 505/243-5500; FAX 505/247-8288.* 105 rms, 3 story. S $69; D $75; each addl $8; suites $105; under 18 free. Crib free. Pet accepted, some restrictions. TV; cable (premium). Pool. Continental bkfst. Restaurant adj 6 am-10 pm. Ck-out noon. Coin lndry. Business servs avail. Valet serv. Free airport transportation. Downhill ski 20 mi. Microwave in suites. Cr cds: A, C, D, DS, MC, V. D ⮞ ☒ ⊠ ⟨ ☒ ☒ SC

✔ ★ **TRAVELODGE.** *13139 Central Ave NE (87123). 505/292-4878; FAX 505/299-1822.* 41 rms, 2 story. May-Oct: S, D $40-$100; each addl $5; under 17 free; lower rates rest of yr. Crib free. Pet accepted, some restrictions; $5. TV; cable (premium). Complimentary continental bkfst. Complimentary coffee in rms. Restaurant nearby. Ck-out 11 am. Business servs avail. Downhill/x-country ski 8 mi. Cr cds: A, C, D, DS, JCB, MC, V. D ⮞ ☒ ☒ ☒ SC

Motor Hotels

★ ★ **AMBERLY SUITE HOTEL.** *7620 Pan American Frwy NE (87109), I-25 & San Antonio Rd N. 505/823-1300; FAX 505/823-2896; res: 800/333-9806.* Web www.cal av.com/amberly. 170 suites, 3 story. S, D $99-$118; each addl $10; under 16 free; monthly rates. Crib free. Pet accepted; $5. TV; cable (premium). Heated pool; whirlpool. Complimentary full bkfst; afternoon refreshments. Restaurant 6 am-9 pm. Bar 4-11 pm. Ck-out noon. Coin lndry. Meeting rms. Business servs avail. In-rm modem link. Free airport, RR station, bus depot transportation. Downhill ski 5 mi. Exercise equipt; weights, bicycles, sauna. Refrigerators, microwaves. Courtyard; fountain. Cr cds: A, C, D, DS, MC, V.

[D] [icons]

↙★ ★ **PLAZA INN.** *900 Medical Arts Ave NE (87102), I-25 Lomas Blvd exit. 505/243-5693; FAX 505/843-6229; res: 800/237-1307.* 120 rms, 5 story. S, D $70-$90; each addl $5; under 17 free. Pet accepted. TV. Heated pool; whirlpool. Restaurant 6 am-midnight. Bar 11-2 am; Sun noon-midnight. Ck-out noon. Coin lndry. Meeting rms. Business servs avail. Valet serv. Free airport, RR station, bus depot transportation. Downhill ski 14 mi. Exercise equipt; weight machine, stair machine. Some refrigerators. Private patios, balconies. Cr cds: A, C, D, DS, ER, JCB, MC, V. [icons]

Inn

↙★ ★ **W.E. MAUGER ESTATE.** *701 Roma Ave NW (87102). 505/242-8755; FAX 505/842-8835.* Web www.thuntele.net/tcart/mareger. 8 air-cooled rms, shower only, 3 story. S, D $79-$149; each addl $15. Crib free. Pet accepted. TV; cable (premium), VCR avail. Complimentary full bkfst; afternoon refreshments. Complimentary coffee in rms. Restaurant nearby. Ck-out 11 am, ck-in 4-6 pm. Business servs avail. In-rm modem link. Downhill/x-country ski 12 mi. Health club privileges. Sun porch. Restored Queen Anne house (1897). Cr cds: A, C, D, DS, MC, V. [icons]

Carlsbad

Motels

★ ★ **BEST WESTERN STEVENS INN.** *1829 S Canal St. 505/887-2851; FAX 505/887-6338.* 202 rms, 1-2 story. S $50; D, suites $55-$65; each addl $5. Crib $5. Pet accepted. TV; cable (premium), VCR (movies $4). Pool. Playground. Restaurant 5:30 am-10 pm; Sun 6 am-9 pm. Rm serv 7 am-9 pm. Bar 11-2 am; entertainment exc Sun. Ck-out noon. Meeting rms. Business servs avail. Sundries. Some refrigerators. Some patios. Cr cds: A, C, D, DS, MC, V. [icons]

★ ★ **CONTINENTAL INN.** *3820 National Parks Hwy. 505/887-0341; FAX 505/885-1186.* 58 units, 2 story. S $34.95; D $39.95-$44.95; each addl $5; suites $49.95-$79.95. Crib free. Pet accepted, some restrictions; $10. TV; cable (premium). Heated pool. Restaurant nearby. Ck-out 11 am. Business servs avail. In-rm modem link. Free airport, bus depot transportation. Some refrigerators. Cr cds: A, C, D, DS, MC, V. [icons]

★ ★ **HOLIDAY INN.** *601 S Canal. 505/885-8500; FAX 505/887-5999.* 100 rms, 2 story. Mid-June-mid-Aug: S $62-$75; D $67-$82; each addl $5; suites $77-$87; under 19 free; lower rates rest of yr. Crib free. Pet accepted; $25 deposit. TV; cable (premium), VCR avail (movies). Pool; whirlpool, poolside serv. Playground. Complimentary coffee in rms. Restaurants 7-10 am, 11:30 am-2:30 pm, 5-8 pm. Rm serv. Ck-out 11 am. Guest lndry. Meeting rms. Business servs avail. In-rm modem link. Bellhops. Valet serv. Tennis privileges. 36-hole golf privileges, greens fee $21, putting green, driving range. Exercise equipt; weights, bicycle, sauna. Some refrigerators. Picnic tables. Cr cds: A, C, D, DS, JCB, MC, V. [icons]

Chama

Motel

(Because of the altitude, air-conditioning is rarely necessary)

★ **ELK HORN LODGE.** *Rte 1, on US 84. 505/756-2105; FAX 505/756-2638; res: 800/532-8874.* 23 motel rms, 1-2 story, 10 kit. cottages. July-Sept: S $47-$55; D $55-$63; each addl $6; kit cottages $70-$102; wkly & lower rates rest of yr. Crib $6. Pet accepted. TV; cable. Restaurant 6 am-10 pm. Ck-out 11 am. X-country ski 5 mi. Balconies. Porches on cottages. Picnic tables, grills. On Chama River. Cr cds: DS, MC, V. [icons]

Cimarron (See also Raton, Red River)

Motel

✔★ **CIMARRON INN.** US 64 & NM 58. 505/376-2268; res: 800/546-2244. 12 rms, 5 with shower only. S $34-$40; D $36-$46; each addl $3; under 8 free. Crib $3. Pet accepted, some restrictions; $50. TV; cable. Complimentary coffee in lobby. Restaurant nearby. Ck-out 11 am. Business servs avail. Some refrigerators, microwaves. Picnic tables, grills. Cr cds: A, DS, MC, V. 🐾 ⚄ 🐾

Clovis (See also Portales)

Motels

✔★ **BISHOPS INN.** 2920 Mabry Dr (US 60). 505/769-1953; FAX 505/762-8304; res: 800/643-9239. 59 rms, 2 story. S $27-$30; D $31.50-$35; each addl $5; under 12 free. Crib free. Pet accepted. TV; cable. Heated pool; whirlpool. Complimentary continental bkfst. Ck-out 11 am. Coin lndry. Business servs avail. Cr cds: A, C, D, DS, MC, V. D 🐾 ⚄ ⚄ 🐾 SC

✔★ **DAYS INN.** 1720 E Mabry Dr. 505/762-2971; FAX 505/762-2735. 92 rms, 1-2 story. S $31-$37; D $37-$44; each addl $6. Crib free. Pet accepted. TV; cable (premium). Pool; wading pool. Complimentary coffee. Restaurant adj open 24 hrs. Ck-out 11 am. Business servs avail. In-rm modem link. Cr cds: A, C, D, DS, MC, V. 🐾 ⚄ ⚄ 🐾 SC

Deming (See also Las Cruces)

Motels

✔★ **DAYS INN.** 1709 E Spruce St (88030). 505/546-8813; FAX 505/546-7095. 57 rms, 2 story. S $38; D $42; each addl $4; suites $46-$58; under 12 free; wkly rates. Crib free. Pet accepted, some restrictions. TV; cable (premium). Pool. Complimentary continental bkfst. Restaurant 5:30 am-9:30 pm. Ck-out 11 am. Meeting rms. Cr cds: A, C, D, DS, MC, V. D 🐾 ⚄ ⚄ 🐾 SC

★ **GRAND MOTOR INN.** 1721 E Spruce St. 505/546-2632; FAX 505/546-4446. 62 rms, 2 story. S $42; D $45-$50; each addl $6; suites $65; under 12 free. Crib free. Pet accepted. TV; cable (premium). Heated pool; wading pool, poolside serv. Restaurant 6 am-10 pm. Rm serv. Bar noon-12:30 am. Ck-out noon. Meeting rms. Business servs avail. Valet serv. Free airport, RR station, bus depot transportation. Golf privileges. Cr cds: A, C, D, DS, MC, V. D 🐾 🎿 ⚄ ⚄ 🐾 SC

★ **HOLIDAY INN.** Box 1138, I-10 E, exit 85. 505/546-2661; FAX 505/546-6308. 120 rms, 2 story. S, D $59; each addl $6; suites $79; under 19 free; higher rates last wkend Aug. Crib free. Pet accepted. TV; cable (premium). Pool. Restaurant 6 am-2 pm, 4-10 pm. Ck-out 11 am. Coin lndry. Meeting rms. Business servs avail. Sundries. Free airport, RR station, bus depot transportation. Some in-rm whirlpools. Cr cds: A, C, D, DS, JCB, MC, V. D 🐾 ⚄ ⚄ 🐾 SC

Española (See also Los Alamos, Santa Fe)

Motel

★ **CHAMISA INN.** 920 Riverside Dr N (NM 68) (87533). 505/753-7291; FAX 505/753-1218; res: 800/766-7943. 51 rms. S $48; D $53.95; each addl $10. Pet accepted; $10. TV; cable (premium). Heated pool. Continental bkfst. Bar 11 am-2 am; Sun to midnight. Ck-out 11 am. Cr cds: A, DS, MC, V. 🐾 ⚄ 🐾 SC

Farmington

Motels

★ ★ ★ **BEST WESTERN INN & SUITES.** 700 Scott Ave (87401), at Bloomfield Hwy. 505/327-5221; FAX 505/327-1565. 194 rms, 3 story. S $65-$69 D $75-$79; each addl $10; under 12 free; wknd rates; golf plans. Crib free. Pet accepted. TV; cable (premium), VCR avail (movies $2). Indoor pool; whirlpool, poolside serv. Coffee in rms. Restaurant 6-10 am, 11 am-2 pm, 5-10 pm. Rm serv. Bar 11:30 am-midnight. Ck-out noon. Coin lndry. Meeting rms. Business servs avail. Bellhops. Valet serv. Free airport, bus depot transportation. Exercise equipt; weights, bicycles, sauna. Rec rm. Some refrigerators. Cr cds: A, C, D, DS, MC, V. D 🐾 ⚄ 🎿 ⚄ 🐾 SC

★ ★ **COMFORT INN.** *555 Scott Ave (87401). 505/325-2626; FAX 505/325-7675.* 60 rms, 2 story, 18 suites. May-Oct: S $54; D $62; each addl $6; suites $59-$69; under 18 free; lower rates rest of yr. Crib $5. Pet accepted. TV; cable (premium). Pool. Complimentary continental bkfst. Complimentary coffee in rms. Ck-out 11 am. Business servs avail. In-rm modem link. Health club priviliges. Refrigerator in suites. Cr cds: A, D, DS, ER, JCB, MC, V. D ◆ ≈ ⇥ 🐾 SC

★ ★ **HOLIDAY INN.** *600 E Broadway (87499), US 64 at Scott Ave. 505/327-9811; FAX 505/325-2288.* 149 rms, 2 story. S $69; D $77; each addl $8; under 19 free. Crib free. Pet accepted. TV; cable (premium). Pool; whirlpool. Restaurant 6 am-10 pm. Rm serv. Bar. Ck-out noon. Business servs avail. Bellhops. Free airport, bus depot transportation. Exercise equipt; weights, bicycles, sauna. Cr cds: A, C, D, DS, JCB, MC, V. D ◆ ≈ 🏃 ⇥ 🐾 SC

★ ★ **LA QUINTA.** *675 Scott Ave (87401). 505/327-4706; FAX 325/6583.* 106 rms, 2 story. S, D $55-$63; each addl $8; under 18 free. Crib free. Pet accepted. TV; cable (premium). Heated pool. Complimentary continental bkfst. Restaurant adj open 24 hrs. Ck-out noon. Meeting rm. Valet serv. Refrigerators avail. Picnic tables, grills. Cr cds: A, C, D, DS, MC, V. D ◆ ≈ ⇥ 🐾 SC

Gallup

Motels

(Rates may be higher during Inter-Tribal Indian Ceremonial week. All properties listed on US 66 are parallel to the main line of the Santa Fe Railroad.)

★ **ECONO LODGE.** *3101 W US 66. 505/722-3800.* 51 rms, 2 story. May-Oct: S, D $38.95-$51.95; each addl $7; under 18 free; higher rates mid-Aug; lower rates rest of yr. Crib $5. Pet accepted; $10 deposit. TV; cable (premium). Restaurant nearby. Ck-out 11 am. Cr cds: A, D, DS, MC, V. D ◆ ⇥ 🐾 SC

★ ★ **EL RANCHO.** *1000 E US 66. 505/863-9311; FAX 505/722-5917; res: 800/543-6351.* 75 rms, 6 kit. units. S $35-$56; D $47-$59; each addl $5; suites $76. Crib free. Pet accepted. TV. Pool. Restaurant 6:30 am-10 pm. Bar 5 pm-1 am. Ck-out noon. Coin lndry. Meeting rms. Business servs avail. Gift shop. Cr cds: A, C, D, DS, MC, V. ◆ ≈ ⇥ 🐾 SC

Motor Hotels

★ ★ **BEST WESTERN.** *3009 W US 66. 505/722-2221; FAX 505/722-7442.* 126 rms, 2 story, 25 suites. June-Sept: S $64; D $72; each addl $8; suites $70; under 12 free; higher rates special events; lower rates rest of yr. Crib free. Pet accepted, some restrictions. TV; cable (premium). Complimentary coffee in rms. Restaurant 6-10 am, 5-9:30 pm. Rm serv. Bar 4:30-11 pm. Ck-out noon. Meeting rms. Sundries. Gift shop. Coin lndry. Exercise equipt; weight machine, treadmill, sauna. Indoor pool; whirlpool. Game rm. Microwave in suites. Cr cds: A, C, D, DS, MC, V. D ◆ ≈ 🏃 🏃 ⇥ 🐾 SC

★ ★ **HOLIDAY INN HOLIDOME.** *2915 W US 66, near Municipal Airport. 505/722-2201; FAX 505/722-9616.* Web www.Hotel.net.com. 212 rms, 2 story. June-Aug: S, D $65-$73; each addl $5; under 19 free; lower rates rest of yr. Crib free. Pet accepted. TV; cable (premium). Indoor pool; whirlpool. Restaurant 6 am-10 pm. Rm serv. Bar 4 pm-12:30 am; closed Sun; entertainment. Ck-out noon. Coin lndry. Meeting rms. Business servs avail. Bellhops. Valet serv. Sundries. Free airport, RR station, bus depot transportation. Exercise equipt; weights, bicycles, sauna. Game rm. Cr cds: A, C, D, DS, JCB, MC, V. D ◆ ≈ 🏃 🏃 ⇥ 🐾 SC

Grants

Motels

★ ★ **BEST WESTERN.** *1501 E Santa Fe Ave, at I-40, exit 85. 505/287-7901; FAX 505/285-5751.* 126 rms, 2 story. S, D $60-$80; each addl $8; under 12 free; suites $65-$85. Crib free. Pet accepted, some restrictions. TV; cable (premium). Indoor pool; whirlpool, sauna. Restaurant 6:30-9:30 am, 5-9:30 pm. Rm serv. Bar 3:30-11 pm; Fri, Sat to midnight; Sun to 11 pm. Ck-out noon. Coin lndry. Meeting rms. Business servs avail. Valet serv. Sundries, Game rm. Refrigerators avail. Cr cds: A, C, D, DS, MC, V. D ◆ ≈ ⇥ 🐾 SC

✔ ★ **LEISURE LODGE.** *1204 E Santa Fe Ave, I-40 exit 85. 505/287-2991.* 32 rms, 2 story. S $24.95-$26.95; D $30-$34; each addl $3; under 12 free. Crib $3. Pet accepted. TV; cable (premium). Heated pool. Complimentary coffee in lobby. Restaurant adj 11 am-9 pm. Ck-out 11 am. Cr cds: A, C, D, DS, MC, V. ◆ ≈ ⇥ 🐾 SC

Hobbs

Motels

✔ ★ ★ **BEST WESTERN LEAWOOD.** *1301 E Broadway. 505/393-4101.* 72 rms. S $37-$41; D $41-$45; each addl $4. Crib $3. Pet accepted. TV; cable (premium). Pool. Complimentary full bkfst. Restaurant opp 11 am-10 pm. Ck-out noon. Business servs avail. In-rm modem link. Cr cds: A, C, D, DS, MC, V. 🄳 ⬤ ≈ ⬛ ⬛ SC

★ ★ **RAMADA INN.** *501 N Marland Blvd. 505/397-3251; FAX 505/393-3065; res: 800/635-6639.* 75 rms, 2 story. S $49; D $59; each addl $7; suites $95-$119; under 18 free. Crib free. Pet accepted, some restrictions; $25. TV; cable. Heated pool. Restaurant 5 am-8 pm; dining rm 5:30-10 pm. Rm serv 6 am-10 pm. Bar 11-2 am; entertainment exc Sun. Ck-out 1 pm. Guest lndry. Meeting rms. Business servs avail. In-rm modem link. Sundries. Cr cds: A, C, D, DS, MC, V. ⬤ ≈ ⬛ SC

Las Cruces (See also El Paso, TX)

Motels

★ ★ **BEST WESTERN MESILLA VALLEY INN.** *901 Avenida de Mesilla (88005), at jct I-10 exit 140. 505/524-8603; FAX 505/526-8437.* 167 units, 2 story. S, D $58-$75; each addl $7; under 12 free. Crib free. Pet accepted. TV; cable. Heated pool; whirlpool. Restaurant 6 am-10 pm. Rm serv. Bar 11-1:30 am; Sun noon-11 pm; entertainment. Ck-out 11 am. Coin lndry. Meeting rms. Business servs avail. Health club privileges. Some refrigerators; microwaves avail. Cr cds: A, C, D, DS, MC, V. 🄳 ⬤ ≈ ⬛ ⬛ SC

★ ★ **DAYS INN.** *2600 S Valley Dr (88005), at I-10 exit 142. 505/526-4441; FAX 505/526-1980.* 131 rms, 2 story. S $50-$60; D $55-$65; each addl $5; under 18 free. Pet accepted. TV; cable (premium). Indoor pool; sauna, poolside serv. Restaurant 6-10 am, 5:30-9 pm. Bar 11 am-11 pm; Sat, Sun noon-10 pm. Ck-out noon. Coin lndry. Meeting rms. Business servs avail. Health club privileges. Valet serv. Some balconies. Cr cds: A, C, D, DS, MC, V. 🄳 ⬤ ≈ ⬛ ⬛ SC

★ ★ **HAMPTON INN.** *755 Avenida de Mesilla (88004). 505/526-8311; FAX 505/527-2015.* 119 rms, 2 story. S $56-$58; D $61-$63; under 18 free. Crib free. Pet accepted. TV; cable (premium). Pool. Complimentary continental bkfst. Restaurant opp 6 am-10 pm. Ck-out noon. Meeting rm. Business servs avail. In-rm modem link. Health club privileges. Cr cds: A, C, D, DS, MC, V. 🄳 ⬤ ≈ ⬛ ⬛ SC

★ ★ **HOLIDAY INN DE LAS CRUCES.** *201 E University Ave (88001). 505/526-4411; FAX 505/524-0530.* 114 rms, 2 story. S, D $74-$89; suites $150; under 18 free. Crib free. Pet accepted, some restrictions. TV; cable (premium). Indoor pool; wading pool. Restaurant 6 am-10 pm. Rm serv. Bar 11-1 am. Ck-out noon. Coin lndry. Meeting rms. Business center. Bellhops. Valet serv. Free airport, bus depot transportation. Game rm. Enclosed courtyard re-creates Mexican plaza; many antiques. Cr cds: A, C, D, DS, MC, V. 🄳 ⬤ ≈ 🛇 ⬛ ⬛ SC 🛇

Hotel

★ ★ ★ **HILTON.** *705 S Telshor Blvd (88011). 505/522-4300; FAX 505/522-7657.* E-mail lchilton@zianet.com; web www.weblifepro.com/lchilton. 203 units, 7 story. S $89-$109; D $99-$119; each addl $10; suites $115-$300. Crib free. Pet accepted. TV; cable; VCR avail (movies). Pool; whirlpool, poolside serv. Coffee in rms. Restaurant 6 am-2 pm, 5-10 pm. Rm serv. Bar 11-2 am; entertainment. Ck-out 1 pm. Meeting rms. Business servs avail. In-rm modem link. Gift shop. Free airport, bus depot transportation. Tennis privileges. Golf privileges. Exercise equipt; stair machine, bicycle. Some refrigerators. Overlooks valley. Cr cds: A, C, D, DS, MC, V. 🄳 ⬤ 🛇 🏃 ≈ 🛇 ⬛ ⬛ SC

Inn

★ ★ **INN OF THE ARTS.** *618 S Alameda (88005). 505/526-3326; FAX 505/647-1334.* E-mail lundeen@innofthearts.com; web www.innofthearts.com. 21 units, 2 story, 7 suites, 11 kits. S $65; D $70-$95; each addl $15; suites, kit. units $78-$95; wkly rates. Crib $15. Pet accepted. TV in sitting rm; cable (premium), VCR avail. Complimentary full bkfst. Restaurant nearby. Ck-out 11 am, ck-in 4 pm. Business servs avail. Bellhops. Exercise equipt; bicycle, treadmill. Lawn games. Some balconies. Microwaves avail. Picnic tables, grills. Built in 1890; antique furnishings. Library, sitting rm. Art gallery; each rm named for an artist. Cr cds: A, D, DS, MC, V. 🄳 ⬤ 🛇 ⬛ ⬛ SC

Las Vegas (See also Santa Fe)

Motels

★ ★ **INN OF SANTA FE TRAIL.** *1133 Grand Ave. 505/425-6791; FAX 505/425-0417; res: 800/425-6791.* Web www.travamerica.com. 42 rms, 12 suites. Mid-May-mid-Oct: S $54-$64; D $59-$69; each addl $5; suites $69-$85; under 12 free; wkly rates; lower rates rest of yr. Crib free. Pet accepted; deposit & $5/day. TV; cable (premium), VCR avail. Heated pool; whirlpool. Complimentary continental bkfst. Restaurant opp 6:30 am-9 pm. Ck-out 11 am. Business servs avail. In-rm modem link. Health club privileges. Lawn games. Refrigerator in suites; microwaves avail. Picnic tables. Cr cds: A, C, D, DS, MC, V.

D ⌨ ⌦ ⊠ 🐾 SC

★ **REGAL.** *1809 N Grand. 505/454-1456.* 50 rms. Mid-May-mid-Sept: S $30-$39; D $40-$49; under 17 free; higher rates special events; lower rates rest of yr. Crib $5. Pet accepted, some restrictions. TV; cable (premium). Complimentary coffee in lobby. Restaurant adj 6 am-9 pm. Ck-out 11 am. Cr cds: A, C, D, DS, MC, V. D ⌨ ⊠ 🐾 SC

✔ ★ **SCOTTISH INN.** *1216 N Grand Ave. 505/425-9357.* 45 rms, 2 story. May-Aug: S $28-$36; D $38-$60; each addl $3; under 3 free; lower rates rest of yr. Crib $3. Pet accepted, some restrictions. TV; cable (premium). Complimentary coffee in lobby. Restaurant nearby. Ck-out 11 am. Meeting rms. Free airport, RR station, bus depot transportation. Cr cds: A, C, D, DS, MC, V. ⌨ ⊠ 🐾 SC

★ **TOWN HOUSE.** *1215 N Grand Ave. 505/425-6717; res: 800/679-6717.* 42 rms. May-Oct: S $27-$36; D $36-$44; each addl $3; under 8 free; wkly rates; higher rates: graduation, family reunions; lower rates rest of yr. Pet accepted, some restrictions; $2. TV; cable (premium). Restaurant nearby. Ck-out 11 am. Picnic tables. Cr cds: A, C, D, DS, MC, V. D ⌨ ⊠ 🐾

Hotel

★ ★ **PLAZA.** *230 Old Town Plaza. 505/425-3591; FAX 505/425-9659; res: 800/328-1882.* 38 rms, 3 story. S $59-$110; D $65-$110; each addl $6; suites from $110; under 17 free; some wkend rates. Crib free. Pet accepted. TV; cable (premium). Coffee in rms. Restaurant 7 am-2 pm, 5-9 pm. Bar noon-midnight. Ck-out 11 am. Meeting rms. Business servs avail. Airport, RR station, bus depot transportation. X-country ski 5 mi. Historic hotel built 1882 in the Victorian Italianate-bracketed style; interior renovated; period furnishings, antiques. Cr cds: A, D, DS, MC, V. D ⌨ ⌦ ⊠ 🐾 SC

Los Alamos (See also Española, Santa Fe)

Motel

★ ★ **HILLTOP HOUSE & LOS ALAMOS SUITES.** *400 Trinity Dr (NM 502), at Central, near airport. 505/662-2441; FAX 505/662-5913; res: 800/462-0936.* Web www.losalamos.com/hilltophouse. 100 rms, 3 story, 33 kits. S $65-$78; D $73-$83; each addl $10; kit. units $77-$87; suites $98-$275; under 12 free. Crib $10. Pet accepted; $25 deposit. TV; cable (premium). Indoor pool. Complimentary bkfst. Restaurant 6:30-9:30 am, 11:30 am-2 pm, 5-9 pm. Rm serv. Ck-out 11 am. Coin lndry. Meeting rms. Business servs avail. In-rm modem link. Airport transportation. Downhill/x-country ski 10 mi. Exercise equipt; bicycles, treadmill. Cr cds: A, C, D, MC, V. D ⌨ ⌦ ⊠ 🏋 ⊠ 🐾 SC

Portales (See also Clovis)

Motel

✔ ★ **CLASSIC AMERICAN ECONOMY INN.** *1613 W 2nd St, NM 70 W. 505/356-6668; FAX 505/356-6668, ext. 13; res: 800/344-9466.* 40 units. S $28-$38; D $32-$45; each addl $5; suite $35-$45; under 12 free; wkly rates. Crib free. Pet accepted. TV; cable (premium), VCR avail. Heated pool. Playground. Complimentary continental bkfst. Complimentary coffee in rms. Restaurant adj 9:30 am-9 pm. Ck-out noon. In-rm modem link. Coin lndry. Sundries. Airport, bus depot transportation. Refrigerators. Picnic tables, grills. Adj to Eastern New Mexico Univ. Cr cds: A, C, D, DS, MC, V. D ⌨ ⌦ ⊠ 🐾 SC

Hotel

★ ★ **PORTALES INN.** *218 W 3rd. 505/359-1208.* 39 rms, 4 story. S $30-$35; D $36-$40; each addl $4; under 12 free; wkly rates. Pet accepted. TV; cable. Restaurant 6 am-8 pm. Ck-out noon. Meeting rms. Cr cds: A, C, D, DS, MC, V. ⌨ ⊠ 🐾 SC

Raton (See also Cimarron; also see Trinidad, CO)

Motel

(Rates may be higher during racing wkends)

✔★ **MELODY LANE.** 136 Canyon Dr, I-25 N Business Loop exit 454. 505/445-3655; FAX 505/445-3461; res: 800/421-5210. 27 rms. May-early Oct: S $36-$46; D $41-$51; each addl $5; wkly rates; lower rates rest of yr. Crib $5. Pet accepted. TV; cable (premium). Continental bkfst. Ck-out 11 am. Meeting rm. RR station transportation. Some in-rm steam baths; refrigerators, microwaves avail. Cr cds: A, C, D, DS, MC, V. 🖭 ⊠ ⊠ SC

Red River (See also Cimarron, Taos)

Motels

(Because of the altitude, air-conditioning is rarely necessary)

★ **TALL PINE RESORT.** 1¹/₂ mi S on NM 578. 505/754-2241; FAX 505/754-3134; res: 800/573-2241. 19 kit. cabins (1-2-bedrm). No A/C. No rm phones. May-Sept: S $65-$75; D $85-$110. Closed rest of yr. Crib free. Pet accepted. Playground. Ck-out 10 am, ck-in 1 pm. Maid serv wkly. Grocery, package store 1¹/₂ mi. Picnic tables, grills. 27 acres in forest; cabins along Red River. Cr cds: MC, V. D 🖭 ⊠ ⊠

✔★ **TERRACE TOWERS LODGE.** 712 W Main St. 505/754-2962; FAX 505/754-2989; res: 800/695-6343. E-mail hearts@newmex. com; web taoswebb.com/redriver info/hearts. 25 kit. suites, 2 story. S, D $52-$110; under 12 free; higher rates: Spring Break, Dec 25. Pet accepted. TV; cable (premium), VCR avail (movies $3). Playground. Restaurant nearby. Ck-out 10 am. Lndry facilities. Downhill/x-country ski ¹/₂ mi. Whirlpool. View of valley and mountains. Cr cds: DS, MC, V. 🖭 ⊠ ⊠ ⊠ SC

Roswell

Motels

★★ **BEST WESTERN SALLY PORT INN.** 2000 N Main St, US 70, 285. 505/622-6430; FAX 505/623-7631. 124 rms, 2 story. S, studio rms $49-$69; D $59-$79; each addl $10; suites $66-$85; under 18 free. Crib free. Pet accepted. TV; cable (premium). Indoor pool; whirlpool. Restaurant 6-10 am, 11:30 am-2 pm, 5-10 pm; closed Sun. Rm serv. Bar 4 pm-midnight; Fri, Sat to 1 am; closed Sun. Ck-out noon. Coin lndry. Meeting rms. Business servs avail. In-rm modem link. Sundries. Beauty shop. Free airport, bus depot transportation. Tennis. 18-hole golf privileges adj, putting green, driving range. Exercise equipt; weights, rower, sauna. Refrigerators. Cr cds: A, C, D, DS, MC, V.

D 🖭 🏋 🏃 ⊠ 🏃 ⊠ SC

✔★ **BUDGET INN.** 2200 W 2nd St. 505/623-3811. 29 rms, 2 story. S $26-$30; D $32-$35; each addl $4; kit. units $175/wk; under 17 free. Crib free. Pet accepted, some restrictions; $2. TV; cable. Pool. Coffee in lobby. Ck-out noon. Some refrigerators. Cr cds: A, C, D, DS, MC, V. 🖭 ⊠ ⊠ SC

✔★ **FRONTIER.** 3010 N Main St (US 70), US 70, 285. 505/622-1400; FAX 505/622-1405; res: 800/678-1401. 38 rms. S $28-$36; D $32-$40; each addl $4; higher rates NMMI events. Pet accepted. TV; cable (premium). Pool. Complimentary continental bkfst. Restaurant adj 5:30 am-9 pm. Ck-out 11 am. Some refrigerators. Cr cds: A, C, D, DS, MC, V. D 🖭 ⊠ ⊠ ⊠ SC

★★ **RAMADA.** 2803 W 2nd St. 505/623-9440; FAX 505/622-9708. 61 rms, 2 story. S $53; D $58; each addl $5; under 18 free. Crib $5. Pet accepted; $15 deposit. TV; cable. Heated pool. Ck-out noon. Meeting rms. Business servs avail. Cr cds: A, C, D, DS, JCB, MC, V. D 🖭 ⊠ ⊠ ⊠ SC

★★★ **ROSWELL INN.** 1815 N Main St, US 70, 285. 505/623-4920; FAX 505/622-3831; res: 800/323-0913 (exc NM), 800/426-3052 (NM). 121 rms, 2 story. S $62; D $65; each addl $7; suites $95-$145; under 18 free. Crib free. Pet accepted; $10. TV; cable (premium), VCR avail. Heated pool; poolside serv. Complimentary full bkfst. Restaurant 6 am-9 pm. Rm serv. Bar 11-1 am. Ck-out noon. Meeting rms. Business center. In-rm modem link. Free airport transportation. 18-hole golf privileges. Balconies. Cr cds: A, C, D, DS, MC, V. D 🖭 🏋 ⊠ ⊠ SC ⚓

Ruidoso *(See also Alamogordo)*

Motels

(Because of the altitude, air-conditioning is rarely necessary)

★ ★ ★ **BEST WESTERN SWISS CHALET INN.** *1451 Mechem, 3 mi N on NM 48. 505/258-3333; FAX 505/258-5325.* 81 rms, 2 story. June-Sept: S $68-$91; D $76-$91; each addl $6; suites $99-$150; under 12 free; lower rates rest of yr. Pet accepted, some restrictions. TV; cable (premium), VCR avail (movies). Indoor pool; whirlpool, sauna. Restaurant 7-11 am, 5:30-9 pm; closed Mon. Rm serv. Bar 5-10 pm. Ck-out noon. Coin lndry. Meeting rms. Business servs avail. Sundries. Balconies. On hilltop. Cr cds: A, C, D, DS, JCB, MC, V. 🐾 ⊠ ⊠ 🐾 SC

★ **HIGH COUNTRY LODGE.** *(Box 137, Alto 88312) 5 mi N on NM 48. 505/336-4321; res: 800/845-7265.* 32 kit. apts (2-bedrm). No A/C. S, D $119; each addl $10; higher rates hol wkends. Pet accepted. TV; cable (premium). Indoor pool; whirlpool, sauna. Playground. Ck-out 11 am. Meeting rms. Business servs avail. Tennis. Game rm. Lawn games. Fireplaces. Picnic table, grills. Lake opp. Cr cds: A, D, DS, MC, V. 🐾 ⳤ ⊠ 🐾 SC

Santa Fe *(See also Española, Las Vegas, Los Alamos)*

Motels

(Because of the altitude, air-conditioning is rarely necessary)

★ **DAYS INN.** *3650 Cerrillos Rd (87505). 505/438-3822; FAX 505/438-3795.* 97 rms, 2 story. Memorial Day-Labor Day: S $65-$105; D $66-$120; each addl $10; suites $95-$195; under 12 free; higher rates special events; lower rates rest of yr. Crib free. Pet accepted, some restrictions. TV; cable (premium). Indoor pool; whirlpool. Complimentary continental bkfst. Ck-out 11 am. Coin lndry. Business servs avail. Downhill/x-country ski 20 mi. Some refrigerators. Balconies. Cr cds: A, C, D, DS, MC, V. D 🐾 ⊠ ⊠ ⊠ 🐾 SC

★ ★ **DOUBLE TREE.** *3347 Cerrillos Rd (87505). 505/473-2800; FAX 505/473-4905.* E-mail dtreesf@rt66.com. 213 rms, 3 story. May-Oct: S, D $89-$139; each addl $10; under 12 free; ski rates; higher rates: Dec 25, Indian Market; lower rates rest of yr. Crib free. Pet accepted. TV; cable (premium). Indoor pool; whirlpools. Restaurant 7 am-1:30 pm, 5-9:30 pm. Bar. Ck-out 11 am. Coin lndry. Meeting rms. Business center. In-rm modem link. Gift shop. Free airport transportation. Downhill/x-country ski 17 mi. Exercise equipt; weights, bicycles. Refrigerators; microwaves avail. Some private patios, balconies. Cr cds: A, C, D, DS, MC, V. D 🐾 ⊠ ⊠ 🏋 ⊠ 🐾 SC 🛷

★ ★ **HOMEWOOD SUITES.** *400 Griffin St (87501). 505/988-3000; FAX 505/988-4700.* 105 kit. suites, 4 story. Mid-June-Oct: 1-bedrm $150-$170; 2-bedrm $255-$310; wkly, monthly rates; higher rates: Indian Market, hols; lower rates rest of yr. Crib free. Pet accepted; $150 deposit & $10/day. TV; cable, VCR (movies $5). Heated pool; whirlpools. Complimentary bkfst buffet. Complimentary coffee in rms. Restaurant nearby. Ck-out noon. Coin lndry. Meeting rms. Business center. In-rm modem link. Bellhops. Concierge. Exercise equipt; weights, bicycles. Microwaves. Many balconies. Picnic tables. Cr cds: A, C, D, DS, MC, V. D 🐾 ⊠ 🏋 ⊠ 🐾 SC 🛷

★ ★ ★ **INN ON THE ALAMEDA.** *303 E Alameda (87501), 2 blks from Plaza. 505/984-2121; FAX 505/986-8325; res: 800/289-2122.* 67 rms, 2-3 story. July-Oct: S, D $170-$350; each addl $15; suites $240-$350; lower rates rest of yr. Pet accepted. TV; cable (premium), VCR avail. Complimentary continental bkfst. Restaurant nearby. Bar 2:30-11 pm. Ck-out noon. Meeting rms. Business servs avail. In-rm modem link. Valet serv. Downhill/x-country ski 15 mi. Exercise equipt; weights, stair machine. Whirlpools. Massage. Health club privileges. Private patios, balconies. Library. Kiva fireplaces. Cr cds: A, C, D, DS, MC, V. D 🐾 ⊠ 🏋 ⊠ 🐾

★ ★ **LA QUINTA.** *4298 Cerrillos Rd (Business Loop I-25) (87505). 505/471-1142; FAX 505/438-7219.* 130 rms, 3 story. Mid-May-late Oct: S, D $80-$90; each addl $8; suites $121; under 18 free; lower rates rest of yr. Crib free. Pet accepted. TV; cable (premium). Pool. Complimentary continental bkfst. Restaurant adj open 24 hrs. Ck-out noon. Coin lndry. Downhill/x-country ski 14 mi. Microwaves avail. Cr cds: A, C, D, DS, MC, V. D 🐾 ⊠ ⊠ 🐾 SC

✔ ★ **QUALITY INN.** *3011 Cerrillos Rd (I-25 Business Loop) (87501). 505/471-1211; FAX 505/438-9535.* 99 rms, 2 story. May-Oct: S $63-$90; D $70-$90; each addl $10; under 18 free; lower rates rest of yr. Crib free. Pet accepted, some restrictions. TV; cable (premium). Pool. Restaurant 7 am-9 pm. Rm serv. Ck-out noon. Meeting rm. Business servs avail. Airport transportation. Downhill/x-country ski 17 mi. Some refrigerators. Balconies. Cr cds: A, C, D, DS, ER, JCB, MC, V. ⓓ 🏌 ➤ ≈ ⊠ 🔥 SC

★ **RAMADA INN.** *2907 Cerrillos Rd (87505), 3 mi N of I-25 exit 278. 505/471-3000.* 101 rms, 2 story. Mid-June-Oct: S $80; D $90; each addl $5; under 17 free; ski plan; lower rates rest of yr. Crib free. Pet accepted. TV; cable (premium). Pool. Restaurant 7-10:30 am, 11 am-2 pm, 6-9 pm. Bar. Meeting rms. Business servs avail. Downhill/x-country ski 20 mi. Health club privileges. Game rm. Cr cds: A, C, D, DS, ER, JCB, MC, V. ⓓ 🏌 ➤ ≈ ⊠ 🔥 SC

★ ★ **RESIDENCE INN BY MARRIOTT.** *1698 Galisteo St (87501). 505/988-7300; FAX 505/988-3243.* Web www.marriott.com. 120 kit. suites, 2 story. June-late Oct: kit. suites $169; under 12 free; wkly, ski rates; lower rates rest of yr. Crib free. Pet accepted, some restrictions; $150 deposit & $10/day. TV; cable (premium). Heated pool; whirlpools. Complimentary continental bkfst. Ck-out noon. Coin lndry. Meeting rms. Business servs avail. In-rm modem link. Valet serv. Airport transportation. Downhill ski 16 mi. Some private patios, balconies. Picnic tables, grills. Cr cds: A, C, D, DS, JCB, MC, V. ⓓ 🏌 ➤ ≈ ⊠ 🔥 SC

Motor Hotel

★ ★ **HOLIDAY INN.** *4048 Cerrillos Rd (I-25 Business Loop) (87501). 505/473-4646; FAX 505/473-2186.* 130 rms, 4 story. Mid-June-Sept: S $75-$135; D $85-$145; each addl $10; under 18 free; lower rates rest of yr. Crib free. Pet accepted, some restrictions. TV; cable (premium). Heated indoor/outdoor pool; whirlpool, poolside serv. Complimentary coffee in rms. Restaurant 6:30 am-10 pm. Rm serv. Bar from noon. Ck-out noon. Meeting rms. Business servs avail. In-rm modem link. Bellhops. Sundries. Airport, bus depot transportation. Downhill/x-country ski 20 mi. Exercise equipt; treadmill, weight machines, sauna. Refrigerator. Private patios, balconies. Cr cds: A, D, DS, JCB, MC, V. ⓓ 🏌 ➤ ≈ 🏃 ⊠ 🔥 SC

Hotels

★ ★ ★ **ELDORADO.** *309 W San Francisco (87501), 2 blks from the Plaza. 505/988-4455; FAX 505/988-5376; res: 800/955-4455.* E-mail res@eldoradohotel.com; web www.eldoradohotel.com. In this Pueblo revival-style hotel in the town's historic district, all the chic Southwestern guest rooms have views of the Santa Fe mountains. 219 rms, 5 story. S, D $169-$309; suites $280-$750; under 18 free. Crib free. Garage parking $9. Pet accepted. TV; cable (premium), VCR avail (movies). Rooftop pool; whirlpool, poolside serv. Restaurant 7 am-9:30 pm. Bar 11:30-2 am; entertainment. Ck-out 11:30 am. Convention facilities. Business center. In-rm modem link. Concierge. Shopping arcade. Barber, beauty shop. Downhill ski 12 mi; x-country ski 7 mi. Exercise rm; instructor, weight machine, treadmill, sauna. Massage. Refrigerators, minibars. Balconies. Cr cds: A, C, D, DS, MC, V. ⓓ 🏌 ➤ ≈ 🏃 ⊠ 🔥 SC 🎿

★ ★ ★ **INN OF THE ANASAZI.** *113 Washington Ave (87501), just off the Plaza, in the historic Plaza District. 505/988-3030; FAX 505/988-3277; res: 800/688-8100.* Web innoftheanasazi.com. This sophisticated adobe hotel one block from the Plaza embodies Santa Fe style. Contained within are native and Southwestern art and artifacts, four-poster beds and kiva fireplaces in the guest rooms. 59 units, 3 story. Apr-Oct: S, D $235-$395; each addl $20; under 12 free; lower rates rest of yr. Crib free. Valet parking $10/day. Pet accepted, some restrictions; $30. TV; cable (premium), VCR (movies $5). Complimentary coffee in rms. Restaurant 7 am-2:30 pm, 5:30-10 pm. Ck-out noon. Business servs avail. Concierge. Tennis privileges. 18-hole golf privileges, putting green, driving range. Downhill ski 13 mi; x-country ski 7 mi. Exercise equipt; treadmill, bicycle. Massage. Health club privileges. Microwaves avail. Cr cds: A, C, D, DS, ER, JCB, MC, V. ⓓ 🏌 ➤ 🏃 🏃 🏃 ⊠ 🔥 SC

Inns

★ ★ ★ **ALEXANDER'S INN.** *529 E Palace Ave (87501). 505/986-1431.* E-mail alexander@aol.com; web www.collectorsguide.com/ alexandinn. 9 rms, 2 share bath, 2 with shower only, 2 story. Mid-Mar-mid-Nov: S, D $85-$160; each addl $20; higher rates: Indian Market, Dec 25; lower rates rest of yr. Pet accepted, some restrictions. TV; cable, VCR avail. Whirlpool. Complimentary continental bkfst; afternoon refreshments. Ck-out 11 am, ck-in by arrangement. Business servs avail. Luggage handling. Concierge serv. Downhill ski 17 mi; x-country ski 10 mi. Health club privileges. Five rms in renovated house built 1903. Totally nonsmoking. Cr cds: MC, V. 🏌 ➤ ⊠ 🔥

✔ ★ ★ **EL PARADERO.** *220 W Manhattan (87501), near Capitol. 505/988-1177.* Web www.nets.com/santafe/elparadero/index.html. 12 rms, 2 kit. suites. Apr-Oct: S $60-$130; D $70-$130; each addl $15; kit. suites $130; lower rates rest of yr. Children over 4 yrs only. Pet accepted. TV in sitting rm; cable in suites. Complimentary full bkfst. Restaurant nearby. Ck-out 11 am, ck-in 2 pm. Downhill ski 18 mi; x-country ski 9 mi. Balconies.

Renovated Spanish adobe house (ca 1820) with details from 1880 & 1912 remodelings. Library/sitting rm; skylights, fireplaces, antiques. Cr cds: MC, V. 🖐 🐾 🐾 🐾

★ ★ ★ **PRESTON HOUSE.** *106 Faithway St (87501), 4 blks E of the plaza. 505/982-3465; FAX 505/982-3465.* 15 rms, 2 with shower only, 3 story, 2 suites. Some A/C. Mar-Oct, hols: S, D $75-$160; each addl $20; suites $165-$167; lower rates rest of yr. Pet accepted, some restrictions. TV. Complimentary continental bkfst; afternoon refreshments. Restaurant nearby. Ck-out 11 am, ck-in 3 pm. Business servs avail. Downhill/x-country ski 17 mi. Some fireplaces. Queen Anne house (1886) with antique furnishings and sitting rm. Totally nonsmoking. Cr cds: A, MC, V. 🖐 🐾 🐾 🐾

Santa Rosa

Motel

★ ★ **BEST WESTERN ADOBE INN.** *Will Rogers Dr (US 54, 66, 84). 505/472-3446; FAX 505/472-5759.* 58 rms, 2 story. S $38-$52; D $48-$58; each addl $2. Crib $4. Pet accepted. TV; cable. Heated pool. Complimentary continental bkfst. Ck-out 11 am. Business servs avail. In-rm modem link. Sundries. Gift shop. Airport, bus depot transportation. Cr cds: A, C, D, DS, MC, V. 🖐 🐾 🐾 SC

Silver City (See also Deming)

Motel

★ ★ **HOLIDAY MOTOR HOTEL.** *3420 NM 180E. 505/538-3711; res: 800/828-8291.* 79 rms, 2 story. S $42.20-$47.59; D $47.59; each addl $4; under 12 free. Pet accepted. TV; cable (premium). Pool. Restaurant 6 am-2 pm, 5-8:30 pm; Sun 7 am-2:30 pm, 5-8:30 pm. Rm serv. Ck-out noon. Guest lndry. Meeting rms. Business servs avail. Free airport transportation. Cr cds: A, C, D, DS, MC, V. D 🖐 🐾 🐾 SC

Socorro

Motels

★ **BEST WESTERN GOLDEN MANOR.** *507 N California St (US 60). 505/835-0230; FAX 505/835-1993.* 41 rms, 2 story. S $45; D $52; each addl $3. Crib $4. Pet accepted, some restrictions; $50 refundable. TV; cable (premium). Heated pool. Restaurant 6 am-9 pm. Rm serv. Ck-out 11 am. Microwaves. Cr cds: A, C, D, DS, MC, V. 🖐 🐾 🐾 SC

★ **WESTERN.** *(US 60, Magdalena 87825) 20 mi W. 505/854-2415.* Web wnmc.net/jlburson. 6 rms, shower only. No A/C. S $26-$44; D $34-$54; each addl $4; under 12 free; wkly rates. Pet accepted. TV; cable (premium). Complimentary coffee in rms. Restaurant nearby. Ck-out 11 am. Cr cds: A, C, D, DS, MC, V. 🖐 🐾 🐾

Taos (See also Red River)

Motels

✔★ ★ **EL PUEBLO LODGE & CONDOMINIUMS.** *412 Paseo del Pueblo Norte. 505/758-8700; FAX 505/758-7321; res: 800/433-9612.* E-mail elpueblo@newmex.com; web www.taosweb/hotel/elpueblo/. 60 rms, 1-2 story, 16 kits. Mid-June-Oct, mid-Dec-early Apr: S $48; D $65; each addl $7; suites $105-$215; kit. units $75; wkly rates; ski plans; lower rates rest of yr. Crib free. Pet accepted. TV; cable (premium). Heated pool; whirlpool. Complimentary continental bkfst. Ck-out 11:30 am. Business servs avail. Downhill ski 17 mi; x-country ski 5 mi. Refrigerators; some microwaves. Some balconies. Cr cds: A, DS, MC, V. D 🖐 🖐 🐾 🐾 🐾 SC

★ ★ **QUALITY INN.** *Box 2319 1043 Camino del Pueblo Sur, NM 68. 505/758-2200; FAX 505/758-9009.* E-mail Quality@taos.NewMexico. com; web taoswebb.com/nmusa/taos/lodging.html. 99 rms, 2 story. Mid-June-Oct: S, D $55-$99; each addl $7; suites $95-$175; under 18 free; ski plans; higher rates Christmas hols; lower rates rest of yr. Crib free. Pet accepted. TV; cable (premium), VCR avail. Heated pool; poolside serv. Coffee in rms. Restaurant 6:30 am-2 pm, 5-9 pm. Rm serv. Bar 11 am-11 pm. Ck-out 11 am. Meeting rms. Business servs avail. In-rm modem link. Valet serv. Downhill ski 20 mi; x-country ski 5 mi. Health club privileges. Many microwaves; refrigerator, wet bar in suites. Picnic tables. Cr cds: A, C, D, DS, ER, JCB, MC, V. D 🖐 🐾 🐾 🐾 🐾 SC

★ ★ ★ **SAGEBRUSH INN.** *1508 Paseo del Pueblo Sur, 3 mi S of Plaza on NM 68. 505/758-2254; FAX 505/758-5077; res: 800/428-3626.* E-mail sagebrush@taos.new mex.com. 100 rms, 2 story. S, D $70-$115; each addl $10; suites $100-$140; under 12 free.

Crib $7. Pet accepted. TV; cable (premium). Pool; whirlpools. Complimentary full bkfst. Coffee in rms. Restaurant 6:30-11 am, 5:30-10 pm. Bar 3 pm-midnight; entertainment. Ck-out 11 am. Meeting rms. Business center. X-country ski 10 mi. Sundries. Many fireplaces; some refrigerators. Built in 1929 of adobe in pueblo-mission style; extensive art collection, antiques, Navajo rugs, pottery. Cr cds: A, C, D, DS, MC, V.

D ⬚ ⬚ ⬚ ⬚ ⬚ SC ⬚

Motor Hotel

★ ★ ★ **HOLIDAY INN DON FERNANDO DE TAOS.** *1005 Paseo del Pueblo. 505/758-4444; FAX 505/758-0055.* E-mail holiday@tao.new mex.com; web taoswebb.com /nmusa/hotel/holidayinn/. 124 rms, 2 story. S, D $65-$149; under 19 free; wkly rates; ski plans; higher rates Christmas hols. Crib free. Pet accepted; $75 deposit. TV; cable, VCR avail. Indoor/outdoor pool; whirlpool, poolside serv. Restaurant 6:30 am-2 pm, 5-10 pm. Rm serv. Bar 3-11 pm; Fri, Sat to 1 am; Sun noon-11 pm. Ck-out 11 am. Meeting rm. Business servs avail. Free airport transportation. Tennis. 18-hole golf privileges, greens fee $27-$35, pro, putting green, driving range. Downhill ski 20 mi; x-country ski 5 mi. Fireplace in suites. Pueblo-style building; central courtyard. Cr cds: A, C, D, DS, JCB, MC, V.

D ⬚ ⬚ ⬚ ⬚ ⬚ ⬚ ⬚ SC

Inns

★ ★ ★ **ADOBE AND STARS INN.** *AZ 150 & Valdez Rim Rd. 505/776-2776; FAX 505/776-2872; res: 800/211-7076.* E-mail stars@taos.newmex.com; web www.taosnet .com/stars/. 7 rms, 3 with shower only. No A/C. Jan-Apr, June-Oct, Dec: S $115-$175; D $135-$185; each addl $20; wkly rates; 2-day min hols; higher rates Dec 25; lower rates rest of yr. Crib $10. Pet accepted, some restrictions. TV in common rm; VCR (movies). Complimentary full bkfst. Ck-out 11 am, ck-in 4 pm. Luggage handling. Concierge serv. Downhill/x-country ski 8 mi. Southwestern furnishings, regional art, kiva fireplaces. Totally nonsmoking. Cr cds: A, DS, MC, V. D ⬚ ⬚ ⬚ ⬚ SC

★ ★ **AUSTING HAUS.** *(Taos Ski Valley 87525) 5 mi N on US 64, then 13½ mi E on Taos Ski Valley Rd (NM 150). 505/776-2649; FAX 505/776-8751; res: 800/748-2932.* E-mail austing@newmex.com; web taoswebb.com/hotel/austinghaus. 54 rms, 2 story. No A/C. Mid-Nov-mid-Apr: S $98; D $110; each addl $20; under 5 free; ski plans; wkday rates; lower rates mid-May-mid-Nov. Closed mid-Apr-mid-May. Pet accepted. TV; cable. Complimentary continental bkfst. Dining rm 7:30-10 am; winter also 6-9 pm. Ck-out 10 am, ck-in 2 pm. Lndry facilities. Business servs avail. Downhill ski 2 mi. 3 whirlpools. Constructed of oak-pegged heavy timbers with beams exposed inside and out; built by hand entirely without nails or metal plates. Cr cds: C, D, MC, V. ⬚ ⬚ ⬚ ⬚

✔ ★ ★ ★ **EL RINCON.** *114 E Kit Carson. 505/758-4874; FAX 505/758-4541.* 17 rms, 3 story. No rm phones. S, D $59-$125; each addl $10. Crib $5. Pet accepted; $5. TV; VCR (free movies). Complimentary continental bkfst. Complimentary coffee in rms. Restaurant nearby. Ck-out 11 am, ck-in 2-6 pm. Business servs avail. Downhill ski 18 mi; x-country ski 5 mi. Many fireplaces; microwaves avail. Picnic tables. Adobe building (1800); antiques, contemporary & Native American art; fireplaces. Cr cds: A, DS, MC, V. D ⬚ ⬚ ⬚ ⬚

Truth or Consequences

Motels

✔ ★ **ACE LODGE.** *1302 N Date St (I-25 Business). 505/894-2151.* 38 rms. S $29-$32; D $34-$40; each addl $2; suites $50-$60; wkly rates. Crib $2. Pet accepted, some restrictions. TV; cable. Heated pool. Playground. Restaurant 6 am-9 pm. Bar 5 pm-2 am. Ck-out 11 am. Free airport transportation. Golf privileges. Picnic tables. Cr cds: A, C, D, MC, V. ⬚ ⬚ ⬚ ⬚ SC

★ ★ **INN AT THE BUTTE.** *(NM 195, Elephant Butte 87935) 5 mi N on I-25, exit 82. 505/744-5431; FAX 505/744-5044.* 48 rms, 2 story. Apr-Aug: S, D $46-$69; each addl $5; under 12 free; wkly rates; lower rates rest of yr. Crib $2. Pet accepted. TV; cable (premium). Complimentary coffee in rms. Restaurant 7 am-2 pm, 5-9 pm. Rm serv. Bar noon-2 am. Ck-out 11 am. Meeting rms. Business servs avail. Lighted tennis. 18-hole golf privileges. Pool. Playground. Many balconies. Picnic tables. On lake. Cr cds: A, C, D, DS, MC, V.

⬚ ⬚ ⬚ ⬚ ⬚ ⬚ ⬚ SC

Tucumcari

Motels

✔★ **BUDGET HOST ROYAL PALACIO.** *1620 E Tucumcari Blvd (I-40 Business).* *505/461-1212.* 23 rms. S $27; D $35; each addl $3. Pet accepted. TV; cable. Restaurant nearby. Ck-out 11 am. Coin lndry. Sundries. Picnic tables. Cr cds: A, DS, MC, V.
✉ ⊠ 🐾 SC

★★ **COMFORT INN.** *2800 Tucumcari.* *505/461-4094; FAX 505/461-4099.* 59 rms, 2 story. S $54-$60; D $61-$66; each addl $6; suites $66; under 12 free. Crib $6. Pet accepted. TV. Pool. Complimentary continental bkfst. Restaurant nearby. Ck-out noon. Meeting rms. Cr cds: A, C, D, DS, ER, JCB, MC, V. D ✉ ≈ ⊠ 🐾 SC

✔★ **ECONO LODGE.** *3400 E Tucumcari Blvd, I-40 exit 335.* *505/461-4194; FAX 505/461-4911.* 41 rms, 2 story. S $31.95; D $43.95-$48.95; each addl $7; under 17 free. Crib free. Pet accepted. TV; cable. Complimentary coffee in lobby. Restaurant nearby. Ck-out 11 am. Business servs avail. Cr cds: A, C, D, DS, JCB, MC, V. D ✉ ⊠ 🐾 SC

★★ **HOLIDAY INN.** *3716 E Tucumari Blvd, E I-40 at exit 335.* *505/461-3780; FAX 505/461-3931.* 100 rms, 2 story. S $45-$65; D $51-$72; each addl $6; under 18 free. Crib free. Pet accepted. TV; cable. Heated pool. Playground. Restaurant 6 am-9 pm. Rm serv. Bar 5-10 pm. Ck-out noon. Coin lndry. Meeting rms. Business servs avail. In-rm modem link. Sundries. Cr cds: A, D, DS, MC, V. D ✉ ≈ ⊠ 🐾 SC

✔★ **RODEWAY INN.** *1302 Tucumcari Blvd.* *505/461-3140.* 61 rms, 2 story. S $38; D $48; each addl $10; under 18 free. Crib free. Pet accepted. TV; cable (premium). Pool. Complimentary continental bkfst. Restaurant adj 11 am-9 pm. Ck-out noon. Meeting rm. Cr cds: A, D, DS, MC, V. D ✉ ≈ ⊠ 🐾 SC

New York

Albany *(See also Schenectady)*

Motels

(Rates may be higher Saratoga racing season)

★ ★ **HOWARD JOHNSON.** *Southern Blvd (12209), US 9W at I-87 exit 23.* 518/462-6555; FAX 518/462-2547. 135 rms, 1-2 story. S $65; D $75; each addl $8; suites $95; under 18 free. Crib free. Pet accepted, some restrictions. TV; cable (premium). Pool; lifeguard. Restaurant open 24 hrs. Bar 11 am-closing. Ck-out noon. Coin lndry. Meeting rms. Business servs avail. Valet serv. Indoor tennis privileges, pro. Exercise equipt; weight machines, treadmills. Private patios, balconies. Cr cds: A, C, D, DS, ER, JCB, MC, V.
D ⬔ 🏃 ⚓ 🏸 🖎 🐾 SC

★ ★ ★ **INN AT THE CENTURY.** *(997 New Loudon Rd (NY 9), Latham 12110) near I-87N exit 7.* 518/785-0931; FAX 518/785-3274. Web www.centuryhouse.inter.net. 68 rms, 2 story. S $79; D $89; each addl $12; suites $125-$225; higher rates: Aug, special events. Pet accepted, some restrictions; $5. TV; cable (premium). Pool. Complimentary full bkfst buffet. Restaurant 11 am-9:45 pm; Sat 4-10 pm; Sun 11 am-2 pm, 4-9 pm. Rm serv 4-9:30 pm (Mon-Fri). Bar 11 am-11 pm. Ck-out noon. Business servs avail. In-rm modem link. Valet serv. Tennis. Exercise equipt; weight machine, treadmills. Nature trail. Some refrigerators. Microwaves avail. Cr cds: A, D, DS, MC, V. D ⬔ 🏃 ⚓ 🏸 🖎 🐾

✔ ★ **MICROTEL.** *(7 Rensselaer Ave, Latham 12110) 5 mi N on I-87, exit 6.* 518/782-9161; FAX 518/782-9162; res: 800/782-9121. 100 rms, 2 story. S $35.95-$51.95; D $39.95-$55.95; under 14 free. Crib free. Pet accepted, some restrictions. TV; cable (premium). Complimentary coffee in lobby. Restaurant nearby. Ck-out noon. Meeting rm. Business servs avail. In-rm modem link. Sundries. Some refrigerators. Microwaves avail. Cr cds: A, C, D, DS, MC, V. D ⬔

★ ★ **RAMADA LIMITED.** *1630 Central Ave (12205), 8 mi W on NY 5 to I-87 exit 2W, near County Airport.* 518/456-0222; FAX 518/452-1376. 105 rms, 2 story. July-Aug: S, D $79-$99; under 18 free; lower rates rest of yr. Crib free. Pet accepted; $50 deposit. TV; cable (premium), VCR (movies). Complimentary continental bkfst. Complimentary coffee in rms. Restaurant nearby. Ck-out 11 am. Meeting rms. Business servs avail. Beauty shop. Exercise equipt; weights, bicycle. Some in-rm whirlpools, refrigerators, microwaves. Cr cds: A, D, DS, MC, V. D ⬔ 🏸 🖎 🐾 SC

Motor Hotels

✔ ★ ★ **RAMADA INN.** *1228 Western Ave (12203), I-90 exit 24; I-87 exit 1.* 518/489-2981; FAX 518/489-8967. E-mail ramadaonwestern@msn.com; web www.ramada.com/ramada.html. 195 rms, 5 story. S $69-$85; D $69-$95; each addl $10; suites $150-$195; under 18 free; wkend plan; higher rates special events. Crib free. Pet accepted. TV; cable (premium). Indoor pool; lifeguard. Complimentary full bkfst (adults). Coffee in rms. Restaurant 6:30 am-10 pm. Bar. Ck-out noon. Meeting rms. Business servs avail. In-rm modem link. Valet serv. Beauty shop. Free airport, RR station, bus depot transportation (8 am-8 pm.). Exercise equipt; weights, bicycle, sauna. Microwaves avail Cr cds: A, C, D, DS, MC, V. ⬔ ⚓ 🏸 🖎 🐾 SC

Hotels

★ ★ ★ **MARRIOTT.** *189 Wolf Rd (12205), near County Airport, I-87 exit 4.* 518/458-8444; FAX 518/458-7365. 360 rms, 7-8 story. S, D $84-$168; suites $250-$350; wkend rates. Pet accepted. TV; cable (premium), VCR avail (movies). 2 heated pools, 1 indoor; whirlpool, poolside serv, lifeguard. Restaurant 6:30 am-10 pm. Bar; entertainment wkends. Ck-out noon. Coin lndry. Convention facilities. Business center. In-rm modem link. Gift shop. Free airport transportation. Exercise equipt; weights, bicycles, sauna. Health club privileges. Refrigerators avail. Luxury level. Cr cds: A, C, D, DS, ER, JCB, MC, V.
D ⬔ ⚓ 🏸 ✈ 🖎 🐾 SC 🏌

★ ★ ★ **OMNI.** *Ten Eyck Plaza (12207).* 518/462-6611; FAX 518/462-2901. 386 rms, 15 story. S $89-$149; D $89-$179; each addl $20; suites $119-$425; family, wkend rates. Pet accepted; $50. TV; cable, VCR avail. Indoor pool; whirlpool. Coffee in rms. Restaurant 7 am-2 pm, 5-10 pm. Rm serv. Bar 11:30-1 am. Ck-out noon. Meeting rms. Business servs avail. In-rm modem link. Shopping arcade. Covered parking. Free airport, RR station, bus depot transportation. Exercise equipt; weight machine, stair machine. Some refrigerators. Cr cds: A, C, D, DS, MC, V. D ⬔ ⚓ 🏸 🖎 🐾 SC

Inn

★ ★ **MANSION HILL.** *115 Philip St (12202), at Park Ave. 518/465-2038; FAX 518/434-2313.* 8 rms, 2 story. S $115; D $125; under 17 free; wkend rates. Crib free. Pet accepted. TV; cable, VCR avail (movies). Complimentary full bkfst. Restaurant 5-9 pm. Rm serv 5-9 pm. Ck-out 11:30 am, ck-in 3 pm. Luggage handling. Valet serv. Concierge serv. RR station, bus depot transportation. Built in 1861. Cr cds: A, C, D, DS, MC, V.

Amsterdam (See also Johnstown, Schenectady)

Motor Hotel

★ ★ **BEST WESTERN.** *10 Market St, just off NY 30N. 518/843-5760; FAX 518/842-0940.* 125 rms, 5 story. S $55-$72; D $58-$78; each addl $6; under 18 free; wkly rates; higher rates Aug. Crib free. Pet accepted, some restrictions. TV; cable, VCR avail (movies). Indoor pool. Restaurant 6:30 am-9 pm. Rm serv. Bar 11-12:30 am. Ck-out noon. Meeting rms. Business servs avail. In-rm modem link. Valet serv. Sundries. Shopping arcade. Refrigerator avail. Cr cds: A, C, D, DS, JCB, MC, V.

Batavia (See also Buffalo, Rochester)

Motels

★ ★ **BEST WESTERN.** *8204 Park Rd. 716/343-1000; FAX 716/343-8608.* 75 rms, 2 story. Mid-June-mid-Sept: S $74-$84; D $79-$99; each addl $6; under 18 free; lower rates rest of yr. Crib free. Pet accepted, some restrictions. TV; cable (premium), VCR avail. Heated pool; poolside serv, lifeguard. Restaurant 6:30 am-2 pm, 5-9 pm. Rm serv. Bar 11-2 am; entertainment Fri, Sat. Ck-out noon. Meeting rms. Business servs avail. In-rm modem link. Valet serv. Lawn games. Cr cds: A, C, D, DS, MC, V.

★ ★ **DAYS INN.** *200 Oak St, just off I-90. 716/343-1440; FAX 716/343-5322.* 120 rms, 2 story. May-Sept: S $62-$82; D $69-$99; each addl $7; under 18 free; lower rates rest of yr. Crib free. Pet accepted. TV; cable (premium). Pool; lifeguard. Complimentary continental bkfst. Restaurant nearby. Ck-out noon. Meeting rms. Business servs avail. Cr cds: A, C, D, DS, JCB, MC, V.

Hotel

★ ★ **HOLIDAY INN.** *8250 Park Rd. 716/344-2100; FAX 716/344-0238.* 196 rms, 5 story. S $80-$110; D $89.95-$119.95; each addl $10; suites $150-$200; under 18 free; racetrack plans. Crib free. Pet accepted, some restrictions. TV; cable (premium). 2 pools, 1 indoor; whirlpool, poolside serv, lifeguard. Restaurant 6:30 am-11 pm. Bar 11-2 am; entertainment Fri, Sat. Ck-out noon. Meeting rms. Business servs avail. In-rm modem link. Exercise equipt; weights, treadmill, sauna. Some refrigerators. Cr cds: A, C, D, DS, ER, JCB, MC, V.

Bath

Motel

✔ ★ **CABOOSE.** *(8620 NY 415, Avoca 14809) 8 mi NW on NY 415. 607/566-2216.* 23 units, 1 story, 5 caboose rms. Mid-Apr-mid-Oct: S, D $45-$70; each addl $7; higher rates: college events, racing season; lower rates mid-Oct-Nov & May-late June. Closed Dec-Mar. Crib $5. Pet accepted, some restrictions. TV; cable (premium). Heated pool. Playground. Complimentary coffee in rms. Restaurant opp 6 am-8 pm. Ck-out 11 am. Business servs avail. In-rm modem link. Gift shop. Lawn games. Refrigerators avail. Picnic tables, grills. Five antique cabooses (1916), set on track laid adj to motel, provide unique accommodations; interiors, including intact bunks, air brakes, torpedo boxes, are in near-original condition. Cr cds: MC, V.

Motor Hotel

★ ★ **DAYS INN.** *330 W Morris St. 607/776-7644; FAX 607/776-7650.* 104 rms, 5 story. June-Oct: S $54-$69; D $59-$74; each addl $5; under 18 free; lower rates rest of yr. Crib free. Pet accepted. TV; cable (premium), VCR avail (movies). Indoor pool. Restaurant 7-11 am, 5-9:30 pm. Bar. Ck-out 11 am. Meeting rms. Business servs avail. Cr cds: A, C, D, DS, MC, V.

Binghamton (See also Endicott)

Motels

✔ ★ ★ **COMFORT INN.** *1156 Front St (13905), I-81 exit 6N. 607/722-5353; FAX 607/722-1823.* 67 rms, 2 story. S $40-$75; D $45-$85; each addl $10; kit. suites $60-$105; under 18 free; higher rates special events. Crib $8. Pet accepted; deposit. TV; cable (premium). Complimentary continental bkfst. Restaurant adj 7 am-11 pm. Ck-out noon. Coin lndry. Meeting rm. Business servs avail. In-rm modem link. Microwave in suites. Cr cds: A, C, D, DS, ER, JCB, MC, V. D ♥ ⊠ ॐ SC

★ **HoJo INN.** *690 Old Front St (13905), I-81 exit 5. 607/724-1341; FAX 607/773-8287.* 107 rms, 2 story. S $40-$60; D $46-$70; each addl $10; higher rates special events. Crib free. Pet accepted, some restrictions. TV; cable, VCR. Complimentary continental bkfst. Restaurant nearby open 24 hrs. Ck-out noon. Meeting rms. Business servs avail. Balconies. Cr cds: A, C, D, DS, MC, V. D ♥ ⊠ ॐ SC

Hotels

★ ★ ★ **HOLIDAY INN-ARENA.** *2-8 Hawley St (13901), I-88 exit 5; I-81 exit 3; NY 17 exit 72; NY 81 S exit 5. 607/722-1212; FAX 607/722-6063.* 241 rms, 8 story. S, D $93-$99; each addl $10; suites $130; under 19 free; wkend plans. Crib free. Pet accepted; $15. TV; cable (premium). Indoor pool; lifeguard. Coffee in rms. Restaurant 6:30 am-10 pm. Rm serv. Bar noon-1 am; Fri, Sat to 2 am; entertainment wkends. Ck-out noon. Coin lndry. Convention facilities. Business servs avail. In-rm modem link. Shopping arcade. Airport transportation. Health club privileges. Some refrigerators, $15. Cr cds: A, C, D, DS, JCB, MC, V.
D ♥ ≈ ⊠ ॐ SC

★ ★ ★ **HOTEL DE VILLE.** *80 State St (13901). 607/722-0000; res: 800/295-5599; FAX 607/722-7912.* 61 rms, 6 story. S $75-$95; D $85-$95; each addl $7; suites $150; under 18 free. Crib avail. Pet accepted, some restrictions. TV; cable (premium). Complimentary bkfst. Restaurant 7 am-2:30 pm, 5:30-9 pm. Bar. Ck-out noon. Meeting rms. Business servs avail. In-rm modem link. Valet parking. X-country ski 5 mi. Health club privileges. Renovated city hall (1897). Cr cds: A, C, D, DS, ER, JCB, MC, V. D ♥ ⊠ ॐ ⊠ ॐ SC

Boonville (See also Rome)

Motel

✔ ★ ★ **HEADWATERS MOTOR LODGE.** *1/4 mi N on NY 12. 315/942-4493; FAX 315/942-4626.* 37 rms, 1-2 story, 4 kits. S $55; D $65; each addl $8; under 12 free. Crib $5. Pet accepted, some restrictions. TV; cable (premium). Complimentary continental bkfst from 6 am; Sat, Sun, hols from 7 am. Restaurant nearby. Ck-out 11 am. Meeting rms. In-rm modem link. Game rm. Downhill/x-country ski 9 mi. Refrigerators. Cr cds: A, DS, MC, V.
D ♥ ⊠ ⊠ ॐ

Buffalo (See also Niagara Falls, NY; also see Niagara Falls, ON, Canada)

Motels

✔ ★ ★ **HERITAGE HOUSE COUNTRY INN.** *(8261 Main St, Williamsville 14221) I-90 exit 49, E on NY 5, near Intl Airport. 716/633-4900; res: 716/283-3899; FAX 716/633-4900.* Web www.wnybiz.com/heritage. 53 rms, 2 story, 9 kit. units. S $52.95-$68.95; D, kit. units $58.95-$88.95; each addl $7; under 18 free. Crib $7. Pet accepted, some restrictions. TV; cable. Complimentary continental bkfst. Restaurant opp 11:30 am-9:30 pm. Ck-out noon. Business servs avail. Bellhops. Valet serv. Free airport, RR station transportation. Health club privileges. Refrigerator, microwave in kit. units. Picnic tables. Cr cds: A, C, D, DS, MC, V. ♥ ⊠ ॐ SC

★ **MICROTEL.** *(1 Hospitality Centre Way, Tonawanda 14150) I-290 to Delaware Ave exit, Crestmount Ave to motel. 716/693-8100; FAX 716/693-8750; res: 800/227-6346.* 100 rms, 2 story. Mid-June-early Sept: S $39.95; D $43.95; under 18 free; lower rates rest of yr. Crib free. Pet accepted, some restrictions. TV; cable. Complimentary coffee in lobby. Ck-out noon. Cr cds: A, D, DS, MC, V. D ♥ ⊠ ॐ

✔ ★ **RED ROOF INN-AMHERST.** *(42 Flint Rd, Amherst 14226) NE on I-290, Millersport exit 58 to Flint Rd. 716/689-7474; FAX 716/689-2051.* 108 rms. June-Aug: S $69.99-$79.99; D $79.99-$89.99; under 18 free; higher rates special events; lower rates rest of yr. Crib free. Pet accepted, some restrictions. TV; cable (premium). Complimentary coffee. Restaurant nearby. Ck-out noon. Business servs avail. Cr cds: A, C, D, DS, MC, V. D ♥ ⊠ ॐ SC

★ ★ **RESIDENCE INN BY MARRIOTT.** *(100 Maple Rd, Williamsville 14221) NE via I-290, NY 263 exit to Maple Rd.* 716/632-6622; FAX 716/632-5247. 112 kit. suites, 2 story. Kit. suites $120-$150. Crib free. Pet accepted, some restrictions; $6 per day. TV; cable, VCR avail. Heated pool. Complimentary continental bkfst. Ck-out noon. Coin lndry. Business servs avail. In-rm modem link. Valet serv. Free airport transportation. Exercise equipt; bicycles, rower. Microwaves. Cr cds: A, C, D, DS, JCB, MC, V.

D ⟲ ≈ 🕉 ✈ ⊠ 🐾 SC

Motor Hotels

★ ★ **HOLIDAY INN-DOWNTOWN.** *620 Delaware Ave (14202).* 716/886-2121; FAX 716/886-7942. Web www.harthotels.com. 168 rms, 8 story. S, D $84-$99; each addl $10; under 18 free; ski plans. Crib free. Pet accepted, some restrictions. TV; cable (premium). Heated pool; wading pool, lifeguard. Restaurant 6:30 am-10 pm. Rm serv. Bar 11 am-midnight. Ck-out noon. Coin lndry. Meeting rms. Business servs avail. In-rm modem link. Bellhops. Valet serv. Some free indoor parking. Free airport transportation. Health club privileges. Cr cds: A, C, D, DS, JCB, MC, V.   D ⟲ ≈ ✈ ⊠ 🐾 SC

★ **LORD AMHERST.** *(5000 Main St, Amherst 14226) E on NY 5 to jct I-290, near Greater Buffalo Intl Airport.* 716/839-2200; res: 800/544-2200; FAX 716/839-1538. 101 rms, 2 story. May-Sept: S $59-$69; D $69-$85; each addl $7; suites $95-$160; kit. units $75-$150; under 18 free; lower rates rest of yr. Crib free. Pet accepted, some restrictions. TV; cable. Heated pool; lifeguard. Complimentary full bkfst. Restaurant 7 am-midnight. Bar 11 am-2 am. Ck-out 1 pm. Coin lndry. Meeting rms. Business servs avail. In-rm modem link. Valet serv. Game rm. Exercise equipt; stair machine, treadmill. Microwaves avail. Colonial decor. Cr cds: A, C, D, DS, MC, V.   D ⟲ ≈ 🕉 ⊠ 🐾 SC

★ ★ **MARRIOTT.** *(1340 Millersport Hwy, Amherst 14221) N on I-290, exit Millersport.* 716/689-6900; FAX 716/689-0483. 356 rms. S $132; D $142; each addl $10; suites $275; under 18 free; wkend plans. Crib free. Pet accepted, some restrictions; $50. TV; cable (premium), VCR avail. Indoor/outdoor pool; whirlpool, poolside serv. Restaurant 6:30 am-10:30 pm; Fri, Sat 7 am-11 pm; Sun 7 am-10:30 pm. Bar noon-3 am, Tues, Fri, Sat to 4 am, Sun noon-midnight. Ck-out noon. Convention facilities. Business servs avail. In-rm modem link. Bellhops. Valet serv. Concierge. Gift shop. Free airport transportation. Exercise equipt; weights, bicycles, sauna. Game rm. Some bathrm phones. Refrigerators, microwaves avail. Some poolside patios. Luxury level. Cr cds: A, C, D, DS, ER, JCB, MC, V.

D ⟲ ≈ 🕉 ✈ ⊠ 🐾 SC

Canandaigua *(See also Rochester, Victor)*

Motels

✔ ★ ★ **ECONO LODGE.** *170 Eastern Blvd (14424).* 716/394-9000; FAX 716/396-2560. 65 rms, 2 story. May-Oct: S $50.95; D $66.95; each addl $8; under 18 free; lower rates rest of yr. Crib free. Pet accepted, some restrictions. TV; cable (premium), VCR avail (movies). Complimentary coffee in lobby. Restaurant adj open 24 hrs. Ck-out 11 am. Coin lndry. Business servs avail. Downhill ski 12 mi. Opp lake. Cr cds: A, C, D, DS, JCB, MC, V.

D ⟲ ≈ ⊠ 🐾 SC

★ ★ **INN ON THE LAKE.** *770 S Main St (14424), off US 20.* 716/394-7800; FAX 716/394-5003; res: 800/228-2801. 134 rms, 2 story, 44 suites. May-Nov: S $95-$145; D $105-$155; each addl $10; suites $139-$295; under 17 free; package plans; higher rates Hill Cumorah Pageant; lower rates rest of yr. Crib free. Pet accepted. TV; cable, VCR avail (movies). Heated pool; lifeguard. Restaurant 6:30 am-9 pm; wkends to 10 pm. Rm serv. Bar 11-1 am. Ck-out 11 am. Meeting rms. Business servs avail. In-rm modem link. Exercise equipt; bicycle, treadmill. Downhill ski 20 mi. Refrigerators in suites. Some balconies. Picnic tables. On lake. Cr cds: A, D, DS, MC, V. D ⟲ ≈ ≈ 🕉 🐾 ⊠ 🐾 SC

Canton *(See also Ogdensburg)*

Motel

★ ★ **BEST WESTERN UNIVERSITY INN.** *90 Main St E, adj to St Lawrence University.* 315/386-8522; FAX 315/386-1025. 102 rms, 3 story. No elvtr. May-Oct: S $55; D $65-$75; under 12 free; golf plan; lower rates rest of yr. Crib free. Pet accepted. TV; cable (premium). Pool. Coffee in rms. Restaurant 6:30 am-9 pm. Rm serv. Bar 11-2 am. Ck-out noon. Meeting rms. Business servs avail. X-country ski on site. Some refrigerators. Cr cds: A, C, D, DS, ER, MC, V.   D ⟲ ≈ ≈ ⊠ 🐾 SC

Cooperstown (See also Oneonta)

Motel

★ ★ **BEST WESTERN INN AT THE COMMONS.** *50 Commons Dr, 3 mi S on NY 28.* 607/547-9439; FAX 607/547-7082. 62 rms, 2 story, 3 suites. May-Sept: S $79-$149; D, suites $89-$149; each addl $8; under 12 free; 2-day min wkends, hols; higher rates special events; lower rates rest of yr. Crib free. Pet accepted, some restrictions; $8. TV; cable (premium), VCR avail (movies). Indoor pool; whirlpool. Playground. Complimentary continental bkfst. Restaurant adj 6 am-midnight. Ck-out 11 am. Coin lndry. Meeting rm. Business servs avail. In-rm modem link. Shopping arcade adj. Barber shop. Exercise equipt; bicycle, treadmill. Game rm. Refrigerator, microwave in suites. Picnic tables. Cr cds: A, C, D, DS, MC, V. D ⟐ ⌇ ⊁ ⊠ ⚭ SC

Corning

Motel

★ **ECONO LODGE.** *200 Robert Dann (14870).* 607/962-4444. 61 rms, 2 story. May-Oct: S $39-$44; D $55-$57; each addl $5; under 18 free; higher rates (2-day min) race wkends, LPGA; lower rates rest of yr. Crib free. Pet accepted; $10. TV; cable, VCR avail (movies). Complimentary continental bkfst. Restaurant nearby. Ck-out 11 am. Meeting rms. Business servs avail. Some refrigerators. Cr cds: A, D, DS, JCB, MC, V.

D ⟐ ⊠ ⚭ SC

Motor Hotel

★ ★ ★ **RADISSON-CORNING.** *125 Denison Pkwy E, on NY 17 (Denison Pkwy), downtown.* 607/962-5000; FAX 607/962-4166. 177 rms, 3 story. S $107-$141; D $117-$151; each addl $10; suites $150-$225; under 18 free; wkend rates. Crib free. Pet accepted, some restrictions. TV; cable. Indoor pool; lifeguard. Coffee in rm. Restaurant 7 am-9:30 pm. Rm serv. Bar 11-12:30 am; entertainment Fri, Sat. Ck-out 1 pm. Meeting rms. Business servs avail. Bellhops. Cr cds: A, D, DS, MC, V. D ⟐ ⌇ ⊠ ⚭ SC

Dunkirk

Motels

★ ★ **DAYS INN.** *(10455 Bennett Rd, Fredonia 14063)* ¼ mi S, I-90 exit 59. 716/673-1351; FAX 716/672-6909. 132 rms, 2 story. Apr-Sept: S $51-$69; D $59-$79; each addl $7; under 18 free; lower rates rest of yr. Crib free. Pet accepted, some restrictions. TV; cable (premium), VCR avail. Ck-out 11 am. Lndry facilities. Meeting rms. Business servs avail. Valet serv. Downhill/x-country ski 20 mi. Cr cds: A, C, D, DS, JCB, MC, V.

D ⟐ ⌇ ⊠ ⚭ SC

✔ **SOUTHSHORE.** *5040 W Lake Shore Drive.* 716/366-2822. 9 A/C units in motel, 7 kits., 12 kit. cottages. July-Aug: D, kit. units, kit. cottages $48-$95; wkly rates; lower rates rest of yr. Crib $5. Pet accepted, some restrictions. TV; VCR avail. Heated pool. Playground. Ck-out 10 am. Guest lndry. Lawn games. Refrigerators. Picnic tables, grill. Cr cds: MC, V. ⟐ ⌇ ⚭

★ ★ **VINEYARD.** *3929 Vineyard Dr, I-90 exit 59.* 716/366-4400; res: 716/366-2200; FAX 716/366-3375. 38 rms in 2 buildings. July-early Sept: S $55-$65; D $65-$75; each addl $4; under 18 free; lower rates rest of yr. Crib free. Pet accepted. TV; cable (premium). Pool; lifeguard. Playground. Restaurant 6 am-11 pm. Bar 10-midnight, Sun noon-9 pm. Ck-out noon. Meeting rms. Business servs avail. Cr cds: A, D, DS, MC, V.

D ⟐ ⌇ ⊠ ⚭ SC

Elmira (See also Corning)

Motels

✔ ★ ★ **BEST WESTERN MARSHALL MANOR.** *(3527 Watkins Rd, Horseheads 14845) on NY 14, 5 mi N of NY 17 exit 52.* 607/739-3891. 40 rms. S $36-$59; D $38-$66; each addl $5; under 18 free; higher rates special events. Crib $2. Pet accepted; $4. TV; cable, VCR avail. Pool. Complimentary continental bkfst. Complimentary coffee in rms. Restaurant 4-10 pm. Bar to 1 am. Ck-out 11 am. In-rm modem link. Refrigerators, microwaves avail. Cr cds: A, C, D, DS, MC, V. D ⟐ ⌇ ⊠ ⚭ SC

★ **COACHMAN MOTOR LODGE.** *908 Pennsylvania Ave (NY 14S) (14904).* 607/733-5526; FAX 607/733-0961. 18 kit. units, 2 story. Apr-Nov: S $49-$55; D $60-$65; under 18 free; each addl $5; wkly rates; lower rates rest of yr. Crib free. Pet accepted. TV;

cable. Complimentary coffee in rms. Restaurant nearby. Ck-out noon. Coin lndry. Business servs avail. Sundries. Microwaves avail. Some balconies. Picnic table, grill. Cr cds: A, C, DS, MC, V. [D] 🐾 ⊠ 🐾 SC

★ ★ ★ **HOLIDAY INN.** *1 Holiday Plaza (14901). 607/734-4211; FAX 607/734-3549.* 150 rms, 2 story. S, D $70-$100; each addl $5; under 19 free; higher rates special events. Crib free. Pet accepted. TV; cable (premium), VCR avail. 2 pools, 1 indoor (winter); wading pool. Restaurant 6:30 am-2 pm, 5-10 pm; wkends from 7 am. Rm serv. Bar 4 pm-midnight; entertainment Sat. Ck-out noon. Coin lndry. Meeting rms. Business servs avail. In-rm modem link. Valet serv. Sundries. Exercise equipt; bicycles, treadmill. Refrigerators, microwaves avail. Cr cds: A, C, D, DS, ER, MC, V. [D] 🐾 ⊠ 🕺 🐾 ⊠ 🐾 SC

★ ★ **HOWARD JOHNSON.** *(2671 Corning Rd, Horseheads 14845) Off NY 17 exit 52 at NY14. 607/739-5636; FAX 607/739-8630.* 76 rms, 1-2 story. May-mid-Nov: S $48-$70; D $58-$80; each addl $8; studio rms avail; under 18 free; lower rates rest of yr. Crib free. Pet accepted. TV; cable (premium). Pool. Coffee in rms. Restaurant 6:30 am-11 pm; Fri, Sat to midnight. Rm serv. Ck-out noon. In-rm modem link. Valet serv. Sundries. Some refrigerators. Microwaves avail. Private patios, balconies. Cr cds: A, C, D, DS, JCB, MC, V.
🐾 ⊠ 🐾 🐾 SC

Endicott *(See also Binghamton, Owego)*

Motor Hotel

★ **EXECUTIVE INN.** *1 Delaware Ave. 607/754-7570.* 135 rms, 40 suites, 60 kits. S $44-$59; D $54-$59; suites $59-$89; kits. $79-$89; under 16 free; wkly, wkend, hol rates; higher rates special events. Crib free. Pet accepted, some restrictions; $50 refundable. TV; cable (premium), VCR avail (movies). Restaurant adj. Ck-out noon. Meeting rms. Business servs avail. Some refrigerators. Microwaves avail. Cr cds: A, C, D, DS, MC, V.
[D] 🐾 ⊠ 🐾 SC

Fishkill *(See also Newburgh, Poughkeepsie)*

Motels

★ ★ ★ **RESIDENCE INN BY MARRIOTT.** *2481 US 9, at I-84 exit 13, US 9N. 914/896-5210; FAX 914/896-9689.* 136 suites, 2 story. Suites $89-$229. Crib free. Pet accepted. TV; cable (premium), VCR avail (movies). Pool. Complimentary continental bkfst. Restaurant adj. Ck-out noon. Coin lndry. Meeting rms. Business servs avail. In-rm modem link. Valet serv. Sundries. Exercise equipt; weights, bicycle. Health club privileges. Refrigerators, microwaves. Cr cds: A, C, D, DS, ER, JCB, MC, V. [D] 🐾 ⊠ 🕺 🐾 ⊠ 🐾 SC

✔ ★ ★ **WELLESLEY INN.** *US 9, I-84 exit 13. 914/896-4995; FAX 914/896-6631; res: 800/444-8888.* 82 rms, 4 story. Apr-Oct: S, D $60-$85; each addl $2; suites $95-$150; under 17 free; wkly, wkend, hol rates (2-day min wkends, hols); higher rates: West Point graduation, hols; lower rates rest of yr. Crib free. Pet accepted; $5. TV; cable (premium). Complimentary continental bkfst. Complimentary coffee in rms. Restaurant adj open 24 hrs. Bar noon-11 pm. Ck-out 11 am. In-rm modem link. Health club privileges. Sundries. Some refrigerators. Minibar, microwaves avail. Cr cds: A, C, D, DS, MC, V. [D] 🐾 ⊠ 🐾 SC

Fulton *(See also Syracuse)*

Motel

✔ ★ ★ **FULTON MOTOR LODGE.** *163 S 1st St, at Academy St, on river. 315/598-6100; FAX 315/592-4738; res: 800/223-6935.* 70 rms, 2 story. S $48-$79; D $55-$90; each addl $8; suites $72-$92. Crib free. Pet accepted. TV; cable (premium). Pool. Complimentary full bkfst. Ck-out noon. Meeting rms. Business servs avail. Valet serv. Exercise equipt; bicycles, rower. Business servs avail. Bathrm phones, refrigerators. Cr cds: A, D, DS, MC, V. [D] 🐾 🐾 ⊠ 🕺 ⊠ 🐾 SC

Garden City, L.I. *(See also New York City)*

Hotel

★ ★ ★ **LONG ISLAND MARRIOTT.** *(101 James Doolittle Blvd, Uniondale 11553) Off Meadowbrook Pkwy exit M4. 516/794-3800; FAX 516/794-5936.* 617 rms, 11 story. S, D $135-155; each addl $20; suites $400-$650; under 18 free; wkend rates. Crib free. Pet accepted, some restrictions. TV; cable (premium), VCR avail. Indoor pool; whirlpool, sauna, poolside serv, lifeguard. Restaurant 6:30 am-11 pm. Rm serv to midnight. Bar 11-2 am. Ck-out noon. Convention facilities. Business center. In-rm modem link. Bellhops. Barber, beauty shop. Exercise rm; instructor, weights, bicycles. Game rm. Refrigerators avail, microwaves avail. Balconies. Adj Nassau Coliseum. Cr cds: A, C, D, DS, ER, JCB, MC, V.

Herkimer *(See also Utica)*

Motels

★ ★ **BEST WESTERN-LITTLE FALLS.** *(20 Albany St, Little Falls 13365) Approx 7 mi E on NY 5.* 315/823-4954; FAX 315/823-4507. 56 rms, 2 story. May-Sept: S $57; D $63; each addl $6; under 12 free; lower rates rest of yr. Crib free. Pet accepted, some restrictions; $10 refundable. TV; cable. Restaurant 6:30 am-2 pm, 5-9 pm; Sun 7 am-1 pm, 5-9 pm. Bar 11 am-2 pm, 5-11 pm. Ck-out noon. Meeting rms. Business servs avail. Game rm. Cr cds: A, C, D, DS, MC, V.

✔ **HERKIMER.** *100 Marginal Rd, adj I-90 Exit 30.* 315/866-0490; FAX 315/866-0416. 61 rms, 2 story, 16 kits. July-early Sept: S $46-$68; D $66-$73; each addl $7; kit. units, studio rms $75-$83; under 13 free; wkly rates; lower rates rest of yr. Crib free. Pet accepted, some restrictions. TV; cable. Heated pool. Restaurant adj open 24 hrs. Ck-out 11 am. Coin lndry. Meeting rms. Business servs avail. Sundries. Downhill/x-country ski 7 mi. Picnic tables. Cr cds: A, C, D, DS, MC, V.

Hillsdale *(See also Hudson)*

Motel

★ ★ **SWISS HUTTE.** *NY 23, just off NY 23, adj Catamount Ski area.* 518/325-3333; FAX 413/528-6201. E-mail 8057@msn.com; web www.regionet.com/colberk/swiss hutte.html. 15 rms, 2 story. MAP: S $95-$140; D $150-$180; lodge suites $95/person; EP avail; wkly rates; lower rates Mar-Apr, Nov. Pet accepted, some restrictions. TV; cable. Heated pool. Restaurant. Bar noon-11:30 pm. Ck-out 11 am. Ck-in 2 pm. Meeting rms. Business servs avail. Tennis. Downhill/x-country ski adj. Lawn games. Refrigerators avail. Private patios, balconies. Cr cds: MC, V.

Inn

★ ★ ★ **LINDEN VALLEY.** *NY 23, 2 mi E on NY 23.* 518/325-7100. 7 rms, 6 with shower only. July-Aug: S, D $125-$135; 3-day min wknds; lower rates rest of yr. Pet accepted, some restrictions. TV; cable. Complimentary full bkfst. Complimentary coffee in rms. Restaurant adj 6-9 pm. Ck-out 1 pm, ck-in 1 pm. Tennis. Downhill ski adj. Refrigerators, minibars. Some balconies. Large spring-fed pond with sand beach; swimming. Cr cds: MC, V.

Hornell *(See also Bath)*

Motel

✔ ★ **COACHLIGHT.** *Box 486, 1¹/₂ mi N on Old NY 36; ¹/₂ mi S of NY 17 Hornell exit.* 607/324-0800; FAX 607/324-0905; res: 800/698-0801. 78 rms, 2 story. S $31-$45; D $39-$49; each addl $3. Pet accepted. TV; cable, VCR avail (movies). Complimentary bkfst in lobby. Restaurant 5-9 pm; Sun brunch 9 am-1:30 pm. Bar from 4:30 pm. Ck-out 11 am. Meeting rms. Business servs avail. In-rm modem link. Downhill ski 10 mi. Picnic tables. Cr cds: A, D, DS, MC, V.

Howes Cave *(See also Albany, Schenectady, Stamford)*

Motel

★ ★ **BEST WESTERN INN OF COBLESKILL.** *(Box 189, Cobleskill 12043) 3 mi SE on NY 7, Campus Dr extension.* 518/234-4321; FAX 518/234-3869. 76 rms, 2 story. S, D $70-$139; under 12 free. Crib free. Pet accepted, some restrictions. TV; cable (premium), VCR avail (movies $7). Indoor pool; wading pool. Coffee in rms. Restaurant 7 am-9 pm. Rm serv. Bar 4-10 pm. Ck-out 11 am. Meeting rms. Business servs avail. Game rm. Bowling lanes. Refrigerators, microwaves avail. Cr cds: A, C, D, DS, MC, V.

Hudson

Hotel

✔ ★ ★ ★ **ST CHARLES.** *16 Park Pl.* 518/822-9900; FAX 518/822-0835. 34 rms, 3 story, 4 suites. S, D $59-$79; each addl $10; suites $89; under 18 free; ski plans. Pet accepted. TV; cable, VCR avail. Complimentary continental bkfst. Restaurants 11:30 am-10 pm. No rm serv. Bar to midnight; entertainment. Ck-out noon. Meeting rms. Business servs avail. No bellhops. Tennis privileges. Health club privileges. Cr cds: A, C, D, DS, MC, V.

Hunter *(See also Cairo, Catskill Park, Shandaken, Windham, Woodstock)*

Motel

★ ★ **HUNTER INN.** *Main St (NY 23 A). 518/263-3777; FAX 518/263-3981.* 41 rms, 2-3 story. No elvtr. S, D $65-$140; each addl $10-$15; suites $95-$169; under 17 free; 3-day min hols; package plans. Crib free. Pet accepted, $10. TV; cable. Complimentary continental bkfst. Ck-out 11 am. Meeting rm. Business servs avail. Sundries. Exercise equipt: weights, treadmill. Downhill/x-country ski ½ mi. Cr cds: A, DS, MC, V.

Ithaca *(See also Binghamton, Cortland)*

Motels

(Rates may be higher during special college events)

★ ★ ★ **BEST WESTERN UNIVERSITY INN.** *1020 Ellis Hollow Rd, East Hill Plaza. 607/272-6100; FAX 607/272-1518.* 94 rms. S $70-$100; D $80-$110; each addl $5; suites $100-$175; under 12 free; wkly rates. Crib free. Pet accepted, some restrictions; $10. TV; cable, VCR (movies $4). Pool; lifeguard. Restaurant 7 am-8 pm; Sun to 2 pm. Rm serv. Ck-out noon. Meeting rms. Business servs avail. Valet serv. Concierge Apr-Nov. Airport transportation. Health club privileges. Refrigerators; microwaves avail. Cr cds: A, C, D, DS, ER, JCB, MC, V.

✔ ★ **ECONO LODGE.** *2303 N Triphammer Rd, just off NY 13. 607/257-1400; FAX 607/257-6359.* 72 rms, 2 story. May-Sept: S $52-$71; D $59-$74; each addl $5; suites $78-$102; under 18 free; lower rates rest of yr. Crib free. Pet accepted; $10. TV; cable. Complimentary coffee in lobby. Continental bkfst. Restaurant nearby. Ck-out 11 am. Meeting rm. Business servs avail. In-rm modem link. Microwaves avail. Cr cds: A, D, DS, MC, V.

★ ★ **RAMADA INN-AIRPORT.** *2310 N Triphammer Rd. 607/257-3100; FAX 607/257-4425.* 120 rms, 2 story. S, D $55-$95; each addl $5; under 18 free; higher rates: wkends, special events. Crib free. Pet accepted, some restrictions. TV; cable, VCR avail (movies). Indoor pool; wading pool, poolside serv, lifeguard. Restaurant 6:30 am-2 pm, 5-10 pm. Rm serv. Bar 4 pm-1 am. Ck-out noon. Meeting rms. Business servs avail. In-rm modem link. Valet serv. Game rm. Free airport, bus depot, transportation. Exercise equipt; bicycles, treadmills. Refrigerators, microwaves avail. Cr cds: A, D, DS, JCB, MC, V.

Motor Hotel

★ ★ **HOLIDAY INN EXECUTIVE TOWER.** *222 S Cayuga St, downtown. 607/272-1000; FAX 607/277-1275.* Web www.harthotels.com. 178 rms, 10 story. S $76-$106; D $83-$113; each addl $7; suites $175-$255; under 19 free; higher rates special events. Crib free. Pet accepted, some restrictions; $15. TV; cable (premium). Indoor pool. Coffee in rms. Restaurant 7-11 am, 5-10 pm. Rm serv. Bar noon-1 am. Ck-out noon. Meeting rms. Business servs avail. Bellhops. Sundries. Free airport, bus depot transportation. Exercise equipt; weight machines, treadmills. Some bathrm phones. Cr cds: A, C, D, DS, JCB, MC, V.

Inn

★ ★ **LA TOURELLE.** *1150 Danby Rd (NY 96B). 607/273-2734; FAX 607/273-4821; res: 800/765-1492.* 35 units, 3 story. S, D $75-$125. Crib $10. Pet accepted, some restrictions. TV; cable, VCR (free movies). Continental bkfst. Restaurant adj. Ck-out noon, ck-in 3 pm. Meeting rm. Business servs avail. Tennis. X-country ski on site. Hiking trails. Refrigerator avail. European inn atmosphere. Located on 70 acres. Buttermilk Falls State Park adj. Cr cds: A, MC, V.

Jamestown

Motel

★ ★ **COMFORT INN.** *2800 N Main St, I-17 exit 12. 716/664-5920; FAX 716/664-3068.* 101 rms, 2 story. June-mid-Sept: S from $62.95; D from $67.95; each addl $5; under 18 free; lower rates rest of yr. Crib free. Pet accepted, some restrictions. TV; cable (premium), VCR avail. Complimentary continental bkfst. Ck-out noon. Meeting rm. Business servs avail. Downhill ski 20 mi. Some in-rm whirlpools. Microwaves avail. Cr cds: A, C, D, DS, ER, JCB, MC, V.

Motor Hotel

★ ★ ★ **HOLIDAY INN.** *150 W 4th St, I-17 exit 12. 716/664-3400; FAX 716/484-3304.* 149 rms, 8 story. S, D $68-$79; under 18 free; ski plans; wkend packages. Crib free. Pet accepted, some restrictions. TV; cable (premium), VCR avail. Indoor pool. Complimentary coffee in rms. Cafe 6:30 am-2 pm, 5:30-10 pm. Rm serv. Bars 5 pm-midnight. Ck-out noon. Coin lndry. Meeting rms. Business servs avail. In-rm modem link. Bellhops. Sundries. Downhill ski 20 mi. Health club privileges. Cr cds: A, C, D, DS, JCB, MC, V.

Johnstown *(See also Amsterdam, Schenectady)*

Motel

✔ ★ ★ **HOLIDAY INN.** *308 N Comrie Ave (12095-1095), NY 30A N. 518/762-4686; FAX 518/762-4034.* 100 rms, 3 story. No elvtr. S $55-$65; D $55-$72; each addl $6; under 19 free; higher rates Aug. Crib free. Pet accepted. TV; cable (premium), VCR avail (movies). Heated pool. Coffee in rms. Restaurant 6:30 am-10 pm. Rm serv 8 am-10 pm. Bar 11 am-midnight; entertainment. Ck-out noon. Coin lndry. Meeting rms. Business servs avail. In-rm modem link. Valet serv. Downhill/x-country ski 15 mi. Cr cds: A, C, D, DS, JCB, MC, V.

Kingston

Motels

★ ★ ★ **HOLIDAY INN.** *503 Washington Ave, just S of Dewey Thrwy exit 19. 914/338-0400.* E-mail holiday@mhb.net. 212 rms, 2 story. S, D $89-$109; suites $109-$139; under 19 free; higher rates wkend (May-Oct). Crib free. Pet accepted. TV. Indoor pool; whirlpool, wading pool. Sauna. Restaurant 6 am-2 pm, 5-10 pm; Sun 6 am-10 pm. Rm serv. Bar from 11:30 am; entertainment, Wed-Sat. Ck-out noon. Coin lndry. Meeting rms. Business servs avail. Bellhops. Sundries. Game rm. Refrigerators avail, $10. Balconies. Cr cds: A, C, D, DS, JCB, MC, V.

✔ ★ **SUPER 8.** *487 Washington Ave. 914/338-3078.* 84 rms, 2 story. June-Oct: S $54.88; D $58.88-$63.88; each addl $6; under 12 free; lower rates rest of yr. Crib free. Pet accepted, some restrictions. TV; cable, VCR avail (movies). Complimentary continental bkfst. Restaurant adj open 24 hrs. Ck-out 11 am. Coin lndry. Sundries. Valet serv. Business servs avail. Refrigerators, microwaves avail. Cr cds: A, C, D, DS, MC, V.

Lake George Village

Motel

★ ★ **FORT WILLIAM HENRY.** *1 blk S on US 9, 1 mi N of I-87 exit 21, on lake. 518/668-3081; res: 800/221-9211.* E-mail reservations@fortwilliamhenry.com; web www.fortwilliamhenry.com. 99 rms, 2 story. Late June-Labor Day: S, D $140-$159; each addl $15; suite $200-$255; under 12 free; hol wkends (2-night min); lower rates rest of yr. Crib free. Pet accepted, some restrictions. TV; cable, VCR avail (movies). 2 pools, 1 indoor; whirlpool, sauna, poolside serv. Playground. Restaurant in season 7 am-10 pm. Bar noon-1 am, closed off-season. Ck-out 11 am. Meeting rms. Business servs avail. Concierge in season. Downhill ski 20 mi; x-country ski 8 mi. Exercise equipt; bicycle, stair machine. Bicycle rentals. Cr cds: A, C, D, DS, ER, MC, V.

Lake Placid *(See also Saranac Lake, Wilmington)*

Motels

✔ ★ ★ **ART DEVLIN'S OLYMPIC.** *350 Main St, 1 blk S on NY 86, at jct NY 73. 518/523-3700.* 40 rms, 2 story. June-mid-Oct: S, D $48-$108; each addl $5; higher rates special events; lower rates rest of yr. Crib free. Pet accepted. TV; cable. Pool; wading pool. Complimentary continental bkfst. Ck-out 11 am. Airport, bus depot transportation. Downhill ski 8 mi; x-country ski 2 mi. Refrigerators. Some balconies, some in-rm whirlpools. Sun deck. Cr cds: A, DS, MC, V.

★ ★ **HOWARD JOHNSON.** *Saranac Ave, 3/4 mi W on NY 86. 518/523-9555; FAX 518/523-4765.* 92 rms, 2 story. July-mid-Sept & mid-Dec-Mar: S, D $85-$140; each addl $10; suites $110-$150; under 18 free; golf plans; MAP avail; lower rates rest of yr. Crib free. Pet accepted. TV; cable (premium). Indoor pool; whirlpool. Coffee in lobby. Restaurant 7 am-11 pm. Bar from noon. Ck-out noon. Coin lndry. Meeting rms. Business servs avail.

Sundries. Tennis. Downhill ski 10 mi; x-country ski on site. Rec rm. Lawn games. Balconies. Picnic tables, grills. Cr cds: A, C, D, DS, ER, JCB, MC, V.

[D] [⚓] [✈] [⚐] [🏃] [≋] [⋈] [🐾] [SC]

★ ★ **RAMADA INN.** *12 Saranac Ave, on NY 86. 518/523-2587; FAX 518/523-2328.* Web www.lakeplacid.ny.us/ramada. 90 rms, 3 story. Mid-July-early Sept, late Sept-mid-Oct, late Dec-early Jan: S $50-$115; D $60-$125; each addl $10; under 18 free; ski, golf plans; higher rates hols; lower rates rest of yr. Crib free. Pet accepted, some restrictions. TV; cable, VCR avail. Indoor pool; whirlpool. Coffee in rms. Restaurant 7 am-10 pm. Bar 4:30 pm-1 am. Ck-out noon. Business servs avail. In-rm modem link. Downhill ski 10 mi; x-country ski 1 mi. Exercise equipt; weight machine, bicycle. Game rm. Some balconies. Cr cds: A, C, D, DS, MC, V. [D] [⚓] [✈] [≋] [🏃] [⋈] [🐾] [SC]

★ **SCHULTE'S MOTOR INN.** *Cascade Rd (NY 73). 518/523-3532.* 30 units, 14 with shower only, 15 kit. cottages. Some A/C. Some rm phones. Mid-June-mid-Sept, mid-Dec-mid-Mar: S, D $68-$78; each addl $9; kit. cottages $48-$85; under 13 free; wkly rates; higher rates some hols; lower rates rest of yr. Crib free. Pet accepted, some restrictions; $5. TV; cable. Restaurant nearby. Ck-out 11 am. Downhill ski 7 mi; x-country ski 2 mi. Pool. Playground. Lawn games. Many refrigerators. Some balconies. Picnic tables, grills. Cr cds: A, MC, V. [⚐] [✈] [≋] [≋] [🐾]

Lodge

★ ★ ★ **LAKE PLACID LODGE.** *Whiteface Inn Rd. 518/523-2700; FAX 518/523-1124.* Web www.lakeplacidlodge.com. Cedar branches, smooth-painted pine and diamond-paned windows mark the facade of this 1882 Adirondack lodge set in the shadow of Whiteface Mountain. Luxurious, rustic rooms and cabins are tastefully decorated with twig-and-bark furniture, richly colored fabrics and works by local artisans. 35 units, 6 A/C, 5 with shower only, 4 story, 13 cottages. No elvtr. S, D $200-$500; each addl $50; cottages $300-$600; wkends 2-day min, hols 3-day min. Crib free. Pet accepted; $50/day. Complimentary full bkfst. Complimentary coffee in lobby. Restaurant 7:30 am-3 pm, 6-9:30 pm. Box lunches. Bar. Ck-out noon. Meeting rms. Business servs avail. In-rm modem link. Bellhops. Concierge. Gift shop. Tennis privileges. Golf privileges. Downhill ski 10 mi; x-country ski on site. Refrigerators in cottages; some wet bars, fireplaces. Some balconies. Picnic tables, grills. Cr cds: A, MC, V. [D] [⚓] [✈] [≋] [🏃] [🏃] [🐾]

Motor Hotels

★ ★ ★ **BEST WESTERN GOLDEN ARROW.** *150 Main St, on Mirror Lake. 518/523-3353; FAX 518/523-3353, ext. 614.* E-mail info@golden-arrow.com; web www.golden-arrow.com. 125 rms, 2-4 story. July-mid-Oct, late Dec-Mar: S, D $89-$149; each addl $10; suites $99-$195; under 12 free; MAP avail; ski plans; lower rates rest of yr. Crib $6. Pet accepted; $25. TV; cable. Indoor pool; wading pool; whirlpool. Restaurant 7 am-9 pm. Bar 11-2 am; entertainment Wed-Sat (in season). Ck-out 11 am. Meeting rms. Business servs avail. In-rm modem link. Shopping arcade. Covered parking. Free airport transportation. Downhill ski 9 mi; x-country ski on site. Exercise rm; instructor, weights, stair machine, sauna. Racquetball. Paddle boats, canoes. Rec rm. Some fireplaces. Refrigerators avail. Private patios, balconies. Picnic tables, grill. Refrigerators avail. Private beach. Cr cds: A, C, D, DS, ER, MC, V. [D] [⚓] [✈] [≋] [≋] [🏃] [⋈] [🐾] [SC]

★ ★ **HOLIDAY INN SUNSPREE RESORT.** *One Olympic Dr, Olympic Arena adj. 518/523-2556; FAX 518/523-9410.* E-mail info@lpresort.com; web www.lpresort.com. 205 rms, 2-4 story. July-Aug: S, D $79-$229; each addl $10; under 19 free; MAP avail; wkend rates; ski, golf plans; varied lower rates rest of yr. Crib free. Pet accepted. TV; cable. Heated pool; whirlpool. Playground. Coffee in rms. Restaurant 7 am-10 pm. Rm serv. Bar 11-2 am. Ck-out 11 am. Meeting rms. Business servs avail. In-rm modem link. Gift shop. Rec rm. Tennis. Golf privileges, putting green. Downhill ski 9 mi; x-country ski on site. Exercise rm; instructor, weight machine, bicycle, sauna. Refrigerators, microwaves. Many balconies. On hilltop overlooking lake. Cr cds: A, C, D, DS, ER, JCB, MC, V.

[D] [⚓] [✈] [≋] [🏃] [🏃] [≋] [🏃] [⋈] [🐾]

Inn

✔ ★ ★ **INTERLAKEN.** *15 Interlaken Ave. 518/523-3180; FAX 518/523-0117; res: 800/428-4369.* Web www.inbook.com. 11 rms, 3 story. No A/C. No rm phones. S, D $60-$120; each addl $15; MAP avail. 2-day min wkends, 3-day min hol wkends. Children over 5 yrs only. Pet accepted, some restrictions. TV in sitting rm; cable. Complimentary full bkfst; afternoon refreshments. Dining rm 6-8:30 pm; closed Tues, Wed. Ck-out 11 am, ck-in 3 pm. Gift shop. Downhill/x-country ski 8 mi. Some balconies. Picnic tables. Built in 1906; turn-of-the-century furnishings. Cr cds: A, MC, V. [⚐] [≋] [⋈] [🐾]

Letchworth State Park

(Entrances at Castile, Mt Morris, Perry and Portageville)

Inn

➤★ **BROMAN'S GENESEE FALLS.** *NY 436 (14536), E of S park entrance on NY 436.* 716/493-2484. 10 rms, 3 story. No rm phones. S, D $52-$62; each addl $15. Pet accepted. Complimentary full bkfst. Restaurant 8:30-1:30 am. Bar. Ck-out 11 am, ck-in 2 pm. Inn since 1870s. Cr cds: MC, V.

Malone

Motel

★ **ECONO LODGE.** *227 W Main.* 518/483-0500. 45 rms, 1-2 story. S $42-$47; D $48-$52; each addl $5. Crib $5. Pet accepted. TV; cable. Pool. Complimentary continental bkfst. Restaurant nearby. Ck-out 11 am. Meeting rms. Cr cds: A, D, DS, MC, V.

Middletown *(See also Newburgh)*

Motel

★ **SUPER 8 LODGE.** *563 NY 211E, at NY 17 exit 120.* 914/692-5828. 82 rms, 2 story. S $55.88-$65.88; D $64.88-$78.88; each addl $7; under 12 free; higher rates: special events, wkends. Pet accepted. TV. Complimentary continental bkfst. Ck-out 11 am. Downhill/x-country ski 15 mi. Some in-rm whirlpools. Cr cds: A, C, D, DS, MC, V.

Mt Kisco *(See also New York City, Peekskill, White Plains)*

Motel

★★★ **HOLIDAY INN.** *1 Holiday Inn Dr, 1 blk E of Saw Mill River Pkwy, exit 37.* 914/241-2600; FAX 914/241-4742. 122 rms, 2 story. S, D $119-$139; under 12 free; wkend plans. Crib. Pet accepted. TV; VCR avail. Pool. Coffee in rms. Restaurant 6:30 am-10 pm. Rm serv. Bar 2 pm-1 am, wkends to 3 am; entertainment. Ck-out 11 am. Coin lndry. Meeting rms. Business servs avail. In-rm modem link. Beauty shop. Health club privileges. Refrigerators avail. Cr cds: A, C, D, DS, MC, V.

Newburgh *(See also Fishkill, Poughkeepsie)*

Motel

★★ **HOWARD JOHNSON.** *95 Rte NY17K, I-87 exit 17.* 914/564-4000; FAX 914/564-0620. 74 rms, 2 story. May-Nov: S, D $89.95; each addl $8; under 18 free; higher rates special events; lower rates rest of yr. Crib free. Pet accepted. TV; cable (premium). Pool. Complimentary continental bkfst. Restaurant 6 am-11 pm. Ck-out noon. Coin lndry. Meeting rms. Business servs avail. Tennis. Downhill/x-country ski 15 mi. Health club privileges. Microwaves, refrigerators avail. Private patios, balconies. Cr cds: A, C, D, DS, ER, JCB, MC, V.

Niagara Falls
(See also Buffalo; also see Niagara Falls, ON, Canada)

Motels

★★ **BEST WESTERN SUMMIT INN.** *9500 Niagara Falls Blvd (14304).* 716/297-5050; FAX 716/297-0802. 88 rms, 2 story. July-early Oct: S $68-$88; D $88-$98; each addl $10; under 18 free; wkly & wkend rates; lower rates rest of yr. Crib free. Pet accepted, some restrictions. TV; VCR avail (movies). Indoor pool; sauna. Restaurant 7-11 am, 4-9 pm. Bar 4-9 pm. Ck-out 11 am. Meeting rms. Business servs avail. Game rm. Cr cds: A, C, D, DS, MC, V.

★ **CHATEAU MOTOR LODGE.** *(1810 Grand Island Blvd, Grand Island 14072) S on I-190 exit 18A.* 716/773-2868; FAX 716/773-5173. 17 rms, 4 kits. June-Sept: S $59; D $69; under 8 free; wkly rates; lower rates rest of yr. Crib free. Pet accepted, some restrictions. TV. Restaurant nearby. Ck-out 11 am. Refrigerators, microwaves avail. Cr cds: A, DS, MC, V.

Hotels

★ ★ **DAYS INN FALLS VIEW.** *201 Rainbow Blvd (14303), 1 blk E of Falls. 716/285-9321; FAX 716/285-2539.* 200 rms, 12 story. Mid-June-early Sept: S, D $59-$118; each addl $8; under 16 free; lower rates rest of yr. Crib free. Pet accepted. TV; VCR avail (movies). Restaurant 6:30 am-10 pm. Bar 11-2 am. Ck-out 11 am. Meeting rms. Business servs avail. Game rm. Some refrigerators; microwaves avail. Overlooks rapids. Cr cds: A, D, DS, MC, V.

★ ★ ★ **RADISSON.** *3rd & Old Falls St (14303). 716/285-3361; FAX 716/285-3900.* 401 rms, 6 story. Mid-June-mid-Sept: S, D $85-$139; each addl $10; suites $175-$375; lower rates rest of yr. Crib free. Pet accepted, some restrictions; $50 refundable. Free garage parking. TV; cable (premium), VCR avail. Indoor pool. Sauna. Restaurant 6:30 am-11 pm. Bar noon-midnight; Sat to 3 am. Ck-out noon. Convention facilities. Business servs avail. Gift shop. Exercise equipt; weight machines, bicycles. Game rm. Some refrigerators. Walkway to Intl Convention & Civic Center & Rainbow Center. Cr cds: A, C, D, DS, ER, JCB, MC, V.

North Creek

Motel

★ ★ **BLACK MOUNTAIN SKI LODGE.** *4 mi W of jct NY 28, on NY 8. 518/251-2800.* 25 rms. Mid-Dec-mid-May: S, D $41-$55; each addl $5; Apr-May: family, wkly rates; skiing, hiking, canoeing, rafting packages; lower rates rest of yr. Crib $5. Pet accepted. TV; cable. Pool. Playground. Restaurant 7-10 am, 6-9 pm. Ck-out 11 am. Sundries. Downhill/x-country ski 5 mi. Rec rm. Some refrigerators. Cr cds: A, DS, MC, V.

Norwich *(See also Oneonta)*

Motel

★ ★ **HOWARD JOHNSON HOTEL.** *75 N Broad St on NY 12. 607/334-2200; FAX 607/336-5619.* 86 units, 3 story. S $55-$75; D $65-$95; each addl $10; suites $75-$125; some wkend rates; higher rates special events. Crib free. Pet accepted, some restrictions; $5. TV; cable (premium). Indoor pool. Restaurant 8 am-10 pm. Bar. Ck-out 11 am. Meeting rms. Business servs avail. Health club privileges. In-rm whirlpools; some refrigerators; microwaves avail. Cr cds: A, D, DS, MC, V.

Nyack *(See also White Plains)*

Motel

✔ ★ **NYACK MOTOR LODGE.** *(NY 303 & NY 59, West Nyack 10994) NY Thrwy exit 12, S on NY 303. 914/358-4100; FAX 914/358-3938.* 125 rms, 2 story. S $52.55-$63.28; D $56.85-$67.57. Pet accepted. TV; cable. Pool; lifeguard. Complimentary continental bkfst. Restaurant adj noon-11 pm. Ck-out 11:30 am. Sundries. Health club privileges. Refrigerators avail. Cr cds: A, D, ER, MC, V.

Ogdensburg (Thousand Islands)
(See also Canton)

Motel

★ ★ **STONE FENCE.** *[B91 Riverside Dr, Riverside Dr. 315/393-1545; FAX 315/393-1749; res: 800/253-1545.* 31 rms, 8 suites. May-Sept: S $49-$56; D $65-$89; each addl $5; suites $79-$145; wkly rates; lower rates rest of yr. Crib $6. Pet accepted; $12. TV; cable. Pool; whirlpool, sauna. Complimentary coffee in rms. Restaurant 7 am-10 pm. Ck-out 11 am. Coin lndry. Tennis. Many refrigerators; some wet bars. Picnic tables, grills. Gazebo. On river; dockage, boat rentals. Cr cds: A, DS, MC, V.

Old Forge

Motel

★ ★ **BEST WESTERN SUNSET INN.** *1 mi S on NY 28. 315/369-6836.* 52 rms, 1-2 story. Late June-Labor Day, late Dec-early Apr: S, D $69-$125; each addl $10; under 13 free; lower rates rest of yr. Crib $6. Pet accepted. TV; cable. Indoor pool; whirlpool, sauna. Playground. Complimentary coffee in rms. Restaurant nearby. Ck-out 11 am. Lndry facilities. Tennis. Downhill ski 3 mi; x-country ski opp. Some balconies. Picnic tables. Cr cds: A, DS, MC, V.

Oneonta (See also Cooperstown, Norwich, Stamford)

Motels

★ ★ **HOLIDAY INN.** *NY 23, 1 mi E of I-88, exit 15. 607/433-2250; FAX 607/432-7028.* E-mail onhny@digital-marketplace.net; web www.holiday-inn.com/hotel/onhny. 120 rms, 2 story. S, D $72-$169; each addl $6; under 19 free. Crib free. Pet accepted, some restrictions. TV; cable (premium). Pool; wading pool. Coffee in rms. Restaurant 7 am-9 pm. Rm serv. Bar noon-midnight; entertainment Wed, Fri, Sat. Ck-out 11 am. Coin Indry. Meeting rms. In-rm modem link. Game rm. Refrigerators, microwaves avail. Picnic tables. Cr cds: A, C, D, DS, JCB, MC, V. 🅳 📋 🏊 🗙 🐾 SC

★ **SUPER 8.** *4973 NY 23, 1/4 mi S of I-88 exit 15. 607/432-9505.* 60 rms, 2 story. S $54.88-$81.88; D $63-$92; each addl $5; under 12 free; higher rates wkends, special events. Crib $3. Pet accepted, some restrictions. TV; cable, VCR avail (movies). Complimentary continental bkfst. Restaurant adj 7 am-10 pm. Ck-out 11 am. Coin Indry. Business servs avail. Cr cds: A, C, D, DS, JCB, MC, V. 🅳 📋 🗙 🐾 SC

Owego (See also Binghamton, Elmira, Endicott)

Motel

🚼 ★ **SUNRISE.** *3778 Wavery Rd, NY 17C W, exit 64. 607/687-5666.* 20 rms. S $34; D $38-$40; each addl $4. Crib $3. Pet accepted, some restrictions; $3. TV; cable. Ck-out 11 am. Picnic tables. Cr cds: A, DS, MC, V. 📋 🗙 🐾 SC

Peekskill (See also Mt Kisco, Tarrytown)

Motel

★ ★ **PEEKSKILL INN.** *634 Main St. 914/739-1500; res: 800/526-9466; FAX 914/739-7067.* 53 rms, 2 story. S $70-$95; D $80-$105; suite $125-$150; higher rates West Point graduation. Crib free. Pet accepted, some restrictions. TV; cable (premium), VCR avail (movies). Complimentary continental bkfst; full bkfst on wkends. Restaurant 11:30 am-10 pm; wkends 8 am-11 pm. Rm serv. Bar noon to 2 am. Ck-out 11 am. Pool; lifeguard. Refrigerators avail. Some balconies. Grills. Cr cds: A, C, D, DS, MC, V. 📋 🏊 🗙 🐾 SC

Penn Yan (See also Canandaigua, Geneva, Hammondsport, Watkins Glen)

Motel

🚼 ★ ★ **VIKING.** *680 East Lake Rd. 315/536-7061; FAX 315/536-0737.* 31 rms, 2 story, 24 kits. Mid-June-Labor Day: S, D $45-$140; kit. units $70-$140; family, wkly rates; lower rates mid-May-mid-June, Labor Day-mid-Oct. Closed rest of yr. Crib free. Pet accepted; $10. TV; cable. Pool; whirlpool. Restaurant nearby. Ck-out 11 am. Lawn games. Refrigerators. Private patios, balconies. Picnic tables, grills. On Keuka Lake; private beach, daily cruises. Rental boats. No cr cds accepted. 🅳 📋 📋 🏊 🗙 🐾

Plattsburgh

Motel

★ ★ **HOWARD JOHNSON.** *446 NY 3, 1 1/2 mi W at jct NY 3 & I-87. 518/561-7750; FAX 518/561-9431.* 120 rms, 2 story. June-Labor Day: S, D $89-$99; each addl $10; under 18 free; higher rates some special events, hols; lower rates rest of yr. Crib free. Pet accepted. TV; cable (premium), VCR avail. Indoor pool; poolside serv. Coffee in rms. Restaurant 6 am-11 pm. Rm serv. Bar 3 pm-midnight, wkends to 1 am. Ck-out noon. Coin Indry. Meeting rms. Business servs avail. In-rm modem link. Exercise equipt; weight machine, bicycles. Rec rm. Refrigerators avail. Some private patios, balconies. Shopping mall adj. Cr cds: A, C, D, DS, JCB, MC, V. 🅳 📋 🏊 🏋 🗙 🐾 SC

Motor Hotel

★ ★ **RAMADA INN.** *Jct I-87 & NY 3, I-87 exit 37. 518/561-5000; FAX 518/562-2974.* 102 rms, 4 story. Mid-June-mid-Oct: S, D $79-$99; each addl $10; under 19 free; lower rates rest of yr. Crib free. Pet accepted, some restrictions. TV; cable. Indoor pool; wading pool, whirlpool. Complimentary bkfst. Restaurant 6:30 am-1 pm, 5-9 pm. Rm serv. Bar from 4 pm. Ck-out noon. Meeting rms. Business servs avail. In-rm modem link. Sundries. Exercise equipt; weight machines, bicycles. Game rm. Cr cds: A, C, D, DS, JCB, MC, V. 🅳 📋 🏊 🏋 🗙 🐾 SC

Poughkeepsie (See also Fishkill, Newburgh)

Motel

✔ ★ **ECONO LODGE.** *418 South Rd (US 9) (12601). 914/452-6600.* 111 rms, 1-2 story. S, D $42-$52; each addl $3; under 18 free; wkly, monthly rates. Crib free. Pet accepted. TV; cable, VCR avail. Complimentary continental bkfst. Restaurant opp open 24 hrs. Ck-out 11 am. Coin lndry. Meeting rms. Business servs avail. In-rm modem link. Some refrigerators. Cr cds: A, C, D, DS, MC, V. 🐾 ⚛ 🐾 SC

Motor Hotel

★ ★ **HOLIDAY INN EXPRESS.** *US 9 & Sharon Dr (12601), 1¹/₂ mi S of Mid-Hudson Bridge. 914/473-1151; FAX 914/485-8127.* 123 rms, 4 story. S, D $65-$89; each addl $10; under 18 free; higher rates special events. Crib free. Pet accepted. TV; cable (premium), VCR avail (movies). Pool; lifeguard. Complimentary continental bkfst. Ck-out noon. Guest lndry. Meeting rms. Business servs avail. Sundries. Cr cds: A, C, D, DS, JCB, MC, V. D 🐾 ≋ ⚛ 🐾 SC

Inn

★ ★ ★ **OLD DROVERS.** *(Old US 22, Dover Plains 12522) US 44 E to Millbrook, US 343 to Dover Plains, S on US 22. 914/832-9311; FAX 914/832-6356.* 4 rms. No rm phones. D $150-$230; MAP avail wkends $320-$395; higher rates May-Oct (2-night min). Closed Wed. Pet accepted, some restrictions; $25. TV; VCR avail (free movies). Complimentary full bkfst. Restaurant 9:30 am-9 pm. Ck-out noon, ck-in 2 pm. Business servs avail. 18-hole golf privileges, greens fee $18-$24. Downhill ski 9 mi. Originally inn for cattle drovers (1750); antiques, fireplaces. Cr cds: D, MC, V. 🐾 ⚛ 🎿 🐾

Rochester (See also Canandaigua)

Motels

★ ★ **COMFORT INN-WEST.** *1501 Ridge Rd W (14615). 716/621-5700; FAX 716/621-8446.* 83 rms, 5 story. S $51.95-$82.95; D $61.95-$82.95; each addl $5; suites $89.95-$99.95; under 18 free. Crib free. Pet accepted, some restrictions. TV; cable (premium). Continental bkfst. Restaurant nearby. Ck-out noon. Business servs avail. In-rm modem link. Valet serv. Some in-rm whirlpools. Cr cds: A, C, D, DS, ER, JCB, MC, V. D 🐾 ⚛ 🐾 SC

★ ★ **DEPOT INN.** *(41 N Main St, Pittsford 14534) Approx 10 mi S on NY 96. 716/381-9900; FAX 716/381-2907; res: 800/836-3376.* 101 rms, 3 story. S $61-$70; D $68-$77; each addl $7; under 12 free; wkend rates. Crib free. Pet accepted. TV; cable (premium), VCR avail. Indoor pool. Restaurant 6:30-10:30 am, 11:30 am-2:30 pm, 5-10 pm; Sun 8 am-2:30 pm, 4:30-9:30 pm. Rm serv. Bar 4 pm-12:30 am; Fri, Sat to 2 am. Ck-out noon. Guest lndry. Meeting rms. Business servs avail. In-rm modem link. Bellhops. Airport transportation. Exercise equipt; bicycle, treadmill. Some refrigerators, in-rm whirlpools. Cr cds: A, C, D, DS, MC, V. D 🐾 ≋ 🏃 ⚛ ⚛ 🐾 SC

✔ ★ **DORKAT.** *3990 W Henrietta Rd (14623), I-90 exit 46. 716/334-7000.* 52 rms, 2 story. S,D $31.95-$43.95; each addl $5. Pet accepted, some restrictions. TV; cable (premium), VCR avail (movies $7). Restaurant adj 6 am-7 pm. Ck-out 11 am. Cr cds: A, D, MC, V. D 🐾 ⚛ 🐾

✔ ★ **ECONO LODGE.** *940 Jefferson Rd (14623). 716/427-2700; FAX 716/427-8504.* 102 rms, 3 story. S $49.95-$59.95; D $54.95-$63.95; each addl $5; suites $85-$100; under 18 free. Crib free. Pet accepted, some restrictions. TV; cable (premium). Continental bkfst. Restaurant nearby open 24 hrs. Ck-out 11 am. Coin lndry. Business servs avail. Valet serv. Free airport transportation. Some in-rm whirlpools. Cr cds: A, C, D, DS, JCB, MC, V. D 🐾 ⚛ 🐾 SC

★ ★ **HAMPTON INN.** *717 E Henrietta Rd (14623). 716/272-7800; FAX 716/272-1211.* 113 rms, 5 story. S $69-$83; D $72-$86; under 18 free. Crib free. Pet accepted, some restrictions. TV; cable. Complimentary continental bkfst. Restaurant adj 7 am-midnight. Ck-out noon. Meeting rms. Business servs avail. In-rm modem link. Valet serv. Cr cds: A, C, D, DS, MC, V. D 🐾 ⚛ 🐾 SC

★ ★ **MARKETPLACE INN.** *800 Jefferson Rd (14623), I-390 exit 14. 716/475-9190; FAX 716/424-2138; res: 800/888-8102.* 144 rms, 3 story. S $62-$83; D $69-$90; each addl $7; under 18 free. Crib free. Pet accepted, some restrictions. TV; cable (premium), VCR (movies free). Pool; poolside serv, lifeguard. Complimentary bkfst buffet Mon-Fri. Restaurants 6:30 am-midnight. Rm serv. Bar. Ck-out noon. Meeting rms. Business servs avail.

In-rm modem link. Free airport transportation. Health club privileges. Game rm. Micro-brewery. Cr cds: A, C, D, DS, MC, V. 🖐 ⌦ ⌦ 🔥 SC

✔ ★ MICROTEL. *(905 Lehigh Station Rd, Henrietta 14467) I-390 exit 12A. 716/334-3400; FAX 716/334-5042; res: 800/999-2005.* 99 rms, 2 story. S $39.95; D $47.95; under 18 free. Crib free. Pet accepted, some restrictions. TV; cable (premium), VCR avail. Complimentary coffee in lobby. Restaurant nearby. Ck-out noon. Business servs avail. Cr cds: A, D, DS, MC, V. D 🖐 ⌦ 🔥

★ ★ RAMADA INN-AIRPORT. *1273 Chili Ave (14624), I-390 exit 19, near Greater Rochester Intl Airport. 716/464-8800; FAX 716/464-0395.* 155 rms, 2 story. S $80; D $90; each addl $10; under 18 free; wkend rates. Crib free. Pet accepted. TV; cable (premium), VCR avail. Pool; lifeguard. Playground. Restaurant 6 am-10 pm; Sat, Sun from 8 am. Rm serv. Bar. Ck-out noon. Meeting rms. Business servs avail. Bellhops. Valet serv. Free airport transportation. Health club privileges. Cr cds: A, C, D, DS, ER, JCB, MC, V.
D 🖐 ⌦ ✈ ⌦ 🔥 SC

✔ ★ RED ROOF INN. *(4820 W Henrietta Rd, Henrietta 14467) I-90 exit 46. 716/359-1100; FAX 716/359-1121.* 108 rms, 2 story. S $29.99-$54.99; D $34.99-$65.99; each addl $7; under 19 free. Crib $5. Pet accepted. TV; cable (premium). Restaurant nearby. Ck-out noon. Business servs avail. Cr cds: A, C, D, DS, MC, V. D 🖐 ⌦ 🔥

★ ★ RESIDENCE INN BY MARRIOTT. *1300 Jefferson Rd (14623). 716/272-8850; FAX 716/272-7822.* 112 kit. suites, 2 story. S $108-$125; D $138-$158; under 12 free; wkly, monthly rates. Crib free. Pet accepted, some restrictions; $8/day. TV; cable (premium), VCR avail (movies). Pool; whirlpool, lifeguard. Complimentary continental bkfst. Complimentary coffee in rms. Restaurant nearby. Ck-out noon. Coin lndry. Meeting rms. Business servs avail. In-rm modem link. Sundries. Free airport transportation. Downhill ski 20 mi; x-country ski 1 mi. Health club privileges. Picnic tables, grills. Cr cds: A, C, D, DS, ER, JCB, MC, V.
D 🖐 ⌦ ⌦ ⌦ 🔥 SC

★ WELLESLEY INN-NORTH. *1635 W Ridge Rd (14615), Exit 46 on I-39. 716/621-2060; FAX 716/621-7102; res: 800/444-8888.* 99 rms (2 with shower only), 4 story. Apr-Nov: S $49.95-$52.95; D $49.95-$65.95; each addl $5; under 18 free; higher rates some special events; lower rates rest of yr. Crib free. Pet accepted, some restrictions; $3. TV; cable (premium), VCR avail (movies $7). Complimentary coffee in rms. Complimentary continental bkfst. Restaurant adj 11 am-10 pm. Ck-out 11 am. Business servs avail. Health club privileges. Some refrigerators. Cr cds: A, C, D, DS, MC, V. D 🖐 ⌦ 🔥 SC

★ WELLESLEY INN-SOUTH. *797 E Henrietta Rd (NY 15A) (14623). 716/427-0130; FAX 716/427-0903.* 98 rms, 4 story. S $45-$60; D $50-$70; each addl $5; suites $65-$90; under 18 free. Crib free. Pet accepted, some restrictions; $3. TV; cable (premium), VCR (movies). Complimentary continental bkfst. Complimentary coffee in rms. Ck-out 11 am. Meeting rm. Business servs avail. In-rm modem link. Sundries. Health club privileges. Cr cds: A, C, D, DS, MC, V. D 🖐 ⌦ 🔥 SC

Motor Hotels

★ ★ ★ HOLIDAY INN-AIRPORT. *911 Brooks Ave (14624). 716/328-6000; FAX 716/328-1012.* 280 rms, 2 story. S $99-$119; D $109-$129; each addl $10; suites $150-$200; under 19 free. Crib free. Pet accepted, some restrictions. TV; cable (premium). Indoor pool; whirlpool, lifeguard. Restaurant 6 am-2 pm, 5-10 pm. Rm serv. Bar 11-2 am; entertainment. Ck-out noon. Coin lndry. Meeting rms. Business servs avail. In-rm modem link. Bellhops. Concierge. Gift shop. Valet serv. Free airport transportation. Exercise equipt; bicycle, treadmill, sauna. Cr cds: A, C, D, DS, ER, MC, V. D 🖐 ⌦ 🏋 ✈ ⌦ 🔥 SC

★ ★ MARRIOTT-AIRPORT. *1890 W Ridge Rd (14615). 716/225-6880; FAX 716/225-8188.* 210 rms, 7 story. S, D $79-$120; suites $185-$310; under 18 free; wkend rates. Crib free. Pet accepted, some restrictions. TV; cable (premium), VCR avail. Indoor pool; poolside serv. Restaurant 6:30 am-11 pm. Rm serv. Bar 11-2 am, Sun from noon. Ck-out noon. Meeting rms. Business servs avail. In-rm modem linkn. Bellhops. Valet serv. Concierge. Sundries. Free airport transportation. Exercise equipt; treadmill, bicycles, sauna. Cr cds: A, C, D, DS, ER, JCB, MC, V. D 🖐 ⌦ 🏋 ✈ ⌦ 🔥 SC

Hotel

★ ★ FOUR POINTS BY SHERATON. *120 E Main St (14604). 716/546-6400; FAX 716/546-3908.* 466 rms, 15 story. S, D $93-$109; suites $125-$350; under 19 free. Crib free. Pet accepted, some restrictions. TV; cable (premium). Heated pool; poolside serv. Complimentary coffee in rms. Restaurant 7 am-10 pm. Bar 11-2 am. Ck-out noon. Coin lndry. Convention facilities. Business servs avail. In-rm modem link. Shopping arcade. Exercise equipt; bicycle, treadmill, sauna. Some balconies. On river. Cr cds: A, C, D, DS, JCB, MC, V. D 🖐 ⌦ 🏋 ⌦ 🔥 SC

Rome *(See also Boonville, Utica)*

Motel

★ ★ **PAUL REVERE LODGE.** *7900 Turin Rd. 315/336-1776; FAX 315/339-2636; res: 800/765-7251.* Web www.thebeeches.com. 75 rms, 1-2 story, 6 kits. S $56-$63; D $62-$69; each addl $5; kit. units $85; under 12 free; wkly rates; wkend packages. Crib free. Pet accepted, some restrictions; $20 deposit. TV; cable. Pool. Restaurant 6-10 am, Sat, Sun 8 am-noon. Ck-out 11 am. Business center. Downhill/x-country ski 8 mi. Lawn games. Refrigerator, microwaves avail. 52 acres with pond. Cr cds: A, C, D, DS, MC, V.
D ⊕ ⊠ ≈ ⊠ ⊠ SC ⊼

Roscoe

Motel

✔ ★ **ROSCOE.** *Old Route 17, W on Old NY 17. 607/498-5220.* 18 rms. S $40; D $45-$55; each addl $10; kit. units $60; Apr-Oct wkends (2-day min). Crib free. Pet accepted. TV; cable. Pool. Complimentary continental bkfst. Ck-out 11 am. Some refrigerators. Picnic tables, grill. On Beaverkill River. Cr cds: MC, V. ⊕ ⊠ ≈ ⊠

Saranac Lake *(See also Lake Placid, Tupper Lake)*

Motels

★ **ADIRONDACK.** *23 Lake Flower Ave. 518/891-2116; FAX 518/891-1405.* 13 rms, 1-2 story, 4 kits. 13 A/C. Mid-June-mid-Oct: S, D $75; each addl $5; kit. units $70-$95; wkly rates; lower rates rest of yr. Crib $5. Pet accepted. Complimentary continental bkfst. Restaurant nearby. Ck-out 11 am. Refrigerators. Picnic tables, grills. Paddle boats, canoes. On lake. Cr cds: A, C, D, DS, MC, V. ⊕ ⊠ ⊠ SC

★ **LAKE SIDE.** *27 Lake Flower Ave. 518/891-4333.* 22 rms. July-mid-Oct: S $59-$79; D $69-$89; each addl $5; kit. units $79-$99; higher rates: some hol wkends, special events; lower rates rest of yr. Crib free. Pet accepted. TV; cable (premium). Heated pool. Complimentary coffee in lobby. Restaurant nearby. Ck-out 11 am. Downhill ski 20 mi; x-country ski 2 mi. Canoes, rowboats, paddle boats avail. Patio. Picnic tables, grills. Overlooks lake; private sand beach. Cr cds: A, DS, MC, V. ⊕ ⊠ ⊠ ≈ ⊠ ⊠ SC

Saratoga Springs *(See also Glens Falls)*

Motel

(Rates may be higher during racing season)

★ ★ **GRAND UNION.** *92 S Broadway. 518/584-9000.* 64 rms. S,D $45-$71; each addl $10; higher rates special events. Crib free. Pet accepted; $10. TV; cable. Pool; sauna, mineral bath spa. Complimentary coffee in lobby. Restaurant adj 8 am-10 pm. Ck-out 11 am. Bellhops (seasonal). Sundries. Lawn games. Some refrigerators. Grill. Victorian-style lobby. Only private mineral bath spa in NY. Cr cds: MC, V. ⊕ ≈ ⊠ ⊠ SC

Motor Hotel

★ ★ **HOLIDAY INN.** *232 Broadway St. 518/584-4550; FAX 518/584-4417.* 150 rms, 4 story. S $69-$195; D $79-$195; each addl $10; suites $138-$390; under 19 free; wkly, ski rates. Crib free. Pet accepted. TV. Pool; poolside serv. Restaurant 6:30 am-10 pm. Rm serv. Bar 11-2 am; entertainment wkends, dancing. Ck-out 11 am. Coin lndry. Meeting rms. Business servs avail. In-rm modem link. Bellhops. Valet serv. Sundries. Downhill ski 15 mi; x-country ski 1 mi. Health club privileges. Cr cds: A, C, D, DS, JCB, MC, V.
⊕ ⊠ ≈ ⊠ ⊠ SC

Hotel

★ ★ ★ **SHERATON-SARATOGA SPRINGS.** *534 Broadway, at City Center. 518/584-4000; FAX 518/584-7430.* 240 rms, 5 story. S, D $99-$130 each addl $10; suites $125-$275; under 18 free. Crib free. Pet accepted. TV; cable (premium), VCR avail. Indoor pool; lifeguard. Coffee in rms. Restaurant 7 am-10 pm. Bar 11-1 am; entertainment, Wed-Sat (summer). Ck-out noon. Meeting rms. Business center. Concierge. Gift shop. Tennis privileges. 18-hole golf privileges, pro. X-country ski 2 mi. Exercise equipt; weight machines, bicycles. Game rm. Some bathrm phones, refrigerators. Some balconies. Luxury level. Cr cds: A, C, D, DS, ER, JCB, MC, V. D ⊕ ⊠ ⊠ ⊠ ⊠ ≈ ⊼ ⊠ ⊠ SC ⊼

Schenectady *(See also Albany, Amsterdam, Saratoga Springs)*

Motor Hotel

★ ★ ★ **HOLIDAY INN.** *100 Nott Terrace (12308), at Franklin St.* 518/393-4141; FAX 518/393-4174. 182 rms, 4 story. S $69-$100; D $75-$125; suites $245; under 18 free; higher rates: college events, racing season. Crib free. Pet accepted, some restrictions. TV; cable (premium). Indoor pool; whirlpool. Complimentary bkfst. Restaurant 6:30 am-2 pm, 5-10 pm. Rm serv. Bar 11-1 am; wkends noon-1 am. Ck-out noon. Meeting rms. Business servs avail. In-rm modem link. Free airport, RR station transportation. Downhill/x-country ski 20 mi. Exercise equipt; treadmills, bicycles, sauna. Wet bar in suites. Cr cds: A, C, D, DS, JCB, MC, V. [D] 🐾 ⚡ ≈ 🎿 🖼 🐾 SC

Shandaken *(See also Hunter, Kingston)*

Lodge

★ ★ **AUBERGE DES 4 SAISONS.** *NY 42.* 914/688-2223; res: 800/864-1877. 28 air-cooled rms, 12 with shower only. S, D $75-$115; each addl $15; hols (min stay required); higher rates hol wkends. Pet accepted, some restrictions. Complimentary full bkfst. Restaurant 11:30 am-2 pm, 5:30-11 pm. Bar. Ck-out noon. Lighted tennis. Pool. Playground. Rec rm. Lawn games. Many balconies. Picnic tables. On stream. Cr cds: A, MC, V. 🐾 ⚡ 🎿 ≈ 🖼 🐾

Inns

★ ★ **BIRCHCREEK.** *(NY 28, Pine Hill 12465) 8 mi W on NY 28.* 914/254-5222; FAX 914/254-5812. 6 rms, 5 with shower only, 1 cottage, 2 story. No rm phones. Dec-Mar, June-Oct: S, D $75-$150; under 12 free; 2-day min wkends, 3-day min hols; ski plans; lower rates rest of yr. Crib free. Pet accepted. TV in some rms; cable. Complimentary full bkfst. Complimentary coffee in rms. Restaurant nearby. Ck-out 11 am, ck-in 3 pm. Downhill ski 1/2 mi; x-country ski on site. Some refrigerators. Built in 1896; in Catskill Mountain forest. Totally nonsmoking. Cr cds: A, MC, V. 🐾 🐾 ⚡ 🖼 🐾 SC

★ **MARGARETVILLE MOUNTAIN INN.** *(Margaretville Mountain Rd, Margaretville 12455) 15 mi W on NY 28.* 914/586-3933; res: 800/684-5546. 7 air-cooled rms, 3 share bath, 2 story. No rm phones. S, D $50-$85; each addl $15; under 12 free; ski plans; hols (2-3-day min). Crib free. Pet accepted, some restrictions. $10. Premium cable TV in common rm; VCR avail (movies). Complimentary full bkfst. Ck-out 11 am, ck-in 4-6 pm. Downhill ski 9 mi; x-country ski on-site. Playground. Lawn games. Built in 1886; first commercial cauliflower farm in US. Totally nonsmoking. Cr cds: A, MC, V.
🐾 🐾 ⚡ 🖼 🐾

Skaneateles *(See also Syracuse)*

Motel

★ **BIRD'S NEST.** *1601 E Genesee St.* 315/685-5641. 28 rms, 4 kits. Mid-May-Sept: S $40-$60; D $45-$95; each addl $5; kit. units $65-$85; under 5 free; wkly rates; lower rates rest of yr. Crib $5. Pet accepted. TV; cable. Pool. Playground. Complimentary coffee in rms. Restaurant nearby. Ck-out 11 am. Lawn games. Some refrigerators, whirlpools. Picnic tables, grill. Duck pond. Cr cds: A, C, D, DS, MC, V. [D] 🐾 🐾 ≈ 🐾 SC

Southampton, L.I.

Motels

★ **BAYBERRY INN.** *281 County Rd 39A.* 516/283-4220; FAX 516/283-6496; res: 800/659-2020. 30 rms, 3 suites. July-Aug: S $195; D $200; suites $225; under 18 free; wkend rates; higher rates: hol wkends, Hampton Classic; lower rates rest of yr. Pet accepted. TV; cable. Pool. Ck-out 11 am. Business servs avail. Some refrigerators. Cr cds: A, DS, MC, V. 🐾 ≈ 🖼 🐾

★ ★ **CONCORD RESORT.** *161 Hill Station Rd.* 516/283-6100; FAX 516/283-6102. 40 kit. suites, 2 story. Memorial Day-Labor Day: S, D $149; higher rates wkends & horse show; 3-day min hol wkends; wkly rates; golf plan; lower rates rest of yr. Crib free. Pet accepted. TV; cable (premium), VCR avail. Pool; lifeguard. Complimentary continental bkfst. Restaurant nearby. Ck-out 11 am. Coin lndry. Meeting rms. Business servs avail. RR station transportation. Tennis. Golf privileges. Exercise equipt; weight machine, treadmill. Game rm. Lawn games. Balconies. Picnic tables. Cr cds: A, C, D, DS, JCB, MC, V.
🐾 🏄 🎿 ≈ 🎿 🖼 🐾 SC

★ **SOUTHAMPTON RESORT AT COLD SPRING BAY.** *County Rd 39. 516/283-7600; FAX 516/283-4625; res: 800/321-4969.* 65 rms, 2 story, 32 kit. units. July-Aug: S, D, kit. units $115-$550; each addl $25; under 12 free; higher rates: hol wkends, horse show classic; lower rates rest of yr. Crib free. Pet accepted. TV; cable, VCR avail. Pool. Ck-out 10 am. Meeting rms. Business servs avail. Cr cds: A, MC, V. 🐾 ⌤ ⌧ 🐾 SC

Spring Valley *(See also Tarrytown)*

Motel

🚗 ★ **WELLESLEY INN.** *(17 N Airmont Rd, Suffern 10901) I-87/287 exit 14B. 914/368-1900; FAX 914/368-1927.* 95 rms, 4 story. Apr-Oct: S $77-$92; D $75-$90; each addl $10; suites $100-$140; under 18 free; higher rates: West Point graduation, Dec 31; lower rates rest of yr. Crib free. Pet accepted, some restrictions; $5/day. TV; cable. Complimentary continental bkfst. Complimentary coffee in rms. Restaurant nearby. Ck-out 11 am. Business servs avail. Refrigerators, microwaves avail. Cr cds: A, C, D, DS, JCB, MC, V. 🄳 🐾 ⌧ 🐾 SC

Stamford

Motel

★ ★ **REXMERE LODGE.** *Hollytree Rd, at jct NY 10 & NY 23. 607/652-7394; FAX 607/652-4765; res: 800/932-1090.* 37 rms, 2 story. S, D $50-$98; each addl $15; cottage $125; under 12 free. Pet accepted. TV; cable. Pool; whirlpool. Coffee in rms. Restaurant 11:30 am-9 pm; wkends to 10 pm. Rm serv. Bar. Ck-out noon. Meeting rms. Business servs avail. Downhill/x-country ski 3 mi. Private patios, balconies. Refrigerators avail. Cr cds: A, C, D, DS, MC, V. 🄳 🐾 ⌨ ⌤ ⌧ 🐾 SC

Syracuse *(See also Skaneateles)*

Motels

🚗 ★ ★ **ECONO LODGE.** *(401 7th North St, Liverpool 13088) At jct I-81 exit 25 & I-90 exit 36. 315/451-6000; FAX 315/451-0193.* 83 rms, 4 story. May-Sept: S $42-$52; D $50-$57; each addl $4; suites $47-$52; under 18 free; higher rates special events; lower rates rest of yr. Crib free. Pet accepted, some restrictions; $3. TV; cable. Complimentary continental bkfst. Restaurant adj 6 am-11 pm. Ck-out 11 am. Business servs avail. Cr cds: A, C, D, DS, MC, V. 🄳 ⌤ ⌧ 🐾 SC

★ ★ **GENESEE INN HOTEL.** *1060 E Genesee St (13210). 315/476-4212; FAX 315/471-4663; res: 800/365-HOME.* 96 rms, 2 story. S $79-$99; D $89-$109; under 18 free; higher rates university special events. Crib free. Pet accepted. TV; cable. Restaurant 7 am-10 pm. Rm serv. Bar 11:30-1 am. Ck-out 11 am. Meeting rms. Business servs avail. Bellhops. Syracuse University & medical center transportation. Health club privileges. Cr cds: A, C, D, DS, MC, V. 🄳 🐾 ⌧ 🐾 SC

🚗 ★ **JOHN MILTON INN.** *6578 Thompson Rd (13206), I-90 exit 35, Carrier Circle. 315/463-8555; FAX 315/432-9240; res: 800/352-1061.* 54 rms, 2 story. S $25-$70; D $31-$75; each addl $5; under 12 free; higher rates special events. Crib $5. Pet accepted. TV; cable (premium). Complimentary continental bkfst. Restaurant adj open 24 hrs. Ck-out 11:30 am. Business servs avail. Cr cds: A, C, D, DS, MC, V. 🐾 ⌧ 🐾 SC

🚗 ★ **KNIGHTS INN.** *(430 Electronics Pkwy, Liverpool 13088) I-90 exit 37. 315/453-6330; FAX 315/457-9240; res: 800/843-5644.* 82 air-cooled rms, 8 kits. S $35-$65; D $43.95-$75; each addl $5; under 18 free; wkly rates. Crib free. Pet accepted, some restrictions. TV; cable (premium), VCR (movies). Complimentary continental bkfst. Restaurant adj 11 am-10 pm. Ck-out 11 am. Meeting rms. Business servs avail. Downhill ski 20 mi; x-country ski 1 mi. Cr cds: A, C, D, DS, MC, V. 🄳 🐾 ⌤ ⌧ 🐾 SC

🚗 ★ **RED ROOF INN.** *6614 N Thompson Rd (13206). 315/437-3309; FAX 315/437-7865.* 115 rms, 3 story. S $31.99-$64.99; D $35.99-$71.99; under 18 free. Crib free. Pet accepted. TV; cable (premium). Complimentary coffee in lobby. Restaurant opp open 24 hrs. Ck-out noon. Business servs avail. Cr cds: A, C, D, DS, MC, V. 🄳 🐾 ⌧ 🐾

★ ★ **RESIDENCE INN BY MARRIOTT.** *(6420 Yorktown Circle, East Syracuse 13057) I-90 exit exit 35. 315/432-4488; FAX 315/432-1042.* 102 kit. suites, 2 story. S $79-$99; D $89-$139; wkly, wkend rates; higher rates: hols, special events. Crib free. Pet accepted; $100. TV; cable (premium), VCR avail (movies). Pool; whirlpool, lifeguard. Complimentary coffee in rms. Complimentary continental bkfst. Restaurant adj 11:30 am-10 pm. Ck-out noon. Coin lndry. Meeting rms. Business servs avail. Valet serv. Downhill ski 20 mi.

Exercise equipt; weights, bicycles. Health club privileges. Picnic tables. Cr cds: A, C, D, DS, JCB, MC, V. ▯ ▱ ▱ ▱ ▱ ▱ ▱ ▱ SC

Motor Hotels

★ ★ ★ **FOUR POINTS BY SHERATON.** *(Electronics Pkwy & 7th North St, Liverpool 13088)* I-90 exit 37, $^1/_4$ mi NW off I-81 exit 25. 315/457-1122; FAX 315/451-1269. 280 rms, 6 story. S, D $75-$150; each addl $10; under 18 free; wknd rates. Crib free. Pet accepted. TV; cable. Indoor pool; whirlpool, lifeguard. Restaurant 6:30 am-11 pm. Rm serv. Bar 2 pm-2 am; entertainment (seasonal). Ck-out 1 pm. Business servs avail. In-rm modem link. Bellhops. Valet serv Mon-Fri. Sundries. Exercise equipt; weight machine, bicycle. Game rm. Patios. Cr cds: A, C, D, DS, ER, MC, V. ▯ ▱ ▱ ▱ ▱ ▱ ▱ SC

★ ★ ★ **MARRIOTT.** *(6301 NY 298, East Syracuse 13057)* 8 mi NE on NY 298, $^1/_4$ mi E of I-90 exit 35. 315/432-0200; FAX 315/433-1210. 250 units, 4-7 story. S $140; D $165; each addl $10; suites $275; studio rms $140; under 18 free; wknd plan. Crib free. Pet accepted. TV; cable (premium), VCR avail (movies). Indoor/outdoor pool; whirlpool, poolside serv. Restaurant 6 am-11 pm. Rm serv. Bar noon-2 am; entertainment exc Mon. Ck-out noon. Coin lndry. Convention facilities. Business servs avail. In-rm modem link. Bellhops. Valet serv. Sundries. Gift shop. Free airport transportation. Tennis privileges. Golf privileges. Exercise equipt; weights, bicycles, sauna. Game rm. Some refrigerators. Some private patios, balconies. Cr cds: A, C, D, DS, ER, JCB, MC, V.
▯ ▱ ▱ ▱ ▱ ▱ ▱ ▱ ▱ SC

Hotel

★ ★ ★ **EMBASSY SUITES.** 6646 Old Collamer Rd (13057). 315/446-3200; FAX 315/437-3302. 215 kit. suites, 5 story. S $109-$149; D $119-$169; each addl $10; under 18 free; higher rates: university events, state fair. Crib free. Pet accepted, some restrictions. TV; cable (premium). Indoor pool; poolside serv, lifeguard. Complimentary full bkfst. Complimentary coffee in rms. Restaurant 11 am-10 pm. Bar to midnight. Ck-out noon. Coin lndry. Meeting rms. Business servs avail. In-rm modem link. Gift shop. Airport transportation. Exercise equipt; weights, bicycles, sauna. Wet bars. Cr cds: A, C, D, DS, MC, V.
▯ ▱ ▱ ▱ ▱ ▱ ▱ SC

Tarrytown <small>(See also New York City, White Plains, Yonkers)</small>

Motel

★ ★ **RAMADA INN.** *(540 Saw Mill River Rd, Elmsford 10523)* E on NY 287, N on NY 9A. 914/592-3300; FAX 914/592-3381. 101 rms, 5 story. Mar-Oct: S $89-$129; D $99-$139; each addl $10; under 18 free. Crib free. Pet accepted, some restrictions. TV; cable (premium). Indoor/outdoor pool; lifeguard. Complimentary coffee in rms. Restaurant 6:30 am-10 pm. Rm serv. Bar noon-midnight; entertainment Fri, Sat. Ck-out noon. Meeting rms. Business servs avail. Health club privileges. Cr cds: A, C, D, DS, ER, JCB, MC, V.
▯ ▱ ▱ ▱ ▱ SC

Ticonderoga (Lake George Area)

Motel

★ **CIRCLE COURT.** 440 Montcalm St. 518/585-7660. 14 rms. June-mid-Oct: S $51-$55; D $56-$59; each addl $5; wkly rates off-season; lower rates rest of yr. Pet accepted. TV; cable. Complimentary coffee in rms. Restaurant nearby. Ck-out 11 am. Refrigerators. Cr cds: A, MC, V. ▱ ▱ SC

Tupper Lake <small>(See also Lake Placid, Saranac Lake)</small>

Motels

✔ ★ **PINE TERRACE MOTEL & RESORT.** 94 Moody Rd, $2^1/_2$ mi S on NY 30. 518/359-9258; res: 518/359-2146. 18 cottage units, 11 kits. No A/C. D $45-$80; each addl $5; kit. units $250-$450/wk; family rates. Crib avail. Pet accepted. TV; cable. Pool; wading pool. Ck-out 11 am. Lighted tennis. Lawn games. Refrigerators. Boats avail. Picnic tables, grills. Private beach opp. View of lake, mountains. Cr cds: MC, V. ▱ ▱ ▱ ▱

✔ ★ **SUNSET PARK.** 71 De Mars Blvd, $^1/_2$ mi W on NY 3. 518/359-3995. 11 rms, 4 kits. No A/C. Mid-June-Oct: S, D $46-$60; each addl $4; kit. units $56-$62; lower rates rest of yr. Crib free. Pet accepted. TV; cable. Complimentary coffee in rms. Restaurant nearby. Ck-out 11 am. Downhill ski 3 mi. Lawn games. Picnic tables, grills. On Tupper Lake. Private sand beach, dock for small boats. Cr cds: A, DS, MC, V. ▱ ▱ ▱ ▱ ▱

Utica *(See also Herkimer, Rome)*

Motels

★ ★ **BEST WESTERN GATEWAY ADIRONDACK INN.** *175 N Genesee St (13502). 315/732-4121; FAX 315/797-8265.* 89 rms, 1-2 story. S $60-$119; D $70-$129; each addl $10; under 12 free; higher rates special events. Crib free. Pet accepted, some restrictions. TV; cable. Complimentary continental bkfst. Coffee in rms. Restaurant adj 10-2 am. Ck-out noon. Business center. Sundries. Exercise equipt; bicycles, treadmill. Game rm. Refrigerators avail. Cr cds: A, C, D, DS, MC, V. [D] [icons]

★ ★ ★ **HOLIDAY INN.** *(1777 Burrstone Rd, New Hartford 13413) S on NY 12, W on Burrstone Rd. 315/797-2131; FAX 315/797-5817.* 100 rms, 2 story. S, D $92-$129; under 18 free; higher rates some wkends. Crib free. Pet accepted. TV; cable. Pool; whirlpool. Coffee in rms. Restaurant 6:30 am-10 pm. Rm serv. Bar 4 pm-2 am; entertainment Fri, Sat. Ck-out noon. Coin lndry. Meeting rms. Business servs avail. In-rm modem link. Valet serv. Sundries. Gift shop. Exercise equipt; weights, bicycles. Game rm. Refrigerators avail. Cr cds: A, C, D, DS, JCB, MC, V. [D] [icons]

✔ ★ **RED ROOF INN.** *20 Weaver St at N Genesee St (13502). 315/724-7128; FAX 315/724-7158.* 112 rms, 2 story. S $38.99-$62; D $48.99-$74; each addl $7-9; under 18 free. Crib free. Pet accepted, some restrictions. TV; cable (premium). Complimentary coffee in lobby. Restaurant nearby. Ck-out noon. Business servs avail. Sundries. Cr cds: A, C, D, DS, MC, V. [D] [icons]

Hotel

★ ★ ★ **RADISSON-UTICA CENTRE.** *200 Genesee St (13502). 315/797-8010; FAX 315/797-1490.* 158 rms, 6 story. S, D $114-$124; suites $175; under 18 free; wkend rates. Crib free. Pet accepted. TV; cable. Indoor pool; lifeguard. Coffee in rms. Restaurant 6:30 am-2 pm, 5-10 pm; Sun 7 am-2 pm, 5-9 pm. Bar 3 pm-2 am; entertainment Tues-Sat. Ck-out noon. Meeting rms. Business servs avail. In-rm modem link. Shopping arcade. Barber, beauty shop. Garage parking. Downhill ski 10 mi; x-country ski 5 mi. Exercise rm; instructor, weight machines, bicycles. Game rm. Some refrigerators. Cr cds: A, C, D, DS, MC, V. [icons]

Victor *(See also Canandaigua, Rochester)*

Motel

★ ★ **SUNRISE HILL INN.** *(6108 Loomis Rd, Farmington 14425) I-90 exit 44. 716/924-2131; FAX 716/924-1876.* 104 rms, 2 story. Mid-June-mid-Sept: S, D $68-$78; each addl $8; suites $85; under 18 free; lower rates rest of yr. Crib free. Pet accepted, some restrictions. TV; cable, VCR avail (movies). Pool. Bar 5-10 pm Wed-Sat. Ck-out 11 am. Meeting rms. Business servs avail. In-rm modem link. Valet serv Mon-Thurs. Health club privileges. Some balconies. Countryside view. Near race track. Cr cds: A, C, D, DS, ER, JCB, MC, V. [icons]

Waterloo *(See also Canandaigua, Geneva)*

Motel

★ ★ ★ **HOLIDAY INN.** *2468 NY 414, 1 mi E on NY 414, just N of jct US 20, NY 5; 4 mi S of I-90 exit 41. 315/539-5011; FAX 315/539-8355.* 147 rms, 2 story. June-mid-Oct: S, D $65; higher rates special events; under 19 free; package plans; lower rates rest of yr. Crib free. Pet accepted. TV; cable (premium), VCR avail. Heated pool; whirlpool. Coffee in rms. Restaurant 6:30 am-10 pm. Rm serv. Bar 11:30-1 am; Fri, Sat to 2 am; Sun to midnight; entertainment Fri, Sat. Ck-out noon. Coin lndry. Meeting rms. Business servs avail. In-rm modem link. Valet serv (Mon-Fri). Tennis. Exercise equipt; weights, bicycles, sauna. Cr cds: A, C, D, DS, JCB, MC, V. [D] [icons]

Watertown

Motels

★ **ECONO LODGE.** *1030 Arsenal St. 315/782-5500; FAX 315/788-7608.* 60 rms, 2 story. May-Sept: S $59.95-$64.95; D $69.95-$74.95; each addl $5; under 18 free; lower rates rest of yr. Crib free. Pet accepted; $5. TV; cable (premium). Indoor pool. Complimentary continental bkfst in lobby. Restaurant adj 11 am-9 pm. Ck-out 11 am. Coin lndry. Sundries. Refrigerators. Picnic tables, grills. Cr cds: A, C, D, DS, MC, V. [D] [icons]

✔★ **NEW PARROT.** *Outer Washington St, 2 mi S on NY 11, 4 mi N of I-81 exit 44. 315/788-5080; res: 800/479-9889.* 26 rms. June-Oct: S $34-$36; D $45-$55; each addl $5; family rates off-season; lower rates rest of yr. Crib $5. Pet accepted; $3. TV; cable. Indoor pool. Restaurant adj 6 am-9 pm. Ck-out 11 am. Picnic tables, grills. Cr cds: A, D, DS, MC, V.

★★ **QUALITY INN.** *1190 Arsenal St, on NY 3 at I-81 exit 45.* 315/788-6800; FAX 315/788-6800, ext. 298. 96 rms, 2 story. May-Oct: S $48-$56; D $60-$70; each addl $6; under 18 free; lower rates rest of yr. Pet accepted. TV; cable (premium). Pool. Restaurant 6:30-11:30 pm. Ck-out noon. Coin lndry. Meeting rms. Game rm. Private patios, balconies. Cr cds: A, C, D, DS, ER, JCB, MC, V.

White Plains

(See also New Rochelle, New York City, Tarrytown, Yonkers)

Hotel

★★ **RAMADA INN.** *(94 Business Park Dr, Armonk 10504) N on I-684, exit 3 S, in Westchester Business Park.* 914/273-9090; FAX 914/273-4105. 140 rms, 2 story. S, D $99-$189; each addl $10; suites $189; under 18 free; wkend, hol rates; higher rates Dec 31. Pet accepted. TV; cable (premium). Pool; poolside serv, lifeguard. Complimentary continental bkfst. Complimentary coffee in rms. Restaurant 7 am-9:30 pm. Bar noon-2 am; entertainment wkends. Ck-out noon. Coin lndry. Meeting rms. Business servs avail. In-rm modem link. Concierge. Free airport, RR station transportation. Exercise equipt; weights, bicycles. Some refrigerators. Microwaves avail. Picnic tables. Cr cds: A, C, D, DS, ER, JCB, MC, V.

Wilmington *(See also Lake Placid, Saranac Lake)*

Motels

★★ **HUNGRY TROUT.** *2 mi SW on NY 86, W branch of Ausable River.* 518/946-2217; res: 800/766-9137. 20 rms. Dec-mid-Apr, late June-Labor Day: S, D $69-$89; suites $106-$124; ski, golf, fishing plans; lower rates rest of yr. Closed Apr, Nov. Crib $5. Pet accepted; $4. TV; cable. Pool; wading pool. Playground. Coffee in rms. Restaurant opp 7-10 am. Bar 5-10 pm. Ck-out 11 am. Downhill ski 1/2 mi; x-country ski 12 mi. On Ausable River. Cr cds: A, C, D, DS, MC, V.

★★ **LEDGE ROCK AT WHITEFACE MOUNTAIN.** *(Placid Rd, Whiteface Mountain) 2 mi S on NY 86, opp Whiteface Mt Ski Center.* 518/946-2302; res: 800/336-4754. 18 rms, 2 story. Mid-Dec-Mar, mid-June-late Oct: S, D $69-$120. Crib free. Pet accepted; $5. TV; cable. Heated pool; wading pool. Playground. Coffee in rms. Restaurant nearby. Ck-out 11 am. Rec rm. Game rm with fireplace. Refrigerators. Some balconies. Picnic area, grills. Pond with paddleboats. Cr cds: A, DS, MC, V.

Yonkers

Motel

★★ **HOLIDAY INN.** *125 Tuckahoe Rd (10710).* 914/476-3800; FAX 914/423-3555. 103 rms, 3 story. S $89-$94; D $89-$101; each addl $10; suites $195; under 12 free; wkend rates. Crib free. TV; cable (premium). Complimentary coffee in rms. Restaurant 7 am-10 pm. Rm serv. Bar 5 pm-midnight; wkends to 2 am; entertainment Thurs-Sat. Ck-out noon. Meeting rms. Business servs avail. In-rm modem link. Valet serv. Tennis privileges. 18-hole golf privileges. Exercise equipt; weights, bicycles. Health club privileges. Pool; poolside serv, lifeguard. Many balconies. Cr cds: A, D, DS, MC, V.

New York City

Manhattan

Hotels

★ ★ ★ ★ ★ **CARLYLE.** *Madison Ave at E 76th St (10021), Upper East Side.* 212/744-1600; FAX 212/717-4682; res: 800/227-5737. The fabled Carlyle has hosted world leaders and the very, very rich for years and continues to be a symbol of European graciousness. And it's just steps away from the tony boutiques of Madison Avenue. 196 rms, 35 story. S $300-$450; D $330-$480; suites (1-2 bedrm) $500-$2,000. Pet accepted, some restrictions. Garage $39. TV; cable (premium), VCR (movies). Restaurant 7 am-2:30 pm, 6 pm-1 am; Sun from 7:30 am. Rm serv 24 hrs. Bar from noon; Café Carlyle from 6 pm; entertainment (cover charge). Ck-out 1 pm. Meeting rms. Business center. In-rm modem link. Concierge. Exercise rm; instructor, weights, bicycles, sauna, steam rm. Massage. Bathrm phones, refrigerators, wet bars, minibars; microwaves avail. Many in-rm whirlpools, serv pantries. Grand piano in many suites. Some terraces. Cr cds: A, C, D, JCB, MC, V.

★ ★ ★ ★ **FOUR SEASONS.** *57 E 57th St (10022), between Madison & Park Aves, on the East Side.* 212/758-5700; res: 800/332-3442; FAX 212/758-5711. Web www.fshr.com. The elegant, five-year-old, 52-story hotel—New York's tallest—offers large guest rooms, meticulous service and spectacular views of the city skyline and Central Park. The huge, multilevel marble lobby seems almost like an Egyptian monument. 370 rms, 52 story, 61 suites. S $440-$580; D $490-$675; each addl $50; suites $825-$7,000; under 12 free; wkend rates. Crib free. Pet accepted, some restrictions. Garage, valet parking $35. TV; cable (premium), VCR. Restaurant 7 am-10:30 pm. Rm serv 24 hrs. Bar 11:30-1 am. Ck-out noon. Convention facilities. Business center. In-rm modem link. Concierge. Extensive exercise rm; instructor, weight machine, bicycles, whirlpool, sauna, steam rm. Massage. Health club privileges. Bathrm phones, minibars. Some terraces. Cr cds: A, C, D, ER, JCB, MC, V.

★ ★ ★ **HILTON AND TOWERS AT ROCKEFELLER CENTER.** *1335 Avenue of the Americas (10019), between W 53rd & 54th Sts, Midtown.* 212/586-7000; FAX 212/315-1374. Web www.travelweb.com. 2,040 rms, 46 story. S $185-$295; D $215-$325; each addl $30; suites $425-$625; family rates; package plans. Crib free. Pet accepted. Garage $35. TV; cable (premium), VCR avail. Restaurant 6 am-midnight. Bar 11-2 am. Ck-out noon. Convention facilities. Business center. In-rm modem link. Shopping arcade. Barber, beauty shop. Exercise rm; instructor, weights, bicycles, sauna. Minibars. Refrigerators avail. Luxury level. Cr cds: A, C, D, DS, ER, JCB, MC, V.

★ ★ **LOEWS NEW YORK.** *569 Lexington Ave (10022), at E 51st St, Midtown.* 212/752-7000; FAX 212/758-6311. Web www.loweshotels.com. 722 rms, 20 story. S, D $189-$279; each addl $25; suites $250-$850; under 16 free; wkend rates. Crib free. Pet accepted, some restrictions. Garage $25. TV; cable (premium). Restaurant 7 am-midnight. Bar 11-2 am. Ck-out noon. Meeting rms. Business center. In-rm modem link. Barber. Exercise rm; instructor, weight machines, bicycles, sauna. Bathrm phones, refrigerators; microwaves avail. Luxury level. Cr cds: A, C, D, DS, JCB, MC, V.

★ ★ **THE MAYFLOWER.** *15 Central Park West (10023), at 61st St, Upper West Side.* 212/265-0060; FAX 212/265-5098; res: 800/223-4164. 365 rms, 18 story, 200 suites. S $155-$195; D $170-$210; each addl $20; suites $205-$285; under 18 free; wkly, wkend, hol rates; lower rates July, Aug & mid-Dec-Mar 31. Pet accepted. Garage parking, valet $25. TV; cable (premium). Restaurant 7 am-10 pm. Bar 11:30-1 am. Ck-out noon. Meeting rms. Business servs avail. In-rm modem link. Concierge. Exercise equipt; treadmill, stair machine. Many refrigerators. Some terraces. Cr cds: A, C, D, DS, ER, JCB, MC, V.

★ ★ **NOVOTEL.** *226 W 52nd St (10019), at Broadway, Midtown.* 212/315-0100; FAX 212/765-5369; res: 800/221-3185. 474 rms, 33 story. S, D $179-$279; each addl $20; under 16 free. Crib $10. Pet accepted. Parking $12. TV; cable (premium). Complimentary coffee in lobby. Restaurant 6 am-midnight. Bar 3:30 pm-1 am; entertainment exc Sun. Ck-out 1 pm. Meeting rm. Business center. In-rm modem link. Exercise equipt; weights, treadmill. Cr cds: A, C, D, ER, JCB, MC, V.

★ ★ **PARKER MERIDIEN.** *118 W 57th St (10019), between 6th & 7th Aves, Midtown.* 212/245-5000; FAX 212/708-7477; res: 800/543-4300. Web www.parker meridien.com. 700 rms, 42 story. S $300-$340; D $325-$365; each addl $30; suites

$325-$2,500; under 12 free; wkend plan. Crib free. Pet accepted. Garage parking, valet $32. TV; VCR avail. Indoor pool; whirlpool. Restaurant 6:30 am-10:45 pm. Rm serv 24 hrs. Bar 3 pm-midnight. Ck-out 1 pm. Business center. In-rm modem link. Exercise rm; instructor, bicycles, stair machine, sauna. Microwaves avail. French ambience; Italian marble flooring, French tapestries. Cr cds: A, C, D, DS, ER, JCB, MC, V. ▣ ⬤ ⬤ ⬤ ⬤ ⬤ ⬤

★ ★ ★ **ROYALTON.** *44 W 44th St (10036), between Fifth & Sixth ave, Midtown.* 212/869-4400; FAX 212/869-8965; res: 800/635-9013. 205 rms, some with shower only, 16 story. S $295-$390; D $330-$400; each addl $30; suites $450; wkend rates. Crib $25. Pet accepted, some restrictions. Valet parking $38. TV; cable (premium), VCR (movies). Restaurant 7-1 am. Rm serv 24 hrs. Bar. Ck-out 1 pm. Meeting rm. Business servs avail. In-rm modem link. Concierge. Exercise equipt; bicycles, treadmill. Bathrm phones, refrigerators, minibars; some fireplaces. Some balconies. Ultramodern rm decor. Cr cds: A, C, D, ER, JCB, MC, V. ▣ ⬤ ⬤ ⬤ ⬤

★ ★ ★ **SOHO GRAND.** *310 W Broadway (10013), between Grand & Canal St, in SoHo.* 212/965-3000; res: 800/965-3000; FAX 212/965-3200. 367 rms, 17 story. S $209-$349; D $229-$369; each addl $20; suites $949-$1149; under 12 free. Crib free. Pet accepted. Garage parking $25. TV; cable (premium), VCR avail. Restaurant 6 am-midnight; Sat, Sun from 7 am. Rm serv 24 hrs. Bar noon-2 am; Sat, Sun from 1 pm. Ck-out noon. Meeting rms. Business center. In-rm modem link. Concierge. Free valet parking. Exercise equipt; rower, stair machines. Massage. Minibars. Cr cds: A, D, DS, JCB, MC, V. ▣ ⬤ ⬤ ⬤ ⬤

★ ★ ★ **WESTBURY.** *15 E Madison Ave (10021), at 69th St, Upper East Side.* 212/535-2000; FAX 212/535-5058; res: 800/321-1569. 228 rms, 17 story, 52 suites. S $315-$345; D $345-$375; each addl $30; 2, 3-rm suites $525-$1,750; under 12 free; wkend rates. Pet accepted. TV; cable (premium), VCR avail (free movies). Restaurant 7-10 am, noon-2:30 pm, 6-10 pm. Rm serv 24 hrs. Bar noon-midnight. Ck-out 1 pm. Business center. In-rm modem link. Exercise equipt; bicycles, treadmill, sauna. Microwaves avail. Bathrm phones. Cr cds: A, C, D, DS, ER, JCB, MC, V. ▣ ⬤ ⬤ ⬤ ⬤

Queens (La Guardia & JFK Intl Airport Areas)

Hotels

★ ★ ★ **MARRIOTT LAGUARDIA.** *102-05 Ditmars Blvd (11369), opp La Guardia Airport, in East Elmhurst area.* 718/565-8900; FAX 718/898-4995. Web www.marriot.com/lgaap. 436 rms, 9 story. S $150; D $170; suites $350-$650; under 18 free; wkly rates; wkend plans. Crib free. Pet accepted. Covered parking $5. TV; cable (premium), VCR avail. Indoor pool; whirlpool, lifeguard. Restaurants 6:30 am-11 pm. Bar 11-1 am. Ck-out 1 pm. Convention facilities. Business center. In-rm modem link. Gift shop. Free airport transportation. Exercise equipt; weight machines, bicycles, sauna. Microwaves avail. Luxury level. Cr cds: A, C, D, DS, ER, JCB, MC, V. ▣ ⬤ ⬤ ⬤ ⬤ ⬤ ⬤ SC ⬤

North Carolina

Asheville

Motels

★ ★ **COMFORT SUITES.** *890 Brevard Rd (28806), I-26 exit 2. 704/665-4000; FAX 704/665-9082.* 125 suites, 5 story. May-Oct: suites $69-$99; each addl $6; under 18 free; lower rates rest of yr. Crib free. Pet accepted; $20. TV; cable (premium). Pool; whirlpool. Complimentary continental bkfst. Coffee in rms. Restaurant nearby. Ck-out noon. Coin lndry. Meeting rms. Business servs avail. In-rm modem link. Free airport transportation. Exercise equipt; bicycles, stair machine. Refrigerators. Cr cds: A, C, D, DS, ER, JCB, MC, V. D ✦ ⩳ 🏃 🖉 🐾 SC

✔ ★ **RED ROOF INN.** *16 Crowell Rd (28806), I-40 exit 44. 704/667-9803; FAX 704/667-9810.* 109 rms, 3 story. May-Oct: S $56; D $62; under 18 free; lower rates rest of yr. Pet accepted, some restrictions. TV; cable (premium). Complimentary coffee in lobby. Restaurant opp open 24 hrs. Ck-out noon. Business servs avail. Cr cds: A, D, DS, MC, V.

D ✦ 🖉 🐾

Brevard (See also Asheville, Hendersonville)

Motel

★ **SUNSET.** *415 S Broad St. 704/884-9106.* 18 rms. June-Oct: S $50; D $60; each addl $5; lower rates rest of yr. Pet accepted, some restrictions. TV; cable. Restaurant opp 11 am-10 pm. Ck-out 11 am. Refrigerators. Cr cds: A, D, DS, MC, V. ✦ 🖉 🐾 SC

Burlington (See also Greensboro)

Motel

★ **COMFORT INN.** *978 Plantation Dr (27215), I-85, exit 145. 336/227-3681; FAX 336/570-0900.* 127 rms, 2 story. S $57-$88; D $61-$88; each addl $4; under 18 free; higher rates Furniture Market. Crib free. Pet accepted, some restrictions. TV; cable (premium). Pool; wading pool. Complimentary continental bkfst. Complimentary coffee in rms. Restaurant adj 11 am-11 pm. Ck-out noon. Coin lndry. Meeting rms. Business servs avail. Valet serv. Exercise equipt; weight machine, stair machine. Some refrigerators; microwaves avail. Cr cds: A, C, D, DS, JCB, MC, V. D ✦ ⩳ 🏃 🖉 🐾 SC

Cashiers (See also Highlands)

Resort

★ ★ ★ **HIGH HAMPTON INN & COUNTRY CLUB.** *2 mi S on NC 107. 704/743-2411; FAX 704/743-5991; res: 800/334-2551.* Web www.highhamptoninn.com. 34 rms in 3-story inn, 15 cottages, 37 golf villas. No A/C. AP, July-Aug: S $93-$95; D $164-$182; each addl $57; golf villas (3-day min) $195-$356; wkly rates; golf, tennis plans; lower rates Sept-June, Oct, Nov. Closed rest of yr. Crib free. Pet accepted, some restrictions. TV rm; cable. Supervised child's activities (June-Labor Day); ages 3-12. Complimentary afternoon refreshments. Dining rm 7-9:30 am, noon-2:15 pm, 6:30-8:15 pm. Box lunches, buffets. Ck-out 1 pm, ck-in 3 pm. Coin lndry. Business servs avail. Valet serv. Gift shop. Airport transportation. Sports dir. Tennis. 18-hole golf, greens fee $26, pro, 2 putting greens, driving range. Exercise equipt; treadmill, stair machine. Boats, dockage. Archery. Trail guides. Bicycle rentals. Outdoor, indoor games. Soc dir; entertainment, movies. Rec rm, library. Lawn games. Kennels. 1,400-acre mountain estate, 2 lakes. Rustic resort; established 1924. Former hunting lodge of a Civil War general. Cr cds: A, DS, MC, V.

D ✦ 🏊 🏃 🏃 🏃 🎣 🐾

Chapel Hill (See also Durham, Raleigh)

Hotel

★ ★ ★ **SIENA.** *1505 E Franklin St (27514). 919/929-4000; res: 800/223-7379; FAX 919/968-8527.* 80 rms, 4 story, 12 suites. S, D $149; each addl $10; suites $185-$200; under 17 free; higher rates: football games, graduation. Crib free. Pet accepted; $50 refundable. TV; cable (premium), VCR avail. Complimentary full bkfst. Restaurant 6:30-10 am, 11:30 am-2 pm, 6-10 pm. Bar noon-midnight; entertainment. Ck-out noon. Meeting rms. Business servs avail. In-rm modem link. Concierge. Airport transportation. Tennis privileges. Golf privileges, greens fee $60, pro, putting green, driving range. Health club privileges. Bathrm phones; some refrigerators. Picnic tables. Cr cds: A, C, D, JCB, MC, V.

D ⚡ 🏊 🏋 🛶 🐾 SC

Charlotte (See also Rock Hill, SC)

Motels

★ ★ LA QUINTA-SOUTH. 7900 Nations Ford Rd (28217), S via I-77 to exit 4. 704/522-7110; FAX 704/521-9778. Web www.laquinta.com. 118 rms, 3 story. S, D $57-$70; each addl $7; under 18 free; higher rates: auto race wkends, special events. Crib free. Pet accepted, some restrictions. TV; cable (premium). Heated pool. Continental bkfst. Restaurant adj open 24 hrs. Ck-out noon. Business servs avail. Valet serv. Health club privileges. Microwaves avail. Cr cds: A, C, D, DS, MC, V. D ⚡ ≈ 🛶 🐾 SC

✓★ RED ROOF INN-COLISEUM. 131 Red Roof Dr (28217), I-77 S to exit 4 (Nations Ford Rd). 704/529-1020; FAX 704/529-1054. E-mail 124@redroofinn.com. 115 rms, 3 story. S $36-$41; D $41-$47; up to 5, $59; under 18 free. Crib free. Pet accepted, some restrictions. TV; cable (premium). Complimentary coffee in lobby. Ck-out noon. Business servs avail. Health club privileges. Cr cds: A, C, D, DS, MC, V. D ⚡ 🛶 🐾

★ ★ RESIDENCE INN BY MARRIOTT. 5800 Westpark Dr (28217), off I-77S at Tyvola Rd exit 5. 704/527-8110; FAX 704/521-8282. 80 kit. suites, 1-2 story. S, D $139-$169. Crib free. Pet accepted; $100 and $5/day. TV; cable (premium). Heated pool; whirlpool. Complimentary continental bkfst. Restaurant adj 7 am-10 pm. Coin lndry. Ck-out noon. Business servs avail. Valet serv. Health club privileges. Lawn games. Microwaves. Private patios, balconies. Cr cds: A, C, D, DS, MC, V. D ⚡ ≈ 🛶 🐾 SC

Motor Hotels

★ ★ SHERATON AIRPORT PLAZA. 3315 S I-85 (28208), at Billy Graham Pkwy, near Douglas Intl Airport, I-85 exit 33. 704/392-1200; FAX 704/393-2207. 222 rms, 8 story. S, D $119-$135; each addl $10; suites $150-$175; under 16 free; wkend rates. Crib free. Pet accepted. TV; cable (premium). Indoor/outdoor pool; whirlpool, poolside serv. Coffee in rms. Restaurant 6:30 am-10:30 pm. Rm serv. Bar 11 am-midnight; entertainment Thurs-Sat. Ck-out noon. Meeting rms. Business servs avail. Bellhops. Valet serv. Gift shop. Free airport transportation. Exercise equipt; weights, bicycles, sauna. Bathrm phones; microwaves avail. Cr cds: A, C, D, DS, JCB, MC, V. D ⚡ ≈ 🏋 🛶 🐾 SC

★ ★ SUMMERFIELD SUITES. 4920 S Tryon St (28217). 704/525-2600; FAX 704/521-9932. 135 kit. suites, 5 story. Kit. suites $79-$109; under 18 free; wkends (2-day min); higher rates race wkend. Crib free. Pet accepted; $50. TV; cable (premium), VCR (movies). Complimentary continental bkfst. Complimentary coffee in rms. Ck-out noon. Meeting rms. Business center. In-rm modem link. Free airport transportation. Exercise equipt; rowers, stair machine. Pool; whirlpool. Game rm. Refrigerators, microwaves. Picnic tables, grills. Totally nonsmoking. Cr cds: A, C, D, DS, JCB, MC, V.

D ⚡ ≈ 🏋 🛶 🐾 SC 🚶

Hotels

★ ★ ★ HILTON AT UNIVERSITY PLACE. 8629 J M Keynes Dr (28262), off I-85, exit 45A (Harris Blvd). 704/547-7444; FAX 704/549-9708. E-mail hiltonuniversity@travel base.com; web www.travelbase.com/desti nations/charlotte/hilton-univ. 243 rms, 12 story. S, D $84-$159; each addl $15; wkend rates. Crib free. Pet accepted; $50. TV; cable (premium). Heated pool; poolside serv. Restaurant 6:30 am-10 pm. Bar 11-2 am; entertainment. Ck-out noon. Meeting rms. Business servs avail. In-rm modem link. Exercise equipt; bicycles, treadmills. Health club privileges. Microwaves avail. Cr cds: A, C, D, DS, MC, V.

D ⚡ ≈ 🏋 🛶 🐾 SC

★ ★ ★ HILTON EXECUTIVE PARK. 5624 Westpark Dr (28217), I-77 exit 5. 704/527-8000; FAX 704/527-4278. 178 rms, 7 story, 34 suites. S $124; D $134; each addl $10; suites $149; under 18 free. Crib free. Pet accepted; $50 deposit, $15/day. TV; cable (premium), VCR avail. Heated pool; whirlpool. Restaurant 6:30 am-2 pm, 5-10 pm. Bar 2 pm-midnight. Ck-out noon. Meeting rms. Business servs avail. Free airport transportation. Exercise equipt; weight machine, treadmill. Microwaves avail. Refrigerator in suites. Cr cds: A, C, D, DS, MC, V. D ⚡ ≈ 🏋 🛶 🐾 SC

★ ★ ★ HYATT. 5501 Carnegie Blvd (28209), opp South Park Mall. 704/554-1234; FAX 704/554-8319. 262 rms, 7 story. S $170; D $195; suites $350-$750; lower rates wkends; under 18 free. Crib free. Pet accepted. TV; cable (premium). Indoor pool; whirlpool, poolside serv. Restaurant 6 am-10:30 pm. Rm serv 24 hrs. Bar 2 pm-2 am. Ck-out noon. Convention facilities. Business center. Gift shop. Free valet parking. Airport transportation.

Exercise equipt; weights, bicycles, sauna. Health club privileges. Refrigerators, microwaves avail. Some balconies. Luxury level. Cr cds: A, C, D, DS, ER, JCB, MC, V.

D ✷ ≋ ⫟ ⊠ 🔥 SC 🏃

★ ★ **RADISSON PLAZA.** *101 S Tryon (28280), at jct Trade & Tryon Sts.* 704/377-0400; FAX 704/347-0649. 365 rms, 15 story. S, D $135; each addl $10; suites $219-$325; under 18 free; wkend rates. Crib free. Pet accepted, some restrictions. TV; cable (premium), VCR avail. Pool; poolside serv. Coffee in rms. Restaurant 6:30 am-10:30 pm. Bar 11 am-midnight. Ck-out noon. Convention facilities. Business center. Concierge. Shopping arcade. Barber, beauty shop. Covered parking. Exercise equipt; weights, stair machine, sauna. Refrigerator, wet bar in suites. Luxury level. Cr cds: A, C, D, DS, ER, MC, V.

D ✷ ≋ ⫟ ⊠ 🔥 SC 🏃

Cornelius *(See also Charlotte)*

Motel

★ ★ **HOLIDAY INN.** *19901 Holiday Ln, jct NC 73 & I-77 exit 28.* 704/892-9120; FAX 704/892-3854. 119 rms, 2 story. S, D $84; under 18 free; higher rates special events. Crib free. Pet accepted; $25. TV; cable (premium). Pool. Complimentary coffee in rms. Restaurant 6 am-10 pm. Rm serv. Bar 4:30 pm-midnight. Ck-out 11 am. Coin lndry. Meeting rms. Exercise equipt; weight machines, bicycles. Some refrigerators, microwaves. Cr cds: A, C, D, DS, JCB, MC, V. D ✷ ≋ ⫟ ⊠ 🔥 SC

Dunn *(See also Fayetteville, Goldsboro)*

Motel

★ **RAMADA INN.** *1011 E Cumberland St, I-95 Exit 73.* 910/892-8101; FAX 910/892-2836. 100 rms, 2 story. S $39-$59; D $49-$69; each addl $6; under 18 free. Crib free. Pet accepted. TV; cable (premium). Pool. Restaurant 6:30 am-2 pm, 5-9 pm. Rm serv. Ck-out noon. Meeting rms. Business servs avail. Valet serv. Some refrigerators. Cr cds: A, C, D, DS, JCB, MC, V. D ✷ ≋ ⊠ 🔥 SC

Durham *(See also Chapel Hill, Raleigh)*

Motels

(Rates may be higher for graduation, football wkends)

★ **BEST WESTERN SKYLAND.** *5400 US 70 (27705), Jct I-85 exit 170 & US 70W.* 919/383-2508; FAX 919/383-7316. Web www.citysearch.com. 31 rms. S $50; D $62; each addl $10; under 12 free. Crib $10. TV; cable (premium). Pool. Playground. Complimentary continental bkfst. Ck-out noon. Business servs avail. Refrigerators. Picnic tables, grills. Situated atop hill. Cr cds: A, C, D, DS, ER, JCB, MC, V.

D ✷ ≋ ⊠ 🔥 SC

✔ ★ **RED ROOF INN.** *2000 I-85 Service Rd (27705), I-85 exit 175.* 919/471-9882; FAX 919/477-0512. 120 rms, 3 story. S $43.99-$52.99; D $48.99-$58.99. Crib free. Pet accepted, some restrictions. TV; cable (premium). Complimentary coffee in lobby. Restaurant nearby. Ck-out noon. Business servs avail. Cr cds: A, C, D, DS, MC, V.

D ✷ ⊠ 🔥 SC

Fayetteville *(See also Goldsboro)*

Motel

✔ ★ ★ **COMFORT INN.** *1957 Cedar Creek Rd (28301).* 910/323-8333; FAX 910/323-3946. 120 rms, 2 story. S $52-$55; D $57-$62; each addl $6; suites $60-$63; under 18 free. Crib free. Pet accepted. TV; cable (premium). Pool. Complimentary continental bkfst. Restaurant adj 6 am-midnight. Ck-out noon. Meeting rms. Business servs avail. Valet serv. Exercise equipt; bicycles, stair machine. Refrigerators. Cr cds: A, C, D, DS, ER, JCB, MC, V. D ✷ ≋ ⫟ ⊠ 🔥 SC

Motor Hotel

★ ★ **HOWARD JOHNSON.** *1965 Cedar Creek Rd (28302), I-95 exit 49.* 910/323-8282; FAX 910/323-3484. 168 rms, 4 story. S $64.95-$72; D $70.95-$78; each addl $6; suites $78-$100; under 18 free; golf plans. Crib free. Pet accepted. TV; cable (premium). Indoor pool; whirlpool. Restaurant 6 am-2 pm, 5-10 pm. Rm serv 5-10 pm. Bar; dancing. Ck-out noon. Meeting rms. Business center. Bellhops. Free airport transportation. Exercise equipt; weights, bicycles, sauna, steam rm. Some private patios. Luxury level. Cr cds: A, C, D, DS, MC, V. D ✷ ≋ ⫟ ⊠ 🔥 SC 🏃

Goldsboro

Motels

★ ★ **HOLIDAY INN.** *(27530). 1¹/₂ mi NE on US 13, 70 Bypass. 919/735-7901; FAX 919/734-2946.* 108 rms, 2 story. S $58; D $64; each addl $6; suites $85; under 16 free. Pet accepted. TV; cable (premium). Pool. Restaurant 6-9 am, 6-9 pm. Rm serv. Bar 5-11 pm. Ck-out noon. Meeting rms. Business servs avail. In-rm modem link. Exercise equipt; weights, bicycle. Cr cds: A, C, D, DS, JCB, MC, V. [D] [🖊] [≈] [🏋] [⊠] [🐾] [SC]

✔ ★ **RAMADA INN.** *808 W Grantham St (27530), jct US 70 & US 117S. 919/736-4590; FAX 919/735-3218.* 128 rms, 2 story. S $40-$57; D $44-$62; suites from $85; under 18 free. Crib free. Pet accepted. TV; cable (premium). Pool. Restaurant 5 am-10 pm. Rm serv. Bar 5 pm-2 am; entertainment Fri-Sat. Ck-out noon. Coin lndry. Meeting rms. Business servs avail. Valet serv. Sundries. Game rm. Some refrigerators. Picnic tables, grills. Cr cds: A, C, D, DS, JCB, MC, V. [D] [🖊] [≈] [⊠] [🐾] [SC]

Greensboro (See also Burlington)

Motel

(Rates are generally higher during Furniture Market)

★ ★ **HAMPTON INN.** *2004 Veasley St (27407). 336/854-8600; FAX 336/854-8741.* 121 rms, 2 story. S $59; D $65-$73; under 18 free. Crib free. Pet accepted, some restrictions. TV; cable (premium). Pool. Complimentary continental bkfst. Meeting rm. Business servs avail. Cr cds: A, C, D, DS, JCB, MC, V. [D] [🖊] [≈] [⊠] [🐾] [SC]

Hendersonville (See also Asheville, Brevard)

Motel

★ **COMFORT INN.** *206 Mitchell Dr (28792). 704/693-8800.* 85 rms, 2 story. June-Oct: S $55.95; D $60.95; each addl $10; under 18 free; higher rates wkends; lower rates rest of yr. Crib free. Pet accepted. TV; cable, in-rm movies. Pool; whirlpool. Complimentary continental bkfst. Restaurant nearby. Ck-out 11 am. Meeting rm. Business servs avail. In-rm modem link. Refrigerators avail. Cr cds: A, C, D, DS, JCB, MC, V. [D] [🖊] [≈] [⊠] [🐾] [SC]

Hickory

Motel

(Rates are generally higher during Furniture Market)

✔ ★ **RED ROOF INN.** *1184 Lenoir Rhyne Blvd (28602). 704/323-1500; FAX 704/323-1509.* 108 rms, 2 story. S $35-$46; D $47-$56; each addl $6; under 18 free. Crib free. Pet accepted, some restrictions. TV. Complimentary coffee in lobby. Restaurant adj. Ck-out noon. In-rm modem link. Cr cds: A, C, D, DS, MC, V. [D] [🖊] [⊠] [🐾]

Highlands (See also Cashiers)

Motel

★ ★ **MOUNTAIN HIGH.** *Main St. 704/526-2790; FAX 704/526-2750; res: 800/445-7293 (exc NC).* 55 rms, 1-2 story. June-Labor Day, Oct: S, D $93-$175; under 18 free; higher rates: wkends, hols; lower rates rest of yr. Crib $5. Pet accepted. TV; cable (premium). Complimentary continental bkfst. Restaurant opp 7:15 am-9:30 pm. Ck-out noon. Meeting rms. Business servs avail. Downhill ski 7 mi. Some bathrm phones, in-rm whirlpools, refrigerators, fireplaces; microwaves avail. Balconies. Picnic tables. Cr cds: A, DS, MC, V. [D] [🖊] [≈] [🐾]

Kill Devil Hills (Outer Banks)

Motel

★ ★ **RAMADA INN.** *1701 S Virginia Dare Trail, milepost 9.5, NC 12. 919/441-2151; FAX 919/441-1830.* 172 rms, 5 story. Memorial Day-Labor Day: D $135-$169; each addl $10; under 18 free; hol plans; lower rates rest of yr. Crib free. Pet accepted; $10. TV; cable, VCR avail (movies free). Indoor pool; whirlpool. Coffee in rms. Restaurant 7-11:30 am, 5-10 pm; summer 7 am-2 pm, 5-10 pm. Rm serv. Bar 7:30-11:30 am, 5-11 pm; entertainment wkends (in season). Ck-out 11 am. Meeting rms. Business servs avail. In-rm modem link. Refrigerators. Private balconies. Lawn games. Cr cds: A, C, D, DS, JCB, MC, V. ⊡ ⊡ ⊡ ⊡ ⊡ ⊡ ⊡ SC

Motor Hotel

★ ★ **THE NAGS HEAD BEACH HOTEL.** *804 N Virginia Dare Trail. 919/441-0411; FAX 919/441-7811.* 96 rms, 4 story. Mid-June-early Sept: S, D $78-$98; higher rates hol wkends; lower rates rest of yr. Crib free. Pet accepted. TV; cable (premium). Pool. Complimentary continental bkfst. Ck-out 11 am. Refrigerators. Many balconies. Cr cds: A, D, DS, MC, V. ⊡ ⊡ ⊡ ⊡ ⊡ ⊡ SC

Lumberton

Motel

★ ★ **HOLIDAY INN.** *5201 Fayetteville Rd. 910/671-1166.* 108 rms, 2 story. S $58; D $64; each addl $6; under 18 free. Crib free. Pet accepted. TV; cable (premium). Pool. Restaurant. Rm serv. Ck-out noon. Meeting rms. Business servs avail. In-rm modem link. Valet serv. Airport transportation. Health club privileges. Cr cds: A, C, D, DS, MC, V. ⊡ ⊡ ⊡ ⊡ ⊡ SC

Morganton

Motel

★ ★ **HOLIDAY INN.** *2400 South Sterling St, 1 mi SE on NC 18, at I-40. 704/437-0171; FAX 704/437-0171, ext. 297.* 135 rms, 2 story. S, D $50-$69; each addl $7; under 19 free. Crib free. Pet accepted. TV; cable (premium). Pool. Restaurant 6 am-2 pm, 5-10 pm. Rm serv. Bar 5 pm-midnight, Sun from 6 pm. Ck-out noon. Meeting rms. Business servs avail. In-rm modem link. Valet serv. Cr cds: A, C, D, DS, JCB, MC, V. ⊡ ⊡ ⊡ ⊡ ⊡ ⊡ SC

New Bern

Hotel

★ ★ ★ **SHERATON GRAND.** *1 Bicentennial Park (28560). 919/638-3585; FAX 919/638-8112.* 172 rms, 5 story. S, D $75-$104; each addl $10; suites $150; under 17 free. Crib free. Pet accepted. TV; cable (premium). Pool. Restaurant 6:30 am-2 pm, 5-10 pm. Bar noon-2 am; entertainment Fri, Sat. Ck-out noon. Meeting rms. Business center. In-rm modem link. Free airport transportation. Golf privileges. Exercise equipt; weight machine, bicycle. Balconies. On river; marina facilities. Cr cds: A, C, D, DS, MC, V. ⊡ ⊡ ⊡ ⊡ ⊡ ⊡ ⊡ ⊡ ⊡ ⊡ SC ⊡

Raleigh (See also Chapel Hill, Durham)

Motels

✔ ★ **RED ROOF INN.** *3520 Maitland Dr (27610). 919/231-0200; FAX 919/231-0228.* 115 rms, 3 story. S $41.99; D $50.99; each addl $6; under 18 free. Crib $5. Pet accepted. TV; cable (premium). Complimentary coffee in lobby. Restaurant adj 6 am-10 pm. Ck-out noon. Health club privileges. Microwaves avail. Cr cds: A, C, D, DS, MC, V. ⊡ ⊡ ⊡ ⊡

★ ★ **RESIDENCE INN BY MARRIOTT.** *1000 Navaho Dr (27609). 919/878-6100; FAX 919/876-4117.* 144 kit. suites, 1-2 story. S, D $120-$154; wkly, monthly rates. Crib free. Pet accepted, some restrictions; $200. TV; cable (premium). Heated pool; whirlpool. Complimentary continental bkfst. Ck-out noon. Coin lndry. Meeting rm. Business servs avail. In-rm modem link. Valet serv. Health club privileges. Microwaves; some bathrm phones. Private patios, balconies. Picnic tables, grills. Cr cds: A, C, D, DS, JCB, MC, V. ⊡ ⊡ ⊡ ⊡ SC

Motor Hotel

★ ★ ★ **VELVET CLOAK INN.** *1505 Hillsborough St (27605), in university area, west of downtown. 919/828-0333; FAX 919/828-2656; res: 800/334-4372 (exc NC), 800/662-8829 (NC).* 171 rms, 5 story. S, D $67-$107; each addl $10; suites $95-$290; under 18 free; wkend rates. Crib free. Pet accepted; $15. TV; cable (premium), VCR avail. Indoor/outdoor pool. Complimentary afternoon refreshments. Restaurant 6:30 am-10 pm. Rm serv. Bar 4:30 pm-1 am. Ck-out noon. Meeting rms. Business servs avail. Bellhops. Concierge. Sundries. Free airport transportation. Health club privileges. Bathrm phones; microwaves avail. Cr cds: A, C, D, DS, ER, JCB, MC, V. ⊡ ⊡ ⊡ ⊡ ⊡ SC

Salisbury

Motels

★ ★ **HAMPTON INN.** *1001 Klumac Rd, I-85 exit 75. 704/637-8000; FAX 704/639-9995.* 121 rms, 4 story. S $59; D $64; suites $95; under 18 free; higher rates: Furniture Market, auto racing events. Crib free. Pet accepted, some restrictions. TV; cable (premium). Pool. Complimentary continental bkfst. Restaurant adj 11 am-11 pm. Ck-out noon. Meeting rms. Business servs avail. Health club privileges. Refrigerator in suites. Cr cds: A, C, D, DS, MC, V. 🄳 ⬧ ⩰ ⬚ ⬚ SC

★ ★ **HOLIDAY INN.** *530 Jake Alexander Blvd S (28147), I-85 exit 75. 704/637-3100; FAX 704/637-9152.* 181 rms, 2 story. S $63-$88; D $67-$90; each addl $6; suites $95-$125; under 18 free; higher rates special events. Crib free. Pet accepted, some restrictions. TV; cable (premium). Indoor/outdoor pool. Restaurant 7 am-2 pm, 5:30-9 pm. Rm serv. Bar 5 pm-1 am; Sat from 6 pm; entertainment Fri, Sat. Ck-out noon. Business servs avail. Bellhops. Valet serv. Exercise equipt; weights, bicycles. Refrigerator avail in suites. Cr cds: A, C, D, DS, JCB, MC, V. 🄳 ⬧ ⩰ 🏃 ⬚ ⬚ 🔥 SC

Sanford

Motel

✔★ **PALOMINO.** *(27331). 2¹/₂ mi on US 1, US 15/501 Bypass. 919/776-7531; FAX 919/776-9670; res: 800/641-6060.* 92 rms. S $30-$38; D $35-$40; each addl $2. Crib free. Pet accepted. TV; cable (premium). Pool; whirlpool. Playground. Restaurant 6 am-10 pm. Ck-out noon. Meeting rms. Golf privileges. Exercise equipt; weight machines, stair machine, sauna. Picnic tables, grill. Cr cds: A, C, D, DS, MC, V.

🄳 ⬧ ⬧ 🏃 ⩰ 🏃 ⬚ ⬚ SC

Williamston

Motels

✔★ **COMFORT INN.** *Jct US 17 & US 13/64. 919/792-8400; FAX 919/792-9003; res: 800/827-8400.* 59 rms, 2 story. S $43; D $47; each addl $5; suites $46-$51; under 18 free. Crib free. Pet accepted. TV; cable (premium). Complimentary continental bkfst. Restaurant nearby. Ck-out noon. Business servs avail. Exercise equipt; weight machine, bicycles. Cr cds: A, C, D, DS, ER, JCB, MC, V. 🄳 ⬧ 🏃 ⬚ ⬚ SC

★ ★ **HOLIDAY INN.** *1 mi S on US 17. 919/792-3184; FAX 919/792-9003.* 100 rms, 2 story. S, D $49; each addl $4; under 18 free. Crib free. Pet accepted. TV; cable (premium). Pool. Restaurant 6 am-9:30 pm. Rm serv. Bar 5 pm-midnight. Ck-out noon. Meeting rms. Business center. In-rm modem link. Cr cds: A, C, D, DS, JCB, MC, V.

🄳 ⬧ ⩰ ⬚ ⬚ SC ⬧

Wilmington (See also Wrightsville Beach)

Hotel

★ ★ **HAMPTON INN & SUITES-LANDFALL PARK.** *1989 Eastwood Rd (28403), 4 mi E on US 74. 910/256-9600; FAX 910/256-1996.* 120 rms, 4 story, 30 kit. suites. May-Sept: S, D $109; suites $149-$349; under 18 free; wkly rates; golf plans; wkends (2-day min); higher rates special events; lower rates rest of yr. Crib free. Pet accepted; $25. TV; cable (premium). Complimentary continental bkfst. Restaurant adj 11 am-11 pm. Bar 4:30-10 pm. Ck-out 11 am. Meeting rms. Business servs avail. In-rm modem link. Concierge. Gift shop. Drug store. Coin lndry. 18-hole golf privileges, greens fee $75, pro, putting green, driving range. Exercise equipt; bicycles, stair machine. Pool; poolside serv. Some in-rm whirlpools, fireplaces; refrigerator, microwave, wet bar in kit. suites. Picnic tables, grills. Cr cds: A, C, D, DS, MC, V. 🄳 ⬧ 🏃 ⩰ 🏃 ⬚ ⬚ SC

Winston-Salem (See also Greensboro)

Motel

(Rates are generally higher during Furniture Market)

★ ★ **RESIDENCE INN BY MARRIOTT.** *7835 N Point Blvd (27106). 336/759-0777; FAX 336/759-9671.* 88 kit. suites, 2 story. S, D $89-$129; under 18 free; wkly rates. Crib free. Pet accepted; $75-$150. TV; cable (premium). Heated pool; whirlpool. Complimentary continental bkfst. Complimentary coffee in rms. Ck-out noon. Coin lndry. Valet serv. Health club privileges. Refrigerators, microwaves. Picnic tables, grills. Cr cds: A, C, D, DS, JCB, MC, V. [D] [🐾] [≈] [⊠] [🔥] [SC]

Wrightsville Beach *(See also Wilmington)*

Motel

★ **WATERWAY LODGE.** *7246 Wrightsville Ave. 910/256-3771; FAX 910/256-6916; res: 800/677-3771.* 42 units, 3 story. May-Sept: S, D $86-$110; each addl $5; kits. $90-$110; under 12 free; wkly rates; golf plans; higher rates wkends (2-day min); lower rates rest of yr. Pet accepted; $15. TV; cable (premium). Pool. Complimentary coffee in lobby. Restaurant opp 11 am-10 pm. Ck-out 11:30 am. Business servs avail. Refrigerators, microwaves Cr cds: A, D, DS, MC, V. [🐾] [≈] [⊠] [🔥] [SC]

North Dakota

Bismarck

Motels

★ **BEST WESTERN DOUBLEWOOD INN.** *1400 E Interchange Ave (58501), just S of jct US 83, I-94 exit 159.* 701/258-7000; FAX 701/258-2001. 143 rms, 2 story. S $59; D $69; each addl $5; suites $69-$79; under 18 free. Crib free. Pet accepted. TV; cable, VCR avail. Indoor pool; whirlpool, sauna, poolside serv. Restaurant 6:30 am-2 pm, 5-10 pm. Rm serv. Bar 11-1 am. Ck-out noon. Meeting rms. Bellhops. Valet serv. Sundries. Free airport, bus depot transportation. Some refrigerators. Cr cds: A, C, D, DS, ER, MC, V.
D ♣ ☎ ⊠ 🐾 SC

★★ **KELLY INN.** *1800 N 12th St (58501), I-94 exit 159.* 701/223-8001; res: 800/635-3559. 101 rms, 2 story. S $42-$46; D $48-$53; each addl $5; suites $65-$95; under 18 free. Crib free. Pet accepted. TV; VCR avail (movies). Indoor pool; whirlpool, sauna. Restaurant 6:30 am-2 pm, 5-9 pm. Rm serv. Bar 11 am-1:30 pm, 4 pm-1 am. Ck-out noon. Meeting rms. Business servs avail. Valet serv. Free airport transportation. Game rm. Cr cds: A, C, D, DS, ER, MC, V. D ♣ ☎ ⊠ 🐾 SC

★ **SUPER 8.** *1124 E Capitol Ave (58501).* 701/255-1314; FAX 701/255-1314. 60 rms, 3 story. S $36.88; D $43.88-$47.88; each addl $5. Crib free. Pet accepted. TV; cable, in-rm movies avail. Complimentary coffee. Restaurant nearby. Ck-out 11 am. Cr cds: A, C, D, DS, MC, V. ♣ ⊠ 🐾 SC

Hotel

★★★ **HOLIDAY INN.** *605 E Broadway (58501).* 701/255-6000; FAX 701/223-0400. 215 rms, 9 story. S $65-$70; D $71-$78; each addl $7; suites $89-$108; under 19 free; wknd rates. Crib free. Pet accepted. TV; cable, VCR avail. Indoor pool; whirlpool, poolside serv. Restaurant 6 am-10:30 pm. Bar 11:30-1 am. Ck-out noon. Meeting rms. Business servs avail. Beauty shop. Free airport transportation. Exercise equipt; treadmill, stair machine, sauna. Game rm. Refrigerators in suites. Cr cds: A, C, D, DS, ER, JCB, MC, V.
D ♣ ☎ 🏃 ⊠ 🐾 SC

Bottineau

Motel

★ **TURTLE MOUNTAIN LODGE.** *1 Hahn's Bay Rd, 12 mi N on RR 1.* 701/263-4206; res: 800/546-5047. 24 rms, 2 story, some kits. S $29.50-$34; D $49.50-$58; each addl $2. Pet accepted. TV; cable. Indoor pool; whirlpool. Restaurant 7 am-10 pm. Bar 4 pm-midnight; entertainment Fri, Sat. Ck-out noon. Meeting rms. Business servs avail. Downhill/x-country ski 5 mi. On Lake Metigoshe. Cr cds: A, DS, MC, V. ♣ 🚣 ⊠ ☎ 🐾

Devils Lake

Motels

✔★ **COMFORT INN.** *215 US 2E.* 701/662-6760. 60 rms, 2 story. S $39.95-$49.95; D $49.95-$59.95; each addl $5; under 18 free. Crib free. Pet accepted. TV; cable. Indoor pool; whirlpool. Coffee in rms. Complimentary continental bkfst. Restaurant opp 6 am-11 pm. Ck-out 11 am. Business servs avail. Sundries. Game rm. Refrigerators avail. Cr cds: A, C, D, DS, JCB, MC, V. D ♣ ☎ ⊠ 🐾 SC

★ **DAYS INN.** *ND 20S.* 701/662-5381; FAX 701/662-3578. 45 rms, 2 story. S $39-$44; D $49-$54; each addl $5; under 12 free. Crib free. Pet accepted; $3. TV; cable. Complimentary continental bkfst. Restaurant nearby. Ck-out 11 am. Business servs avail. Some refrigerators. Cr cds: A, C, D, DS, MC, V. D ♣ ⊠ 🐾 SC

Dickinson

Motel

✔★ **COMFORT INN.** *493 Elk Dr, off I-94.* 701/264-7300; FAX 701/264-7300. 115 rms, 2 story. June-mid-Sept: S $31-$33; D $40-$44; each addl $3; suites $50.50; under 18 free; higher rates special events; lower rates rest of yr. Crib $2. Pet accepted. TV; cable.

Pool; whirlpool. Complimentary continental bkfst. Ck-out 11 am. Coin Indry. Free airport transportation. Cr cds: A, C, D, DS, ER, MC, V. ✒ ≈ ⊠ 🖾 SC

Fargo

Motels

✔★★ **AMERICINN.** *1423 35th St SW (58103). 701/234-9946; FAX 701/234-9946.* 43 rms, 2 story. May-Sept: S $47.90-$64.90; D $53.90-$109.90; each addl $4; under 18 free; lower rates rest of yr. Crib free. Pet accepted. TV; cable (premium), VCR avail (movies). Indoor pool; whirlpool, sauna. Complimentary continental bkfst. Restaurant nearby. Ck-out 11 am. Business servs avail. Valet serv. Coin Indry. Some refrigerators. Cr cds: A, C, D, DS, MC, V. D ✒ ≈ ⊠ 🖾 SC

✔★★ **COMFORT INN.** *1407 35th St S (58103). 701/280-9666; FAX 701/235-1174.* 66 rms, 2 story. June-Sept: S $49.95-$59.95; D $59.95; each addl $5; suites $54.95-$64.95; family rates; higher rates special events; lower rates rest of yr. Crib free. Pet accepted. TV; cable. Indoor pool; whirlpool. Complimentary continental bkfst. Restaurant nearby. Ck-out 11 am. Business servs avail. Game rm. Refrigerators in suites. Cr cds: A, C, D, DS, ER, MC, V. D ✒ ≈ ⊠ 🖾 SC

★★ **COMFORT INN-WEST.** *3825 9th Ave S (58103), I-29 exit 64. 701/282-9596.* 56 rms, 2 story, 14 suites. S $40-$60; D $44-$70; each addl $5; suites $66-$76; under 18 free. Crib free. Pet accepted. TV; cable. Indoor pool; whirlpool. Complimentary continental bkfst. Restaurant nearby. Ck-out 11 am. Business servs avail. In-rm modem link. Sundries. Game rm. Refrigerator in suites. Cr cds: A, C, D, DS, ER, JCB, MC, V.
D ✒ ≈ ⊠ 🖾 SC

★★ **COMFORT SUITES.** *1415 35th St S (58103), I-29 exit 13th Ave. 701/237-5911.* 66 rms, 2 story. June-Aug: S $58.95-$73.95; D $63.95-$78.95; each addl $5; under 18 free; higher rates special events; lower rates rest of yr. Crib free. Pet accepted; $5. TV; cable. Indoor pool; whirlpool. Complimentary continental bkfst. Restaurant nearby. Ck-out 11 am. Business servs avail. In-rm modem link. Valet serv. Game rm. Refrigerators. Cr cds: A, C, D, DS, ER, JCB, MC, V. D ✒ ≈ ⊠ 🖾 SC

★★ **COUNTRY SUITES BY CARLSON.** *3316 13th Ave S (58013), I-29 exit 64. 701/234-0565; FAX 701/234-0565, ext. 408; res: 800/456-4000.* 99 rms, 3 story, 42 suites. S $65-$71; D $68-$74; suites $75-$139; under 18 free. Crib free. Pet accepted. TV; cable. Indoor pool; whirlpool. Complimentary continental bkfst. Coffee in rms. Restaurant adj 6 am-11 pm. Bar 4:30 pm-1 am. Ck-out noon. Meeting rms. Business servs avail. In-rm modem link. Valet serv. Sundries. Free airport transportation. Exercise equipt; weight machine, bicycles. Game rm. Refrigerators, wet bars. Cr cds: A, C, D, DS, MC, V.
D ✒ ≈ 🏃 ⊠ 🖾 SC

✔★ **ECONO LODGE.** *1401 35th St S (58103). 701/232-3412.* 44 rms, 2 story. S $28.96-$33.96; D $38.96-$44.96; each addl $5; under 16 free. Crib free. Pet accepted. TV; cable. Complimentary continental bkfst. Restaurant adj open 24 hrs. Ck-out 11 am. Business servs avail. In-rm modem link. Cr cds: A, C, D, DS, ER, JCB, MC, V.
D ✒ ⊠ 🖾 SC

✔★★ **HOLIDAY INN EXPRESS.** *1040 40th St S (58103). 701/282-2000; FAX 701/282-4721.* 77 rms, 4 story. S, D $45-$59; under 18 free. Crib free. Pet accepted. TV; cable. Indoor pool; whirlpool. Complimentary continental bkfst. Restaurant adj 6 am-11 pm. Ck-out noon. Business servs avail. Sundries. Valet serv. Coin Indry. Game rm. Cr cds: A, C, D, DS, JCB, MC, V. D ✒ ≈ ⊠ 🖾 SC

★★ **KELLY INN-13TH AVENUE.** *4207 13th Ave SW (58103). 701/277-8821; FAX 701/277-0208.* 59 rms, 2 story. S $46; D $51; each addl $5; suites $80-$100; under 18 free. Crib free. Pet accepted. TV; cable (premium). Indoor pool; whirlpool, sauna. Complimentary continental bkfst. Restaurant adj 6 am-11 pm. Ck-out 11 am. Business servs avail. Valet serv. Coin Indry. Game rm. Some refrigerators. Cr cds: A, C, D, DS, ER, MC, V.
D ✒ ≈ ⊠ 🖾 SC

✔★ **SLEEP INN.** *1921 44th St SW (58103). 701/281-8240; FAX 701/281-2041.* 61 rms, shower only, 2 story. Mid-May-Sept: S $43.95-$49.95; D $49.95-$55.95; each addl $4; under 18 free; lower rates rest of yr. Crib $6. Pet accepted. TV; cable (premium). Complimentary continental bkfst. Restaurant opp open 24 hrs. Ck-out 11 am. Business servs avail. Valet serv. Free airport transportation. Exercise equipt; bicycle, weight machine. Cr cds: A, C, D, DS, MC, V. D ✒ 🏃 ⊠ 🖾 SC

★ **SUPER 8.** *3518 Interstate Blvd (58103). 701/232-9202; FAX 701/232-4543.* 135 units, 1-2 story, 25 suites. S $32.88-$40.88; D $42.88-$60.88; suites $45-$95; each addl $2-$5. Crib $2. Pet accepted. TV; cable (premium). Indoor pool; whirlpool. Complimentary continental bkfst. Restaurant nearby. Ck-out 11 am. Coin lndry. Business servs avail. Some in-rm whirlpools. Cr cds: A, C, D, DS, MC, V. [D] 🐾 🏊 🖳 🔥 [SC]

Motor Hotel

★ ★ ★ **HOLIDAY INN.** *(58106). at I-29 13th Ave S exit. 701/282-2700; FAX 701/281-1240.* 309 rms, 2-7 story. S, D $64-$99; suites $95-$145; under 19 free; wkend rates; package plans. Crib free. Pet accepted. TV; cable (premium). Indoor pool; wading pool, whirlpool, poolside serv. Restaurant 6 am-11 pm; Sat from 7 am; Sun 7 am-10 pm. Rm serv. Bar 11-1 am; Sat from 10 am; Sun 7 am-10 pm; entertainment. Ck-out noon. Convention facilities. Business servs avail. In-rm modem link. Bellhops. Valet serv. Concierge. Sundries. Free airport, RR station, bus depot transportation. Exercise equipt; weight machines, bicycles, sauna. Rec rm. Casino. Cr cds: A, C, D, DS, JCB, MC, V.

[D] 🐾 🏊 🍴 🖳 🔥 [SC]

Grand Forks

Motels

★ ★ **COMFORT INN.** *3251 30th Ave S (58201), adj to Columbia Mall. 701/775-7503.* 67 rms, 2 story. June-Aug: S $43.95-$54.95; D $43.95-$65.95; each addl $6; suites $55.95-$65.95; under 19 free; lower rates rest of yr. Crib free. Pet accepted. TV; cable. Indoor pool; whirlpool. Complimentary continental bkfst. Restaurant nearby. Ck-out 11 am. Business servs avail. Game rm. Refrigerator in suites. Cr cds: A, C, D, DS, ER, JCB, MC, V. [D] 🐾 🏊 🖳 🔥 [SC]

✔ ★ **SELECT INN.** *1000 N 42nd St (58203), at jct I-29, US 2. 701/775-0555; res: 800/641-1000.* 120 rms. S $27.95-$35.95; D $36.95-$45.95; each addl $4; under 13 free. Crib free. Pet accepted. TV; cable (premium), VCR avail (movies). Complimentary continental bkfst. Restaurant nearby. Ck-out noon. Coin lndry. Business servs avail. Valet serv. Cr cds: A, D, DS, MC, V. 🐾 🖳 🔥

Motor Hotel

✔ ★ **BEST WESTERN FABULOUS WESTWARD HO.** *ND 2 (58206), 1/2 mi W on US 2. 701/775-5341; FAX 701/775-3703.* 108 rms, 1-2 story. S $40; D $45-$49; each addl $5; suites $80; under 12 free. Crib free. Pet accepted. TV; cable, VCR avail (movies). Heated pool; sauna. Restaurant 6:30 am-10 pm; Sun 8 am-10 pm. Bars 11-1 am; entertainment Wed-Sat evenings. Ck-out noon. Meeting rms. Business servs avail. In-rm modem link. Bathrm phones. Picnic tables. Old West motif; model Western village. Casino. Cr cds: A, C, D, DS, ER, MC, V. 🐾 🏊 🖳 🔥 [SC]

Jamestown

Motels

✔ ★ ★ **COMFORT INN.** *811 20th St SW, at jct I-94 & US 281. 701/252-7125.* 52 rms, 2 story, 8 suites. S $49.95; D $55.95; each addl $5; suites $61.95; under 18 free; wkly rates; higher rates: county fair, stockcar stampede. Crib free. Pet accepted. TV; cable. Indoor pool; whirlpool. Complimentary continental bkfst. Restaurant adj 6 am-10 pm. Ck-out 11 am. Business servs avail. Game rm. Refrigerator in suites. Cr cds: A, C, D, DS, ER, JCB, MC, V. [D] 🐾 🏊 🖳 🔥 [SC]

★ ★ **DAKOTA INN.** *at jct I-94, US 281S. 701/252-3611; FAX 701/251-1212; res: 800/726-7924.* 120 rms, 2 story. S $40-$50; D $45-$60; each addl $5; under 16 free. Crib $5. Pet accepted. TV; cable. Indoor pool; whirlpool. Restaurant 7 am-10 pm. Rm serv. Bar 3 pm-1 am; entertainment Fri, Sat. Ck-out 11 am. Meeting rms. Business servs avail. Bellhops. Valet serv. Free airport, bus depot transportation. Game rm. Lawn games. Cr cds: A, C, D, DS, MC, V. 🐾 🏊 🖳 🔥 [SC]

Minot

Motels

★ ★ **BEST WESTERN SAFARI INN.** *1510 26th Ave SW. 701/852-4300; FAX 701/838-1234.* 100 rms, 2 story. S $49-$59; D $59-$69; each addl $6; suites $69-$85; under 18 free; higher rates special events. Crib avail. Pet accepted. TV; cable (premium), VCR (movies). Indoor pool; whirlpool. Complimentary continental bkfst. Bar 5 pm-1 am. Ck-out 11 am. Meeting rm. Business servs avail. Game rm. Cr cds: A, D, DS, ER, MC, V.

[D] 🐾 🏊 🖳 🔥 [SC]

★ ★ **COMFORT INN.** *1515 22nd Ave SW, adj to Dakota Square Mall. 701/852-2201; FAX 701/852-2201.* 142 rms, 3 story. S $39.95; D $44.95-$49.95; each addl $5; under 18 free. Crib free. Pet accepted. TV; cable. Indoor pool; whirlpool. Complimentary continental bkfst. Restaurant adj 6-1 am. Ck-out noon. Meeting rms. Business servs avail. Valet serv. Sundries. Game rm. Cr cds: A, C, D, DS, ER, JCB, MC, V. 🄳 🐾 ⊠ 🖾 🖾 SC

✔ ★ **DAKOTA INN.** *Bypass US 2. 701/838-2700; FAX 701/839-7792; res: 800/862-5003.* 129 rms, 3 story. S $29.95; D $39.95-$48.95; each addl $3. Crib free. Pet accepted. TV; cable. Indoor pool; whirlpool. Complimentary continental bkfst. Restaurant adj 6 am-10 pm. Ck-out noon. Coin lndry. Sundries. Game rm. Cr cds: A, D, DS, MC, V. 🐾 ⊠ 🖾 🖾 SC

✔ ★ **DAYS INN.** *2100 4th St SW. 701/852-3646; FAX 701/852-0501.* 82 rms, 2 story. S $38-$42; D $44-$59; each addl $3; under 18 free. Crib free. Pet accepted. TV; cable, VCR avail. Indoor pool; whirlpool, sauna. Complimentary continental bkfst. Ck-out noon. Business servs avail. Cr cds: A, C, D, DS, MC, V. 🄳 🐾 ⊠ 🖾 🖾 SC

✔ ★ **SUPER 8.** *1315 N Broadway (US 83). 701/852-1817; FAX 701/852-1817.* 60 rms, 3 story. No elvtr. S $33.88-$36.88; D $40.88-$45.88; each addl $5; under 12 free; higher rates: state fair, Norsk Hostfest. Crib free. Pet accepted. TV; cable (premium). Complimentary coffee. Restaurant nearby. Ck-out 11 am. Coin lndry. Cr cds: A, C, D, DS, MC, V. 🐾 🖾 🖾 SC

Ohio

Akron (See also Aurora, Canton, Cleveland, Kent)

Motels

★ ★ **HOLIDAY INN-SOUTH.** *I-77 & Arlington Rd (44312), exit 120.* 330/644-7126; *FAX 330/644-1776.* 131 rms, 2 story. S $59-$65; D $60-$65; each addl $6; suites $130-$185; under 18 free. Crib free. Pet accepted. TV; cable. Pool; poolside serv. Restaurant 6 am-10 pm; Sat, Sun from 7 am. Rm serv. Bar 11-2:30 am; entertainment Tues-Sat. Ck-out noon. Meeting rms. Business servs avail. Bellhops. Valet serv. Sundries. Airport transportation. Cr cds: A, C, D, DS, JCB, MC, V. [D] [⌖] [⇌] [⌖] [⌖] [SC]

✔ ★ **RED ROOF INN.** *99 Rothrock Rd (44321), OH 18 & I-77.* 330/666-0566; *FAX 330/666-6874.* 108 rms, 2 story. S $35.99-$41.99; D $39.99-$49.99; each addl $7; under 18 free. Crib free. Pet accepted. TV; cable (premium). Complimentary coffee. Restaurant adj 6 am-10 pm. Ck-out noon Business servs avail. Cr cds: A, C, D, DS, MC, V. [D] [⌖] [⇌] [⌖] [SC]

Hotel

★ ★ **HILTON INN-WEST.** *3180 W Market St (44333).* 330/867-5000; *FAX 330/867-1648.* 204 rms, 4 story. S $79-$115; D $89-$125; each addl $10; suites $110-$140; studio rms $75; family rates. Crib free. Pet accepted. TV; cable. 2 pools, 1 indoor; poolside serv. Restaurant 6:30 am-10 pm; Fri, Sat from 7:30 am. Rm serv. Bar 11:30-2 am, Sun 4 pm-midnight; entertainment Fri, Sat. Ck-out noon. Coin lndry. Meeting rms. Business center. In-rm modem link. Bellhops. Valet serv. Sundries. Gift shop. Airport transportation. Exercise equipt; weights, bicycles, sauna, whirlpool. Some refrigerators. Cr cds: A, C, D, DS, MC, V. [D] [⌖] [⇌] [⋇] [⌖] [⌖] [SC] [⋇]

Alliance (See also Akron, Canton, Kent, Youngstown)

Motor Hotel

★ ★ **COMFORT INN.** *2500 W State St.* 330/821-5555; *FAX 330/821-4919.* 113 rms, 5 story. S $50; D $54; each addl $5; suites $80-$115; under 18 free. Crib free. Pet accepted, some restrictions; $10. TV; cable (premium), VCR avail (movies). Indoor pool; whirlpool. Complimentary continental bkfst. Ck-out noon. Coin lndry. Meeting rms. Business servs avail. Bellhops. Exercise equipt; weight machine, bicycles. Cr cds: A, C, D, DS, JCB, MC, V. [D] [⌖] [⇌] [⋇] [⌖] [⌖] [SC]

Beachwood (See also Brecksville, Cleveland)

Motor Hotel

★ ★ ★ **MARRIOTT-EAST.** *3663 Park East Dr.* 216/464-5950; *FAX 216/464-6539.* 403 rms, 4-7 story. S, D $79-$165; suites $225-$500; under 18 free. Crib free. Pet accepted; fee. TV; cable (premium), VCR avail. Indoor/outdoor pool; lifeguard, poolside serv; whirlpool. Restaurant 6:30 am-11 pm; Sat, Sun from 7 am. Rm serv. Bar 11:30-2 am. Ck-out noon. Coin lndry. Convention facilities. Business center. Bellhops. Concierge. Gift shop. Downhill ski 15 mi; x-country ski 10 mi. Exercise equipt; weights, bicycles, sauna. Game rm. Rec rm. Some refrigerators. Luxury level. Cr cds: A, C, D, DS, ER, JCB, MC, V. [D] [⌖] [⇌] [⇌] [⋇] [⌖] [⌖] [SC] [⋇]

Bellefontaine (See also Lima, Sidney)

Motels

★ ★ **COMFORT INN.** *260 Northview Dr, 3 mi N of OH 68 at US 33.* 513/599-6666; *FAX 513/599-2300.* 73 rms, 2 story. S $58-$77; D $47.70-$82; each addl $5; suites $82-$96; under 18 free. Crib free. Pet accepted; $10. TV; cable (premium), VCR avail (movies). Heated pool. Complimentary continental bkfst. Restaurant nearby. Bar; entertainment. Ck-out noon. Coin lndry. Meeting rms. In-rm modem link. Sundries. Downhill ski 8 mi. Exercise equipt; stair machine, treadmill. Some refrigerators, microwaves. Cr cds: A, C, D, DS, JCB, MC, V. [D] [⌖] [⇌] [⇌] [⋇] [⌖] [⌖] [SC]

★ ★ **HOLIDAY INN.** *1134 N Main St, 2 mi N on OH 68 at US 33.* 513/593-8515; *FAX 513/593-4802.* 103 rms, 2 story. S, D $69; each addl $5; under 18 free. Crib free. Pet accepted, some restrictions. TV; cable (premium), VCR avail. Indoor pool. Restaurant 6 am-2 pm, 5-10 pm; Sun to 8 pm. Rm serv. Bar 4 pm-1 am; entertainment Tues-Sat. Ck-out noon. Coin lndry. Meeting rms. In-rm modem link. Downhill ski 5 mi. Exercise equipt; weights, stair machine. Cr cds: A, C, D, DS, JCB, MC, V. 🅳 💳 ⊠ ≋ 🕴 ⊠ ⊠ SC

Brecksville (See also Beachwood, Cleveland)

Motor Hotel

★ ★ ★ **HILTON-SOUTH.** (6200 Quarry Ln, Independence 44131) N on I-77, at Rockside Rd. 440/447-1300; FAX 440/642-9334. 195 rms, 5 story. S $105-$115; D $110-$140; each addl $12; wkend, family rates. Crib free. Pet accepted; some restrictions. TV; cable. Indoor/outdoor pool; poolside serv (summer), lifeguard. Playground. Coffee in rms. Restaurant 6 am-10 pm; Fri, Sat to 11 pm. Rm serv. Entertainment. Ck-out noon. Meeting rms. Business servs avail. In-rm modem link. Bellhops. Gift shop. Free airport transportation. Tennis. Exercise equipt; weights, bicycle, whirlpool, sauna. Cr cds: A, C, D, DS, ER, JCB, MC, V. 🅳 💳 🏌 ≋ 🕴 ⊠ ⊠ SC

Cambridge (See also Zanesville)

Motels

(Rates may be higher during Jamboree in the Hills Festival)

✔ ★ **BEST WESTERN.** 1945 Southgate Pkwy, I-70 exit 178. 614/439-3581; FAX 614/439-1824. 95 rms, 2 story. S, D $79-$110; each addl $10; under 18 free; higher rates special events. Crib $1. Pet accepted. TV; cable, VCR avail (movies). Pool. Restaurant adj. Bar 11-2 am. Ck-out 11 am. Business servs avail. Cr cds: A, C, D, DS, MC, V. 🅳 💳 ≋ ⊠ ⊠ SC

✔ ★ **HOLIDAY INN.** Southgate Pkwy, 1 mi SW on OH 209, 1/4 mi N of jct I-70 exit 178. 614/432-7313; FAX 614/432-2337. 109 rms, 2 story. May-Nov: S $49-$139; D $57-$147; each addl $8; under 18 free; lower rates rest of yr. Crib free. Pet accepted. TV; cable. Pool. Restaurant 6 am-10 pm; Sat, Sun 7 am-11 pm. Rm serv. Bar 4 pm-midnight, Sun 5-10 pm. Ck-out noon. Coin lndry. Meeting rms. Business servs avail. Health club privileges. Cr cds: A, C, D, DS, JCB, MC, V. 🅳 💳 ≋ ⊠ ⊠ SC

Canton (See also Akron, Alliance, New Philadelphia, Wooster)

Motels

★ ★ **HOLIDAY INN-BELDON VILLAGE.** 4520 Everhard Rd NW (44718), I-77 exit 109. 330/494-2770; FAX 330/494-6473. 196 rms, 2-3 story. S $79-$86; D $87-$94; each addl $8; suites $150; under 19 free; higher rates Hall of Fame wkend. Crib free. Pet accepted. TV. Pool; poolside serv. Restaurant 6:30 am-10 pm; Sun from 7 am. Rm serv. Bar 2 pm-2:30 am; entertainment. Ck-out noon. Meeting rms. Business servs avail. In-rm modem link. Free airport transportation. Health club privileges. Cr cds: A, C, D, DS, JCB, MC, V. 🅳 💳 ≋ ⊠ ⊠ SC

✔ ★ **RED ROOF INN.** 5353 Inn Circle Ct NW (44720), I-77 exit 109. 330/499-1970; FAX 330/499-1975. 108 rms, 2 story. S $37.99-$40.99; D $44.95-$51.99; each addl $7; under 18 free. Crib free. Pet accepted. TV. Restaurant adj 6 am-10 pm. Ck-out noon. Business servs avail. Cr cds: A, C, D, DS, MC, V. 🅳 💳 ⊠ ⊠ SC

Chillicothe

Motels

★ **COMFORT INN.** 20 North Plaza Blvd. 614/775-3500; FAX 614/775-3588. 109 rms, 2 story. S, D $65-$75; each addl $5; under 17 free. Crib free. Pet accepted. TV; cable. Heated pool. Coffee in rms. Complimentary continental bkfst. Restaurant nearby. Bar; entertainment Fri, Sat. Ck-out noon. Meeting rms. Business servs avail. Valet serv. Complimentary health club privileges. Cr cds: A, C, D, DS, ER, JCB, MC, V. 🅳 💳 ≋ ⊠ ⊠ SC

★ ★ **DAYS INN.** 1250 N Bridge St. 614/775-7000; FAX 614/773-1622. 155 rms, 2 story. S, D $62-$75; each addl $6; under 19 free. Crib free. Pet accepted. TV; cable (premium). Heated pool; poolside serv. Complimentary coffee in rms. Restaurant 6 am-2 pm, 4-9 pm; Sun 7 am-2 pm, brunch 10 am-2 pm. Rm serv. Bar 4 pm-2 am; closed Sun; entertainment Fri, Sat. Ck-out noon. Coin lndry. Meeting rms. Business servs avail. Valet serv. Cr cds: A, C, D, DS, JCB, MC, V. 🅳 💳 ⊠ ⊠ ⊠ SC

Cincinnati *(See also Hamilton, Mason)*

Motels

(Rates may be higher during Kool Jazz Festival)

★ ★ **AMERISUITES.** *11435 Reed Hartman Hwy (45241). 513/489-3666; FAX 513/489-4187.* 127 suites, 6 story. May-Sept: S, D $99-$149; each addl $10; under 18 free; lower rates rest of yr. Crib avail. Pet accepted. TV; cable (premium), VCR (movies). Heated pool. Complimentary continental bkfst. Restaurant nearby. Ck-out noon. Meeting rms. Business center. Valet serv. Coin lndry. Exercise equipt; treadmill, stair machine. Health club privileges. Microwaves. Cr cds: A, C, D, DS, MC, V. D ⊮ ≈ 🕂 🖎 🖎 SC 🖎

✔ ★ **RED ROOF INN.** *11345 Chester Rd (45246), I-75 Sharon Rd exit 15, north of downtown. 513/771-5141; FAX 513/771-0812.* 108 rms, 2 story. S $45.99-$55.99; D $50.99-$69.99; each addl $7; under 18 free; higher rates special events. Crib $5. Pet accepted. TV; cable (premium). Restaurant adj 11-2 am. Ck-out noon. Business servs avail. Valet serv. Health club privileges. Cr cds: A, C, D, DS, MC, V. ⊮ 🖎 🖎

★ ★ **RESIDENCE INN BY MARRIOTT.** *11689 Chester Rd (45246), north of downtown. 513/771-2525; FAX 513/771-3444.* 144 kit. suites, 1-2 story. 1 bedrm $89-$129; 2 bedrm $109-$159; higher rates July. Pet accepted; $75-$95. TV; cable (premium). Pool; whirlpool. Complimentary continental bkfst. Ck-out noon. Coin lndry. Business servs avail. Valet serv. Health club privileges. Microwaves. Picnic tables, grills. Cr cds: A, C, D, DS, JCB, MC, V. D ⊮ ≈ 🖎 🖎 SC

★ **SUPER 8.** *11335 Chester Rd (45246), I-75 Sharon Rd exit 15, north of downtown. 513/772-3140; FAX 513/772-1931.* 144 rms, 2 story. S $46-$73; D $53-$80; each addl $7; under 18 free; higher rates: wkends, special events. Crib free. Pet accepted, some restrictions. TV; cable (premium). Pool. Complimentary continental bkfst. Restaurant adj 11 am-11 pm. Ck-out noon. Coin lndry. Meeting rms. Business servs avail. Valet serv. Cr cds: A, C, D, DS, MC, V. D ⊮ ≈ 🖎 🖎 SC

Motor Hotels

★ ★ **QUALITY HOTEL & SUITES CENTRAL.** *4747 Montgomery Rd (45212), north of downtown, OH 42 at Norwood Lateral. 513/351-6000; FAX 513/351-0215.* 146 rms, 8 story. S, D $76-$99; each addl $5; under 18 free; wkend rates. Pet accepted. TV; cable (premium), VCR avail. Pool; poolside serv. Complimentary continental bkfst. Restaurant 11 am-2:30 pm, 5-10:30 pm; Sat 7-10 am, 5-11:30 pm; Sun 7-10 am, 4-9 pm. Rm serv. Bar 11-2 am, Sat from 1 pm, Sun 4-11 pm. Ck-out noon. Meeting rms. Business center. In-rm modem link. Bellhops. Free airport transportation. Health club privileges. Some bathrm phones; refrigerators, microwaves in suites. Some private patios, balconies. Picnic tables, grills. Cr cds: A, C, D, DS, ER, JCB, MC, V. D ⊮ ≈ 🖎 🖎 SC 🖎

★ ★ **WOODFIELD SUITES.** *(11029 Dowlin Dr, Sharonville 45241) 12 mi N on I-75 exit 15. 513/771-0300; res: 800/338-0008; FAX 513/771-6411.* 151 suites, 7 story. May-Oct: S, D $89-$189; each addl $10; under 17 free; lower rates rest of yr. Crib free. Pet accepted, some restrictions; $10. TV; cable (premium), VCR avail. Complimentary continental bkfst. Coffee in rms. Restaurant nearby. Ck-out noon. Meeting rms. Business servs avail. In-rm modem link. Bellhops. Valet serv (Mon-Fri). Coin lndry. Exercise equipt; treadmills, stair machines. Indoor pool; whirlpool. Rec rm. Refrigerators, microwaves; some wet bars, in-rm whirlpools. Cr cds: A, C, D, DS, MC, V. D ⊮ ≈ 🕂 🖎 🖎 SC

Hotels

★ ★ **GARFIELD HOUSE.** *2 Garfield Place (45202), 2 blks W of Fountain Square, downtown. 513/421-3355; FAX 513/421-3729; res: 800/367-2155.* 133 kit. suites, 16 story. 1-bedrm $165-$185; 2-bedrm $175-$200; penthouse suites $425-$1,200; monthly rates. Crib free. Pet accepted; $75. Garage parking $4-$8. TV; cable (premium), VCR avail. Complimentary continental bkfst. Complimentary coffee in rms. Restaurant 11 am-9 pm; wkends from 5 pm. Rm serv 5-10 pm. Bar. Ck-out noon. Coin lndry. Meeting rms. Business servs avail. Exercise equipt; weight machine, stair machine. Health club privileges. Microwaves. Some balconies. Cr cds: A, C, D, DS, MC, V. D ⊮ 🕂 🖎 🖎 SC

★ ★ **HOLIDAY INN-QUEENSGATE.** *800 W Eighth St (45203), I-75 at Linn, west of downtown. 513/241-8660; FAX 513/241-9057.* 246 rms, 11 story. S, D $99-$119; suites $189-$210; under 18 free. Crib free. Pet accepted. TV; cable (premium). Pool. Coffee in rms. Restaurant 6:30 am-2 pm, 5-9 pm. Bar 4 pm-2 am; closed Sun. Ck-out noon. Coin lndry. Meeting rms. Business servs avail. In-rm modem link. Exercise equipt; stair machine, bicycle. Health club privileges. Refrigerators avail. Cr cds: A, C, D, DS, ER, JCB, MC, V. D ⊮ ≈ 🕂 🖎 🖎 SC

Cleveland

Motels

★ ★ **COMFORT INN.** *(17550 Rosbough Dr, Middleburg Heights 44130) approx 13 mi S on I-71 exit 235.* 216/234-3131; FAX 216/234-6111. 136 rms, 3 story. S, D $79-$99; each addl $5; under 18 free; wkend rates. Crib free. Pet accepted, some restrictions. TV; cable (premium). Pool. Complimentary continental bkfst. Coffee in rms. Restaurant nearby. Ck-out noon. Meeting rms. Business center. Valet serv. Sundries. Free airport transportation. Microwaves avail. Cr cds: A, C, D, DS, ER, JCB, MC, V. 🅳 🐾 ≋ 📶 🐾 SC 🛶

✔ ★ **RED ROOF INN.** *(17555 Bagley Rd, Middleburg Heights 44130) 13 mi SW via I-71 exit 235.* 216/243-2441; FAX 216/243-2474. 117 rms, 3 story. S $42.99-$54.99; D $47.99-$56.99; each addl $10; under 18 free. Crib free. Pet accepted. TV; cable (premium). Complimentary coffee. Restaurant nearby. Ck-out noon. Cr cds: A, C, D, DS, MC, V. 🅳 🐾 📶 🐾

★ ★ ★ **RESIDENCE INN BY MARRIOTT.** *(17525 Rosbough Dr, Middleburg Heights 44130) 16 mi S on I-71 exit 235.* 216/234-6688; FAX 216/234-3459. 158 kit. suites, 2 story. S, D $109-$169; wkend, wkly, monthly rates. Crib free. Pet accepted, some restrictions. TV; cable (premium), VCR avail (movies). Heated pool; whirlpool. Complimentary continental bkfst. Complimentary coffee in rms. Restaurant adj 6 am-midnight. Ck-out noon. Coin lndry. Business servs avail. Valet serv. Sundries. Airport transportation. Downhill ski 15 mi; x-country ski 5 mi. Lawn games. Exercise equipt; bicycles, treadmill. Microwaves; many fireplaces. Picnic tables, grills. Cr cds: A, C, D, DS, JCB, MC, V. 🅳 🐾 ≋ 📶 🍴 📶 🐾 SC

Hotels

★ ★ ★ **EMBASSY SUITES.** *1701 E 12th St (44114), downtown.* 216/523-8000; FAX 216/523-1698. Web www.embassy-suites.com. 268 suites, 10 story. S, D $119-$169; under 18 free; kit. units $119-$169; wkend rates. Crib free. Pet accepted. Valet parking $12. TV; cable. Indoor pool. Complimentary coffee in rms. Restaurant 6:30 am-10:30 pm. Bar 11-1 am. Ck-out noon. Coin lndry. Meeting rms. In-rm modem link. Concierge. Lighted tennis. Exercise equipt; weights, bicycles, sauna. Minibars, microwaves. Balconies. Cr cds: A, C, D, DS, ER, JCB, MC, V. 🅳 🐾 🏃 ≋ 🍴 📶 🐾 SC

★ ★ ★ **MARRIOTT AIRPORT.** *4277 W 150th St (44135), west of downtown.* 216/252-5333; FAX 216/251-1508. Web www.marriott.com. 371 rms, 4-9 story. S $139; D $159; suites $175-$350; under 18 free; wkend package. Crib free. Pet accepted; $50. TV; cable (premium), VCR avail (movies). Indoor pool; whirlpool; poolside serv. Restaurant 6 am-11 pm. Bar 11:30-2 am. Ck-out noon. Coin lndry. Convention facilities. Business servs avail. In-rm modem link. Gift shop. Free airport transportation. Exercise equipt; weights, bicycles, sauna. Cr cds: A, C, D, DS, ER, JCB, MC, V. 🅳 🐾 ≋ 🍴 🏃 📶 🐾 SC

★ ★ ★ ★ **THE RITZ-CARLTON, CLEVELAND.** *1515 W Third St (44113), at Tower City Center, downtown.* 216/623-1300; FAX 216/623-0515. Web www.ritzcarlton.com. China cabinets in the halls and guest rooms with easy chairs add Victorian flourish to the modern elegance of this hotel. 208 rms, 7 story, 21 suites. S, D $149-$209; suites $259-$359; under 12 free; wkend rates. Pet accepted. Valet parking (fee). TV; cable, VCR avail (movies). Indoor pool; whirlpool; poolside serv. Restaurant 6:30 am-10 pm. Afternoon tea. Rm serv 24 hrs. Bar 11:30-1 am; pianist. Ck-out noon. Meeting rms. Business center. In-rm modem link. Concierge. Exercise equipt; weight machine, bicycles, sauna. Massage. Health club privileges. Bathrm phones, minibars. Luxury level. Cr cds: A, C, D, DS, ER, JCB, MC, V. 🅳 🐾 🏃 🍴 📶 🐾 🛶

Columbus *(See also Delaware, Lancaster, Newark)*

Motels

★ **BEST WESTERN-EAST.** *(2100 Brice Rd, Reynoldsburg 43068) E on I-70, exit 110.* 614/864-1280; FAX 614/864-1280, ext. 388. 143 rms, 2 story. S $60-$72; D $69-$79; under 18 free; higher rates special events. Crib free. Pet accepted. TV; cable (premium). Pool; poolside serv. Restaurant 6 am-11 pm. Rm serv. Bar 11 am-midnight. Ck-out noon. Meeting rms. Businesss servs avail. Free airport transportation. Cr cds: A, C, D, DS, MC, V. 🅳 🐾 ≋ 📶 🐾 SC

★ ★ **HOMEWOOD SUITES.** *115 Hutchinson Ave (43235), jct I-270 & US 23N.* 614/785-0001; FAX 614/785-0143; res: 800/225-5466. 99 kit. units, 3 story, 99 suites. S, D $99-$115; wkend rates. Crib free. Pet accepted; from $10/day. TV; cable (premium), VCR (movies $5). Heated pool; whirlpool. Complimentary bkfst. Complimentary coffee in rms. Restaurant adj 6 am-midnight. Ck-out noon. Coin lndry. Meeting rms. Business center. In-rm modem link. Sundries. Tennis privileges. Exercise equipt; weight machine, stair machine. Lawn games. Microwaves. Grills. Cr cds: A, C, D, DS, JCB, MC, V.

[D] [🐾] [🏃] [🏊] [🍴] [🐾] [🐾] [SC] [🏌]

✔ ★ **RED ROOF INN-MORSE ROAD.** *750 Morse Rd (43229), I-71 Morse-Sinclair exit 16.* 614/846-8520; FAX 614/846-8526. 107 rms, 2 story. S $42.99-$52.99; D $49.99-$59.99; under 18 free. Crib free. Pet accepted. TV. Complimentary coffee in lobby. Restaurant adj 7 am-11 pm. Ck-out noon. Business servs avail. Cr cds: A, C, D, DS, MC, V.

[D] [🐾] [🐾] [🐾] [SC]

Motor Hotels

★ ★ ★ **HOLIDAY INN.** *175 Hutchinson Ave (43235), I-270 exit 23.* 614/885-3334; FAX 614/846-4353. 316 rms, 6 story. S, D $99-$115; suites $205-$220; under 17 free. Crib free. Pet accepted. TV; cable (premium), VCR avail. Indoor pool. Complimentary coffee in rms. Restaurant 6 am-11 pm. Rm serv. Bar. Ck-out noon. Coin lndry. Convention facilities. Business servs avail. In-rm modem link. Bellhops. Gift shop. Free airport transportation. Exercise equipt; weight machine, stair machine. Refrigerator in suites. Cr cds: A, C, D, DS, MC, V. [D] [🐾] [🐾] [🍴] [🐾] [🐾] [SC]

★ **HOLIDAY INN-AIRPORT.** *750 Stelzer Rd (43219), near Port Columbus Airport.* 614/237-6360; FAX 614/237-2978. 236 rms, 3 story. S $89.95-$109.95; D $108.95-$119.95; each addl $10; suites $135-$175; under 18 free; wkend rates. Crib free. Pet accepted. TV; cable. Indoor pool; whirlpool. Complimentary coffee in rms. Restaurant 6:30 am-2 pm, 5:30-10 pm. Rm serv. Bar 1 pm-midnight. Ck-out noon. Coin lndry. Meeting rms. Business servs avail. In-rm modem link. Sundries. Gift shop. Airport transportation. Exercise equipt; weights, bicycles, sauna. Cr cds: A, C, D, DS, JCB, MC, V.

[D] [🐾] [🐾] [🍴] [🍴] [🐾] [🐾] [SC]

✔ ★ ★ **LENOX INN.** *(I-70E at OH 256, Reynoldsburg 43086) exit 112B.* 614/861-7800; FAX 614/759-9059; res: 800/821-0007. 151 rms, 2 story. S, D $49-$77; each addl $6; suites $109-$134; under 18 free. Crib free. Pet accepted; $10. TV; cable (premium). Pool. Restaurant 6:30 am-10 pm. Rm serv. Bar. Ck-out 11 am. Meeting rms. Business servs avail. In-rm modem link. Valet serv. Sundries. Free airport transportation. Health club privileges. Cr cds: A, C, D, DS, MC, V. [D] [🐾] [🐾] [🐾] [🐾] [SC]

Hotels

★ ★ **HOLIDAY INN-CITY CENTER.** *175 E Town St (43215).* 614/221-3281; FAX 614/221-2667. 240 rms, 12 story. S, D $119-$150; under 18 free. Crib free. Pet accepted. TV; cable (premium). Pool. Complimentary coffee in rms. Restaurant 6:30 am-2 pm, 5-10 pm; Sat, Sun from 7 am. Bar 4 pm-midnight. Ck-out noon. Meeting rms. Business servs avail. Free airport transportation. Health club privileges. Cr cds: A, C, D, DS, ER, JCB, MC, V. [D] [🐾] [🐾] [🐾] [SC]

★ ★ **RADISSON-NORTH.** *4900 Sinclair Rd (43229), near jct I-71 & Morse Rd.* 614/846-0300; FAX 614/847-1022. 268 rms, 5-6 story. S, D $138; each addl $10; suites $125-$175; under 18 free; wkend rates. Pet accepted, some restrictions. TV; cable (premium), VCR avail. 2 pools, 1 indoor; wading pool, whirlpool, poolside serv. Restaurant 6:30 am-2 pm, 5-11 pm. Bar 11-2 am; entertainment Thurs-Sat. Ck-out noon. Convention facilities. Business center. In-rm modem link. Gift shop. Free airport transportation. Exercise equipt; weight machines, bicycles. Game rm. Cr cds: A, C, D, DS, JCB, MC, V.

[D] [🐾] [🐾] [🍴] [🐾] [🐾] [SC] [🏌]

Dayton *(See also Miamisburg, Middletown)*

Motels

★ ★ **HAMPTON INN.** *(2550 Paramount Place, Fairborn 45324) N on I-675, exit 17 to Fairfield Rd to Colonel Glen Hwy.* 937/429-5505; FAX 937/429-6828. 63 rms, 3 story, 8 suites. S, D $70-$79; suites $75-$85; under 18 free; higher rates special events; lower rates winter. Crib free. Pet accepted, some restrictions. TV; cable (premium), VCR avail. Indoor pool; whirlpool. Complimentary continental bkfst. Restaurant adj 5 am-11 pm. Ck-out noon. Business servs avail. In-rm modem link. Valet serv. Health club privileges. Refrigerator, microwave in suites. Cr cds: A, C, D, DS, MC, V. [D] [🐾] [🐾] [🐾] [🐾]

★ ★ **HOMEWOOD SUITES.** *(2750 Presidential Dr, Fairborn 45324) 8 mi NE on I-675 exit 17.* 937/429-0600; FAX 937/429-6311; res: 800/225-5466. Web www.homewood.suites.com. 128 suites, 3 story. S, D $109-$119; family, wkly, monthly rates. Crib free. Pet accepted. TV; cable (premium), VCR (movies $6). Heated pool; whirlpool, poolside serv. Complimentary continental bkfst. Complimentary coffee in rms. Restaurant adj 6 am-11 pm. Ck-out noon. Coin lndry. Meeting rms. Business center. In-rm modem link. Bellhops. Valet serv. Sundries. Gift shop. Grocery store. Exercise equipt; weight machine, stair machine.

Lawn games. Refrigerators, microwaves. Picnic tables, grills. Cr cds: A, C, D, DS, JCB, MC, V. 🅳 ✦ 🖾 🏋 🏖 🔥 SC 🏃

★ **HOWARD JOHNSON.** *7575 Poe Ave (45414). 937/454-0550; FAX 937/454-5566.* 121 rms, 2 story. S $52-$59; D $59-$66; each addl $7; under 18 free. Crib free. Pet accepted, some restrictions; $50 deposit. TV; cable (premium), VCR avail (movies). Pool. Complimentary continental bkfst. Bar 5 pm-midnight. Ck-out noon. Guest lndry. Meeting rms. Business servs avail. Valet serv. Free airport transportation. Health club privileges. Cr cds: A, C, D, DS, MC, V. 🅳 ✦ 🖾 🏖 🔥 SC

✔ ★ **RED ROOF INN-NORTH.** *7370 Miller Ln (45414), I-75 exit 60. 937/898-1054; FAX 937/898-1059.* 109 rms, 2 story. S $37.95-$45.99; D $42.99-$58.99; each addl $5; under 18 free. Crib free. Pet accepted. TV; cable (premium). Complimentary coffee in lobby. Restaurant nearby. Ck-out noon. Business servs avail. Cr cds: A, C, D, DS, MC, V. 🅳 ✦ 🏖 🔥

Hotels

★ ★ ★ **CROWNE PLAZA DAYTON.** *Fifth & Jefferson Sts (45402), opp Convention Ctr. 937/224-0800; FAX 937/224-3913.* 284 rms, 14 story. S $142-$162; D $157-$177; each addl $15; suites $249-$394; under 12 free. Crib free. Pet accepted, some restrictions. TV; cable (premium). Heated pool; poolside serv. Complimentary coffee in rms. Restaurant 6:30 am-11 pm. Rm serv 24 hrs. Bar; entertainment. Ck-out noon. Meeting rms. Business servs avail. Gift shop. Exercise equipt; weight machines, stair machine. Some refrigerators. Luxury level. Cr cds: A, C, D, DS, ER, JCB, MC, V. 🅳 ✦ 🖾 🏋 🏖 🔥 SC

★ ★ ★ **MARRIOTT.** *1414 S Patterson Blvd (45409). 937/223-1000; FAX 937/223-7853.* 399 rms, 6 story. S, D $120-$140; suites $200-$400; under 18 free; wkend rates. Crib free. Pet accepted, some restrictions. TV; cable (premium), VCR avail. Indoor/outdoor pool; whirlpool, poolside serv. Restaurant 7 am-10 pm. Bar 11-2 am; entertainment. Ck-out noon. Coin lndry. Convention facilities. Business center. In-rm modem link. Gift shop. Exercise equipt; weights, treadmill, sauna. Balconies. Luxury level. Cr cds: A, C, D, DS, ER, JCB, MC, V. 🅳 ✦ 🖾 🏋 🏖 🔥 SC 🏃

Defiance

Motel

★ **PARAMOUNT HOTEL.** *(2395 N Scott St, Napoleon 43545) 18 mi W on US 24 & OH 6, exit 108. 419/592-5010; res: 800/827-8641; FAX 419/592-6618.* 79 rms, 2 story. S, D $53-$57; each addl $6; suites $75-$80; under 18 free; wkend rates. Crib free. Pet accepted, some restrictions. TV; cable (premium). Complimentary coffee in lobby. Restaurant 6:30 am-10 pm. Rm serv. Bar 11-1:30 am. Ck-out noon. Meeting rms. Business servs avail. Sundries. Coin lndry. Pool. Microwaves avail. Cr cds: A, C, D, DS, MC, V. 🅳 ✦ 🖾 🏖 🔥 SC

Delaware <small>(See also Columbus, Marion, Mount Vernon)</small>

Motels

★ ★ **HOLIDAY INN EXPRESS.** *(16510 Square Dr, Marysville 43040) 16 mi W on US 36. 513/644-8821.* 74 rms, 2 story, 12 kit. units. S, D $65; each addl $5; suites $94; kit. units $65; under 19 free. Crib free. Pet accepted, some restrictions. TV; cable (premium), VCR avail. Complimentary bkfst. Restaurant adj 6 am-10 pm. Ck-out noon. Business center. In-rm modem link. Whirlpool in some suites. Cr cds: A, C, D, DS, MC, V. 🅳 ✦ 🏖 🔥 SC 🏃

✔ ★ **TRAVELODGE.** *1001 US 23N. 614/369-4421.* 32 rms, 1-2 story. S $42-$48; D $47-$59; each addl $6; under 18 free; higher rates: Little Brown Jug harness race, wkends during peak season. Crib $6. Pet accepted. TV; cable. Complimentary coffee in rms. Restaurant open 24 hrs. Ck-out noon. Meeting rms. Business servs avail. Sundries. Cr cds: A, C, D, DS, MC, V. ✦ 🏖 🔥 SC

Gallipolis

Motels

✔ ★ **BEST WESTERN WILLIAM ANN.** *918 Second Ave. 614/446-3373; FAX 614/446-1337.* 56 rms, 1-2 story. S $35-$40; D $40-$45; each addl $5; suites $50-$65; under 12 free. Crib $5. Pet accepted. TV; cable. Restaurant nearby. Ck-out 11 am. Business servs avail. Cr cds: A, C, D, DS, MC, V. ✦ 🏖 🔥 SC

★ ★ **HOLIDAY INN.** *577 OH State Rt 7.* 614/446-0090. 100 rms, 2 story. S, D $59; suites $59; under 20 free. Crib free. Pet accepted. TV; cable. Pool; wading pool. Restaurant 6 am-10 pm. Rm serv. Bar 4 pm-midnight. Ck-out noon. Coin lndry. Meeting rms. Business servs avail. Sundries. Cr cds: A, C, D, DS, JCB, MC, V. [D] 🏊 ⛱ 🐾 SC

Hamilton *(See also Cincinnati, Mason, Middletown)*

Hotel

★ ★ **HAMILTONIAN.** *1 Riverfront Plaza (45011).* 513/896-6200; FAX 513/896-9463; res: 800/522-5570. 120 rms, 6 story. S, D $77-$84; each addl $8; suites $130-$135; wkend rates. Crib free. Pet accepted. TV; cable (premium), VCR avail. Pool. Coffee in rms. Restaurant 6:30 am-10 pm. Bar 11-1 am; Fri, Sat to 2 am. Ck-out noon. Meeting rms. Business servs avail. In-rm modem link. Indoor tennis privileges. Health club privileges. Refrigerator avail. On river. Luxury level. Cr cds: A, C, D, DS, MC, V.

[D] 🏊 ⛱ 🐾 SC

Kent *(See also Akron, Alliance, Aurora, Cleveland)*

Motels

(Rates may be higher for special university wkends)

★ ★ **HOLIDAY INN.** *4363 OH 43, 3 mi S on OH 43 at jct I-76.* 330/678-0101; FAX 330/677-5001. 152 rms, 2 story. May-Sept: S, D $99; under 19 free; lower rates rest of yr. Crib free. Pet accepted. TV; cable (premium). Heated pool. Restaurant 6:30 am-2 pm, 5-10 pm. Rm serv. Bar. Ck-out noon. Coin lndry. Meeting rms. Business servs avail. Exercise equipt; weight machine, bicycles. Cr cds: A, C, D, DS, JCB, MC, V.

[D] 🏊 ⛱ 🏋 🐾 SC

★ **INN OF KENT.** *303 E Main St, OH Tpke exit 13.* 330/673-3411; FAX 330/673-9878. 57 rms, 2 story, some kits. June-Labor Day: S, D $55-$70; each addl $3; under 12 free; lower rates rest of yr. Crib free. Pet accepted, some restrictions. TV; cable. Indoor pool. Restaurant 7 am-2:30 pm; Fri, Sat to 9 pm. Rm serv. Ck-out noon. Coin lndry. Meeting rm. Business servs avail. Cr cds: A, C, D, DS, MC, V. [D] 🏊 ⛱ 🐾

✔ ★ **KNIGHTS INN.** *4423 OH 43, at jct I-76.* 330/678-5250; FAX 330/678-7014. 99 rms, 30 kit. units. May-Sept: S, D $44.95-$49.95; each addl $6; kit. units $49.95-$54.95; under 18 free; some lower rates rest of yr. Crib free. Pet accepted. TV; cable. Pool. Restaurant adj open 24 hrs. Ck-out noon. Meeting rm. Business servs avail. Some refrigerators. Cr cds: A, DS, MC, V. 🏊 ⛱ 🐾 SC

Lancaster *(See also Columbus, Newark)*

Motels

★ ★ **BEST WESTERN.** *1858 N Memorial Dr.* 614/653-3040; FAX 614/653-1172. 168 rms, 2 story. S, D $52-$80; each addl $7; under 19 free. Crib free. Pet accepted. TV; cable. Pool. Complimentary coffee in rms. Restaurant 6 am-10 pm. Rm serv. Bar to 1 am. Ck-out noon. Meeting rms. Business servs avail. Valet serv. Coin lndry. Health club privileges. Some refrigerators. Cr cds: A, C, D, DS, JCB, MC, V. [D] 🏊 ⛱ 🐾 SC

✔ ★ **KNIGHTS INN.** *1327 River Valley Blvd, at OH 33.* 614/687-4823; FAX 614/687-6276; res: 800/843-5644. 60 units, 7 kits. S, D $39-$49; each addl $6; under 18 free. Crib free. Pet accepted. TV; VCR avail (movies). Complimentary coffee in lobby. Restaurant adj 7 am-10 pm. Ck-out noon. Business servs avail. Cr cds: A, C, D, DS, ER, MC, V. [D] ⛱ 🐾 SC

Lima *(See also Wapakoneta)*

Motor Hotel

★ ★ ★ **HOLIDAY INN.** *1920 Roschman Ave (45804).* 419/222-0004; FAX 419/222-2176. 150 rms, 4 story. S, D $86-$100; under 18 free. Crib free. Pet accepted. TV. Indoor pool; whirlpool. Playground. Restaurant 6:30 am-10 pm; Sat to 11 pm. Rm serv. Bar; entertainment Fri, Sat. Ck-out noon. Meeting rms. In-rm modem link. Sundries. Exercise equipt; weight machine, bicycles, sauna. Game rm. Rec rm. Microwaves avail. Balconies. Cr cds: A, C, D, DS, ER, JCB, MC, V. [D] 🏊 ⛱ 🏋 🐾 SC

Mansfield *(See also Mount Vernon)*

Motels

★ **BEST WESTERN INN.** *880 Laver Rd (44905), I-71 exit 176. 419/589-2200; FAX 419/589-5624.* 105 rms, 2 story. S $47-$65; D $47-$77; each addl $6; under 18 free; higher rates: special events, summer wkends. Crib free. Pet accepted. TV; cable (premium). Pool. Restaurant 6-11 am, 5-9 pm. Rm serv. Bar 5 pm-2 am. Ck-out noon. Meeting rms. Business servs avail. Cr cds: A, C, D, DS, MC, V. 🄳 🕊 ⛱ 🏮 🔥 SC

★ ★ **COMFORT INN NORTH.** *500 N Trimble Rd (44906). 419/529-1000; FAX 419/529-2953.* 114 rms, 2 story, 22 suites. S $58-$63; D $63-$68; each addl $5; suites $72-$88; under 18 free; higher rates auto racing wkends. Crib free. Pet accepted, some restrictions. TV; cable. Indoor pool. Complimentary continental bkfst. Restaurant adj 11 am-10 pm; Fri, Sat to 11 pm. Rm serv. Bar. Ck-out noon. Coin lndry. Meeting rms. Business servs avail. In-rm modem link. Sundries. Downhill/x-country ski 20 mi. Refrigerators in suites. Cr cds: A, C, D, DS, ER, JCB, MC, V. 🄳 🕊 ⛱ ⛱ 🏮 🔥 SC

✔ ★ **KNIGHTS INN.** *555 N Trimble Rd (44906), just off US 30. 419/529-2100; FAX 419/529-6679; res: 800/843-5644.* 110 rms. S $35-$45; D $47-$55; each addl $5; kit. units $57-$65; under 16 free; higher rates auto races. Crib free. Pet accepted. TV; cable (premium); VCR (movies). Pool. Complimentary continental bkfst. Restaurant adj 6 am-midnight. Ck-out noon. Business servs avail. Valet serv. Sundries. Cr cds: A, C, D, DS, MC, V. 🄳 🕊 ⛱ 🏮 🔥 SC

✔ ★ **TRAVELODGE.** *90 Hanley Rd (OH 13) (44904). 419/756-7600.* 93 rms, 2 story. S $40-$47; D $42-$59; each addl $5; kit. units $52-$62; higher rates auto racing wkends; under 18 free. Crib free. Pet accepted. TV; cable. Pool. Coffee in rms. Restaurant open 24 hrs. Ck-out noon. Meeting rms. Business servs avail. Downhill/x-country ski 2 mi. Cr cds: A, C, D, DS, ER, JCB, MC, V. 🕊 ⛱ ⛱ 🏮 🔥 SC

Marion *(See also Delaware)*

Motels

★ **COMFORT INN.** *256 Jamesway, 3 mi E on OH 95 exit 95. 614/389-5552.* 56 rms, 2 story. May-Oct: S $54-$80; D $54-$90; each addl $6; suites $65-$95; under 18 free; higher rates special events; lower rates rest of yr. Crib $6. Pet accepted, some restrictions; $6. TV; cable (premium). Complimentary continental bkfst. Restaurant opp 5 am-11 pm. Ck-out 11 am. Business servs avail. Indoor pool; whirlpool. Game rm. Refrigerator, microwave in suites. Cr cds: A, D, DS, MC, V. 🕊 ⛱ 🏮 🔥 SC

★ **HARDING MOTOR LODGE.** *1065 Delaware Ave. 614/383-6771; FAX 614/383-6733; res: 800/563-4399.* 99 rms, 2 story. S, D $45; each addl $6; suites $71.25; under 18 free. Crib free. Pet accepted; $5. TV; cable (premium). Complimentary coffee in lobby. Ck-out noon. In-rm modem link. Coin lndry. Valet serv. Microwaves avail. Cr cds: A, C, D, DS, MC, V. 🄳 🕊 🏮 🔥 SC

✔ ★ **TRAVELODGE.** *1952 Marion-Mt Gilead Rd. 614/389-4671; FAX 614/389-4671, ext. 101.* 90 rms, 2 story. S $45-$60; D $47-$65; each addl $6; suites $60-$79; under 18 free. Crib free. Pet accepted; $3-$6. TV; cable (premium), VCR avail. Pool. Complimentary coffee in rms. Restaurant nearby. Ck-out noon. Meeting rms. Business servs avail. In-rm modem link. Valet serv. Health club privileges. Microwaves avail. Picnic tables. Cr cds: A, C, D, DS, ER, JCB, MC, V. 🕊 ⛱ 🏮 🔥 SC

Mason *(See also Cincinnati, Dayton, Hamilton, Middletown)*

Motels

✔ ★ **DAYS INN KINGS ISLAND.** *9735 Mason-Montgomery Rd, at I-71 exit 19. 513/398-3297; FAX 513/398-3297, ext. 302.* 124 rms, 2 story. S, D $39-$129; higher rates for special events. Crib free. Pet accepted, some restrictions. TV; cable (premium). Pool. Playground. Complimentary continental bkfst. Restaurant adj. Ck-out 11 am. Meeting rms. Business servs avail. Game rm. Cr cds: A, C, D, DS, MC, V. 🄳 🕊 ⛱ 🏮 🔥 SC

★ ★ **HOLIDAY INN-NORTHEAST.** *9845 Escort Dr, at I-71 exit 19. 513/398-8015; FAX 513/398-0822.* 104 rms, 2 story. S, D $79-$110; under 19 free. Crib free. Pet accepted. TV; cable (premium). Pool. Playground. Restaurant 6:30 am-2 pm, 5-10 pm. Rm serv. Bar 6-11 pm; closed Sun. Ck-out noon. Meeting rms. Business servs avail. In-rm modem link. Cr cds: A, C, D, DS, JCB, MC, V. 🄳 🕊 ⛱ 🏮 🔥 SC

Miamisburg (See also Dayton)

Motels

★ **KNIGHTS INN.** *185 Byers Rd, just W of I-75 exit 44. 937/859-8797; FAX 937/746-9109; res: 800/843-5644.* 161 rms, 22 kit. units. S $37.95-$41.95; D $42.95-$46.95; kit. units $46.95-$48.95; under 18 free. Crib free. Pet accepted, some restrictions. TV; cable (premium). Pool. Complimentary continental bkfst. Restaurant adj open 24 hrs. Ck-out noon. Meeting rms. Some refrigerators. Cr cds: A, C, D, DS, MC, V. 🅳 🐾 ≈ ⊠ 🖐 SC

✔★ **RED ROOF INN-DAYTON SOUTH.** *222 Byers Rd, just off I-75 exit 44. 937/866-0705; FAX 937/866-0700.* 107 rms, 2 story. S $35.99-$55.99; D $48.99-$56.99; each addl $7; under 18 free. Crib free. Pet accepted, some restrictions. TV; cable (premium). Ck-out noon. Business servs avail. In-rm modem link. Cr cds: A, C, D, DS, MC, V. 🅳 🐾 ⊠ 🖐

★★ **RESIDENCE INN BY MARRIOTT.** *155 Prestige Place, E of I-75 exit 44. 937/434-7881; FAX 937/434-9308.* 96 suites, 2 story. 1-bedrm suites $97-$125; 2-bedrm suites $120-$150. Crib free. Pet accepted; $10. TV; cable (premium), VCR avail (movies). Heated pool; whirlpool. Complimentary continental bkfst. Restaurant nearby. Ck-out noon. Coin lndry. Business servs avail. Valet serv. Health club privileges. Fireplaces. Balconies. Picnic tables, grills. Cr cds: A, C, D, DS, JCB, MC, V. 🅳 🐾 ≈ ⊠ 🖐 SC

Middletown (Butler Co)

(For accommodations see Cincinnati, Dayton, Mason)

Motor Hotel

★★ **MANCHESTER INN AND CONFERENCE CENTER.** *1027 Manchester Ave, downtown. 513/422-5481; res: 800/523-9126; FAX 513/422-4615.* Web www.middle town.com/maninn. 79 rms, some with shower only, 5 story, 16 suites. S, D $64-$98; each addl $8; suites $84-$149; under 18 free; hol rates. Crib free. Pet accepted; $8/day. TV; cable, VCR avail. Complimentary coffee in rms. Restaurant 6:30 am-10 pm; Sat 8 am-11 pm; Sun 8 am-9 pm. Rm serv. Bar; entertainment Fri. Ck-out noon. Meeting rms. Business servs avail. In-rm modem link. Bellhops. Valet serv (Mon-Fri). Gift shop. Health club privileges. Refrigerator, microwave in suites. Microwaves avail. Cr cds: A, C, D, DS, MC, V. 🅳 🐾 ⊠ 🖐 SC

Milan (See also Sandusky)

Motel

★★ **COMFORT INN.** *11020 Milan Rd (US 250), N of Tpke exit 7. 419/499-4681; FAX 419/499-3159.* 102 rms, 2 story. May-Sept: S, D $58-$180; under 18 free; lower rates rest of yr. Crib $10. Pet accepted, some restrictions. TV; cable. 2 pools, 1 indoor; whirlpools. Continental bkfst. Complimentary coffee. Restaurant nearby. Ck-out noon. Coin lndry. Business servs avail. Sundries. Sauna. Cr cds: A, C, D, DS, JCB, MC, V. 🅳 🐾 ≈ ⊠ 🖐 SC

Mount Vernon (See also Mansfield, Newark)

Motel

✔★★ **CURTIS.** *12 Public Sq. 614/397-4334; res: 800/934-6835.* 72 rms, 2 story. S, D $46-$52; each addl $5; under 13 free. Crib free. Pet accepted. TV; cable, VCR avail (movies). Complimentary coffee in rms. Restaurant 6:30 am-2 pm, 5-9 pm. Rm serv. Bar 11-1 am. Ck-out noon. Coin lndry. Business servs avail. Valet serv. Refrigerators. Some minibars. Cr cds: A, C, D, DS, MC, V. 🐾 ⊠ 🖐

Newark (See also Columbus, Zanesville)

Motel

★★ **HOWARD JOHNSON.** *775 Hebron Rd, I-70 exit 129B. 614/522-3191; FAX 614/522-4396.* 72 rms, 2 story. S $55-$65; D $70-$80; each addl $8; suites $100-$125; under 18 free; higher rates special events. Crib free. Pet accepted. TV; cable (premium), VCR avail (movies). Indoor pool. Complimentary continental bkfst Mon-Fri. Bar 6 pm-1 am; closed Sun. Ck-out noon. Meeting rms. Business servs avail. In-rm modem link. Exercise equipt; treadmill, stair machine. Private patios, balconies. Cr cds: A, C, D, DS, JCB, MC, V. 🅳 🐾 ≈ ⊠ 🖐 SC

New Philadelphia (See also Canton)

Motel

★ ★ **HOLIDAY INN.** *131 Bluebell Dr, I-77 exit 81. 330/339-7731; FAX 330/339-1565.* 150 rms, 2 story. S, D $79 wkdays, $89 wkends; higher rates: Hall of Fame Week, Ohio Swiss Festival. Crib free. Pet accepted. TV; cable, VCR avail. 2 pools, 1 indoor; whirlpool. Restaurant 6:30 am-10 pm. Bar 4 pm-1 am. Ck-out 11 am. Meeting rms. Business servs avail. Valet serv. Sundries. Exercise equipt; weights, bicycles, sauna. Cr cds: A, C, D, DS, MC, V. [D] 🐾 ⊠ 🏋 ⊠ 🐾 [SC]

Painesville (See also Cleveland)

Inn

★ ★ **RIDER'S 1812 INN.** *792 Mentor Ave. 216/354-8200.* 10 rms, 2 story. S, D $75-$99; each addl $10. Crib free. Pet accepted. TV; cable, VCR avail (movies $2). Complimentary full bkfst in rm. Restaurant 11:30 am-9 pm. Rm serv. Ck-out, ck-in flexible. Business servs avail. Bellhops. Concierge. Airport transportation. 18-hole golf privileges. Health club privileges. Original stagecoach stop (1812); historic stop on the underground railroad, some original antiques. Cr cds: A, DS, MC, V. 🐾 🏋 ⊠ 🐾

Portsmouth

Motel

★ ★ **HOLIDAY INN.** *Box 1190, 4 mi N on US 23. 614/354-2851; FAX 614/353-2084.* 100 rms, 2 story. S, D $59; under 18 free; higher rates special events. Crib free. Pet accepted, some restrictions. TV; cable. Pool. Restaurant. Rm serv. Bar 5 pm-2 am. Ck-out noon. Meeting rms. Business servs avail. In-rm modem link. Valet serv. Cr cds: A, C, D, DS, MC, V. [D] 🐾 ⊠ ⊠ 🐾 [SC]

Motor Hotel

✔ ★ ★ **RAMADA INN.** *711 2nd St, at jct US 23, 52. 614/354-7711; FAX 614/353-1539.* 119 rms, 5 story. S $49-$59; D $53-$69; each addl $7; under 18 free. Crib free. Pet accepted, some restrictions. TV; cable (premium). Indoor pool; wading pool, whirlpool, poolside serv. Complimentary continental bkfst. Restaurant 11 am-11 pm; Fri, Sat to midnight. Rm serv. Ck-out noon. Meeting rms. Business servs avail. Valet serv. Sundries. Health club privileges. Dockage. Some refrigerators. Cr cds: A, C, D, DS, MC, V. [D] 🐾 ⊠ ⊠ 🐾 [SC]

St Clairsville (See also Steubenville)

Motel

✔ ★ **KNIGHTS INN.** *51260 National Rd, I-70 exit 218. 614/695-5038; FAX 614/695-3014; res: 800/835-9628.* 104 rms, 16 kits. S $36.95-$44.95; D $38.95-$54.95; each addl $7; kit. units $44.95-$69.95; under 18 free. Crib free. Pet accepted, some restrictions. TV; cable (premium), VCR avail (movies). Pool. Complimentary coffee. Restaurant nearby. Ck-out noon. Business servs avail. In-rm modem link. Some in-rm whirlpools; microwaves avail. Cr cds: A, D, DS, ER, MC, V. [D] 🐾 ⊠ ⊠ 🐾 [SC]

Sandusky (See also Milan, Port Clinton)

Motor Hotels

★ ★ ★ **FOUR POINTS BY SHERATON.** *1119 Sandusky Mall Blvd. 419/625-6280; FAX 419/625-9080.* 143 rms, 2 story. May-Sept: S, D $75-$140; suites $80-$200; under 18 free; lower rates rest of yr. Crib free. Pet accepted. TV; cable (premium). Indoor pool; whirlpool, poolside serv. Restaurant 7 am-10 pm. Rm serv. Bar 5 pm-2 am; entertainment Wed-Sat. Ck-out 11 am. Meeting rms. Business servs avail. In-rm modem link. Sundries. Game rm. Exercise equipt; bicycles, treadmill, sauna. Atrium. Cr cds: A, C, D, DS, MC, V. 🐾 ⊠ 🏋 ⊠ 🐾 [SC]

★ ★ ★ **RADISSON HARBOUR INN.** *2001 Cleveland Rd, at Cedar Point Causeway. 419/627-2500; FAX 419/627-0745.* 237 rms, 4 story, 49 suites. May-mid-Sept: S, D $99-$239; suites $109-$359; under 18 free; lower rates rest of yr. Crib free. Pet accepted, some restrictions. TV; cable (premium), VCR avail. Indoor pool; whirlpool, poolside serv. Supervised child's activities (May-mid-Sept); ages 4-13. Restaurant 6:30 am-11 pm. Rm serv. Bars 11-2 am; entertainment wkends. Ck-out noon. Coin lndry. Meeting rms. Business center. In-rm modem link. Bellhops. Valet serv. Gift shop. Airport, RR station, bus depot transportation. Exercise equipt; weights, bicycles. Game rm. Rec rm. Some refrigerators; microwaves avail. Private patios, balconies. Waterfront views of Sandusky Bay. Cr cds: A, C, D, DS, ER, JCB, MC, V. 🄳 🛉 ≋ 🏌 🎿 🔥 SC 🚶

Sidney *(See also Bellefontaine, Wapakoneta)*

Motel

★ ★ **HOLIDAY INN.** *400 Folkerth Ave, OH 47 & I-75 exit 92.* 513/492-1131; FAX *513/498-4655.* 134 rms, 2 story. S $65-$67; D $70-$77; each addl $5; suites $75-$77; under 19 free; package plans. Crib free. Pet accepted, some restrictions. TV; cable (premium), VCR avail. Pool. Restaurant 6:30 am-10 pm; Sat from 7 am; Sun to 9 pm. Rm serv. Bar 11 am-midnight, Fri, Sat to 1 am. Ck-out noon. Coin lndry. Meeting rms. Business servs avail. In-rm modem link. Valet serv. Sundries. Exercise equipt; weights, bicycles, sauna. Game rm. Microwaves in suites. Cr cds: A, C, D, DS, JCB, MC, V. 🄳 🛉 ≋ 🏌 🔥 🔥 SC

Steubenville

Motor Hotel

★ ★ ★ **HOLIDAY INN.** *1401 University Blvd, ³/₄ mi W of OH 7.* 614/282-0901; FAX *614/282-9540.* 120 rms, 2 story. No elvtr. S, D $65; each addl $5; under 18 free. Pet accepted, some restrictions. TV; cable (premium), VCR avail. Heated pool. Restaurant 6 am-midnight. Rm serv. Bar 7 am-10 pm. Ck-out noon. Coin lndry. Business servs avail. In-rm modem link. Bellhops. Valet serv. Cr cds: A, C, D, DS, JCB, MC, V.
🄳 🛉 ≋ 🔥 🔥 SC

Toledo

Motels

★ ★ **COMFORT INN.** *3560 Secor Rd (43606), at I-475 exit 17.* 419/531-2666; FAX *419/531-4757.* 70 rms, 2 story. S, D $60-$65. Crib free. Pet accepted, some restrictions. TV; cable (premium). Complimentary continental bkfst. Restaurant adj. Ck-out noon. Health club privileges. Picnic tables. Cr cds: A, C, D, DS, JCB, MC, V. 🄳 🛉 ≋ 🔥 SC

✔ ★ ★ **DAYS INN.** *(150 Dussel Dr, Maumee 43537) 1 mi S off I-80/90 exit 4.* 419/893-9960; FAX 419/893-9559. 120 units, 2 story, 6 suites, 4 kits. S $34-$47; D $49-$68; each addl $6; suites, kit. units $47-$68; under 18 free; wkly rates. Crib free. Pet accepted. TV; cable (premium). Pool. Complimentary continental bkfst. Restaurant adj 6 am-11 pm. Ck-out noon. Business servs avail. Valet serv. Some refrigerators; microwaves avail. Cr cds: A, C, D, DS, JCB, MC, V. 🄳 🛉 ≋ 🏌 🔥 SC

Motor Hotels

★ ★ ★ **CLARION-WESTGATE.** *3536 Secor Rd (43606).* 419/535-7070; FAX *419/536-4836.* 305 rms, 3 story. S, D $79-$99; suites $99-$275; under 18 free. Crib free. Pet accepted, some restrictions. TV; cable. Indoor pool; whirlpool. Restaurant 6:30 am-2:30 pm, 6-11 pm. Rm serv. Bar. Ck-out noon. Convention facilities. Business center. In-rm modem link. Valet serv. Sundries. Gift shop. Exercise equipt; treadmill, stair machines. Game rm. Landscaped enclosed courtyard. Cr cds: A, C, D, DS, MC, V.
🄳 🛉 ≋ 🏌 🎿 🔥 🔥 SC 🚶

★ ★ **HOLIDAY INN.** *2340 S Reynolds Rd (43614).* 419/865-1361; FAX 419/865-6177. 218 rms, 11 story. S, D $99; each addl $10; suites $109-$119; under 18 free; family, wkend rates. Crib free. Pet accepted. TV; cable (premium). Indoor pool. Restaurant 6:30 am-2 pm, 5-10 pm; Sat, Sun from 7 am. Rm serv. Bar 4:30 pm-midnight, Sat from 4 pm, closed Sun. Ck-out noon. Meeting rms. Business servs avail. In-rm modem link. Bellhops. Gift shop. Beauty shop. Free airport transportation. Exercise equipt; bicycles, rowers. Cr cds: A, C, D, DS, JCB, MC, V. 🄳 🛉 ≋ 🏌 🔥 🔥 SC

★ ★ **RAMADA.** *2429 S Reynolds Rd (43614).* 419/381-8765; FAX 419/381-0129. 264 rms, 6 story. S $59-$78; D $63-$86; each addl $8; under 18 free; wkend rates. Crib free. Pet accepted, some restrictions. TV; cable (premium), VCR avail. Indoor pool; whirlpool, poolside serv. Playground. Restaurant 6 am-2 pm, 5-10 pm. Rm serv. Bar 11-2:30 am, Sun to 11 pm. Ck-out 11 am. Convention facilities. In-rm modem link. Bellhops. Valet serv. Sundries. Gift shop. Free airport transportation. Microwaves avail. Cr cds: A, C, D, DS, JCB, MC, V. 🄳 🛉 ≋ 🔥 🔥 SC

Hotel

★ ★ ★ **CROWNE PLAZA.** *2 Seagate (43604).* 419/241-1411; FAX 419/241-8161. Web www.meettoledo.org/crownehtml. 241 rms, 12 story. S, D $139; suites $149; under 18 free; wkend rates. Crib free. Pet accepted. Garage parking $10, valet. TV; cable (premium). Indoor pool; whirlpool. Restaurant 6:30 am-11 pm; Sat from 7 am. Bar from 11 am; Sun from 1 pm. Ck-out noon. Meeting rms. Business center. In-rm modem link. Gift shop. Exercise equipt; weights, bicycles, sauna. On river. Cr cds: A, C, D, DS, MC, V.

Wapakoneta *(See also Bellefontaine, Lima)*

Motor Hotel

★ ★ **HOLIDAY INN.** *1510 Saturn Dr. 419/738-8181; FAX 419/738-6478.* 100 rms, 4 story. S, D $59; each addl $5; suites $69; under 18 free. Crib free. Pet accepted. TV; cable (premium), VCR avail. Pool. Complimentary continental bkfst. Complimentary coffee in rms. Restaurant 6 am-9 pm; Sat from 7 am; Sun 7 am-8 pm. Rm serv. Bar 11-1 am; Sat 5 pm-1 am. Ck-out noon. Coin lndry. Meeting rms. Business servs avail. In-rm modem link. Valet serv. Sundries. Exercise equipt; treadmill, stair machine. Neil Armstrong Museum adj. Cr cds: A, C, D, DS, JCB, MC, V.

Warren *(See also Kent, Youngstown)*

Motel

★ ★ **BEST WESTERN-DOWNTOWN.** *777 Mahoning Ave (44483), just off OH 45. 330/392-2515; FAX 330/392-7099.* 73 rms, 2 story. S $50-$60; D $62-$72; each addl $3; under 16 free. Pet accepted. TV; cable (premium). Pool. Complimentary continental bkfst. Restaurant 3-11 pm. Bar to 2 am. Ck-out 11 am. Business servs avail. Valet serv. Some refrigerators. Cr cds: A, C, D, DS, ER, MC, V.

Hotel

★ ★ **PARK.** *136 N Park Ave (44481). 330/393-1200; FAX 330/399-2875; res: 800/397-7275.* 55 rms, 4 story, 11 suites. S $60; D $70; each addl $10; suites $77; under 16 free. Crib free. Pet accepted. TV. Restaurant 6:30 am-10 pm. Bars. Ck-out noon. Meeting rms. Business servs avail. Airport transportation. Health club privileges. Restored brick hotel (1887). Cr cds: A, C, D, DS, MC, V.

Wauseon *(See also Toledo)*

Motel

★ ★ **BEST WESTERN DEL-MAR.** *8319 SH 108, OH Tpke exit 3. 419/335-1565; FAX 419/335-1828.* 40 rms. June-Sept: S $52-$66; D $54-$66; each addl $10; suites $99-$109; under 18 free; lower rates rest of yr. Crib $6. Pet accepted. TV; cable (premium). Heated pool. Playground. Complimentary continental bkfst. Restaurant nearby. Ck-out 11 am. Cr cds: A, C, D, DS, ER, MC, V.

Wooster *(See also Akron, Canton, Mansfield)*

Motel

✔ ★ **ECONO LODGE.** *2137 Lincoln Way E. 330/264-8883; FAX 330/264-8883, ext. 301; res: 800/248-8341.* 98 rms, 2 story. Apr-Oct: S $36.95-$39.95; D $40.95-$50; each addl $4; under 18 free; lower rates rest of yr. Crib free. Pet accepted. TV; cable. Indoor pool; whirlpool. Continental bkfst. Complimentary coffee in lobby. Restaurant adj 7 am-9 pm; closed Sun. Ck-out 11 am. Coin lndry. Meeting rm. Business center. Sundries. Airport transportation. Picnic tables. Cr cds: A, D, DS, MC, V.

Inn

★ ★ ★ **WOOSTER INN.** *801 E Wayne Ave. 330/264-2341; FAX 330/264-9951.* 16 rms, 2 story. S, D $70-$95; each addl $15; suite $95-$130; 3-12 yrs, $5. Closed Jan 2-9, Dec 25, 26. Crib free. Pet accepted, some restrictions. TV; cable. Restaurant 7 am-2 pm, 6-8:30 pm. Ck-out noon. Meeting rms. Business servs avail. Tennis privileges. 9-hole golf, greens fee $8-$9, putting green, driving range. Picnic tables. Colonial decor. Owned, operated by College of Wooster; on campus. Cr cds: A, C, D, DS, MC, V.

Youngstown *(See also Warren)*

Motel

★ ★ **BEST WESTERN MEANDER INN.** *870 N Canfield-Niles Rd (44515). 330/544-2378; FAX 330/544-7926.* 57 rms, 2 story. S $54-$62; D $68-$74; each addl $4; suites $85-$95; under 18 free. Crib free. Pet accepted. TV; cable. Pool. Complimentary

continental bkfst. Restaurant 3-10 pm. Rm serv. Bar. Ck-out noon. Coin Indry. Meeting rm.
Cr cds: A, C, D, DS, MC, V. [D] [⬤] [≈] [⬤] [⬤] [SC]

Zanesville *(See also Cambridge, Newark)*

Motel

★ ★ **HOLIDAY INN.** *4645 E Pike, off I-70 exit 160.* 614/453-0771. 130 rms, 2 story.
S $69-$77; D $71-$99; each addl $5; under 19 free. Crib free. Pet accepted. TV; cable
(premium). Indoor pool; whirlpool, poolside serv. Playground. Complimentary coffee in rms.
Restaurant 6 am-2 pm, 5-10 pm; Sat, Sun 6:30 am-10 pm. Rm serv. Bars 2 pm-midnight.
Ck-out noon. Coin Indry. Meeting rms. Business servs avail. In-rm modem link. Bellhops.
Sundries. Exercise equipt; bicycles, stair machine, sauna. Cr cds: A, C, D, DS, ER, JCB,
MC, V. [D] [⬤] [≈] [🏃] [⬤] [⬤] [SC]

Oklahoma

Altus

Motels

★ ★ **BEST WESTERN.** *2804 N Main (73521). 405/482-9300; FAX 405/482-2245.* 100 rms, 2 story. S, D $50-$54.50; each addl $6; under 12 free. Crib free. Pet accepted. TV; cable (premium), VCR (movies). Indoor/outdoor pool; sauna. Complimentary continental bkfst. Ck-out noon. Coin lndry. Meeting rms. Business servs avail. In-rm modem link. Some bathrm phones, refrigerators. Cr cds: A, C, D, DS, JCB, MC, V. 🄳 ☚ ⩪ ⨾ 🅰 SC

✔ ★ **DAYS INN.** *3202 N Main (73521). 405/477-2300; FAX 405/477-2379.* 36 rms, 2 story. S $37; D $42; each addl $5; under 18 free. Crib free. Pet accepted. TV; cable (premium). Complimentary continental bkfst. Ck-out 11 am. Business servs avail. Cr cds: A, C, D, DS, ER, MC, V. ☚ ⨾ 🅰 SC

★ **RAMADA INN.** *2515 E Broadway (73521). 405/477-3000; FAX 405/477-0078.* 121 units, 12 suites, 2 story. S $47-$53; D $53-$59; each addl $6; suites $86-$102. Crib free. Pet accepted. TV; cable (premium). Indoor pool. Restaurant 6:30 am-2 pm, 5-10 pm. Rm serv. Bar 5 pm-2 am; dancing. Ck-out noon. Meeting rms. Business servs avail. Valet serv. Refrigerators. Balconies. Cr cds: A, C, D, DS, MC, V. 🄳 ☚ ⩪ ⨾ 🅰 SC

Alva

Motel

★ **RANGER INN.** *420 E Oklahoma Blvd (US 64). 405/327-1981; FAX 405/327-1981, ext. -142.* 41 rms. S $34-$36; D $38; up to 2 addl free; under 16 free. Pet accepted, some restrictions. TV; cable (premium). Complimentary coffee. Ck-out 11 am. Microwaves avail. Cr cds: A, C, D, DS, MC, V. 🄳 ☚ ⨾ 🅰

Ardmore

Motels

★ **DORCHESTER INN.** *2614 W Broadway. 580/226-1761; FAX 580/223-3131.* 50 rms, 2 story. S $27.95-$30.95; D $30.95-$35; under 12 free. Crib free. Pet accepted, some restrictions. TV; cable (premium). Complimentary continental bkfst. Restaurant adj open 24 hrs. Ck-out 11 am. Refrigerators avail. Cr cds: A, C, D, DS, MC, V. 🄳 ☚ ⨾ 🅰

✔ ★ **GUEST INN.** *2519 W OK 142. 580/223-1234; FAX 580/223-1234, ext. 33; res: 800/460-4064.* 126 rms, 2 story. S $34; D $38; suites $67; each addl $5; under 12 free; wkly rates. Crib $2. Pet accepted, some restrictions. TV; cable (premium), VCR avail (movies). Pool. Complimentary coffee in lobby. Restaurant adj 6 am-9 pm. Ck-out 1 pm. Coin lndry. Business servs avail. Valet serv. Airport transportation. Cr cds: A, C, D, DS, MC, V. 🄳 ☚ ⩪ ⨾ 🅰 SC

★ ★ **HOLIDAY INN.** *2705 Holiday Dr, at jct I-35 & US 70. 580/223-7130; FAX 580/223-7130, ext. 390.* 171 rms, 2 story. S, D $52-$64; each addl $6; suites $95-$150. Crib free. Pet accepted. TV; cable. Pool; wading pool. Playground. Restaurant open 24 hrs. Ck-out noon. Coin lndry. Valet serv. Business servs avail. In-rm modem link. Sundries. Cr cds: A, C, D, DS, JCB, MC, V. 🄳 ☚ ⩪ ⨾ 🅰 SC

Atoka

Motel

★ ★ **BEST WESTERN ATOKA INN.** *2101 S Mississippi Ave. 405/889-7381; FAX 405/889-6695.* 54 rms, 2 story. S $49-$54; D $54-$59; each addl $5; under 12 free. Pet accepted. TV; cable. Pool. Restaurant open 6 am-2 pm, 6-10 pm. Ck-out noon. Meeting rms. Business servs avail. Cr cds: A, C, D, DS, MC, V. 🄳 ☚ ⩪ ⨾ 🅰 SC

Bartlesville

Motel

★ ★ **HOLIDAY INN.** *1410 SE Washington Blvd (US 75) (74006). 918/333-8320; FAX 918/333-8979.* 104 rms, 3 story, 6 kits. S $55-$75; D $62-$80; each addl $6; suites $75; under 18 free. Crib free. Pet accepted; $15 deposit. TV; cable (premium). Indoor pool. Complimentary coffee in rms. Restaurant 6-11 am, 5-9 pm; Sun to 2 pm. Rm serv. Bar. Ck-out noon. Coin lndry. Meeting rm. Business servs avail. In-rm modem link. Valet serv. Free local airport transportation. Exercise equipt; weight machine, bicycle, sauna. Cr cds: A, C, D, DS, MC, V. 🄳 🐾 ≋ 🏋 🖎 🔥 SC

Chickasha

Motels

✔ ★ ★ **BEST WESTERN INN.** *2101 S 4th (73018), on US 81, 7 blks N of H.E. Bailey Tpke. 405/224-4890; FAX 405/224-3411.* 154 rms, 2 story. S $39-$49; D $44-$55; each addl $5; under 18 free. Crib free. Pet accepted. TV; cable. Heated pool; whirlpool, sauna, poolside serv. Restaurant 6 am-9 pm. Rm serv. Ck-out noon. Meeting rms. Business servs avail. Valet serv. Refrigerator in suites. Cr cds: A, C, D, DS, MC, V. 🄳 🐾 ≋ 🖎 🔥 SC

✔ ★ ★ **DAYS INN.** *2701 S 4th St (73018). 405/222-5800.* 86 rms, 2 story. S $37; D $42; each addl $5; under 18 free. Crib free. Pet accepted. TV; cable (premium). Pool. Restaurant 5:30 am-9 pm. Rm serv. Ck-out 11 am. Meeting rms. Business servs avail. In-rm modem link. Valet serv. Some refrigerators. Cr cds: A, C, D, DS, JCB, MC, V. 🄳 🐾 ≋ 🖎 🔥 SC

Claremore *(See also Pryor, Tulsa)*

Motel

✔ ★ ★ **BEST WESTERN WILL ROGERS INN.** *940 S Lynn Riggs Blvd (OK 66). 918/341-4410; FAX 918/341-6045.* 52 rms. S $44; D $54; each addl $4. Crib $5. Pet accepted. TV; cable (premium). Pool. Coffee in rms. Restaurant adj 6 am-9:30 pm; closed Sun. Bar noon-1:30 am, closed Sun, hols. Ck-out noon. Coin lnry. Meeting rm. Business servs avail. Many refrigerators; microwaves avail. Cr cds: A, C, D, DS, ER, JCB, MC, V. 🄳 🐾 ≋ 🖎 🔥 SC

Duncan *(See also Lawton)*

Motels

✔ ★ **DUNCAN INN.** *3402 N US 81. 405/252-5210; FAX 405/252-5210, ext. 336.* 92 rms, 2 story. S $25-$30; D $30-$36; each addl $4; wkly, monthly rates. Pet accepted. TV; cable (premium). Pool. Complimentary coffee in lobby. Restaurant. Ck-out 11 am. Coin lndry. Meeting rm. Cr cds: A, C, D, DS, MC, V. 🄳 🐾 ≋ 🖎 🔥 SC

★ ★ **HOLIDAY INN.** *1015 N US 81. 405/252-1500; FAX 405/255-1851.* 138 rms, 2 story. S $51-$61; D $57-$68; under 18 free. Crib free. Pet accepted, some restrictions. TV; cable (premium). Indoor pool; wading pool, sauna. Complimentary coffee in lobby. Restaurant 6 am-10 pm; Sat to 11 pm; Sun to 9 pm. Rm serv. Bar 5 pm-2 am. Ck-out noon. Meeting rms. Business servs avail. In-rm modem link. Valet serv. Sundries. Picnic tables. Cr cds: A, C, D, DS, JCB, MC, V. 🄳 🐾 ≋ 🖎 🔥 SC

Elk City

Motels

★ **DAYS INN.** *1100 OK 34, I-40 exit 41. 580/225-9210; FAX 580/225-1278.* 135 rms, 63 kits. S $35-$45; D $40-$50; kit. Crib free. Pet accepted. TV; cable. Pool. Complimentary continental bkfst. Restaurant opp open 24 hrs. Ck-out noon. Business servs avail. Gift shop. Some refrigerators. Cr cds: A, C, D, DS, MC, V. 🄳 🐾 ≋ 🖎 🔥 SC

★ ★ **HOLIDAY INN.** *Box 782 (73648), I-40 at OK 6, exit 38. 580/225-6637.* 151 rms, 2 story. S $57-$65; D $63-$71; each addl $6; suites $85-$105; under 19 free. Crib free. Pet accepted. TV; cable (premium), VCR avail (movies). Indoor pool; whirlpool. Complimentary coffee in rms. Restaurant 6 am-2 pm, 5-10 pm. Rm serv. Bar 5 pm-midnight; Fri & Sat to 2 am. Ck-out noon. Meeting rms. Business servs avail. In-rm modem link. Valet serv. Exercise equipt; stair machine, treadmill, sauna. Holidome. Lawn games. Wet bar in suites. Cr cds: A, C, D, DS, JCB, MC, V. 🄳 🐾 ≋ 🏋 🖎 🔥 SC

★ **QUALITY INN.** *102 Hughes Access Rd, I-40 exit 38.. 580/225-8140; FAX 580/225-8233.* 50 rms, 2 story. S $32; D $44; family, wkly rates. Pet accepted. TV; cable (premium). Indoor pool; whirlpool. Complimentary continental bkfst. Restaurant opp 6-9:30 am. Ck-out 11 am. Business servs avail. Game rm. Cr cds: A, C, D, DS, ER, JCB, MC, V.
⊷ ⋈ ⋈ ⋈ SC

El Reno

Motel

★ **BEST WESTERN HENSLEY'S.** *Country Club Rd, I-40 exit 123. 405/262-6490; FAX 405/262-7642.* 60 rms, 2 story. S $40-$45; D $45-$48; each $4; under 12 free. Crib $2. Pet accepted, some restrictions. TV; cable (premium). Heated pool. Complimentary continental bkfst. Restaurant adj. Ck-out 11 am. Meeting rms. Business servs avail. Cr cds: A, C, D, DS, MC, V. D ⊷ ⋈ ⋈ ⋈ SC

Enid

Motels

↙★ ★ **HOLIDAY INN.** *2901 S Van Buren (US 81) (73703). 580/237-6000; FAX 580/237-6000, ext. 177.* 100 rms, 2 story. S $46-$50; D $52-$56; each addl $6. Crib free. Pet accepted. TV; cable (premium). Pool. Restaurant 6 am-9 pm; Sun to 2 pm. Rm serv. Bar 4 pm-2 am, closed Sun. Ck-out noon. Meeting rms. Business servs avail. Sundries. Cr cds: A, C, D, DS, JCB, MC, V. D ⊷ ⋈ ⋈ ⋈ SC

★ ★ **RAMADA INN.** *3005 W Owen K. Garriott Rd (73703). 580/234-0440; FAX 580/233-1402.* 125 rms, 2 story. S $53; D $61; each addl $8; under 18 free. Crib free. Pet accepted. TV; cable (premium). Pool. Restaurant 6 am-2 pm, 5-9 pm. Rm serv. Ck-out noon. Coin lndry. Meeting rms. Microwaves avail. Cr cds: A, C, D, DS, JCB, MC, V.
D ⊷ ⋈ ⋈ ⋈ SC

Guthrie (See also Oklahoma City)

Motel

★ ★ **BEST WESTERN TERRITORIAL INN.** *2323 Territorial Dr, OK 33 at jct I-35, exit 157. 405/282-8831.* 84 units, 2 story. S $51-$65; D $61-$69; each addl $6; under 12 free. Crib free. Pet accepted, some restrictions. TV; cable. Pool. Restaurant 6 am-2 pm, 5-9 pm. Rm serv. Bar 5 pm-2 am. Ck-out 11 am. Meeting rms. Cr cds: A, C, D, DS, MC, V.
D ⊷ ⋈ ⋈ ⋈ SC

Guymon

Motel

(Rates vary during pheasant season, Pioneer Days)

★ ★ **AMBASSADOR INN.** *PO Box 5, US 64 at 21st St. 580/338-5555; FAX 580/338-1784.* 70 rms, 2 story. S $45-$55; D $48-$58; each addl $4; under 12 free. Crib free. Pet accepted, some restrictions. TV; cable (premium). Pool. Restaurant 6 am-9 pm. Bar; dancing. Ck-out 11 am. Meeting rms. Business servs avail. Valet serv. Cr cds: A, C, D, DS, MC, V. D ⊷ ⋈ ⋈ ⋈ SC

Henryetta (See also Okmulgee)

Motels

★ **GUEST HOUSE INN & DOME.** *Box 789, E Trudgeon & US 75, 1/2 mi N of jct I-40. 918/652-2581.* 84 rms, 2 story. S $55.95-$62.95; D $61-$68; each addl $7; under 19 free. Crib free. Pet accepted. TV; cable. Indoor pool. Restaurant 6 am-10 pm. Rm serv. Bar 5 pm-2 am; closed Sun. Ck-out noon. Coin lndry. Meeting rms. Business servs avail. Sundries. Rec rm. Cr cds: A, C, D, DS, JCB, MC, V. D ⊷ ⋈ ⋈ ⋈ SC

↙★ **LE BARON.** *Rte 2, Box 170, E Main & US 75. 918/652-2531; res: 800/868-3562.* 24 rms, 2 story. S $29.95; D $36.85-$39.95. Crib free. Pet accepted. TV; cable (premium). Cafe nearby. Ck-out noon. Sundries. Some in-rm whirlpools. Cr cds: A, C, D, DS, MC, V. ⊷ ⋈ ⋈ SC

Lake Murray State Park (See also Ardmore)

(7 mi SE of Ardmore, off I-35 exit 24 or 29)

Resort

✔★ **LAKE MURRAY.** *(3310 S Lake Murray Dr, #12A, Ardmore 73401) 7 mi S of Ardmore on Scenic US 77, 2 mi E of I-35, Lake Murray exit 24.* 580/223-6600; FAX 580/223-6154; res: 800/654-8240. 55 rms in lodge, 88 cottages. Mid-May-mid-Sept: S, D $58-$78; each addl $10; suites $150; lower rates rest of yr; kit. cottages (no equipt) $53-$98; cottages for 6-12, $110-$250; 1-2 bedrm cottages $78-$98; under 18 free in lodge rms; golf plans. Crib free. Pet accepted. TV in lodge rms, lobby; VCR avail (movies). Pool; lifeguard. Playgrounds. Free supervised child's activities; ages 6-18. Dining rm 7 am-10 pm. Take outs, snacks. Rm serv. Bar 1 pm-midnight. Ck-out noon, ck-in 3 pm. Meeting rms. Business servs avail. Airport transportation. Gift shop. Grocery. Tennis. 18-hole golf privileges. Miniature golf. Paddleboats. Sport facilities of Lake Murray State Park. Lawn games. Soc dir. Rec rm. Movies. Chapel; services Sun. Some refrigerators, fireplaces. Cottages widely spaced. 2,500-ft lighted, paved airstrip. On Lake Murray. State operated. Cr cds: A, C, D, DS, MC, V. 🄳 💺 🐕 🏊 🎿 🚶 🎣 📠 ⛵ 🚴 🐾 SC

Lawton (See also Duncan)

Motels

★ **DAYS INN.** *3110 NW Cache Rd (US 62) (73505).* 580/353-3104; FAX 580/353-0992; res: 800/241-3952. 96 rms, 2 story. S, D $40-$54; each addl $6; under 16 free. Crib free. Pet accepted. TV; cable. Indoor/outdoor pool; whirlpool. Complimentary full bkfst. Ck-out noon. Business servs avail. Free airport, bus depot transportation. Some bathrm phones, refrigerators. Cr cds: A, C, D, DS, MC, V. 🄳 💺 ⛵ 🚴 🐾 SC

★★ **HOWARD JOHNSON.** *1125 E Gore Blvd (73501), off I-44.* 580/353-0200; FAX 580/353-6801. 142 rms, 2 story. S, D $44-$49; suites $110-$140; each addl $5; under 16 free. Crib free. Pet accepted; $25. TV; cable (premium), VCR avail. 3 pools, 1 indoor; wading pool, sauna, poolside serv. Complimentary coffee in lobby. Restaurant 6 am-9 pm. Rm serv. Bar 4 pm-2 am. Ck-out noon. Meeting rms. Business center. In-rm modem link. Free airport transportation. Lighted tennis. Exercise equipt; weight machine, bicycle. Some refrigerators. Private patios, balconies. Picnic tables. Cr cds: A, C, D, DS, JCB, MC, V. 🄳 💺 🏖 ⛵ 🎿 🚶 🚴 🐾 SC 🛶

★★ **RAMADA INN.** *601 N 2nd St (73507).* 580/355-7155; FAX 580/353-6162. 98 rms, 2 story. S $44-$48; D $50-$54; each addl $6; under 18 free. Crib free. Pet accepted, some restrictions; $10. TV; cable (premium), VCR avail (movies). Pool. Complimentary coffee in rms. Restaurant 6 am-10 pm. Rm serv. Bar. Ck-out noon. Meeting rms. Business servs avail. Cr cds: A, C, D, DS, JCB, MC, V. 🄳 💺 ⛵ 🚴 🐾 SC

McAlester

Motels

✔★★ **COMFORT INN.** *1215 George Nigh Expy (74502), 4 mi S of jct US 270 & US 69 Bypass.* 918/426-0115; FAX 918/426-3634. 61 rms, 2 story. S $36-$40; D $44-$50; each addl $4; suite $75; under 18 free. Crib free. Pet accepted. TV; cable (premium). Pool. Restaurant 6 am-10 pm. Ck-out noon. Business servs avail. Some refrigerators. Cr cds: A, C, D, DS, MC, V. 💺 ⛵ 🚴 🐾 SC

★★ **DAYS INN.** *1217 George Nigh Expy.* 918/426-5050. 100 rms, 2 story. S $49; D $54; each addl $5; under 18 free. Crib free. Pet accepted. TV; cable (premium), VCR avail (movies $5). Indoor pool; whirlpool. Coffee in rms. Restaurant 6-10 am, 5-10 pm. Rm serv. Bar 6 pm-midnight, closed Sun. Ck-out noon. Meeting rm. Business servs avail. Some refrigerators. Near Municipal Airport. Cr cds: A, C, D, DS, JCB, MC, V. 🄳 💺 ⛵ 🚴 🐾 SC

★★ **HOLIDAY INN.** *Box 430 (74502), 2 mi SE on US 69 Bypass S.* 918/423-7766; FAX 918/426-0068. 161 rms, 2 story. S $47-$52; D $52-$57; each addl $5; suites $98-$197; under 19 free. Crib free. Pet accepted. TV; cable. Heated pool. Restaurant 6 am-10 pm. Rm serv. Bar 4 pm-2 am, closed Sun. Ck-out noon. Coin lndry. Meeting rms. Business servs avail. Bellhops. Valet serv. Sundries. Miniature golf. Exercise equipt; weight machine, bicycle, whirlpool, sauna. Game rm. Near Municipal Airport. Cr cds: A, C, D, DS, JCB, MC, V. 🄳 💺 🏊 🚶 ⛵ 🐾 SC

Miami

Motel

✔ ★ ★ **BEST WESTERN.** *2225 E Steve Owens Blvd. 918/542-6681; FAX 918/542-3777.* 80 rms. S $48-$54; D $56-$62; each addl $4; under 12 free. Crib $3. Pet accepted. TV; cable (premium). Pool. Restaurant 6 am-10 pm. Rm serv. Bar 5 pm-midnight. Ck-out noon. Airport transportation. Valet serv. Refrigerators. Cr cds: A, C, D, DS, MC, V.

✦ ⬚ ⬚ ⬚ SC

Muskogee

Motels

★ **BEST WESTERN TRADE WINDS.** *534 S 32nd St (US 64/69) (74401). 918/683-2951.* 109 rms, 2 story. S $42; D $51; each addl $5; suites $70; under 12 free. Crib $5. Pet accepted, some restrictions. TV; cable (premium). Pool; poolside serv. Bar 5 pm-2 am, closed Sun. Ck-out 11 am. Meeting rms. Business servs avail. In-rm modem link. Valet serv. Cr cds: A, C, D, DS, MC, V. ✦ ⬚ ⬚ ⬚ SC

★ ★ **RAMADA INN.** *800 S 32nd St (US 69) (74401). 918/682-4341; FAX 918/682-7400.* 135 rms, 2 story. S $52; D $58; each addl $5; suites $95-$125; under 18 free. Crib free. Pet accepted; some restrictions. TV; cable (premium), VCR avail. Indoor pool; whirlpool, sauna. Restaurant 6 am-2 pm, 5-10 pm; Sun to 2 pm. Rm serv. Bar 5 pm-2 am; closed Sun; entertainment. Ck-out noon. Meeting rms. Business servs avail. Exercise equipt; weight machine, bicycle. Game rm. Microwaves avail. Cr cds: A, C, D, DS, MC, V.

D ✦ ⬚ ✕ ⬚ ⬚ SC

Norman

Motels

★ **DAYS INN.** *609 N Interstate Dr (73069), I-35, exit 110B S; exit 109 N. 405/360-4380; FAX 405/321-5767.* 72 rms, 2 story. S $40; D $45-$50; each addl $5; suites $55; under 12 free. Pet accepted, some restrictions. TV; cable (premium). Pool. Ck-out 11 am. Some refrigerators. Business servs avail. Cr cds: A, C, D, DS, MC, V.

D ✦ ⬚ ⬚ ⬚ SC

★ **GUEST INNS.** *2543 W Main (73069). 405/360-1234; res: 800/460-4619.* 110 units, 2 story. S $42-$47; D $52-$55; suites $95; wkly plans. Crib $2. Pet accepted; $10. TV; cable (premium), VCR avail. Pool. Complimentary coffee in lobby. Restaurant open 24 hrs. Rm serv. Ck-out noon. Coin lndry. Meeting rms. Business servs avail. Valet serv. Game rm. Refrigerators, microwaves avail. Picnic tables, grills. Cr cds: A, C, D, DS, MC, V.

D ✦ ⬚ ⬚ ⬚ SC

★ ★ **RESIDENCE INN BY MARRIOTT.** *2681 Jefferson St (73072). 405/366-0900; FAX 405/360-6552.* Web www.aol.ok.whg. 126 kit. suites, 2 story. Kit. suites from $99; family, wkly, monthly rates. Crib free. Pet accepted; $75. TV; cable (premium). Pool; whirlpool. Complimentary continental bkfst. Complimentary coffee in rms. Ck-out noon. Coin lndry. Meeting rms. Business servs avail. In-rm modem link. Lighted tennis. Health club privileges. Microwaves. Cr cds: A, C, D, DS, JCB, MC, V. D ✦ ⬚ ⬚ ⬚ ⬚ SC

Oklahoma City

Motels

✔ ★ **COMFORT INN.** *4017 NW 39th Expy (US 66/270) (73112), north of downtown. 405/947-0038; FAX 405/946-7450.* 112 rms, 2 story, 15 kit. units. S, D $51-$62; each addl $6; kit. units $59-$71; under 18 free. Crib free. Pet accepted, some restrictions. TV; cable (premium), VCR avail (movies). Pool. Complimentary continental bkfst. Coffee in rms. Restaurant adj open 24 hrs. Ck-out noon. Coin lndry. Meeting rms. Business servs avail. Valet serv. Health club privileges. Some refrigerators; microwaves avail. Cr cds: A, C, D, DS, ER, JCB, MC, V. D ✦ ⬚ ⬚ ⬚ SC

✔ ★ **DAYS INN-NORTHWEST.** *2801 NW 39th St (73112), north of downtown. 405/946-0741; FAX 405/942-0181.* E-mail gertysocks@msn.com. 117 rms, 2 story. S $45-$51; D $46-$55; each addl $6; suites $150; under 16 free; wkend rates. Crib free. Pet accepted. TV; cable (premium). Coffee in rms. Pool. Restaurant 6:30 am-1 pm, 5-9 pm. Rm serv. Bar 2 pm-2 am. Ck-out 11 am. Coin lndry. Meeting rms. Business center. Valet serv. Sundries. Free airport transportation. Some bathrm phones, refrigerators. Cr cds: A, C, D, DS, JCB, MC, V. D ✦ ⬚ ⬚ ⬚ SC ✕

✔★ **HOWARD JOHNSON.** *400 S Meridian (73108), west of downtown.* 405/943-9841; FAX 405/942-1869. 96 rms, 2 story. S $49-$60; D $49-$63; each addl $6; under 17 free. Crib free. Pet accepted, some restrictions. TV; cable (premium). Pool. Complimentary continental bkfst. Complimentary coffee in rms. Restaurant adj 10:30 am-11 pm. Ck-out noon. Coin lndry. Business servs avail. Many refrigerators; microwaves avail. Cr cds: A, C, D, DS, MC, V. 🐾 ≈ ⊠ 🏋 SC

★★ **LA QUINTA.** *800 S Meridian Ave (73108), west of downtown.* 405/942-0040; FAX 405/942-0638. 168 rms, 2 story. S $69-$89; D $79-$99; each addl $10; under 18 free. Pet accepted, some restrictions. TV; cable (premium), VCR avail. Pool; wading pool, poolside serv. Complimentary continental bkfst. Restaurant 6:30 am-midnight. Rm serv. Bar from 10 am. Ck-out noon. Meeting rms. Business servs avail. In-rm modem link. Free airport, bus depot transportation. Refrigerators, microwaves avail. Cr cds: A, C, D, DS, MC, V. D 🐾 ≈ ⊠ 🏋 SC

★★ **RESIDENCE INN BY MARRIOTT.** *4361 W Reno Ave (73107), 2 blks NE of I-40 Meridian exit, west of downtown.* 405/942-4500; FAX 405/942-7777. 135 kit. suites, 1-2 story. 1-bedrm suites $105; 2-bedrm suites $135. Crib free. Pet accepted, some restrictions. TV; cable (premium), VCR avail (movies). Heated pool; whirlpool. Complimentary continental bkfst. Complimentary coffee in rms. Ck-out noon. Coin lndry. Meeting rms. Business servs avail. In-rm modem link. Valet serv. Airport transportation. Health club privileges. Refrigerators, microwaves, fireplaces. Private patios, balconies. Picnic tables, grills. Cr cds: A, C, D, DS, JCB, MC, V. D 🐾 ≈ ⊠ 🏋 SC

★★ **RICHMOND SUITES HOTEL.** *1600 Richmond Square (73118), north of downtown.* 405/840-1440; FAX 405/843-4272; res: 800/843-1440. 51 suites, 2 story. S, D $88-$150; under 18 free; wknd, hol rates. Crib $5. Pet accepted, some restrictions; $50. TV; cable (premium). Pool. Complimentary continental bkfst. Complimentary coffee in rms. Restaurant 11:30 am-2 pm, 6-9:30 pm; Fri, Sat to 10 pm; closed Sun. Rm serv. Bar; closed Sun; pianist. Meeting rms. Business servs avail. In-rm modem link. Free airport transportation. Health club privileges. Refrigerators, microwaves. Cr cds: A, C, D, DS, MC, V. D 🐾 ≈ ⊠ 🏋 SC

Motor Hotel

★★ **RADISSON.** *401 S Meridian Ave (73108), at I-40, Meridian Ave exit, west of downtown.* 405/947-7681; FAX 405/947-4253. 509 rms, 2 story. S $65-$88; D $75-$91; each addl $10; suites $89-$195; family, wknd rates. Crib free. Pet accepted, some restrictions. TV; cable (premium), VCR avail. 4 pools, 1 indoor; whirlpool, poolside serv. Restaurants 6 am-11 pm. Rm serv. Bars 11:30-2 am; entertainment. Ck-out noon. Meeting rms. Business servs avail. In-rm modem link. Bellhops. Sundries. Gift shop. Barber shop. Free airport transportation. Tennis. Exercise equipt; weights, bicycles, sauna. Rec rm. Bathrm phone, microwave, wet bar in townhouse suites; whirlpool in some suites. Cr cds: A, C, D, DS, ER, JCB, MC, V. D 🐾 🎿 ≈ 🎿 🏃 ⊠ 🏋 SC

Hotels

★★★ **EMBASSY SUITES.** *1815 S Meridian Ave (73108), west of downtown.* 405/682-6000; FAX 405/682-9835. 236 suites, 6 story. S, D $129; each addl $10; under 12 free; wkend rates. Crib free. Pet accepted; some restrictions. TV; cable (premium). Indoor pool; whirlpool. Complimentary bkfst. Complimentary coffee in rms. Restaurant 6 am-10 pm. Bar 4 pm-2 am. Ck-out noon. Meeting rms. Business center. In-rm modem link. Gift shop. Airport transportation. Exercise equipt; weights, bicycles, steam rm, sauna. Refrigerators, microwaves, wet bars. Some balconies. Atrium. Cr cds: A, C, D, DS, MC, V. D 🐾 ≈ 🎿 ⊠ 🏋 SC 🏊

★★ **FIFTH SEASON.** *6200 N Robinson Ave (73118), north of downtown.* 405/843-5558; FAX 405/840-3410; res: 800/682-0049 (exc OK), 800/522-9458 (OK). 202 rms, 3 story, 27 suites. S, D $89-$99; each addl $10; suites $95-$105; under 12 free; wkend rates; package plans. Crib free. Pet accepted, some restrictions. TV; cable (premium). Indoor pool; poolside serv. Complimentary full bkfst. Complimentary coffee in rms. Restaurant 6:30 am-2 pm, 5-10 pm. Bar 4 pm-midnight. Ck-out noon. Coin lndry. Meeting rms. Business servs avail. Gift shop. Free airport transportation. Health club privileges. Refrigerator, minibar in suites. Cr cds: A, C, D, DS, JCB, MC, V. D 🐾 ≈ ⊠ 🏋 SC

★★★ **MARRIOTT.** *3233 Northwest Expy (OK 3) (73112), west of downtown.* 405/842-6633; FAX 405/840-5338. Web www.marriott.com. 354 rms, 15 story. S, D $139-$149; suites $175-$350; studio rms $99; under 18 free; wknd rates. Crib free. Pet accepted, some restrictions. TV; cable (premium). Indoor/outdoor pool. Restaurant 6-10 pm. Bar 3 pm-2 am; Sun to midnight; entertainment Sat. Ck-out noon. Coin lndry. Convention facilities. Business servs avail. In-rm modem link. Concierge. Gift shop. Exercise equipt; weights, bicycles. Health club privileges. Some balconies. Luxury level. Cr cds: A, C, D, DS, ER, JCB, MC, V. D 🐾 ≈ 🎿 ⊠ 🏋 SC

Okmulgee *(See also Henryetta)*

Motel

★ ★ **BEST WESTERN.** *3499 N Wood Dr. 918/756-9200.* 50 units, 2 story, 6 suites. S $50-$60; D $55-$65; suites $80-$90; under 18 free. Crib avail. Pet accepted. TV; cable (premium). Pool. Restaurant 7 am-9 pm. Bar 4 pm-2 am; entertainment. Ck-out 11 am. Meeting rms. Business servs avail. In-rm modem link. Refrigerators. Cr cds: A, C, D, DS, JCB, MC, V. ⒹＰＮＮＮＮＮ

Pauls Valley

Motel

✔ ★ **DAYS INN.** *I-35 & US 19. 405/238-7548; FAX 405/238-1262.* 54 rms, 2 story. May-Sept: S $38; D $48; each addl $5; under 12 free. Crib free. Pet accepted, some restrictions. TV; cable. Complimentary continental bkfst. Restaurant nearby. Ck-out noon. Meeting rooms. Cr cds: A, C, D, DS, MC, V. ⒹＮＮＮＮＮ

Perry *(See also Stillwater)*

Motel

★ ★ **BEST WESTERN CHEROKEE STRIP.** *2819 US 77W, 2 mi W at I-35, US 77, Exit 185. 405/336-2218; FAX 405/336-9753.* 90 rms. S $45-$51; D $51-$57; each addl $5. Crib free. Pet accepted, some restrictions. TV; cable (premium), VCR avail. Indoor pool. Restaurant 6 am-10 pm. Bar 5-11 pm; closed Sun. Ck-out noon. Cr cds: A, C, D, DS, MC, V. ⒹＮＮＮＮＮＮ

Ponca City

Motel

✔ ★ **DAYS INN.** *1415 E Bradley (74604). 580/767-1406; FAX 580/762-9589.* 59 rms, 3 story. No elvtr. S $34; D $36; each addl $5; under 12 free. Crib free. Pet accepted, some restrictions. TV; cable (premium). Complimentary continental bkfst. Restaurant nearby. Ck-out noon. Microwaves avail. Cr cds: A, C, D, DS, MC, V. ⒹＮＮＮＮＮ

Inn

★ **ROSE STONE.** *120 S Third St (74601). 580/765-5699; res: 800/763-9922.* 25 rms, 2 story, 3 suites. S $54; D $64; each addl $5; suites $79; under 16 free; wkend, hol rates. Crib free. Pet accepted, some restrictions. TV; cable (premium), VCR avail (movies). Complimentary full bkfst; afternoon refreshments. Restaurant nearby. Ck-out 11 am, ck-in 3 pm. Business servs avail. In-rm modem link. Luggage handling. Concierge serv. Guest lndry. Health club privileges. Some refrigerators; microwave in suites. Former home of one of the first S & L west of the Mississippi. Totally nonsmoking. Cr cds: A, C, D, DS, ER, MC, V. ⒹＮＮＮＮ

Pryor *(See also Claremore, Miami)*

Motel

★ **PRYOR HOUSE MOTOR INN.** *123 S Mill St (US 69). 918/825-6677.* 35 rms, 2 story. S $35; D $40; each addl $5; suites $40-$42; under 12 free. Pet accepted. TV; cable (premium). Pool. Complimentary continental bkfst. Restaurant opp open 24 hrs. Ck-out 11 am. Cr cds: A, C, D, MC, V. ＮＮＮＮＮ

Sallisaw *(See also Fort Smith, AR)*

Motels

★ ★ **BEST WESTERN-BLUE RIBBON.** *706 S Kerr Blvd, at jct I-40 & US 59. 918/775-6294.* 81 rms, 2 story. June-Aug: S $39; D $45; each addl $5; suites $60-$75; under 12 free; lower rates rest of yr. Crib $5. Pet accepted; $5. TV; cable (premium). 2 pools, 1 indoor; whirlpool. Restaurant adj 6 am-10 pm. Ck-out 11 am. Lndry facilities. Meeting rms. Gift shop. Exercise equipt; weights, bicycles. Some refrigerators. Cr cds: A, C, D, DS, MC, V. ⒹＮＮＮＮＮＮ

✔ ★ **DAYS INN.** *Rte 2, On US 64W at jct US 59. 918/775-4406; FAX 918/775-4406.* 33 rms, 2 story, 3 kits. S, kits. $34; each addl $5; suites $44-$46; under 12 free. Crib $5. Pet accepted, some restrictions. TV; cable (premium). Complimentary coffee in lobby.

Restaurant adj 6 am-8:30 pm. Ck-out 11 am. Some refrigerators. Cr cds: A, C, D, DS, JCB, MC, V. [D] 🐾 ⛵ 🐾 [SC]

✔ ★ **MAGNOLIA INN.** *I-40 & US 59. 918/775-4443.* 29 rms, 2 story. S $30; D $32-$34; each addl $5; under 12 free. Crib $3. Pet accepted, some restrictions. TV; cable (premium). Pool. Complimentary coffee in lobby. Ck-out 11 am. Cr cds: A, C, D, DS, MC, V. 🐾 ⛵ ⛵ 🐾 [SC]

Shawnee

Motels

★ ★ **BEST WESTERN CINDERELLA.** *623 Kickapoo Spur, 2¹/₂ mi S of I-40.* *405/273-7010.* 92 rms, 2 story. S $46-$56; D $60-$67; each addl $5; under 18 free. Crib free. Pet accepted. TV; cable (premium). Indoor pool; poolside serv, whirlpool. Restaurant 6 am-10 pm. Rm serv. Bar 4 pm-midnight; closed Sun. Ck-out noon. Coin lndry. Meeting rms. Business servs avail. Sundries. Cr cds: A, C, D, DS, MC, V. 🐾 ⛵ ⛵ 🐾 [SC]

★ ★ **HOLIDAY INN.** *Harrison St & I-40 (74802). 405/275-4404; FAX 405/275-4998.* 106 rms, 2 story. S $55; D $65; each addl $5; suites $125; under 18 free. Crib free. Pet accepted; $20 deposit. TV; cable (premium). Pool; poolside serv. Complimentary coffee in rms. Restaurant 6 am-10 pm. Rm serv. Bar 4 pm-midnight; Fri, Sat to 2 am; entertainment Fri, Sat. Coin lndry. Meeting rms. Business servs avail. In-rm modem link. Sundries. Game rm. Some refrigerators. Minibars. Cr cds: A, C, D, DS, JCB, MC, V. [D] 🐾 ⛵ 🐾 🐾 [SC]

Stillwater *(See also Perry)*

Motor Hotels

✔ ★ ★ **BEST WESTERN.** *600 E McElroy (74075). 405/377-7010; FAX 405/743-1686.* 122 rms, 4 story. S $46-$65; D $51-$70; each addl $5; suites $95-$120; under 12 free. Crib free. Pet accepted, some restrictions. TV; cable (premium). Indoor pool. Restaurant 6 am-11 am, 4-9 pm; Sat, Sun 6 am-9 pm. Rm serv. Bar 4 pm-2 am; closed Sun. Ck-out noon. Coin lndry. Meeting rms. Business center. In-rm modem link. Valet serv. Health club privileges. Game rm. Some refrigerators. Balconies. Cr cds: A, C, D, DS, ER, JCB, MC, V. [D] 🐾 ⛵ 🐾 🐾 [SC] 🛩

★ ★ **HOLIDAY INN.** *2515 W 6th (OK 51) (74074). 405/372-0800; FAX 405/377-8212.* 141 rms, 2 story. S $46-$65; D $53-$70; each addl $7; suites from $69; town house $128; under 19 free. Crib free. Pet accepted. TV; cable (premium). Indoor pool; whirlpool, steam rm. Restaurant 6 am-8 pm. Rm serv. Bar from 4 pm. Ck-out noon. Coin lndry. Meeting rms. Valet serv. Exercise equipt; weight machines, stair machines. Game rm. Lawn games. Cr cds: A, C, D, DS, JCB, MC, V. [D] 🐾 ⛵ 🏃 🐾 🐾 [SC]

Tenkiller Ferry Lake *(See also Muskogee)*

Resort

★ ★ ★ **FIN AND FEATHER.** *(Rte 1, Box 194, Gore 74435) 8 mi N of Gore on OK 10A; I-40 Webbers Falls exit. 918/487-5148; FAX 918/487-5025.* 82 units (1-8 bedrm), 35 kits. Easter-Sept (wkends, 2-day min; kit. units, 3-day min): 1-bedrm $56-$62; 2-bedrm kit. units $95-$142; 3-5-bedrm $285; 8-bedrm $570. Closed rest of yr. Crib $5. Pet accepted, some restrictions. TV; cable (premium), VCR avail (movies). Pool; wading pool, whirlpool. Playground. Dining rms 8 am-2 pm, 6-8 pm. Box lunch, snacks. Ck-out noon, ck-in 2 pm. Grocery. Coin lndry. Convention facilities. Business servs avail. Gift shop. Tennis. Private pond. Basketball. Volleyball. Roller-skating. Lawn games. Theater. Rec rm. Game rm; mini golf. Refrigerators. Picnic tables, grills. Cr cds: A, DS, MC, V. 🐾 🐾 🎿 ⛵ ⛵ 🐾

Tulsa

Motels

★ ★ **BEST WESTERN GLENPOOL.** *(14831 S Casper, Glenpool 74033) 15 mi S, just off US 75. 918/322-5201; FAX 918/322-9604.* 63 rms, 2 story. S $45-$50; D $50-$60; each addl $5; under 18 free; higher rates special events. Crib free. Pet accepted. TV; cable (premium). Pool. Complimentary continental bkfst. Restaurant adj 6 am-9 pm. Ck-out 11 am. Coin lndry. Business servs avail. In-rm modem link. Refrigerators, microwaves. Cr cds: A, C, D, DS, JCB, MC, V. [D] 🐾 ⛵ 🐾 🐾 [SC]

★ ★ **BEST WESTERN TRADE WINDS CENTRAL INN.** *3141 E Skelly Dr (74105), I-44 Harvard exit. 918/749-5561; FAX 918/749-6312.* 167 rms, 2 story. S $64; D $68-$74; each addl $4; studio rms $71-$83; under 18 free; wkend rates. Crib free. Pet accepted, some restrictions. TV; cable (premium), VCR avail (movies). Heated pool; poolside serv. Complimentary continental bkfst. Restaurant 6 am-10 pm. Rm serv. Bar 11-2 am; closed Sun; entertainment. Ck-out noon. Coin lndry. Meeting rms. Business servs avail. In-rm modem link. Valet serv. Sundries. Airport transportation. Exercise equipt; weight machine, treadmill. Wet bar, whirlpool in suites. Some balconies. Cr cds: A, C, D, DS, MC, V.

★ ★ HAWTHORN SUITES. *3509 S 79th East Ave (74145), at jct I-44 & Broken Arrow Expy. 918/663-3900; FAX 918/664-0548.* 131 units, 3 story. S, D $69-$99; 1-bedrm kit. suites $89-$129; 2-bedrm kit. suites $139-$189; wknd rates. Pet accepted, some restrictions. Crib free. TV; cable (premium). Heated pool; whirlpool. Complimentary full bkfst; evening refreshments Mon-Thurs. Coin lndry. Meeting rms. Business servs avail. Free airport transportation. Bellhops. Valet serv. Game court. Health club privileges. Microwaves, fireplaces. Private patios, balconies. Cr cds: A, C, D, DS, MC, V.

★ ★ HOLIDAY INN-EAST/AIRPORT. *1010 N Garnett Rd (74116), near Intl Airport. 918/437-7660; FAX 918/438-7538.* 158 rms, 2 story. S, D $75; each addl $5; under 19 free. Pet accepted. TV; cable (premium). Indoor pool. Playground. Restaurant 6 am-2 pm, 5-10 pm; Sat, Sun from 7 am. Rm serv. Bar 4 pm-2 am; Sat from 4 pm. Ck-out noon. Meeting rms. Business servs avail. In-rm modem link. Bellhops. Valet serv. Free airport transportation. Health club privileges. Game rm. Microwaves avail. Cr cds: A, C, D, DS, ER, JCB, MC, V.

★ ★ LA QUINTA INN. *35 N Sheridan Rd (74115), jct I-244 & Sheridan Rd. 918/836-3931; FAX 918/836-5428.* 101 rms, 2 story. S, D $63; each addl $7; units for 6, $73; suites $89-$110; under 18 free. Crib free. Pet accepted, some restrictions. TV; cable (premium). Heated pool. Complimentary continental bkfst. Coffee in rms. Restaurant adj open 24 hrs. Ck-out noon. Business servs avail. In-rm modem link. Valet serv. Free airport transportation. Cr cds: A, C, D, DS, JCB, MC, V.

★ ★ RESIDENCE INN BY MARRIOTT. *8181 E 41st St (74145). 918/664-7241; FAX 918/622-0314.* 135 kit. units, 2 story. S, D $99-$125; under 12 free. Crib free. Pet accepted, some restrictions. TV; cable (premium), VCR avail. Pool; whirlpool. Complimentary continental bkfst. Complimentary coffee in rms. Ck-out noon. Coin lndry. Meeting rms. Business servs avail. In-rm modem link. Sundries. Valet serv. Free airport transportation. Health club privileges. Microwaves. Balconies. Picnic tables. Cr cds: A, C, D, DS, ER, JCB, MC, V.

Motor Hotel

★ ★ ★ RAMADA. *5000 E Skelly Dr (74135). 918/622-7000; FAX 918/664-9353.* 318 rms, 4 story. S, D $75-$95; each addl $6; suites from $100; under 12 free. Crib free. Pet accepted. TV; cable (premium). Pool. Restaurant 6:30 am-2 pm, 5-10 pm. Rm serv. Bar 5 pm-midnight. Ck-out noon. Coin lndry. Convention facilities. Business servs avail. Bellhops. Valet serv. Gift shop. Free airport transportation. Exercise equipt; weight machine, stair machine. Health club privileges. Private patios; balcony on suites. Cr cds: A, C, D, DS, MC, V.

Hotels

★ ★ ★ DOUBLETREE DOWNTOWN. *616 W 7th St (74127). 918/587-8000; FAX 918/587-1642.* Web www.doubletreehotels.com. 417 rms, 18 story. S, D $79-$140; each addl $15; suites $400-$700; under 18 free; wkend rates. Crib free. Pet accepted; $50 deposit ($25 refundable). Valet parking, garage. TV; cable (premium), VCR avail. Indoor pool; whirlpool, poolside serv. Coffee in rms. Restaurant 6:30 am-10:30 pm. Bar; entertainment. Ck-out noon. Convention facilities. Business center. In-rm modem link. Gift shop. Free airport transportation. Exercise equipt; weight machine, treadmill, sauna. Microwaves avail. Cr cds: A, C, D, DS, JCB, MC, V.

★ ★ ★ DOUBLETREE HOTEL AT WARREN PLACE. *6110 S Yale (74136). 918/495-1000; FAX 918/495-1944.* Web www.doubletree hotels.com. 370 rms, 10 story. S $130-$153; D $140-$173; each addl $15; suites $200-$500; under 18 free; wkend rates. Crib free. Pet accepted. Valet parking $6. TV; cable (premium), VCR avail. Indoor pool; whirlpool. Coffee in rms. Restaurants 6:30 am-11 pm. Bar 3 pm-1 am. Ck-out noon. Convention facilities. Business centers. In-rm modem link. Concierge. Gift shop. Free covered parking. Free airport transportation. Exercise equipt; weight machines, stair machines, sauna, steam rm. Health club privileges. Refrigerator, wet bar in suites. Some balconies. Elaborate landscaping. Common rms decorated with Chippendale, Hepplewhite furniture. Luxury level. Cr cds: A, C, D, DS, ER, JCB, MC, V.

★ ★ ★ SHERATON. *10918 E 41st St (74146), at Garnett Rd, at jct Broken Arrow Expy & OK 169. 918/627-5000; FAX 918/627-4003.* 325 rms, 11 story. S, D $110; suites $250-$500; under 18 free; wkend plans. Crib free. Pet accepted, some restrictions. TV;

cable (premium), VCR avail (movies). Indoor/outdoor pool; whirlpool, poolside serv. Restaurant 6 am-10 pm. Bar. Ck-out 11 am. Coin lndry. Convention facilities. Business center. In-rm modem link. Concierge. Gift shop. Free parking. Free airport transportation. Exercise equipt; weights, bicycles, sauna. Health club privileges. Luxury level. Cr cds: A, C, D, DS, JCB, MC, V. 🄳 🏕 🌊 🏋 🖿 🐾 SC 🛫

Weatherford

Motel

↙ ★ ★ **BEST WESTERN-THE MARK.** *525 E Main St. 580/772-3325; FAX 580/772-8950.* 63 rms, 1-2 story. S $45-$49; D $49-$52; each addl $3. Crib $4. Pet accepted. TV; cable (premium), VCR avail. Pool. Complimentary coffee in rms. Restaurant opp 6 am-10 pm. Ck-out noon. Meeting rms. Business servs avail. In-rm modem link. Refrigerators. Cr cds: A, C, D, DS, MC, V. 🏕 🌊 🖿 🐾 SC

Woodward

Motels

↙ ★ **HOSPITALITY INN.** *4120 Williams Ave (73801), off US 270S. 405/254-2964; FAX 405/254-2964, ext. 101.* 60 rms, 2 story. S $27; D $32; under 12 free; wkly rates. Crib avail. Pet accepted; $7. TV; cable (premium). Pool. Complimentary continental bkfst. Restaurant nearby. Ck-out 11 am. Business servs avail. Lawn games. Picnic table. Cr cds: A, DS, MC, V. 🄳 🏕 🌊 🖿 🐾

★ ★ **NORTHWEST INN.** *US 270S (73802), US 270 & 1st St. 405/256-7600; FAX 405/254-2274; res: 800/727-7606.* 124 rms, 2 story. S, D $52-$62; each addl $7; under 18 free. Crib free. Pet accepted. TV; cable (premium). Indoor pool. Restaurant 6 am-11 am, 5-10 pm. Rm serv. Bar 5 pm-2 am; closed Sun; entertainment. Ck-out noon. Coin lndry. Meeting rms. Business servs avail. Some in-rm modem links. Exercise equipt; treadmills, bicycles. Game rm. Some refrigerators. Cr cds: A, C, D, DS, MC, V.
🄳 🏕 🌊 🏋 🖿 🐾 SC

Oregon

Albany *(See also Corvallis, Salem)*

Motel

★ ★ **COMFORT INN.** *251 Airport Rd SE. 541/928-0921; FAX 541/928-8055.* 50 rms, 3 story. Apr-Aug: S $60-$75; D $67-$82; each addl $7; suites $150; kit. units $70-$107; under 18 free; wkly, monthly rates; higher rates special events; lower rates rest of yr. Crib free. Pet accepted. TV; cable. Indoor pool; whirlpool. Complimentary continental bkfst. Restaurant opp 5 am-11 pm. Ck-out noon. Coin lndry. Meeting rms. Business servs avail. Gift shop. Exercise equipt; stair machine, weights, sauna. Refrigerators avail. Cr cds: A, C, D, DS, JCB, MC, V. 🄳 🐾 ⚓ 🕴 🖊 🐾 SC

Ashland *(See also Medford)*

Motels

(Rates are generally higher during Shakespeare Festival)

★ ★ **BEST WESTERN BARD'S INN.** *132 N Main St. 541/482-0049; FAX 541/488-3259.* 92 rms, 2-3 story. June-Oct: S $92-$115; D $106-$128; each addl $10; lower rates rest of yr. Crib $10. Pet accepted; $10. TV; cable (premium). Pool; whirlpool. Ck-out 11 am. Business servs avail. Airport transportation. Downhill/x-country ski 15 mi. Refrigerators. Near Shakespeare Festival theater. Cr cds: A, C, D, DS, MC, V. 🄳 🐾 ⚓ ⚓ 🖊 🐾

★ ★ **CEDARWOOD INN.** *1801 Siskiyou Blvd. 541/488-2000; res: 800/547-4141; FAX 541/482-2000.* 59 rms, 14 with shower only, 2-3 story, 24 kit. units. Mid-May-mid-Oct: S $68; D $72; each addl $6; kit. units $78-$125; under 2 free; ski plans; lower rates rest of yr. Crib $6. Pet accepted, some restrictions. TV; cable, VCR avail (movies). Complimentary coffee in rms. Restaurant nearby. Bar. Ck-out 11 am. Business servs avail. Downhill/x-country ski 15 mi. 2 pools, 1 indoor; whirlpool. Microwaves avail. Picnic tables, grills. Cr cds: A, D, DS, MC, V. 🄳 🐾 ⚓ ⚓ 🐾 SC

✔ ★ **KNIGHTS INN.** *2359 OR 66, at I-5 exit 14. 541/482-5111; res: 800/547-4566.* 40 rms, 1-2 story. June-Sept: S $38-$51; D $42-$62; each addl $6; ski plans; lower rates rest of yr. Crib $6. Pet accepted, some restrictions; $6. TV; cable. Heated pool; whirlpool. Complimentary coffee in lobby. Restaurant 7 am-10 pm. Bar 11 am-midnight. Ck-out 11 am. Downhill ski 15 mi. Cr cds: A, D, DS, MC, V. 🄳 🐾 ⚓ ⚓ 🖊 🐾

★ ★ **QUALITY INN FLAGSHIP.** *2520 Ashland St. 541/488-2330; FAX 541/482-1068.* E-mail fsi@cdsnet.net; web www.flagshipinn.com. 60 rms, 2 story, 5 kit. units. Mid-May-Sept: S $60.75-$93.75; D $65.75-$93.75; each addl $6; kit. units $93.75-$103.75; lower rates rest of yr. Crib $6. Pet accepted, some restrictions; $6. TV; cable, VCR (movies). Heated pool. Complimentary continental bkfst. Restaurant adj open 24 hrs. Ck-out 1 pm. Business servs avail. Airport transportation. Downhill/x-country ski 13 mi. Microwaves in suites. Cr cds: A, C, D, DS, ER, JCB, MC, V. 🄳 🐾 ⚓ ⚓ 🖊 🐾 SC

✔ ★ **RODEWAY INN.** *1193 Siskiyou Blvd. 541/482-2641; FAX 541/488-1650.* 64 rms, 1-3 story. S $72-$80; D $72-$82; each addl $6. Crib $6. Pet accepted, some restrictions; $6. TV; cable (premium). Heated pool. Coffee in rms. Restaurant adj. Ck-out 11 am. Business servs avail. Downhill/x-country ski 18 mi. Microwaves avail. College opp. Cr cds: A, C, D, DS, MC, V. 🄳 🐾 ⚓ ⚓ 🖊 🐾

Motor Hotel

★ ★ ★ **WINDMILL'S ASHLAND HILLS INN & SUITES.** *2525 Ashland St, just E of I-5 exit 14. 541/482-8310; FAX 541/488-1783; res: 800/547-4747.* 230 rms, 3 story. June-Sept: S, D $94-$125; each addl $6-$11; suites $142-$260; under 18 free; lower rates rest of yr. Crib $3.50. Pet accepted. TV; cable. Heated pool; whirlpool. Restaurant 6:30 am-9 pm. Rm serv. Bar. Ck-out 11 am. Meeting rms. Business servs avail. Bellhops. Valet serv. Sundries. Beauty shop. Airport transportation. Tennis. Downhill/x-country ski 13 mi. Exercise equipt; weight machine, bicycles. Some refrigerators; microwaves avail. Balconies. Cr cds: A, C, D, DS, MC, V. 🄳 🐾 ⚓ 🕴 ⚓ 🖊 🐾 SC

Hotel

★ **MARK ANTONY.** *212 E Main St. 541/482-1721.* 79 rms, 9 story. June-Oct: S, D $65-$105; each addl $5. Pet accepted, some restrictions. Heated pool. Complimentary continental bkfst. Restaurant 7 am-11 pm. Bar. Ck-out noon. Meeting rms. Business servs avail. Airport transportation. Downhill/x-country ski 20 mi. Microwaves avail. Built 1925; some antiques. Cr cds: A, C, D, DS, ER, MC, V. 🐾 ⛷ ⛱ 🔥 SC

Astoria *(See also Cannon Beach, Seaside)*

Motels

★ **BAYSHORE MOTOR INN.** *555 Hamburg. 503/325-2205; FAX 503/325-5550; res: 800/621-0641.* 76 rms, 4 story. Some A/C. June-Oct: S $55-$80; D $65-$85; each addl $7; under 10 free; lower rates rest of yr. Crib avail. Pet accepted, some restrictions; $5. TV; cable. Indoor pool; whirlpool, sauna. Complimentary coffee. Ck-out 11 am. Coin lndry. Meeting rm. Business servs avail. In-rm modem link. Sundries. Some refrigerators. On river. Cr cds: A, C, D, DS, MC, V. D 🐾 ⛱ ⛷ 🔥 SC

★ ★ **CREST.** *5366 Leif Erickson Dr. 503/325-3141; res: 800/421-3141.* 40 rms, 1-2 story. No A/C. Mid-May-mid-Oct: S, D $48.50-$82.50; each addl $7; under 10 free; lower rates rest of yr. Crib free. Pet accepted. TV; cable (premium). Continental bkfst 8-10 am. Complimentary coffee in rms. Ck-out noon. Coin lndry. Business servs avail. Whirlpool. Some refrigerators. Balconies. On high bluff overlooking Columbia River. Cr cds: A, C, D, DS, MC, V. D 🐾 ⛷ 🔥

★ ★ **RED LION INN.** *400 Industry St, just W of bridge, on US 101. 503/325-7373; FAX 503/325-8727.* 124 rms, 2 story. No A/C. May-early Oct: S $65-$88; D $79-$92; each addl $15; under 18 free; lower rates rest of yr. Crib free. Pet accepted, some restrictions; $10. TV; cable. Restaurant 6 am-10 pm. Rm serv. Bar 11-2 am; entertainment exc Sun, Mon. Ck-out noon. Meeting rms. Business servs avail. Free airport, bus depot transportation. Private patios, balconies. Overlooks harbor; on Columbia River. Cr cds: A, C, D, DS, ER, JCB, MC, V. 🐾 ⛷ 🔥 SC

★ ★ **SHILO INN.** *(1609 E Harbor Dr, Warrenton 97146) 2 mi S on US 101, near airport. 503/861-2181; FAX 503/861-2980.* 62 rms, 4 story, 11 kit. units. May-Sept: S, D $79-$135; each addl $10; kit. units $109-$159; under 12 free; lower rates rest of yr. Crib free. Pet accepted; $7. TV; cable (premium), VCR (movies). Indoor pool; whirlpool. Restaurant 7 am-10:30 pm. Rm serv. Bar. Ck-out noon. Coin lndry. Meeting rms. Business servs avail. Sundries. Free airport transportation. Exercise equipt; weight machine, bicycle, sauna. Refrigerators. Cr cds: A, C, D, DS, ER, JCB, MC, V. D 🐾 ⛱ 🏋 ⛷ 🔥 SC

Baker City *(See also La Grande)*

Motels

✔ ★ ★ **EL DORADO.** *695 E Campbell St, at I-84 N City Center exit. 541/523-6494; FAX 541/523-6494; res: 800/537-5756.* 56 rms, 2 story. S, D $43-$50; family rates. Crib $3. Pet accepted; $2/day. TV; cable, VCR avail. Indoor pool; whirlpool. Restaurant open 24 hrs. Ck-out noon. Business servs avail. Cr cds: A, C, D, DS, MC, V. 🐾 ⛱ ⛷ 🔥 SC

★ **QUALITY INN.** *810 Campbell St. 541/523-2242; FAX 541/523-2242, ext. 400.* 54 rms, 2 story. Mid-May-mid-Sept: S $43-$47; D $46-$51; each addl $5; under 19 free; lower rates rest of yr. Crib $3. Pet accepted; $2/day. TV; cable. Pool privileges. Complimentary continental bkfst, coffee. Restaurant nearby. Ck-out noon. Meeting rms. Some refrigerators. Cr cds: A, C, D, DS, ER, JCB, MC, V. D 🐾 ⛷ 🔥 SC

Bandon *(See also Coos Bay, North Bend)*

Motel

★ **SUNSET.** *1755 Beach Loop Rd, 1/2 mi W of US 101. 541/347-2453; FAX 541/347-3636; res: 800/842-2407.* E-mail sunset@harborside.com; web www.harborside .com/home/s/sunset/sunset.htm. 58 rms, 1-3 story, 8 kits. S, D $45-$105; suites $110-$215; kit. units $66-$120; cottages w/kits $125-$215. Crib free. Pet accepted, some restrictions; $5/day. TV; cable. Restaurant 11 am-3 pm, 5-9 pm. Ck-out 11 am. Coin lndry. Business servs avail. Free airport transportation. Whirlpool. Ocean view; beach access. Cr cds: A, D, DS, MC, V. D 🐾 ⛷ 🔥

Beaverton *(See also Oregon City, Portland)*

Motor Hotel

★ ★ **GREENWOOD INN.** *10700 SW Allen Blvd. 503/643-7444; FAX 503/626-4553; res: 800/289-1300.* 250 rms, 2 story, 24 kits. S $91-$115; D $106-$130; each addl $15; kit. suites $170-$400; under 12 free; wkend rates. Crib free. Pet accepted; $10. TV; cable (premium). Pools; whirlpool. Complimentary coffee in rms. Restaurant 6:30 am-10 pm.

Rm serv. Bar 11-2 am; entertainment exc Sun. Ck-out 1 pm. Meeting rms. Business servs avail. Sundries. Gift shop. Exercise equipt; weights, bicycles, sauna. Some refrigerators. Cr cds: A, C, D, DS, MC, V. [D] 🏃 ⌦ 🏊 🏌 🏊 🐾 SC

Bend *(See also Redmond)*

Motels

★ ★ **BEST WESTERN ENTRADA LODGE.** *19221 Century Dr (97702).* 541/382-4080. 79 rms. S, D $49-$89; each addl $5; ski plans; some higher rates major hols. Crib $5. Pet accepted; $5/day. TV; cable. Pool; whirlpool. Complimentary continental bkfst. Ck-out noon. Meeting rm. Business servs avail. In-rm modem link. Downhill/x-country ski 17 mi. On 31 acres. Whitewater rafting. Cr cds: A, D, DS, MC, V. [D] 🏃 ⌦ 🏊 🐾 SC

✔ ★ **CIMARRON MOTOR INN.** *201 NE Third St (97701).* 541/382-8282; FAX 541/388-6833; res: 800/304-4050. 60 rms, 2 story. S $44; D $49-$61; each addl $5. Pet accepted, some restrictions; $5. TV; cable (premium). Heated pool. Complimentary continental bkfst. Restaurant nearby. Ck-out noon. Business servs avail. Downhill/x-country ski 20 mi. Some microwaves. Cr cds: A, D, DS, MC, V. 🏃 ⌦ 🏊 🐾 SC

★ ★ **HAMPTON INN.** *15 NE Butler Market Rd (97701).* 541/388-4114; FAX 541/389-3261. 99 rms, 2 story. S, D $71-$95; under 18 free. Crib free. Pet accepted. TV; cable (premium). Heated pool; whirlpool. Complimentary continental bkfst. Ck-out noon. Business servs avail. In-rm modem link. Cr cds: A, C, D, DS, MC, V.
[D] 🏃 ⌦ 🐾 SC

★ ★ **RED LION-NORTH.** *1415 NE Third St (97701).* 541/382-7011; FAX 541/382-7934. 75 rms, 2 story. S, D $79; each addl $10; under 18 free. Crib free. Pet accepted. TV; cable (premium). Heated pool; whirlpool. Restaurant 6 am-10 pm. Rm serv. Ck-out noon. Meeting rms. Business servs avail. In-rm modem link. Sundries. Saunas. Cr cds: A, C, D, DS, ER, MC, V. [D] 🏃 ⌦ 🐾 SC

✔ ★ ★ **RIVERHOUSE MOTOR INN.** *3075 N US 97 (97701).* 541/389-3111; FAX 541/389-0870; res: 800/547-3928 (exc OR), 800/452-6878 (OR). 220 rms, 2 story, 29 suites, 39 kits. S $55-$68; D $65-$74; each addl $6; suites $85-$175; kit. units $75-$105; under 6 free; ski, golf plans. Crib $10. Pet accepted. TV; cable (premium), VCR (movies). 2 heated pools, 1 indoor; poolside serv. Coffee in rms. Restaurant 6 am-10 pm. Rm serv. Ck-out noon. Coin lndry. Meeting rms. Business servs avail. In-rm modem link. Bellhops. Sundries. Ski area transportation. 18-hole golf, greens fee $33, pro, putting green, driving range. Exercise equipt; stair machine, rower. Some microwaves. Balconies. On the Deschutes River. Cr cds: A, C, D, DS, MC, V. [D] 🏃 🏌 ⌦ 🏊 🐾

★ ★ ★ **SHILO INN SUITES HOTEL.** *3105 O.B. Riley Rd (97701), opp Bend River Mall.* 541/389-9600; FAX 541/382-4130. 151 rms, 2 story, 54 kit. units. S, D $89-$165; each addl $10; suites $165; kit. units $105-$135; under 12 free. Crib free. Pet accepted; $7. TV; cable (premium), VCR avail. 2 pools, 1 indoor; whirlpools. Complimentary bkfst buffet. Restaurant adj 7 am-10 pm. Bar. Ck-out noon. Coin lndry. Meeting rms. Business servs avail. Sundries. Free airport transportation. Downhill ski 20 mi; x-country ski 15 mi. Exercise equipt; weight machine, bicycles, sauna. Bathrm phones, refrigerators, microwaves; some wet bars. Some balconies. On Deschutes River. Cr cds: A, C, D, DS, ER, JCB, MC, V.
[D] 🏃 ⌦ 🏊 🏌 🐾 SC

Burns

Motel

✔ ★ **BEST WESTERN PONDEROSA.** *577 W Monroe.* 541/573-2047; FAX 541/573-3828. 52 rms, 2 story. S $36-$50; D $42-$55; each addl $5. Pet accepted. TV; cable (premium), VCR avail. Pool. Complimentary coffee in lobby. Restaurant nearby. Ck-out 11 am. Business servs avail. Free airport transportation. Cr cds: A, C, D, DS, MC, V.
🏃 ⌦ 🐾 SC

Cannon Beach *(See also Astoria, Seaside)*

Motels

★ ★ ★ **SURFSAND RESORT.** *S on Hemlock St, at Gower St.* 503/436-2274; FAX 503/436-9116; res: 800/547-6100. 86 rms, 2 story, 38 kits. No A/C. June-mid-Oct: S, D $124-$165; suites, kit. units $149-$219; lower rates rest of yr. Crib $5. Pet accepted; $5/day. TV; cable (premium), VCR (movies $3). Indoor pool; whirlpool. Coffee in rms. Restaurant 8 am-midnight. Bar to 1 am. Ck-out noon. Lndry facilities. Meeting rms. Free airport transportation. Gift shop. Refrigerators, fireplaces. Balconies. On ocean, beach. View of Haystack Rock. Cr cds: A, C, D, DS, MC, V. 🅳 ♿ ⊠ ⊠ 🐾 SC

★ ★ **TOLOVANA INN.** *(Tolovana Park 97145) 1¹/₂ mi S; ¹/₄ mi W of US 101. 503/436-2211; FAX 503/436-0134; res: 800/333-8890.* 180 rms, 3 story, 96 kits. No A/C. No elvtr. S, D $68-$145; suites $154-$225; kit. units $145-$225; studio rms $131-$145. Crib free. Pet accepted; $7. TV; cable, VCR avail (movies). Indoor pool; whirlpool. Ck-out 11 am. Coin lndry. Meeting rms. Business servs avail. Game rm. Refrigerators. Some fireplaces. Private patios, balconies. Overlooks Haystack Rock. Cr cds: A, DS, MC, V. ♿ ⊠ ⊠ 🐾 SC

Motor Hotel

★ ★ **HALLMARK RESORT.** *1400 S Hemlock. 503/436-1566; FAX 503/436-0324; 800 888/448-4449.* 132 rms, 3 story, 63 kits., 5 cottages. July-Sept: S, D $99-$189; suites $125-$229; kit. units $125-$229; cottages $265-$425; lower rates rest of yr. Crib free. Pet accepted; $8/day. TV; cable (premium), VCR avail (movies). Indoor pool; wading pool; whirlpool. Complimentary coffee. Restaurant adj 8 am-9 pm. Ck-out noon, ck-in 4 pm. Coin lndry. Meeting rms. Business servs avail. Gift shop. Free local airport, bus depot transportation. Exercise equipt; weight machine, bicycles, sauna. Refrigerators. Some fireplaces, in-rm whirlpools. Balconies. On beach. Cr cds: A, C, D, DS, JCB, MC, V. 🅳 ♿ ⊠ 🏋 ⊠ 🐾 SC

Coos Bay *(See also Bandon, North Bend, Reedsport)*

Motel

★ ★ ★ **RED LION INN.** *1313 N Bayshore Dr, on US 101. 541/267-4141; FAX 541/267-2884.* 143 rms, 1-2 story. S $69-$85; D $79-$100; each addl $15; under 18 free. Crib free. Pet accepted, some restrictions. TV; cable (premium). Pool. Coffee in rms. Restaurant 6 am-10 pm. Rm serv. Bar 11-2 am; entertainment Fri, Sat. Ck-out noon. Meeting rms. Business servs avail. In-rm modem link. Free airport transportation. Microwaves avail. On Coos Bay. Cr cds: A, C, D, DS, ER, JCB, MC, V. 🅳 ♿ ⊠ ⊠ 🐾 SC

Corvallis *(See also Albany, Eugene, Salem)*

Motels

✔ ★ **ORLEANS.** *935 NW Garfield (97330). 541/758-9125; res: 800/626-1900; FAX 541/758-0544.* 61 rms, 3 story. No elvtr. S $45-$50; D $51-$54; each addl $4; suites $56-$64; under 12 free. Crib $5. Pet accepted, some restrictions. TV; cable. Pool privileges. Complimentary coffee in lobby. Restaurant nearby. Ck-out 11 am. Coin lndry. Whirlpool. Microwaves avail. Cr cds: A, D, DS, MC, V. 🅳 ♿ ⊠ 🐾 SC

✔ ★ ★ **SHANICO INN.** *1113 NW 9th (97330). 541/754-7474; FAX 541/754-2437; res: 800/432-1233.* Web www.sdl.com/shanicoinn.html. 76 rms, 3 story. S $48; D $55-$65; each addl $5; suites $64; under 12 free. Crib free. Pet accepted, some restrictions. TV. Heated pool. Continental bkfst. Restaurant adj open 24 hrs. Ck-out noon. Meeting rm. Cr cds: A, C, D, DS, MC, V. 🅳 ♿ ⊠ ⊠ 🐾 SC

Cottage Grove *(See also Eugene)*

Motel

★ ★ ★ **BEST WESTERN VILLAGE GREEN.** *725 Row River Rd, just off I-5 exit 174. 541/942-2491; FAX 541/942-2386.* 96 rms. June-Oct: S $69-$99; D $79-$110; each addl $5; suites $99-$165; under 12 free; lower rates rest of yr. Crib free. Pet accepted. TV; cable (premium). Heated pool; whirlpool. Playground. Restaurant 6:30 am-9 pm. Bar 4 pm-midnight. Ck-out 11 am. Coin lndry. Meeting rms. Business servs avail. Sundries. Covered parking. Tennis. Some refrigerators. Private patios. 18-hole golf course adj. Cr cds: A, C, D, DS, MC, V. 🅳 ♿ 🏌 ⊠ 🎿 ⊠ 🐾 SC

Eugene *(See also Corvallis, Cottage Grove)*

Motels

✔ ★ **BARRON'S TRAVELODGE.** *1859 Franklin Blvd (97403), near University of Oregon. 541/342-6383.* 60 rms, 2-3 story. S $52-$61; D $70-$80; each addl $5; suites $80-$85; under 12 free. Crib free. Pet accepted, some restrictions. TV; cable. Complimentary continental bkfst. Coffee in rms. Restaurant adj 7 am-11 pm. Ck-out 11 am. Business servs avail. Sauna. Whirlpool. Microwaves avail; refrigerators in suites. Cr cds: A, D, DS, MC, V. 🅳 ♿ ⊠ 🐾 SC

★ ★ **BEST WESTERN NEW OREGON.** *1655 Franklin Blvd (97403), opp University of Oregon.* 541/683-3669; FAX 541/484-5556. E-mail neworegon@aol.com. 129 rms, 1-2 story. S $54-$62; D $68-$78; each addl $2; suites $89-$125. Crib free. Pet accepted, some restrictions; $25 deposit. TV; cable (premium). Indoor pool; whirlpool. Complimentary coffee in lobby. Restaurant adj 6 am-11 pm. Ck-out noon. Coin lndry. Business servs avail. In-rm modem link. Exercise equipt; bicycle, stair machine, saunas. Health club privileges. Refrigerators. Cr cds: A, C, D, DS, ER, JCB, MC, V. 🄳 🖚 🌊 🏋 🖂 🐾 SC

✔ ★ **CAMPUS INN.** *390 E Broadway (97401).* 541/343-3376; res: 800/888-6313. 58 rms, 2 story. S $46; D $48-$70; each addl $8. Pet accepted; $20 refundable. TV; cable (premium). Complimentary continental bkfst. Restaurant nearby. Ck-out 11 am. In-rm modem link. Cr cds: A, C, D, DS, MC, V. 🖚 🖂 🐾 SC

★ ★ **RODEWAY INN.** *(3480 Hutton St, Springfield 97477) just off I-5 exit 195A.* 541/746-8471; FAX 541/747-1541. 58 rms, 3 story. S $60-$70; D $70-$82; each addl $6; under 18 free. Pet accepted; $10. TV; cable; VCR avail (movies). Indoor pool; whirlpool. Complimentary continental bkfst. Restaurant adj open 24 hrs. Ck-out noon. Coin lndry. Meeting rms. Business servs avail. In-rm modem link. Exercise equipt; bicycles, stair machine. Microwaves avail. Cr cds: A, C, D, DS, ER, JCB, MC, V.
🄳 🖚 🌊 🏋 🖂 🐾 SC

★ ★ **SHILO INN.** *(3350 Gateway St, Springfield 97477) 3¹/₂ mi NE, just E of I-5 exit 195A.* 541/747-0332; FAX 541/726-0587. 143 rms, 2 story, 43 kits. S, D $65-$75; each addl $10; kit. units $79-$89; under 12 free; wkly, monthly rates. Pet accepted, some restrictions; $7/day. TV; cable (premium), VCR avail (movies). Pool. Complimentary continental bkfst. Restaurant 6 am-11 pm. Rm serv. Bar 11-2 am. Ck-out noon. Coin lndry. Meeting rms. Business servs avail. Free airport transportation. Some microwaves. Cr cds: A, C, D, DS, ER, JCB, MC, V. 🄳 🖚 🌊 🖂 🐾 SC

Motor Hotels

★ ★ **RED LION INN.** *205 Coburg Rd (97401), I-5 exit 194B, then I-105 1 mi to exit 1.* 541/342-5201; FAX 541/485-2314. 137 rms, 2 story. S $80-$85; D $95-$100; each addl $15; studio rms $80-$100; under 18 free. Crib free. Pet accepted, some restrictions. TV; cable, VCR avail. Heated pool; whirlpool. Restaurant 6 am-10 pm; closed Sun. Rm serv. Bar 3 pm-2 am, Sun to midnight; entertainment. Ck-out noon. Meeting rms. Business servs avail. In-rm modem link. Bellhops. Sundries. Free airport, RR station, bus depot transportation. Exercise equipt; weight machine, bicycle. Some private patios, balconies. Cr cds: A, C, D, DS, ER, JCB, MC, V. 🄳 🖚 🌊 🏋 🖂 🐾

★ ★ **VALLEY RIVER INN.** *1000 Valley River Way (97440), off I-5 exit 194B, northbound and southbound, follow signs to Valley River Center.* 541/687-0123; FAX 541/683-5121; res: 800/543-8266. E-mail reserve@valleyriverinn.com; web www.valleyriverinn.com. 257 rms, 2-3 story. S, D $135-$180; suites $175-$300; under 18 free. Crib free. Pet accepted, some restrictions. TV; cable (premium), VCR avail. Heated pool; whirlpool, wading pool, poolside serv. Restaurant 6:30 am-2 pm, 5:30-9:30 pm. Rm serv. Bar 11:30 am-midnight, Sun 9 am-11 pm; entertainment. Ck-out 11 am. Meeting rms. Business servs avail. In-rm modem link. Bellhops. Valet serv. Concierge. Free airport, RR station, bus depot transportation. Exercise equipt; bicycles, stair machine, sauna. Health club privileges. Private patios, balconies. Logging memorabilia. Some rms have views of Willamette River. Cr cds: A, C, D, DS, MC, V. 🄳 🖚 🌊 🏋 🖂 🐾 SC

Hotel

★ ★ ★ **HILTON.** *66 E Sixth Ave (97401).* 541/342-2000; FAX 541/302-6660. 272 rms, 12 story. S $130; D $145; each addl $15; suites $290-$360; under 18 free. Pet accepted, some restrictions; $25. TV; cable (premium). Indoor pool; whirlpool. Restaurant 6:30 am-10 pm. Rm serv to 1 am. Bar; entertainment. Ck-out noon. Convention facilities. Business center. Concierge. Gift shop. Free covered parking. Free airport, RR station, bus depot transportation. Exercise equipt; weights, treadmills. Health club privileges. Some refrigerators; microwaves avail. Balconies. Luxury level. Cr cds: A, C, D, DS, ER, JCB, MC, V.
🄳 🖚 🌊 🏋 🖂 🐾 SC 🏌

Florence *(See also Reedsport, Yachats)*

Motel

✔ ★ **MONEY SAVER.** *170 US 101, just N of bridge.* 541/997-7131. 40 rms, 2 story. No A/C. June-Sept: S $46-$48; D $52-$60; each addl $6; lower rates rest of yr. Crib $6. Pet accepted, some restrictions; $5. TV; cable. Complimentary coffee in lobby. Restaurant nearby. Ck-out 11 am. Cr cds: A, DS, MC, V. 🄳 🖚 🖂 🐾 SC

Grants Pass *(See also Medford)*

Motels

★ ★ **BEST WESTERN INN AT THE ROGUE.** *8959 Rogue River Hwy (97527).* *541/582-2200; FAX 541/582-1415.* 54 rms, 2 story. June-Sept: S, D $69.50-$159; each addl $5; suites $129-$179; under 12 free; lower rates rest of yr. Crib $5. Pet accepted, some restrictions; $10. TV; cable (premium), VCR avail. Heated pool; whirlpool. Complimentary continental bkfst. Restaurant adj 6 am-10 pm. Bar 5-10 pm. Ck-out 11 am. Coin lndry. Meeting rms. Business servs avail. Exercise equipt; weights, bicycles. Some refrigerators, microwaves, minibars. Balconies. Cr cds: A, C, D, DS, MC, V.
🅳 🐾 ➤ ⛭ 🏋 🏊 🐾 SC

★ ★ **HOLIDAY INN EXPRESS.** *105 NE Agness Ave (97526), I-5 exit 55.* 541/471-6144; FAX 541/471-9248. Web www.rogueweb.com/holiday. 80 rms, 4 story. Mid-May-mid-Sept: S $74; D $79-$84; each addl $5; suites $129; under 19 free; higher rates Boatnik Festival; lower rates rest of yr. Crib free. Pet accepted, some restrictions; $5/day. TV; cable (premium). Heated pool; whirlpool. Complimentary continental bkfst. Restaurant adj 6 am-11 pm. Ck-out 11 am. Guest lndry. Meeting rms. Business center. In-rm modem link. Sundries. Health club privileges. Cr cds: A, C, D, DS, JCB, MC, V. 🅳 🐾 ➤ ⛭ 🐾 SC 🏊

★ ★ **REDWOOD.** *815 NE Sixth St (97526).* 541/476-0878; FAX 541/476-1032. E-mail redwood@chatlink.com; web www.chatlink.com/~red wood. 26 rms, 9 kits. Mid-May-Sept: S $55-$80; D $79-$84; each addl $5; kit. units $68-$95; lower rates rest of yr. Crib $5. Pet accepted, some restrictions; $10. TV; cable (premium). Heated pool. Playground. Complimentary continental bkfst. Restaurant opp 6 am-10 pm. Guest lndry. Ck-out 11 am. Microwaves avail. Picnic tables. Cr cds: A, C, D, DS, MC, V. 🅳 🐾 ➤ ⛭ 🐾 SC

★ **ROGUE VALLEY.** *7799 Rogue River Hwy (97527), I-5 exit 48.* 541/582-3762. 8 rms, 6 with shower only, 1 story. June-Sept: S $45-49; D $72; each addl $5; lower rates rest of yr. Crib free. Pet accepted, some restrictions. TV; cable. Heated pool. Complimentary coffee in rms. Ck-out 11 am. Refrigerators; many microwaves. Picnic tables. On river. Cr cds: MC, V. 🅳 🐾 ➤ ⛭

✔ ★ **ROYAL VUE.** *110 NE Morgan Lane (97526).* 541/479-5381; res: 800/547-7555 (exc OR), 800/452-1452 (OR). 60 rms, 2 story. S $40-$44; D $49-$66; suites $64. Crib $4. Pet accepted. TV; cable (premium), VCR avail. Heated pool; whirlpool, poolside serv. Coffee in rms. Restaurant 6 am-10 pm. Rm serv. Bar 11-2 am; entertainment Thur-Sun. Ck-out noon. Coin lndry. Sauna, steam rm. Refrigerator, minibar in suites. Balconies. Cr cds: A, C, D, DS, MC, V. 🐾 ➤ ⛭ 🐾 SC

★ ★ **SHILO INN.** *1880 NW Sixth St (97526).* 541/479-8391; FAX 541/474-7344. 70 rms, 2 story. May-Sept: S, D $59-$79; each addl $10; under 12 free; lower rates rest of yr. Crib free. Pet accepted; $7. TV; cable (premium). Pool. Continental bkfst. Restaurant adj open 24 hrs. Ck-out noon. Meeting rm. Sauna, steam rm. Microwaves avail. Cr cds: A, C, D, DS, ER, JCB, MC, V. 🅳 🐾 ➤ ⛭ 🐾 SC

Motor Hotel

★ ★ ★ **RIVERSIDE INN RESORT & CONFERENCE CENTER.** *971 SE Sixth St (97526).* 541/476-6873; FAX 541/474-9848; res: 800/334-4567. Web www.riversideinn .com. 174 rms, 3 story. S, D $65-$105; each addl $10; suites $140-$275; cottage $350; under 11 free. Crib $10. Pet accepted, some restrictions; $15. TV; cable, VCR avail (movies). 2 heated pools. Complimentary coffee in rms. Restaurant 6 am-10 pm. Bar 11-1 am. Ck-out 11 am. Meeting rms. Business servs avail. Sundries. Gift shop. Some in-rm whirlpools; microwaves avail. Balconies. Jet boat trips May-Sept. Cr cds: A, C, D, DS, MC, V. 🅳 🐾 ➤ ⛭ 🐾 SC

Hermiston *(See also Pendleton)*

Motel

★ **SANDS.** *835 N First St.* 541/567-5516; FAX 541/567-5516. 39 rms, 3 kit, 1-2 story. S $35; D $42; each addl $5; suites $58; wkly rates. Crib $3. Pet accepted; $5. TV; cable (premium). Pool. Restaurant adj 5 am-10 pm. Bar adj. Ck-out 11 am. Business servs avail. Cr cds: A, D, DS, MC, V. 🐾 ➤ ⛭ 🐾

Hood River *(See also The Dalles)*

Motel

✔★★ **VAGABOND LODGE.** *4070 Westcliff Dr. 541/386-2992; FAX 541/386-3317.* 40 rms, 23 A/C, 5 suites. S $41-$61; D $47-$77; each addl $6; suites $61-$82; lower rates winter. Crib $5. Pet accepted. TV; cable. Playground. Restaurant adj 7 am-9 pm. Ck-out 11 am. Picnic tables. On 5 wooded acres; overlooks Columbia River Gorge. Cr cds: A, C, D, MC, V. 🐾 ⊠ ⊠

Hotel

★★★ **COLUMBIA GORGE.** *4000 Westcliff Dr, I-84 exit 62. 541/386-5566; FAX 541/387-5414; res: 800/345-1921.* 40 rms, 3 story. No A/C. S $125; D $150-$270; each addl $30. Pet accepted. TV; cable, VCR avail. Complimentary bkfst. Restaurant 8 am-10 pm. Bar to midnight. Ck-out noon. Business servs avail. Free RR station, bus depot transportation. Restored building (1920s) with formal gardens; "Jazz Age" atmosphere. Windsurfing nearby. Overlooks river, waterfall. Cr cds: A, C, D, DS, MC, V. 🐾 ⊠ ⊠

Inn

★★ **INN OF THE WHITE SALMON.** *(172 W Jewett, White Salmon 98672) I-84 E to exit 64, E on WA 14 for 1½ mi, left at flashing light, 1.6 mi to inn. 509/493-2335; res: 800/972-5226.* 16 rms, 2 story, 5 suites. S $75; D $89-$115; suites $99-$115. Crib free. Pet accepted. TV. Complimentary full bkfst; coffee in common rm. Restaurant nearby. Ck-out noon, ck-in 3 pm. Luggage handling. Picnic tables. European-style inn built in 1937; antique decor, original art. Cr cds: A, C, D, DS, MC, V. 🐾 ⊠ ⊠

John Day

Motels

✔★ **DREAMERS LODGE.** *144 N Canyon Blvd, just N of jct US 26, 395. 541/575-0526; FAX 541/575-2733; res: 800/654-2849.* 25 rms, 2 story. S $40-$42; D $46-$48; each addl $2; suites $45-$60. Crib $3. Pet accepted. TV; cable (premium). Complimentary coffee in rms. Restaurant nearby. Ck-out 11 am. Business servs avail. Free airport transportation. X-country ski 20 mi. Refrigerators. Cr cds: A, C, D, DS, MC, V. 🐾 ⊠ ⊠ ⊠ SC

★ **SUNSET INN.** *390 W Main St. 541/575-1462; FAX 541/575-1471; res: 800/452-4899.* 43 rms, 2 story. S $45-$48.50; D $65; each addl $5; suites $110. Crib $5. Pet accepted, some restrictions. TV, cable (premium). Indoor pool; whirlpool. Restaurant 5 am-11 pm. Bar. Ck-out 11 am. Meeting rms. Business servs avail. Free airport transportation. Cr cds: A, D, DS, MC, V. D 🐾 ⊠ ⊠ ⊠ SC

Klamath Falls

Motels

★★ **BEST WESTERN KLAMATH INN.** *4061 S Sixth St (97603), near Kingsley Field Airport. 541/882-1200; FAX 541/882-2729.* 52 rms, 2 story. S, D $59-$79; each addl $8. Crib $4. Pet accepted, some restrictions. TV; cable (premium), VCR avail. Indoor pool. Complimentary continental bkfst. Restaurant adj 6 am-10:30 pm. Ck-out noon. Meeting rms. Microwaves; some in-rm whirlpools, refrigerators. Cr cds: A, C, D, DS, MC, V. D 🐾 ⊠ ⊠ ⊠ SC

✔★ **CIMARRON MOTOR INN.** *3060 S Sixth St (97603). 541/882-4601; FAX 541/882-6690; res: 800/742-2648.* 163 rms, 2 story. S $45; D $50-$55; each addl $5. Pet accepted; $5. TV; cable (premium). Heated pool. Continental bkfst. Restaurant adj open 24 hrs. Ck-out noon. Meeting rm. Business servs avail. Cr cds: A, D, DS, MC, V. D 🐾 ⊠ ⊠ ⊠ SC

★★ **QUALITY INN.** *100 Main St (97601). 541/882-4666; FAX 541/883-8795; res: 800/732-2025.* Web www.multi.com/molatore. 80 rms, 2 story, 4 suites. S $63; D $63-$95.50; each addl $5; suites $93.50; under 18 free. Crib free. Pet accepted, some restrictions. TV; cable (premium). Heated pool. Complimentary continental bkfst. Coffee in rms. Restaurant adj. Ck-out noon. Coin lndry. Meeting rms. Business servs avail. In-rm modem link. Some in-rm whirlpools, microwaves. Cr cds: A, C, D, DS, JCB, MC, V. D 🐾 ⊠ ⊠ ⊠ SC

✔★ **TRAVELODGE.** *11 Main St (97601). 541/882-4494; FAX 541/882-8940.* 47 rms, 2 story. May-Oct: S $38-$42; D $48-$58; each addl $5; under 17 free. Pet accepted, some restrictions. TV; cable. Heated pool. Complimentary continental bkfst. Complimentary coffee in rms. Restaurant nearby. Ck-out 11 am. Some refrigerators, microwaves. Cr cds: A, C, D, DS, MC, V. 🐾 🌊 🐾 SC

Motor Hotel

★ ★ ★ **SHILO INN SUITES.** *2500 Almond St (97601), 2 mi NW on US 97 N (Business), exit OIT.* 541/885-7980; FAX 541/885-7959. 143 suites, 4 story. June-Sept: S, D $99-$119; each addl $10; kit. units $149; under 12 free; golf plans; lower rates rest of yr. Crib free. Pet accepted, some restrictions; $7. TV; cable (premium), VCR (movies). Complimentary continental bkfst. Complimentary coffee in rms. Restaurant 6 am-11 pm. Rm serv. Bar 11-2 am. Ck-out noon. Meeting rms. Business center. In-rm modem link. Bellhops. Valet serv. Sundries. Coin lndry. Free airport, RR station transportation. Exercise equipt; bicycle, stair machine, sauna. Health club privileges. Indoor pool; whirlpool. Bathrm phones, refrigerators, microwaves, wet bars. Cr cds: A, D, DS, MC, V. D 🐾 🌊 🕺 🌊 🐾 SC 🚶

La Grande *(See also Baker City, Pendleton)*

Motel

★ ★ **HOWARD JOHNSON.** *2612 Island Ave, 1 mi E on OR 82, just E of I-84N, exit 261.* 541/963-7195; FAX 541/963-4498. 146 rms, 2 story. S, D $70-$77; each addl $5; under 12 free; lower rates rest of yr. Crib $3.50. Pet accepted. TV; cable (premium). Heated pool; whirlpool. Complimentary continental bkfst. Restaurant adj open 24 hrs. Ck-out noon. Free lndry. Meeting rms. Business servs avail. Exercise equipt; weights, bicycles, sauna. Refrigerators. Private patios, balconies. Cr cds: A, C, D, DS, ER, MC, V.

D 🐾 🌊 🕺 🌊 🌊 🐾 SC

Lakeview

Motel

✔ ★ **LAKEVIEW LODGE.** *301 North G St, just S of jct US 395, OR 140.* 541/947-2181; FAX 541/947-2572. Web bobkings@triax.com. 40 rms. S $38-$46; D $42-$50; each addl $4; family units $42-$60; kit. units $4-$6 addl; higher rates Labor Day wknd. Crib free. Pet accepted. TV; cable (premium). Complimentary coffee in rm. Restaurant nearby. Ck-out 11 am. Downhill/x-country ski 8 mi. Exercise equipt; bicycle, stair machine, sauna. Whirlpool. Microwaves avail. Cr cds: A, C, D, DS, MC, V. D 🐾 🐾 🕺 🌊 🐾 SC

Lincoln City *(See also Newport, Tillamook)*

Motels

★ ★ **BEST WESTERN LINCOLN SANDS INN.** *535 NW Inlet Ave.* 541/994-4227; FAX 541/994-2232. 33 kit. suites, 3 story. Suites $89-$349. Crib $10. Pet accepted, some restrictions. TV; cable (premium), VCR. Heated pool; whirlpool. Complimentary continental bkfst. Complimentary coffee in rms. Restaurant nearby. Ck-out 11 am. In-rm modem link. Sauna. Microwaves. Balconies. Picnic table. On beach. Cr cds: A, C, D, DS, MC, V.

D 🐾 🌊 🌊 🐾 SC

★ **COHO INN.** *1635 NW Harbor Ave, just W of US 101.* 541/994-3684; FAX 541/994-6244; res: 800/848-7006. 50 rms, 3 story, 31 kits. No A/C. No elvtr. June-Oct: S, D $96; each addl $6; suites $104-$116; lower rates rest of yr. Pet accepted, some restrictions; $6. TV; cable (premium). Complimentary coffee in lobby. Ck-out 11 am. Business servs avail. Sauna. Whirlpool. Some fireplaces. Some private patios, balconies. Oceanfront; beach nearby. Cr cds: A, DS, MC, V. 🐾 🌊 🐾

★ ★ **SHILO INN-OCEANFRONT RESORT.** *1501 NW 40th Place.* 541/994-3655; FAX 541/994-2199. 247 rms, 3-4 story. Mid-June-mid-Sept: S $49-$102; D $84-$110; suites $169-$240; kit. unit $125-$160; under 12 free; lower rates rest of yr. Crib free. Pet accepted, some restrictions; $6/day. TV; cable (premium), VCR avail. Indoor pool; whirlpool. Restaurant adj 7-2 am. Rm serv. Bar 11-1 am. Ck-out noon. Coin lndry. Meeting rms. Business center. Free local airport, bus depot transportation. Exercise equipt; weight machine, stair machine, sauna. Health club privileges. Refrigerators, microwaves; some bathrm phones. Picnic tables. On beach. Cr cds: A, C, D, DS, ER, JCB, MC, V.

D 🐾 🌊 🕺 🌊 🌊 🐾 SC 🚶

Lodge

★ ★ ★ **SALISHAN.** *(US 101, Gleneden Beach 97388) 1 blk E of US 101.* 541/764-2371; FAX 541/764-3681; res: 800/452-2300. Web www.dolce.com. Nestled on a 700-acre hillside forest preserve on the Oregon coast, Salishan comprises multiple buildings connected by bridges and walkways. Views of the ocean, forest and golf course are available. Rooms feature wood-burning fireplaces, balconies and prints and lithographs by Oregon artists. 205 rms, 2-3 story. No elvtr. May-Oct: S, D $175-$265; each addl $15; under 6 free; lower rates rest of yr. Crib $10. Pet accepted, some restrictions; $15. TV; cable (premium), VCR avail. Indoor pool; whirlpool, hydrotherapy pool. Dining rm 7 am-10 pm. Rm serv. Bar noon-1:30 am; entertainment. Ck-out noon. Meeting rms. Business servs avail. Bellhops. Valet serv. Concierge. Shopping mall. Indoor/outdoor lighted tennis, pro. 18-hole golf, greens fee $50-$55, pro, putting green, covered driving range. Self-guided nature trail. Exercise rm; instructor, weights, bicycles, sauna. Massage. Game rm. Art gallery. Refrigerators. Library. Cr cds: A, C, D, DS, MC, V. [D] [symbols]

Madras *(See also Redmond)*

Motel

✔ ★ ★ **SONNY'S.** *1539 SW US 97. 541/475-7217; FAX 541/475-6547; res: 800/624-6137.* 44 rms, 2 story, 2 suites, 2 kits. S $47; D $55; each addl $7; suites $80-$105; kit. units $95; under 6 free. Crib $4. Pet accepted; $7. TV; cable (premium). Heated pool; whirlpool. Complimentary continental bkfst. Restaurant 11 am-10 pm. Bar 11 am-midnight. Ck-out 11 am. Coin lndry. Business servs avail. Lawn games. Some microwaves; refrigerators avail. Cr cds: A, C, D, DS, MC, V. [D] [symbols]

Resort

★ ★ ★ **KAH-NEE-TA.** *(Box K, Warm Springs 97761) 14 mi NW on US 26 to Warm Springs, then 11 mi N. 541/553-1112; FAX 541/553-1071; res: 800/554-4786.* 139 rms in 3-4 story lodge, 32 condos, 20 unfurnished teepees in village. Lodge: S, D $115-$140; suites $170-$275; condos: `$109.95`; village teepees for 5, $55; under 6 free in lodge; mid-wk packages (off season). Pet accepted. TV; cable (premium). 2 heated pools; whirlpools, poolside serv, private hot mineral baths at village. Dining rm 7 am-10 pm. Snacks. Salmon Bake Sat (Memorial Day-Labor Day). Bars 11 am-2 pm. Ck-out 11:30 am, ck-in 4:30 pm. Lodge meeting rms. Gift shop. Tennis. 18-hole golf, greens fee $32, pro, putting green, driving range. Exercise rm; instructor, weights, bicycles, sauna. Massage. Kayak float trips. Trails. Bicycles. Rec dir; entertainment. Game rm. Authentic Native American dances Sun May-Sept. Varied accommodations. Owned by Confederated Tribes of Warm Springs Reservation. RV and trailer spaces avail. Cr cds: A, C, D, DS, MC, V.

[D] [symbols]

McMinnville *(See also Newberg, Oregon City, Salem)*

Motel

✔ ★ **PARAGON.** *2065 S OR 99W. 503/472-9493; FAX 503/472-8470; res: 800/525-5469.* 55 rms, 2 story. S $36; D $43; each addl $3; suites $86. Crib $2. Pet accepted; $5. TV; cable (premium), VCR avail. Heated pool. Complimentary continental bkfst. Restaurant nearby. Ck-out noon. Coin lndry. Meeting rm. Business servs avail. Refrigerators. Cr cds: A, D, DS, MC, V. [symbols]

Guest Ranch

★ ★ **FLYING M RANCH.** *(23029 NW Flying M Rd, Yamhill 97148) N on OR 47 to Yamhill, left on Oak Ridge Rd, left on Fairdale Rd, left on NW Flying M Rd. 503/662-3222; FAX 503/662-3202.* 28 rms in main building, 8 kit. cottages. S, D $50-$70; kit. cottages $75-$200. Pet accepted. TV in lounge. Dining rm 8 am-8 pm; Fri, Sat & hols to 10 pm. Box lunches. Picnics. Bar; entertainment Sun, dancing Fri, Sat. Ck-out 11 am, ck-in 4 pm. Grocery, coin lndry, package store 10 mi. Meeting rms. Business servs avail. Gift shop. Tennis. Swimming pond. X-country ski adj. Snowmobiling, sleighing. Hiking. Overnight trail rides. Lawn games. Fishing/hunting. Balconies. Picnic tables, grills. Cr cds: A, D, DS, MC, V. [D] [symbols]

Medford *(See also Ashland, Grants Pass)*

Motels

★ ★ **BEST WESTERN PONY SOLDIER.** *2340 Crater Lake Hwy (97504), just E of I-5 exit 30. 541/779-2011; FAX 541/779-7304.* 72 rms, 2 story. May-Sept: S $75-$82; D $90-$96; each addl $5; under 12 free; lower rates rest of yr. Crib $3. Pet accepted, some restrictions. TV; cable (premium). Heated pool; whirlpool. Complimentary continental bkfst. Restaurant adj open 24 hrs. Ck-out noon. Free guest lndry. In-rm modem link. Downhill/x-country ski 20 mi. Health club privileges. Refrigerators, microwaves. Cr cds: A, C, D, DS, MC, V. [D] [symbols]

✔ ★ **CEDAR LODGE.** *518 N Riverside Ave (97501). 541/773-7361; FAX 541/776-1033; res: 800/282-3419.* Web www.prairieweb.j/arrons/hotel/usa/or/cedarlodge.htm. 79 rms, 1-2 story. May-Oct: S $32-$37; D $38-$45; each addl $5; suites $45-$62; kit. unit $52;

under 12 free; wkly rates; lower rates rest of yr. Crib $5. Pet accepted, some restrictions. TV; cable. Heated pool. Restaurant adj 6 am-10 pm. Bar 10-2 am. Ck-out 11 am. Downhill/x-country ski 20 mi. Some microwaves. Cr cds: A, C, D, DS, MC, V. 🐾 🏊 🏊 🎿 🎿 🐾 SC

★ ★ **HORIZON MOTOR INN.** *1154 E Barnett Rd (97504), E of I-5 exit 27.* 541/779-5085; *res:* 800/452-2255. Web www.horizoninns.com. 129 rms, 2 story. S $50-$58; D $55-$61; each addl $5; suites $100-$150; under 17 free. Crib $5. Pet accepted; $10. TV; cable (premium). Heated pool; whirlpool. Complimentary coffee in lobby. Restaurant 6 am-midnight. Bar. Ck-out noon. Airport transportation. Downhill/x-country ski 20 mi. Sauna. Some microwaves. Cr cds: A, C, D, MC, V. D 🐾 🏊 🎿 🎿 🐾 SC

★ ★ **WINDMILL INN.** *1950 Biddle Rd (97504), I-5 exit 30, near Medford-Jackson County Airport.* 541/779-0050; *res:* 800/547-4747. 123 rms, 2 story. S $72; D $85; kit. units $95; under 18 free. Crib $3.50. Pet accepted. TV; cable (premium). Heated pool; whirlpool. Complimentary continental bkfst. Restaurant adj 6 am-11 pm. Meeting rm. Business servs avail. Valet serv. Sundries. Free airport, bus depot transportation. Sauna. Health club privileges. Bicycles. Microwaves avail. Library. Cr cds: A, C, D, DS, MC, V. D 🐾 🏊 ✈ 🎿 🐾 SC

Motor Hotels

★ ★ ★ **DOUBLETREE.** *200 N Riverside Ave (97501).* 541/779-5811; FAX 541/779-7961. Web www.doubletreehotel.com. 186 rms, 2 story. S $76-$86; D $79-$89; each addl $10; suites $250; under 18 free. Crib free. Pet accepted; $50 deposit. TV; cable. 2 heated pools. Restaurant 6 am-10 pm; dining rm 11:30 am-2 pm, 5-10 pm; Sun 10 am-2 pm. Rm serv. Bar 3 pm-midnight; Fri, Sat to 2 am; entertainment. Ck-out noon. Coin lndry. Meeting rms. Business servs avail. In-rm modem link. Bellhops. Sundries. Free airport transportation. Downhill/x-country ski 20 mi. Health club privileges. Some private patios, balconies. Cr cds: A, C, D, DS, ER, MC, V. D 🐾 🏊 🎿 ✈ 🎿 🐾 SC

🛏 ★ ★ **RESTON.** *2300 Crater Lake Hwy (97504), E of I-5 exit 30, near Medford-Jackson County Airport.* 541/779-3141; FAX 541/779-2623; *res:* 800/779-7829. E-mail maryc@restonhotel.com; web www.restonhotel.com. 164 rms, 2 story. S, D $65; each addl $5; suites $120; under 18 free. Crib free. Pet accepted, some restrictions; $10. TV; cable. Indoor pool. Restaurant 6:30 am-1 pm, 5-10 pm. Rm serv. Bar 5 pm-midnight, Thurs-Sat to 2 am. Ck-out noon. Meeting rms. Business servs avail. Sundries. Airport transportation. Microwaves avail. Cr cds: A, C, D, DS, ER, MC, V. D 🐾 🏊 ✈ 🎿 🐾 SC

Mount Hood National Forest (See also Hood River, The Dalles)

Motel

★ **MT HOOD INN.** *(Box 400, 87450 Government Camp Loop, Government Camp 97028)* On US 26. 503/272-3205; FAX 503/272-3307; *res:* 800/443-7777. 56 rms, 2 story, 4 suites. No A/C. S, D $95-$135; each addl $10; suites $115; under 12 free. Crib $5. Pet accepted; $5. TV; cable (premium), VCR avail. Complimentary continental bkfst. Restaurant nearby. Ck-out noon. Coin lndry. Meeting rms. Business servs avail. Downhill ski 1/4 mi; x-country ski adj. Whirlpool. Some refrigerators, wet bars. Picnic tables. Cr cds: A, D, DS, MC, V. D 🐾 🏊 🎿 🐾

Newberg (See also Beaverton, McMinnville, Oregon City, Portland, Salem)

Motel

★ ★ **SHILO INN.** *501 Sitka Ave.* 503/537-0303; FAX 503/537-0442. 60 rms, 3 story. S, D $65-$79; each addl $10; suites $75; kit. units $79; under 12 free. Crib free. Pet accepted; $7/day. TV; cable (premium), VCR avail. Heated pool; whirlpool. Complimentary continental bkfst, coffee. Restaurant nearby. Ck-out noon. Coin lndry. Meeting rms. Business servs avail. Valet serv. Sundries. Exercise equipt; weights, bicycles, sauna. Bathrm phones, refrigerators, wet bars. Cr cds: A, C, D, DS, ER, JCB, MC, V. D 🐾 🏊 🎿 🎿 🐾 SC

Newport (See also Lincoln City, Yachats)

Motels

★ ★ **SHILO INN OCEAN FRONT RESORT.** *536 SW Elizabeth St, just W of US 101.* 541/265-7701; FAX 541/265-5687. 179 rms, 4 story, 10 kits. Mid-June-mid-Sept: S, D $149-$205; each addl $15; kit. suites $199-$395; lower rates rest of yr. Pet accepted, some restrictions; $7/day. TV; cable (premium), VCR. Indoor pools. Restaurant 7 am-10 pm. Rm serv. Bar 11-2 am; entertainment Fri, Sat. Ck-out noon. Meeting rms. Coin lndry. Business servs avail. Free airport transportation. Refrigerators, microwaves. On beach. Cr cds: A, C, D, DS, ER, JCB, MC, V. 🄳 💺 ⊠ ⊠ 🐾 SC

★ **WHALER.** *155 SW Elizabeth St. 541/265-9261; FAX 541/265-9515; res: 800/433-9444.* 73 rms, 3 story. No elvtr. S, D $91-$135; package plans off-season. Crib $5. Pet accepted, some restrictions. TV; cable (premium). Continental bkfst. Restaurant nearby. Ck-out noon. Coin lndry. Free airport, bus depot transportation. Some refrigerators, microwaves. Ocean view. Cr cds: A, D, DS, MC, V. 🄳 💺 ⊠ 🐾 SC

North Bend (See also Bandon, Coos Bay, Reedsport)

Motel

✔ ★ **BAY BRIDGE.** *33 US 101. 541/756-3151; res: 800/557-3156.* 16 rms, 3 kit. units. May-Oct: S $42-$52; D $52-$60; each addl $5; kit. units $59-$65; under 3 free; lower rates rest of yr. Crib $2. Pet accepted, some restrictions; $5/day. TV; cable. Complimentary coffee in lobby. Restaurant nearby. Ck-out 11 am. Some refrigerators. On Pacific Bay. Cr cds: A, C, D, DS, MC, V. 💺 ⊠ 🐾

Ontario (See also Caldwell, ID)

Motel

★ **HOLIDAY.** *615 E Idaho Ave, I-84, exit 376. 541/889-9188; FAX 541/889-4303.* 72 rms, 2 story. S $28.95; D $38.95; each addl $5. Crib $5. Pet accepted. TV; cable (premium). Heated pool. Restaurant open 24 hrs. Ck-out 11 am. Meeting rm. Business servs avail. Cr cds: A, D, DS, MC, V. 🄳 💺 ⊠ ⊠ 🐾 SC

Oregon City (See also Beaverton, Newberg, Portland, Salem)

Motor Hotel

★ **VAL-U INN.** *1900 Clackamette Dr at McLoughlin Blvd, just off I-205. 503/655-7141; FAX 503/655-1927; res: 800/443-7777.* 120 rms, 4 story. S $61; D $71-$76; each addl $5; suites $120; under 12 free. Crib $5. Pet accepted, some restrictions; $5. TV; cable (premium). Heated pool; whirlpool. Restaurant 6 am-10 pm; Sun 7 am-9 pm. Rm serv. Bar noon-1 am. Ck-out noon. Most balconies overlook river. Cr cds: A, C, D, DS, MC, V.
🄳 💺 ⊠ ⊠ 🐾 SC

Pendleton (See also Hermiston, La Grande)

Motels

(Rates are higher during Pendleton Roundup)

★ **CHAPARRAL.** *SW 620 Tutuilla Rd, just S of I-84 exit 209. 541/276-8654; FAX 541/276-5808.* 51 rms, 1-3 story, 2 kits. S $39-$46; D $45-$48; each addl $5; kit. units $57-$60. Crib $4. Pet accepted; $5. TV; cable (premium). Complimentary coffee in rms, lobby. Restaurant adj open 24 hrs. Ck-out 11 am. Cr cds: A, D, DS, MC, V. 💺 ⊠ 🐾 SC

★ **TAPADERA INN.** *105 SE Court Ave. 541/276-3231; FAX 541/276-0754; res: 800/722-8277.* 47 rms, 2 story. Mid-May-mid-Sept: S $32.50-$42; D $38-$47; each addl $5; under 13 free; lower rates rest of yr. Crib $5. Pet accepted; $5. TV; cable (premium). Restaurant 6:30 am-9 pm. Rm serv. Bar 11-2 am. Ck-out noon. Meeting rms. Business servs avail. Cr cds: A, C, D, DS, MC, V. 🄳 💺 ⊠ 🐾 SC

✔ ★ **VAGABOND INN.** *201 SW Court Ave. 541/276-5252; FAX 541/278-1213.* 51 rms, 2 story. June-Sept: S $32-$36; D $40-$46; each addl $5; under 16 free; lower rates rest of yr. Closed during Pendleton Roundup. Crib free. Pet accepted; $5. TV; cable, VCR avail. Pool. Complimentary continental bkfst. Restaurant nearby. Ck-out noon. Cr cds: A, C, D, DS, MC, V. 💺 ⊠ ⊠ 🐾 SC

Motor Hotel

★ ★ ★ **DOUBLETREE AT INDIAN HILLS.** *304 SE Nye Ave, at I-84N exit 210. 541/276-6111; FAX 541/278-2413.* 168 rms, 3 story. S $71; D $71-$81; each addl $10; under 18 free; wknd rates. Crib free. Pet accepted. TV. Heated pool. Restaurant 6 am-10:30 pm. Rm serv. Bar; entertainment. Ck-out noon. Meeting rms. Business servs avail. Free airport, RR station, bus depot transportation. Private patios, balconies. Cr cds: A, C, D, DS, ER, MC, V. 🄳 💺 ⊠ ⊠ 🐾

Portland

Motels

★ ★ **HOLIDAY INN EXPRESS.** *(2323 NE 181st Ave, Gresham 97230) I-84 exit 13.* 503/492-4000; FAX 503/492-3271. 71 rms, 3 story, 23 suites. May-Sept: S $70; D $77; each addl $7; suites $80-$120; under 18 free; lower rates rest of yr. Crib free. Pet accepted, some restrictions. TV; cable (premium), VCR avail (movies). Indoor pool; whirlpool. Complimentary continental bkfst. Coffee in rms. Restaurant adj 7 am-10 pm. Ck-out 1 pm. Coin lndry. Meeting rms. Business servs avail. Sundries. Valet serv. Exercise equipt; rower, stair machine, sauna. Some refrigerators. Cr cds: A, D, DS, JCB, MC, V.

D 🐾 ≋ 🏋 ✕ ⊠ 🐾 SC

★ ★ **PHOENIX INN.** *(477 NW Phoenix Dr, Troutdale 97060) 503/669-6500; FAX* 503/669-3500; res: 800/824-6824. 73 rms, 3 story. Mid-May-Sept: S $65-$75; D $79-$85; each addl $7; suites $115; under 17 free; lower rates rest of yr. Crib free. Pet accepted; $10. TV; cable (premium). Indoor pool; whirlpool. Complimentary continental bkfst. Restaurant adj open 24 hrs. Bar 11-2 am. Ck-out noon. Meeting rms. Business servs avail. Free airport transportation. Exercise equipt; bicycle, stair machine. Cr cds: A, D, DS, MC, V.

D 🐾 ≋ 🏋 ✈ ⊠ 🐾 SC

★ ★ **RESIDENCE INN BY MARRIOTT-SOUTH.** *(15200 SW Bangy Rd, Lake* Oswego 97035) S on I-5, exit 292. 503/684-2603; FAX 503/620-6712. 112 kit. units, 2 story. 1 & 2-bedrm suites $120-$175. Crib $5. Pet accepted; $10/day. TV; cable (premium), VCR avail (movies free). Heated pool; whirlpool. Complimentary continental bkfst. Restaurant adj. Ck-out noon. Coin lndry. Business servs avail. Valet serv. Health club privileges. Fireplace in suites. Private patios, balconies. Picnic tables, grills. Cr cds: A, C, D, DS, JCB, MC, V.

D 🐾 ≋ ⊠ 🐾 SC

★ ★ **SHILO INN-WASHINGTON SQUARE.** *(10830 SW Greenburg Rd, Tigard* 97223) S on OR 217, Greenburg Rd exit. 503/620-4320; FAX 503/620-8277. 77 rms, 4 story, 6 kits. S, D $59-$89; each addl $10; kit. units $85; under 12 free; wkly, monthly rates. Crib free. Pet accepted; $7/day. TV; cable (premium), VCR avail (movies). Complimentary continental bkfst. Restaurant nearby. Ck-out noon. Coin lndry. Meeting rm. Business servs avail. Valet serv. Free airport transportation. Exercise equipt; weight machines, bicycles, sauna, steam rm. Cr cds: A, C, D, DS, ER, JCB, MC, V. D 🐾 🏋 ⊠ 🐾 SC

✔ ★ **SUPER 8.** *(25438 SW Parkway Ave, Wilsonville 97070) I-5 exit 286.* 503/682-2088; FAX 503/682-0453. 72 rms, 4 story. S $48.88; D $57.88-$65.88; each addl $4. Crib free. Pet accepted; $25 refundable. TV; cable (premium). Complimentary coffee in lobby. Restaurant opp open 24 hrs. Ck-out noon. Coin lndry. Meeting rm. Business servs avail. Cr cds: A, C, D, DS, MC, V. D 🐾 ⊠ 🐾

Motor Hotels

✔ ★ **DELTA INN.** 9930 N Whitaker Rd (97217), I-5 exit 306B, north of downtown. 503/289-1800; FAX 503/289-3778; res: 800/833-1800. 212 rms, 4 story. S, D $55-$65; each addl $5; under 12 free; wkly rates. Crib free. Pet accepted; $10/day. TV; cable (premium). Complimentary coffee. Restaurant adj 6 am-11 pm. Ck-out noon. Coin lndry. Meeting rm. Business servs avail. In-rm modem link. Sundries. Free airport, RR station, bus depot transportation. Park adj. Cr cds: A, C, D, DS, MC, V. D 🐾 ⊠ 🐾

★ ★ **DOUBLETREE-COLUMBIA RIVER.** 1401 N Hayden Island Dr (97217), just W of I-5, Jantzen Beach exit, north of downtown. 503/283-2111; FAX 503/283-4718. 351 rms, 3 story. S, D $150; each addl $15; suites $225-$350; under 18 free. Crib free. Pet accepted; $15. TV; cable, VCR avail. Heated pool. Restaurants 6 am-10 pm. Rm serv. Bars 11-2 am; entertainment. Ck-out noon. Convention facilities. Business servs avail. In-rm modem link. Bellhops. Valet serv. Gift shop. Barber, beauty shop. Free airport, RR station, bus depot transportation. Tennis adj. Putting green. Some refrigerators, bathrm phones. Whirlpool in some suites. Private patios, balconies. On Columbia River. Cr cds: A, C, D, DS, ER, JCB, MC, V. D 🐾 ≋ ⊠ 🐾

★ ★ **DOUBLETREE-JANTZEN BEACH.** 909 N Hayden Island Dr (97217), just E of I-5 exit Jantzen Beach, north of downtown. 503/283-4466; FAX 503/283-4743. 320 rms, 4 story. S, D $99-$109; each addl $15; suites $195-$350; under 18 free; package plans; wkend rates. Crib free. Pet accepted; $20. TV; cable, VCR avail. Heated pool; whirlpool. Coffee in rms. Restaurant 6 am-10 pm. Rm serv. Bar 10-2:30 am; entertainment. Ck-out noon. Convention facilities. Business servs avail. Bellhops. Valet serv. Sundries. Free airport transportation. Lighted tennis. Exercise equipt; weights, stair machine. Some bathrm phones, in-rm whirlpools. Private patios, balconies. On river; boat dock. Cr cds: A, C, D, DS, ER, JCB, MC, V. D 🐾 🐾 ≋ 🏋 ⊠ 🐾 SC

★ ★ **RIVERSIDE INN.** *50 SW Morrison St (97204), downtown.* 503/221-0711; FAX *503/274-0312; res: 800/899-0247.* 140 rms, 5 story. S $130-$145; D $140-$155; each addl $10; under 17 free. Crib free. Pet accepted, some restrictions; $10/day. TV. Coffee in rms. Restaurant 6:30-10 am, 4-11 pm; Sat, Sun 7 am-noon, 4-11 pm. Rm serv 5 pm-1 am. Bar 4 pm-2 am. Ck-out noon. Meeting rm. Business servs avail. Health club privileges. Balconies. Cr cds: A, C, D, DS, ER, MC, V. 🄳 ✔ 🏊 🐾

★ ★ **SWEETBRIER INN.** *(7125 SW Nyberg, Tualatin 97062) approx 10 mi S on I-5, exit 289.* 503/692-5800; FAX 503/691-2894; res: 800/551-9167. 100 rms, 32 suites. S $63-$83; D $73-$93; suites $90-$165; under 18 free; wknd rates. Crib free. Pet accepted; $100 refundable. TV; cable (premium). Heated pool. Playground. Complimentary coffee in rms. Restaurant 6:30 am-10 pm. Rm serv. Bar; entertainment Wed-Sat. Ck-out noon. Meeting rms. Business servs avail. In-rm modem link. Sundries. Valet serv. Refrigerator in suites. Some balconies, patios. Picnic tables. Cr cds: A, C, D, DS, JCB, MC, V. 🄳 ✔ 🏊 🍽 🐾 SC

Hotels

★ ★ ★ ★ **5TH AVENUE SUITES.** *506 SW Washington (97205), downtown.* 503/222-0001; FAX 503/222-0004; res: 800/711-2971. Built in 1912, this former department store has been completely renovated and redecorated in turn-of-the-century, American country-home style. Rooms are comfortable, light and airy. There are on-site business and fitness centers and the Red Star Tavern is open daily for breakfast, lunch and dinner. 221 rms, 10 story, 139 suites. S $150-$165; D $165-$180; each addl $15; suites $160-$225; under 18 free; wknd, hol rates. Crib free. Pet accepted, some restrictions. Garage/valet parking $13. TV; cable (premium), VCR avail (movies). Pool privileges. Complimentary continental bkfst. Restaurant 6:30 am-10 pm. Rm serv 24 hrs. Bar 11-1 am. Ck-out noon. Meeting rms. Business center. In-rm modem link. Concierge. Exercise equipt; weights, treadmill. Refrigerators. Cr cds: A, C, D, DS, JCB, MC, V. 🄳 ✔ 🏋 🍽 🐾 🏃

★ ★ ★ **THE BENSON.** *309 SW Broadway (97205), at Oak St, downtown.* 503/228-2000; FAX 503/226-4603; res: 800/426-0670. 286 units, 13 story, 44 suites. S $145-$190; D $185-$210; each addl $25; suites $180-$600; under 18 free; wknd rates. Crib $25. Pet accepted; $50. Garage, valet $12/day. TV; cable, VCR avail. Restaurant 6:30 am-2 pm, 5-10 pm. Rm serv 24 hrs. Bar 11-1 am; entertainment. Ck-out noon. Convention facilities. Business center. In-rm modem link. Concierge. Gift shop. Airport transportation. Exercise equipt; weights, treadmills. Minibars. Bathrm phone in suites. Cr cds: A, C, D, DS, ER, JCB, MC, V. 🄳 ✔ 🏋 🍽 🐾 🏃

★ ★ ★ **CROWNE PLAZA.** *(14811 SW Kruse Oaks Blvd, Lake Oswego 97035)* 503/624-8400; FAX 503/684-8324. 161 rms, 6 story. June-Aug: S $134; D $149; suites $150-$265; under 18 free; lower rates rest of yr. Crib free. Pet accepted. Valet parking $5. TV; cable (premium). Indoor/outdoor pool; whirlpool, sauna. Complimentary coffee in rms. Restaurant 6 am-2 pm, 5-10 pm. Rm serv to midnight. Bar 2 pm-midnight. Ck-out noon. Meeting rms. Business servs avail. Sundries. Gift shop. Valet serv. Free RR transportation. Tennis privileges. Exercise equipt; bicycle, treadmill. Cr cds: A, D, DS, ER, JCB, MC, V. 🄳 ✔ 🏊 🍽 🏋 🐾 SC

★ ★ ★ **DOUBLETREE-LLOYD CENTER.** *1000 NE Multnomah St (97232), I-84 exit 1 (Lloyd Blvd), east of downtown.* 503/281-6111; FAX 503/284-8553. 476 rms, 15 story. S, D $99-$149; each addl $15; suites $269-$575; under 18 free. Crib free. Pet accepted. TV; cable, VCR avail. Pool; poolside serv. Coffee in rms. Restaurant 6 am-midnight. Bar; entertainment. Ck-out noon. Convention facilities. Business center. Valet parking. Free airport transportation. Exercise equipt; weights, bicycles. Some bathrm phones, in-rm whirlpools, refrigerators. Many private patios, balconies. Cr cds: A, C, D, DS, ER, JCB, MC, V. 🄳 ✔ 🏊 🏋 🍽 🐾 🏃

★ ★ **IMPERIAL.** *400 SW Broadway (97205), at Stark St, downtown.* 503/228-7221; FAX 503/223-4551; res: 800/452-2323. 136 rms, 9 story. S $75-$90; D $80-$100; each addl $5; under 12 free. Crib free. TV; cable (premium). Pet accepted; $10. Restaurants 6:30 am-9 pm. Bar 11-1 am, Sat & Sun 1-9 pm. Ck-out 2 pm. Meeting rms. Business servs avail. In-rm modem link. Valet parking. Cr cds: A, C, D, DS, MC, V. 🄳 ✔ 🏊 🐾

✔ ★ **MALLORY.** *729 SW 15th Ave (97205), just W of I-405, downtown.* 503/223-6311; FAX 503/223-0522; res: 800/228-8657. 143 rms, 8 story. S $65-$100; D $70-$110; each addl $5; suites $110-$120. Crib free. Pet accepted; $10. TV; cable (premium), VCR avail. Restaurant 6:30 am-9 pm; Sun from 7 am. Bar 11:30-1 am, Sun 1-9 pm. Ck-out 2 pm. Business servs avail. Some refrigerators. Cr cds: A, C, D, DS, MC, V. 🄳 ✔ 🐾

★ **MARK SPENCER.** *409 SW 11th Ave (97205), downtown.* 503/224-3293; FAX 503/223-7848; res: 800/548-3934. 101 kit. units, 6 story. S, D $69-$105; each addl $10; suites $95-$110; studio rms $69; under 12 free; monthly rates. Crib free. Pet accepted; $200 refundable. Parking lot 1 blk $7. TV; cable, VCR avail. Complimentary coffee in lobby. Complimentary continental bkfst. Restaurant nearby. Ck-out noon. Coin lndry. Business servs avail. Health club privileges. Refrigerators. Rooftop garden. Cr cds: A, C, D, DS, MC, V. 🐾 ⚡ 🏊 🔥 SC

★ ★ ★ **MARRIOTT.** *1401 SW Front Ave (97201), downtown.* 503/226-7600; FAX 503/221-1789. 503 rms, 15 story. S $170-$190; D $180-$200; suites $350-$500; under 18 free. Crib free. Pet accepted. Valet parking in/out $14/day. TV; cable (premium), VCR avail. Indoor pool; whirlpool, poolside serv. Restaurant 6 am-11 pm; Fri, Sat to midnight. Bar 11:30-2 am; entertainment. Ck-out noon. Coin lndry. Convention facilities. Business center. Concierge. Gift shop. Barber, beauty shop. Exercise equipt; bicycles, rower, sauna. Massage. Game rm. Some bathrm phones, refrigerators; wet bar in suites. Some private patios, balconies. Japanese garden at entrance. Luxury level. Cr cds: A, C, D, DS, ER, JCB, MC, V. D 🐾 ⚡ 🏋 🏊 🔥 SC 🏃

★ ★ ★ **RIVERPLACE.** *1510 SW Harbor Way (97201), downtown.* 503/228-3233; FAX 503/295-6161; res: 800/227-1333. 84 rms, 4 story. S, D $185-$245; condos $375-$475; suites $205-$700; under 18 free. Valet, garage parking in/out $15. Crib free. Pet accepted, some restrictions; $100. TV; cable (premium), VCR avail. Complimentary continental bkfst. Restaurant 6:30 am-2 pm, 5-10 pm. Rm serv 24 hrs. Bar 11-1 am; entertainment Wed-Sun evenings. Ck-out 1 pm. Meeting rms. Business servs avail. In-rm modem link. Concierge. Shopping arcade. Whirlpool, sauna. Health club privileges. Minibars; some bathrm phones. Some refrigerators, fireplaces in suites. Balconies. On river. Skyline, marina views. Cr cds: A, C, D, DS, ER, JCB, MC, V. D 🐾 ⚡ 🏊

Redmond *(See also Bend, Madras)*

Motels

✓ ★ **REDMOND INN.** *1545 US 97S.* 541/548-1091; res: 800/833-3259. 46 rms, 3 story, 6 kits. No elvtr. Mid-May-Sept: S $55; D $64; each addl $5; kit. units $63; under 12 free; lower rates rest of yr. Crib free. Pet accepted, some restrictions; $5. TV; cable. Heated pool. Complimentary continental bkfst. Restaurant opp 7 am-11 pm. Ck-out 11 am. Refrigerators, microwaves. Cr cds: A, D, DS, MC, V. D 🐾 ⚡ 🏊 🔥 SC

★ **VILLAGE SQUIRE.** *629 S 5th St.* 541/548-2105; res: 800/548-2102. 24 rms, 2 story. S $55; D $55-$60; each addl $5. Crib $5. Pet accepted. TV; cable (premium), VCR avail. Complimentary coffee in lobby. Restaurant nearby. Ck-out 11 am. Some refrigerators, microwaves. Cr cds: A, D, DS, MC, V. D 🐾 ⚡ 🔥 SC

Reedsport *(See also Coos Bay, Florence, North Bend)*

Motels

✓ ★ **ANCHOR BAY INN.** *1821 Hwy 101.* 541/271-2149; FAX 541/271-1802; res: 800/767-1821. E-mail anchorbay@presys.com; web www.presys.com/chwy/r/reedspor.htm. 21 rms, 2 story, 4 kits. S $43-$48; D $51-$59; kit. units $60-$65. Pet accepted, some restrictions; $5/day. TV; cable (premium), VCR avail. Pool. Complimentary continental bkfst. Restaurant nearby. Ck-out 10 am. Coin lndry. Business servs avail. Some refrigerators, microwaves. Cr cds: A, DS, MC, V. 🐾 ⚡ 🏊 🔥 SC

★ ★ **BEST WESTERN SALBASGEON INN.** *1400 Highway Ave (US 101).* 541/271-4831; FAX 541/271-4832. 56 rms, 2 story, 9 suites, 2 kit. units. Late May-mid-Sept: S $64-$79; D $78-$98; each addl $5; suites $95-$130; kit. units $95-$120; lower rates rest of yr. Crib free. Pet accepted; $5. TV; cable (premium), VCR avail. Indoor pool; whirlpool. Complimentary continental bkfst. Restaurant nearby. Ck-out 11 am. Coin lndry. Meeting rms. Business servs avail. Exercise equipt; stair machine, bicycle. Minibars; refrigerators. Near Scholfield River. Cr cds: A, C, D, DS, MC, V. D 🐾 ⚡ 🏋 🏊 🔥 SC

★ **SALBASGEON INN OF THE UMPQUA.** *45209 OR 38.* 541/271-2025. 12 rms, 2 story, 1 suite, 4 kit. units. Late May-mid-Sept: S $52-$68; D $65-$78; each addl $5; suite $71-$94; kit. units $73-$99; lower rates rest of yr. Pet accepted, some restrictions; $5/day. TV; cable (premium). Ck-out 11 am. Picnic tables. On Umpqua River. All rooms have river views. Cr cds: A, C, D, DS, MC, V. D 🐾 ⚡ 🏊 🔥 SC

Rockaway *(See also Cannon Beach, Seaside, Tillamook)*

Motel

★ **SURFSIDE.** *101 NW 11th Ave.* 503/355-2312; res: 800/243-7786. 79 units, 1-2 story. No A/C. Mid-May-mid-Sept: S $44.50-$98.50; D $98.50-$149.50; kit. units $79.50-$149.50; lower rates rest of yr. Crib $5. Pet accepted; $10. TV; cable. Indoor pool.

Complimentary coffee. Restaurant nearby. Ck-out 11 am. Some fireplaces. On ocean; beach access. Cr cds: A, DS, MC, V. [D] [⬆] [≈] [◿] [🔥] [SC]

Roseburg

Motels

★ ★ **BEST WESTERN GARDEN VILLA.** *760 NW Garden Valley Blvd. 541/672-1601; FAX 541/672-1316.* 122 rms, 2 story. June-Sept: S $64-$70; D $68-$88; each addl $7; under 12 free; lower rates rest of yr. Crib $5. Pet accepted, some restrictions. TV; cable (premium). Heated pool. Complimentary continental bkfst. Restaurant adj 5 am-midnight. Ck-out noon. Coin lndry. Meeting rms. Sundries. Exercise equipt; weight machine, treadmill. Microwaves avail. Cr cds: A, C, D, DS, ER, JCB, MC, V. [D] [⬆] [≈] [🏃] [◿] [🔥] [SC]

★ ★ **WINDMILL INN.** *1450 Mulholland Dr. 541/673-0901; res: 800/547-4747.* Web www.mind.net/windmills. 128 rms, 2 story. June-Sept: S $65-$71; D $71-$88; each addl $6; under 18 free; lower rates rest of yr. Crib $3.50. Pet accepted, some restrictions. TV; cable (premium). Pool; whirlpool. Complimentary continental bkfst. Restaurants 6 am-midnight. Bar. Ck-out 11 am. Guest lndry. Meeting rms. Business servs avail. In-rm modem link. Valet serv. Sundries. Free airport, bus depot transportation. Exercise equipt; bicycles, treadmill, sauna. Microwaves avail. Some balconies. Cr cds: A, C, D, DS, MC, V.
[D] [⬆] [≈] [🏃] [◿] [🔥] [SC]

Salem *(See also Albany, McMinnville, Newberg, Oregon City, Portland)*

Motels

(Rates may be higher during state fair)

✔ ★ **PHOENIX INN.** *4370 Commercial St SE (97302), I-5 exits 249 & 252. 503/588-9220; FAX 503/585-3616; res: 800/445-4498.* 89 rms, 4 story. June-Sept: S $56-$70; D $56-$77; each addl $5; suites $92-$110; under 17 free. Crib free. Pet accepted, some restrictions; $10. TV; cable (premium). Indoor pool; whirlpool. Complimentary continental bkfst. Restaurant adj 11 am-11 pm. Ck-out noon. Coin lndry. Meeting rms. Business servs avail. Exercise equipt; weight machine, treadmill. Refrigerators. Some suites with whirlpool. Cr cds: A, C, D, DS, MC, V. [D] [⬆] [≈] [🏃] [◿] [🔥] [SC]

★ **TIKI LODGE.** *3705 Market St (97301), I-5 Market St exit. 503/581-4441; FAX 503/581-4442.* 50 rms, 20 with shower only, 2 story. Mid-May-Sept: S $49-$52; D $52-$58; each addl $4; under 12 free; wkly rates; lower rates rest of yr. Crib $2. Pet accepted. TV; cable (premium). Heated pool; sauna. Playground. Complimentary coffee in lobby. Restaurant adj open 24 hrs. Ck-out noon. Meeting rms. Business servs avail. Cr cds: A, D, DS, MC, V. [⬆] [≈] [🔥] [SC]

Motor Hotel

★ ★ **QUALITY INN.** *3301 Market St (97301), I-5 exit 256. 503/370-7888; FAX 503/370-6305.* 150 rms, 4 story. S $73-$78; D $78-$83; each addl $5; suites $107-$112; under 18 free. Crib free. Pet accepted; $10. TV; cable (premium), VCR avail. Indoor pool; whirlpool, sauna. Complimentary coffee in rms. Restaurant 6:30 am-10 pm. Rm serv. Bar 11-1 am; entertainment Sat. Ck-out 11 am. Coin lndry. Meeting rms. Business servs avail. Bellhops. Sundries. Valet serv. Balconies. Cr cds: A, C, D, DS, ER, JCB, MC, V.
[D] [⬆] [≈] [◿] [🔥] [SC]

Seaside *(See also Astoria, Cannon Beach)*

Motels

★ **ALOHA INN.** *441 2nd Ave, just W of US 101. 503/738-9581; res: 800/448-5544.* 48 rms, 3 story, 10 kit. units. May-Oct: S $64; D $68; each addl $8; suites $106-$135; kit. units $77-$135; lower rates rest of yr. Crib free. Pet accepted; $10. TV; cable (premium). Indoor pool; whirlpool, sauna. Complimentary continental bkfst. Restaurant nearby. Ck-out 11 am. Coin lndry. Meeting rm. Business servs avail. Some refrigerators. Cr cds: A, C, D, DS, MC, V. [D] [⬆] [≈] [◿] [🔥] [SC]

★ ★ **EBB TIDE.** *300 N Promenade, at 3rd Ave. 503/738-8371; FAX 503/738-0938; res: 800/468-6232.* 83 rms, 3 story, 45 kits. No A/C. No elvtr. May-Sept: S, D $80-$120; kit. units $70-$120; lower rates rest of yr. Crib $5. Pet accepted; $10/day. TV; cable (premium), VRC avail. Indoor pool; whirlpool. Restaurant nearby. Business servs avail. In-rm modem link. Refrigerators. On beach. Cr cds: A, C, D, DS, MC, V. [⬆] [≈] [◿] [🔥] [SC]

Motor Hotel

★ ★ **BEST WESTERN OCEANVIEW RESORT.** *414 N Promenade. 503/738-3334; FAX 503/738-3264.* 104 rms, 5 story, 20 suites, 45 kit. units. No A/C. June-Aug: S, D, kit. units $69-$172; suites $195-$265; under 18 free; lower rates rest of yr. Crib free. Pet accepted, some restrictions; $15. TV. Indoor pool; whirlpool. Restaurant 7 am-10 pm. Rm serv. Bar 4 pm-midnight. Ck-out 11 am. Coin lndry. Meeting rms. Business servs avail. In-rm modem link. Many refrigerators. Balconies. On beach. Cr cds: A, C, D, DS, MC, V.

D 🖰 🖾 🖾 🖍 🐾 SC

The Dalles *(See also Hood River)*

Motels

★ ★ **LONE PINE VILLAGE.** *351 Lone Pine Dr, I-84, exit 87, at US 197. 541/298-2800; FAX 541/298-8282; res: 800/955-9626.* 56 rms, 2 story. June-Sept: S $52.20-$58; D $60.30-$67; each addl $6; suites $72-$81; under 12 free; lower rates rest of yr. Crib free. Pet accepted, some restrictions; $6. TV; cable (premium). Indoor pool; whirlpool. Complimentary full bkfst; coffee in lobby. Restaurant adj 6 am-10 pm. Bar. 3-11 pm. Ck-out noon. Coin lndry. Meeting rms. Business servs avail. Sundries. Gift shop. Free airport transportation. Golf privileges (par 3), pro, driving range. Exercise equipt; bicycle, stair machine. Lawn games. Refrigerators. Cr cds: A, D, DS, MC, V.

D 🖰 🏋 🖾 🏋 🖾 🐾 SC

★ ★ **QUALITY INN.** *2114 W 6th St. 541/298-5161; FAX 541/298-6411.* 85 rms, 2 story, 16 kits. S $59; D $65; kit. units $72-$79; each addl $5. Crib $2. Pet accepted; $2. TV; cable. Heated pool; whirlpool. Restaurant 6 am-10 pm; Fri, Sat to 11 pm. Ck-out 11 am. Coin lndry. Meeting rms. Business servs avail. In-rm modem link. Health club privileges. Some fireplaces. Cr cds: A, D, DS, MC, V. 🖰 🖾 🖾 🐾 SC

Motor Hotel

↙ ★ ★ **BEST WESTERN TAPADERA.** *112 W 2nd St, at Liberty St. 541/296-9107; FAX 541/296-3002.* 65 rms, 2-4 story. S $51-$56; D $59-$63; each addl $7; under 12 free. Crib $7. Pet accepted. TV; cable (premium). Heated pool. Restaurant 6:30 am-9 pm. Rm serv. Bar 11 am-11 pm. Ck-out noon. Meeting rms. Business servs avail. In-rm modem link. Some refrigerators. Cr cds: A, C, D, DS, ER, JCB, MC, V.

🖰 🖾 🖾 🐾 SC

Tillamook *(See also Lincoln City, Rockaway)*

Motor Hotel

★ ★ ★ **SHILO INN.** *2515 N Main. 503/842-7971; FAX 503/842-7960.* 100 rms, 2 story. July-Oct: S, D $69-$110; each addl $10; kit. units $110; under 12 free; higher rates during County Fair; lower rates rest of yr. Crib free. Pet accepted, some restrictions; $7. TV; cable (premium), VCR avail (movies). Indoor pool; whirlpool. Restaurant 6 am-11 pm. Bar 11-2 am. Ck-out noon. Coin lndry. Meeting rms. Business servs avail. Exercise equipt; weights, bicycle. Refrigerators. Cr cds: A, D, DS, MC, V.

D 🖰 🖾 🏋 🖾 🐾 SC

Yachats *(See also Florence, Newport)*

Motels

★ ★ **ADOBE.** *1555 US 101. 541/547-3141; FAX 541/547-4234; res: 800/522-3623 (western US).* 93 rms, 2-3 story, 5 kits. S, D $58-$100; each addl $8; suites $150; kit. units $110-$135. Crib $8. Pet accepted, some restrictions. TV; cable (premium), VCR. Complimentary coffee in rms. Restaurant 8 am-2:30 pm, 5-9 pm. Bar. Ck-out 11 am. Meeting rm. Business servs avail. Gift shop. Exercise equipt; weight machine, bicycle, sauna. Whirlpool. Refrigerators; some fireplaces. Whirlpool in suites. Some balconies. On ocean. Cr cds: A, C, D, DS, MC, V. D 🖰 🖾 🏋 🖾 🐾 SC

↙ ★ **FIRESIDE.** *1881 US 101N. 541/547-3636; FAX 541/547-3152; res: 800/336-3573.* 43 rms, 2 story. Mid-May-Sept: S, D $60-$130; each addl $7; kit. cottages $99-$135; some lower rates rest of yr. Crib $5. Pet accepted, some restrictions; $7/day. TV; cable, VCR avail. Complimentary coffee in rms. Restaurant nearby. Ck-out 11 am. Refrigerators; some fireplaces, microwaves. View of ocean. Cr cds: DS, MC, V.

D 🖰 🖾 🖾 🐾 SC

★ ★ **SHAMROCK LODGETTES.** $1/4$ *mi S on US 101. 541/547-3312; FAX 541/547-3843; res: 800/845-5028.* Web www.o-t-b.com. 19 rms, 11 kit. cottages. Mid-May-Sept: S, D, kit. units $70-$100; each addl $7; kit. cottages $91-$112; wkly rates; lower rates rest of yr. Crib $7. Pet accepted, some restrictions; $3/day. TV; cable (premium). Complimentary coffee in rms. Restaurant nearby. Ck-out 11 am. Massage. Refrigerators; some in-rm whirlpools; microwaves avail. Some private patios, balconies. Beach adj. Cr cds: A, D, DS, MC, V.

Pennsylvania

Allentown *(See also Bethlehem)*

Motels

★ **ALLENWOOD.** *1058 Hausman Rd (18104), E on US 22 to PA 309S to Hausman Rd. 610/395-3707.* 21 rms. S, D, studio rms $40-$45; each addl $3. Crib free. Pet accepted. TV; cable. Restaurant nearby. Ck-out 11 am. Cr cds: A, DS, MC, V. 🐾 ▨ 🔥 ▨

✔★ **HOLIDAY INN EXPRESS.** *15th St & US 22 (18103). 610/435-7880; FAX 610/432-2555.* 84 rms, 4 story. S, D $74-$95; each addl $5; under 18 free. Crib free. Pet accepted; $5. TV; cable. Complimentary continental bkfst. Restaurant nearby. Ck-out 11 am. Business servs avail. Cr cds: A, C, D, DS, MC, V. D 🐾 ▨ ▨ SC

Motor Hotel

★★ **SHERATON INN JETPORT.** *3400 Airport Rd (18103), 5 mi E on US 22. 610/266-1000.* 147 rms, 3 story, 30 suites. S $99, D $109, each addl $10, suites $115-$130, under 13 free; higher rates NASCAR races. Crib free. Pet accepted. TV; cable (premium), VCR avail. Indoor pool; sauna, whirlpool, lifeguard. Complimentary coffee in rms. Complimentary continental bkfst. Restaurant 6:30 am-10 pm. Rm serv. Bar 11-2 am, entertainment Tues-Sun. Ck-out noon. Meeting rm. Business servs avail. In-rm modem link. Bellhops. Sundries. Valet serv. Free airport transportation. Exercise equipt; stair machine, treadmill. Some refrigerators. Cr cds: A, D, DS, MC, V. D 🐾 ≈ 🏃 ✈ ▨ 🔥

Altoona

Motor Hotel

★★★ **RAMADA.** *1 Sheraton Dr (16601), 5 mi S on US 220. 814/946-1631; FAX 814/946-0785.* 215 rms, 2-3 story. S, D $55-$85; each addl $5; suites $80-$140; under 18 free; some wkend rates; higher rates: football games, ski season. Crib $5. Pet accepted. TV; cable (premium), VCR avail. Indoor pool; wading pool, whirlpool, lifeguard. Complimentary continental bkfst. Restaurants 6:30 am-2:30 pm, 5:30-10 pm; Sat to 11 pm. Rm serv. Bar 11-2 am. Ck-out noon. Meeting rms. Business center. In-rm modem link. Bellhops. Valet serv. Gift shop. Airport transportation. 18-hole golf privileges. Downhill ski 20 mi. Exercise rm; instructor, weights, bicycles. Rec rm. Microwaves avail. Cr cds: A, C, D, DS, JCB, MC, V. D 🐾 ≈ 🏃 ≈ ✈ ▨ ▨ SC 🏃

Beaver Falls

Motel

★ **CONLEY'S MOTOR INN.** *Big Beaver Blvd, on PA 18, 1/4 m S of PA Tpke exit 2. 724/843-9300.* 54 rms, 4 kits. S $49; D $59; each addl $10; under 12 free; wkly, monthly rates. Pet accepted. TV; cable. Restaurant 7 am-10 pm. Bar. Ck-out 11 am. Meeting rms. Business servs avail. Refrigerators. Cr cds: A, C, D, DS, MC, V. 🐾 ▨ 🔥 SC

Motor Hotel

★★★ **HOLIDAY INN.** *PA 18N at PA Tpke exit 2. 724/846-3700.* 156 rms, 3 story. S, D $74-$83; each addl $8; under 18 free; wkend rates. Crib free. Pet accepted. TV. Indoor pool; whirlpool, sauna, poolside serv, lifeguard. Restaurant 6:30 am-10 pm. Rm serv. Bar 11-2 am. Ck-out noon. Meeting rms. Business servs avail. In-rm modem link. Valet serv. Miniature golf. Game rm. Cr cds: A, C, D, DS, JCB, MC, V. D 🐾 ≈ ▨ ▨ SC

Bedford

Motels

✔★★★ **BEST WESTERN HOSS'S INN.** *RD 2, Box 33B, 2 mi N via US 220 Business, PA Tpke exit 11. 814/623-9006; FAX 814/623-7120.* Web www.best western.com/best.html. 105 rms, 2 story. Apr-Oct: S $48.50; D $56.50; suites $65; each addl $8; under 18 free; lower rates rest of yr. Crib free. Pet accepted, some restrictions; $50. TV; cable (premium), VCR avail (movies). Pool; lifeguard. Restaurant 6:30-11 am, 5-10 pm; Sat, Sun 6:30 am-10 pm. Bar 5 pm-midnight. Ck-out noon. Meeting rms. Gift shop. Exercise equipt; weight machine, treadmill, sauna. Game rm. Cr cds: A, C, D, DS, MC, V. D 🐾 ≈ 🏃 ▨ ▨ SC

★ **ECONOLODGE.** *US 220 Business. 814/623-5174; FAX 814/623-5455.* Web www.hotelchoice. 32 rms, 2 story. May-Oct: S $42; D $46-$48; each addl $6; under 18 free; ski plans; higher rates special events; lower rates rest of yr. Crib free. Pet accepted. TV; cable (premium). Restaurant 6 am-10 pm. Rm serv. Bar 4 pm-midnight. Ck-out 11 am. Downhill ski 15 mi. Game rm. Cr cds: A, C, D, DS, JCB, MC, V.

★ ★ **QUALITY INN.** *RD 2, Box 171, 2 mi N on US 220 Business, 1 blk N of PA Tpke exit 11. 814/623-5188; FAX 814/623-0814.* Web www.quality inn.com. 66 rms. May-Nov: S $57-$63; D $63-$69; each addl $6; under 18 free; lower rates rest of yr. Crib $4. Pet accepted, some restrictions. TV; cable (premium). Pool. Restaurant 7 am-10 pm. Bar 11 am-11 pm. Ck-out 11 am. Meeting rms. Business servs avail. Downhill ski 20 mi. Cr cds: A, C, D, DS, ER, JCB, MC, V.

Bethlehem *(See also Allentown)*

Motel

★ ★ **COMFORT INN.** *3191 Highfield Dr (18017), US 22 exit 191.* 610/865-6300. 116 rms, 2½ story. S $56-$75; D $65-$85; each addl $6; under 18 free; ski plan. Crib free. Pet accepted. TV; cable, VCR (movies $5). Complimentary continental bkfst. Restaurant adj. Bar noon-2 am; entertainment Fri, Sat. Ck-out noon. Business servs avail. Valet serv. Cr cds: A, C, D, DS, ER, JCB, MC, V.

Bloomsburg

Motel

★ ★ **QUALITY INN-BUCKHORN PLAZA.** *1 Buckhorn Rd, I-80 at Buckhorn exit 34.* 717/784-5300; FAX 717/387-0367. 120 rms, 2 story. S $45-$65; D $50-$70; each addl $5; under 18 free. Crib $5. Pet accepted. TV; cable. Coffee in lobby. Restaurant adj 6 am-10 pm. Bar 7-2 am, Sun from 11 am. Ck-out 11 am. Business servs avail. Sundries. Balconies. Cr cds: A, C, D, DS, ER, JCB, MC, V.

Inns

★ ★ ★ **INN AT TURKEY HILL.** *991 Central Rd, at I-80 exit 35.* 717/387-1500; FAX 717/784-3718. 18 rms, 2 story. S $87, D $92; each addl $15; suites $115-$185; under 12 free. Pet accepted; $15. TV; cable. Complimentary continental bkfst. Dining rm 5-9 pm. Rm serv. Bar. Ck-out noon, ck-in 2 pm. Business servs avail. In-rm modem link. Airport, bus depot transportation. Fireplace in some rms. Elegant antiques. Old homestead (1839); guest rooms overlook landscaped courtyard; gazebo, lily pond. Cr cds: A, C, D, DS, MC, V.

★ ★ **MAGEE'S MAIN STREET.** *20 W Main St.* 717/784-3200; FAX 717/784-5517; res: 800/331-9815. 43 rms, 3 story. S $57-$79; D $66-$87; each addl $3.95-$7.95; under 6 free. Pet accepted. TV; cable. Complimentary full bkfst. Dining rm 7 am-midnight. Bar 11-1 am, Sun to 11 pm. Ck-out noon. Meeting rms. Business servs avail. Cr cds: A, C, D, DS, MC, V.

Breezewood *(See also Bedford, Chambersburg)*

Motel

★ ★ **RAMADA INN.** *I-70 & US 30.* 814/735-4005; FAX 814/735-3228. 125 rms, 2 story. Apr-Oct: S $57; D $79; under 18 free; lower rates rest of yr. Crib avail. Pet accepted, some restrictions. TV; cable (premium), VCR avail (movies). Indoor pool. Playground. Restaurant 6:30 am-10 pm. Rm serv. Bar 4 pm-midnight. Ck-out noon. Meeting rms. Business center. In-rm modem link. Gift shop. Golf privileges. Exercise equipt; weight machine, treadmill. Game rm. Lawn games. Picnic tables. Cr cds: A, C, D, DS, JCB, MC, V.

Brookville *(See also Clarion)*

Motels

★ ★ **DAYS INN.** *PA 36 & I-80, I-80 exit 13.* 814/849-8001; FAX 814/849-8001. 124 rms, 3 story. S $40-$60; D $45-$85; each addl $5; under 18 free; higher rates hunting season. Crib free. Pet accepted. TV; cable. Heated pool; wading pool, poolside serv, lifeguard. Restaurant 6-10 am, 4:30-10 pm; winter from 7 am. Bar 5 pm-midnight, closed Sun. Ck-out noon. Coin lndry. Business servs avail. X-country ski 17 mi. Game rm. Cr cds: A, D, DS, MC, V.

✔ ★ **HOLIDAY INN EXPRESS.** *235 Allegheny Blvd, I-80 exit 13. 814/849-8381; FAX 814/849-8386.* 69 rms, 3 story. S $38-$53; D $43-$66; each addl $5; under 12 free; higher rates hunting season. Crib free. Pet accepted. TV; cable (premium). Pool; lifeguard. Complimentary continental bkfst. Restaurant adj 11 am-11 pm. Ck-out noon. Coin lndry. Meeting rm. Business servs avail. Sundries. Private patios, balconies. Cr cds: A, C, D, DS, MC, V. 🅳 ⟋ ⩯ ⬚ 🔥 SC

Carlisle *(See also Harrisburg)*

Motels

★ ★ ★ **EMBERS INN & CONVENTION CENTER.** *1700 Harrisburg Pike (US 11), I-81 exit 17, I-76 exit 16. 717/243-1717; FAX 717/243-6648; res: 800/692-7315.* 270 rms. S $62; D $67; each addl $5; suites $110-$173; under 18 free. Crib $10. Pet accepted. TV; cable (premium), VCR avail (movies). Indoor pool; wading pool, whirlpool, sauna, poolside serv, lifeguard. Restaurant 7 am-9 pm; Sat to 9:30 pm. Rm serv. Bar 11-2 am. Ck-out 11 am. Meeting rms. Business servs avail. In-rm modem link. Bellhops. Sundries. Gift shop. Airport transportation. Tennis. Putting green. Lawn games. Refrigerators; microwaves avail. Cr cds: A, C, D, DS, ER, MC, V. 🅳 ⟋ 🎿 ⩯ ⬚ 🔥 SC

★ ★ ★ **HOLIDAY INN.** *1450 Harrisburg Pike (US 11), just off I-81, exit 17. 717/245-2400; FAX 717/245-9070.* 100 rms, 2 story. S, D $79; each addl $10; under 18 free; higher rates special events. Crib free. Pet accepted. TV; cable (premium), VCR avail. Pool; lifeguard. Restaurant 6:30 am-2 pm, 5-10 pm. Rm serv. Bar 11 am-midnight. Ck-out noon. Coin lndry. Meeting rms. Business servs avail. In-rm modem link. Valet serv. Health club privileges. Cr cds: A, D, DS, JCB, MC, V. 🅳 ⟋ ⩯ ⬚ 🔥 SC

★ ★ **QUALITY INN.** *1255 Harrisburg Pike, US 11 at I-81. 717/243-6000; FAX 717/258-4123.* 96 rms, 2 story. S, D $59.99; each addl $5; under 18 free; higher rates special events. Crib free. Pet accepted. TV; cable (premium). Pool; wading pool. Continental bkfst. Coffee in rms. Restaurant adj open 24 hrs. Bar 5 pm-midnight. Ck-out noon. Coin lndry. Business servs avail. Valet serv. Microwaves avail. Cr cds: A, C, D, DS, MC, V. 🅳 ⟋ ⩯ ⬚ 🔥 SC

Chambersburg

Motels

✔ ★ **DAYS INN.** *30 Falling Spring Rd, I-81 exit 6. 717/263-1288; FAX 717/263-6514.* E-mail cha33chm@attmail.com; web www.daysinn.com. 107 rms, 3 story. Apr-Oct: S $46-$60; D $51-$65; each addl $7; suites $70-$85; under 17 free; lower rates rest of yr. Crib free. Pet accepted. TV; cable (premium). Complimentary continental bkfst. Restaurant adj 6 am-11 pm. Ck-out 11 am. Meeting rms. Business servs avail. Downhill ski 15 mi. Cr cds: A, C, D, DS, JCB, MC, V. 🅳 ⟋ ⩯ ⬚ 🔥 SC

★ ★ **HOLIDAY INN.** *1095 Wayne Ave, I-81 exit 5. 717/263-3400.* 139 rms, 2 story. Apr-Oct: S $59; D $66; each adl $7; under 19 free; wkend rates; golf plan; lower rates rest of yr. Crib free. Pet accepted, some restrictions. TV; cable, VCR avail. Pool; poolside serv, lifeguard. Restaurant 6 am-2 pm, 5-10 pm. Rm serv. Bar. Ck-out noon. Meeting rms. Business servs avail. Some in-rm modem links. Bellhops. Sundries. Valet serv. 18-hole golf privileges. Health club privileges. Cr cds: A, D, DS, JCB, MC, V. · 🅳 ⟋ 🎿 ⩯ ⬚ 🔥 SC

✔ ★ **TRAVELODGE.** *565 Lincoln Way E (US 30), I-81 exit 6. 717/264-4187; FAX 717/264-2446.* 52 rms, 3 story. S $49-$51; D $53-$57; each addl $7; under 18 free. Crib free. Pet accepted, some restrictions. TV; cable (premium). Coffee in rms. Restaurant 6 am-2 pm, 4:30-9:30 pm. Rm serv. Bar 11 am-2 pm, 4:30-9:30 pm. Ck-out noon. Meeting rm. Health club privileges. Refrigerators avail. Some balconies. Cr cds: A, C, D, DS, ER, JCB, MC, V. 🅳 ⟋ ⬚ 🔥 SC

Inn

★ ★ **PENN NATIONAL INN.** *(3809 Anthony Hwy, Mont Alto 17237) E on PA 30, then S on PA 997. 717/352-2400; FAX 717/352-3926; res: 800/231-0080.* 36 rms, 4 in manor house, 2 story. Mid-Apr-Oct: S $80-$100; D $90-$110; each addl $10-$15; under 18 free; golf plan; monthly rates; lower rates rest of yr. Crib free. Pet accepted, some restrictions. TV; cable. Heated pool. Playground. Complimentary full bkfst. Coffee in rms. Restaurant (Apr-Oct) 7 am-7 pm. Ck-out 11 am, ck-in 2 pm. Business servs avail. Lighted tennis. 18-hole golf; greens fee $25-$45, putting green, driving range. Refrigerators; microwaves avail. Federalist-style manor house built in 1847, additions built in 1989. Cr cds: A, MC, V. 🅳 ⟋ ➤ 🎿 ⛷ ⩯ 🎣 ⬚ 🔥 SC

Clarion

Motels

★ ★ **DAYS INN.** *PA 68 & I-80, exit 9N. 814/226-8682; FAX 814/226-8372.* 150 rms, 2 story. S $46-$56; D $51-$61; each addl $5; under 18 free; tennis, golf, ski plans; higher rates: Autumn Leaf Festival, hunting season. Crib free. Pet accepted. TV; cable (premium), VCR avail (movies). Heated pool; lifeguard. Complimentary continental bkfst. Restaurant 6 am-2 pm, 5-10 pm. Rm serv. Bar 4 pm-2 am; entertainment. Ck-out noon. Coin lndry. Meeting rms. Business servs avail. Sundries. Golf privileges. Health club privileges. Cr cds: A, C, D, DS, JCB, MC, V. 🅳 📶 🎿 ⚊ 🛇 🐾 SC

✔ ★ **SUPER 8.** *RD 3, I-80 exit 9. 814/226-4550; FAX 814/227-2337.* 99 rms, 9 kits. S, D $45-$80; each addl $5; kit. units avail; wkly, monthly rates (winter); under 18 free. Crib free. Pet accepted. TV; cable (premium), VCR avail (movies). Pool; lifeguard. Complimentary continental bkfst. Restaurant adj 6 am-10 pm. Ck-out noon. Business servs avail. In-rm modem link. Cr cds: A, C, D, DS, ER, MC, V. 🅳 📶 ⚊ 🛇 🐾 SC

Clearfield (Clearfield Co)

Motel

★ ★ **DAYS INN.** *R R 2, PA 879 & I-80 exit 19. 814/765-5381; FAX 814/765-7885.* 119 rms, 2 story. S $40-$60; D $46-$80; each addl $6; under 18 free; higher rates special events. Crib free. Pet accepted. TV, VCR avail (movies). Pool; lifeguard. Complimentary continental bkfst. Bar 4 pm-2 am. Ck-out noon. Meeting rms. Business servs avail. In-rm modem link. Exercise equipt; treadmill, bicycles, weight machine. Cr cds: A, C, D, DS, MC, V. 🅳 📶 ⚊ 🏃 🛇 🐾 SC

Connellsville *(See also Uniontown)*

Motel

★ **MELODY MOTOR LODGE.** *1607 Morrell Ave (US 119). 724/628-9600.* 46 rms. S, D $34-$47; higher rates Labor Day wkend. Crib $5. Pet accepted, some restrictions. TV; cable. Restaurant adj 6 am-10 pm. Bar 4 pm-midnight. Ck-out 11 am. Picnic tables. Cr cds: A, DS, MC, V. 📶 🐾

Denver/Adamstown *(See also Lancaster, Reading)*

Motel

★ ★ ★ **BLACK HORSE LODGE.** *(2180 N Reading Rd, Denver 17517) jct PA Tpke exit 21 & US 272. 717/336-7563; FAX 717/336-1110.* 74 rms, 2 story. Mid-Apr-mid-Nov: S $59-$129; D $69-$139; under 13 free; suites $100-$250; wkly, monthly rates; golf plans; lower rates rest of yr. Crib free. Pet accepted, some restrictions. TV; cable. Pool. Complimentary full bkfst. Complimentary coffee in rms. Restaurant 11:30 am-2:15 pm, 5-10 pm. Bar to 11 pm. Ck-out noon. Coin lndry. Business servs avail. Golf privileges. Many refrigerators, microwaves avail; some bathrm phones. Private patios, balconies. Picnic tables, grills. Cr cds: A, C, D, DS, MC, V. 📶 🏃 ⚊ 🛇 🐾 SC

Downingtown *(See also West Chester)*

Motor Hotel

★ ★ **HOLIDAY INN.** *(815 N Pottstown Pike, Exton 19341) N on PA 113 to PA 100, 1 mi S of PA Tpke exit 23. 610/363-1100; FAX 610/524-2329.* 225 rms, 4 story. S, D $99; under 18 free. Crib free. Pet accepted. TV; cable (premium). 2 pools, 1 indoor; poolside serv, lifeguard. Coffee in rms. Restaurant 6:30 am-10 pm; Sat from 7 am; Sun 7 am-1 pm. Rm serv. Bar 2 pm-2 am; entertainment exc Sun. Ck-out 11 am. Coin lndry. Meeting rms. Business servs avail. In-rm modem link. Valet serv. Gift shop. Airport transportation. Health club privileges. Refrigerators, microwaves avail. Picnic tables. Cr cds: A, C, D, DS, ER, JCB, MC, V. 🅳 📶 ⚊ 🛇 🐾 SC

Du Bois *(See also Clearfield)*

Motels

★ ★ **HOLIDAY INN.** *US 219 & I-80 exit 16. 814/371-5100; FAX 814/375-0230.* 161 rms, 2 story. S $62-$79; D $68-$85; each addl $6; studio rms $75; under 18 free. Pet accepted. TV; cable (premium), VCR avail. Pool; wading, poolside serv, lifeguard. Complimentary coffee in rms. Restaurant 7 am-2 pm, 5-10 pm. Rm serv. Bar 5 pm-1 am. Ck-out noon. Coin lndry. Meeting rms. Business servs avail. In-rm modem link. Bellhops. Free airport transportation. Health club privileges. Cr cds: A, C, D, DS, JCB, MC, V.

D ⬚ ⬚ ⬚ ⬚ ⬚ SC

★ ★ **RAMADA INN.** *Jct I-80 exit 17 & PA 255N. 814/371-7070; FAX 814/371-1055.* 96 rms, 2-3 story. No elvtr. S $53-$65; D $59-$75; each addl $10; suites $80-$150; under 18 free. Crib free. Pet accepted. TV; cable (premium), VCR avail. Indoor pool; poolside serv. Restaurant 6:30 am-2 pm, 5-10 pm. Rm serv. Bar 5 pm-2 am; entertainment exc Sun. Ck-out noon. Meeting rms. Business servs avail. Airport transportation. Golf privileges, pro. Cr cds: A, C, D, DS, JCB, MC, V. D ⬚ ⬚ ⬚ ⬚ ⬚ ⬚ SC

Erie

Motel

★ ★ ★ **RAMADA INN.** *6101 Wattsburg Rd (16509). 814/825-3100; FAX 814/825-0857.* 122 rms, 2 story. July-Sept: S, D $75-$85; each addl $8; suites $65-$95; under 16 free; ski, wkend plans; lower rates rest of yr. Crib free. Pet accepted. TV; cable (premium), VCR (movies avail). Heated pool; wading pool, lifeguard. Restaurant 6:30 am-10 pm. Rm serv. Bar 5 pm-2 am. Ck-out noon. Meeting rms. Business center. In-rm modem link. Sundries. Downhill ski 15 mi. Game rm. Cr cds: A, C, D, DS, JCB, MC, V.

D ⬚ ⬚ ⬚ ⬚ ⬚ ⬚ SC ⬚

Franklin (Venango Co) (See also Meadville)

Motor Hotel

★ ★ **INN AT FRANKLIN.** *1411 Liberty St. 814/437-3031; FAX 814/432-7481; res: 800/535-4052.* 85 rms, 6 story. Apr-Sept: S $65; D $70; each addl $5; under 18 free; wkly, monthly rates; lower rates rest of yr. Pet accepted. TV; cable, VCR avail (movies). Complimentary continental bkfst. Restaurant 6 am-2 pm, 5-10 pm; Sun 7 am-8 pm. Bar. Ck-out 11 am. Business servs avail. Valet serv. Barber, beauty shop. Free airport, bus depot transportation. Cr cds: A, C, D, DS, MC, V. D ⬚ ⬚ ⬚ ⬚ ⬚ SC

Gettysburg (See also York)

Motels

✔ ★ ★ **HOWARD JOHNSON LODGE.** *301 Steinwehr Ave. 717/334-1188.* Web www.gettysburg.com. 77 rms, 2 story. Apr-Oct: S, D $59-$99; under 18 free; lower rates rest of yr. Crib free. Pet accepted, some restrictions. TV; cable (premium), VCR avail. Pool; lifeguard. Complimentary coffee in lobby. Restaurant adj 6:30 am-11 pm. Bar 4 pm-1 am, closed Sun. Ck-out noon. Sundries. Free bus depot transportation. Downhill ski 9 mi; x-country ski adj. Private patios. Sun deck. Cr cds: A, C, D, DS, MC, V.

D ⬚ ⬚ ⬚ ⬚ ⬚ ⬚ SC

★ ★ ★ **QUALITY INN.** *380 Steinwehr Ave. 717/334-1103.* E-mail gbur gqi@mail .cvn.net; web www.gettysburg.com. 109 rms, 2 story. Apr-Oct: S, D $69-$104; suite $97-$135; under 16 free; lower rates rest of yr. Crib free. Pet accepted, some restrictions. TV; cable (premium), VCR avail. 2 pools; 1 indoor, lifeguard. Coffee in rm. Restaurant opp 6 am-11 pm. Bar 6 pm-1 am. Ck-out noon. Coin lndry. Meeting rm. Gift shop. Free bus depot transportation. Putting green. Downhill/x-country ski 8 mi. Exercise equipt; weight machines, bicycle, sauna. Balconies. Cr cds: A, C, D, DS, MC, V. D ⬚ ⬚ ⬚ ⬚ ⬚ ⬚ SC

Harrisburg (See also Carlisle, Hershey, York)

Motels

★ ★ **BEST WESTERN.** *300 N Mountain Rd (17112), I-81 exit 26. 717/652-7180; FAX 717/541-8991.* Web www.bestwestern.com/best.html. 49 rms, 2 story. S $50-$80; D $50-$85; each addl $3; under 13 free. Crib $5. Pet accepted. TV; cable (premium). Restaurant 6:30 am-9 pm. Bar 11 am-11 pm. Ck-out 11 am. Business servs avail. In-rm modem link. Sundries. Microwaves avail. Cr cds: A, C, D, DS, MC, V. ⬚ ⬚ ⬚ SC

★ **BUDGETEL INN.** *200 N Mountain Rd (17112), I-81 exit 26. 717/540-9339; FAX 717/540-9486.* Web www.budgetel.com. 66 rms, 3 story, 8 suites. Apr-Oct: S $56.95-$64.95; D $62.95-$71.95; suites $65.95-$72.95; under 19 free; lower rates rest of yr. Crib free. Pet accepted. TV; cable (premium), VCR avail. Complimentary continental bkfst. Complimentary coffee in rms. Restaurant nearby. Ck-out noon. Coin lndry. Meeting rms. Business center. In-rm modem link. Sundries. Refrigerator in suites; microwaves avail. Cr cds: A, C, D, DS, MC, V. D ⬚ ⬚ ⬚ SC ⬚

★ ★ **COMFORT INN.** *4021 Union Deposit Lane (17109), I-83 exit 29. 717/561-8100; FAX 717/561-1357.* 115 rms, 5 story. June-Oct: S, D $79-$99; under 18 free; higher rates car shows; lower rates rest of yr. Crib free. Pet accepted. TV; cable (premium). Heated pool; lifeguard. Complimentary continental bkfst. Restaurant adj 6 am-10 pm. Ck-out noon. Coin lndry. Meeting rms. Business servs avail. Free airport, RR station transportation. Health club privileges. Microwaves avail. Cr cds: A, C, D, DS, ER, JCB, MC, V.

D 🐾 🌊 🏊 🐕 SC

✔ ★ ★ ★ **HOLIDAY INN.** *(I-83 & PA Tpke, New Cumberland 17070) S on I-83, W on I-283. 717/774-2721; FAX 717/774-2485.* 196 rms, 2 story. May-Oct: S, D $59-$99; each addl $10; suites $160; under 18 free; family, wknd, hol rates; ski plans; higher rates special events; lower rates rest of yr. Crib free. Pet accepted, some restrictions; $10. TV; cable (premium). Restaurant 6:30 am-2 pm, 5-9 pm; Fri, Sat to 10 pm. Rm serv. Bar 5 pm-2 am; entertainment. Ck-out 11 am. Meeting rms. Business center. In-rm modem link. Bellhops. Valet serv. Coin lndry. Free airport, RR station transportation. Exercise equipt; treadmill, stair machine. Indoor pool; whirlpool. Game rm. Some balconies. Refrigerators, microwaves avail. Picnic tables, grills. Luxury level. Cr cds: A, C, D, DS, JCB, MC, V.

D 🐾 🌊 🍴 🏊 🐕 SC 🏌

★ ★ **HOLIDAY INN-WEST.** *(5401 Carlisle Pike, Mechanicsburg 17055) W on I-81 exit 18 S. 717/697-0321; FAX 717/697-7594.* 218 rms, 2 story. Feb-Oct: S $93; D $103; each addl $10; suites $125-$200; under 18 free; wkly rates; higher rates special events; lower rates rest of yr. Crib free. Pet accepted, some restrictions; $50 deposit. TV; cable (premium). Complimentary continental bkfst. Complimentary coffee in rms. Restaurant 6:30 am-9 pm. Rm serv. Bar 5 pm-2 am; entertainment. Ck-out noon. Meeting rms. Business servs avail. Coin lndry. Exercise equipt; weight machine, bicycle. Miniature golf. Heated indoor/outdoor pool; lifeguard. Some in-rm whirlpools; microwaves avail. Picnic tables, grills. Cr cds: A, C, D, DS, JCB, MC, V. D 🐾 🌊 🍴 🏊 🐕 SC

★ ★ ★ **RADISSON PENN HARRIS.** *(1150 Camp Hill Bypass, Camp Hill 17011) S on US 15, Camp Hill Bypass; 6 mi N of PA Turnpike exit 17. 717/763-7117; FAX 717/763-4518; res: 800/345-7366.* 250 rms, 2-3 story. No elvtr. S $69-$119; D $79-$139; each addl $10; suites $225-$400; under 18 free. Crib free. Pet accepted. TV; cable (premium). Pool; poolside serv, lifeguard. Restaurant 6:30 am-10 pm. Rm serv. Bar 3 pm-2 am. Ck-out noon. Convention facilities. Business center. In-rm modem link. Valet serv. Bellhops. Free airport transportation. Exercise equipt; bicycles, stair machines. Cr cds: A, C, D, DS, MC, V.

D 🐾 🌊 🍴 🏊 🐕 SC 🏌

✔ ★ **RED ROOF INN.** *400 Corporate Circle (17110), I-81 exit 24. 717/657-1445; FAX 717/657-2775.* 110 rms, 2 story. S $40-$44; D $45-$57; under 18 free. Crib free. Pet accepted. TV; cable (premium). Complimentary coffee in lobby Mon-Fri. Restaurant nearby. Ck-out noon. Business servs avail. In-rm modem link. Cr cds: A, D, DS, MC, V.

D 🐾 🐕 🔥

Motor Hotel

★ ★ ★ **SHERATON HARRISBURG EAST.** *800 East Park Dr (17111), I-83 exit 29. 717/561-2800; FAX 717/561-8398.* 174 rms, 3 story. S $86-$105; D $96-$115; each addl $10; suites $145-$165; under 18 free. Crib free. Pet accepted, some restrictions. TV; cable (premium). Heated pool; whirlpool, lifeguard. Restaurant 6:30 am-10 pm. Rm serv. Bar 11-2 am. Ck-out noon. Meeting rms. Business servs avail. In-rm modem link. Bellhops. Valet serv. Shopping arcade. Free airport transportation. Golf privileges. Exercise rm; instructor, weights, bicycles, sauna. Game rm. Cr cds: A, C, D, DS, MC, V.

D 🐾 🍴 🌊 🏊 🐕 SC

Hotel

★ ★ ★ **WYNDHAM GARDEN.** *765 Eisenhower Blvd (17111), I-283 exit 1. 717/558-9500; FAX 717/558-8956.* 167 rms, 6 story. May-Oct: S, D $89-$119; each addl $10; suites $150; under 19 free; ski plans; wknd rates; higher rates car shows; lower rates rest of yr. Crib free. Pet accepted. TV; cable (premium). Heated pool; lifeguard. Coffee in rms. Restaurant 6 am-10 pm. Bar 5 pm-2 am. Ck-out noon. Meeting rms. Business servs avail. In-rm modem link. Concierge. Free airport, RR station, bus depot transportation. Downhill ski 20 mi. Exercise equipt; weight machine, stair machine. Refrigerator, wet bar in suites; microwaves avail. Cr cds: A, C, D, DS, ER, JCB, MC, V. D 🐾 🌊 🍴 🏊 🐕 SC

Hazleton *(See also Bloomsburg, Wilkes-Barre)*

Motel

★ ★ **HOLIDAY INN.** *1¹/₂ mi N on PA 309. 717/455-2061; FAX 717/455-9387.* 107 rms, 2 story. S, D, studio rms $72; under 18 free. Crib free. Pet accepted. TV; cable. Pool; lifeguard. Restaurant 6 am-10 pm. Rm serv. Bar 5 pm-2 am. Ck-out noon. Meeting rms.

Business servs avail. In-rm modem link. Bellhops. Sundries. Cr cds: A, C, D, DS, ER, JCB, MC, V. [D] [symbols]

Hershey *(See also Harrisburg)*

Motor Hotel

★ ★ ★ **HOLIDAY INN HARRISBURG-HERSHEY.** *(604 Station Rd, Grantville 17028)* *N on PA 743 to I-81, exit 28.* 717/469-0661; FAX 717/469-7755. E-mail info@stayholiday .com; web www.stayholiday.com. 195 rms, 4 story. Memorial Day-mid-Oct: S $119-$149; D $129-$159; each addl $10; suites $175-$275; under 19 free; lower rates rest of yr. Crib free. Pet accepted. TV; cable, VCR avail. 2 pools, 1 indoor; whirlpool, wading pool. Restaurant 6:30 am-10 pm. Rm serv. Bar 11-2 am; entertainment. Ck-out noon. Coin lndry. Meeting rms. Business center. In-rm modem link. Bellhops. Valet serv. Shopping arcade. Airport, RR station, bus depot transportation. Exercise equipt; weight machine, bicycles, sauna. Lawn games. Microwaves avail. Balconies. Cr cds: A, C, D, DS, ER, JCB, MC, V.

[D] [symbols]

Huntingdon *(See also Altoona)*

Motels

★ ★ **DAYS INN.** *RD 1, Box 353, 4th St at US 22.* 814/643-3934; FAX 814/643-3005. 76 rms, 3 story. S $44-$56; D $49-$61; each addl $5; under 13 free; higher rates special events. Crib free. Pet accepted; $5. TV; cable. Restaurant 6 am-10 pm; Fri, Sat to 11 pm. Bar 4:30 pm-2 am. Ck-out 11 am. Meeting rms. Business servs avail. In-rm modem link. Valet serv. Sundries. Microwaves avail. Cr cds: A, C, D, DS, MC, V.

[D] [symbols]

✔ ★ ★ **HUNTINGDON MOTOR INN.** *US 22 & PA 26.* 814/643-1133; FAX 814/643-1331. 48 rms, 2 story. S $37-$40; D $46-$52; each addl $4. Crib free. Pet accepted, some restrictions. TV; cable. Restaurant 7 am-9 pm. Bar 4:30 pm-2 am. Ck-out 11 pm. Meeting rms. Business servs avail. In-rm modem link. Microwaves avail. Balconies. Cr cds: A, C, D, DS, MC, V. [symbols]

Indiana *(See also Johnstown)*

Motel

★ ★ ★ **HOLIDAY INN.** *1395 Wayne Ave.* 724/463-3561; FAX 724/463-8006. 159 rms, 2 story. S, D $79; suites $125; family, wkend rates; golf plans; higher rates university events. Crib free. Pet accepted. TV; cable (premium). Indoor pool, sauna, poolside serv, lifeguard. Complimentary full bkfst. Restaurant 6:30 am-10 pm; Sat, Sun from 7 am. Rm serv. Bar 2 pm-2 am; entertainment. Ck-out noon. Meeting rms. Business servs avail. In-rm modem link. Miniature golf. Game rm. Cr cds: A, C, D, DS, MC, V.

[D] [symbols]

Johnstown

Motels

✔ ★ ★ **COMFORT INN.** *455 Theatre Dr (15904), US 219 exit Elton.* 814/266-3678; FAX 814/266-9783. 117 rms, 5 story, 27 suites. S $57-$63; D $63-$69; each addl $6; suites $84-$91; kit. units $94-$99; under 18 free; monthly rates; higher rates special events. Crib free. Pet accepted; $6. TV; cable, VCR (movies). Indoor pool; whirlpool, lifeguard. Complimentary continental bkfst. Restaurant nearby. Ck-out noon. Coin lndry. Meeting rms. Business center. In-rm modem link. Sundries. Free airport transportation. Exercise equipt; weights, bicycles. Health club privileges. Refrigerator, wet bar in suites; microwaves avail. Picnic table, grill. Cr cds: A, C, D, DS, ER, JCB, MC, V. [D] [symbols]

✔ ★ **SLEEP INN.** *453 Theatre Dr (15904).* 814/262-9292; FAX 814/262-0486. 62 rms, 59 with shower only, 3 story. S $49-$55; D $55-$61; under 18 free; wkly rates; higher rates: Labor Day, sporting events. Crib free. Pet accepted, some restrictions; $6. TV; cable (premium), VCR avail. Complimentary continental bkfst. Restaurant adj 11 am-9 pm. Ck-out noon. Meeting rm. Business servs avail. In-rm modem link. Airport transportation. Microwaves avail. Cr cds: A, C, D, DS, ER, JCB, MC, V. [D] [symbols]

Hotel

★ ★ **HOLIDAY INN-DOWNTOWN.** *250 Market St (15901), US 219 exit 56W.* 814/535-7777; FAX 814/539-1393. 164 rms, 6 story. S, D $72-$89; suites $238-$290; under 18 free. Crib free. Pet accepted, some restrictions. TV; cable (premium). Indoor pool; whirlpool, sauna, poolside serv, lifeguard. Coffee in rms. Restaurant 7 am-10 pm. Bar 4 pm-midnight. Ck-out noon. Meeting rms. Business center. In-rm modem link. Airport transportation. Exercise equipt; bicycles, treadmills. Health club privileges. Cr cds: A, C, D, DS, JCB, MC, V. [D] [≈] [≈] [🏃] [≈] [🐾] [SC] [🏌]

Kennett Square (See also West Chester; also see Wilmington, DE)

Inn

★ ★ ★ **BRANDYWINE RIVER HOTEL.** *(Box 1058, US 1 & PA 100, Chadds Ford 19317) Approx 6 mi E on US 1.* 610/388-1200; FAX 610/388-1200. 40 rms, 2 story, 10 suites. S, D $119; each addl $10; suites $140. Crib free. Pet accepted, some restrictions. TV; cable. Complimentary continental bkfst. Restaurant adj 11:30 am-10 pm. Ck-out 11 am, ck-in 2 pm. Meeting rms. Business servs avail. Airport, RR station, bus depot transportation. Exercise equipt; stair machine, treadmill. Bathrm phones; refrigerator in suites. Specialty shops on site. Cr cds: A, C, D, DS, MC, V. [D] [≈] [🏃] [≈] [≈] [🐾] [SC]

Kulpsville (See also Philadelphia)

Motor Hotel

★ ★ **HOLIDAY INN.** *1750 Sumneytown Pike, at exit 31 of PA Tpke NE extension.* 215/368-3800; FAX 215/368-7824. 183 rms, 4 story. S $79-$84; D $84-$89; each addl $5; suites $89-$99; under 18 free. Crib free. Pet accepted. TV; cable (premium), VCR avail. Pool; poolside serv, lifeguard. Coffee in rms. Restaurant 6:45 am-2 pm, 5:30-10 pm. Rm serv. Bar 4 pm-2 am; entertainment Wed-Sat. Ck-out noon. Meeting rms. Business servs avail. In-rm modem link. Valet serv. Airport transportation. Exercise equipt; weights, treadmill. Cr cds: A, C, D, DS, JCB, MC, V. [D] [≈] [≈] [🏃] [≈] [🐾] [SC]

Lancaster (See also Reading, York)

Motel

★ ★ **RAMADA.** *2250 Lincoln Hwy E (17602), Rte 30 E.* 717/393-5499; FAX 717/293-1014. Web www.ramada.com/ramada.html. 166 rms, 5 story. Mid-June-Oct: S, D $84-$129; each addl $10; under 18 free; lower rates rest of yr. Crib free. Pet accepted, some restrictions. TV; cable. 2 pools, 1 indoor; sauna. Playground. Ck-out 11 am. Coin lndry. Meeting rms. Business servs avail. In-rm modem link. Free airport transportation. Tennis. 27-hole golf privileges, pro, putting green, driving range. Health club privileges. Game rm. Lawn games. Refrigerators. Balconies. Picnic tables. Cr cds: A, C, D, DS, ER, JCB, MC, V. [D] [≈] [🎱] [🏌] [≈] [≈] [🐾] [SC]

Motor Hotel

★ ★ ★ **BEST WESTERN EDEN RESORT INN.** *222 Eden Rd (17601).* 717/569-6444; FAX 717/569-4208. E-mail eden@edenresort.com; web www.edenresort.com. 274 rms, 3 story. June-Nov: S, D $125-$139; each addl $10; suites $129-$249; under 18 free; varied lower rates rest of yr. Crib free. Pet accepted. TV; cable (premium). 2 pools, 1 indoor; whirlpool, poolside serv, lifeguard. Playground. Restaurant 6:30 am-11 pm; wkends to midnight. Rm serv. Bar 11-2 am; entertainment. Ck-out noon. Meeting rms. Business center. In-rm modem link. Valet serv. Free airport transportation. Gift shop. Lighted tennis. Exercise equipt; weights, bicycles, saunas. Lawn games. Microwaves avail. Some balconies. Cr cds: A, C, D, DS, MC, V. [D] [≈] [🎱] [≈] [🏃] [≈] [🐾] [SC] [🏌]

Hotel

✔ ★ ★ **HOTEL BRUNSWICK.** *(17603), at jct Chestnut & Queen Sts.* 717/397-4801; FAX 717/397-4991; res: 800/233-0182. E-mail hblanc@lancnews.info.net; web www.hotel brunswick.com. 222 rms, 7 story. S $62-$78; D $72-$86; each addl $6; under 17 free; monthly, wkly, wkend rates; golf plan; lower rates Nov-Apr. Crib free. Pet accepted; $100. TV; cable, VCR avail (movies). Indoor pool; lifeguard. Restaurant 7 am-1:30 pm, 5:30-9 pm. Bar; entertainment. Ck-out noon. Coin lndry. Meeting rms. Business servs avail. Free garage parking. Exercise equipt; weights, bicycles. Refrigerators avail. Cr cds: A, C, D, DS, MC, V. [D] [≈] [≈] [🏃] [≈] [🐾] [SC]

Inns

★ ★ ★ **GENERAL SUTTER.** *(14 E Main St, Lititz 17543) 6 mi N via PA 501, on the Square.* 717/626-2115; FAX 717/626-0992. 14 rms, 3 story. S, D $75-$100. Crib $5. Pet accepted. TV; cable. Dining rm 7 am-9 pm; Sun 8 am-8 pm. Bar 11 am-11 pm. Ck-out noon, ck-in 3 pm. Spacious brick-lined patio. Built in 1764; antique country and Victorian furniture. Fireplace in parlor. Cr cds: A, DS, MC, V. [≈] [🐾]

★ ★ ★ **HISTORIC STRASBURG.** *(PA 896, Strasburg 17579) 8 mi SE via US 30, PA 896.* 717/687-7691; FAX 717/687-6098; res: 800/872-0201. Web www.800padutch.com/.

strasinn.html. 101 rms in 5 buildings, 2 story. Apr-Nov: S, D $119-$129; each addl $15; suites $159-$199; under 12 free; lower rates rest of yr. Crib $7. Pet accepted; $15. TV; cable, VCR avail (movies). Heated pool; whirlpool. Playground. Complimentary full bkfst. Restaurant 7 am-2 pm, 5-9 pm. Bar 11:30 am-11 pm. Ck-out noon. Meeting rms. Business servs avail. Sundries. Gift shop. Exercise equipt; treadmill, bicycle. Lawn games. Balconies. Petting zoo and hot air balloon rides on property (58 acres). Cr cds: A, C, D, DS, MC, V.

Lewistown

Motel

✔ ★ ★ **CLARION INN.** *(US 322, Burnham 17009) just off US 322 at Burnham exit.* *717/248-4961; FAX 717/242-3013.* 119 rms, 2 story. S, D $59; each addl $5; under 18 free. Crib free. Pet accepted. TV; cable (premium). Pool; poolside serv, lifeguard. Restaurant 6 am-2 pm, 5-10 pm. Rm serv. Bar 4 pm-midnight. Ck-out noon. Meeting rms. In-rm modem link. Valet serv. Cr cds: A, C, D, DS, MC, V.

Mansfield *(See also Wellsboro)*

Motel

★ ★ **COMFORT INN.** *300 Gateway Dr. 717/662-3000; FAX 717/662-2551.* 100 rms, 2 story. S $49-$75; D $59-$85; each addl $6; under 18 free; golf plans; higher rates seasonal events. Crib avail. Pet accepted. TV; cable. Complimentary continental bkfst. Ck-out noon. Business servs avail. Exercise equipt; stair machines, bicycles. Cr cds: A, C, D, DS, ER, JCB, MC, V.

Meadville *(See also Franklin)*

Motel

★ ★ **DAYS INN.** *240 Conneaut Lake Rd, I-79 exit 36A. 814/337-4264; FAX 814/337-7304.* 163 rms, 2 story. S $65-$85; D $70-$85; each addl $6; under 18 free; higher rates special events. Crib free. Pet accepted. TV; cable (premium), VCR avail (movies). Indoor pool; whirlpool, lifeguard. Restaurant 7 am-2 pm, 5-10 pm; Sun 7 am-2 pm. Bar 3 pm-2 am. Ck-out 11 am. Coin lndry. Meeting rms. Business servs avail. Cr cds: A, D, DS, JCB, MC, V.

Mercer *(See also Franklin)*

Motel

★ ★ ★ **HOWARD JOHNSON.** *835 Perry Hwy, US 19 S, just off I-80 exit 2. 724/748-3030; FAX 724/748-3484.* 102 rms, 2 story. S $67; D $71-$74; each addl $6; suites $105-$125; under 18 free; higher rates special events. Crib free. Pet accepted. TV; cable (premium), VCR avail. Heated pool; lifeguard. Playground. Restaurant 6 am-11 pm; Fri, Sat open 24 hrs. Rm serv. Bar. Ck-out noon. Coin lndry. Meeting rms. Business servs avail. In-rm modem link. Bellhops. Bus depot transportation. Exercise equipt; weights, bicycles, sauna. Private patios, balconies. Amish craft shop in lobby. Cr cds: A, C, D, DS, JCB, MC, V.

Milford

Motels

★ ★ ★ **BEST WESTERN INN AT HUNTS LANDING.** *(900 US 6 & US 209, Matamoras 18336) 6 mi E on I-84, exit 11. 717/491-2400; FAX 717/491-2422.* 108 rms, 4 story. May-Oct: S $69-$75; D $77-$85; each addl $6; suites $115-$125; under 12 free; lower rates rest of yr. Crib free. Pet accepted. TV; cable. Indoor pool; sauna, lifeguard. Restaurant 6:30 am-9 pm; Fri, Sat to 10 pm; Sun from 7 am. Bar 4-11 pm; entertainment. Ck-out 11 am. Coin lndry. Meeting rms. Business servs avail. In-rm modem link. Sundries. Gift shop. Game rm. Lawn games. Cr cds: A, C, D, DS, MC, V.

✔ ★ ★ **MYER.** *RD 4, Box 8030, 1/4 mi E on US 6, PA 209. 717/296-7223; res: 800/764-6937.* 19 cottages, 1 kit. S $40-$50; D $45-$70; each addl $5; kit. unit $90. Crib free. Pet accepted, some restrictions. TV; cable. Restaurant nearby. Ck-out 11 am. Lawn games. Refrigerators. Picnic tables, grills. Cr cds: A, C, D, DS, MC, V.

New Castle (See also Beaver Falls)

Motel

✔ ★ ★ **COMFORT INN.** *1740 New Butler Rd (16101), 11 mi W on US 422 Business.* 724/658-7700; FAX 724/658-7727. 79 rms, 2 story, 13 suites. S $59-$69; D $64-$79; each addl $5; suites $90-$119; under 18 free. Wkly rates; higher rates July 4, Dec 31. Crib free. Pet accepted, some restrictions; $6/day. TV; cable. Complimentary continental bkfst. Restaurant nearby. Ck-out noon. Meeting rm. Business servs avail. Valet serv. Exercise equipt; weight machine, bicycle, sauna. Some refrigerators. Cr cds: A, C, D, DS, JCB, MC, V.

[D] [symbols] [SC]

New Hope (Bucks Co) (See also Trenton, NJ)

Inns

★ ★ ★ **AARON BURR HOUSE.** *80 W Bridge St.* 215/862-2343; FAX 215/862-2343. 6 rms, 2 story, 2 suites. S, D $75-$150; each addl $20; suite $150-$195; wkly rates; lower rates mid-wk. Pet accepted. TV in sitting rm; cable, VCR avail. Complimentary full bkfst; afternoon refreshments. Restaurant nearby. Ck-out 11 am, ck-in 2 pm. Meeting rm. Business servs avail. Concierge. Free bus depot transportation. Downhill ski 2 mi; x-country ski adj. Lawn games. Fireplace in suites. Built in 1854, some antiques. Screened flagstone patio. Totally nonsmoking. Cr cds: MC, V. [D] [symbols] [SC]

★ ★ ★ **GOLDEN PHEASANT INN.** *(763 River Rd, Erwinna 18920) 13 mi N on PA 32.* 610/294-9595; FAX 610/294-9882. 6 rms, 3 with shower only, 2 story, kit. suite. No rm phones. MAP: S, D $85-$155; each addl $10; suite $125-$155; wkly rates; hols (3-day min). Pet accepted; $10. Complimentary continental bkfst. Coffee in rms. Restaurant 5:30-10 pm. Ck-out 11 am, ck-in 2 pm. Meeting rms. Cr cds: A, C, D, DS, MC, V. [symbols]

✔ ★ ★ ★ **WEDGWOOD.** *111 W Bridge St.* 215/862-2520; FAX 215/862-2570. 12 rms, 2 story. Some rm phones. S $75-$120; D $95-$165; each addl $20; suites $150-$210. Pet accepted. Complimentary full bkfst; afternoon refreshments. Ck-out 11 am, ck-in 2 pm. Concierge serv. Meeting rm. Business servs avail. Health club privileges. Lawn games. Microwaves avail. Picnic tables, grills. Built 1870; antiques, many Wedgwood pieces, some fireplaces. Totally nonsmoking. Cr cds: MC, V. [D] [symbols] [SC]

Philadelphia

Motel

✔ ★ ★ **COMFORT INN.** *(3660 Street Rd, Bensalem 19020) N on I-95 to Street Rd W exit, 3 mi W.* 215/245-0100; FAX 215/245-1851. 141 units, 3 story. S $75-$109; D $85-$125; each addl $10; suites $125; family rates. Crib free. Pet accepted, some restrictions. TV; cable (premium). Complimentary continental bkfst. Restaurant nearby. Bar 4 pm-2 am; entertainment. Ck-out noon. Meeting rms. Business servs avail. In-rm modem link. Gift shop. Exercise equipt; weights, bicycles. Game rm. Some in-rm whirlpools. Cr cds: A, C, D, DS, ER, JCB, MC, V. [D] [symbols] [SC]

Motor Hotels

✔ ★ ★ **BEST WESTERN-CENTER CITY.** *501 N 22nd St (19130), in Center City.* 215/568-8300; FAX 215/557-0259. 183 rms, 3 story. Apr-Oct: S $99-$119.50; D $109-$129; each addl $10; suites $150; under 18 free; family rates. Pet accepted, some restrictions. TV; cable (premium), VCR avail. Complimentary coffee in lobby. Restaurant 6:30 am-10:30 pm. Bar 11-2 am. Ck-out noon. Meeting rms. Business servs avail. In-rm modem link. Bellhops. Valet serv. Gift shop. Exercise equipt; treadmill, stair machine. Pool; lifeguard. Refrigerators, microwaves avail. Cr cds: A, C, D, DS, MC, V. [D] [symbols] [SC]

★ ★ ★ **HILTON-PHILADELPHIA AIRPORT.** *4509 Island Ave (19153), at Intl Airport, south of downtown.* 215/365-4150; FAX 215/937-6382. 330 rms, 9 story. S, D $109-$149; suites $325; studio rms $150; under 18 free; wkend rates. Crib free. Pet accepted, some restrictions. TV; cable (premium). Indoor pool; whirlpool. Restaurant 6 am-11 pm. Rm serv 24 hrs. Bar 11-2 am. Ck-out noon. Meeting rms. Business center. In-rm modem link. Bellhops. Valet serv. Gift shop. Free airport transportation. Exercise equipt; weights, bicycles. Luxury level. Cr cds: A, C, D, DS, ER, MC, V. [D] [symbols] [SC]

Hotels

★ ★ ★ ★ **FOUR SEASONS HOTEL PHILADELPHIA.** *1 Logan Square (19103), on Logan Circle, downtown.* 215/963-1500; FAX 215/963-9506. Web www.fshr.com. This elegant eight-story hotel has a magnificent setting on Logan Circle, reminiscent of the Place de la Concorde in Paris. Guest rooms are large and uncluttered, and the spacious marble lobby has an indoor garden with a fountain that makes it easy to forget that this is the heart of a large city. 371 rms, 8 story. S $250-$325; D $280-$355; each addl $30; suites $540-$1,290; under 18 free; wkend rates. Pet accepted. Garage $12-$24. TV; cable (premium), VCR avail. Indoor pool; whirlpool, poolside serv, lifeguard. Restaurants 6:30-1 am; Sat, Sun from 7 am. Rm serv 24 hrs. Bar 11-2 am; pianist. Ck-out 1 pm. Convention facilities. Business center. In-rm modem link. Concierge. Beauty shop. Exercise rm; instructor, weights, bicycles, sauna. Massage. Minibars; microwaves avail. Some balconies. Cr cds: A, C, D, ER, JCB, MC, V. D 🐾 ≈ 🏋 🏃 🐾 🏊

★ ★ ★ **MARRIOTT.** *1201 Market St (19107), in Center City. 215/625-2900; FAX 215/625-6000.* E-mail 74161.1366@compuserv.com. 1,200 rms, 23 story, 56 suites. S $159-$208; D $179-$228; suites $350-$1,000; under 12 free; wkend, hol rates. Crib free. Pet accepted. Valet parking $21. TV; cable (premium), VCR avail. Indoor pool; wading pool, whirlpool, poolside serv. Restaurants 6-1:30 am. 24 hr rm serv. Bar 5 pm-2 am. Ck-out 12:30 pm. Coin lndry. Convention facilities. Business center. In-rm modem link. Concierge. Shopping arcade. Beauty shop. Exercise equipt; weight machine, stair machine, sauna. Refrigerator in suites; microwaves avail. Connected to shopping mall. Luxury level. Cr cds: A, C, D, DS, ER, JCB, MC, V. D 🐾 ≈ 🏋 🏃 🐾 🐾 SC 🏊

★ ★ ★ ★ **THE RITTENHOUSE.** *210 W Rittenhouse Square (19103), downtown. 215/546-9000; FAX 215/732-3364; res: 800/635-1042.* E-mail hotel@rittenhouse.com. Subdued elegance and superior, intimate service are the hallmarks of the lower floors of a residential building on fashionable Rittenhouse Square, a verdant park in central Philadelphia. The hotel is suitable for business travelers, family vacationers and honeymooners. 133 rms, 9 story. S, D $315-$340; suites $475-$1,200; wkend rates. Crib free. Pet accepted. Garage; valet parking $23. TV; cable (premium), VCR (movies avail). Indoor pool; poolside serv. Restaurants 6:30-2 am. Rm serv 24 hrs. Bar; entertainment. Ck-out 1 pm. Meeting rms. Business center. In-rm modem link. Concierge. Barber, beauty shop. Exercise rm; instructor, weight machine, bicycles, sauna, steam rm. Massage. Bathrm phones, minibars; microwaves avail. Cr cds: A, C, D, DS, MC, V. D 🐾 ≈ 🏋 🏃 🐾 🏊

★ ★ ★ **SHERATON SOCIETY HILL.** *1 Dock St (19106), in Society Hill. 215/238-6000; FAX 215/922-2709.* Web www.ITTsheraton.com. 365 units, 4 story. S, D $169-$225; suites $375-$3,000; under 17 free; wkend rates. Crib free. Pet accepted. Covered parking (fee). TV; cable (premium), VCR avail. Indoor pool; whirlpool, wading pool, poolside serv. Coffee in rms. Restaurants 6:30 am-2 pm, 5-10 pm. Rm serv 24 hrs. Bar noon-2 am. Ck-out noon. Convention facilities. Business servs avail. In-rm modem link. Concierge. Shopping arcade. Exercise rm; instructor, weights, bicycles, sauna. Massage. Minibars; some refrigerators. Cr cds: A, C, D, DS, ER, JCB, MC, V. D 🐾 ≈ 🏋 🏃 🐾 SC

★ ★ **TRAVELODGE.** *2015 Penrose Ave (19145), in Packer Park subdivision, near Intl Airport, south of downtown. 215/755-6500; FAX 215/465-7517.* 208 rms, 17 story. S $79-$99; D $89-$109; each addl $6; under 18 free; wkly, wkend, hol rates; higher rates special events. Crib free. Pet accepted, some restrictions; $35. TV; cable (premium). Heated pool; wading pool, poolside serv. Complimentary continental bkfst. Complimentary coffee in rms. Restaurant 6:30 am-10 pm. Bar 7-2 am. Ck-out noon. Coin lndry. Meeting rms. Business servs avail. In-rm modem link. Gift shop. Free airport, RR station transportation. Tennis privileges. 18-hole golf privileges. Exercise equipt; weights, bicycle. Some refrigerators; microwaves avail. Cr cds: A, C, D, DS, JCB, MC, V.
D 🐾 🏃 🏌 ≈ 🏋 🏃 🐾 SC

★ ★ ★ **THE WARWICK.** *1701 Locust St (19103), downtown. 215/735-6000; FAX 215/790-7766; res: 800/523-4210 (exc PA).* 180 rms, 20 story, 20 kits. S $165-$185; D $195-$200; each addl $15; suites $185-$390; studio rms $185; apt $195; under 12 free; wkend plans. Crib free. Pet accepted, some restrictions. Garage (fee). TV; cable (premium), VCR avail. Restaurant 6:30 am-midnight. Bar 11-2 am. Ck-out noon. Meeting rms. Business servs avail. In-rm modem link. Concierge. Barber, beauty shop. Health club privileges. Cr cds: A, C, D, MC, V. D 🐾 🐾 🐾 SC

★ ★ ★ **WYNDHAM FRANKLIN PLAZA.** *2 Franklin Plaza (19103), jct 17th & Race Sts, downtown. 215/448-2000; FAX 215/448-2864.* E-mail franklinplaza@wyndham.com; web www.wyndham.com. 758 rms, 26 story. S $165-$200; D $175-$210; each addl $20; suites $300-$1,000; under 18 free; wkend rates. Crib free. Pet accepted; some restrictions. Garage $15. TV; cable (premium), VCR avail. Indoor pool; whirlpool, poolside serv. Complimentary coffee in rms. Restaurant 6 am-11 pm. Bars 11-1 am. Ck-out noon. Convention facilities. Business center. In-rm modem link. Drugstore. Barber, beauty shop. Tennis. Exercise rm; instructor, weights, bicycles, sauna, steam rm. Massage. Refrigerators; microwaves avail. Cr cds: A, C, D, DS, ER, JCB, MC, V. D 🐾 🏌 ≈ 🏋 🏃 🐾 SC 🏊

Pittsburgh *(See also Beaver Falls, Connellsville, Washington)*

Motels

✔★ ★ **HAMPTON INN.** *555 Trumbull Dr (15205), across river, west of downtown.* 412/922-0100; FAX 412/921-7631. 135 rms, 6 story. June-Nov: S $69-$75; D $79; under 18 free; wkend rates; lower rates rest of yr. Crib free. Pet accepted. TV; cable (premium). Complimentary continental bkfst. Restaurant nearby. Ck-out noon. Meeting rms. Business servs avail. In-rm modem link. Valet serv. Free airport transportation. Health club privileges. Picnic tables. Cr cds: A, C, D, DS, MC, V. 🅓 ⏻ ✕ ⊠ ⚲ SC

★ ★ **HAWTHORN SUITES.** *700 Mansfield Ave (15205), at Noblestown Rd, or I-279 exit 4, south of downtown.* 412/279-6300; FAX 412/279-4993. E-mail tn009665@psi net.com; web www.hawthorn.com. 151 suites, 2 story. S $89-$119; D $119-$149; wkly, monthly rates. Crib free. Pet accepted, some restrictions; $50 and $6/day. TV; cable (premium). Pool; whirlpool, lifeguard. Complimentary full bkfst. Ck-out noon. Meeting rms. Business servs avail. Airport, RR station, bus depot transportation. Health club privileges. Refrigerators, microwaves, fireplaces. Private patios, balconies. Picnic tables, grills. Chalet-style buildings. Cr cds: A, C, D, DS, JCB, MC, V. 🅓 ⏻ ≋ ⊠ ⚲ SC

★ ★ **HOLIDAY INN GREENTREE-CENTRAL.** *401 Holiday Dr (15220), west of downtown.* 412/922-8100; FAX 412/922-6511. 200 rms, 4 story. S, D $104-$148; each addl $10; under 18 free. Crib free. Pet accepted. TV; cable, VCR avail. Heated pool; poolside serv, lifeguard. Restaurant 6:30 am-10 pm; Fri, Sat to 11 pm. Rm serv. Bar 11-2 am, Sun from 1 pm; entertainment. Ck-out noon. Meeting rms. Business servs avail. In-rm modem link. Valet serv. Sundries. Free airport transportation. Tennis privileges. Golf privileges. Health club privileges. Exercise equipt; weight machine, bicycles. Private patios. Cr cds: A, C, D, DS, JCB, MC, V. 🅓 ⏻ 🏋 🏌 ≋ 🚶 ✕ ⊠ ⚲ SC

✔ ★ **RED ROOF INN.** *6404 Steubenville Pike (PA 60) (15205), south of downtown.* 412/787-7870; FAX 412/787-8392. 120 rms, 2 story. S, D $53.99-$59.99; under 18 free. Crib free. Pet accepted, some restrictions. TV; cable (premium). Complimentary morning coffee. Restaurant adj open 24 hrs. Ck-out noon. Business servs avail. Cr cds: A, C, D, DS, MC, V. 🅓 ⏻ ⊠ ⚲

Motor Hotels

★ ★ **HOLIDAY INN.** *4859 McKnight Rd (15237), 5 mi N on I-279, exit 18, north of downtown.* 412/366-5200; FAX 412/366-5682. 147 rms, 7 story, 19 suites. S, D $99-$109; each addl $10; suites $109-$139; under 18 free. Crib free. Pet accepted. TV; cable (premium). Heated pool; poolside serv, lifeguard. Complimentary coffee in rms. Restaurant 6:30 am-10 pm; Sun from 7 am. Rm serv. Bar 11 am-11 pm; entertainment Fri, Sat. Ck-out noon. Coin lndry. Meeting rms. Business servs avail. In-rm modem link. Valet serv. Sundries. Health club privileges. Refrigerator in suites; microwaves avail. Cr cds: A, C, D, DS, MC, V. 🅓 ⏻ ≋ ⊠ ⚲ SC

★ ★ **HOLIDAY INN.** *164 Fort Couch Rd (15241), south of downtown.* 412/833-5300; FAX 412/831-8539. 210 rms, 8 story. S, D $75; each addl $10; suites $120-$130; under 18 free; wkend rates. Crib free. Pet accepted, some restrictions. TV; cable (premium), VCR avail. Pool; poolside serv, lifeguard. Restaurant 6:30 am-11 pm; Sat, Sun from 7 am. Rm serv. Bar 11-2 am; entertainment Tues-Sat. Ck-out noon. Meeting rms. Business servs avail. In-rm modem link. Bellhops. Valet serv. Shopping arcade. Airport transportation. Health club privileges. Game rm. Gift shop. Microwaves avail. Balconies. Cr cds: A, C, D, DS, ER, JCB, MC, V. 🅓 ⏻ ≋ ⊠ ⚲ SC

★ ★ **HOLIDAY INN-MONROEVILLE.** *(2750 Mosside Blvd, Monroeville 15146) approx 7 mi E on I-376, exit 16A, at PA 48 & US 22 Business.* 412/372-1022; FAX 412/373-4065. 189 rms, 4 story. S, D $79-$119; each addl $10; under 19 free; wkly, monthly, wkend rates. Crib free. Pet accepted. TV; cable (premium). Pool. Complimentary coffee in rms. Restaurant 6:30 am-2 pm, 5-10 pm. Rm serv. Bar 11-2 am; entertainment Wed-Sun. Ck-out noon. Coin lndry. Meeting rms. Business servs avail. In-rm modem link. Valet serv. Sundries. Exercise equipt; weight machine, stair machines. Health club privileges. Microwaves avail. Cr cds: A, C, D, DS, ER, MC, V. 🅓 ⏻ 🚶 ≋ ⊠ ⚲ SC

★ ★ **HOLIDAY INN-PARKWAY EAST.** *915 Brinton Rd (15221), east of downtown.* 412/247-2700; FAX 412/371-9619. 180 rms, 11 story. Apr-Oct: S, D $99-$119; suites $150; under 18 free; wkend, hol rates; lower rates rest of yr. Crib free. Pet accepted. TV; cable (premium). Indoor pool; lifeguard. Coffee in rms. Restaurant 6:30 am-10 pm. Rm serv. Bar 11-1 am; entertainment Fri, Sat. Ck-out noon. Coin lndry. Meeting rms. Business servs avail. Bellhops. Valet serv. Health club privileges. Some refrigerators, microwaves avail. Cr cds: A, D, DS, ER, JCB, MC, V. 🅓 ⏻ ≋ ⊠ ⚲ SC

★ ★ ★ **MARRIOTT GREENTREE.** *101 Marriott Dr (15205), across river, west of downtown.* 412/922-8400; FAX 412/922-8981. Web www.marriott.com. 467 rms, 7 story. S $99-$164; D $114-$179; each addl $15; suites $200-$375; under 18 free; wkend rates; package plans. Crib free. Pet accepted. TV; cable (premium), VCR avail. 3 pools, 1 indoor; whirlpool, poolside serv, lifeguard. Restaurant 6:30 am-midnight. Rm serv. Bar 11-2 am; entertainment. Ck-out noon. Meeting rms. Business servs avail. In-rm modem link. Bellhops. Valet serv. Sundries. Gift shop. Barber, beauty shop. Free airport transportation. Indoor tennis privileges. Exercise equipt; weight machines, bicycles, sauna, steam rm. Health club privileges. Rec rm. Many minibars. Luxury level. Cr cds: A, C, D, DS, ER, MC, V.

🄳 ✸ 🏊 🍴 ✈ ▨ 🐾 SC

Hotels

★ ★ ★ **DOUBLETREE.** *1000 Penn Ave (15222), downtown.* 412/281-3700; FAX 412/227-4500. 616 rms, 26 story. S $125-$180; D $145-$215; each addl $20; suites $255-$1,550; family rates; wkend rates. Crib free. Pet accepted. TV; cable (premium). Indoor pool; whirlpool. Coffee in rms. Restaurants 6:30 am-10:30 pm. Rm serv 24 hrs. Bar 11-2 am. Ck-out noon. Convention facilities. Business center. In-rm modem link. Concierge. Shopping arcade. Courtesy limo downtown. Exercise rm; instructor, weights, bicycles, sauna, steam rm. Refrigerators; many bathrm phones. Cr cds: A, C, D, DS, ER, JCB, MC, V. 🄳 ✸ 🏊 🍴 ▨ 🐾 SC 🛬

★ ★ ★ **HILTON.** *Gateway Center (15222), at Point State Park, downtown.* 412/391-4600; FAX 412/594-5161. 711 rms, 24 story. S $139-$196; D $159-$206; each addl $20; suites $325; studio rms $109; children free; wkend plans. Crib free. Pet accepted, some restrictions. TV; cable (premium), VCR avail. Coffee in rms. Restaurant 6:30 am-11:30 pm. 2 bars 11-2 am; entertainment. Ck-out noon. Meeting rms. Business center. In-rm modem link. Concierge. Drugstore. Barber, beauty shop. Garage avail; valet parking. Airport transportation. Exercise equipt; weights, treadmill. Minibars; some bathrm phones, refrigerators. Luxury level. Cr cds: A, C, D, DS, ER, JCB, MC, V. 🄳 ✸ 🍴 ▨ 🐾 SC 🛬

★ ★ ★ **WESTIN WILLIAM PENN.** *530 Wm Penn Place (15219), on Mellon Square, downtown.* 412/281-7100; FAX 412/553-5252. 595 rms, 24 story. S, D $179-$189; each addl $20; suites $398-$1,200; under 18 free; wkend rates. Crib free. Pet accepted. Valet parking $19.50. TV; cable (premium), VCR avail. Restaurant 6:30 am-11 pm. Rm serv 24 hrs. Bar 11-2 am; entertainment. Ck-out 1 pm. Convention facilities. Business center. Gift shop. Barber shop. Airport, RR station, bus depot transportation. Exercise equipt; bicycles, treadmill. Health club privileges. Historic, landmark hotel. Cr cds: A, C, D, DS, ER, JCB, MC, V.

🄳 ✸ 🍴 ✈ ▨ 🐾 SC 🛬

Pittsburgh Intl Airport Area (See also Pittsburgh)

Motels

★ **HAMPTON INN-NORTHWEST.** *(1420 Beers School Rd, Coraopolis 15108) N on PA Business 60.* 412/264-0020; FAX 412/264-3220. 129 rms, 5 story. S $64; D $74; under 18 free. Crib free. Pet accepted. TV; cable (premium). Complimentary continental bkfst. Restaurant adj 6 am-10 pm. Ck-out noon. Meeting rms. Business servs avail. Valet serv. Free airport transportation. Health club privileges. Cr cds: A, C, D, DS, ER, MC, V.

🄳 ✸ ✈ ▨ 🐾 SC

★ ★ **LA QUINTA.** *(1433 Beers School Rd, Coraopolis 15108) N on Business PA 60.* 412/269-0400; FAX 412/269-9258. 127 rms, 3 story. S $64-$78; D $71-$85; under 19 free. Crib free. Pet accepted. TV; cable. Heated pool; lifeguard. Complimentary continental bkfst. Coffee in rms. Restaurant adj 6 am-11 pm. Ck-out noon. Coin lndry. Meeting rms. Business servs avail. In-rm modem link. Valet serv. Sundries. Free airport transportation. Exercise equipt; treadmill, rower. Cr cds: A, D, DS, MC, V. 🄳 ✸ 🏊 🍴 ✈ ▨ 🐾 SC

✔ ★ ★ **PITTSBURGH PLAZA.** *(1500 Beers School Rd, Coraopolis 15108) I-79 Bus 60 exit to Beers School Rd.* 412/264-7900; FAX 412/262-3229; res: 800/542-8111. 193 rms, 2 story. S, D $49.99-$59.99; under 18 free. Pet accepted; $50 refundable. TV; cable (premium), VCR avail. Complimentary continental bkfst 5-9 am in lobby. Restaurant adj open 24 hrs. Ck-out noon. Meeting rms. Business servs avail. In-rm modem link. Valet serv. Sundries. Free airport transportation. Exercise equipt; weights, bicycles, sauna. Some refrigerators. Some balconies. Cr cds: A, C, D, DS, MC, V. ✸ 🍴 ✈ ▨ 🐾 SC

✔ ★ **RED ROOF INN.** *(1454 Beers School Rd, Coraopolis 15108) N on Bus PA 60.* 412/264-5678; FAX 412/264-8034. 119 rms, 3 story. S $47.99-$58.99; D $61.99-$66.99; each addl $6; under 18 free. Crib free. Pet accepted. TV; cable (premium). Coffee in lobby 6-10 am. Restaurant opp 6 am-10 pm. Ck-out noon. Coin lndry. Meeting rm. Business servs avail. Valet serv. Free airport transportation. Cr cds: A, C, D, DS, MC, V.

🄳 ✸ ✈ ▨ 🐾

Hotels

★ ★ ★ **CLARION-ROYCE.** *(1160 Thorn Run Rd Extension, Coraopolis 15108)* N on Bus Rte 60, exit Thorn Run Rd. 412/262-2400; FAX 412/264-9373. 193 rms, 9 story. S $69-$119; D $69-$129; each addl $10; suites $109-$139; under 18 free; wkend rates. Crib free. Pet accepted. TV; cable (premium). Pool; lifeguard. Restaurant 6 am-2 pm, 5-11 pm; Sat, Sun 7 am-11 pm. Bar 11-2 am; entertainment. Ck-out noon. Meeting rms. Business center. In-rm modem link. Concierge. Airport transportation. Exercise equipt; weight machines, bicycles. Luxury Level. Cr cds: A, C, D, DS, MC, V.

[D] [icons]

★ ★ ★ **MARRIOTT.** *(100 Aten Rd, Coraopolis 15108)* S on PA 60, exit Montour Run Rd. 412/788-8800; FAX 412/788-6299. 314 rms, 14 story. S, D $69-$169; each addl $15; suites $175-$425; family, wkly rates. Crib free. Pet accepted. TV; cable (premium). 2 pools, 1 indoor; whirlpool, poolside serv, lifeguard. Restaurant 6:30 am-11 pm. Bar 11-1 am; pianist Wed-Sat. Ck-out noon. Convention facilities. Business center. In-rm modem link. Concierge. Shopping arcade. Free airport, bus depot transportation. Exercise equipt; weights, bicycles, sauna. Some refrigerators. Luxury level. Cr cds: A, C, D, DS, ER, JCB, MC, V.

[D] [icons]

Pottstown *(See also Reading)*

Motels

★ ★ **COMFORT INN.** PA 100 & Shoemaker Rd. 610/326-5000; FAX 610/970-7230. 121 rms, 4 story, 30 suites. S, D $59-$92; each addl $7; suites $63-$95; under 18 free; golf plans; wkend rates. Crib free. Pet accepted. TV; cable (premium). Heated pool; lifeguard. Complimentary continental bkfst. Restaurant adj 6 am-11 pm. Rm serv. Ck-out noon. Coin lndry. Meeting rms. Business servs avail. In-rm modem link. Free bus depot transportation. Refrigerator in suites. Cr cds: A, C, D, DS, ER, JCB, MC, V.

[D] [icons]

★ ★ **HOLIDAY INN EXPRESS.** 1600 Industrial Hwy (US 422), at Armand Hammer Blvd exit. 610/327-3300; FAX 610/327-9447. 120 rms, 4 story. S, D $69; each addl $5; suites $122; under 19 free; wkly, hol rates; higher rates special events. Crib free. Pet accepted. TV; cable (premium), VCR avail (movies). Pool. Complimentary continental bkfst. Complimentary coffee in rms. Restaurant adj open 24 hrs. Rm serv 24 hrs. Ck-out noon. Meeting rms. Business servs avail. In-rm modem links. Sundries. Valet serv. Health club privileges. Some refrigerators; microwaves avail. Cr cds: A, D, DS, JCB, MC, V. [D] [icons]

Reading *(See also Denver/Adamstown, Lancaster, Pottstown)*

Motels

★ ★ **BEST WESTERN DUTCH COLONY INN.** 4635 Perkiomen Ave (19606). 610/779-2345; FAX 610/779-8348; res: 800/828-2830. 71 rms, 2 story. May-Nov: S $58-$83; D $63-$88; each addl $5; under 18 free; lower rates rest of yr. Crib $5. Pet accepted, some restrictions; $5. TV; cable. Pool; lifeguard. Restaurant 7 am-3 pm, 5-9:30 pm. Rm serv. Bar 11-2 am. Ck-out noon. Coin lndry. Meeting rms. Business servs avail. Valet serv. Sundries. Health club privileges. Lawn games. Microwaves avail. Balconies. Cr cds: A, C, D, DS, ER, MC, V. [D] [icons]

✔ ★ **ECONO LODGE.** 635 Spring St (19610). 610/378-5105; FAX 610/373-3181. 84 rms, 4 story. Mar-Nov: S, D $48-$65; each addl $5; under 18 free; higher rates Keystone Nationals, Antique Wkends; lower rates rest of yr. Crib free. Pet accepted; $5 daily. TV; cable (premium). Complimentary continental bkfst. Restaurant adj 7 am-10 pm. Ck-out 11 am. Business servs avail. Sundries. Coin lndry. Exercise equipt; bicycles, treadmill. Many refrigerators, microwaves. Cr cds: A, DS, MC, V. [D] [icons]

★ ★ **HOLIDAY INN-NORTH.** 2545 N 5th St Hwy (19605), at Warren St Bypass. 610/929-4741; FAX 610/929-5237. 138 rms, 2 story. S $55-$175; D $60-$175; each addl $10; under 18 free; some wkend rates. Crib free. Pet accepted. TV; cable (premium), VCR avail. Pool. Restaurant 6:30 am-1 pm, 5-10 pm. Rm serv. Bar 5-11:30 pm, Sun to 11 pm. Ck-out noon. Meeting rms. Business servs avail. In-rm modem link. Valet serv. Sundries. Cr cds: A, C, D, DS, MC, V. [D] [icons]

★ ★ ★ **INN AT READING.** *(1040 Park Rd, Wyomissing 19610)* 3 mi W, just off US 422 at Warren St Bypass. 610/372-7811; FAX 610/372-4545; res: 800/383-9713. 250 rms, 1-2 story. S $79-$109; D $89-$119; suites $99-$129; each addl $7; under 18 free; some wkend rates. Crib free. Pet accepted, some restrictions. TV; cable (premium). Pool; poolside serv, lifeguard. Playground. Restaurant 6:30 am-10 pm. Rm serv. Bar 11-1 am; entertainment. Ck-out 11 am. Meeting rms. Business center. In-rm modem link. Bellhops. Valet serv.

Sundries. Gift shop. Free airport, bus depot transportation. Tennis privileges. Golf privileges. Exercise equipt; weight machine, bicycles. Picnic tables. Cr cds: A, C, D, DS, MC, V.

Motor Hotels

★ ★ ★ **HOLIDAY INN.** *(230 Cherry S (Rte 10), Morgantown 19543)* PA Tpke exit 22. *610/286-3000; FAX 610/286-0520.* 192 rms, 4 story. S $79-$99; D $89-$109; each addl $10; under 18 free. Crib free. Pet accepted, some restrictions. TV; cable (premium). Indoor pool; whirlpool. Free supervised child's activities, wkends (Jan-Mar); ages 2-12. Restaurant 6:30 am-2 pm, 5-10 pm; Sat, Sun from 5 pm. Rm serv. Bar 5 pm-1 am. Ck-out noon. Meeting rms. Business servs avail. In-rm modem link. Sundries. Exercise equipt; weight machine, bicycles. Some refrigerators. Cr cds: A, C, D, DS, JCB, MC, V.

★ ★ ★ **SHERATON BERKSHIRE.** *1741 Papermill Rd (19610), US 422 W, Papermill Rd exit. 610/376-3811; FAX 610/375-7562.* 254 rms, 5 story. S, D $79-$199; each addl $10; suites $185-$195; studio rms $140-$150; under 18 free; some wkend rates. Crib free. Pet accepted; $50. TV; cable (premium), VCR avail. Indoor pool; whirlpool, poolside serv, lifeguard. Coffee in rms. Restaurant 6:30 am-10:30 pm. Rm serv. Bar 11:30-2 am; entertainment. Ck-out noon. Meeting rms. Business servs avail. In-rm modem link. Bellhops. Valet serv. Gift shop. Free airport, bus depot transportation. Putting green. Exercise equipt; weights, bicycles, sauna. Some bathrm phones; microwaves avail. Cr cds: A, C, D, DS, JCB, MC, V.

Scranton (See also Wilkes-Barre)

Motels

★ ★ **DAYS INN.** *(1226 O'Neill Hwy, Dunmore 18512) 4 mi N on I-81, exit 55A. 717/348-6101; FAX 717/348-5064.* 90 rms, 4 story. S $59.99-$83.99; D $61.99-$99.99; suites $78.99-$99.99; under 17 free; wkend, hol rates; higher rates Pocono NASCAR. Crib free. Pet accepted; $3. TV; cable (premium), VCR avail. Complimentary continental bkfst. Restaurant adj open 24 hrs. Ck-out 11 am. Business servs avail. Valet serv. Refrigerators. Cr cds: A, C, D, DS, ER, MC, V.

★ ★ ★ **HOLIDAY INN-EAST.** *(200 Tigue St, Dunmore 18512) I-380 exit 1, just E of I-81. 717/343-4771; FAX 717/343-5171.* 139 rms, 2-3 story. S, D $79-$89; each addl $10; suites $145-$175; under 18 free; some wkend rates; ski plan. Crib free. Pet accepted. TV; cable. Pool. Restaurant 6:30 am-10 pm. Rm serv. Bar noon-2 am. Ck-out noon. Meeting rms. Business servs avail. In-rm modem link. Valet serv. Cr cds: A, C, D, DS, ER, JCB, MC, V.

Shamokin Dam

Motel

★ **DAYS INN.** *On US 15, 11. 717/743-1111; FAX 717/743-1190.* 151 rms, 2 story. S $50-$60; D $55-$70; each addl $5; under 18 free. Crib free. Pet accepted. TV; cable. Pool; lifeguard. Restaurant 7 am-9 pm. Bar from 5 pm; Ck-out noon. Meeting rms. Business servs avail. In-rm modem link. Valet serv. Sundries. Cr cds: A, C, D, DS, JCB, MC, V.

Somerset (See also Johnstown)

Motels

✔ ★ **BUDGET HOST INN.** *799 N Center Ave. 814/445-7988.* 28 rms, 2 story. S $40-$50; D $45-$55; each addl $5. Crib $4. Pet accepted. TV; cable (premium). Complimentary coffee in lobby. Restaurant nearby. Ck-out 11 am. Downhill ski 10 mi; x-country ski 13 mi. Cr cds: A, C, D, DS, MC, V.

✔ ★ **DOLLAR INN.** *1146 N Center Ave, PA 601. 814/445-2977; FAX 814/443-6205.* 15 rms. S $25-$40; D $30-$50; each addl $5; under 10 free; wkly, wkend rates; higher rates special events. Crib $5. Pet accepted, some restrictions; $5. TV; cable (premium). Complimentary coffee in lobby. Restaurant nearby. Ck-out 11 am. Business servs avail. Some refrigerators. Cr cds: A, D, DS, MC, V.

✔ ★ **KNIGHTS INN.** *585 Ramada Rd, exit 10 off I-70/76, at PA Tpke entrance. 814/445-8933; FAX 814/443-9745; res: 800/843-5644.* 112 rms, 10 kit. units. S $39.95-$59.95; D $46.95-$69.95; each addl $10; kit. units $43.95-$52.95; under 18 free; wkly rates; higher rates Dec-Mar wkends. Crib free. Pet accepted, some restrictions. TV; cable (premium), VCR avail (movies). Pool. Complimentary coffee in lobby. Restaurant nearby. Ck-out noon. Coin lndry. Business servs avail. Downhill ski 15 mi. Cr cds: A, C, D, DS, MC, V.

Motor Hotel

★ ★ ★ **RAMADA INN.** *At PA Tpke exit 10. 814/443-4646; FAX 814/445-7539.* 152 rms, 2 story. S $64-$78; D $74-$88; each addl $10; suites $95-$125; under 18 free; some wkend rates. Crib free. Pet accepted. TV; cable (premium). Indoor pool; whirlpool, sauna, poolside serv, lifeguard. Restaurant 6:30 am-2 pm, 5-10 pm; Sun 7-11 am. Rm serv. Bar 2 pm-2 am; Sun to 9 pm; entertainment Tues-Sat. Ck-out noon. Meeting rms. Business servs avail. Bellhops. Valet serv. Sundries. Downhill/x-country ski 12 mi. Health club privileges. Game rm. Cr cds: A, C, D, DS, JCB, MC, V.

Inn

★ ★ ★ **THE INN AT GEORGIAN PLACE.** *800 Georgian Place Dr. 814/443-1043; FAX 814/445-3047.* 11 rms, 3 story, 2 suites. S, D $95-$140; each addl $10; suites $165-$180. Children over 5 yrs only. Pet accepted, some restrictions. TV; cable (premium), VCR (movies). Complimentary full bkfst. Restaurant noon-4 pm. Rm serv. Ck-out noon, ck-in 3 pm. Business servs avail. Luggage handling. Valet serv. Concierge serv. Downhill/x-country ski ski 12 mi. Some fireplaces. Georgian mansion built in 1915; chandeliers, marble foyer. Cr cds: A, D, DS, MC, V.

State College

Motel

(Rates higher football, art festival & special wkends; may be 2-day min)

★ ★ ★ **RAMADA INN.** *1450 S Atherton St (US 322 Business) (16801). 814/238-3001; FAX 814/237-1345.* 28 rms, 2 story. S $65-$72; D $72-$79; each addl $7; suites $95; under 19 free. Crib free. Pet accepted. TV; cable (premium), VCR avail. 2 pools; lifeguard. Restaurant 7 am-2 pm, 5-10 pm. Rm serv. Bar 2 pm-2 am. Ck-out noon. Coin lndry. Meeting rms. Business servs avail. In-rm modem link. Exercise equipt; treadmill, bicycle. Health club privileges. Game rm. Microwaves avail. Cr cds: A, C, D, DS, JCB, MC, V.

Motor Hotel

★ ★ **DAYS INN-PENN STATE.** *240 S Pugh St (16801). 814/238-8454; FAX 814/234-3377.* 184 rms, 6 story. S $50-$95; D $60-$105; each addl $10; suites $150; under 18 free; some wkend rates; higher rates special events. Crib free. Pet accepted, some restrictions; $8. TV; cable Indoor pool; lifeguard. Complimentary continental bkfst Mon-Fri. Restaurant 6:30 am-midnight; Sun from 8 am. Rm serv. Bar 11-2 am; entertainment. Ck-out noon. Meeting rms. Business center. In-rm modem link. Bellhops. Valet serv. Sundries. Free airport transportation. Exercise rm; instructor, weight machine, bicycles, sauna. Rec rm. Game rm. Refrigerators avail. Cr cds: A, C, D, DS, MC, V.

Stroudsburg

Motel

✔ ★ **BUDGET.** *(E Stroudsburg 18301) E on I-80, exit 51. 717/424-5451; FAX 717/424-0389; res: 800/233-8144.* 115 rms, 2-3 story. No elvtr. S $33.90-48; D $48-$66; higher rates: special events, hols, some wkends. Crib free. Pet accepted; $20 deposit. TV; cable, VCR avail (movies). Restaurant 7-11 am, 5-10 pm. Bar 4 pm-midnight. Ck-out 11 am. Business servs avail. In-rm modem link. Game rm. Cr cds: A, C, D, DS, MC, V.

Towanda *(See also Mansfield, Scranton)*

Motel

✔ ★ **TOWANDA.** *383 York Ave (US 6). 717/265-2178; FAX 717/265-9060.* 48 rms. S $39-$65; D $43-$70; each addl $5; under 12 free. Crib $3.50. Pet accepted. TV; cable. Pool. Restaurant 6 am-9:30 pm; Sat, Sun from 7 am. Bar 3 pm-2 am. Ck-out noon. Meeting rms. Business servs avail. Sundries. Cr cds: A, C, D, DS, MC, V.

Uniontown (See also Connellsville)

Motels

★ ★ ★ **HOLIDAY INN.** *700 W Main St (US 40).* 724/437-2816; FAX 724/437-3505. 179 rms, 2 story. S $75-$97; D $77-$97; suites $145-$175; under 18 free; ski, wkend plan in winter; higher rates Labor Day wkend. Crib free. Pet accepted, some restrictions. TV; cable (premium), VCR avail. Indoor pool; whirlpool, sauna, poolside serv, lifeguard. Restaurant 6:30 am-2 pm, 4:30-10 pm. Rm serv from 7 am. Bar 11-2 am; entertainment. Ck-out 11 am. Meeting rms. Business servs avail. In-rm modem link. Valet serv. Sundries. Lighted tennis. Miniature golf. Rec rm. Game rm. Lawn games. Microwaves avail. Some balconies. Cr cds: A, C, D, DS, JCB, MC, V. 🄳 ⮐ 🏌 ≋ 🏊 🐾 SC

✔ ★ ★ **LODGE AT CHALK HILL.** *(Box 240, US 40E, Chalk Hill 15421) 9 mi E on US 40.* 724/438-8880; FAX 724/438-1685; res: 800/833-4283. Web it.pulsenet.com/~thelodge. 60 units, 6 suites, 6 kit. units. May-Nov: S $53.95-$70; D $64.95-$75.95; each addl $10; suites $128.95-$162.95; kit. units $69.95-$90.95; under 14 free; higher rates: July 4, Memorial Day, Labor Day, Dec 31; lower rates rest of yr. Crib free. Pet accepted, some restrictions; $5. TV; cable (premium), VCR avail. Complimentary continental bkfst. Restaurant opp 7 am-11 pm. Ck-out noon. Meeting rms. Business servs avail. Balconies. Picnic tables. On Lake Lenore. Cr cds: A, DS, MC, V. 🄳 ⮐ ➡ 🏃 ≋ 🐾 SC

Washington

Motels

★ **MOTEL 6.** *1283 Motel 6 Dr, I-70 at US 19, exit 7A.* 724/223-8040; res: 800/843-5644; FAX 724/228-6445. 102 rms. S $35.99; D $42.39; each addl $6; under 18 free. Crib free. Pet accepted. TV; cable (premium). Pool. Complimentary coffee in lobby. Restaurant adj open 24 hrs. Ck-out noon. Cr cds: A, C, D, DS, ER, MC, V.
🄳 ⮐ ≋ 🐾 SC

✔ ★ **RED ROOF INN.** *1399 W Chestnut St.* 724/228-5750; FAX 724/228-5865. 110 rms, 2 story. May-Oct: S $35.99-$45.99; D $42.99-$64.99; each addl $6; under 18 free; lower rates rest of yr. Crib free. Pet accepted, some restrictions. TV; cable (premium). Complimentary coffee in lobby. Restaurant adj open 24 hrs. Ck-out noon. Cr cds: A, C, D, DS, MC, V. 🄳 ⮐ 🐾

Motor Hotel

★ ★ ★ **HOLIDAY INN-MEADOW LANDS.** *340 Race Track Rd, I-79 exit 8B.* 724/222-6200; FAX 724/228-1977. 138 rms, 7 story. S, D $99-$109; each addl $6; under 18 free. Crib free. Pet accepted, some restrictions. TV; cable (premium), VCR avail. Pool; whirlpool, poolside serv, lifeguard. Restaurant 6:30 am-10 pm. Rm serv. Bars 11-2 am; entertainment. Ck-out noon. Meeting rms. Business servs avail. In-rm modem link. Airport transportation. Exercise equipt; weight machines, bicycles, sauna. Microwaves avail. Private patios. Meadows Racetrack adj. Cr cds: A, C, D, DS, ER, JCB, MC, V. 🄳 ⮐ ≋ 🏃 🐾 SC

Wellsboro (See also Mansfield)

Motels

✔ ★ **CANYON.** *18 East Ave.* 717/724-1681; FAX 717/724-5202; res: 800/255-2718. 28 rms. S $28-$45; D $32-$49; each addl $5; under 12 free; golf, ski package plans. Crib $5. Pet accepted. TV; cable. Heated pool; lifeguard. Playground. Complimentary continental bkfst. Restaurant nearby. Ck-out 11 am. Business servs avail. In-rm modem link. Downhill/x-country ski 17 mi. Refrigerators. Picnic tables, grills. Cr cds: A, C, D, DS, MC, V. 🄳 ⮐ ➤ ≋ 🐾 SC

★ **SHERWOOD.** *2 Main St.* 717/724-3424; FAX 717/724-5658; res: 800/626-5802. 32 rms, 1-2 story. S $37; D $49-$54; each addl $5; under 10 free; golf, ski package plans. Crib $5. Pet accepted; $5. TV; cable. Heated pool; lifeguard. Playground. Complimentary coffee. Restaurant nearby. Ck-out 11 am. Business servs avail. In-rm modem link. Downhill/x-country ski 17 mi. Refrigerators. Cr cds: A, C, D, DS, MC, V.
⮐ ➤ ≋ 🐾 SC

West Chester (See also Kennett Square, Philadelphia)

Motel

✔★ **ABBEY GREEN MOTOR LODGE.** *1036 Wilmington Pike (PA 202) (19382).* *610/692-3310; FAX 610/431-0811.* E-mail ireland@epix.net; web www.abbeygreen.com. 18 rms. S $39-$49; D $55-$65; each addl $5; cottages with kit. $55-$65; under 12 free; wkly rates. Crib free. Pet accepted. TV; cable (premium). Restaurant nearby. Ck-out 11 am. Business servs avail. Gift shop. Airport, RR station, bus depot transportation. Refrigerators; some fireplaces; microwaves avail. Picnic tables, grill. Cr cds: A, C, D, DS, MC, V.

D ✔ 🏊 🐾 SC

West Middlesex

Motels

★ ★ **HOLIDAY INN.** *(3200 S Hermitage Rd, Hermitage)* N on PA 60, at jct I-80 exit 1N. *724/981-1530; FAX 724/981-1518.* 180 rms, 3 story. S, D $74; each addl $6; under 19 free; golf plans. Crib free. Pet accepted. TV; cable (premium). Heated pool; poolside serv, lifeguard. Playground. Restaurant 6:30 am-10 pm; Dec-Mar 6:30 am-2 pm, 5-10 pm. Rm serv. Bar 11-2 am; entertainment. Ck-out 11 am. Coin lndry. Meeting rms. Business servs avail. In-rm modem link. Valet serv. Sundries. Game rm. Cr cds: A, C, D, DS, ER, JCB, MC, V. D ✔ 🏊 🚂 🐾 SC

★ ★ **RADISSON SHARON.** *On PA 18 at I-80 exit 1N.* *724/528-2501; FAX 724/528-2306.* 153 rms, 3 story. S $80-$90; D $88-$98; each addl $8; suites $150-$200; under 12 free; wkend rates. Crib free. Pet accepted. TV; cable. Indoor pool; whirlpool, poolside serv, lifeguard. Restaurant 6:30 am-10 pm. Rm serv. Bar 11-2 am; entertainment Wed, Fri, Sat. Ck-out noon. Coin lndry. Meeting rms. Business servs avail. Bellhops. Valet serv. Gift shop. Sundries. Exercise equipt; treadmill, stair machine, sauna. Game rm. In-rm whirlpools; refrigerator in suites. Cr cds: A, C, D, DS, MC, V. D ✔ 🏊 🚴 🐾 SC

White Haven (See also Hazleton, Wilkes-Barre)

Motel

★ ★ **RAMADA INN.** *PA 940 (18624), 4 mi E on I-80, exit 42.* *717/443-8471.* 138 rms, 4 story, 2 suites. Jan-Feb & mid-June-Columbus Day: S $90-$120; D $95-$130; each addl $10; under 18 free; higher rates NASCAR races; lower rates rest of yr. Crib free. Pet accepted; $450 deposit. TV; cable. Heated indoor pool; sauna, poolside serv, lifeguard. Complimentary coffee in lobby. Restaurant 7 am-10 pm. Rm serv. Bar 4 pm-midnight. Ck-out noon. Meeting rm. Business servs avail. Gift shop. Valet serv. Coin lndry. Airport transportation. Golf privileges, greens fee $40, pro, putting green, driving range. Downhill/x-country ski 4 mi. Game rm. Lawn games. Some refrigerators. Picnic tables. Cr cds: A, C, D, DS, JCB, MC, V. ✔ 🚴 🏊 🐾 SC

Wilkes-Barre (See also Hazleton, Scranton, White Haven)

Motels

★ ★ **HAMPTON INN.** *1063 PA 315 (18702).* *717/825-3838; FAX 717/825-8775.* 123 rms, 5 story. May-Oct: S $55-$65; D $65-$75; under 18 free; ski plans; higher rates: car races, Dec 31; lower rates rest of yr. Crib free. Pet accepted. TV; cable. Complimentary continental bkfst. Restaurant adj 7 am-11 pm. Ck-out noon. Meeting rm. Business servs avail. In-rm modem link. Valet serv Mon-Fri. Downhill ski 10 mi. Cr cds: A, C, D, DS, ER, MC, V. D ✔ 🏊 🐾 SC

★ ★ **HOLIDAY INN.** *880 Kidder St (18702), at PA 309.* *717/824-8901; FAX 717/824-9310.* 120 rms, 2 story. S, D $69-$120; each addl $10; studio rms $75; family plan; ski packages. Pet accepted. TV; cable. Pool; wading pool, poolside serv. Restaurant 6:30-1 am. Rm serv. Bar noon-2 am. Ck-out noon. Meeting rms. Business servs avail. In-rm modem link. Bellhops. Sundries. Downhill ski 10 mi. Cr cds: A, C, D, DS, ER, JCB, MC, V.

D ✔ 🏊 🐾 SC

Hotel

★ ★ **BEST WESTERN GENETTI.** *77 E Market St (18701).* *717/823-6152; FAX 717/820-8502; res: 800/833-6152.* 72 rms, 5 story, 16 suites. Apr-Dec: S $74-$79; D $79-$89; each addl $10; suites $89-$99; under 12 free; higher rates NASCAR races; lower rates rest of yr. Crib free. Pet accepted; $25. TV; cable, VCR avail (movies). Pool; poolside serv. Complimentary coffee in lobby. Restaurant 7 am-2 pm, 5-9 pm. Rm serv. Bar 4 pm-2 am; entertainment. Ck-out 11 am. Coin lndry. Meeting rms. Business servs avail. Bellhops. Valet serv. Downhill/x-country ski 12 mi. Cr cds: A, C, D, DS, MC, V.

D ✦ ⊠ ⊠ ⊠ ⊠

Williamsport *(See also Lewisburg)*

Motels

✔★ **ECONO LODGE.** *2401 E 3rd St, at US 220.* 717/326-1501; FAX 717/326-9776. 99 rms, 2 story. S $45-$50; D $50-$55; each addl $5; higher rates Little League World Series. Crib free. Pet accepted. TV; cable (premium). Complimentary coffee in lobby. Restaurant 6 am-8 pm. Bar 6 pm-2 am; entertainment Tues-Sat. Ck-out noon. Meeting rms. Business servs avail. Valet serv. Cr cds: A, C, D, DS, ER, JCB, MC, V. D ✦ ⊠ ⊠ SC

★★ **HOLIDAY INN.** *1840 E 3rd St (US 220).* 717/326-1981; FAX 717/323-9590. 170 rms, 2 story. S, D $64-$79; each addl $10; under 18 free; higher rates Little League World Series. Crib free. Pet accepted, some restrictions. TV; cable. Pool; lifeguard. Restaurant 6:30-1 am. Rm serv. Bar 11-1:30 am. Ck-out 11 am. Coin lndry. Meeting rms. Business servs avail. In-rm modem link. Cr cds: A, C, D, DS, JCB, MC, V. D ✦ ⊠ ⊠ ⊠ SC

Motor Hotel

★★★ **SHERATON INN.** *100 Pine St, at jct PA 220 & US 15.* 717/327-8231; FAX 717/322-2957. 148 rms, 5 story. S, D $85-$95; suites $150; under 18 free. Crib free. Pet accepted. TV; cable. Indoor pool. Restaurant 6:30 am-10 pm. Rm serv. Bar 11:30-2 am; DJ Tues-Sat. Ck-out noon. Meeting rms. Business servs avail. Bellhops. Free airport transportation. Downhill/x-country ski 18 mi. Some refrigerators. Whirlpool in suites. Cr cds: A, C, D, DS, MC, V. D ✦ ⊠ ⊠ ⊠ ⊠ SC

Hotel

✔★★★ **GENETTI HOTEL.** *200 W 4th St (17704), downtown.* 717/326-6600; FAX 717/326-5006; res: 800/321-1388. 206 rms, 10 story, 42 suites. S $29.95-$59, D $35.95-$65.95, each addl $6; suites $75.95-$139; under 10 free; higher rates Little League World Series. Wkly rates; golf plans. Crib free. Pet accepted. TV; cable (premium), VCR avail. Pool; poolside serv. Restaurant 6:30 am-10 pm. Bar 11-2 am; entertainment Fri, Sat. Ck-out 11 am. Meeting rm. Business servs avail. Barber, beauty shop. Coin lndry. Free airport transportation. Downhill ski, 20 mi. Exercise equipt; weight machine, stair machine. Some refrigerators. Cr cds: A, D, MC, V. D ✦ ⊠ ⊠ 🕱 ⊠ SC

York *(See also Harrisburg, Lancaster)*

Motor Hotel

★★★ **HOLIDAY INN.** *2000 Loucks Rd (17404), at West Manchester Mall.* 717/846-9500. 181 rms, 2 story. S, D $72-$98; under 18 free. Crib $10. Pet accepted. TV; cable (premium). 2 pools, 1 indoor; whirlpool, poolside serv, lifeguard. Playground. Restaurant 6:30 am-9:30 pm. Rm serv. Bar 3 pm-2 am. Ck-out 11 am. Meeting rms. Business servs avail. Bellhops. Valet serv. Miniature golf. Exercise equipt; weight machine, rowers, sauna. Holidome. Cr cds: A, C, D, DS, JCB, MC, V. D ✦ ⊠ 🕱 ⊠ ⊠ SC

Rhode Island

Kingston (See also Newport)

Inn

✔ ★ ★ **LARCHWOOD.** *(521 Main St, Wakefield 02879) 401/783-5454; FAX 401/783-1800; res: 800/275-5450.* 18 rms, 12 with bath, 3 story. Some A/C. Some rm phones. S, D $35-$110; each addl $10. Crib $10. Pet accepted; $5. TV in sitting rm. Restaurant 7:30 am-2:30 pm, 5:30-9 pm. Bar 11-1 am; entertainment. Ck-out, ck-in noon. Meeting rms. Business servs avail. Private patio. Built 1831. Cr cds: A, C, D, DS, MC, V.

Newport

Motels

✔ ★ ★ **HOWARD JOHNSON LODGE.** *(351 W Main Rd, Middletown 02842) On RI 138 at jct RI 114. 401/849-2000; FAX 401/849-6047.* 155 rms, 2 story. Late May-mid-Oct: S $59-$134; D $63-$139; each addl $5; suites $138-$268; studio rms $84-$164; under 18 free; some wkend rates; lower rates rest of yr. Crib free. Pet accepted. TV; cable (premium), VCR avail. Heated pool; lifeguard, sauna. Restaurant. Bar 5 pm-1 am. Ck-out 11 am. Meeting rms. Business servs avail. Valet serv. Sundries. Tennis. Some refrigerators. Private patios, balconies. Cr cds: A, C, D, DS, MC, V.

★ ★ **QUALITY INN SUITES.** *(936 W Main Rd, Middletown) 3 mi N on RI 114. 401/846-7600; FAX 401/849-6919.* 155 rms, 2 story. Mid-June-Sept: S, D $125; under 18 free; lower rates rest of yr. Crib free. Pet accepted; $10. TV; cable (premium). Indoor pool. Complimentary continental bkfst. Bar 2-11 pm. Ck-out noon. Coin lndry. Meeting rms. Business servs avail. In-rm modem link. Gift shop. Cr cds: A, C, D, DS, ER, JCB, MC, V.

Providence (See also Warwick)

Motor Hotel

★ ★ ★ **MARRIOTT.** *1 Orms St (02904). 401/272-2400; FAX 401/273-2686.* 345 rms, 6 story. S $99-$149; D $99-$169; suites $250; family, wkend rates; higher rates special events. Crib free. Pet accepted. TV; cable (premium), VCR avail. Indoor/outdoor pool; whirlpool, poolside serv, lifeguard. Coffee in rms. Restaurant 6:30 am-11 pm. Rm serv. Bar; entertainment. Ck-out noon. Convention facilities. Business center. In-rm modem link. Bellhops. Concierge. Sundries. Gift shop. Airport transportation. Exercise equipt; weights, bicycles, sauna. Game rm. Balconies; some private patios. Cr cds: A, C, D, DS, ER, JCB, MC, V.

Warwick (See also Providence)

Motel

★ ★ **COMFORT INN.** *1940 Post Rd (02886), near T.F. Green State Airport. 401/732-0470; res: 800/228-5150.* 196 rms, 4 story. May-Oct: S $79-$89; D $89-$99; each addl $10; under 18 free; lower rates rest of yr. Pet accepted, some restrictions; $50. TV; cable (premium). Complimentary continental bkfst. Restaurant nearby. Ck-out noon. Bellhops. Business center. In-rm modem link. Free airport transportation. Health club privileges. Game rm. Cr cds: A, C, D, DS, MC, V.

Westerly (See also Mystic, CT)

Inn

★ ★ ★ **THE VILLA.** *190 Shore Rd. 401/596-1054; FAX 401/596-6268; res: 800/722-9240.* Web www.thevillaatwesterly.com. 6 suites, 3 story. Some rm phones. Late May-Columbus Day: S, D $95-$166; each addl $25; wkly rates; higher rates wkends & hols (2-day min); lower rates rest of yr. Pet accepted, some restrictions. TV; cable (premium), VCR avail. Pool; whirlpool. Complimentary continental bkfst. Complimentary coffee in rms. Restaurant adj 6 am-midnight. Ck-out 11 am, ck-in 1 pm. Business servs avail. Luggage handling. RR station transportation. Lawn games. Some fireplaces, whirlpools. Refrigerators. Picnic tables. Some antiques. Mediterranean-style grounds. Cr cds: A, MC, V.

South Carolina

Aiken

Motel

✔★★ **RAMADA INN.** *(29802). At jct SC 19, I-20 exit 18. 803/648-4272; FAX 803/648-3933.* 110 units, 2 story. S, D $49-$53; each addl $6; under 18 free; higher rates Masters Golf Tournament. Crib free. Pet accepted, some restrictions. TV; cable (premium), VCR avail. Pool; wading pool. Restaurant 6-9:30 am, 5-9:30 pm; Sat from 7 am; Sun 7-10 am. Rm serv. Bar 5-10 pm. Ck-out noon. Meeting rms. Business servs avail. Valet serv. Refrigerators, microwaves avail. Cr cds: A, C, D, DS, ER, JCB, MC, V.

D ✔ 🏊 🚫 🐾 SC

Anderson (See also Clemson, Greenville)

Motel

★★ **HOLIDAY INN.** *3025 N Main St (29621), I-85 exit 19A, on US 76. 864/226-6051; FAX 864/964-9145.* 130 rms, 2 story. S $59-$64; D $65-$70; each addl $6; under 18 free; higher rates Clemson Univ football games. Crib free. Pet accepted, some restrictions. TV; cable. Pool. Complimentary coffee in rms. Restaurant 6:30 am-10 pm. Rm serv. Bar 4:30 pm-midnight; entertainment Fri, Sat. Ck-out noon. Coin lndry. Meeting rms. Business servs avail. In-rm modem link. Valet serv. Health club privileges. Refrigerators avail. Cr cds: A, C, D, DS, JCB, MC, V. D ✔ 🏊 🚫 🐾 SC

Camden (See also Columbia, Sumter)

Motel

✔★★ **COLONY INN.** *2020 W DeKalb St. 803/432-5508; res: 800/356-9801; FAX 803/432-0920.* 53 rms, 2 story. S $35-$39; D $45-$52; each addl $3. Crib $5. Pet accepted, some restrictions. TV; cable. Pool. Restaurant 5:30-10:30 am. Ck-out 11 am. Valet serv. Cr cds: A, C, D, DS, MC, V. D ✔ 🏊 🚫 🐾 SC

Charleston (See also Walterboro)

Motels

★ **DAYS INN-AIRPORT.** *2998 W Montague Ave (29418), near Intl Airport. 843/747-4101; FAX 843/566-0378.* 147 rms, 2 story. S $42-$62; D $48-$68; each addl $6; under 12 free. Crib free. Pet accepted; $6. TV; cable (premium). Pool. Playground. Restaurant 6 am-9 pm. Ck-out noon. Coin lndry. Business servs avail. Some refrigerators. Cr cds: A, D, DS, ER, MC, V. D ✔ 🏊 🚫 🐾 SC

✔★★ **HAMPTON INN.** *11 Ashley Pointe Dr (29407). 843/556-5200; FAX 843/571-5499.* 177 rms, 4 story. S $75-$99; D $85-$115; under 18 free; higher rates: wkends, special events. Crib free. Pet accepted. TV; cable (premium). Pool. Complimentary continental bkfst. Restaurant adj 11 am-11 pm. Ck-out noon. Coin lndry. Meeting rm. Business servs avail. In-rm modem link. Valet serv. Golf privileges. Health club privileges. Opp Ashley River; marina. Cr cds: A, C, D, DS, MC, V. D ✔ 🍴 🏊 🚫 🐾 SC

★ **LA QUINTA.** *2499 La Quinta Lane (29420), at I-26N exit 209. 843/797-8181; FAX 843/569-1608.* Web www.laquinta.com. 122 rms, 2 suites, 2 story. S $55-$66; D $65-$76; each addl $10; suites $85-$95; under 18 free; higher rates wkends. Crib free. Pet accepted. TV; cable (premium). Heated pool. Complimentary continental bkfst. Restaurant adj 6 am-11 pm. Rm serv. Ck-out noon. Business servs avail. In-rm modem link. Valet serv. Refrigerators, microwaves avail. Picnic tables, grill. Cr cds: A, D, DS, MC, V. D ✔ 🏊 🐾 SC

✔★ **MASTERS INN.** *(300 Wingo Way, Mt Pleasant 29464) 3 mi E on US 17. 843/884-2814; FAX 843/884-2958; res: 800/633-3434.* 120 units, 2 story, 26 kits. S $42.95-$55.95; D $48.95-$61.95; each addl $6; kit. units $53.95-$66.95; under 18 free; wkend rates. Pet accepted, some restrictions; $6. TV; cable (premium). Pool. Continental bkfst. Complimentary coffee. Restaurant nearby. Ck-out noon. Coin lndry. Meeting rm. Business servs avail. Cr cds: A, C, D, DS, MC, V. D ✔ 🏊 🚫 🐾 SC

✔ ★ **RED ROOF INN.** *7480 Northwoods Blvd (29406), I-26 to exit 209. 843/572-9100; FAX 843/572-0061.* 109 rms, 2 story. S $37-$51; D $43-$57; each addl $7-$8; under 18 free. Crib free. Pet accepted, some restrictions. TV; cable (premium). Complimentary coffee in lobby. Restaurant nearby. Ck-out noon. Cr cds: A, C, D, DS, MC, V.

[D] [✔] [≈] [🐾] [SC]

Motor Hotel

★ ★ **HAWTHORN SUITES.** *181 Church St (29401). 843/577-2644; FAX 843/577-2697.* E-mail hawthorne@awod.com; web www.hawthorne.com. 182 rms, 5 story, 125 kit. suites. Mar-mid-June, Sept-mid-Nov: S, D $129-$189; wkly rates; higher rates wkends; lower rates rest of yr. Crib free. Pet accepted, some restrictions; $125 and $10/day. TV; cable (premium), VCR. Complimentary full bkfst. Complimentary coffee in rms. Restaurant nearby. Ck-out noon. Coin lndry. Meeting rms. Business servs avail. In-rm modem link. Bellhops. Valet serv. Sundries. Exercise equipt; weight machine, bicycles. Whirlpool. Microwaves; some wet bars. In historic market area. Cr cds: A, C, D, DS, JCB, MC, V.

[D] [✔] [🏋] [≈] [🐾] [SC]

Inn

★ ★ ★ **INDIGO.** *1 Maiden Lane (29401). 843/577-5900; FAX 843/577-0378; res: 800/845-7639.* E-mail IndigoInn@crabnet.net; web www.aesir.com/indigoinn. 40 rms, 3 story. Mar-June, Sept-Nov: S $140; D $155; each addl $10; under 12 free; lower rates rest of yr. Crib $10. Pet accepted; $10. TV; cable (premium). Complimentary continental bkfst; afternoon refreshments. Restaurant nearby. Ck-out noon, ck-in 3 pm. Business servs avail. In-rm modem link. Luggage handling. Valet serv. Health club privileges. Parking. Built in 1850; antique furnishings; courtyard. Cr cds: A, D, DS, MC, V. [✔] [≈]

Cheraw (See also Camden, Florence)

Motel

★ **INN CHERAW.** *321 Second St. 803/537-2011; FAX 803/537-1398; res: 800/535-8709.* 50 rms, 2 story. S $36-$60; D $40-$65; each addl $5; kit. units $45-$60; under 6 free; golf plans; higher rates NASCAR races. Crib free. Pet accepted, some restrictions. TV; cable (premium), VCR. Complimentary continental bkfst. Complimentary coffee in rms. Restaurant adj 11 am-9 pm. Ck-out 11 am. Meeting rms. Valet serv. Refrigerators; microwaves avail. Cr cds: A, D, DS, MC, V. [D] [✔] [≈] [🐾] [SC]

Clemson (See also Anderson, Greenville)

Motel

★ ★ **HOLIDAY INN.** *894 Tiger Blvd (29633), 1½ mi E on US 123. 864/654-4450; FAX 864/654-8451.* 220 rms, 2 story. S, D $49-$54; each addl $5; suites $129; under 19 free; higher rates football wkends. Crib free. Pet accepted. TV; cable (premium). Pool. Coffee in rms. Restaurant 6:30 am-2 pm, 5:30-8:30 pm. Bar 4 pm-midnight; closed Sun. Ck-out noon. Coin lndry. Meeting rms. Business servs avail. In-rm modem link. Valet serv. Golf privileges. On lake. Cr cds: A, C, D, DS, JCB, MC, V. [D] [✔] [🏋] [≈] [≈] [🐾] [SC]

Clinton (See also Greenville, Spartanburg)

Motel

✔ ★ **DAYS INN.** *Jct I-26 & SC 56, exit 52. 864/833-6600.* 58 rms, 2 story. S $42-$45; D $49-$50; each addl $5; suites $80; under 12 free. Crib free. Pet accepted. TV; cable. Pool. Complimentary continental bkfst. Restaurant adj 6:30 am-10 pm. Ck-out 11 am. Coin lndry. Meeting rms. Exercise equipt; weight machine, bicycles. Some refrigerators. Cr cds: A, C, D, DS, MC, V. [D] [✔] [≈] [🏋] [≈] [🐾] [SC]

Columbia (See also Camden, Sumter)

Motel

★ ★ **RESIDENCE INN BY MARRIOTT.** *150 Stoneridge Dr (29210), off I-126 Greystone Blvd exit. 803/779-7000; FAX 803/779-0408.* 128 kit. suites, 2 story. S $99; D $109-$134; family rates. Crib free. Pet accepted, some restrictions. TV; cable (premium). Pool; whirlpool. Complimentary continental bkfst. Complimentary coffee in rms. Ck-out noon. Coin lndry. Meeting rms. Business servs avail. In-rm modem link. Valet serv. Exercise equipt; bicycle, stair machine. Microwaves; some fireplaces. Some grills. Cr cds: A, C, D, DS, JCB, MC, V. [D] [✔] [≈] [🏋] [≈] [🐾] [SC]

Motor Hotel

★ ★ ★ **RAMADA PLAZA HOTEL.** *8105 Two Notch Rd (29223), at I-77. 803/736-5600; FAX 803/736-1241.* 187 units, 6 story. S $79; D $89; suites $130-$220; under 18 free; golf plan. Crib $6. Pet accepted, some restrictions. TV; cable (premium). Pool; whirlpool. Restaurant 6:30 am-10 pm. Rm serv. Bar 4:30 pm-2 am. Ck-out noon. Convention facilities. Business servs avail. In-rm modem link. Bellhops. Valet serv. Tennis privileges. 18-hole golf privileges. Exercise equipt; weight machine, bicycles, sauna. Refrigerator, microwave in suites. Cr cds: A, C, D, DS, ER, MC, V. D ⊡ ⊡ ⊡ ⊡ ⊡ ⊡ ⊡ ⊡ SC

Hotel

★ ★ ★ **ADAM'S MARK.** *1200 Hampton St (29201). 803/771-7000; FAX 803/254-8307.* 301 rms, 13 story. S $129; D $139; each addl $10; suites $225-$450; under 18 free; wkend rates. Crib free. Pet accepted; $50 deposit. TV; cable. Indoor pool; whirlpool. Restaurants 6 am-midnight. Bar 11:30-1 am. Ck-out noon. Convention facilities. Business servs avail. In-rm modem link. Airport transportation. Exercise equipt; treadmills, bicycles. Some refrigerators. Some balconies. Cr cds: A, C, D, DS, ER, JCB, MC, V.

D ⊡ ⊡ ⊡ ⊡ ⊡ SC

Florence

Motels

✓ ★ **DAYS INN.** *2111 W Lucas St (29501), jct I-95 & US 52. 843/665-4444.* 103 rms, 2 story. S, D $38-$75; under 12 free; higher rates: race wkends, hols. Crib free. Pet accepted, some restrictions. TV; cable (premium). Pool; whirlpool. Complimentary continental bkfst. Restaurant adj 6 am-midnight. Ck-out 11 am. Meeting rms. Business servs avail. Exercise equipt; weights, bicycles, sauna. Some in-rm whirlpools, refrigerators, microwaves. Cr cds: A, C, D, DS, MC, V. D ⊡ ⊡ ⊡ ⊡ ⊡ SC

★ ★ **RAMADA INN.** *2038 W Lucas (29501). 843/669-4241; FAX 843/665-8883.* 179 rms, 2 story. S, D $54-$75; each addl $6; suites $70-$150; under 18 free; higher rates special events. Crib free. Pet accepted, some restrictions. TV; cable (premium). Pool; whirlpool. Restaurant 6:30 am-2 pm, 5-10 pm. Rm serv. Bar; entertainment. Ck-out noon. Meeting rms. Business servs avail. Bellhops. Free airport transportation. Exercise equipt; weights, bicycles. Refrigerators, microwaves avail. Cr cds: A, C, D, DS, ER, JCB, MC, V.

D ⊡ ⊡ ⊡ ⊡ ⊡ SC

✓ ★ **RED ROOF INN.** *2690 David McLeod Blvd (29501). 843/678-9000; FAX 843/667-1267.* 112 rms, 2 story. S $36.99; D $43.99-$52.99; each addl $7; under 18 free; higher rates special events. Crib free. Pet accepted. TV; cable (premium). Complimentary coffee in lobby. Restaurant adj open 24 hrs. Ck-out noon. Business servs avail. Cr cds: A, C, D, DS, MC, V. D ⊡ ⊡ ⊡

Greenville *(See also Anderson, Clemson, Clinton, Spartanburg)*

Motels

★ ★ **LA QUINTA.** *31 Old Country Road (29607). 864/297-3500; FAX 864/458-9818.* 122 rms, 2 story. S $53; D $59; under 18 free. Crib free. Pet accepted. TV; cable, VCR avail. Pool. Complimentary continental bkfst. Restaurant adj 6 am-10 pm. Ck-out noon. Coin lndry. Meeting rms. Business servs avail. Valet serv. Health club privileges. Cr cds: A, C, D, DS, MC, V. D ⊡ ⊡ ⊡ ⊡ SC

★ ★ **RESIDENCE INN BY MARRIOTT.** *48 McPrice Ct (29615). 864/297-0099; FAX 864/288-8203.* 96 kit. suites, 2 story. S, D $99-$119; wkly, monthly rates. Crib free. Pet accepted, some restrictions; $100. TV; cable (premium). Pool; whirlpool. Complimentary continental bkfst. Restaurant adj 11:30 am-11 pm. Ck-out noon. Meeting rms. Business servs avail. Private patios, balconies. Cr cds: A, C, D, DS, JCB, MC, V.

D ⊡ ⊡ ⊡ ⊡ SC

Hardeeville

Motel

✓ ★ ★ **HOWARD JOHNSON.** *US 17 at jct I-95. 803/784-2271.* 126 rms, 2 story. S $33-$50; D $37-$55; each addl $5; under 18 free. Crib free. Pet accepted; $5. TV; cable (premium). Pool; wading pool. Restaurant 7-10 am, 11 am-2 pm, 5-9 pm. Ck-out noon. Business servs avail. Private patios, balconies. Cr cds: A, C, D, DS, MC, V.

D ⊡ ⊡ ⊡ ⊡ ⊡ SC

Myrtle Beach

Motor Hotel

★★ **ST JOHN'S INN.** *6803 N Ocean Blvd (29572). 803/449-5251; FAX 803/449-3306; res: 800/845-0624.* 90 rms, 3 story, 28 kits. June-Labor Day: D $87; each addl $5; kit. units $94; under 12 free; golf plan; higher rates hols; varied lower rates rest of yr. Crib avail. Pet accepted, some restrictions. TV; cable. Pool; whirlpool. Restaurant 7-11 am. Ck-out 11 am. Meeting rm. Lawn games. Refrigerators. Private patios, balconies. Bathrm phones. Beach opp. Cr cds: A, DS, MC, V. 🅳 📳 🏊 🖵 🔥 SC

Rock Hill (See also Charlotte, NC)

Motels

★ **DAYS INN CHARLOTTE SOUTH/CAROWINDS.** *(3482 US 21, Ft Mill 29715) Approx 5 mi N on I-77 exit 90. 803/548-8000; FAX 803/548-6058.* 119 rms, 2 story. Apr-Sept: S $45-$70; D $50-$75; each addl $5; higher rates special events; lower rates rest of yr. Crib free. Pet accepted. TV; cable, VCR (movies). Pool. Complimentary continental bkfst. Restaurant adj open 24 hrs. Ck-out 11 am. Cr cds: A, C, D, DS, MC, V. 🅳 📳 🏊 🖵 🔥 SC

★★ **HOLIDAY INN.** *2640 Cherry Rd (29730), at jct I-77, US 21N. 803/329-1122; FAX 803/329-1072.* 125 rms, 2 story. S, D $55; each addl $5; suites $95-$125; under 16 free. Crib free. Pet accepted, some restrictions. TV; cable (premium). Pool. Complimentary full bkfst. Coffee in rms. Restaurant 6:30 am-11 am; 5:30 pm-10 pm. Bar 3 pm-2 am, Sat to midnight. Ck-out noon. Coin lndry. Business servs avail. In-rm modem link. Airport transportation. Cr cds: A, C, D, DS, JCB, MC, V. 🅳 📳 🏊 🖵 🔥 SC

✔★★ **HOWARD JOHNSON.** *2625 Cherry Rd (29730), I-77 exit 82B, jct US 21. 803/329-3121; FAX 803/366-1043.* 140 rms, 2 story. S $46-$53; D $48-$59; each addl $6; suites $125; under 12 free. Crib free. Pet accepted. TV; cable. Pool. Complimentary continental bkfst. Restaurant open 24 hrs. Rm serv 6 am-9 pm. Bar 5-10 pm, closed Sun. Ck-out noon. Meeting rm. Valet serv. Private patios, balconies. Cr cds: A, C, D, DS, JCB, MC, V. 🅳 📳 🏊 🖵 🔥 SC

Hotel

★★ **RAMADA.** *(225 Carowinds Blvd, Ft Mill 29715) I-77 Carowinds exit. 803/548-2400; FAX 803/548-6382.* 208 rms, 11 story. S, D $71-$85; each addl $10; under 18 free. Crib free. Pet accepted. TV; cable (premium). Pool. Complimentary bkfst. Restaurant 6:30 am-2 pm, 5-10 pm; Fri, Sat to 11 pm. Bar 4:30-11 pm. Ck-out noon. Coin lndry. Meeting rms. Business servs avail. In-rm modem link. Free airport transportation. Cr cds: A, D, DS, JCB, MC, V. 🅳 📳 🏊 🖵 🔥 SC

Santee

Motel

✔★ **DAYS INN.** *Jct I-95 & SC 6. 803/854-2175; FAX 803/854-2835.* 119 rms, 2 story. S $30-$50; D $40-$60; each addl $6; under 12 free; golf plans. Crib free. Pet accepted, some restrictions; $6. TV; cable (premium). Complimentary full bkfst. Restaurant 6-10 am, 5-9 pm. Ck-out noon. Guest lndry. Business servs avail. 18-hole golf privileges. Refrigerators avail. Cr cds: A, C, D, DS, MC, V. 📳 🚴 🏊 🖵 🔥 SC

Spartanburg (See also Clinton, Greenville)

Motor Hotel

★★ **QUALITY HOTEL AND CONFERENCE CENTER.** *7136 Asheville Hwy (29303). 864/503-0780.* 143 rms, 6 story. S $52-$62; D $62-$75; each addl $10; under 18 free. Crib free. Pet accepted. TV; cable (premium). Pool; poolside serv. Restaurant 6:30 am-2 pm, 5-10 pm. Bar 4 pm-midnight. Ck-out noon. Meeting rms. Business servs avail. In-rm modem link. Valet serv. Exercise equipt; weight machine, treadmill. Cr cds: A, C, D, DS, JCB, MC, V. 📳 🏊 🏋 🖵 🔥 SC

Sumter (See also Camden, Columbia)

Motel

★★ **RAMADA INN.** *226 N Washington St (29150), on US 76/378/521. 803/775-2323; FAX 803/773-9500.* 125 rms in 2 buildings, 2-3 story. S $49-$69; D $56-$76; each addl $9; under 18 free; golf plans. Crib free. Pet accepted, some restrictions. TV; cable (premium). Pool. Complimentary bkfst buffet. Coffee in rms. Restaurant 6:30 am-2 pm, 6-9 pm. Rm serv. Bar 5 pm-midnight; closed Sun. Ck-out noon. Meeting rms. Business servs avail. In-rm modem link. Health club privileges. Refrigerators, microwaves avail. Cr cds: A, C, D, DS, ER, JCB, MC, V. 🅳 ⟵ 🏊 ⊠ 🐾 🆂🅲

Walterboro *(See also Charleston)*

Motel

★ ★ **HOLIDAY INN.** *I-95 & SC 63. 843/538-5473.* 171 rms, 2 story. S, D $65; under 18 free. Crib free. Pet accepted. TV, cable (premium). Pool; wading pool. Complimentary full bkfst. Restaurant 6 am-2 pm, 5-10 pm. Rm serv. Ck-out noon. Meeting rms. Business servs avail. Valet serv. Cr cds: A, C, D, DS, MC, V. 🅳 ⟵ 🏊 ⊠ 🐾 🆂🅲

South Dakota

Aberdeen

Motels

★ **BREEZE INN.** *1216 6th Ave SW. 605/225-4222; res: 800/288-4248.* 20 rms, 3 kits. S $24; D $34.95-$36.95; each addl $2. Crib $2. Pet accepted. TV; cable. Restaurant adj. Ck-out 11 am. X-country ski 1 mi. Cr cds: C, D, DS, MC, V. 🐾 🖼 🛏 🛠

✔ ★ ★ **WHITE HOUSE INN.** *500 6th Ave SW. 605/225-5000; FAX 605/225-6730; res: 800/225-6000.* 96 rms, 3 story. S $32; D $36-$38; each addl $3; suites $40-$55; under 12 free. Crib free. Pet accepted. TV; cable. Complimentary continental bkfst. Restaurant nearby. Ck-out 11 am. Business servs avail. Airport, RR station, bus depot transportation. X-country ski 1¹/₂ mi. Cr cds: A, C, D, DS, MC, V. 🄳 🐾 🖼 🛏 🛠 🆂🅲

Motor Hotels

★ ★ ★ **BEST WESTERN RAMKOTA INN.** *1400 8th Ave NW. 605/229-4040; FAX 605/229-0480.* 154 rms, 2 story. S, D $55.75-$63.75; each addl $6; suites $75-$150; under 18 free. Crib free. Pet accepted. TV; cable. Indoor pool; wading pool, whirlpool, sauna. Restaurant 6:30 am-10 pm. Bar 11-2 am. Ck-out noon. Meeting rms. Business servs avail. Free airport, RR station, bus depot transportation. X-country ski 2 mi. Cr cds: A, C, D, DS, ER, JCB, MC, V. 🄳 🐾 🖼 🛏 🛠 🆂🅲

✔ ★ ★ **HOLIDAY INN.** *Box 1007, 2727 6th Ave SE, near Municipal Airport. 605/225-3600; FAX 605/225-6704.* 153 rms, 2 story. S $40-$60; D $50-$65; each addl $8; under 18 free. Crib free. Pet accepted, some restrictions. TV; cable. Indoor pool. Playground. Restaurant 6 am-10 pm. Rm serv. Bar 4 pm-2 am. Ck-out 11 am. Meeting rms. Business servs avail. Valet serv. Sundries. Free airport, bus depot transportation. X-country ski 1 mi. Rec rm. Cr cds: A, C, D, DS, JCB, MC, V. 🄳 🐾 🖼 🏊 ✈ 🏊 🛏 🛠 🆂🅲

Beresford *(See also Sioux Falls, Vermillion)*

Motel

✔ ★ **CROSSROADS.** *On SD 46, ¹/₄ mi E of I-29 exit 46. 605/763-2020.* 32 rms. S $20-$24; D $28-$34.50; each addl $3. Crib $5. Pet accepted. TV. Restaurant adj 6 am-10 pm. Ck-out 11 am. Cr cds: C, D, DS, MC, V. 🐾 🛏 🛠

Brookings *(See also Madison, Watertown)*

Motels

✔ ★ ★ **BEST WESTERN STAUROLITE INN.** *2515 E 6th St, 1¹/₄ mi E at jct US 14, I-29 exit 132. 605/692-9421; FAX 605/692-9429.* 102 rms, 2 story. S $43-$49; D $48-$56; each addl $2; suites $90; under 18 free. Crib free. Pet accepted. TV; cable. Indoor pool; wading pool, whirlpool. Restaurant 6 am-9 pm. Rm serv. Bar 4 pm-2 am; entertainment exc Sun. Ck-out 11 am. Meeting rms. Business servs avail. In-rm modem link. Bellhops. Valet serv. Sundries. Free airport, bus depot transportation. X-country ski 1 mi. Private patios, balconies. Picnic tables. Cr cds: A, C, D, DS, ER, MC, V. 🐾 🖼 🏊 🛏 🛠 🆂🅲

★ ★ **HOLIDAY INN.** *2500 E 6th St, near Municipal Airport. 605/692-9471; FAX 605/692-5807.* 125 rms, 2 story. S $49-$61; D $54-$61; each addl $4; under 18 free. Crib free. TV; cable. Indoor pool; whirlpool, sauna. Restaurant 6:30 am-10 pm. Rm serv. Bar 4 pm-2 am, closed Sun; entertainment. Ck-out noon. Coin lndry. Meeting rms. Business center. In-rm modem link. Bellhops. Valet serv. Sundries. Free airport transportation. X-country ski 1¹/₂ mi. Rec rm. Exercise equipt; stair machine, bicycles. Some balconies. Cr cds: A, C, D, DS, JCB, MC, V. 🄳 🐾 🖼 🏊 🏋 ✈ 🛏 🆂🅲 🏋

Chamberlain *(See also Platte, Winner)*

Motel

✔ ★ ★ **OASIS INN.** *(SD 16, Oacoma 57365) 2 mi W of Missouri River Bridge at I-90 exit 260. 605/734-6061; FAX 605/734-4161; res: 800/341-8000 (exc SD), 800/635-3559 (SD).* 69 rms, 2 story. June-mid-Oct: S $39-$50; D $60-$70; each addl $5; under 12 free; lower rates rest of yr. Crib free. Pet accepted. TV; cable. Restaurant adj 6 am-10:30 pm. Bar 5 pm-midnight. Ck-out 11 am. Coin lndry. Meeting rms. Sundries. Airport, bus depot transportation. Miniature golf. Whirlpool. Sauna. Picnic tables, grills. Pond. On river. Cr cds: A, C, D, DS, MC, V. 🅓 ⊡ ⊠ ⊠ SC

Custer *(See also Keystone, Rapid City)*

Motel

★ **BAVARIAN INN.** *Box 152, 1 mi N on US 16, 385. 605/673-2802; FAX 605/673-4777; res: 800/657-4312.* 64 rms, 2 story. June-late Aug: S $65; D $68-$78; each addl $5; suites $90-$115; lower rates rest of yr. Crib free. Pet accepted. TV; cable (premium). 2 pools, 1 indoor; whirlpool, sauna. Playground. Coffee in rms. Restaurant 6:30-10:30 am, 4-10 pm. Bar 4:30 pm-2 am. Ck-out noon. Meeting rms. Gift shop. Lighted tennis. Game rm. Lawn games. Patios, balconies. Cr cds: A, C, D, DS, MC, V.
⊡ ⊡ ⊠ ⊠ ⊠ SC

Custer State Park *(See also Custer, Keystone)*

Lodge

★★ **STATE GAME LODGE.** *(HC 83, Box 74, Custer 57730) 15 mi E of Custer on US 16A in park. 605/255-4541; FAX 605/255-4706; res: 800/658-3530.* 68 rms, 3 story, 21 cabins, 8 kits. No A/C in cabins, lodge, motel units. Some rm phones. Mid-May-mid-Oct: S, D $65-$230; 2 bedrm house $175-$250; 4 bedrm house $315; kit. cabins for 2-8, $85-$115. Closed rest of yr. Pet accepted. TV; cable. Dining rm 7 am-9 pm. Snack bar, box lunches. Bar noon-10 pm. Ck-out 10 am. Meeting rms. Gift shop. Grocery $1/4$ mi, package store. Jeep rides into buffalo area. Hiking trails. Fireplace in lobby. Picnic tables. Served as "summer White House" for Presidents Coolidge and Eisenhower. Cr cds: A, DS, MC, V. ⊡ ⊡ ⊠

Cottage Colony

★ **LEGION LAKE RESORT.** *(HCR 83, Box 67, Custer 57730) 7 mi E of Custer. 605/255-4521; FAX 605/255-4753; res: 800/658-3530.* 25 cabins, 12 kits. May-Sept: S, D $67; kits. $90-$110; each addl $5. Closed rest of yr. Crib $5. Pet accepted; $5. Playground. Restaurant 7 am-9 pm. Ck-out 10 am. Grocery. Swimming beach; boating. Hiking. Bicycle rentals. On lake. Cr cds: A, DS, MC, V. ⊡ ⊡ ⊠ ⊠

Huron *(See also Brookings, Mitchell)*

Motels

★★★ **CROSSROADS.** *100 4th St, at Wisconsin. 605/352-3204; FAX 605/352-3204, ext. 177.* 100 rms, 3 story. S $51-$61; D $56-$69; each addl $5; suites $130; family rates. Crib free. Pet accepted. TV; cable. Indoor pool; whirlpool, poolside serv. Sauna. Restaurants 6:30 am-10 pm. Rm serv. Bar 4 pm-2 am. Ck-out 11 am. Meeting rms. Business servs avail. In-rm modem link. Valet serv. Airport, RR station, bus depot transportation. Some refrigerator. Cr cds: A, C, D, DS, MC, V. 🅓 ⊡ ⊠ ⊠ ⊠ SC

✔★★ **DAKOTA PLAINS INN.** *Box 1433, US 14E. 605/352-1400; res: 800/648-3735.* 77 rms, 2 story. S $39; D $44; each addl $5; under 12 free. Crib free. Pet accepted. TV; cable. Pool. Restaurant adj 6-10 pm. Bar 11:30-2 am. Ck-out 11 am. Meeting rm. Business servs avail. In-rm modem link. X-country ski $1 1/2$ mi. Cr cds: A, DS, MC, V.
⊡ ⊡ ⊠ ⊠ ⊠ SC

Keystone *(See also Custer, Rapid City)*

Motels

★ **BEST WESTERN FOUR PRESIDENTS.** *Box 690, on US 16A. 605/666-4472; FAX 605/666-4574.* 30 rms, 3 story. No elvtr. Mid-June-Sept: S $82; D $92; each addl $5; lower rates Apr-mid-June & Oct-Nov. Closed rest of yr. Crib $5. Pet accepted, some restrictions. TV. Complimentary coffee in rms. Restaurant adj 7 am-10 pm. Ck-out 10 am. Cr cds: A, C, D, DS, MC, V. ⊡ ⊠ ⊠ SC

★ **FIRST LADY INN.** *702 US 16A. 605/666-4990; FAX 605/666-4676; res: 800/252-2119.* 39 rms, 3 story. No elvtr. Late May-early Sept: S $75; D $81; each addl $5; suites $125; lower rates rest of yr. Crib $5. Pet accepted. TV; cable. Complimentary coffee in rms. Ck-out 10 am. Whirlpool. Cr cds: A, DS, MC, V. 🅓 ⊡ ⊠ ⊠ SC

Madison *(See also Brookings, Sioux Falls)*

Motels

★ **LAKE PARK.** *1515 NW 2nd, 1 mi W on US 81, SD 34.* 605/256-3524. 40 rms. S $30; D $35; each addl $5. Crib $7. Pet accepted. TV; cable (premium). Heated pool. Restaurant adj. Ck-out 11 am. X-country ski 1 mi. Some refrigerators. Cr cds: A, C, D, DS, MC, V. 🄳 🗨 🗨 🏊 🎿 🐾 SC

✔★ **SUPER 8.** *Box 5, at jct US 81, SD 34.* 605/256-6931. 34 rms, 2 story. S $31.88; D $35.88-$38.88; each addl $3-$4; under 12 free. Crib free. Pet accepted. TV; cable. Restaurant adj 6 am-10 pm. Ck-out 11 am. Cr cds: A, C, D, DS, MC, V. 🄳 🗨 🎿 🐾 SC

Milbank *(See also Watertown)*

Motel

★★ **MANOR.** *Box 26, on US 12, 3/4 mi E of jct SD 15.* 605/432-4527; res: 800/341-8000. 30 rms, 1-2 story. S $30-$32; D $36-$42; each addl $4; under 16 free; higher rates Oct hunting season. Crib free. Pet accepted. TV. Indoor pool; whirlpool. Sauna. Restaurant 6 am-11 pm. Ck-out 11 am. X-country ski 1 mi. Cr cds: A, C, D, DS, MC, V. 🗨 🏊 🎿 🐾 SC

Mitchell

Motels

✔★ **COACH LIGHT.** *1000 W Havens St, 1 1/2 mi SW on I-90 Business.* 605/996-5686. 20 rms. June-Oct: S $30; D $36-$38; each addl $3; lower rates rest of yr. Crib free. Pet accepted. TV; cable. Restaurant nearby. Ck-out 11 am. Airport, bus depot transportation. X-country ski 1 1/2 mi. Cr cds: A, DS, MC, V. 🗨 🏊 🎿

✔★ **MOTEL 6.** *1309 S Ohlman St, N of I-90 exit 330.* 605/996-0530; FAX 605/995-2019. 122 rms. Mid-June-mid-Sept: S $29.95; D $35.95; under 17 free; lower rates rest of yr. Crib free. Pet accepted. TV. Heated pool. Restaurant nearby. Ck-out noon. X-country ski 2 mi. Cr cds: A, C, D, DS, MC, V. 🄳 🗨 🏊 🎿 🐾 SC

★ **SIESTA.** *1210 W Havens St.* 605/996-5544; FAX 605/996-4946; res: 800/424-0537. 23 rms. Memorial Day-Labor Day: S $38; D $38-$48; each addl $4; lower rates rest of yr. Crib free. Pet accepted. TV; cable. Pool. Restaurant nearby. Ck-out 10 am. Cr cds: A, DS, MC, V. 🗨 🏊 🎿 🐾 SC

Motor Hotel

★★★ **HOLIDAY INN.** *1525 W Havens St, I-90 Business exit 330.* 605/996-6501; FAX 605/996-3228. 153 rms, 2 story. June-Oct: S $74-$79; D $79-$84; each addl $5; under 19 free; lower rates rest of yr. Crib free. Pet accepted. TV; cable. Indoor pool; wading pool, whirlpool, sauna, poolside serv. Restaurant 6 am-10 pm. Rm serv. Bar 11-2 am. Ck-out noon. Coin lndry. Meeting rms. Business servs avail. In-rm modem link. Bellhops. Free airport, bus depot transportation. Putting green. Rec rm. Lawn games. Private patios, balconies. Cr cds: A, C, D, DS, JCB, MC, V. 🄳 🗨 🏊 🎿 🐾 SC

Murdo

Motel

✔★ **HOSPITALITY INN.** *302 W 5th St.* 605/669-2425; res: 800/328-0529. 29 rms, 1-2 story. June-Aug: S $35-$55; D $45-$75; each addl $4; wkly rates; lower rates rest of yr. Crib $1. Pet accepted. TV; cable. Complimentary coffee. Restaurant nearby. Ck-out 11 am. Cr cds: A, C, D, DS, MC, V. 🗨 🎿 🐾

Pierre

Motels

★ **BEST WESTERN KINGS INN.** *220 S Pierre St.* 605/224-5951; FAX 605/224-5301. 104 rms, 2 story. S $44; D $49-$52; each addl $5; under 12 free. Crib free. Pet accepted. TV; cable. Restaurant 6 am-11 pm. Rm serv. Bar 11-2 am. Ck-out noon. Business servs avail. Sundries. X-country ski 1 mi. Whirlpool, sauna. Some refrigerators. Cr cds: A, C, D, DS, ER, MC, V. 🗨 🏊 🎿 🐾 SC

★ ★ ★ **BEST WESTERN RAMKOTA INN.** *920 W Sioux, adj to River Centre convention facility.* 605/224-6877; FAX 605/224-1042. 151 rms, 2 story. S $57; D $64; each addl $6; suites $150; under 17 free. Crib avail. Pet accepted. TV; cable. Indoor pool; wading pool; whirlpool. Restaurant 6 am-10 pm. Rm serv. Bar. Ck-out noon. Coin lndry. Meeting rms. Business servs avail. Bellhops. Valet serv. Free airport, RR station, bus depot transportation. Exercise equipt; bicycles, stair machine, sauna. Game rm. Some refrigerators. Balconies. At Missouri River. Cr cds: A, C, D, DS, ER, MC, V. 🄳 🐾 ➿ 🏋 ⛱ 🔥 SC

★ **CAPITOL INN.** *815 Wells Ave.* 605/224-6387; FAX 605/224-8083; res: 800/658-3055. 81 rms, 2 story. S $19.95; D $21.95-$23.95; each addl $2; suites $58-$76. Crib free. Pet accepted. TV; cable. Pool. Restaurant nearby. Ck-out 11 am. Business servs avail. Some refrigerators. Balconies. Cr cds: A, C, D, DS, MC, V. 🄳 🐾 ➿ ⛱ 🔥

Platte

Motel

✔ ★ **KING'S INN.** *Box 54, ¼ mi E on SD 44, 45, 50.* 605/337-3385. 34 rms. S $24-$28; D $31.95-$35.95. Crib $3. Pet accepted. TV; cable. Playground. Complimentary continental bkfst. Restaurant nearby. Ck-out 10 am. Cr cds: A, DS, MC, V. 🐾 ⛱ 🔥

Rapid City *(See also Keystone, Sturgis)*

Motels

★ **RAMADA INN.** *1721 LaCrosse St (57701).* 605/342-1300; FAX 605/342-0663. 139 rms, 4 story. June-Aug: S $79-$119; D $89-$139; each addl $10; suites $119-$159; under 18 free; higher rates special events; lower rates rest of yr. Crib free. Pet accepted. TV; cable (premium), VCR (movies). Indoor pool; whirlpool. Restaurant adj. Bar 7-12:30 am. Ck-out noon. Meeting rms. Business servs avail. Bellhops. Game rm. Some bathrm phones, refrigerators. Cr cds: A, C, D, DS, MC, V. 🐾 ➿ ⛱ 🔥 SC

★ **SUPER 8.** *2124 LaCrosse St (57701), at I-90 exit 59.* 605/348-8070; FAX 605/348-0833. 119 rms, 3 story. No elvtr. June-Aug: S $75; D $85; lower rates rest of yr. Crib free. Pet accepted. TV; cable (premium), VCR avail (movies). Complimentary coffee in lobby. Restaurant adj open 24 hrs. Ck-out 11 am. Sundries. Game rm. Cr cds: A, C, D, DS, JCB, MC, V. 🄳 🐾 ➿ 🔥

Sioux Falls

Motels

★ **BUDGET HOST PLAZA INN.** *2620 E 10th St (57103).* 605/336-1550; FAX 605/339-0616; res: 800/283-4678. 38 rms. June-Sept: S $38.95; D $46.95-$55.95; each addl $4; under 10 free; lower rates rest of yr. Crib $3. Pet accepted. TV; cable. Heated pool. Restaurant adj open 24 hrs. Ck-out 11 am. Meeting rm. Cr cds: A, C, D, DS, ER, MC, V. 🐾 ➿ ⛱ 🔥 SC

✔ ★ **BUDGETEL.** *3200 Meadow Ave (57106), Empire Mall.* 605/362-0835; FAX 605/362-0835. 82 rms, 3 story. Late-May-Sept: S $46.99-$59.99; D $56.99-$69.99; suites $70.99-$84.99; under 18 free; lower rates rest of yr. Crib free. Pet accepted. TV; cable (premium). Indoor pool; whirlpool. Complimentary coffee in rms. Restaurant adj open 24 hrs. Ck-out 11 am. Meeting rms. X-country ski 2 mi. Some refrigerators. Cr cds: A, C, D, DS, MC, V. 🄳 🐾 🏊 ➿ ⛱ 🔥 SC

✔ ★ **COMFORT INN.** *3216 S Carolyn Ave (57106), Empire Mall.* 605/361-2822; FAX 605/361-2822. 67 rms, 2 story. Mid-May-mid-Sept: S $45.95-$65.95; D $50.95-$75.95; each addl $5; under 18 free; lower rates rest of yr. Crib free. Pet accepted. TV; cable (premium). Indoor pool; whirlpool. Complimentary continental bkfst. Restaurant adj open 24 hrs. Ck-out 11 am. Meeting rms. Game rm. Some refrigerators. Cr cds: A, C, D, DS, ER, JCB, MC, V. 🄳 🐾 ➿ ⛱ 🔥 SC

★ ★ **COMFORT SUITES.** *3208 S Carolyn Ave (57106).* 605/362-9711; FAX 605/362-9711. 61 rms, 3 story. Mid-May-mid-Sept: S $59.95-$79.95; D $63.95-$89.95; each addl $5; under 18 free; lower rates rest of yr. Crib free. Pet accepted. TV; cable (premium). Indoor pool; whirlpool. Complimentary continental bkfst. Restaurant adj open 24 hrs. Ck-out 11 am. Business servs avail. X-country ski 1 mi. Cr cds: A, C, D, DS, ER, JCB, MC, V. 🄳 🐾 ➿ ⛱ 🔥 SC

✔ ★ **EXEL INN.** *1300 W Russell St (57104).* 605/331-5800; FAX 605/331-4074. 105 rms, 2 story. S $31.99-$34.99; D $39.99-$41.99; each addl $4; under 18 free. Crib free.

Pet accepted. TV; cable. Complimentary continental bkfst. Restaurant nearby. Ck-out noon. Coin lndry. X-country ski 1¹/₂ mi. Cr cds: A, C, D, DS, MC, V. [D] [icons]

★ ★ KELLY INN. *Box 84711 (57118), 3101 W Russell St. 605/338-6242; res: 800/635-3559.* 42 rms, 2 story. June-Aug: S $44-$65; D $49-$70; each addl $5; under 12 free; lower rates rest of yr. Crib free. Pet accepted. TV; cable. Restaurant adj 6 am-11 pm. Ck-out 11 am. Coin lndry. Meeting rm. Airport transportation. Whirlpool, sauna. Cr cds: A, C, D, DS, ER, MC, V. [D] [icons]

★ MOTEL 6. *3009 W Russell St (57104). 605/336-7800; FAX 605/330-9273.* 87 rms, 2 story. May-Sept: S $29.99; D $35.99; each addl $6; under 17 free; lower rates rest of yr. Crib free. Pet accepted, some restrictions. TV; cable. Heated pool. Restaurant adj 6 am-11 pm. Ck-out noon. Business servs avail. Cr cds: A, C, D, DS, MC, V. [icons]

✔ ★ SELECT INN. *3500 Gateway Blvd (57106). 605/361-1864; FAX 605/361-9287.* 100 rms, 2 story. S $29.90-$39.90; D $35.90-$39.90; each addl $3; under 12 free. Crib $3. Pet accepted. TV; cable, VCR avail (movies). Complimentary continental bkfst. Ck-out 11 am. Cr cds: A, C, D, DS, MC, V. [D] [icons]

✔ ★ SUPER 8. *1508 W Russell St (57104), SE of I-29 exit 81. 605/339-9330.* 95 rms, 3 story. No elvtr. S $27.29-$38.88; D $29.59-$47.88; each addl $5; under 12 free. Crib free. Pet accepted. TV; cable (premium). Restaurant adj open 24 hrs. Ck-out 11 am. Business servs avail. In-rm modem link. X-country ski 1 mi. Cr cds: A, C, D, DS, MC, V. [icons]

Motor Hotels

★ ★ ★ BEST WESTERN RAMKOTA INN. *2400 N Louise (57107), 2 mi NW on SD 38, at jct I-29 exit 81. 605/336-0650; FAX 605/336-1687.* 227 rms, 2 story. S $67-$77; D $75-$85; each addl $8; suites $130-$180; under 18 free. Crib free. Pet accepted. TV; cable (premium), VCR avail. 2 pools, 1 indoor; wading pool, whirlpool, sauna, poolside serv. Playground. Restaurant 6 am-10 pm. Rm serv. Bar 11-2 am. Ck-out 11 am. Coin lndry. Convention facilities. Business servs avail. Bellhops. Valet serv. Sundries. Free airport, bus depot transportation. X-country ski 2 mi. Game rm. Rec rm. Cr cds: A, C, D, DS, ER, MC, V. [D] [icons]

★ ★ ★ RAMADA INN CONVENTION CENTER. *1301 Russell St (57104), E of I-29 exit 81, near Joe Foss Field Airport. 605/336-1020; FAX 605/336-3030.* 200 rms, 2 story. S $57-$74; D $69-$84; each addl $8; under 18 free; Crib free. Pet accepted. TV; cable. Indoor pool; whirlpool, sauna. Restaurant 6 am-10 pm. Rm serv. Bar 4 pm-2 am, Sun to 10 pm; entertainment. Ck-out noon. Coin lndry. Meeting rms. Business servs avail. In-rm modem link. Bellhops. Valet serv. Sundries. Free airport, bus depot transportation. Putting green. X-country ski 2 mi. Cr cds: A, C, D, DS, ER, JCB, MC, V. [D] [icons]

Sisseton

Motel

✔ ★ HOLIDAY. *1¹/₂ mi E at jct US 127, SD 10. 605/698-7644.* 19 rms. S $22-$28; D $30-$34; each addl $3. Crib free. Pet accepted. TV; cable. Complimentary coffee. Restaurant nearby. Ck-out 11 am. Cr cds: A, C, D, DS, MC, V. [D] [icons]

Spearfish *(See also Rapid City, Sturgis)*

Motels

(Advance reservations advised during Passion Play season)

★ COMFORT INN. *2725 1st Ave, I-90 exit 14. 605/642-2337; FAX 605/642-0866.* 40 rms, 2 story. June-Aug: S $72; D $80; each addl $5; under 18 free; ski plan; higher rates special events; lower rates rest of yr. Pet accepted, some restrictions. TV; cable (premium). Indoor pool; whirlpool. Complimentary continental bkfst. Restaurant nearby. Ck-out 11 am. Coin lndry. Meeting rm. Cr cds: A, C, D, DS, JCB, MC, V. [D] [icons]

★ ★ FAIRFIELD INN BY MARRIOTT. *2720 1st Ave E, I-90 exit 14. 605/642-3500; FAX 605/642-3500.* 57 rms, 3 story. May-Sept: S $65.95-$73.95; D $78.95; each addl $5; suites $85.95-$150; under 18 free; ski plan; lower rates rest of yr. Crib free. Pet accepted, some restrictions; $25 deposit. TV; cable (premium). Indoor pool; whirlpool. Complimentary continental bkfst. Ck-out 11 am. Meeting rm. Downhill/x-country ski 16 mi. Refrigerator in suites. Cr cds: A, D, DS, MC, V. [D] [icons]

★ ★ **KELLY INN.** *540 E Jackson. 605/642-7795; res: 800/635-3559.* 50 rms, 2 story. June-Aug: S $60; D $65; each addl $5; under 12 free; lower rates rest of yr. Crib free. Pet accepted. TV; cable (premium). Complimentary coffee. Restaurant adj open 24 hrs. Ck-out 11 am. Coin lndry. Whirlpool, sauna. Some in-rm whirlpools. Cr cds: A, D, DS, MC, V. D 🏊 🎿 🏖 🔥

Sturgis *(See also Rapid City, Spearfish)*

Motel

★ **SUPER 8.** *Box 703, 1/2 blk SW of I-90 exit 30. 605/347-4447; FAX 605/347-2334.* 59 rms, 3 story. June-Sept: S $59.88; D $63.88-$68.88; each addl $3; lower rates rest of yr. Crib $5. Pet accepted. TV; cable (premium). Complimentary coffee in lobby. Restaurant adj open 24 hrs. Ck-out 11 am. Coin lndry. Exercise equipt; weights, bicycles, sauna. Whirlpool. Some balconies. Cr cds: A, C, D, DS, MC, V. D 🏊 🏃 🏖 🔥 SC

Vermillion *(See also Beresford, Yankton; also see Sioux City, IA)*

Motel

★ **COMFORT INN.** *701 W Cherry St (SD 50). 605/624-8333.* 46 rms, 2 story. S $38.95-$43.95; D $43.95-$59.95; each addl $5; under 18 free; higher rates some special events. Crib free. Pet accepted. TV; cable (premium). Indoor pool; whirlpool. Complimentary continental bkfst. Ck-out 11 am. Meeting rms. Business servs avail. Exercise equipt; bicycle, weights, sauna. Outdoor patio. Cr cds: A, C, D, DS, ER, JCB, MC, V. D 🏊 🏊 🏃 🏖 🔥 SC

Wall *(See also Rapid City)*

Motel

★ **BEST WESTERN PLAINS.** *Box 393, 712 Glenn St, I-90 Business exit 110. 605/279-2145; FAX 605/279-2977.* 74 rms, 1-2 story, 8 (2-rm) units. August: S, D $85; each addl $5; lower rates rest of yr. Crib $5. Pet accepted. TV; cable. Heated pool. Complimentary coffee in rms. Restaurant nearby. Ck-out 10:30 am. Gift shop. Rec rm. Cr cds: A, C, D, DS, MC, V. 🏊 🏊 🏖 🔥 SC

Watertown *(See also Brookings)*

Motel

✔ ★ **TRAVEL HOST.** *1714 9th Ave SW, 1 mi W on US 212. 605/886-6120; FAX 605/886-5352; res: 800/658-5512.* 29 units, 2 story. S $28.90-$32.90; D $36.90-$41.90; each addl $5; under 12 free. Crib free. Pet accepted. TV; cable (premium). Complimentary continental bkfst. Restaurant adj 7 am-10 pm. Ck-out 11 am. Cr cds: A, C, D, DS, MC, V. D 🏖 🔥 SC

Winner

Motel

✔ ★ **BUFFALO TRAIL.** *950 W First St, located at jct W US 18/183 & SD 44. 605/842-2212; FAX 605/842-3199; res: 800/341-8000.* 31 rms. S $30-$38; D $38-$42; each addl $5; higher rates hunting season. Crib $5. Pet accepted. TV; cable. Pool. Complimentary continental bkfst. Restaurant nearby. Ck-out 11 am. Free airport transportation. 9-hole golf privileges, putting green, driving range. Rec rm. Picnic tables, grills. Cr cds: A, C, D, DS, MC, V. D 🏌 🏊 🏖 🔥

Yankton *(See also Beresford, Vermillion)*

Motels

★ **BEST WESTERN YANKTON INN.** *1607 E SD 50. 605/665-2906; FAX 605/665-4318.* 124 rms, 2 story. S $45-$66; D $49-$66; each addl $4; under 14 free. Crib free. Pet accepted. TV; cable, VCR avail (movies). Indoor pool; wading pool, whirlpool. Complimentary continental bkfst. Restaurant adj 6 am-10 pm. Ck-out 11 am. Meeting rms. Business servs avail. Bellhops. X-country ski 1 mi. Exercise equipt; bicycle, treadmill, sauna. Game rm. Some refrigerators. Opp lake. Cr cds: A, C, D, DS, ER, MC, V. D 🏊 🏊 🏃 🏖 🔥 SC

✔ ★ **BROADWAY.** *1210 Broadway, on US 81 at jct 15th St. 605/665-7805.* 37 rms. S $30.95-$39.95; D $35.95-$49.95; each addl $3. Crib $4. Pet accepted. TV; cable, VCR avail. Pool. Restaurant nearby. Bar 11-2 am. Ck-out 11 am. X-country ski 1 mi. Cr cds: A, DS, MC, V. 🏕 🏊 ➿ ⛳ 🐾 SC

★ **COMFORT INN.** *2118 Broadway, US 81 N. 605/665-8053; FAX 605/665-8165.* 45 rms, 2 story. S $39.95; D $47.95-$65.95; each addl $4; under 19 free. Crib $5. Pet accepted, some restrictions. TV; cable. Whirlpool. Complimentary continental bkfst. Restaurant nearby. Ck-out 11 am. Business servs avail. In-rm modem link. Cr cds: A, C, D, DS, JCB, MC, V. **D** 🏕 ⛳ 🐾 SC

Tennessee

Caryville

Motel

★ ★ **HOLIDAY INN.** *At jct US 25W, TN 63, I-75 exit 134.* 423/562-8476; *FAX 423/562-8870.* 102 rms, 2 story. S $45-$52; D $50-$64; each addl $5; family rates. Crib free. Pet accepted. TV; cable (premium). Pool; wading pool. Playground. Restaurant 6:30 am-2 pm, 5-10 pm. Rm serv. Ck-out noon. Meeting rms. Business servs avail. Cr cds: A, C, D, DS, ER, JCB, MC, V. 🄳 🏷 🌊 🐾 🐾 SC

Celina

Resort

★ **CEDAR HILL.** *2371 Cedar Hill Rd, 3¹/₂ mi N on TN 53.* 931/243-3201; *res: 800/872-8393.* 37 1-4 rm kit. cottages; 10 motel rms, 4 kits. Memorial Day wkend-Labor Day: cottages (no towels; maid serv avail) for 2-6, $50-$170; motel S, D $50-$60; each addl $6; kit. units $55-$65; wkly rates; lower rates rest of yr. Pet accepted. TV. Pool (open to public); lifeguard. Dining rm 6 am-8:30 pm. Box lunches, snack bar. Ck-out 10 am, ck-in 1 pm. Grocery ¹/₄ mi. Sports dir. Boats, motors, guides; waterskiing. Lawn games. Houseboats (drive your own) for 6-14 (3-day min) $125-$500; $450-$3,495 wkly. On Dale Hollow Lake. Cr cds: MC, V. 🐾 🏷 🌊 🐾

Chattanooga

Motels

★ ★ **COMFORT INN.** *7717 Lee Hwy (37421).* 423/894-5454; *FAX 423/499-9597.* 64 rms, 2 story. S, D $40-$58; each addl $5; under 18 free; higher rates: hol wkends, special events. Crib free. Pet accepted; $5. TV; cable (premium). Pool. Complimentary continental bkfst. Restaurant adj open 24 hrs. Ck-out 11 am. Microwaves avail. Cr cds: A, C, D, DS, ER, JCB, MC, V. 🄳 🏷 🌊 🐾 🐾 SC

✔ ★ ★ **DAYS INN AIRPORT.** *7725 Lee Hwy (37421).* 423/899-2288. Web www.daysinn.com. 80 rms, 2 story. June-Aug: S $48-$58; D $58-$78; each addl $5; under 12 free; lower rates rest of yr. Crib avail. Pet accepted, some restrictions; $5. TV; cable (premium). Indoor pool; whirlpool. Complimentary continental bkfst. Restaurant nearby. Ck-out 11 am. Microwaves avail. Cr cds: A, C, D, DS, ER, MC, V. 🄳 🏷 🌊 🐾 🐾 SC

✔ ★ **ECONO LODGE.** *1417 St Thomas (37412), I-75 exit 1.* 423/894-1417. 89 rms, 2 story. S $29.95-$59.95; D $34.95-$59.95; each addl $5; under 12 free. Crib $4. Pet accepted, some restrictions. TV; cable (premium). Pool. Complimentary continental bkfst. Restaurant nearby. Ck-out 11 am. Cr cds: A, C, D, DS, MC, V. 🄳 🏷 🌊 🐾 🐾 SC

✔ ★ ★ **KING'S LODGE.** *2400 West Side Dr (37404), 4 mi NE at jct US 41, I-24 East Ridge, 4th Ave exit.* 423/698-8944; *FAX 423/698-8949; res: 800/251-7702.* 138 rms, 2 story, 24 suites. S, D $40-$65; each addl $5; suites $60-$95; under 12 free. Crib free. Pet accepted, some restrictions. TV; cable (premium). Pool. Coffee in rms. Restaurant 7 am-11 pm. Rm serv. Bar 1 pm-3 am. Ck-out 11 am. Business servs avail. Refrigerators. Some balconies. Cr cds: A, C, D, DS, MC, V. 🄳 🏷 🌊 🐾 🐾 SC

★ ★ **LA QUINTA.** *7015 Shallowford Rd (37421), at I-75.* 423/855-0011; *FAX 423/855-0011, ext. 72.* 132 rms, 2 story. May-Oct: S $59-$66; D $65-$85; each addl $10; suites $92-$125; under 18 free; higher rates special events; lower rates rest of yr. Crib free. Pet accepted, some restrictions. TV; cable (premium). Pool. Complimentary continental bkfst. Ck-out noon. Health club privileges. Some refrigerators; microwaves avail. Cr cds: A, C, D, DS, MC, V. 🄳 🏷 🌊 🐾 🐾 SC

★ **RED ROOF INN.** *7014 Shallowford Rd (37421), I-75 exit 5.* 423/899-0143; *FAX 423/899-8384.* 112 rms, 2 story. Mar-Aug: S, D $41.99-$64.99; each addl $7; under 18 free; higher rates special events; lower rates rest of yr. Crib free. Pet accepted, some restrictions. TV; cable (premium). Complimentary coffee in lobby. Restaurant adj open 24 hrs. Ck-out noon. Cr cds: A, C, D, DS, MC, V. 🄳 🏷 🐾 🐾

★ **SUPER 8.** *20 Birmingham Hwy (37419), I-24 exit 174.* 423/821-8880. 74 rms, 3 story. Apr-Sept: S $42.88-$45.88; D $47.88-$55.88; each addl $5; under 12 free; lower rates rest of yr. Crib free. Pet accepted, some restrictions. TV; cable (premium). Complimentary coffee in lobby. Restaurant adj open 24 hrs. Ck-out 11 am. Coin lndry. Picnic tables. Cr cds: A, C, D, DS, MC, V. [D] [♦] [≈] [⋈] [🔥] [SC]

Clarksville (See also Hopkinsville, KY)

Motels

✔ ★ ★ **DAYS INN.** *1100 Connector Rd (TN 76) (37043), I-24 exit 11.* 931/358-3194; FAX 931/358-9869. 84 rms, 2 story. S $36-$50; D $45-$60; each addl $6; under 16 free. Crib free. Pet accepted. TV; cable (premium). Pool. Complimentary continental bkfst. Restaurant adj 6 am-9 pm; wkends to 10 pm. Ck-out 11 am. Business servs avail. Microwaves avail. Cr cds: A, C, D, DS, MC, V. [D] [♦] [≈] [⋈] [🔥] [SC]

★ ★ **QUALITY INN.** *803 N 2nd St (37040), 1¹/₂ mi NW on US 41A, 79.* 931/645-9084; FAX 931/645-9084, ext. 340. 134 rms, 2 story. S $45-$61; D $55-$61; each addl $6; under 18 free. Crib free. Pet accepted, some restrictions. TV; cable (premium), VCR avail. Indoor pool; whirlpool, sauna. Complimentary continental bkfst. Bar 4-11 pm. Ck-out noon. Coin lndry. Meeting rms. Business servs avail. Valet serv. Microwaves in suites. Cr cds: A, C, D, DS, JCB, MC, V. [D] [♦] [≈] [⋈] [🔥] [SC]

Motor Hotels

★ ★ **RAMADA INN RIVERVIEW.** *50 College St (37040).* 931/552-3331; FAX 931/647-5005. 154 rms, 7 story. S, D $54-$85; each addl $5; under 18 free. Crib free. Pet accepted, some restrictions. TV; cable (premium). Indoor pool. Restaurant 6 am-2 pm, 5-10 pm; Sat, Sun 7am-2 pm. Bar from 5 pm. Ck-out noon. Meeting rms. In-rm modem link. Microwaves in suites. Cr cds: A, C, D, DS, JCB, MC, V. [D] [♦] [≈] [⋈] [🔥] [SC]

✔ ★ ★ **TRAVELODGE.** *3075 Wilma Rudolph Blvd (37040), US 79 & I-24 exit 4.* 931/645-1400; FAX 931/551-3917. E-mail Travel@Knight wave.com. 125 rms, 4 story. S,D $50-$60; suites $65; under 18 free. Crib free. Pet accepted. TV; cable (premium). Heated pool; whirlpool. Complimentary full bkfst. Coffee in rms. Restaurant 6 am-9 pm. Rm serv. Bar 5:30 pm-midnight. Ck-out noon. Meeting rms. Business servs avail. Game rm. Microwaves avail. Cr cds: A, C, D, DS, MC, V. [D] [♦] [≈] [⋈] [🔥] [SC]

Cleveland (See also Chattanooga)

Motels

✔ ★ ★ **BUDGETEL INN.** *107 Interstate Dr NW (37312).* 423/339-1000; FAX 423/339-2760. 102 rms, 3 story, 14 suites. Apr-Sept: S, D, suites $45.75-$80.95; each addl $7; under 18 free; higher rates special events; lower rates rest of yr. Crib free. Pet accepted, some restrictions. TV; cable (premium). Pool. Complimentary continental bkfst. Complimentary coffee in rms. Restaurant adj open 24 hrs. Ck-out noon. Coin lndry. Meeting rm. Business servs avail. Health club privileges. Cr cds: A, C, D, DS, MC, V. [D] [♦] [≈] [⋈] [🔥] [SC]

★ ★ **HOLIDAY INN-NORTH.** *2400 Executive Park Dr (37312), jct TN 60 & I-75 exit 25.* 423/472-1504; FAX 423/479-5962. 146 rms, 2 story. S $58-$80; D $65-$89; each addl $7; under 18 free; higher rates special events. Crib free. Pet accepted, some restrictions. TV; cable (premium). Pool. Restaurant 6 am-2 pm, 5-10 pm. Rm serv 7 am-9:30 pm. Ck-out noon. Meeting rms. Business servs avail. Sundries. Health club privileges. Cr cds: A, C, D, DS, JCB, MC, V. [D] [♦] [≈] [⋈] [SC]

★ ★ **QUALITY INN CHALET.** *2595 Georgetown Rd (37311), jct TN 60 & I-75 exit 25.* 423/476-8511. 97 rms, 2-3 story. No elvtr. May-Sept: S, D $52-$64; each addl $5; under 18 free; lower rates rest of yr. Crib $5. Pet accepted, some restrictions. TV; cable (premium). Pool; wading pool. Coffee in rms. Restaurant 11 am-10 pm. Ck-out noon. Coin lndry. Meeting rms. Some refrigerators; microwaves avail. Cr cds: A, C, D, DS, ER, MC, V. [D] [♦] [≈] [⋈] [🔥] [SC]

Columbia (See also Franklin)

Motel

★ ★ **RAMADA INN.** *1208 Nashville Hwy, 2¹/₂ mi N on US 31.* 931/388-2720; FAX 931/388-2360. 155 rms, 2 story. S $42-$52; D $47-$57; each addl $5. Crib free. Pet accepted. TV; cable (premium), VCR avail. Pool. Restaurant 6 am-2 pm, 5-10 pm. Rm serv. Bar 4 pm-midnight. Ck-out noon. Meeting rms. Cr cds: A, C, D, DS, JCB, MC, V. [D] [♦] [≈] [⋈] [🔥] [SC]

Cookeville

Motels

✔★★ **BEST WESTERN THUNDERBIRD.** *900 S Jefferson Ave, ¹/₂ mi N of I-40 Sparta Rd exit 287.* 931/526-7115. 60 rms, 2 story. S $30-$45; D $35-$47; each addl $4; under 12 free. Crib $6. Pet accepted. TV; cable. Pool. Complimentary continental bkfst. Restaurant adj 6 am-midnight. Ck-out noon. Meeting rms. Business servs avail. Cr cds: A, C, D, DS, JCB, MC, V. ✊ ≈ 🖾 🐾 SC

★★ **ECONO LODGE.** *1100 S Jefferson Ave, I-40 exit 287.* 931/528-1040; FAX 931/528-5227. 71 air-cooled rms, 2 story. May-Oct: S $39.95-$49.95; D $44.95-$54.95; each addl $5; suites $59.95-$69.95; under 10 free; lower rates rest of yr. Crib $5. Pet accepted; $5. TV; cable (premium). Pool. Complimentary continental bkfst. Ck-out 11 am. Business servs avail. Many refrigerators. Cr cds: A, C, D, DS, ER, JCB, MC, V. D ✊ ≈ 🖾 🐾 SC

✔★★ **HOWARD JOHNSON.** *2021 E Spring St (38506), on US 70N at I-40 exit 290.* 931/526-3333; FAX 931/528-9036. 64 rms, 2 story. S $40-$44; D $48-$55; each addl $5; under 18 free. Crib free. Pet accepted; $5/day. TV; cable (premium), VCR avail (movies $2). Pool; wading pool, whirlpool. Complimentary continental bkfst. Restaurant 11 am-10 pm. Ck-out noon. Coin lndry. Business servs avail. In-rm modem link. Sundries. Free local airport transportation. Refrigerators. Private patios, balconies. Picnic tables. Cr cds: A, C, D, DS, ER, JCB, MC, V. D ✊ ≈ 🖾 🐾 SC

Motor Hotel

★★ **HOLIDAY INN.** *970 S Jefferson Ave, at jct I-40 & TN 136, exit 287.* 931/526-7125. 200 rms, 2-3 story. S, D $67-$77; suites $127-$200; family rates. Crib avail. Pet accepted. TV; cable (premium). Indoor/outdoor pool; whirlpool. Restaurant 6 am-2 pm, 5-10 pm. Rm serv. Lounge 4 pm-1 am. Ck-out noon. Meeting rms. Business center. In-rm modem link. Bellhops. Valet serv. Sundries. Exercise equipt; weight machine, stair machine. Holidome. Game rm. Cr cds: A, C, D, DS, JCB, MC, V. D ✊ ≈ 🕇 🖾 🐾 SC 🕱

Crossville

Motel

✔★ **GUEST HOUSE INN.** *3114 N Main St.* 931/484-9691; res: 800/626-9432. 61 rms, 2 story. Mid-May-Oct: S $30.60-$39; D $37-$50; each addl $5; under 18 free; lower rates rest of yr. Crib free. Pet accepted, some restrictions. TV; cable (premium), VCR avail (movies $4). Pool. Complimentary continental bkfst. Restaurant adj. Ck-out 11 am. Business servs avail. On river. Cr cds: A, C, D, DS, MC, V. ✊ ✊ ≈ 🖾 🐾 SC

Franklin (See also Columbia, Nashville)

Motel

✔★★ **BEST WESTERN FRANKLIN INN.** *1308 Murfreesboro Rd, TN 96 at I-65 exit 65.* 615/790-0570; FAX 615/790-0512. Web www.bestwest ern.com/best.httm. 142 rms, 2 story. S, D $50-$60; each addl $5; under 12 free; higher rates Fan Fair. Crib free. Pet accepted. TV; cable (premium). Pool. Complimentary continental bkfst. Restaurant adj 6 am-11 pm. Ck-out noon. Meeting rms. Business servs avail. Cr cds: A, C, D, DS, MC, V. D ✊ ≈ 🖾 🐾 SC

Gatlinburg (See also Pigeon Forge, Townsend)

Motels

★ **ALTO.** *404 Airport Rd.* 423/436-5175; FAX 423/430-7342; res: 800/456-4336. 21 rms, 2 story. Late May-Oct: S, D $60-$70; each addl $6; under 16 free; lower rates rest of yr. Crib free. Pet accepted. TV; cable (premium). Pool; wading pool. Playground. Restaurant adj 7 am-11 pm. Ck-out 11 am. Downhill ski 4 mi. Refrigerators. Picnic tables, grills. Cr cds: A, DS, MC, V. ✊ ≈ 🖾 🐾

✔★ **BON AIR MOUNTAIN INN.** *950 Parkway, 950 Parkway.* 423/436-4857; FAX 423/436-8942; res: 800/848-4857. 74 rms, 3 story, 1 kit. chalet. Apr-Oct: S, D $43-$106; each addl $5; chalet $125; under 16 free; lower rates rest of yr. Crib free. Pet accepted. TV; cable. Pool. Restaurant nearby. Ck-out 11 am. Business servs avail. Downhill ski 1 mi. Refrigerators. Balconies. Cr cds: A, DS, MC, V. D ✊ ≈ ≈ 🖾 🐾 SC

Motor Hotel

★ ★ **HOLIDAY INN SUNSPREE.** *520 Airport Rd. 423/436-9201; FAX 423/436-7974.* 402 rms, 2-8 story. May-Oct: S, D $60-$139; suites $150-$250; under 19 free; lower rates rest of yr. Crib free. Pet accepted. TV; cable (premium). 3 pools, 2 indoor; wading pool, whirlpools. Supervised child's activities (summer); ages 3-12. Restaurant 7 am-10 pm. Rm serv. Bar 4 pm-midnight. Ck-out 11 am. Coin lndry facilities. Convention facilities. Business servs avail. Bellhops. Gift shop. Downhill ski 4 mi. Exercise equipt; weight machine, bicycle. Holidome. Rec rm. Picnic tables, grills. Cr cds: A, C, D, DS, JCB, MC, V.

[D] 🐾 🏊 🏊 🏊 🎿 ⊠ 📷 SC

Harrogate

Motor Hotel

★ ★ **HOLIDAY INN.** *(Cumberland Gap 37724)* $1/2$ *mi E on US 25E. 423/869-3631; FAX 423/869-5953.* 147 rms, 4 story. S $54; D $60; each addl $6; under 19 free. Crib free. Pet accepted, some restrictions; $25 fee. TV; cable (premium), VCR avail. Pool. Playground. Restaurant 6:30 am-2 pm, 5:30-9:30 pm. Rm serv. Bar 5 pm-midnight exc Sun. Ck-out 11 am. Coin lndry. Meeting rms. Valet serv. Sundries. Balconies. Cr cds: A, C, D, DS, MC, V.

[D] 🐾 🏊 ⊠ 📷 SC

Hurricane Mills

Motel

✔ ★ ★ **BEST WESTERN.** *15542 TN 13S, On TN 13; I-40 exit 143. 931/296-4251; FAX 931/296-9104.* 89 rms, 2 story. May-Aug: S $56-$62; D $60-$68; each addl $4; under 12 free; higher rates special events; lower rates rest of yr. Crib $2. Pet accepted, some restrictions. TV; cable (premium), VCR avail (movies). Pool; whirlpool. Playground. Restaurant 6 am-9 pm. Ck-out noon. Coin lndry. Meeting rm. Some refrigerators; microwaves avail. Cr cds: A, C, D, DS, ER, MC, V. [D] 🐾 🏊 ⊠ 📷 SC

Jackson

Motel

★ ★ **BEST WESTERN OLD HICKORY INN.** *1849 US 45 Bypass (38305),* $1/2$ *mi S of I-40, exit 80A. 901/668-4222; FAX 901/664-8536.* 141 rms, 2 story. S $45-$52, D $49-$57; each addl $4; under 12 free. Crib $2. Pet accepted; some restrictions. TV; cable (premium). Pool; wading pool. Restaurant 6 am-10 pm. Rm serv. Bar 4 pm-1 am; entertainment exc Sun. Ck-out noon. Meeting rms. Business servs avail. Cr cds: A, C, D, DS, MC, V.

[D] 🐾 ⊠ 📷 SC

Johnson City

Motel

★ ★ **DAYS INN.** *2312 Brown's Mill Rd (37601). 423/282-2211; FAX 423/282-6111.* 102 rms, 2 story. S $38-$42; D $42-$48; each addl $5; under 12 free. Pet accepted. TV; cable, VCR avail (movies). Pool. Restaurant 6-10 am, 5-10 pm. Rm serv. Bar 3 pm-midnight. Ck-out 11 am. Coin lndry. Meeting rm. Business servs avail. Cr cds: A, D, DS, MC, V.

🐾 🏊 ⊠ 📷 SC

Motor Hotel

★ ★ **GARDEN PLAZA.** *211 Mockingbird Ln (37604). 423/929-2000; res: 800/342-7336.* 187 rms, 5 story. S, D $83-$91; each addl $8; suites $125-$135; under 18 free; higher rates special events. Crib free. Pet accepted. TV; cable, VCR avail (movies). Indoor/outdoor pool; whirlpool, poolside serv. Restaurant 6:30 am-2 pm, 5-10 pm. Rm serv. Bar 5 pm-1 am. Ck-out noon. Meeting rms. Business servs avail. Bellhops. Free airport transportation. Health club privileges. Wet bar in suites. Cr cds: A, C, D, DS, MC, V.

[D] 🐾 🏊 ⊠ 📷 SC

Knoxville

Motels

(Rates may be higher during football wkends)

★ ★ **BEST WESTERN HIGHWAY HOST.** *118 Merchants Dr (37912), I-75N exit 108. 423/688-3141; FAX 423/687-4645.* 214 rms, 6 story. S, D $59-$85; each addl $7; under 18 free; higher rates special events. Crib free. Pet accepted; $25 deposit. TV; cable (premium). Indoor pool; whirlpool. Complimentary coffee in rms. Restaurant open 24 hrs.

Bar 11 am-midnight. Ck-out noon. Coin lndry. Gift shop. Meeting rms. Business servs avail. Valet serv. Game rm. Microwaves avail. Balconies. Cr cds: A, C, D, DS, ER, MC, V.
🄳 ✦ ≈ ⊠ 🐾 SC

✔★★ BUDGETEL INN. 11341 Campbell Lakes Dr (37922), I-40/75 exit 373. 423/671-1010; FAX 423/675-5039. 100 rms, 3 story. S, D $57.95-$99.95; each addl $7; under 18 free; lower rates rest of yr. Crib free. Pet accepted, some restrictions. TV; cable (premium), VCR avail. Pool. Complimentary continental bkfst. Complimentary coffee in rms. Restaurant adj 6 am-10 pm. Ck-out noon. Coin lndry. Meeting rms. Business servs avail. Exercise equipt; weight machine, bicycles, sauna. Some refrigerators; microwaves avail. Cr cds: A, C, D, DS, MC, V. 🄳 ✦ ≈ 🍴 ⊠ 🐾 SC

✔★★ DAYS INN. 200 Lovell Rd (37922), I-40 exit 374. 423/966-5801; FAX 423/966-1755. 120 rms, 2 story. S, D $43-$75; each addl $6; under 13 free; higher rates special events. Crib free. Pet accepted, some restrictions; $6. TV; cable (premium). Pool. Complimentary full bkfst. Restaurant adj 6 am-11 pm. Ck-out noon. Cr cds: A, C, D, DS, JCB, MC, V. 🄳 ✦ ≈ ⊠ 🐾 SC

★★ LA QUINTA MOTOR INN. 258 Peters Rd N (37923). 423/690-9777; FAX 423/531-8304. 130 rms, 3 story. S $54-$61; D $61-$68; each addl $10; under 18 free. Crib free. Pet accepted, some restrictions. TV; cable, VCR avail. Pool. Complimentary continental bkfst. Restaurant adj open 24 hrs. Ck-out noon. Coin lndry. Meeting rms. Business servs avail. Health club privileges. Microwaves avail. Cr cds: A, C, D, DS, MC, V.
🄳 ✦ ≈ ⊠ 🐾 SC

✔★★ RAMADA INN. 323 Cedar Bluff Rd (37923). 423/693-7330; FAX 423/693-7383. 178 rms, 2 story. S, D $52-$58; each addl $10; under 16 free; higher rates special events. Pet accepted, some restrictions. TV; cable (premium). Indoor pool. Restaurant 7 am-2 pm, 5-10 pm. Rm serv. Bar 5 pm-2:30 am. Ck-out noon. Meeting rms. Business servs avail. Cr cds: A, C, D, DS, MC, V. 🄳 ✦ ≈ ⊠ 🐾 SC

★ RED ROOF INN. 5640 Merchants Center Blvd (37912), at I-75 exit 108. 423/689-7100; FAX 423/689-7974. 84 rms, 2 story. S $34-$52; D $36-$64; each addl $7. Crib free. Pet accepted, some restrictions. TV; cable (premium). Ck-out noon. Business servs avail. Health club privileges. Cr cds: A, C, D, DS, MC, V. 🄳 ✦ ⊠ 🐾

★ SUPER 8. 6200 Paper Mill Rd (37919). 423/584-8511. 139 rms, 2-3 story. No elvtr. S $44-$75; D $54-$95; each addl $5; under 18 free. Crib free. Pet accepted, some restrictions. TV; cable (premium). Pool; wading pool, whirlpool. Ck-out 11 am. Meeting rm. Business servs avail. Exercise equipt; bicycle, treadmill. Cr cds: A, C, D, DS, JCB, MC, V. 🄳 ✦ ≈ 🍴 ⊠ 🐾 SC

Motor Hotels

✔★★ DAYS INN. 1706 W Cumberland (37916), on Univ of TN campus. 423/521-5000. 119 rms, 7 story. S, D $55-$65; each addl $5; under 12 free; higher rates special events. Crib free. Pet accepted; $15. TV; cable (premium). Ck-out noon. Meeting rms. Business servs avail. Cr cds: A, C, D, DS, JCB, MC, V. 🄳 ✦ ⊠ 🐾 SC

★★ HOLIDAY INN WEST. 1315 Kirby Rd (37909), jct I-40 & I-75. 423/584-3911; FAX 423/588-0920. 242 rms, 4 story. S, D $80-$119; under 19 free. Crib free. Pet accepted. TV; cable (premium). Pool; whirlpool. Restaurant 6:30 am-10 pm. Rm serv. Bar 4 pm-1 am; entertainment wkends. Ck-out noon. Coin lndry. Meeting rms. Business servs avail. Bellhops. Free airport transportation. Health club privileges. Balconies. Picnic tables. Cr cds: A, C, D, DS, MC, V. 🄳 ✦ ≈ ⊠ 🐾 SC

★★ LA QUINTA INN. 5634 Merchants Center Blvd (37912). 423/687-8989; FAX 423/687-9351. 123 rms, 5 story. S, D $49-$75; each addl $5; higher rates special events. Crib free. Pet accepted. TV; cable (premium). Pool. Complimentary continental bkfst. Coffee in rms. Ck-out noon. Meeting rms. Health club privileges. Cr cds: A, C, D, DS, MC, V. 🄳 ✦ ≈ ⊠ 🐾 SC

★★ QUALITY INN WEST. 7621 Kingston Pike (37919). 423/693-8111; FAX 423/690-1031. 162 rms, 4 story. S, D $60.50-$70.50; each addl $10; suites $100-$175; studio rms $65-$90; under 18 free. Crib free. Pet accepted, some restrictions; $5. TV; cable (premium). Pool. Restaurant 7 am-1 pm, 5-10 pm. Rm serv. Bar 4 pm-2 am; entertainment. Ck-out noon. Meeting rms. Business servs avail. Cr cds: A, C, D, DS, ER, JCB, MC, V. 🄳 ✦ ≈ ⊠ 🐾 SC

Hotels

★★★ HYATT REGENCY. 500 Hill Ave SE (37915). 423/637-1234; FAX 423/637-1193. 385 rms, 11 story. S, D $130-$160; each addl $25; suites $175-$425; under 18 free; wkend rates; higher rates special events. Crib free. Pet accepted, some restrictions; $25.

TV; cable (premium), VCR avail. Pool; poolside serv. Playground. Restaurants 6:30 am-midnight. Bar 4 pm-1 am. Ck-out noon. Convention facilities. Business center. Barber, beauty shop. Gift shop. Airport transportation. Exercise equipt; bicycles, treadmills, sauna. Many balconies. Contemporary decor; 8-story lobby with atrium. On hill above Tennessee River. Cr cds: A, C, D, DS, ER, JCB, MC, V. 🄳 🖅 ≋ 🏂 🖎 🖘 SC 🎿

Lebanon (See also Murfreesboro, Nashville)

Motels

✔ ★ **DAYS INN.** *914 Murfreesboro Rd. 615/444-5635.* 52 rms, 2 story. May-Oct: S $32-$40; D $42-$52; each addl $5; under 18 free; higher rates special events; lower rates rest of yr. Crib free. Pet accepted. TV; cable (premium). Pool. Complimentary continental bkfst. Restaurant nearby. Ck-out 11 am. Coin lndry. Business servs avail. Some refrigerators. Cr cds: A, C, D, DS, ER, JCB, MC, V. 🖅 ≋ 🖎 🖘 SC

★ ★ **HAMPTON INN.** *704 S Cumberland, I-40 exit 238. 615/444-7400; FAX 615/449-7969.* 87 rms, 2 story. S $50-$85; D $55-$90; under 18 free; higher rates Fan Fair. Crib free. Pet accepted. TV; cable. Pool. Complimentary continental bkfst. Restaurant nearby. Ck-out 11 am. Lndry facilities avail. Meeting rms. Business servs avail. Exercise equipt; treadmill, bicycle, whirlpool, sauna. Cr cds: A, D, DS, MC, V.
🄳 🖅 ≋ 🏂 🖎 🖘 SC

Manchester (See also Monteagle)

Motels

★ ★ **HOLIDAY INN I-24.** *126 Expy Dr, I-24 exit 114. 931/728-2208; res: 800/465-4329.* 141 rms, 2 story. S, D $61-$70; each addl $5; suites $72-$84; under 18 free. Crib free. Pet accepted. TV; cable (premium), VCR avail. Pool. Restaurant 6 am-2 pm, 5-10 pm. Rm serv. Bar 5 pm-midnight. Ck-out noon. Free lndry facilities. Meeting rms. Business servs avail. In-rm modem link. Some refrigerators, microwaves. Cr cds: A, C, D, DS, JCB, MC, V. 🄳 🖅 ≋ 🖎 🖘 SC

✔ ★ **SUPER 8.** *2430 Hillsboro Hwy, 1 mi S on US 41 at I-24 exit 114. 931/728-9720.* 50 rms, 2 story. S $24-$36; D $31-$45; each addl $5; under 12 free; higher rates special events. Crib free. Pet accepted, some restrictions. TV; cable (premium). Pool. Complimentary continental bkfst. Ck-out 11 am. Cr cds: A, D, DS, MC, V.
🄳 🖅 ≋ 🖎 🖘 🖘 SC

McMinnville

Motel

✔ ★ **SHONEY'S INN.** *(508 Sunnyside Heights, McMinnville) 931/473-4446.* 61 rms, 3 story. S $42-$46; D $46; under 18 free. Crib free. Pet accepted, some restrictions. TV; cable (premium). Complimentary continental bkfst. Restaurant nearby. Ck-out noon. Meeting rms. Business servs avail. Pool. Some refrigerators, microwaves. Cr cds: A, C, D, DS, MC, V. 🄳 🖅 ≋ 🖎 🖘 SC

Memphis

Motels

✔ ★ **RED ROOF INN.** *6055 Shelby Oaks Dr (38134), I-40 exit 12, east of downtown. 901/388-6111; FAX 901/388-6157.* 108 rms, 2 story. S $43.99; D $51.99; each addl $8; under 18 free; higher rates special events. Crib free. Pet accepted, some restrictions. TV; cable (premium). Complimentary coffee in lobby. Restaurant adj open 24 hrs. Ck-out noon. Microwaves avail. Cr cds: A, C, D, DS, MC, V. 🄳 🖅 🖎 🖘

✔ ★ **RED ROOF INN SOUTH.** *3875 American Way (38118), east of downtown. 901/363-2335; FAX 901/363-2822.* 109 rms, 3 story. S $38.99-$54.99; D $41.99-$49.99; each addl $8; under 18 free. Pet accepted. TV; cable (premium). Complimentary coffee in lobby. Ck-out noon. Cr cds: A, C, D, DS, MC, V. 🄳 🖅 🖎 🖘

★ ★ **RESIDENCE INN BY MARRIOTT.** *6141 Poplar Pike (38119), east of downtown. 901/685-9595; FAX 901/685-1636.* 105 kit. suites, 4 story. Kit. suites $109-$154. Crib free. Pet accepted, some restrictions; $100-$200. TV; cable, (premium). Pool; whirlpool. Complimentary continental bkfst. Restaurant nearby. Ck-out noon. Coin lndry. Meeting rms. Business servs avail. Health club privileges. Microwaves. Private patios, balconies. Cr cds: A, C, D, DS, JCB, MC, V. 🄳 🖅 ≋ 🖎 🖘 SC

Motor Hotels

★ ★ **COMFORT INN-POPLAR EAST.** *5877 Poplar Ave (38119), east of downtown. 901/767-6300; FAX 901/767-0098.* 126 rms, 5 story. S, D $68-$79; each addl $6; under 18 free; higher rates special events. Crib free. Pet accepted, some restrictions, $20. TV; cable (premium). Pool. Complimentary continental bkfst. Rm serv. Ck-out noon. Meeting rms. Bellhops. Sundries. Free airport transportation. Exercise equipt; weight machine, bicycles. Cr cds: A, D, DS, MC, V. 🄳 🏧 🏊 🏋 🖎 🐾 SC

★ ★ **COUNTRY SUITES BY CARLSON.** *4300 American Way (38118), east of downtown. 901/366-9333; FAX 901/366-7835; res: 800/456-4000.* 120 kit. suites, 3 story. Kit. suites $69-$99; under 16 free. Crib free. Pet accepted; $100. TV; cable (premium). Pool; whirlpool. Complimentary continental bkfst. Complimentary coffee in rms. Restaurant adj open 24 hrs. Ck-out noon. Coin lndry. Meeting rms. Business servs avail. Valet serv. Sundries. Free airport transportation. Health club privileges. Microwaves. Cr cds: A, C, D, DS, MC, V. 🄳 🏧 🏊 🖎 🐾 SC

Hotel

★ ★ ★ **CROWNE PLAZA.** *250 N Main (38103), downtown. 901/527-7300; FAX 901/526-1561.* Web www.crownplaza.com. 402 rms, 18 story. S $125-$155; D $125-$175; each addl $10; suites $250-$400; under 18 free. Crib free. Pet accepted, some restrictions. Valet parking $10, garage $5. TV; cable (premium). Indoor pool; whirlpool, sauna. Restaurant 6 am-11 pm. Bar 11-2 am. Ck-out noon. Convention facilities. Business center. Concierge. Shopping arcade. Exercise equipt; weight machine, bicycles. Some refrigerators. Cr cds: A, C, D, DS, JCB, MC, V. 🄳 🏧 🏊 🏋 🖎 🐾 SC 🏃

Monteagle *(See also Manchester)*

Motel

🛏 ★ ★ **JIM OLIVER'S SMOKE HOUSE MOTOR LODGE.** *I-24 exit 134. 931/924-2091; res: 800/489-2091.* 97 rms, 2 story. S $28-$43; D $35-$47; each addl $5; suites $80-$120; 1-2-bedrm cabins $99-$166; under 13 free. Crib $3. Pet accepted. TV; cable (premium). Pool. Playground. Restaurant 6 am-10 pm. Rm serv. Ck-out 11 am. Meeting rms. Business servs avail. Sundries. Tennis. Microwaves avail. Cr cds: A, DS, MC, V.
🄳 🏧 🐾 🏊 🎣 🖎 🐾 SC

Morristown

Motel

★ ★ **RAMADA INN.** *(37815). 6 mi S at I-81 & US 25E exit 8. 423/587-2400; FAX 423/581-7344.* 112 rms, 3 story. No elvtr. S, D $52-$84; under 19 free. Crib free. Pet accepted. TV; cable. 2 pools; wading pool. Complimentary coffee in lobby. Restaurant 6 am-2 pm, 5-9 pm. Ck-out noon. Meeting rms. Business servs avail. Private patios, balconies. Exercise equipt; treadmill, bicycles. Cr cds: A, C, D, DS, JCB, MC, V.
🄳 🏧 🏊 🏋 🖎 🐾 SC

Murfreesboro *(See also Lebanon, Nashville)*

Motels

(Rates may be higher during horse shows)

🛏 ★ ★ **HAMPTON INN.** *2230 Old Fort Pkwy (37129). 615/896-1172; FAX 615/895-4277.* 119 rms, 2 story. S, D $59-$66; each addl $5; under 18 free. Crib free. Pet accepted, some restrictions. TV; cable, VCR avail. Pool. Complimentary continental bkfst. Restaurant adj open 24 hrs. Ck-out noon. Meeting rm. Business servs avail. Microwaves avail. Cr cds: A, C, D, DS, MC, V. 🄳 🏧 🏊 🖎 🐾 SC

★ ★ **HOWARD JOHNSON.** *2424 S Church St (37130), at jct US 231 & I-24. 615/896-5522; FAX 615/890-0024.* 79 rms, 2 story. S $39-$69; D $39.95-$79; each addl $5; under 12 free; higher rates special events. Crib free. Pet accepted, some restrictions; $5. TV; cable (premium). Pool. Complimentary continental bkfst. Restaurant adj 11 am-8 pm. Ck-out 11 am. Coin lndry. Meeting rm. Business servs avail. Microwaves avail. Cr cds: A, C, D, DS, MC, V. 🄳 🏧 🏊 🖎 🐾 SC

★ ★ **RAMADA LIMITED.** *1855 S Church St (37130), I-24 exit 81. 615/896-5080.* 81 rms, 2 story. Mar-Dec: S, D $39.95-$75; each addl $5; under 18 free; lower rates rest of yr. Crib free. Pet accepted. TV; cable (premium). Complimentary continental bkfst. Restaurant adj open 24 hrs. Ck-out noon. Meeting rms. Business servs avail. Sundries. Pool; wading pool. Cr cds: A, C, D, DS, MC, V. 🄳 🏧 🏊 🖎 🐾 SC

Motor Hotels

★ ★ ★ **GARDEN PLAZA.** *1850 Old Fort Pkwy (37129). 615/895-5555; FAX 615/895-5555, ext. 165; res: 800/342-7336.* 170 rms, 5 story. S $69-$79; D $79-$89; each addl $10; suites $119; under 12 free. Crib free. Pet accepted, some restrictions. TV; cable (premium), VCR avail. Indoor/outdoor pool; whirlpool, poolside serv. Restaurant 6:30 am-2 pm, 5-10 pm. Rm serv. Bar 4 pm-midnight. Ck-out noon. Meeting rms. Health club privileges. Refrigerators; some wet bars; microwaves avail. Cr cds: A, C, D, DS, MC, V.

D 🐾 ≊ ⊠ 🐾 SC

★ ★ **WINGATE INN.** *165 Chaffin Pl (37129). 615/849-9000; res: 800/228-1000; FAX 615/849-9066.* Web www.wingateinns.com. 86 rms, 4 story. S, D $65-$85; each addl $5; under 18 free; higher rates Fanfare. Crib free. Pet accepted, some restrictions. TV; cable (premium). Complimentary continental bkfst. Complimentary coffee in rms. Restaurant adj 6 am-10 pm. Ck-out 11 am. Meeting rms. Business center. In-rm modem link. Sundries. Coin lndry. Exercise equipt; bicycle, treadmill. Pool; whirlpool. In-rm whirlpool, minibar, wet bar in suites. Cr cds: A, D, DS, MC, V. D 🐾 ≊ 🏃 ⊠ 🐾 SC 🏄

Nashville (See also Franklin, Lebanon, Murfreesboro)

Motels

(Rates may be higher during Fan Fair Week)

✔ ★ ★ **BUDGETEL INN GOODLETTSVILLE.** *(120 Cartwright Court, Goodlettsville 37072) 14 mi N on I-65, at exit 97. 615/851-1891; FAX 615/851-4513.* 102 rms, 3 story. Apr-Oct: S, D $45.95-$60.95; each addl $6; under 18 free; lower rates rest of yr. Crib free. Pet accepted, some restrictions. TV; cable (premium). Pool. Complimentary continental bkfst. Restaurant adj. 6 am-10 pm. Ck-out noon. Meeting rm. Business servs avail. Valet serv. Sundries. Cr cds: A, C, D, DS, MC, V. D 🐾 ≊ ⊠ 🐾 SC

★ ★ **COMFORT INN-NORTH.** *2306 Brick Church Pike (37207), I-65 exit 87B, north of downtown. 615/226-9560.* 95 rms, 4 story. S $42.95-$50.95; D $48.95-$56.95; each addl $5; under 16 free; higher rates special events. Crib free. Pet accepted, some restrictions. TV; cable (premium). Pool. Complimentary continental bkfst. Restaurant adj open 24 hrs. Ck-out noon. Business servs avail. Cr cds: A, C, D, DS, MC, V. D 🐾 ≊ ⊠ 🐾 SC

★ ★ **ECONO LODGE OPRYLAND.** *2460 Music Valley Dr (37214), in Opryland Area. 615/889-0090; FAX 615/889-0086.* 86 rms, 3 story. May-Oct: S, D $69.95-$74.95; each addl $10; under 18 free; higher rates special events; lower rates rest of yr. Crib free. Pet accepted, some restrictions. TV; cable (premium). Pool. Complimentary coffee in lobby. Restaurant nearby. Ck-out noon. Gift shop. Cr cds: A, C, D, DS, MC, V.

D 🐾 ≊ ⊠ 🐾 SC

★ ★ **RAMADA INN SUITES-SOUTH.** *2425 Atrium Way (37214), near International Airport, east of downtown. 615/883-5201; FAX 615/883-5594.* Web wwwramada.com /ramada.html. 120 suites, 3 story. S, D $75-129; each addl $10; under 18 free. Crib free. Pet accepted, some restrictions. TV; cable (premium), VCR avail. Pool. Complimentary continental bkfst. Coffee in rms. Ck-out noon. Coin lndry. Meeting rms. Business servs avail. Valet serv. Free airport transportation. Health club privileges. Refrigerators; microwaves avail. Cr cds: A, C, D, DS, JCB, MC, V. D 🐾 ≊ 🏃 ⊠ 🐾 SC

★ ★ **RAMADA LIMITED.** *(5770 Old Hickory Blvd, Hermitage 37076) 6 mi E on I-40, exit 221. 615/889-8940; FAX 615/871-4444.* Web www.rds2. com/motels/ramadsltd. 100 rms, 3 story. June-Aug: S $35-$55; D $40-$70; each addl $6; under 18 free; lower rates rest of yr. Crib free. Pet accepted, some restrictions; $5. TV; cable. Pool. Complimentary continental bkfst. Restaurant nearby. Ck-out noon. Business servs avail. Microwaves avail. Cr cds: A, C, D, DS, MC, V. D 🐾 ≊ ⊠ 🐾 SC

✔ ★ **RED ROOF INN.** *510 Claridge St (37214), I-40 exit 216, near International Airport, east of downtown. 615/872-0735; FAX 615/871-4647.* 120 rms, 3 story. Mar-Sept: S $39.99-$49.99; D $45.99-$55.99; each addl $6; under 17 free; higher rates special events; lower rates rest of yr. Crib avail. Pet accepted, some restrictions. TV; cable (premium). Complimentary coffee in lobby. Restaurant nearby. Ck-out 11 am. Free airport transportation. Cr cds: A, C, D, DS, MC, V. D 🐾 🏃 ⊠ 🐾

✔ ★ **RED ROOF INN-SOUTH.** *4271 Sidco Dr (37204), at jct I-65 & Harding Pl, south of downtown. 615/832-0093; FAX 615/832-0097.* 85 rms, 3 story. Mar-Sept: S $43.99-$69.99; D $46.99-$69.99; each addl $8; under 18 free; lower rates rest of yr. Crib free. Pet accepted. TV; cable. Complimentary coffee in lobby. Restaurant nearby. Ck-out 11 am. Business servs avail. Cr cds: A, C, D, DS, MC, V. D 🐾 ⊠ 🐾

★ **SUPER 8.** *412 Robertson Ave (37209), I-40 exit 204, west of downtown.* 615/356-0888. 73 rms, 3 story. June-July: S $50-$57; D $59.88-$69.88; each addl $5; suites $69-$75; under 12 free; higher rates for special events; lower rates rest of yr. Crib free. Pet accepted. TV; cable (premium). Complimentary continental bkfst. Restaurant adj open 24 hrs. Ck-out 11 am. Business servs avail. Cr cds: A, C, D, DS, MC, V. 🅳 ⊡ ⊠ ⊠ SC

Motor Hotels

★ ★ **AMERISUITES.** *(202 Summit View Dr, Brentwood 37027) Approx 9 mi S on I-65, exit 74A.* 615/661-9477; FAX 615/661-9936. Web www.travelbase.com/destination/nashville/amerisuites-brentwood. 126 kit. suites, 6 story. Mar-Oct: S, D $80-$150; each addl $10; under 18 free; higher rates special events; lower rates rest of yr. Crib free. Pet accepted, some restrictions; $10. TV; cable (premium), VCR (movies). Heated pool. Complimentary continental bkfst. Complimentary coffee in rms. Restaurant nearby. Ck-out noon. Coin lndry. Meeting rms. Business center. Valet serv. Sundries. Exercise equipt; bicycle, weight machine. Refrigerators. Cr cds: A, C, D, DS, ER, JCB, MC, V.
🅳 ⊡ ⊠ ✕ ⊠ ⊠ SC ⊿

★ ★ **HILTON SUITES-BRENTWOOD.** *(9000 Overlook Blvd, Brentwood 37027) S on I-65, exit 74B.* 615/370-0111; FAX 615/370-0272. Web www.hiltons.com. 203 suites, 4 story. S, D $115-$155; each addl $15; family rates. Crib free. Pet accepted, some restrictions. TV; cable (premium), VCR (movies $2). Indoor pool; whirlpool. Complimentary full bkfst. Coffee in rms. Restaurant 6-9:30 am, 11:30 am-1:30 pm, 5-10 pm; Sat, Sun 7-11 am, 5-10 pm. Rm serv from 5 pm. Bar 4 pm-midnight. Ck-out noon. Free lndry facilities. Meeting rms. Business center. Gift shop. Exercise equipt; weight machine, bicycles. Rec rm. Refrigerators, wet bars. Balconies. Cr cds: A, C, D, DS, ER, JCB, MC, V.
🅳 ⊡ ⊠ ✕ ⊠ ⊠ SC ⊿

✔ ★ **WILSON INN.** *600 Ermac Dr (37214), east of downtown.* 615/889-4466; res: 800/945-7667; FAX 615/889-0464. 80 rms, 5 story. S, D $54.95-$76.95; each addl $7; suites $69.95-$86.95; under 19 free; higher rates special events. Crib free. Pet accepted. TV; cable (premium). Complimentary continental bkfst. Restaurant adj open 24 hrs. Ck-out noon. Meeting rms. Business servs avail. Free airport transportation. Refrigerators; wet bar in suites; microwaves avail. Cr cds: A, C, D, DS, JCB, MC, V. 🅳 ⊡ ⊠ ⊠ SC

Hotels

★ ★ ★ **EMBASSY SUITES.** *10 Century Blvd (37214), near International Airport, east of downtown.* 615/871-0033; FAX 615/883-9245. Web www.embassysuites.com. 296 suites, 9 story. Suites $129-$169; each addl $10; under 17 free; wkend plans. Crib free. Pet accepted, some restrictions. TV; cable (premium), VCR avail. Indoor pool; whirlpool. Complimentary full bkfst. Restaurant 6:30-9:30 am, 11 am-2 pm, 5-10 pm; Fri, Sat to 11 pm. Rm serv 11 am-11 pm. Bar 5 pm-midnight. Ck-out noon. Convention facilities. Business servs avail. Concierge. Gift shop. Free airport transportation. Exercise equipt; weights, bicycles, sauna. Game rm. Refrigerators, microwaves, wet bars. Atrium. Cr cds: A, C, D, DS, JCB, MC, V. 🅳 ⊡ ⊠ ✕ ✈ ⊠ ⊠ SC

★ ★ ★ **LOEWS VANDERBILT PLAZA.** *2100 West End Ave (37203), downtown.* 615/320-1700; FAX 615/320-5019. 340 rms, 12 story. S $159-$209; D $179-$229; each addl $20; suites $400-$750; under 18 free. Crib free. Pet accepted. Garage $8; valet parking $10. TV; cable (premium), VCR avail. Restaurants 6:30 am-10 pm. Rm serv to midnight; Fri-Sat to 1 am. Bars 3 pm-1 am; entertainment exc Sun. Ck-out noon. Convention facilities. Business center. In-rm modem link. Concierge. Shopping arcade. Barber, beauty shop. Exercise equipt; weights, treadmill. Minibars; microwaves avail. Luxury level. Cr cds: A, C, D, DS, JCB, MC, V. 🅳 ⊡ ✕ ⊠ ⊠ SC ⊿

★ ★ ★ **SHERATON-MUSIC CITY.** *777 McGavock Pike (37214), near International Airport, east of downtown.* 615/885-2200; FAX 615/231-1134. Web www.tenn.com/sheraton. 412 rms, 4 story. S, D $148-$168; each addl $15; suites $170-$550; under 17 free; wkend rates. Pet accepted. TV; cable (premium), VCR avail. Indoor/outdoor pools; wading pool, whirlpool, poolside serv. Restaurants 6 am-11 pm. Bar 11-3 am; entertainment. Ck-out noon. Convention facilities. Business center. Concierge. Beauty shop. Gift shop. Free airport transportation. Lighted tennis. Golf privileges. Exercise rm; instructor, weight machine, bicycles, sauna. Bathrm phones; some refrigerators. Private balconies. On 23 landscaped acres on top of hill. Semiformal decor. Cr cds: A, C, D, DS, ER, JCB, MC, V.
🅳 ⊡ ✕ ⚓ ⊡ ✕ ✈ ⊠ ⊠ SC ⊿

★ ★ ★ **UNION STATION.** *1001 Broadway (37203), downtown.* 615/726-1001; res: 800/331-2123; FAX 615/248-3554. Web www.GrandHeritage.com. 124 rms, 7 story, 12 suites. S, D $129-$215; each addl $10; suites $215-$400; under 13 free; wkend rates. Crib free. Pet accepted. Valet parking $10. TV; cable (premium), VCR avail (movies). Coffee in rms. Restaurant 6:30 am-11 pm. Bar 11 am-11 pm. Ck-out 11 am. Business center.

Concierge. Valet parking. Gift shop. Airport transportation. Tennis, 18-hole golf privileges. In renovated historic train station (1897); stained-glass roof. Cr cds: A, C, D, DS, MC, V.

[D] 🐾 🏃 🚶 ⛷ 🏊 🔥 SC 🎿

Oak Ridge *(See also Knoxville)*

Motels

★ ★ **COMFORT INN.** *433 S Rutgers Ave.* 423/481-8200; FAX 423/483-6142. 122 rms, 5 story, 26 suites. S, D $59-$79; each addl $7; suites $69-$89; under 18 free. Crib free. Pet accepted. TV; cable. Pool. Complimentary continental bkfst. Restaurant nearby. Ck-out noon. Coin lndry. Meeting rms. Business servs avail. Valet serv. Free local transportation. Health club privileges. Refrigerators in suites. Cr cds: A, C, D, DS, ER, JCB, MC, V.

[D] 🐾 🏊 🚶 🔥 SC

✔ ★ **DAYS INN.** *206 S Illinois Ave.* 423/483-5615. 80 rms, 2 story. S $47-$53; D $53-$59; each addl $3; under 12 free. Crib free. Pet accepted. TV; cable. Heated pool. Playground. Complimentary continental bkfst. Restaurant adj 6:30 am-midnight; Fri, Sat to 2 am. Ck-out 11 am. Meeting rms. Business servs avail. Refrigerators. Cr cds: A, C, D, DS, MC, V. [D] 🐾 🏊 🚶 🔥 SC

Pigeon Forge *(See also Gatlinburg)*

Motel

(Rates may be higher Univ of Tennessee football wkends)

★ ★ **ECONO LODGE.** *2440 Parkway.* 423/428-1231; FAX 423/453-6879. 202 rms, 3 story. June-Oct: S, D $79-$89; each addl $6; under 12 free; higher rates wkends, hols, special events; lower rates rest of yr. Crib free. Pet accepted. TV. Pool; wading pool, whirlpool. Restaurant nearby. Ck-out 11 am. Business servs avail. Downhill ski 10 mi. View of river, mountains. Cr cds: A, C, D, DS, MC, V. [D] 🐾 🏊 🚶 🔥 SC

Motor Hotels

★ ★ **GRAND RESORT HOTEL AND CONVENTION CENTER.** *3171 Parkway (US 441).* 423/453-1000; FAX 423/428-3944; res: 800/362-1188. 425 rms, 5 story. May-Oct: S, D $70-$100; each addl $10; suites $80-$199; under 12 free; higher rates special events; lower rates rest of yr. Crib free. Pet accepted. TV; cable. Pool; whirlpool. Restaurant 7 am-10 pm. Rm serv. Ck-out 11 am. Convention facilities. Business servs avail. Gift shop. Downhill ski 10 mi. Some fireplaces. Cr cds: A, D, DS, MC, V.

[D] 🐾 🏊 🚶 🔥 SC

★ ★ **HEARTLANDER COUNTRY RESORT.** *2385 Parkway (US 441).* 423/453-4106; FAX 423/429-0159. 160 rms, 5 story. Late May-early Nov: S, D $59-$119; each addl $5; under 12 free; lower rates rest of yr. Crib free. Pet accepted. TV; cable. 2 pools, 1 indoor; whirlpool. Continental bkfst. Ck-out 11 am. Meeting rms. Business servs avail. Sundries. Game rm. Balconies. Cr cds: A, C, D, DS, ER, JCB, MC, V. [D] 🐾 🏊 🚶 🔥 SC

Shelbyville

Motel

★ ★ **SHELBYVILLE INN.** *317 N Cannon Blvd.* 931/684-6050; FAX 931/684-2714; res: 800/684-0466. 72 rms, 2 story. S $49-$55; D $56-$65; each addl $6; under 12 free; higher rates special events. Crib free. Pet accepted, some restrictions. TV; cable (premium). Pool. Restaurant 6 am-2 pm, 5-9 pm. Ck-out noon. Meeting rms. Cr cds: A, C, D, DS, JCB, MC, V. [D] 🐾 🏊 🚶 🔥 SC

Sweetwater

Motels

★ **BUDGET HOST.** *207 TN 68.* 423/337-9357; FAX 423/337-7436. 61 rms, 2 story. Mar-Nov: S $29.95-$39.95; D $33.95-$43.95; each addl $5; under 10 free; weekly rates; higher rates football games; lower rates rest of yr. Crib $5. Pet accepted; $2. TV; cable (premium), VCR avail (movies). Complimentary coffee in lobby. Restaurant adj open 24 hrs. Ck-out 11 am. Coin lndry. Some refrigerators. Cr cds: A, C, D, DS, MC, V. [D] 🐾 🔥 SC

✔ ★ **COMFORT INN.** *803 South Main St, 803 S Main St, 1/2 mi S on US 11.* 423/337-6646; FAX 423/337-5409. 60 rms, 2 story. S $30-$55; D $36-$55; each addl $4. Crib $5. Pet accepted. TV; cable. Pool; wading pool. Complimentary continental bkfst.

Restaurant nearby. Ck-out 11 am. Business servs avail. Pond, picnic area. Cr cds: A, C, D, DS, ER, MC, V. [D] [icons]

Townsend *(See also Gatlinburg)*

Motels

★★ **BEST WESTERN VALLEY VIEW LODGE.** *7726 Lamar Alexander Pkwy. 423/448-2237; FAX 423/448-9957.* 91 rms, 2 story, 39 suites. May-Oct: S, D $49.50-$89.50; each addl $5; suites $64.50-$125.50; lower rates rest of yr. Crib $5. Pet accepted. TV; cable (premium). 3 pools, 1 indoor; whirlpools. Complimentary continental bkfst. Coffee in rms. Restaurant nearby. Ck-out 11 am. Meeting rms. Business servs avail. Lawn games. Refrigerators; some fireplaces; minibar in suites. Private patios, balconies. Covered picnic area, grill. Cr cds: A, C, D, DS, MC, V. [D] [icons]

Texas

Abilene (See also Sweetwater)

Motels

✔ ★ ★ BEST WESTERN COLONIAL INN. *3210 Pine St (79601). 915/677-2683; FAX 915/677-8211.* 100 rms. S $43-$48; D $48-$53; each addl $5; under 12 free. Crib free. Pet accepted, some restrictions. TV; cable (premium). Pool; wading pool. Restaurant 6 am-10 pm. Rm serv. Ck-out noon. Meeting rms. Business servs avail. Cr cds: A, C, D, DS, ER, MC, V.

✔ ★ ★ BEST WESTERN MALL SOUTH. *3950 Ridgemont Dr (79606). 915/695-1262; FAX 915/695-2593.* 61 rms, 2 story. S $47-$55; D $53-$63; under 12 free. Pet accepted, some restrictions. TV; cable (premium). Pool. Complimentary continental bkfst. Restaurant adj open 24 hrs. Ck-out noon. Meeting rm. In-rm modem link. Airport, bus depot transportation. Refrigerators. Cr cds: A, C, D, DS, MC, V.

★ ★ CLARION HOTEL AND CONFERENCE CENTER. *5403 S 1st St (79605). 915/695-2150; FAX 915/698-6742.* 178 rms, 3 story. S, D $54-$69; each addl $5; suites $120-$159; under 16 free. Crib free. Pet accepted; some restrictions. TV; cable (premium), VCR avail. 2 pools, 1 indoor; wading pool, whirlpool, sauna. Restaurant 6 am-2 pm, 5-9 pm. Rm serv. Bar 4:30 pm-midnight; Sat to 1 am. Ck-out noon. Coin lndry. Meeting rms. Business center. Sundries. Some refrigerators. Microwaves avail. Cr cds: A, C, D, DS, MC, V.

★ ★ HOLIDAY INN EXPRESS. *1625 TX 351 (79601), 1 blk N of I-20. 915/673-5271; FAX 915/673-8240.* 161 rms, 2 story. S $56; D $62. Crib free. Pet accepted, some restrictions. TV; cable (premium). Pool. Ck-out noon. Coin lndry. Business servs avail. Free airport transportation. Cr cds: A, C, D, DS, JCB, MC, V.

★ ★ LA QUINTA. *3501 W Lake Rd (79601). 915/676-1676; FAX 915/672-8323.* 106 rms, 2 story. S $59-$63; D $66-$73; each addl $7; suites $100; under 18 free. Crib avail. Pet accepted; some restrictions. TV; cable (premium). Pool. Complimentary continental bkfst. Ck-out noon. Cr cds: A, C, D, DS, MC, V.

★ ★ QUALITY INN. *505 Pine St (79601). 915/676-0222; FAX 915/676-0513.* Web hotel/moteltex.assn. 118 rms, 2 story. S $51-$58; D $56-$63; each addl $5; suites $75-$200; under 18 free. Crib free. Pet accepted, some restrictions; $10. TV; cable (premium). Pool. Complimentary full bkfst. Restaurant 6 am-9 pm. Rm serv. Bar noon-11 pm. Ck-out noon. Meeting rms. Business servs avail. Sundries. Free airport transportation. Health club privileges. Cr cds: A, C, D, DS, JCB, MC, V.

✔ ★ ROYAL INN. *5695 S 1st St (79605). 915/692-3022; FAX 915/692-3137; res: 800/588-4386.* 150 rms. S $24.95; D $30-$40; each addl $4; suites $40. Crib $5. Pet accepted, some restrictions. TV; cable (premium). Pool. Restaurant 6 am-10 pm. Rm serv. Bar 10 am-midnight. Ck-out noon. Meeting rms. Business servs avail. Sundries. Microwaves avail. Cr cds: A, C, D, DS, MC, V.

Motor Hotel

★ ★ ★ EMBASSY SUITES. *4250 Ridgemont Dr (79606). 915/698-1234; FAX 915/698-2771.* 176 suites, 3 story. S, D $92; each addl $10; under 12 free. Crib free. Pet accepted, some restrictions. TV; cable (premium). Indoor pool; whirlpool, sauna, steam rm. Complimentary full bkfst. Coffee in rms. Restaurant 11 am-2 pm, 5-10 pm. Bar to midnight; entertainment. Ck-out noon. Coin lndry. Meeting rms. Business servs avail. Bellhops. Sundries. Airport, RR station, bus depot transportation. Game rm. Refrigerators, wet bars, microwaves. Garden atrium. Cr cds: A, C, D, DS, JCB, MC, V.

Alpine (See also Fort Stockton)

Motel

★ ★ HOTEL LIMPIA. *(Main St on the Square, Fort Davis 79734) Approx 20 mi N on TX 118. 915/426-3237; FAX 915/426-3983; res: 800/662-5517.* 36 rms, 2 story, 8 with kit., 14 suites, 1 cottage. No rm phones. S, D $68; each addl $10; suites, kit. units $84-$125; cottage $99; under 12 free. Pet accepted; $10. TV; cable (premium). Complimentary coffee in lobby. Restaurant nearby. Ck-out noon. Business servs avail. Some refrigerators. Microwaves in suites. Balconies. Picnic tables. Built in 1912 of locally mined pink limestone. Cr cds: A, DS, MC, V. D ✐ ≈ ☒ ⊠ SC

Amarillo

Motel

★ ★ **HAMPTON INN.** *1700 I-40 E (79103). 806/372-1425; FAX 806/379-8807.* 116 rms, 2 story. June-Sept: S, D $61-$70; under 18 free; lower rates rest of yr. Crib free. Pet accepted. TV; cable (premium). Pool. Complimentary continental bkfst. Restaurant adj open 24 hrs. Ck-out noon. Business servs avail. Cr cds: A, C, D, DS, MC, V.

D ✐ ≈ ☒ ⊠ SC

Motor Hotel

★ ★ **HOLIDAY INN.** *1911 I-40 (79102), at Ross & Osage. 806/372-8741; FAX 806/372-2913.* 247 rms, 4 story. S $79.95; D $89.95; each addl $10; under 19 free. Crib free. Pet accepted. TV; cable (premium). Indoor pool; wading pool. Restaurants 6 am-1 pm, 5:30-10 pm. Rm serv. Bar 4 pm-2 am. Ck-out noon. Coin lndry. Meeting rms. Business servs avail. In-rm modem link. Bellhops. Sundries. Free airport transportation. Exercise equipt; weight machine, bicycle. Holidome. Game rm. Balconies. Cr cds: A, C, D, DS, JCB, MC, V.

D ✐ ≈ 🏋 ☒ ⊠ SC

Arlington-Grand Prairie
(See also Dallas, Dallas/Fort Worth Airport Area, Fort Worth)

Motor Hotel

★ ★ **HAWTHORN SUITES.** *(2401 Brookhollow Plaza Dr, Arlington 76006) I-30 at Lamar Blvd exit. 817/640-1188; FAX 817/640-1188; res: 800/527-1133.* 26 rms, 130 suites, 3 story, 104 kit. suites. S, D $110; Suites $110-$180; wknd rates. Crib free. Pet accepted, some restrictions; $50. TV; cable (premium), VCR avail (movies). Pool. Complimentary full bkfst. Restaurant nearby. Ck-out noon. Coin lndry. Meeting rms. Business servs avail. Valet serv. Exercise equipt; weight machine, treadmill. Microwaves. Private patios, balconies. Cr cds: A, C, D, DS, MC, V. D ✐ ≈ 🏋 ☒ ⊠ SC

Austin *(See also Georgetown, San Antonio, San Marcos)*

Motels

★ ★ **HAWTHORN SUITES-SOUTH.** *4020 I-35 S (78704). 512/440-7722; FAX 512/440-4815.* Web www.hawthorn.com. 120 suites, 2 story. S $99-$139; D $109-$159; each addl $10; under 18 free; wknd rates. Crib free. Pet accepted; $50. TV; cable (premium). Heated pool; whirlpool. Complimentary continental bkfst. Complimentary coffee in rms. Restaurant nearby. Bar. Ck-out noon. Coin lndry. Meeting rms. Business servs avail. Valet serv. Refrigerators; microwaves avail. Picnic tables, grills. Cr cds: A, C, D, DS, JCB, MC, V. D ✐ ≈ ☒ ⊠ SC

★ ★ **LA QUINTA.** *(2004 N I-35, Round Rock 78681) 15 mi N on I-35, exit 254. 512/255-6666; FAX 512/388-3635.* 115 units. S $70-$80; D $80-$90; each addl $10, suite $114-$124. Crib free. Pet accepted, some restrictions. TV; cable (premium). Pool; whirlpool. Complimentary continental bkfst. Restaurant nearby. Ck-out noon. Meeting rm. In-rm modem link. Exercise equipt; stair machine, bicycle, sauna. Some refrigerators; microwaves avail. Cr cds: A, C, D, MC, V. D ✐ ≈ 🏋 ☒ ⊠ SC

★ ★ **LA QUINTA-NORTH.** *7100 I-35N (78752). 512/452-9401; FAX 512/452-0856.* Web www.laquinta.com. 115 rms, 2 story. S $72-82; D $82-$92; each addl $10; suites $102-$122; under 18 free. Crib free. Pet accepted, some restrictions. TV; cable (premium). Pool. Restaurant adj open 24 hrs. Ck-out noon. Business servs avail. In-rm modem link. Free airport transportation. Health club privileges. Cr cds: A, C, D, DS, MC, V.

D ✐ ≈ ☒ ⊠ SC

✔ ★ **QUALITY INN-AIRPORT.** *909 E Koenig Lane (78751), near jct I-35 & US 290. 512/452-4200; FAX 512/374-0652.* 91 rms, 2 story. S $50-$60; D $55-65; each addl $5; under 17 free. Crib free. Pet accepted; $25. TV; cable (premium). Pool. Complimentary continental bkfst. Ck-out noon. Meeting rm. Free airport transportation. Cr cds: A, C, D, DS, MC, V. D ✐ ≈ ☒ ⊠ SC

✔ ★ **RED ROOF INN.** *8210 N I-35 (78753). 512/835-2200; FAX 512/339-9043.* 143 rms, 4 story. S $42-$47; D $44-$56; each addl $8; suites $65-$72; under 18 free. Crib free. Pet accepted. TV; cable (premium). Pool. Complimentary coffee in lobby. Restaurant nearby. Ck-out noon. Some refrigerators. Cr cds: A, D, DS, MC, V. D ✐ ≈ ☒ ⊠ SC

Motor Hotels

★ **DRURY INN.** *6711 I-35N (78752). 512/467-9500.* 154 rms, 4 story. S $65-$76; D $75-$86; each addl $10; under 18 free. Pet accepted, some restrictions. TV; cable (premium) Pool. Complimentary continental bkfst. Restaurant adj 6 am-midnight. Ck-out noon. Meeting rms. Business servs avail. In-rm modem link. Valet serv. Sundries. Some refrigerators; microwaves avail. 4-story atrium lobby. Cr cds: A, C, D, DS, MC, V.
D ✦ ≈ ✕ ✕ SC

✔ ★ **EXEL INN.** *2711 I-35 S (78741). 512/462-9201; FAX 512/462-9371.* 90 rms, 3 story. S $38.99; D $45.99; each addl $5; under 18 free. Pet accepted, some restrictions. TV; cable (premium). Pool. Complimentary continental bkfst. Restaurant adj open 24 hrs. Ck-out noon. Coin lndry. Health club privileges. Game rm. Microwaves avail. Cr cds: A, C, D, DS, MC, V. D ✦ ≈ ✕ ✕ SC

★ ★ **HOLIDAY INN-SOUTH.** *3401 I-35S (78741). 512/448-2444; FAX 512/448-4999.* 210 rms, 5 story. S $99-$119; D $109-$139; each addl $10; suites $129-$149; under 18 free; wkend rates. Crib free. Pet accepted. TV; cable (premium). Pool; whirlpool, poolside serv. Restaurant 6:30 am-10 pm; Sat, Sun from 7 am. Rm serv. Bar 4 pm-midnight; Sat from 4:30 pm. Ck-out noon. Coin lndry. Meeting rms. Business servs avail. In-rm modem link. Bellhops. Gift shop. Free airport transportation. Exercise equipt; bicycle, stair machine. Refrigerators; many bathrm phones; microwaves avail. Private patios. Cr cds: A, C, D, DS, MC, V. D ✦ ≈ ✗ ✕ ✕ SC

★ ★ **RED LION.** *6121 I-35N (78752), at US 290. 512/323-5466; FAX 512/453-1945.* 300 rms, 7 story. S $119-$139; D $129-$149; each addl $10; suites $250-$300; under 18 free; wkend rates. Crib free. Pet accepted. TV; cable (premium). Heated pool; whirlpool, poolside serv. Restaurant 6 am-10 pm. Rm serv. Bar 3 pm-midnight; Fri, Sat to 2 am. Ck-out noon. Coin lndry. Meeting rms. Business servs avail. In-rm modem link. Bellhops. Gift shop. Sundries. Free airport transportation. Exercise equipt; weights, bicycle, sauna. Some refrigerators. Private patios. Cr cds: A, C, D, DS, ER, MC, V. D ✦ ≈ ✗ ✕ ✕ SC

Hotels

★ ★ **DOUBLETREE GUEST SUITES.** *303 W 15th St (78701). 512/478-7000; FAX 512/478-3562.* Web www.doubletreehotels.com. 189 suites, 15 story. S, D $129-$159; each addl $10; 2-bedrm suites $195-$275; under 18 free; wkly, wkend rates. Crib free. Pet accepted, some restrictions. Valet parking $7. TV; cable (premium), VCR avail. Heated pool; whirlpool, poolside serv. Complimentary coffee in rms. Restaurant 6:30 am-10 pm. Rm serv 24 hrs. Bar 11 am-midnight. Ck-out noon. Coin lndry. Meeting rms. Business servs avail. In-rm modem link. Exercise equipt; stair machines, bicycles, sauna. Health club privileges. Refrigerators; microwaves avail. Balconies. Cr cds: A, C, D, DS, MC, V.
D ✦ ≈ ✗ ✕ ✕ SC

★ ★ ★ **FOUR SEASONS.** *98 San Jacinto Blvd (78701), downtown. 512/478-4500; FAX 512/478-3117.* Web www.fshr.com. Queen Elizabeth II has stayed at this property. Facilities combine European tone with Texas Hill Country comfort; many rooms have lovely Town Lake views. 291 units, 9 story. S $175-$220; D $195-$240; each addl $20; suites $245-$1,200; under 18 free; wkend rates. Crib free. Covered parking $7; valet parking $12. Pet accepted, some restrictions. TV; cable (premium), VCR avail. Heated pool; whirlpool, poolside serv. Restaurant 6:30 am-11 pm. Rm serv 24 hrs. Bar 11-2 am. Ck-out 1 pm. Convention facilities. Business center. In-rm modem link. Concierge. Gift shop. Exercise rm; instructor, weights, bicycles, sauna. Massage. Bathrm phones; some refrigerators; microwaves avail. Balconies. Cr cds: A, C, D, ER, JCB, MC, V. D ✦ ≈ ✗ ✗ ✕ ✕ ✦

★ ★ **HILTON-NORTH.** *6000 Middle Fiskville Rd (78752). 512/451-5757; FAX 512/467-7644.* E-mail 74161.1562@compuserv.com. 237 rms, 9 story. S $134-$154, D $144-$164; each addl $12; suites $195-$310; family, wkend rates. Crib avail. Pet accepted, some restrictions. TV; cable (premium). Pool. Restaurant 6:30 am-11 pm; Sat, Sun from 7 am. Bar 11 am-midnight. Ck-out noon. Meeting rms. Business servs avail. In-rm modem link. Gift shop. Free airport transportation. Exercise equipt; bicycles, treadmill. Health club privileges. Balconies. Luxury level. Cr cds: A, C, D, DS, MC, V. D ✦ ≈ ✗ ✗ ✕ ✕ SC

★ ★ **RENAISSANCE.** *9721 Arboretum Blvd (78759), jct US 183, TX 360, north of downtown. 512/343-2626; FAX 512/346-7953.* Web www.renaissancehotels.com. 478 units, 9 story, 16 suites. S, D $167-$227; each addl $20; suites $275-$1,500; under 18 free; package plans. Crib free. Pet accepted, some restrictions; $50 refundable. TV; cable (premium), VCR avail. 2 pools, 1 indoor; whirlpool, poolside serv. Restaurant open 24 hrs. Bar noon-2 am; entertainment. Ck-out 1 pm. Convention facilities. Business center. In-rm modem link. Concierge. Shopping arcade. Airport transportation. Exercise equipt, weight machines, bicycles, sauna. Some refrigerators; microwaves avail. Balconies. Elegant skylit atrium lobby. Luxury level. Cr cds: A, C, D, DS, ER, JCB, MC, V.

[D] 🛒 ⛵ 🏋️ 🔥 🖳 🐾 SC 🏃

Beaumont *(See also Orange, Port Arthur)*

Motels

✔ ★ ★ **BEST WESTERN-JEFFERSON INN.** *1610 I-10S (77707). 409/842-0037; FAX 409/842-0057.* 120 rms, 12 kits. S $52; D $58; each addl $6; kit. units $57-$63; under 18 free. Crib free. Pet accepted, some restrictions. TV; cable (premium). Pool. Complimentary continental bkfst. Ck-out noon. Coin lndry avail. Meeting rms. Business servs avail. In-rm modem link. Some refrigerators. Cr cds: A, C, D, DS, MC, V. [D] 🛒 ⛵ 🖳 🐾 SC

★ ★ **LA QUINTA.** *220 I-10N (77702). 409/838-9991; FAX 405/832-1266.* 122 rms, 2 story. S $59-$69; D $69-$79; under 18 free. Crib free. Pet accepted, some restrictions. TV; cable (premium), VCR avail. Pool. Complimentary continental bkfst. Ck-out noon. Meeting rms. Business servs avail. In-rm modem link. Valet serv. Sundries. Microwaves avail. Cr cds: A, C, D, DS, JCB, MC, V. [D] 🛒 ⛵ 🖳 🐾 SC

Motor Hotel

★ **HOLIDAY INN-MIDTOWN.** *2095 N 11th St (77703). 409/892-2222; FAX 409/892-2231.* 190 rms, 6 story. S, D $89; each addl $7; under 18 free; wkend rates. Crib free. Pet accepted, some restrictions. TV; cable (premium). Pool; poolside serv. Restaurant 6 am-10 am, 5:30-10 pm. Rm serv. Bar. Ck-out noon. Coin lndry. Meeting rms. Business servs avail. In-rm modem link. Bellhops. Free airport transportation. Health club privileges. Cr cds: A, C, D, DS, JCB, MC, V. [D] 🛒 ⛵ 🖳 🐾 SC

Hotel

★ ★ **HOLIDAY INN-BEAUMONT PLAZA.** *3950 I-10S (77705), Walden exit. 409/842-5995; FAX 409/842-0315.* 253 rms, 80 suites, 8 story. S $110; D $120; each addl $10; suites $120-$275; under 20 free; wkend rates. Crib free. Pet accepted; $15 refundable. TV; cable (premium), VCR avail. Indoor pool; whirlpool; poolside serv. Restaurant 6 am-10 pm. Bar. Ck-out noon. Business center. In-rm modem link. Gift shop. Free airport transportation. Exercise equipt; bicycles, treadmills, sauna. Game rm. Some refrigerators. Microwaves avail. 3-story waterfall in lobby. Convention center adj. Cr cds: A, C, D, DS, JCB, MC, V. [D] 🛒 ⛵ 🏋️ 🖳 🐾 SC 🏃

Big Spring *(See also Midland)*

Motel

★ **DAYS INN.** *300 Tulane Ave. 915/263-7621; FAX 915/263-2790.* 102 rms. S $42; D $48; under 18 free. Crib free. Pet accepted. TV; cable (premium). Pool. Bar 5 pm-midnight. Coin lndry. Meeting rms. Business servs avail. Cr cds: A, C, D, DS, MC, V. 🛒 ⛵ 🖳 🐾 SC

Brazosport *(See also Houston)*

Motels

✔ ★ ★ **LA QUINTA.** *(1126 TX 332W, Clute 77531) 2 mi W on TX 332. 409/265-7461; FAX 409/265-3804.* 136 rms, 2 story. S $49-$56; D $56-$63; each addl $7; suites $66-$73; under 18 free. Pet accepted, some restrictions. TV; cable (premium). Pool. Complimentary continental bkfst. Coffee in rms. Restaurant adj open 24 hrs. Ck-out noon. Meeting rm. In-rm modem link. Cr cds: A, C, D, DS, ER, JCB, MC, V. [D] 🛒 ⛵ 🖳 🐾 SC

★ **RAMADA INN.** *(925 TX 332W, Lake Jackson 77566) 6 mi W on TX 332. 409/297-1161; FAX 409/297-1249.* 147 rms, 2 story. S, D $77-$125; each addl $10; family, wkend, wkly rates. Crib free. Pet accepted, some restrictions. TV; cable. Indoor pool. Restaurant 6 am-2 pm, 5-10 pm. Rm serv. Bar 4 pm-midnight. Ck-out 1 pm. Meeting rms. 8 mi from Gulf. Cr cds: A, C, D, DS, JCB, MC, V. [D] 🛒 ⛵ 🖳 🐾 SC

Brownsville *(See also Harlingen, South Padre Island)*

Motor Hotels

★ ★ **FOUR POINTS BY SHERATON.** *3777 N Expy (78520). 956/350-9191; FAX 956/350-4153.* 142 rms. S $80-$91; D $90-$101; each addl $10; suites $225; under 17 free; wkend rates. Pet accepted, some restrictions. TV; cable. Indoor/outdoor pool; whirlpool. Coffee in rms. Restaurant 6 am-11 pm. Rm serv. Bar 4 pm-2 am; entertainment. Ck-out noon. Meeting rms. Business servs avail. In-rm modem link. Refrigerator, whirlpool in suites. Cr cds: A, C, D, DS, MC, V.

★ ★ **HOLIDAY INN FORT BROWN.** *1900 E Elizabeth (78520), 2 blks E of Gateway Bridge.* 956/546-2201; FAX 956/546-0756. 168 rms, 2 story. S $78; D $83; each addl $8; suites $95-$200; under 19 free. Crib free. Pet accepted, some restrictions. TV; cable (premium). Pool; poolside serv. Restaurant 6 am-10 pm. Rm serv. Bar noon-2 am; entertainment. Ck-out noon. Convention facilities. Business servs avail. In-rm modem link. Bellhops. Valet serv. Gift shop. Lighted tennis. Balconies. Intl Gateway Bridge nearby. Cr cds: A, C, D, DS, MC, V.

Brownwood

Motel

★ ★ **GOLD KEY INN.** *515 E Commerce (76801), ¼ mi W of jct US 183, US 377.* 915/646-2551; FAX 915/643-6064. 140 rms, 2 story. S, D $42-$48; under 18 free. Crib $5. Pet accepted. TV; cable (premium). Pool; whirlpool. Ck-out noon. Coin lndry. Meeting rms. Business servs avail. In-rm modem link. Exercise equipt; weight machine, treadmill, sauna. Microwaves avail. Cr cds: A, D, DS, MC, V.

Bryan/College Station *(See also Huntsville)*

Motels

★ ★ **HOLIDAY INN.** *(1503 Texas Ave S, College Station 77840)* 409/693-1736; FAX 409/693-1736. 126 rms, 6 story. S, D $53-$59; each addl $6; under 19 free. Crib free. Pet accepted, some restrictions. TV; cable. Pool; poolside serv. Restaurant 6 am-2 pm, 5-9 pm; Sun 7 am-2 pm. Rm serv. Bar. Ck-out noon. Meeting rms. Free airport transportation. Health club privileges. Some refrigerators. Cr cds: A, C, D, DS, JCB, MC, V.

★ ★ **LA QUINTA.** *(607 Texas Ave S, College Station 77840)* 409/696-7777; FAX 409/696-0531. 176 rms. S $64-$84; D $72-$92; each addl $10; under 18 free. Crib free. Pet accepted. TV; cable (premium). Pool. Complimentary continental bkfst. Restaurant adj open 24 hrs. Ck-out noon. In-rm modem link. Free airport transportation. Texas A & M Univ opp. Picnic tables. Cr cds: A, C, D, DS, MC, V.

✔ ★ **MANOR HOUSE.** *(2504 Texas Ave S, College Station 77840)* 409/764-9540; FAX 409/693-2430; res: 800/231-4100. 117 rms, 2 story. S, D $46-$90; under 12 free; higher rates: hols, special events. Crib $7. Pet accepted; $10/day. TV; cable (premium). Pool. Complimentary continental bkfst. Restaurant adj open 24 hrs. Ck-out noon. Meeting rms. In-rm modem link. Valet serv. Free airport transportation. Health club privileges. Refrigerators. Cr cds: A, C, D, DS, MC, V.

Hotel

★ ★ **HILTON-COLLEGE STATION.** *(801 University Dr E, College Station 77840)* 409/693-7500; FAX 409/846-7361. E-mail stayathiltonics.com. 303 rms, 11 story. S $72-$125; D $82-$135; each addl $10; suites $110-$250; family rates. Crib free. Pet accepted, some restrictions; $50 refundable. TV; cable (premium). Pool; poolside serv. Restaurant 6 am-10 pm; Fri, Sat to 11 pm. Bar 11 am-midnight; Fri, Sat to 1 am; Sun noon-midnight; entertainment. Meeting rms. Business servs avail. In-rm modem link. Gift shop. Free airport transportation. Exercise equipt; weights, bicycle. Some refrigerators, in-rm whirlpools. Microwaves avail. Private patios, balconies. Cr cds: A, C, D, DS, ER, JCB, MC, V.

Childress *(See also Vernon)*

Motel

✔ ★ ★ **ECONO LODGE.** *1612 Avenue F NW, US 287.* 940/937-3695; FAX 940/937-6956; res: 800/542-4229. 28 rms, 2 story. S $38-$46; D $48; each addl $3. Crib free. Pet accepted. TV; cable. Pool. Complimentary coffee in lobby. Restaurant 6-10 am, 5-10 pm. Ck-out 11 am. Business servs avail. Cr cds: A, D, DS, JCB, MC, V.

Clarendon *(See also Amarillo)*

Motel

✔ ★ **WESTERN SKIES.** *800 W 2nd St, 6 blks NW on US 287, TX 70.* 806/874-3501; FAX 806/874-5303. 23 rms. S $35-$38; D $36-$42; each addl $3. Crib $5. Pet accepted, some restrictions. TV; cable. Heated pool. Playground. Complimentary coffee. Restaurant nearby. Ck-out 11 am. Business servs avail. Cr cds: A, C, D, DS, MC, V.

D ✎ ≋ 🐾

Corpus Christi

(See also Kingsville, Port Aransas, Rockport)

Motels

★ ★ **DRURY INN.** *2021 N Padre Island Dr (78408).* 512/289-8200. 105 units, 4 story, 10 suites. S $59-$67; D $67-$75; suites $67-$75; under 18 free. Crib free. Pet accepted. TV; cable (premium), VCR avail. Pool. Complimentary continental bkfst. Ck-out noon. Meeting rms. Business servs avail. In-rm modem link. Valet serv. Free airport transportation. Refrigerator in suites. Cr cds: A, C, D, DS, MC, V. D ✎ ≋ ⊠ 🐾 SC

✔ ★ ★ **LA QUINTA NORTH.** *5155 I-37N (78408), at Navigation Blvd.* 512/888-5721. 122 rms, 2 story. S $46-$59; D $56-$69; each addl $7; suites $75-$85; under 18 free. Crib free. Pet accepted. TV; cable. Pool. Complimentary continental bkfst. Restaurant open 24 hrs. Ck-out noon. Meeting rms. Business servs avail. In-rm modem link. Valet serv. Health club priviliges. Cr cds: A, C, D, DS, ER, JCB, MC, V. D ✎ ≋ ⊠ 🐾 SC

Motor Hotels

★ ★ ★ **HOLIDAY INN-EMERALD BEACH.** *1102 S Shoreline Blvd (78401).* 512/883-5731; FAX 512/883-9079. 368 rms, 2-7 story. S, D $89-$129; each addl $5; under 19 free; some wkend rates. Pet accepted. TV; cable. Heated pool; wading pool, whirlpool, poolside serv (summer). Playground. Restaurant 6 am-2 pm, 5-10 pm. Rm serv. Bar 11 am-midnight. Ck-out noon. Meeting rms. Business servs avail. In-rm modem link. Bellhops. Exercise equipt; weights, bicycles, sauna. Game rm. Some private patios, balconies. On beach. Cr cds: A, C, D, DS, ER, JCB, MC, V. D ✎ ≋ 🏋 ⊠ 🐾 SC

★ ★ **HOLIDAY INN-GULF BEACH RESORT.** *15202 Windward Dr (78418), on Padre Island.* 512/949-8041; FAX 512/949-9139. 148 rms, 6 story. Mar-early Sept: S, D $99.95-$159.95; each addl $10; under 19 free; wkly rates; lower rates rest of yr. Crib free. Pet accepted; $10. TV; cable (premium), VCR avail (movies). 2 pools; poolside serv. Playground. Restaurant 6:30 am-2 pm, 5-10 pm. Rm serv. Bar 5 pm-2 am. Ck-out 11 am. Meeting rms. Business center. In-rm modem link. Tennis privileges, pro. 18-hole golf privileges, greens fee $35, pro. Exercise equipt: weights, stair machine, sauna. Game rm. Refrigerators avail. Some balconies. Picnic tables. Swimming beach. Cr cds: A, C, D, DS, MC, V. D ✎ ⛳ 🏌 🎿 ≋ 🏋 ⊠ 🐾 SC ⛷

Hotel

★ ★ ★ **EMBASSY SUITES.** *4337 S Padre Island Dr (78411).* 512/853-7899; FAX 512/851-1310. 150 kit. suites, 3 story. S $89-$119; D $99-$129; each addl $10; under 17 free; wkend rates. Crib free. Pet accepted, some restrictions; $100. TV; cable (premium). Indoor pool; whirlpool. Complimentary bkfst. Restaurant 11 am-11 pm. Coin lndry. Meeting rms. Business servs avail. In-rm modem link. Free airport transportation. Exercise equipt; weights, treadmill, sauna. Game rm. Refrigerators. Atrium lobby with fountain, plants. Cr cds: A, C, D, DS, MC, V. D ✎ ≋ 🏋 ⊠ 🐾 SC

Dalhart *(See also Amarillo)*

Motel

✔ ★ ★ **DAYS INN.** *701 Liberal St, E on US 87.* 806/249-5246; FAX 806/249-0805. 40 rms, 2 story. S $38-$84; D $48-$94; each addl $5. Crib free. Pet accepted, some restrictions. TV; cable. Indoor pool; whirlpool. Complimentary continental bkfst. Restaurant nearby. Ck-out noon. Business servs avail. Cr cds: A, C, D, DS, MC, V. D ✎ ≋ ⊠ 🐾 SC

Dallas

Motels

(Rates may be higher State Fair, Cotton Bowl, Texas/OU wkend and city-wide conventions. Most accommodations near Six Flags Over Texas have higher rates when the park is open daily.)

★ ★ **BEST WESTERN PARK SUITES.** *(640 E Park Blvd, Plano 75074) 10 mi N on US 75.* 972/578-2243; FAX 972/578-0563. 84 suites, 3 story. Suites $88-$95; family rates. Crib free. Pet accepted, some restrictions. TV; cable (premium). Complimentary continental bkfst. Complimentary coffee in rms. Restaurant nearby. Bar. Ck-out noon. Meeting rms. Business servs avail. In-rm modem link. Valet serv. Sundries. Coin lndry. Exercise equipt; weight machines, treadmill. Pool; whirlpool. Refrigerators, microwaves; some in-rm whirlpools. Cr cds: A, C, D, DS, JCB, MC, V. D ✎ ≋ 🏋 ⊠ 🐾 SC

✔★★ **BEST WESTERN-NORTH.** *13333 N Stemmons Frwy (75234), I-35E, exit at Valwood, north of downtown.* 972/241-8521; FAX 972/243-4103. 186 rms, 2 story. S $65-$69, D $75; each addl $6; suites $125; under 12 free; wkend rates. Pet accepted; $20 deposit. TV; cable (premium). Pool; whirlpool, sauna. Coffee in rms. Restaurant 6:30 am-10 pm; hrs vary Sat, Sun. Rm serv. Bar 5 pm-midnight. Ck-out 11 am. Coin lndry. Meeting rms. Business servs avail. In-rm modem link. Valet serv. Airport transportation. Health club privileges. Microwaves avail. Cr cds: A, C, D, DS, MC, V. 🄳 🏄 🌊 🖾 🖾 SC

★ **HAWTHORN SUITES.** *7900 Brookriver Dr (75247), north of downtown.* 214/688-1010; FAX 214/638-5215; res: 800/527-1133. Web www.hawthorn.com. 97 kit. suites, 2 story. S $130; D $168; wkend, wkly, hol rates. Crib free. Pet accepted, some restrictions; $25. TV; cable (premium). Pool. Complimentary full bkfst. Complimentary coffee in rms. Ck-out noon. Coin lndry. Meeting rms. Business servs avail. In-rm modem link. Valet serv Mon-Fri. Sundries. Free airport transportation. Health club privileges. Lawn games. Microwaves avail. Balconies, patios. Cr cds: A, C, D, DS, MC, V. 🄳 🏄 🌊 🐾 🖾 🖾

★★ **LA QUINTA INN-EAST.** *8303 E RL Thornton Frwy (I-30) (75228), I-30 exit Jim Miller, east of downtown.* 214/324-3731; FAX 214/324-1652. 102 rms, 2 story. Mar-Oct: S $59-$65; D $66-$73; suites $135; each addl $10; under 18 free; higher rates wkends; lower rates rest of yr. Crib free. Pet accepted, some restrictions. TV; cable (premium). Pool. Complimentary continental bkfst. Restaurant adj 6 am-midnight. Ck-out noon. Business servs avail. In-rm modem link. Sundries. Valet serv Mon-Fri. Microwaves avail. Cr cds: A, C, D, DS, MC, V. 🄳 🏄 🌊 🖾 🖾 SC

✔★★ **LA QUINTA NORTHWEST-FARMERS BRANCH.** *13235 Stemmons Frwy N (75234), I-35E exit Valleyview, north of downtown.* 972/620-7333; FAX 972/484-6533. 121 rms, 2 story. S, D $64; each addl $6; under 18 free. Crib free. Pet accepted, some restrictions. TV; cable (premium). Pool. Complimentary continental bkfst. Coffee in rms. Restaurant adj 6 am-11 pm. Ck-out noon. Meeting rms. Business servs avail. In-rm modem link. Free airport transportation. Some refrigerators; microwaves avail. Cr cds: A, C, D, DS, MC, V. 🄳 🏄 🌊 🖾 🖾 SC

★★ **RESIDENCE INN BY MARRIOTT.** *13636 Goldmark Dr (75240), US 75 exit Midpark, W to Goldmark, north of downtown.* 972/669-0478; FAX 972/644-2632. 70 kit. suites, 1-2 story. Suites $129-$149; wkend rates. Crib free. Pet accepted, some restrictions; $60. TV; cable (premium). Pool; whirlpool. Complimentary continental bkfst. Ck-out noon. Coin lndry. Business servs avail. In-rm modem link. Valet serv. Health club privileges. Refrigerators, microwaves, fireplaces. Private patios, balconies. Grill. Cr cds: A, C, D, DS, MC, V. 🄳 🏄 🌊 🖾 🖾 SC

★★ **RESIDENCE INN BY MARRIOTT.** *6950 N Stemmons (75247), north of downtown.* 214/631-2472; FAX 214/634-9645. 142 kit. suites, 3 story. S $120; D $160; wkend rates. Crib free. Pet accepted; $50. TV; cable (premium). Pool; whirlpool. Complimentary continental bkfst. Complimentary coffee in rms. Ck-out noon. Coin lndry. Meeting rms. Business servs avail. Valet serv. Exercise equipt; weight machine, treadmill. Health club privileges. Microwaves avail. Picnic tables. Cr cds: A, D, DS, JCB, MC, V. 🄳 🏄 🌊 🏋 🖾 🖾 SC

★ **SLEEP INN.** *(4801 W Plano Pkwy, Plano 75093) 20 mi N on North Dallas Tollway, Plano Pkwy exit.* 972/867-1111; FAX 972/612-6753. 104 rms, 2 story. S $65-$80; D $70-$80; each addl $6; under 19 free; wkend rates. Crib free. Pet accepted. TV; cable. Heated pool. Complimentary continental bkfst. Restaurant nearby. Ck-out noon. Meeting rms. Business servs avail. In-rm modem link. Valet serv. Cr cds: A, C, D, DS, ER, JCB, MC, V. 🄳 🏄 🌊 🖾 🖾 SC

Motor Hotels

★★ **HARVEY HOTEL-ADDISON.** *14315 Midway Rd (75244), I-635 exit Midway Rd, north of downtown.* 972/980-8877; FAX 972/788-2758. 429 rms, 3 story. Feb-May: S $99-$120; D $109-$135; each addl $10; under 12 free; wkly, wkend, hol rates. Crib free. Pet accepted, some restrictions; $125 ($100 refundable). TV; cable (premium), VCR avail. Pool; whirlpool. Restaurant 10:30 am-10 pm. Rm serv. Coin lndry. Business center. In-rm modem link. Garage parking. Airport transportation. Exercise equipt; weight machine, treadmill. Health club privileges. Some refrigerators. Microwaves. Cr cds: A, C, D, DS, ER, MC, V. 🄳 🏄 🌊 🏋 🖾 🖾 SC 🦽

★★ **HARVEY HOTEL.** *7815 LBJ Frwy (75240), I-635 exit 19A Coit Rd, north of downtown.* 214/960-7000; FAX 214/788-4227; res: 800/922-9222. 313 rms, 3 story. S $99-$129; D $109-$139; each addl $10; suites $125-$250; under 17 free. Crib free. Pet accepted; $125 ($100 refundable). TV; cable. Pool. Restaurant 6:30 am-11 pm. Rm serv 24 hours. Bar 11 am-midnight. Ck-out 1 pm. Meeting rms. Business servs avail. In-rm modem link. Health club privileges. Valet serv. Gift shop. Covered parking. Microwaves avail. Cr cds: A, C, D, DS, JCB, MC, V. [D] [⟟] [≈] [⟟] [⟟] [SC]

★ ★ **HARVEY HOTEL-PLANO.** *(1600 N Central Expy, Plano 75074) 12 mi N on Central Expy (US 75), 15th St exit.* 972/578-8555; FAX 972/578-9720. 279 rms, 3 story. S $109-$159; D $119-$169; each addl $10; suites $159; under 16 free. Crib free. Pet accepted; $125 ($100 refundable). TV; cable, VCR avail. Pool; whirlpool, poolside serv. Restaurants 6:30 am-11 pm. Rm serv. Bar 10 am-midnight; Sat to 1 am. Ck-out 1 pm. Coin lndry. Meeting rms. Business servs avail. In-rm modem link. Bellhops. Valet serv. Sundries. Gift shop. Game rm. Exerise equipt; weight machine, treadmill. Microwaves avail; refrigerator, wet bar in suites. Cr cds: A, C, D, DS, MC, V. [D] [⟟] [≈] [⟟] [⟟] [⟟] [SC]

Hotels

★ ★ ★ **BRISTOL SUITES.** *7800 Alpha Rd (75240), I-635 exit 19A to Coit Rd, north of downtown.* 972/233-7600; FAX 972/701-8618; res: 800/922-9222. 295 suites, 10 story. Suites $149-$239; each addl $15; under 17 free; some lower rates summer. Crib free. Pet accepted; $125 ($100 refundable). TV; cable. Indoor/outdoor pool; whirlpool, poolside serv. Complimentary full bkfst. Restaurant 6:30 am-10 pm. Bar 11 am-midnight. Ck-out 1 pm. Coin lndry. Convention facilities. Business center. In-rm modem link. Gift shop. Exercise equipt; weights, bicycle. Refrigerators, microwaves; some bathrm phones. Cr cds: A, D, DS, MC, V. [D] [⟟] [≈] [⟟] [⟟] [⟟] [SC] [⟟]

★ ★ ★ ★ **CRESCENT COURT.** *400 Crescent Court (75201), at Maple & McKinney Ave, in the Crescent area, north of downtown.* 214/871-3200; FAX 214/871-3272; res: 800/654-6541. Web www.rosewood-hotels.com. Modeled after the Royal Crescent spa in Bath, England, this hotel is part of a castle-like complex that includes a posh retail gallery. Furnishings are reminiscent of those in an English manor house; all the suites have hardwood floors and some have lofts. 216 rms, 7 story. S $270-$360; D $300-$390; each addl $30; suites $580-$1,600; under 12 free; wkend rates. Crib free. Pet accepted, some restrictions; $25. Garage $5.50; valet $12. TV; cable (premium), VCR avail. Pool; whirlpool, poolside serv. Restaurant 6:30 am-midnight. Afternoon tea 3-5 pm. Rm serv 24 hrs. Bar 11:30-2 am. Ck-out 1 pm. Meeting rms. Business center. In-rm modem link. Concierge. Shopping arcade. Free airport transportation. Exercise rm; instructor, weights, bicycles, sauna, steam rm. Spa. Bathrm phones, refrigerators. Cr cds: A, C, D, DS, ER, JCB, MC, V. [D] [⟟] [≈] [⟟] [⟟] [⟟] [⟟]

★ ★ **HAMPTON INN-WEST END.** *1015 Elm St (75202), in West End Historic District.* 214/742-5678; FAX 214/744-6167. 311 rms, 23 story. S $86; D $93; under 16 free; wkend rates; higher rates special events. Crib free. Pet accepted; $125 ($100 refundable). In/out parking $5. TV; cable (premium). Complimentary continental bkfst. Restaurant nearby. No rm serv. Ck-out noon. Business servs avail. In-rm modem link. Concierge. Barber. Coin lndry. Exercise equipt; treadmill, stair machine. Pool. Cr cds: A, C, D, DS, MC, V. [D] [⟟] [≈] [⟟] [⟟] [⟟] [SC]

★ ★ **HOLIDAY INN SELECT.** *1241 W Mockingbird Lane (75247), near Love Field Airport, north of downtown.* 214/630-7000; FAX 214/638-6943. 348 rms, 13 story. S $139; D $149; each addl $10; suites $225-$550; under 18 free; wkend, hol rates. Crib free. Pet accepted, some restrictions; $50. TV; cable (premium). Pool; wading pool, poolside serv. Coffee in rms. Restaurant 6:30 am-2 pm, 5-10 pm. Bar 11-2 am. Rm serv 6 am-11 pm. Ck-out noon. Coin lndry. Convention facilities. Business servs avail. In-rm modem link. Gift shop. Free airport transportation. Exercise equipt; weight machine, stair machine. Health club privileges. Cr cds: A, C, D, DS, ER, JCB, MC, V. [D] [⟟] [≈] [⟟] [⟟] [⟟] [⟟] [SC]

★ ★ **RADISSON.** *2330 W Northwest Hwy (75220), north of downtown.* 214/351-4477; FAX 214/351-4499. 198 rms, 8 story. S $119-$139; D $129-$159; each addl $10; suites $129-$149; under 18 free; wkly, wkend, hol rates. Crib free. Pet accepted, some restrictions; $25 deposit. TV; cable (premium), VCR avail. Pool; whirlpool, poolside serv. Coffee in rms. Restaurant 6:30 am-10 pm. Bar 11-1 am. Ck-out noon. Coin lndry. Meeting rms. Business servs avail. In-rm modem link. Concierge. Gift shop. Free airport transportation. Exercise equipt; weight machine, treadmill. Health club privileges. Microwaves avail. Some balconies. Cr cds: A, C, D, DS, ER, JCB, MC, V. [D] [⟟] [≈] [⟟] [⟟] [⟟] [SC]

✔ ★ ★ **RAMADA PLAZA CONVENTION CENTER.** *1011 S Akard (75215), downtown.* 214/421-1083; FAX 214/428-6827. 236 rms, 12 story. S $69-$140; D $79-$150; each addl $10; suites $350-$450; under 18 free; wkend rates. Crib free. Pet accepted. TV; cable (premium). Indoor pool; whirlpool. Restaurant 6 am-11 pm. Bar 4 pm-2 am. Ck-out noon. Meeting rms. Business center. In-rm modem link. Free garage parking. Airport transportation. Exercise equipt; weights, bicycles. Health club privileges. Balconies. Cr cds: A, C, D, DS, ER, JCB, MC, V. [D] [⟟] [≈] [⟟] [⟟] [⟟] [SC] [⟟]

✓ ★ **RAMADA-MARKET CENTER.** *1055 Regal Row (75247), north of downtown. 214/634-8550; FAX 214/634-8418.* 322 units, 12 story. S, D $89-$109; each addl $10; suites $125-$350; under 16 free. Pet accepted, some restrictions. TV; cable, VCR avail. Pool; poolside serv. Restaurant 6:30 am-2 pm, 5-10 pm. Bar 4 pm-1 am. Ck-out noon. Convention facilities. Business servs avail. Valet serv. Gift shop. Free covered parking. Free airport transportation. Game rm. Tennis. Exercise equipt; bicycle, treadmill. Some refrigerators. Cr cds: A, C, D, DS, JCB, MC, V. 🄳 ⟟ 🏊 🍴 🚫 🔥 🆂🅲

★ ★ **RENAISSANCE.** *2222 Stemmons Frwy (I-35E) (75207), near Market Center, I-35E exit 430C, north of downtown. 214/631-2222; FAX 214/634-9319.* 538 rms, 30 story. S $174-$194; D $194-$214; each addl $20; suites $214-$1,000; under 18 free; wkend rates. Crib free. Pet accepted, some restrictions. TV; cable (premium), VCR avail. Heated pool; whirlpool. Complimentary coffee. Restaurant 6:30 am-10 pm. Bar 3 pm-2 am; entertainment. Ck-out 1 pm. Convention facilities. Business center. In-rm modem link. Gift shop. Exercise equipt; weights, bicycles, sauna, steam rm. Some refrigerators. Three-story chandelier; art objects. Luxury level. Cr cds: A, C, D, DS, ER, JCB, MC, V. 🄳 ⟟ 🏊 🍴 🚫 🔥 🧍

Dallas/Fort Worth Airport Area *(See also Dallas, Fort Worth)*

Motels

★ ★ **DRURY INN.** *(4210 W Airport Frwy, Irving 75062) TX 183 & Esters Rd. 972/986-1200.* Web www.DruryInn.org. 129 rms, 4 story. S $71-$81; D $81-$91; each addl $10; under 18 free. Crib free. Pet accepted, some restrictions. TV; cable (premium). Pool. Complimentary continental bkfst. Restaurant adj 11-2 am. Ck-out noon. Meeting rms. Business servs avail. In-rm modem link. Sundries. Free airport transportation. Cr cds: A, C, D, DS, MC, V. 🄳 ⟟ 🏊 🍴 🚫 🔥 🆂🅲

★ ★ **HAMPTON INN.** *(4340 W Airport Frwy, Irving 75062) on TX 183, exit Esters Rd. 972/986-3606; FAX 972/986-6852.* 81 rms, 4 story. S $75; D $85; suites $87; under 18 free. Crib free. Pet accepted. TV; cable (premium). Pool. Complimentary continental bkfst. Restaurant adj 11-2 am. Ck-out noon. Sundries. Valet serv. Free airport transportation. Some refrigerators; microwaves avail. Cr cds: A, C, D, DS, MC, V.
🄳 ⟟ 🏊 🍴 🚫 🔥 🆂🅲

✓ ★ ★ **LA QUINTA-DFW.** *(4105 W Airport Frwy, Irving 75062) TX 183 & Esters Rd. 972/252-6546; FAX 972/570-4225.* 169 rms, 2 story. S $68-$78; D $78-$88; each addl $10; suites $87-$108; under 18 free. Crib free. Pet accepted. TV; cable (premium). Pool. Complimentary continental bkfst. Restaurant adj open 24 hrs. Ck-out noon. Meeting rm. Business servs avail. In-rm modem link. Free airport transportation. Health club privileges. Cr cds: A, C, D, DS, MC, V. 🄳 ⟟ 🏊 🍴 🚫 🔥 🆂🅲

Motor Hotels

★ ★ ★ **HARVEY SUITES.** *(4550 W John Carpenter Frwy, Irving 75063) TX 114 off Esters Blvd exit. 972/929-4499; FAX 972/929-0774; res: 800/922-9222.* 164 suites, 3 story. S, D $129-$139; under 18 free; wkend rates. Crib free. Pet accepted; $25 deposit. TV; cable, VCR avail (movies). Pool; whirlpool, poolside serv. Complimentary continental bkfst. Complimentary coffee in rms. Restaurant 6:30-11 am; Sat, Sun from 7 am. Bar 4 pm-midnight. Ck-out 1 pm. Coin lndry. Meeting rms. Business servs avail. In-rm modem link. Valet serv. Sundries. Gift shop. Free airport transportation. Exercise equipt; treadmill, bicycles. Health club privileges. Refrigerators, wet bars; microwaves avail. Picnic tables, grills. Cr cds: A, C, D, DS, JCB, MC, V. 🄳 ⟟ 🏊 🍴 🚫 🔥 🆂🅲

★ **WILSON WORLD.** *(4600 W Airport Frwy, Irving 75062) 972/513-0800; FAX 972/513-0106.* 200 rms, 5 story, 96 suites. S, D $79-$119; suites $89-$129; under 18 free; wkend rates. Crib free. Pet accepted, some restrictions. TV; cable (premium). Indoor pool; whirlpool. Restaurant 6 am-1:30 pm, 5:30-10 pm. Bar 5 pm-midnight. Ck-out noon. Meeting rms. Business center. In-rm modem link. Gift shop. Free airport transportation. Exercise equipt; weight machine, stair machine. Refrigerators; microwaves avail. Cr cds: A, C, D, DS, MC, V. 🄳 ⟟ 🏊 🍴 🚫 🔥 🆂🅲 🧍

Hotels

★ ★ ★ ★ **FOUR SEASONS RESORT & CLUB.** *(4150 N MacArthur Blvd, Irving 75038) NW via TX 114, exit MacArthur Blvd, S 2 mi. 972/717-0700; FAX 972/717-2550.* This property combines top-notch resort amenities—including a superb health center and spa—and state-of-the-art conference facilities with the comforts of an elegant hotel. 357 rms, 9 story. S, D $290-$340; suites $500-$1,100; under 18 free; golf, spa, wkend plans. Pet accepted, some restrictions. Valet parking $5. TV; cable (premium), VCR avail. 4 pools, 2 heated, 1 indoor & 1 child's; whirlpool, poolside serv, lifeguard (wkends in season). Supervised child's activities; ages 6 months-8 yrs. Restaurant 6:30 am-11 pm. Rm serv 24 hrs. Bar 11-2 am. Ck-out noon. Convention facilities. Business center. In-rm modem link.

Concierge. Gift shop. Barber, beauty shop. 12 tennis courts, 4 indoor, pro. 18-hole golf, greens fee $130 (incl cart), pro, 2 putting greens, driving range. Exercise rm; instructor, weight machines, bicycles, sauna, steam rm. Massage. Lawn games. Minibars; microwaves avail. Private patios, balconies. Cr cds: A, C, D, JCB, MC, V.

★ ★ **MARRIOTT-DFW AIRPORT.** *(8440 Freeport Pkwy, Irving 75063) TX 114 at N entrance to airport. 972/929-8800; FAX 972/929-6501.* Web www.marriott.com/marriott/dfwap. 491 rms, 20 story. S, D $159-$189; suites $200-$425; under 12 free; wkend rates. Crib free. Pet accepted, some restrictions. TV; cable (premium). Indoor/outdoor pool; whirlpool, poolside serv. Restaurants 6 am-11 pm. Bar 11-2 am. Ck-out 1 pm. Coin lndry. Convention facilities. Business center. In-rm modem link. Sundries. Gift shop. Free airport transportation. Tennis privileges. Golf privileges. Exercise equipt; weights, bicycles, sauna. Some refrigerators. Luxury level. Cr cds: A, C, D, DS, ER, JCB, MC, V.

Del Rio *(See also Eagle Pass, Uvalde)*

Motels

★ ★ **BEST WESTERN INN.** *810 Ave F. 830/775-7511; FAX 830/774-2194.* 62 rms, 2 story. S $51; D $60; each addl $9; under 13 free. Pet accepted; $5. TV; cable (premium). Pool; whirlpool. Complimentary full bkfst. Ck-out noon. Coin lndry. Business servs avail. In-rm modem link. Health club privileges. Cr cds: A, C, D, DS, MC, V.

★ ★ **LA QUINTA.** *2005 Ave F. 830/775-7591; FAX 830/774-0809.* 101 rms, 2 story. S $54-$70; D $62-$77; under 18 free. Crib free. Pet accepted. TV; cable (premium). Pool. Complimentary continental bkfst. Coffee in rms. Ck-out noon. Coin lndry. In-rm modem link. Cr cds: A, C, D, DS, MC, V.

★ ★ **RAMADA INN.** *2101 Ave F. 830/775-1511.* 127 rms. S $55-$70; D $62-$80; each addl $8; suites $123; under 18 free; higher rates special events. Crib free. Pet accepted, some restrictions. TV; cable (premium), VCR (movies). Pool; whirlpool, poolside serv. Complimentary coffee in rms. Restaurant 6 am-2 pm, 5-10 pm; Sun 6 am-3 pm, 5-10 pm. Rm serv. Bar 4 pm-2 am. Ck-out noon. Coin lndry. Valet serv. Exercise equipt; weight machine, bicycle, sauna. Refrigerators. Cr cds: A, C, D, DS, MC, V.

Denton *(See also Arlington-Grand Prairie, Dallas, Fort Worth, Gainesville)*

Motel

✔ ★ ★ **LA QUINTA.** *700 Ft Worth Dr (76201), I-35E, Ft Worth Dr exit 465B. 940/387-5840; FAX 940/387-2493.* 99 rms, 2 story. S $60-$70; D $70-$80; each addl $8; under 18 free. Crib free. Pet accepted. TV; cable (premium). Pool. Restaurant adj open 24 hrs. Ck-out noon. Meeting rms. Business servs avail. In-rm modem link. Cr cds: A, C, D, DS, MC, V.

Hotel

★ ★ **RADISSON.** *2211 I-35 E North (76205), at University of North Texas. 940/565-8499; FAX 940/387-4729.* 150 rms, 8 story. S, D $89-$109; each addl $10; suites $189-$340; under 18 free; golf plans. Pet accepted; $100 refundable. TV; cable (premium), VCR avail. Pool. Complimentary coffee in rms. Restaurant 6 am-10 pm. Rm serv. Bar 11 am-midnight. Meeting rms. Business center. Tennis privileges. 18-hole golf, pro, putting green, driving range. Exercise equipt; weights, treadmill. Cr cds: A, C, D, DS, ER, MC, V.

Dumas *(See also Amarillo)*

Motels

★ ★ **BEST WESTERN DUMAS INN.** *1712 S Dumas Ave. 806/935-6441; FAX 806/935-9331.* 102 rms, 2 story. S $49-$89; D $53-$97; each addl $8; suites $125. Crib $8. Pet accepted. TV; cable (premium). Indoor pool; whirlpool. Restaurant 6 am-10 pm. Rm serv. Private club 5 pm-2 am. Ck-out noon. Meeting rms. Business servs avail. In-rm modem link. Exercise equipt; treadmill, bicycle. Game rm. Cr cds: A, C, D, DS, MC, V.

✔ ★ **ECONO LODGE OLD TOWN INN.** *1719 S Dumas Ave. 806/935-9098; FAX 806/935-7483.* 40 rms, 2 story. Mar-July: S $38.95-$50; D $47.95-$70; each addl $3; under 18 free; wkly, wkend rates; lower rates rest of yr. Crib $5. Pet accepted. TV; cable (premium). Heated pool; whirlpool. Complimentary continental bkfst. Restaurant nearby.

Ck-out 11 am. Business servs avail. Coin lndry. Some refrigerators. Cr cds: A, C, D, DS, MC, V. [D] 🐾 ⛱ ➤ 🐾 SC

★ **SUPER 8.** *119 W 17th St. 806/935-6222.* 30 rms, 2 story. Apr-Sept, Dec: S $39-$49; D $52-$62; each addl $5; under 10 free; lower rates rest of yr. Pet accepted, some restrictions; $5. TV; cable. Complimentary continental bkfst. Restaurant nearby. Ck-out 11 am. Business servs avail. Refrigerators. Cr cds: A, C, D, DS, MC, V. [D] 🐾 ➤ 🐾 SC

Eagle Pass (See also Del Rio, Uvalde)

Motels

★ **BEST WESTERN.** *1923 Loop 431 (78852). 830/758-1234; FAX 830/758-1235.* 40 rms, 2 story, 14 suites. S $64; D $70; suites $70-$80; under 12 free; family rates. Crib free. Pet accepted, some restrictions. TV; cable (premium). Restaurant opp open 24 hrs. Ck-out noon. Meeting rms. Business servs avail. In-rm modem link. Pool. Refrigerators, microwaves. Cr cds: A, D, DS, MC, V. [D] 🐾 ⛱ ➤ 🐾 SC

★ ★ **LA QUINTA.** *2525 Main St (78852). 830/773-7000; FAX 830/773-8852.* 130 rms, 2 story. S $60-$67; D $68-$75; each addl $8; under 18 free; wkend rates. Crib free. Pet accepted. TV; cable (premium). Pool. Complimentary continental bkfst. Complimentary coffee in rms. Restaurant adj open 24 hrs. Ck-out noon. Valet serv. Meeting rms. In-rm modem link. Microwaves, refrigerators avail. Cr cds: A, C, D, DS, MC, V.
[D] 🐾 ⛱ ➤ 🐾 SC

El Paso (See also Las Cruces, NM)

Motels

✔★ ★ **COMFORT INN.** *900 N Yarbrough (79915). 915/594-9111; FAX 915/590-4364.* 200 units, 3 story. S $49 D $56; each addl $10; under 18 free. Crib free. Pet accepted. TV; cable (premium). Pool; whirlpool. Complimentary continental bkfst. Restaurant adj 10 am-8 pm. Ck-out noon. Coin lndry. Airport transportation. Balconies. Cr cds: A, C, D, DS, JCB, MC, V. [D] 🐾 ⛱ ➤ 🐾 SC

★ ★ **HOWARD JOHNSON.** *8887 Gateway W (79925), I-10 exit 26. 915/591-9471; FAX 915/591-5602.* 140 rms, 1-2 story. S $57-$61; D $61-$65; each addl $3. Crib free. Pet accepted. TV; cable (premium). Pool; wading pool. Restaurant adj open 24 hrs. Ck-out 2 pm. Coin lndry. Meeting rms. Business servs avail. In-rm modem link. Bellhops. Valet serv. Free airport transportation. Exercise equipt; weight machine, treadmills. Some refrigerators. Private patios, balconies. Cr cds: A, C, D, DS, JCB, MC, V. [D] 🐾 ⛱ 🏋 ➤ 🐾 SC

★ ★ **LA QUINTA.** *6140 Gateway E (79905). 915/778-9321.* 121 rms, 2 story. S $61; D $69; each addl $8; suites $95; under 18 free. Crib free. Pet accepted. TV; cable (premium). Pool. Restaurant adj open 24 hrs. Ck-out noon. Business servs avail. In-rm modem link. Free airport transportation. Cr cds: A, C, D, DS, ER, JCB, MC, V.
[D] 🐾 ⛱ ➤ 🐾 SC

★ ★ **QUALITY INN.** *6201 Gateway W (79925), near Intl Airport. 915/778-6611; FAX 915/779-2270.* 307 rms, 2-3 story. No elvtr. S $48; D $52; suites $74-$95. Crib. Pet accepted. TV; cable, VCR avail. Pool; wading pool. Restaurant 6 am-10 pm. Rm serv. Bar 4 pm-1:30 am; entertainment. Ck-out 2 pm. Convention facilities. Business servs avail. Bellhops. Gift shop. Free airport transportation. Cr cds: A, C, D, DS, JCB, MC, V.
🐾 ⛱ 🏋 ➤ 🐾 SC

Motor Hotel

★ ★ **HILTON-AIRPORT.** *2027 Airway Blvd (79925), near Intl Airport. 915/778-4241; FAX 915/772-6871.* 272 rms, 4 story. S $97-$102; D $102-$107; each addl $10; suites $117-$127; family, wkend rates. Pet accepted. TV; cable (premium), VCR avail. Heated pool; whirlpool, poolside serv. Bkfst buffet. Restaurant 6 am-11 pm. Rm serv. Bar noon-2 am. Ck-out noon. Convention facilities. Business center. In-rm modem link. Bellhops. Valet serv. Sundries. Barber, beauty shop. Free airport transportation. Exercise equipt; stair machine, weight machine. Microwaves avail. Cr cds: A, C, D, DS, ER, JCB, MC, V.
[D] 🐾 ⛱ 🏋 ➤ 🐾 SC 🏌

Hotels

★ ★ **CAMINO REAL.** *101 S El Paso St (79901). 915/534-3000; FAX 915/534-3024; res: 800/769-4300.* E-mail elp@caminoreal.com; web www.caminoreal.com. 359 units, 17 story. S, D $130-$145; each addl $15; suites $155-$990; under 12 free. Crib free. Pet accepted, some restrictions; $50. TV; cable. Pool. Restaurants 6 am-11:30 pm. Rm serv 24 hrs. Bar 11-1 am; entertainment. Ck-out noon. Convention facilities. Business center.

In-rm modem link. Free airport transportation. Exercise equipt; weights, rower, sauna. Renovated historic hotel (1912). Luxury level. Cr cds: A, C, D, DS, ER, JCB, MC, V.

D ✦ ≋ ✕ ⊠ 🔥 SC 🛷

★ ★ **EMBASSY SUITES.** *6100 Gateway E (79905). 915/779-6222; FAX 915/779-8846.* E-mail elpgw.com@aol.com. 185 suites, 8 story. S, D $119; under 18 free; wkend rates. Pet accepted, some restrictions; $50. TV; cable (premium), VCR avail. Indoor pool; whirlpool. Complimentary bkfst. Ck-out 1 pm. Coin lndry. Meeting rms. Business servs avail. In-rm modem link. Free airport transportation. Exercise equipt; weight machine, treadmill, sauna. Refrigerators, microwaves. Large atrium with fountain, pools, plants. Cr cds: A, C, D, DS, JCB, MC, V. D ✦ ≋ ✕ ⊠ 🔥

✔ ★ ★ **INTERNATIONAL.** *113 W Missouri (79901). 915/544-3300; FAX 915/544-9990; res: 800/668-3466.* 200 rms, 17 story. S, D $45-$55; each addl $5; suites $85-$125; under 16 free. Crib free. Pet accepted; $10. TV; cable. Pool. Complimentary continental bkfst. Restaurant 11:30 am-10 pm. Bar 4 pm-2 am; closed Sun, Mon. Ck-out noon. Meeting rms. Business servs avail. Free airport, RR station, bus depot transportation. Balconies. Cr cds: A, C, D, DS, MC, V. D ✦ ≋ ⊠ 🔥 SC

★ ★ **MARRIOTT.** *1600 Airway Blvd (79925), near Intl Airport. 915/779-3300; FAX 915/772-0915.* Web www.marriott.com/marriott/tx177.htm. 296 rms, 6 story. S $124; D $139; each addl $15; suites $300-$500; wkend rates. Crib free. Pet accepted, some restrictions. TV; cable (premium). Indoor/outdoor pool; whirlpool, poolside serv. Restaurant 6:30 am-11 pm. Bar noon-1 am. Ck-out 1 pm. Coin lndry. Convention facilities. Business servs avail. In-rm modem link. Valet serv. Shopping arcade. Free airport transportation. Exercise equipt; weight machines, bicycles, sauna. Private patios. Southwestern decor and art. Luxury level. Cr cds: A, C, D, DS, ER, JCB, MC, V. D ✦ ≋ ✕ ✈ ⊠ 🔥 SC

Fort Stockton *(See also Alpine)*

Motels

✔ ★ ★ **BEST WESTERN SWISS CLOCK INN.** *3201 W Dickinson. 915/336-8521; FAX 915/336-6513.* 112 rms, 2 story. S $44-$48; D $45-$54; each addl $6; studio rms $60; under 12 free. Crib free. Pet accepted. TV; cable (premium). Pool. Restaurant 6 am-2 pm, 5-10 pm. Rm serv. Private club 5-10 pm. Ck-out noon. Meeting rms. Business servs avail. Valet serv. Some private patios. Cr cds: A, C, D, DS, JCB, MC, V. D ✦ ≋ ⊠ 🔥 SC

★ ★ **LA QUINTA.** *2601 I-10W, Near jct I-10 & US 285. 915/336-9781; FAX 915/336-3634.* 97 rms, 2 story. S $54; D $61; each addl $7; suite $64; under 18 free. Crib free. Pet accepted, some restrictions. TV; cable (premium), VCR avail. Pool. Restaurant opp 8:30 am-11 pm. Ck-out noon. Guest lndry. Business servs avail. Cr cds: A, C, D, DS, JCB, MC, V. D ✦ ≋ ⊠ 🔥 SC

Fort Worth

Motels

✔ ★ **BEST WESTERN-WEST BRANCH INN.** *7301 W Frwy (76116), I-30 at TX 183, west of downtown. 817/244-7444; FAX 817/244-7902.* 118 rms, 2 story. S $46-$76; D $59.95-$89.95; each addl $5; suites $69.95-$109.95; under 12 free. Crib free. Pet accepted, some restrictions. TV; cable (premium), VCR avail. Pool. Complimentary continental bkfst. Restaurant adj 4 pm-2 am; closed Sun-Tues. Ck-out noon. Coin lndry. Meeting rms. Business servs avail. In-rm modem link. Some refrigerators; microwaves avail. Cr cds: A, C, D, DS, JCB, MC, V. ✦ ≋ ⊠ 🔥 SC

✔ ★ ★ **LA QUINTA-WEST.** *7888 I-30W (76108), west of downtown. 817/246-5511; FAX 817/246-8870.* 106 rms, 3 story. S $65; D $72; each addl $8; under 18 free. Crib $5. Pet accepted. TV; cable (premium). Pool. Complimentary continental bkfst. Restaurant adj open 24 hrs. Meeting rms. In-rm modem link. Microwaves avail. Cr cds: A, C, D, DS, MC, V. D ✦ ≋ ⊠ 🔥 SC

★ ★ **RESIDENCE INN BY MARRIOTT.** *1701 S University Dr (76107), west of downtown. 817/870-1011; FAX 817/877-5500.* 120 kit. suites, 2 story. Suites: $112-$155; wkend rates. Crib free. Pet accepted; $5/day. TV; cable (premium). Heated pool; whirlpool. Complimentary continental bkfst. Restaurant nearby. Ck-out noon. Coin lndry. Meeting rm. Business servs avail. In-rm modem link. Valet serv. Microwaves. Private patios, balconies. Picnic tables, grills. Cr cds: A, C, D, DS, ER, JCB, MC, V. D ✦ ≋ ⊠ 🔥

Motor Hotel

★ ★ **GREEN OAKS PARK HOTEL.** *6901 W Frwy (76116), I-30 at TX 183, west of downtown. 817/738-7311; FAX 817/377-1308; res: 800/433-2174 (exc TX), 800-772-2341*

(TX). E-mail greenoak@onramp.net. 284 rms, 2-3 story. S $86-$99; D $96-$114; suites $96-$135; each addl $10; under 18 free; wkend rates; package plans. Crib free. Pet accepted. TV; cable (premium). 2 pools; poolside serv. Restaurant 6 am-2 pm, 5-10 pm. Rm serv. Bars 4 pm-2 am; entertainment exc Sun. Ck-out noon. Convention facilities. Business servs avail. In-rm modem link. Sundries. Lighted tennis. Exercise equipt; weights, bicycles, sauna. Adj Naval Air Station, Carswell Joint Reserve Base, 18-hole golf course. Cr cds: A, D, DS, MC, V. 🄳 💺 🏋 ⊠ 🏃 ⊠ 🐾 SC

Fredericksburg *(See also Johnson City, Kerrville)*

Motels

★ **BEST WESTERN SUNDAY HOUSE.** *501 E Main St. 830/997-4484; FAX 830/997-5607.* 124 rms, 2-3 story. Mar-Nov: S $64-$70; D $70-$90; each addl $8; suites $95-$125; under 12 free; lower rates rest of yr. Crib $6. Pet accepted, some restrictions. TV; cable. Pool. Restaurant 7 am-9 pm; Sat, Sun to 10 pm. Ck-out noon. Business servs avail. In-rm modem link. Cr cds: A, C, D, DS, MC, V. 🄳 💺 ⊠ ⊠ 🐾 SC

★ **COMFORT INN.** *908 S Adams. 830/997-9811; FAX 830/997-2068.* 46 rms, 2 story. S $59-$69; D $64-$74; each addl $5. Crib free. Pet accepted, some restrictions. TV; cable. Pool. Complimentary continental bkfst. Ck-out noon. Bus depot transportation. Tennis. Picnic tables, grills. Cr cds: A, C, D, DS, ER, JCB, MC, V. 🄳 💺 🏋 ⊠ ⊠ 🐾 SC

✔ ★ **DIETZEL.** *909 W Main St. 830/997-3330.* 20 rms. S $35-$45; D $42-$52; each addl $5. Crib free. Pet accepted, some restrictions; $3. TV; cable (premium). Pool. Complimentary coffee in lobby. Restaurant adj 11 am-10 pm. Ck-out 11 am. Picnic tables. Cr cds: A, DS, MC, V. 💺 ⊠ 🐾

✔ ★ ★ **FREDERICKSBURG INN & SUITES.** *201 S Washington St. 830/997-0202; res: 800/446-0202; FAX 830/997-5740.* Web www.texaslodging.ads/4685.html. 51 rms, 2 story, 6 suites. S $59; D $65; each addl $6; suites $75-$80; under 13 free; wkends (2-day min). Pet accepted; $10. TV; cable (premium). Complimentary continental bkfst. Complimentary coffee in rms. Restaurant nearby. Ck-out noon. Playground. Bathrm phones; refrigerator, microwave, wet bar in suites. Cr cds: A, DS, MC, V. 💺 💺 ⊠

★ ★ **PEACH TREE INN.** *401 S Washington (US 87S). 830/997-2117; FAX 830/997-0827; res: 800/843-4666.* 34 rms, some with shower only. S $29.25-$66.50; D $35.40-$66.50; kit. suites $73-$97.50; under 12 free. Crib free. Pet accepted, some restrictions. TV; cable (premium). Pool. Playground. Complimentary continental bkfst. Restaurant nearby. Ck-out 11 am. Lawn games. Some refrigerators, microwaves. Picnic tables. Cr cds: A, DS, MC, V. 💺 ⊠ ⊠ 🐾

Gainesville *(See also Denton)*

Motel

★ **HOLIDAY INN.** *600 Fair Pk Blvd, I-35 California St exit. 940/665-8800; FAX 940/665-8709.* 118 rms, 2 story. S, D $55; each addl $5; under 18 free. Crib $3. Pet accepted. TV; cable (premium). Pool. Restaurant 6:30 am-9 pm. Rm serv. Bar 5 pm-midnight, Sat to 1 am, closed Sun. Ck-out noon. Coin lndry. Meeting rms. Business servs avail. Game rm. Cr cds: A, C, D, DS, ER, JCB, MC, V. 🄳 💺 ⊠ ⊠ 🐾 SC

Galveston *(See also Houston)*

Motel

★ ★ **LA QUINTA.** *1402 Seawall Blvd (77550). 409/763-1224; FAX 409/765-8663.* 117 rms, 3 story. May-mid-Sept: S, D $99-$125; each addl $10; under 18 free; higher rates wkends; lower rates rest of yr. Crib free. Pet accepted, some restrictions. TV; cable (premium). Pool. Complimentary continental bkfst. Restaurant adj open 24 hrs. Ck-out noon. Business servs avail. In-rm modem links. Microwaves avail. Cr cds: A, C, D, DS, MC, V. 🄳 💺 💺 ⊠ ⊠ 🐾 SC

Motor Hotel

★ ★ **HARBOR HOUSE.** *No. 28, Pier 21 (77550). 409/763-3321; FAX 409/765-6421; res: 800/874-3721.* 42 rms, 3 story. S $120; D $135; each addl $15; suites $175; under 18 free; package plans; higher rates Mardi Gras. Crib free. Pet accepted. TV; cable (premium). Ck-out noon. Meeting rms. Business servs avail. In-rm modem link. Shopping arcade. Marina for guests' boats. Cr cds: A, C, D, MC, V. 🄳 💺 ⊠ 🐾 SC

Hotel

★ ★ **HOTEL GALVEZ.** *2024 Seawall Blvd (77550).* 409/765-7721; FAX 409/765-5780; res: 800/392-4285. 228 rms, 7 story. S, D $129-$150; suites $175-$350; under 18 free. Valet parking $5. Pet accepted. TV; cable (premium). Pool; wading pool, whirlpool. Restaurant 6:30 am-2 pm, 5:30-10 pm. Bar noon-1 am; entertainment Fri, Sat. Ck-out noon. Meeting rms. Business servs avail. In-rm modem link. Gift shop. Health club privileges. Refrigerator in suites. Cr cds: A, C, D, MC, V. 🄳 🐾 ⊠ ⊠ 🐾 SC

Georgetown *(See also Austin)*

Motel

✔ ★ **COMFORT INN.** *1005 Leander Rd (78628).* 512/863-7504; FAX 512/819-9016. Web www.comfortinn.com. 55 rms. S $54-$72; D $59-$77; each addl $5; under 12 free. Crib free. Pet accepted, some restrictions. TV; cable, VCR avail (movies). Pool. Complimentary continental bkfst. Restaurant nearby. Ck-out noon. Microwaves avail. Cr cds: A, C, D, DS, JCB, MC, V. 🄳 🐾 ⊠ ⊠ 🐾

Graham

Motel

✔ ★ ★ **GATEWAY INN.** *1401 TX 16S, SE of downtown.* 940/549-0222; FAX 940/549-4301. 77 rms, 2 story. S $35; D $36-$40; each addl $4. Pet accepted; $5. TV; cable (premium). Pool; whirlpool. Complimentary coffee in rms. Restaurant 6 am-10 pm. Rm serv. Private club 11 am-midnight, Sat to 1 am. Ck-out noon. Coin lndry. Free airport transportation. Cr cds: A, C, D, DS, MC, V. 🄳 🐾 ⊠ ⊠ 🐾 SC

Granbury *(See also Arlington-Grand Prairie, Fort Worth)*

Motels

★ **BEST WESTERN CLASSIC INN.** *1209 N Plaza Dr.* 817/573-8874. 42 rms. S $59; D $64; each addl $5; under 12 free. Crib $4. Pet accepted, some restrictions. TV; cable (premium). Pool. Complimentary continental bkfst. Restaurant adj open 24 hrs. Ck-out 11 am. Business servs avail. Refrigerators, microwaves. Lake 1/4 mi; swimming beach. Cr cds: A, D, DS, JCB, MC, V. 🄳 🐾 ⊠ ⊠ 🐾 SC

★ **LODGE OF GRANBURY.** *401 E Pearl St.* 817/573-2606; FAX 817/573-2077. 58 suites, 3 story. May-Oct: suites $89-$165; lower rates rest of yr. Pet accepted. TV; cable (premium). Pool; whirlpool. Complimentary coffee in rms. Private club 4 pm-midnight. Ck-out noon. Business servs avail. Lighted tennis. 18-hole golf privileges. Refrigerators, microwaves. Private patios, balconies. Picnic tables. On lake. Cr cds: A, C, D, DS, MC, V.

🄳 🐾 🏊 🕺 🎿 ⊠ ⊠ 🐾 SC

★ ★ **PLANTATION INN.** *1451 E Pearl St.* 817/573-8846; FAX 817/579-0917; res: 800/422-2402. E-mail planinn@hcnews.com; web www.hcnews.com/~planinn. 53 rms, 2 story. S $60, D $65; each addl $5; suites $75-$80; under 6 free. Pet accepted, some restrictions. TV; cable (premium). Pool; wading pool. Complimentary continental bkfst. Ck-out 11 am. Meeting rms. In-rm modem link. Health club privileges. Refrigerators; microwaves avail. Some private patios, balconies. Cr cds: A, C, D, DS, MC, V.

🐾 ⊠ ⊠ 🐾 SC

Greenville *(See also Dallas)*

Motels

✔ ★ ★ **BEST WESTERN INN.** *1216 I-30W (75401).* 903/454-1792. 99 rms, 2 story. S $36-$42; D $45-$49; each addl $4; suites $55-$65; under 12 free. Crib free. Pet accepted. TV; cable (premium), VCR avail (movies $4). Pool. Complimentary continental bkfst. Restaurant adj open 24 hrs. Bar 2 pm-midnight, closed Sun. Ck-out noon. Coin lndry. Meeting rm. Business servs avail. Valet serv. Health club privileges. Cr cds: A, C, D, DS, JCB, MC, V. 🄳 🐾 ⊠ ⊠ 🐾 SC

★ ★ **HOLIDAY INN.** *1215 I-30 (75402), at US 69 Business.* 903/454-7000. 138 rms, 2 story. S, D $48; under 18 free. Crib free. Pet accepted. TV; cable (premium). Pool; whirlpool, sauna. Complimentary coffee. Restaurant 6 am-9 pm. Rm serv. Private club 5 pm-midnight. Ck-out noon. Coin lndry. Meeting rm. Business servs avail. In-rm modem link. Valet serv. Sundries. Cr cds: A, D, DS, MC, V. 🄳 🐾 ⊠ ⊠ 🐾 SC

Harlingen (See also Brownsville, McAllen)

Motels

✔★ **DAYS INN.** *1901 W Tyler (48550). 956/425-1810; FAX 956/425-7227.* 148 rms, 2 story. S $49-$64; D $61-$71; each addl $5; under 18 free. Crib free. Pet accepted. TV; cable (premium). Heated pool. Complimentary coffee in lobby. Restaurant 7 am-2 pm, 5-9 pm. Rm serv. Bar noon-2 am. Ck-out noon. Coin lndry. Meeting rms. Business servs avail. Free airport transportation. Refrigerators avail. Picnic tables. Cr cds: A, C, D, DS, JCB, MC, V. [D] [✎] [≈] [⊠] [🐾] [SC]

★★ **LA QUINTA.** *1002 S US 83 (78550). 956/428-6888; FAX 956/425-5840.* 130 rms, 2 story. S $49-$56; D $59-$66; each addl $8; under 18 free. Crib free. Pet accepted. TV; cable (premium). Pool. Complimentary full bkfst. Restaurant adj open 24 hrs. Ck-out noon. Coin lndry. Meeting rms. Business servs avail. In-rm modem link. Valet serv. Free airport transportation. Cr cds: A, C, D, DS, MC, V. [D] [✎] [≈] [⊠] [🐾] [SC]

Hereford (See also Amarillo)

Motel

✔★★ **BEST WESTERN RED CARPET INN.** *830 W First. 806/364-0540; FAX 806/364-0540.* 90 rms, 2 story. S $36-$40; D $40-$48; each addl $4; under 12 free. Pet accepted. TV; cable. Pool. Complimentary coffee in lobby. Restaurant adj 11 am-9 pm. Ck-out noon. Some refrigerators. Cr cds: A, C, D, DS, ER, JCB, MC, V.
[D] [✎] [≈] [⊠] [🐾] [SC]

Hillsboro (See also Arlington-Grand Prairie, Dallas, Waco)

Motel

★ **RAMADA INN.** *Jct I-35 & TX 22. 254/582-3493; FAX 254/582-2755.* 94 rms, 2 story. S $50-$60; D $55-$65; each addl $8; under 18 free; wkend rates. Crib free. Pet accepted, some restrictions. TV; cable (premium). Pool. Ck-out noon, ck-in 2 pm. Business servs avail. Cr cds: A, C, D, DS, MC, V. [D] [✎] [≈] [⊠] [🐾] [SC]

Houston (See also Galveston)

Motels

(Rates may be higher for sports & special events in Astrodome.)

★★ **DRURY INN.** *1000 N TX 6 (77079), I-10 exit 751, west of downtown. 281/558-7007; FAX 281/558-7007.* 120 rms, 5 story. S $65-$81; D $75-$91; each addl $10; under 18 free; wkend rates. Crib free. Pet accepted. TV; cable (premium). Indoor pool; whirlpool. Complimentary continental bkfst. Restaurant adj 11 am-10 pm. Ck-out noon. Meeting rm. In-rm modem link. Some refrigerators; microwaves avail. Cr cds: A, C, D, DS, MC, V.
[D] [✎] [≈] [⊠] [🐾] [SC]

★★ **DRURY INN.** *1615 West Loop 610 S (77027), in Galleria Area. 713/963-0700; FAX 713/963-0700.* 134 rms, 5 story. S $77-$90; D $87-$100; each addl $10; under 12 free; wkend rates. Crib avail. Pet accepted. TV; cable (premium). Heated indoor/outdoor pool; whirlpool. Complimentary continental bkfst. Ck-out noon. Meeting rm. Business servs avail. In-rm modem link. Health club privileges. Some refrigerators; microwaves avail. Cr cds: A, C, D, DS, MC, V. [D] [✎] [≈] [⊠] [🐾] [SC]

✔★ **FAIRFIELD INN BY MARRIOTT.** *3131 W Loop S (77027), west of downtown. 713/961-1690; FAX 713/627-8434.* 107 rms, 2 story. S, D $44-$79; under 18 free; wkend rates. Crib free. Pet accepted; $225 ($200 refundable). TV; cable (premium). Complimentary continental bkfst. Restaurant adj 6 am-2 pm, 5-11 pm. Rm serv from 5 pm. Bar from 5 pm. Ck-out noon. Business servs avail. In-rm modem link. Valet serv. Coin lndry. Exercise equipt; weight machine, bicycle. Pool; wading pool, whirlpool. Refrigerators, microwaves avail. Cr cds: A, C, D, DS, MC, V. [D] [✎] [≈] [🏋] [⊠] [🐾] [SC]

★ **FAIRFIELD INN BY MARRIOTT.** *10155 I-10E (77029), east of downtown. 713/675-2711; FAX 713/674-6853.* 160 rms, 2 story. S $53; D $58; each addl $5; under 16 free. Crib free. Pet accepted, some restrictions. TV; cable (premium). Complimentary continental bkfst. Restaurant adj 6-2 am. Bar from 11 am. Ck-out noon. Meeting rms. Business servs avail. In-rm modem link. Valet serv. Coin lndry. Pool; wading pool. Picnic tables. Cr cds: A, D, DS, MC, V. [D] [✎] [≈] [⊠] [🐾] [SC]

✔ ★ **HAMPTON INN.** *828 Mercury Dr (I-10 E) (77013), east of downtown.* 713/673-4200; FAX 713/674-6913. 90 rms, 6 story. S $65-$69; D $71-$75; under 18 free; wkend rates. Crib free. Pet accepted; $25 deposit. TV; cable (premium). Pool. Complimentary continental bkfst. Restaurant adj open 24 hrs. Ck-out noon. Coin lndry. Business servs avail. In-rm modem link. Valet serv. Some refrigerators. Cr cds: A, C, D, DS, MC, V.
D ✔ ≈ ⊠ ◼ SC

★ ★ **HOLIDAY INN SELECT-INTERNATIONAL AIRPORT.** *15222 JFK Blvd (77032), near Intercontinental Airport, north of downtown.* 281/449-2311; FAX 281/449-6726. 402 rms, 5 story. S, D $89-$135; each addl $10; under 18 free; wkend, wkly rates. Crib $10. Pet accepted; $125 ($100 refundable). TV; cable (premium), VCR avail. Complimentary coffee in lobby. Restaurant 6 am-10:30 pm. Rm serv. Bar from 11 am. Ck-out noon. Convention facilities. Business servs avail. In-rm modem link. Bellhops. Valet serv. Gift shop. Coin lndry. Free airport transportation. Lighted tennis. Exercise equipt; weight machine, bicycle. Pool; wading pool, poolside serv. Lawn games. Some refrigerators; microwaves avail. Cr cds: A, D, DS, JCB, MC, V. D ✔ ≈ ⊠ 🏃 ✈ ⊠ ◼ SC

★ ★ **LA QUINTA-GREENWAY PLAZA.** *4015 SW Frwy (77027), Weslayan Rd exit, south of downtown.* 713/623-4750; FAX 713/963-0599. 131 rms, 2-3 story. S, D $66-$74; each addl $8; suites $82-$90; under 18 free; family units. Crib free. Pet accepted, some restrictions. TV; cable (premium). Pool. Complimentary continental bkfst. Ck-out noon. Coin lndry. Meeting rms. Microwaves avail. Cr cds: A, C, D, DS, MC, V. D ✔ ≈ ⊠ ◼ SC

★ ★ **LA QUINTA-WEST.** *11113 Katy Frwy (77079), west of downtown.* 713/932-0808; FAX 713/973-2352. 176 rms, 2 story. S $60-$70; D $68-$78; each addl $8; under 18 free. Crib free. Pet accepted. TV; cable (premium). Pool. Complimentary continental bkfst. Restaurant adj open 24 hrs. Ck-out noon. Coin lndry. Meeting rms. In-rm modem link. Microwaves avail. Cr cds: A, C, D, DS, MC, V. D ✔ ≈ ⊠ ◼ SC

✔ ★ **RED ROOF INN.** *15701 Park Ten Place (77084), west of downtown.* 281/579-7200; FAX 281/579-0732. 123 rms, 3 story. S $39.99-$59.99; D $52.99-$69.99; under 17 free; wkend rates. Pet accepted. TV; cable (premium). Complimentary coffee in lobby. Restaurant nearby. Meeting rm. Business servs avail. In-rm modem link. Cr cds: A, C, D, DS, MC, V. D ✔ ⊠ ◼ SC

★ ★ **RESIDENCE INN BY MARRIOTT.** *525 Bay Area Blvd (77058), off I-45, south of downtown.* 281/486-2424; FAX 281/488-8179. 110 kit. units, 2 story. S, D $110-$150; under 16 free; wkend rates. Crib free. Pet accepted; $50 and $6/day. TV; cable (premium), VCR avail. Heated pool. Complimentary continental bkfst; evening refreshments. Complimentary coffee in rms. Restaurant adj 11 am-11 pm. Ck-out noon. Coin lndry. Meeting rm. Business servs avail. In-rm modem link. Exercise equipt; weight machine, stair machine. Microwaves. Grills. Cr cds: A, C, D, DS, JCB, MC, V. D ✔ ≈ 🏃 ⊠ ◼ SC

★ ★ **RESIDENCE INN BY MARRIOTT-ASTRODOME.** *7710 S Main St (77030), S edge of medical center, in Hermann Park Area.* 713/660-7993; FAX 713/660-8019. 285 kit. suites. Kit. suites $95-$125; family rates. Crib free. Pet accepted; $25 and $5/day. TV; cable (premium). Heated pool; whirlpool. Complimentary continental bkfst. Bar. Ck-out noon. Meeting rms. Business servs avail. In-rm modem link. Valet serv. Lawn games. Private patios, balconies. Picnic tables, grills. Cr cds: A, C, D, DS, MC, V. D ✔ ≈ ⊠ ◼ SC

Motor Hotel

★ ★ **RAMADA HOTEL.** *12801 NW Frwy (77040), north of downtown.* 713/462-9977; FAX 713/460-8725. 296 rms, 10 story. S $85; D $95; each addl $10; suites $119-$148; under 12 free; wkend rates. Pet accepted, some restrictions. TV; cable (premium). Pool; poolside serv. Coffee in rms. Restaurant 6 am-10 pm. Rm serv. Bar 4 pm-2 am. Ck-out noon. Meeting rms. In-rm modem link. Bellhops. Valet serv. Sundries. Gift shop. Free bus depot transportation. Exercise equipt; weights, stair machine, sauna. Health club privileges. Some bathrm phones; refrigerator, wet bar in suites. Balconies. Cr cds: A, C, D, DS, MC, V. D ✔ ≈ 🏃 ⊠ ◼ SC

Hotels

★ ★ ★ **DOUBLETREE AT ALLEN CENTER.** *400 Dallas St (77002), downtown.* 713/759-0202; FAX 713/752-2734. 341 rms, 20 story. S $145-$185; D $160-$195; each addl $10; suites $225-$675; under 17 free; wkend rates. Crib free. Pet accepted, some restrictions; $75 refundable. TV; cable (premium). Restaurants 6 am-10 pm. Bar 11-2 am; entertainment Mon-Fri. Ck-out noon. Meeting rms. Business center. In-rm modem link. Concierge. Gift shop. Exercise equipt; weights, treadmill. Elegant hanging tapestries. Cr cds: A, C, D, DS, ER, JCB, MC, V. D ✔ 🏃 ⊠ ◼ SC 🏊

★ ★ ★ **DOUBLETREE GUEST SUITES.** *5353 Westheimer Rd (77056), in Galleria Area.* 713/961-9000; FAX 713/877-8835. 335 kit. suites, 26 story. S, D $210; each addl $20;

2-bedrm suites $310; under 18 free; wkend rates. Crib free. Garage $8, valet parking $12. Pet accepted, some restrictions. TV; cable (premium). Pool; whirlpool, poolside serv. Restaurant 6:30 am-2 pm, 5-10 pm; Sat, Sun 6:30 am-1 pm, 5-10 pm. Rm serv 24 hrs. Bar 5 pm-midnight. Ck-out noon. Business servs avail. In-rm modem link. Coin lndry. Tennis privileges. Exercise equipt; weights, bicycles. Health club privileges. Game rm. Refrigerators. Some balconies. Cr cds: A, C, D, DS, MC, V. 🄳 👣 🛌 🏌 🎿 🔥 🆂🄲

★ ★ ★ ★ **FOUR SEASONS HOTEL-HOUSTON CENTER.** *1300 Lamar St (77010), downtown.* 713/650-1300; FAX 713/652-6293. This toney high-rise with etched-glass doors and thick carpeting is all marble, fresh flowers and antiques. Ten of the 30 stories are occupied by apartments that are home to well-to-do Houstonians. 399 rms, 30 story. S $195-$235; D $225-$265; each addl $25; suites $550-$1,200; under 18 free; wkend rates. Crib free. Pet accepted. Valet & covered parking $13/day. TV; cable (premium), VCR avail. Heated pool; whirlpool, poolside serv. Restaurant 6:30 am-1:30 pm, 6-10 pm. Rm serv 24 hrs. Bar 11-1 am; entertainment. Ck-out 1 pm. Meeting rms. Business center. In-rm modem link. Concierge. Shopping arcade. Beauty shop. Exercise rm; instructor, bicycles, rowing machine, sauna. Massage. Health club privileges. Bathrm phones, minibars; some refrigerators; microwaves avail. Cr cds: A, C, D, ER, JCB, MC, V. 🄳 👣 🛌 🏌 🎿 🔥 🏃

★ ★ **HOLIDAY INN-HOBBY AIRPORT.** *9100 Gulf Frwy (I-45) (77017), near Hobby Airport, south of downtown.* 713/943-7979; FAX 713/943-2160. 288 rms, 10 story. S $99-$115; D $109-$129; each addl $10; under 12 free; wkend rates. Crib avail. Pet accepted. TV; cable (premium). Indoor pool; whirlpool, poolside serv. Restaurant 5:30 am-10 pm. Bar; pianist. Ck-out noon. Meeting rms. Business servs avail. In-rm modem link. Concierge. Gift shop. Free airport transportation. Exercise equipt; weight machine, stair machine, sauna. Game rm. Luxury level. Cr cds: A, C, D, DS, ER, JCB, MC, V. 🄳 👣 🛌 🏌 🎿 🔥 🆂🄲

★ ★ **HOUSTON MEDALLION.** *3000 North Loop W (77092), north of downtown.* 713/688-0100; FAX 713/688-9224; res: 800/688-3000. 382 rms, 10 story. S, D $160-$250; family, wkend rates. Crib free. Pet accepted, some restrictions. TV; cable (premium), VCR avail. Pool; whirlpool, poolside serv. Restaurant 6 am-2 pm, 5 pm-midnight. Rm serv to 1 am. Bar 11 am- midnight. Ck-out 1 pm. Meeting rms. In-rm modem link. Gift shop. Free garage parking. Exercise equipt; weight machine, bicycles, sauna. Refrigerators avail. Luxury level. Cr cds: A, C, D, DS, ER, JCB, MC, V. 🄳 👣 🛌 🏌 🎿 🔥 🆂🄲

★ ★ **HYATT REGENCY-HOUSTON AIRPORT.** *15747 JFK Blvd (77032), north of downtown.* 281/987-1234; FAX 281/590-8461. Web www.hyatt.com. 309 rms, 7 story. S $119-$149; D $144-$174; each addl $10; under 18 free; package plans; wkend rates. Crib free. Pet accepted; $25. TV; cable (premium). Pool; whirlpool, poolside serv. Restaurant 6 am-2 pm, 5-11 pm. Bar 11 am-midnight. Ck-out noon. Meeting rms. Business servs avail. In-rm modem link. Gift shop. Free airport transportation. Exercise equipt; weight machine, stair machine. Cr cds: A, C, D, DS, ER, JCB, MC, V. 🄳 👣 🛌 🏌 🎿 🔥 🆂🄲

★ ★ **MARRIOTT-AIRPORT.** *18700 JFK Blvd (77032), at Intercontinental Airport, north of downtown.* 281/443-2310; FAX 281/443-5294. 566 rms, 3 & 7 story. S, D $134-$149; suites $250-$350; studio rms $150-$250; under 18 free; wkend rates. Crib free. Pet accepted, some restrictions. Valet parking $16. TV; cable (premium). Pool; poolside serv. Restaurant 6 am-10:30 pm. Bar 11-2 am; Sat from 4 pm; Sun noon-midnight. Ck-out 1 pm. Free lndry facilities. Convention facilities. Business center. In-rm modem link. Shopping arcade. Exercise equipt; weights, stair machine. Some bathrm phones, refrigerators. Some private patios. Luxury level. Cr cds: A, C, D, DS, ER, JCB, MC, V. 🄳 👣 🛌 🏌 ✈ 🎿 🔥 🆂🄲 🏃

★ ★ **MARRIOTT-WESTSIDE.** *13210 Katy Frwy (77079), west of downtown.* 281/558-8338; FAX 281/558-4028. 400 rms, 5 story. S, D $139-$160; under 18 free; wkend rates. Crib free. Pet accepted; $25. TV; cable (premium). Pool; whirlpool, poolside serv. Restaurant 6 am-3 pm, 5-11 pm. Bar; pianist Mon-Fri. Ck-out noon. Convention facilities. Business center. In-rm modem link. Gift shop. Free garage parking. Lighted tennis. Exercise equipt; weight machine, rowers. Health club privileges. Cr cds: A, C, D, DS, MC, V. 🄳 👣 🛌 🏌 🎿 🔥 🆂🄲 🏃

★ ★ **RED LION.** *2525 West Loop South (77027), in Galleria area.* 713/961-3000; FAX 713/961-1490. 319 rms, 14 story. S $136-$159; D $146-$169; each addl $10; suites $325-$500; under 18 free; wkend rates. Crib free. Pet accepted; $10. Valet parking $9; garage free. TV; cable (premium), VCR avail. Pool; whirlpool, poolside serv. Coffee in rms. Restaurant 6 am-10 pm. Bar 4 pm-midnight. Ck-out 1 pm. Convention facilities. Business center. In-rm modem link. Gift shop. Exercise equipt; weight machine, treadmill, sauna. Microwaves avail. Luxury level. Cr cds: A, C, D, DS, ER, JCB, MC, V. 🄳 👣 🛌 🏌 🎿 🔥 🆂🄲 🏃

★ ★ ★ **RENAISSANCE.** *6 Greenway Plaza E (77046), west of downtown.* 713/629-1200; FAX 713/629-4702. 389 rms, 20 story. S $129-$159; D $139-$169; each addl $10; suites $300-$750; under 18 free; wknd rates. Crib free. Pet accepted, some restrictions. Garage parking; valet $10, self-park free. TV; cable (premium). Heated pool; poolside serv. Complimentary coffee in rms. Restaurant 6 am-10 pm. Rm serv 24 hrs. Bar 11:30-2 am. Ck-out 1 pm. Convention facilities. Business servs avail. In-rm modem link. Tennis privileges. Exercise equipt; weights, bicycles, sauna. Health club privileges. Bathrm phones; some refrigerators. Cr cds: A, C, D, DS, ER, JCB, MC, V. ▢ ⬟ ⬟ ⬟ ⬟ ⬟ ⬟ SC

★ ★ **SHERATON ASTRODOME.** *8686 Kirby Dr (77054), south of downtown.* 713/748-3221; FAX 713/796-9371. 631 rms, 9 story. S $69-$150; D $69-$165; each addl $10; suites $225-$375; under 18 free. Crib free. Pet accepted, some restrictions. TV; cable (premium). 2 pools; whirlpool. Coffee in rms. Restaurant 6:30 am-10:30 pm. Bar 11-2 am. Ck-out noon. Meeting rms. Business servs avail. In-rm modem link. Valet serv. Gift shop. Exercise equipt; weights, bicycles, sauna. Game rm. Some refrigerators. Cr cds: A, C, D, DS, JCB, MC, V. ▢ ⬟ ⬟ ⬟ ⬟ ⬟ SC

Huntsville *(See also Bryan/College Station)*

Motel

★ **LA QUINTA.** *1407 I-45, exit 116.* 409/295-6454; FAX 409/295-9245. 120 rms, 2 story. S $54-$62; D $61-$69; each addl $7; under 18 free. Crib free. Pet accepted. TV; cable (premium). Pool; wading pool. Complimentary continental bkfst. Ck-out noon. Meeting rms. Some refrigerators. Cr cds: A, C, D, DS, MC, V. ▢ ⬟ ⬟ ⬟ ⬟ ⬟ SC

Motor Hotel

↙★ **UNIVERSITY HOTEL.** *1600 Ave H (77341).* 409/291-2151; FAX 409/294-1683. 95 rms, 4 story. S $37; D $42; each addl $3; under 18 free; monthly rates. Crib free. Pet accepted, some restrictions. TV; cable. Ck-out noon. Meeting rm. Health club privileges. Refrigerators; microwaves avail. On Sam Houston State Univ campus. Totally nonsmoking. Cr cds: A, C, D, MC, V. ▢ ⬟ ⬟ ⬟ SC

Jasper

Motel

↙★ **RAMADA INN.** *239 E Gibson.* 409/384-9021; FAX 409/384-9021, ext. 309. 100 rms. S, D $50-$55; each addl $4. under 18 free. Pet accepted. TV; cable (premium). VCR avail. Pool. Restaurant 6 am-2 pm, 5 pm-9 pm; Sun to 2 pm. Rm serv. Bar 4 pm-midnight. Ck-out noon. Coin lndry. Meeting rms. Business servs avail. In-rm modem link. Valet serv. Some refrigerators. Picnic tables. Cr cds: A, C, D, DS, JCB, MC, V. ▢ ⬟ ⬟ ⬟ ⬟ SC

Jefferson *(See also Marshall)*

Motel

↙★ ★ **BEST WESTERN INN OF JEFFERSON.** *400 S Walcott (US 59).* 903/665-3983. 65 rms, 2 story. S $48-$58; D $54-$64; each addl $6; suites $79-$100; under 16 free; higher rates: Mardi Gras, hol wknds, Pilgrimage, Candlelight Tour. Pet accepted, some restrictions; $20 refundable. TV; cable (premium). Pool. Restaurant adj 6 am-9 pm; Fri, Sat to 10 pm. Ck-out noon. Business servs avail. Some in-rm whirlpools. Cr cds: A, C, D, DS, MC, V. ▢ ⬟ ⬟ ⬟ ⬟ SC

Johnson City *(See also Austin, Fredericksburg)*

Motel

★ **SAVE INN MOTEL.** *107 US 281, jct US 281 & US 290.* 210/868-4044; FAX 210/868-7888. 53 rms, 2 story. S $36-$39.95; D $41-$46; under 6 free; higher rates wknds. Crib $5. Pets accepted; $5. TV; cable (premium). Pool. Continental bkfst. Restaurant 6:30 am-2 pm; wknds to 9 pm. Ck-out 11 am. Microwaves avail. Cr cds: A, C, DS, MC, V. ▢ ⬟ ⬟ ⬟ ⬟ SC

Kerrville *(See also Fredericksburg, San Antonio)*

Motels

★ ★ **BEST WESTERN SUNDAY HOUSE INN.** *2124 Sidney Baker St.* 830/896-1313; FAX 830/896-1336. 97 rms, 2 story. S $60-$70; D $62-$92; each addl $6; studio,

family rms $92-$116; under 12 free. Crib $6. Pet accepted; $10. TV; cable (premium). Pool. Restaurant 6 am-9 pm. Bar 5-9 pm. Ck-out noon. Meeting rms. Cr cds: A, C, D, DS, MC, V.
🏃 ≈ 📷 SC

★ ★ ★ **HOLIDAY INN-Y.O. RANCH HOTEL & CONFERENCE CENTER.** *2033 Sidney Baker, jct I-10, TX 16. 830/257-4440; FAX 830/896-8189.* E-mail holinnyo@ktc.com. 200 rms, 2 story. S $79-$109; D $89-$119; suites $150-$259; each addl $10; parlors $79; family rates; package plans. Crib free. Pet accepted. TV; cable (premium). Pool; wading pool, whirlpool. Coffee in rms. Restaurant 6 am-2 pm, 5-10 pm; Fri, Sat to 11 pm. Rm serv. Bar 4 pm-2 am. Ck-out noon. Meeting rms. Business servs avail. In-rm modem link. Airport transportation. Tennis. 18-hole golf privileges, greens fee $35-$50. Lawn games. Some bathrm phones, refrigerators. Microwaves avail. Private patios, balconies. Western decor; Mexican tile floors. Cr cds: A, C, D, DS, ER, JCB, MC, V.
D 🏃 🏊 🎿 ≈ 🏃 📷 🐾 SC

Resort

★ ★ **INN OF THE HILLS.** *1001 Junction Hwy. 830/895-5000; FAX 830/895-1277; res: 800/292-5690.* Web www.innofthehills.com. 228 units, 2-6 story, 37 kit. units. May-Oct: S $60-$80; D $65-$85; each addl $6; suites $100-$250; kits. $125-$130; under 12 free; wkly rates; lower rates rest of yr. Crib $10. Pet accepted. TV; cable (premium). 6 pools, 2 indoor; wading pool; whirlpool, sauna, poolside serv (summer). Playground. Complimentary coffee in rms. Restaurant 6 am-10 pm. Rm serv. Bar 3 pm-1 am; entertainment, dancing exc Mon. Ck-out noon. Coin lndry. Meeting rms. In-rm modem link. Valet serv. Gift shop. Barber, beauty shop. Free bus depot transportation. Lighted tennis. 18-hole golf privileges, greens fee $75, pro, putting green. Canoes, paddleboats. Exercise rm; instructor, weights, stair machine. Game rm. Microwaves. Some balconies. Cr cds: A, C, D, DS, MC, V.
D 🏃 🚲 🏊 🎿 ≈ 🏃 🐾 📷 SC

Killeen *(See also Temple)*

Motel

★ ★ **LA QUINTA.** *1112 Ft Hood St (76541), US 190 exit TX 95. 254/526-8331; FAX 254/526-0394.* 105 rms, 3 story. No elvtr. S $64-$78; D $71-$78; each addl $7; suites $76-$97; under 18 free. Crib free. Pet accepted, some restrictions. TV; cable (premium). Pool. Complimentary continental bkfst. Restaurant adj open 24 hrs. Ck-out noon. In-rm modem link. Valet serv. Free airport transportation. Health club privileges. Microwaves avail. Cr cds: A, C, D, DS, MC, V. D 🏃 ≈ 📷 🐾 SC

Kingsville *(See also Corpus Christi)*

Motel

✔ ★ **QUALITY INN.** *2502 E Kenedy St. 512/592-5251; FAX 512/592-6197.* 117 rms, 2 story. S $45; D $45-$52; each addl $4; under 12 free. Pet accepted. TV; cable (premium). Pool; wading pool. Complimentary continental breakfast. Ck-out noon. Meeting rms. Business servs avail. Exercise equipt; treadmill, bicycle. Refrigerators. Cr cds: A, C, D, DS, JCB, MC, V. D 🏃 ≈ 📷 🐾 SC 🏃

Laredo

Motels

✔ ★ **BEST WESTERN FIESTA INN.** *5240 San Bernardo (78041). 956/723-3603; FAX 956/724-7697.* 150 rms, 2 story. S $49-$65; D $55-$65; each addl $10; suites $65; under 12 free. Crib free. Pet accepted; some restrictions. TV; cable (premium). Pool. Complimentary continental bkfst. Restaurant adj open 24 hrs. Ck-out noon. Meeting rms. Business servs avail. Coin lndry. Free airport transportation. Some refrigerators. Cr cds: A, C, D, DS, MC, V. D 🏃 📷 🐾 SC

✔ ★ **LA QUINTA.** *3610 Santa Ursula Ave (78040). 956/722-0511; FAX 956/723-6642.* 152 rms, 2 story. S $66-$73; D $76-$86; each addl $10; suites $76-$96; under 18 free. Crib free. Pet accepted. TV; cable (premium). Pool. Complimentary continental bkfst. Restaurant adj open 24 hrs. Ck-out noon. Business servs avail. In-rm modem link. Cr cds: A, C, D, DS, MC, V. D 🏃 ≈ 📷 🐾 SC

Hotel

★ ★ **HOLIDAY INN ON THE RIO GRANDE.** *1 S Main St (78040). 956/722-2411; FAX 956/722-4578.* 207 rms, 15 story. S $82-$88; D $88-$98; each addl $10; under 19 free. Crib avail. Pet accepted. TV; cable (premium). Complimentary coffee in rms. Restaurant 6 am-10 pm. Bar 11 am-11 pm. Ck-out noon. Coin lndry. Meeting rms. Business servs avail.

In-rm modem link. Free airport transportation. Refrigerators avail. On river, overlooking Mexico. Cr cds: A, C, D, DS, MC, V. ⎡D⎤ 🐾 ⌦ ⍐ ⍈ SC

Longview *(See also Marshall, Tyler)*

Motels

★ ★ **HOLIDAY INN.** *3119 Estes Pkwy (75602), I-20 Exit 596. 903/758-0700; FAX 903/758-8705.* 193 rms, 2-4 story. S, D $69-$75; each addl $7; suites $77-$175; under 18 free; wkend rates. Crib free. Pet accepted, some restrictions. TV; cable (premium). Indoor/outdoor pool; whirlpool, poolside serv. Restaurant 6 am-2 pm, 5:30-10 pm. Rm serv. Private club 4 pm-2 am, closed Sun. Ck-out 1 pm. Coin lndry. Meeting rms. Business servs avail. In-rm modem link. Sundries. Free airport transportation. Game rm. Holidome. Cr cds: A, C, D, DS, MC, V. ⎡D⎤ 🐾 ⌦ ⍐ ⍈ SC

★ ★ **LA QUINTA INN.** *502 S Access Rd (75602), I-20 at Estes Pkwy. 903/757-3663; FAX 903/753-3780.* 106 rms, 2 story. S $57-$60; D $60-$71; each addl $6; under 18 free. Crib free. Pet accepted, some restrictions. TV; cable (premium). Pool. Complimentary continental bkfst. Complimentary coffee in lobby. Restaurant adj open 24 hrs. Ck-out noon. Meeting rms. Business servs avail. In-rm modem link. Valet serv. Cr cds: A, C, D, DS, MC, V. ⎡D⎤ 🐾 ⌦ ⍐ ⍈ SC

Lubbock *(See also Plainview)*

Motels

✔ ★ ★ **LA QUINTA MOTOR INN.** *601 Avenue Q (79401). 806/763-9441; FAX 806/747-9325.* 137 rms, 2 story. S $64-$76; D $69-$81; each addl $5; under 18 free. Crib free. Pet accepted. TV; cable. Pool. Complimentary continental bkfst. Restaurant adj open 24 hrs. Ck-out noon. Business servs avail. In-rm modem link. Cr cds: A, C, D, DS, MC, V. ⎡D⎤ 🐾 ⌦ ⍐ ⍈ SC

★ ★ **RESIDENCE INN BY MARRIOTT.** *2551 S Loop 289 (79423), 3 mi S on Loop 289, exit Indiana. 806/745-1963; FAX 806/748-1183.* 80 kit. suites, 2 story. S $85; D $85-$125; wkly rates. Pet accepted. TV; cable (premium). Heated pool; whirlpools. Complimentary continental bkfst. Ck-out noon. Coin lndry. Meeting rms. Business servs avail. In-rm modem link. Valet serv. Free airport transportation. Tennis. Refrigerators. Private patios, balconies. Picnic tables, grills. Cr cds: A, C, D, DS, JCB, MC, V. ⎡D⎤ 🐾 🏃 ⌦ ⍐ ⍈ SC

Motor Hotel

★ ★ ★ **HOLIDAY INN.** *3201 Loop 289 S (79423), at Indiana Ave. 806/797-3241; FAX 806/793-1203.* 202 rms, 2 story. S, D $59-$89.50; each addl $10; suites $99-$225; under 18 free; seasonal rates. Crib free. Pet accepted. TV; cable (premium). Indoor pool; wading pool. Restaurant 6 am-10 pm. Rm serv. Bars 4 pm-midnight; Fri, Sat to 2 am. Ck-out noon. Coin lndry. Meeting rms. Business servs avail. In-rm modem link. Bellhops. Free airport transportation. Health club privileges. Cr cds: A, C, D, DS, ER, JCB, MC, V. ⎡D⎤ 🐾 ⌦ ⍐ ⍈ SC

Hotel

★ ★ **HOLIDAY INN-CIVIC CENTER.** *801 Avenue Q (79401). 806/763-1200; FAX 806/763-2656.* 295 rms, 6 story. S $76; D $86; each addl $10; suites $90; under 19 free. Crib free. Pet accepted. TV; cable. Indoor pool; whirlpool, poolside serv. Restaurant 6 am-10 pm. Bar 4 pm-2 am; Sun noon-midnight. Ck-out noon. Coin lndry. Convention facilities. Business servs avail. Free airport transportation. Exercise equipt; weight machines, bicycles, sauna. Cr cds: A, C, D, DS, ER, JCB, MC, V. ⎡D⎤ 🐾 ⌦ 🏋 ⍈ SC

Lufkin *(See also Nacogdoches)*

Motels

✔ ★ **DAYS INN.** *2130 S 1st St, I-59S. 409/639-3301; FAX 409/634-4266.* 126 rms, 2 story. S $46; D $42-$47; each addl $5; suites $65-$75; under 18 free; wkend rates. Crib free. Pet accepted, some restrictions. TV; cable (premium). Pool; wading pool. Complimentary continental bkfst. Restaurant 6 am-2 pm, 5-9 pm; closed Sun. Rm serv. Bar 5 pm-midnight, Sat to 1 am, closed Sun. Ck-out noon. Coin lndry. Meeting rms. Business servs avail. Some refrigerators. Whirlpool in some suites. Cr cds: A, C, D, DS, MC, V. ⎡D⎤ 🐾 ⌦ ⍐ ⍈ SC

★ ★ **HOLIDAY INN.** *4306 S 1st St. 409/639-3333; FAX 409/639-3382.* 102 rms, 2 story. S $55; D $60; each addl $7; suites $65-$75; under 19 free; wkend rates (min stay required). Crib free. Pet accepted, some restrictions; $5. TV; cable (premium). Pool; poolside serv. Restaurant 6 am-2 pm, 5-10 pm. Rm serv. Bar. Ck-out noon. Coin lndry. Meeting rms. Business servs avail. In-rm modem link. Sundries. Valet serv. Free airport transportation. Health club privileges. Some refrigerators; minibar in suites. Cr cds: A, C, D, DS, ER, JCB, MC, V. [D] 🐾 🏊 🦵 🔥 [SC]

✔★★ **LA QUINTA.** *2119 S 1st St. 409/634-3351; FAX 409/634-9475.* 106 rms, 2 story. S $51-$58; D $58-$65; each addl $7; suites $67; under 18 free. Crib free. Pet accepted, some restrictions. TV; cable. Pool. Complimentary continental bkfst. Restaurant adj. Ck-out noon. Meeting rms. Business servs avail. In-rm modem link. Valet serv. Cr cds: A, C, D, DS, MC, V. [D] 🐾 🏊 🦵 🔥 [SC]

Marshall *(See also Longview; also see Shreveport, LA)*

Motel

✔★★ **DAYS INN.** *4911 E End Blvd. 903/927-1718; FAX 903/927-1747.* 46 rms, 2 story. S $45-$50; D $50-$60; each addl $4; suites $65-$75; under 16 free. Crib free. Pet accepted. TV; cable (premium). Pool. Complimentary continental bkfst. Restaurant adj 10 am-9 pm. Ck-out 11 am. Sundries. Valet serv. Some refrigerators. Cr cds: A, C, D, DS, MC, V. [D] 🐾 🏊 🦵 🔥 [SC]

McAllen *(See also Harlingen)*

Motels

(Rates may be higher dove-hunting season)

★ **DRURY INN.** *612 W US 83 (78501). 956/687-5100.* 89 units. S $65-$75; D $75-$80; each addl $10; under 18 free. Crib free. Pet accepted, some restrictions. TV; cable (premium), VCR avail. Pool. Complimentary continental bkfst. Restaurant adj. Ck-out noon. Meeting rm. Business servs avail. In-rm modem link. Refrigerator in suites. Cr cds: A, C, D, DS, MC, V. [D] 🐾 🏊 🦵 🔥 [SC]

★★ **HAMPTON INN.** *300 W US 83 (78501). 956/682-4900; FAX 956/682-6823.* 91 rms, 4 story. S $62-$72; D $67-$77; under 18 free. Crib free. Pet accepted. TV; cable. Pool. Complimentary continental breakfast. Restaurant adj. Ck-out noon. Business servs avail. In-rm modem link. Near airport. Cr cds: A, C, D, DS, MC, V. [D] 🐾 🏊 🦵 🔥 [SC]

✔★★ **LA QUINTA MOTOR INN.** *1100 S 10th St (78501), near Miller Intl Airport. 956/687-1101; FAX 956/687-9265.* 120 rms, 3 story. S $59-$65; D $61-$66; each addl $5; under 18 free. Crib free. Pet accepted. TV; cable. Pool. Complimentary continental bkfst. Restaurant adj open 24 hrs. Bar 11-2 am. Ck-out 1 pm. Meeting rm. Business servs avail. In-rm modem link. Free airport, bus depot transportation. Convention Center adj. Cr cds: A, C, D, DS, MC, V. [D] 🐾 🏊 ✈ 🦵 🔥 [SC]

Motor Hotel

★★ **HOLIDAY INN-CIVIC CENTER.** *200 W US 83 (78501), at 2nd St, near Miller Intl Airport. 956/686-2471; FAX 956/686-2038.* 173 rms, 2 story. S $65-$85; D $75-$95; each addl $10; under 18 free. Crib free. Pet accepted, some restrictions. TV; cable (premium), VCR avail. 2 pools, 1 indoor; whirlpool. Coffee in rms. Restaurant 6 am-10 pm. Rm serv. Bar noon-2 am; Sun to midnight. Ck-out noon. Coin lndry. Meeting rms. Business servs avail. In-rm modem link. Bellhops. Free airport transportation. Lighted tennis. Exercise equipt; bicycle, stair machine, sauna. Game rm. Rec rm. Cr cds: A, C, D, DS, JCB, MC, V. [D] 🐾 🏋 🏊 🎾 ✈ 🦵 🔥 [SC]

Midland *(See also Big Spring, Odessa)*

Motels

★★ **BEST WESTERN.** *3100 W Wall (79701). 915/699-4144; FAX 915/699-7639.* 200 rms, 3 story. S, D $59; under 12 free. Crib $6. Pet accepted, some restrictions. TV; cable (premium). Indoor pool. Restaurant 6-9 am, 5-9 pm. Rm serv. Bar 4 pm-midnight. Ck-out noon. Meeting rms. Business servs avail. Free airport transportation. Exercise equipt; bicycle, treadmill. Cr cds: A, C, D, DS, MC, V. [D] 🐾 🏊 🏋 🦵 🔥 [SC]

★★ **HOLIDAY INN.** *4300 W Wall (79703). 915/697-3181; FAX 915/694-7754.* 252 rms, 2 story, 31 suites. S $55-$71; D $65-$79; each addl $10; suite $132-$159; under 18 free. Crib free. Pet accepted. TV; cable (premium). Indoor pool; whirlpool. Restaurant 6 am-9 pm. Rm serv. Bar 4-11 pm. Ck-out noon. Coin lndry. Meeting rms. Business center. Free airport transportation. Exercise equipt; weight machine, bicycles, sauna. Holidome. Cr cds: A, C, D, DS, JCB, MC, V. [D] 🐾 🏊 🏋 🦵 🦽

★ ★ **LA QUINTA.** *4130 W Wall (79703). 915/697-9900; FAX 915/689-0617.* 146 rms, 2 story. S $55-$62; D $62-$69; under 18 free. Crib free. Pet accepted. TV; cable (premium). Pool. Complimentary continental bkfst. Ck-out noon. Coin lndry. Business servs avail. Valet serv. Cr cds: A, C, D, DS, MC, V. 🄳 ⮐ ≈ ⊠ 🐾 SC

★ ★ **LEXINGTON HOTEL SUITES.** *1003 S Midkiff (79701). 915/697-3155; FAX 915/699-2017.* 182 kit. units, 2 story. 1-bedrm $54-$65; 2-bedrm $80-$108. Crib free. Pet accepted, some restrictions; $75 deposit. TV; cable (premium). Heated pool; whirlpool. Complimentary continental bkfst. Restaurant nearby. Ck-out noon. Coin lndry. Business servs avail. Airport transportation. Cr cds: A, C, D, DS, MC, V. 🄳 ⮐ ≈ ⊠ 🐾 SC

Hotel

★ ★ ★ **HILTON.** *117 W Wall (79701), Wall & Loraine Sts. 915/683-6131; FAX 915/683-0958.* 249 rms, 2-11 story. S, D $125; each addl $10; suites $190-$265; wkend rates. Crib $10. Pet accepted, some restrictions; $100 refundable. TV; cable (premium), VCR avail. Pool; whirlpool, poolside serv. Restaurant 6:30 am-10 pm. Bar 4 pm-midnight; Sun from 7 pm. Ck-out noon. Meeting rms. Business servs avail. In-rm modem link. Gift shop. Free airport transportation. Exercise equipt; bicycles, stair machines. Health club privileges. Luxury level. Cr cds: A, C, D, DS, MC, V. 🄳 ⮐ ≈ 🕴 ⊠ 🐾 SC

Nacogdoches *(See also Lufkin)*

Motel

★ ★ **LA QUINTA.** *3215 South St. 409/560-5453; FAX 409/560-4372.* 106 rms, 2 story. S $48-$56; D $54-$62; each addl $6; suites $65-$77; under 18 free. Crib free. Pet accepted, some restrictions. TV; cable (premium). Pool. Complimentary continental bkfst. Complimentary coffee in lobby. Restaurant adj open 24 hrs. Ck-out noon. Meeting rms. Business servs avail. In-rm modem link. Valet serv. Cr cds: A, C, D, DS, MC, V. 🄳 ⮐ ≈ ⊠ 🐾 SC

Hotel

★ **FREDONIA.** *200 N Fredonia St. 409/564-1234; FAX 409/564-1234, ext. 240.* 113 rms, 6 story. S $54-$64; D $59-$69; each addl $10; suites $150-$175; under 18 free. Crib free. Pet accepted. TV; cable. Pool; poolside serv. Complimentary full bkfst. Restaurant 6:30 am-2 pm, 5:30-9 pm. Private club 5 pm-midnight; closed Sun. Ck-out 1 pm. Meeting rms. Business center. In-rm modem link. Gift shop. Some private patios. Cr cds: A, C, D, DS, MC, V. 🄳 ⮐ ≈ ⊠ 🐾 SC 🛫

New Braunfels *(See also San Antonio, San Marcos)*

Motel

★ **HOLIDAY INN.** *1051 I-35 E (78130), exit 189. 830/625-8017; FAX 830/625-3130.* 140 rms, 2 story. Memorial Day-Labor Day: S, D $85; each addl $5; suites $125-$150; under 18 free; lower rates rest of yr. Crib free. Pet accepted; $15. TV; cable (premium). Pool; wading pool. Complimentary coffee in rms. Restaurant 6-11 am, 5:30-10 pm. Rm serv. Bar 4 pm-midnight. Ck-out noon. Meeting rms. Business servs avail. In-rm modem link. Coin lndry. Exercise equipt; weight machine, bicycles. Cr cds: A, C, D, DS, JCB, MC, V. 🄳 ⮐ ≈ 🕴 ⊠ 🐾 SC

Motor Hotel

★ **BEST WESTERN INN & SUITES.** *1493 I-35N (78130). 830/625-7337.* 60 rms, 2 story, 20 suites. S, D $39-$89; each addl $5; suites $79-$99; under 18 free. Crib free. Pet accepted; $20 deposit. TV; cable (premium). Complimentary continental bkfst. Restaurant nearby. Ck-out noon. Meeting rms. Business servs avail. Coin lndry. Pool; wading pool. Refrigerator, microwave in suites. Cr cds: A, D, DS, MC, V. ⮐ ≈ ⊠ 🐾 SC

Odessa *(See also Midland)*

Motels

★ ★ **BEST WESTERN GARDEN OASIS.** *110 W I-20 (79761), at Grant Ave. 915/337-3006; FAX 915/332-1956.* 118 rms, 2 story. S, D $48-$58; each addl $5; suites $85-$95; under 12 free. Crib $8. Pet accepted, some restrictions. TV; cable (premium), VCR avail (movies). Indoor pool; whirlpool, sauna, poolside serv. Restaurant 6 am-10 pm. Rm serv. Ck-out noon. Meeting rms. Business servs avail. Lndry facilities. Gift shop. Free airport, bus depot transportation. Cr cds: A, C, D, DS, ER, JCB, MC, V. 🄳 ⮐ ≈ ⊠ 🐾 SC

★ ★ **HOLIDAY INN CENTRE.** *6201 E I-20 (79760), exit loop 338. 915/362-2311; FAX 915/362-9810.* 244 rms, 3 story. S $64-$69; D $74-$79; suites $87-$150. Crib free. Pet accepted, some restrictions. TV; cable. Indoor/outdoor pool; whirlpool, poolside serv. Restaurant 6 am-9 pm. Rm serv. Bar 4-11 pm. Coin lndry. Business servs avail. In-rm modem link. Bellhops. Valet serv. Free airport, bus depot transportation. Putting green. Exercise equipt; weight machines, bicycles, sauna. Microwave in suites. Cr cds: A, C, D, DS, MC, V.
D ⟨⟩ ≋ 🏋 ⊠ 🔥 SC

★ ★ **LA QUINTA.** *5001 E US 80 (79761). 915/333-2820; FAX 915/333-4208.* 122 rms. S $55; D $62; each addl $7; under 18 free. Crib free. Pet accepted, some restrictions. TV; cable (premium). Pool. Restaurant adj open 24 hrs. Ck-out noon. Business servs avail. Picnic tables, grills. Cr cds: A, C, D, DS, MC, V. D ⟨⟩ ≋ ⊠ 🔥 SC

Orange (See also Beaumont, Port Arthur)

Motels

✔ ★ ★ **BEST WESTERN.** *2630 I-10, exits 876 & 877. 409/883-6616; FAX 409/883-3427.* 60 rms, 2 story. S $45-$53; D $51-$53; each addl $5; under 18 free. Crib avail. Pet accepted, some restrictions. TV; cable (premium). Pool. Complimentary coffee. Restaurant adj 6 am-10 pm; Sun 6 am-9 pm. Ck-out noon. In-rm modem link. Some refrigerators. Near Orange County Airport. Cr cds: A, C, D, DS, MC, V. ⟨⟩ ≋ ⊠ 🔥 SC

★ ★ **RAMADA INN.** *2610 I-10. 409/883-0231; FAX 409/883-8839.* 125 rms, 2 story. S, D $66; each addl $8; studio rms $66-$76; suites $73-$135; under 18 free. Crib free. Pet accepted. TV; cable (premium). Pool; wading pool. Restaurant 6 am-10 pm. Rm serv. Bar 4 pm-2 am; Sat from 5 pm; closed Sun; entertainment Fri, Sat. Ck-out noon. Meeting rms. Business servs avail. In-rm modem link. Some refrigerators, microwaves. Wet bar in some suites. Cr cds: A, C, D, DS, MC, V. D ⟨⟩ ≋ ⊠ 🔥 SC

Palestine

Motel

✔ ★ **BEST WESTERN PALESTINE INN.** *1601 W Palestine Ave (75801). 903/723-4655; FAX 903/723-2519.* 66 rms, 2 story. S $39.95; D $46; under 16 free. Crib $3. Pet accepted. TV; cable (premium). Pool. Playground. Restaurant 6 am-9 pm. Ck-out 1 pm. Business servs avail. In-rm modem link. Cr cds: A, C, D, DS, MC, V.
D ⟨⟩ ≋ ⊠ 🔥 SC

Paris

Motel

★ ★ **HOLIDAY INN.** *3560 NE Loop 286. 903/785-5545; FAX 903/785-9510.* 124 rms, 2 story. S $69; D $75-$79; each addl $6; under 19 free; wkend rates. Crib free. Pet accepted. TV; cable (premium). Pool; whirlpool. Coffee in rms. Restaurant 6 am-1 pm, 5-10 pm. Rm serv. Private club. Ck-out noon. Coin lndry. Meeting rms. Business servs avail. In-rm modem link. Valet serv. Cr cds: A, C, D, DS, ER, JCB, MC, V.
D ⟨⟩ ≋ ⊠ 🔥 SC

Plainview (See also Lubbock)

Motels

★ ★ **BEST WESTERN-CONESTOGA.** *600 N I-27. 806/293-9454.* 83 rms, 2 story. S $44; D $51; each addl $7; suites $90; under 12 free. Crib free. Pet accepted, some restrictions. TV; cable (premium), VCR avail (movies). Pool. Complimentary continental bkfst. Restaurant adj open 24 hrs. Private club 5 pm-midnight; closed Sun. Ck-out noon. Meeting rm. Business servs avail. In-rm modem link. Some bathrm phones. Some refrigerators. Cr cds: A, C, D, DS, MC, V. D ⟨⟩ ≋ ⊠ 🔥 SC

✔ ★ ★ **HOLIDAY INN EXPRESS.** *4005 Olton Rd. 806/293-4181.* 95 rms, 2 story. S $48-$50; D $56-$60; each addl $8; under 12 free; higher rates pheasant season. Crib free. Pet accepted. TV; cable (premium), VCR avail (movies). Pool. Complimentary continental bkfst. Ck-out noon. Meeting rms. Business servs avail. In-rm modem link. Some refrigerators. Picnic tables. Cr cds: A, C, D, DS, MC, V. D ⟨⟩ ≋ ⊠ 🔥 SC

Port Aransas (See Corpus Christi, Rockport)

Motel

★ **DAYS INN SUITES.** *(US 361E, Aransas Pass 78336) 6 mi N on US 361. 512/758-7375.* 32 rms, 18 suites. S $55-$100; D $65-$100; each addl $8-$10; suites $70-$150. Crib free. Pet accepted, some restrictions. TV; cable. Pool. Complimentary continental bkfst. Restaurant nearby. Ck-out noon. Meeting rms. Business servs avail. In-rm modem link. Exercise equipt; bicycles, treadmill. Refrigerators. Cr cds: A, C, D, DS, MC, V.

Port Arthur (See also Beaumont, Orange)

Motor Hotel

★ ★ **RAMADA INN.** *3801 TX 73 (77643). 409/962-9858; FAX 409/962-3685.* 125 rms, 2 story. S, D $57-$73; each addl $8; suites $120-$135; studio rms $63-$71; under 18 free; wkend rates. Pet accepted, some restrictions. TV; cable (premium). Pool; wading pool. Restaurant 6 am-10 pm. Rm serv. Bar 4 pm-2 am. Ck-out noon. Meeting rms. Business servs avail. Free airport transportation. Lighted tennis. Some refrigerators. Cr cds: A, C, D, DS, MC, V.

Port Lavaca (See also Victoria)

Motel

★ **DAYS INN.** *2100 N TX 35 Bypass. 512/552-4511.* 99 rms, 2 story. S $51.05; D $55.05; each addl $6; suites $72-$78; under 12 free. Crib free. Pet accepted. TV. Pool. Complimentary continental bkfst. Restaurant 6:30 am-2 pm. Bar 5 pm-midnight Mon-Fri. Ck-out noon. Coin lndry. Meeting rms. Business servs avail. In-rm modem link. Some refrigerators. Cr cds: A, C, D, DS, MC, V.

Rockport (See also Corpus Christi)

Motel

✔ ★ **BEST WESTERN INN BY THE BAY.** *(3902 N TX 35, Fulton 78358) N on US 35N. 512/729-8351; FAX 512/729-0950.* 72 rms, 2 story. S $50-$58; D $60-$68; under 11 free. Pet accepted. TV; cable (premium). Pool. Complimentary continental bkfst. Restaurant nearby. Ck-out 11 am. Coin lndry. Some refrigerators. Cr cds: A, C, D, DS, MC, V.

San Angelo

Motels

★ ★ **BEST WESTERN INN OF THE WEST.** *415 W Beauregard (76903). 915/653-2995.* 75 rms, 3 story. S $43; D $55; each addl $6; under 12 free. Crib $6. Pet accepted, some restrictions. TV; cable (premium), VCR avail. Indoor pool. Restaurant 6 am-8 pm. Rm serv. Ck-out noon. Meeting rms. Business servs avail. In-rm modem link. Sun deck. Cr cds: A, C, D, DS, MC, V.

✔ ★ **EL PATIO.** *1901 W Beauregard St (76901). 915/655-5711; res: 800/677-7735; FAX 915/653-2717.* 100 rms, 2 story. S $34; D $38; under 12 free; wkly rates; higher rates rodeo. Crib avail. Pet accepted; $5/day. TV; cable (premium), VCR avail. Complimentary coffee in lobby. Ck-out noon. Business servs avail. Pool. Cr cds: A, DS, MC, V.

★ ★ **INN OF THE CONCHOS.** *2021 N Bryant (76903). 915/658-2811; FAX 915/653-7560.* Web www.inn-of-the-conchos.com. 125 rms, 2 story. S $40-$44; D $44-$50; each addl $6; suites $85-$100; under 12 free. Crib $6. Pet accepted, some restrictions. TV; cable (premium). Pool. Restaurant adj 6 am-9 pm; Sun 7 am-2 pm. Rm serv. Bar 4 pm-2 am. Ck-out noon. Meeting rms. Sundries. Grill. Cr cds: A, C, D, DS, ER, MC, V.

★ ★ **LA QUINTA.** *2307 Loop 306 (76904). 915/949-0515; FAX 915/944-1187.* 170 rms, 2 story. S $59-$66; D $66-$81; each addl $7; suites $74; under 18 free. Crib free. Pet accepted, some restrictions. TV; cable (premium). Pool. Complimentary continental bkfst. Ck-out noon. Guest lndry. Meeting rms. Business servs avail. In-rm modem link. Health club privileges. Cr cds: A, C, D, DS, MC, V.

Hotel

★ ★ ★ **HOLIDAY INN-CONVENTION CENTER.** *441 Rio Concho Dr (76903). 915/658-2828; FAX 915/658-8741.* 148 rms, 6 story. S, D $57-$81; each addl $8; suites $140-$160; under 12 free. Crib free. Pet accepted, some restrictions. TV; cable (premium). Indoor pool; whirlpool, poolside serv. Restaurant 6:30 am-2 pm, 5:30-10 pm. Bar 4-11:30 pm. Ck-out noon. Meeting rms. Business servs avail. Some refrigerators. Microwaves in suites. Cr cds: A, C, D, DS, JCB, MC, V. [D] [⌨] [≋] [⊠] [⊠] [SC]

San Antonio (See also New Braunfels)

Motels

★ ★ **HAWTHORN SUITES.** *4041 Bluemel Rd (78240), at I-10, Huebner exit. 210/561-9660; FAX 210/561-9663.* 128 kit. suites, 2 story. S, D $89-$138; under 12 free; wkly, wkend rates. Crib free. Pet accepted, some restrictions; $50. TV; cable (premium). Heated pool; whirlpool. Complimentary bkfst; evening refreshments. Ck-out noon. Coin lndry. Meeting rm. Business servs avail. In-rm modem link. Valet serv. Health club privileges. Microwaves; fireplace in most suites. Private patios, balconies. Picnic table. Cr cds: A, C, D, DS, MC, V. [D] [⌨] [≋] [⊠] [⊠] [SC]

★ ★ **LA QUINTA-INGRAM PARK.** *7134 NW Loop I-410 (78238). 210/680-8883; FAX 210/681-3877.* Web www.laquinta.com. 195 rms, 3 story. S $59-$76; D $69-$76; suites $80-$122; under 18 free. Crib free. Pet accepted, some restrictions. TV; cable (premium). Pool. Complimentary continental bkfst. Restaurant adj open 24 hrs. Ck-out noon. Meeting rms. In-rm modem link. Refrigerator, microwave in suites. Cr cds: A, C, D, DS, MC, V. [D] [⌨] [≋] [⊠] [⊠] [SC]

★ ★ **LA QUINTA-MARKET SQUARE.** *900 Dolorosa St (78207), downtown. 210/271-0001; FAX 210/228-0663.* 124 rms, 2 story. S, D $84-$91; each addl $10; suites $126; under 18 free; higher rates Fiesta wk. Crib free. Pet accepted, some restrictions. TV; cable (premium). Pool. Continental bkfst. Complimentary coffee. Restaurant opp open 24 hrs. Ck-out noon. Business servs avail. In-rm modem link. Valet serv. Cr cds: A, C, D, DS, MC, V. [D] [⌨] [≋] [⊠] [⊠] [SC]

Motor Hotels

★ ★ **DRURY INN AND SUITES.** *8811 Jones Maltsberger Rd (78216), near Intl Airport, north of downtown. 210/366-4300; FAX 210/308-8100.* E-mail mail@druryinns.com; web www.drury-inns.com. 139 rms, 6 story. S $60-$77; D $67-$87; each addl $10; under 18 free. Crib free. Pet accepted, some restrictions. TV; cable (premium). Pool; whirlpool. Complimentary continental bkfst. Restaurant opp 6 am-midnight. Ck-out noon. Meeting rm. Business servs avail. In-rm modem link. Free airport transportation. Refrigerators, microwaves. Picnic tables. Cr cds: A, C, D, DS, MC, V. [D] [⌨] [≋] [✈] [⊠] [⊠] [SC]

★ ★ **EXECUTIVE GUESTHOUSE.** *12828 US 281N (78216), 12 mi N on US 281, exit Bitters, north of downtown. 210/494-7600; FAX 210/545-4314; res: 800/362-8700.* 124 rms, 4 story. S $99-$170; D $109-$180; each addl $10; under 12 free; wkend rates. Crib free. Pet accepted, some restrictions; $100 ($50 refundable). TV; cable (premium). Indoor pool. Complimentary full bkfst; evening refreshments. Complimentary coffee in rms. Ck-out noon. Meeting rms. In-rm modem link. Valet serv. Free airport transportation. Exercise equipt; weight machine, bicycle, sauna. Bathrm phones, refrigerators, microwaves; some in-rm whirlpools. Atrium. Cr cds: A, C, D, DS, MC, V. [D] [⌨] [≋] [✈] [⊠] [⊠] [SC]

★ ★ **HOLIDAY INN EXPRESS-AIRPORT.** *91 NE Loop I-410 (78216), near Intl Airport, north of downtown. 210/308-6700.* 154 rms, 10 story. S $75-$85; D $85-$99; under 19 free. Crib free. Pet accepted, some restrictions. TV; cable (premium). Pool. Complimentary continental bkfst. Restaurant adj 11 am-midnight. Ck-out noon. Meeting rms. Business servs avail. In-rm modem link. Coin lndry. Free airport transportation. Microwaves avail. Cr cds: A, C, D, DS, MC, V. [D] [⌨] [✈] [⊠] [⊠] [SC]

★ ★ **PEAR TREE INN.** *143 NE Loop 410 (78216), at I-410 & Airport Blvd, near Intl Airport, north of downtown. 210/366-9300.* 125 rms, 4 story. S $49.95-$56.95; D $57.95-$64.95; each addl $8; under 18 free. Crib free. Pet accepted, some restrictions. TV; cable (premium). Pool. Complimentary bkfst. Restaurant adj 6 am-midnight. Serv bar. Ck-out noon. Coin lndry. Meeting rms. Business servs avail. In-rm modem link. Free airport transportation. Some refrigerators; microwaves avail. Cr cds: A, C, D, DS, MC, V. [D] [⌨] [≋] [✈] [⊠] [⊠] [SC]

✔ **RED ROOF INN.** *333 Wolfe Rd (78216), near Intl Airport, north of downtown. 210/340-4055.* 135 rms, 3 story. S, D $39.95-$99; each addl $5; under 18 free. Crib free. Pet accepted. TV; cable (premium). Complimentary continental bkfst. Restaurant nearby. Ck-out noon. Meeting rms. Business servs avail. In-rm modem link. Free airport transportation. Cr cds: A, C, D, DS, MC, V. [D] 🏃 ✈ 🏊 🐾 SC

Hotels

★ ★ ★ **HILTON PALACIO DEL RIO.** *200 S Alamo St (78205), on Riverwalk.* 210/222-1400; FAX 210/270-0761. 481 rms, 22 story. S $155-$205; D $175-$225; each addl $20; suites $425-$650; package plans. Crib free. Pet accepted, some restrictions. Garage $8, valet $18. TV; cable (premium), VCR avail. Pool; whirlpool, poolside serv. Complimentary coffee in rms. Restaurant 6:30-1 am. Bars 11:30-1:30 am; wkends to 2 am; entertainment. Ck-out 11 am. Convention facilities. Business servs avail. In-rm modem link. Concierge. Gift shop. Tennis privileges. Golf privileges. Exercise equipt; weights, bicycles. Some bathrm phones, refrigerators; microwaves avail. Balconies. Luxury level. Cr cds: A, C, D, DS, ER, JCB, MC, V. [D] 🏃 🎿 🏊 🐾 SC

★ ★ **HOLIDAY INN-RIVERWALK.** *217 N St Mary's St (78205), on Riverwalk.* 210/224-2500; FAX 210/223-1302. 313 rms, 23 story. S, D $119-$159; suites $179-$350; under 18 free. Crib free. Pet accepted, some restrictions. Valet parking $8; in/out $6. TV; cable (premium). Heated pool; whirlpool, poolside serv. Restaurant 6:30 am-2 pm, 5:30-10 pm. Rm serv 6 am-midnight. Bar noon-12:30 am; Fri, Sat to 2 am; entertainment exc Sun & Mon. Ck-out noon. Convention facilities. Business servs avail. In-rm modem link. Exercise equipt; bicycles, treadmill. Refrigerator in suites. Balconies. View of river. Cr cds: A, C, D, DS, JCB, MC, V. [D] 🏃 🎿 🏊 🐾 SC

★ ★ ★ **LA MANSION DEL RIO.** *112 College St (78205), on River Walk.* 210/225-2581; FAX 210/226-0389; res: 800/323-7500. Web www.lamansion.com. 337 rms, 7 story. S $185-$280; D $210-$305; each addl $25; suites $475-$1,900; under 18 free; wkend rates; special packages. Crib free. Pet accepted. Valet parking $12. TV; cable, VCR avail. Pool; poolside serv. Restaurants 6:30 am-11 pm. Rm serv 24 hrs. Bar 11-2 am; entertainment. Ck-out noon. Convention facilities. Business servs avail. In-rm modem link. Concierge. Gift shop. Airport transportation. Minibars. Private patios, balconies. Overlooks San Antonio River, courtyard. Cr cds: A, C, D, DS, JCB, MC, V. [D] 🏃 🏊 🐾 SC

★ ★ **MARRIOTT PLAZA.** *555 S Alamo St (78205), in La Villita.* 210/229-1000; FAX 210/229-1418. Web www.plazasa.com. 252 rms, 5-7 story. S $205-$220; D $225-$240; each addl $20; suites $340-$725; under 18 free; wkend rates. Crib free. Pet accepted, some restrictions. Valet parking $11. TV; cable (premium), VCR avail. Pool; whirlpool, poolside serv. Restaurant 7 am-2 pm, 6-10 pm. Rm serv 24 hrs. Bar noon-1 am; entertainment Thurs-Sat. Ck-out noon. Meeting rms. Business center. In-rm modem link. Concierge. Lighted tennis. Golf privileges. Exercise equipt; weights, bicycles, sauna. Massage. Complimentary bicycles. Microwaves avail. Private patios. Balconies. Cr cds: A, C, D, DS, ER, MC, V. [D] 🏃 🎿 🏊 🐾 SC

★ ★ **MARRIOTT RIVERCENTER.** *101 Bowie St (78205), opp convention Center, on Riverwalk.* 210/223-1000; FAX 210/223-6239. 1,000 units, 38 story. S $185; D $205; each addl $20; suites $325-$1,200; under 18 free. Crib free. Pet accepted. Garage $9, valet $11. TV; cable (premium), VCR avail. Indoor/outdoor pool; whirlpool, poolside serv. Coffee in rms. Restaurant 6 am-midnight. Rm serv 24 hrs. Bar. Ck-out noon. Free lndry facilities. Convention facilities. Business center. In-rm modem link. Concierge. Shopping arcade. Barber, beauty shop. 18-hole golf privileges, greens fee $65-$85, pro, putting green, driving range. Exercise equipt; weight machine, bicycles, sauna. Some refrigerators, wet bars. Balconies. Located on the banks of the San Antonio River and adj Rivercenter shopping complex. Luxury level. Cr cds: A, C, D, DS, MC, V. [D] 🏃 🎿 🏊 🐾 SC

★ ★ **MARRIOTT RIVERWALK.** *711 E River Walk (78205), on Riverwalk.* 210/224-4555; FAX 210/224-2754. 500 rms, 30 story. S $134-$219; D $144-$229; each addl $20; suites $550; under 17 free; wkend rates. Crib free. Pet accepted. Garage parking $9, valet $12. TV; cable (premium), VCR avail. Indoor/outdoor pool; whirlpool. Restaurant 6:30 am-11 pm. Rm serv 24 hrs. Bar 11:30-2 am; entertainment Tues-Sat. Ck-out noon. Meeting rms. Business center. In-rm modem link. Gift shop. Golf privileges. Exercise equipt; weights, bicycles, sauna. Some bathrm phones, refrigerators. Balconies. Many rms overlook San Antonio River. Luxury level. Cr cds: A, C, D, DS, ER, JCB, MC, V.
[D] 🏃 🎿 🏊 🐾 SC

★ ★ **RADISSON DOWNTOWN MARKET SQUARE.** *502 W Durango (78207), downtown.* 210/224-7155; FAX 210/224-9130. E-mail zip@txdirect.net. 250 rms, 6 story. S $69-$119; D $79-$129; each addl $10; suites $135-$195; under 12 free. Crib free. Pet accepted; $50 deposit. TV; cable (premium). Pool; whirlpool. Restaurant 6:30 am-10 pm. Bar noon-midnight. Ck-out noon. Coin lndry. Meeting rms. Business servs avail. Free garage parking. Gift shop. Exercise equipt; weights, stair machine. Game rm. Refrigerator in suites. Balconies. Cr cds: A, C, D, DS, MC, V. [D] 🏃 🏊 🐾 SC

★ ★ **RESIDENCE INN BY MARRIOTT.** *425 Bonham (78205), downtown. 210/212-5555; FAX 210/212-5554.* 220 kit. suites, 13 story. Kit. suites $159; wkend, wkly, hol rates. Crib free. Pet accepted; $6/day. Garage parking $7. TV; cable (premium). Complimentary continental bkfst. Complimentary coffee in rms. Restaurant nearby. No rm serv. Ck-out noon. Meeting rms. Business servs avail. In-rm modem link. Coin lndry. Exercise equipt; weight machine, bicycle, sauna. Pool; whirlpool. Refrigerators, microwaves. Grills. Cr cds: A, C, D, DS, JCB, MC, V. [D] [✦] [≈] [✗] [⊠] [⋔] [SC]

San Marcos *(See also New Braunfels)*

Motels

★ **BEST WESTERN.** *917 I-35N. 512/754-7557.* 50 rms, 2 story. S $55-$89; D $59-$95; each addl $5; under 12 free. Crib free. Pet accepted, some restrictions. TV; cable (premium). Complimentary continental bkfst. Restaurant adj 10:30 am-midnight. Ck-out noon. Meeting rms. Business servs avail. In-rm modem link. Coin lndry. Pool; wading pool. Some refrigerators, microwaves. Cr cds: A, C, D, DS, JCB, MC, V. [D] [✦] [≈] [⊠] [⋔] [SC]

★ **HOWARD JOHNSON.** *1635 Aquarena Springs Dr. 512/353-8011; FAX 512/396-8062.* 100 rms, 2 story. S $59-$79; D $69-$89; under 18 free. Pet accepted. TV; cable (premium). Pool. Complimentary continental bkfst. Ck-out noon. Meeting rms. Business servs avail. In-rm modem link. Cr cds: A, C, D, DS, JCB, MC, V. [D] [✦] [≈] [⊠] [⋔] [SC]

★ ★ **LA QUINTA.** *1619 I-35 N, I-35 exit 206. 512/392-8800; FAX 512/392-0324.* 117 rms, 2 story. S $59-$89; D $69-$89; under 18 free. Crib free. Pet accepted, some restrictions. TV; cable (premium). Heated pool. Complimentary continental bkfst. Coffee in rms. Restaurant adj open 24 hrs. Ck-out noon. Meeting rm. In-rm modem link. Some refrigerators. Cr cds: A, C, D, DS, MC, V. [D] [✦] [≈] [⊠] [⋔] [SC]

Shamrock *(See also Amarillo)*

Motels

★ ★ **BEST WESTERN IRISH INN.** *301 I-40E. 806/256-2106.* 157 rms, 2 story. S $40-$60; D $44-$62; each addl $4; under 12 free. Crib $3. Pet accepted. TV; cable, VCR (movies). Indoor pool; whirlpool. Restaurant open 24 hrs. Private club 5 pm-midnight. Ck-out 1 pm. Coin lndry. Meeting rm. Business servs avail. In-rm modem link. Gift shop. Cr cds: A, C, D, DS, MC, V. [D] [✦] [≈] [⊠] [⋔] [SC]

✔ **WESTERN.** *104 E 12th St. 806/256-3244; FAX 806/256-3244, ext. 128.* 24 rms, 2 story. S $28-$30; D $32-$38; each addl $5. Crib $2. Pet accepted. TV; cable. Pool. Restaurant 6 am-9 pm. Ck-out 11 am. Cr cds: A, C, D, DS, MC, V. [✦] [≈] [⊠] [⋔] [SC]

Snyder *(See also Big Spring)*

Motel

★ ★ **PURPLE SAGE.** *1501 E Coliseum Dr, 1³/₄ mi E on US 84 Business, TX 180. 915/573-5491; FAX 915/573-9027; res: 800/545-5792.* 45 rms. S $40-$50; D $48-$58; each addl $3-$5; under 14 free. Crib free. Pet accepted. TV; cable (premium), VCR avail (movies). Pool. Playground. Complimentary continental bkfst. Ck-out noon. Business servs avail. Gift shop. Refrigerators. Picnic tables. Health club privileges. Cr cds: A, C, D, DS, MC, V. [D] [✦] [≈] [⊠] [⋔] [SC]

Sonora

Motel

✔ ★ ★ **DAYS INN DEVIL'S RIVER.** *I-10 & Golf Course Rd/US 277. 915/387-3516; FAX 915/387-2854.* 99 rms, 2 story. S $36-$38; D $46-$49; each addl $3. Crib $4. Pet accepted, some restrictions; $2. TV; cable. Pool. Restaurant 6 am-2 pm, 5-10 pm; Sun to 2 pm. Ck-out noon. Coin lndry. Meeting rm. Business servs avail. 9-hole golf privileges. Cr cds: A, C, D, DS, MC, V. [D] [✦] [🏌] [≈] [⊠] [⋔] [SC]

South Padre Island *(See also Brownsville, Harlingen)*

Motel

✔ ★ **DAYS INN.** *3913 Padre Blvd. 956/761-7831; FAX 956/761-2033.* 57 rms, 2 story. Mar-Labor Day: S, D $89-$130; each addl $10; under 12 free; lower rates rest of yr.

Crib free. Pet accepted; $25. TV; cable (premium). Pool; whirlpool. Ck-out noon. Coin lndry. Refrigerators. Opp ocean. Cr cds: A, C, D, DS, MC, V. [D] [←] [≈] [⌐] [🔥] [SC]

Motor Hotel

★ **BEST WESTERN FIESTA ISLES.** *5701 Padre Blvd. 956/761-4913; FAX 956/761-2719.* 58 rms, 3 story, 52 kits. Apr-Aug: S, D $84-$94; each addl $10; under 13 free; wkly rates; higher rates Mar; lower rates rest of yr. Crib free. Pet accepted. TV; cable (premium). Pool; whirlpool. Complimentary coffee. Restaurant adj 7 am-3 pm. Ck-out noon. Meeting rm. Balconies. Cr cds: A, C, D, DS, MC, V. [D] [←] [≈] [↙] [⌐] [🔥] [SC]

Stephenville

Motels

✔ ★ **DAYS INN.** *701 S Loop, jct US 281 & 377. 254/968-3392; FAX 254/968-3527.* 65 rms, 2 story. S $34-$65; D $40-$80; each addl $5; under 12 free. Crib free. Pet accepted, some restrictions; $10. TV; cable (premium). Pool. Ck-out 11 am. Meeting rms. Business servs avail. In-rm modem link. Cr cds: A, C, D, DS, MC, V. [D] [←] [≈] [⌐] [🔥] [SC]

★ ★ **HOLIDAY INN.** *2865 W Washington. 254/968-5256; FAX 254/968-4255.* 100 rms, 2 story. S $60-$65; D $70-$75; each addl $5; suites $125-$175; under 18 free. Crib free. Pet accepted. TV; cable (premium). Coffee in rms. Pool. Restaurant 6 am-9 pm; Sun to 3 pm. Rm serv. Private club 5 pm-midnight; closed Sun. Ck-out noon. Meeting rms. Business servs avail. In-rm modem link. Valet serv. Sundries. Cr cds: A, C, D, DS, JCB, MC, V. [D] [←] [≈] [⌐] [🔥] [SC]

★ **TEXAN MOTOR INN.** *3030 W Washington. 254/968-5003; FAX 817/968-5060.* 30 rms. Mid-Apr-Sept: S $37.50; D $43.50; each addl $6; under 12 free. Crib avail. Pet accepted, some restrictions; $3. TV; cable (premium). Complimentary continental bkfst. Restaurant nearby. Ck-out 11 am. Business servs avail. Bus depot transportation. Microwaves avail. Cr cds: A, DS, MC, V. [D] [←] [⌐] [🔥] [SC]

Sulphur Springs *(See also Greenville)*

Motel

★ ★ ★ **HOLIDAY INN.** *1495 E Industrial. 903/885-0562; FAX 903/885-0562.* 98 rms, 2 story. S, D $49-$52; each addl $5; suites $75-$80; under 18 free. Crib free. Pet accepted, some restrictions. TV; cable (premium), VCR avail (movies). Pool. Complimentary coffee in rms. Restaurant open 24 hrs. Rm serv 6 am-10 pm. Bar 4 pm-midnight. Ck-out noon. Coin lndry. Meeting rms. Business servs avail. In-rm modem link. Valet serv. Sundries. Some refrigerators. Cr cds: A, C, D, DS, ER, JCB, MC, V. [D] [←] [≈] [⌐] [🔥] [SC]

Sweetwater *(See also Abilene)*

Motels

★ ★ **HOLIDAY INN.** *500 NW Georgia St, at I-20. 915/236-6887.* 107 rms, 2 story. S, D $46-$65; each addl $5; under 19 free. Crib $5. Pet accepted. TV; cable (premium). Pool. Playground. Restaurant open 24 hrs. Rm serv. Private club 4 pm-midnight; Sat to 1 am. Ck-out noon. Coin lndry. Meeting rms. Business servs avail. Some refrigerators. Cr cds: A, C, D, DS, MC, V. [D] [←] [≈] [⌐] [🔥] [SC]

★ **MOTEL 6.** *510 NW Georgia, off I-20. 915/235-4387.* 79 rms, 2 story. S $27.99; D $31.99; each $2; under 17 free. Crib avail. Pet accepted. TV; cable (premium). Pool. Complimentary coffee in lobby. Restaurant opp open 24 hrs. Ck-out noon. Coin lndry. Cr cds: A, C, D, DS, MC, V. [←] [≈] [⌐] [🔥] [SC]

Temple *(See also Killeen, Waco)*

Motels

★ ★ **BEST WESTERN INN AT SCOTT & WHITE.** *2625 S 31st St (76504), I-35 at Loop 363 (exit 299). 254/778-5511; FAX 254/773-3161.* 129 rms, 1-2 story. S $56-$66; D $66-$70; each addl $8; suites $135; under 18 free; wkly, wkend rates. Crib free. Pet accepted, some restrictions. TV; cable. Pool. Restaurant 6 am-10 pm. Rm serv. Private club 4-9 pm. Ck-out noon. Meeting rms. Business servs avail. Valet serv. Sundries. Barber. Gift shop. RR station, bus depot transportation. Microwaves avail. Private patios, balconies. Near Scott & White Hospital. Cr cds: A, C, D, DS, MC, V. [D] [←] [≈] [↙] [🔥] [SC]

✔ ★ **GUEST HOUSE INN.** *400 SW H.K. Dodgen Loop (76504), 3 mi S on I-35, E at exit 299. 254/773-1515; res: 800/214-8378.* 100 rms, 2 story. S $40-$45; D $46-$52; each addl $6; under 18 free; wkly, wkend rates. Crib free. Pet accepted. TV; cable (premium). Complimentary coffee in rms. Restaurant open 24 hrs. Rm serv 7 am-10 pm. Ck-out 1 pm. Meeting rms. Business servs avail. In-rm modem link. Health club privileges. Pool. Some refrigerators. Cr cds: A, C, D, DS, MC, V. ⊡ 🖙 ⩲ ⩲ ⩲ SC

★ ★ **LA QUINTA.** *1604 W Barton Ave (76504), I-35 exit 301.* 254/771-2980; FAX 254/778-7565. 106 rms, 3 story. S $59; D $66; each addl $7; suites $85-$125; under 18 free. Crib free. Pet accepted, some restrictions. TV; cable (premium). Pool. Continental bkfst. Complimentary coffee in rms. Restaurant adj open 24 hrs. Ck-out noon. Business servs avail. Microwaves avail. Sundries. Cr cds: A, C, D, DS, MC, V. ⊡ 🖙 ⩲ ⩲ ⩲ SC

★ **RAMADA INN.** *802 N General Bruce Dr (76504-2337), I-35 exit 302.* 254/778-4411; FAX 254/778-8086. 132 rms, 2 story. S, D $48-$52; each addl $6; under 18 free. Crib free. Pet accepted, some restrictions. TV; cable (premium). Pool. Coffee in rms. Restaurant 6:30 am-2 pm, 5:30-10 pm; wkend hrs vary. Bar. Ck-out noon. Meeting rms. Business servs avail. In-rm modem link. Valet serv. Coin lndry. Picnic tables. Cr cds: A, C, D, DS, MC, V. ⊡ 🖙 ⩲ ⩲ ⩲ SC

Texarkana

Motels

(All directions are given from the jct of US 67, 7th St, and the state line)

✔ ★ ★ **BEST WESTERN KINGS ROW INN.** *(4200 State Line Ave, Texarkana AR 71854) at I-30 exit 223A.* 501/774-3851; FAX 501/772-8440; res: 800/643-5464. 116 rms, 2 story. S $44; D $48; each addl $5; under 12 free. Crib $2. Pet accepted, some restrictions. TV; cable (premium). Pool. Restaurant 6 am-2:30 pm, 5:30-9:30 pm. Ck-out noon. Lndry facilities. Meeting rms. Free airport transportation. Some balconies. Cr cds: A, D, DS, MC, V. ⊡ 🖙 ⩲ ⩲ ⩲ SC

★ ★ **LA QUINTA.** *5201 State Line Ave (75503), at I-30 exit 223A.* 903/794-1900; FAX 903/792-5506. 130 rms, 2 story. May-Aug: S $65, D $65-$74; each addl $9; suites $82-$91; under 18 free; lower rates rest of yr. Crib free. Pet accepted. TV; cable (premium). Pool. Complimentary continental bkfst. Restaurant adj open 24 hrs. Ck-out noon. In-rm modem link. Sundries. Free airport, RR station, bus depot transportation. Cr cds: A, C, D, DS, MC, V. ⊡ 🖙 ⩲ ⩲ ⩲ SC

Texas City *(See also Galveston, Houston)*

Motel

★ ★ **LA QUINTA.** *1121 TX 146 N (77590).* 409/948-3101; FAX 409/945-4412. 121 rms, 2 story. S $59-$67; D $67-$75; each addl $8; under 18 free. Crib free. Pet accepted. TV; cable (premium). Pool. Complimentary continental bkfst. Restaurant adj open 24 hrs. Ck-out noon. Meeting rms. Coin lndry. Business servs avail. Microwaves avail. Cr cds: A, C, D, DS, MC, V. ⊡ 🖙 ⩲ ⩲ ⩲ SC

Tyler *(See also Longview)*

Motels

✔ ★ **DAYS INN.** *3300 Mineola (75702), US 69, Loop 323.* 903/595-2451; FAX 903/595-2261. 139 rms, 2 story. S $38-$48; D $40-$50; each addl $6; suites $65-$90; under 18 free. Crib free. Pet accepted. TV; cable (premium), VCR avail. Pool. Complimentary continental bkfst. Restaurant open 24 hrs. Rm serv 8 am-8 pm. Private club 4 pm-midnight. Ck-out noon. Coin lndry. Meeting rms. Business servs avail. Valet serv. Sundries. Barber, beauty shop. Exercise equipt; weights, bicycles. Some refrigerators. Cr cds: A, C, D, DS, ER, MC, V. 🖙 ⩲ 🏋 ⩲ ⩲ SC

✔ ★ **ECONO LODGE.** *3209 W Gentry Pkwy (75702), US 69.* 903/593-0103. 50 rms. S $32.95-$40.95; D $37.95-$41.95; each addl $5; under 18 free; higher rates: Canton Days, 1st wkend of month. Pet accepted; $5/day. TV; cable (premium), VCR avail (movies $4). Pool. Complimentary coffee in lobby. Restaurant nearby. Ck-out noon. Business servs avail. Cr cds: A, C, D, DS, MC, V. 🖙 ⩲ ⩲ ⩲ SC

★ ★ ★ **HOLIDAY INN-SOUTHEAST CROSSING.** *3310 Troup Hwy (75701), jct TX 110, Loop 323.* 903/593-3600; FAX 903/533-9571. 160 rms, 2 story. S, D $69-$75; suites $125; under 18 free; wkend rates. Crib free. Pet accepted. TV; cable (premium), VCR avail. Pool; poolside serv. Coffee in rms. Restaurant 6 am-1 pm, 5:30-10 pm; Sat, Sun 7 am-1 pm, 5:30-10 pm. Rm serv. Private club 5-10 pm; closed Sun. Ck-out noon. Coin lndry. Meeting rms. Business servs avail. In-rm modem link. Valet serv. Sundries. Free airport transportation. Health club privileges. Cr cds: A, C, D, DS, JCB, MC, V. 🄳 💺 🏊 🖹 🐾 SC

★ ★ **LA QUINTA.** *1601 W Southwest Loop 323 (75701). 903/561-2223; FAX 903/581-5708.* 130 rms, 2 story. S $60-$67; D $70-$77; each addl $10. Crib free. Pet accepted, some restrictions. TV; cable (premium). Pool. Complimentary continental bkfst. Restaurant adj open 24 hrs. Ck-out noon. Meeting rms. In-rm modem link. Valet serv. Sundries. Free airport transportation. Cr cds: A, C, D, DS, MC, V. 🄳 💺 🏊 🖹 🐾 SC

★ ★ **RESIDENCE INN BY MARRIOTT.** *3303 Troup Hwy (75701). 903/595-5188; FAX 903/595-5719.* 128 kit. suites, 2 story. Kit. suites $86-$125; wkend rates. Pet accepted; $50. TV; cable (premium). Heated pool; whirlpool. Complimentary continental bkfst. Ck-out noon. Coin lndry. Meeting rms. Business servs avail. In-rm modem link. Valet serv. Sundries. Free airport transportation. Health club privileges. Sport court. Balconies. Picnic tables, grills. Cr cds: A, C, D, DS, JCB, MC, V. 🄳 💺 🏊 🖹 🐾 SC

Hotel

★ **TYLER INN.** *2843 NW Loop 323 (75702). 903/597-1301; FAX 903/597-9437.* 139 rms, 4 story. S $47-$49; D $53-$57; each addl $6; under 18 free. Crib free. Pet accepted, some restrictions. TV; cable (premium). Pool. Complimentary continental bkfst. Restaurant 5-10 pm. Private club 5-11 pm; Sat to midnight. Ck-out 1 pm. Meeting rms. Business servs avail. Free airport, RR station, bus depot transportation. Balconies. Cr cds: A, C, D, DS, MC, V. 🄳 💺 🏊 🖹 🐾 SC

Uvalde *(See also Eagle Pass)*

Motel

★ **HOLIDAY INN.** *920 E Main. 830/278-4511.* 150 rms, 2 story. S, D $56.95-$59.95; each addl $8; suites $113.90-$119.90; under 18 free. Pet accepted, some restrictions. TV; cable (premium). Pool. Restaurant 6 am-2 pm, 5-9 pm. Rm serv. Bar 4:30-11:45 pm; closed Sun. Ck-out noon. Coin lndry. Meeting rms. Valet serv. Cr cds: A, C, D, DS, JCB, MC, V. 🄳 💺 🏊 🖹 🐾 SC

Van Horn

Motels

★ ★ **BEST WESTERN INN OF VAN HORN.** *1705 Broadway, 6 blks W on US 80 Business. 915/283-2410; FAX 915/283-2143.* 60 rms. S $39-$42; D $42-$55; each addl $4; suites $60; under 18 free. Crib $2. Pet accepted, some restrictions. TV; cable (premium). Pool. Complimentary continental bkfst. Restaurant 6:15 am-10 pm. Private club 5-11 pm; closed Sun. Ck-out noon. Business servs avail. Lndry facilities. Gift shop. 9-hole golf privileges. Cr cds: A, C, D, DS, JCB, MC, V. 🄳 💺 🏌 🏊 🖹 🐾 SC

✔ ★ **HOWARD JOHNSON.** *200 Golf Course Dr, 1 mi W on US 80 Business. 915/283-2780; FAX 915/283-2804.* 98 rms, 2 story. S $40-$47; D $47-$50; each addl $5; under 18 free. Crib free. Pet accepted, some restrictions. TV; cable (premium), VCR avail. Pool; wading pool. Ck-out 1 pm. Bar; entertainment. Coin lndry. Meeting rms. Business servs avail. Sundries. Cr cds: A, C, D, DS, MC, V. 🄳 💺 🏊 🖹 🐾 SC

Vernon *(See also Wichita Falls)*

Motels

★ **DAYS INN.** *3110 Frontage Rd, off US 287 Bentley St exit. 940/552-9982; FAX 940/552-7851.* 50 rms, 2 story. S $42; D $47. Pet accepted. TV; cable, VCR avail (movies). Pool. Restaurant adj 6 am-9 pm. Ck-out noon. Business servs avail. Cr cds: A, C, D, DS, MC, V. 💺 🏊 🖹 🐾 SC

✔ ★ **GREEN TREE INN.** *3029 Morton, off US 287, Bentley St exit. 940/552-5421; res: 800/600-5421.* 30 rms. S $30-$34; D $34-$42; each addl $4; under 12 free. Pet accepted. TV; cable (premium). Pool. Complimentary continental bkfst. Ck-out 11 am. In-rm modem link. Cr cds: A, C, D, DS, MC, V. 💺 🏊 🖹 🐾 SC

Victoria *(See also Port Lavaca)*

Motels

✔ ★ ★ **HAMPTON INN.** *3112 Houston Hwy (77901). 512/578-2030; FAX 512/573-1238.* 102 rms, 2 story. S, D $52-$56; suites $60-$62; under 18 free. Crib free. Pet accepted. TV; cable (premium). Pool. Complimentary continental bkfst. Restaurant nearby. Ck-out 1 pm. Meeting rms. Business servs avail. In-rm modem link. Valet serv. Free airport transportation. Health club privileges. Cr cds: A, C, D, DS, MC, V. [D] [⌨] [≈] [⊠] [⚒] [SC]

★ ★ **HOLIDAY INN.** *2705 E Houston Hwy (77901). 512/575-0251; FAX 512/575-8362.* 226 rms, 2 story. S $48-$64; D $55-$71; each addl $7; suites $64-$71; under 18 free; wkend rates. Crib free. Pet accepted. TV; cable (premium). Indoor/outdoor pool; whirlpool. Restaurant 6 am-10 pm. Rm serv. Bar 3 pm-12:30 am; closed Sun. Ck-out 1 pm. Coin lndry. Meeting rms. Business servs avail. In-rm modem link. Bellhops. Valet serv. Sundries. Free airport transportation. Exercise equipt; weight machine, bicycle, sauna. Game rm. Cr cds: A, C, D, DS, JCB, MC, V. [D] [⌨] [≈] [✕] [⊠] [⚒] [SC]

★ ★ **LA QUINTA.** *7603 N Navarro Hwy (77904). 512/572-3585; FAX 512/576-4617.* 130 rms, 2 story. S $58-$65; D $58-$76; each addl $10; under 18 free. Crib free. Pet accepted. TV; cable (premium). Pool. Complimentary continental bkfst. Restaurant adj open 24 hrs. Ck-out noon. Meeting rms. Business servs avail. In-rm modem link. Cr cds: A, C, D, DS, MC, V. [D] [⌨] [≈] [⊠] [⚒] [SC]

✔★ ★ **RAMADA INN.** *3901 Houston Hwy (77901). 512/578-2723.* 126 rms, 2 story. S $42-$47; D $44-$49; each addl $10; family, wkend rates. Crib free. Pet accepted. TV; cable. Pool; whirlpool, sauna, poolside serv. Restaurant 6 am-2 pm, 5-10 pm. Rm serv to 9:30 pm. Bar 4 pm-midnight; closed Sun. Ck-out 1 pm. Meeting rms. Business servs avail. In-rm modem link. Free airport, bus depot transportation. Cr cds: A, C, D, DS, JCB, MC, V. [D] [⌨] [≈] [⊠] [⚒] [SC]

Waco *(See also Temple)*

Motels

★ ★ **BEST WESTERN OLD MAIN LODGE.** *I-35 at 4th St (76703), I-35 exit 335A. 254/753-0316; FAX 254/753-3811.* 84 rms. S $62; D $68; each addl $6; under 18 free; higher rates special events. Crib free. Pet accepted, some restrictions. Pool. TV; cable (premium). Complimentary coffee in rms. Restaurant adj open 24 hrs. Ck-out 1 pm. Meeting rms. Business servs avail. Valet serv. Some refrigerators; microwaves avail. Near Baylor Univ. Cr cds: A, C, D, DS, MC, V. [⌨] [≈] [⊠] [⚒] [SC]

★ ★ **LA QUINTA MOTOR INN.** *1110 S 9th St (76706), I-35 exit 18th St. 254/752-9741; FAX 254/757-1600.* 102 rms, 2 story. S $68-$76; D $76-$84; each addl $8; suites $88-$96; under 18 free. Crib free. Pet accepted, some restrictions. TV; cable (premium). Pool. Complimentary continental bkfst. Coffee in rms. Restaurant adj open 24 hrs. Ck-out noon. Business servs avail. In-rm modem link. Valet serv. Sundries. Microwaves avail. Baylor Univ nearby. Cr cds: A, C, D, DS, MC, V. [D] [⌨] [≈] [⊠] [⚒] [SC]

Wichita Falls *(See also Vernon)*

Motel

★ ★ **LA QUINTA.** *1128 Central Frwy N (76305). 940/322-6971; FAX 940/723-2573.* 139 rms, 2 story. S $55; D $63; each addl $8; suites $72-$88; under 18 free. Crib free. Pet accepted. TV; cable (premium). Pool. Complimentary continental bkfst. Restaurant adj open 24 hrs. Ck-out noon. Coin lndry. Meeting rm. Business servs avail. In-rm modem link. Valet serv. Cr cds: A, C, D, DS, MC, V. [D] [⌨] [≈] [⊠] [⚒] [SC]

Utah

Beaver *(See also Cedar City, Richfield)*

Motels

★ ★ **BEST WESTERN PAICE INN.** *161 S Main St. 435/438-2438.* 24 rms, 2 story. Mid-May-Oct: S $46-$52; D $48-$58; each addl $2; lower rates rest of yr. Crib $2. Pet accepted. TV; cable (premium). Heated pool; whirlpool, sauna. Restaurant 7 am-10 pm. Ck-out 11 am. Business servs avail. In-rm modem link. Downhill ski 18 mi. Cr cds: A, C, D, DS, MC, V. 🐾 🐟 🌊 ⊠ ⊠ 🔥 SC

✔ ★ **DE LANO.** *480 N Main St. 435/438-2418; FAX 435/438-2115; res: 800/288-3171.* 10 rms. May-Oct: S $34-$36; D $36-$39; each addl $4; wkly rates; lower rates rest of yr. Crib $3. Pet accepted. TV; cable. Restaurant nearby. Ck-out 11 am. Coin lndry. Business servs avail. Covered parking. Downhill ski 18 mi. Some refrigerators. Cr cds: A, DS, MC, V. D 🐾 🐟 ⊠ ⊠ 🔥 SC

Brigham City *(See also Ogden)*

Motel

✔ ★ **HOWARD JOHNSON.** *1167 S Main St. 435/723-8511.* 44 rms, 2 story. S $40-$45; D $49-$56; each addl $4; under 18 free. Crib free. Pet accepted, some restrictions. TV; cable (premium). Indoor pool; whirlpool. Complimentary continental bkfst. Restaurant adj 7 am-9 pm; closed Tues. Business servs avail. Ck-out noon. Cr cds: A, C, D, DS, ER, JCB, MC, V. D 🐾 ⊠ ⊠ 🔥 SC

Bryce Canyon National Park

Motel

(Air conditioning is rarely necessary at this elevation)

★ ★ ★ **BEST WESTERN RUBY'S INN.** *(Bryce 84764)* $1/2$ mi N of park entrance on UT 63. 435/834-5341. 369 rms, 1-2 story. June-Sept: S, D $83; each addl $5; suites, $125; lower rates rest of yr. Crib free. Pet accepted; $100 deposit. TV; cable, VCR (movies). 2 indoor pools. Restaurant 6:30 am-9 pm; winter hrs vary. Coin lndry. Business servs avail. Shopping arcade. Game rm. X-country ski opp. Picnic tables. Rodeo in summer; general store. Lake on property. Trailer park. Cr cds: A, C, D, DS, MC, V. D 🐾 🐟 🎿 🐟 🌊 ⊠ 🔥 SC

Capitol Reef National Park

Motel

★ **CAPITOL REEF INN.** *(360 W Main St, Torrey 84775)* 10 mi W of park on UT 24, $1/2$ mi W of Torrey. 435/425-3271. 10 rms. Apr-Oct: S $36, D $40; each addl $4. Closed rest of yr. Pet accepted. TV; cable (premium). Playground. Restaurant 7-11 am, 5-9 pm. Ck-out 11 am. Gift shop. Cr cds: DS, MC, V. 🐾 ⊠ 🔥

Cedar City

Motels

★ ★ **COMFORT INN.** *250 N 1100 West. 435/586-2082; FAX 435/586-3193.* 94 rms, 2 story. June-Sept: S $59; D $68; each addl $5; under 12 free; lower rates rest of yr. Crib free. Pet accepted. TV; cable. Indoor pool. Complimentary continental bkfst. Restaurant adj 6 am-11 pm. Ck-out 11 am. Business servs avail. Free airport transportation. Exercise equipt; weight machine, bicycle. Cr cds: A, C, D, DS, ER, MC, V. 🐾 🌊 🏋 ⊠ 🔥 SC

✔ ★ **RODEWAY INN.** *281 S Main St. 435/586-9916.* 48 rms, 2 story. June-Sept: S $54 D $62; suites $66-$74; under 18 free; lower rates rest of yr. Crib free. Pet accepted. TV; cable. Heated pool; sauna. Restaurant adj 6 am-10 pm; winter to 9:30 pm. Ck-out noon. Meeting rm. Business servs avail. Free airport transportation. Game rm. Cr cds: A, C, D, DS, ER, JCB, MC, V. 🐾 🌊 ⊠ 🔥 SC

Fillmore *(See also Nephi, Richfield)*

Motel

✔★ **BEST WESTERN PARADISE INN.** *1025 N Main St.. 435/743-6895; FAX 435/743-6892.* 80 rms, 2 story. Mid-May-Oct: S $46; D $52; each addl $2; lower rates rest of yr. Crib $6. Pet accepted. TV; cable. Heated pool; whirlpool. Restaurant 6 am-10 pm; summer to 11 pm. Ck-out 11 am. Business servs avail. Cr cds: A, C, D, DS, JCB, MC, V.

Heber City *(See also Provo, Salt Lake City)*

Motel

✔★ **DANISH VIKING LODGE.** *989 S Main St. 435/654-2202; FAX 435/654-2770; res: 800/544-4066 (exc UT).* 34 rms, 1-2 story, 3 kits. Mid-May-mid-Sept & Christmas season: S $40-$65; D $49-$85; each addl $5; kit. units $65-$95; package plans; lower rates rest of yr. Crib $3. Pet accepted, some restrictions. TV; cable (premium), VCR avail. Pool; whirlpool, sauna. Playground. Complimentary coffee in lobby. Restaurant nearby. Ck-out 11 am. Coin lndry. Downhill ski 12 mi; x-country ski 7 mi. Refrigerators, microwaves. Picnic tables, grills. Cr cds: A, D, DS, MC, V.

Kanab

Motel

✔★★ **PARRY LODGE.** *89 E Center St. 435/644-2601; FAX 435/644-2605; res: 800/748-4104.* 89 rms, 1-2 story. May-Oct: S $43-$57; D $57-$65; each addl $6; family rates; lower rates rest of yr. Pet accepted. TV; cable. Heated pool. Restaurant 7 am-noon, 5-10 pm. Ck-out 11 am. Coin lndry. Business servs avail. Autographed pictures of movie stars displayed in lobby. Cr cds: A, DS, MC, V.

Moab

Guest Ranch

★★ **PACK CREEK RANCH.** *8 mi S on US 191 to La Sal Mt Loop Rd, head E to "T" intersection, then right 6 mi to Pack Creek turnoff. 435/259-5505; FAX 435/259-8879.* 10 kit. cottages (1, 2 & 3 bedrm). No rm phones. Apr-Oct, AP: $125 per person; lower rates rest of yr. Crib $10 (one-time fee). Pet accepted. Pool; whirlpool, sauna. Dining rm 7-10 am, 6:30-8:30 pm. Ck-out 11 am, ck-in 3 pm. Grocery, package store 16 mi. X-country ski on site. Hiking. Picnic tables. A 300-acre ranch at foot of La Sal Mts; features trail rides, pack trips. Cr cds: A, DS, MC, V.

Nephi *(See also Fillmore, Payson)*

Motel

★ **BEST WESTERN PARADISE INN.** *1025 S Main St. 435/623-0624.* 40 rms, 2 story. Mid-May-Oct: S $46; D $52 each addl $2; lower rates rest of yr. Crib $6. Pet accepted, some restrictions. TV; cable. Heated pool; whirlpool. Complimentary continental bkfst. Restaurant nearby. Ck-out 11 am. Exercise equipt; bicycle, ski machine. Cr cds: A, C, D, DS, ER, MC, V.

Ogden *(See also Brigham City, Salt Lake City)*

Motel

✔★ **MOTEL 6.** *1500 W Riverdale Rd (84405). 801/627-2880; FAX 801/392-1713.* 109 rms, 2 story. June-Aug: S, D $39.99-$45.99; each addl $6; suites $79.98; under 17 free; lower rates rest of yr. Crib free. Pet accepted, some restrictions. TV; cable (premium). Heated pool. Restaurant 8 am-10 pm. Bar 5:30 pm-1 am Tues-Sat; private club Sun, Mon. Ck-out noon. Coin lndry. Business servs avail. Some in-rm whirlpools. Cr cds: A, C, D, DS, MC, V.

Motor Hotel

★★ **DAYS INN.** *3306 Washington Blvd (84401). 801/399-5671; FAX 801/621-0321.* 109 rms, 2 story. S $65-$70; D $80-$88; each addl $8; under 18 free. Crib free. Pet accepted, some restrictions. TV; cable (premium). Indoor pool; whirlpool. Complimentary continental bkfst. Ck-out noon. Coin lndry. Business servs avail. In-rm modem link. Exercise equipt; weight machine, rower. Downhill/x-country ski 15 mi. Microwaves avail. Cr cds: A, C, D, DS, JCB, MC, V. 🄳 ⬚ ⬚ ⬚ ⬚ ⬚ ⬚ SC

Hotels

★ ★ ★ **BEST WESTERN OGDEN PARK.** *247 24th St (84401). 801/627-1190; FAX 801/394-6312.* 288 rms, 8 story, 18 suites. S $85-$95; D $95-$105; suites $105-$159; wkend rates; ski plans. Pet accepted, some restrictions. TV; cable. Indoor pool; whirlpool. Coffee in rms. Restaurant 6 am-10 pm. Private club noon-1 am. Ck-out noon. Coin lndry. Convention facilities. Business servs avail. Bellhop. Gift shop. Free parking. Exercise equipt; weight machine, bicycles. Massage. Game rm. Refrigerator in suites. Microwaves avail. Cr cds: A, D, DS, JCB, MC, V. 🄳 ⬚ ⬚ ⬚ ⬚ ⬚ ⬚ SC

★ ★ ★ **RADISSON SUITE.** *2510 Washington Blvd (84401). 801/627-1900; FAX 801/394-5342.* 144 rms, 11 story, 122 suites. S $139-$159; D $149-$169; each addl $12; suites $129-$169; under 17 free; ski packages. Crib free. Pet accepted, some restrictions. TV; cable (premium). Complimentary bkfst buffet. Complimentary coffee in rms. Restaurant 6 am-9 pm; Sat 6:30 am-10 pm; Sun 7 am-11 pm. Ck-out noon. Coin lndry. Meeting rms. Business center. Free covered parking. Downhill/x-country ski 16 mi. Exercise equipt; bicycles, treadmill. Health club privileges. Refrigerator, microwave, wet bar in suites. Cr cds: A, C, D, DS, ER, JCB, MC, V. 🄳 ⬚ ⬚ ⬚ ⬚ ⬚ ⬚ SC ⬚

Payson *(See also Nephi, Provo)*

Motel

★ ★ **COMFORT INN.** *830 N Main St. 435/465-4861.* 62 rms, 2 story, 6 kits. (no equipt). S $55-$65; D $60-$80; each addl $6; suites $110; under 18 free. Crib free. Pet accepted; $10 deposit. TV; cable (premium), VCR avail (movies). Indoor pool; whirlpool. Complimentary continental bkfst. Restaurant adj open 24 hrs. Ck-out 11 am. Coin lndry. Meeting rms. Business servs avail. Exercise equipt; weight machine, bicycles, sauna. Cr cds: A, C, D, DS, ER, JCB, MC, V. 🄳 ⬚ ⬚ ⬚ ⬚ ⬚ ⬚ SC

Provo *(See also Heber City, Payson, Salt Lake City)*

Motels

★ **DAYS INN.** *1675 North 200 West (84604). 801/375-8600; FAX 801/374-6654.* 49 rms, 2 story. S $65; D $70; each addl $5; kit. unit $65-$70; under 18 free. Crib free. Pet accepted, some restrictions. TV; cable. Heated pool. Complimentary continental bkfst. Coffee in rms. Restaurant 11 am-11 pm. Ck-out noon. Business servs avail. Some in-rm modem links. Downhill/x-country ski 15 mi. Some refrigerators, microwaves. Cr cds: A, C, D, DS, MC, V. 🄳 ⬚ ⬚ ⬚ ⬚ ⬚ SC

✔ ★ **NATIONAL 9 COLONY INN SUITES.** *1380 S University Ave (84601). 801/374-6800; FAX 801/374-6803; res: 800/524-9999.* 80 kit. suites, 2 story. May-Oct: S $42-$52; D $58-$72; each addl $5; wkly, monthly rates; lower rates rest of yr. Crib $5. Pet accepted, some restrictions; $15 refundable & $5/day. TV; cable (premium). Heated pool. Complimentary continental bkfst. Restaurant adj. Ck-out noon. Coin lndry. Business servs avail. In-rm modem link. Downhill ski 20 mi. Cr cds: A, DS, MC, V. ⬚ ⬚ ⬚ ⬚ ⬚ SC

★ ★ **UNIVERSITY COMFORT INN.** *1555 N Canyon Rd (84604). 801/374-6020; FAX 801/374-0015.* 101 rms, 2 story, 6 suites. S, D $85; each addl $5; suites $99-$155; kit. unit $135; under 18 free. Crib free. Pet accepted, some restrictions. TV; cable (premium), VCR avail (movies $5). Indoor pool; whirlpool. Complimentary continental bkfst. Restaurant nearby. Ck-out 1 pm. Coin lndry. Meeting rms. Business servs. In-rm modem link. Sundries. Downhill/x-country ski 15 mi. Some refrigerators, microwaves. Cr cds: A, C, D, DS, ER, MC, V. 🄳 ⬚ ⬚ ⬚ ⬚ ⬚ SC

Hotel

★ ★ ★ **PROVO PARK.** *101 West 100 North (84601). 801/377-4700; FAX 801/377-4708; res: 800/777-7144.* 333 rms, 9 story. S $80-$125; D $95-$130; each addl $8; suites $125-$410; under 18 free; ski, honeymoon packages. Crib free. Pet accepted, some restrictions. TV; cable (premium). Heated pool; whirlpool. Complimentary coffee in rms. Restaurant 6:30 am-10 pm. Private club 4 pm-midnight. Ck-out noon. Meeting rms. Business center. In-rm modem link. Gift shop. Free covered parking. Airport transportation avail, free RR station, bus depot transportation. Downhill ski 14 mi. Exercise equipt; bicycles, treadmill; sauna. Some refrigerators, microwvaves, wet bars. Cr cds: A, C, D, DS, JCB, MC, V. 🄳 ⬚ ⬚ ⬚ ⬚ ⬚ ⬚ SC ⬚

Richfield (See also Beaver, Fillmore, Salina)

Motel

✔★ **ROMANICO INN.** *1170 S Main St. 435/896-8471.* 29 rms, 2 story. S, D $36-$64; each addl $4; kit.; under 12 free. Crib free. Pet accepted. TV; cable. Restaurant adj 5:30-10 pm. Ck-out noon. Coin lndry. Whirlpool. Some refrigerators. Cr cds: A, C, D, DS, ER, MC, V. [D] [✔] [≋] [▨] [SC]

Roosevelt

Motel

✔★ **FRONTIER.** *75 South 200 East. 435/722-2201; FAX 435/722-2212.* 54 units, 2 kits. S $30-$40; D $34-$59; each addl $3; kit. units $36-$45. Crib $2.50. Pet accepted. TV; cable (premium). Pool. Restaurant 6 am-9:30 pm; Sun to 9 pm. Ck-out 11 am. Business servs avail. Cr cds: A, D, DS, MC, V. [✔] [≋] [▨] [▨] [SC]

St George

Motel

✔★ **TRAVELODGE EAST.** *175 North 1000 East. 435/673-4621.* 40 rms, 2 story. S $36-$49; D $44-$59; each addl $4; suites $76; under 18 free. Crib free. Pet accepted. TV; cable. Heated pool. Coffee in rms. Restaurant adj open 24 hrs. Ck-out noon. Business servs avail. Some refrigerators. Cr cds: A, C, D, DS, ER, JCB, MC, V. [✔] [≋] [▨] [SC]

Salina (See also Richfield)

Motel

★ **SAFARI.** *1425 S State St. 435/529-7447.* 28 rms, 2 story. June-mid-Oct: S $44-$56; D $52-$56; each addl $6; under 12 free; lower rates rest of yr. Crib $6. Pet accepted. TV; cable. Heated pool. Restaurant 6 am-10 pm. Ck-out 11 am. Business servs avail. Cr cds: A, C, D, DS, MC, V. [✔] [≋] [≋] [▨] [▨] [SC]

Salt Lake City (See also Heber City, Ogden, Provo)

Motels

(Rates may be higher during state fair)

✔★ **DAYS INN AIRPORT.** *1900 W North Temple St (84116), west of downtown. 801/539-8538.* 110 rms, 2 story. S, D $58-$105; each addl $7; suites $98-$125; under 12 free. Crib free. Pet accepted. TV; cable (premium). Complimentary continental bkfst. Restaurant nearby. Ck-out 11 am. Business servs avail. In-rm modem link. Valet serv. Free airport, RR station, bus depot transportation. Health club privileges. Microwaves avail. Cr cds: A, C, D, DS, JCB, MC, V. [D] [✔] [✗] [▨] [▨] [SC]

★★ **HAMPTON INN.** *(2393 S 800 W, Woods Cross 84087) 801/296-1211; FAX 801/296-1222.* 60 rms, 3 story. S, D $71-$79; suites $125-$160; under 18 free. Crib free. Pet accepted. TV; cable (premium). Indoor pool; whirlpool. Complimentary continental bkfst. Restaurant nearby. Ck-out noon. Meeting rms. Business servs avail. In-rm modem link. Coin lndry. Free airport transportation. Health club privileges. Microwaves avail. Cr cds: A, C, D, DS, MC, V. [D] [✔] [≋] [▨] [▨] [SC]

✔★★ **LA QUINTA.** *(530 Catalpa Rd, Midvale 84047) 8 mi S on I-15, 72nd South St exit, E to Catalpa Rd. 801/566-3291; FAX 801/562-5943.* 122 rms, 2 story. S $75; D $83; each addl $8; under 18 free. Crib free. Pet accepted. TV; cable (premium). Heated pool. Continental bkfst. Complimentary coffee in lobby. Restaurant adj open 24 hrs. Ck-out noon. Coin lndry. Business servs avail. In-rm modem link. Downhill ski 15 mi; x-country ski 20 mi. Health club privileges. Microwaves avail. Cr cds: A, C, D, DS, MC, V. [D] [✔] [≋] [≋] [▨] [SC]

★ **RAMADA INN-DOWNTOWN.** *230 West 600 South (84102), downtown. 801/364-5200; FAX 801/364-0974.* Web www.accommidations.com. 160 rms, 2 story. S, D $59-$79; each addl $10; under 19 free. Crib free. Pet accepted; some restrictions; $10 deposit. TV; cable. Indoor pool; whirlpool. Restaurant 6:00 am-10 pm; Sun 6:30 am-9 pm. Rm serv. Private club from 5 pm. Ck-out noon. Coin lndry. Meeting rms. Business servs avail. In-rm modem link. Valet serv. Free airport, RR station, bus depot transportation. Exercise equipt; weight machine, bicycles, sauna. Game rm. Rec rm. Microwaves avail. Cr cds: A, C, D, DS, MC, V. [D] [✔] [≋] [✗] [▨] [▨] [SC]

★ ★ **RESIDENCE INN BY MARRIOTT.** *765 East 400 South (84102), east of downtown.* 801/532-5511; FAX 801/531-0416. 128 kit. suites (1-2-bedrm), 2 story. Suites $159-$199; wkly, monthly rates; ski packages. Pet accepted. TV; cable (premium), VCR avail (movies). Heated pool. Complimentary continental bkfst. Ck-out noon. Coin lndry. Business servs avail. In-rm modem link. Bellhops. Valet serv. Free airport, RR station, bus depot transportation. Exercise equipt; weights, stair machine. Microwaves; many fireplaces. Sport court. Cr cds: A, C, D, DS, JCB, MC, V. 🄳 💺 ⛖ 🏃 ⊠ 🐾 SC

★ **TRAVELODGE CITY CENTER.** *524 S West Temple (84101).* 801/531-7100; FAX 801/359-3814. 60 rms, 3 story. S $50-72; D $58-$75; each addl $6; under 18 free; ski plan. Crib free. Pet accepted; deposit. TV; cable (premium). Heated pool; whirlpool. Complimentary coffee in rms. Restaurant nearby. Ck-out noon. Business servs avail. Cr cds: A, C, D, DS, MC, V. 💺 ⛖ ⊠ 🐾 SC

Motor Hotels

★ ★ **BEST WESTERN-SALT LAKE PLAZA.** *122 W South Temple St (84101), downtown.* 801/521-0130; FAX 801/322-5057; res: 800/366-3684. E-mail sales@plaza-hotel.com; web www.plaza-hotel.com. 226 rms, 13 story. S $89-$129; D $99-$149; each addl $10; suites $265; under 18 free. Crib free. Pet accepted; $10. TV; cable (premium), VCR avail. Heated pool; whirlpool. Restaurant 6 am-11 pm. Rm serv. Ck-out 11 am. Lndry facilities. Meeting rms. Business servs avail. In-rm modem link. Bellhops. Gift shop. Free airport, RR station, bus depot transportation. Exercise equipt; bicycles, stair machine. Some refrigerators. Cr cds: A, C, D, DS, ER, JCB, MC, V. 🄳 💺 ⛖ 🏃 ⊠ 🐾 SC

★ ★ **COMFORT INN.** *200 N Admiral Byrd Rd (84116), in Salt Lake Intl Center, near Intl Airport, west of downtown.* 801/537-7444; FAX 801/532-4721. 154 rms, 4 story. S, D $69-$129; each addl $10; under 18 free. Crib free. Pet accepted; $25 deposit. TV. Heated pool; whirlpool. Restaurant 6 am-midnight. Rm serv. Ck-out 11 am. Meeting rms. Business servs avail. Valet serv. Free airport transportation. Some refrigerators; microwaves avail. Balconies. Cr cds: A, DS, MC, V. 🄳 💺 ⛖ 🏃 ⊠ 🐾 SC

Hotel

★ ★ ★ **HILTON.** *150 W 500 South St (84101), downtown.* 801/532-3344; FAX 801/531-0705. 351 rms, 10 story. S, D $119-$189; each addl $20; suites $159-$350; family rates; ski plans. Crib free. Pet accepted, some restrictions; $50 deposit. TV; cable (premium), VCR avail. Pool; whirlpool, poolside serv. Restaurant 6 am-11:30 pm. Private club 11:30 am-midnight, Sun 5-10 pm; entertainment. Ck-out noon. Convention facilities. Business center. In-rm modem link. Barber, beauty shop. Free airport transportation. Exercise equipt; weight machine, bicycles, sauna. Health club privileges. Ski rentals avail. Balconies. Luxury level. Cr cds: A, C, D, DS, ER, JCB, MC, V. 🄳 💺 ⛖ 🏃 ⊠ 🐾 SC 🏊

Zion National Park *(See also Cedar City, Kanab, St George)*

Motels

★ ★ **BEST WESTERN DRIFTWOOD LODGE.** *(Springdale 84767) On UT 9, 2 mi S of park entrance.* 435/772-3262. 47 rms, 1-2 story. S $70; D $80; each addl $4. Crib $2. Pet accepted. TV. Heated pool; whirlpool. Complimentary continental bkfst. Ck-out 11 am. Business servs avail. Gift shop. Private patios, balconies. Shaded grounds; good views of park. Cr cds: A, C, D, DS, MC, V. 🄳 💺 ⛖ ⊠ 🐾 SC

★ ★ **CLIFFROSE LODGE & GARDENS.** *(281 Zion Park Blvd, Springdale 84767)* 435/772-3234; FAX 435/772-3900; res: 800/243-8824. 36 rms, 2 story. May-mid-Oct: S, D $99-$119; suites $145; under 18 free; lower rates rest of yr. Crib $10. Pet accepted; $10. TV; cable (premium), VCR avail. Pool. Playground. Complimentary coffee in lobby. Restaurant nearby. Ck-out 11 am. Meeting rms. Cr cds: A, DS, MC, V. 🄳 💺 ⛖ 🏃 ⊠ 🐾

Vermont

Bennington *(See also Williamstown, MA)*

Motels

(Rates may be higher fall foliage season)

✔ ★ ★ **FIFE 'N DRUM.** *VT 7S, 1¹/₂ mi S on US 7. 802/442-4074.* 18 rms, 1-2 story, 4 kits. May-Oct: S $39-$61; D $42-$74; each addl $6-$7; kit. units $48-$78; wkly rates off-season; lower rates rest of yr. Crib free. Pet accepted, some restrictions; $5. TV; cable (premium). Heated pool; whirlpool. Playground. Complimentary coffee in rms. Ck-out 11 am. Sundries. Gift shop. Free bus depot transportation. Downhill ski 20 mi; x-country ski 6 mi. Lawn games. Refrigerators. Picnic tables; some grills. Cr cds: A, DS, MC, V.

✔ ★ **SERENITY.** *(VT 7A, Shaftsbury 05262) 7 mi N on VT 7A. 802/442-6490; res: 800/644-6490.* 8 units (all with shower only). S $35-$40; D $35-$50; each addl $5; under 18 free; wkly rates. Closed Nov-Apr. Crib free. Pet accepted. TV; cable. Complimentary coffee in rms. Ck-out 11 am. Grills, picnic tables. Cr cds: A, D, MC, V.

Brandon *(See also Middlebury)*

Inn

★ ★ **MOFFETT HOUSE.** *69 Park St. 802/247-3843; res: 800/752-5794.* 6 rms, 3 with shower only, 2 story. No A/C. No rm phones. S $65-$70; D $70-$110; each addl $15; under 2 free; ski plans; hols (2-day min); higher rates fall foliage. Closed Apr. Crib free. Pet accepted. TV; cable in some rms. Complimentary full bkfst. Restaurant nearby. Ck-out 11 am, ck-in 2 pm. Downhill ski 20 mi; x-country ski 5 mi. Built in 1856. Totally nonsmoking. Cr cds: MC, V.

Brattleboro *(See also Marlboro, Newfane; also see Keene, NH)*

Motel

★ **QUALITY INN.** *VT 5N, off I-91 exit 3. 802/254-8701; FAX 802/257-4727.* 92 rms, 2 story. June-Oct: S, D $89-$109; each addl $10; under 18 free; lower rates rest of yr. Crib free. Pet accepted. TV; cable. 2 pools, 1 indoor; whirlpool, sauna. Complimentary full bkfst. Restaurant 6:30-10:30 am, 5-9:30 pm. Rm serv. Bar 4:30-11:30 pm. Ck-out 11 am. Meeting rms. Business servs avail. In-rm modem link. Cr cds: A, D, DS, MC, V.

Burlington

Motels

✔ ★ **DAYS INN.** *(23 College Pkwy, Colchester 05446) N on I-89, exit 15. 802/655-0900; FAX 802/655-6851.* 73 rms, 4 story. July-mid Oct: S $49-$69; D $59-$85; under 16 free; suites $75-$120; lower rates rest of yr. Crib free. Pet accepted; $25 deposit. TV; cable (premium). Indoor pool. Complimentary continental bkfst. Ck-out 11 am. Business servs avail. Sundries. X-country ski 5 mi. Refrigerators; some in-rm whirlpools. Some balconies. Cr cds: A, D, DS, MC, V.

★ ★ **ECONO LODGE.** *1076 Williston Rd (US 2). 802/863-1125; FAX 802/658-1296.* Web www.econolodge.com. 177 rms, 2 story. May-Labor Day: S $60-$90; D $70-$99; each addl $5; suites $80-$109; under 18 free; higher rates fall foliage; lower rates rest of yr. Crib free. Pet accepted; $5. TV; cable (premium). Pool; whirlpool. Complimentary continental bkfst. Restaurant 11:30 am-2:30 pm, 5-10 pm; Sun 10 am-2:30, 4-9 pm. Ck-out 11 am. Coin lndry. Meeting rms. Business servs avail. Free airport transportation. Exercise equipt; weight machines, bicycle, sauna. Nature trail. Cr cds: A, C, D, DS, ER, JCB, MC, V.

★ ★ **RESIDENCE INN BY MARRIOTT.** *(One Hurricane Lane, Williston 05495) Jct I-89 exit 12 & VT 2A. 802/878-2001.* 96 kit. suites, 2 story. S, D $89-$149; wkly rates; higher rates: graduation, fall foliage. Crib free. Pet accepted. TV; cable (premium). Indoor pool; whirlpool. Playground. Complimentary continental bkfst. Ck-out noon. Coin lndry. Meeting rms. Business servs avail. In-rm modem link. Valet serv. Free airport transportation. Downhill/x-country ski 15 mi. Exercise equipt; weight machine, bicycles. Many fireplaces. Balconies. Cr cds: A, D, DS, MC, V. [D] [icons] [SC]

Motor Hotels

★ ★ **HAMPTON INN & CONFERENCE CENTER.** *(8 Mountain View Dr, Colchester 05446)* N on I-89 exit 16. 802/655-6177; FAX 802/655-4962. Web www.hamptoninn.com. 188 rms, 5 story. Aug-Oct: S $95; D $105; suites $119-$139; under 18 free; lower rates rest of yr. Crib free. Pet accepted. TV; cable (premium), VCR avail. Indoor pool; whirlpool. Complimentary continental bkfst. Restaurant 11:30-10 pm. Ck-out 11 am. Coin lndry. Meeting rms. Business servs avail. In-rm modem link. Free airport transportation. Downhill ski 20 mi; x-country ski 5 mi. Exercise equipt; weights, stair machine. Refrigerators avail. Cr cds: A, C, D, DS, ER, MC, V. [D] [icons] [SC]

★ ★ **HOLIDAY INN.** *(1068 Williston Rd, S Burlington 05403)* 1½ mi E on US 2, at I-89 exit 14E. 802/863-6363; FAX 802/863-3061. Web www.holiday-inn.com/hotels/btvvt. 174 rms, 4 story. May-Oct: S, D $83-$129; under 19 free; varied lower rates rest of yr. Crib free. Pet accepted. TV; cable. 2 pools, 1 indoor; whirlpool. Restaurant 6 am-10 pm. Rm serv. Bar noon-2 am, Sat to 1 am, Sun to 10 pm; entertainment Thur-Sat. Ck-out noon. Meeting rm. Business servs avail. In-rm modem link. Bellhops. Sundries. Free airport transportation. Exercise equipt; weights, bicycles. Cr cds: A, C, D, DS, JCB, MC, V.
[D] [icons] [SC]

★ ★ ★ **SHERATON HOTEL & CONFERENCE CENTER.** *(870 Williston Rd, S Burlington 05403)* 1½ mi E on US 2, at I-89 exit 14W, near Intl Airport. 802/865-6600; FAX 802/865-6670. Web www.ITTsheraton.com. 309 rms, 2-4 story. May-Oct: S $99-$130; D $99-$145; each addl $10; suites $200; under 17 free; wknd rates; ski plan; lower rates rest of yr. Crib free. Pet accepted. TV; cable (premium), VCR avail. Indoor pool; whirlpool. Coffee in rms. Restaurant 6:30 am-2:30 pm, 5-10:30 pm. Rm serv. Bar 11 am-midnight; entertainment Fri-Sat. Ck-out noon. Meeting rms. Business center. In-rm modem link. Bellhops. Gift shop. Free airport transportation. X-country ski 6 mi. Exercise rm; instructor, weights, bicycles. Game rm. Some refrigerators. Tennis nearby. Luxury level. Cr cds: A, C, D, DS, ER, JCB, MC, V. [D] [icons]

Dorset

Inn

★ ★ **BARROWS HOUSE.** *Rte 30, 1 blk S on VT 30.* 802/867-4455; FAX 802/867-0132; res: 800/639-1620. 28 rms in 9 houses, inn, 3 kits. No rm phones. June-Oct, MAP: S $125-$190; D $185-$235; each addl $30-$50; EP avail; lower rates rest of yr. Crib free. Pet accepted. TV in some rms; VCR avail. Heated pool; sauna, poolside serv. Restaurant 7:30-9 am, 6-9 pm. Bar 5-11 pm. Ck-out 11 am, ck-in early afternoon. Bus depot transportation. Meeting rm. Business servs avail. Tennis. Downhill ski 12 mi; x-country ski 6 mi. Bicycles. Lawn games. Game rm. Some refrigerators, fireplaces. Private patios. Picnic tables. Library. Antiques. Gardens. Built in 1804. Cr cds: A, DS, MC, V. [icons]

Fairlee *(See also White River Junction)*

Lodge

✔ ★ **SILVER MAPLE.** *S Main St (VT 5).* 802/333-4326; res: 800/666-1946. 8 lodge rms, 2 share bath, no A/C; 8 cottages. No rm phones. S $48-$74; D $52-$78; each addl $6; cottages $69-$78; kit. cottages $72-$78. Pet accepted in cottages. TV in cottages. Complimentary continental bkfst. Restaurant nearby. Ck-out 11 am. Lodge built as farmhouse in 1790s. Wrap-around porch. Cr cds: A, DS, MC, V. [D] [icons] [SC]

Killington *(See also Woodstock)*

Motel

(Rates may be higher during fall foliage season)

✔ ★ ★ **VAL ROC.** *On US 4, ½ mi W of jct VT 100S.* 802/422-3881; res: 800/238-8762. Web www.killingtoninfo.com/valrock. 24 rms, 16 A/C, 1-2 story, 2 kits. Mid-Dec-mid-Apr: D $54-$92; each addl $12; kit. units $74-$98; under 12 free; family, wkly rates; higher rates wk of Dec 25; lower rates rest of yr. Crib free. Pet accepted. TV; cable (premium), VCR avail. Heated pool; whirlpool. Complimentary continental bkfst. Complimentary coffee in rms. Ck-out 11 am. Tennis. Downhill ski ¼ mi; x-country ski 3 mi. Game rm. Lawn games. Refrigerators. Some balconies. Picnic tables. Cr cds: A, C, D, MC, V.
[icons] [SC]

Ludlow *(See also Springfield)*

Inn

★ ★ **COMBES.** *RFD 1, Box 275, 5 mi N via VT 103, VT 100, follow signs.* 802/228-8799. Web www.vermontlodging.com. 11 units, 2 story. No rm phones. Mid-Sept-mid-Apr: S $58-$69; D $68-90; each addl $10-$21; MAP avail; family, wkly rates; golf, ski, theater package plans; higher rates last wk of Dec 25, hols; lower rates mid-May-mid-Sept. Closed rest of yr. Pet accepted. Dining rm (public by res) 8-9:30 am, 7 pm sitting. Rm serv 8-9:30 am. Ck-out 11 am, ck-in 2 pm. Bus depot transportation. Downhill ski 4 mi; x-country ski 3 mi. Game rm. Rec rm. Lawn games. Picnic tables, grills. Restored farmhouse (1850) on 50 acres; near Lake Rescue. Cr cds: A, DS, MC, V.

Lyndonville *(See also St Johnsbury)*

Inn

✔ ★ **OLD CUTTER.** *(RR 1, Box 62, East Burke 05832) 1 mi N on US 5 to VT 114, then 4 mi N to Burke Mountain Rd.* 802/626-5152. 10 rms, 2 story. S $44-$56; D $54-$66; each addl $10-$12; kit. suite $120-$140; under 12 free; MAP avail. Closed Apr, Nov. Crib free. Pet accepted. TV in lobby. Pool. Dining rm 5:30-9 pm. Ck-out 11 am, ck-in 1 pm. Downhill/x-country ski ¹/₂ mi. Lawn games. Picnic tables. Sitting rm. In restored farmhouse (ca 1845) & renovated turn-of-the-century carriage house. Cr cds: MC, V.

Marlboro *(See also Brattleboro)*

Inn

✔ ★ **WHETSTONE.** *¹/₂ mi off VT 9 (South Rd), follow Marlboro College signs.* 802/254-2500. 11 rms, 3 share bath, 2 story, 3 kits. No A/C. S $35-$60; D $55-$80; each addl $10; kit. units $75-$85; wkly rates. Crib $2. Pet accepted. Restaurant 8-10 am, 7-8 pm (public by res). Ck-out 2 pm, ck-in after 2 pm. Some refrigerators. Picnic tables. 18th-century country inn was originally a stagecoach stop; fireplaces in public rms. Swimming pond. No cr cds accepted.

Middlebury *(See also Brandon, Vergennes)*

Inn

★ ★ **MIDDLEBURY.** *Box 798, Court Square, on US 7.* 802/388-4961; FAX 802/388-4563; res: 800/842-4666. E-mail midinnut@sover.net; web www. middleburyinn .com. 45 rms in inn, 20 motel rms, 2-3 story. S $86-$160; D $90-$160; each addl $8; suites $144-$190. Crib free. Pet accepted, some restrictions; $8. TV; cable. Complimentary continental bkfst; afternoon refreshments. Coffee in motel rms. Restaurants 7:30-10 am, 11:30 am-2 pm, 5:30-9 pm (winter to 8 pm); Sun brunch 10:30 am-2 pm. Bar. Ck-out 11 am, ck-in 3 pm. Meeting rms. Business servs avail. Bellhops. Gift shop. Downhill/x-country ski 13 mi. Bathrm phones. Antiques. Porch dining in summer. Established in 1827. Cr cds: A, C, D, DS, MC, V.

Montpelier *(See also Waitsfield, Waterbury)*

Inn

★ ★ ★ **INN ON THE COMMON.** *(Main St, Craftsbury Common 05827) 7 mi E on US 2, 30 mi N on VT 14.* 802/586-9619; FAX 802/586-2249; res: 800/521-2233. 16 rms in 3 bldgs, 2 story. No A/C. No rm phones. MAP: S $135-$145; D $220-$240; suites $240; ski, package plans; higher rates: fall foliage. Serv charge 15%. Crib free. Pet accepted. TV, VCR in sitting rm. Heated pool. Afternoon refreshments. Dining rm 8-9:30 am, dinner (2 sittings) 6:30, 8 pm. Bar. Ck-out 11 am, ck-in 1 pm. Business servs avail. Tennis on site. Golf privileges. X-country ski on site. Bicycles (rentals). Health club privileges. Lawn games. Antiques. Library. Fireplace in 5 rms. Restored Federal-period houses in scenic Vermont village; landscaped gardens. Extensive film collection. Cr cds: MC, V.

Newfane *(See also Brattleboro)*

Inn

★ ★ ★ **FOUR COLUMNS.** *230 West St, On Village Green.* 802/365-7713. 15 rms, 4 suites. S, D $110-$125; each addl $25; suites $140-$200. Pet accepted. TV in lounge; cable (premium). Pool. Complimentary full bkfst. Dining rm (guests only) 8-9:30 am. Bar from 6 pm. Ck-out 11 am, ck-in 2 pm. Business servs avail. Stately 19th-century house; colonial furnishings. On 150 wooded acres; walking paths, gardens. Totally nonsmoking. Cr cds: A, DS, MC, V.

North Hero

Motel

★ ★ SHORE ACRES INN AND RESTAURANT. *US 2. 802/372-8722.* Web www.shoreacres.com. 23 rms, 6 A/C. Mid-June-mid-Oct: S, D $77.50-$97.50; lower rates rest of yr; limited rms avail mid-Oct-May. Pet accepted. TV; cable. Restaurant 7:30-10 am, 5-9 pm. Bar. Ck-out 10:30 am. Driving range. Lawn games. Two tennis courts. Some refrigerators. 50 acres on Lake Champlain; panoramic view. Cr cds: DS, MC, V.

St Johnsbury *(See also Lyndonville)*

Motel

✔ ★ AIME'S. *RFD 1, Box 332, 3 mi E at jct US 2, VT 18; I-93 exit 1. 802/748-3194.* 17 rms. D $35-$60; each addl $5. Crib free. TV; cable. Continental bkfst avail. Ck-out noon. Screened porches. Near brook. Cr cds: A, DS, MC, V.

Springfield

Motel

★ ★ HOLIDAY INN EXPRESS. *818 Charlestown Rd. 802/885-4516; FAX 802/885-4595.* 88 rms, 2 story. July-mid-Oct: S, D $79-$84; each addl $5; suites $150; under 19 free; higher rates graduation wk; lower rates rest of yr. Crib free. Pet accepted. TV; cable. Indoor pool. Complimentary continental bkfst. Restaurant 6 am-11 pm. Bar 4-11 pm. Ck-out noon. Meeting rms. Business servs avail. In-rm modem link. Valet serv. Downhill ski 20 mi; x-country ski 14 mi. Exercise equipt; weight machine, bicycle. Refrigerators, microwaves avail. Picnic tables. Cr cds: A, C, D, DS, JCB, MC, V.

Stowe *(See also Waterbury)*

Motels

(Rates may be higher during fall foliage season)

✔ ★ ★ COMMODORES INN. *PO Box 970, VT 100S. 802/253-7131; FAX 802/253-2360; res: 800/44-STOWE.* 50 rms, 2 story. Mid-Sept-mid-Oct, mid-Dec-mid-Mar: S $70-$100; D $84-$120; each addl $10; under 12 free; wkend rates; higher rates wk of Dec 25; lower rates rest of yr. Crib free. Pet accepted; $10. TV; cable, VCR avail. 2 pools, heated, 1 indoor; wading pool, whirlpools. Complimentary continental bkfst off season. Restaurant 7-10:30 am, 6-9:30 pm. Ck-out 11 am. Meeting rm. Business servs avail. In-rm modem link. Downhill ski 9 mi; x-country ski 6 mi. Exercise equipt; weight machine, bicycle, saunas. Game rm. Refrigerators avail. Cr cds: A, C, D, DS, MC, V.

★ ★ INNSBRUCK INN. *Mt Mansfield Rd, 4 mi W on VT 108. 802/253-8582; FAX 802/253-2260; res: 800/225-8582.* 28 rms, 2 story, 4 kits. Mid-Dec-mid-Apr: S $65-$79; D $74-$99; each addl $15; under 12 free; higher rates hol wks; lower rates rest of yr. Crib $7. Pet accepted, some restrictions; $7. TV; cable, VCR avail (movies $3). Heated pool; whirlpool. Restaurant 7:30-9:30 am. Bar (fall, winter only) 3:30 pm-1 am. Ck-out 11 am. Business servs avail. Ski shuttle. Indoor tennis privileges. Downhill ski 2 mi; x-country ski adj. Exercise equipt; stair machine, bicycle, sauna. Game rm. Refrigerators. Balconies. Picnic tables. Cr cds: A, DS, MC, V.

★ ★ ★ MOUNTAIN ROAD. *VT 108, 1 mi NW on VT 108. 802/253-4566; FAX 802/253-7397; res: 800/367-6873.* E-mail stowevt@aol.com; web www. stowevtusa.com. 30 rms, 7 suites (some with kit.), 7 kit. units. June-Oct, late Dec-Mar: D $89-$175; each addl $12-$20; suites $185-$295; kits. $115-$155; MAP avail; family, wkly rates; golf, ski plans; higher rates: hols, special events; lower rates rest of yr. Crib $5. Pet accepted; $15. TV; cable (premium), VCR avail. 2 pools, 1 indoor; whirlpool. Playground. Coffee in rms. Restaurant opp 7 am-9 pm. Ck-out 11 am. Business servs avail. Coin lndry. Sundries. RR station, bus depot, free ski lift transportation. Tennis. Downhill ski 4 mi; x-country ski 2½ mi. Bicycles. Exercise equipt; bicycles, rower, saunas. Rec rm. Lawn games. Some balconies. Refrigerators; some in-rm whirlpools; microwaves avail. Picnic tables, grills. Cr cds: A, C, D, DS, MC, V.

★ ★ **NOTCH BROOK.** *1229 Notch Brook Rd, 6 mi N; 1¹/₂ mi N of VT 108.* 802/253-4882; FAX 802/253-4882; res: 800/253-4882. E-mail nbrook@sover.net. 66 units, 33 kits. No A/C. Mid-Dec-Apr: S, D $69-$97; each addl $15; kit. units $85-$175; studio rms $119; townhouse $179; wkly rates; ski plan; higher rates winter hols; lower rates rest of yr. Crib $5. Pet accepted. TV; cable. Heated pool; saunas. Complimentary continental bkfst (in season). Ck-out 11 am. Coin lndry. Business servs avail. Some garage parking. Tennis. Downhill/x-country ski 4 mi. Some fireplaces. Balconies. On 16 acres. Cr cds: A, C, D, MC, V.

✔ ★ ★ **STOWE INN & TAVERN AT LITTLE RIVER.** *123 Mountain Rd, Mt Mansfield Rd at Bridge St, just N on VT 108.* 802/253-4836; FAX 802/253-7308; res: 800/227-1108 *(eastern US).* 43 rms in motel, lodge, 4 kits. Dec-Apr: D $55-$150; each addl $10; ski plan; higher rates special events; lower rates rest of yr. Crib $10. Pet accepted, some restrictions. TV; cable. Pool; whirlpool. Continental bkfst. Restaurant 11:30 am-9 pm. Bar. Ck-out 11 am. Business servs avail. Downhill ski 6 mi; x-country ski 4 mi. Rec rm. Some refrigerators. Cr cds: A, MC, V.

✔ ★ **WALKABOUT CREEK.** *199 Edson Hill Rd.* 802/253-7354; FAX 802/253-8429; res: 800/426-6697. Web www.stoweinfo.com/saa/walkabout. 20 rms, 5 with shower only, 2 story. Mid-Dec-mid-Mar, mid-June-Labor Day: S $55-$65; D $90-$110; each addl $35; 3-bdrm townhouse $350; family, wkly, wkend rates; ski plans; higher rates hols (2-day min); lower rates rest of yr. Crib free. Pet accepted; $10/day. 5 TVs; cable (premium). Pool; whirlpool. Complimentary full bkfst. Complimentary coffee in lobby. Restaurant 4-9 pm mid-June-Labor Day. Bar 4-11 am. Ck-out 11 am. Business servs avail. Tennis. Downhill ski 3 mi; x-country ski on site. Rec rm. Some balconies. Picnic tables. Totally nonsmoking. Cr cds: A, MC, V.

Inns

★ ★ **GREEN MOUNTAIN.** *PO Box 60, Main St, on VT 100.* 802/253-7301; FAX 802/253-5096; res: 800/786-9346. E-mail grnmtinn@aol.com; web www.greenmountain inne.com. 64 rms in inn, motel, 1-3 story, 1 carriage house. S, D $89-$139; suites $125-$189; each addl $15; MAP avail; under 12 free; higher rates: hols, Fall foliage. Crib free. Pet accepted. TV; cable, VCR (movies $3.50). Pool; whirlpool. Dining rm 7:30 am-9:30 pm. Rm serv. Bar noon-1 am. Ck-out 11 am, ck-in 2 pm. Meeting rm. Business servs avail. Downhill ski 6 mi; x-country ski 5 mi. Exercise equipt; weight machines, bicycles, sauna. Massage. Some fireplaces. Some balconies. Historic inn (1833); antiques, library, paintings by Vermont artist. Cr cds: A, DS, MC, V.

Stratton Mountain

Motel

★ ★ **LIFTLINE LODGE.** *(Stratton Mountain Rd, Stratton)* 802/297-2600; FAX 802/297-2949; res: 800/597-5438. 91 rms, 2 story, 69 with A/C. Mid-Dec-mid-Mar: S, D $125-$135; each addl $15; kit. units $225-$275; under 16 free; wkly rates; ski, golf plans; higher rates fall foliage season; lower rates rest of yr. Crib free. Pet accepted. TV; cable, VCR avail. Pool; whirlpools, saunas. Complimentary coffee in lobby. Restaurant 7:30-10:30 am, 5:30-9 pm; wkends 6-10 pm. Bar 4 pm-1 am; entertainment ski season. Ck-out 11 am. Meeting rms. Business servs avail. In-rm modem link. Lighted tennis. 27-hole golf privileges, greens fee $63, putting green, driving range. Downhill ski adj; x-country ski 1 mi. Exercise equipt; weight machine, bicycle. Rec rm. Cr cds: A, MC, V.

Vergennes *(See also Middlebury)*

Resort

★ ★ **BASIN HARBOR CLUB.** *Basin Harbor Rd, 6 mi W of US 7, VT 22A.* 802/475-2311; FAX 802/475-6545; res: 800/622-4000. E-mail res@basinharbor.com; web www.basinharbor.com. 40 rms in lodges, 77 cottages (1-3 bedrm). Mid-May-mid-Oct, AP: S $165; D $220-$375; each addl $5-$70; EP avail mid-May-mid-June, Sept-Oct; wkly rates. Closed rest of yr. Crib avail. Pet accepted, some restrictions. TV avail. Heated pool; poolside serv, lifeguard. Free supervised child's activities (July-Aug); ages 3-13. Dining rm 8 am-10 pm. Box lunches. Bar 11 am-midnight. Ck-out noon, ck-in 4 pm. Coin lndry. Business servs avail. Concierge. Gift shop. Airport, RR station, bus depot transportation. Rec dirs. Exercise rm; instructor, treadmill, rower. Massage. Tennis. 18-hole golf, greens fee $42, putting green. Beach; motorboats, sailboats, canoes, cruise boat; windsurfing, waterskiing. Fitness, nature trails. Lawn games. Bicycles. Rec rm. Refrigerator in cottages. Family-owned since 1886; colonial architecture. Located on 700 acres, on Lake Champlain; dockage. 3,200-ft airstrip avail. Cr cds: MC, V.

Waitsfield *(See also Montpelier, Warren, Waterbury)*

Inn

★ **WHITE HORSE INN.** *German Flats Rd. 802/496-3260; res: 800/323-3260; FAX 802/496-2476.* 24 rms, 16 with shower only, 2 story. No A/C. No rm phones. Dec-Mar: S $50-$70; D $64-$94; each addl $15; ski plans; hols, wkends (2-day min); lower rates rest of yr. Pet accepted. Premium cable TV in some rms. Complimentary full bkfst. Ck-out noon, ck-in 3 pm. Downhill ski ½ mi; x-country ski 2 mi. Picnic tables, grill. Totally nonsmoking. Cr cds: A, DS, MC, V. 🐾 ⛷ ⬛ 🐕

Warren *(See also Waitsfield, Waterbury)*

Motel

✔★ **GOLDEN LION RIVERSIDE INN.** *VT 100, 1 mi N. 802/496-3084.* 12 rms, 2 kit. units. No A/C. Mid-Sept-mid-Apr: S, D $55-$65; each addl $10; under 6 free; higher rates wkends, hols; lower rates rest of yr. Crib free. Pet accepted. TV; cable. Complimentary full bkfst. Restaurant nearby. Ck-out 11 am. Downhill/x-country ski 3 mi. Picnic table, grill. Cr cds: A, DS, MC, V. 🐾 ⛷ 🐕 SC

★ **POWDERHOUND INN.** *Rte 100, 1¼ mi N on VT 100, at jct Sugarbush Access Rd. 802/496-5100; FAX 802/496-5163; res: 800/548-4022.* 48 units, 44 kit. units, 1-2 story. No A/C. Dec-late Mar: S, D $80-$115; higher rates: wk of Washington's birthday, wk of Dec 25; lower rates rest of yr. Crib $5. Pet accepted; $5. TV; cable. Pool; whirlpool. Restaurant (in season only) 7:30-9:30 am. Ck-out 10 am. Tennis. Downhill/x-country ski 3 mi. Game rm. Lawn games. Balconies. Picnic tables, grills. Restored, 19th-century farmhouse. Cr cds: A, DS, MC, V. 🐾 ⛷ 🏂 ⬛ 🐕

Waterbury *(See also Montpelier, Stowe, Waitsfield, Warren)*

Motel

★★ **HOLIDAY INN.** *Blush Hill Rd, at jct of I-89 exit 10 & VT 100 N. 802/244-7822; FAX 802/244-7822.* 79 rms, 2 story. S, D $70-$135; each addl $8; under 12 free; higher rates fall foliage. Crib free. Pet accepted. TV; cable (premium); VCR avail (movies). Pool; sauna. Restaurant 6:30 am-2 pm, 5:30-9 pm; Sat, Sun 7 am-2 pm, 5:30-10 pm. Rm serv. Bar; entertainment Fri, Sat, dancing. Ck-out noon. Meeting rms. Coin lndry. Tennis. Business servs avail. In-rm modem link. Downhill/x-country ski 12 mi. Game rm. Picnic tables. Covered bridge. Cr cds: A, C, D, DS, ER, JCB, MC, V. D 🐾 ⛷ 🏂 ⬛ 🐕 SC

White River Junction
(See also Woodstock; also see Hanover, NH)

Motels

✔★★ **BEST WESTERN AT THE JUNCTION.** *1 mi S on US 5, 1 blk E of jct I-89, I-91. 802/295-3015; FAX 802/296-2581.* 112 rms, 2 story. Mid-May-Mid-Sept: S $59-$76; D $71-$110; each addl $10; under 18 free; higher rates: fall foliage, special events; lower rates rest of yr. Crib free. Pet accepted; $10. TV; cable (premium). Indoor pool; wading pool, whirlpool. Playground. Restaurant adj 6 am-10 pm; Sat to 1 am. Bar 4 pm-1 am. Ck-out 11 am. Coin lndry. Meeting rms. Sundries. Downhill ski 20 mi; x-country ski 14 mi. Exercise equipt; bicycles, rower, sauna. Game rm. Microwaves avail. Private patios, balconies. Cr cds: A, C, D, DS, ER, JCB, MC, V. D 🐾 ⛷ ⬛ 🏋 🐕 SC

★★ **HOLIDAY INN.** *Sykes Ave & Holiday Inn Dr, 2 mi SW on US 5; off Sykes Ave at jct I-89, I-91. 802/295-3000; FAX 802/295-3774.* 140 rms, 2 story. S $59-$81; D $59-$97; each addl $6; under 19 free; ski plan; wkend rates; higher rates: fall foliage. Crib free. Pet accepted. TV; cable (premium). Indoor pool; whirlpool. Coffee in rms. Restaurants 7 am-10 pm. Rm serv. Bar 4 pm-1 am; entertainment. Ck-out noon. Meeting rms. Business servs avail. Bellhops. Sundries. Putting green. Downhill ski 15 mi. Exercise equipt; bicycle, treadmill, sauna. Game rm. Balconies. Cr cds: A, C, D, DS, ER, JCB, MC, V.
D 🐾 ⛷ ⬛ 🏋 🐕 SC

Woodstock *(See also Killington, White River Junction)*

Inns

★★★ **KEDRON VALLEY.** *South Woodstock (05071), 5 mi S on VT 106. 802/457-1473; res: 800/836-1193; FAX 802/457-4469.* E-mail kedroninn@aol.com. 26 inn rms, 1-3 story. 8 with A/C. No elvtr. No rm phones. S, D $120-$215; each addl $5; MAP avail; mid-wk rates; wkend riding plan; higher rates: fall foliage, Dec 25. Closed Apr. Crib free. Pet accepted. TV. Restaurant 8-9:30 am, 6-9 pm. Bar 5-11 pm. Ck-out 11:30 am, ck-in 3:30 pm. Business servs avail. Downhill ski 7 mi; x-country ski 3 mi. Some fireplaces, wood stoves. Some private patios. Natural pond. Cr cds: DS, MC, V. 🖔 🖘 🐟 ⛷ 🞣 🐾

★ ★ **WINSLOW HOUSE.** *38 US 4, W on US 4.* 802/457-1820. 4 rms, 2 story. S $55; D $75-$85; each addl $15; under 6 free; 2-day min hols; higher rates fall foliage. Pet accepted. TV; cable (premium). Complimentary full bkfst. Ck-out 11 am, ck-in 2 pm. Downhill ski 8 mi; x-country ski 3 mi. Lawn games. Refrigerators. Farmhouse built 1872; period furnishings. Totally nonsmoking. Cr cds: C, D, DS, MC, V. 🖔 ⛷ 🞣 🐾

Virginia

Alexandria
(See also Arlington County, Fairfax; also see District of Columbia)

Motels

★ ★ **BEST WESTERN OLD COLONY INN.** *615 1st St (22314), near National Airport. 703/739-2222; FAX 703/549-2568.* 151 rms, 2 story. Apr-June: S $89; D $99; each addl $10; kits. $99-$109; under 18 free; wkend, hol rates; lower rates rest of yr. Crib free. Pet accepted; $50 deposit & $10/day. TV; cable (premium). Pool; lifeguard. Complimentary continental bkfst. Restaurant adj 6:30 am-10 pm. Ck-out noon. Meeting rms. Business servs avail. In-rm modem link. Sundries. Valet serv. Free airport transportation. Health club privileges. Cr cds: A, C, D, DS, MC, V. [D] 🐾 ➰ ✈ ➰ 🐾 SC

✔ ★ **COMFORT INN-MT VERNON.** *7212 Richmond Hwy (US 1) (22306). 703/765-9000; FAX 703/765-2325.* 92 rms, 2 story. S $50-$65; D $55-$75; each addl $7; under 17 free; wkly, wkend rates. Crib free. Pet accepted, some restrictions. TV; cable (premium), VCR avail (movies $5). Pool; lifeguard. Complimentary continental bkfst. Restaurant nearby. Ck-out noon. Meeting rm. Business servs avail. In-rm modem link. Valet serv. Refrigerators, microwaves avail. Cr cds: A, C, D, DS, MC, V. [D] 🐾 ➰ ➰ 🐾 SC

★ **ECONO LODGE OLD TOWN.** *700 N Washington St (22314). 703/836-5100; FAX 703/519-7015.* 39 rms, 2 story. S $54.95; D $64.95; each addl $5; under 18 free. Crib free. Pet accepted, some restrictions. TV; cable. Restaurant nearby. Ck-out 11 am. Business servs avail. Free airport transportation. Microwaves avail. Cr cds: A, D, DS, MC, V. 🐾 ➰ 🐾 SC

✔ ★ **RED ROOF INN.** *5975 Richmond Hwy (US 1) (22303). 703/960-5200; FAX 703/960-5209.* Web www.redroofinn.com. 115 rms, 3 story. Apr-Oct: S, D $63.99-$75.99; each addl $7; under 18 free; higher rates special events; lower rates rest of yr. Crib free. Pet accepted, some restrictions. TV; cable (premium). Complimentary coffee in lobby. Restaurant nearby. Ck-out noon. Business servs avail. In-rm modem link. Coin lndry. Valet serv. Cr cds: A, C, D, DS, MC, V. [D] 🐾 ➰ 🐾 SC

Motor Hotels

★ ★ **EXECUTIVE CLUB SUITES.** *610 Bashford Ln (22314). 703/739-2582; FAX 703/548-0266; res: 800/535-2582.* 78 kit. suites, 3 story. No elvtr. S, D $179-$199; wkend, hol rates. Crib free. Pet accepted, some restrictions. TV; cable (premium). Pool; lifeguard. Complimentary continental bkfst. Complimentary coffee in rms. Restaurant nearby. Ck-out noon. Coin lndry. Meeting rms. Business center. In-rm modem link. Valet serv. Sundries. Free airport transportation. Exercise equipt; weight machine, treadmill, sauna. Microwaves. Picnic tables. Cr cds: A, C, D, DS, ER, MC, V. 🐾 ➰ 🏃 ➰ 🐾 🏃

★ ★ **HOWARD JOHNSON-OLDE TOWNE.** *5821 Richmond Hwy (US 1) (22303). 703/329-1400; FAX 703/329-1424.* E-mail 74664.2275@compuserv. 156 rms, 7 story. Mar-June: S $55-$91; D $65-$99; each addl $10; under 18 free; lower rates rest of yr. Crib free. Pet accepted, some restrictions. TV; cable (premium), VCR avail. Indoor pool. Restaurant 6 am-10 pm; Fri, Sat to 11 pm. Rm serv. Bar. Ck-out noon. Meeting rms. Business servs avail. In-rm modem link. Valet serv. Gift shop. Beauty shop. Free airport transportation. Exercise equipt; weights, bicycles, sauna. Some in-rm whirlpools; microwaves avail. Cr cds: A, C, D, DS, JCB, MC, V. [D] 🐾 ➰ 🏃 ➰ 🐾 SC

Hotels

★ ★ **DOUBLETREE GUEST SUITES.** *100 S Reynolds St (22304). 703/370-9600; FAX 703/370-0467.* 225 kit. suites, 9 story. Mid-Mar-Oct: S $79-$140; D $89-$180; each addl $20; under 18 free; wkend rates; lower rates rest of yr. Crib free. Pet accepted; $10/day. TV; cable. Pool; lifeguard. Complimentary continental bkfst. Restaurant 6:30-9:30 am, 11 am-3 pm, 5-10 pm. Bar from 4 pm. Ck-out noon. Coin lndry. Meeting rms. Business center. In-rm modem link. Exercise equipt; weight machine, treadmills. Health club privileges. Microwaves. Some balconies. Cr cds: A, C, D, DS, MC, V. [D] 🐾 ➰ 🏃 ➰ 🐾 🏃

★ ★ **HOLIDAY INN SELECT OLD TOWN.** *480 King St (22314). 703/549-6080; FAX 703/684-6508.* E-mail othismta@erols.com; web www.hiselect.com. 227 rms, 6 story. S $120-$170; D $135-$190; each addl $20; suites $225-$300; under 18 free; wkend rates. Crib free. Pet accepted, some restrictions. Garage $7. TV; cable (premium). Indoor pool; lifeguard. Complimentary continental bkfst (Mon-Fri). Complimentary coffee in rms. Restaurant 6:30 am-11 pm. Bars 11 am-midnight. Ck-out noon. Coin lndry. Meeting rms. Business center. In-rm modem link. Concierge. Gift shop. Barber, beauty shop. Free airport transportation. Exercise equipt; bicycles, stair machines, sauna. Refrigerators, minibars, microwaves avail. Some balconies. Cr cds: A, C, D, DS, ER, JCB, MC, V.

★★ **RAMADA PLAZA HOTEL-OLD TOWN.** *901 N Fairfax St (22314). 703/683-6000; FAX 703/683-7597.* 258 rms, 12 story. S, D $125-$150; each addl $10; under 18 free; wkend rates. Crib free. Pet accepted, some restrictions. TV; cable (premium). Pool; lifeguard. Coffee in rms. Restaurant 6 am-10 pm. Bar 11-1 am. Ck-out 1 pm. Business servs avail. In-rm modem link. Gift shop. Free airport transportation. Health club privileges. Refrigerators, microwaves avail. Cr cds: A, C, D, DS, MC, V.

★★★ **SHERATON SUITES.** *801 N St Asaph St (22314). 703/836-4700; FAX 703/548-4514.* Web www.ittsheraton.com. 247 suites, 10 story. Apr-May: S, D $170; under 12 free; wkend, hol rates; lower rates rest of yr. Crib free. Pet accepted. Garage parking $8. TV; cable (premium). Indoor pool; whirlpool, lifeguard. Complimentary coffee in rms. Restaurant 6:30 am-10 pm; wkends from 7 am. Bar. Ck-out 1 pm. Guest lndry. Meeting rms. Business servs avail. In-rm modem link. Gift shop. Free airport transportation. Exercise equipt; weight machine, treadmill. Health club privileges. Refrigerators; microwaves avail. Cr cds: A, C, D, DS, ER, JCB, MC, V.

Arlington County (National Airport Area)

(See also Alexandria, Fairfax; also see District of Columbia)

Motel

★★ **EXECUTIVE CLUB SUITES.** *108 S Courthouse Rd (22204). 703/522-2582; FAX 703/486-2694.* 74 kit. suites, 2-3 story. Mar-Sept: kit. suites: $159-$179; wkend, wkly, hol rates; higher rates Cherry Blossom Festival; lower rates rest of yr. Crib free. Pet accepted, some restrictions; $250 deposit ($25 nonrefundable). TV; cable (premium), VCR avail. Complimentary continental bkfst. Complimentary coffee in rms. Ck-out noon. Meeting rms. Business servs avail. Valet serv. Sundries. Coin lndry. Free airport transportation. Exercise equipt; weights, weight machine, sauna. Health club privileges. Pool; whirlpool, lifeguard. Refrigerators, microwaves. Picnic tables, grills. Cr cds: A, C, D, DS, MC, V.

Hotels

★★ **BEST WESTERN KEY BRIDGE.** *1850 N Fort Myer Dr (22209). 703/522-0400; FAX 703/524-5275.* 178 rms, 11 story. S $113; D $123; suites $125-$155; under 12 free. Crib free. Pet accepted. TV; cable (premium). Pool. Restaurant 6:30 am-2 pm, 5-10 pm. Ck-out noon. Meeting rms. Business servs avail. Exercise equipt; bicycles, treadmill. Some refrigerators; microwaves avail. Cr cds: A, C, D, DS, MC, V.

★★ **DOUBLETREE.** *300 Army/Navy Dr (22202). 703/416-4100; FAX 703/416-4126.* Web www.doubletreehotels.com. 632 rms, 15 story, 265 suites. S, D $190; suites $200-$400; under 18 free; wkend rates. Crib free. Pet accepted. Garage $10; valet $12. TV; cable (premium). Indoor pool; sauna, lifeguard. Restaurant 6:30 am-11 pm. Bar 11-2 am; entertainment. Ck-out noon. Convention facilities. Business servs avail. In-rm modem link. Gift shop. Free airport transportation. Health club privileges. Bathrm phones; some refrigerators; microwaves avail. Some balconies. Luxury level. Cr cds: A, C, D, DS, ER, JCB, MC, V.

★★★ **HOLIDAY INN NATIONAL AIRPORT.** *1489 Jefferson Davis Hwy (22202). 703/416-1600; FAX 703/416-1615.* 306 rms, 11 story. S, D $145; each addl $10; suites $159-$165; under 20 free; wkend, hol rates. Crib free. Pet accepted, some restrictions. Garage $6. TV; cable (premium), VCR avail. Pool; lifeguard. Restaurant 6 am-10 pm; Sat, Sun from 7 am. Bar 11 am-midnight. Ck-out noon. Meeting rms. Business servs avail. In-rm modem link. Gift shop. Free airport transportation. Health club privileges. Game rm. Refrigerators avail. Cr cds: A, C, D, DS, JCB, MC, V.

★★★ **HOLIDAY INN ROSSLYN WESTPARK.** *1900 N Ft Myer Dr (22209). 703/807-2000; FAX 703/522-8864.* 306 rms, 20 story. S, D $109-$119; suites $135-$150; under 18 free; wkly, wkend, hol rates. Crib free. Pet accepted. TV; cable (premium). Indoor pool; lifeguard. Restaurant 6:30 am-11 pm. Bar 11:30 am-midnight. Ck-out noon. Coin lndry. Convention facilities. Business center. In-rm modem link. Garage parking. Exercise equipt: stair machine, treadmill. Health club privileges. Some refrigerators. Balconies. Overlooking Potomac River. Cr cds: A, C, D, DS, ER, JCB, MC, V.

★★★ **HYATT ARLINGTON.** *1325 Wilson Blvd (22209), near Key Bridge at Nash St & Wilson. 703/525-1234; FAX 703/875-3393.* 302 rms, 16 story. S $185; D $210; each addl $25; suites $275-$575; under 12 free; wkend rates. Crib free. Pet accepted, some restrictions. Garage $10 (Sun-Thurs). TV; cable (premium), VCR avail. Restaurant 6:30 am-mid-night. Bars 11 am-midnight. Ck-out noon. Free guest lndry. Meeting rms. Business center. In-rm modem link. Gift shop. Exercise equipt; bicycles, treadmill. Health club privileges. Metro adj. Cr cds: A, C, D, DS, ER, JCB, MC, V. [D] [▼] [✕] [♒] [✕] [✕] [✕] [SC] [✕]

★ ★ ★ MARRIOTT CRYSTAL GATEWAY. *1700 Jefferson Davis Hwy (US 1) (22202), entrance on S Eads St, between 15th & 17th Sts, near National Airport.* 703/920-3230; FAX 703/271-5212. 700 units, 16 story. S, D $192-$220; suites $199-$700; under 18 free; wkend rates. Crib free. Pet accepted, some restrictions. Garage $12. TV; cable (premium). Indoor/outdoor pool; whirlpool, lifeguard. Restaurant 6:30-2 am. Bar 11-2 am. Ck-out 1 pm. Convention facilities. Business center. In-rm modem link. Concierge. Free airport transportation. Tennis privileges. Exercise equipt; weights, bicycles, sauna. Health club privileges. Original artwork. Luxury level. Cr cds: A, C, D, DS, ER, JCB, MC, V. [D] [▼] [✕] [♒] [✕] [✕] [✕] [✕] [SC] [✕]

✔ ★ ★ QUALITY HOTEL COURTHOUSE PLAZA. *1200 N Courthouse Rd (22201).* 703/524-4000; FAX 703/522-6814. Web www.qualityhotelarlington.com. 391 rms, 1-10 story. S $59.95-$125.95; D $65.95-$135.95; each addl $10; suites $109.95-$169.95; under 18 free; wkend, wkly rates. Crib free. Pet accepted, some restrictions. TV; cable (premium). Pool; lifeguard. Coffee in rms. Restaurant 6:30 am-2 pm, 5-9:30 pm. Bar 4-10 pm. Ck-out noon. Coin lndry. Convention facilities. Business servs avail. In-rm modem link. Concierge. Gift shop. Exercise equipt; weight machine, rowers, sauna. Microwaves avail. Balconies. Luxury level. Cr cds: A, C, D, DS, ER, JCB, MC, V. [D] [▼] [♒] [✕] [✕] [✕] [SC]

Ashland *(See also Richmond)*

Motel

✔ ★ ★ COMFORT INN. *101 Cottage Green Dr.* 804/752-7777; FAX 804/798-0327. 126 rms, 2 story. Memorial Day-Labor Day: S, D $59-$73; each addl $5; suites $120; under 18 free; lower rates rest of yr. Crib free. Pet accepted. TV; cable. Pool. Complimentary continental bkfst. Restaurant adj open 24 hrs. Ck-out noon. Coin lndry. Business servs avail. Exercise equipt; weight machine, bicycles, sauna. Some refrigerators. Cr cds: A, C, D, DS, JCB, MC, V. [D] [▼] [♒] [✕] [✕] [✕] [SC]

Basye *(See also Luray, Woodstock)*

Motel

✔ ★ ★ BEST WESTERN-MT JACKSON. *(250 Conicville Rd, Mt Jackson 22842) at I-81 exit 273.* 540/477-2911; FAX 540/477-2392. 98 rms, 2 story. June-Oct: S $49-$53; D $53-$61; each addl $5; lower rates rest of yr. Crib free. Pet accepted. TV; cable. Pool; wading pool. Playground. Restaurant open 24 hrs. Bar 5-10 pm. Ck-out 11 am. Meeting rms. Business servs avail. Sundries. Gift shop. Tennis. Game rm. Cr cds: A, C, D, DS, MC, V. [D] [▼] [✕] [♒] [✕] [✕] [SC]

Inn

★ ★ ★ WIDOW KIP'S. *(355 Orchard Dr, Mt Jackson 22842) approx 9 mi E via VA 263E, then S on VA 698.* 540/477-2400; res: 800/478-8714. 5 rms, 2 cottages. No rm phones. S $55-$75; D $65-$85; each addl $15, lower rates mid-wk. Pet accepted in cottages. TV in sitting rm, cottages; cable (premium). Pool. Complimentary full bkfst. Picnic lunches avail. Ck-out 11 am, ck-in 3 pm. Some fireplaces. Bicycles. Grill. Federal-style saltbox house (1830) on 7 acres. Victorian furnishings. Totally nonsmoking. Cr cds: MC, V. [▼] [♒] [✕] [✕] [SC]

Blacksburg *(See also Radford, Roanoke)*

Motels

★ ★ COMFORT INN. *3705 S Main St.* 540/951-1500; FAX 540/951-1530. 80 rms, 4 story. S $57-$65; D $62-$67; each addl $5; suite $85; under 18 free; higher rates special events. Crib free. Pet accepted. TV; cable (premium), VCR avail. Pool. Complimentary continental bkfst. Restaurant adj 6 am-10 pm. Ck-out 11 am. Business servs avail. In-rm modem link. Valet serv. Exercise equipt; weight machine, rowers. Microwaves avail. Cr cds: A, C, D, DS, ER, JCB, MC, V. [D] [▼] [♒] [✕] [✕] [✕] [SC]

✔ ★ ★ DAYS INN. *(US 11, Christianburg 24073) 6 mi S, 1 blk NE of I-81 exit 118.* 540/382-0261; FAX 540/382-0365. 122 rms, 2 story. S $39-$84; D $44-$84; each addl $5; under 18 free; higher rates: Radford Univ graduation, football games. Crib free. Pet ac-

cepted. TV; cable (premium). Pool. Playground. Complimentary continental bkfst. Ck-out noon. In-rm modem link. Microwaves avail. Cr cds: A, C, D, DS, JCB, MC, V.
D ⌨ ≋ ⊠ 🐾 SC

★ ★ **HOLIDAY INN.** *3503 Holiday Ln. 540/951-1330; FAX 540/951-4847.* 98 rms, 2 story. S $55-$65; D $60-$70; each addl $5; suites $135; under 12 free; higher rates: univ graduation, football wkends. Crib free. Pet accepted. TV; cable (premium). Pool; wading pool. Restaurant 6:30 am-2 pm, 5-10 pm. Rm serv. Bar. Ck-out noon. Coin lndry. Meeting rm. Business servs avail. Valet serv. Sundries. X-country ski 20 mi. Some in-rm steam baths. Cr cds: A, C, D, DS, JCB, MC, V. D ⌨ ≋ ⊠ ⊠ 🐾 SC

Blue Ridge Parkway *(See also Roanoke, Waynesboro)*

Lodge

★ ★ ★ **DOE RUN.** *(Milepost 189, Fancy Gap 24328)* ¹⁄₈ *mi S of Blue Ridge Pkwy. 540/398-2212; FAX 540/398-2833; res: 800/325-6189.* Web www.hillsville.com/doerun. 47 kit. suites, 1-2 story. No elvtr. May-Oct: kit. suites $119-$250; each addl $18; under 15 free; wkly rates; hunting, golf plans; lower rates rest of yr. Crib free. Pet accepted; $45 deposit. TV; VCR (movies $3). Heated pool; sauna, poolside serv. Complimentary coffee in rms. Restaurant 8 am-10 pm. Bar; entertainment Fri, Sat. Ck-out noon. Meeting rms. Business servs avail. Sundries. Lighted tennis. 18-hole golf privileges, greens fee, pro, putting green, driving range. Rec rm. Lawn games. Balconies. Picnic tables. Cr cds: A, MC, V.
D ⌨ ⊿ 🏌 🎿 ≋ ⊠ 🐾 SC

Bristol

Motels

(Most rates higher race weekends)

✔ ★ **RED CARPET INN.** *15589 Lee Hwy (24202), I-81 exit 10. 540/669-1151.* 60 rms, 2 story. June-Oct: S $35-$74; D $38-$80; each addl $6; lower rates rest of yr. Crib free. Pet accepted, some restrictions. TV; cable (premium). Pool. Ck-out noon. Business servs avail. Microwaves avail. Cr cds: A, D, DS, MC, V. ⌨ ≋ ⊠ 🐾 SC

★ **SUPER 8.** *2139 Lee Hwy, I-81 exit 5. 540/466-8800; FAX 540/466-8800, ext. 400.* 62 rms, 3 story. S, D $43-$61; each addl $6; under 12 free. Crib free. Pet accepted. TV; cable. Complimentary coffee in lobby. Restaurant nearby. Ck-out 11 am. Business servs avail. Some refrigerators, microwaves. Picnic tables. Cr cds: A, C, D, DS, JCB, MC, V.
D ⌨ ⊠ 🐾 SC

Charlottesville *(See also Waynesboro)*

Motels

✔ ★ ★ **BEST WESTERN-MOUNT VERNON.** *1613 Emmet St (22901), Jct US 29 Business and US 250 Bypass. 804/296-5501; FAX 804/977-6249.* 110 rms, 1-2 story. Mar-Oct: S $51-$55; D $58-$65; each addl $6; under 18 free; family, wkly rates; higher rates graduation; lower rates rest of yr. Crib free. Pet accepted, some restrictions. TV; cable (premium). Complimentary coffee in rms. Restaurant adj 6-10 am. Ck-out noon. Meeting rms. Business servs avail. Bellhops. Sundries. Pool; wading pool. Microwaves, refrigerators avail. Cr cds: A, C, D, DS, ER, JCB, MC, V. D ⌨ ≋ ⊠ 🐾 SC

★ ★ **HOLIDAY INN.** *1600 Emmet St (22901), near jct US 29 Business & US 250 Bypass. 804/293-9111; FAX 804/977-2780.* 129 rms, 3 story. S $64-$68; D $74-$78; each addl $10; under 18 free; higher rates special univ events. Crib free. Pet accepted. TV; cable (premium), VCR avail. Pool; wading pool. Restaurant 6:30 am-10 pm; Fri, Sat to 11 pm. Rm serv. Bar 10-1 am. Ck-out noon. Meeting rms. Business servs avail. In-rm modem link. Bellhops. Valet serv. Free airport, RR station, bus depot transportation. Exercise equipt; bicycle, stair machine, sauna. Health club privileges. Cr cds: A, C, D, DS, JCB, MC, V.
D ⌨ ≋ 🏃 ⊠ 🐾 SC

✔ ★ **KNIGHTS INN.** *1300 Seminole Trail (22901), US 29N. 804/973-8133; FAX 804/973-1168.* 115 units. S, D $39-$58; each addl $6; kits. $63; under 18 free; wkly rates. Crib free. Pet accepted, some restrictions. TV; cable (premium), VCR avail (movies). Pool. Complimentary coffee in lobby. Restaurant nearby. Ck-out noon. Meeting rm. Business servs avail. Cr cds: A, C, D, DS, MC, V. D ⌨ ≋ ⊠ 🐾 SC

Motor Hotel

★ **BEST WESTERN CAVALIER INN.** *105 Emmet St (22903), jct US Business 29, US 250. 804/296-8111; FAX 804/296-3523.* 118 rms, 5 story. S $63-$79; D $73-$89;

each addl $8; suites $125; under 18 free; 2-day packages; higher rates univ events. Crib free. Pet accepted. TV; cable (premium). Pool. Complimentary continental bkfst. Coffee in rms. Restaurant 11:30 am-10 pm. Rm serv. Bar to 1 am. Ck-out 1 pm. Meeting rms. Business servs avail. Bellhops. Valet serv. Free airport, RR station, bus depot transportation. Univ of VA opp. Cr cds: A, C, D, DS, MC, V. [D] 🐾 🏊 ✕ 🎿 🐾 [SC]

Hotel

★ ★ OMNI. *235 W Main St (22902). 804/971-5500; FAX 804/979-4456.* 204 rms, 7 story. S $144-$154; D $139-$174; each addl $15; under 18 free; suites $200-$295; wkend rates; higher rates univ events. Crib free. Pet accepted, some restrictions. TV; cable (premium), VCR avail. 2 pools, 1 indoor; whirlpool, poolside serv. Coffee in rms. Restaurant 6:30 am-10 pm. Bar 11-1 am. Ck-out noon. Convention facilities. Business servs avail. Gift shop. Free covered parking. Free airport, RR station, bus depot transportation. Exercise equipt; weights, bicycles, sauna. Refrigerators avail. Ultra-modern architecture; 7-story atrium lobby. Cr cds: A, C, D, DS, JCB, MC, V. [D] 🐾 🏊 ✕ 🎿 🐾 [SC]

Chesapeake *(See also Norfolk, Portsmouth, Virginia Beach)*

Motels

✔ ★ COMFORT INN-BOWERS HILL. *4433 S Military Hwy (23321). 757/488-7900; FAX 757/488-6152.* 93 rms, 2 story, 7 kit. units. May-Sept: S, D $65; each addl $5; kits. $70; wkly rates; higher rates major summer hols; lower rates rest of yr. Crib free. Pet accepted; $5. TV; cable (premium). Pool. Complimentary continental bkfst. Ck-out 11 am. Business servs avail. Cr cds: A, C, D, DS, ER, JCB, MC, V. [D] 🐾 🏊 🎿 🐾 [SC]

★ WELLESLEY INN. *1750 Sara Dr (23320). 757/366-0100; FAX 757/366-0396.* 106 rms, 4 story. S $55-$70; D $60-$75; each addl $10; suites $65-$85; under 18 free. Crib free. Pet accepted; $5. TV; cable (premium). Pool. Complimentary continental bkfst. Coffee in rms. Restaurant adj 6:30 am-10:30 pm. Ck-out 11 am. Meeting rms. Business servs avail. Valet serv. Coin lndry. Health club privileges. Refrigerators, microwaves. Cr cds: A, C, D, DS, ER, JCB, MC, V. [D] 🐾 🏊 🎿 🐾 [SC]

Clarksville *(See also South Hill)*

Motel

✔ ★ LAKE. *101 Virginia Ave. 804/374-8106; FAX 804/374-0108.* 76 rms, 2 story, 3 suites. Mid-May-mid-Sept: S, D $49-$65; each addl $5; suites $65-$85; under 12 free; lower rates rest of yr. Pet accepted. TV; cable. Pool. Restaurant adj 6 am-10 pm. Bar 5 pm-1 am. Ck-out 11 am. Meeting rms. Business servs avail. Free airport transportation. Refrigerators avail. Picnic tables, grills. On lake; swimming. Cr cds: A, MC, V.
[D] 🐾 🏊 🐾 [SC]

Clifton Forge *(See also Covington, Lexington)*

Inn

★ ★ LONGDALE INN. *6209 Longdale Furnace Rd, I-64 exit 35. 540/862-0892; FAX 540/862-3554.* 10 rms, 3 with shower only, 4 share bath, 3 story, 2 suites. No A/C. Rm phones avail. S, D $75-$95; each addl $25; suites $95-$120; wkly rates. Crib $25. Pet accepted. TV in common rm; VCR. Complimentary full bkfst. Ck-out 11 am, ck-in 3 pm. Business servs avail. Gift shop. X-country ski 2 mi. Playground. Game rm. Lawn games. Many fireplaces. Picnic tables, grills. Virginia countryside setting; Victorian inn built in 1873. Totally nonsmoking. Cr cds: A, DS, MC, V. 🐾 🏊 🎿 🐾

Covington *(See also Clifton Forge, Hot Springs)*

Motels

✔ ★ ★ BEST WESTERN-MOUNTAIN VIEW. *820 E Madison, on US 60 at jct I-64 exit 16. 540/962-4951; FAX 540/965-5714.* 79 rms, 2 story. S $52-$69; D $66-$79; each addl $8; under 18 free. Crib free. Pet accepted; $10. TV; cable (premium). Pool; wading pool. Coffee in rms. Restaurant 6 am-2 pm, 5-10 pm. Rm serv. Ck-out 11 am. Meeting rms. Business servs avail. In-rm modem link. Bellhops. Valet serv. Some refrigerators. Cr cds: A, C, D, DS, ER, JCB, MC, V. [D] 🐾 🏊 🎿 🐾 [SC]

★ ★ COMFORT INN. *203 Interstate Dr, I-64 exit 16. 540/962-2141; FAX 540/965-0964.* 99 units, 2 story, 32 suites. S $50-$64; D $69-$74; each addl $8; suites $68-$81; under 18 free. Crib free. Pet accepted; $10. TV; cable (premium), VCR (movies $4). Pool;

whirlpool. Restaurant 7 am-midnight. Bar 4 pm-2 am. Ck-out 11 am. Business servs avail. Guest lndry. Sundries. Some refrigerators. Cr cds: A, C, D, DS, ER, JCB, MC, V.

[D] 🐾 ⚏ ⊠ 🖎 [SC]

Inn

★ ★ ★ **MILTON HALL BED & BREAKFAST.** *207 Thorny Lane.* 540/965-0196. 6 rms, 2 with shower only, 2 story, 1 suite. Some rm phones. S $75; D $85; each addl $10; suite $130-$140; under 10 free; hunting, fishing plans. Crib free. Pet accepted. TV in some rms, sitting rm; cable (premium). Complimentary full bkfst. Ck-out noon, ck-in 2 pm. Lawn games. Historic country manor house (1874) on 44 acres adj George Washington National Forest. Cr cds: MC, V. 🐾 🖎 [SC]

Culpeper (See also Warrenton)

Motels

★ ★ **COMFORT INN.** *890 Willis Ln.* 540/825-4900; FAX 540/825-4904. 49 rms, 2 story. Apr-Oct: S $58; D $65; each addl $8; under 18 free. Crib free. Pet accepted; $10. TV; cable (premium). Pool. Complimentary continental bkfst. Complimentary coffee in rms. Ck-out 11 am. Business servs avail. In-rm modem link. Refrigerators avail. Cr cds: A, C, D, DS, JCB, MC, V. [D] 🐾 ⚏ ⊠ 🖎 [SC]

✔ ★ ★ **HOLIDAY INN.** *US 29, 2¹/₂ mi S on US 29.* 540/825-1253; FAX 540/825-7134. 159 rms, 2 story. S, D $59; under 19 free. Crib free. Pet accepted, some restrictions. TV; cable. Pool; wading pool. Restaurant 6 am-2 pm, 5-10 pm. Rm serv. Bar 4 pm-12:30 am; entertainment. Ck-out noon. Coin lndry. Meeting rms. Business sersv avail. In-rm modem link. Valet serv. Sundries. Refrigerators avail. Cr cds: A, C, D, DS, JCB, MC, V.

[D] 🐾 ⚏ ⊠ 🖎 [SC]

Guest Ranch

★ ★ **GRAVES' MOUNTAIN LODGE.** *(VA 670, Syria 22743) 20 mi W via US 29, VA 609 & VA 231 to VA 670.* 540/923-4231; FAX 540/923-4312. 40 rms, 13 cottages, 8 kits. AP, mid-Mar-Nov: S $57-$92; D $65-$98/person; kit. cottages $110-$230; higher rates Oct. Closed rest of yr. Crib free. Pet accepted. Pool; wading pool, lifeguard. Playground. Dining rm (public by res) 8:30-9:30 am, 12:30-1:30 pm, 6:30-7:30 pm. Box lunches. Ck-out 11 am, ck-in 3 pm. Coin lndry. Grocery ¹/₄ mi. Meeting rms. Business servs avail. Tennis. Golf privileges, greens fee $45. Lawn games. Rec·rm. Some fireplaces. Picnic tables, grills. Cr cds: DS, MC, V. 🐾 🖘 📄 👣 🖋 ⚏ ⊠ 🖎

Danville (See also Martinsville)

Motel

(Rates may be higher during sports car races in Martinsville)

★ ★ **STRATFORD INN.** *2500 Riverside Dr (US 58) (24540).* 804/793-2500; FAX 804/793-6960; res: 800/326-8455. 152 rms, 2 story. S $43-$48; D $48-$55; each addl $7; suites $88-$150; under 18 free. Crib free. Pet accepted. TV; cable (premium), VCR avail. Heated pool; wading pool; whirlpool. Complimentary full bkfst. Restaurant 6 am-10 pm. Rm serv. Bar to midnight. Ck-out noon. Coin lndry. Meeting rms. Business servs avail. Valet serv. Sundries. Exercise equipt; treadmill, stair machine. Cr cds: A, C, D, DS, MC, V.

[D] 🐾 ⚏ 🖋 ⊠ 🖎 [SC]

Dulles Intl Airport Area (See also Fairfax)

Motels

★ ★ **HOLIDAY INN EXPRESS.** *(485 Elden St, Herndon 20170) Dulles Toll Rd exit 10, then E on Elden St.* 703/478-9777; FAX 703/471-4624. E-mail disales@bfsaulco.com. 115 rms, 4 story. S, D $84-$99; each addl $6; under 19 free. Crib free. Pet accepted, some restrictions. TV; cable (premium). Complimentary continental bkfst. Complimentary coffee in rms. Restaurant nearby. Ck-out 11 am. Meeting rm. Business servs avail. Valet serv. Free airport transportation. Exercise equipt; weights, bicycles. Refrigerators, microwaves avail. Cr cds: A, C, D, DS, JCB, MC, V. [D] 🐾 🖋 ⊠ ⚏ 🖎 [SC]

★ ★ **RESIDENCE INN BY MARRIOTT.** *(315 Elden St, Herndon 20170) Dulles Toll Rd exit 12, then left on Baron Cameron Rd (VA 606).* 703/435-0044; FAX 703/437-4007. Web www.marriott.com. 168 kit. units, 2 story. S, D $135-$169; wkend rates. Crib free. Pet accepted; $100 nonrefundable, $6/day. TV; cable (premium), VCR avail (movies). Pool; whirlpool, lifeguard. Playground. Complimentary continental bkfst. Complimentary coffee in rms. Restaurant opp 6:30 am-10 pm. Ck-out noon. Coin lndry. Business servs avail. In-rm modem link. Valet serv. Sundries. Lighted tennis. Health club privileges. Microwaves. Picnic tables. Cr cds: A, C, D, DS, JCB, MC, V. [symbols]

Motor Hotel

★ ★ ★ **HOLIDAY INN.** *(1000 Sully Rd, Sterling 20166) Dulles Toll Rd exit 9B (US 28/Sully Rd), then 1 mi N.* 703/471-7411. 296 rms, 2 story. S, D $125; suites $130-$160; each addl $10; under 18 free; wknd rates. Crib free. Pet accepted, some restrictions. TV; cable (premium). Indoor pool; whirlpool, lifeguard. Restaurant 6:30 am-10:30 pm. Rm serv to midnight. Bars 11-1:30 am, Sun to midnight; entertainment. Ck-out noon. Coin lndry. Meeting rms. Business center. In-rm modem link. Bellhops. Gift shop. Valet serv. Free airport transportation. Exercise equipt; weights, bicycles, sauna. Refrigerators avail. Rec rm. Cr cds: A, C, D, DS, JCB, MC, V. [symbols]

Hotel

✔ ★ ★ ★ **HILTON.** *(13869 Park Center Rd, Herndon 22171) On Sully Rd (VA 28), Dulles Toll Rd exit 9A, then 1 mi S to McLearen Rd.* 703/478-2900; FAX 703/834-1996. Web www.alma.net/hilton-wda. 301 rms, 5 story. S, D $110-$165; suites $360-$690; under 18 free; wkend rates. Crib free. Pet accepted, some restrictions. TV; cable (premium), VCR avail. 2 pools, 1 indoor; poolside serv, lifeguard. Coffee in rms. Restaurant 6 am-11 pm; Sat, Sun from 6:30 am. Rm serv 24 hrs. Bars 11:30 am-midnight; entertainment. Ck-out noon. Convention facilities. Business center. In-rm modem link. Gift shop. Barber, beauty shop. Free airport transportation. Tennis. Exercise equipt; weight machines, bicycles. Some bathrm phones, refrigerators. Luxury level. Cr cds: A, C, D, DS, ER, JCB, MC, V.

Resort

★ ★ ★ **WESTFIELDS MARRIOTT.** *(14750 Conference Center Dr, Chantilly 20151) 8 mi S on VA 28.* 703/818-0300; FAX 703/818-3655. Web www.marriott.com. 340 rms, 4 story. S $195; D $215; each addl $20; suites $295-$695; under 12 free; MAP avail; wkend rates. Crib free. Pet accepted, some restrictions. TV; cable (premium), VCR avail (movies). 2 pools, 1 indoor; whirlpool, poolside serv, lifeguard. Complimentary coffee in lobby. Restaurant 7 am-2 pm, 6-10 pm. Rm serv 6-1 am. Box lunches, picnics. Bar 11-1 am; entertainment. Ck-out 1 pm, ck-in 3 pm. Bellhops. Valet serv. Concierge. Gift shop. Convention facilities. Business center. In-rm modem link. Valet parking. Free airport transportation. Sports dir. Lighted tennis, pro. 18-hole golf, greens fee $75. Hiking. Bicycles. Lawn games. Basketball. Exercise rm; instructor, weights, bicycles, sauna, steam rm. Massage. Health club privileges. Minibars. Balconies. Picnic tables. Cr cds: A, C, D, DS, JCB, MC, V.
[symbols]

Emporia

Motels

★ **COMFORT INN.** *1411 Skipper's Rd (10960), at I-95 exit 8.* 804/348-3282. 96 rms, 2 story. S $48.95; D 56.95; each addl $4; family rates. Crib $2. Pet accepted. TV; cable (premium). Heated pool. Playground. Complimentary continental bkfst. Restaurant adj 5:30 am-11 pm. Business servs avail. In-rm modem link. Cr cds: A, C, D, DS, ER, MC, V.
[symbols]

★ ★ **HAMPTON INN.** *1207 W Atlantic St, (10960), off I-95 exit 11B.* 804/634-9200; FAX 804/348-0071. 115 rms, 2 story. S $54-$65; D $62-$65; under 18 free. Crib free. Pet accepted. TV; cable (premium). Pool. Complimentary continental bkfst. Restaurant nearby. Ck-out 11 am. Cr cds: A, C, D, DS, MC, V. [symbols]

Fairfax

(See also Alexandria, Arlington County; also see District of Columbia)

Hotels

★ **HOLIDAY INN.** *3535 Chain Bridge Rd (22030).* 703/591-5500; FAX 703/591-7483. 127 rms, 3 story. Mar-Oct: S $79-$99; D $89-$109; each addl $10; suites $99-$129; under 18 free; lower rates rest of yr. Crib free. Pet accepted, some restrictions. TV; cable (premium). Pool. Complimentary coffee in lobby. Restaurant 6:30-10 am, 5-10 pm. Ck-out noon. Meeting rms. Business servs avail. Valet serv. Coin lndry. Health club privileges. Some refrigerators; microwaves avail. Cr cds: A, C, D, DS, JCB, MC, V.
[symbols]

★ ★ ★ **HOLIDAY INN FAIR OAKS MALL.** *11787 Lee Jackson Hwy (22033), I-66, exit 57B.* 703/352-2525; FAX 703/352-4471. E-mail hifo@erols.com. 312 rms, 6 story. S, D $129-$149; each addl $10; under 19 free; wknd, hol rates. Crib free. Pet accepted. TV; cable (premium), VCR avail. Indoor pool; lifeguard. Complimentary coffee in rms. Restaurant 6:30 am-midnight. Bar; entertainment. Ck-out noon. Coin lndry. Convention facilities. Business center. In-rm modem link. Concierge. Gift shop. Airport transportation. Exercise equipt; weight machine, bicycle, sauna. Health club privileges. Game rm. Microwaves avail. Balconies. Luxury level. Cr cds: A, C, D, DS, ER, JCB, MC, V.

Fredericksburg

Motels

✔ ★ ★ **BEST WESTERN THUNDERBIRD.** *3000 Plank Rd (22401), I-95, exit 130B.* *540/786-7404; FAX 540/785-7415.* 76 rms, 2-3 story. Mar-Oct: S $42; D $48-$55; each addl $4; under 12 free. Crib $2. Pet accepted, some restrictions. TV; cable (premium). Complimentary continental bkfst. Restaurant nearby. Ck-out noon. Coin lndry. Business servs avail. Sundries. Valet serv. Refrigerators avail. Cr cds: A, C, D, DS, ER, MC, V.

✔ ★ ★ **DAYS INN-NORTH.** *14 Simpson Rd (22406), jct I-95 & US 17N, exit 133/133B. 540/373-5340; FAX 540/373-5340.* 120 rms, 2 story. S $38-$41; D $48-$51; each addl $5; under 12 free. Crib free. Pet accepted; $5. TV; cable (premium). Pool. Complimentary continental bkfst. Ck-out noon. Business servs avail. Cr cds: A, C, D, DS, MC, V.

★ ★ **HAMPTON INN.** *2310 William St (22401), E of I-95 exit 130A. 540/371-0330; FAX 540/371-1753.* 166 rms, 2 story. S $50; D $72; under 18 free; higher wkend rates. Crib free. Pet accepted, some restrictions. TV; cable (premium). Pool. Complimentary continental bkfst. Ck-out noon. Coin lndry. Meeting rms. Business servs avail. In-rm modem link. Cr cds: A, C, D, DS, MC, V.

✔ ★ **RAMADA INN-SPOTSYLVANIA MALL.** *2802 Plank Rd (22404), Jct I-95, VA 3W, exit 130B. 540/786-8361; FAX 540/786-8811.* 130 rms, 2 story. S $45-$57; D $50-$62; each addl $5; suites $75-$100; under 18 free. Crib free. Pet accepted. TV; cable (premium). Pool. Complimentary coffee in lobby. Restaurant 6 am-10 pm. Rm serv 11 am-9 pm. Ck-out 1 pm. Meeting rms. Business servs avail. In-rm modem link. Valet serv. Sundries. Cr cds: A, C, D, DS, ER, JCB, MC, V.

Motor Hotel

★ ★ **HOLIDAY INN SOUTH.** *5324 Jefferson Davis Hwy (22408), I-95 exit 126. 540/898-1102; FAX 540/898-2017.* 195 rms, 2 story. S, D $61-$80; each addl $6; under 18 free; golf plans. Crib free. Pet accepted. TV; cable (premium), VCR avail (movies). Indoor pool; whirlpool. Coffee in lobby. Restaurant 6:30 am-1 pm, 5-9:30 pm. Rm serv. Bar 4 pm-2 am; entertainment Wed-Sat. Ck-out noon. Coin lndry. Meeting rms. Business servs avail. In-rm modem link. Bellhops. Sundries. Valet serv. Exercise equipt; bicycles, rowers. Game rm. Cr cds: A, C, D, DS, JCB, MC, V.

Hampton *(See also Newport News, Norfolk, Portsmouth, Virginia Beach)*

Motels

✔ ★ **ARROW INN.** *7 Semple Farm Rd (23666), I-64 exit 261B or 262B, 2 mi N on VA 134, E on Semple Farm Rd. 757/865-0300; FAX 757/766-9367; res: 800/833-2520.* E-mail mb@arrowinn.com; web www.arrowinn.com. 60 rms, 3 story, 21 kit. units. No elvtr. Memorial Day-Labor Day: S $43.90-$53.90; D $47.90-$57.90; each addl $5; kit. units $51.90-$59.90; under 18 free; wkly rates; higher rates jazz festival; lower rates rest of yr. Crib free. Pet accepted; $5-$30 per day. TV; cable (premium). Complimentary coffee in lobby. Restaurant adj 6-1 am. Ck-out noon. Business servs avail. Coin lndry. Refrigerators; many microwaves. Cr cds: A, C, D, DS, MC, V.

✔ ★ **HAMPTON INN.** *1813 W Mercury Blvd (23666). 757/838-8484; FAX 757/826-0725.* 132 rms, 6 story. S, D $69. Crib free. Pet accepted, some restrictions. TV; cable (premium). Pool privileges. Complimentary continental bkfst. Complimentary coffee in rms. Restaurant adj 6 am-10 pm. Ck-out noon. Business servs avail. In-rm modem link. Cr cds: A, C, D, DS, MC, V.

Harrisonburg *(See also Luray, Staunton)*

Motels

★ ★ **DAYS INN.** *1131 Forest Hill Rd, I-81 exit 245. 540/433-9353; FAX 540/433-5809.* 89 rms, 4 story. June-Oct: S $55; D $68; each addl $5; under 17 free; ski plan; higher rates for special events, wkends (2-day min); lower rates rest of yr. Crib free. Pet accepted; $5 per day. TV; cable (premium). Indoor pool; whirlpool. Complimentary continental bkfst.

Restaurant adj 11 am-11 pm. Ck-out 11 am. Meeting rms. Business servs avail. Sundries. Valet serv. 27-hole golf privileges; greens fee $30, pro, putting green, driving range. Downhill ski 12 mi. Health club privileges. Refrigerators avail. Cr cds: A, C, D, DS, MC, V.

⊡ 🐾 🏊 🏋 🛏 🍽 ⚡ 🔥 SC

✓ ★ **ECONO LODGE.** *1703 E Market St , ¹/₂ mi E of I-81 exit 247A.* 540/433-2576. 88 rms, 2 story. S $42.95; D $45-$55.95; each addl $5; suites $74.95; under 18 free. Crib free. Pet accepted. TV; cable (premium), VCR avail (movies). Pool. Complimentary continental bkfst. Restaurant adj open 24 hrs. Ck-out 11 am. Business servs avail. Some in-rm whirlpools. Cr cds: A, C, D, DS, JCB, MC, V. ⊡ 🐾 🏊 ⚡ 🔥 SC

✓ ★ ★ **HOWARD JOHNSON.** *605 Port Republic Rd, I-81 exit 245.* 540/434-6771; FAX 540/434-0153. 134 rms, 2 story. Mar-Nov: S $44.95-$54.95; D $44.95-$59.95; each addl $5; higher rates some univ events; lower rates rest of yr. Crib free. Pet accepted. TV; cable (premium). Pool; wading pool. Restaurant 6 am-10:30 pm. Ck-out noon. Business servs avail. Refrigerators avail. Private patios, balconies. Cr cds: A, C, D, DS, ER, JCB, MC, V. ⊡ 🐾 🏊 ⚡ 🔥 SC

✓ ★ ★ **THE VILLAGE INN.** *Rte 1, Box 76, on VA 11, 1¹/₂ N of I-81 exit 240.* 540/434-7355; res: 800/736-7355. 36 rms. S $37; D $43-$53; each addl $5; kit. units $58. Crib $2. Pet accepted. TV; cable; VCR avail (movies). Pool. Playground. Restaurant 7-10 am, 5:30-9 pm; closed Sun. Ck-out noon. Meeting rm. Business servs avail. Sundries. Lawn games. Some in-rm whirlpools. Picnic tables. Cr cds: A, C, D, DS, MC, V.

⊡ 🐾 🏊 ⚡ 🔥

Motor Hotel

★ ★ **FOUR POINTS BY SHERATON.** *1400 E Market St, off I-81 exit 247A.* 540/433-2521; FAX 540/434-0253. 138 rms, 5 story. S $68-$104; D $80-$104; each addl $12; under 18 free. Crib free. Pet accepted. TV; cable (premium). 2 pools, 1 indoor; wading pool, whirlpool, sauna, poolside serv. Restaurant 6:30-11 am, 5-10:30 pm. Rm serv. Bar 11-2 am; entertainment. Ck-out noon. Meeting rms. Business servs avail. In-rm modem link. Bellhops. Valet serv. Bathrm phones; refrigerators avail. Cr cds: A, C, D, DS, ER, JCB, MC, V. ⊡ 🐾 🏊 ⚡ 🔥 SC

Hot Springs *(See also Clifton Forge, Covington)*

Motel

✓ ★ **ROSELOE.** *Rte 2, Box 590, 3 mi N on US 220.* 540/839-5373. 14 rms, 6 kits. S $36; D $46; each addl $4; kits. $40-$53; family rates. Crib free. Pet accepted; $5. TV; cable (premium). Complimentary coffee in rms. Restaurant nearby. Ck-out noon. Business servs avail. Downhill ski 3 mi. Refrigerators; microwaves avail. Cr cds: A, D, DS, MC, V.

🐾 🏊 🔥

Irvington

Resort

★ ★ ★ **TIDES LODGE RESORT & COUNTRY CLUB.** *N on VA 200, then W on VA 646, then SW on County 709, follow signs.* 804/438-6000; FAX 804/438-5950; res: 800/248-4337. 60 units. Mid-Mar-Dec: S, D $108-$198; each addl $30; cottages to 2 persons $300; under 18 free; AP, MAP avail; golf packages; higher rates some wkends. Closed rest of yr. Crib free. Pet accepted, some restrictions; $10. TV; cable (premium), VCR avail (free movies). 2 pools, 1 saltwater, 1 heated; poolside serv. Playground. Free supervised child's activities (late June-Labor Day); ages 5-12. Coffee in rms. Dining rm 8-9:30 am, noon-2 pm, 6-10 pm. Bar noon-11 pm. Ck-out 1 pm, ck-in after 3:30 pm. Coin lndry. Meeting rms. Business servs avail. Bellhops. Valet serv. Gift shop. Lighted tennis. 45-hole golf, greens fee $25-$40, pro, putting greens, driving range. Exercise equipt; weight machine, bicycles. Marina, cruises, boat rental. Bicycles. Lawn games. Game rm. Rec rm. Exercise equipt; weights, bicycles, sauna. Refrigerators. Balconies. Cr cds: DS, MC, V.

⊡ 🐾 🐎 🏌 🏋 🏊 🎿 ⚓ 🔥

Keysville

Motel

✓ ★ **SHELDON'S.** *RFD 2, Box 189, 1¹/₂ mi N on US 15 Business.* 804/736-8434; FAX 804/736-9402. 40 rms, 2 story. S $35.95-$50; D $41.95-$50; each addl $6. Crib $6. Pet accepted. TV; cable (premium). Restaurant 6:30 am-10 pm. Ck-out noon. Business servs avail. Some refrigerators; microwaves avail. Cr cds: A, DS, MC, V. ⊡ 🐾 ⚡ 🔥

Leesburg *(See Arlington County; also see District of Columbia)*

Motel

✔ ★ **DAYS INN.** *721 E Market St (20175), near Prosperity Shopping Center.* 703/777-6622; FAX 703/777-4119. 81 rms, 2 story. Mar-Oct: S $49; D $53; each addl $3; under 12 free; lower rates rest of yr. Crib free. Pet accepted, some restrictions; $6. TV; cable (premium). Complimentary continental bkfst. Restaurant nearby. Ck-out noon. Coin lndry. Business servs avail. Cr cds: A, C, D, DS, JCB, MC, V. **D** 🛇 🛏 🐾 **SC**

Inn

★ ★ **COLONIAL.** *19 S King St (20175).* 703/777-5000; res: 800/392-1332. 10 rms, 3 story. S $58-$150; D $68-$150; under 10 free. Crib free. Pet accepted, some restrictions. TV; cable. Complimentary full bkfst; afternoon refreshments in library. Restaurant 11:30 am-4 pm, 5-10 pm. Rm serv. Ck-out noon, ck-in 2 pm. Luggage handling. Free airport transportation. Tennis privileges. Golf privileges. Health club privileges. Picnic tables. Historic building (1759) built of same stone as Capital in DC. Fireplaces; some in-rm whirlpools. Cr cds: A, C, D, DS, MC, V. 🐾 🏃 ⛷ 🛇 🐾 **SC**

Lexington *(See also Clifton Forge, Natural Bridge)*

Motels

★ ★ ★ **BEST WESTERN INN AT HUNT RIDGE.** *Willow Springs Rd at VA 39.* 540/464-1500. 100 rms, 3 story, 10 suites. Apr-Oct: S $69-$82; D $74-$86; each addl $8, suites $81-$90; under 12 free; higher rates special events; lower rates rest of yr. Crib free. Pet accepted, some restrictions. TV; cable (premium). Indoor/outdoor pool. Complimentary coffee in rms. Restaurant 7 am-10 pm. Rm serv. Bar to midnight. Ck-out 11 am. Coin lndry. Meeting rms. Business servs avail. In-rm modem link. Refrigerator, microwave in suites. Cr cds: A, C, D, DS, JCB, MC, V. **D** 🛇 ≈ 🛏 🐾 **SC**

✔ ★ ★ **DAYS INN KEYDET-GENERAL.** *325 W Midland Trail.* 540/463-2143. 53 rms, 10 kit. units. S $47.95-$57.95; D $55.95-$65.95; each addl $5. Crib free. Pet accepted, some restrictions. TV; cable (premium). Ck-out 11 am. Business servs avail. Some bathrm phones, refrigerators. Picnic tables. View of mountains. Cr cds: A, C, D, DS, ER, JCB, MC, V. **D** 🛇 🛏 🐾 **SC**

★ ★ **HOLIDAY INN EXPRESS.** *1 mi N on US 11.* 540/463-7351. E-mail dominion @rockbridge.net; web www.rockbridge.net/anderson/index.htp. 72 rms, 2 story. S $75; D $85; each addl $10; under 18 free. Crib free. Pet accepted. TV; cable (premium). Pool. Complimentary continental bkfst. Ck-out 11 am. Business servs avail. In-rm modem link. Valet serv. View of mountains. Cr cds: A, C, D, DS, ER, JCB, MC, V. **D** 🛇 ≈ 🛏 🐾 **SC**

★ ★ **RAMADA INN.** *US 11N.* 540/463-6400; FAX 540/464-3639. 80 rms, 4 story. May-Oct: S $60; D $70; each addl $6; under 19 free; wkly, wkend rates; higher rates special events; lower rates rest of yr. Crib free. Pet accepted. TV; cable (premium). Indoor pool. Restaurant 6 am-2 pm, 5-10 pm. Rm serv. Bar 5-10 pm. Ck-out noon. Meeting rms. Business servs avail. Sundries. Cr cds: A, C, D, DS, ER, JCB, MC, V. **D** 🛇 ≈ 🛏 🐾 **SC**

Motor Hotels

★ ★ **COMFORT INN.** *US 11S, at I-64 exit 55, I-81 exit 191.* 540/463-7311; FAX 540/463-4590. E-mail Dominion@Rockbridge.net; web www.rock bridge.net/anderson/in dex.htp. 80 rms, 4 story. Apr-Nov: S, D $80-$85; each addl $5; under 18 free; lower rates rest of yr. Crib free. Pet accepted. TV; cable (premium). Indoor pool. Complimentary continental bkfst. Restaurant adj 6 am-11 pm. Ck-out 11 am. Coin lndry. Business servs avail. Sundries. Cr cds: A, C, D, DS, ER, JCB, MC, V. **D** 🛇 ≈ 🛏 🐾 **SC**

✔ ★ ★ **HOWARD JOHNSON.** *US 11N, I-81 exit 195.* 540/463-9181; FAX 540/464-3448. 100 rms, 5 story. S $45-$63; D $50-$68; each addl $7; under 18 free; higher rates special events. Crib free. Pet accepted. TV; cable (premium). Pool. Restaurant 6 am-10 pm. Ck-out noon. Coin lndry. Meeting rm. Business servs avail. Gift shop. Microwaves avail. Balconies. Private patios. On hill; panoramic view of mountains. Cr cds: A, C, D, DS, ER, JCB, MC, V. **D** 🛇 ≈ 🛏 🐾 **SC**

Inn

★ ★ ★ **HUMMINGBIRD INN.** *(30 Wood Ln, Goshen 24439) US 11 N to VA 39 N, turn left, S on Wood Ln.* 540/997-9065; res: 800/397-3214; FAX 540/997-0289. E-mail hmgbird@cfw.com; web www.humingbird.inn.com. 5 rms, 2 story. No rm phones. May-Nov: S $75-$105; D $80-$110; wkend rates; MAP avail; wkends (2-day min); lower rates rest of yr. Children over 12 yrs only. Pet accepted; $20. TV in common rm. Complimentary full bkfst. Restaurant nearby. Ck-out 11 am, ck-in 4 pm. Business servs avail. Rec rm. Lawn games. Some in-rm whirlpools, fireplaces. Picnic tables. On river. Victorian Carpenter Gothic villa built in 1780; wraparound verandahs. Totally nonsmoking. Cr cds: A, DS, MC, V.

⊷ ⋈ ⋈ SC

Luray *(See also Basye, Harrisonburg)*

Motels

✔★ **BEST WESTERN INTOWN.** *410 W Main St (US 211). 540/743-6511; FAX 540/743-2917.* 40 rms, 2 story. Apr-Nov: S, D $32.50-$73.50; each addl $5; under 18 free; higher rates foliage season; lower rates rest of yr. Crib $4. Pet accepted; $10 per day. TV; cable (premium). Pool. Playground. Restaurant 6 am-2 pm, 5-9 pm. Rm serv. Ck-out noon. Business servs avail. Lawn games. Cr cds: A, C, D, DS, MC, V. ⊷ ≋ ⋈ ⋈ SC

★★ **MIMSLYN INN.** *401 W Main St (US 211 Business). 540/743-5105; FAX 540/743-2632; res: 800/296-5105.* 49 rms, 2 with shower only, 3 story, 11 suites. Mid-June-Oct: S $59-$85; D $74-$95; suites $99-$139; under 18 free; lower rates rest of yr. Crib $7. Pet accepted. TV; cable. Restaurant 7-10 am, 11:30 am-2 pm, 5-9 pm. Rm serv. Ck-out noon. Business servs avail. Art gallery, antique shop. Built 1930 in style of antebellum mansion. Cr cds: A, C, D, DS, MC, V. ⊷ ⋈ SC

Lynchburg

Hotel

★★ **HOLIDAY INN SELECT.** *601 Main St (24504). 804/528-2500; FAX 804/528-4782.* 243 units, 8 story. S, D $72; each addl $10; suites $85-$110; under 17 free. Crib free. Pet accepted. TV; cable (premium). Pool; poolside serv. Restaurant 6:30 am-10 pm. Bar 3 pm-1 am. Ck-out noon. Meeting rms. Business servs avail. In-rm modem link. Free airport, RR station, bus depot transportation. Exercise equipt; weights, bicycles. Some bathrm phones, refrigerators; microwaves avail. Cr cds: A, C, D, DS, ER, JCB, MC, V.

D ⊷ ≋ 🕴 ⋈ ⋈ SC

Manassas

(See also Arlington County, Fairfax; also see District of Columbia)

Motels

★★ **BEST WESTERN BATTLEFIELD INN.** *10820 Balls Ford Rd (20109), I-66 exit 47A. 703/361-8000.* 121 rms, 2 story. S $54-$69; D $64-$75; each addl $10; under 18 free. Crib free. Pet accepted, $10/day. TV; cable (premium). Pool. Complimentary continental bkfst. Restaurant 5-10 pm; closed Sun. Rm serv. Bar to midnight, Fri, Sat to 2 am; entertainment Tues-Sat. Ck-out 11 am. Meeting rms. Business servs avail. In-rm modem link. Valet serv. Sundries. Health club privileges. Refrigerators, microwaves avail. Cr cds: A, C, D, DS, MC, V. D ⊷ ≋ ⋈ ⋈ SC

✔★ **RED ROOF INN.** *10610 Automotive Dr (20109), I-66 exit 47A. 703/335-9333; FAX 703/335-9342.* 119 rms, 3 story. S $47.99-$63.99; D $53.99-$67.99; under 18 free; higher rates: Cherry Blossom, hol wkends. Crib free. Pet accepted, some restrictions. TV; cable (premium). Complimentary coffee in lobby. Restaurant adj 6-2 am. Ck-out noon. Business servs avail. Sundries. Health club privileges. Cr cds: A, C, D, DS, MC, V.

D ⊷ ⋈ ⋈ SC

Motor Hotel

★★ **HOLIDAY INN.** *10800 Vandor Ln (20109), I-66 exit 47B. 703/335-0000; FAX 703/361-8440.* 159 rms, 5 story. S $125; D $130; under 12 free. Crib free. Pet accepted; deposit. TV; cable (premium). Pool. Complimentary coffee in lobby. Restaurant 6-11 am, 5-10 pm; Sat, Sun 6-11 am. Rm serv. Bar 4 pm-2 am. Ck-out noon. Coin lndry. Meeting rms. Business servs avail. In-rm modem link. Valet serv. Exercise equipt; weight machines, bicycle. Health club privileges. Refrigerators, microwaves avail. Near Manassas (Bull Run) Battlefield. Cr cds: A, C, D, DS, ER, MC, V. D ⊷ ≋ 🕴 ⋈ ⋈ SC

Martinsville *(See also Danville)*

Motels

✔★★ **BEST WESTERN.** *Business US 220N (24112). 540/632-5611; FAX 540/632-1168; res: 800/388-3934.* 97 rms, 2 story, 20 suites. S $48; D $54; each addl $10; suites $49-$59; under 12 free; wkly, monthly rates. Crib free. Pet accepted. TV, cable (premium). Pool; wading pool. Complimentary coffee in rms. Restaurant 6 am-10 pm; Sat, Sun from 7 am. Rm serv. Bar 4 pm-midnight. Ck-out noon. Coin lndry. Meeting rms. Business servs avail. In-rm modem link. Valet serv. Sundries. Exercise equipt; weight machine, treadmill. Microwave avail. Cr cds: A, C, D, DS, ER, MC, V. [D] 🐾 ≋ 🛪 🖂 🖎 SC

✔★★ **DUTCH INN.** *(2360 Virginia Ave, Collinsville 24078) 1¹/₄ mi N on US 220 Business.* 540/647-3721; FAX 540/647-4857; res: 800/800-3996. E-mail sgrodens@neo comm.net; web www.dutch-inn.com. 150 rms, 2 story. S $48-$60; D $56-$66; each addl $6; suites $88-$125; studio rms $55-$75; under 16 free; higher rates race wks. Crib free. Pet accepted. TV; cable (premium). Pool; whirlpool, poolside serv. Restaurant 6 am-10:30 pm. Rm serv. Bar 4 pm-midnight; Fri, Sat to 2 am. Ck-out noon. Meeting rms. Business servs avail. In-rm modem link. Valet serv. Sundries. 18-hole golf privileges. Exercise equipt; bicycle, treadmill, sauna. Many bathrm phones, refrigerators; microwaves avail. Cr cds: A, C, D, DS, MC, V. [D] 🐾 🛪 ≋ 🛪 🖂 🖎 SC

Natural Bridge *(See also Lexington)*

Motel

★ **WATTSTULL.** *(Rte 1, Box 21, Buchanan 24066) 8 mi S on US 11; I-81 exit 168.* 540/254-1551. 26 rms. S, D $40-$48; each addl $3. Crib $4. Pet accepted. TV. Pool; wading pool. Restaurant 6 am-10 pm. Ck-out 11 am. Panoramic view of Shenandoah Valley. Cr cds: MC, V. 🐾 ≋ 🖎

Newport News

(See also Hampton, Norfolk, Portsmouth, Virginia Beach)

Motels

★★ **COMFORT INN.** *12330 Jefferson Ave (23602), I-64 exit 255A.* 757/249-0200; FAX 757/249-4736. 124 rms, 3 story. S $64; D $71; each addl $7; under 18 free. Crib free. Pet accepted. TV; cable (premium). Pool. Complimentary continental bkfst. Complimentary coffee in rms. Restaurant adj 11 am-midnight. Ck-out noon. Coin lndry. Meeting rms. Business servs avail. In-rm modem link. Free airport transportation. Health club privileges. Some refrigerators. Cr cds: A, C, D, DS, ER, JCB, MC, V. [D] 🐾 ≋ 🖂 🖎 SC

✔★★ **DAYS INN.** *14747 Warwick Blvd (23602).* 757/874-0201. 117 rms, 2 story. June-Sept: S $42-$59; D $48-$66; each addl $5; kit. units $48-$65; under 18 free; lower rates rest of yr. Crib free. Pet accepted, some restrictions; $5. TV; cable (premium). Pool. Playground. Complimentary continental bkfst. Restaurant 6 am-11 pm. Ck-out 11 am. Coin lndry. Business servs avail. Free airport transportation. Refrigerators avail. Picnic tables, grills. Cr cds: A, C, D, DS, MC, V. 🐾 ≋ 🖂 🖎 SC

Norfolk

Motels

✔★ **ECONO LODGE-OCEANVIEW BEACH.** *9601 4th View St (23503).* 757/480-9611; FAX 757/480-1307. 71 units, 3 story, 22 kits. Mid-May-Labor Day: S $54.95; D $64.95; each addl $5; kit. units $69.95; under 18 free; wkly rates; higher rates: some hols, special events; lower rates rest of yr. Pet accepted, some restrictions; $50 deposit. TV; cable (premium), VCR avail (movies). Complimentary continental bkfst. Restaurant nearby. Ck-out 11 am. Business servs avail. Coin lndry. Refrigerators. Ocean; fishing pier. Beach adj. Cr cds: A, C, D, DS, JCB, MC, V. [D] 🐾 🖂 🖎 SC

★★ **QUALITY INN LAKE WRIGHT.** *6280 Northampton Blvd (23502).* 757/461-6251; FAX 757/461-5925. 304 rms, 2 story. May-Sept: S, D $74; each addl $7; suites $125; under 18 free; lower rates rest of yr. Crib $7. Pet accepted; $25. TV; cable (premium). Pool. Complimentary coffee in rms. Restaurant 6:30 am-2 pm, 5-10 pm. Bar 11:30 am-midnight. Ck-out 11 am. Meeting rms. Business servs avail. Barber, beauty shop. Coin lndry. Free airport transportation. Some refrigerators. Cr cds: A, C, D, DS, ER, MC, V. [D] 🐾 ≋ 🛪 🖂 🖎 SC

Hotels

★★★ **MARRIOTT-WATERSIDE.** *235 E Main St (23510).* 757/627-4200; FAX 757/628-6466. 404 rms, 24 story. S, D $109-$165; suites $250-$600. Crib free. Pet accepted; $35. Garage parking $8; valet $10. TV; cable (premium). Indoor pool; whirlpool, poolside serv. Restaurant 6-11 am, 5:30-11 pm. Bar 11-1 am. Ck-out noon. Coin lndry. Convention facilities. Business center. In-rm modem link. Concierge. Gift shop. Exercise equipt; weight machine, treadmill, sauna. Game rm. Refrigerator, wet bar in suites. Luxury level. Cr cds: A, C, D, DS, ER, JCB, MC, V. [D] 🐾 ≋ 🛪 🖂 🖎 SC 🖎

★ ★ ★ **OMNI WATERSIDE.** *777 Waterside Dr (23510), at St Paul's Blvd and I-264.* 757/622-6664; FAX 757/625-8271. 446 rms, 10 story. S, D $99-$129; each addl $15; suites $150-$600; under 17 free; wkend packages. Crib free. Pet accepted. Valet parking $9.50. TV, cable (premium), VCR avail. Pool; poolside serv. Restaurant 6:30 am-10 pm. Rm serv to 12:30 am. Bars 11-2 am; entertainment wkends. Ck-out noon. Convention facilities. Business center. In-rm modem link. Gift shop. Free airport transportation. Health club privileges. Dockage. Some refrigerators. Balconies. Atrium-like lobby. On harbor. Luxury level. Cr cds: A, C, D, DS, JCB, MC, V. 🄳 💳 🏊 🏖 🖃 🛅 🐾 SC 🏃

Petersburg *(See also Richmond)*

Motels

★ ★ **DAYS INN.** *12208 S Crater Rd (23805), I-95 exit 45.* 804/733-4400; FAX 804/861-9559. 154 rms, 2 story. S, D $44.95-$55.95; each addl $5; kit. suites $55-$59; family rates. Crib free. Pet accepted. TV; cable (premium). Pool; wading pool. Playground. Restaurant adj 5:30 am-10 pm. Ck-out 11 am. Coin lndry. Meeting rms. Business servs avail. In-rm modem link. Bellhops. Sundries. Putting green. Exercise equipt; weights, bicycles. Some refrigerators. Cr cds: A, C, D, DS, ER, JCB, MC, V.

🄳 💳 🏊 🎿 🛅 🖃 🐾 SC

✔ ★ ★ ★ **QUALITY INN-STEVEN KENT.** *12205 S Crater Rd (23805), 6 mi S, I-95 exit 45.* 804/733-0600; FAX 804/862-4549. 138 rms, 1-2 story. S $35.95-$59.95; D $37.95-$59.95; each addl $5; under 18 free. Crib $5. Pet accepted. TV; cable (premium). Pool; wading pool. Playground. Restaurant 5:30 am-10 pm. Bar noon-midnight. Ck-out 11 am. Coin lndry. Business servs avail. In-rm modem link. Sundries. Lighted tennis. Game rm. Lawn games. Miniature golf. Some refrigerators. Picnic tables. Cr cds: A, C, D, DS, ER, JCB, MC, V. 🄳 💳 🎾 🏊 🖃 🛅 🐾 SC

Portsmouth
(See also Chesapeake, Hampton, Newport News, Norfolk, Virginia Beach)

Motel

★ ★ **HOLIDAY INN OLD TOWN-PORTSMOUTH.** *8 Crawford Pkwy (23704), on waterfront at Elizabeth River.* 757/393-2573; FAX 757/399-1248. Web www.holiday portsmouth.com. 268 rms, 4 story. S $60-$89; D $60-$99; each addl $10; suites $130-$161; studio rms $75-$150; under 19 free; wkend packages; higher rates Harborfest. Crib free. Pet accepted; $10. TV; cable (premium). Pool. Coffee in rms. Restaurant 6:30 am-10 pm. Rm serv. Bar noon-2 am. Ck-out noon. Coin lndry. Meeting rms. Business servs avail. In-rm modem link. Exercise equipt; weights, stair machine. Refrigerators avail. Dockage, marina adj. Cr cds: A, C, D, DS, JCB, MC, V. 🄳 💳 🏊 🎿 🖃 🐾 SC

Radford *(See also Blacksburg)*

Motels

★ ★ ★ **BEST WESTERN RADFORD INN.** *1501 Tyler Ave.* 540/639-3000; FAX 540/639-3000, ext. 412. 72 rms, 2 story. S $75-$80; D $80-$90; each addl $5; under 12 free; higher rates univ events. Crib free. Pet accepted. TV; cable (premium). Indoor pool; wading pool, whirlpool. Restaurant 6:30 am-1:30 pm, 5-9 pm; wkends from 7 am. Ck-out noon. Business servs avail. Sundries. Exercise equipt; bicycles, stair machine, sauna. Bathrm phones; some refrigerators. Cr cds: A, C, D, DS, MC, V. 🄳 💳 🏊 🖃 🐾 SC

✔ ★ **EXECUTIVE.** *7498 Lee Hwy.* 540/639-1664; res: 888/393-8483. 27 rms, 13 with shower only, 2 story. Apr-Nov: S $32.50-$36.50; D $36.50-$46.50; under 12 free; higher rates special events; lower rates rest of yr. Crib free. Pet accepted, some restrictions; $4. TV; cable (premium), VCR. Complimentary coffee in lobby. Restaurant adj 6 am-11 pm. Ck-out 11 am. Refrigerators. Microwaves avail. Cr cds: D, DS, MC, V. 🄳 💳 🖃 🐾 SC

Richmond *(See also Ashland, Petersburg)*

Motels

★ **LA QUINTA.** *6910 Midlothian Pike (US 60W) (23225), at VA 150.* 804/745-7100; FAX 804/276-6660. 130 rms, 3 story. S $52-$59; D $59-$66; each addl $7; under 18 free. Crib free. Pet accepted, some restrictions. TV; cable (premium). Heated pool. Complimentary continental bkfst. Restaurant adj 6 am-11 pm. Ck-out noon. Meeting rms. Business servs avail. In-rm modem link. Cr cds: A, C, D, DS, ER, JCB, MC, V.

🄳 💳 🏊 🖃 🐾 SC

✔ ★ **RED ROOF INN.** *4350 Commerce Rd (23234), south of downtown.* 804/271-7240; FAX 804/271-7245. 108 rms, 2 story. S $33.99-$49.99; D $39.99-$49.99; under 18 free; higher rates race wkends. Pet accepted. TV; cable (premium). Complimentary coffee in lobby. Restaurant nearby. Ck-out noon. Business servs avail. Some refrigerators. Cr cds: A, C, D, DS, MC, V. 🔲 ⊡ 🔳 🔳

★ ★ **RESIDENCE INN BY MARRIOTT.** *2121 Dickens Rd (23230).* 804/285-8200; FAX 804/285-2530. 80 kit. suites, 2 story. S, D $109-$159; monthly, wkly, wkend rates. Crib free. Pet accepted, some restrictions; $50 and $5/day. TV; cable (premium), VCR avail (movies). Pool. Complimentary continental bkfst. Ck-out noon. Coin lndry. Meeting rm. Business servs avail. In-rm modem link. Valet serv. Health club privileges. Microwaves; many fireplaces. Private patios, balconies. Picnic tables, grills. Cr cds: A, C, D, DS, ER, JCB, MC, V. 🔲 ⊡ 🔳 🔳 🔳 SC

Motor Hotels

★ ★ **HOLIDAY INN AIRPORT.** *(5203 Williamsburg Rd, Sandston 23150) near Intl Airport.* 804/222-6450; FAX 804/226-4305. 230 rms, 3-6 story. S, D $76-$90; suites $86-$101; under 12 free. Pet accepted, some restrictions. TV; cable (premium). Pool; lifeguard. Complimentary continental bkfst. Restaurant 6 am-3 pm, 5-10:30 pm. Rm serv. Bar noon-1 am; entertainment. Ck-out noon. Meeting rms. Business servs avail. In-rm modem link. Bellhops. Free airport transportation. Refrigerators, microwaves avail. Cr cds: A, C, D, DS, JCB, MC, V. 🔲 ⊡ 🔳 ✗ 🔳 🔳 SC

★ ★ ★ **SHERATON INN-AIRPORT.** *4700 S Laburnum Ave (23231), near Intl Airport.* 804/226-4300; FAX 804/226-6516. 151 rms, 4 story. S $98-$118; D $105-$125; each addl $10; suites $115-$205; under 17 free; wkend rates. Crib free. Pet accepted. TV; cable (premium), VCR avail. Indoor pool; whirlpool. Restaurant 6-1 am. Rm serv. Bar 11-2 am. Ck-out noon. Business servs avail. In-rm modem link. Bellhops. Valet serv. Gift shop. Barber, beauty shop. Free airport transportation. Exercise equipt; weights, bicycles, sauna. Bathrm phones. Some private patios, balconies. Cr cds: A, C, D, DS, ER, JCB, MC, V. 🔲 ⊡ 🔳 ✗ ✗ 🔳 🔳 SC

Roanoke

Motels

★ ★ **RAMADA INN.** *1927 Franklin Rd SW (24014).* 540/343-0121; FAX 540/342-2048. 127 rms, 4 story. S $58; D $64; each addl $7; under 18 free; higher rates special events. Pet accepted. TV; cable. Pool. Complimentary full bkfst. Coffee in rms. Restaurant 11:30 am-2:30 pm, 4:30-9:30 pm. Bar 4:30 pm-2 am. Ck-out noon. Coin lndry. Meeting rms. Business servs avail. In-rm modem link. Health club privileges. Sundries. Near river. Cr cds: A, C, D, DS, ER, JCB, MC, V. 🔲 ⊡ 🔳 🔳 🔳 SC

✔ ★ **TRAVELODGE-NORTH.** *(2444 Lee Hwy S, Troutville 24175) I-81 exit 150-A.* 540/992-6700; FAX 540/992-3991. 109 rms. S $45; D $52; each addl $6; kit. units $45; under 18 free; wkly rates. Crib free. Pet accepted; $6. TV; cable (premium). Pool. Playground. Complimentary continental bkfst. Coffee in rms. Restaurant nearby. Ck-out 11 am. Meeting rms. Business servs avail. Cr cds: A, D, DS, MC, V. 🔲 ⊡ 🔳 🔳 🔳 SC

Motor Hotels

★ ★ ★ **CLARION-AIRPORT.** *2727 Ferndale Dr (24017), near Municipal Airport.* 540/362-4500; FAX 540/362-4506. 154 rms, 5 story. S $89-$109; D $99-$115; each addl $10; under 18 free; wkend rates. Crib free. Pet accepted; $50 deposit. TV; cable (premium). Indoor/outdoor pool; whirlpool. Restaurant 6 am-10:30 pm. Rm serv. Complimentary coffee in rms. Bar 11:30 am-11 pm. Ck-out noon. Meeting rms. Business servs avail. In-rm modem link. Bellhops. Valet serv. Sundries. Free airport transportation. Lighted tennis. 18-hole golf privileges. Exercise equipt; weight machine, bicycles. Bathrm phones. Picnic tables, grills. Cr cds: A, C, D, DS, ER, JCB, MC, V. 🔲 ⊡ ✗ 🔳 🔳 ✗ ✗ 🔳 SC

★ ★ **HOLIDAY INN-TANGLEWOOD.** *4468 Starkey Rd SW (24014).* 540/774-4400; FAX 540/774-1195. 196 rms, 5 story. S, D $88-$102; suites $128-$153; under 18 free; wkend rates. Crib free. Pet accepted; $10. TV; cable (premium). Pool; poolside serv. Restaurant 6:30 am-10 pm. Rm serv. Bar 4 pm-2 am; entertainment. Ck-out noon. Meeting rms. Business servs avail. In-rm modem link. Bellhops. Valet serv. Concierge. Free airport, bus depot transportation. Golf privileges. Health club privileges. Some wet bars; microwaves avail. Luxury level. Cr cds: A, C, D, DS, JCB, MC, V. 🔲 ⊡ ✗ 🔳 🔳 🔳 SC

Hotel

★ ★ ★ **MARRIOTT-ROANOKE AIRPORT.** *2801 Hershberger Rd NW (24017), I-581 exit 3W, near Municipal Airport.* 540/563-9300; FAX 540/366-5846. Web www.swva.net/roanoke.marriott/. 320 rms, 8 story. S, studio rms $74-$134; D $84-$150; each addl $10;

suites $210-$250; under 18 free; golf, wkend rates. Crib free. Pet accepted, some restrictions; $10. TV; cable (premium), VCR avail. 2 pools, 1 indoor; whirlpool, poolside serv. Restaurant 6:30 am-10 pm. Bars 11-1 am. Ck-out noon. Convention facilities. Business servs avail. Concierge. Gift shop. Free airport transportation. Lighted tennis. Exercise equipt; weights, bicycles, sauna. Some refrigerators. Private patios, balconies. Luxury level. Cr cds: A, C, D, DS, ER, JCB, MC, V. 🄳 👆 🏄 🏊 🏋 ✈ 🏊 🐾 SC

South Hill *(See also Clarksville)*

Motel

★ ★ **BEST WESTERN.** *Box 594, Jct I-85, US 58. 804/447-3123; FAX 804/447-4237.* 152 rms, 2 story. S $52-$59; D $58-$65; each addl $6; under 19 free. Crib free. Pet accepted. TV; cable (premium). Heated pool; wading pool. Restaurant adj open 24 hrs. Bar 5 pm-1 am. Ck-out 11 am. Coin lndry. Meeting rms. Valet serv. Free airport, bus depot transportation. Health club privileges. Game rm. Cr cds: A, C, D, DS, JCB, MC, V. 🄳 👆 🏊 🐾 SC

Springfield

(See also Alexandria, Arlington County, Fairfax; also see District of Columbia)

Motels

★ ★ **COMFORT INN.** *6560 Loisdale Court (22150), I-95 exit 169A. 703/922-9000; FAX 703/971-6944.* 112 rms, 5 story. S, D $69-$89; each addl $6; under 18 free. Pet accepted. TV; cable (premium). Complimentary continental bkfst. Ck-out noon. Meeting rms. Business servs avail. In-rm modem link. Valet serv. Health club privileges. Microwaves avail. Cr cds: A, C, D, DS, MC, V. 🄳 👆 🐾 SC

★ ★ **DAYS INN-POTOMAC MILLS.** *(14619 Potomac Mills Rd, Woodbridge 22192) 10 mi S on I-95, exit 156. 703/494-4433; FAX 703/385-2627.* E-mail daysinn@pwcweb.com; web www.pwcweb.com/daysinn. 176 rms, 9 story. S $68-$78; D $75-$85; each addl $7; suites $89; under 13 free. Crib free. Pet accepted, some restrictions. TV; cable. Pool; lifeguard. Complimentary continental bkfst. Restaurant adj 6 am-midnight. Ck-out noon. Coin lndry. Meeting rms. Business servs avail. In-rm modem link. Valet serv. Sundries. Exercise equipt: stair machine, bicycle. Some refrigerators, minibars. Cr cds: A, C, D, DS, MC, V. 🄳 👆 🏊 🏋 🐾 SC

★ ★ **HAMPTON INN.** *6550 Loisdale Ct (22150). 703/924-9444; FAX 703/924-0324.* 153 rms, 7 story. Apr-June: S, D $89-$99; each addl $10; under 18 free; lower rates rest of yr. Crib free. Pet accepted. TV; cable (premium). Pool. Complimentary continental bkfst. Restaurant nearby. Ck-out noon. Valet serv. Health club privileges. Some refrigerators. Cr cds: A, C, D, DS, MC, V. 🄳 👆 🏊 🐾 SC

Staunton *(See also Harrisonburg, Waynesboro)*

Motels

★ ★ **COMFORT INN.** *1302 Richmond Ave. 540/886-5000; FAX 540/886-6643.* 98 rms, 5 story. May-Oct: S $49-$75; D $57-$75; each addl $8; under 18 free; higher rates special events; lower rates rest of yr. Crib avail. Pet accepted, some restrictions. TV; cable (premium). Pool. Complimentary continental bkfst. Complimentary coffee in rms. Restaurant adj open 24 hrs. Ck-out 11 am. Business servs avail. Some refrigerators. Cr cds: A, C, D, DS, ER, JCB, MC, V. 🄳 👆 🏊 🐾 SC

✔ ★ **ECONO LODGE-HESSIAN HOUSE.** *Rte 2, Box 364, 1/2 mi S of jct I-81 & 64 exit 213/213A Greenville. 540/337-1231; FAX 540/337-0821.* 32 rms, 2 story. May-Nov: S $32-$35.95; D $35.95-$55; each addl $5; under 12 free; wkly rates; lower rates rest of yr. Crib free. Pet accepted, some restrictions; $5. TV; cable (premium). Pool; wading pool. Playground. Complimentary continental bkfst. Restaurant nearby. Ck-out 11 am. Refrigerators. Private patios, balconies. Picnic tables. Cr cds: A, DS, MC, V. 👆 🏊 🐾 SC

Tysons Corner *(See also Arlington County, Fairfax; also see District of Columbia)*

Motels

★ ★ **COMFORT INN.** *(1587 Spring Hill Rd, Vienna 22182) 1 1/2 mi W of I-495, exit 10B. 703/448-8020; FAX 703/448-0343.* 250 rms, 3 story. S, D $89-$109; each addl $5; suites $109-$114; under 18 free. Crib free. Pet accepted, some restrictions. TV; cable (premium). Pool; lifeguard. Complimentary continental bkfst. Coffee in rms. Ck-out noon. Coin lndry. Meeting rms. Business servs avail. In-rm modem link. Valet serv. Free airport transportation. Health club privileges. Refrigerators, microwaves avail. Cr cds: A, C, D, DS, ER, JCB, MC, V. [D] [✦] [≋] [▨] [▨] [SC]

★ ★ **RESIDENCE INN BY MARRIOTT.** *(8616 Westwood Center Dr, Vienna 22182) I-495 exit 10B to VA 7, then 2 mi W. 703/893-0120; FAX 703/790-8896.* 96 kit. suites, 2 story. Kit. suites $149-$199; each addl $10; under 18 free; wknd rates. Crib free. Pet accepted; $85 and $5/day. TV; cable (premium), VCR avail (movies). Pool; whirlpool, lifeguard. Complimentary continental bkfst 6:30-9 am; Sat, Sun 7:30-10 am. Restaurant nearby. Ck-out noon. Coin lndry. Meeting rm. Business servs avail. In-rm modem link. Valet serv. Lighted tennis. Health club privileges. Many fireplaces. Picnic tables, grills. Cr cds: A, C, D, DS, MC, V. [D] [✦] [▨] [≋] [✦] [▨] [▨] [SC]

Virginia Beach
(See also Chesapeake, Hampton, Newport News, Norfolk, Portsmouth)

Motor Hotel

★ ★ **DAYS INN-OCEANFRONT.** *32nd St & Atlantic Ave (23451). 757/428-7233; FAX 757/491-1936.* 121 units, 8 story. Late June-early Sept: S, D $135-$225; each addl $10; under 12 free; golf plans; lower rates rest of yr. Crib free. Pet accepted; $10. TV; cable (premium). Indoor pool; whirlpool. Restaurant 7-11 am, noon-2 pm, 6-10 pm. Rm serv. Bar from 5 pm. Ck-out 11 am. Coin lndry. Meeting rms. Business servs avail. In-rm modem link. Golf privileges. Game rm. Some refrigerators; microwaves avail. Balconies. On ocean; beach. Cr cds: A, C, D, DS, MC, V. [D] [✦] [▨] [≋] [▨] [▨] [SC]

Warrenton *(See also Culpeper, Fairfax, Manassas)*

Motel

★ ★ **COMFORT INN.** *7379 Comfort Inn Dr (20187), US 29 Bypass N. 540/349-8900; FAX 540/347-5759.* 97 rms. May-Oct: S, D $59-$79; each addl $8; suites $99-$125; under 18 free; mid-wk rates; lower rates rest of yr. Crib free. Pet accepted, some restrictions; $10/day. TV; cable (premium). Pool. Complimentary continental bkfst. Coffee in rms. Ck-out 11 am. Coin lndry. Meeting rm. Business servs avail. In-rm modem link. Exercise equipt; weight machine, treadmill. Refrigerators; microwaves avail. Whirlpool in some suites. Cr cds: A, C, D, DS, MC, V. [D] [✦] [≋] [✦] [▨] [▨] [SC]

Waynesboro *(See also Charlottesville)*

Motels

✔ ★ ★ **COMFORT INN.** *640 W Broad St. 540/942-1171; FAX 540/942-4785.* 75 rms. S $45-$59; D $52-$69; each addl $5; under 18 free. Crib free. Pet accepted, some restrictions. TV; cable (premium). Pool; wading pool. Coffee in rms. Ck-out noon. Business servs avail. Valet serv. Downhill ski 20 mi. Health club privileges. Microwaves avail. Cr cds: A, C, D, DS, ER, JCB, MC, V. [D] [✦] [▨] [≋] [▨] [▨] [SC]

★ **DAYS INN.** *2060 Rosser Ave, I-64 exit 94. 540/943-1101; FAX 540/949-7586.* 98 rms, 2 story. May-Oct: S $45-$75; D $50-$85; each addl $5; higher rates fall foliage, graduation; lower rates rest of yr. Crib free. Pet accepted; $6. TV; cable (premium). Pool. Restaurant adj 6 am-midnight. Ck-out 11 am. Meeting rms. Business servs avail. Valet serv. Game rm. Lawn games. Microwaves avail. Picnic tables. Cr cds: A, C, D, DS, MC, V. [D] [✦] [≋] [▨] [▨] [SC]

★ ★ **INN AT AFTON.** *US 250 & I-64, 4 mi E on US 250 at jct Skyline Dr & I-64 exit 99. 540/942-5201; res: 800/860-8559; FAX 540/943-8746.* Web www.comet.net/nelsoncty. 118 rms, 2-3 story. No elvtr. May-Oct: S $60-$76; D $63-$81; each addl $7; under 18 free; higher rates special events; lower rates rest of yr. Crib free. Pet accepted. TV. Heated pool. Restaurant 7 am-2 pm, 5-10 pm. Rm serv. Bar 5 pm-12:30 am; entertainment Fri, Sat. Ck-out noon. Meeting rms. Business servs avail. Valet serv. Downhill ski 18 mi. Cr cds: A, C, D, DS, JCB, MC, V. [D] [✦] [≋] [≋] [▨] [▨] [SC]

Williamsburg *(See also Newport News)*

Motels

(Rates may be higher holiday seasons)

★ **GOVERNOR'S INN.** *506 N Henry St (23185). 757/229-1000, ext. 6000; FAX 757/220-7019; res: 800/447-8679.* 200 rms, 3 story. May-Aug: S, D $89; family rates; lower rates rest of yr. Closed Jan-mid-Mar. Crib $8. Pet accepted. TV; cable (premium). Pool.

Complimentary coffee. Restaurant nearby. Business servs avail. Sundries. Gift shop. Tennis privileges. Golf privileges. Game rm. Cr cds: A, D, DS, MC, V.

★ **HERITAGE INN.** *1324 Richmond Rd (23185). 757/229-6220; FAX 757/229-2774; res: 800/782-3800.* 54 rms, 3 story. Mid-June-Labor Day: S, D $74; 2-day min hols, special events; lower rates rest of yr. Crib avail. Pet accepted. TV; cable. Pool. Continental bkfst. Ck-out noon. Business servs avail. Cr cds: A, C, D, DS, MC, V.

★ **QUARTERPATH INN.** *620 York St (23185). 757/220-0960; FAX 757/220-1531; res: 800/446-9222.* 130 rms, 2 story. Apr-Oct: S, D $62-$75; each addl $6; under 18 free; packages avail; lower rates rest of yr. Crib free. Pet accepted, some restrictions. TV, cable (premium). Pool. Restaurant adj 4-10 pm. Ck-out noon. Meeting rm. Business servs avail. Some in-rm whirlpools. Cr cds: A, C, DS, MC, V.

Winchester

Motels

(Rates may be higher during Apple Blossom Festival)

★ ★ **BEST WESTERN LEE-JACKSON MOTOR INN.** *711 Millwood Ave (22601). 540/662-4154; FAX 540/662-2618.* 140 rms, 2 story. Apr-Oct: S $48.50; D $53.50; each addl $5; suites $60-$65; kit. units $35 (14-day min); under 13 free; lower rates rest of yr. Crib avail. Pet accepted. TV; cable (premium). Pool. Restaurant 6 am-10 pm. Rm serv. Bar 4-10:30 pm. Ck-out noon. Coin lndry. Meeting rms. Business servs avail. Valet serv. Free airport transportation. Health club privileges. Some refrigerators. Picnic tables, grills. Cr cds: A, C, D, DS, MC, V.

★ ★ **HOLIDAY INN.** *1017 Millwood Pike (22602), at jct I-81 & US 50E, exit 313. 540/667-3300; FAX 540/722-2730.* 175 rms, 2 story. S, D $49-$69; each addl $6; under 18 free. Crib free. Pet accepted, some restrictions. TV; cable. Pool. Restaurant 6:30 am-10 pm. Rm serv. Bar 5:30 pm-midnight. Ck-out noon. Meeting rms. Business servs avail. In-rm modem link. Bellhops. Valet serv. Sundries. Tennis. Health club privileges. Some refrigerators. Balconies. Cr cds: A, C, D, DS, JCB, MC, V.

✔ ★ ★ **TRAVELODGE.** *160 Front Royal Pike (22602), I-81 exit 313. 540/665-0685; FAX 540/665-0689.* 149 rms, 3 story. S $41-$57; D $47-$63; each addl $5; suites $95; under 17 free. Crib free. Pet accepted. TV; cable (premium), VCR avail (movies). Heated pool. Complimentary continental bkfst. Complimentary coffee in rms. Restaurant nearby. Ck-out 11 am. Coin lndry. Business servs avail. In-rm modem link. Health club privileges. Refrigerators avail. Cr cds: A, C, D, DS, ER, JCB, MC, V.

Woodstock (See also Basye, Luray)

Motel

✔ ★ **BUDGET HOST INN.** *US 11 S & I-81, I-81 exit 283. 540/459-4086; FAX 540/459-4043.* 43 rms, 1-2 story. S $30; D $34-$40; each addl $4; under 6 free; wkly rates. Crib $5. Pet accepted, some restrictions. TV; cable. Pool. Restaurant 6:30 am-9 pm; Sun from 7 am. Ck-out 11 am. Coin lndry. Business servs avail. Downhill ski 20 mi. Picnic tables. Cr cds: A, C, D, DS, MC, V.

Wytheville

Motels

★ ★ **HOLIDAY INN.** *1800 and Main St, I-81 exit 73. 540/228-5483; FAX 540/228-5417.* 199 rms, 1-4 story. Mar-Oct: S $49-$70; D $54-$70; each addl $5; suites $104-$150; under 18 free; wkly rates; higher rates auto races; lower rates rest of yr. Crib free. Pet accepted. TV; cable (premium). Pool; wading pool. Restaurant 6 am-2 pm, 5-9 pm. Rm serv. Bar. Ck-out 11 am. Meeting rms. Business servs avail. Cr cds: A, C, D, DS, JCB, MC, V.

★ ★ **RAMADA INN.** *955 Pepper's Ferry Rd, I-77 exit 41 & I-81 exit 72. 540/228-6000.* Web www.naxs.com/wytheville/ramada. 154 rms, 2 story. S $64-$70; D $69-$75; each addl $5; under 18 free. Crib free. Pet accepted. TV; cable (premium). Pool. Coffee in rms. Restaurant 6 am-10 pm. Rm serv. Bar 5-11 pm; Sun 5 pm-midnight. Ck-out noon. Coin lndry. Meeting rms. Business servs avail. Cr cds: A, C, D, DS, ER, JCB, MC, V.

★ **THE SHENANDOAH.** *140 Lithia Rd. 540/228-3188; FAX 540/228-6458; res: 800/273-0935.* 100 rms, 1-2 story. S $35-$45; D $43-$60; each addl $6; under 16 free; wkly, wkend, hol rates; higher rates some special events. Crib free. Pet accepted; $5. TV; cable. Complimentary coffee in lobby. Restaurant nearby. Ck-out 11 am. Balconies. Cr cds: A, C, D, DS, MC, V. **D** 🔁 🛏 🐾 **SC**

Washington

Aberdeen *(See also Ocean Shores)*

Motel

★★ **RED LION INN.** *52 W Wishkah. 360/532-5210; FAX 360/533-8483.* 67 rms, 2 story. June-Sept: S $68-$78; D $78-$98; each addl $10; under 18 free; lower rates rest of yr. Crib free. Pet accepted. TV; cable. Complimentary continental bkfst. Restaurant nearby. Ck-out noon. Sundries. Cr cds: A, C, D, DS, ER, MC, V. 🄳 ⬥ ⊠ 🅰 SC

Anacortes *(See also Coupeville, La Conner, Mount Vernon, Oak Harbor)*

Motel

★★ **ANACORTES INN.** *3006 Commercial Ave. 360/293-3153; FAX 360/293-0209; res: 800/327-7976.* 44 rms, 2 story, 5 kits. May-mid-Oct: S $65; D $70-$85; each addl $5; kit. units $10 addl; under 12 free. Pet accepted. TV; cable (premium). Heated pool. Coffee in rms. Restaurant nearby. Ck-out 11 am. Business servs avail. Refrigerators, microwaves. Cr cds: A, D, DS, MC, V. ⬥ ⊠ ⊠ 🅰 SC

Bellevue *(See also Seattle)*

Motels

★★ **BEST WESTERN BELLEVUE INN.** *11211 Main St (98004), just W of I-405 exit 12. 425/455-5240; FAX 425/455-0654.* 180 rms, 2 story. S $120; D $130; under 18 free; wkend rates. Crib free. Pet accepted; $30. TV; cable (premium), VCR avail. Heated pool; poolside serv. Coffee in rms. Restaurant 6:30 am-2 pm, 5-10 pm. Rm serv. Bar; entertainment Thurs-Sat. Ck-out noon. Meeting rms. Business servs avail. In-rm modem link. Bellhops. Valet serv. Sundries. Exercise equipt; treadmill, bicycle. Refrigerators; microwaves avail. Balconies. Cr cds: A, C, D, DS, ER, JCB, MC, V. 🄳 ⬥ ⊠ 🛪 ⊠ 🅰 SC

★★★ **RESIDENCE INN BY MARRIOTT.** *14455 NE 29th Place (98007), off WA 520 148th Ave N exit. 425/882-1222; FAX 425/885-9260.* 120 suites, 2 story. S, D $160-$240. Crib $5. Pet accepted; $10/day. TV; cable (premium), VCR avail (free movies). Heated pool. Complimentary continental bkfst. Complimentary coffee in rms. Ck-out noon. Coin lndry. Meeting rms. Business servs avail. In-rm modem link. Valet serv. Lawn games. Refrigerators, microwaves. Private patios, balconies. Picnic tables, grills. Cr cds: A, C, D, DS, JCB, MC, V. 🄳 ⬥ ⊠ ⊠ 🅰

Bellingham *(See also Blaine; also see Vancouver, BC Canada)*

Motels

✔★ **DAYS INN.** *125 E Kellogg Rd (98226), I-5 exit 256, near Intl Airport. 360/671-6200; FAX 360/671-9491.* 70 rms, 3 story. July-Sept: S $49.95; D $54.95; each addl $5; suites $79-$99; under 12 free; lower rates rest of yr. Crib free. Pet accepted; $5. TV; cable (premium). Heated pool; whirlpool. Complimentary continental bkfst. Restaurant nearby. Ck-out 11 am. Coin lndry. Meeting rms. Health club privileges. Some refrigerators; microwaves avail. Cr cds: A, D, DS, MC, V. 🄳 ⬥ ⊠ ⊠ 🅰 SC

★ **VAL-U INN.** *805 Lakeway Dr (98226), I-5 exit 253. 360/671-9600; FAX 360/671-8323.* 82 rms, 3 story. June-Sept: S, D $51.50-$61.50; each addl $5; suites $75-$90; under 12 free; lower rates rest of yr. Crib $5. Pet accepted; $5. TV; cable (premium), VCR avail. Whirlpool. Complimentary continental bkfst. Restaurant nearby. Ck-out noon. Coin lndry. Meeting rms. Business servs avail. Valet serv. Free airport, RR station, ferry terminal transportation. Some refrigerators; microwaves avail. Cr cds: A, C, D, DS, MC, V. 🄳 ⬥ ⊠ 🅰 SC

Motor Hotel

★★★ **BEST WESTERN LAKEWAY INN.** *714 Lakeway Dr (98226), just off I-5 Lakeway Dr exit 253. 360/671-1011; FAX 360/676-8519.* 132 rms, 4 story. S $64-$74; D $74-$84; each addl $10; suites $99-$119; under 13 free. Crib $5. Pet accepted, some restrictions. TV; cable (premium). Indoor pool; whirlpool. Complimentary full bkfst buffet. Coffee in rms. Restaurant 6 am-10 pm. Rm serv. Bar; entertainment Tues-Sat. Ck-out noon. Coin lndry. Meeting rms. Business center. Valet serv. Beauty shop. Free airport, bus depot transportation. Exercise equipt; weights, bicycles, sauna. Microwaves avail. Cr cds: A, C, D, DS, ER, JCB, MC, V. 〔D〕〔⦿〕〔≋〕〔ⵊ〕〔⤓〕〔🏊〕〔SC〕〔⛷〕

Blaine *(See also Bellingham; also see Vancouver, BC Canada)*

Resort

★ ★ ★ **INN AT SEMI-AH-MOO, A WYNDHAM RESORT.** *9565 Semiahmoo Pkwy (98230), 3 mi S of downtown, across Drayton Harbor; follow signs.* 360/371-2000; FAX 360/371-5490. Web www.semi.ah.moo.com. 198 units, 4 story, 14 suites. May-Oct: S, D $189-$419; each addl $20; suites $269-$499; under 19 free; golf plans; lower rates rest of yr. Crib free. Pet accepted; $50. TV; cable. Indoor/outdoor pool; whirlpool, poolside serv. Complimentary coffee in rms. Dining rms 6:30 am-2:30 pm, 5:30-11 pm. Box lunches, snack bar. Rm serv 6:30 am-11 pm. Bar 11-1 am; entertainment. Ck-out noon, ck-in 4 pm. Grocery 2 blks. Coin lndry, package store 7 mi. Meeting rms. Business servs avail. In-rm modem link. Concierge. Beauty shop. Sports dir. Indoor & outdoor tennis courts, pro. 18-hole golf, greens fee $75, pro, putting green, driving range. Beachcombing. 300-slip marina; boat & water sports. San Juan Island cruise yacht. Charter fishing, clam digging, oyster picking (seasonal). Bicycle rentals. Lawn games. Game rm. Exercise rm; instructor, weights, bicycles, sauna, steam rm. Spa. Some fireplaces. Some private patios, balconies. On 1,100-acre wildlife preserve. Cr cds: A, C, D, DS, ER, JCB, MC, V.

〔D〕〔⦿〕〔⦿〕〔ⵊ〕〔ⵊ〕〔≋〕〔ⵊ〕〔⤓〕〔🏊〕〔SC〕

Bremerton *(See also Seattle)*

Motels

✓ ★ ★ **MID WAY INN.** *2909 Wheaton Way (98310).* 360/479-2909; FAX 360/479-1576; res: 800/231-0575. 60 rms, 3 story, 12 kit. units. S $59; D $63; each addl $7; kit. units $65; under 10 free; wkly rates. Crib $5. Pet accepted, some restrictions; $10. TV; cable (premium), VCR (free movies). Complimentary continental bkfst. Complimentary coffee in rms. Restaurant adj 4 pm-midnight. Ck-out 11 am. Coin lndry. Meeting rm. Business servs avail. Refrigerators. Cr cds: A, C, D, DS, MC, V. 〔D〕〔⦿〕〔≋〕〔🏊〕〔SC〕

★ ★ **QUALITY INN.** *4303 Kitsap Way (98312).* 360/405-1111; FAX 360/377-0597. 103 rms, 2-3 story, 77 kits. No elvtr. S $65-$80; D $80-$95; each addl $5; suites $75-$150. Crib free. Pet accepted; $50 refundable. TV; cable (premium), VCR avail (movies $5). Heated pool; whirlpool. Playground. Complimentary continental bkfst. Ck-out 11 am. Coin lndry. Meeting rm. Business servs avail. In-rm modem link. Exercise equipt; bicycles, weight machine. Picnic tables, grills. Cr cds: A, C, D, DS, ER, MC, V. 〔D〕〔⦿〕〔≋〕〔ⵊ〕〔⤓〕〔🏊〕〔SC〕

Cheney *(See also Spokane)*

Motel

✓ ★ **WILLOW SPRING.** *5 B Street, I-90 exit 270.* 509/235-5138; FAX 509/235-4528. 44 rms, 3 story, 12 kits. No elvtr. S $37; D $41-$52; each addl $4; kit. units $5 addl. Pet accepted; $5/day. TV; cable. Restaurant opp 7 am-10 pm. Ck-out 11 am. Coin lndry. Cr cds: A, D, DS, MC, V. 〔⦿〕〔≋〕〔🏊〕〔SC〕

Coulee Dam

Motel

✓ ★ **COULEE HOUSE.** *110 Roosevelt Way.* 509/633-1101; FAX 509/633-1416; res: 800/715-7767. 61 units, 2 story, 15 kits. S, D $50-$70; each addl $4; suites $98-$115; kit. units $62-$98. Crib $4. Pet accepted. TV; cable (premium). Heated pool; whirlpool. Restaurant adj 6 am-10 pm. Ck-out 11 am. Coin lndry. Business servs avail. Sundries. Some refrigerators, balconies. View of dam. Cr cds: A, D, DS, MC, V. 〔⦿〕〔≋〕〔≋〕〔🏊〕

Coupeville *(See also Oak Harbor, Port Townsend)*

Motel

★ **HARBOUR INN.** *(1606 E Main, Freeland 98249) 20 mi S of Coupeville; 1 blk N off WA 525.* 360/331-6900. E-mail harborinn@whid bey.com. 20 rms, 2 story. No A/C. S $49-$72; D $54-$77; each addl $6. Crib $6. Pet accepted, some restrictions; $6. TV; cable. Complimentary continental bkfst. Restaurant nearby. Ck-out 11 am. Refrigerators; microwaves avail. Cr cds: A, MC, V. 〔⦿〕〔≋〕〔🏊〕

Ellensburg *(See also Yakima)*

Motel

★ ★ **BEST WESTERN ELLENSBURG INN.** *1700 Canyon Rd. 509/925-9801; FAX 509/925-2093.* 105 rms, 2 story. S $59; D $64; each addl $5; suites $75; under 12 free; higher rates rodeo. Crib free. Pet accepted. TV; cable (premium). Indoor pool; wading pool; whirlpool. Restaurant 7 am-10 pm. Rm serv. Bar 11-2 am; entertainment. Ck-out noon. Meeting rms. Business servs avail. Valet serv. Exercise equipt; weights, treadmill. Cr cds: A, C, D, DS, JCB, MC, V. 🄳 🖛 ⊠ 🏋 ⊠ 🖎 SC

Enumclaw *(See also Tacoma)*

Motel

★ ★ **BEST WESTERN PARK CENTER HOTEL.** *1000 Griffin Ave. 360/825-4490; FAX 360/825-3686.* 40 rms, 2 story. June-Oct: S, D $63; each addl $5; under 12 free; lower rates rest of yr. Crib $10. Pet accepted; $10. TV; cable. Complimentary coffee in lobby. Restaurant 7 am-9 pm. Rm serv. Bar from 4 pm. Ck-out 11 am. Meeting rms. Business servs avail. In-rm modem link. Whirlpool. Some refrigerators, microwaves. Picnic tables. Cr cds: A, D, DS, MC, V. 🄳 🖛 ⊠ 🖎 SC

Forks

Resort

★ ★ **KALALOCH LODGE.** *157151 WA 101, 35 mi S on US 101. 360/962-2271; FAX 360/962-3391.* 8 rms in lodge, 10 motel rms, 2 story, 40 cabins, 34 kits. No A/C. No rm phones. June 7-Oct 5: lodge rms $76-$100; cabins $126-$176; suites $106; varied lower rates off season. Crib free. Pet accepted. Dining rm (public by res) 5-9 pm. Coffee shop 7 am-9 pm. Box lunches. Bar 4-10:45 pm; Sat, Sun from noon. Ck-out 11 am, ck-in 4 pm. Grocery. Gift shop. Fish/hunt guides. Some refrigerators, fireplaces. Some balconies. Cr cds: A, MC, V. 🄳 🖛 ⊠ 🖎

Goldendale

Motel

★ **PONDEROSA.** *775 E Broadway St. 509/773-5842; FAX 509/773-4049.* 28 rms, 2 story, 4 kits. S $34; D $40-$43; each addl $5; kit. units $5 addl. Pet accepted. TV; cable. Ck-out 11 am. Business servs avail. Cr cds: A, C, D, DS, MC, V. 🖛 ⊠ 🖎 SC

Kelso

Motels

★ ★ **DOUBLETREE.** *510 Kelso Dr, I-5 exit 39. 360/636-4400; FAX 360/425-3296.* 162 rms, 2 story. S, D $79; each addl $20; suites $175; under 18 free; wkend rates. Crib free. Pet accepted. TV; cable (premium), VCR avail. Heated pool; wading pool, poolside serv. Restaurant 6 am-10 pm; Fri, Sat to 11 pm. Rm serv. Bar 11-1:30 am; entertainment Fri, Sat. Ck-out noon. Meeting rms. Business servs avail. Cr cds: A, C, D, DS, ER, JCB, MC, V. 🄳 🖛 ⊠ 🖎 SC

✔ ★ **MOUNT ST HELENS.** *(1340 Mt St Helens, Castle Rock 98611) 10 mi N on I-5, exit 49. 360/274-7721.* 32 rms, 2 story, AC upper level only. S $35; D $38-$48; each addl $6; under 6 free. Crib free. Pet accepted; $6. TV; cable. Complimentary coffee in lobby. Restaurant adj 6:30 am-11 pm. Ck-out 11 am. Coin lndry. Meeting rms. Some refrigerators. Cr cds: A, C, D, DS, MC, V. 🄳 🖛 ⊠ 🖎

Kennewick *(See also Pasco, Richland)*

Motels

★ ★ ★ **CAVANAUGH'S AT COLUMBIA CENTER.** *1101 N Columbia Center Blvd (99336). 509/783-0611; FAX 509/735-3087; res: 800/843-4667.* 162 rms, 2 story. S $77, D $87; each addl $5; suites $90-$280; studio rms $75-$85; golf plans. Crib free. Pet accepted. TV; cable (premium), VCR avail. Pool; whirlpool. Restaurant 6:30 am-9 pm. Rm serv. Bar 11-2 am; entertainment Tues-Sat. Ck-out noon. Meeting rms. Business servs avail. Sundries. Airport, RR station, bus depot transportation. Private patios, balconies. Cr cds: A, C, D, DS, MC, V. 🄳 🖛 ⊠ 🖎 🖎 SC

★ **NENDELS INN.** *2811 W 2nd (99336). 509/735-9511; FAX 509/735-1944; res: 800/547-0106.* 104 rms, 3 story, 19 kits. S $45; D $50-$53; each addl $5; kit. units $50; under 12 free; higher rates boat race wkends. Crib free. Pet accepted; $5. TV; cable. Heated pool. Restaurant nearby. Ck-out noon. Business servs avail. Some refrigerators. Cr cds: A, C, D, DS, MC, V. 🐾 ⚞ ⚟ 🔥 SC

★ **TAPADARA INN.** *300 N Ely (99336), on WA 395. 509/783-6191; FAX 509/735-3854.* 61 rms, 2 story. May-Sept: S $40; D $47-$50; each addl $7; under 13 free; higher rates hydro races; lower rates rest of yr. Crib free. Pet accepted; $5. TV; cable (premium), VCR avail. Heated pool. Complimentary coffee in lobby. Restaurant adj 6 am-11 pm. Bar 11-2 am. Ck-out noon. Some refrigerators. Cr cds: A, C, D, DS, MC, V. 🐾 ⚞ ⚟ 🔥 SC

La Conner *(See also Anacortes, Mount Vernon)*

Inn

★ ★ **THE HERON.** *117 Maple Ave. 360/466-4626; FAX 360/466-3254.* 12 rms, 3 story, 3 suites. No A/C. S, D $75-$95; suites $120-$160. Pet accepted, some restrictions. TV. Complimentary continental bkfst. Restaurant nearby. Ck-out 11 am, ck-in 3 pm. Whirlpool. Victorian-style inn. Stone fireplace in parlor. Cr cds: A, MC, V. D 🐾 ⚟ 🔥

Leavenworth *(See also Wenatchee)*

Motel

★ ★ **DER RITTERHOF.** *190 US 2. 509/548-5845; res: 800/255-5845.* 51 rms, 2 story, 5 kits. S, D $68-$74; each addl $8; kit. units $74. Crib free. Pet accepted. TV; cable, VCR avail. Heated pool; whirlpool. Restaurant opp 7 am-11 pm. Ck-out 11 am. Business servs avail. Putting green. X-country ski 1 mi. Lawn games. Private patios, balconies. Picnic table, grill. Cr cds: A, MC, V. D 🐾 ⚞ ⚞ ⚟ 🔥 SC

Long Beach

Motels

★ **ANCHORAGE MOTOR COURT.** *22nd NW & Boulevard N. 360/642-2351; FAX 360/642-8730; res: 800/646-2351.* 9 kit. units (1-2 bedrm). No A/C. July-Sept: S $58.50-$68.50; D $88.50; each addl $10; lower rates rest of yr. Crib free. Pet accepted, some restrictions; $5-$10. TV; cable. Playground. Restaurant nearby. Ck-out 11 am. Lawn games. Fireplaces (free firewood). Most units overlook ocean. Cr cds: A, DS, MC, V. 🐾 🔥

★ ★ **BREAKERS.** *Box 428, 1 mi N on WA 103. 360/642-4414; FAX 360/642-8772; res: 800/288-8890.* 114 rms, 3 story, 53 kits. No A/C. June-Labor Day: S, D $65-$77; suites $115-$175; kit. units $65-$77; lower rates rest of yr. Crib free. Pet accepted; $7. TV; cable, VCR avail. Heated pool; whirlpool. Restaurant nearby. Ck-out 11 am. Meeting rm. Business servs avail. Some refrigerators. Private patios, balconies. Public golf adj. Cr cds: A, D, DS, MC, V. D 🐾 ⚞ ⚟ 🔥 SC

✔ ★ **CHAUTAUQUA LODGE.** *304 14th St NW. 360/642-4401; FAX 360/642-2340; res: 800/869-8401.* 180 units, 3 story, 60 kits. No A/C. June-Sept: S, D $55-$100; each addl $5; suites $115-$160; kit. units $85-$115; lower rates rest of yr. Crib $2. Pet accepted, some restrictions; $8. TV; VCR avail. Indoor pool; whirlpool, sauna. Restaurant adj 8 am-10 pm; winter from 11 am. Bar 4 pm-1 am. Ck-out 11 am. Coin lndry. Meeting rms. Business servs avail. Sundries. Rec rm. Refrigerators. Private patios, balconies. On beach. Cr cds: A, D, DS, MC, V. D 🐾 ⚞ ⚟ 🔥 SC

★ **NENDELS EDGEWATER INN.** *409 10th St SW. 360/642-2311; FAX 360/642-8018; res: 800/547-0106.* 84 rms, 3 story. Mid-May-Sept: S, D $70-$108; lower rates rest of yr. Crib $3. Pet accepted, some restrictions. TV; cable (premium), VCR avail. Coffee in rms. Ck-out 11 am. Ocean view. Cr cds: A, D, DS, MC, V. D 🐾 ⚟ 🔥 SC

✔ ★ **OUR PLACE AT THE BEACH.** *1309 South Blvd. 360/642-3793; FAX 360/642-3896; res: 800/538-5107.* 25 rms, 1-2 story, 4 kits. May-Oct: S, D $45-$59; each addl $5; kit. units $64-$75; some lower rates rest of yr. Crib $1. Pet accepted; $5. TV. Coffee in rms. Restaurant nearby. Ck-out 11 am. Meeting rms. Business servs avail. Exercise equipt; bicycles, rowers, sauna. Whirlpool. Refrigerators. Picnic tables. Pathway to beach. Cr cds: A, C, D, DS, MC, V. 🐾 🏋 🔥 SC

★ ★ **SHAMAN.** *115 3rd St SW, 1 blk W off WA 103. 360/642-3714; FAX 360/642-8599; res: 800/753-3750.* 42 rms, 2 story, 20 kits. No A/C. Mid-May-Sept: S $59-$84; D, kit.

units $59-$79; lower rates rest of yr. Crib free. Pet accepted, some restrictions; $5. TV; cable, VCR avail (movies). Heated pool. Restaurant adj 7 am-11 pm. Ck-out 11 am. Business servs avail. Some refrigerators, fireplaces (log supplied). Cr cds: A, C, D, DS, MC, V. 🐾 ⛱ ⛷ 🐕

Marysville

Motel

✔★ **VILLAGE MOTOR INN.** *235 Beach Ave (98270).* 360/659-0005; *FAX 360/658-0866.* 45 rms, 3 story, 6 suites. S $50-$57; D $55-$62; each addl $5; suites $75-$130; under 12 free; monthly rates. Pet accepted, some restrictions. TV; cable (premium). Complimentary continental bkfst. Complimentary coffee in rms. Restaurant adj. Ck-out 11 am. Meeting rms. Business servs avail. In-rm modem link. Valet serv. Refrigerators avail. Cr cds: A, C, D, DS, MC, V. **D** 🐾 ⛷ 🐕 **SC**

Moclips

Motel

★ **HI-TIDE OCEAN BEACH RESORT.** *3 mi N of Pacific Beach just off WA 109, on Pacific Ocean.* 360/276-4142; *res: 800/662-5477 (WA).* 25 kit. suites, 2 story. No A/C. Mid-June-mid-Oct: kit. suites $84-$159; each addl $10; under 5 free; wkly rates; lower rates rest of yr. Crib free. Pet accepted; $10/day. TV; cable, VCR avail. Restaurant nearby. Ck-out 11 am. Business servs avail. Lawn games. Fireplaces. Health club privileges. Private patios, balconies. Cr cds: A, DS, MC, V. **D** 🐾 🎣 ⛷ 🐕 **SC**

Moses Lake

Motels

★ **EL RANCHO.** *1214 S Pioneer Way, I-90 exit 179, then 1½ mi N.* 509/765-9173; *FAX 509/765-1137; res: 800/341-8000.* 21 rms, 9 kits. S $30-$40; D $40-$46; each addl $3; kit. units $4 addl; higher rates: Spring Festival, Grant County Fair. Crib $3.50. Pet accepted, some restrictions. TV; cable (premium). Heated pool. Restaurant nearby. Ck-out 11 am. Refrigerators. Cr cds: A, D, DS, MC, V. 🐾 ⛱ ⛷ 🐕 **SC**

✔★ **INTERSTATE INN.** *2801 W Broadway, at I-90 Business exit 176.* 509/765-1777; *FAX 509/766-9452; res: 800/777-5889.* 30 rms, 2 story. S $39-$42; D $49-$54; each addl $3; family, wkly rates. Crib $3.50. Pet accepted. TV; cable (premium), VCR avail. Indoor pool; whirlpool, sauna. Restaurant adj open 24 hrs. Ck-out 11 am. Business servs avail. Some refrigerators. Cr cds: A, C, D, DS, MC, V. 🐾 ⛱ ⛷ 🐕 **SC**

Motor Hotel

★ ★ **BEST WESTERN HALLMARK INN.** *3000 Marina Dr, I-90 exit 176.* 509/765-9211; *FAX 509/766-0493.* 160 rms, 2-3 story. S, D $75-$95; each addl $5; suites $100-$150; under 12 free. Crib free. Pet accepted, some restrictions. TV; cable (premium), VCR avail. Pool; wading pool, whirlpool, sauna. Restaurant 7 am-10 pm. Rm serv. Bar 11:30-2 am; entertainment exc Sun. Ck-out noon. Coin lndry. Meeting rms. Business servs avail. Valet serv. Free airport transportation. Tennis. Refrigerators. Many private patios, balconies. On lake; dock. Cr cds: A, C, D, DS, JCB, MC, V. 🐾 🎣 ⛱ ⛷ 🐕 **SC**

Mount Vernon (See also Anacortes, La Conner)

Motels

✔★ **BEST WESTERN COLLEGE WAY INN.** *300 W College Way, I-5 exit 227, then 1 blk W.* 360/424-4287; *FAX 360/424-6036.* 66 rms, 56 A/C, 2 story, 10 kits. Mid-June-Sept: S $55; D $60-$65; each addl $5; kit. units $10 addl; under 12 free; lower rates rest of yr. Crib free. Pet accepted. TV; cable (premium). Heated pool; whirlpool. Complimentary continental bkfst. Coffee in rms. Restaurant adj 7 am-11 pm. Ck-out noon. Meeting rm. Business servs avail. In-rm modem link. Health club privileges. Some refrigerators; microwaves avail. Private patios, balconies. Cr cds: A, C, D, DS, ER, MC, V. **D** 🐾 ⛱ ⛷ 🐕 **SC**

★ ★ **BEST WESTERN COTTON TREE INN.** *2300 Market St, I-5 exit 229.* 360/428-5678; *FAX 360/428-1844.* 120 rms, 3 story. S $69; D $74; each addl $5; under 18 free; wkly rates, golf plan. Crib free. Pet accepted. TV; cable (premium). Pool. Complimentary continental bkfst. Complimentary coffee in rms. Restaurant opp 4 am-9 pm. Bar noon-2 am. Ck-out noon. Coin lndry. Meeting rms. Business servs avail. In-rm modem link. Sundries.

Valet serv. Health club privileges. Some refrigerators; microwaves avail. Cr cds: A, C, D, DS, ER, JCB, MC, V. [D] 🛏 🖴 📶 🔥 [SC]

North Bend *(See also Seattle)*

Lodge

★ ★ ★ ★ **SALISH LODGE AND SPA.** *(6501 Railroad Ave, Snoqualmie 98065) NW via WA 202. 425/888-2556; FAX 425/888-2533; res: 800/826-6124.* Web www.salish.com. Located at the crest of spectacular 268-foot Snoqualmie Falls, the lodge was used in filming the TV series *Twin Peaks.* Salish is dotted with antiques, and most rooms have a view of river, valley or falls. 91 units, 4 story. S, D $129-$269; each addl $25; suites $500-$575; higher rates Fri, Sat & hols June-Sept. Crib free. Pet accepted, some restrictions. TV; cable (premium), VCR. Complimentary coffee in rms. Restaurant 7 am-10 pm. Rm serv. Bar 11-2 am. Ck-out noon. Meeting rms. Business servs avail. In-rm modem link. Concierge. Gift shop. Golf privileges. Downhill/x-country ski 20 mi. Exercise equipt; weight machines, bicycles, saunas. Spa. Refrigerators, whirlpools, minibars, bathrm phones, fireplaces. Private patios, balconies. Library. Cr cds: A, C, D, DS, JCB, MC, V.

[D] 🛏 🖴 📶 🏋 🎿 🖴 🔥

Oak Harbor *(See also Anacortes, Coupeville, Port Townsend)*

Motel

★ ★ ★ **BEST WESTERN HARBOR PLAZA.** *33175 WA 20. 360/679-4567; FAX 360/675-2543.* 80 rms, 3 story. July-Sept: S $89; D $99; each addl $10; under 18 free; lower rates rest of yr. Crib free. Pet accepted, some restrictions. TV; cable (premium). Heated pool; whirlpool. Complimentary continental bkfst. Coffee in rms. Restaurant adj 6 am-11 pm. Bar. Ck-out noon. Meeting rms. Business servs avail. In-rm modem link. Bellhops. Valet serv. Concierge. Exercise equipt; weight machine, bicycle. Refrigerators, microwaves. Balconies. Cr cds: A, C, D, DS, MC, V. [D] 🛏 🖴 🏋 🖴 🔥 [SC]

Ocean Shores *(See also Aberdeen)*

Motel

★ ★ **GREY GULL.** *Ocean Shores Blvd. 360/289-3381; res: 800/562-9712 (WA).* 36 kit. apts, 3 story. No A/C. Apr-Sept, hols & wkends in winter: kit. apts $98-$115; each addl $5; suites $110-$315; under 16 free; some lower rates rest of yr. Crib free. Pet accepted, some restrictions. TV; cable. Heated pool; whirlpool, sauna. Complimentary coffee. Restaurant nearby. Ck-out noon. Ck-in 4 pm. Coin lndry. Business servs avail. Refrigerators, fireplaces. Lanais, balconies. Cr cds: A, D, DS, MC, V. [D] 🛏 🖴 🖴 🔥 [SC]

Olympia *(See also Tacoma)*

Motel

★ ★ **BEST WESTERN TUMWATER.** *(5188 Capitol Blvd SE, Tumwater 98501) S on I-5, exit 102. 360/956-1235.* 89 rms, 2 story. June-Sept: S $54-$62; D $58-$73; each addl $2; under 18 free; lower rates rest of yr. Crib $5. Pet accepted, some restrictions; $5. TV; cable. Complimentary continental bkfst. Restaurant opp open 24 hrs. Ck-out 11 am. Guest lndry. Meeting rms. Business servs avail. In-rm modem link. Exercise equipt; weight machine, bicycles, sauna. Refrigerators. Cr cds: A, C, D, DS, JCB, MC, V.

[D] 🛏 🏋 🖴 🔥 [SC]

Olympic National Park *(See also Forks, Port Angeles, Sequim)*

Resort

★ **SOL DUC HOT SPRINGS.** *(Port Angeles 98362) 30 mi W of Port Angeles on US 101, then South 12 mi on Sol Duc Rd. 360/327-3583; FAX 360/327-3593.* 32 cottages (1-bedrm), 6 kits. No A/C. Mid-May-Sept 23 & Apr, Oct wkends: S, D $83; each addl $12.50; kit. cabins $93; under 4 free. Closed rest of yr. Crib free. Pet accepted. Pool; wading pool, mineral pools. Dining rm 7:30-10:30 am, 5-9 pm. Ck-out 11 am, ck-in 4 pm. Grocery. Gift shop. Massage therapy. Picnic tables. Originally conceived as a European-style health spa (ca 1912). Mineral pools range in temperature from 98-106. Cr cds: A, DS, MC, V.

[D] 🛏 🖴 🖴 🖴 🔥

Omak

Motel

✔ ★ **CEDARS INN.** *(1 Apple Way, Okanogan 98840) S on WA 215 to jct WA 20 & US 97. 509/422-6431; FAX 509/422-4214.* 78 rms, 3 story, 6 kits. No elvtr. S $46-$52; D, kit. units $52-$57; each addl $5; under 13 free; higher rates Stampede. Crib free. Pet accepted. TV; cable, VCR avail (movies $2). Pool. Restaurant 6:30 am-10 pm. Bar 11 am-11:30 pm. Ck-out noon. Coin lndry. Meeting rms. Business servs avail. Cr cds: A, C, D, DS, MC, V.

D 🐾 🏊 ➰ ✕ 🏋 🐕 SC

Packwood

Motel

✔ ★ ★ **TIMBERLINE VILLAGE RESORT.** *13807 US 12. 360/494-9224.* 21 rms, 3 story. Some A/C. July-mid-Sept: S, D $50-$55; each addl $5; suites $70; under 10 free; lower rates rest of yr. Crib free. Pet accepted. TV; cable. Complimentary coffee in rms. Restaurant adj 8 am-10 pm. Ck-out 11 am. Downhill ski 18 mi. Cr cds: A, MC, V.

D 🐾 🏊 🐕

Pasco *(See also Kennewick, Richland)*

Motel

✔ ★ **VINEYARD INN.** *1800 W Lewis St, near Tri-Cities Airport. 509/547-0791; FAX 509/547-8632; res: 800/824-5457.* 165 rms, 2 story, 45 kits. S $40.50-$48; D $50-$60; each addl $5; kit. units, studio rms $50-$60; under 12 free; some wkend rates; higher rates hydro races. Crib $6. Pet accepted; $5/day. TV; cable (premium), VCR avail. Indoor pool; whirlpool. Complimentary continental bkfst. Restaurant 11 am-9 pm. Bar 11-2 am. Ck-out noon. Coin lndry. Business servs avail. Valet serv. Airport, RR station, bus depot transportation. Cr cds: A, C, D, DS, MC, V. D 🐾 🏊 ✈ ➰ 🐕 SC

Motor Hotel

★ ★ **DOUBLETREE MOTOR INN.** *2525 N 20th St, north of downtown. 509/547-0701; FAX 509/547-4278.* 279 rms, 2-3 story. S, D $89; each addl $10; under 18 free; some wkend rates. Crib free. Pet accepted. TV; cable. 2 heated pools; whirlpool, poolside serv. Restaurants 6 am-11 pm. Rm serv 7 am-10 pm. Bar 11-2 am; entertainment. Ck-out noon. Convention facilities. Business center. In-rm modem link. Bellhops. Valet serv. Sundries. Gift shop. Free airport, RR station, bus depot transportation. Exercise equipt; weight machine, bicycle. Refrigerator, wet bar in some suites. Private patios, balconies. Cr cds: A, C, D, DS, ER, JCB, MC, V. D 🐾 🏊 🏋 ➰ 🐕 🏃

Port Angeles *(See also Sequim)*

Motels

★ ★ **DOUBLETREE.** *221 N Lincoln. 360/452-9215; FAX 360/452-4734.* 187 rms, 2 story. No A/C. May-Sept: S $100-$130; D $115-$145; suites $145-$160; each addl $10; under 18 free; some lower rates rest of yr. Crib free. Pet accepted. TV; cable. Heated pool; whirlpool. Complimentary coffee in rms. Restaurant 5:30 am-midnight. Ck-out noon. Business center. Sundries. Health club privileges. Private balconies. Overlooks harbor. Cr cds: A, D, DS, ER, MC, V. D 🐾 🏊 ➰ 🐕 SC 🏃

★ ★ **UPTOWN.** *101 E Second St. 360/457-9434; res: 800/858-3812.* 35 rms, 1-3 story, 4 kits. No A/C. June-Oct: S, D $89-$130; each addl $5; kit. units $125; under 12 free; wkly, monthly rates; lower rates rest of yr. Crib free. Pet accepted, some restrictions. TV; cable (premium). Complimentary continental bkfst. Complimentary coffee in rms. Restaurant nearby. Ck-out 11 am. Refrigerators, microwaves. Scenic view. Cr cds: A, C, D, DS, MC, V. 🐾 ➰ 🐕 SC

Inn

★ ★ **MAPLE ROSE.** *112 Reservoir Rd (98363), near Intl Airport. 360/457-7673; res: 800/570-2007.* E-mail maplerose@tenforward.com; web www.northolympic.com/maple rose. 5 rms, 4 story, 3 suites. No A/C. No elvtr. May-Sept: S, D $79-$89; each addl $15; suites $127-$147; under 9 free; wkends, hols (2-day min); lower rates rest of yr. Pet accepted; $15. TV; cable (premium), VCR (movies). Complimentary full bkfst. Complimentary coffee in rms. Restaurant nearby. Ck-out 11 am, ck-in 3-6 pm. Business center. In-rm modem link. Luggage handling. Free airport transportation. Putting green. Exercise equipt; weight machine, bicycle. Massage. Whirlpool. Some in-rm whirlpools, refrigerators, microwaves. Some balconies. Picnic tables, grills. Contemporary country inn. Totally nonsmoking. Cr cds: A, MC, V. 🐾 🏋 ✈ ⊠ 📶 SC 🏊

Port Ludlow *(See also Sequim)*

Inn

★ ★ ★ **INN AT LUDLOW BAY.** *1 Heron Rd. 360/437-0411; FAX 360/437-0310.* 37 rms, 3 story, 3 suites. No A/C. May-Sept: S, D $165-$200; each addl $35; suites $300-$450; lower rates rest of yr; under 18 free; golf plan; hol rates; 2-day min summer wknds. Crib avail. Pet accepted, some restrictions; $50 deposit. TV; VCR (free movies). Complimentary continental bkfst. Complimentary coffee in rms. Restaurant 5:30-9:30 pm. Ck-out noon, ck-in after 3 pm. Luggage handling. Meeting rms. Business servs avail. In-rm modem link. 27-hole golf privileges; greens fee $50-$55, putting green, driving range. Lawn games. Refrigerators, some minibars. Balconies. Built in 1994 to resemble estate in Maine. Views of Olympics & Cascades Mts. On shore, beach. Totally nonsmoking. Cr cds: A, D, DS, MC, V.
D 🐾 🐀 🏋 ⊠ 📶

Port Townsend *(See also Coupeville, Oak Harbor)*

Lodge

✔ ★ ★ **THE OLD ALCOHOL PLANT.** *(310 Alcohol Loop Rd, Port Hadlock 98339)* 9 mi S. *360/385-7030; FAX 360/385-6955; res: 800/735-7030.* 28 rms, 3 story. Mid-May-mid-Oct: S $49-$99; D $79-$99; each addl $10; suites $90-$250; under 14 free; wkly, monthly rates; lower rates rest of yr. Crib free. Pet accepted; $10. TV; cable (premium), VCR (movies $6). Restaurant 7 am-10 pm. Fri, Sat to 11 pm. Bar. Ck-out 11 am. Meeting rms. Exercise equipt. Game rm. Picnic tables. Former alcohol plant built 1910. Marina. Cr cds: A, D, DS, MC, V. **D** 🐾 🐀 🏋 ⊠ 📶 SC

Hotel

★ ★ **PALACE.** *1004 Water St. 360/385-0773; FAX 360/385-0780; res: 800/962-0741 (WA).* E-mail palace@olympus.net; web www.olympus.net/palace. 15 rms, 2 story. No A/C. No rm phones. May-mid-Sept: S, D $69-$139; each addl $10; suites $109-$129; under 13 free; lower rates rest of yr. Crib free. Pet accepted. TV; cable. Complimentary continental bkfst. Restaurant 6:30 am-10 pm. Ck-out noon. Meeting rms. Coin lndry. Some refrigerators. Cr cds: A, DS, MC, V. 🐾 ⊠ 📶 SC

Inns

★ ★ **BISHOP VICTORIAN GUEST SUITES.** *714 Washington St. 360/385-6122; res: 800/824-4738.* E-mail bishop@waypt.com; web www.waypt.com/bishop. 14 kit. suites, 7 with shower only, 3 story. No A/C. No elvtr. May-Sept: kit. suites $71-$139; under 12 free; wkly rates; hols (2-day min); higher rates special events; lower rates rest of yr. Crib free. Pet accepted, some restrictions; $15. TV; cable, VCR avail (movies). Complimentary continental bkfst. Restaurant nearby. Ck-out 11 am, ck-in 3 pm. Business center. In-rm modem link. Luggage handling. Health club privileges. Refrigerators, microwaves; many fireplaces. Built in 1890 as an office/warehouse; converted to English inn. Totally nonsmoking. Cr cds: A, DS, MC, V. 🐾 ⊠ 📶 SC 🏊

★ ★ **THE SWAN HOTEL.** *222 Monroe St. 360/385-1718; res: 800/776-1718; FAX 360/379-1010.* E-mail swan@waypt.com; web www.waypt.com/bishop. 9 rms, 3 story, 5 kit. suites, 4 kit. cottages. May-Sept: kit. suites $105-$400; kit. cottages $85-$95; under 12 free; wkly rates; higher rates special events; lower rates rest of yr. Crib free. Pet accepted, some restrictions; $15 and daily fees. TV; cable, VCR avail (movies). Complimentary coffee in rms. Restaurant nearby. Ck-out 11 am, ck-in 3 pm. Meeting rms. Business servs avail. In-rm modem link. Free airport transportation. Refrigerators; microwaves avail. Some balconies. Cr cds: A, D, MC, V. **D** 🐾 ⊠ 📶 SC

Quincy *(See also Ellensburg, Wenatchee)*

Motel

✔ ★ **TRADITIONAL INNS.** *500 SW F Street (WA 28). 509/787-3525; FAX 509/787-3528.* 24 rms, 2 story. S, D $43-$67; under 13 free; wkly rates; higher rates Concerts in the Gorge. Pet accepted. TV; cable. Complimentary coffee in lobby. Ck-out 11 am. Coin lndry. Refrigerators. Cr cds: A, C, D, DS, MC, V. **D** 🐾 ⊠ 📶 SC

Richland *(See also Kennewick, Pasco)*

Motels

★ ★ ★ **DOUBLETREE.** *802 George Washington Way. 509/946-7611; FAX 509/943-8564.* 150 rms, 2 story. S, D $72; each addl $10; under 18 free. Crib free. Pet accepted. TV. Heated pool; poolside serv. Coffee in rms. Restaurant 6 am-2 pm, 5-10 pm. Rm serv. Bar. Ck-out noon. Meeting rms. Bellhops. Valet serv. Sundries. Free airport, RR station, bus depot transportation. Boat dock; waterskiing. Private patios, balconies. Most rms with private lanais. Cr cds: A, C, D, DS, ER, JCB, MC, V. 🐾 ⌨ 🏊 🐾 SC

★ ★ **SHILO INN RIVERSHORE.** *50 Comstock St, at George Washington Way. 509/946-4661; FAX 509/943-6741.* 150 rms, 2 story, 12 kits. Mid-May-mid-Sept: S, D $79-$99; each addl $9; kit. units $139-$155; under 13 free; higher rates hydroplane races; lower rates rest of yr. Crib free. Pet accepted; $7/day. TV; cable (premium), VCR (movies $3). Heated pool; wading pool, whirlpool. Restaurant 6 am-10 pm. Bar. Ck-out noon. Coin lndry. Meeting rms. Business servs avail. Valet serv. Airport, RR station, bus depot transportation. Tennis privileges, Golf privileges. Boats, waterskiing. Exercise equipt; treadmill, bicycle. Refrigerator in suites. On 12 acres. Cr cds: A, C, D, DS, ER, JCB, MC, V. 🐾 🏋 ⛷ ⌨ 🍴 🏊 🐾 SC

★ **VAGABOND INN.** *515 George Washington Way. 509/946-6117; FAX 509/943-2463.* 40 rms, 2 story. S $35-$55; D $38-$85; each addl $6; under 18 free. Crib free. Pet accepted; $10. TV; cable (premium), VCR avail. Heated pool. Restaurant nearby. Ck-out 11 am. Some refrigerators. Cr cds: A, C, D, DS, MC, V. 🐾 ⌨ 🏊 🐾 SC

Ritzville *(See also Moses Lake)*

Motel

★ ★ **BEST WESTERN HERITAGE INN.** *1405 Smitty's Blvd. 509/659-1007.* 42 rms, 2 story. May-mid-Nov: S $55; D $64-$70; each addl $8; suites $95-$145; under 18 free; lower rates rest of yr. Crib free. Pet accepted. TV; cable (premium), VCR avail. Heated pool; whirlpool. Complimentary continental bkfst. Restaurant adj open 24 hrs. Ck-out noon. Coin lndry. Meeting rms. Business servs avail. Gift shop. Cr cds: A, C, D, DS, ER, JCB, MC, V. D 🐾 ⌨ 🏊 🐾 SC

Seattle

Motel

★ **QUALITY INN CITY CENTER.** *2224 8th Ave (98121), downtown. 206/624-6820; FAX 206/467-6926.* 72 rms, 7 story. May-Oct: S $105-$115; D $115-$125; each addl $10; suites $145-$185; under 18 free; lower rates rest of yr. Crib free. Pet accepted. TV; cable (premium), VCR avail (movies). Continental bkfst. Coffee in rms. Ck-out 1 pm. Meeting rms. Business servs avail. In-rm modem link. Valet serv. Sundries. Exercise equipt; weight machine, treadmill, sauna. Whirlpool. Some refrigerators; microwaves avail for suites. Balconies. Cr cds: A, C, D, DS, ER, JCB, MC, V. D 🐾 🏋 🍴 🏊 🐾 SC

Hotels

★ ★ ★ **ALEXIS HOTEL.** *1007 1st Ave (98104), downtown. 206/624-4844; FAX 206/621-9009; res: 800/426-7033.* Web www.alexishotel.com. A charming small hotel, the Alexis is in an artfully restored 1901 building near the waterfront, the Public Market and the Seattle Art Museum. Each room is individually decorated. 109 rms, 6 story. S, D $210-$235; suites $245-$550; under 12 free; some wkend rates. Crib free. Pet accepted. Covered valet parking $18/day. TV; cable (premium), VCR avail. Restaurant 6:30 am-10 pm. Rm serv 24 hrs. Bar 11 am-midnight. Ck-out 1 pm. Meeting rms. Business servs avail. In-rm modem link. Concierge. Shopping arcade. Exercise equipt; treadmill, stair machine, steam rm. Massage. Refrigerators; some bathrm phones; microwaves avail. Wet bar, minibar, beverages, whirlpool in suites. Eight wood-burning fireplaces. Some balconies. Cr cds: A, C, D, DS, MC, V. D 🐾 🍴 🐾

HOTEL MONACO. *(Too new to be rated) 1101 Fourth Ave (98101), downtown. 206/621-1770; res: 800/945-2240; FAX 206/621-7779.* Web www.monaco-seattle.com. 189 rms, 11 story, 45 suites. May-Sept: S $195; D $210; suites $240-$900; under 18 free; wkly, hol plans; lower rates rest of yr. Crib free. Pet accepted. Valet parking $18. TV; cable (premium), VCR. Complimentary coffee in rms. Restaurant 6:30 am-10 pm. Rm serv 24 hrs. Bar 11:30 am-midnight. Ck-out noon. Meeting rms. Business center. In-rm modem link. Valet serv. Concierge. Gift shop. Exercise equipt; weights, treadmill. Massage. Health club privileges. Bathrm phones, refrigerators, minibars; some in-rm whirlpools; microwaves avail. Luxury level. Whimsical yet elegant decor with vibrant color scheme throughout. Cr cds: A, D, DS, MC, V. 🄳 ⏐ 🏋 ⊠ 🐾 SC ⚓

★ ★ ★ **SHERATON.** *1400 6th Ave (98101), downtown. 206/621-9000; FAX 206/621-8441.* Web www.ITTsheraton.com. 840 units, 35 story. S $200, D $220; suites $275-$600; under 17 free; wkend rates. Crib free. Pet accepted, some restrictions. Valet parking $18. TV; cable (premium), VCR avail. Indoor pool; whirlpool. Complimentary coffee in rms. Restaurant 6 am-midnight. Rm serv 24 hrs. Bar 11-2 am; entertainment. Ck-out noon. Convention facilities. Business center. In-rm modem link. Concierge. Drugstore. Barber. Exercise rm: instructor, weight machine, stair machine, sauna. Minibars; some bathrm phones. Rms with original Northwest art. Luxury level. Cr cds: A, C, D, DS, ER, JCB, MC, V. 🄳 ⏐ ≈ 🏋 ⊠ 🐾 SC ⚓

★ ★ ★ ★ **SORRENTO.** *900 Madison St (98104), I-5 N James, S Madison exits, downtown. 206/622-6400; FAX 206/343-6155; res: 800/426-1265 (exc WA).* Web usa.nia.com/sorrento. Designed in 1909 to resemble an Italian villa, this deluxe hotel offers wonderful views of downtown and the waterfront. Standard rooms are quiet and comfortable; spacious corner suites have antiques and oversize baths. 76 rms, 6 story, 42 suites. S, D $180-$240; each addl $15; suites $220-$1,200; under 16 free. Crib free. Pet accepted. Covered parking; valet $17. TV; cable (premium), VCR avail. Restaurant 7 am-2:30 pm, 5:30-10 pm. Bar 11:30-2 am. Ck-out noon. Meeting rms. Business servs avail. In-rm modem link. Concierge. Airport transportation. Exercise equipt; weight machines, treadmill. Massage. Refrigerators; many bathrm phones; microwaves avail. Cr cds: A, C, D, DS, JCB, MC, V.
🄳 ⏐ 🏋 ⊠ 🐾

Inn

✔ ★ ★ **BEECH TREE MANOR.** *1405 Queen Anne Ave N (98109), in Queen Anne. 206/281-7037; FAX 206/284-2350.* 7 rms, 2 share bath, 2 story. No A/C. No rm phones. Mid-May-mid-Oct: S $64-$94; D $74-$94; suite $110; each addl $10; wkly rates; lower rates rest of yr. Pet accepted. TV in sitting rm; cable (premium), VCR. Complimentary full bkfst. Restaurant nearby. Ck-out 11 am, ck-in 4-7 pm. Business servs avail. Street parking. Turn-of-the-century mansion (1903) furnished with many antiques. Totally nonsmoking. Cr cds: MC, V. ⏐ ⊠ 🐾

Seattle-Tacoma Intl Airport Area (See also Seattle, Tacoma)

Motels

✔ ★ ★ **LA QUINTA.** *(2824 S 188th St, Seattle 98188) 1 mi S on WA 99. 206/241-5211; FAX 206/246-5596.* 142 rms, 6 story. Late May-Sept: S $74; D $82; each addl $8; lower rates rest of yr; under 18 free. Crib free. Pet accepted, some restrictions. TV; cable (premium). Pool; whirlpool. Complimentary continental bkfst. Restaurant opp. Ck-out noon. Coin lndry. Meeting rm. Business servs avail. In-rm modem link. Sundries. Free airport transportation. Exercise equipt; weights, stair machine. Luxury level. Cr cds: A, D, DS, MC, V. 🄳 ⏐ ≈ 🏋 ✈ ⊠ 🐾 SC

★ ★ **RAMADA INN-SEATAC EAST.** *(16838 International Blvd, Seattle 98188) ¼ mi S on WA 99, at S 168th St. 206/248-0901; FAX 206/242-3170; res: 800/845-2968.* 150 rms, 3 story. June-Sept: S, D $78-$87; each addl $10; suites $80; under 12 free; lower rates rest of yr. Crib free. Pet accepted. TV; cable (premium). Restaurant 7 am-10 pm. Ck-out noon. Meeting rm. Business servs avail. In-rm modem link. Sundries. Free airport transportation. Exercise equipt; weight machine, rower. Balconies. Cr cds: A, C, D, DS, ER, JCB, MC, V. 🄳 ⏐ 🏋 ✈ ⊠ 🐾 SC

Motor Hotels

★ ★ **BEST WESTERN EXECUTEL.** *(31611 20th Ave S, Federal Way 98003) I-5 exit 143 S. 253/941-6000; FAX 253/941-9500.* E-mail execute1@ricochet.net. 112 rms, 3 story. Mid-June-mid-Sept: S, D $99-$129; each addl $10; under 18 free; lower rates rest of yr. Crib free. Pet accepted; $20. TV; cable (premium). Heated pool; whirlpool. Restaurant 6 am-11 pm. Rm serv. Bar. Ck-out noon. Meeting rms. Business center. In-rm modem link. Bellhops. Valet serv. Free airport transportation. Health club privileges. Cr cds: A, C, D, DS, JCB, MC, V. 🄳 ⏐ ≈ ⊠ 🐾 SC ⚓

★ ★ ★ **HILTON SEATTLE AIRPORT.** *(17620 International Blvd, Seattle 98188) at S 176th St. 206/244-4800; FAX 206/248-4495.* E-mail debra_ noonan@hilton.com; web www.hilton.com. 178 rms, 2-3 story. S, D $109-$159; suites $275-$350; under 18 free; wkend rates. Crib free. Pet accepted. TV; cable (premium), VCR avail. Heated pool; whirlpool, poolside serv. Complimentary coffee in rms. Restaurant 6 am-11 pm. Rm serv 24 hrs. Bar 11 am-midnight. Ck-out 1 pm. Meeting rms. Business center. In-rm modem link.

Bellhops. Valet serv. Sundries. Free airport transportation. Exercise equipt; weight machine, bicycles. Private patios. Garden setting. Cr cds: A, C, D, DS, ER, JCB, MC, V.

[D] [♿] [≋] [🕆] [✈] [⊠] [🐾] [SC] [♨]

★ ★ ★ **MARRIOTT SEA-TAC.** *(3201 S 176th St, Seattle 98188) International Blvd (WA 99) to S 176th St.* 206/241-2000; FAX 206/248-0789. 459 rms. S, D $111-$132; suites $200-$450; under 18 free; wkly, wkend rates. Crib free. Pet accepted. TV; cable (premium), VCR avail. Indoor pool; whirlpool, poolside serv. Restaurant 6 am-11 pm. Rm serv. Bar 11-2 am. Ck-out 1 pm. Convention facilities. Business center. In-rm modem link. Bellhops. Valet serv. Shopping arcade. Free airport transportation. Exercise equipt; weight machines, bicycles, sauna. Game rm. Microwaves avail. 21,000-sq ft atrium with trees, plants, totem poles, waterfall. Luxury level. Cr cds: A, C, D, DS, ER, JCB, MC, V.

[D] [♿] [≋] [🕆] [✈] [⊠] [🐾] [SC] [♨]

Sequim (See also Port Angeles, Port Townsend)

Motel

✔ ★ ★ **BEST WESTERN BAY LODGE.** *268522 US 101.* 360/683-0691; FAX 360/683-3748. E-mail sbl@olympus.net. 54 rms, 1 with shower only, 36 with A/C, 3 story, 14 suites. No elvtr. May-Sept: S $75-$100; D $85-$110; each addl $8; suites $95-$145; under 12 free; lower rates rest of yr. Crib free. Pet accepted; $25 refundable. TV; cable (premium). Heated pool. Complimentary coffee in lobby. Complimentary continental bkfst Mid-Oct-mid Mar. Restaurant adj 7 am-9 pm. Ck-out noon. Meeting rms. Business servs avail. 9-hole putting course. Lawn games. Refrigerators in suites. Balconies. Picnic tables. Cr cds: A, C, D, DS, ER, JCB, MC, V. [D] [♿] [≋] [⊠] [🐾] [SC]

Soap Lake (See also Coulee Dam)

Motel

✔ ★ ★ **NOTARAS LODGE.** *231 Main St.* 509/246-0462; FAX 509/246-1054. 20 kit. units, 2 story. S $48; D $55; each addl $7; suites $90-$110. Pet accepted; $50 refundable and $10/day. TV; cable. Restaurant 11 am-10 pm. Ck-out 11 am. Refrigerators. Some in-rm whirlpools. Balconies. Picnic tables. Some rms with skylights. Cr cds: MC, V. [♿] [⊠] [🐾]

Spokane (See also Cheney; also see Coeur d'Alene & Sandpoint, ID)

Motels

★ **COMFORT INN SPOKANE VALLEY.** *N 905 Sullivan Rd (99037), 15 mi E on I-90, exit 291.* 509/924-3838; FAX 509/921-6976. 76 rms, 2 story, 13 suites. May-Sept: S, D $63-$68; each addl $5; suites $80-$125; under 19 free; higher rates special events; lower rates rest of yr. Crib free. Pet accepted, some restrictions; $15. TV; cable, VCR avail. Pool; whirlpool. Complimentary continental bkfst. Restaurant nearby. Ck-out 11 am. Coin lndry. Meeting rms. Business servs avail. Valet serv. Refrigerator in suites. Cr cds: A, C, D, DS, JCB, MC, V. [D] [♿] [≋] [⊠] [🐾] [SC]

✔ ★ **DAYS INN.** *1919 Hutchinson Rd (99212).* 509/926-5399; FAX 509/928-5974. 92 rms, 2 story. S, D $55-$70; each addl $5; suites $75-$80; family rates. Crib free. Pet accepted; $10. TV; cable. Complimentary continental bkfst, coffee. Restaurant adj. Ck-out noon. Meeting rms. Business servs avail. Cr cds: A, C, D, DS, MC, V. [D] [♿] [⊠] [🐾] [SC]

★ ★ **RAMADA INN.** *Box 19228 (99219), opp Intl Airport.* 509/838-5211; FAX 509/838-1074. 168 rms, 2 story. S $65-$85; D $75-$95; each addl $8; suites $95-$150; kit units $150; studio rms $85; under 18 free; some wkend rates. Crib free. Pet accepted. TV; cable. 2 pools, 1 indoor; whirlpool, sauna. Restaurant 6 am-11 pm. Rm serv. Bar; entertainment exc Sun. Ck-out noon. Business servs avail. Bellhops. Valet serv. Sundries. Free airport transportation. Cr cds: A, C, D, DS, ER, JCB, MC, V. [D] [♿] [≋] [🕆] [⊠] [🐾] [SC]

✔ ★ **RODEWAY INN.** *W 827 1st Ave (99204).* 509/838-8271; FAX 509/838-0525. 81 rms, 4 story. Mid-May-Sept: S $40-$55; D $46-$65; each addl $10; suites $95; under 18 free; higher rates Bloomsday; lower rates rest of yr. Crib free. Pet accepted, some restrictions. TV. Heated pool. Complimentary continental bkfst. Restaurant 6 am-10 pm. Bar to 2 am. Ck-out 1 pm. Meeting rms. Business servs avail. Airport, RR station, bus depot transportation. Cr cds: A, D, DS, JCB, MC, V. [♿] [≋] [⊠] [🐾] [SC]

Motor Hotels

★ **CAVANAUGH'S FOURTH AVENUE.** *E 110 4th Ave (99202), I-90 exit 281.* 509/838-6101; FAX 509/624-0733. 151 rms, 6 story. S $54-$78; D $58-$78; each addl $8; suites $78; under 18 free. Crib free. Pet accepted. TV; cable. Pool. Restaurant 6 am-10 pm.

Rm serv. Bar. Ck-out noon. Coin lndry. Meeting rms. Business servs avail. Free airport, RR station, bus depot transportation. Minibar in suites. Cr cds: A, C, D, DS, ER, MC, V.
[D] [symbols] [SC]

★ ★ ★ **CAVANAUGH'S RIVER INN.** *N 700 Division St (99202). 509/326-5577; FAX 509/326-1120; res: 800/843-4667.* 241 rms, 2 story. S $77-$94; D $82-$99; each addl $10; suites $160; under 17 free. Crib free. Pet accepted, some restrictions. TV; cable, VCR avail. 2 heated pools; wading pool, whirlpool, sauna, poolside serv. Restaurant 7 am-10 pm. Rm serv. Bar 11-2 am; entertainment exc Sun. Ck-out noon. Meeting rms. Business servs avail. Bellhops. Valet serv. Sundries. Gift shop. Airport, RR station, bus depot transportation. Tennis. On river. Cr cds: A, C, D, DS, ER, MC, V. [D] [symbols] [SC]

★ ★ ★ **DOUBLETREE.** *N 1100 Sullivan Rd (99220), I-90 exit 291. 509/924-9000; FAX 509/922-4965.* 237 rms, 2-3 story. S, D $79-$99; each addl $15; under 18 free. Crib free. Pet accepted, some restrictions. TV; cable. Heated pool; whirlpool. Coffee in rms. Restaurant 6 am-11 pm. Rm serv. Bar 11-2 am; entertainment Tues-Sat. Ck-out noon. Meeting rms. Bellhops. Valet serv. Sundries. Barber, beauty shop. Free airport transportation. Some bathrm phones, refrigerators. Private patios, balconies. Cr cds: A, C, D, DS, ER, JCB, MC, V. [symbols]

★ **SHILO INN.** *E 923 3rd Ave (99202). 509/535-9000; FAX 509/535-5740; res: 800/222-2244.* 105 rms, 5 story. S $65; D $65-$69; each addl $8; under 12 free; some wknd rates. Crib free. Pet accepted; $7/day. TV; cable (premium), VCR (movies). Indoor pool. Coffee in rms. Complimentary full bkfst. Restaurant 6:30 am-10 pm. Rm serv. Bar 11:30 am-11 pm. Ck-out noon. Meeting rms. Business servs avail. In-rm modem link. Free airport transportation. Exercise equipt; weight machine, bicycle, sauna. Refrigerators. Cr cds: A, C, D, DS, ER, JCB, MC, V. [symbols]

Tacoma

Motels

★ ★ **BEST WESTERN TACOMA INN.** *8726 S Hosmer St (98444), I-5 at 84th St exit. 253/535-2880; FAX 253/537-8379.* 149 rms, 2 story, 8 kits. S $64-$72; D $70-$80; each addl $6; kit. units $78-$84; under 18 free. Crib free. Pet accepted, some restrictions; $20. TV; cable (premium). Heated pool; poolside serv. Playground. Complimentary coffee in rms. Restaurant 6:30 am-10:30 pm. Rm serv. Bar 11-2 am; entertainment. Ck-out noon. Coin lndry. Meeting rms. Business servs avail. In-rm modem link. Valet serv. Putting green. Exercise equipt; weight machine, bicycles. Some refrigerators; microwaves avail. Private patios, balconies. Cr cds: A, C, D, DS, ER, JCB, MC, V. [D] [symbols] [SC]

★ ★ **DAYS INN.** *6802 Tacoma Mall Blvd (98409), I-5 exit 129. 253/475-5900; FAX 253/475-3540.* 123 rms, 2 story. S, D $70-$89; each addl $10; suites $165; under 12 free. Crib free. Pet accepted. TV; cable (premium). Heated pool. Complimentary coffee in lobby. Restaurant 6:30 am-10 pm; Sat from 8 am; Sun 8 am-9 pm. Ck-out 11 am. Ck-in 3 pm. Meeting rms. Business center. In-rm modem link. Valet serv. Health club privileges. Refrigerator; microwaves avail. Cr cds: A, C, D, DS, ER, JCB, MC, V. [D] [symbols] [SC]

★ ★ **ROYAL COACHMAN MOTOR INN.** *5805 Pacific Hwy E (98424). 253/922-2500; FAX 253/922-6443; res: 800/422-3051.* 94 rms, 2 story. S $56-$65; D $68-$75; each addl $7; suites $140; kit. units $95-$120; under 12 free. Crib free. Pet accepted; $25 refundable. TV; cable (premium), VCR avail. Coffee in rms. Restaurant 6:30 am-9 pm. Ck-out noon. Coin lndry. Meeting rms. Business servs avail. Valet serv. Some refrigerators, microwaves, in-rm whirlpools. Cr cds: A, C, D, DS, ER, JCB, MC, V. [D] [symbols] [SC]

Motor Hotels

★ ★ **BEST WESTERN EXECUTIVE INN.** *(5700 Pacific Hwy E, Fife 98424) I-5 exit 137. 253/922-0080; FAX 253/922-6439.* 140 rms, 4 story. May-Sept: S $79-$99; D $109-$129; each addl $8; suites $150-$175; under 19 free; hol rates; lower rates rest of yr. Crib free. Pet accepted, some restrictions; $25 deposit. TV; cable (premium), VCR avail. Indoor pool; whirlpool. Complimentary coffee in rms. Restaurant 6 am-10 pm. Rm serv from 7 am. Bar 11-2 am. Ck-out noon. Meeting rms. Business center. In-rm modem link. Bellhops. Sundries. Valet serv. Free airport, RR station, bus depot transportation. Health club privileges. Some refrigerators; microwaves avail. Cr cds: A, D, DS, JCB, MC, V.
[D] [symbols] [SC]

★ ★ **LA QUINTA.** *1425 E 27th St (98421), exit I-5 exits 134S, 135N. 253/383-0146; FAX 253/627-3280.* 158 rms, 7 story. S $68-$78; D $76-$88; each addl $8; under 18 free. Crib free. Pet accepted. TV; cable (premium). Heated pool; whirlpool. Complimentary continental bkfst. Restaurant 6:30 am-10 pm. Rm serv. Bar. Ck-out noon. Coin lndry. Meeting rms. Business center. In-rm modem link. Valet serv. Sundries. Exercise equipt;

bicycles, treadmill. Microwaves avail. View of both Mt Rainier and Commencement Bay. Cr cds: A, C, D, DS, MC, V. 🄳 💺 🌊 🏋 ⛷ 🛁 SC 🎣

★ ★ ★ **SHILO INN.** *7414 S Hosmer (98408), S on I-5, exit 72nd St. 253/475-4020; FAX 253/475-1236.* 132 rms, 4 story, 11 kits. S $79; D $85-$89; each addl $10; kit. units $99; under 12 free. Crib avail. Pet accepted; $7. TV; cable (premium), VCR (movies $3). Indoor pool; whirlpool. Complimentary continental bkfst. Restaurant opp 6 am-11 pm. Ck-out noon. Coin lndry. Meeting rms. Business servs avail. In-rm modem link. Valet serv. Exercise equipt; weight machine, treadmill, sauna, steam rm. Bathrm phones, refrigerators, microwaves. Cr cds: A, D, DS, ER, JCB, MC, V. 🄳 💺 🌊 🏋 ⛷ 🛁 SC

Vancouver *(See also Portland, OR)*

Motels

★ **BEST WESTERN FERRYMAN'S INN.** *7901 NE 6th Ave (98665), I-5 exit 4. 360/574-2151; FAX 360/574-9644.* 134 rms, 2 story, 9 kit. S $54-$65; D $63-$78; each addl $5; suites $65-$90.50; kit. units $65-$70; under 12 free. Crib free. Pet accepted; $3. TV; cable (premium). Heated pool. Complimentary continental bkfst. Restaurant adj open 24 hrs. Ck-out noon. Coin lndry. Meeting rms. Business servs avail. Cr cds: A, C, D, DS, MC, V. 🄳 💺 🌊 ⛷ 🛁 SC

✔ ★ **QUALITY INN.** *7001 NE WA 99 (98665), I-5 exit 4. 360/696-0516; FAX 360/693-8343.* 72 kit. suites, 2 story. S $62.50-$67.50; D $69.50-$74.50; each addl $5; under 18 free. Crib $5. Pet accepted, some restrictions; $5. TV; cable (premium). Heated pool; whirlpool. Complimentary continental bkfst. Restaurant nearby. Ck-out noon. Coin lndry. Business servs avail. Some balconies. Cr cds: A, C, D, DS, MC, V. 💺 🌊 ⛷ 🛁 SC

✔ ★ **RODEWAY INN.** *221 NE Chkalov Dr (98684), I 205 exit 28. 360/256-7044; FAX 360/256-1231; res: 800/426-5110.* 118 rms, 2 story. S $52; D $58; each addl $6; suites $85-$100; under 18 free. Crib free. Pet accepted; $15. TV; cable (premium). Indoor pool; whirlpool. Complimentary continental bkfst. Restaurant 6 am-10 pm. Ck-out noon. Meeting rms. Business servs avail. Valet serv. Free airport transportation. Health club privileges. Cr cds: A, C, D, DS, MC, V. 🄳 💺 🌊 ⛷ 🛁 SC

★ **SHILO INN-HAZEL DELL.** *13206 WA 99 (98686), I-5 exit 7. 360/573-0511; FAX 360/573-0396.* 66 rms, 2 story, 6 kits. S, D $75; each addl $10; kit. units $55-$79; under 13 free. Crib free. Pet accepted; $7. TV; cable (premium). Indoor pool; whirlpool. Complimentary continental bkfst. Restaurant adj 6:30 am-10:30 pm. Bar. Ck-out noon. Coin lndry. Meeting rms. Business servs avail. Valet serv. Free airport transportation. Sauna, steam rm. Refrigerators. Cr cds: A, C, D, DS, ER, JCB, MC, V. 💺 🌊 ⛷ 🛁 SC

Walla Walla

Motel

★ ★ **COMFORT INN.** *520 N 2nd Ave. 509/525-2522; FAX 509/522-2565.* 61 rms, 3 story. May-Sept: S $57; D $62-$67; each addl $8; suites $100-$125; under 18 free; higher rates special events; lower rates rest of yr. Crib free. Pet accepted, some restrictions. TV; cable (premium). Indoor pool. Complimentary continental bkfst. Restaurant adj 11 am-10 pm. Ck-out 1 pm. Meeting rm. Business servs avail. Gift shop. Some refrigerators. Cr cds: A, C, D, DS, MC, V. 🄳 💺 🌊 ⛷ 🛁 SC

Wenatchee *(See also Leavenworth)*

Motel

★ **CHIEFTAIN.** *1005 N Wenatchee Ave (98801). 509/663-8141; FAX 509/663-8176; res: 800/572-4456 (WA).* 105 rms, 1-2 story. S $45; D $65-$80; each addl $5. Crib free. Pet accepted. TV; cable (premium). Heated pool; whirlpool. Restaurant 6 am-midnight. Bar; entertainment Tues-Sat. Ck-out noon. Meeting rms. Business servs avail. Private patios, balconies. Cr cds: A, C, D, DS, MC, V. 🄳 💺 🌊 ⛷ 🛁 SC

Motor Hotel

★ ★ ★ **DOUBLETREE.** *1225 N Wenatchee Ave (98801). 509/663-0711; FAX 509/662-8175.* 149 rms, 3 story. S, D $79-$89; each addl $10; under 18 free; wkend rates. Crib free. Pet accepted. TV; cable. Heated pool; poolside serv. Restaurant 6 am-10 pm. Rm serv. Bar 11-2 am, Sun 4 pm-midnight; entertainment exc Sun. Ck-out 1 pm. Meeting rms. Business servs avail. In-rm modem link. Valet serv. Sundries. Free airport, bus depot transportation. Balconies. Cr cds: A, C, D, DS, JCB, MC, V. 💺 🌊 ⛷ 🛁

Hotel

★ ★ ★ **WESTCOAST WENATCHEE CENTER.** *201 N Wenatchee Ave (98801). 509/662-1234; FAX 509/662-0782.* 147 rms, 9 story. S $87-$92; D $97-$102; each addl $10; suites $125-$200; under 18 free; ski rates; higher rates Apple Blossom Festival. Crib free. Pet accepted; $50 deposit. TV. Indoor/outdoor pool; whirlpool, poolside serv. Restaurant 6:30 am-10:30 pm. Bar 11-2 am; entertainment Tues-Sat. Ck-out noon. Meeting rms. Business servs avail. Free airport, RR station, bus depot transportation. Downhill ski 12 mi. Exercise equipt; weights, bicycles. Some refrigerators. Cr cds: A, C, D, DS, ER, JCB, MC, V. 🄳 💺 🐾 ➰ 🏋 🖾 🖢 SC

Yakima *(See also Ellensburg)*

Motels

★ ★ ★ **HOLIDAY INN.** *9th St & Yakima Ave (98901), I-82 City Center exit. 509/452-6511; FAX 509/457-4931.* 171 rms, 2-3 story, 8 kits. S, D, kit. units $69-$95; each addl $10; suites $110-$195; under 19 free. Crib free. Pet accepted. TV; cable (premium), VCR avail. Heated pool; poolside serv. Complimentary continental bkfst. Restaurant 6:30 am-10 pm. Rm serv. Bar. Ck-out noon. Coin lndry. Meeting rms. Business servs avail. In-rm modem link. Free airport transportation. Some refrigerators. Some private patios, balconies. Cr cds: A, C, D, DS, JCB, MC, V. 🄳 💺 ➰ 🖾 🖢 SC

✔ ★ **QUALITY INN.** *12 Valley Mall Blvd (98903), I-82 Union Gap exit. 509/248-6924; FAX 509/575-8470.* 85 rms, 2 story. S $52-$57; D $66-$69; each addl $8; under 18 free. Pet accepted. TV; cable, VCR avail. Heated pool. Complimentary continental bkfst. Restaurant adj open 24 hrs. Ck-out 11 am. Business servs avail. Valet serv. Free airport transportation. Sun deck. Cr cds: A, C, D, DS, MC, V. 💺 ➰ 🖾 🖢 SC

★ ★ **RED LION INN.** *818 N 1st St (98901), I-82 exit N 1st St. 509/453-0391; FAX 509/453-8348.* 58 rms, 2 story. S $64-$79; D $74-$89; each addl $10; suites $120-$150; under 18 free. Crib free. Pet accepted, some restrictions. TV; cable (premium). Heated pool. Coffee avail. Restaurant adj open 24 hrs. Ck-out noon. Business servs avail. Cr cds: A, C, D, DS, ER, MC, V. 💺 ➰ 🖾 🖢

West Virginia

Beckley

Motel

✔★ **COMFORT INN.** *1909 Harper Rd (WV 3) (25801). 304/255-2161.* Web wvweb.com/www/cibeckley.html. 130 rms, 3 story. S $56-$84; D $61-$89; under 19 free. Crib free. Pet accepted; $10. TV; cable (premium), VCR avail (movies). Complimentary continental bkfst. Restaurant nearby. Ck-out noon. Coin lndry. Business servs avail. Sundries. Downhill ski 15 mi. Exercise equipt; weights, bicycle. Some refrigerators, microwaves. Cr cds: A, C, D, DS, ER, JCB, MC, V. 🄳 🛉 ≋ 🏋 ⊠ 🐾 SC

Bluefield (See also Princeton)

Motels

✔★ **ECONO LODGE.** *3400 Cumberland Rd. 304/327-8171.* 48 rms, 2 story. S $39; D $45; each addl $5; under 18 free. Crib free. Pet accepted; $5. TV; cable. Coffee in lobby. Restaurant nearby. Ck-out 11 am. Business servs avail. Cr cds: A, C, D, DS, MC, V. 🄳 🛉 ⊠ 🐾 SC

★★ **HOLIDAY INN.** *US 460/52 Bypass, 3 mi W of I-77, Bluefield exit 1, via US 460/52. 304/325-6170.* Web www.com.holidayinnonthehill.com. 118 rms, 2 story. S, D $85; each addl $10; suites $170; under 18 free. Crib free. Pet accepted. TV; cable (premium), VCR avail. Heated pool; poolside serv. Saunas. Restaurant 6 am-10 pm. Ck-out noon. Meeting rms. In-rm modem link. Gift shop. Valet serv Mon-Fri. Golf privileges. Cr cds: A, C, D, DS, JCB, MC, V. 🄳 🛉 🏋 ≋ ⊠ 🐾 SC

Buckhannon (See also Weston)

Motel

✔★ **CENTENNIAL.** *22 N Locust St. 304/472-4100.* 24 rms. S $27.95-$39.95, D $39.95; each addl $6; apt. $175/wk; under 12 free. Crib free. Pet accepted. TV; cable. Complimentary coffee. Restaurant nearby. Ck-out noon. Cr cds: A, C, D, DS, MC, V. 🛉 ⊠ 🐾 SC

Charleston (See also Nitro)

Motel

✔★ **RED ROOF INN.** *6305 MacCorkle Ave SE (25304). 304/925-6953; FAX 304/925-8111.* E-mail i0059@redroof.com; web www.redroofinns.com. 108 rms, 2 story. Apr-Oct: S $49.99; D $59.99; each addl $7; under 18 free; higher rates special events; lower rates rest of yr. Crib free. Pet accepted. TV; cable (premium). Complimentary coffee in lobby. Restaurant adj 6 am-10:30 pm. Ck-out noon. Business servs avail. Cr cds: A, C, D, DS, MC, V. 🄳 🛉 ⊠ 🐾

Hotel

★★★ **HOLIDAY INN-CHARLESTON HOUSE.** *600 Kanawha Blvd E (25301). 304/344-4092; FAX 304/345-4847.* Web wvweb.com/www/holiday_inn_charleston_house. 256 rms, 12 story. S, D $99-$109; each addl $6; under 18 free; suites $200-$375; 4-day min Labor Day wkend; wkend rates; package plans. Crib free. Pet accepted. TV; cable (premium), VCR avail. Heated pool. Restaurant 6:30 am-2 pm; dining rm 5-10 pm. Bar 4 pm-2 am, closed Sun; pianist. Ck-out noon. Convention facilities. Business servs avail. In-rm modem link. Barber, beauty shop. Gift shop. Garage. Free airport transportation. Exercise equipt; weights, bicycles. Some wet bars. Some rms with river view. Cr cds: A, C, D, DS, JCB, MC, V. 🄳 🛉 ≋ 🏋 ⊠ 🐾 SC

Charles Town (See also Martinsburg; also see Winchester, VA)

Motel

★ **TURF.** *608 E Washington St, 1 mi E on WV 51. 304/725-2081; FAX 304/728-7605; res: 800/422-8873.* 46 rms, 2 story, 6 kits. June-Labor Day: S $32-$56; D $46-$56; each addl $2-$5; suites $75-$150; kit. units $55-$75; lower rates rest of yr. Crib $5. Pet accepted. TV; cable (premium). Pool. Restaurant 6:30 am-9 pm; Fri, Sat to 10 pm. Rm serv.

Bar 10-2 am. Ck-out noon. Meeting rms. Business servs avail. Free RR station transportation. Microwaves avail. Cr cds: A, C, D, DS, MC, V. [D] 🐾 ≈ ⊠ 🐾 SC

Huntington

Motels

✔ ★ **RED ROOF INN.** *5190 US 60E (25705). 304/733-3737; FAX 304/733-3786.* 108 rms, 2 story. S $45-$55; D $52-$57; each addl $7; under 18 free. Crib free. Pet accepted. TV; cable. Business servs avail. Microwaves avail. Cr cds: A, C, D, DS, MC, V. [D] 🐾 ⊠ 🐾

★ **TRAVELODGE.** *5600 US 60E (25705). 304/736-3451; FAX 304/736-3451, ext. 706.* 120 rms, 3 story. S $42-$54; D $47-$60; each addl $5; suites $54; under 18 free. Crib free. Pet accepted. TV; cable (premium). Pool. Restaurant 5-9 pm. Private club 5 pm-2 am. Ck-out noon. Meeting rms. Business servs avail. Sundries. Free airport transportation. Exercise equipt; weight machine, stair machines. Private patios, balconies. Cr cds: A, C, D, DS, JCB, MC, V. [D] 🐾 ≈ 🏋 ⊠ 🐾 SC

Motor Hotel

★ ★ **UPTOWNER INN.** *1415 4th Ave (25701). 304/525-7741; res: 800/828-9016; FAX 304/525-3508.* 138 rms, 4 story. S, D $63-$70; each addl $5; suites $90-$100; under 18 free. Crib free. Pet accepted. TV; cable. Pool; wading pool. Restaurants 6:30 am-10 pm. Rm serv. Bar 4 pm-midnight, Fri, Sat to 1 am. Ck-out noon. Meeting rms. Business servs avail. In-rm modem link. Free airport transportation. Exercise equipt; weights, bicycle. Cr cds: A, C, D, DS, JCB, MC, V. [D] 🐾 ≈ 🏋 ⊠ 🐾 SC

Lewisburg *(See also White Sulphur Springs)*

Motels

(Rates are generally higher during state fair)

★ ★ **BRIER INN.** *540 N Jefferson, jct US 219 & I-64 exit 169. 304/645-7722; FAX 304/645-7865.* 162 units, 2 story. S $42; D $47; each addl $5; suites $70-$75; kit. units $62-$67; under 12 free; higher rates state fair. Crib $5. Pet accepted, some restrictions; $10. TV; cable, VCR avail (movies). Pool. Restaurant 11 am-10 pm; Fri, Sat to 11 pm. Rm serv. Bar 10-2 am; entertainment Fri. Ck-out 11 am. Meeting rms. Business servs avail. In-rm modem link. Health club privileges. Cr cds: A, D, DS, MC, V. [D] 🐾 ≈ ⊠ 🐾 SC

✔ ★ **BUDGET HOST-FORT SAVANNAH INN.** *204 N Jefferson St. 304/645-3055; FAX /; res: 800/678-3055.* E-mail omb00827.@mall.wunit.edu. 66 rms, 2 story. S $36-$50; D $42-$65; each addl $5; under 18 free. Crib free. Pet accepted; $5. TV; cable. Pool; whirlpool. Restaurant 6 am-10 pm. Rm serv. Ck-out noon. Business servs avail. Airport transportation. Balconies. Cr cds: A, C, D, DS, MC, V. [D] 🐾 ≈ ⊠ 🐾 SC

★ **DAYS INN.** *635 N Jefferson St. 304/645-2345; FAX 304/645-5501; res: 800/325-2525.* 26 rms. S $48-$65; D $48-$85; each addl $5; higher rates special events. Crib free. Pet accepted, some restrictions; $10. TV; cable (premium). Complimentary coffee in lobby. Restaurant nearby. Ck-out 11 am. Business servs avail. Airport transportation. Cr cds: A, D, DS, MC, V. 🐾 ⊠ 🐾 SC

Martinsburg *(See also Hagerstown, MD)*

Motels

★ **KNIGHTS INN.** *1599 Edwin Miller Blvd, I-81 exit 16E. 304/267-2211; FAX 304/267-9606.* 59 rms, 1-2 story, 6 kits. Apr-Dec: S $46.95; D $55; each addl $5; kits. $46.95-$55; under 17 free; lower rates rest of yr. Crib free. Pet accepted. TV; cable (premium), VCR avail. Complimentary coffee in lobby. Restaurant adj 6 am-11 pm. Ck-out noon. Meeting rms. Business servs avail. Sundries. Refrigerators, microwaves avail. Cr cds: A, C, D, DS, MC, V. [D] 🐾 ⊠ 🐾 SC

★ **SUPER 8.** *1602 Edwin Miller Blvd, I-81, exit 16E. 304/263-0801.* 43 rms, 3 story. June-Sept: S, D $43.88-$49.88; each addl $6; under 16 free; wkly, wkend rates; higher rates special events; lower rates rest of yr. Crib free. Pet accepted; $20 deposit. TV; cable (premium). Complimentary continental bkfst. Restaurant adj 6 am-11 pm. Ck-out 11 am. Meeting rms. Cr cds: A, C, D, DS, JCB, MC, V. [D] 🐾 ⊠ 🐾 SC

Hotel

★ ★ **HOLIDAY INN.** *301 Foxcroft Ave, I-81 exit 13. 304/267-5500; FAX 304/264-9157.* 120 rms, 5 story. Apr-Oct: S, D $79-$90; each addl $10; under 17 free; lower rates rest of yr. Crib free. Pet accepted, some restrictions. TV; cable (premium), VCR avail. 2 pools, 1 indoor; whirlpool, lifeguard. Restaurant 6:30 am-10 pm; Sun 7 am-9 pm. Bar 4 pm-1 am. Ck-out noon. Meeting rms. Business servs avail. In-rm modem link. Lighted tennis, pro. Exercise rm; instructor, weight machines, bicycles, saunas. Lawn games. Some refrigerators. Cr cds: A, C, D, DS, ER, JCB, MC, V. 🄳 ⛄ 🏃 🏊 🏹 📶 🐾 SC

Morgantown

Motels

✔★ **ECONO LODGE-COLISEUM.** *3506 Monongahela Blvd.* 304/599-8181; FAX 304/599-4866. 71 rms, 2 story. S, D $59; each addl $5; higher rates: football wkends, graduation. Crib $5. Pet accepted. TV; VCR avail. Restaurant adj 6 am-midnight. Ck-out 11 am. Meeting rm. Business servs avail. Sundries. Cr cds: A, D, DS, MC, V.
🄳 ⛄ 📶 🐾 SC

✔★ **FRIENDSHIP INN-MOUNTAINEER.** *452 Country Club Rd, near University Medical Center.* 304/599-4850; FAX 304/599-4866. 30 rms, 1-2 story. S, D $34-$44; each addl $5; higher rates: football wkends, graduation. Crib $5. Pet accepted. TV; cable. Restaurant adj 7 am-11 pm. Ck-out 11 am. Business servs avail. Cr cds: A, D, DS, MC, V.
🄳 ⛄ 📶 🐾 SC

★★ **HOLIDAY INN.** *1400 Saratoga Ave.* 304/599-1680; FAX 304/598-0989. 147 rms, 2 story. S, D $45-$66; under 18 free; higher rates: graduation, athletic events. Crib free. Pet accepted. TV; cable. Pool. Restaurant 6 am-2 pm, 5-10 pm. Rm serv. Bar 4 pm-2 am. Ck-out noon. Meeting rms. Business servs avail. Balconies. Cr cds: A, C, D, DS, ER, MC, V. 🄳 ⛄ 🏊 📶 🐾 SC

Nitro *(See also Charleston)*

Motel

✔★★ **RAMADA LIMITED.** *(419 Hurricane Creek Rd, Hurricane 25526) W on US 60.* 304/562-3346; FAX 304/562-7408. 147 rms, 2 story. Apr-Sept: S, D $45-$55; each addl $5; under 16 free; wkly rates; higher rates special events; lower rates rest of yr. Crib free. Pet accepted, some restrictions; $5. TV; cable (premium). Complimentary continental bkfst. Restaurant adj 7 am-10 pm. Ck-out noon. Meeting rms. Business servs avail. Sundries. Pool. Some refrigerators. Microwaves avail. Picnic tables, grills. Cr cds: A, C, D, DS, JCB, MC, V. 🄳 ⛄ 🏊 📶 🐾 SC

Parkersburg

Motel

★ **RED ROOF INN.** *3714 7th St.* 304/485-1741; FAX 304/485-1746. 107 rms, 2 story. S $36.99-$45.99; D $41.99-$48.99; each addl $5; under 18 free. Crib free. Pet accepted. TV; cable (premium). Ck-out noon. Meeting rms. Business servs avail. In-rm modem link. Cr cds: A, C, D, DS, MC, V. 🄳 ⛄ 📶 🐾 SC

Princeton *(See also Bluefield)*

Motel

★ **DAYS INN.** *347 Meadowfield Ln.* 304/425-8100; FAX 304/487-1734. 122 rms, 2 story. S $58-$63; D $63-$68; kit. units $67-$75; under 16 free. Crib free. Pet accepted. TV; cable. Indoor pool; whirlpool. Complimentary continental bkfst. Restaurant adj 6 am-10 pm. Ck-out 11 am. Business servs avail. Sundries. Downhill ski 15 mi. Cr cds: A, C, D, DS, JCB, MC, V. 🄳 ⛄ 🏊 🏊 📶 🐾 SC

Summersville

Motels

✔★ **BEST WESTERN SUMMERSVILLE LAKE.** *1203 Broad St.* 304/872-6900; FAX 304/872-6908. 59 rms, 3 story. April-Oct: S $42-$48; D $47-$53; each addl $5; under 12 free; lower rates rest of yr. Crib free. Pet accepted, some restrictions. TV; cable, VCR avail (movies avail). Complimentary continental bkfst. Restaurant 11 am-10 pm. Rm serv. Bar. Ck-out 11 am. Business servs avail. Microwave avail. Cr cds: A, C, D, DS, ER, JCB, MC, V. 🄳 ⛄ 📶 🐾 SC

★★ **COMFORT INN.** *903 Industrial Dr, 2 mi N on US 19 at jct WV 41.* 304/872-6500; FAX 304/872-3090. Web wvweb.com/www/comfort.inn-summersville. 99 rms, 2 story.

June-Oct: S $47-$62; D $52-$69; each addl $5-$7; suites $62-$114; under 18 free; lower rates rest of yr. Crib free. Pet accepted, some restrictions; $5. TV; cable (premium), VCR avail (movies avail). Heated pool; wading pool. Complimentary continental bkfst. Restaurant nearby. Ck-out 11 am. Coin lndry. Meeting rms. Bellhops. Exercise equipt; weight machine, bicycles, sauna. Refrigerator in suites. Microwave avail. Picnic tables. Cr cds: A, C, D, DS, ER, JCB, MC, V. [D] [☞] [≈] [✕] [⊠] [🔥] [SC]

★ **SLEEP INN.** *701 Professional Park Dr, off US 19. 304/872-4500; FAX 304/872-0288; res: 800/872-1751.* 97 rms, 2 story. June-Oct: S $40-$53; D $45-$65; each addl $5; under 18 free; higher rates special events; lower rates rest of yr. Crib free. Pet accepted, some restrictions. TV; cable (premium), VCR avail (movies). Heated pool. Complimentary continental bkfst. Restaurant adj 11 am-10 pm. Ck-out 11 am. Coin lndry. Meeting rms. Business servs avail. Sundries. Lawn games. Refrigerators, microwaves avail. Cr cds: A, C, D, DS, ER, JCB, MC, V. [D] [☞] [≈] [⊠] [🔥] [SC]

Weston *(See also Buckhannon)*

Motel

🚫 ★ ★ **COMFORT INN.** *Box 666, At jct US 33 & I-79. 304/269-7000.* 60 rms, 2 story. S $40-$52; D $46-$58; each addl $6; under 18 free. Crib free. Pet accepted. TV; cable. Heated pool. Restaurant 6 am-9 pm. Bar 5-11 pm. Ck-out noon. Meeting rm. Balconies. Cr cds: A, C, D, DS, ER, JCB, MC, V. [D] [☞] [≈] [⊠] [🔥] [SC]

Wheeling

Motel

(Rates are usually higher for Jamboree in the Hills)

★ ★ **DAYS INN.** *(RD 1, Box 292, Triadelphia 26059) 9 mi E, at I-70 exit 11. 304/547-0610; FAX 304/547-9029.* 106 rms, 2 story. S, D $45-$55; each addl $6; under 18 free. Crib free. Pet accepted. TV; cable (premium), VCR avail. Pool. Bar 5 pm-1 am, closed Sun. Ck-out noon. Meeting rm. Business servs avail. Valet serv. Some in-rm whirlpools. Cr cds: A, C, D, DS, MC, V. [D] [☞] [≈] [⊠] [🔥] [SC]

White Sulphur Springs *(See also Lewisburg; also see Covington, VA)*

Motel

(Rates are generally higher during state fair)

🚫 ★ ★ **OLD WHITE.** *865 E Main St. 304/536-2441; res: 800/867-2441.* 26 rms. S $36; D $44; each addl $3; higher rates special events. Crib free. Pet accepted, some restrictions. TV; cable (premium). Pool. Coffee in lobby. Restaurant adj 7:30 am-9 pm. Ck-out noon. Cr cds: A, C, D, DS, MC, V. [☞] [≈] [⊠] [🔥]

Wisconsin

Algoma *(See also Green Bay, Sturgeon Bay)*

Motel

✔★ **RIVER HILLS.** *820 N Water St (WI 42N). 920/487-3451; FAX 920/487-2031; res: 800/236-3451.* E-mail rhmotel@itol.com. 30 rms. D $40-$60. Crib $3. Pet accepted, some restrictions; $3. TV; cable (premium). Ck-out 11 am. Business servs avail. Some refrigerators. Boat dock, ramps nearby. Cr cds: MC, V. 🆔 ♿ 🐾 🔥

Appleton *(See also Green Bay, Neenah-Menasha, Oshkosh)*

Motels

★★ **BEST WESTERN MIDWAY HOTEL.** *3033 W College Ave (WI 125) (54914). 414/731-4141; FAX 414/731-6343.* 105 rms, 2 story. S $67-$86; D $78-$98; each addl $12; under 18 free; wkend rates. Crib free. Pet accepted, some restrictions; $10. TV; cable. Indoor pool; whirlpool. Complimentary full bkfst (Mon-Fri). Coffee in rms. Restaurant 6:30 am-11 pm. Rm serv. Bar 11-1 am. Ck-out 11 am. Meeting rms. Business servs avail. In-rm modem link. Bellhops. Sundries. Free airport, bus depot transportation. Exercise equipt; bicycles, weights, sauna. Health club privileges. Rec rm. Cr cds: A, C, D, DS, MC, V. 🆔 ♿ 🏊 🍴 🔥 🐾 SC

✔★ **EXEL INN.** *210 N Westhill Blvd (54914), off College Ave (WI 125). 414/733-5551; FAX 414/733-7199.* 105 rms, 2 story. S $37.99; D $45.99-$105; each addl $4; under 18 free. Crib free. Pet accepted, some restrictions. TV; cable (premium). Complimentary continental bkfst. Restaurant adj 6 am-11 pm. Ck-out noon. Business servs avail. In-rm modem link. Health club privileges. Refrigerator, microwave, in-rm whirlpool avail. Cr cds: A, C, D, DS, MC, V. 🆔 ♿ 🐾 🔥 SC

★★ **RAMADA INN.** *200 N Perkins St (54914). 920/735-2733; FAX 920/735-5588.* 91 units, 2 story. S $60-$80; D $70-$90; each addl $5; suites $80-$100; under 18 free. Crib free. Pet accepted, some restrictions. TV; cable (premium), VCR avail (movies). Indoor pool; whirlpool. Complimentary bkfst buffet 6-10 am. Restaurant adj. Bar 11-1 am. Ck-out noon. Coin lndry. Meeting rms. Business servs avail. Valet serv. Sundries. Free airport, bus depot transportation. Exercise equipt; bicycle, stair machine. Some refrigerators. Cr cds: A, C, D, DS, JCB, MC, V. 🆔 ♿ 🏊 🍴 🐾 🔥 SC

✔★ **ROAD STAR INN.** *3623 W College Ave (WI 125) (54914). 414/731-5271; FAX 414/731-0227; res: 800/445-4667.* 102 rms, 2 story. S $35; D $41; each addl $5; suites $42.95-$44.95; under 15 free; higher rates special events. Pet accepted. TV; cable (premium). Complimentary continental bkfst. Restaurant adj 7 am-9 pm. Ck-out noon. Sundries. Cr cds: A, C, D, DS, MC, V. 🆔 ♿ 🐾 🔥 SC

Ashland *(See also Bayfield)*

Motels

★★ **BEST WESTERN HOLIDAY HOUSE.** *Rte 3, Box 24, Lakeshore Dr (US 2/63/WI 13). 715/682-5235; FAX 715/682-4730.* 65 rms, 2 story. Mid-May-early Oct: S $44-$56; D $48-$90; each addl $5; winter wkend packages; lower rates rest of yr. Crib free. Pet accepted, some restrictions. TV; cable (premium). Sauna. Indoor pool; whirlpool. Coffee in rms. Restaurants 6 am-2 pm, 4:30-10 pm. Bar. Ck-out 11 am. Business servs avail. Downhill ski 15 mi; x-country ski opp. Many balconies. Overlooks Chequamegon Bay. Cr cds: A, C, D, DS, ER, MC, V. 🆔 ♿ 🏊 🍴 🐾 🔥 SC

✔★ **SUPER 8.** *1610 Lake Shore Dr. 715/682-9377; FAX 715/682-5593.* 70 rms, 2 story. Mid-June-Sept: S $58.88-$65.88; D $59.88-$74.88; each addl $5; under 12 free; lower rates rest of yr. Crib free. Pet accepted, some restrictions. TV; cable (premium), VCR avail. Indoor pool; whirlpool. Complimentary coffee in lobby. Ck-out 11 am. Coin lndry. Business servs avail. In-rm modem link. X-country ski 10 mi. Microwaves avail. Opp Lake Superior. Cr cds: A, C, D, DS, MC, V. 🆔 ♿ 🐾 🔥 SC

Baraboo *(See also Portage, Wisconsin Dells)*

Motel

↙★ **SPINNING WHEEL.** *809 8th St, 2 mi E of US 12 on WI 33. 608/356-3933.* 25 rms. S $33-$53; D $35-$63; each addl $6; under 12 free. Crib $6. Pet accepted. TV; cable (premium). Restaurant nearby. Downhill ski 10 mi; x-country ski 5 mi. Cr cds: A, DS, MC, V.

D ⬤ ⬤ ⬤ ⬤ ⬤ SC

Bayfield *(See also Ashland)*

Motel

★ **SUPER 8.** *(Harbor View Dr, Washburn 54891) 12 mi S on WI 13. 715/373-5671; FAX 715/373-5674.* 35 rms, 2 story. July-Sept: S $69.98-$75.98; D $79.98-$84.98; each addl $5; suite $89.98-$99.98; under 12 free; wkly & hol rates; higher rates Apple Fest; lower rates rest of yr. Crib free. Pet accepted, some restrictions; $25. TV; cable. Complimentary continental bkfst. Restaurant adj 4-10 pm. Ck-out 11 am. Business servs avail. Downhill/x-country ski 8 mi. Sauna. Whirlpool. Game rm. On lake. Cr cds: A, D, DS, MC, V.

D ⬤ ⬤ ⬤ ⬤ ⬤ SC

↙★ **WINFIELD INN.** *Rte 1, Box 33, 4 blks N on WI 13. 715/779-3252; FAX 715/779-5180.* 31 rms, 26 A/C, 1-2 story, 6 kit. apts (1-2 bedrm). June-Oct: S, D $66; kit. apts $95-$125; lower rates rest of yr. Crib free. Pet accepted. TV; cable. Complimentary coffee in rms. Restaurant nearby. Ck-out 11 am. Downhill/x-country ski 8 mi. Some balconies. Sun deck. Overlooks Lake Superior. Cr cds: A, DS, MC, V. D ⬤ ⬤ ⬤ ⬤

Beaver Dam

Motel

↙★ **GRAND VIEW.** *1510 N Center. 414/885-9208; FAX 414/887-8706.* 22 rms. S $26-$29; D $35-$39; each addl $4. Crib $3. Pet accepted, some restrictions. TV; cable (premium). Ck-out 11 am. Cr cds: DS, MC, V. ⬤ ⬤

Beloit *(See also Janesville; also see Rockford, IL)*

Motel

★★ **COMFORT INN.** *2786 Milwaukee Rd. 608/362-2666.* 56 rms, 2 story, 16 suites. June-Sept: S $45-$65; D $50-$70; each addl $5; suites $55-$75; under 18 free; wkly rates; higher rates special events; lower rates rest of yr. Crib free. Pet accepted. TV; cable (premium), VCR avail (movies). Indoor pool; whirlpool. Complimentary continental bkfst. Restaurant nearby. Ck-out 11 am. Business servs avail. Game rm. Refrigerator in suites. Cr cds: A, C, D, DS, JCB, MC, V. D ⬤ ⬤ ⬤ ⬤ SC

Black River Falls *(See also Sparta, Tomah)*

Motels

↙★★ **AMERICAN HERITAGE INN.** *919 WI 54E, at jct I-94 exit 116. 715/284-4333; FAX 715/284-9068; res: 800/356-8018.* 86 rms, 2 story. S $36.99-$61.99; D $47.99-$63.99; suites $75-$110; under 12 free. Crib free. Pet accepted. TV; cable, VCR avail. Sauna. Indoor pool; whirlpool. Complimentary continental bkfst. Restaurant adj 6 am-11 pm. Ck-out noon. Coin lndry. Meeting rm. Business servs avail. In-rm modem link. Downhill ski 15 mi; x-country ski 1 mi. Game rm. Cr cds: A, C, D, DS, MC, V. D ⬤ ⬤ ⬤ ⬤ ⬤ SC

★★ **BEST WESTERN ARROWHEAD LODGE.** *600 Oasis Rd, 1 mi E on WI 54 at I-94. 715/284-9471; FAX 715/284-9664; res: 800/284-9471.* 144 rms, 3 story, 30 suites. S $43-$64.50; D $53-$74.95; each addl $5; suites $59.95-$149.95; under 12 free. Crib $3. Pet accepted. TV; cable, VCR avail. Sauna. Indoor pool; whirlpool. Playground. Restaurant 6:30 am-2 pm, 5-10 pm. Bar; entertainment Sat. Ck-out noon. Meeting rms. Business servs avail. In-rm modem link. Sundries. Snowmobile trails. Nature/fitness trail. Cr cds: A, C, D, DS, MC, V. D ⬤ ⬤ ⬤ ⬤ ⬤ SC

Boulder Junction

(See also Eagle River, Land O'Lakes, Manitowish Waters, Minocqua)

Cottage Colonies

★★ **WHITE BIRCH VILLAGE.** *1¹/₂ mi S on County M, then 6 mi E on County K. 715/385-2182; FAX 715/385-2537.* 11 kit. cottages (1-4 bedrm), 1-2 story. No A/C. Late

May-early Oct: $550-$875/wk. Closed rest of yr. Crib free. Pet accepted. TV in sitting rm. Playground. Ck-out 9 am, ck-in 2 pm. Grocery. Coin lndry. Package store 8 mi. Business servs avail. Sand beach; dock, launching ramp, boats, canoes, sailboats, paddleboats. Lawn games. Tandem bicycles. Rec rm. Fishing guides, clean & store area. Library. Fireplaces. Private decks. Grills. Woodland setting on White Birch Lake. No cr cds accepted.

⬛🦆➡🏊🔥🖐

★ **ZASTROW'S LYNX LAKE LODGE.** *4 mi N on County M, then 4 mi W on County B.* 715/686-2249; FAX 715/686-2257; res: 800/882-5969. 11 cottages (1-4 bedrm), 7 with kit. No A/C. MAP, May-Oct: $279/wk/person; family rates; EP off-season; 3-day min some wkends; lower rates Dec-Feb. Closed Mar-Apr & late Oct-Dec 26. Crib avail. Pet accepted. TV; cable. Playground. Dining rm 8-9:30 am, 5-9:30 pm. Box lunches. Bar 4:30 pm-2 am. Ck-out 10 am, ck-in 2 pm. Business servs avail. Grocery 4 mi. Coin lndry 8 mi. Package store. Gift shop. Free airport, bus depot transportation. Private beach, swimming; boats, rowboats, canoes, sailboats, paddleboats, motors. X-country ski on site. Snowmobiles. Bicycles. Lawn games. Movies. Rec rm. Fish/game clean & store area. Some fireplaces. No cr cds accepted. ⬛🦆➡🏊🔥🖐

Cedarburg *(See also Milwaukee, Port Washington)*

Motels

★ ★ **BEST WESTERN QUIET HOUSE SUITES.** *(10330 N Port Washington Rd, Mequon 53092) 6 mi S on I-43, exit 85.* 414/241-3677; FAX 414/241-3707. 54 rms, 2 story. S $81-$150; D $91-$160; each addl $10; suites, kit. units $140-$160. Pet accepted; $15. TV; cable (premium). Indoor/outdoor pool; whirlpool. Complimentary continental bkfst. Restaurant adj 11 am-11 pm. Ck-out 11 am. Business servs avail. In-rm modem link. Exercise equipt; stair machine, treadmill. Cr cds: A, C, D, DS, MC, V. ⬛🦆🏊✈🚫🖐

★ **BREEZE INN TO THE CHALET.** *(10401 N Port Washington Rd, Mequon 53092) 6 mi S on I-43.* 414/241-4510; FAX 414/241-5542; res: 800/343-4510. 41 rms, 2 story. May-Oct: S $40-$67; D $47-$67; each addl $7; suites $85-$125; under 12 free; wkly rates; higher rates special events, hols; lower rates rest of yr. Crib free. Pet accepted, some restrictions. TV; cable (premium). Restaurant 6 am-2 pm; Fri to 9:30 pm; Sat, Sun from 7 am. Bar. Ck-out 11 am. Meeting rm. Business servs avail. Many refrigerators. Cr cds: A, C, D, DS, MC, V. 🦆🚫🖐 SC

Chippewa Falls *(See also Eau Claire, Menomonie)*

Motels

✔★ **AMERICINN.** *11 W South Ave, 1 mi S on US 53.* 715/723-5711; FAX 715/723-5254. 62 rms, 2 story. S $49.90-$69.90; D $56.90-$69.90; suites $58.90-$104.90. Pet accepted; $25 deposit. TV; cable (premium). Complimentary coffee in lobby. Ck-out 11 am. Business servs avail. In-rm modem link. Indoor pool; whirlpool. Some refrigerators. Cr cds: A, C, D, DS, MC, V. ⬛🦆🏊🚫 SC

✔★ **INDIANHEAD.** *501 Summit Ave (WI 29/124).* 715/723-9171; FAX 715/723-6142; res: 800/341-8000. 27 rms. S, D $42-$47.25; each addl $5. Crib avail. Pet accepted. TV; cable (premium), VCR avail. Complimentary coffee in lobby. Restaurant adj. Ck-out 11 am. Valet serv. Some refrigerators. On bluff overlooking city. Cr cds: A, C, D, DS, MC, V. ⬛🦆🚫🖐 SC

★ ★ **PARK INN INTERNATIONAL.** *1009 W Park Ave (County J), 1 blk N of WI 124.* 715/723-2281; FAX 715/723-2283; res: 800/446-9320. 67 rms. S $50-$57; D $57-$64; each addl $7. Crib avail. Pet accepted, some restrictions. TV; cable. Indoor pool; whirlpool. Restaurants 6:30 am-1:30 pm, 5-9:30 pm. Rm serv. Bar. Ck-out noon. Meeting rms. Business servs avail. Valet serv. Sundries. Some wet bars. Cr cds: A, C, D, DS, MC, V. ⬛🦆🏊🚫 SC

Eagle River *(See also Land O'Lakes, Rhinelander, Three Lakes)*

Motels

★ ★ **AMERICAN HERITAGE INN.** *844 Railroad St N.* 715/479-5151; FAX 715/479-8259; res: 800/356-8018. 93 rms, 2 story. June-Oct: S $49-$74; D $59-$79.99; each addl $5; under 18 free; 2-day min wkends; higher rates for special events; lower rates rest of yr. Crib free. Pet accepted. TV; cable, VCR (movies). Sauna. Indoor pool; whirlpool. Complimentary coffee in lobby. Complimentary continental bkfst. Restaurant adj 5 am-9 pm. Ck-out 11 am. Coin lndry. Meeting rm. Business servs avail. X-country ski 1/2 mi. Game rm. Some in-rm whirlpools. Some refrigerators. Cr cds: A, C, D, DS, MC, V.

⬛🦆🏊🏊🚫🖐 SC

✔★ **WHITE EAGLE.** *4948 WI 70W. 715/479-4426; res: 800/782-6488.* 22 rms. No A/C. Mid-June-mid-Oct: S, D $37-$71; lower rates rest of yr. Crib free. Pet accepted; $5. TV; cable. Sauna. Heated pool; whirlpool. Complimentary coffee. Restaurant nearby. Ck-out 10:30 am. X-country ski 3 mi. Snowmobile trails. Paddleboat. Picnic tables. On Eagle River; private piers. Driving range, miniature golf opp. Cr cds: DS, MC, V.

D ✔ ➡ ➷ ☁ ⊠ 🐾

Resort

★ **GYPSY VILLA.** *950 Circle Dr. 715/479-8644; FAX 715/479-8644; res: 800/232-9714.* 21 kit. cottages (1-4-bedrm), 4 A/C. Phone avail. Kit. cottages $345-$1,681/wk (2-6 persons); daily rates; MAP avail. Crib free. Maid serv $20/day. Pet accepted. TV; VCR avail. Wading pool; whirlpool. Playground. Free supervised child's activities (June-Aug). Ck-out noon, ck-in 3 pm. Coin lndry. Meeting rms. Business servs avail. Grocery, package store 2 mi. Garage parking avail (fee). Tennis. Private swimming beach. Boats, waterskiing. Bicycles. Lawn games. Soc dir. Game rm. Exercise equipt; bicycles, rower, sauna. Fish/hunt guides. Fireplaces; some in-rm whirlpools. Private patios. Picnic tables, grills. Most cottages on Cranberry Island. Cr cds: A, DS, MC, V.

✔ ➡ 🎿 ☁ 🎿 🐾 SC

Eau Claire *(See also Chippewa Falls, Menomonie)*

Motels

★★ **COMFORT INN.** *3117 Craig Rd (54701). 715/833-9798.* 56 rms, 2 story. June-Aug: S $62.95-$70.95; D $67.95-$75.95; each addl $5; under 18 free; lower rates rest of yr. Crib avail. Pet accepted. TV; cable (premium). Indoor pool. Complimentary continental bkfst. Restaurant nearby. Ck-out 11 am. Business servs avail. In-rm modem link. X-country ski 2 mi. Cr cds: A, C, D, DS, ER, JCB, MC, V. D ✔ 🎿 ☁ ⊠ 🐾 SC

✔★ **EXEL INN.** *2305 Craig Rd (54701). 715/834-3193; FAX 715/839-9905.* 101 rms, 2 story. S $31.99-$43.99; D $42.99-$49.99; each addl $4. Crib free. Pet accepted. TV; cable (premium). Complimentary continental bkfst. Restaurant adj open 24 hrs. Ck-out noon. Business servs avail. Cr cds: A, C, D, DS, MC, V. D ✔ ⊠ 🐾 SC

★ **HEARTLAND INN.** *4075 Commonwealth Ave (54701). 715/839-7100; FAX 715/839-7050; res: 800/334-3277, ext. 40.* 88 rms, 2 story. S $44-$51; D $52-$59; each addl $5; under 17 free. Crib avail. Pet accepted. TV; cable (premium), VCR avail. Indoor pool; whirlpool. Complimentary continental bkfst. Restaurant nearby. Ck-out noon. Meeting rms. Business servs avail. In-rm modem link. Sundries. X-country ski 5 mi. Sauna. Cr cds: A, C, D, DS, MC, V. D ✔ 🎿 ☁ ⊠ 🐾 SC

✔★ **MAPLE MANOR.** *2507 S Hastings Way (US 53) (54701). 715/834-2618; FAX 715/834-1148; res: 800/624-3763.* 36 rms. S $29.95; D $39.95-$49.95; each addl $5; wkly rates. Crib $3. Pet accepted. TV; cable (premium). Complimentary full bkfst. Restaurant 6:30 am-1:30 pm. Bar to 11 pm. Ck-out 11:30 am. Sundries. Many refrigerators. Picnic tables. Cr cds: A, C, D, DS, MC, V. ✔ ⊠ 🐾 SC

★★ **QUALITY INN.** *809 W Clairemont (54702), US 12. 715/834-6611.* 120 rms, 2 story. S $52-$75; D $60-$75; each addl $10; suites $69-$139; under 18 free; Sun rates. Crib free. Pet accepted. TV; cable (premium), VCR avail. 2 pools, 1 indoor; whirlpool. Complimentary full bkfst Mon-Fri. Restaurant 6 am-10 pm; Fri, Sat to 10:30 pm. Rm serv. Bar 11-2 am; entertainment Tues-Sat. Ck-out noon. Meeting rms. Business servs avail. In-rm modem link. Valet serv. Sundries. Sauna. Rec rm. Private patios, balconies. Cr cds: A, C, D, DS, ER, JCB, MC, V. D ✔ ☁ ⊠ 🐾 SC

Egg Harbor (Door Co)

Motel

★★ **ALPINE RESORT.** *¾ mi SW on County G. 920/868-3000.* 52 motel rms, 3 story, 5 suites; 30 kit. cottages. No elvtr. No rm phones. Mid-June-Labor Day: S $59-$79; D $69-$93; each addl $10; suites $93; kit. cottages $101-$265 or $605-$1,115/wk; MAP avail; family, wkly rates; golf plan; lower rates Memorial Day-mid-June, Labor Day-mid-Oct. Closed rest of yr. Crib $5. Pet accepted, some restrictions. TV. Heated pool. Playground. Supervised child's activities (July & Aug); ages 3-8. Restaurant 7:30-11 am, 5:45-8:30 pm. Bar to midnight. Ck-out 10 am. Meeting rms. Business servs avail. Bellhops. Gift shop. Tennis. 27-hole golf, greens fee, putting green. Game rm. Rec rm. Some refrigerators; microwaves avail; wet bar in cottages. Picnic tables, grills. Swimming beach. Cr cds: A, DS, MC, V. D ✔ ➡ 🎿 🎿 ☁ 🐾

Ellison Bay (Door Co)

Inn

★ ★ **HARBOR HOUSE.** *(12666 WI 42, Ellison Bay) at Gills Rock.* 920/854-5196; *FAX 920/854-9717.* 14 units, 8 with shower only, 13 with A/C, 2 story. No rm phones. July-Aug: S, D $55-$95; each addl $15; cabins $105-$110; wkly rates; 3-day min wkends; some lower rates May-June, Sept-Oct. Closed rest of yr. Pet accepted, some restrictions. TV. Playground. Complimentary continental bkfst. Restaurant nearby. Ck-out 10 am, ck-in 2 pm. Sauna. Whirlpool. Refrigerators; microwaves avail. Balconies. Picnic tables, grills. Lake view, beach access. Victorian-style house built 1904; many antiques. Totally nonsmoking. Cr cds: A, MC, V.

Fond du Lac (See also Oshkosh)

Motels

✔ ★ **DAYS INN.** *107 N Pioneer Rd (54935), on US 41 at jct WI 23.* 414/923-6790; *FAX 414/923-6790.* 59 rms, 2 story. S $39.95-$45.95; D $55.95-$60.95; each addl $6; under 17 free. Crib free. Pet accepted; $3. TV; cable (premium). Complimentary continental bkfst. Ck-out noon. Business servs avail. In-rm modem link. Cr cds: A, D, DS, MC, V.

★ ★ **HOLIDAY INN.** *625 W Rolling Meadows Dr (54937), at jct US 41 & 151.* 414/923-1440; FAX 414/923-1366. 141 rms, 2 story. S $69-$109; D $79-$119; under 19 free. Crib free. Pet accepted. TV; cable (premium), VCR avail. Indoor pool; whirlpool. Coffee in rms. Restaurant 6:30 am-10 pm. Rm serv. Bar 11-1 am. Ck-out 11 am. Coin lndry. Meeting rms. In-rm modem link. Bellhops. Valet serv. Sundries. Free airport transportation. Putting green. Exercise equipt; bicycle, treadmill, sauna. Rec rm. Golf course opp. Microwaves avail. Cr cds: A, C, D, DS, JCB, MC, V.

★ **NORTHWAY.** *301 North Pioneer Rd (54935), off WI 41.* 414/921-7975; FAX 414/921-7983. E-mail folcvv@visitwisconsin.com; web www.visit wisconsin.com/fondulac. 19 rms. June-Oct: S $30-$35; D $49-$55; each addl $5; under 12 free; wkly rates; higher rates special events; lower rates rest of yr. Crib $4. Pet accepted; $7. TV; cable. Complimentary continental bkfst. Coffee in rms. Ck-out 11 am. X-country ski 10 mi. Refrigerators, microwaves avail. Picnic tables, grills. Cr cds: A, DS, MC, V.

Green Bay (See also Appleton)

Motels

(Rates may be higher for special football wkends)

★ **BUDGETEL INN.** *2840 S Onieda (54304).* 920/494-7887; FAX 920/494-3370. Web www.budgetel.com. 80 rms, 2 story. S $55.95-$66.95; D $55.95-$73.95; under 18 free; higher rates: wkends, special events, football games. Crib free. Pet accepted, some restrictions. TV; cable (premium), VCR avail (movies). Complimentary continental bkfst. Complimentary coffee in rms. Restaurant adj. Ck-out noon. Meeting rms. Business center. X-country ski 10 mi. Health club privileges. Microwaves avail. Cr cds: A, C, D, DS, MC, V.

★ **COMFORT INN.** *2841 Ramada Way (54304).* 920/498-2060; FAX 920/498-2060; res: 800/228-5150. Web www.comfortinn.com. 60 rms, 2 story. S $46.95-$64.95; D $52.95-$74.95; each addl $5; under 18 free; higher rates: Packers football games, EAA Fly-in, Dec 31; lower rates wkdays. Crib free. Pet accepted, some restrictions. TV; cable (premium). Indoor pool; whirlpool. Complimentary continental bkfst. Restaurant nearby. Ck-out 11 am. Business servs avail. In-rm modem link. Valet serv. X-country ski 5 mi. Health club privileges. Cr cds: A, C, D, DS, ER, JCB, MC, V.

✔ ★ **EXEL INN.** *2870 Ramada Way (54304), US 41 Oneida St exit.* 920/499-3599; FAX 920/498-4055. 105 rms, 2 story. S $38-$41; D $44-$51; each addl $5; under 18 free. Crib free. Pet accepted, some restrictions. TV; cable. Complimentary continental bkfst. Restaurant adj open 24 hrs. Ck-out noon. Business servs avail. In-rm modem link. Health club privileges. Cr cds: A, C, D, DS, MC, V.

✔ ★ **ROAD STAR INN.** *1941 True Lane (54304), 1/4 mi E of US 41 Lombardi exit.* 920/497-2666; FAX 920/497-4754; res; 800/445-4667. 63 rms, 2 story. July-Oct: S $34; D $40; each addl $3; under 15 free; higher rates: special events, wkends; lower rates rest of yr. Pet accepted. TV; cable. Complimentary continental bkfst. Restaurant nearby. Ck-out 11 am. Some refrigerators, wet bars. Cr cds: A, C, D, DS, MC, V.

✔ ★ **SKY-LIT.** *2120 S Ashland Ave (US 41 Business/WI 32) (54304).* 920/494-5641; FAX 920/494-4032. 23 rms, some kits. S $29.50-$35; D $39.50-$56; under 12 free. Crib $5. Pet accepted, some restrictions. TV; cable (premium). Restaurant nearby. Ck-out 11 am. Coin lndry. Sundries. Microwaves avail. Picnic tables. Cr cds: DS, MC, V.

D ✔ ⊠ ⊠

★ **SUPER 8.** *2868 S Oneida St (54304).* 920/494-2042; FAX 920/494-6959. 84 rms, 2 story. Mid-June-Oct: S $53.88-$57.88; D $63.88-$67.88; lower rates rest of yr. Crib free. Pet accepted. TV; cable, VCR avail. Complimentary continental bkfst. Restaurant nearby. Ck-out 11 am. Coin lndry. Meeting rm. Business servs avail. Sauna. Whirlpool. Microwaves avail. Cr cds: A, D, DS, MC, V. D ✔ ⊠ ⊠ SC

Motor Hotels

★ ★ **DAYS INN.** *406 N Washington St (54301), at Main St, adj to Port Plaza.* 920/435-4484; FAX 920/435-3120. 98 rms, 5 story. S $55-$85; D $65-$95; suites $70-$100; each addl $5; under 18 free. Crib free. Pet accepted. TV. Indoor pool. Restaurant 6:30 am-2 pm, 5-9 pm. Rm serv. Bar 3 pm-midnight. Ck-out noon. Meeting rms. Business servs avail. In-rm modem link. Valet serv. Sundries. Health club privileges. Microwaves avail. Overlooks Fox River. Cr cds: A, C, D, DS, ER, MC, V. D ✔ ≈ ⊠ ⊠ SC

★ ★ **HOLIDAY INN-CITY CENTRE.** *200 Main St (US 141/WI 29) (54301).* 920/437-5900; FAX 920/437-1199. 149 rms, 7 story. S, D $89; family rates. Crib free. Pet accepted, some restrictions. TV; cable (premium). Indoor pool; whirlpool. Coffee in rms. Restaurant 6 am-10 pm. Rm serv. Bar 10-1 am; entertainment. Ck-out noon. Coin lndry. Meeting rms. Business servs avail. Bellhops. Valet serv. Sundries. Sauna. Health club privileges. On Fox River; marina. Luxury level. Cr cds: A, C, D, DS, JCB, MC, V.

D ✔ ≈ ⊠ ⊠ SC

Hayward *(See also Spooner)*

Motels

★ ★ **AMERICINN.** *620 E First St.* 715/634-2700; res: 800/634-3444; FAX 715/634-3958. 41 rms, 2 story. S $58.90-$68.90; each addl $71.90-$81.90; each addl $6; suites $81.90-$99.90; under 11 free; higher rates special events. Crib free. Pet accepted, some restrictions; $6. TV; cable (premium), VCR avail. Complimentary continental bkfst. Restaurant nearby. Ck-out 11 am. Meeting rms. Business servs avail. Downhill ski 20 mi; x-country ski adj. Sauna. Indoor pool; whirlpool. Game rm. Rec rm. Some in-rm whirlpools, refrigerators, microwaves. Picnic tables. Cr cds: A, C, D, DS, MC, V. D ✔ ≥ ≈ ⊠ ⊠ SC

★ ★ **COUNTRY INN & SUITES.** *WI 27S.* 715/634-4100; FAX 715/634-2403. 66 rms, 2 story, 8 suites. June-Sept: S, D $68-$78; each addl $6; suites $78-$113; under 18 free; wkend rates; higher rates special events; lower rates rest of yr. Crib free. Pet accepted, some restrictions. TV; cable (premium). Complimentary continental bkfst. Coffee in rms. Restaurant 11 am-10:30 pm; closed Sun. Rm serv. Bar 11 am-midnight. Ck-out noon. Meeting rms. Business servs avail. In-rm modem link. X-country ski 4 mi. Indoor pool; whirlpool. Game rm. Bathrm phones, refrigerators, microwaves, wet bars; some in-rm whirlpools. Cr cds: A, C, D, DS, MC, V. D ✔ ≥ ≈ ⊠ ⊠ SC

★ **NORTHWOODS.** *Rte 6, Box 6453, 1¹/₂ mi S on WI 27.* 715/634-8088; res: 800/232-9202. 9 rms. S $41; D $46; each addl $5; kit. suite $65; family rates; higher rates special events (3-day min). Crib free. Pet accepted. TV; cable. Complimentary coffee in lobby. Ck-out 10 am. Downhill ski 19 mi; x-country ski 3 mi. Cr cds: A, C, D, DS, MC, V.

D ✔ ≥ ⊠ ⊠

★ **SUPER 8.** *317 South Dakota Ave, On WI 27.* 715/634-2646; FAX 715/634-6482. 46 rms, 1-2 story. Apr-Sept: S $49.88; D $55.88-$58.88; each addl $5; under 12 free; higher rates special events; lower rates rest of yr. Crib $5. Pet accepted. TV; cable (premium). Indoor pool; whirlpool. Complimentary coffee in lobby. Restaurant adj 5:30 am-9 pm. Ck-out 11 am. X-country ski 2 mi. Game rm. Cr cds: A, C, D, DS, MC, V.

D ✔ ≥ ≈ ⊠ ⊠ SC

Hudson

Motel

✔ ★ **COMFORT INN.** *811 Dominion Dr, 1 mi SE, just off I-94 exit 2.* 715/386-6355; FAX 715/386-9778. 60 rms, 2 story. S $44.95-$62.95; D $47.95-$72.95; each addl $5; under 18 free. Crib free. Pet accepted, some restrictions; $50. TV; cable (premium), VCR avail. Indoor pool; whirlpool. Complimentary continental bkfst. Restaurant nearby. Ck-out 11 am. Guest lndry. Business servs avail. Cr cds: A, C, D, DS, ER, JCB, MC, V.

D ✔ ≈ ⊠ ⊠ SC

Hurley *(See also Manitowish Waters)*

Motel

★ ★ **HOLIDAY INN.** *1000 10th Ave, S of jct US 2, 51. 715/561-3030; FAX 715/561-4280.* 100 rms, 2 story. S $48-$65; D $62-$77; each addl $6; under 19 free; higher rates some winter hol wks & winter wkends. Crib free. Pet accepted. TV; cable. Indoor pool; whirlpool. Restaurant 7 am-2 pm, 5:30-10 pm. Rm serv. Bar 11-1 am. Ck-out noon. Coin lndry. Meeting rms. Business servs avail. Valet serv. Downhill/x-country ski 15 mi. Snowmobile trails. Game rm. Cr cds: A, C, D, DS, JCB, MC, V.

Janesville *(See also Beloit, Madison)*

Motel

✔ ★ **BEST WESTERN JANESVILLE MOTOR LODGE.** *3900 Milton Ave (53546), jct I-90, WI 26. 608/756-4511.* 106 rms, 3 story. May-Sept: S, D $65-$80; each addl $5; suites $95-$140; under 12 free; lower rates rest of yr. Crib free. Pet accepted. TV; cable. Indoor pool; whirlpool. Complimentary coffee in rms. Restaurant 6-9 pm; wkends 7 am-10 pm. Rm serv. Bar 4 pm-1 am. Ck-out noon. Meeting rms. Business servs avail. Airport transportation. Exercise equipt; treadmill, weight machine. Game rm. Cr cds: A, C, D, DS, JCB, MC, V.

Kenosha *(See also Milwaukee, Racine; also see Waukegan, IL)*

Motels

✔ ★ **BUDGETEL INN.** *7540 118th Ave (53142), at jct I-94, WI 50. 414/857-7911; FAX 414/857-2370.* 95 rms, 2 story. S $43.95; D $46.95-$48.95; each addl $7; higher rates wkends; under 18 free. Crib free. Pet accepted. TV; cable (premium). Complimentary continental bkfst. Complimentary coffee in rms. Restaurant adj open 24 hrs. Ck-out noon. Business servs avail. In-rm modem link. Valet serv. Downhill ski 15 mi. Cr cds: A, C, D, DS, MC, V.

★ **KNIGHTS INN.** *7221 122nd Ave (53142), off I-94 exit 344 (WI 50). 414/857-2622; FAX 414/857-2375.* 113 rms, 14 kits. June-Oct: S, D $47.95-$69.95; each addl $5; kit. units $62.95-$68.95; under 18 free; higher rates wkends; lower rates rest of yr. Crib free. Pet accepted. TV. Complimentary coffee in lobby. Restaurant nearby. Ck-out noon. Business servs avail. Cr cds: A, C, D, DS, MC, V.

Lac du Flambeau *(See also Manitowish Waters, Minocqua)*

Resort

★ ★ **DILLMAN'S SAND LAKE LODGE.** *3¹/₂ mi NE on County D. 715/588-3143; FAX 715/588-3110.* 17 units, 18 cottages. No A/C. EP, mid-May-mid-Oct: daily, from $68/person; wkly, from $455/person; MAP avail; family rates. Closed rest of yr. Crib free. Pet accepted. TV in lobby, some rms. Playground. Dining rm (public by res) 8-9:30 am. Box lunches, cookouts. Serv bar. Ck-out 10 am, ck-in 2 pm. Package store. Meeting rms. Sports dir in summer. Tennis. Practice fairway. Sand beaches; waterskiing; windsurfing; scuba diving; boats, motors, kayaks, sailboats, canoes; private launch, covered boathouse. Archery. Bicycles. Lawn games. Hiking trails. Soc dir; wine & cheese party Sun. Nature study, photography, painting workshops. Rec rm. Fishing clean & store area. Some fireplaces; refrigerator in suites & cottages. On 250 acres. No cr cds accepted.

La Crosse *(See also Sparta)*

Hotel

★ ★ **RADISSON.** *200 Harborview Plaza (54601). 608/784-6680; FAX 608/784-6694, ext. 490.* 170 units, 8 story. S $89-$99; D $99-$109; each addl $10; suites $185-$420; under 18 free. Pet accepted. TV; cable. Indoor pool; whirlpool. Restaurant 6:30 am-11 pm. Bar 11-1 am; entertainment Fri-Sat. Ck-out noon. Meeting rms. Business servs avail. Free airport, bus depot transportation. Downhill/x-country ski 8 mi. Exercise equipt; weights, bicycles. Overlooks Mississippi River. Cr cds: A, C, D, DS, ER, JCB, MC, V.

Ladysmith

Motels

★★ **BEST WESTERN EL RANCHO.** *8500 W Flambeau Ave. 715/532-6666; FAX 715/532-7551.* 27 rms. S $44-$48; D $52-$60; each addl $4; under 12 free. Crib $9. Pet accepted. TV; cable (premium). Restaurant 11 am-2 pm, 4:30-9:30 pm. Bar to 1 am. Ck-out 11 am. Business servs avail. Downhill ski 15 mi; x-country ski on site. Cr cds: A, C, D, DS, MC, V. 🐕 D 🐾 ⊠ ⊠ 🐾 SC

✔★ **EVERGREEN.** *On US 8, 2 blks W of WI 27. 715/532-5611.* 20 rms. S $34; D $38-$42; each addl $4. Crib $4. Pet accepted, some restrictions. TV; cable (premium). Complimentary coffee in rms. Restaurant nearby. Ck-out 11 am. Downhill/x-country ski 7 mi. Picnic tables. Cr cds: A, DS, MC, V. 🐾 ⊠ ⊠ 🐾 SC

Land O' Lakes *(See also Boulder Junction, Eagle River)*

Motel

★ **PINEAIRE.** *1 mi N on US 45. 906/544-2313.* 9 cottages (7 with shower only). No A/C, rm phones. Cottages $35-$45; each addl $3; under 8 free. Crib free. Pet accepted. TV. Restaurant nearby. Ck-out 10 am. X-country ski on site. Picnic tables. No cr cds accepted. 🐕 🐾 ⊠ 🐾

Resort

★★ **SUNRISE LODGE.** *5894 W Shore Dr, N off County E. 715/547-3684; FAX 715/547-6110; res: 800/221-9689.* 22 units in 21 cottages, 18 kits. No A/C in cottages. May-Oct, AP: S $80; D $150; EP: S $49; D $59; wkly, family rates; fall plan; Nov-Apr, EP only: D $55-$125. Crib avail. Pet accepted. Playground. Dining rm 7:30-10 am, 11:30 am-2 pm, 5-7:30 pm; Sun 7:30-11 am, noon-3 pm; wkends only in winter. Box lunches. Meeting rm. Business servs avail. Airport, bus depot transportation. Tennis. Miniature golf. Private beach; boats, motors, canoes. X-country ski on site. Lawn games. Exercise trail. Nature trail. Bicycles. Rec rm. Fish/hunt guides; clean & store area. Refrigerators. Picnic tables, grills. Spacious grounds. On Lac Vieux Desert. Cr cds: DS, MC, V. D 🐾 🐾 ⊠ 🏃 ⊠ 🐾

Madison *(See also Mt Horeb, New Glarus)*

Motels

★★ **BEST WESTERN WEST TOWNE SUITES.** *650 Grand Canyon Dr (53719). 608/833-4200; FAX 608/833-5614.* 101 suites, 2 story. Suites $60-$80; each addl $5; under 19 free. Crib free. Pet accepted. TV; cable. Complimentary full bkfst. Ck-out noon. Coin lndry. Meeting rms. Business servs avail. In-rm modem link. Exercise equipt; bicycles, treadmills. Health club privileges. Refrigerators, wet bars; microwaves avail. Cr cds: A, C, D, DS, JCB, MC, V. D 🐾 🏃 ⊠ 🐾 SC

★★ **BUDGETEL INN.** *8102 Excelsior Dr (53717). 608/831-7711; FAX 608/831-1942.* 129 rms, 2 story, 14 suites. S, D $65.95; each addl $7; suites $70.95-$114.95; under 18 free; higher rates special events. Crib free. Pet accepted, some restrictions. TV; cable. Indoor pool; whirlpool. Complimentary continental bkfst. Complimentary coffee in rms. Bar from 5 pm. Coin lndry. Meeting rms. Business servs avail. Bellhops. Valet serv. Free airport transportation. Exercise equipt; rower, bicycles, sauna. Game rm. Refrigerator, wet bar in suites. Cr cds: A, C, D, DS, MC, V. D 🐾 🏃 ⊠ 🐾 SC

✔★ **EXEL INN.** *4202 E Towne Blvd (53764). 608/241-3861; FAX 608/241-9752.* 102 rms, 2 story. May-Sept: S $39.99-$54; D $48.99-$63; each addl $4; under 18 free; wkly rates; higher rates special events; lower rates rest of yr. Crib free. Pet accepted, some restrictions. TV; cable (premium). Complimentary continental bkfst. Coffee in rms. Restaurant nearby. Ck-out noon. Business servs avail. In-rm modem link. Sundries. Coin lndry. X-country ski 3 mi. Exercise equipt; bicycle, treadmill. Health club privileges. Game rm. Some refrigerators; microwaves avail. Cr cds: A, C, D, DS, MC, V.
D 🐾 ⊠ 🏃 ⊠ 🐾 SC

★★ **RAMADA CAPITAL CONFERENCE CENTER.** *3902 Evan Acres Rd (53704), at I-90 East Cambridge exit 142B. 608/222-9121; FAX 608/222-5332.* 186 rms, 2 story. S, D $59-$69; each addl $8; suites $95-$125; under 19 free. Crib free. Pet accepted, some restrictions. TV; cable. Indoor pool; poolside serv. Restaurant 6 am-1:30 pm, 5-9:30 pm. Rm serv. Bar 11-1 am. Ck-out noon. Meeting rms. Business center. Free airport transportation. Sauna. Game rm. 36-hole golf course adj. Some in-rm whirlpools; microwaves avail. Cr cds: A, C, D, DS, JCB, MC, V. D 🐾 ⊠ ⊠ 🐾 SC 🏃

★ ★ **RAMADA LIMITED.** *3841 E Washington (53704). 608/244-2481; FAX 608/244-0383.* 194 rms, 2 story. Mid-May-Oct: S $59-$79; D $69-$89; each addl $10; suites $89-$163; under 18 free; lower rates rest of yr. Crib free. Pet accepted; $10. TV; cable (premium). Indoor pool; whirlpool. Complimentary bkfst. Ck-out noon. Meeting rms. Business servs avail. Valet serv. Airport transportation. Cr cds: A, C, D, DS, MC, V.

★ ★ **RESIDENCE INN BY MARRIOTT.** *501 D'Onofrio Dr (53719). 608/833-8333; FAX 608/833-2693.* 80 kit. suites, 2 story. Kit. suites $110-$140; higher rates special events. Crib free. Pet accepted, some restrictions. TV; cable, VCR. Heated pool; whirlpool. Complimentary continental bkfst. Restaurant nearby. Ck-out noon. Coin lndry. Meeting rms. Valet serv. Exercise equipt; bicycle, treadmill. Health club privileges. Microwaves. Private patios, balconies. Picnic tables, grills. Cr cds: A, C, D, DS, JCB, MC, V.

★ **SELECT INN.** *4845 Hayes Rd (53704), I-90/94 exit 151S. 608/249-1815; res: 800/641-1000.* Web www.selectinn.com. 96 rms, 2 story. June-mid-Sept: S $33.90-$53.90; D $41.90-$53.90; each addl $4; under 13 free. Pet accepted; $25 deposit. TV; cable. Complimentary continental bkfst. Restaurant nearby. Ck-out 11 am. Business servs avail. Sundries. Whirlpool. Some refrigerators, minibars. Cr cds: A, C, D, DS, MC, V.

Motor Hotel

★ ★ ★ **EDGEWATER.** *666 Wisconsin Ave (53701). 608/256-9071; FAX 608/256-0910; res: 800/922-5512.* 116 rms, 8 story. S, D $79-$160; suites $189-$389. Crib free. Pet accepted, some restrictions. TV; cable (premium). Restaurant. Rm serv 6:30 am-10:30 pm. Bar 11-12:30 am. Ck-out noon. Meeting rms. Business servs avail. Bellhops. Valet serv. Free garage. Free airport transportation. Massage. Health club privileges. Some microwaves. On Lake Mendota; swimming beach. Cr cds: A, C, D, MC, V.

Hotel

★ ★ **BEST WESTERN INN ON THE PARK.** *22 S Carroll (53703), downtown. 608/257-8811; FAX 608/257-5995.* 213 rms, 9 story. S $82-$98; D $94-$108; each addl $10; suites $126-$136; under 12 free; higher rates special events. Crib free. Pet accepted. TV; cable (premium). Heated pool; whirlpool. Restaurants 6 am-9 pm. Bar 11 am-midnight. Ck-out noon. Meeting rms. Business servs avail. In-rm modem link. Gift shop. Free covered parking; valet. Free airport transportation. Exercise equipt; weights, bicycles. Some in-rm whirlpools. Cr cds: A, C, D, DS, MC, V.

Manitowish Waters
(See also Boulder Junction, Lac du Flambeau, Minocqua)

Motel

✔ ★ **GREAT NORTHERN.** *(US 51 S, Mercer 54547) 715/476-2440; FAX 715/476-2205.* 80 rms, 2 story. No A/C. S, D $49-$59; each addl $10; higher winter rates; under 10 free. Pet accepted. TV; cable (premium). Sauna. Indoor pool; whirlpool. Complimentary continental bkfst. Restaurant. Bar 5 pm-2 am. Ck-out 11 am. Meeting rms. Business servs avail. Gift shop. X-country ski 1 mi. Game rm. On lake; swimming beach. Cr cds: DS, MC, V.

Resort

★ ★ **VOSS' BIRCHWOOD LODGE.** *3 mi SE on US 51. 715/543-8441.* 2 rms, 4 suites in 2-story lodge, 12 kits, 20 cottages (1-3 bedrm). Memorial Day-Oct: D $65-$85; cottages $525-$850/wk; monthly rates. Closed rest of yr. Crib avail. Pet accepted. TV in some cottages. Playground. Dining rm (public by res) 8-10 am, 5:30-8 pm. Serv bar. Ck-out 10 am, ck-in 2 pm. Grocery, coin lndry, package store 1 1/2 mi. Airport, bus depot transportation. Marina. Private beach; waterskiing. Bicycles avail. Fishing guides, store area. Many fireplaces, refrigerators. Sun deck. Tea room 11 am-4 pm. Art gallery; antiques. Spacious grounds on Spider Lake. No cr cds accepted.

Manitowoc *(See also Green Bay, Sheboygan)*

Motor Hotel

★ ★ ★ **INN ON MARITIME BAY.** *101 Maritime Dr. 920/682-7000; FAX 920/682-7013; res: 800/654-5353.* 107 rms, 3 story. S, D $96; each addl $10; suites $119-$140; under 18 free; package plans. Crib free. Pet accepted, some restrictions; $25. TV; cable. Indoor pool; whirlpool, poolside serv. Coffee in rms. Restaurant 6 am-10 pm; Fri, Sat from 7 am. Rm serv. Bar 11-1 am. Ck-out 11 am. Meeting rms. Business servs avail. In-rm modem link. Valet serv. Free airport transportation. Downhill ski 10 mi; x-country ski 5 mi. Sauna. Game rm. Refrigerators, microwaves avail. On lake. Cr cds: A, C, D, DS, MC, V.

Marinette

Motel

✔ ★ **SUPER 8.** *1508 Marinette Ave. 715/735-7887; FAX 715/735-7455.* 68 rms, 2 story. May 16-Sept 30: S $44; D $49; under 12 free; lower rates rest of yr. Crib free. Pet accepted, some restrictions. TV; cable (premium). Complimentary continental bkfst. Ck-out 11 am. Meeting rms. Business servs avail. X-country ski 5 mi. Sauna. Whirlpool. Cr cds: A, C, D, DS, MC, V.

Mauston *(See also Wisconsin Dells)*

Guest Ranch

★ ★ **WOODSIDE RANCH.** *W 4015 WI 82, 4¹/₂ mi E. 608/847-4275; res: 800/626-4275.* 14 rms in 2-story lodge, 23 cottages (1-, 2- & 3-bedrm). No rm phones. AP, late June-late Sept, late Dec-late Feb: S $210-$545/wk; D $370-$980/wk; each addl $175-$420/wk; lower rates rest of yr. Crib free. Pet accepted. TV in lobby. Sauna. Pool; wading pool, poolside serv. Playground. Free supervised child's activities. Complimentary coffee in lobby. Dining rm; sittings at 8 am, 12:30 & 5:30 pm. Snack bar, picnics. Bar 8-2 am; entertainment Tues, Sat. Ck-out 10 am, ck-in 1:30 pm. Coin lndry. Grocery, package store 5 mi. Gift shop. Sports dir. Tennis. Swimming. Boats. Downhill/x-country ski on site. Sleighing, sledding. Hiking. Soc dir. Rec rm. Game rm. Fireplace in cottages. On 1,400 acres. Cr cds: DS, MC, V.

Menomonee Falls *(See also Milwaukee, Wauwatosa)*

Motel

★ **SUPER 8.** *(N 96 W 17490 County Line Rd, Germantown 53022) US 41/45 at County Q. 414/255-0880; FAX 414/255-7741.* 81 rms, 2 story. June-Sept: S $55; D $62-$72; each addl $5; suites $60-$65; under 12 free; lower rates rest of yr. Crib free. Pet accepted; $50 refundable. TV; cable (premium). Complimentary continental bkfst. Restaurant adj open 24 hrs. Ck-out 11 am. Coin lndry. Business servs avail. Cr cds: A, C, D, DS, MC, V.

Menomonie *(See also Chippewa Falls, Eau Claire)*

Motel

★ **BOLO COUNTRY INN.** *207 Pine Ave, just S of I-94, Memomonie exit 41A. 715/235-5596.* 25 rms. S $45-$60; D $60-$80. Pet accepted. TV; cable (premium). Complimentary bkfst. Restaurant 11:30 am-10 pm. Bar 11-1 am. Ck-out noon. Meeting rms. Picnic tables. Cr cds: C, D, MC, V.

Milwaukee

Motels

(Rates may be higher during state fair)

★ **BUDGETEL INN.** *5442 N Lovers Lane Rd (53225), just E of I-45 Silver Spring Dr exit E, north of downtown. 414/535-1300; FAX 414/535-1724.* 140 rms, 3 story. S $45-$52; D $51-$58; each addl $7; suites $57.95-$67; under 18 free. Pet accepted, some restrictions. TV; cable (premium), VCR avail. Complimentary continental bkfst. Complimentary coffee in rms. Restaurant nearby. Ck-out noon. Meeting rm. Business servs avail. In-rm modem link. Valet serv. Microwaves avail. Cr cds: A, C, D, DS, MC, V.

★ **EXEL INN-NORTHEAST.** *(5485 N Port Washington Rd, Glendale 53217) N on I-43, exit Silver Spring Dr. 414/961-7272; FAX 414/961-1721.* 125 rms, 3 story. S $39.99-$63.99; D $49.99-$76.99; each addl $7; under 17 free; wknd rates; higher rates special events. Crib free. Pet accepted, some restrictions. TV; cable (premium). Complimentary continental bkfst. Restaurant adj open 24 hrs. Ck-out noon. Coin lndry. Business servs avail. In-rm modem link. Sundries. Game rm. Some in-rm whirlpools; microwaves avail. Cr cds: A, C, D, DS, MC, V.

✔ ★ **EXEL INN-SOUTH.** *1201 W College Ave (53154), just E of I-94 College Ave exit E, south of downtown. 414/764-1776; FAX 414/762-8009.* 110 rms, 2 story. S $33.99-$59.99; D $34.99-$69.99; each addl $4; under 18 free. Crib free. Pet accepted. TV; cable (premium). Complimentary continental bkfst. Complimentary coffee in lobby. Restaurant opp 6 am-noon. Ck-out noon. Coin lndry. Business servs avail. In-rm modem link. Free airport transportation. Microwaves avail. Cr cds: A, C, D, DS, MC, V. 🅳 🏃 🏊 🐾 SC

✔★ **RED ROOF INN.** *(6360 S 13th St, Oak Creek 53154) At jct College Ave, I-94 exit 319 E.* 414/764-3500; FAX 414/764-5138. 108 rms, 2 story. S $36.99-$58.99; D $41.99-$69.99; under 18 free. Crib free. Pet accepted. TV; cable (premium). Complimentary coffee in lobby. Ck-out noon. Business servs avail. Cr cds: A, C, D, DS, MC, V. 🅳 🏃 🏊 🐾

Motor Hotels

★★★ **HOLIDAY INN AIRPORT.** 6331 S 13th St (53221), I-94 exit 319, south of downtown. 414/764-1500; FAX 414/764-6531. 159 rms, 3 story. S $69-$90; D $79-$110; each addl $10; under 18 free. Crib free. Pet accepted. TV. Indoor pool. Playground. Restaurant 6 am-1 pm, 5-10 pm; Sat, Sun from 7 am. Rm serv. Bar. Ck-out 11 am. Coin lndry. Meeting rms. Business servs avail. Bellhops. Sundries. Free airport transportation. Exercise equipt; weight machine, treadmill, saunas. Game rm. Balconies. Cr cds: A, C, D, DS, JCB, MC, V. 🅳 🏃 🏊 🍴 🏊 🐾 SC

★★ **RAMADA INN-WEST.** 201 N Mayfair Rd (53226), just N of I-94 Mayfair Rd (WI 100) exit, west of downtown. 414/771-4400; FAX 414/771-4517. 230 rms, 3 story. May-Sept: S $84; D $99; under 18 free; lower rates rest of yr. Crib free. Pet accepted, some restrictions. TV; cable (premium). Indoor pool; whirlpool. Playground. Restaurant 6 am-1 pm, 5-9 pm. Rm serv. Bar 3 pm-1 am; Fri, Sat to 2 am. Ck-out noon. Coin lndry. Meeting rms. Business servs avail. Valet serv. Exercise equipt; weights, bicycles, sauna. Picnic tables. Cr cds: A, C, D, DS, ER, JCB, MC, V. 🅳 🏃 🏊 🍴 🏊 🐾 SC

Hotels

★★★ **EMBASSY SUITES-WEST.** *(1200 S Moorland Rd, Brookfield 53008) 10 mi W via I-94, Moorland Rd S exit.* 414/782-2900; FAX 414/796-9159. 203 suites, 5 story. S, D, suites $99-$500; each addl $20; under 12 free; wkend rates; package plans. Crib free. Pet accepted, some restrictions. TV; cable (premium). Indoor pool; whirlpool. Complimentary full bkfst. Complimentary coffee in rms. Restaurant 11 am-11 pm. Bar to 1 am. Ck-out noon. Meeting rms. Business center. In-rm modem link. Concierge. Free airport transportation. Tennis privileges. Golf privileges. Exercise equipt; weight machine, bicycles, sauna, steam rm. Game rm. Refrigerators, microwaves, wet bars. Cr cds: A, C, D, DS, ER, JCB, MC, V. 🅳 🍴 🏃 🏊 🍴 🏊 🐾 SC 🏃

★★ **HOTEL WISCONSIN.** 720 N Old World 3rd St (53203), downtown. 414/271-4900; FAX 414/271-9998. 234 rms, 11 story. Mid-June-Sept: S, D $69-$76; each addl $8; suites $85; kit. units $69-$82; under 17 free; lower rates rest of yr. Crib free. Pet accepted. TV; cable (premium), VCR avail. Restaurant 6 am-10 pm. Ck-out 11 am. Meeting rm. Business servs avail. Concierge. Sundries. Valet serv. Coin lndry. Game rm. Health club privileges. Some refrigerators; microwaves avail. Cr cds: A, C, D, DS, ER, JCB, MC, V. 🅳 🏃 🏊 🐾 SC

Minocqua

(See also Boulder Junction, Eagle River, Lac du Flambeau, Rhinelander)

Motels

★ **AQUA AIRE.** 806 US 51 N. 715/356-3433; FAX 715/356-3433. 10 rms (with shower only), 1 story. June-Aug: S $32-$59; D $59-$79; each addl $5; under 3 free; wkly rates; higher rates special events; lower rates rest of yr. Crib free. Pet accepted, some restrictions. TV; cable (premium). Restaurant opp 7 am-2:30 pm. Ck-out 11 am. Business servs avail. X-country ski 7 mi. Refrigerators. Picnic tables. Cr cds: MC, V. 🏃 🏃 🏊 🐾 SC

★★ **BEST WESTERN LAKEVIEW MOTOR LODGE.** 3 blks S on US 51. 715/356-5208; FAX 715/356-1412. 41 rms, 2 story. June-Sept, also hols: S $73-$103; D $79-$109; each addl $6; 2-story chalet units avail; lower rates rest of yr. Pet accepted; $6. TV; cable (premium). Continental bkfst. Restaurant nearby. Ck-out 11 am. Business servs avail. X-country ski 10 mi. Snowmobiling. Some in-rm whirlpools. Some balconies. Picnic tables. On Lake Minocqua; dock. Cr cds: A, C, D, DS, MC, V. 🏃 🏃 🏊 🏊 🐾 SC

★ **CROSS TRAILS.** 8644 US 51N. 715/356-5202; FAX 715/356-1104; res: 800/842-5261. 17 rms. Mid-June-mid-Aug: S, D $59-$69; each addl $4-$5; lower rates rest of yr. Crib $4. Pet accepted. TV; cable (premium). Restaurant 6 am-8 pm; off-season to 7 pm. Ck-out 11 am. Business servs avail. In-rm modem link. X-country ski 8 mi. Snowmobiling. Small wildlife refuge. Cr cds: A, C, D, DS, MC, V. 🅳 🏃 🏊 🐾

Mt Horeb *(See also Madison, New Glarus)*

Motel

★ ★ **BEST WESTERN KARAKAHL INN.** *1405 US 18 Business/151 E. 608/437-5545; FAX 608/437-5908.* 75 rms, 1-2 story. Mid-May-mid-Oct: S $59-$64; D $69-$174; each addl $5; suites $119; under 12 free; lower rates rest of yr; Crib $4. Pet accepted, some restrictions; $5. TV; cable. Saunas. Indoor pool. Complimentary coffee in lobby. Restaurant 7 am-2 pm, 5-8 pm; Fri, Sat to 10 pm; closed Sun eve. Bar 5 pm-1 am. Ck-out noon. Business servs avail. X-country ski 2 blks. Cr cds: A, C, D, DS, MC, V.

Neenah-Menasha *(See also Appleton, Green Bay, Oshkosh)*

Motel

★ **PARKWAY.** *(1181 Gillingham Rd, Neenah 54956) 2 mi N on WI 47, across bridge. 920/725-3244.* 19 rms, 8 with shower only, 1-2 story. June-Sept: S $27-$30; D $32-$34; each addl $5; under 5 free; wkly rates; higher rates special events; lower rates rest of yr. Crib $3. Pet accepted, some restrictions. TV; cable. Complimentary continental bkfst. Restaurant adj 11 am-10:30 pm. Ck-out 11 am. Heated pool. Playground. Picnic tables, grills. Cr cds: A, DS, MC, V.

New Glarus *(See also Madison, Mt Horeb)*

Motels

★ ★ **CHALET LANDHAUS.** *at jct WI 69, 39. 608/527-5234; FAX 608/527-2365.* 67 rms, 3-4 story. May-Oct: S $49-$60; D $68-$75; each addl $12; suites $130; family rms $100; under 8 free; lower rates rest of yr. Crib $12. Pet accepted. TV; cable. Restaurant 7-11 am, 5:30-9 pm; Sun, Mon to 11 am. Ck-out 11 am. Meeting rms. Business servs avail. X-country ski 2 mi. Whirlpool in suites. Some balconies. Cr cds: A, MC, V.

✔ ★ **SWISS-AIRE.** *1200 WI 69. 608/527-2138; res: 800/798-4391.* 26 rms. May-Oct: S $45-$49; D $45-$65; each addl $6; under 5 free; lower rates rest of yr. Crib free. Pet accepted. TV; cable. Heated pool. Complimentary continental bkfst. Ck-out 11 am. Meeting rms. Picnic tables. Cr cds: DS, MC, V.

Oconomowoc *(See also Milwaukee)*

Inn

★ ★ **INN AT PINE TERRACE.** *351 E Lisbon Rd. 414/567-7463; res: 800/421-4667.* 13 rms, 3 story. S, D $60-$120; each addl $15. Pet accepted, some restrictions. TV; cable (premium). Heated pool. Complimentary continental bkfst. Restaurant nearby. Ck-out 10:30 am, ck-in 3 pm. Restored mansion (1879); antique furnishings. Cr cds: A, C, D, DS, MC, V.

Oshkosh

Motel

(Rates higher EAA Intl Fly-in Convention)

✔ ★ **HOWARD JOHNSON.** *1919 Omro Rd (54901), at jct US 41 & WI 21. 920/233-1200; FAX 920/233-1135.* 100 rms, 2 story. May-Aug: S $45-$55; D $50-$80; each addl $5; under 18 free; lower rates rest of yr. Crib free. Pet accepted, some restrictions. TV; cable (premium). Indoor pool; whirlpool. Restaurant adj 6 am-10 pm. Bar 4 pm-1 am. Ck-out noon. Meeting rms. Business servs avail. Private patios, balconies. Cr cds: A, C, D, DS, ER, MC, V.

Hotel

★ ★ ★ **HILTON.** *1 N Main St (54901). 920/231-5000; FAX 920/231-8383.* E-mail www.hiltonnet.com; web hilton, 8 story. S, D $65-$95; suites $125; under 18 free. Pet accepted, some restrictions. TV; cable (premium), VCR avail. Indoor pool; whirlpool, poolside serv. Restaurant 6:30 am-10 pm. Bar 11-1 am. Ck-out noon. Meeting rms. Business center. In-rm modem link. Concierge. Free covered parking. Free airport transportation. Exercise equipt; bicycles, treadmills. Health club privileges. Some refrigerators; microwaves avail. View of river. Luxury level. Cr cds: A, C, D, DS, MC, V.

Platteville

Motels

★ ★ **BEST WESTERN GOVERNOR DODGE MOTOR INN.** *West US 151, 5 blks S on US 151, ¹/₄ mi W of jct WI 80, 81. 608/348-2301; FAX 608/348-8579.* 74 rms, 2 story. S $45-$64; D $69-$75; each addl $5-$7; suites $105-$140; under 12 free. Crib $3. Pet accepted, some restrictions. TV; cable, VCR avail (movies). Indoor pool; whirlpool. Complimentary coffee in lobby. Restaurant 6 am-10 pm; Sun to 7 pm; winter to 9 pm. Ck-out noon. Meeting rms. Business servs avail. Exercise equipt; rower, stair machine, saunas. Game rm. State university 5 blks. Cr cds: A, C, D, DS, MC, V.

✔ ★ **SUPER 8.** *100 WI 80/81S. 608/348-8800.* 73 rms, 2 story. S $34-$47; D $47-$64; each addl $5; suites $125. Crib $4. Pet accepted; $10. TV; cable (premium). Complimentary continental bkfst. Restaurant adj open 24 hrs. Ck-out 11 am. Coin lndry. Meeting rms. Sauna. Whirlpool. Some bathrm phones, refrigerators. Balconies. Overlooks stream. Gazebo. Cr cds: A, D, DS, MC, V.

Portage *(See also Baraboo, Wisconsin Dells)*

Motel

✔ ★ ★ **RIDGE MOTOR INN.** *2900 New Pinery Rd, 2 mi N on US 51. 608/742-5306.* 113 rms, 3 story, 9 kit. suites. June-Aug: S $50-$75; D $70-$90; each addl $5; kit. suites $100-$125; under 12 free; wkend rates; package plans; lower rates rest of yr. Crib $4. Pet accepted. TV; cable (premium), VCR avail (movies). Indoor pool; whirlpool. Complimentary coffee in rms. Restaurant 6 am-10 pm. Rm serv. Bar. Ck-out noon. Coin lndry. Meeting rms. Business servs avail. Downhill ski 4 mi; x-country ski 16 mi. Exercise rm; instructor, weight machine, bicycles, sauna, steam rm. Massage. Health club privileges. Game rm. Cr cds: A, C, D, DS, MC, V.

Port Washington *(See also Cedarburg, Milwaukee, Sheboygan)*

Motel

★ **BEST WESTERN HARBORSIDE MOTOR INN.** *135 E Grand Ave. 414/284-9461; FAX 414/284-3169.* 96 rms, 5 story. S $64-$107; D $74-$117; each addl $10; under 12 free. Crib free. Pet accepted. TV; cable (premium). Sauna. Indoor pool; whirlpool. Bkfst 7-10 am. Bar 4 pm-1 am. Ck-out noon. Meeting rms. Business servs avail. Valet serv. Game rm. On Lake Michigan; dock. Some whirlpools. Cr cds: A, C, D, DS, MC, V.

Prairie du Chien

Motels

★ ★ **BEST WESTERN-QUIET HOUSE SUITES.** *US 18S & WI 35/60. 608/326-4777; FAX 608/326-4787.* 42 suites, 2 story. S $63-$125; D $73-$135; each addl $10. Pet accepted. TV; cable (premium). Indoor pool; whirlpool. Restaurant opp 5 am-10 pm. Ck-out 11 am. Business servs avail. In-rm modem link. Sundries. Exercise equipt; bicycles, stair machine. Some in-rm whirlpools. Cr cds: A, C, D, DS, ER, MC, V.

★ **HOLIDAY.** *1010 S Marquette Rd. 608/326-2448; FAX 608/326-2413; res: 800/962-3883.* 18 rms, 1-2 story. May-Oct: S $38-$45; D $50-$56; suite $70-$76; each addl $5; under 16 free; lower rates rest of yr. Crib free. Pet accepted, some restrictions. TV; cable (premium). Complimentary coffee. Restaurant nearby. Ck-out 11 am. Business servs avail. Cr cds: A, DS, MC, V.

✔ ★ **PRAIRIE.** *1616 S Marquette Rd. 608/326-6461; res: 800/526-3776.* 32 rms. May-Oct: S $35-$49; D $49-$59; family rates; lower rates rest of yr. Crib $3. Pet accepted. TV; cable (premium). Heated pool. Playground. Complimentary coffee in rms. Ck-out 11 am. X-country ski 2 mi. Miniature golf. Lawn games. Some refrigerators. Picnic tables, grills. Cr cds: A, D, DS, MC, V.

Racine *(See also Kenosha, Milwaukee)*

Motels

✔ ★ **KNIGHTS INN.** *1149 Oakes Rd (53406). 414/886-6667; FAX 414/886-1501; res: 800/843-5644.* 107 rms, 1 story. June-Labor Day: S, D $48.95-$52.95; each addl $3; suites $51.95-$55.95; kit. units $58.95-$62.95; under 18 free; lower rates rest of yr. Crib free. Pet accepted. TV; cable (premium), VCR avail (movies). Complimentary continental bkfst. Restaurant adj 10 am-11 pm. Ck-out noon. Cr cds: A, C, D, DS, ER, MC, V.

★ ★ **QUALITY INN.** *3700 Northwestern Ave (53405), off Green Bay Rd.* 414/637-9311; FAX 414/637-4575. 112 rms, 2 story. S $54-$89; D $62-$99; each addl $6; under 18 free. Crib free. Pet accepted. TV; cable (premium). Heated pool. Complimentary coffee in rms. Restaurant 6 am-2 pm, 5:30-9 pm. Rm serv. Bar 4 pm-2 am. Ck-out noon. Coin lndry. Meeting rms. Business servs avail. In-rm modem link. Bellhops. Valet serv. Sundries. X-country ski 3 mi. Game rm. Lawn games. Picnic tables. On Root River. Cr cds: A, C, D, DS, JCB, MC, V.

Rhinelander *(See also Eagle River, Minocqua, Three Lakes)*

Motels

★ ★ **AMERICINN.** *648 W Kemp (US 8W).* 715/369-9600; FAX 715/369-9613. 52 rms (3 with shower only), 2 story. Mid-June-Labor Day: S $56.90-$61.90; D $58.90-$63.90; each addl $6; suites $84.90-$98.90; under 12 free; lower rates rest of yr. Pet accepted. TV; cable (premium), VCR avail. Sauna. Indoor pool; whirlpool. Complimentary continental bkfst. Restaurant opp 6 am-11 pm. Ck-out 11 am. Meeting rm. Business servs avail. Sundries. Valet serv. Coin lndry. X-country ski 1 mi. Some refrigerators. Cr cds: A, C, D, DS, MC, V.

★ ★ **BEST WESTERN CLARIDGE.** *70 N Stevens St.* 715/362-7100; FAX 715/362-3883. 81 rms, 2-4 story. S $49-$63; D $53-$73; each addl $8; under 18 free. Pet accepted. TV; cable. Indoor pool; whirlpool. Restaurant 6:30 am-2 pm, 5-10 pm; Sun, hols to 9 pm. Rm serv 5-9 pm. Bar 11 am-2 pm, 4 pm-midnight. Ck-out 11 am. Lndry facilities. Meeting rms. Business servs avail. Valet serv. Sundries. Free airport transportation. X-country ski 5 mi. Exercise equipt: stair machine, weight machine, treadmill. Cr cds: A, C, D, DS, MC, V.

Resort

★ **HOLIDAY ACRES.** *Lake George Rd, 4 mi E on US 8, then 2 mi N on Lake George Rd.* 715/369-1500; FAX 715/369-3665; res: 800/261-1500. 28 rms in 2-story lodge, 28 kit. cottages (1-4 bedrm; boat incl; maid serv avail). Lodge, mid-June-late Aug, also Fri & Sat Dec 24-mid-Mar: S, D $85-$109; each addl $11.50; cottages for 2-8, $99-$239; winter wkend package; lower rates rest of yr. Pet accepted; $6. TV; cable, VCR avail (movies). Indoor pool. Playground. Coffee in rms. Dining rm 5 am-10 pm. Box lunches, coffee shop. Rm serv. Bar 4 pm-1 am. Ck-out 11 am (cottages in summer, 10 am). Meeting rms. Business servs avail. Grocery, package store 3 mi. Gift shop in season. Airport transportation. Tennis. Sand beach; boats, motors, rafts, canoes, sailboat, windsurfing. Downhill ski 20 mi; x-country ski on site. Snowmobile trails. Bicycles. Lawn games. Fireplace in 24 cottages, 2 lodge rms; some screened porches. 1000 acres on Lake Thompson. Cr cds: A, C, D, DS, MC, V.

Rice Lake *(See also Spooner)*

Motels

★ ★ **CURRIER'S LAKEVIEW.** *2010 E Sawyer, east shore of Rice Lake.* 715/234-7474; res: 800/433-5253. 19 rms, 2 story, 8 kits. Mid-May-mid-Sept: S, D $50-$98; kit. units for 2-8, $4 addl; lower rates rest of yr. Crib $2. Pet accepted. TV; cable (premium). Continental bkfst. Ck-out 11 am. Meeting rm. Free airport transportation. Downhill/x-country ski 18 mi. Snowmobile trails. Refrigerators. Private beach; boats, motors, dockage; paddle boats, sailboats, canoes, pontoons. Picnic tables, grill. Wooded grounds; on lake; park adj. Cr cds: A, DS, MC, V.

✔ ★ **EVERGREEN.** *1801 W Knapp.* 715/234-1088. 21 rms. S $35-$51; D $40-$55; each addl $5; under 12 free. Pet accepted. TV; cable (premium). Complimentary continental bkfst. Restaurant nearby. Ck-out 10:30 am. Business servs avail. Cr cds: MC, V.

St Croix Falls

Motel

★ ★ **DALLES HOUSE.** *Box 664, ³/₄ mi S on WI 35, 1 blk S of jct US 8.* 715/483-3206; FAX 715/483-3207; res: 800/341-8000. 50 rms, 2 story. S, D $39-$85; each addl $5. Crib $7. Pet accepted. TV; cable (premium). Sauna. Indoor pool; whirlpools. Restaurant 8 am-11 pm. Ck-out 11 am. Coin lndry. Meeting rm. Business servs avail. In-rm modem link. Downhill ski 3 mi; x-country ski ¹/₄ mi. Interstate State Park adj. Cr cds: A, C, D, DS, MC, V.

Sayner *(See also Boulder Junction, Eagle River, Minocqua)*

Resort

★ ★ **FROELICH'S SAYNER LODGE.** ¹/₂ mi NE of WI 155. 715/542-3261; res: 800/553-9695. 11 lodge rms, 2 story, 25 cottages (1-3 bedrm). No A/C exc public rms. Late May-Oct: S, D $40-$60; cabana: $70; cottage $70-$180; under 5, $26. Closed rest of yr. Pet accepted. TV; VCR avail. Heated pool. Playground. Bar 4 pm-1 am, closed Tues. Ck-out 10 am, ck-in 2 pm. Grocery, coin lndry, package store ³/₄ mi. Airport transportation. Tennis. Boats, motors, canoe, pontoon boat; waterskiing. Lawn games. Hiking trails. Rec rm. Fishing guides. Library. Screened porch in most cottages; some fireplaces. On Plum Lake. Cr cds: MC, V.

Sheboygan *(See also Manitowoc, Port Washington)*

Motels

✔ ★ **BUDGETEL INN.** 2932 Kohler Memorial Dr (53081), E of I-43 exit 126 N. 920/457-2321; FAX 920/457-0827. Web www.budgetel.com. 97 rms, 2 story. S $40.95-$51.95; D $43.95-$55.95; under 18 free. Crib free. Pet accepted, some restrictions. TV; cable. Complimentary continental bkfst. Complimentary coffee in rms. Restaurant adj 6 am-11 pm. Ck-out noon. Business servs avail. Cr cds: A, C, D, DS, MC, V.

★ **PARKWAY.** 3900 Motel Rd (53081), 6 mi S on I-43 exit 120, at jct County OK, V. 920/458-8338; FAX 920/459-7470; res: 800/341-8000. Web www.imalodging.com. 32 rms. June-Sept: S, D $59.90-$81.90; each addl $3; higher rates special events; lower rates rest of yr. Crib $6. Pet accepted. TV, cable (premium). Complimentary coffee in rms. Restaurant nearby. Ck-out 11 am. Business servs avail. Sundries. X-country ski 2 mi. Refrigerators; microwaves avail. Picnic table, grill. Cr cds: A, C, D, DS, MC, V.

Sister Bay (Door Co)

Motel

★ **EDGE OF TOWN.** 11092 WI 42. 920/854-2012. 10 rms. No rm phones. Mid-June-Oct: S, D $62-$65; each addl $7; family rates; lower rates rest of yr. Crib free. Pet accepted, some restrictions; $7. TV; cable (premium). Complimentary coffee in lobby. Restaurant nearby. Ck-out 11 am. Refrigerators, microwaves. Cr cds: DS, MC, V.

Sparta *(See also Black River Falls, La Crosse, Tomah)*

Motels

✔ ★ **BEST NIGHTS INN.** 303 Wisconsin St. 608/269-3066; FAX 608/269-3175. 28 rms. Mid-May-Oct: S $30-$69; D $35-$89; each addl $7; under 16 free; lower rates rest of yr. Crib avail. Pet accepted. TV; cable. Complimentary continental bkfst (wkends). Restaurant opp open 24 hrs. Ck-out 11 am. Refrigerators. Totally nonsmoking. Cr cds: A, C, D, DS, MC, V.

★ ☆ **COUNTRY INN.** 737 Avon Rd. 608/269-3110; FAX 608/269-6726; res: 800/456-4000. 61 rms, 2 story. S $50.95-$58.95; D $57.95-$67.95; suites $60.95-$112.90; under 18 free. Crib avail. Pet accepted. TV; cable (premium), VCR avail (movies). Indoor pool; whirlpool. Complimentary continental bkfst. Restaurant adj 6 am-11 pm. Bar from 4 pm. Ck-out noon. Coin lndry. Meeting rms. Business servs avail. Downhill ski 7 mi; x-country ski 1 mi. Some refrigerators. Cr cds: A, C, D, DS, MC, V.

★ **HERITAGE.** 704 W Wisconsin St, at jct US 16 & WI 27. 608/269-6991; res: 800/658-9484. 22 rms, 2 story. S $31; D $37-$45; each addl $3. Crib $5. Pet accepted. TV; cable (premium). Pool; whirlpool. Restaurant adj open 24 hrs. Ck-out 11 am. Cr cds: A, C, D, DS, MC, V.

Spooner (See also Hayward, Rice Lake)

Motel

★ **GREEN ACRES.** *N 4809 US 63S, 1 mi S on US 63. 715/635-2177; res: 800/373-5293; FAX 715/635-6305.* 21 rms. Late May-Aug: S, D $59; each addl $5; higher rates rodeo; lower rates rest of yr. Crib $5. Pet accepted, some restrictions; $5. TV; cable (premium). Complimentary coffee in lobby. Ck-out 10 am. Business servs avail. X-country ski 2 mi. Playground. Lawn games. Microwaves avail. Picnic tables, grills. Cr cds: A, C, D, DS, MC, V.

Stevens Point

Motels

★ **BUDGETEL INN.** *4917 Main St, jct US 51 & US 10. 715/344-1900; FAX 715/344-1254.* 80 rms, 3 story. S $39.95-$44.95; D $47.95-$51.95; under 19 free. Crib free. Pet accepted. TV; cable (premium). Complimentary continental bkfst. Complimentary coffee in rms. Restaurant adj open 24 hrs. Ck-out noon. Coin lndry. Meeting rms. Business servs avail. In-rm modem link. X-country ski 1 mi. Cr cds: A, C, D, DS, MC, V.

✔ ★ **POINT.** *209 Division St. 715/344-8312; res: 800/344-3093.* 44 rms, 2 story. S $33; D $37-$42; each addl $4. Crib $4. Pet accepted. TV; cable, VCR avail. Coffee in lobby. Complimentary continental bkfst. Ck-out 11 am. Meeting rm. Cr cds: A, C, D, DS, MC, V.

✔ ★ **TRAVELER.** *3350 Church (US Business 51). 715/344-6455; FAX 715/344-6455; res: 800/341-8000.* 17 units. S $24.95-$36.95; D $28.95-$45.95; each addl $4; under 18 free. Crib $5. Pet accepted, some restrictions. TV; cable (premium). Complimentary coffee in rms. Ck-out 11 am. Downhill ski 12 mi. Cr cds: A, DS, MC, V.

Motor Hotel

★ ★ ★ **HOLIDAY INN.** *1501 N Point Dr, exit 161 on US 51. 715/341-1340; FAX 715/341-9446.* 295 rms, 2-6 story. S $79; D $89; each addl $10; suites $99-$168; under 18 free. Crib free. Pet accepted. TV; cable (movies). Indoor pool; whirlpool, poolside serv. Restaurant 6:30 am-10 pm; Fri, Sat to 11 pm. Rm serv. Bar 11-1 am; entertainment. Ck-out 11 am. Coin lndry. Convention facilities. Business servs avail. In-rm modem link. Valet serv. Sundries. Gift shop. Free airport transportation. Downhill ski 20 mi; x-country ski 1 mi. Exercise equipt; weight machine, bicycle, sauna. Cr cds: A, C, D, DS, JCB, MC, V.

Sturgeon Bay (Door Co)

(See also Algoma, Green Bay)

Motel

✔ ★ **HOLIDAY.** *(29 N Second Ave, Sturgeon Bay) 920/743-5571; FAX 920/743-5395.* 18 rms, 2 story. July-Aug: S $49; D $65; each addl $5; under 18 free; wkly rates; higher rates: wkends Sept, Oct; 2-day min wkends; lower rates rest of yr. Crib free. Pet accepted, some restrictions; $5. TV; cable, VCR avail (free movies). Complimentary continental bkfst. Restaurant nearby. Ck-out 11 am. Business servs avail. X-country ski 4 mi. Refrigerators; microwaves avail. Cr cds: A, D, DS, MC, V.

Superior

Motels

★ ★ **BEST WESTERN BAY WALK INN.** *1405 Susquehanna. 715/392-7600; FAX 715/392-7680.* 50 rms, 2 story. June-Sept: S $50-$75; D $55-$81; each addl $6; suites $80-$125; under 16 free; higher rates special events; lower rates rest of yr. Crib free. Pet accepted, some restrictions. TV; cable (premium), VCR avail (movies). Sauna. Indoor pool; whirlpool. Complimentary continental bkfst. Restaurant adj 11 am-9 pm. Ck-out 11 am. Coin lndry. Business servs avail. Downhill ski 7 mi; x-country ski 1 mi. Game rm. Some refrigerators. Cr cds: A, C, D, DS, MC, V.

★ ★ **BEST WESTERN BRIDGEVIEW MOTOR INN.** *415 Hammond Ave, at jct 5th St, near foot of Duluth-Superior Bridge. 715/392-8174; FAX 715/392-8487.* 96 rms, 2 story. Mid-June-Sept: S $50-$100; D $60-$100; each addl $5; under 18 free; lower rates rest of yr. Pet accepted. TV; cable (premium). Sauna. Indoor pool; whirlpool. Complimentary continental bkfst. Restaurant nearby. Bar 5-10:30 pm, to midnight wkends. Ck-out noon. Coin lndry.

Meeting rm. Business servs avail. Sundries. Downhill/x-country ski 8 mi. Some refrigerators, microwaves. Cr cds: A, C, D, DS, ER, JCB, MC, V. [D] ✦ ⅀ ⅀ ⅀ ⅀ [SC]

Three Lakes (See also Eagle River, Rhinelander)

Motel

✓ ★ **ONEIDA VILLAGE INN.** *1785 Superior St. 715/546-3373; FAX 715/546-8060; res: 800/374-7443.* 47 rms, 2 story. June-Aug & mid-Dec-Feb: S $45; D $55; each addl $7; suites $65-$75; kits. $48; under 12 free; wkend, wkly rates; higher rates special events; lower rates rest of yr. Crib $5. Pet accepted; $10. TV; cable. Complimentary coffee in lobby. Restaurant 5-10 pm. Bar; entertainment (summer). Ck-out 11 am. Meeting rms. Business servs avail. X-country ski ½ mi. Game rm. Cr cds: DS, MC, V. [D] ✦ ⅀ ⅀ [SC]

Tomah (See also Sparta)

Motels

✓ ★ **BUDGET HOST DAYBREAK.** *215 E Clifton, WI 12, 16. 608/372-5946; FAX 608/372-5947; res: 800/999-7088.* 32 rms, 1-2 story. Mid-May-mid-Oct: S $36-$48; D $58-$63; each addl $7; lower rates rest of yr. Crib $4. Pet accepted. TV; cable (premium). Restaurant opp 10 am-midnight. Ck-out 10:30 am. Business servs avail. Downhill ski 10 mi; x-country ski 1 mi. Snowmobile trails. Business servs avail. Refrigerators. Municipal park, pool opp. Cr cds: A, C, D, DS, MC, V. [D] ✦ ⅀ ⅀ ⅀ [SC]

★ **COMFORT INN.** *305 Wittig Rd. 608/372-6600; FAX 608/372-6600.* 52 rms, 2 story. May-Aug: S, D $52.95-$79.95; each addl $5; under 18 free; lower rates rest of yr. Crib avail. Pet accepted. TV; cable (premium). Indoor pool; whirlpool. Complimentary continental bkfst. Restaurant adj. Ck-out 11 am. Business servs avail. Downhill ski 15 mi; x-country ½ mi. Some refrigerators. Cr cds: A, C, D, DS, MC, V. [D] ✦ ⅀ ⅀ ⅀ ⅀ [SC]

★ **LARK INN.** *229 N Superior Ave. 608/372-5981; res: 800/447-LARK.* 25 rms, 1-2 story, 3 kits. S $45-$55; D $50-$60; each addl $5; kits. $60-$70; under 16 free. Crib $3. Pet accepted. TV; cable (premium), VCR avail (movies $2.50). Restaurant 6 am-11 pm. Rm serv. Ck-out 11 am. Coin lndry. Sundries. Downhill ski 10 mi; x-country ski 1 mi. Some refrigerators. Picnic tables. Cr cds: A, C, D, DS, MC, V. [D] ✦ ⅀ ⅀ ⅀ [SC]

✓ ★ **REST WELL.** *E on US 12 (WI 16). 608/372-2471.* 12 rms (10 with shower only). No rm phones. S $20-$36; D $30-$50. Pet accepted. TV. Ck-out 10 am. Downhill ski 10 mi; x-country 1 mi. Cr cds: MC, V. ✦ ⅀

★ **SUPER 8.** *I-94 & WI 21, exit 143. 608/372-3901; FAX 608/372-5792.* 64 rms, 2 story. Mid-June-late Sept: S, D $42.98-$104.98; each addl $5; under 19 free; lower rates rest of yr. Crib free. Pet accepted. TV; cable. Complimentary continental bkfst. Restaurant adj open 24 hrs. Ck-out 11 am. Coin lndry. Business servs avail. Downhill ski 12 mi; x-country ski 1 mi. Some refrigerators. Cr cds: A, C, D, DS, MC, V. [D] ✦ ⅀ ⅀ ⅀ [SC]

Washington Island (Door Co)

Motel

★ **VIKING VILLAGE.** *2 mi NE of ferry dock. 920/847-2551; res: 800/522-5469.* E-mail jfindlay@mail.wisenet.net; web www.holidayinn.net. 12 kit units. No A/C. S $55-$75; D $66-$95; each addl $6; suites $85-$110; under 6 free; wkly rates. Crib free. Pet accepted. TV. Coffee in rms. Restaurant 7 am-1:30 pm, 5:30-7:30 pm. Ck-out 10 am. Health club privileges. Refrigerators; some microwaves, fireplaces. Cr cds: MC, V. [D] ✦ ✦ ⅀

Waukesha (See also Milwaukee)

Motel

✓ ★ **SELECT INN.** *2510 Plaza Court (53186), at jct I-94 exit 297, County JJ. 414/786-6015; FAX 414/786-5784.* 101 rms, 2-3 story. No elvtr. S, D $39-$51; under 12 free. Pet accepted; $25 refundable. TV; cable. Complimentary continental bkfst. Ck-out 11 am. Meeting rm. Business servs avail. X-country ski 5 mi. Some refrigerators. Cr cds: A, C, D, DS, MC, V. [D] ✦ ⅀ ⅀ ⅀ [SC]

Wausau *(See also Stevens Point)*

Motels

★ ★ **BEST WESTERN MIDWAY HOTEL.** *2901 Martin Ave, on US 51 & WI 29 at exit 190. 715/842-1616; FAX 715/845-3726.* 98 rms, 2 story. S $75-$87; D $85-$97; each addl $12; under 18 free. Crib free. Pet accepted. TV; cable. Sauna. Indoor pool; whirlpool. Playground. Coffee in rms. Restaurant 6 am-10 pm. Rm serv. Bar; entertainment. Ck-out noon. Meeting rms. Business servs avail. In-rm modem link. Valet serv. Free airport, Rib Mt ski slope transportation. Downhill ski 1 mi; x-country ski 3 mi. Rec rm. Lawn games. Picnic tables. Cr cds: A, C, D, DS, MC, V. 🅓 👄 🏊 🌊 🐾 🐾 **SC**

✔ ★ **BUDGETEL INN.** *1910 Stewart Ave. 715/842-0421; FAX 715/845-5096.* 96 rms, 2 story. S $43.95; D $50.95; under 18 free. Crib free. Pet accepted. TV; cable. Spa. Indoor pool. Continental bkfst. Coffee in rms. Restaurant nearby. Ck-out noon. Business servs avail. In-rm modem link. Downhill/x-country ski 2 mi. Cr cds: A, C, D, DS, MC, V. 🅓 👄 🏊 🌊 🐾 **SC**

✔ ★ **EXEL INN.** *116 S 17th Ave. 715/842-0641; FAX 715/848-1356.* 123 rms, 2 story. S $35.99-$45.99; D $44.99-$51.99; each addl $4; under 18 free. Crib free. Pet accepted. TV. Complimentary continental bkfst. Restaurant nearby. Ck-out noon. Business servs avail. Lndry facilities. Downhill ski 3 mi; x-country ski 3 mi. Game rm. View of Rib Mt. Cr cds: A, C, D, DS, MC, V. 🅓 👄 🏊 🌊 🐾 🐾 **SC**

★ **RIB MOUNTAIN INN.** *2900 Rib Mountain Way. 715/848-2802; FAX 715/848-1908.* 16 rms, 2 story, 4 villas, 4 townhouses. S $48-$71; D $55-$78; villas $95-$155; townhomes $125-$155; wkly, monthly rates; ski plan; higher rates: ski season, wkends. Pet accepted. TV; cable (premium), VCR (movies). Continental bkfst. Ck-out 11 am. Business servs avail. Driving range. Downhill ski ¼ mi; x-country ski 7 mi. Sauna. Lawn games. Refrigerators, fireplaces. Patios, balconies. Picnic tables, grills. On Rib Mountain. Adj to state park. Cr cds: A, C, D, DS, MC, V. 👄 🌊 🐾 **SC**

★ **SUPER 8.** *2006 Stewart Ave. 715/848-2888; FAX 715/842-9578.* 88 rms, 2 story. S $44-$47; D $56-$59; each addl $5-10; under 18 free. Crib free. Pet accepted. TV; cable. Indoor pool; whirlpool. Complimentary continental bkfst. Ck-out noon. Business servs avail. Valet serv. Sundries. Cr cds: A, C, D, DS, MC, V. 🅓 👄 🌊 🌊 🐾 🐾 **SC**

Wauwatosa *(See also Menomonee Falls, Milwaukee)*

Motel

✔ ★ **EXEL INN-WEST.** *115 N Mayfair Rd (US 100) (53226). 414/257-0140; FAX 414/475-7875.* 123 rms, 2 story. S $35.99-$46.99; D $37.99-$56.99; suites $85-$125; each addl (up to 4) $4; under 17 free. Crib free. Pet accepted, some restrictions. TV; cable (premium). Complimentary continental bkfst in lobby. Restaurant adj 6 am-10 pm. Ck-out noon. Business servs avail. Cr cds: A, C, D, DS, MC, V. 🅓 👄 🌊 🐾 **SC**

Wisconsin Dells *(See also Baraboo, Mauston, Portage)*

Motel

★ **INTERNATIONAL.** *1311 E Broadway. 608/254-2431.* 45 rms. July-Labor Day: S $55; D $80; lower rates May-June, after Labor Day-mid-Oct. Closed rest of yr. Crib $5. Pet accepted, some restrictions. TV; cable (premium). Heated pool; wading pool. Playground. Complimentary coffee in lobby. Restaurant adj 7 am-midnight. Ck-out 11 am. Game rm. Refrigerators avail. Balconies. Picnic tables on patio. Cr cds: A, C, D, DS, MC, V. 🅓 👄 🌊 🌊 🐾 **SC**

Wyoming

Afton *(See also Alpine)*

Motels

(Air conditioning is rarely needed at higher altitudes)

★ **BEST WESTERN HI COUNTRY INN.** *689 S Washington, ¹/₄ mi S on US 89.* 307/886-3856; FAX 307/886-9318. 30 rms. No A/C. S $45-$50; D $50-$55; each addl $5. Crib free. Pet accepted, some restrictions. TV; cable. Heated pool; whirlpool. Restaurant adj 6 am-10 pm. Ck-out 11 am. X-country ski 12 mi. Cr cds: A, C, D, DS, MC, V.
🐕 🏊 ⛷ 🖭 🔥 SC

✔ ★ **CORRAL.** *161 Washington (US 89).* 307/886-5424. 15 rms, 2 kits. No A/C. Apr-Oct: S $35; D $40-$45; each addl $5; kits. $5 addl. Closed rest of yr. Crib $2. Pet accepted, some restrictions. TV; cable (premium). Restaurant nearby. Ck-out 10 am. Some refrigerators. Picnic tables, grills. Cr cds: A, C, D, DS, MC, V. 🐕 🖭 🔥

★ **MOUNTAIN INN.** *1 mi S on US 89.* 307/886-3156; res: 800/682-5356. 20 rms. No A/C. Mid-May-mid-Oct: S $55; D $60; each addl $5; lower rates rest of yr. Crib $5. Pet accepted. TV. Heated pool; whirlpool. Sauna. Restaurant nearby. Ck-out 11 am. Cr cds: A, C, D, DS, MC, V. 🐕 🏊 🖭 🔥

Alpine *(See also Afton, Jackson)*

Motor Hotel

★ **ALPEN HAUS.** *Box 258, jct of US 26, 89.* 307/654-7545; FAX 307/654-7287, ext. 331; res: 800/343-6755 (exc WY). 45 rms, 3 story. S $58-$64; D $65-$71; each addl $7; under 12 free. Crib $10. Pet accepted. TV; cable (premium); VCR avail (movies). Playground. Restaurant 7 am-10 pm. Bar 11-1 am. Ck-out 11 am. Coin lndry. Meeting rm. Gift shop. X-country ski on site. Whirlpool. Some refrigerators, minibars. Some balconies. Ice cream parlor. Cr cds: A, C, D, DS, MC, V. D 🐕 🏊 🖭 🔥 SC

Buffalo *(See also Sheridan)*

Motels

✔ ★ **CANYON.** *997 Fort St.* 307/684-2957; res: 800/231-0742. 18 rms, 3 kits. S $38, D $40-$48; each addl $3; kit. units $50-$55. Crib free. Pet accepted. TV; cable. Complimentary coffee in rms. Restaurant nearby. Ck-out 11 am. Airport transportation. Picnic tables. Cr cds: A, DS, MC, V. 🐕 🖭 🔥 SC

★ **COMFORT INN.** *65 Hwy 16 E.* 307/684-9564. 41 rms, 2 story. Late June-mid-Aug: S, D $79.95-$94.95; each addl $5; under 18 free; lower rates rest of yr. Crib $5. Pet accepted, some restrictions. TV; cable (premium). Complimentary continental bkfst. Restaurant nearby. Ck-out 11 am. Whirlpool. Cr cds: A, D, DS, MC, V.
D 🐕 🖭 🔥 SC

✔ ★ **WYOMING.** *610 E Hart St, ¹/₂ mi NE on US 16.* 307/684-5505; FAX 307/684-5442; res: 800/666-5505. 27 rms, 5 kit. June-Oct: S $36-$62; D $46-$91; each addl $8; kit. unit $60-$145; lower rates rest of yr. Pet accepted. TV; cable (premium). Heated pool; whirlpool. Restaurant adj 6 am-10:30 pm. Ck-out 11 am. Picnic tables. Cr cds: A, C, D, DS, MC, V. 🐕 🏊 🖭 🔥

Lodge

★ ★ **THE RANCH AT UCROSS.** *(2673 US 14E, Clearmont 82835)* 307/737-2281; FAX 307/737-2211; res: 800/447-0194. 31 rms, 2 story. S $95; D $115; each addl $20; under 19 free. Pet accepted. Heated pool. Complimentary full bkfst. Restaurant 6:30-9 am, 11:30 am-1 pm, 7-9 pm. Bar 5-9 pm. Ck-out 1 pm. Meeting rm. Business servs avail. Bellhops. Sundries. Gift shop. Tennis. On creek. Cr cds: MC, V.
🐕 🎾 ⛷ 🏊 🖭 🔥

Casper *(See also Douglas)*

Motels

★ ★ **HAMPTON INN.** *400 West F Street (82601), I-25 exit Poplar St.* 307/235-6668; FAX 307/235-2027. 122 rms, 2 story. S $59; D $67; under 18 free. Crib free. Pet accepted; $6. TV; cable (premium). Heated pool; sauna. Complimentary continental bkfst. Coffee in rms. Ck-out 11 am. Business servs avail. In-rm modem link. Valet serv. Free airport transportation. Downhill ski 7 mi. Cr cds: A, C, D, DS, MC, V.

[D] [✦] [✈] [≈] [⊠] [🐾] [SC]

✔ ★ **KELLY INN.** *821 N Poplar (82601).* 307/266-2400; FAX 307/266-1146; res: 800/635-3559. 103 rms, 2 story. S $35-$43; D $41-$51; each addl $5; under 16 free. Crib free. Pet accepted. TV; cable (premium), VCR avail (movies). Complimentary coffee in lobby. Restaurant nearby. Ck-out 11 am. Coin lndry. Meeting rms. Whirlpool. Sauna. Cr cds: A, C, D, DS, MC, V. [D] [✦] [⊠] [🐾] [SC]

Motor Hotels

★ ★ ★ **HILTON INN.** *PO Box 224 (82602), 1 blk N of I-25, N Poplar exit.* 307/266-6000; FAX 307/473-1010. 228 rms, 6 story. S $65; D $65-$75; suites $85-$175; under 18 free. Crib free. Pet accepted. TV; cable (premium). Indoor pool; whirlpool. Restaurant 6 am-10 pm. Rm serv. Bar 11-1:30 am. Ck-out noon. Meeting rms. Business servs avail. Sundries. Beauty shop. Free airport transportation. Downhill/x-country ski 7 mi. Some in-rm whirlpools. Cr cds: A, C, D, DS, MC, V. [D] [✦] [✈] [≈] [⊠] [🐾] [SC]

★ ★ **HOLIDAY INN.** *300 West F Street (82602), (US 20/26).* 307/235-2531; FAX 307/266-0160. 200 rms, 2 story. S, D $69; each addl $5; suites $75-$150; under 18 free. Crib $6. Pet accepted, some restrictions. TV; cable (premium). Indoor pool; whirlpool. Restaurant 6 am-2 pm, 5-10 pm. Rm serv. Bar. Ck-out noon. Coin lndry. Meeting rms. Business servs avail. In-rm modem link. Sundries. Free airport, bus depot transportation. Downhill/x-country ski 7 mi. Exercise equipt; weights, bicycle, sauna. Game rm. Picnic tables. On river. Cr cds: A, C, D, DS, MC, V. [D] [✦] [✈] [≈] [🕴] [🏋] [⊠] [🐾] [SC]

Cheyenne *(See also Laramie)*

Motels

(Rates may be higher during Frontier Days)

✔ ★ **COMFORT INN.** *2245 Etchepare Dr.* 307/638-7202; FAX 307/635-8560. 77 rms, 2 story. June-Aug: S, D $60; under 18 free. Crib free. Pet accepted. TV; cable (premium). Heated pool. Complimentary continental bkfst. Restaurant opp open 24 hrs. Ck-out noon. Ck-in 3 pm. Coin lndry. Meeting rm. Business servs avail. Cr cds: A, C, D, DS, MC, V. [D] [✦] [≈] [⊠] [🐾] [SC]

★ **LA QUINTA.** *2410 W Lincolnway (US 30 Business).* 307/632-7117; FAX 307/638-7807. 105 rms, 3 story. June-Aug: S $55; D $63; each addl $5; under 18 free; lower rates rest of yr. Crib free. Pet accepted. TV; cable (premium). Pool. Complimentary continental bkfst. Restaurant adj open 24 hrs. Ck-out noon. Meeting rms. In-rm modem link. Sundries. Cr cds: A, C, D, DS, MC, V. [D] [✦] [≈] [⊠] [🐾] [SC]

Motor Hotel

★ ★ ★ **BEST WESTERN HITCHING POST INN.** *Box 1769, 1700 W Lincolnway (US 30, I-80 Business), 1/2 mi E at I-25 & I-80.* 307/638-3301; FAX 307/778-7194. 175 rms, 1-2 story. June-Labor Day: S $70-$80; D $80-$100; each addl $6; suites $85-$150; under 12 free; lower rates rest of yr. Crib free. Pet accepted. TV; cable (premium). Indoor pool; whirlpool. Playground. Restaurants 5:30 am-11 pm. Rm serv. Bar noon-2 am; entertainment. Ck-out noon. Coin lndry. Meeting rms. Business center. In-rm modem link. Bellhops. Gift shop. Free airport, RR station, bus depot transportation. Exercise equipt; weights, bicycles, sauna. Game rm. Bathrm phones, refrigerators. Private patios, balconies. Cr cds: A, C, D, DS, ER, JCB, MC, V. [D] [✦] [≈] [🕴] [⊠] [🐾] [SC] [⛷]

Cody

Motel

✔ ★ **KELLY INN.** *US 16 & 26th St, near Regional Airport.* 307/527-5505; res: 800/635-3559. 50 rms, 2 story. June-mid-Sept: S $69; D $82; each addl $5; lower rates rest of yr. Crib free. Pet accepted. TV; cable. Complimentary coffee in lobby. Restaurant nearby. Ck-out 11 am. Business servs avail. Coin lndry. Whirlpool, sauna. Cr cds: A, D, DS, MC, V.

[D] [✦] [⊠] [🐾]

Lodges

✔★ ABSAROKA MOUNTAIN. *(1231 E Yellowstone Hwy, Wapiti 82450) 40 mi W on US 14, 16, 20, on Gunbarrel Creek in Shoshone Natl Forest; 12 mi E of Yellowstone Natl Park. 307/587-3963.* 16 cabins. No A/C. AP, June-Sept: S, D $60-$84; each addl $6; lower rates May. Closed rest of yr. Crib $10. Pet accepted, some restrictions. Playground. Dining rm 7:30-9:30 am, 6-8 pm. Bar 6-10 pm. Ck-out 11 am, ck-in 2 pm. Airport transportation. Lawn games. Picnic tables. Log cabins; western decor. Cr cds: DS, MC, V.

★★ ELEPHANT HEAD. *(1170 Yellowstone Hwy, Wapiti 82450) 41 mi W on US 14, 16, 20; 11 mi E of Yellowstone Natl Park. 307/587-3980; FAX 307/527-7922.* 11 cabins. No A/C. Mid-May-mid-Oct: S $54-$64; D $54-$84; AP avail. Closed rest of yr. Pet accepted. Playground. Western movies nightly. Dining rm 7:30-9:30 am, 11:30 am-1:30 pm, 6:30-8:30 pm. Bar 5:30-10 pm. Ck-out, ck-in noon. Picnic tables, grills. On river in Shoshone Natl Forest. Trail rides avail. Cr cds: A, DS, MC, V.

★ GOFF CREEK. *Box 155, 42 mi W on US 14, 16, 20; 10 mi E of Yellowstone Natl Park. 307/587-3753; res: 800/859-3985.* 14 cabins. No A/C. Mid-May-mid-Oct: S $85; D $90; each addl $5; duplex cabins $100-$180; lower rates rest of yr. Crib $5. Pet accepted. TV; VCR avail. Dining rm 7-9:30 am, 5-8 pm. Bar noon-11 pm. Ck-out 11 am. Sundries. White water rafting. Lawn games. Private patios. Picnic tables. Trail rides avail. Cr cds: MC, V.

★ SHOSHONE. *349 Yellowstone Hwy, 46 mi W on US 14, 16, 20; 4 mi E of Yellowstone Natl Park. 307/587-4044; FAX 307/587-2681.* 16 cabins, 3 kits. (no equipt). No A/C. No rm phones. May-Oct: S $60-$70; D $66-$86; each addl $10; kit. units $20 addl. Closed rest of yr. Crib $2. Pet accepted. Dining rm 7-9 am, noon-1:30 pm, 6-8 pm. Ck-out 10 am. Coin lndry. Sundries. Lawn games. Downhill ski opp, X-country ski. Cookouts. Fireplace, trophies in lodge. Most cabins have porches. Scenic location on Grinnell Creek. Cr cds: A, DS, MC, V.

Guest Ranch

★★★ HIDDEN VALLEY RANCH RESORT. *153 Hidden Valley Rd. 307/587-5090; FAX 307/587-5265; res: 800/894-7262.* 9 cabins, shower only. June-Sept, AP: S $95-$195; D $190-$290; each addl $75; under 3 free; wkly rates; lower rates rest of yr. Crib free. Pet accepted. Heated pool; whirlpool. Box lunches, picnics. Bar; entertainment. Ck-out noon, ck-in 3 pm. Coin lndry. Bellhops. Gift shop. Meeting rms. Business servs avail. Free airport transportation. X-country ski on site. Horse stables. Hiking. Fishing/hunting guides, clean & store. Lawn games. Picnic tables. On creek. Totally nonsmoking. Cr cds: A, DS, MC, V.

Douglas (See also Casper)

Motel

(Rates may be higher during state fair)

★★ BEST WESTERN DOUGLAS INN. *1450 Riverbend Dr. 307/358-9790; FAX 307/358-6251.* 116 rms, 2 story. S $65-$75; D $73-$85; each addl $8; under 19 free. Crib free. Pet accepted, some restrictions. TV; cable (premium). Indoor pool; whirlpool. Complimentary coffee in lobby. Restaurant 6 am-2 pm, 5-10 pm. Rm serv. Bar 4:30 pm-2 am, Sun noon-10 pm. Ck-out 11 am. Coin lndry. Meeting rms. Business servs avail. Valet serv. Sundries. Exercise equipt; weights, star machine, sauna. Game rm. Cr cds: A, C, D, DS, MC, V.

Dubois (See also Grand Teton National Park)

Motel

(Air conditioning is rarely needed at higher altitudes)

✔★ SUPER 8. *1414 Warm Springs Dr. 307/455-3694; FAX 307/455-3640.* 32 rms, 2 story. July-Aug: S $40.88; D $44.88-$49.88; suite $85; each addl $5; under 12 free; higher rates July 4 wknd; lower rates rest of yr. Crib free. Pet accepted. TV; cable (premium). Whirlpool. Complimentary coffee. Ck-out 11 am. Cr cds: A, D, DS, MC, V.

Guest Ranch

★★★ LAZY L & B RANCH. *1072 E Fork Rd, 10 mi E on Fork Rd, follow ranch sign 12 mi to ranch. 307/455-2839; FAX 307/455-2634; res: 800/453-9488.* 12 cabins. AP (1-wk min), Memorial Day-Sept: S $970 person; D $895/person; under 13 yrs $795. Closed rest of yr. Pet accepted. Heated pool. Supervised child's activities (May-Aug). Dining rm. Cookouts. Ck-out Sat 10 am, ck-in Sun 1 pm. Gift shop. Airport transportation. River swimming. Hiking. Hayrides. Children's petting farm. Lawn games. Rec rm. 1,800 acres on mountain range bordering Shoshone National Forest. Totally nonsmoking. No cr cds accepted.

🐾 💤 ⛷ ≋ 🎿 📶 🐾

Gillette *(See also Buffalo)*

Motor Hotel

★ **HOLIDAY INN.** *2009 S Douglas Hwy (82718). 307/686-3000; FAX 307/686-4018.* 158 rms, 3 story. July-mid-Sept: S $85; D $93; each addl $8; suites $120-$150; under 18 free; lower rates rest of yr. Crib free. Pet accepted. TV; cable (premium). Indoor pool; whirlpool. Restaurant 6 am-10 pm. Rm serv. Bar 4:30 pm-2 am; entertainment Mon-Sat. Ck-out noon. Coin lndry. Meeting rms. Business servs avail. Valet serv. Gift shop. Free airport transportation. Exercise equipt; weights, bicycles, sauna. Holidome. Game rm. Rec room. Cr cds: A, C, D, DS, MC, V. 🅳 🐾 ≋ 🏋 📶 🐾 **SC**

Grand Teton National Park *(See also Dubois, Jackson)*

Motel

(Reservations advised for accommodations within the national park; air conditioning is rarely needed at higher altitudes)

↙ ★ **HATCHET.** *(US 26/287, Moran 83013) 7¹/₂ mi E of Moran jct. 307/543-2413; FAX 307/543-2413.* 22 cabins. No A/C. Memorial Day-Labor Day: S, D $80; each addl $5. Closed rest of yr. Pet accepted; $20 deposit. Restaurant 6:30 am-9:30 pm. Ck-out 11 am. Gift shop. Sundries. Picnic tables. Totally nonsmoking. Cr cds: DS, MC, V. 🐾 📶 🐾

Lodge

★ ★ **SIGNAL MOUNTAIN.** *(Moran 83013) 4¹/₂ mi W on Interpark Rd, 3 mi SW of jct US 89/287 in park. 307/543-2831; FAX 307/543-2569.* E-mail 102547.1642@compuserv.com. 79 cabins, 1-2 story, 30 kits. No A/C. S, D $78-$160; each addl $8; kit. units $155. Pet accepted, some restrictions. Crib free. Restaurant 7 am-10 pm in season. Bar noon-midnight. Ck-out 11 am. Meeting rms. Gift shop. Some refrigerators, fireplaces; microwaves avail. Private patios, balconies. Marina; boat rentals; guided fishing trips. Scenic float trips on Snake River. On lake; campground adj. Cr cds: A, DS, MC, V.

🐾 💤 📶 🐾

Cottage Colony

★ **COLTER BAY CABINS.** *(83013). 10 mi N of Moran Jct. 307/543-3100; res: 800/628-9988; FAX 307/543-3046.* 208 cabins, 192 with shower only, 9 share bath. No A/C. No rm phones. S $32-$85; D $32-$110; each addl $8; under 12 free. Closed mid-Oct-mid-May. Crib free. Pet accepted, some restrictions. Restaurant 6:30 am-10 pm. Ck-out 11 am, ck-in 4 pm. Airport transportation. Boat rentals, lake cruises. On Jackson Lake. Cr cds: A, D, MC, V. 🐾 💤 ≋ 📶 🐾

Jackson *(See also Alpine, Grand Teton National Park, Pinedale)*

Motels

(Reservations advised June-Aug)

★ ★ **FRIENDSHIP INN-49ER.** *330 W Pearl St. 307/733-7550; FAX 307/733-2002; res: 800/451-2980.* 148 rms, 1-2 story. June-Sept: S $102; D $106; each addl $4; suites $130-$170; lower rates rest of yr. Crib free. Pet accepted, some restrictions. TV; cable (premium). Complimentary continental bkfst. Restaurant nearby 6 am-10 pm. Ck-out 11 am. Meeting rm. Downhill/x-country ski 12 mi. Exercise equipt; weight machines, treadmill. Health club privileges. Whirlpool. Some in-rm whirlpools, refrigerators, microwaves, fireplaces. Cr cds: A, C, D, DS, JCB, MC, V. 🅳 🐾 ≋ 🏋 📶 🐾

★ **FRIENDSHIP INN-ANTLER.** *43 W Pearl St. 307/733-2535; FAX 307/733-4158; res: 800/522-2406.* 104 rms, 1-2 story, 2 suites. June-mid-Sept: S $76-$92; D $82-$96; each addl $5; suites $120; family rm (up to 6 persons) $112; lower rates rest of yr. Crib free. Pet accepted, some restrictions. TV; cable (premium). Restaurant opp 7 am-10 pm. Ck-out 11 am. Meeting rm. Downhill/x-country ski 12 mi. Exercise equipt; treadmill, stair machine. Whirlpool. Some fireplaces, in-rm whirlpools; microwaves avail. Cr cds: A, C, D, DS, MC, V. 🅳 🐾 ≋ 📶 🐾

★ ★ **WYOMING INN.** *930 W Broadway. 307/734-0035; FAX 307/734-0037; res: 800/844-0035.* 73 rms, 3 story, 4 kit. units. July-Aug: S, D $179-$219; each addl $10; kit. units $199; under 13 free; lower rates rest of yr. Pet accepted. TV; cable. Complimentary continental bkfst. Coffee in rms. Restaurant nearby. Ck-out 11 am. Free guest lndry. Meeting rm. Business servs avail. Free airport transportation. Some refrigerators, fireplaces, whirlpools. Totally nonsmoking. Cr cds: A, DS, MC, V. ⒹⒺ🗙🗙🗙 SC

Motor Hotel

★ ★ ★ **SNOW KING RESORT.** *400 E Snow King Ave. 307/733-5200; FAX 307/733-4086; res: 800/522-5464.* 204 rms, 7 story. Late May-late Sept: S $170; D $180; each addl $10; suites $200-$420; under 14 free; ski plan; lower rates rest of yr. Crib free. Pet accepted, some restrictions. TV; cable. Heated pool; whirlpools, poolside serv. Restaurants 6:30 am-10 pm. Rm serv. Bar noon-2 am. Ck-out noon. Coin lndry. Meeting rms. Business servs avail. Bellhops. Valet serv. Concierge. Sundries. Gift shop. Barber, beauty shop. Free airport transportation; free shuttle to Jackson Hole ski area. Alpine Slide. Exercise equipt; treadmill, stair machine, sauna. Massage. Downhill ski adj; x-country ski 5 mi. Game rm. Located at foot of Snow King Mountain. Cr cds: A, C, D, DS, MC, V.

ⒹⒺ⚡🗙🗙🗙🗙🗙🗙 SC

Lander *(See also Riverton)*

Motel

✔ ★ **BUDGET HOST PRONGHORN.** *150 E Main St. 307/332-3940; FAX 307/332-2651.* 54 rms, 2 story. May-Sept: S $39-$43; D $42-$53; each addl $5; suites $61; under 12 free; lower rates rest of yr. Crib $5. Pet accepted, some restrictions. TV; cable (premium). Complimentary continental bkfst. Restaurant 6 am-11 pm. Ck-out 11 am. Coin lndry. Meeting rms. Whirlpool. Some refrigerators. On river. Cr cds: A, C, D, DS, MC, V.

ⒹⒺ🗙🗙🗙 SC

Laramie *(See also Cheyenne)*

Motels

★ **BEST WESTERN FOSTER'S COUNTRY INN.** *1561 Jackson St, (WY 130, 230) at jct I-80 Snowy Range exit 311. 307/742-8371; FAX 307/742-0884.* 112 rms, 2 story. Mid-May-mid-Sept: S $54; D $60; each addl $6; under 12 free; higher rates special events; lower rates rest of yr. Crib $6. Pet accepted. TV; cable. Indoor pool; whirlpool. Restaurant open 24 hrs. Bar 8-2 am. Ck-out noon. Coin lndry. Meeting rms. Gift shop. Free airport, RR station, bus depot transportation. Cr cds: A, C, D, DS, MC, V. ⒹⒺ🗙🗙🗙🗙 SC

★ **ECONO LODGE.** *1370 McCue St. 307/745-8900; FAX 307/745-5806.* 51 rms, 2 story. June-Aug: S, D $89-$189; each addl $10; under 13 free; lower rates rest of yr. Crib free. Pet accepted. TV; cable, VCR avail (movies). Indoor pool. Complimentary coffee in lobby. Restaurant nearby. Ck-out noon. Meeting rm. Some refrigerators. Cr cds: A, C, D, DS, MC, V. ⒹⒺ🗙🗙 SC

★ **HOLIDAY INN.** *2313 Soldier Springs Rd, at jct US 30, 287; I-80 exit 313. 307/742-6611; FAX 307/745-8371.* 100 rms, 2 story. Mid-May-mid-Sept: S $60; D $68; each addl $8; under 12 free; lower rates rest of yr. Crib free. Pet accepted. TV; cable (premium). Indoor pool; whirlpool. Restaurant 6 am-10 pm. Rm serv. Bar. Ck-out noon. Coin lndry. Meeting rms. Gift shop. Free airport transportation. Game rm. Cr cds: A, C, D, DS, MC, V.

ⒹⒺ🗙🗙🗙 SC

Pinedale *(See also Jackson)*

Motels

★ ★ **BEST WESTERN PINEDALE INN.** *850 W Pine. 307/367-6869; FAX 307/367-6897.* 58 rms, 2 story. June-Labor Day: S, D $85; suites $95; under 12 free; lower rates rest of yr. Crib $5. Pet accepted. TV; cable. Indoor pool; whirlpool. Sauna. Complimentary continental bkfst. Restaurant nearby. Ck-out 11 am. Meeting rms. Exercise equipt; bicycle, treadmill. Some refrigerators. Cr cds: A, D, DS, MC, V. Ⓔ🗙🗙🗙🗙 SC

★ **THE ZZZZ INN.** *327 S Pine. 307/367-2121.* 34 rms. No A/C. May-Oct: S $50-$65; D $55-$75; each addl $5. Closed rest of yr. Pet accepted. TV; cable. Restaurant nearby. Ck-out 11 am. Cr cds: A, C, D, DS, MC, V. Ⓔ🗙🗙

Rawlins

Motel

★ **DAYS INN.** *2222 E Cedar St. 307/324-6615.* 121 rms, 2 story. June-mid-Sept: S $50; D $50-$55; each addl $5; under 13 free; lower rates rest of yr. Crib free. Pet accepted. TV; cable. Indoor pool. Restaurant 6-9 am, 11 am-2 pm, 5-9 pm. Rm serv. Bar 5 pm-2 am. Ck-out noon. Coin lndry. Meeting rms. Business servs avail. Game rm. Cr cds: A, C, D, DS, MC, V. 🄳 🖇 🏊 ⊠ 🐾 SC

Riverton *(See also Lander)*

Motel

★ ★ **SUNDOWNER STATION.** *1616 N Federal, (US 26, WY 789). 307/856-6503; res: 800/874-1116.* 60 rms, 2 story. S $42-$44; D $44-$48; each addl $4; under 12 free. Crib free. Pet accepted. TV; cable. Heated pool; sauna. Restaurant 5:30 am-10 pm. Bar 4 pm-11 pm. Ck-out 11 am. Meeting rms. Sundries. Free airport transportation. Balconies. Cr cds: A, C, D, DS, MC, V. 🖇 🏊 ⊠ 🐾 SC

Motor Hotel

★ ★ **HOLIDAY INN.** *900 E Sunset. 307/856-8100; FAX 307/856-0266.* 121 rms, 2 story. S $59; D $65; each addl $6; under 19 free. Pet accepted. TV; cable. Indoor pool; whirlpool, poolside serv. Restaurant 6 am-10 pm. Rm serv. Bar 4 pm-2 am. Ck-out noon. Coin lndry. Meeting rms. Sundries. Beauty shop. Airport transportation. Game rm. Bathrm phones. Cr cds: A, C, D, DS, JCB, MC, V. 🄳 🖇 🏊 ⊠ 🐾 SC

Rock Springs *(See also Green River)*

Motels

★ **COMFORT INN.** *1670 Sunset Dr (US 30), at I-80 Dewar exit. 307/382-9490; FAX 307/382-7333.* 103 rms. Mid-May-mid-Sept: S $60.80; D $66.80; each addl $6; lower rates rest of yr. Crib $5. Pet accepted; $6. TV; cable (premium). Heated pool; whirlpool. Playground. Complimentary continental bkfst. Restaurant adj. Ck-out 11 am. Coin lndry. Business servs avail. In-rm modem link. Exercise equipt; weights, treadmill. Bathrm phones. Cr cds: A, C, D, DS, MC, V. 🄳 🖇 🏊 🏋 ⊠ 🐾 SC

✔ ★ ★ **LA QUINTA.** *2717 Dewar Dr. 307/362-1770; FAX 307/362-2830.* 130 rms, 2 story. June-Aug: S $46; D $52; each addl $5; under 18 free; lower rates rest of yr. Crib free. Pet accepted. TV; cable (premium). Heated pool. Complimentary continental bkfst. Restaurant adj open 24 hrs. Ck-out noon. Meeting rms. Business servs avail. In-rm modem link. Valet serv. Cr cds: A, C, D, DS, MC, V. 🄳 🖇 🏊 ⊠ 🐾 SC

Motor Hotel

★ ★ **HOLIDAY INN.** *1675 Sunset Dr (US 187). 307/382-9200; FAX 307/362-1064.* 114 rms, 4 story. May-Sept: S, D $56-$70; each addl $6; under 18 free; lower rates rest of yr. Crib free. Pet accepted. TV; cable (premium). Indoor pool; wading pool, whirlpool, poolside serv. Restaurant 6 am-2 pm, 5-10 pm. Rm serv. Bar 11-2 am, Sun noon-10 pm. Ck-out noon. Coin lndry. Meeting rms. Business servs avail. Bellhops. Airport transportation. Balconies. Cr cds: A, C, D, DS, MC, V. 🖇 🏊 ⊠ 🐾 SC

Sheridan *(See also Buffalo)*

Motor Hotel

★ ★ ★ **HOLIDAY INN.** *1809 Sugarland Dr, I-90 exit 25. 307/672-8931; FAX 307/672-6388.* 212 rms, 5 story. S $76-$86; D $86-$108; each addl $10; suites $135-$200; under 19 free. Crib free. Pet accepted. TV; cable. Indoor pool; whirlpool, poolside serv. Restaurant 6 am-10 pm. Rm serv. Bar 4 pm-1:45 am. Ck-out noon. Coin lndry. Meeting rms. Business servs avail. In-rm modem link. Bellhops. Sundries. Gift shop. Beauty shop. Airport, bus depot transportation. Exercise equipt; stair machine, treadmill, sauna. Holidome. Game rm. Putting green. Some refrigerators. Picnic area. Cr cds: A, C, D, DS, JCB, MC, V.
🄳 🖇 🏊 🏋 🏃 🛪 ⊠ 🐾 SC

Wheatland *(See also Cheyenne)*

Motel

✔★ **BEST WESTERN TORCHLITE MOTOR INN.** *1809 N 16th. 307/322-4070; FAX 307/322-4072.* 50 rms, 2 story. S $40-$75; D $45-$75; each addl $5. Crib $8. Pet accepted. TV; cable (premium). Ck-out 11 am. Business servs avail. Airport transportation. Refrigerators. Cr cds: A, C, D, DS, MC, V. **D** 🐾 ⊠ 🐾 **SC**

Canada

Banff, Alberta *(See also Calgary, Lake Louise)*

Motels

★ **BEST WESTERN SIDING 29 LODGE.** *(453 Marten St, Banff AB T0L 0C0)* *451 Marten St. 403/762-5575; FAX 403/762-8866.* 57 rms, 3 story, 10 suites. No A/C. June-Sept: S, D $140-$170; suites $175-$250; lower rates rest of yr. Crib $10. Pet accepted. TV; cable. Indoor pool; whirlpool. Complimentary coffee in lobby. Restaurant adj 7-11 am, 5-11 pm. Ck-out 11 am. Business servs avail. Downhill ski 5 mi; x-country ski 2 mi. Some refrigerators. Some balconies. Cr cds: A, C, D, DS, ER, JCB, MC, V. 🐾 ⛷ 🏊 ⛸ 🐾

✔ ★ **RED CARPET INN.** *(425 Banff Ave, Banff AB T0L 0C0)* *403/762-4184; FAX 403/762-4894; res: 800/563-4609 (CN only).* 52 rms, 3 story. No A/C. June-mid-Oct: S $100-$125; D $140-$150; lower rates rest of yr. Crib avail. Pet accepted. TV; VCR avail. Restaurant adj 7 am-11 pm. Business servs avail. Free garage parking. Whirlpool (winter only). Balconies. Cr cds: A, MC, V. 🐾 ⛸ 🐾

Motor Hotel

★ ★ **BANFF ROCKY MOUNTAIN RESORT.** *(Box 100, Banff AB T0L 0C0)* Banff Ave at Tunnel Mt Rd, just off Trans-Canada Hwy 1. *403/762-5531; FAX 403/762-5166; res: 800/661-9563.* 171 condo units, 2 story. Mid-June-mid-Sept: condos $200-$275; each addl $15; under 16 free; higher rates Christmas hol; lower rates rest of yr. Crib free. Pet accepted. TV, cable. Indoor pool; whirlpool. Playground. Restaurant 7-11 am, 6-9:30 pm. Rm serv 3-10 pm. Bar 11-1 am. Ck-out 11 am. Meeting rms. Business servs avail. Tennis. Downhill/x-country ski 2 mi. Exercise equipt; weight machine, bicycle, sauna. Refrigerators, fireplaces. Balconies. Picnic tables, grill. Cr cds: A, C, D, ER, JCB, MC, V.
🅳 🐾 ⛷ 🏊 🏋 🚴 🎾 🍴 🐾 SC

Hotels

★ ★ **BANFF SPRINGS.** *(Box 960, Banff AB T0L 0C0)* Spray Ave. *403/762-2211; FAX 403/762-5755; res: 800/441-1414.* 815 rms, 9 story. No A/C. Mid-May-mid-Oct: S, D $190-$425; each addl $21; suites $425-$975; under 18 free; lower rates rest of yr. Crib free. Pet accepted; $20. Garage $6.50/day, valet $11. TV; cable. 2 pools, 1 indoor; whirlpool. Restaurant 7-10 am, 6-9 pm. Bar 11:30-1 am. Ck-out noon. Convention facilities. Business servs avail. In-rm modem link. Concierge. Shopping arcade. Beauty shop. Tennis, pro. 27-hole golf, greens fee $90, pro, putting green, driving range. Downhill ski 2 mi. Exercise equipt; weights, bicycles, sauna. Bowling. Rec rm. Minibars. Picnic tables. Antiques throughout. Located in wooded area overlooking Bow River Valley. Elaborate landscaping. Cr cds: A, C, D, DS, ER, JCB, MC, V. 🅳 🐾 ⛷ 🏊 🏋 🚴 🎾 🍴 🐾 🐾

★ ★ **MOUNT ROYAL.** *(138 Banff Ave, Banff AB T0L 0C0)* 138 Banff Ave. *403/762-3331; FAX 403/762-8938; res: 800/267-3035.* 136 rms, 3-4 story. Late June-Sept: S, D $185; each addl $18; suites $245; under 16 free; ski plans; lower rates rest of yr. Crib free. Pet accepted, some restrictions. TV; cable. Restaurant 7 am-10 pm. Bar 11:30-1 am. Ck-out 11 am. Meeting rms. Beauty shop. Airport transportation. Downhill/x-country ski 5 mi. Exercise equipt; weight machine, bicycles, sauna. Whirlpool. Cr cds: A, D, ER, JCB, MC, V. 🐾 ⛷ 🏋 🍴 🐾

★ ★ **PTARMIGAN INN.** *(337 Banff Ave, Banff AB T0L 0C0)* *403/762-2207; FAX 403/762-3577; res: 800/661-8310.* 167 rms, 3 story. No A/C. June-Sept: S $133; D $140; each addl $12; suites $210; under 16 free; ski plans; lower rates rest of yr. Pet accepted, some restrictions; $25. Free garage. TV; cable. Restaurant 7 am-11 pm. Bar 5 pm-midnight; entertainment wkends. Ck-out 11 am. Meeting rms. Business servs avail. Gift shop. Downhill/x-country ski 2 mi. Sauna. Whirlpool. Balconies. Cr cds: A, D, DS, ER, JCB, MC, V. 🅳 🐾 ⛷ ⛸ 🐾 SC

Inn

✔ ★ ★ **LADY MACDONALD COUNTRY INN.** *(1201 Bow Valley Trail, Canmore AB T0L 0M0)* 15 mi E on Hwy 1A. *403/678-3665; FAX 403/678-9714; res: 800/567-3919.* 11 rms, 2 story. No A/C. June-Sept & Dec hols: D $100-$160; each addl $10; under 6 free; lower rates rest of yr. Pet accepted, some restrictions; $10. TV; cable (premium). Complimentary full bkfst. Restaurant adj open 24 hrs. Ck-out 11 am. Business servs avail. In-rm modem link. Luggage handling. Downhill ski 10 mi; x-country ski 2 blks. Picnic tables. Victorian-style architecture; Shaker pine furniture. Cr cds: A, MC, V. 🅳 🐾 ⛷

Calgary, Alberta *(See also Banff)*

Motel

(Rates may be higher Stampede Week)

★ **QUALITY INN.** *(2359 Banff Trail NW (1A), Calgary AB T2M 4L2) 1 blk N of Trans-Canada Hwy 1.* 403/289-1973; FAX 403/282-1241. 101 rms, 2 story. July-Sept: S, D $69-$129; suites $89-$249; under 18 free; lower rates rest of yr. Crib free. Pet accepted. TV; cable, VCR avail (movies). Sauna. Indoor pool. Restaurant 7 am-2 pm, 5-10 pm. Rm serv. Bar 11-2 am. Ck-out 11 am. Meeting rms. Business servs avail. In-rm modem link. Balconies. Cr cds: A, C, D, DS, ER, MC, V. 🐾 ⩳ ⩨ 🏃 SC

Motor Hotels

★ ★ ★ **BLACKFOOT INN.** *(5940 Blackfoot Trail SE, Calgary AB T2H 2B5)* 403/252-2253; FAX 403/252-3574; res: 800/661-1151. 200 rms, 7 story. S $135; D $145; each addl $10; suites $150; under 16 free; monthly rates. Crib free. Pet accepted. TV; cable, VCR avail. Heated pool; whirlpool, poolside serv. Restaurant 7 am-midnight. Rm serv. Bar 11:30-1:30 am; entertainment Mon-Fri. Ck-out 1 pm. Meeting rms. Business servs avail. In-rm modem link. Bellhops. Sundries. Gift shop. Exercise equipt; bicycles, rowers, sauna. Minibars. Cr cds: A, D, ER, MC, V. D 🐾 ⩳ 🏋 ⩨ 🏃

★ ★ **HIGHLANDER.** *(1818 16th Ave NW (Trans-Canada Hwy 1), Calgary AB T2M 0L8)* 403/289-1961; FAX 403/289-3901; res: 800/661-9564 (CAN). 130 rms, 4 story. Mid-June-Sept: S $79; D $99; suites $125; each addl $6; under 16 free; higher rates special events; lower rates rest of yr. Crib free. Pet accepted. TV; cable (premium), VCR avail. Heated pool; poolside serv. Restaurant 6:30 am-11:30 pm; pianist in dining rm Thurs-Sun. Rm serv. Bar 11-1:30 am. Ck-out noon. Meeting rms. Business servs avail. Bellhops. Gift shop. Airport transportation. Balconies. Cr cds: A, C, D, ER, JCB, MC, V.
D 🐾 ⩳ ⩨ 🏃 SC

★ ★ **HOLIDAY INN.** *(4206 Macleod Trail SE, Calgary AB T2G 2R7)* 403/287-2700; FAX 403/243-4721. 154 rms, 4 story. May-Sept: S $104-$109; D $109-$114; each addl $5; under 19 free; wkend, wkly rates; lower rates rest of yr. Crib free. Pet accepted. TV; cable (premium), VCR avail. Heated pool. Restaurant 7 am-10 pm. Rm serv. Bar 11 am-midnight. Ck-out noon. Coin lndry. Meeting rms. Business servs avail. Bellhops. Valet serv. Some refrigerators. Cr cds: A, C, D, DS, ER, JCB, MC, V. D 🐾 ⩳ ⩨ 🏃 SC

★ ★ **HOLIDAY INN CALGARY AIRPORT.** *(1250 McKinnon Dr NE, Calgary AB T2E 7T7) Trans-Canada Hwy 1 & 19th St NE.* 403/230-1999; FAX 403/277-2623. 170 rms, 5 story. S $94-$105; D $94-$125; each addl $10; under 18 free. Pet accepted. TV; cable. Sauna. Indoor pool. Restaurant 6:30 am-10 pm. Rm serv. Bar 11-1 am. Ck-out 11 am. Meeting rms. Business servs avail. Gift shop. Free airport transportation. Cr cds: A, C, D, DS, ER, JCB, MC, V. D 🐾 ⩳ ⩨ 🏃 SC

✔ ★ **NITE INN.** *(4510 Macleod Trail S, Calgary AB T2G 0A4)* 403/243-1700; FAX 403/243-4719. 60 rms, 6 story. D $99; each addl $10; under 18 free. Pet accepted. TV; cable. Complimentary coffee in rms. Restaurant 7 am-9 pm. Rm serv. Bar 11-2 am. Meeting rms. Business servs avail. Cr cds: A, C, D, DS, ER, MC, V. D 🐾 ⩳ ⩨ 🏃 SC

✔ ★ ★ **QUALITY AIRPORT INN.** *(4804 Edmonton Trail NE, Calgary AB T2E 3V8)* 403/276-3391; FAX 403/230-7267. 117 rms, 7 story. S, D $85-$90; each addl $5; suites $114; under 18 free. Crib $10. Pet accepted, some restrictions. TV; cable. Restaurant 6:30 am-10 pm. Rm serv. Bar 11-2 am; entertainment. Ck-out 11 am. Meeting rms. Business servs avail. In-rm modem link. Free airport transportation. Sauna. Cr cds: A, D, DS, ER, MC, V. 🐾 ⩳ ⩨ 🏃 SC

✔ ★ **STAMPEDER INN.** *(3828 Macleod Trail S, Calgary AB T2G 2R2)* 403/243-5531; FAX 403/243-6962; res: 800/361-3422. 102 rms, 3 story. S, D $70-$140; suites $95-$150; each addl $10; under 16 free. Crib free. Pet accepted. TV; cable. Heated pool; whirlpool. Coffee in rms. Restaurants 7 am-10 pm. Rm serv. Bar 11-2 am, closed Sun. Ck-out 11 am. Meeting rms. Business servs avail. Bellhops in summer. Valet serv. Gift shop. Cr cds: A, C, D, DS, ER, MC, V. D 🐾 ⩳ ⩨ 🏃 SC

Hotels

★ ★ ★ **CALGARY AIRPORT.** *(2001 Airport Rd NE, Calgary AB T2E 6Z8) at Intl Airport.* 403/291-2600; FAX 403/291-3419; res: 800/441-1414. 296 rms, 8 story. S $155-$195; D $165-$205; each addl $15; suites $270-$370; under 18 free. Pet accepted, some restrictions. TV; cable, VCR avail. Indoor pool; whirlpool. Restaurant 6:30 am-10 pm. Rm serv 24 hrs. Bar 11:30-1 am. Ck-out noon. Convention facilities. Business servs avail. Gift shop. Exercise equipt; weights, bicycles, sauna. Minibars. Atrium. Cr cds: A, C, D, DS, ER, JCB, MC, V. D ⛵ ≈ 🏋 🚫 🐾 SC

★ ★ **CARRIAGE HOUSE INN.** *(9030 Macleod Trail S, Calgary AB T2H 0M4) 403/253-1101; FAX 403/259-2414; res: 800/661-9566 (CAN).* 175 rms, 10 story. S, D $100-$121; each addl $5; suites $170; under 16 free; wkly rates. Crib free. Pet accepted, some restrictions; $5. TV; cable (premium), VCR avail. Heated pool (in season); whirlpool, poolside serv. Restaurant 6:30 am-11 pm. Bar 11-2 am; entertainment. Ck-out noon. Meeting rms. Business servs avail. In-rm modem link. Gift shop. Sauna. Health club privileges. Game rm. Bathrm phones, minibars. Cr cds: A, C, D, DS, ER, JCB, MC, V. D ⛵ ≈ 🚫 🐾 SC

★ ★ ★ **THE COAST PLAZA AT CALGARY.** *(1316 33rd St NE, Calgary AB T2A 6B6) 403/248-8888; FAX 403/248-0749; res: 800/661-1464.* 248 rms, 7 & 12 story. S, D $125-$140; each addl $10; suites $250; under 18 free. Crib free. Pet accepted; $10. TV; cable, VCR avail. Heated pool; whirlpool. Sauna. Complimentary coffee, tea in rms. Restaurant 6:30 am-11 pm. Bar 11-2 am; entertainment. Ck-out noon. Convention facilities. Business servs avail. Gift shop. Free airport transportation. Luxury level. Cr cds: A, C, D, DS, ER, MC, V. D ⛵ ≈ 🚫 🐾 SC

★ ★ ★ **LODGE AT KANANASKIS.** *(Kananaskis Village, Calgary AB T0L 2H0)* 60 mi SW on Trans-Canada Hwy 1 and Kananaskis Trail (Hwy 40). *403/591-7711; FAX 403/591-7770; res: 800/441-1414.* 251 air-cooled rms, 3 story. S, D $185-$260; each addl $20; suites $300-$550; under 18 free; ski plans. Crib free. Pet accepted; $20/day. Covered parking $4. TV; cable, VCR avail (movies). Indoor/outdoor pool; whirlpool. Restaurant 6-4 am. Bar; entertainment. Ck-out noon. Convention facilities. Business center. In-rm modem link. Concierge. Shopping arcade. Barber, beauty shop. Tennis. 36-hole golf course; greens fee, pro, putting green, driving range. Downhill ski 1 mi; x-country ski on site. Exercise equipt; weights, sauna, steam rm. Game rm. Rec rm. Minibars; some bathrm phones. Private patios, balconies. Cr cds: A, C, D, DS, ER, JCB, MC, V. D ⛵ ⛳ 🏓 🏋 🎿 ≈ 🏋 🎣 🚫 🐾 SC ⛷

★ ★ ★ **PALLISER.** *(133 9th Ave SW, Calgary AB T2P 2M3) 403/262-1234; FAX 403/260-1260; res: 800/441-1414.* 405 rms, 12 story. S, D $260; each addl $25; suites $300-$600; under 18 free. Crib free. Pet accepted, some restrictions. TV; cable (premium), VCR avail. Restaurant 6:30 am-10 pm. Rm serv 24 hrs. Bar 11-2 am. Ck-out noon. Convention facilities. Business center. In-rm modem link. Concierge. Shopping arcade. Barber, beauty shop. Airport transportation. Exercise equipt; weight machine, bicycles. Minibars. Luxury level. Cr cds: A, C, D, ER, JCB, MC, V. D ⛵ 🏋 🚫 🐾 SC ⛷

★ ★ ★ **SHERATON CAVALIER.** *(2620 32nd Ave NE, Calgary AB T1Y 6B8) 403/291-0107; FAX 403/291-2834.* 306 rms, 8 story. S $195; D $205; each addl $10; suites $250-$280; under 18 free. Crib free. Pet accepted, some restrictions. TV; cable (premium). Sauna. Indoor pool; wading pool, whirlpools, poolside serv, 2 water slides. Coffee in rms. Restaurant 6:30 am-10 pm. Bar 11-12:30 am. Ck-out noon. Convention facilities. Business servs avail. In-rm modem link. Gift shop. Free airport transportation. Game rm. Minibars. Cr cds: A, C, D, ER, MC, V. D ⛵ ≈ 🚫 🐾 SC

★ ★ ★ **THE WESTIN.** *(320 4th Ave SW, Calgary AB T2P 2S6) 403/266-1611; FAX 403/233-7471; res: 800/228-3000.* 525 rms, 17 & 19 story. S $119-$178; D $129-$188; each addl $10; suites $285-$660; under 18 free; wknd rates. Crib free. Pet accepted, some restrictions. TV; cable (premium), VCR avail. Indoor pool; poolside serv. Restaurant 6:30 am-11 pm. Rm serv 24 hrs. Bar 11:30-1 am. Ck-out 1 pm. Lndry facilities. Convention facilities. Business servs avail. In-rm modem link. Concierge. Barber. Indoor valet parking. Exercise equipt; weights, bicycles, sauna. Minibars. Downtown; skywalk to adj shopping mall. Cr cds: A, C, D, DS, ER, JCB, MC, V. D ⛵ ≈ 🏋 🚫 🐾 SC

Edmonton, Alberta

Motor Hotels

★ ★ **BEST WESTERN CEDAR PARK INN.** *(5116 Calgary Trail N (Hwy 2), Edmonton AB T6H 2H4) 403/434-7411; FAX 403/437-4836.* 190 rms, 5 story. S, D $72-$92; each addl $5; suites $135-$150; family rates. Crib free. Pet accepted, some restrictions. TV; cable. Sauna. Heated pool. Restaurant 7 am-11 pm; also 24-hr snack shop. Rm serv. Bar 11:30-1 am. Ck-out noon. Meeting rms. Business servs avail. In-rm modem link. Gift shop. Free airport transportation. Cr cds: A, D, DS, ER, JCB, MC, V. ⛵ ≈ 🚫 🐾 SC

✔ ★ ★ **CHATEAU LOUIS.** *(11727 Kingsway Ave, Edmonton AB T5G 3A1) 403/452-7770; FAX 403/454-3436; res: 800/661-9843.* 147 rms, 3 story. S $65; D $70; each addl $6; suites $100-$125; wkend rates; under 12 free. Crib $3. Pet accepted, some restrictions. TV; cable, VCR (movies $5). Complimentary coffee in rms. Restaurant 6 am-midnight; Sat from

7 am; Sun, hols from 8 am. Rm serv 24 hrs. Bars 11-2 am; entertainment. Ck-out noon.
Meeting rms. Business servs avail. In-rm modem link. Valet serv. Airport transportation.
Some minibars. Outdoor patio dining. Some in-rm whirlpools in suites. Cr cds: A, C, D, ER,
MC, V. 🖕 🔄 🐾 SC

★ ★ NISKU INN. *(Edmonton Intl Airport AB T5J 2T2) off Hwy 2, opp Intl Airport.*
403/955-7744; FAX 403/955-7743; res: 800/661-6966. 160 rms, 2 story. S $89; D $99; each
addl $8; suites $129-$189; under 18 free; wkend rates. Crib free. Pet accepted, some
restrictions. TV; cable, VCR avail (movies). Indoor pool; whirlpool. Restaurant 6 am-11 pm.
Rm serv. Bar 11:30-2 am. Ck-out noon. Meeting rms. Business center. In-rm modem link.
Sundries. Gift shop. Free airport transportation 24 hrs. Downhill ski 10 mi. Sauna. Some
in-rm whirlpools. Courtyard atrium. Cr cds: A, D, ER, MC, V.
D 🖕 🔄 ✈ 🔄 🐾 SC 🎣

✔ ★ ★ ROYAL INN. *(10010 178th St, Edmonton AB T5S 1T3) 403/484-6000; FAX*
403/489-2900; res: 800/661-4879 (CAN). 194 rms, 4 story. S $59-$95; D $59-$103; each
addl $8; wkend rates. Crib free. Pet accepted. TV; cable, VCR. Restaurants 6:30 am-10 pm.
Rm serv. Bar noon-1 am. Meeting rms. Business servs avail. In-rm modem
link. Bellhops. Valet serv. Sundries. Gift shop. Exercise equipt; bicycles, treadmill, steam rm.
Whirlpool. Refrigerator in suites; some in-rm whirlpools. Cr cds: A, ER, MC, V.
D 🖕 ✗ 🔄 🐾 SC

Hotels

★ ★ COAST TERRACE INN. *(4440 Calgary Trail North, Edmonton AB T6H 5C2)*
403/437-6010; FAX 403/431-5801; 800 888/837-7223. 223 rms, 4 story. S, D $90-$180;
suites $99-$199; under 18 free; wkend rates; package plans. Pet accepted, some restrictions. TV; cable. Heated pool; whirlpool. Restaurant 6:30 am-10 pm. Rm serv 24 hrs. Bar
11:30-1 am; entertainment. Ck-out 1 pm. Meeting rms. Business servs avail. In-rm modem
link. Bellhops. Gift shop. Barber, beauty shop. Underground parking. Exercise equipt;
weights, bicycles, steam rm, sauna. Minibars. Balconies. Luxury level. Cr cds: A, D, DS, ER,
JCB, MC, V. D 🖕 🔄 ✗ ✗ 🔄 🐾 SC

★ ★ CROWNE PLAZA CHATEAU LACOMBE. *(10111 Bellamy Hill, Edmonton AB*
T5J 1N7) 403/428-6611; FAX 403/425-6564. 307 rms, 24 story. S $150; D $165; each addl
$15; suites $180-$275; under 18 free; wkend rates. Crib free. Pet accepted, some restric-
tions. TV; cable, VCR avail. Restaurant 6:30 am-9 pm, Fri, Sat to 11 pm. Bar 11-1 am.
Ck-out 1 pm. Meeting rms. Business servs avail. In-rm modem link. Garage parking; valet.
Exercise equipt; weights, bicycles. Minibars. Some balconies. Luxury level. Cr cds: A, C, D,
DS, ER, MC, V. D 🖕 ✗ 🔄 🐾 SC

★ ★ EDMONTON INN. *(11830 Kingsway Ave, Edmonton AB T5G 0X5) 403/454-*
9521; FAX 403/453-7360; res: 800/661-7264 (CAN). 431 rms, 6-9 & 15 story. S, D $110-
$120; each addl $10; suites to $385; under 18 free; wkend rates. Crib free. Pet accepted,
some restrictions. TV; cable. Restaurants 6:30 am-midnight; Sat, Sun from 7 am. Bar;
entertainment. Ck-out 11 am. Convention facilities. Business servs avail. In-rm modem link.
Gift shop. Beauty shop. Local airport transportation. Some refrigerators. Balconies. Cr cds:
A, D, DS, ER, MC, V. D 🖕 🔄 🐾 SC

★ ★ ★ HOTEL MACDONALD. *(10065 100th St, Edmonton AB T5J 0N6) 403/424-*
5181; FAX 403/424-8017; res: 800/441-1414. Restored to its 1915 glory, this chateau-like
property on the North Saskatchewan River features ornamental plasterwork and original
artwork in the lobby. Gardens and gazebos grace the spacious grounds. 198 rms, 8
story. S $139-$220; D $159-$240; each addl $20; suites $300-$2,500; under 18 free;
wkend rates. Crib free. Pet accepted, some restrictions. Valet parking. TV; cable (premium). Indoor pool; wading pool, whirlpool, poolside serv. Restaurant 6:30 am-10 pm.
Rm serv 24 hrs. Bar 11-1 am. Ck-out 1 pm. Meeting rms. Business servs avail. In-rm
modem link. Concierge. Gift shop. Exercise rm; instructor, weight machine, bicycles,
sauna. Massage. Sun deck. Game rm. Minibars. Cr cds: A, C, D, DS, ER, JCB, MC, V.
D 🖕 🔄 ✗ 🔄 🐾 SC

★ ★ INN ON 7TH. *(10001 107th St, Edmonton AB T5J 1J1) 403/429-2861; FAX*
403/426-7225; res: 800/661-7327 (AB). 172 rms, 14 story. S $118; D $128; suites $170;
each addl $10; under 12 free. Crib free. Pet accepted. TV; cable (premium). Restaurant 6:30
am-9 pm. Bar 11 am-11 pm. Ck-out 11 am. Meeting rms. Business servs avail. Cr cds: A, D,
DS, ER, MC, V. D 🖕 🔄 🐾 SC

★ ★ TOWER ON THE PARK. *(9715 110th St, Edmonton AB T5K 2M1) 403/488-*
1626; FAX 403/488-0659; res: 800/661-6454 (CAN). 98 kit. suites, 14 story. 1-bedrm $79;
2-bedrm $89; wkly, monthly rates. Crib $5. Pet accepted. TV; cable. Complimentary conti-

nental bkfst. Coffee, tea in rms. Ck-out noon. Meeting rms. Business servs avail. Covered parking. Lndry facilities. Balconies. Italian marble, mirrored lobby. Cr cds: A, D, ER, MC, V. 🖘 ⊠ 🔥

Fort Macleod, Alberta (See also Lethbridge)

Motel

✔★ **SUNSET.** *(104 Hwy 3W, Fort Macleod AB T0L 0Z0) at W edge of town. 403/553-4448; res: 888/554-2784; FAX 403/553-2784.* E-mail sunsetmo@telusplanet.net. 22 rms, 3 kits. June-Sept: S $46; D $52; each addl $4; kit. units $74-$85; varied lower rates rest of yr. Crib free. Pet accepted. TV; cable. Coffee in office. Restaurant nearby. Ck-out 11 am. Refrigerators. Cr cds: A, D, DS, ER, MC, V. 🖘 ⊠ 🔥 SC

Jasper National Park, Alberta

Motels

(Because of the altitude, air conditioning is rarely necessary)

★★ **AMETHYST LODGE.** *(200 Connaught Dr, Jasper National Park AB T0E 1E0) 200 Connaught Dr. 403/852-3394; FAX 403/852-5198; res: 800/661-9935 (W CAN).* 97 rms, 3 story. June-Sept: S, D $151-$205; each addl $10; under 15 free; lower rates rest of yr. Pet accepted, some restrictions. TV; cable (premium). Complimentary coffee in rms. Restaurant 7-10 am, 5-10 pm; also noon-2 pm in season. Bar 4 pm-midnight. Ck-out 11 am. Meeting rms. Business center. Bellhops. Free RR station, bus depot transportation. Downhill/x-country ski 15 mi. 2 whirlpools. Balconies. Cr cds: A, D, ER, JCB, MC, V. D 🖘 🏊 ⊠ 🔥 🎿

★★ **LOBSTICK LODGE.** *(Box 1200, Jasper National Park AB T0E 1E0) Juniper at Geikie St. 403/852-4431; FAX 403/852-4142; res: 800/661-9317 (W CAN).* 138 rms, 3 story, 43 kits. No A/C. June-Sept: S, D $151; each addl $10; suites, kit. units $166; under 15 free; MAP avail; ski plans; lower rates rest of yr. Crib free. Pet accepted, some restrictions. TV; cable (premium). Sauna, steam rm. Heated pool; 2 whirlpools. Restaurant 7-11 am, 5-10 pm; summer 6:30-11 am, 5-11 pm. Bar 5 pm-midnight. Ck-out 11 am. Coin lndry. Business servs avail. Downhill/x-country ski 15 mi. Cr cds: A, D, ER, JCB, MC, V. D 🖘 🏊 ⊠ ⊠ 🔥

★★ **MARMOT LODGE.** *(86 Connaught Dr, Jasper National Park AB T0E 1E0) 86 Connaught Dr. 403/852-4471; FAX 403/852-3280; res: 800/661-6521 (W CAN).* 107 rms, 47 A/C, 2 story. June-Sept: S, D $131-$178; each addl $10; suites $178-$325; under 16 free; ski plan; lower rates rest of yr. Pet accepted, some restrictions. TV; cable. Heated pool; whirlpool, sauna. Complimentary coffee. Restaurant 6:30-11 am, 5-10 pm. Bar 4:30 pm-1 am. Ck-out 11 am. Coin lndry. Meeting rm. Business servs avail. Valet serv. RR station, bus depot transportation. Downhill/x-country ski 15 mi. Fireplace in some kit. units. Private patios, balconies. Grills. Ski waxing rm & lockers in winter. Cr cds: A, D, JCB, MC, V. D 🖘 🏊 ⊠ ⊠ 🔥

Lodge

★★ **OVERLANDER MOUNTAIN.** *(Hinton AB T7V 1X5) 403/866-2330.* 29 rms, 2 story. No A/C. No rm phone. May-Oct: S, D $100-$140; each addl $20; kit. units $125; lower rates rest of yr. Crib free. Pet accepted. Complimentary coffee in rms. Restaurant 7:30-10:30 am, 5:30-9:30 pm. Ck-out noon. Meeting rms. Business servs avail. X-country ski 15 mi. Some refrigerators. Some balconies. Cr cds: A, MC, V. 🖘 ➡ 🏊

Resort

★★★ **JASPER PARK LODGE.** *(Box 40, Jasper National Park AB T0E 1E0) 2 mi E off Hwy 16. 403/852-3301; FAX 403/852-5107; res: 800/441-1414.* 442 units, 5 cabins. No A/C. Late May-mid-Oct: S, D $364-$544; each addl $22; under 18 free; MAP avail; lower rates rest of yr. Crib free. Pet accepted, some restrictions. TV; cable. Heated pool; whirlpool, lifeguard. Supervised child's activities; ages 2 and up. Dining rm 6-9 pm. Box lunches. Rm serv. Bar 11-1 am. Ck-out noon, ck-in 4:30 pm. Business servs avail. In-rm modem link. Shopping arcade. Airport, RR station, bus depot transportation. Tennis, pro. 18-hole golf, greens fee $45-$75, putting green, driving range. Swimming. Rowboats, canoes, sailboats. Whitewater rafting. Downhill ski 15 mi; x-country ski on site. Bicycles. Lawn games. Soc dir; entertainment, dancing, movies. Rec rm. Game rm. Exercise rm; instructor, weights, bicycles, sauna, steam rm. Massage. Fishing guides. Minibars; some refrigerators, fireplaces. Some private patios, balconies. Cr cds: A, C, D, DS, ER, JCB, MC, V. D 🖘 ➡ 🎿 🏊 🏋 🎿 ➡ 🎣 ⊠ ⊠ 🔥

Lake Louise, Alberta *(See also Banff)*

Motel

(Because of the altitude, air conditioning is rarely necessary)

★ ★ **CASTLE MOUNTAIN VILLAGE.** *(Lake Louise AB T0L 1E0) 18 mi (29 km) E on Trans-Canada Hwy 1, just N of Castle Junction, in Banff National Park.* 403/522-2783; FAX 403/762-8629. 21 kit. cottages, 8 with shower only, 7 suites. No A/C. No rm phones. S, D $150-$210. Crib $5. Pet accepted; $10. TV. Restaurant nearby. Ck-out 10:30 am. Coin lndry. Gift shop. Grocery store. Downhill ski 20 mi; x-country ski on site. Exercise equipt; weights, rowers. Some in-rm whirlpools, fireplaces. Cr cds: MC, V. 🐾 🏂 ✕ 🛶

Hotel

★ ★ ★ **CHATEAU LAKE LOUISE.** *(2¹/₂ mi SE off Trans-Canada Hwy 1, Lake Louise AB T0L 1E0)* 403/522-3511; FAX 403/522-3834; res: 800/441-1414. 511 rms, 8 story. Mid-May-mid-Oct: S $275; D $445; each addl $20; suites $560-$1,350; under 18 free; lower rates rest of yr. Pet accepted; $20. Covered parking $5/day. TV; cable, VCR avail. Steam rm. Indoor pool; whirlpool. 6 dining rms. Bars noon-2 am; entertainment. Ck-out noon. Convention facilities. Business servs avail. In-rm modem link. Shopping arcade. Airport transportation. Downhill ski 5 mi; x-country ski on site. Sleigh rides, ice-skating. Minibars. Some balconies. Resort-like hotel on Lake Louise, surrounded by rolling lawns and large flower gardens. Cr cds: A, C, D, DS, ER, JCB, MC, V. 🅳 🐾 ⚕ 🏂 ⛵ 🎣 🛶 🛶

Lethbridge, Alberta *(See also Fort Macleod)*

Hotel

★ ★ ★ **LETHBRIDGE LODGE.** *(320 Scenic Dr, Lethbridge AB T1J 4B4)* 403/328-1123; FAX 403/328-0002; res: 800/661-1232. 191 rms, 4 story. S $81-$88; D $83-$90; each addl $7; suites $106-$130; under 18 free. Crib free. Pet accepted, some restrictions. TV; cable. Heated pool; whirlpool. Restaurant 6:30 am-11 pm. Bar 11 am-midnight; entertainment exc Sun. Ck-out noon. Meeting rms. Business servs avail. Health club privileges. Some refrigerators. Overlooks gorge & Univ of Lethbridge. Cr cds: A, D, ER, MC, V.
🐾 ⛵ 🛶 🛶 SC

Medicine Hat, Alberta

Motels

★ ★ **BEST WESTERN INN.** *(722 Redcliff Dr, Medicine Hat AB T1A 5E3) 1¹/₂ mi W, 3 blks N of Hwy 3, near Municipal Airport.* 403/527-3700; FAX 403/526-8689. 110 rms, 2 story, 24 suites, 11 kits. S $69; D $75-$79; suites $119; kit. units $73-$83. Crib $3. Pet accepted. TV; cable (premium). 2 indoor pools; 2 whirlpools. Complimentary continental bkfst. Restaurant adj 6 am-10:30 pm. Bar. Ck-out 11 am. Coin lndry. Meeting rms. Business servs avail. Sundries. Exercise equipt; weight machine, stair machine, sauna. Game rm. Refrigerators, microwaves. Cr cds: A, C, D, DS, ER, MC, V. 🅳 🐾 ⛵ 🛶 🛶 SC

★ **SUPER 8.** *(1280 Transcanada Way SE, Medicine Hat ON T1B 1J5) opp Southview Mall.* 403/528-8888; FAX 403/526-4445. 70 rms, 3 story, 8 kit. units. Late June-early Sept: S $59.88; D $63.88-$68.88; each addl $4; suite $114.88; kit. units $78.88; under 12 free; wkly rates; higher rates Exhibition and Stampede; lower rates rest of yr. Crib free. Pet accepted. TV; cable. Indoor pool; whirlpool. Complimentary continental bkfst. Restaurant opp open 24 hrs. Ck-out 11 am. Business servs avail. Cr cds: A, D, DS, ER, MC, V. 🅳 🐾 ⛵ 🛶 🛶 SC

Motor Hotel

★ ★ ★ **MEDICINE HAT LODGE.** *(1051 Ross Glen Dr SE, Medicine Hat AB T1B 3T8) at jct Trans-Canada Hwy 1 & Dunmore Rd.* 403/529-2222; FAX 403/529-1538; res: 800/661-8095. 190 rms, 4 story. S, D $79-$87; suites $109-$239; under 18 free. Crib free. Pet accepted. TV; cable, VCR avail. Indoor pool; wading pool, whirlpool. Coffee in rms. Restaurant 6:30 am-11 pm. Rm serv. Bar noon-1 am. Ck-out noon. Meeting rms. Business servs avail. In-rm modem link. Bellhops. Sundries. Gift shop. Barber, beauty shop. Exercise equipt; bicycles, treadmill, sauna. Game rm. Balconies. Cr cds: A, C, D, DS, ER, MC, V.
🅳 🐾 ⛵ ✕ 🛶 🛶 SC

Red Deer, Alberta

Motels

✔★★ **NORTH HILL INN.** *(7150 50th Ave (Hwy 2A), Red Deer AB T4N 6A5)* *403/343-8800; FAX 403/342-2334; res: 800/662-7152 (AB).* 98 rms, 3 story. S $62; D $66; under 12 free; wknd rates; golf plans. Crib free. Pet accepted, some restrictions. TV; cable (premium), VCR avail. Heated pool; whirlpool, sauna. Restaurant 6 am-10 pm. Rm serv. Bar; entertainment. Ck-out 11 am. Meeting rms. Business center. In-rm modem link. Downhill ski 10 mi; x-country ski 3 mi. Luxury level. Cr cds: A, D, ER, MC, V.

🐾 ⊁ ≈ 🦮 SC 🏌

✔★ **RAINBOW MOTOR INN.** *(2803 50th Ave (Hwy 2A), Red Deer AB T4R 1H1)* *403/343-2112; FAX 403/340-8540; res: 800/223-1993 (AB, BC, SK).* 88 rms, 2 story, 12 kits. S, D $47-$55; each addl $6; kit. units $53-$68; under 12 free. Crib free. Pet accepted, some restrictions. TV; cable (premium), VCR avail (movies). Restaurant 6:30 am-9 pm; wkends from 7 am. Ck-out noon. Meeting rm. Business servs avail. In-rm modem link. Downhill ski 10 mi; x-country ski 3 mi. Refrigerators. Picnic tables. Courtyard. Cr cds: A, C, D, ER, MC, V. 🐾 ⊁ ≈ 🦮 SC

✔★ **TRAVELODGE.** *(2807 50th Ave, Red Deer AB T4R 1H1)* *403/346-2011; FAX 403/346-1075; res: 800/578-7878.* 136 rms, 3 story, 10 kits. S $59; D $64; suites $90; under 12 free. Crib avail. Pet accepted. TV; cable. Indoor pool; whirlpool. Restaurant 6:30 am-1 pm, 5-10 pm. Rm serv. Ck-out 11 am. Business servs avail. Coin lndry. Downhill ski 10 mi; x-country ski 3 mi. Cr cds: A, D, ER, MC, V. 🐾 ⊁ ≈ 🦮 SC

Hotels

✔★★★ **CAPRI CENTRE.** *(3310 Gaetz Ave, Red Deer AB T4N 3X9) at the top of the South Hill.* *403/346-2091; FAX 403/346-4790; res: 800/662-7197 (AB).* 175 rms, 14 story, 22 kits. S $70-$85; D $70-$100; each addl $15; suites, kit. units $145-$300; under 16 free. Pet accepted, some restrictions. TV; cable, VCR avail. Heated pool; whirlpool. Restaurant 7 am-midnight. Bar 11-2 am; entertainment. Ck-out noon. Meeting rms. Business center. In-rm modem link. Shopping arcade. Barber, beauty shop. Airport transportation. Downhill ski 10 mi; x-country ski 3 mi. Exercise equipt; weights, bicycles, sauna, steam rm. Some refrigerators. Some balconies. Cr cds: A, C, D, ER, MC, V. D 🐾 ⊁ ≈ 🏌 🦮 SC 🏌

★★ **HOLIDAY INN.** *(6500 67th St, Red Deer AB T4P 1A2)* *403/342-6567; FAX 403/343-3600.* 97 rms, 4 story. S, D $70-$89; suites from $140; under 10 free; golf packages. Crib free. Pet accepted. TV; cable (premium). Complimentary coffee in rms. Restaurant 6 am-11 pm; Bar 11-2 am. Ck-out 11 am. Business center. In-rm modem link. Barber, beauty shop. Downhill ski 10 mi; x-country ski 2 mi. Exercise equipt; weights, bicycles, sauna. Whirlpool. Cr cds: A, C, D, DS, ER, JCB, MC, V.

D 🐾 ⊁ 🏌 🦮 SC 🏌

Waterton Lakes National Park, Alberta

(Because of the altitude, air conditioning is rarely necessary)

Lodge

★★ **CRANDELL MOUNTAIN.** *(102 Mount View Rd, Waterton Lakes National Park AB T0K 2M0)* *403/859-2288.* 17 rms, 2 story, 8 kit. units. No A/C. No rm phones. June-Sept: S $99-$149; D $104-$149; each addl $10; kit. units $119-$169; 2-day min hols; lower rates rest of yr. Crib $7. Pet accepted, some restrictions. TV. Coffee in rms. Restaurant opp 7:30 am-10 pm. Ck-out 10 am. Meeting rms. Some fireplaces. Cr cds: A, DS, ER, MC, V.

D 🐾 🦮

Kamloops, British Columbia

Motel

★★ **STAY 'N SAVE.** *(1325 Columbia St W, Kamloops BC V2C 2P4)* *250/374-8877; FAX 604/372-0507.* 83 rms, 3 story, 25 kit. units. S $89; D $99; each addl $10; suites $120; kit. units $99-$130; under 17 free; ski plans. Crib free. Pet accepted. TV; cable. Heated pool; whirlpool. Complimentary coffee in lobby. Restaurant adj open 24 hrs. Ck-out 11 am. Coin lndry. Meeting rms. Business servs avail. In-rm modem link. Valet serv. X-country ski 15 mi. Exercise equipt; bicycle, stair machine, sauna. Picnic tables. Cr cds: A, D, ER, MC, V. D 🐾 ⊁ ≈ 🏌 🦮 SC

Motor Hotel

★ ★ **DAYS INN.** *([B85 W Trans-Canada Hwy 1, Kamloops BC V2E 2J7)* 250/374-5911; FAX 250/374-6922; res: 800/561-5002 (AB, BC).* 60 rms. June-Sept: S $99; D $109; each addl $10; suites $125-$250; kits. $150-$250; under 12 free; lower rates rest of yr. Crib free. Pet accepted, some restrictions. TV; cable (premium), VCR avail. Heated pool; whirlpool. Restaurant 7 am-9 pm. Ck-out noon. Meeting rms. Business servs avail. Refrigerators. Cr cds: A, D, ER, MC, V. 🐾 ⚏ ⊠ 🐾 SC

Kelowna, British Columbia *(See also Penticton)*

Motel

★ **SANDMAN HOTEL.** *(2130 Harvey Ave (Hwy 97N), Kelowna BC V1Y 6G8)* 250/860-6409; FAX 250/860-7377; res: 800/726-3626.* 120 rms, 3 story. S $77-$87; D $85-$89; each addl $5; kit. units $10 addl; under 12 free. Crib free. Pet accepted, some restrictions. TV; cable. Sauna. Pool; whirlpool. Restaurant open 24 hrs. Bar 11-1 am. Ck-out noon. Meeting rms. Business servs avail. Sundries. Refrigerators. Balconies. Cr cds: A, C, D, DS, ER, JCB, MC, V. 🐾 ⚏ ⊠ 🐾 SC

Nanaimo, British Columbia *(See also Vancouver, Victoria)*

Motel

★ **DAYS INN HARBOURVIEW.** *(809 Island Hwy S, Nanaimo BC V9R 5K1)* 250/754-8171; FAX 250/754-8557.* 79 rms, 2 story, 16 kits. June-Sept: S $83; D $93; each addl $10; suites $120; kit. units $85-$115; under 13 free; lower rates rest of yr. Crib $5. Pet accepted; $7/day. TV; cable (premium), VCR avail. Indoor pool; whirlpool. Restaurant 6 am-10 pm. Rm serv. Ck-out 11 am. Coin lndry. Meeting rms. Business servs avail. Sundries. Some refrigerators. Overlooking Nanaimo's inner harbour. Cr cds: A, D, DS, ER, JCB, MC, V. D 🐾 ➤ ⚏ ⊠ 🐾 SC

Hotel

★ ★ **COAST BASTION INN.** *(11 Bastion St, Nanaimo BC V9R 2Z9)* 250/753-6601; FAX 250/753-4155; res: 800/663-1144.* 179 rms, 14 story. Mid-May-mid-Sept: S, D $120-$130; each addl $10; suites $198-$208; under 18 free; package plans; lower rates rest of yr. Crib free. Pet accepted. TV; cable (premium). Restaurant 6:30 am-9 pm. Bar 11:30-1 am; entertainment exc Sun. Ck-out 1 pm. Meeting rms. Business servs avail. Gift shop. Barber, beauty shop. Exercise equipt; weight machine, bicycles, sauna. Whirlpool. Many minibars. Balconies. Ocean 1 blk; swimming. Cr cds: A, D, MC, V. 🐾 ➤ 🏃 ⊠ 🐾 SC

Penticton, British Columbia *(See also Kelowna)*

Motel

★ ★ **RAMADA COURTYARD INN.** *(1050 Eckhardt Ave W, Penticton BC V2A 2C3)* 250/492-8926; FAX 250/492-2778.* 50 rms. Mid-May-mid-Sept: S, D $95; each addl $10; under 12 free; lower rates rest of yr. Pet accepted, some restrictions. TV; cable (premium). Heated pool. Restaurant nearby open 24 hrs. Bar. Ck-out 11 am. Coin lndry. Meeting rms. Business servs avail. Valet serv. Lawn games. Some refrigerators, fireplaces. Private patios. Picnic tables, grill. Cr cds: A, D, DS, ER, MC, V. 🐾 ⚏ ⊠ 🐾

Hotel

★ ★ ★ **CLARION LAKESIDE RESORT.** *(21 Lakeshore Dr W, Penticton BC V2A 7M5)* 250/493-8221; FAX 250/493-0607; res: 800/663-1144.* 204 rms, 6 story. July-Aug: S, D $175-$195; each addl $15; under 16 free; golf plans; lower rates rest of yr. Crib free. Pet accepted, some restrictions. TV; cable (premium), VCR avail. Indoor pool; whirlpool. Supervised child's activities (late May-Labor Day); ages 3-17. Restaurant 7 am-11 pm. Bar noon-2 am; seasonal entertainment. Meeting rms. Business servs avail. In-rm modem link. Gift shop. Beauty shop. Tennis. Golf privileges. Downhill/x-country ski 20 mi. Exercise rm; instructor, weights, bicycles, sauna. Game rm. Balconies. On Okanagan Lake; swimming, boat rides. Cr cds: A, D, ER, MC, V. D 🐾 ➤ 🏃 ⚏ ⊠ 🏃 ⊠ 🐾 SC

Revelstoke, British Columbia

Motel

✔ ★ **CANYON MOTOR INN.** *(Box 740, Revelstoke BC V0E 2S0) Trans-Canada Hwy 1 & Columbia River Bridge.* 250/837-5221.* 40 rms, 1-2 story, 12 kits. May-Oct: S $44-$76; D $50-$100; each addl $7; kit. units $7 addl; lower rates rest of yr. Crib free. Pet accepted. TV; cable. Restaurant 6 am-10 pm. Rm serv. Ck-out noon. Coin lndry. Meeting rms. Sundries. Downhill/x-country ski 5 mi. Sauna. Whirlpool. Refrigerators. Private patios, balconies. Picnic tables. On riverbank. RV park on property. Cr cds: A, D, DS, ER, MC, V.

[icons]

Vancouver, British Columbia

(See also Nanaimo, Victoria; also see Bellingham, WA)

Motor Hotels

★ ★ **QUALITY HOTEL-DOWNTOWN.** *(1335 Howe St, Vancouver BC V6Z 1R7)* downtown. *604/682-0229; FAX 604/662-7566.* 157 units, 7 story, 25 suites. May-Sept: S $140; D $160; each addl $16; suites $170-$190; under 18 free; lower rates rest of yr. Crib free. Pet accepted. Garage $6. TV; cable. Pool. Restaurant 7 am-10 pm. Rm serv. Bar 11:30-1 am. Ck-out 11 am. Meeting rms. Business servs avail. Bellhops. Valet serv. Some refrigerators. Cr cds: A, C, D, DS, ER, JCB, MC, V. [icons]

↙ ★ ★ **STAY 'N SAVE-AIRPORT.** *(10551 St Edward Dr, Richmond BC V6X 3L8)* Hwy 99 exit 39, near Vancouver Airport. *604/273-3311; FAX 604/273-9522; res: 800/663-0298.* 206 rms, 3 story. Mid-May-Sept: S $104; D $114; each addl $10; suites $120-$130; kits. $10 addl; under 16 free; lower rates rest of yr. Crib free. Pet accepted. TV; cable, VCR avail (movies free). Complimentary coffee in rms. Restaurant 6:30 am-11 pm. Ck-out 11 am. Coin lndry. Meeting rms. Business servs avail. Valet serv. Free airport transportation. Exercise equipt; stair machine, bicycles. Whirlpool. Cr cds: A, C, D, ER, MC, V.

[icons]

Hotels

★ ★ ★ **DELTA PACIFIC.** *(10251 St Edwards Dr, Richmond BC V6X 2M9)* 8 mi S via Hwy 99. *604/278-9611; FAX 604/276-1121; res: 800/877-1133 (US), 800/268-1133 (CAN).* 460 rms, 2, 11 & 17 story. Apr-Oct: S, D $155-$185; each addl $15; suites $250-$350; under 18 free; lower rates rest of yr. Crib free. Pet accepted. TV; cable. 3 pools, 1 indoor; whirlpool, poolside serv. Playground. Supervised child's activities; ages 5-12. 2 restaurants 6:30 am-11 pm. Rm serv 24 hrs. Bar 11-1 am. Ck-out noon. Convention facilities. Business center. In-rm modem link. Gift shop. Beauty shop. Golf privileges. Lighted & indoor tennis. Exercise rm; instructor, weight machine, treadmill, sauna. Massage. Squash courts. Private patios, balconies. Cr cds: A, C, D, DS, ER, JCB, MC, V.

[icons]

★ ★ ★ **FOUR SEASONS.** *(791 W Georgia St, Vancouver BC V6C 2T4)* downtown. *604/689-9333; FAX 604/684-4555.* Web www.fshr.com. Tasteful pastel-hued decor, outstanding service and large, luxurious rooms create an atmosphere of calm in this bustling high-rise above the Pacific Centre shopping mall and adjacent to the Vancouver Stock Exchange. Notable are the glamorous atrium bar/restaurant and a partially covered pool on a sun terrace. 385 rms, 28 story. May-Oct: S, D $280-$495; each addl $25; suites $450-$2,200; under 18 free; wknd rates; lower rates rest of yr. Crib free. Pet accepted. Garage $20/day. TV; cable (premium), VCR (movies). Heated pool; whirlpool. Restaurant 6:30 am-11 pm. Rm serv 24 hrs. Bar 11:30-1 am. Ck-out noon. Meeting rms. Business center. In-rm modem link. Concierge. Shopping arcade. Tennis privileges. Downhill ski 10 mi. Exercise rm; instructor, weights, bicycles, sauna. Shuffleboard. Minibars. Cr cds: A, C, D, ER, JCB, MC, V. [icons]

★ ★ ★ **GEORGIAN COURT.** *(773 Beatty St, Vancouver BC V6B 2M4)* downtown. *604/682-5555; FAX 604/682-8830; res: 800/663-1155.* 180 rms, 12 story. May-Oct: S $170; D $190; each addl $20; suites $195-$450; under 18 free; lower rates rest of yr. Crib free. Pet accepted, some restrictions. Parking $7. TV; cable (premium). Restaurant 6:30 am-9:30 pm. Bar. Ck-out 1 pm. Meeting rms. Business servs avail. In-rm modem link. Concierge. Gift shop. Exercise equipt; weight machine, bicycles, sauna. Whirlpool. Bathrm phones, minibars. Balconies. Italian marble in bathrms. Cr cds: A, C, D, ER, JCB, MC, V.

[icons]

★ ★ **HOLIDAY INN VANCOUVER CENTER.** *(711 W Broadway, Vancouver BC V5Z 3Y2)* at Heather St, south of downtown. *604/879-0511; FAX 604/872-7520.* 200 rms, 16 story. May-Oct: S $179; D $199; each addl $20; suites $275-$325; under 19 free; wkend rates; lower rates rest of yr. Crib free. Pet accepted, some restrictions. TV; cable. Indoor pool. Restaurant 7 am-10 pm. Bar 11-1 am. Ck-out noon. Meeting rms. Business servs avail. In-rm modem link. Gift shop. Exercise rm; instructor, weights, bicycles, sauna. Massage. Refrigerator in suites. Balconies. Cr cds: A, C, D, DS, ER, JCB, MC, V.

[icons]

★ ★ **HOTEL VANCOUVER.** *(900 W Georgia St, Vancouver BC V6C 2W6)* downtown. *604/684-3131; FAX 604/662-1929; res: 800/441-1414.* 550 rms, 14 story. Late Apr-early Oct: S $180-$340; D $205-$365; each addl $25; suites $305-$1,830; family, wknd rates; lower rates rest of yr. Pet accepted. TV; cable (premium), VCR avail. Indoor pool; wading pool; whirlpool. Restaurant 6 am-10 pm. Rm serv 24 hrs. Bars 11-1 am; entertainment. Ck-out noon. Meeting rms. Business center. In-rm modem link. Concierge. Shopping arcade. Beauty shop. Exercise rm; instructor, weights, bicycles, sauna. Refrigerator in suites. Luxury level. Cr cds: A, C, D, DS, ER, JCB, MC, V.

★ ★ ★ **THE METROPOLITAN.** *(645 Howe St, Vancouver BC V6C 2Y9) downtown.* 604/687-1122; FAX 604/689-7044; res: 800/667-2300. 197 units, 18 story. May-Oct: S $325; D $345; each addl $20; suites $425-$1,500; under 18 free; wkend rates. Crib free. Pet accepted. Covered parking $16. TV; cable (premium), VCR avail. Indoor pool; whirlpool, poolside serv. Complimentary coffee, tea in rms. Restaurant 6:30 am-11 pm. Rm serv 24 hrs. Bar 11:30-1 am. Ck-out 1 pm. Convention facilities. Business center. In-rm modem link. Concierge. Exercise rm; instructor, weights, bicycles, sauna, steam rm. Bathrm phones, refrigerators. Private patios, balconies. Library. Artwork, antiques; elaborate floral arrangements. Elegant Oriental touches. Cr cds: A, C, D, DS, ER, JCB, MC, V.

★ ★ ★ ★ **PAN PACIFIC VANCOUVER.** *(300-999 Canada Place, Vancouver BC V6C 3B5) adj trade & convention center, downtown.* 604/662-8111; FAX 604/685-8690; res: 800/663-1515. Dramatically positioned at the cruise-ship complex, looking over the bay toward Stanley Park and the mountains, this ultra-modern luxury hotel has comfortable Asian-accented rooms with fine views. There's a well-equipped gym and sports center and several bars, cafes and restaurants. 506 rms, 23 story. Mid-Apr-late Oct: S, D, studios $400-$430; each addl $30; suites $525-$2,000; under 18 free; wkend rates; lower rates rest of yr. Crib free. Pet accepted. Garage $20; valet. TV; cable, VCR avail. Heated pool; whirlpool. Restaurant 6:30 am-11 pm. Rm serv 24 hrs. Bar 11:30-1 am. Ck-out 1 pm. Convention facilities. Business center. In-rm modem link. Concierge. Shopping arcade. Barber, beauty shop. Exercise rm; instructor, weights, bicycles, sauna, steam rm. Massage. Bathrm phones, refrigerators; some in-rm steam baths. Cr cds: A, C, D, ER, JCB, MC, V.

★ ★ ★ **RENAISSANCE HARBOURSIDE-VANCOUVER.** *(1133 W Hastings, Vancouver BC V6E 3T3) downtown.* 604/689-9211; FAX 604/689-4358. 439 rms, 19 story. May-Oct: S $205-$305; D $230-$330; each addl $25; suites $350-$1,000; under 19 free; lower rates rest of yr. Crib free. Pet accepted. Covered parking $12. TV; cable (premium). Indoor pool. 2 restaurants 6:30 am-11 pm. 2 bars; entertainment exc Sun. Ck-out noon. Convention facilities. Business servs avail. In-rm modem link. Exercise equipt; weights, bicycles, sauna. Minibars; refrigerators. Balconies. Cr cds: A, C, D, DS, ER, JCB, MC, V.

★ ★ ★ **WATERFRONT CENTRE.** *(900 Canada Place Way, Vancouver BC V6C 3L5) at Burrard Inlet, in the West End.* 604/691-1991; FAX 604/691-1838. 489 units, 23 story. May-Oct: S, D $280-$395; each addl $25; suites $465-$1,700; under 18 free; lower rates rest of yr. Crib free. Pet accepted; $50. Garage parking $15.70. TV; cable, VCR avail. Heated pool; whirlpool, poolside serv. Restaurant 6:30 am-midnight. Rm serv 24 hrs. Bar from 11 am; entertainment exc Sun. Ck-out noon. Convention facilities. Business center. In-rm modem link. Concierge. Shopping arcade. Exercise equipt; weight machine, bicycles. Minibars. Waterfront hotel, flanked by terraced gardens, is linked by an enclosed walkway to Trade and Convention Centre & cruise ship terminal. Luxury level. Cr cds: A, C, D, DS, ER, JCB, MC, V.

Inn

★ ★ ★ **RIVER RUN COTTAGES.** *(4551 River Rd W, Ladner BC V4K 1R9)* 604/946-7778; FAX 604/940-1970. 4 cottages, 1 story. Apr-Dec: S, D $80-$160; each addl $20; under 5 free; lower rates rest of yr. Pet accepted. Complimentary full bkfst; afternoon refreshments. Restaurant nearby. Ck-out noon, ck-in 3 pm. Luggage handling. Business servs avail. On river. Totally nonsmoking. Cr cds: MC, V.

Victoria, British Columbia *(See also Nanaimo, Vancouver)*

Motels

★ ★ **QUALITY INN HARBOURVIEW.** *(455 Belleville St, Victoria BC V8V 1X3)* 250/386-2421; FAX 250/383-7603. E-mail grandpac@octonet.com; web www.victoriabc .com/accom/quality. 86 rms, 3 story, 11 kit. units. No A/C. June-Sept: S, D $145-$165; kit. units $160-$180; under 18 free; golf plans; lower rates rest of yr. Crib free. Pet accepted, some restrictions. TV; cable, VCR avail. Complimentary coffee in rms. Restaurant 7 am-10 pm. Bar 11-1 am. Ck-out 11 am. Meeting rms. Business servs avail. In-rm modem link. Bellhops. Valet serv. Sundries. Coin lndry. Free garage parking. Exercise equipt; weights, rowers, sauna. Massage. Indoor pool; wading pool, whirlpool. Opp ocean. Cr cds: A, D, DS, ER, JCB, MC, V. [D] [♦] [≈] [⅄] [⅃] [⅂] [SC]

✔ ★ **STAY 'N SAVE.** *(3233 Maple St, Victoria BC V8X 4Y9) at Mayfair Shopping Center.* 250/475-7500; FAX 250/475-7599; res: 800/663-0298. 117 rms, 3 story. July-Aug: S, D $99-$119; each addl $10; suites $120-$130; under 16 free; golf plans; lower rates rest of yr. Crib free. Pet accepted, some restrictions. TV; cable. Complimentary coffee in rms. Restaurant 6:30 am-10 pm. Ck-out 11 am. Coin lndry. Meeting rms. Business servs avail. In-rm modem link. Health club privileges. Cr cds: A, D, ER, MC, V. [D] [♦] [⅄] [⅂] [SC]

Hotels

★ ★ ★ **CLARION GRAND PACIFIC.** *(540 Quebec St, Victoria BC V8V 1W5)* 250/386-0450; FAX 250/383-7603. E-mail grandpac@octonet.com; web www.victoriabc .com/accom/clarion. 145 rms, 8 story, 19 suites. June-Sept: S, D $289-$349; suites $369-$589; under 18 free; golf plans; lower rates rest of yr. Crib free. Pet accepted, some restrictions. TV; cable, VCR avail. Complimentary coffee in rms. Restaurant 7 am-10 pm. Rm serv 24 hrs. Bar 11-1 am. Ck-out 11 am. Meeting rms. Business center. In-rm modem link. Concierge. Coin lndry. Free garage parking. 18-hole golf privileges. Exercise rm; instructor, weights, weight machine, sauna. Massage. Indoor pool; wading pool, whirlpool. Refrigerators, minibars. Opp ocean. Cr cds: A, D, DS, ER, JCB, MC, V.

[D] [♦] [⅄] [≈] [⅄] [⅃] [⅂] [SC] [⅄]

★ ★ ★ **COAST VICTORIA HARBOURSIDE.** *(146 Kingston, Victoria BC V8V 1V4)* 250/360-1211; FAX 250/360-1418. 132 rms, 8 story. May-Oct: S $220; D $250; each addl $30; suites $270-$560; under 18 free; lower rates rest of yr. Crib free. Pet accepted. TV; cable, VCR avail. 2 pools, 1 indoor; whirlpool. Complimentary coffee in rms. Restaurant 6:30 am-10 pm. Rm serv 24 hrs. Bar. Ck-out noon. Meeting rms. Business servs avail. In-rm modem link. Concierge. Sundries. Valet serv. Exercise equipt; bicycles, weight machine, sauna. Refrigerators; microwaves avail. Balconies. Cr cds: A, C, D, DS, ER, JCB, MC, V.

[D] [♦] [≈] [⅄] [⅃] [⅂] [SC]

★ ★ **EXECUTIVE HOUSE.** *(777 Douglas St, Victoria BC V8W 2B5)* 250/388-5111; FAX 250/385-1323; res: 800/663-7001. E-mail executivehouse@executivenhouse.com; web www.executivehouse.com. 179 rms, 17 story, 100 kits. No A/C. May-mid-Oct: S, D $99-$195; each addl $15; kit. units $15 addl; suites $195-$595; under 18 free; lower rates rest of yr. Pet accepted; $15/day. Garage $2. TV; cable. Complimentary coffee. Restaurant 7 am-10 pm. Bars 11-1 am; entertainment. Ck-out noon. Meeting rm. Business servs avail. Exercise equipt; weights, bicycles, sauna, steam rm. Massage. Whirlpool. Many refrigerators; some bathrm phones. Private patios, balconies. Cr cds: A, D, DS, ER, JCB, MC, V.

[♦] [⅄] [⅃] [⅂] [SC]

★ ★ ★ **OCEAN POINTE RESORT, HOTEL & SPA.** *(45 Songhees Rd, Victoria BC V9A 6T3) across Johnson St bridge.* 250/360-2999; FAX 250/360-1041; res: 800/667-4677. E-mail ocean_pointe@pinc.com; web www.oprhotel. com. 250 rms, 143 with A/C, 8 story, 27 suites. Mid-May-mid-Oct: S, D $219-$279; each addl $15; suites $395-$650; kits. avail; under 13 free; wkly, wkend, hol rates; lower rates rest of yr. Crib free. Pet accepted; $75. TV; cable, VCR avail. Indoor pool; whirlpool, poolside serv. Restaurants 7 am-10 pm. Rm serv 24 hrs. Bar 11-1 am. Ck-out noon. Meeting rms. Business center. In-rm modem link. Concierge. Gift shop. Beauty shop. Lighted tennis. Exercise rm; instructor, weight machines, treadmill, sauna. Spa. Minibars; microwaves avail. Balconies. On harbor. Cr cds: A, C, D, ER, JCB, MC, V. [D] [♦] [⅄] [⅄] [≈] [⅄] [⅂] [⅄] [SC] [⅄]

Inn

★ ★ ★ ★ **SOOKE HARBOUR HOUSE.** *(1528 Whiffen Spit Rd, Sooke Harbour BC V0S 1N0) 23 mi NW via Hwy 1A & Hwy 14, thru Sooke, left on Whiffen Spit Rd.* 250/642-3421; res: 800/889-9688; FAX 250/642-6988. E-mail shh@islandnet.com; web sookenet.com/shh. This elegant country inn by the sea offers all the amenities of an exclusive resort with a homey, yet elegant, atmosphere. All 13 rooms have an ocean view, balcony or terrace and fireplace. Staff will arrange everything from scuba diving excursions to fishing charters. 13 rms, 1 with shower only, 2 story. No A/C. Apr-Oct, MAP: S, D $290-$360; each addl $35; under 12 free; lower rates rest of yr. Closed 3 wks Jan. Crib free. Pet accepted; $20. TV avail; cable (premium), VCR avail (movies). Whirlpool. Restaurant 5:30-9:30 pm. Rm serv 24 hrs. Ck-out noon, ck-in 3 pm. Luggage handling. Business servs avail. Free airport transportation. Massage. Lawn games. Refrigerators; microwaves avail. Balconies. Picnic tables. On ocean. Totally nonsmoking. Cr cds: A, D, ER, JCB, MC, V. [D] [♦] [⅄] [⅂]

Whistler, British Columbia (See also Vancouver)

Hotels

★ ★ ★ **CHATEAU WHISTLER RESORT.** *(4599 Chateau Blvd., Whistler BC V0N 1B4)* 604/938-8000; FAX 604/938-2020; res: 800/441-1414. 342 rms, 10-12 story. Mid-Dec-mid-May: S, D $350-$375; each addl $30; suites $475-$1,100; under 17 free; ski, golf plans; higher rates Christmas hols; lower rates rest of yr. Crib free. Pet accepted; $10. Valet parking $15. TV; cable. Indoor/outdoor pool; whirlpool, poolside serv. Supervised child's activities (June-Sept). Restaurants 7 am-11 pm. Rm serv 24 hrs. Bar 11 am-midnight; entertainment, dancing. Ck-out 11 am. Meeting rms. Concierge. Shopping arcade. Tennis, pro. 18-hole golf, greens fee $109 (incl cart), pro, putting green. Downhill/x-country ski adj. Exercise equipt; weights, rowers, sauna. Refrigerators avail. Minibars; some bathrm phones. Large, chateau-style hotel at foot of Blackcomb Mt. Cr cds: A, D, DS, ER, JCB, MC, V. 🄳 🏄 ⛷ 🏋 🏌 🛎 🏊 🕴 🐾 SC

★ ★ ★ **DELTA WHISTLER RESORT.** *(4050 Whistler Way, Whistler BC V0N 1B0)* 604/932-1982; FAX 604/932-7332; res: 800/268-1133. 292 rms, 8 story, 99 kit. units. Early Dec-mid-Apr: S, D $335; each addl $30; suites $470-$595; kit. units $390; family rates; ski, golf plans; higher rates Christmas hols; lower rates rest of yr. Crib free. Pet accepted. Garage parking $12. TV; cable (premium). Pool; whirlpool, poolside serv. Complimentary tea, coffee. Restaurant 6 am-10 pm. Bar 11-1 am. Ck-out 11 am. Coin lndry. Convention facilities. Business servs avail. Concierge. Shopping arcade. Indoor tennis, pro. Downhill/x-country ski adj. Exercise equipt; weights, stair machine, steam rm. Minibars; some bathrm phones. Rms overlook valley, mountains. Cr cds: A, C, D, ER, JCB, MC, V. 🄳 🏄 ⛷ 🏋 🏌 🛎 🏊 🕴 🐾 SC

Brandon, Manitoba

Motel

★ **COMFORT INN.** *(925 Middleton Ave, Brandon MB R7C 1A8)* 204/727-6232; FAX 204/727-2246. 81 rms, 2 story. Apr-Oct: S $56.99-$78.99; D $64.99-$86.99; each addl $4; under 18 free; wkend rates; lower rates rest of yr. Crib free. Pet accepted. TV; cable. Complimentary coffee in lobby. Complimentary continental bkfst. Restaurant nearby. Ck-out 11 am. Business servs avail. In-rm modem link. Sundries. Valet serv. Cr cds: A, D, DS, ER, JCB, MC, V. 🄳 🏄 🕴 🐾 SC

Motor Hotels

★ ★ **ROYAL OAK INN.** *(3130 Victoria Ave W, Brandon MB R7B 0N2)* 204/728-5775; FAX 204/726-5828; res: 800/852-2709 (MB). 96 rms, 2 story. S $64-$82; D, suites $72-$82; each addl $10; under 17 free; package plans. Pet accepted. TV; cable, VCR avail (movies). Indoor pool; wading pool, poolside serv. Restaurant 7 am-10 pm; Sun 8 am-10 pm. Bar 11:30 am-midnight. Ck-out noon. Coin lndry. Meeting rms. Business servs avail. Valet serv. Sundries. RR station, bus depot transportation. Exercise equipt; bicycles, rower, whirlpool. Cr cds: A, C, D, ER, MC, V. 🄳 🏄 🏊 🏌 🕴 🐾 SC

★ ★ **VICTORIA INN.** *(3550 Victoria Ave W, Brandon MB R7B 2R4)* 204/725-1532; FAX 204/727-8282; res: 800/852-2710 (MB). 131 rms, 2 story. S $60.95-$75.95; D $68.95-$85.95; suites $75.95; studio rms $75-$125; under 18 free; package plans. Crib free. Pet accepted. TV; cable. Indoor pool; whirlpool, poolside serv. Restaurant 7 am-10 pm; Sun 8 am-9 pm. Rm serv. Bar 11:30-2 am. Ck-out noon. Meeting rms. Business servs avail. In-rm modem link. Sundries. Exercise equipt; weights, bicycles, sauna. Poolside balconies. Cr cds: A, D, ER, MC, V. 🄳 🏄 🏊 🏌 🕴 🐾 SC

Inn

✔ ★ **THE CASTLE.** *(149 2nd Ave, Minnedosa MB R0J 1E0)* 204/867-2830. 4 rms (1 shared bath), 2 story. S $45; D $55-$60; each addl $10; suites $90; under 5 free. Pet accepted. TV in sitting rm. Complimentary full bkfst. Restaurant nearby. Ck-out noon, ck-in 1 pm. Downhill ski 5 mi; x-country 2 mi. Built in 1901; antiques, art collection. Totally nonsmoking. Cr cds: MC. 🏄 🏊 🕴

Winnipeg, Manitoba

Motels

★ **COMFORT INN.** *(1770 Sargent Ave, Winnipeg MB R3H 0C8)* near Intl Airport. 204/783-5627. 81 rms, 2 story. Mid-June-mid-Sept: S $57.99-$63.99; D $65.99-$71.99; each addl $4; under 18 free; wkend rates; lower rates rest of yr. Crib free. Pet accepted. TV;

cable. Complimentary coffee in lobby. Continental bkfst avail. Restaurant nearby. Ck-out 11 am. Business servs avail. In-rm modem link. Valet serv. Cr cds: A, D, JCB, MC, V.

[D] [⮌] [⊠] [⊠] [SC]

✔ ★ ★ **COUNTRY INN & SUITES BY CARLSON.** *(730 King Edward St, Winnipeg MB R3H 1B4) near Intl Airport.* 204/783-6900; FAX 204/775-7197. 77 units, 3 story, 36 suites. S $65-$95; D $75-$105; each addl $10; under 18 free; wkend rates. Crib free. Pet accepted, some restrictions. TV; cable (premium), VCR (free movies). Complimentary coffee in rms. Complimentary continental bkfst. Restaurant adj 7 am-11 pm. Ck-out noon. Coin lndry. Business servs avail. Sundries. Valet serv. Refrigerators. Cr cds: A, C, D, DS, ER, MC, V. [D] [⮌] [⊠] [⊠] [SC]

Motor Hotels

★ ★ **BEST WESTERN INTERNATIONAL INN.** *(1808 Wellington Ave, Winnipeg MB R3H 0G3) near Intl Airport.* 204/786-4801; FAX 204/786-1329. 288 rms, 5 story. S $78; D $83; each addl $5; suites $175; under 16 free; wkend rates. Crib $5. Pet accepted. TV; cable, VCR avail (movies free). 2 pools, 1 indoor; whirlpool, sauna, poolside serv. Restaurant 7 am-midnight; dining rms 5:30-midnight. Rm serv. Bar 11:30-2 am. Ck-out 2 pm. Meeting rms. Business servs avail. In-rm modem link. Bellhops. Gift shop. Free airport transportation. Game rm. Some refrigerators. Cr cds: A, D, DS, ER, JCB, MC, V.
[⮌] [≋] [✈] [⊠] [SC]

★ ★ **HOLIDAY INN-SOUTH.** *(1330 Pembina Hwy, Winnipeg MB R3T 2B4)* 204/452-4747; FAX 204/284-2751. 169 rms, 11 story. S $125; D $136; each addl $11; suites $200; under 19 free; wkend rates. Crib free. Pet accepted. TV; cable, VCR avail. Indoor pool; wading pool, whirlpool, poolside serv. Coffee in rms. Restaurant 6:30 am-11 pm; wkend hrs vary. Rm serv. Bar from 11:30 am. Ck-out noon. Coin lndry. Meeting rms. Business servs avail. In-rm modem link. Bellhops. Valet serv. Sundries. Free airport transportation. Cr cds: A, C, D, DS, ER, JCB, MC, V. [D] [⮌] [≋] [⊠] [⊠] [SC]

Hotels

✔ ★ ★ **CHARTER HOUSE.** *(330 York Ave, Winnipeg MB R3C 0N9)* 204/942-0101; FAX 204/956-0665. 90 rms, 5 story. S, D $75-$125; under 18 free; wkly, wkend rates. Crib avail. Pet accepted. TV; cable, VCR avail (movies). Heated pool; poolside serv. Restaurant 7 am-11 pm. Dining rm 11:30 am-2:30 pm, 5-11 pm; Sat from 5 pm; Sun 5-9 pm. Bar 11-1 am. Ck-out noon. Meeting rms. Business servs avail. In-rm modem link. Health club privileges. Balconies. Cr cds: A, C, D, DS, ER, MC, V. [D] [⮌] [≋] [⊠] [⊠] [SC]

★ ★ **DELTA.** *(288 Portage Ave, Winnipeg MB R3C 0B8)* 204/956-0410; FAX 204/947-1129; res: 800/268-1133 (CAN), 800/877-1133 (US). 272 rms, 29 story. S, D $129-$199; each addl $15; suites $229; under 18 free; wkend rates. Crib free. Pet accepted. Garage parking $3.75-$7; valet $3. TV; cable (premium), VCR avail (movies). Indoor pool; whirlpool, poolside serv. Supervised child's activities. Coffee in rms. Restaurant 6:30 am-10 pm; Sat, Sun from 7 am. Rm serv 24 hrs. Bars 11:30-1 am. Ck-out 1 pm. Meeting rms. Business center. In-rm modem link. Concierge. Gift shop. Exercise equipt; weights, rowers, sauna. Minibars. Adj to skywalks major downtown businesses & shopping. Cr cds: A, D, ER, JCB, MC, V. [D] [⮌] [≋] [✈] [⊠] [⊠] [SC] [⚓]

★ ★ **SHERATON.** *(161 Donald St, Winnipeg MB R3C 1M3)* 204/942-5300; FAX 204/943-7975. 266 rms, 21 story. S $130-$145; D $140-$155; each addl $15; under 18 free; wkend rates. Crib free. Pet accepted. Underground parking, valet $7.50/day. TV; cable (premium). Indoor pool; whirlpool, poolside serv. Coffee in rms. Restaurant 6:30 am-11 pm. Rm serv 24 hrs. Bar 11-1 am. Ck-out noon. Convention facilities. Business servs avail. In-rm modem link. Concierge. Gift shop. Airport transportation avail. Sauna. Health club privileges. Many refrigerators. Many balconies. Cr cds: A, D, ER, MC, V. [D] [⮌] [≋] [⊠] [⊠] [SC]

Fredericton, New Brunswick

Motels

★ ★ **FREDERICTON MOTOR INN.** *(1315 Regent St, Fredericton NB E3C 1A1)* 506/455-1430; FAX 506/458-5448; res: 800/561-8777. 199 rms, 1-3 story. July-Sept: S $65-$105; D $75-$105; each addl $10; suites $105; kit. unit $115; lower rates rest of yr. Crib $6. Pet accepted. TV; cable, VCR avail. Heated pool; wading pool, whirlpool, poolside serv. Restaurant 6:30 am-11 pm. Rm serv. Bar 4 pm-1 am. Ck-out 11 am. Meeting rms. Business servs avail. In-rm modem link. Bellhops. Sundries. Some in-rm whirlpools. Refrigerators avail. Balconies. Cr cds: A, C, D, DS, ER, MC, V. [D] [⮌] [≋] [⊠] [⊠] [SC]

★ ★ **HOWARD JOHNSON.** *(Fredericton NB E3B 5E3) N side of Princess Margaret Bridge, 1/8 mi E on Trans-Can Hwy 2.* 506/472-0480; FAX 506/472-0170. 116 rms, 2 story. S $65-$76; D $74-$79; each addl $8; suites $136; under 18 free. Crib free. Pet accepted, some restrictions. TV; cable (premium), VCR avail. Heated pool; whirlpool; poolside serv. Restaurant 7 am-10 pm. Rm serv. Bar 4 pm-1 am. Ck-out noon. Coin lndry. Meeting rms. Business servs avail. In-rm modem link. Valet serv. Airport transportation. Indoor tennis (fee & res). Downhill ski 10 mi; x-country ski 5 mi. Exercise equipt; bicycle, rower, sauna. Rec rm. Lawn games. Balconies. Cr cds: A, C, D, DS, ER, JCB, MC, V.

🅓 ⚟ 🏊 🏃 🛌 🎿 🈁 🐾 SC

   ✔★ **KEDDY'S INN.** *(368 Forest Hill, Fredericton NB·E3B 5G2) 1 blk N of Trans-Can Hwy 2 exit 295.* 506/454-4461; FAX 506/452-6915. 120 rms, 3 story. S $61.95; D $67.95; each addl $8; under 18 free. Pet accepted. TV; cable, VCR avail. Heated pool; sauna. Restaurant 7 am-2 pm, 5-10 pm. Rm serv. Bar 11:30 am-midnight, Sun 4 pm-midnight. Ck-out noon. Meeting rms. Business servs avail. Valet serv. Downhill ski 15 mi; x-country ski 10 mi. Balconies. Picnic tables. Cr cds: A, C, D, DS, ER, MC, V.

⚟ 🏊 🛌 🈁 🐾 SC

Motor Hotel

   ★★ **AUBERGES WANDLYN INN.** *(58 Prospect St W, Fredericton NB E3B 4Y9) 1 blk N of Hwy 2 Smyth St exit.* 506/452-8937; FAX 506/452-7658. 99 rms, 3 story. S, D $70-$85; studio rms $75-$100; each addl $8; suites $105-$150; under 18 free. Crib free. Pet accepted. TV; cable (premium), VCR avail. 2 pools, 1 indoor; whirlpool, sauna, poolside serv. Restaurant 7 am-2 pm, 5-9:30 pm. Bar 11-1 am. Ck-out 11 am. Coin laundry. Meeting rms. Business servs avail. Valet serv. Sundries. Refrigerators avail. Cr cds: A, C, D, ER, MC, V. ⚟ 🏊 🈁 🐾 SC

Hotels

   ★★★ **LORD BEAVERBROOK.** *(659 Queen St, Fredericton NB E3B 5A6)* 506/455-3371; FAX 506/455-1441; res: 800/561-7666. 168 rms, 7 story. S $80; D $85; each addl $10; suites $90-$150; under 19 free; package plans. Crib free. Pet accepted. TV; cable, VCR avail. Heated pool; wading pool; whirlpool; poolside serv. Sauna. Playground. Supervised child's activities. Restaurant 6 am-10 pm. Bar 11 am-2 am; entertainment, dancing; also sun deck bar. Ck-out noon. Meeting rms. Business servs avail. In-rm modem link. Concierge. Gift shop. Airport transportation. Bicycle, boat, canoe rentals. Docking facilities. Rec rm. Game rm. Minibars. Picnic tables. Cr cds: A, C, D, DS, ER, MC, V.

🅓 ⚟ 🏊 🛌 🐾 SC

Moncton, New Brunswick

Motels

   ★★ **COLONIAL INN.** *(42 Highfield St, Moncton NB E1C 8T6) 42 Highfield St, 1/2 blk off Hwy 6.* 506/382-3395; FAX 506/858-8991; res: 800/561-4667. 61 rms, 1-2 story. S $62 D $68; each addl $6; studio rms $75; under 16 free. Crib $6. Pet accepted, some restrictions. TV; cable. Heated pool; whirlpool. Sauna. Complimentary continental bkfst Mon-Fri. Restaurant open 24 hrs. Rm serv. Bar 11-2 am; entertainment. Ck-out noon-2 pm. Meeting rms. Business servs avail. Valet serv. Sundries. Some refrigerators. Cr cds: A, D, ER, MC, V. ⚟ 🏊 🛌 🐾 SC

   ✔★ **MONCTON MOTOR INN.** *(1905 W Main St (Rte 6), Moncton NB E1E 1H9)* 506/382-2587; FAX 506/858-5998; res: 800/465-7666. 71 rms, 5 kit. units, 2 story. S $50; D $65; each addl $5; studio rms $55; kit. units $89; each addl $5; under 12 free; wkly rates. Pet accepted, some restrictions. TV; cable. Heated pool. Restaurant 7 am-9 pm. Bar. Ck-out 11 am. Business servs avail. Cr cds: A, C, D, DS, ER, MC, V. ⚟ 🏊 🛌 🐾 SC

Hotel

   ★★★ **BEAUSEJOUR.** *(750 Main St, Moncton NB E1C 1E6)* 506/854-4344; FAX 506/858-0957; res: 800/441-1414. 314 rms, 9 story. S $106-$150; D $106-$172; each addl $15; suites $204-$465; studio rms $89-$145; under 18 free; wkend rates. Crib free. Pet accepted. TV; cable (premium). Pool; poolside serv, lifeguard. Coffee in rms. Restaurants 6:30 am-11 pm. Rm serv 24 hrs. Bar 4:30 pm-1 am, wknds from 6 pm, closed Sun; entertainment wknds. Ck-out noon. Meeting rms. Business servs avail. In-rm modem link. Concierge. Gift shop. Barber. Minibars; many bathrm phones; some refrigerators. Cr cds: A, C, D, DS, ER, JCB, MC, V. 🅓 ⚟ 🏊 🛌 🐾 SC

St Andrews, New Brunswick

Motels

   ✔★ **BLUE MOON.** *(300 Mowatt Dr, St Andrews NB E0G 2X0)* 506/529-3245; FAX 506/529-3245. 39 air-cooled rms, 2 kits. May-Oct: S $50-$55; D $50-$75; each addl $7; kit. units $5 addl; under 6 free. Closed rest of yr. Crib free. Pet accepted, some restrictions. TV;

cable. Ck-out 11 am. Business servs avail. 18-hole golf privileges. Cr cds: A, D, DS, ER, MC, V. 🐾 🛅 ⊠ 🛥️

★ **PICKET FENCE.** *(102 Reed Ave, St Andrews NB E0G 2X0) 506/529-8985; FAX 506/529-8985.* 17 rms, 1 kit. unit. No A/C. May-Oct: S $50; D $65; each addl $5; under 6 free. Closed rest of yr. Crib free. Pet accepted, some restrictions. TV; cable. Restaurant nearby. Ck-out 11 am. Picnic tables. Cr cds: A, D, DS, MC, V. 🐾 ⊠ 🛥️

✔★ **SEASIDE BEACH RESORT.** *(339 Water St, St Andrews NB E0G 2X0) 506/529-3846; FAX 506/529-4479.* E-mail davidsu@nbnet.nb.ca; web www.seaside.nb .com. 24 kit. units, 19 with shower only, 1-2 story, 4 cottages. No A/C. No rm phones. June-Labor Day: S, D $65-$75; each addl $5; wkly rates; lower rates May, early Sept-Oct. Closed rest of yr. Crib $5. Pet accepted. TV; cable. Restaurant nearby. Ck-out 11 am. Coin lndry. Microwaves avail. Balconies. Picnic tables, grills. Overlooks St Andrews Harbour. Cr cds: MC, V. 🐾 🛥️ 🛥️

★ **ST STEPHEN INN.** *(99 King St, St Stephen NB E3L 2C6) N via Hwy 127, W via Hwy 1 (King St).* 506/466-1814; FAX 506/466-6148. 52 rms, 2 story. July-Dec: S $65; D $80; each addl $8; under 17 free; lower rates rest of yr. Crib free. Pet accepted. TV; cable, VCR avail. Restaurant 7 am-10 pm. Meeting rms. Business servs avail. Cr cds: A, C, D, ER, MC, V. 🄳 🐾 ⊠ 🛥️ 🆂🅲

Motor Hotel

★★ **HISTORIC SHIRETOWN INN.** *(218 Water St, St Andrews NB E0G 2X0) 506/529-8877; FAX 506/529-3044.* 34 rms, 3 story. No A/C. Mid-May-Oct: S, D $85-$110; each addl $10; suites, studio rms $95-$125; under 16 free; wkly rates; lower rates rest of yr. Crib free. Pet accepted, some restrictions. TV; cable. Restaurant 7:30 am-10 pm; hrs vary off season. Bar noon-11:30 pm. Ck-out noon. Meeting rm. Business servs avail. Old World atmosphere; built in 1881. Cr cds: A, C, D, ER, MC, V. 🐾 🛥️ ⊠ 🛥️ 🆂🅲

Inn

★★★ **KINGSBRAE ARMS.** *(219 King St, St Andrews NB E0G 2X0) 506/529-1897; FAX 506/529-1197.* E-mail kingsbrae@nbnet.nb.ca; web www.kingsbrae-arms.com. This 1897 manor house was built for the pleasures of merchants working the trade routes betweeen North America and Shanghai. Spacious suites and grand guest rooms offer sweeping bay and garden views. Rooms are impeccably furnished in period detail and feature fireplaces, marble baths and many other comforts and luxuries. 9 rms, 3 story, 3 suites. Mid-Mar-mid-Oct: S, D $225; suites $250-$350; wkends 2-day min; lower rates rest of yr. Children over 9 yrs only. Pet accepted, some restrictions. TV; cable, VCR avail (movies). Heated pool. Complimentary full bkfst; afternoon refreshments. Rm serv 24 hrs. Ck-out noon, ck-in 2 pm. In-rm modem link. Luggage handling. Valet serv. Concierge serv. Airport transportation. Tennis privileges. Health club privileges. Lawn games. Fireplaces; some in-rm whirlpools. Some balconies. Totally nonsmoking. Cr cds: MC, V.
🐾 🏃 🛥️ ⊠ 🛥️

Resort

★★★ **ALGONQUIN.** *(184 Adolphus St, St Andrews NB E0G 2X0) 506/529-8823; FAX 506/529-7162; res: 800/441-1414.* 250 rms, 54 A/C, 4 story, 42 kit. units. Mid-May-mid-Oct: S, D $115-$205; each addl $20; suites $185-$275; under 19 free. Crib free. Pet accepted. TV; cable, VCR avail. Heated pool; whirlpool, lifeguard. Playground. Supervised child's activities (mid-May-Oct); ages 12 and under. Coffee in rms. Restaurant 7 am-10 pm. Rm serv. Bar; entertainment. Ck-out 11 am, ck-in 4 pm. Coin lndry. Business servs avail. Bellhops. Valet serv. Concierge. Gift shop. Free valet parking. Tennis. 9, 18-hole golf, greens fee $25-$39, pro, putting green. Bicycle rentals. Exercise equipt; weight machines, bicycles, sauna. Lawn games. Aerobics. Some in-rm whirlpools, microwaves, minibars, fireplaces. On hill; view of water from most rms. Cr cds: A, C, D, DS, ER, JCB, MC, V.
🄳 🐾 🛅 🏃 🛥️ 🛅 ⊠ 🛥️ 🆂🅲

Saint John, New Brunswick

Motel

✔★★ **COLONIAL INN.** *(175 City Rd, Saint John NB E2L 3T5) 506/652-3000; FAX 506/658-1664.* 94 rms, 82 A/C, 2 story. S $51.95; D $57.95-$59.95; each addl $6; suites $85; under 18 free. Crib free. Pet accepted. TV; cable. Heated pool; whirlpool, sauna. Restaurant open 24 hrs. Rm serv. Bar 6 pm-2 am. Ck-out noon-2 pm. Meeting rms. Business servs avail. Valet serv. Cr cds: A, D, ER, MC, V. 🄳 🐾 🛥️ ⊠ 🛥️ 🆂🅲

Motor Hotel

★ ★ **HOTEL COURTENAY BAY.** *(350 Haymarket Sq, Saint John NB E2L 3P1)* *506/657-3610; FAX 506/633-1773; res: 800/563-2489.* 125 rms, 5 story. S $59-$69; D $69-$79; each addl $8; under 18 free. Pet accepted. TV; cable (premium). Heated pool. Restaurant 7 am-11 pm. Rm serv. Bar 11 am-11 pm. Ck-out 1 pm. Coin lndry. Meeting rms. Business servs avail. Bellhops. Valet serv. Sundries. Minibars. Some private patios, balconies. Cr cds: A, C, D, ER, JCB, MC, V. 🐾 ⚓ 🏊 🖎 🐾 SC

Hotels

★ ★ ★ **DELTA BRUNSWICK.** *(39 King St, Saint John NB E2L 4W3) above Brunswick Square Shopping Mall. 506/648-1981; FAX 506/648-9670; res: 800/268-1133.* 255 units, 5 story. Mid-May-mid-Oct: S, D $125-$135; each addl $10; suites $135-$500; studio rms $135-$145; under 18 free; lower rates rest of yr. Crib free. Pet accepted. Covered parking $9; valet $12. TV; cable. Indoor pool; whirlpool. Free supervised child's activities (wkends), over age 2. Restaurant 6:30 am-10 pm (June-Sept). Rm serv 24 hrs. Bar 11-1 am. Ck-out 1 pm. Convention facilities. Business servs avail. Shopping arcade. Exercise equipt; weights, bicycles, sauna, steam rm. Game rm. Rec rm. Minibars; refrigerators avail. Covered walkway to downtown offices, Market Square. Cr cds: A, D, ER, MC, V.

D 🐾 ⚓ 🏊 🖎 🐾 SC

★ ★ ★ **HILTON.** *(1 Market Square, Saint John NB E2L 4Z6) 506/693-8484; FAX 506/657-6610.* 197 rms, 12 story. May-Sept: S, D $99-$135; each addl $12; suites $305-$439; lower rates rest of yr. Crib free. Pet accepted, some restrictions. Garage parking $8.25. TV; cable. Indoor pool; whirlpool. Complimentary coffee in rms. Restaurant 6:30 am-11 pm. Bar 11:30-1 am; entertainment. Ck-out noon. Meeting rms. Business center. Concierge. Shopping arcade. Barber, beauty shop. X-country ski 2 mi. Exercise equipt; weights, bicycle, sauna. Game rm. Rec rm. Refrigerators, minibars. Harbor view. Underground access to Market Square shopping mall. Cr cds: A, C, D, DS, ER, JCB, MC, V.

D 🐾 ⚓ 🏊 🖎 🐾 SC 🎣

Antigonish, Nova Scotia *(See also Baddeck)*

Motels

★ ★ **AUBERGES WANDLYN MOTOR INN.** *(158 Main St, Antigonish NS B2B 2B7) 902/863-4001; FAX 902/863-2672.* 34 rms, 2 story. Mid-June-mid-Oct: S $70; D $80; each addl $8; suites $90-$140; under 18 free; lower rates rest of yr. Crib free. Pet accepted. TV; cable. Restaurant 7 am-9 pm. Bar 4 pm-midnight. Ck-out 11 am. Sundries. Tennis privileges. Downhill ski 7 mi. Cr cds: A, D, ER, MC, V. D 🐾 ⚓ 🦅 🖎 🐾 SC

★ ★ **HEATHER.** *(Foord St, Stellarton NS B0K 1S0) just off Trans-Canada Hwy 104 exit 24. 902/752-8401; FAX 902/755-4580.* 76 rms, 2 story. S $62; D $74; each addl $6; studio rms $68; under 12 free. Crib free. Pet accepted. TV; cable. Restaurant 7 am-11 pm. Rm serv. Bar 11 am-11:30 pm. Ck-out 2 pm. Meeting rms. 18-hole golf privileges. X-country ski 5 mi. Refrigerators; minibars. Cr cds: A, D, ER, MC, V. 🐾 ⚓ 🦅 🐾 SC

Baddeck, Nova Scotia

Motel

★ ★ ★ **GISELE'S COUNTRY INN.** *(387 Shore Rd (Hwy 205), Baddeck NS B0E 1B0) 902/295-2849; FAX 902/295-2033; res: 800/304-0466.* 63 rms, 47 A/C, 3 story. Late June-Dec: S, D $65-$95; each addl $8; suites for 4, $125-$150; kit. units $150 (up to 4); under 10 free; lower rates rest of yr. Crib free. Pet accepted. TV. Restaurant 7:30-9:30 am, 5:30-10 pm. Bar. Ck-out 10 am. Lndry facilities. Sauna. Cr cds: A, C, D, ER, MC, V.

D 🐾 🖎 🐾 SC

Dartmouth, Nova Scotia *(See also Halifax)*

Motel

✔ ★ **SEASONS MOTOR INN.** *(40 Lakecrest Dr, Dartmouth NS B2X 1V1) 902/435-0060; FAX 902/454-6110.* 42 rms, 2 story. Mid-May-mid-Oct: S, D $42; each addl $3; under 12 free; wkly rates in winter; lower rates rest of yr. Pet accepted. TV; cable, VCR avail (movies). Ck-out 11 am. Business servs avail. X-country ski 5 mi. Refrigerators avail. Cr cds: A, DS, ER, MC, V. D 🐾 🦅 🐾 SC

Motor Hotel

✔ ★ ★ **KEDDY'S DARTMOUTH INN.** *(9 Braemer Dr, Dartmouth NS B2Y 3H6) 902/469-0331; FAX 902/466-6324; res: 800/561-7666.* E-mail keddys @nbnet.nb.ca; web www.keddys.nb.ca. 115 rms, 3 story, 14 kits. S, D $62-$80; each addl $8; suites $150;

studio rms $75; kit. units $65; under 18 free. Crib free. Pet accepted. TV; cable (premium), VCR avail (movies). Restaurant 6:30 am-10 pm. Bar 10-2 am. Ck-out noon. Meeting rms. Business servs avail. Valet serv. X-country ski 5 mi. Some refrigerators. Balconies. Picnic tables. Lake opp. Cr cds: A, C, D, DS, ER, MC, V. 🄳 🐾 ⛾ 🏊 🐾 SC

Hotels

★ ★ ★ HOLIDAY INN. *(99 Wyse Rd, Dartmouth NS B3A 1L9) on Plaza of MacDonald Bridge.* 902/463-1100; FAX 902/464-1227. 196 rms, 7 story. May-Oct: S $89, D $99; each addl $10; suites $195-$395; under 19 free; wkend rates; lower rates rest of yr. Crib free. Pet accepted, some restrictions. TV; cable. Heated pool. Restaurant 7 am-10:30 pm. Bar 11-1 am. Ck-out noon. Business center. In-rm modem link. Airport transportation. X-country ski 15 mi. Health club privileges. Microwaves avail. Some balconies. Cr cds: A, C, D, DS, ER, JCB, MC, V. 🄳 🐾 ⛾ 🏊 🐾 SC 🏊

★ ★ ★ RAMADA RENAISSANCE. *(240 Brownlow Ave, Dartmouth NS B3B 1X6)* 902/468-8888; FAX 902/468-8765. E-mail ramadartc@fox.nstn.ca. 178 rms, 5 story, 31 suites. May-Oct: S, D $89; each addl $10; suites $129; under 15 free; wkly, wkend, hol rates; lower rates rest of yr. Crib $10. Pet accepted, some restrictions; $50 deposit. TV; cable. Indoor pool; wading pool, whirlpool, lifeguard. Complimentary coffee in rms. Restaurant 6:30 am-10 pm. Bar 11-1 am. Meeting rms. Business center. Gift shop. X-country ski 1 mi. Exercise equipt; weights, rower. Sauna. Many minibars; microwaves avail. Cr cds: A, D, DS, ER, MC, V. 🄳 🐾 ⛾ 🏊 🏊 🐾 SC 🏊

Digby, Nova Scotia

Motels

★ ★ ADMIRAL DIGBY INN. *(Shore Rd, Digby NS B0V 1A0)* 902/245-2531; FAX 902/245-2533; res: 800/465-6262. 46 air-cooled rms, 2 A/C kit. cottages. Mid-June-mid-Sept: S $71-$89, D $89-$143; each addl $6; kit. cottages $110; under 12 free; lower rates Apr-mid-June & mid-Sept-Oct. Closed rest of yr. Crib $6. Pet accepted. TV; cable, VCR avail (movies). Heated pool. Restaurant 7:30-10:30 am, 5:30-9:30 pm. Bar 5-10 pm. Ck-out 11 am. Coin lndry. Business servs avail. Sundries. Gift shop. X-country ski 2 mi. Overlooks Bay of Fundy. Cr cds: A, C, D, DS, ER, MC, V. 🄳 🐾 ⛾ 🏊 🐾

✔ ★ ★ COASTAL INN KINGFISHER. *(111 Warwick St, Digby NS B0V 1A0) off Hwy 101 exit Z6, near St John Ferry.* 902/245-4747; FAX 902/245-4866. 36 rms, 25 A/C. S $55; D $65; each addl $7; under 10 free; some lower rates. Crib free. Pet accepted. TV; cable. Playground. Restaurant 7 am-8:30 pm; Sat, Sun 8 am-8:30 pm. Ck-out noon. Coin lndry. Meeting rm. Business servs avail. Microwaves avail. Picnic tables. Beach 4 mi. Cr cds: A, C, D, DS, ER, MC, V. 🐾 🏊 🐾

Resort

★ ★ MOUNTAIN GAP RESORT. *(Digby NS B0V 1A0) 4 mi E on Rte 1; Hwy 101 exits 24, 25.* 902/245-5841; FAX 902/245-2277; res: 800/565-5020. E-mail mtngap@marina.istar.ca. 96 rms, 12 cottages. No A/C. Mid-May-mid-Oct: S $69; D $69-$180; each addl $10; kit. units, kit. cottages $149-$189; under 18 free; wkly rates. Closed rest of yr. Crib free. Pet accepted. TV; cable, VCR avail (movies). Heated pool (seasonal). Playground. Dining rms 7-10 am, noon-2 pm, 5:30-9 pm. Bar 5:30 pm-midnight. Ck-out 11 am, ck-in 2 pm. Grocery, package store 1 mi. Business servs avail. Gift shop. Private beach. Tennis. 18-hole golf privileges. Lawn games. Bicycle rentals. Soc dir. Game rm. Private patios, grills. Rustic setting on 45 acres. Cr cds: A, C, D, DS, ER, MC, V. 🄳 🐾 🏊 🏊 🏊 🏊 🐾 SC

Fortress of Louisbourg National Historic Site, Nova Scotia *(See also Baddeck)*

Motel

✔ ★ ★ LOUISBOURG. *(1225 Main st (Hwy 22), Fortress of Louisbourg National Historic Site NS B0A 1M0)* 902/733-2280. 44 rms. No A/C. S $43-$49; D $55-$67; each addl $6. Pet accepted. TV; cable. Restaurant 7 am-10:30 pm. Bar 11:30 am-midnight; entertainment. Ck-out 11 am. Tennis privileges. X-country ski 2 mi. Cr cds: A, D, MC, V. 🐾 🏊 🏊 🐾

Grand Pré, Nova Scotia

Motel

★ ★ GREENSBORO INN. *(9016 Commercial St, New Minas NS B4N 3E2) 8 mi W on Hwy 101, exit 12.* 908/681-3201; res: 800/561-3201 NS & PEI; FAX 908/681-3399. Web www.valleyweb.com/greensboro. 26 rms. 1 kit. unit. Mid-May-Oct: S $59; D $69-$79, kit. unit $100; under 18 free; lower rates rest of yr. Pet accepted. TV; cable. Indoor pool. Complimentary coffee in lobby. Restaurant adj 11 am-10 pm. Ck-out 11 am. Golf privileges. Downhill/x-country ski 20 mi. Picnic tables. Cr cds: A, D, ER, MC, V.

★ ★ ★ **AUBERGES WANDLYN INN.** *(Hwy 101 at exit 14 & Hwy 1, Kentville NS B0P 1K0)* 902/678-8311; FAX 902/679-1253; res: 800/561-0000. 70 units, 3 story. Mid-June-Oct: S $68-$88; D $88-$100; each addl $10; suites $88-$100; under 18 free; lower rates rest of yr. Crib free. Pet accepted. TV; cable, VCR avail. Indoor pool. Restaurant 7 am-9:30 pm. Bar 10-1:30 am. Ck-out noon. Meeting rms. Business servs avail. Some refrigerators, minibars. Picnic tables. Cr cds: A, C, D, DS, ER, MC, V. [D]

Halifax, Nova Scotia

Motels

★ ★ **AUBERGES WANDLYN MOTOR INN.** *(50 Bedford Hwy, Halifax NS B3M 2J2)* 3 1/2 mi N on Hwy 2 outbound. 902/443-0416; FAX 902/457-0665; res: 800/261-0000. 66 rms, 2 story. June-Sept: S $60-$85; D $65-$85; each addl $10; suites $95-$135; under 18 free; lower rates rest of yr. Pet accepted. TV, VCR avail (movies). Restaurant 7-11 am, 5-9 pm. Bar 4-11 pm. Ck-out noon. Meeting rms. Business servs avail. Sundries. Exercise equipt; weight machines, bicycles. Microwaves avail. Ocean view from some rms. Cr cds: A, D, ER, MC, V. [D]

★ ★ **DAYS INN.** *(636 Bedford Hwy, Halifax NS B3M 2L8)* 902/443-3171; FAX 902/443-9368. E-mail carton@istar.ca. 51 units, 1-2 story, 17 kit. suites. June-Oct: S, D $65; each addl $7; kit. suites $89; some wkly rates; lower rates rest of yr. Crib free. Pet accepted. TV; cable, VCR avail. Playground. Restaurant 7-11 pm. Bar. Ck-out 11 am. Meeting rms. Balconies. Picnic tables. Cr cds: A, D, DS, ER, MC, V. [D]

✔ ★ **GRAND VIEW.** *(Black Point, Halifax County NS B0J 1B0)* W on Hwy 103, exit 5, then left 1/4 mi on Hwy 213, turn right at flashing light and continue 10 mi on Hwy 3. 902/857-9776; FAX 902/857-9776; 800 888/591-5122. 14 rms, 10 kit. units, 2 cottages. No A/C. No rm phones. Mid-June-early Sept: S $47-$55; D $50-$60; each addl $7; cottages $85; under 5 free; wkly rates; lower rates rest of yr. Crib avail. Pet accepted. TV; cable. Playground. Coffee in rms. Ck-out 10:30 am. Near swimming beach; all rms have view of St Margaret's Bay. Cr cds: MC, V. [D]

★ **SEASONS MOTOR INN.** *(4 Melrose Ave, Halifax NS B3N 2E2)* 902/443-9321; res: 800/792-2498. 36 rms, 32 air-cooled, 4 story. June-Oct: S $48-$57; D $51-$59; each addl $2; under 11 free; lower rates rest of yr. Crib free. Pet accepted, some restrictions. TV; cable, VCR avail (movies). Complimentary continental bkfst. Ck-out 11 am. Meeting rm. Cr cds: A, D, ER, MC, V.

✔ ★ ★ **STARDUST.** *(1067 Bedford Hwy, Bedford NS B4A 2X3)* 9 mi E on Hwy 2. 902/835-3316; FAX 902/835-4973. 50 rms, 25 A/C, 3 story, 32 kits. June-Oct: S $40; D $45; each addl $10; family rms $55; 2-bedrm apts $95; kit. units $35-$45 (equipt $10 addl); under 12 free; lower rates rest of yr. Crib $5. Pet accepted. TV; cable, VCR avail. Restaurant 7 am-10 pm. Serv bar. Ck-out 11 am. Sundries. Some refrigerators. On Bedford Basin. Cr cds: A, ER, MC, V.

★ ★ **WINDJAMMER.** *(Box 240, Chester NS B0J 1J0)* approx 45 mi W on Hwy 3. 902/275-3567; FAX 902/275-5867. 18 rms, 6 A/C. Mid-June-mid-Sept: S $39-$47; D $45-$55 each addl $6; under 12 free; lower rates rest of yr. Crib $5. Pet accepted. TV; cable, VCR avail. Restaurant adj 7:30 am-9 pm. Ck-out 11 am. Miniature golf. Some refrigerators, microwaves avail. Picnic tables. On lake; swimming beach. Cr cds: A, C, D, DS, ER, MC, V.

Motor Hotels

★ ★ ★ **AIRPORT HOTEL.** *(60 Bell Blvd, Enfield NS B2T 1K3)* Off Hwy 102 exit 6, near International Airport. 902/873-3000; FAX 902/873-3001; res: 800/667-3333. Web www.jwg.com/atlific/. 156 rms, 3 story. No elvtr. May-Nov: S $98-$110; D, kit. units $97-$144; each addl $10; suites $140; under 18 free; lower rates rest of yr. Crib avail. Pet accepted. TV; cable. 2 pools, 1 indoor; whirlpool, sauna. Restaurant 6:30 am-10 pm. Rm serv. Bar. Ck-out noon. Meeting rms. Business servs avail. In-rm modem link. Free airport transportation. Exercise equipt; weight machine, stair machine. Some refrigerators, minibars; microwaves avail. Cr cds: A, C, D, DS, ER, JCB, MC, V.

[D]

★ ★ ★ **DELTA BARRINGTON.** *(1875 Barrington St, Halifax NS B3J 3L6) 902/429-7410; FAX 902/420-6524.* Web www.deltahotels.com. 202 rms, 4 story. S, D $131-$142; each addl $15; suites $289-$475; under 18 free; wkend rates; some lower rates. Crib free. Pet accepted, some restrictions. Parking $14. TV; cable, VCR avail. Indoor pool; wading pool, whirlpool. Free supervised child's activities (2 days/wk); ages 3-16. Restaurant 6:30 am-2:30 pm, 5-10 pm. Rm serv to 1 am. Bar. Ck-out 1 pm. Meeting rms. Business servs avail. In-rm modem link. Bellhops. Valet serv. Shopping arcade. Barber, beauty shop. Exercise equipt; weights, bicycles, sauna. Minibars; microwaves avail. Cr cds: A, C, D, ER, JCB, MC, V. 🄳 📞 ⚯ 🕱 🖾 🐾 SC

★ ★ **HOLIDAY INN.** *(1980 Robie St, Halifax NS B3H 3G5) jct Quinpool St. 902/423-1161; FAX 902/423-9069.* E-mail hiselect@ holinnselect.hfx.com. 232 rms, 14 story. S, D $115-$125; each addl $10; suites $175-$225; under 19 free; wkend rates. Crib free. Pet accepted. TV; cable, VCR avail. Heated pool; wading pool, whirlpool, poolside serv, lifeguard. Complimentary coffee in lobby. Restaurant 6 am-11 pm. Rm serv. Bars noon-1 am. Ck-out 1 pm. Meeting rms. Business center. In-rm modem link. Sundries. Free indoor parking. Exercise equipt; weights, bicycles, sauna. Health club privileges. Microwaves avail. Cr cds: A, C, D, DS, ER, JCB, MC, V. 🄳 📞 ⚯ 🕱 🖾 🐾 SC 🛧

★ ★ **KEDDY'S.** *(20 St Margaret's Bay Rd, Armdale NS B3N 1J4)* On Hwy 3, ¹/₂ mi W of Armdale Traffic Circle. *902/477-5611; FAX 902/479-2150; res: 800/561-7666.* 135 rms, 9 story, 14 kits. June-Oct: S $73; D $78; each addl $8; suites $85-$125; kit. units $54-$85; under 18 free; lower rates rest of yr. Pet accepted. TV; cable, VCR avail (movies). Indoor pool; whirlpool. Restaurant 7 am-10 pm. Bar 11-2 am. Ck-out 11 am. Meeting rms. Business servs avail. In-rm modem link. Valet serv. Sundries. Exercise equipt; weight machine, rower, sauna. Microwaves avail. Cr cds: A, C, D, DS, ER, MC, V. 🄳 📞 ⚯ 🕱 🖾 🐾 SC

Hotels

★ ★ ★ **CITADEL INN.** *(1960 Brunswick St, Halifax NS B3J 2G7) at foot of Citadel Hill. 902/422-1391; FAX 902/429-6672; res: 800/565-7162 (CAN).* Web centennialhotels .com/citadel. 264 rms, 7-11 story. S, D $89-$150; each addl $15; suites $250-$305; wkend rates; under 18 free. Crib free. Pet accepted, some restrictions. TV; cable, VCR avail. Indoor pool; whirlpool, poolside serv. Complimentary continental bkfst. Restaurant 7 am-3 pm, 5-11 pm. Bar 11-1 am. Ck-out 1 pm. Meeting rms. Business center. In-rm modem link. Exercise equipt; weight machine, treadmill, sauna. Minibars; some refrigerators. Private patios, balconies. Cr cds: A, C, D, DS, ER, MC, V. 🄳 📞 ⚯ 🕱 🖾 🐾 SC 🛧

★ ★ ★ **HOTEL HALIFAX.** *(1990 Barrington St, Halifax NS B3J 1P2) in Scotia Square. 902/425-6700; FAX 902/425-6214; res: 800/441-1414.* Web www.cphotels.ca. 300 rms, 8 story. S $115-$145; D $135-$165; each addl $20; suites $195-$400; under 17 free. Crib free. Pet accepted, some restrictions. Valet parking $12. TV; cable, VCR avail. Heated pool; whirlpool. Restaurant 6:30 am-10 pm. Bars 11-1 am. Ck-out noon. Meeting rms. Business center. Shopping arcade. Barber, beauty shop. Exercise equipt; weight machine, bicycle, sauna. Minibars. On Halifax Harbour. Cr cds: A, C, D, DS, ER, JCB, MC, V. 🄳 📞 ⚯ 🕱 🖾 🐾 SC 🛧

★ ★ ★ **PRINCE GEORGE.** *(1725 Market St, Halifax NS B3J 3N9) 902/425-1986; res: 800/565-1567; FAX 902/429-6048.* Web centennial hotels.com/princegeorge. 206 rms, 6 story. S, D $119-$160; suites $225-$350; under 18 free; wkend rates. Crib free. Pet accepted, some restrictions. Garage $9/night. TV; cable (premium), VCR avail. Indoor pool; poolside serv. Restaurant 6:30 am-11 pm. Rm serv 24 hrs. Bar 11-2 am. Ck-out 1 pm. Convention facilities. Business center. Concierge. Gift shop. Exercise equipt; weight machine, bicycles. Minibars; microwaves avail. Directly connected to the World Trade & Convention Centre and the Metro Centre by shuttle elvtr and underground walkway. Cr cds: A, C, D, DS, ER, JCB, MC, V. 🄳 📞 ⚯ 🕱 🖾 🐾 SC 🛧

★ ★ ★ **SHERATON.** *(1919 Upper Water St, Halifax NS B3J 3J5) downtown. 902/421-1700; FAX 902/422-5805.* 351 rms, 6 story. S, D $139-$200; each addl $20; suites $225-$850; under 18 free. Crib free. Pet accepted. Parking $10. TV; cable, VCR avail (movies). Indoor pool; whirlpool, poolside serv. Complimentary coffee in rms. Restaurant 6:30 am-midnight. Bars 11-2 am; entertainment, disc jockey, pianist. Ck-out noon. Convention facilities. Business center. In-rm modem link. Concierge. Shopping arcade. Barber, beauty shop. Exercise equipt; weights, bicycles, sauna. Some bathrm phones; microwaves avail. On ocean, Halifax Harbor. Cr cds: A, C, D, DS, ER, JCB, MC, V. 🄳 📞 ⚯ 🕱 🖾 🐾 SC 🛧

Inn

✔ ★ **FRESH START.** *(2720 Gottingen St, Halifax NS B3K 3C7) 902/453-6616; FAX 902/453-6617; 800 888/453-6616.* 8 rms, 6 share baths, 2-3 story. No A/C. Rm phones avail. May-Oct: S $55-$70; D $70; each addl $10; wkly rates; lower rates rest of yr. Pet accepted, some restrictions. TV in sitting rm; cable, VCR avail. Complimentary full bkfst. Ck-out 1 pm, ck-in 4 pm. Business servs avail. Microwaves avail. Victorian house (1880); antiques. Maritime Museum opp. Totally nonsmoking. Cr cds: A, D, ER, MC, V.

🐾 ⊠ 🐾

Resort

★ ★ ★ **OAK ISLAND COASTAL INN & MARINA.** *(Western Shore NS B0J 3M0) 45 mi W on Hwy 103, exit 9.* 902/627-2600; FAX 902/627-2020; res: 800/565-5075. E-mail oakislnd@istar.ca; web home.istar.ca /oakislnd. 70 rms, 3 story. No A/C. No elvtr. June-Sept: S, D $69-$89; each addl $10; suites $115-$140; under 16 free; wkend rates; lower rates rest of yr. Crib free. Pet accepted. TV; cable (premium), VCR avail. Indoor pool; whirlpool, poolside serv. Dining rm 7 am-2 pm, 5-9 pm. Rm serv. Bar. Ck-out 1 pm, ck-in 3 pm. Convention facilities. Business center. Tennis. 18-hole golf privileges. Swimming beach. X-country ski 1 mi. Hiking. Lawn games. Exercise equipt; weights, bicycles, sauna. Fishing guides, charter boats. Balconies. Oceanfront resort overlooking Oak Island. Cr cds: A, D, ER, MC, V. 🄳 🐾 🐾 ⊁ 🏌 🏃 ≈ 🏃 ⊠ 🆂🅲 🐾

Truro, Nova Scotia

Motels

★ ★ **BEST WESTERN GLENGARRY.** *(150 Willow St, Truro NS B2N 4Z6)* 902/893-4311; FAX 902/893-1759. 90 rms, 3 story. June-Oct: S $86.96-$97.39; D $97.39-115; each addl $10; suites $180; under 18 free; lower rates rest of yr. Pet accepted. TV; cable, VCR avail (movies). 2 pools, 1 indoor; wading pool, whirlpool, poolside serv. Restaurant 7 am-9 pm; Sun 8 am-8 pm. Rm serv. Bar 5 pm-1 am; entertainment. Ck-out 11 am. Meeting rms. Cr cds: A, C, D, DS, ER, JCB, MC, V. 🄳 🐾 ≋ ⊠ 🐾 🆂🅲

✔ ★ **PALLISER.** *(Tidal Bore Rd, Truro NS B2N 5G6)* Hwy 102 exit 14. 902/893-8951; FAX 902/895-8475. E-mail palliser@auracom.com. 42 rms. No A/C. No rm phones. Early May-late-Oct: S $39; D $47; each addl $5; under 10, $5. Closed rest of yr. Crib $5. Pet accepted. TV; cable. Complimentary continental bkfst. Restaurant 7:30 am-8:30 pm. Bar from 11 am. Ck-out 11 am. Meeting rm. Business servs avail. Gift shop. Cr cds: A, D, ER, MC, V. 🄳 🐾 🐾

✔ ★ **WILLOW BEND.** *(277 Willow St, Truro NS B2N 5N3)* 902/895-5325; FAX 902/893-8375; 800 888/594-5569. 27 rms, 9 kits. Mid-June-mid-Sept: S $40-$45; D $42-$55; each addl $5; kits. $39-$49; wkly rates; lower rates rest of yr. Pet accepted. TV; cable (premium), VCR avail. Pool; poolside serv. Bar from 5 pm. Ck-out 11 am. Business servs avail. 18-hole golf privileges. Cr cds: MC, V. 🐾 🏌 ≈ ⊠ 🐾

Yarmouth, Nova Scotia

Motels

★ ★ **BEST WESTERN MERMAID.** *(545 Main St, Yarmouth NS B5A 1J6)* 902/742-7821; FAX 902/742-2966. E-mail kelley@fox.nstn.ca. 45 rms, 2 story, 5 kits. No A/C. June-Oct: S, D $89-$99; each addl $8; kit. units $99-$135; under 18 free; lower rates rest of yr. Crib $6. Pet accepted, some restrictions. TV; cable. Heated pool. Restaurant nearby. Ck-out 11 am. Coin lndry. Business center. Some refrigerators, microwaves. Deep-sea fishing arranged. Cr cds: A, C, D, DS, ER, JCB, MC, V. 🐾 ≈ ⊠ 🐾 🆂🅲 🐾

★ ★ **RODD COLONY HARBOUR INN.** *(6 Forest St, Yarmouth NS B5A 3K7) at ferry terminal.* 902/742-9194; FAX 902/742-6291; res: 800/565-7633. 65 rms, 4 story, 8 suites. May-Sept: S $75; D $85; under 16 free; suites $95; lower rates rest of yr. Pet accepted. TV; cable, VCR avail (movies). Restaurant 7 am-11 pm. Rm serv. Bar noon-midnight. Meeting rms. Business servs avail. Valet serv. Gift shop. Airport transportation. Health club privileges. Sauna. Game rm. Microwaves avail. Cr cds: A, D, DS, ER, MC, V. 🄳 🐾 ⊠ 🐾 🆂🅲

Hotel

★ ★ ★ **RODD GRAND HOTEL.** *(417 Main St, Yarmouth NS B5A 4B2) near Municipal Airport.* 902/742-2446; FAX 902/742-4645; res: 800/565-7633. Web www.rodd-hotels.ca/rodds 138 air-cooled rms, 7 story. June-Oct: S, D $89-$99; each addl $15; suites $104-$114; under 16 free; lower rates rest of yr. Crib free. Pet accepted. TV; cable. Indoor pool. Restaurants 6:30 am-9 pm. Bar 11-1 am. Ck-out 11 am. Meeting rms. Business center. In-rm modem link. Shopping arcade. Free airport, bus depot transportation. Exercise equipt; weights, bicycles. Microwaves avail. Cr cds: A, C, D, ER, MC, V. 🄳 🐾 ≈ 🏌 🏃 ⊠ 🐾 🆂🅲 🐾

Inn

★ ★ ★ **THE MANOR.** *(Hebron NS B0W 1X0) 5 mi N on Hwy 1E. 902/742-2487; res: 888/626-6746; FAX 902/742-8094.* E-mail manor inn@fox.nstn.ca. 54 rms, 2 story. Mid-June-Sept: S, D $73-$139; under 12 free; lower rates rest of yr. Crib $12. Pet accepted. TV; cable, VCR avail (movies). Heated pool; whirlpool, poolside serv. Complimentary continental bkfst. Dining rm 7-11 am, 5:30-9:30 pm. Rm serv. Ck-out 11 am, ck-in 4 pm. Business servs avail. Tennis. Lawn games. Microwaves avail. Some balconies. Picnic tables. Rms in colonial-style inn (ca 1920), coach house and motel building; antiques. Nine landscaped acres on Doctor's Lake; private dock. Cr cds: A, D, DS, ER, MC, V.

D ⟨symbols⟩ SC

Brantford, Ontario *(See also Hamilton, Stratford)*

Motels

★ ★ ★ **BEST WESTERN-BRANT PARK INN.** *(19 Holiday Dr, Brantford ON N3T 5W5) Park Rd exit. 519/753-8651; FAX 519/753-2619.* E-mail kbrown@bfree.on.ca. 115 rms, 2 story. June-Sept: S $64.95; D $71.95; each addl $7; under 12 free. Crib free. Pet accepted. TV; cable. Heated pool; wading pool, whirlpool, lifeguard. Playground. Restaurant 6:30 am-9:30 pm. Rm serv. Ck-out noon. Meeting rms. Business servs avail. In-rm modem link. Bellhops. Valet serv. Exercise equipt; stair machine, bicycle, sauna. Private patios; some balconies. Cr cds: A, D, DS, ER, MC, V. D ⟨symbols⟩ SC

✔ ★ ★ **DAYS INN.** *(460 Fairview Dr, Brantford ON N3R 7A9) 519/759-2700; FAX 519/759-2089; res: 800/329-7466.* Web www.daysinn.com/ daysinn.html. 75 rms, 2 story. Apr-Oct: S $52.95; D $59.95-$76.95; each addl $7; under 12 free; wkly, wkend rates; lower rates rest of yr. Crib free. Pet accepted. TV; cable (premium). Pool privileges. Restaurant 7-1 am. Ck-out 11 am. Meeting rms. Business servs avail. In-rm modem link. Health club privileges. Cr cds: A, D, DS, ER, JCB, MC, V. D ⟨symbols⟩ SC

Cornwall, Ontario *(See also Morrisburg)*

Motel

★ ★ ★ **BEST WESTERN PARKWAY INN.** *(1515 Vincent Massey Dr (Hwy 2), Cornwall ON K6H 5R6) 613/932-0451; FAX 613/938-5479.* 91 rms, 2 story. S $86; D $110-$145; each addl $6; suites $200; under 18 free. Crib free. Pet accepted. TV; cable (premium). Pool; whirlpool. Coffee in rms. Restaurant 6:30 am-10 pm; Sun to 9 pm. Bar 11-2 am. Ck-out noon. Meeting rms. Business servs avail. In-rm modem link. Valet serv. X-country ski 2 mi. Exercise equipt; weights, bicycles, sauna. Refrigerators, some fireplaces. Cr cds: A, C, D, ER, MC, V. ⟨symbols⟩ SC

Hamilton, Ontario *(See also Brantford, Mississauga, St Catharines, Toronto)*

Motor Hotel

★ ★ **VENTURE INN-BURLINGTON.** *(2020 Lakeshore Rd, Burlington ON L7S 1Y2) N via Hwy 2/6 or QEW. 905/681-0762; FAX 905/634-4398; res: 800/486-8873.* Web www.jwg.com/ventureinns. 122 rms, 7 story. S $89; D $99; each addl $10; suites $150; under 19 free. Crib free. Pet accepted, some restrictions. TV. Indoor pool; whirlpool, sauna. Continental bkfst. Restaurant adj 7-2 am; Sat, Sun 9-2 am. Bar; live band. Meeting rms. Business servs avail. Valet serv. Sun deck. Picnic tables. Opp lake, beach. Cr cds: A, D, DS, ER, MC, V. D ⟨symbols⟩ SC

Hotels

★ ★ **HOWARD JOHNSON ROYAL CONNAUGHT.** *(112 King St E, Hamilton ON L8N 1A8) 905/546-8111; FAX 905/546-8144.* 206 rms, 11 story. S $89-$99, D $99-$109; each addl $10; suites from $139; under 18 free; wkend package. Crib free. Pet accepted. TV; cable (premium), VCR avail. Indoor pool; whirlpool. Coffee in rms. Restaurant 24 hrs. Rm serv 24 hrs. Bars 11-2 am. Ck-out noon. Meeting rms. Business servs avail. Barber, beauty shop. Exercise equipt; weight machine, bicycle, sauna. Some refrigerators, minibars; microwaves avail. 124-ft (38-m) pool slide. Cr cds: A, C, D, DS, ER, MC, V.

D ⟨symbols⟩ SC

✔ ★ ★ **RAMADA.** *(150 King St E, Hamilton ON L8N 1B2) 905/528-3451; FAX 905/522-2281.* 215 rms, 12 story. S, D $69-$110; each addl $10; suites $195-$400; under 19 free. Crib free. Pet accepted. TV; cable, VCR avail. Heated pool; wading pool, whirlpool. Restaurant 7:30 am-10 pm. Bar Fri-Sat 5:30 pm- 2 am. Ck-out 11 am. Meeting rms. Business servs avail. Shopping arcade. Barber, beauty shop. Exercise equipt; weights, bicycles, sauna. Health club privileges. Cr cds: A, C, D, DS, ER, JCB, MC, V.

D ⟨symbols⟩ SC

★ ★ ★ **SHERATON.** *(116 King St W, Hamilton ON L8P 4V3)* in Lloyd D Jackson Sq. *905/529-5515; FAX 905/529-8266.* E-mail shsales@netaccess.on.ca. 299 units, 18 story. S, D $175-$195; each addl $18; suites from $225; under 17 free; wkend rates. Crib free. Pet accepted. Parking $7.99. TV; cable (premium). Indoor pool; whirlpool. Complimentary coffee in rms. Restaurant 6:30 am-10.30 pm. Rm serv to 1 am. Bar 11-2 am; entertainment. Ck-out noon. Convention facilities. Business center. In-rm modem link. Shopping arcade. Barber, beauty shop. Exercise equipt; weights, bicycles, sauna. Downhill/x-country ski 4 mi. Health club privileges. Bathrm phones; microwaves avail. Direct access to Convention Centre & Hamilton Place Concert Hall. Cr cds: A, C, D, DS, ER, JCB, MC, V.

🄳 🌊 🐾 ➳ 🏋️ 🔅 🔥 SC 🏃

Kenora, Ontario

Motels

★ **COMFORT INN.** *(1230 Hwy 17E, Kenora ON P9N 1L9) 807/468-8845; FAX 807/468-1588.* 77 rms, 2 story. Mid-June-mid-Sept: S $70-$90; D $75-$100; each addl $4; under 18 free; lower rates rest of yr. Crib free. Pet accepted. TV; cable (premium). Restaurant nearby. Ck-out 11 am. Business servs avail. Cr cds: A, D, DS, ER, MC, V.

🄳 🌊 🔅 🔥 SC

★ ★ **TRAVELODGE.** *(800 Hwy 17E, Kenora ON P9N 1L9) 807/468-3155; FAX 807/468-4780.* 42 rms, 1-2 story, 5 kits. Mid-June-mid-Sept: S $75-$80; D $75-$104; lower rates rest of yr. Crib $6. Pet accepted. TV; cable (premium). 2 pools, 1 indoor; whirlpool. Playground. Restaurant 6 am-11 pm. Rm serv. Bar 11-1 am. Ck-out noon. Meeting rms. Business servs avail. Valet serv. Downhill/x-country ski 6 mi. Exercise equipt; bicycles, weight machine, sauna. Picnic tables. Cr cds: A, D, DS, ER, JCB, MC, V.

🄳 🌊 🐾 ➳ 🏋️ 🔅 🔥 SC

Hotel

★ ★ **BEST WESTERN LAKESIDE INN.** *(470 1st Ave S, Kenora ON P9N 1N5)* just off Hwy 17 on Lake of the Woods. *807/468-5521; FAX 807/468-4734.* 94 rms, 9 story. S $93; D $103; each addl $10; suites $175-$225; under 14 free. Crib avail. Pet accepted. TV; cable (premium), VCR avail. Indoor pool. Complimentary coffee in rms. Restaurant 7 am-10 pm. Bar 11:30-1 am. Ck-out 11 am. Meeting rms. Business servs avail. Downhill/x-country ski 4 mi. Exercise rm; instructor, treadmills, stair machines, sauna. Game rm. Rec rm. Refrigerators avail. Minibar in suites. On lakeshore. Cr cds: A, C, D, DS, ER, JCB, MC, V.

🄳 🌊 🐾 ➳ 🏋️ 🔅 🔥 SC

Kingston, Ontario

Motels

✔★ **ECONO LODGE.** *(2327 Princess St (Hwy 2), Kingston ON K7M 3G1) 613/531-8929.* 32 rms, 8 kits. May-Labour Day: S $48; D $58-$78; each addl $4; kit. units $4 addl; lower rates rest of yr. Crib $4. Pet accepted; $12/day. TV; cable. Heated pool. Playground. Complimentary coffee in lobby. Restaurant adj 7 am-9 pm. Ck-out 11 am. Refrigerators. Picnic tables. Grills. Cr cds: A, C, D, ER, MC, V. 🄳 🌊 ➳ 🔅 🔥 SC

★ ★ **FIRST CANADA INN.** *(First Canada Court, Kingston ON K7K 6W2)* Hwy 401 exit 617 S. *613/541-1111; FAX 613/549-5735; res: 800/267-7899.* 74 rms, 2 story. June-Oct 1: S $53.95-$69.95; D $60.95-$76.95; each addl $5; suites $85.95-$125.95; under 12 free; lower rates rest of yr. Crib free. Pet accepted. TV; cable, VCR avail (movies). Complimentary continental bkfst. Complimentary coffee in rms. Restaurant opp 10-2 am. Bar 4 pm-1 am. Coin lndry. Meeting rms. Business servs avail. Refrigerators. Cr cds: A, D, ER, MC, V.

🄳 🌊 🔅 🔥 SC

★ **SEVEN OAKES.** *(2331 Princess St (Hwy 2), Kingston ON K7M 3G1) 613/546-3655; FAX 613/549-5677.* 40 rms. June-Oct 1: S $64; D $68-$74; each addl $5; package plans; lower rates rest of yr. Crib free. Pet accepted. Heated pool; whirlpool. Sauna. Playground. Bar. Ck-out 11 am. Coin lndry. Sundries. Lighted tennis. Refrigerators; some in-rm whirlpools. Picnic tables, grills. Cr cds: A, D, DS, ER, MC, V. 🌊 🎾 ➳ 🔅 🔥 SC

Motor Hotel

★ ★ **HOWARD JOHNSON CONFEDERATION PLACE.** *(237 Ontario St, Kingston ON K7L 2Z4) 613/549-6300; FAX 613/549-1508.* 94 rms, 6 story. May-late Sept: S, D $99-$160; each addl $10; suites $225-$250; under 18 free; higher rates special events; lower rates rest of yr. Crib free. Pet accepted. TV; cable. Heated pool; whirlpool, poolside serv. Restaurant 7 am-10 pm. Rm serv. Ck-out 11 am. Meeting rms. Business servs avail. Underground free parking. Exercise equipt; weight machine, bicycles. X-country ski 3 mi. On waterfront. Cr cds: A, D, DS, ER, MC, V. 🌊 ➳ 🏋️ 🔅 🔥 SC

Kitchener-Waterloo, Ontario

Motels

★ **COMFORT INN.** *(220 Holiday Inn Dr, Cambridge ON N3C 1Z4) ON 401 exit ON 24 N.* 519/658-1100; FAX 519/658-6979; res: 800/228-5150. 84 rms, 2 story. S $59-$80; D $67-$95; each addl $4; under 18 free. Crib free. Pet accepted. TV; cable (premium), VCR avail. Complimentary coffee in lobby. Ck-out 11 am. Business servs avail. Sundries. Downhill/x-country ski 4 mi. Cr cds: A, C, D, DS, ER, JCB, MC, V. 🦮 🏊 ➰ 🐾 SC

★ **DAYS INN.** *(650 Hespeler Rd, Cambridge ON N1R 6J8) S on ON 24, off Hwy 401.* 519/622-1070; FAX 519/622-1512. 119 rms, 2 story. S $69.95; D $74.95; each addl $7; under 18 free. Crib free. Pet accepted. TV; cable (premium), VCR avail. Heated pool. Playground. Ck-out 11 am. Meeting rms. Business servs avail. Valet serv. Sundries. Microwaves avail. Cr cds: A, D, ER, MC, V. 🦮 🏊 ➰ 🐾 SC

Motor Hotels

★★ **CLARION INN.** *(1333 Weber St E, Kitchener ON N2A 1C2)* 519/893-1234; FAX 519/893-2100. 102 rms, 2-4 story. S $89-$109; D $99-$129; each addl $8; under 18 free; higher rates Oktoberfest. Crib free. Pet accepted, some restrictions; $50 refundable. TV; cable, VCR avail. Heated pool; whirlpool, sauna, poolside serv. Complimentary coffee in rms. Retaurant 7 am-9 pm. Rm serv. Bar 11-1 am; entertainment Thurs-Sat. Ck-out 11:30 am. Meeting rms. Business center. Sundries. Some refrigerators; microwaves avail. Balconies. Cr cds: A, C, D, DS, ER, MC, V. D 🦮 🏊 ➰ 🐾 SC 🎿

★★ **HOLIDAY INN.** *(30 Fairway Rd S, Kitchener ON N2A 2N2)* 519/893-1211; FAX 519/894-8518. 182 rms, 2-6 story. S $119.95-$139.95, D $129.95-$149.95; each addl $10; suites $195.95-$295.95; under 19 free. Crib free. Pet accepted. TV; cable (premium). Indoor/outdoor pool; poolside serv. Supervised child's activities (July-Aug). Restaurant 6:30 am-10 pm. Bar 11-1 am. Ck-out noon. Meeting rms. Business center. In-rm modem link. Valet serv. Downhill/x-country ski 2 mi. Exercise equipt; weight machine, bicycles. Microwaves avail. Private patios, balconies. Cr cds: A, C, D, DS, ER, JCB, MC, V.
D 🦮 🏊 🏊 🎿 ➰ 🐾 SC 🎿

★★★ **WATERLOO INN.** *(475 King St N, Waterloo ON N2J 2Z5) 1 mi N on ON 86.* 519/884-0220; FAX 519/884-0321; res: 800/361-4708. Web www.nrzone.com/waterlooinn/. 160 rms, 4 story. S $93; D $103; each addl $12; suites from $165; under 16 free. Crib free. Pet accepted. TV; cable. Indoor pool; whirlpool, poolside serv. Complimentary coffee in rms. Restaurant 7 am-10 pm. Rm serv. Bar 11-1 am. Convention facilities. Business servs avail. In-rm modem link. Valet serv. Sundries. Downhill ski 10 mi; x-country ski 1/2 mi. Exercise equipt; weights, bicycles, sauna. Game rm. Balconies. Landscaped courtyard. Cr cds: A, D, DS, ER, MC, V. D 🦮 🏊 ➰ 🎿 ➰ 🐾 SC

Hotels

★★★ **FOUR POINTS BY SHERATON.** *(105 King St E, Kitchener ON N2G 2K8) at Benton.* 519/744-4141; FAX 519/578-6889. 202 rms, 9 story. S, D $119-$139; each addl $10; suites $130-$269; studio rms $79; under 18 free; wkend package. Crib free. Pet accepted, some restrictions. TV; cable, VCR avail. Pool; whirlpool, poolside serv. Supervised child's activities; ages 6-16. Complimentary coffee in rms. Restaurant 6:30 am-2 pm, 5:30-10:30 pm. Bar 5 pm-1 am; entertainment. Ck-out noon. Meeting rms. Business center. In-rm modem link. Free covered parking. Downhill/x-country ski 4 mi. Exercise rm; instructor, weights, treadmill, sauna. Game rm. Miniature golf. Rec rm. Minibars; microwaves avail. Some balconies. Cr cds: A, C, D, ER, MC, V. D 🦮 🏊 🏊 🎿 ➰ 🐾 SC 🎿

★★★ **LANGDON HALL.** *(RR 33, Cambridge ON N3H 4R8) E on Hwy 8 to Fountain St, turn right to Blair Rd then left to Langdon.* 519/740-2100; FAX 519/740-8161; res: 800/268-1898. E-mail langdon@golden.net. 43 rms, 3 story. 2-day min: S, D $199-$269; suites $369. Crib $25. Pet accepted, some restrictions; $25. TV; cable (premium), VCR avail. Heated pool; whirlpool, poolside serv. Complimentary continental bkfst. Restaurant 7-10 am, noon-2 pm, 6-9 pm. Rm serv 24 hrs. Bar. Ck-out noon. Meeting rms. Business servs avail. In-rm modem link. Gift shop. Tennis. Downhill ski 4 mi; x-country ski on site. Hiking trail. Exercise equipt; weights, bicycles, sauna, steam rm. Massage. Rec rm. Lawn games. Balconies. Antebellum-style building in rural setting. Cr cds: A, D, ER, MC, V.
D 🦮 🏊 🎿 ➰ 🎿 🐾 🐾

London, Ontario

Motel

★★ **BEST WESTERN LAMPLIGHTER INN.** *(591 Wellington Rd, London ON N6C 4R3)* 519/681-7151; FAX 519/681-3271. 126 rms, 2 story. S $67-$150; D $78-$150; each addl $8; suites $85-$200; under 12 free. Pet accepted, some restrictions. TV; cable. Pool. Complimentary coffee in rms. Restaurant 6:30 am-9 pm; Sun to 8 pm. Bar 4 pm-midnight. Ck-out 11 am. Meeting rms. Business servs avail. Some in-rm whirlpools. Private patios, balconies. Picnic tables. Cr cds: A, D, DS, ER, MC, V. D ☕ ≈ ⌨ 🐾 SC

Hotels

★ ★ ★ **DELTA LONDON ARMOURIES.** *(325 Dundas St, London ON N6B 1T9)* *519/679-6111; FAX 519/679-3957.* 250 rms, 20 story. S $155-$175; D $165-$185; each addl $10; suites $250-$450; under 18 free; wkend rates. Crib free. Pet accepted. TV; cable (premium), VCR avail (movies). Indoor pool; whirlpool, wading pool. Supervised child's activities (July & Aug, daily; rest of yr, Sat, Sun); ages 5-12. Coffee in rms. Restaurant 6:30 am-10 pm. Bar to 1 am. Ck-out noon. Meeting rms. Business center. Concierge. Valet parking. Putting green. Exercise equipt; weights, bicycles, sauna. Health club privileges. Rec rm. Minibars. Some balconies. Luxury level. Cr cds: A, C, D, DS, ER, MC, V.
D ☕ ≈ ✗ ⌨ 🐾 SC ⛷

★ ★ ★ **WESTIN.** *(300 King St, London ON N6B 1S2)* *519/439-1661; FAX 519/439-9672.* Web www.westin.com. 322 rms, 22 story. S, D $110-$130; suites $240; under 18 free; wkend rates. Crib free. Pet accepted. TV; cable, VCR avail. Heated pool; wading pool, whirlpool, poolside serv. Restaurant 7 am-11 pm. Bar 11:30-1 am; entertainment. Ck-out 1 pm. Convention facilities. Business servs avail. In-rm modem link. Concierge. Gift shop. Exercise equipt; weights, bicycles, sauna. Health club privileges. Minibars. Luxury level. Cr cds: A, C, D, DS, ER, JCB, MC, V. D ☕ ≈ ✗ ⌨ 🐾 SC

Mississauga, Ontario *(See also Hamilton, Toronto)*

Motels

✔ ★ **DAYS INN.** *(4635 Tomken Rd, Mississauga ON L4W 1J9)* *905/238-5480; FAX 905/238-1031.* 61 rms, 3 story. No elvtr. S, D $60-$80; each addl $5; suites $135; under 18 free; wkly rates. Crib free. Pet accepted. TV; cable, VCR (movies). Complimentary continental bkfst. Restaurant opp 11:30 am-midnight. Ck-out 11:30 am. Business servs avail. Some refrigerators. Cr cds: A, C, D, DS, ER, JCB, MC, V. D ☕ ≈ ⌨ SC

★ **HOWARD JOHNSON.** *(2420 Surveyor Rd, Mississauga ON L5N 4E6)* *905/858-8600; FAX 905/858-8574.* 117 rms, 2 story. June-Sept: S $64-$69; D $69-$79; each addl $5; under 18 free; wkly, wkend, hol rates; lower rates rest of yr. Crib free. Pet accepted, some restrictions. TV; cable (premium). Complimentary continental bkfst. Complimentary coffee in rms. Restaurant opp open 24 hrs. Ck-out 1 pm. Coin lndry. Meeting rms. Business servs avail. Downhill/x-country ski 15 mi. Game rm. Some refrigerators. Picnic tables. Cr cds: A, D, DS, ER, MC, V. ☕ ≈ ⌨ 🐾 SC

Motor Hotels

★ ★ **DAYS INN-TORONTO AIRPORT.** *(6257 Airport Rd, Mississauga ON L4V 1E4)* near Lester B. Pearson Intl Airport. *905/678-1400; FAX 905/678-9130.* Web www.vsamota@cara.com. 202 rms, 7 story. S $140; D $150; each addl $10; suites $150; under 18 free; wkend rates. Crib free. Pet accepted, some restrictions; $10. TV; cable (premium). Indoor pool; whirlpool. Coffee in rms. Restaurant 6:30 am-11 pm. Rm serv. Bar noon-1 am. Ck-out noon. Meeting rms. Business servs avail. Bellhops. Gift shop. Barber, beauty shop. Valet serv. Airport transportation. 18-hole golf privileges. Downhill/x-country ski 20 mi. Exercise equipt; weight machine, stair machine, sauna. Balconies. Cr cds: A, C, D, DS, ER, JCB, MC, V. D ☕ ≈ 🏌 ≈ ✗ ⌨ 🐾 SC

★ ★ **HOLIDAY INN-TORONTO WEST.** *(100 Britannia Rd, Mississauga ON L4Z 2G1)* *905/890-5700; FAX 905/568-0868.* Web www.holi day-inn.com. 132 air-cooled rms, 6 story. S, D $125; each addl $8; under 20 free. Crib free. Pet accepted, some restrictions. TV; cable (premium), VCR avail. Complimentary bkfst buffet. Coffee in rms. Restaurant from 6:30 am. Rm serv. Bar. Ck-out noon. Meeting rms. Business servs avail. In-rm modem link. Valet serv. Free airport transportation. Exercise equipt; weight machine, bicycles, sauna. Whirlpool. Refrigerators avail. Cr cds: A, D, DS, ER, JCB, MC, V. D ☕ ✗ ⌨ 🐾 SC

★ **TRAVELODGE-TORONTO WEST.** *(5599 Ambler Dr, Mississauga ON L4W 3Z1)* SW of jct ON 401, Dixie Rd. *905/624-9500; FAX 905/624-1382.* 225 rms, 6 story. S $59; D $68; under 18 free; suites $86.95. Crib free. Pet accepted. TV; cable. Indoor pool; whirlpool. Complimentary coffee in rms. Restaurant 7-1 am. Bar from noon. Ck-out 11 am. Guest lndry. Meeting rms. Business servs avail. Valet serv. Sundries. Cr cds: A, D, DS, ER, JCB, MC, V. D ☕ ≈ ⌨ 🐾 SC

Hotels

★ ★ ★ **DELTA MEADOWVALE RESORT & CONFERENCE CENTER.** *(6750 Mississauga Rd, Mississauga ON L5N 2L3)* in Meadowvale Business Park. *905/821-1981; FAX*

905/542-4036; res: 800/268-1133 (CAN), 800/877-1133 (US). 374 rms, 15 story. S $195-$205; D $205-$220; each addl $15; suites $150-$300; under 18 free. Crib free. Pet accepted. TV; cable (premium), VCR avail. 2 pools, 1 indoor; whirlpool, poolside serv. Supervised child's activities; ages 2-14. Restaurant 6:30 am-10:30 pm. Rm serv 24 hrs. Bar 11-2 am; entertainment. Ck-out noon. Meeting rms. Business servs avail. Barber, beauty shop. Free airport transportation. Indoor tennis, pro shop. Golf privileges. Exercise rm; instructor, weight machine, bicycles. Lawn games. Minibars; some fireplaces. Microwaves avail. Balconies. Extensive grounds. Cr cds: A, D, DS, JCB, MC, V.

D ✦ ⛵ ✕ ≋ ✕ ⊠ SC

★ ★ ★ **FOUR POINTS BY SHERATON.** *(5444 Dixie Rd, Mississauga ON L4W 2L2)* ¹/₄ *mi S of ON 401 Dixie Rd S exit.* 905/624-1144; FAX 905/624-9477. Web www.shera ton.com/863. 296 rms, 10 story. S, D $89-$178; each addl $10; suites $225-$395; under 18 free; wkend package plans. Crib free. Pet accepted, some restrictions. TV; cable (premium), VCR avail. Heated pool. Supervised child's activities; ages 2-12. Complimentary coffee in rms. Restaurant 6:30 am-10 pm; Sat, Sun from 7 am. Bars 11:30-1 am. Ck-out 1 pm. Meeting rms. Business center. In-rm modem link. Gift shop. Beauty shop. Garage parking. Free airport transportation. Exercise equipt; weights, bicycles, sauna. Game rm. Refrigerators, minibars. Cr cds: A, C, D, DS, ER, JCB, MC, V. D ✦ ⛵ ≋ ✕ ⊠ ▨ SC ⚹

★ ★ ★ **HILTON INTERNATIONAL-TORONTO AIRPORT.** *(5875 Airport Rd, Mississauga ON L4V 1N1) 1 mi W of jct ON 427, Dixon Rd, near Lester B. Pearson Intl Airport.* 905/677-9900; FAX 905/677-5073. Web www.hilton.com. 413 rms, 11 story. S, D $139-$179; each addl $20; suites $159-$189; family rates; wkend packages. Crib free. Pet accepted, some restrictions. TV. Heated pool; poolside serv. Coffee in rms. Restaurant 6:30 am-11 pm. Bars 11-2 am; entertainment. Ck-out noon. Meeting rms. Business center. Barber. Free garage parking. Free airport transportation. Exercise equipt; weights, bicycle, sauna. Minibars; many bathrm phones. Cr cds: A, D, DS, ER, JCB, MC, V.

D ✦ ⚹ ≋ ✕ ✕ ⊠ ▨ SC ⚹

★ ★ **NOVOTEL.** *(3670 Hurontario St, Mississauga ON L5B 1P3) jct ON 10 & Burnhamthorpe Rd.* 905/896-1000; res: 800/668-6835; FAX 905/896-2521. E-mail missmail @aol.com. 325 air-cooled rms, 14 story. S, D $160; each addl $15; suite $250; under 16 free; wkend rates. Crib free. Pet accepted. TV; cable (premium). Indoor pool. Restaurant 6 am-midnight. Bar 11-1 am. Ck-out 1 pm. Meeting rms. Business servs avail. In-rm modem link. Shopping arcade. Beauty shop. Covered parking. Free airport transportation. Health club privileges. Minibars; some bathrm phones. Shopping center opp. Cr cds: A, C, D, DS, ER, JCB, MC, V. D ✦ ≋ ✕ ▨ SC

★ ★ **STAGE WEST.** *(5400 Dixie Rd, Mississauga ON L4W 4T4) 905/238-0159; FAX 905/238-9820; res: 800/668-9887.* Web www.mississa loga.com/stage_west.htm. 224 suites, 16 story. Suites $129; family, wkly rates; package plans. Crib free. Pet accepted. TV; cable (premium), VCR avail. Indoor pool; whirlpool, lifeguard, water slide. Supervised child's activities; ages 1-12. Restaurant 6:30 am-midnight. Bar 11-1 am. Ck-out noon. Meeting rms. Business center. In-rm modem link. Concierge. Shopping arcade. Barber, beauty shop. Valet parking $5/day. Free airport transportation. Downhill/x-country ski 20 mi. Exercise equipt; weights, rower. Health club privileges. Microwaves avail. Complex includes Stage West Dinner Theatre. Cr cds: A, D, ER, MC, V. D ✦ ⚹ ⛵ ≋ ✕ ✕ ⊠ ▨ SC ⚹

Morrisburg, Ontario *(See also Cornwall; also see Ogdensburg, NY)*

Motel

★ **LOYALIST HOTEL.** *(Hwy 2 & 31, Morrisburg ON K0C 1X0)* 613/543-2932; FAX 613/543-3316. 31 rms, 1-2 story. S $39-$49; D $49-$69; wkend rates. Pet accepted. TV; cable. Heated pool. Restaurant 11:30 am-2 pm, 5-9:30 pm. Bar noon-1 am. Ck-out 11 am. Cr cds: A, MC, V. ✦ ≋ ✕ ▨ SC

Niagara Falls, Ontario
(See St Catharines; also see Buffalo & Niagara Falls, NY)

Motels

(Rates are usually higher on holiday wkends)

✔ ★ ★ **FLAMINGO MOTOR INN.** *(7701 Lundy's Lane (ON 20), Niagara Falls ON L2H 1H3) 1¹/₂ mi W of Falls.* 905/356-4646. 95 rms, 2 story. Mid-June-Labour Day: S, D $52-$84; each addl $8; suite $80-$200; lower rates rest of yr. Crib free. Pet accepted, some restrictions. TV; cable. Heated pool. Restaurant adj 7 am-10 pm. Ck-out 11 am. Gift shop. Picnic tables. Cr cds: A, C, D, DS, MC, V. ✦ ≋ ✕ ▨ SC

★ ★ **HONEYMOON CITY.** *(4943 Clifton Hill, Niagara Falls ON L2G 3N5)* 905/357-4330; FAX 905/357-0423; res: 800/668-8840. Web www.niagara. com/falls. 77 rms, 2 story. Mid-June-early Sept: S, D $49.50-$149.50; suites, kits. $79.50-$269.50; under 12 free; wkend, hol rates; lower rates rest of yr. Crib free. Pet accepted, some restrictions. TV; cable, VCR avail (movies). Heated pool. Restaurant 7 am-11 pm. Ck-out 11 am. Business servs avail. Shopping arcade. X-country ski 2 mi. Some balconies. Cr cds: A, DS, MC, V.
🐾 ⚓ 🛏 🖐 SC

Motor Hotels

★ ★ **BEST WESTERN FALLSVIEW.** *(5551 Murray St, Niagara Falls ON L2G 2J4)* 1 blk to Falls. 905/356-0551; FAX 905/356-7773. 244 rms, 4-6 story. June-Sept: S, D $79-$169; each addl $10; lower rates rest of yr. Crib $5. Pet accepted. TV; cable. Indoor pool; whirlpool. Sauna. Restaurant 6 am-10 pm. Bar 11-1 am. Ck-out 11 am. Coin lndry. Meeting rms. Business center. Bellhops. Gift shop. Sundries. Game rm. Some in-rm whirlpools. Cr cds: A, C, D, DS, ER, JCB, MC, V. D 🐾 ⚓ 🛏 🖐 SC 🛷

★ ★ **HOLIDAY INN BY THE FALLS.** *(5339 Murray St, Niagara Falls ON L2G 2J3)* 2 blks W of Falls. 905/356-1333; FAX 905/356-7128. E-mail res@holi dayinn.com; web www.holidayinn.com. 122 rms, 6 story. Mid-June-mid-Sept: S, D $95-$195; each addl $10; bridal suite $175-$225; lower rates rest of yr. Crib $5. Pet accepted. TV. 2 pools, 1 indoor; whirlpool. Restaurant 7 am-10 pm; winter from 8 am. Rm serv. Bar noon-2 am. Ck-out noon. Meeting rm. Business servs avail. Sundries. Sauna. Some in-rm whirlpools. Balconies. Cr cds: A, C, D, DS, ER, JCB, MC, V. D 🐾 ⚓ 🛏 🖐 SC

★ ★ **RAMADA-CORAL INN RESORT.** *(7429 Lundy's Lane (ON 20), Niagara Falls ON L2H 1G9)* 2 mi W of Falls. 905/356-6116; FAX 905/356-7204. E-mail ramada.niagara @sympatico.ca; web ourismniagara.com/ramcoral. 130 units, 2-4 story. Mid-June-early Sept: S, D $79-$129.50; each addl $8; suites, studio rms $119.50-$159; under 18 free; package plans; higher rates: Sat in season, hols, special events; lower rates rest of yr. Crib free. Pet accepted, some restrictions; $8. TV. 2 heated pools, 1 indoor; whirlpool. Restaurant 7 am-10 pm. Ck-out 11 am. Meeting rms. Business center. Valet serv. Gift shop. 9-hole golf privileges. Sauna. Health club privileges. Playground. Game rm. Refrigerators, in-rm whirlpools; fireplace in suites. Cr cds: A, C, D, DS, ER, JCB, MC, V.
🐾 🕴 ⚓ 🛏 🖐 SC 🛷

Ottawa, Ontario

Hotels

★ ★ ★ **DELTA.** *(361 Queen St, Ottawa ON K1R 7S9)* off Lyon St. 613/238-6000; FAX 613/238-2290; res: 800/268-1133. Web www.deltahotels. com. 328 units, 18 story. May-June, Sept-Oct: S $140-$155; D $155-$175; each addl $15; suites $175-$190; under 18 free; wkend rates; special summer rates; lower rates rest of yr. Crib free. Pet accepted. Garage $11.50. TV; cable. Indoor pool; whirlpool. Restaurant 6:30 am-10 pm; dining rm 5-10 pm. Rm serv 6 am-11 pm. Bars 11-2 am. Ck-out noon. Meeting rms. Business center. In-rm modem link. Barber, beauty shop. Downhill/x-country ski 12 mi. Exercise rm; instructor, weights, bicycles, saunas. Minibars. Some balconies. Cr cds: A, D, ER, MC, V.
D 🐾 ⚓ 🛏 🕴 🖐 SC 🛷

★ ★ **LORD ELGIN.** *(100 Elgin St, Ottawa ON K1P 5K8)* at Laurier Ave. 613/235-3333; FAX 613/235-3223; res: 800/267-4298. 311 rms, 11 story. S $109-$135; D $115-$141; each addl $5; suites $225-$300; under 18 free; wkend rates. Crib free. Pet accepted, some restrictions. Garage; valet, in/out $11. TV; cable. Coffee in rms. Restaurant 7 am-11 pm. Bar 11:30-1 am. Ck-out 1 pm. Meeting rms. Business servs avail. In-rm modem link. Gift shop. Downhill/x-country ski 12 mi. Exercise equipt; weight machines, treadmill. Originally opened 1941; completely renovated. Cr cds: A, C, D, ER, JCB, MC, V.
D 🐾 ⚓ 🕴 🛏 🖐 SC

★ ★ ★ **RADISSON-OTTAWA CENTRE.** *(100 Kent St, Ottawa ON K1P 5R7)* 613/238-1122; FAX 613/783-4229. 478 rms, 26 story. S, D $125-$155; each addl $10; suites $300-$400; under 19 free; wkend rates. Crib free. Pet accepted. Garage (fee). TV; cable (premium). Indoor pool; whirlpool. Restaurant 6:30 am-11 pm; revolving rooftop dining rm 11:30 am-2:30 pm, 6-11 pm; Sat from 6 pm. Bar 11-1 am. Ck-out 1 pm. Meeting rms. Business servs avail. In-rm modem link. Downhill ski 15 mi. Exercise rm; instructor, weights, bicycles, sauna. Minibars. Many balconies. Adj underground shopping mall. Luxury level. Cr cds: A, C, D, DS, ER, JCB, MC, V. D 🐾 ⚓ 🛏 🕴 🖐 SC

★ ★ ★ **SHERATON.** *(150 Albert St, Ottawa ON K1P 5G2)* 613/238-1500; FAX 613/235-2723. 236 rms, 18 story. S $175; D $185; each addl $20; suites $180-$390; family rates; wkend package plan. Crib free. Garage (fee). Pet accepted. TV; cable. Indoor pool; whirlpool; poolside serv. Coffee in rms. Restaurant 6:30 am-11 pm. Ck-out noon. Meeting rms. Business center. In-rm modem link. Downhill/x-country ski 12 mi. Exercise equipt; weights, bicycles, sauna. Minibars. Luxury level. Cr cds: A, D, DS, ER, JCB, MC, V.

⊡ 🐾 🏊 🏊 🏋 🖾 🐾 SC 🏄

★ ★ ★ **THE WESTIN.** *(11 Colonel By Dr, Ottawa ON K1N 9H4) connects with Ottawa Congress Center, Rideau Center.* 613/560-7000; FAX 613/560-7359. 484 rms, 24 story. Mid-Apr-June, mid-Sept-mid-Nov: S, D $175-$195; each addl $20; suites $265-$700; under 18 free; wkend rates; lower rates rest of yr. Crib free. Pet accepted, some restrictions. TV; cable. Indoor pool; whirlpool. Restaurants 6:30 am-11 pm. Rm serv 24 hrs. Bar 11:30-2 am. Ck-out 1 pm. Convention facilities. Business center. Concierge. Shopping arcade adj. Barber, beauty shop. Valet parking. Downhill/x-country ski 12 mi. Exercise rm; instructor, weights, bicycles, sauna. Massage. Minibars; some bathrm phones. Opp Rideau Canal; near Parliament Hill. Cr cds: A, C, D, DS, ER, JCB, MC, V.

⊡ 🐾 🏊 🏊 🏋 🖾 🐾 SC 🏄

Resort

★ ★ ★ **LE CHÂTEAU MONTEBELLO.** *(392 Rue Notre Dame, Montebello, Quebec QE J0V 1L0) 40 mi E on Hwy 148.* 819/423-6341; FAX 819/423-5283; res: 800/441-1414. 210 rms, 3 story. Mid-May-mid-Oct, MAP: S $176.50; D $228; each addl $71.50; under 4 free; lower rates rest of yr. Crib free. Pet accepted. TV; cable. 2 pools, 1 indoor; whirlpool, lifeguard. Playground. Supervised child's activities (mid-June-early Sept); ages 3-12. Dining rm 7 am-3 pm, 5:30-10 pm. Rm serv 7 am-11 pm. Bar 11-1 am; entertainment Fri-Sat. Ck-out noon, ck-in 3 pm. Meeting rms. Business center. In-rm modem link. Bellhops. Valet serv. Gift shop. Sports dir. Indoor & outdoor tennis. 18-hole golf, greens fee (incl cart) $54, pro, putting green. X-country ski on site (rentals). Sleighing. Curling. Bicycles. Horseback riding. Lawn games. Soc dir. Rec rm. Game rm. Squash courts. Exercise rm; instructor, weight machines, bicycles, sauna, steam rm. Massage. Fishing, hunting guides. Minibars. Marina. On 65,000 acres. Cr cds: A, C, D, DS, JCB, MC, V.

⊡ 🐾 🏊 🏋 🏊 🏋 🏊 🏋 🖾 🐾 🏄

St Catharines, Ontario (See also Hamilton, Niagara Falls, NY & ON)

Motel

★ ★ ★ **HOLIDAY INN.** *(2 N Service Rd, St Catharines ON L2N 4G9) at QEW Lake St exit.* 905/934-8000; FAX 905/934-9117. E-mail holiday@niagra.com. 140 rms, 2 story. July-Sept: S $99-$129; D $109-$139; each addl $10; under 18 free; lower rates rest of yr. Crib free. Pet accepted. TV; cable (premium) VCR avail (movies). Indoor/outdoor pool; poolside serv, lifeguard. Playground. Restaurant 7 am-11 pm. Rm serv. Bar noon-1 am. Ck-out 1 pm. Business servs avail. In-rm modem link. Bellhops. Valet serv. Gift shop. Exercise rm; instructor, weights, rower, sauna. Balconies. Cr cds: A, C, D, DS, ER, JCB, MC, V. ⊡ 🐾 🏊 🏋 🖾 🐾 SC

Motor Hotels

★ ★ ★ **EMBASSY SUITES.** *(3530 Schmon Pkwy, Thorold ON L2V 4Y6)* 905/984-8484; FAX 905/984-6691. Web www.embassy-suites.com. 128 kit. suites, 4 story. S, D $94-$200; each addl $10; under 18 free. Crib free. Pet accepted. TV; cable, VCR avail. Indoor pool. Complimentary full bkfst. Restaurant 11 am-11 pm. Rm serv. Bar. Ck-out noon. Meeting rms. Business center. In-rm modem link. Valet serv. Sundries. Exercise equipt; weights, rowers, sauna. Lawn games. Microwaves. Cr cds: A, D, DS, ER, MC, V.

⊡ 🐾 🏊 🏋 🖾 🐾 SC 🏄

✔ ★ ★ **HOWARD JOHNSON.** *(89 Meadowvale Dr, St Catharines ON L2N 3Z8) just off QEW Lake St N exit.* 905/934-5400; FAX 905/646-8700. 96 rms, 5 story. S $59-$89; D $69-$99; each addl $10; under 18 free. Crib free. Pet accepted. TV. Indoor pool; sauna. Coffee in rms. Restaurant open 24 hrs. Bar 11-2 am. Ck-out noon. Coin lndry. Meeting rm. Business servs avail. In-rm modem link. X-country ski 10 mi. Exercise equipt; weights, rower. Microwaves avail. Cr cds: A, C, D, DS, ER, MC, V. ⊡ 🐾 🏊 🏋 🖾 🐾 SC

Sarnia, Ontario (See also London)

Motels

★ ★ ★ **DRAWBRIDGE INN.** *(283 N Christina St, Sarnia ON N7T 5V4)* 519/337-7571; FAX 519/332-8181; res: 800/663-0376. 97 rms, 3 story. S, D $82; each addl $9; suites $115-$135; under 12 free; wkend rates. Crib free. Pet accepted. TV; cable. Indoor pool; sauna. Restaurant 7 am-2 pm, 5-9 pm; Fri-Sun 8 am-2 pm, 5-9 pm. Rm serv. Bar noon-11 pm. Ck-out noon. Meeting rms. Business center. In-rm modem link. Bellhops. Valet serv. Health club privileges. Cr cds: A, D, DS, ER, MC, V. 🐾 🏊 🏋 🐾 SC 🏄

✔★★ **HARBOURFRONT INN.** (505 Harbour Rd, Sarnia ON N7T 5R8) ½ mi SW of Bluewater Bridge. 519/337-5434; FAX 519/332-5882; res: 800/787-5010. 105 rms, 2 story. S $51-$58; D $59-$67; each addl $4; under 16 free. Crib free. Pet accepted, some restrictions. TV; cable, VCR avail. Restaurant adj 11-1 am. Ck-out 11 am. Valet serv. Picnic tables. On river. Cr cds: A, D, ER, JCB, MC, V. 🄳 🐾 🔊 ⛱ 🐾 SC

★★★ **HOLIDAY INN.** (1498 Venetian Blvd, Sarnia ON N7T 7W6) 519/336-4130; FAX 519/332-3326. 151 rms, 2 story. S, D $69-$89; suites $180-$240; under 19 free; wkend rates. Crib free. Pet accepted. TV; cable (premium). 2 pools, 1 indoor; whirlpool. Playground. Restaurant 6:30 am-10:30 pm. Rm serv. Bar 11-1 am. Ck-out 1 pm. Meeting rms. Bellhops. Valet serv. Golf privileges, greens fee $10, putting green. Exercise equipt; weight machine, treadmill, sauna. Lawn games. Balconies. Cr cds: A, C, D, DS, ER, JCB, MC, V.
🄳 🐾 🎿 ⛱ 🏋 🔊 🐾 SC

Sault Ste Marie, Ontario

Motor Hotels

★★★ **ALGOMA'S WATER TOWER INN.** (360 Great Northern Rd, Sault Ste Marie ON P6A 5N3) 705/949-8111; FAX 705/949-1912. E-mail awtinn@age.net; web watertower inn.com. 180 rms, 5 story. S, D $79-$99; each addl $7; suites $130-$290; under 18 free; ski plans. Crib free. Pet accepted. TV; cable (premium), VCR avail. Heated pool; whirlpool. Restaurant 7 am-11 pm. Rm serv 7-11 am, 5-10 pm. Bar noon-1 am, dancing. Ck-out noon. Meeting rms. Bellhops. Valet serv. Airport transportation. Sundries. X-country ski 5 mi. Exercise equipt; weights, treadmill. Some refrigerators, microwaves; whirlpool in suites. Cr cds: A, C, D, DS, ER, JCB, MC, V. 🄳 🐾 🔊 ⛱ 🏋 🔊 🐾 SC

★★ **HOLIDAY INN.** (208 St Mary's River Dr, Sault Ste Marie ON P6A 5V4) 705/949-0611; FAX 705/945-6972. 195 rms, 9 story. June-mid-Oct: S $89-$115; D $99-$120; each addl $10; suites $175-$275; under 12 free; wkend rates; lower rates rest of yr. Crib free. Pet accepted. TV; cable (premium). Indoor pool; whirlpool, poolside serv in season. Supervised child's activities (June-Aug). Restaurant 6 am-11 pm; off-season from 7 am. Rm serv. Bars noon-1 am. Ck-out 1 pm. Meeting rms. Business center. In-rm modem link. Bellhops. Valet serv. Sundries. Gift shop. Airport transportation. Downhill ski 20 mi; x-country ski 10 mi. Exercise equipt; weight machine, rowers, sauna. Game rm. Refrigerator in some suites. Cr cds: A, C, D, DS, ER, JCB, MC, V. 🄳 🐾 🔊 ⛱ 🏋 🎿 🐾 SC 🛷

★★ **RAMADA INN & CONVENTION CENTRE.** (229 Great Northern Rd (Hwy 17 N), Sault Ste Marie ON P6B 4Z2) 705/942-2500; FAX 705/942-2570. 210 units, 2-7 story. S $70-$92; D $80-$112; each addl $10; suites $84-$250; studio rms $90; under 18 free; ski, package plans. Crib free. Pet accepted. TV; cable, VCR avail. 2 pools, 1 indoor; whirlpool. Restaurant 7 am-11 pm. Rm serv. Bar 11-1 am. Ck-out noon. Meeting rms. Business servs avail. Bellhops. Valet serv (Mon-Fri). Sundries. Downhill ski 20 mi; x-country ski 3 mi. Exercise equipt; weight machine, treadmill. Miniature golf; water slide. Carousel. Bowling. Game rms. Some refrigerators. Cr cds: A, C, D, ER, MC, V. 🄳 🐾 🔊 ⛱ 🏋 🔊 🐾 SC

Stratford, Ontario (See also Brantford, Kitchener-Waterloo)

Inn

★★★ **QUEEN'S INN.** (161 Ontario St, Stratford ON N5A 3H3) 519/271-1400; res: 800/461-6450; FAX 519/271-7373. 32 rms, 3 story, 7 suites. May-Oct: S $100-$110; D $85-$120; each addl $25; suites $130-$200; kit. units $190-$200; under 12 free; ski plans; lower rates rest of yr. Crib free. Pet accepted, some restrictions. TV; cable, VCR avail (movies). Restaurant 7 am-10 pm. Rm serv. Ck-out 11 am, ck-in 2 pm. Business servs avail. Luggage handling. Valet serv. Concierge serv. Downhill ski 20 mi; x-country ski 10 mi. Exercise equipt; weights, bicycle. Microwaves avail. Built in 1850. Cr cds: A, D, ER, MC, V.
🄳 🐾 🏋 🔊 🐾 SC

Thunder Bay, Ontario

Motels

✔★ **COMFORT INN.** (660 W Arthur St, Thunder Bay ON P7E 5R8) near Thunder Bay Airport. 807/475-3155; FAX 807/475-3816. 80 rms, 2 story. S $70-$85; D $75-$93; each addl $8; under 19 free. Crib free. Pet accepted. TV; cable. Complimentary coffee in lobby. Restaurant adj 7 am-11 pm. Ck-out 11 am. Business servs avail. In-rm modem link. Cr cds: A, D, DS, ER, MC, V. 🄳 🐾 🔊 🐾 SC

★★ **VICTORIA INN.** (555 W Arthur St, Thunder Bay ON P7E 5R5) near airport. 807/577-8481; res: 800/387-3331; FAX 807/475-8961. E-mail vicinn@tbaytel.net. 182 rms, 3 story. S $76.95-$155; D $86.95-$155; each addl $10; suites $179-$229; under 16 free.

Crib free. Pet accepted; $15. TV; cable, VCR avail (movies). Complimentary coffee in rms. Restaurant 7 am-11 pm. Rm serv. Bar 11:30-1 am. Ck-out noon. Meeting rms. Business servs avail. In-rm modem link. Valet serv. Sundries. Coin Indry. Free airport transportation. Downhill ski 8 mi; x-country ski 5 mi. Exercise equipt; treadmill, stair machine, sauna. Indoor pool; wading pool, whirlpool, poolside serv, lifeguard. Some refrigerators. Cr cds: A, C, D, DS, ER, MC, V. [D] [🛏] [⛷] [≋] [🍴] [✈] [📶] [🐾] [SC]

Motor Hotels

★ ★ ★ **AIRLANE HOTEL.** *(698 W Arthur St, Thunder Bay ON P7C 5R8) at jct ON 11/17 & ON 61, near Thunder Bay Airport.* 807/577-1181; FAX 807/475-4852; res: 800/465-5003. E-mail inquire@airline.com; web www.airline.com. 160 rms, 2-3 story. S $79-$105; D $85-$110; each addl $5; wkend rates. Crib free. Pet accepted. TV; cable (premium), VCR avail. Indoor pool; whirlpool. Restaurants 7 am-11 pm. Rm serv. Bar 4 pm-1 am, closed Sun; entertainment. Ck-out 11 am. Meeting rms. Business center. In-rm modem link. Bellhops. Valet serv. Sundries. Free airport transportation. Exercise equipt; weights, stair machine, sauna. Minibars. Cr cds: A, C, D, ER, MC, V. [D] [🛏] [⛷] [🍴] [✈] [📶] [🐾] [🦽]

★ **BEST WESTERN CROSSROADS.** *(655 W Arthur St, Thunder Bay ON P7E 5R6) at jct ON 11/17 & ON 61, near Thunder Bay Airport.* 807/577-4241; FAX 807/475-7059. 60 rms, 2 story. May-Oct: S $73; D $78; under 12 free; lower rates rest of yr. Crib free. Pet accepted. TV; cable. Complimentary coffee. Restaurant opp 7 am-midnight. Ck-out 11 am. Business servs avail. In-rm modem link. Valet serv. Free airport transportation. Some refrigerators. Cr cds: A, C, D, DS, ER, MC, V. [🛏] [🍴] [📶] [🐾] [SC]

★ ★ **LANDMARK INN.** *(1010 Dawson Rd, Thunder Bay ON P7B 5J4) jct Hwy 11/17 & 102, County Fair Plaza.* 807/767-1681; FAX 807/767-1439; res: 800/465-3950 (CAN & MI, WI, IN). 106 rms, 4 story. S $80; D $86; each addl $8; under 12 free. Crib free. Pet accepted; $50. TV; cable. Indoor pool; whirlpool, sauna, water slide, poolside serv. Complimentary continental bkfst. Coffee in rms. Restaurant 7-1 am. Rm serv. Bar 11-1 am. Ck-out 11 am. Meeting rms. Business servs avail. In-rm modem link. Valet serv. Sundries. Free airport transportation. Downhill ski 20 mi. Cr cds: A, DS, ER, MC, V. [D] [🛏] [⛷] [≋] [🍴] [🐾] [SC]

↙ ★ ★ **PRINCE ARTHUR.** *(17 N Cumberland, Thunder Bay ON P7A 4K8)* 807/345-5411; FAX 807/345-8565; res: 800/267-2675. E-mail pahotel@tbaytel.net; web www.tradenet.ca/prince_arthur. 121 rms, 6 story. S $59-$75; D $65-$79; each addl $8; suites $105-$135; under 16 free. Crib free. Pet accepted. TV; cable. Indoor pool; wading pool, whirlpool, saunas. Coffee in rms. Restaurant 6:30 am-10 pm. Bar 11-1 am. Rm serv. Ck-out noon. Meeting rms. Business servs avail. In-rm modem link. Valet serv. Sundries. Free airport transportation. Health club privileges. Some refrigerators; microwaves avail. Downhill ski 10 mi. Overlooks harbor. Shopping mall opp. Cr cds: A, C, D, ER, MC, V. [D] [🛏] [⛷] [≋] [🍴] [🐾] [SC]

★ ★ **VALHALLA INN.** *(1 Valhalla Inn Rd, Thunder Bay ON P7E 6J1) at jct ON 11/17 & ON 61, near Thunder Bay Airport.* 807/577-1121; res: 800/964-1121; FAX 807/475-4723. E-mail valvay@baynet.net; web www.valhalla inn.com. 267 rms, 5 story. S $175-$190; D $185-$200; each addl $10; suites $295-$305; under 18 free; ski, wkend plans. Crib free. Pet accepted; $10. TV. Indoor pool; whirlpool. Complimentary coffee in rms. Restaurant 6:30 am-11:30 pm. Rm serv. Bar 4:30 pm-2 am. Ck-out 1 pm. Meeting rms. Business servs avail. In-rm modem link. Bellhops. Valet serv. Sundries. Free airport transportation. Downhill ski 3 mi; x-country ski 4 mi. Exercise equipt; weights, bicycles, sauna. Bicycle rentals. Game rm. Some bathrm phones, minibars; microwaves avail. Luxury level. Cr cds: A, C, D, DS, ER, MC, V. [D] [🛏] [⛷] [≋] [🍴] [✈] [📶] [🐾] [SC]

★ ★ **VENTURE INN.** *(450 Memorial Ave, Thunder Bay ON P7B 3Y7) adj to auditorium.* 807/345-2343; FAX 807/345-3246; 800 888/483-6887. Web www.jwg.com/ventureinns/. 93 rms, 3 story. S $75; D $85; each addl $10; under 20 free. Crib free. Pet accepted. TV; cable. Indoor pool; sauna. Complimentary continental bkfst. Restaurant adj 11-1 am. Ck-out 1 pm. Meeting rms. Business servs avail. In-rm modem link. Sun deck. Downhill ski 15 mi. Cr cds: A, C, D, DS, ER, MC, V. [🛏] [⛷] [≋] [📶] [🐾] [SC]

Toronto, Ontario *(See also Hamilton, Mississauga)*

(Rates will be higher during Canadian National Exhibition)

Motor Hotels

★ ★ **HOWARD JOHNSON-EAST.** *(940 Progress Ave, Scarborough ON M1G 3T5)* 416/439-6200; FAX 416/439-5689. 186 rms, 6 story. S $99; D $109; each addl $10; under 18 free; wkend package plan. Crib free. Pet accepted. TV; cable (premium). Heated pool; whirlpool. Restaurant 6:30 am-2 pm, 5-10 pm. Rm serv. Bar 4:30 pm-1 am. Ck-out noon. Coin Indry. Meeting rms. Business servs avail. Valet serv. Sundries. Gift shop. Exercise equipt; weight machine, bicycle, sauna. Health club privileges. Microwaves avail. Cr cds: A, C, D, DS, ER, JCB, MC, V. [D] [♥] [≈] [✗] [✗] [🐾] [SC]

★ ★ **RAMADA HOTEL-TORONTO AIRPORT.** *(2 Holiday Dr, Etobicoke ON M9C 2Z7) near Lester B Pearson Intl Airport. 416/621-2121; FAX 416/621-9840.* 179 rms, 2-6 story. June-Aug: S, D $140-$150; each addl $10; suites $250-$350; under 19 free; wkly, wkend rates; lower rates rest of yr. Crib free. Pet accepted. TV; cable (premium). Indoor/outdoor pool; whirlpool, lifeguard. Complimentary coffee in rms. Restaurant 6 am-11 pm. Rm serv. Bar 11:30-1 am. Ck-out noon. Business servs avail. In-rm modem link. Bellhops. Valet serv. Free airport transportation. Exercise equipt; weights, sauna. Some minibars; microwaves avail. Cr cds: A, C, D, DS, ER, JCB, MC, V. [D] [♥] [≈] [✗] [✗] [🐾] [SC]

★ ★ **TRAVELODGE-NORTH.** *(50 Norfinch Dr, North York ON M3N 1X1) N on Hwy 400 to Finch Ave, then E to Norfinch Dr. 416/663-9500; FAX 416/663-8480.* Web www .travelodge.com. 184 rms, 6 story. S $76; D $84; each addl $8; under 17 free. Crib free. Pet accepted, some restrictions. TV; cable (premium). Indoor pool; whirlpool. Coffee in rms. Restaurant 7-1 am. Rm serv. Bar. Ck-out 11 am. Meeting rms. Business servs avail. Sundries. Cr cds: A, D, DS, ER, MC, V. [D] [♥] [≈] [✗] [🐾] [SC]

★ **TRAVELODGE-TORONTO EAST.** *(20 Milner Business Ct, Scarborough ON M1B 3C6) 416/299-9500; FAX 416/299-6172.* Web www.travel odge.com. 156 rms, 6 story. S, D $66-$76; each addl $6; suites $75-$81; under 17 free. Pet accepted. TV; cable (premium), VCR. Indoor pool; whirlpool. Complimentary coffee in rms. Restaurant 11-2 am. Rm serv noon-11 pm. Ck-out 11 am. Meeting rms. Business servs avail. Sundries. Health club privileges. Microwaves avail. Cr cds: A, D, DS, ER, JCB, MC, V. [D] [♥] [≈] [✗] [SC]

★ ★ **VALHALLA INN.** *(1 Valhalla Inn Rd, Etobicoke ON M9B 1S9) 416/239-2391; FAX 416/239-8764; res: 800/268-2500.* 236 rms, 2-12 story. S $140; D $150; each addl $10; suites $189-230; under 18 free; AP avail; wkend packages. Crib free. Pet accepted. TV; cable (premium). Heated pool. Coffee in rms. Restaurant 6 am-11 pm; dining rm noon-2:30 pm, 5:30-10 pm. Rm serv 6 am-11 pm. Bars 11-1 am; entertainment. Ck-out 1 pm. Meeting rms. Business servs avail. In-rm modem link. Bellhops. Valet serv. Sundries. Free airport transportation. Health club privileges. Some bathrm phones. Private patios, balconies. Grills. Cr cds: A, C, D, DS, ER, MC, V. [♥] [≈] [✗] [🐾] [SC]

★ **VENTURE INN-YORKVILLE.** *(89 Avenue Rd, Toronto ON M5R 2G3) downtown. 416/964-1220; FAX 416/964-8692; res: 800/387-3933.* 71 rms, 8 story. S $124; D $134; each addl $10; under 19 free; wkend rates off-season. Crib free. Pet accepted, some restrictions. Parking $6.50/day. TV; cable (premium), VCR avail. Complimentary continental bkfst. Ck-out 1 pm. Meeting rms. Business servs avail. Health club privileges. Cr cds: A, D, DS, ER, MC, V. [♥] [✗] [🐾] [SC]

Hotels

★ ★ ★ **BEST WESTERN CARLTON PLACE.** *(33 Carlson Court, Etobicoke ON M9W 6H5) near Lester B. Pearson Intl Airport. 416/675-1234; FAX 416/675-3436.* 524 rms, 12 story. S $160-175; D $175-$190; each addl $15; suites $250-$350; under 18 free; wkend, mid-wk rates. Crib free. Parking in/out $4/day. Pet accepted. TV; cable (premium). Indoor pool; whirlpool. Complimentary coffee in rms. Restaurant 6:30-1 am. Rm serv 24 hrs. Bar 11-1 am. Ck-out 1 pm. Meeting rms. Business center. Gift shop. Airport transportation. Exercise equipt; bicycles, treadmill, sauna. Health club privileges. Minibars. Cr cds: A, D, DS, ER, JCB, MC, V. [D] [♥] [≈] [✗] [✗] [🐾] [SC] [✦]

★ **DAYS INN-DOWNTOWN.** *(30 Carlton St, Toronto ON M5B 2E9) adj to Maple Leaf Gardens, between Yonge & Church Sts, downtown. 416/977-6655; FAX 416/977-0502.* Web www.daysinn.com/daysinn.html. 536 rms, 23 story. S, D $89-$129; each addl $15; under 16 free. Crib free. Pet accepted, some restrictions. Covered parking $13/day. TV; cable. Indoor pool; sauna. Restaurant 7 am-10 pm. Bar 11:30-2 am. Ck-out 11 am. Coin lndry. Meeting rms. Business servs avail. Sundries. Barber, beauty shop. Some refrigerators. Sun deck. Cr cds: A, D, DS, ER, JCB, MC, V. [♥] [≈] [✗] [🐾] [SC]

★ ★ **DELTA CHELSEA INN.** *(33 Gerrard St W, Toronto ON M5G 1Z4) between Bay & Yonge Sts, downtown. 416/595-1975; FAX 416/585-4362; res: 800/268-1133.* E-mail reservations@deltachelsea .com; web www.deltahotels. com. 1,594 rms, 26 story. S $225-$235; D $240-$250; each addl $15; suites, kit. units $240-$345; under 18 free; wkend rates. Crib free. Pet accepted, some restrictions. Valet parking $21 in/out. TV; cable, VCR avail. 2 heated pools; whirlpool. Supervised child's activities; ages 2-13. Restaurant 6:30-1 am. Rm serv 24 hrs. Bar 11-1 am; entertainment. Ck-out 11 am. Convention facilities. Business center. Gift shop. Exercise equipt; weights, bicycles, sauna. Health club privileges. Game rm. Refrigerator in some suites. Microwaves avail. Many balconies. Cr cds: A, C, D, DS, ER, JCB, MC, V. [D] [♥] [≈] [✗] [✗] [🐾] [SC] [✦]

★ ★ ★ **DELTA-TORONTO AIRPORT.** *(801 Dixon Rd, Etobicoke ON M9W 1J5) near Lester B. Pearson Intl Airport. 416/675-6100; FAX 416/675-4022; res: 800/668-1444.* E-mail delta@nbnet.nb.ca; web www. deltahotels.com. 251 rms, 8 story. S, D $105-$155; each addl $15; suites $155-$205; under 18 free; wkend package plan. Crib free. Pet accepted, some restrictions. TV; cable (premium). Indoor pool; sauna. Supervised child's activities (June-Aug). Restaurant 6 am-11 pm. Rm serv 24 hrs. Bar 11:30-2 am. Ck-out 1 pm. Convention facilities. Business center. Bellhops. Valet serv. Gift shops. Exercise equipt; bicycles, treadmill. Health club privileges. Minibars. Microwave avail. Cr cds: A, C, D, DS, ER, JCB, MC, V. 🄳 ⬗ ⛱ 🏋 ⊠ 🐾 SC 🏃

★ ★ ★ ★ **FOUR SEASONS.** *(21 Avenue Rd at Bloor St, Toronto ON M5R 2G1) downtown. 416/964-0411; FAX 416/964-2302; res: 800/268-6282 (CAN & NY).* Web www.fshr.com. This fashionable, elegant hotel has a prime location in Toronto. 380 rms, 32 story. S $250-$280; D $280-$315; each addl $25; suites $375-$2,400; under 18 free; wkend rates. Crib free. Pet accepted. Garage $18.75/day. TV; cable (premium), VCR avail (movies). Indoor/outdoor pool; whirlpool, poolside serv, lifeguard. Restaurants 6:30 am-11 pm. Rm serv 24 hrs. Bar 11:30-2 am; entertainment exc Sun. Ck-out 1 pm. Convention facilities. Business center. In-rm modem link. Concierge. Barber, beauty shop. Valet parking. Exercise rm; instructor, weights, bicycles, sauna. Massage. Bathrm phones, minibars; microwaves avail. Some balconies. Cr cds: A, C, D, ER, JCB, MC, V.

🄳 ⬗ ⛱ 🏋 ⊠ 🐾 SC 🏃

★ ★ ★ **HOLIDAY INN.** *(1100 Eglinton Ave E, Toronto ON M3C 1H8) north of downtown. 416/446-3700; FAX 416/446-3701.* 298 rms, 14 story. S $75-$115; D $85-$125; each addl $10; suites $175-$325; family, wkend, wkly rates. Crib free. Pet accepted, some restrictions. TV; cable (premium), VCR avail (movies). Complimentary coffee in lobby. Restaurant 6:30 am-11 pm. Rm serv from 5 pm. Bar 11:30-1 am; entertainment Thurs-Sat. Ck-out noon. Convention facilities. Business servs avail. In-rm modem link. Concierge. Shopping arcade. Barber, beauty shop. Free valet parking. Airport, RR station transportation. Indoor tennis, pro. X-country ski 1/4 mi. Exercise equipt; weights, stair machine, sauna. Indoor/outdoor pool; whirlpool, poolside serv, lifeguard. Playground. Supervised child's activities (May-Sept); ages 5-12. Game rm. Lawn games. Bathrm phones, refrigerators. Many balconies. Cr cds: A, C, D, DS, ER, JCB, MC, V.

🄳 ⬗ ⛱ 🎿 ⊠ 🏋 ⊠ 🐾 SC

★ ★ **HOLIDAY INN.** *(970 Dixon Rd, Etobicoke ON M9W 1J9) near Lester B. Pearson Intl Airport. 416/675-7611; FAX 416/674-4364.* 444 rms, 12 story. S, D $160-$175; suites $230-$430; wkend rates. Crib free. Pet accepted. TV; cable (premium). 2 heated pools, 1 indoor; whirlpool. Playground. Coffee in rms. Restaurant 6 am-10:30 pm. Rm serv to 1 am. Bar 11-2 am; Sun noon-11 pm. Ck-out 1 pm. Meeting rms. Business center. Concierge. Barber, beauty shop. Free airport transportation. Exercise equipt; weights, bicycles, sauna. Rec rm. Minibars. Cr cds: A, C, D, DS, ER, JCB, MC, V.

🄳 ⬗ ⛱ 🏋 ✈ ⊠ 🐾 SC 🏃

★ ★ ★ **HOWARD JOHNSON PLAZA.** *(2737 Keele St, North York ON M3M 2E9) N on Hwy 401, exit Keele St, then 1 blk N. 416/636-4656; FAX 416/633-5637.* Web www.hojo.com. 367 rms, most A/C, 10 story, 27 suites. S, D $129-$179; each addl $10; suites $175-$375; family, wkly, wkend, hol rates. Crib free. Pet accepted. TV; cable (premium), VCR avail. Indoor pool. Supervised child's activities (June-Sept); ages 4-12. Complimentary coffee in rms. Restaurant 6:30 am-11 pm, Sun to 10 pm. Bar 11-1 am; entertainment. Ck-out 1 pm. Meeting rms. Business servs avail. Free garage parking. Downhill/x-country ski 10 mi. Exercise equipt; weight machine, treadmill, sauna. Game rm. Rec rm. Some minibars; microwaves avail. Cr cds: A, C, D, DS, ER, JCB, MC, V.

🄳 ⬗ ⛱ 🏋 ⊠ 🐾 SC

★ ★ ★ **INTERNATIONAL PLAZA.** *(655 Dixon Rd, Toronto ON M9W 1J4) near Lester B. Pearson Intl Airport, west of downtown. 416/244-1711; FAX 416/244-8031; res: 800/668-3656.* 415 rms, 12 story. S, D $150; each addl $10; suites $250-$450; under 18 free; wkly, wkend, hol rates. Crib free. Pet accepted. Valet parking $6. TV; cable (premium). Indoor pool; wading pool, poolside serv, lifeguard. Supervised child's activities; ages 3-12. Restaurant 6:30 am-11 pm. Rm serv 24 hrs. Bar 11-2 am. Ck-out noon. Convention facilities. Business center. Concierge. Gift shop. Beauty, barber shop. Exercise equipt; weight machine, treadmill, sauna. Massages. Game rm. Refrigerators. Minibars in suites. Cr cds: A, D, DS, ER, MC, V. 🄳 ⬗ ⛱ 🏋 ⊠ 🏃

★ ★ ★ **METROPOLITAN.** *(108 Chestnut St, Toronto ON M5G 1R3) downtown. 416/977-5000; res: 800/668-6600; FAX 416/977-9513.* E-mail reservations@metropolitan.com; web www.metropolitan.com. 480 rms, 26 story. S $160; D $180; each addl $20; suites $195-$850; wkend rates. Crib free. Parking, in/out $15.87. Pet accepted, some restrictions. TV; cable (premium), VCR avail (free movies). Indoor pool; whirlpool. Restaurant 6:30 am-midnight. Rm serv 24 hrs. Bar 11-1 am. Ck-out noon. Meeting rms. Business center.

In-rm modem link. Concierge. Gift shop. Exercise equipt; treadmill, bicycles, sauna. Bathrm phones, minibars. Adj to City Hall. Eatons Centre 2 blks. Cr cds: A, C, D, DS, ER, JCB, MC, V. 🅳 🐾 🏊 🏄 🎿 🏂 🖼 🐾 SC 🛠

★ ★ **NOVOTEL-AIRPORT.** *(135 Carlingview Dr, Etobicoke ON M9W 5E7) near Lester B. Pearson Intl Airport. 416/798-9800; FAX 416/798-1237; res: 800/668-6835.* E-mail tairmail@aol.com. 192 rms, 7 story. S $165; D $175; suites $175; family, wkly, wkend rates. Crib free. Pet accepted. TV; cable (premium), VCR avail. Indoor pool; whirlpool. Restaurant 6 am-11 pm. Bar 11-1 am. Ck-out 1 pm. Meeting rms. Business center. In-rm modem link. Gift shop. Free garage parking. Free airport transportation. Downhill/x-country ski 20 mi. Exercise equipt; weights, treadmill, sauna. Minibars. Cr cds: A, D, DS, ER, JCB, MC, V. 🅳 🐾 🏊 🏄 🎿 🏂 🖼 🐾 SC

★ ★ ★ **NOVOTEL-TORONTO CENTRE.** *(45 The Esplanade, Toronto ON M5E 1W2) downtown. 416/367-8900; FAX 416/360-8285; res: 800/668-6835.* Web novotel northamerica.com/welcome. 262 rms, 9 story. S, D $135-$185; each addl $15; suites $215; under 16 free; wkend rates. Crib free. Pet accepted. Garage (fee). TV; cable (premium). Indoor pool; whirlpool. Restaurant 6 am-midnight. Bar 11-1 am. Ck-out 1 pm. Meeting rms. Business servs avail. Exercise equipt; weights, rowers, sauna. Minibars. Cr cds: A, D, DS, ER, JCB, MC, V. 🅳 🐾 🏊 🎿 🖼 🐾 SC

★ ★ ★ **PARK PLAZA.** *(4 Avenue Rd, Toronto ON M5R 2E8) at Bloor St, downtown. 416/924-5471; FAX 416/924-6693; res: 800/977-4197.* 261 rms, 12-18 story; 40 suites. S, D $225-$260; each addl $15; suites $350-$750; family, wkend rates. Crib free. Pet accepted. Garage in/out $18. TV; cable (premium), VCR avail. Restaurant 7 am-10:30 pm. Bar 11:30-2 am. Ck-out noon. Meeting rms. Business center. Concierge. Health club privileges. Minibars. Many antique furnishings in public areas. Royal Ontario Museum opp. Cr cds: A, C, D, DS, ER, JCB, MC, V. 🅳 🐾 🖼 🐾 SC 🛠

★ **QUALITY.** *(111 Lombard St, Toronto ON M5C 2T9) downtown. 416/367-5555; FAX 416/367-3470; res: 800/228-5151.* 196 rms, 16 story. S $129; D $139; each addl $10; under 18 free. Crib free. Pet accepted. Garage $11.75/day. TV; cable. Ck-out 11 am. Business servs avail. Health club privileges. Cr cds: A, D, DS, JCB, MC, V. 🅳 🐾 🖼 🐾 SC

★ **QUALITY.** *(280 Bloor St W, Toronto ON M5S 1V8) downtown. 416/968-0010; FAX 416/968-7765.* 210 rms, 14 story. Mid-Mar-Oct: S $115-$130; D $127-$152; under 18 free; wkend rates; higher rates special events; lower rates rest of yr. Crib free. Pet accepted, some restrictions. Garage in/out $11.50. TV; cable. Restaurant 7 am-11 pm. Bar 11 am-11 pm. Ck-out 11 am. Meeting rms. Business servs avail. No bellhops. Health club privileges. Cr cds: A, D, DS, JCB, MC, V. 🅳 🐾 🖼 🐾 SC

✔ ★ ★ **QUALITY SUITES.** *(262 Carlingview Dr, Etobicoke ON M9W 5G1) near Lester B. Pearson Intl Airport. 416/674-8442; FAX 416/674-3088.* Web hotelchoice.com. 254 suites, 12 story. S, D $120-$145; each addl $5; under 18 free; wkend, hol rates. Crib free. Pet accepted. TV; cable (premium), VCR avail (movies). Complimentary coffee in rms. Restaurant 6:30-1 am. Bar. Ck-out 11 am. Meeting rms. Business servs avail. No bellhops. Gift shop. Downhill/x-country ski 15 mi. Exercise equipt; bicycles, stair machine. Health club privileges. Game rm. Minibars; microwaves avail. Cr cds: A, D, DS, ER, JCB, MC, V. 🅳 🐾 🏊 🎿 🏂 🖼 🐾 SC

★ **QUALITY-AIRPORT EAST.** *(2180 Islington Ave, Toronto ON M9T 3P1) west of downtown. 416/240-9090; FAX 416/240-9944.* Web www.qualityinn.com. 214 rms, 12 story. S, D $85-135; each addl $5; under 18 free; wkly, wkend rates; higher rates special events. Crib free. Pet accepted. TV; cable (premium). Restaurant 7 am-10 pm. Bar from 11 am. Ck-out 11 am. Meeting rms. In-rm modem link. Microwaves avail. Near airport. Cr cds: A, D, DS, ER, JCB, MC, V. 🅳 🐾 🖼 🐾 SC

★ ★ **RADISSON SUITE-TORONTO AIRPORT.** *(640 Dixon Rd, Etobicoke ON M9W 1J1) near Lester B. Pearson Intl Airport. 416/242-7400; FAX 416/242-9888.* Web www.radisson.com. 215 suites, 14 story. S, D $204-216; under 18 free. Crib free. Pet accepted, some restrictions. TV; cable, VCR avail. Complimentary continental bkfst. Restaurant 6:30 am-11 pm. Bar 11-1 am. Ck-out noon. Meeting rms. Business center. In-rm modem link. Concierge. Gift shop. Free valet parking. Exercise equipt; weights, bicycles. Minibars, microwaves avail. Cr cds: A, C, D, DS, ER, JCB, MC, V. 🅳 🐾 🎿 🏂 🖼 🐾 SC 🛠

★ ★ **REGAL CONSTELLATION.** *(900 Dixon Rd, Etobicoke ON M9W 1J7) near Lester B. Pearson Intl Airport. 416/675-1500; FAX 416/675-1737; res: 800/268-4838.* Web www.dms-destination.com/regal/regal.htm. 710 rms, 8-16 story. S, D $95-$165; each addl $15; suites from $275; under 18 free; wkend package plan. Crib free. Pet accepted, some restrictions. Valet parking $7.50/day. TV; cable (premium), VCR avail. 2 heated pools, 1 indoor/outdoor; whirlpool, poolside serv in season. Restaurant 6:30 am-11 pm; dining rm 11 am-2 pm, 5:30-10 pm. Rm serv 24 hrs. Bar 11-2 am; entertainment Thurs-Sat. Ck-out noon. Concierge. Convention facilities. Business center. Gift shop. Barber, beauty shop. Airport transportation. Exercise equipt; weights, bicycles, sauna. Some balconies. Cr cds: A, C, D, DS, ER, MC, V. [D] ⬡ ⬡ ⬡ ⬡ ⬡ ⬡ [SC] ⬡

★ ★ ★ **ROYAL YORK.** *(100 Front St W, Toronto ON M5J 1E3) opp Union Station, downtown. 416/368-2511; FAX 416/368-2884; res: 800/828-7447 (US).* E-mail reserve @ryh.mhs.compuserve.com; web www.cphotels.ca. 1,365 rms, 22 story. S, D $189-$289; each addl $20; suites $295-$1,750; under 18 free; wkend packages. Crib free. Pet accepted. Garage (fee). TV; cable. Pool; wading pool, whirlpool. Restaurant 6:30 am-10:30 pm. Rm serv 24 hrs. Bars noon-2 am; entertainment. Ck-out noon. Convention facilities. Business center. Concierge. Shopping arcade. Barber, beauty shop. Exercise rm; instructor, weight machines, rower, sauna. Massage. Health club privileges. Minibars; refrigerators, microwaves avail. Luxury level. Cr cds: A, C, D, DS, ER, JCB, MC, V.
[D] ⬡ ⬡ ⬡ ⬡ ⬡ [SC] ⬡

★ ★ ★ **SHERATON GATEWAY.** *(PO Box 3000, Toronto ON L5P 1C4) at Lester B. Pearson Intl Airport, west of downtown. 905/672-7000; FAX 905/672-7100.* 474 rms, 8 story. S, D $180-$210; each addl $15; suites $270-$695; under 18 free; wkly, wkend rates. Crib free. Pet accepted. Garage parking $8; valet $18. TV; cable (premium), VCR avail. Indoor pool; whirlpool. Restaurant 6 am-11 pm. Rm serv 24 hrs. Bar 11-1 am. Ck-out noon. Convention facilities. Business center. Concierge. Shopping arcade. Barber, beauty shop. Free airport transportation. Exercise equipt; weights, rowers, sauna. Massage. Minibars. Modern facility connected by climate-controlled walkway to Terminal 3. Cr cds: A, C, D, DS, ER, JCB, MC, V. [D] ⬡ ⬡ ⬡ ⬡ ⬡ ⬡ [SC] ⬡

★ ★ ★ **SHERATON-TORONTO EAST.** *(2035 Kennedy Rd, Scarborough ON M1T 3G2) 416/299-1500; FAX 416/299-8959.* E-mail sheraton@maple.net; web www.sheraton .com/toronto. 371 rms, 13 story. S, D $198; each addl $15; suites $350-$595; under 18 free; wkend rates. Crib free. Pet accepted. TV; cable. Indoor pool; wading pool; whirlpool. Free supervised child's activities (mid-Mar & mid-June-Aug, daily; rest of yr, Sat, Sun & hols); ages 3-15. Restaurants 6:30-2 am. Rm serv 24 hrs. Bar 11-2 am. Ck-out noon. Convention facilities. Business servs avail. In-rm modem link. Concierge. Gift shop. Barber, beauty shop. Covered valet parking. Putting green. Exercise rm; instructor, weights, bicycles, sauna. Game rm. Microwaves avail. Luxury level. Cr cds: A, C, D, DS, ER, JCB, MC, V.
[D] ⬡ ⬡ ⬡ ⬡ ⬡ [SC]

★ ★ ★ **SKYDOME.** *(1 Blue Jays Way, Toronto ON M5V 1J4) adj CN Tower, downtown. 416/341-7100; FAX 416/341-5090; res: 800/441-1414.* E-mail mgeorge@sky.mhs.compuserv.com; web www.cphotels.ca. 346 rms, 11 story, 70 suites. Apr-Oct: S, D $139-$179; each addl $30; suites from $300; under 18 free; wkend rates; package plans. Crib avail. Pet accepted. Garage parking $16; valet $22. TV; cable, VCR avail. Indoor pool. Complimentary coffee in rms. Supervised child's activities (June-Sept). Restaurant 7-1 am. Rm serv 24 hrs. Bar. Ck-out 9:30 am-noon. Convention facilities. Business center. Concierge. Gift shop. Health club privileges. Massage. Minibars. Modern facility within SkyDome complex; lobby and some rms overlook playing field. Cr cds: A, C, D, DS, ER, JCB, MC, V. [D] ⬡ ⬡ ⬡ ⬡ [SC] ⬡

★ ★ **TOWN INN.** *(620 Church St, Toronto ON M4Y 2G2) downtown. 416/964-3311; FAX 416/924-9466; res: 800/387-2755.* E-mail mitch@towninn.com; web towninn .com/. 200 kit. units (1-2 bedrm), 26 story. June-Dec: S $95-$125; D $110-$135; each addl $15; under 12 free; monthly rates; lower rates rest of yr. Crib free. Pet accepted. Garage $13. TV; cable (premium). Heated pool; saunas. Complimentary continental bkfst. Restaurant 7-10 am. Ck-out noon. Meeting rms. Business servs avail. Tennis. Exercise equipt; bicycles. Health club privileges. Refrigerators, microwaves. Balconies. Cr cds: A, C, D, ER, MC, V. [D] ⬡ ⬡ ⬡ ⬡ [SC]

★ **VENTURE INN-AIRPORT.** *(925 Dixon Rd, Etobicoke ON M9W 1J8) near Lester B. Pearson Intl Airport. 416/674-2222; FAX 416/674-5757; res: 888/4-VENTURE.* Web www.jwg.com/ventureinns/. 283 rms, 17 story. S $95; D $105; each addl $10; suites $140-$275; under 19 free; wkend rates. Crib free. Pet accepted. TV, cable (premium). Indoor pool; whirlpool. Complimentary continental bkfst. Restaurant 11-2 am. Bar. Ck-out 1 pm. Convention facilities. Business servs avail. In-rm modem link. Airport transportation. Sauna. Health club privileges. Gift shop. Cr cds: A, D, DS, ER, MC, V.
[D] ⬡ ⬡ ⬡ ⬡ ⬡ [SC]

Windsor, Ontario

Motels

★ ★ **COMFORT INN.** *(1100 Richmond St, Chatham ON N7M 5J5) E on HWY 401 to exit 81.* 519/352-5500; FAX 519/352-2520. 81 rms, 2 story. May-Sept: S $57-$95; D $65-$105; each addl $4; under 19 free; wkend rates; lower rates rest of yr. Crib free. Pet accepted. TV; cable. Complimentary coffee in lobby. Restaurant adj 9 am-10 pm. Ck-out 11 am. Cr cds: A, C, D, DS, ER, JCB, MC, V. 🄳 🛋 ⬛ 🐾 SC

↙★ ★ **MARQUIS PLAZA.** *(2530 Ouellette Ave, Windsor ON N8X 1L7)* 519/966-1860; FAX 519/966-6619; res: 800/265-5021. 97 rms, 2 story. S $48-$150; D $60; each addl $5; suites $90-$150. Crib $5. Pet accepted, some restrictions; $10. TV; cable (premium), VCR avail. Ck-out noon. Meeting rms. Cr cds: A, D, ER, MC, V. 🄳 🛋 ⬛ 🐾 SC

★ ★ **ROYAL MARQUIS.** *(590 Grand Marais E, Windsor ON N8X 3H4) near Intl Airport.* 519/966-1900; FAX 519/966-4689. 99 rms, 5 story, 14 suites. S $70; D $80; each addl $5; suites $90-$175; under 12 free; wkend rates; higher rates prom. Crib $5. Pet accepted, some restrictions; $10. TV; cable (premium), VCR avail. Indoor pool. Supervised child's activities; ages 5-10. Restaurant 6:30 am-10 pm. Rm serv. Bar; entertainment Thurs-Sun. Ck-out noon. Meeting rms. Valet serv. Concierge. Barber, beauty shop. X-country ski 5 mi. Exercise equipt; stair machine, treadmill, sauna. Luxurious furnishings, atmosphere. Cr cds: A, D, ER, MC, V. 🄳 🛋 ⬛ 🏊 🐾 🏃 🐾 SC

Hotel

★ **COMPRI.** *(333 Riverside Dr W, Windsor ON N9A 5K4)* 519/977-9777; FAX 519/977-1411. 207 rms, 19 story. S, D $95; under 12 free. Crib free. Pet accepted, some restrictions. Garage avail. TV; cable (premium). Indoor pool; whirlpool. Complimentary full bkfst. Restaurant nearby. Ck-out noon. Meeting rms. In-rm modem link. Exercise equipt; weight machine, bicycle, saunas. Minibars. Cr cds: A, D, DS, ER, MC, V.
🄳 🛋 ⬛ 🏃 ⬛ 🐾 SC

Charlottetown, Prince Edward Island

Motels

★ ★ **ISLANDER.** *(146-148 Pownal St., Charlottetown PE C1A 3W6)* 902/892-1217; FAX 902/566-1623. 49 rms, 2 story, 3 kits. Mid-May-mid-Oct: S, D $86-$96; each addl $8; suites, kit. units $96-$120; under 12 free; lower rates rest of yr. Crib $7. Pet accepted. TV; cable. Restaurant 7 am-8 pm. Ck-out 11 am. Meeting rms. Sundries. Microwaves avail. Cr cds: A, ER, MC, V. 🄳 🛋 🐾

★ ★ **RODD'S THRIFT LODGE.** *(Charlottetown PE C1A 7L3) 2 mi W on Hwy 1.* 902/892-2481; FAX 902/368-3247; res: 800/565-9077 (Eastern US), 800/565-0207 (Maritimes), 800/565-0241 (NF, ON, PQ). E-mail rodds@roddhotels.com; web www.roddhotels .com. 61 rms, 2 story, 34 suites. July-Aug: S, D $82; suites $90-$98; under 16 free; lower rates rest of yr. Crib free. Pet accepted. TV; cable. Heated pool. Restaurant 7-10 am, 5-9 pm. Bar 11-1 am; closed Sun. Ck-out noon. Meeting rm. Bellhops. Health club privileges. Microwaves avail. Cr cds: A, C, D, DS, ER, JCB, MC, V. 🛋 ⬛ 🐾 SC

Motor Hotels

★ ★ **BEST WESTERN MacLAUCHLAN'S.** *(238 Grafton St, Charlottetown PE C1A 1L5)* 902/892-2461; FAX 902/566-2979. 143 rms, 2-3 story, 26 kits. June-mid-Oct: S $119-$139; D $129-$149; each addl $10; studio rms $149-$149; suites $169-$209; kit. units $139-$149; under 19 free; lower rates rest of yr. Pet accepted, some restrictions. TV; cable. Indoor pool; whirlpool. Complimentary coffee in rms. Restaurants 7 am-9 pm; Sun from 8 am. Bar 11:30 am-midnight, closed Sun. Ck-out noon. Meeting rms. Valet serv. Exercise equipt; weight machines, bicycles, sauna. Sundries. Microwaves avail. Cr cds: A, C, D, DS, ER, JCB, MC, V. 🄳 🛋 🏊 🏃 ⬛ 🐾 SC

★ ★ **QUALITY INN ON THE HILL.** *(150 Euston St, Charlottetown PE C1A 1W5)* 902/894-8572; FAX 902/368-3556. 48 rms, 5 story. Late June-mid-Oct: S $111; D $120; each addl $9; studio rms $123-$140; suites $138-$153; under 16 free; lower rates rest of yr. Pet accepted. TV; cable. Coffee in rms. Restaurant 11 am-8 pm. Rm serv. Bar 11-1 am. Ck-out noon. Meeting rms. Bellhops. Health club privileges. Sundries. Microwaves avail. Cr cds: A, C, D, ER, MC, V. 🛋 ⬛ 🐾

Hotels

★ ★ **THE PRINCE EDWARD.** *(18 Queen St, Charlottetown PE C1A 8B9)* 902/566-2222; FAX 902/566-1745. E-mail vdown@peh.mhs.compu serve.com; web www.cphotels

.ca. 211 rms, 10 story. May-mid-Oct: S $170-$200; D $190-$220; each addl $20; suites $275-$750; lower rates rest of yr. Crib avail. Pet accepted. TV; cable, VCR avail (movies). Indoor pool; wading pool, whirlpool. Restaurants 6:30 am-11 pm. Bar; entertainment. Ck-out noon. Meeting rms. Business center. Exercise rm; instructor, weight machines, bicycles, sauna. Massage. On waterfront in "Olde Charlottetown." Cr cds: A, D, DS, MC, V.

[D] [♦] [≈] [🏋] [🖫] [🖑] [SC] [🛩]

★ ★ **RODD'S CHARLOTTETOWN.** (Charlottetown PE C1A 7K4) Corner Kent & Pownal Sts. 902/894-7371; FAX 902/368-2178; res: 800/566-7633 (US), 800/565-0207 (PE). E-mail rodds@rodd-hotels.ca; web www.Rodd-Ho tels.ca/. 110 rms, 5 story. June-mid-Oct: S, D $99-$130; each addl $10; under 16 free; lower rates rest of yr. Crib free. Pet accepted. TV; cable. Indoor pool; whirlpool. Restaurant 7 am-2 pm, 5-10 pm. Bar 4 pm-1 am; closed Sun. Ck-out noon. Meeting rms. Valet serv. Exercise equipt; bicycle, rower, sauna. Cr cds: A, D, DS, ER, JCB, MC, V. [D] [♦] [≈] [🏋] [🖫] [🖑] [SC]

Drummondville, Québec (See also Montréal, Sherbrooke)

Motor Hotel

★ ★ **HÔTEL UNIVERSEL.** (915 Hains St, Drummondville QE J2C 3A1) 819/478-4971; FAX 819/477-6604; res: 800/668-3521. 119 rms, 4 story. S $72.95; D $82.95; each addl $10; suites $120-$150; under 15 free. Crib free. Pet accepted. TV; cable. Indoor pool; poolside serv. Restaurant 7 am-10 pm. Rm serv. Bar 11-3 am; entertainment Wed-Sat. Ck-out noon. Meeting rms. Business servs avail. Cr cds: A, C, D, DS, ER, MC, V.

[D] [♦] [≈] [🖫]

Montréal, Québec

Motor Hotel

★ **DAYS INN-MONTRÉAL AIRPORT.** (4545 Côte-Vertu W, Montréal QE H4S 1C8) 8 mi N on Hwy 40, exit 62W. 514/332-2720; FAX 514/332-4512. 91 rms, 3 story. S, D $55-$95; wkend rates. Crib free. Pet accepted. TV; VCR avail. Pool; lifeguard. Coffee in rms. Restaurant 7 am-11 pm. Rm serv. Bar 4-11 pm. Ck-out 1 pm. Coin lndry. Meeting rms. Business servs avail. In-rm modem link. Cr cds: A, C, D, DS, ER, JCB, MC, V.

[♦] [≈] [🖫] [🖑] [SC]

Hotels

★ ★ ★ **BONAVENTURE HILTON.** (1 Place Bonaventure, Montréal QE H5A 1E4) 514/878-2332; FAX 514/878-3881. Web www.travelweb.com/ hiltnint.html. 395 rms, 3 story. S $135-$244; D $145-$268; each addl $25; suites $360-$1,100; wkend package. Crib free. Pet accepted. TV; cable, VCR avail. Heated pool; poolside serv in summer, lifeguard. Restaurant 6:30 am-11 pm. Bar 11:30-1 am. Ck-out noon. Meeting rms. Business center. In-rm modem link. Garage; valet parking. Exercise equipt; bicycles, stair machine. Massage. Minibars. 17th-floor garden courtyard; pheasants, ducks, goldfish ponds. Access to subway via underground mall. Cr cds: A, C, D, DS, ER, JCB, MC, V. [D] [♦] [≈] [🏋] [🖫] [🖑] [SC] [🛩]

★ ★ ★ **DELTA.** (475 President Kennedy, Montréal QE H3A 1V7) 514/286-1986; FAX 514/284-4342; res: 800/268-1133 (CN); 800/877-1133 (US). 453 rms, 23 story. S, D $195-$210; each addl $15; suites $315-$880; under 18 free; wkend packages. Crib free. Pet accepted. Covered parking $12. TV; cable, VCR avail. 2 pools, 1 indoor; whirlpool. Supervised child's activities; ages 2-17, wkends only. Coffee in rms. Restaurant 7 am-9:30 pm. Rm serv to 1 am. Bar 11:30-1:30 am; entertainment exc Sun. Ck-out noon. Convention facilities. Business center. In-rm modem link. Concierge. Barber, beauty shop. Exercise rm; instructor, weights, bicycles, sauna. Massage. Minibars. Balconies. Cr cds: A, C, D, ER, JCB, MC, V. [D] [♦] [≈] [🏋] [🖫] [🖑] [SC] [🛩]

★ ★ ★ **HOTEL DU PARC.** (3625 Parc Ave, Montréal QE H2X 3P8) 514/288-6666; FAX 514/288-2469. 449 rms, 16 story. May-Oct: S, D $99-$129; each addl $10; suites $150-$350; under 18 free; wkend rates; lower rates rest of yr. Crib free. Garage (fee). Pet accepted, some restrictions. TV; cable, VCR avail. Free coffee in rms. Restaurant 7 am-10:30 pm. Bar from 4 pm. Ck-out noon. Meeting rms. Business servs avail. Exercise equipt; weights, bicycles. Health club privileges. Shopping arcade. Barber, beauty shop. Luxury level. Cr cds: A, C, D, DS, ER, JCB, MC, V. [D] [♦] [🏋] [🖫] [🖑] [SC] [🛩]

★ **HOWARD JOHNSON-PLAZA.** (475 Sherbrooke St W, Montréal QE H3A 2L9) 514/842-3961; FAX 514/842-0945. 194 rms, 20 story, 89 suites. May-Oct: S $95-$105; D $110-$120; each addl $15; suites $125-$400; under 12 free; package plans; lower rates rest of yr. Crib $15. Pet accepted. Parking (fee). TV; cable. Restaurant 7 am-10 pm. Bar from 10 am. Ck-out noon. Meeting rms. Business center. In-rm modem link. Concierge. Exercise equipt; weights, bicycles, sauna. Some minibars. Cr cds: A, C, D, ER, MC, V.

★ ★ ★ **INTER-CONTINENTAL.** *(360 rue St-Antoine W, Montréal QE H2Y 3X4) at the World Trade Centre.* 514/987-9900; FAX 514/847-8550. 357 rms, 17 story. May-mid-Oct: S, D $235-$315; each addl $25; suites $360-$2,000; under 14 free; family, wkend rates; lower rates rest of yr. Crib free. Pet accepted. Garage parking $16; valet. TV; cable, VCR avail. Indoor pool. Restaurant 6:30 am-11:30 pm. Rm serv 24 hrs. Bar 11:30-1 am; entertainment. Ck-out 1 pm. Convention facilities. Business center. In-rm modem link. Concierge. Shopping arcade. Barber, beauty shop. Exercise rm; instructor; treadmill, saunas, steam rm. Massage. Bathrm phones, minibars. Located on 10th-26th floors of 26-story building. Cr cds: A, C, D, DS, ER, JCB, MC, V.

★ ★ ★ **LE WESTIN MONT-ROYAL.** *(1050 Sherbrooke St W, Montréal QE H3A 2R6) at Peel St, downtown.* 514/284-1110; FAX 514/845-3025. 300 rms, 32 story. May-Oct: S $175-$225; D $200-$250; each addl $25; suites $375-$1,180; under 18 free; wkend rates; lower rates rest of yr. Crib free. Pet accepted, some restrictions. Garage (fee). TV; cable, VCR avail (movies). Heated pool; whirlpool, poolside serv, lifeguard. Complimentary continental bkfst. Restaurants 11:30 am-2:30 pm, 5:30-10 pm. Rm serv 24 hrs. Bar noon-1 am; pianist. Ck-out 1 pm. Meeting rms. Business center. In-rm modem link. Concierge. Shopping arcade. Barber, beauty shop. Exercise rm; instructor, weights, bicycles, sauna, steam rm. Massage. Bathrm phones, minibars. Cr cds: A, C, D, DS, ER, JCB, MC, V.

★ ★ ★ **LOEWS HÔTEL VOGUE.** *(1425 rue de la Montagne, Montréal QE H3G 1Z3)* 514/285-5555; FAX 514/849-8903. This small luxury hotel in the heart of Montréal has an elegant facade of polished rose granite, trimmed in aqua, with tall windows. Guest rooms are decorated with satiny duvets on the beds and striped silk. 126 rms, 9 story, 16 suites. Mid-May-mid-Oct: S, D $195-$285; each addl $20; suites $405-$1,260; under 18 free; wkend rates; lower rates rest of yr. Crib free. Pet accepted. Garage; valet parking $15. TV; cable, VCR (movies). Restaurant 7 am-11 pm. Rm serv 24 hrs. Bar 3 pm-1 am. Ck-out 1 pm. Meeting rms. Business servs avail. In-rm modem link. Concierge. Gift shop. Exercise equipt; weights, rower. Massage. Health club privileges. In-rm whirlpools, minibars. Cr cds: A, C, D, ER, JCB, MC, V.

★ ★ ★ **NOVOTEL.** *(1180 rue de la Montagne, Montréal QE H3G 1Z1)* 514/861-6000; FAX 514/861-0992; res: 800/221-4542. 199 rms, 9 story. May-Oct: S, D $160-$170; each addl $15; suites $200; family, wkend & hol rates; higher rates during Grand Prix; lower rates rest of yr. Crib free. Pet accepted, some restrictions. Parking garage $9.75. TV; cable (premium). Restaurant 6:30 am-10:30 pm. Bar noon-midnight. Ck-out 1 pm. Meeting rms. Business servs avail. In-rm modem link. Exercise equipt; weights, bicycles. Health club privileges. Indoor playground. Minibars. Cr cds: A, C, D, DS, ER, MC, V.

Mont Tremblant Provincial Park, Québec

(Approx 15 mi or 24 km N of Saint-Jovite on PQ 327)

Resort

★ ★ ★ **AUBERGE GRAY ROCKS.** *(525 Chemin Principal, Mont Tremblant, QE J0T 1Z0) on Hwy 327, 4 mi N of Hwy 117.* 819/425-2771; FAX 819/425-3474; res: 800/567-6767. E-mail grayrocks@tremblant.com; web www.tremblant.com/grayrocks/. 56 rms in 5-story inn, 18 chalet suites, 39 deluxe rms, 5 cottages, 56 condos; 21 rms share bath, some A/C. AP: S $165-$230; D $125-$198/person; suites $198/person (4 min); condos$180-$420; family, wkly, wkend rates; ski, golf, tennis, package plans. Crib free. Pet accepted. TV; cable, VCR avail. Indoor pool; whirlpool, lifeguard. Playground. Supervised child's activities (late June-early Sept & late Nov-Mar). Dining rm (public by res) 7:30-9:30 am, noon-1:30 pm, 6:30-8:30 pm. Bar noon-1 am. Snack bar. Ck-out 1 pm. Ck-in 3 pm. Coin lndry. Meeting rms. Business servs avail. Gift shop. Bellhops. Tennis. 18-hole golf; greens fee $25-$42; 2 putting greens; driving range. Private beach; beachside serv. Rowboats, canoes, sailboats, paddleboats, kayaks. Windsurfing lessons. Downhill/x-country ski on site. Lawn games. Guides. Entertainment. Movies. Rec rm. Exercise equipt; weight machines, bicycles, sauna. Fireplace in some rms. Many private patios, balconies. Terrace. Sea plane base. Cr cds: A, D, DS, ER, MC, V.

Québec City, Québec

Motels

(Rates may be higher during Carnaval de Québec)

✔★ **MOTEL SPRING.** *(8520 Boul Ste Anne, Chateau-Richer QE G0A 1N0) N on Hwy 138. 418/824-4953; FAX 418/824-4117; 800 888/824-4953.* E-mail bcj@mail.accent .net; web www.accent.net/bcj. 25 rms, 12 with shower only. No rm phones. July-early Sept: S $40-$50; D $40-$70; wkly rates; higher rates major hols; lower rates mid-May-June, early Sept-late Oct. Closed rest of yr. Crib free. Pet accepted. TV; cable. Restaurant 7 am-9 pm. Ck-out noon. Picnic tables. On river. Family-owned. Cr cds: MC, V.

D 🐾 🐾 SC

✔★ **ONCLE SAM.** *(7025 W Hamel Blvd, Ste-Foy QE G2G 1B6) 5¹/₂ mi W on Hwy 138, jct Hwy 540. 418/872-1488; FAX 418/871-5519; res: 800/414-1488.* 44 rms, 1-2 story. Mid-June-mid-Sept: S, D $49-$69; each addl $10; under 14 free; lower rates rest of yr. Crib free. Pet accepted. TV; cable, VCR avail. Heated pool. Playground. Ck-out noon. Coin lndry. Business servs avail. X-country ski 5 mi. Picnic table. Cr cds: A, C, D, ER, MC, V.

D 🐾 🐾 🏊 🐾 🐾 SC

★ **PAVILLON BONNE ENTENTE.** *(3400 Chemin Ste-Foy, Québec City QE G1X 1S6) 6 mi W on Hwy 73, Duplessis exit, then Chemin Ste-Foy exit W, on grounds of Château Bonne Entente Motel. 418/653-5221; FAX 418/653-3098; res: 800/463-4390.* 46 rms, 1-2 story, 3 kit. units; ck-in/ck-out service at Château Bonne Entente Motel. Mid-May-mid-Oct: S $114; D $124; each addl $10; kit. units $114-$124; under 18 free; wkly, wknd rates; higher rates Carnaval de Québec; lower rates rest of yr. Crib free. Pet accepted. TV; cable, VCR avail. Supervised child's activities (June-Sept); ages 6 mo and up. Ck-out 1 pm. Business servs avail. Airport transportation. X-country ski 5 mi. Exercise equipt; bicycles, stair machines. Massage. Minibars. Shares facilities of Château Bonne Entente Motel, including heated pool, playground, restaurant, tennis, stocked fishing pond. Cr cds: A, C, D, DS, ER, MC, V.

🐾 🐾 🐾 🏊 🐾 🐾 🐾 🐾 SC

Motor Hotel

★★ **HOTEL CHÂTEAU LAURIER.** *(695 E Grand-Allée, Québec City QE G1R 2K4) 418/522-8108; FAX 418/524-8768; res: 800/463-4453 (E CAN, NE US).* 57 rms, 4 story. May-Oct: S $69-$89; D $79-$99; each addl $10; under 12 free; lower rates rest of yr. Crib free. Pet accepted, some restrictions. TV; cable, VCR avail. Restaurant 7:30 am-3:30 pm. Bar 11-3 am. Ck-out noon. Business servs avail. Cr cds: A, C, D, DS, ER, MC, V.

🐾 🐾 🐾

Hotels

★★★ **HILTON.** *(1100 Blvd René Lévesque E, Québec City QE G1K 7M9) 418/647-2411; FAX 418/647-3737.* 565 rms, 23 story. Mid-May-mid-Oct: S $138-$187; D $160-$209; each addl $22; suites $355-$835; wkend rates. Crib free. Pet accepted, some restrictions. Parking $16. TV; cable. Pool; whirlpool, poolside serv, lifeguard. Coffee in rms. Restaurant 7 am-midnight. Bars 11 am-midnight. Ck-out noon. Meeting rms. Business center. Shopping arcade. Barber, beauty shop. Downhill ski 11 mi; x-country ski nearby. Exercise rm; instructor, weights, bicycles, sauna. Massage. Quebec convention center opp. Luxury level. Cr cds: A, C, D, DS, ER, JCB, MC, V.

D 🐾 🐾 🏊 🐾 🐾 🐾 🐾 SC 🐾

★★★ **LOEWS LE CONCORDE.** *(1225 place Montcalm, Québec City QE G1R 4W6) on Grande Allée. 418/647-2222; FAX 418/647-4710.* Web www.loewshotels.com. 404 rms, 26 story. May-Oct: S, D $135-$215; each addl $20; suites $220-$750; wknd, ski plans; lower rates rest of yr. Crib free. Pet accepted. Garage $14; valet parking $18. TV; cable. Heated pool; whirlpool, poolside serv, lifeguard. Restaurant 6:45 am-midnight. Bars 11-3 am. Ck-out 1 pm. Meeting rms. Business center. In-rm modem link. Concierge. Downhill ski 11 mi; x-country ski on site. Tennis privileges. Exercise rm; instructor, weights, bicycles, sauna. Health club privileges. Refrigerators, minibars; fireplace in 2 bi-level suites. Luxury level. Cr cds: A, C, D, DS, ER, JCB, MC, V.

D 🐾 🐾 🐾 🐾 🐾 🐾 SC 🐾

Trois-Rivières, Québec

Hotel

★★★ **DELTA.** *(1620 Notre Dame St, Trois-Rivières QE G9A 6E5) 819/376-1991; FAX 819/372-5975; res: 800/877-1133 (US), 800/268-1133 (CAN).* 159 rms, 12 story. S, D $69-$154; each addl $15; suites $150-$300; under 18 free; higher rates Formula Grand Prix

(Aug). Crib free. Pet accepted. TV; cable, VCR avail. Indoor pool; whirlpool, lifeguard. Coffee in rms. Restaurant 6:30 am-9:30 pm. Bar 4 pm-midnight. Ck-out noon. Meeting rms. Business servs avail. In-rm modem link. Gift shop. Free garage parking. Downhill ski 15 mi; x-country ski 5 mi. Exercise rm; instructor, weights, rowers, sauna. Massage. Minibars; some bathrm phones. Cr cds: A, D, DS, ER, MC, V. ⓓ 🐾 🏊 🏊 ✕ ✕ ✕ SC

Appendix A: Pet First-Aid

by Andrea Arden

A to Z of Health Concerns

Following is a brief list of pet health concerns you may encounter while traveling. It is by no means meant to be a comprehensive list or treated as a substitute for good veterinary care.

Allergies. Many animals suffer from allergies, and traveling can make them worse. Be sure to discuss your travel plans with your vet prior to departure, so he can send you off fully prepared to deal with any allergic onsets.

Bites and Stings

Other animals. If your pet has been in a fight with another animal, take him to a vet. On the way you should check for any wounds. If he is bleeding, try to stop it by applying pressure to the wound.

Insects. If your pet has been bitten by an insect, you will most likely hear him yelp and see him begin to frantically lick the affected area. Have someone hold and in some cases muzzle him, and gently pull the stinger out, if there is one. Cool water, ice or rubbing alcohol is usually all that need be applied to the area. If you know your pet is allergic to certain insects, consult a veterinarian.

Snakebites. Symptoms of snakebites are swelling, vomiting, difficulty breathing, weakness and convulsion. If you suspect your pet has been bitten by a snake, get to a veterinarian immediately. Try not to let the animal walk. Do not attempt to capture the snake; in most cases clear identification of the type of snake is not necessary for the vet to treat the bite.

Bleeding. If your pet has been injured and blood is pumping out of the wound with each beat of his pulse, slow or stop the bleeding as soon as possible and get him to a veterinarian immediately. As a temporary measure, try covering the wound with one hand while wrapping a finger and thumb around the limb to constrict blood flow. Release the finger and thumb every 15 seconds—do not close off blood flow for more than one minute at a time. If two people are available, one should drive while the other tends to the injured animal. If only one person is available, bandage the wound and get to the vet immediately.

Bloating. Bloat is especially dangerous in large breed dogs. The symptoms include a distended abdomen and whining or moaning sounds. Call a veterinarian immediately if you notice these symptoms.

Burns. Burns can be caused by heat, electric shock or chemicals. A superficial burn is indicated by redness of the skin and in some cases mild swelling. Most burns should be looked at by a veterinarian because shock can set in quickly. In the meantime, for mild burns, apply cold water or an ice pack to cool the skin and ease the pain. Neosporin (a topical antibiotic) can be applied, and you may want to wrap the area in a light gauze to protect it until the vet can take a look.

Car accident. If your pet has been in a car accident, gently move him to a safe place, changing his position as little as possible. It's a good idea to leash the injured animal immediately following the accident and to tie the leash to a stationary object. It's a disaster when an injured and disoriented animal jumps up and runs loose at an accident site. You may want to use a blanket to carry him to a vet immediately.

Coughing. If coughing persists for more than a few moments, it may be due to an obstruction in the throat. Call your veterinarian immediately.

Dehydration. Dehydration can be caused by a lack of fluid intake, fever, prolonged vomiting and diarrhea. Symptoms are a dry mouth and lack of skin elasticity. When you pick up the fold of skin on your pet's back, it should spring back. If it doesn't, your pet might be dehydrated. Sunken eyes are also an indication of dehydration. If your pet is noticeably dehydrated, consult a vet immediately. In mild cases, fluids can be given.

Diarrhea. One loose stool is usually not enough to cause major concern. Loose stools are often caused by stress, overeating or a deviation from the normal diet. However, if there is any blood in the stool, if the diarrhea is accompanied by any other symptoms, such as vomiting, or if it persists for more than 24 hours, call a veterinarian immediately.

Drooling. Travel or motion sickness is a common cause of excessive drooling. Some drugs, especially tranquilizers, can also cause this. Foreign objects (for example, sticks) in the mouth can also cause drooling. If drooling persists, contact your vet.

Fever. Before you leave for your trip have your vet write down all of your pet's normal vital signs (body temperature, pulse, etc.). This record will serve as a baseline for comparison. If your pet is feverish, take him to a vet.

Heartworm. Heartworm is an infestation of the heart chambers by a parasitic worm. It is passed to your dog by mosquitoes. Every US state has reported cases of heartworm. If you haven't already, you should talk to your vet about putting your dog on preventative medication.

Heatstroke. If you suspect your pet is suffering from heatstroke, get her to a vet immediately. If possible, immerse the animal in cold water or an ice bath. Apply ice packs to her head and/or towels soaked in water around her body on the way to the vet. Symptoms of heatstroke are uncontrollable panting, foaming at the mouth and unconsciousness. The color of your pet's lips is an indication of her health. Normally, lips are a light pink, and if you press them the white spot caused by the pressure should fade back to pink within a couple of seconds. If the animal is suffering from heatstroke, the gums will be dark pink and it will take a bit longer for the white pressure spot to refill with color.

Hypothermia. Prolonged shivering is indicative of hypothermia. Hypothermia is especially serious if your dog or cat is wet. Vigorously rub her dry and keep her warm by wrapping her in a blanket and snuggling her close to you. Call a vet who will advise you whether or not to bring your pet in for emergency care.

Minor Cuts and Scrapes. Clean cuts and scrapes with peroxide and apply an over-the-counter antibacterial ointment (such as Neosporin) to prevent infection. If bleeding persists, apply direct pressure with a clean cloth. Seek veterinary care if the scrape is to the eye or if there is any discharge. Any wound inflicted by another animal should also be seen by a veterinarian.

Panting (excessive). Excessive panting can be due to overexertion or excitement. If fever, sneezing, racing pulse, vomiting or diarrhea are also present, consult your vet. These symptoms can indicate a cold, fluid in the lungs, poisoning or internal bleeding.

Paws (licking). If your pet is constantly licking his paw(s) it could be a sign of a foreign body (splinter, etc.) or other trauma to the paws. In some cases, persistent licking is a sign of an allergy or a behavioral disorder. In either case you should consult a vet.

Poisons. If you suspect your pet has been poisoned, contact a vet or the poison control hotline immediately (see APPENDIX B). The most obvious symptoms of poisoning are excessive/profuse salivation, vomiting and convulsions. It is a good idea to keep activated charcoal tablets in your first-aid kit, which can be used to help absorb the poisons, if recommended by a vet. Some common poisons are car antifreeze, rat poison and insecticides.

Pulse. The pulse is a reflection of the heartbeat. Have your pet stand or lay on his back and gently feel along the inside of the thigh or gently press along the rib cage just over the heart. Count the number of beats per minute. At rest, most dogs have a rate in the range of 60 to 160. Generally speaking, the smaller the dog the faster the heart rate.

Shock. Symptoms of shock are a racing pulse, fast breathing, a lower-than-normal temperature and in some cases a loss of consciousness. In cases of shock, lay the animal on its side and be sure the breathing passages are not obstructed. Do not give your pet anything to drink. Keep your pet warm and get him to a veterinarian immediately.

Skunks. If your pet has been sprayed by a skunk, soaking his coat in tomato juice may help to dilute the odor.

Staggering. If your pet shows prolonged difficulty getting up or laying down, or if he looks as if he has an aching back, you should contact a veterinarian immediately. This could indicate a herniated disc, damage to a joint, or any one of numerous neurological conditions.

Stool (streaked with blood). Constipation is most often due to a lack of exercise and not enough water. In some cases it is due to an obstruction or stones in the bladder or urethra. Call your veterinarian if it persists for more than a day. If there is blood in the stool contact a vet immediately.

Ticks. Ticks can carry potentially dangerous diseases to both dogs and humans. If you find one on your pet—they usually attach near the neck and ears—drip a little rubbing alcohol on the tick and use tweezers to grab it as near to the head as possible and pull it out. After extracting the tick, soak the area with a bit of peroxide to clean the area. If infection occurs, consult your vet.

Urination (frequent). Frequent urination is most often a result of drinking large quantities of water after exertion. However, it may be a bladder infection or a sign of some sort of hormonal problem. If the condition persists, consult a vet.

Urine (blood in). Any sign of blood in the urine requires immediate attention from a vet.

Vomiting. Regurgitation—marked by repeated gulping sounds and production of a pile of semi-digested food—is normal for dogs. Vomiting, however, is much more violent and usually produces a yellow, viscous solution. If vomiting occurs more than once in a day or is accompanied by any other symptoms, consult a vet immediately. This is especially true if any blood is present in the vomit.

Appendix B: Pet Resources

by Andrea Arden

National Pet Resources

Air Transport Association of America. 1301 Pennsylvania Ave NW, Suite 1100 Washington, DC 20004-1707. Web www.air-transport.org/press/96-033.htm. This organization sets the guidelines for pet air travel.

American Animal Hospital Association (AAHA). PO Box 150899, Denver, CO 80215-0899 or 12575 W Bayaud Ave, Lakewood, CO 80228. 303/986-2800; 800/252-2242. Hrs: 9 am-5 pm, Mountain Time, Mon-Fri. Web www.healthy-pet.com. This is an association of more than 16,000 veterinary care providers founded in 1933. You can call them for veterinary referrals; their web site is full of lots of tips on pet health and safety.

American Boarding Kennels Association. 4575 Galley Rd #400A, Colorado Springs, CO 80915. 719/591-1113. Referrals for boarding kennels.

American Cat Association. 8101 Katherine Ave, Panorama City, CA 91402. 818/782-6080. This is the oldest registry for purebred cats in the US. Call for some basic tips on cat health or referrals to cat breeders.

American Cat Fancier's Association. PO Box 203, Point Lookout, MO 65726. 417/334-5430. A registry for purebred cats.

American Humane Association. 63 Inverness Dr E, Englewood, CO 80112. 800/227-4645. Hrs: 8:30 am-5 pm, Mountain Time. This is a national federation of concerned individuals and agencies dedicated to the prevention of cruelty, neglect, abuse and exploitation of animals. Contact them for information on how to report any of the above.

American Kennel Club. 51 Madison Ave, New York, NY 10010. 212/696-8336; 919/233-9767. A national registry for purebred dogs. The AKC offers free brochures on traveling with your dog as well as free packets on responsible dog ownership.

American Veterinary Medical Association. 930 N Meacham Rd, Schaumburg, IL 60196. 800/233-2862 in IL; 800/248-2862 other states. Hrs: Mon-Fri 8:30 am-4:45 pm, Central Time. This association can provide veterinarian referrals from a list that includes more than 50,000 vets in the US.

Animal Behavior Systems. 5910-F Breckenridge Pkwy, Tampa, FL 33610. 800/627-9447. Hrs: 8 am-6 pm Eastern Time, after hours answering service. ABS offers a collar that stops barking using an innovative and humane method. When the dog barks a small squirt of citronella is automatically emitted. The dog associates barking with this unpleasant smell. They also offer a shampoo that aids in the reduction of nonseasonal hair shedding. One of their best products is a very effective clean-up aid called Petzorb.

ASPCA Education Department. 424 E 92nd St, New York, NY 10128. 212/876-7700, ext 4650. Web www.ASPCA.org. The ASPCA web site has several pages on traveling trips and advice.

Association of Pet Dog Trainers. PO Box 385, Davis, CA 95617. 800/PET-DOGS. E-mail apdtbod@aol.com; web www.apdt.com. If you are interested in learning more about dog training, this is the group to contact. The APDT can refer you to trainers and to educational seminars and conferences about dogs and dog training throughout the US. Their web site is clear and informative.

Canadian Cat Association. 83 Kennedy Rd S, Unit 1805, Brampton, ON Canada L6W 3P3. 905/459-1481. This is the registry body for purebred cats in Canada. They offer a magazine for members that includes tips on cat care.

Canadian Veterinary Medical Association. 339 Booth St, Ottawa, ON Canada K1R 7K1. 613/236-1162. A good source for veterinary referrals if you are traveling in Canada.

Cherry Brook. Rte 57, PO Box 15, Broadway, NJ 08808. 908/689-7979; 800/524-0820. A wholesale pet-supply catalog.

Chicago Veterinary Medical Associations Dial-Pet Line. 161 S Lincolnway, North Aurora, IL 60542. 312/342-5738. Call to hear pre-recorded information from vets who are members of the association. Topics discussed include veterinary and training tips.

Cool Paw Productions. 708 E Solana Dr, Tempe, AZ 85281. 800/650-PAWS. This mail-order catalogs offer collapsible water bowls for $15.

Delta Society. Pet Partners Program, PO Box 1080, Renton, WA 98057. 206/226-7357. This organization promotes all aspects of the human and companion animal bond. Includes pet partners therapy programs and service-animal training and education.

DGNY Magazine (the magazine for New York City dog owners). 981 First Ave, Suite 140, New York, NY 10022. 212/832-2828. A source for things to do with your pet when visiting New York City.

Dog and Cat Book Catalogue. PO Box 2778, Wenatchee, WA 98807-2778. 509/663-9115; 800/776-2665. Web dgctbook@cascade.net. One of the best places to find just about any dog or cat book you are looking for, including rare and hard-to-find volumes. The staff are very friendly and helpful.

Doggone Good! 6429 Pelham Court, San Jose, CA 95123. 800/660- 2665. Web www.doggone.com. Mail-order catalog of dog travel and gift items, including collapsible bowls.

Good Dog! Magazine & Catsumer Report. PO Box 10069, Austin, TX 78766. 800/968-1738. The consumer magazines for dog and cat owners. Covers health, behavior and nutrition. Exclusive product test reports look at everything for your pet. Six issues a year.

Help 4 Pets. 800/Help-4-Pets (435-7473). Services include a national vet referral system and 24-hour pet-recovery system. The more pets you register, the lower the registration fees. Help 4 Pets is endorsed by the Los Angeles SPCA.

Humane Society of the United States. 2100 L St NW, Washington, DC 20037. 202/452-1100. Information regarding the humane treatment of animals.

In the Company of Dogs. PO Box 7071, Dover, DE 19903. 800/924-5050. A wide selection of unique gift items for dog lovers. Call for a free catalog.

James & Kenneth Publishers. 2140 Shattuck Ave #2406, Berkeley, CA 94704. 510/658-8588. A great source for cutting-edge books and videos on cat and dog training and behavior.

JB Wholesale. 5 Raritan Rd, Oakland, NJ 07436. 800/526-0388. Hrs: Mon-Fri 8:30 am-10 pm, Sat 11 am-4 pm, Sun 9:30 am-4:30 pm. Web www.JBPet.com. wholesale pet-supply catalog. Call to request a free catalog.

K9 Cruiser. 4640 Desoto St, San Diego, CA 92109. 800/592-7847. A wonderful device designed to make taking your pet along on bike rides a safe and fun prospect. If you intend to go biking with your dog at home or while traveling, the K9 Cruiser is indispensable.

Meblo. 2250 Rd "E" Redwood, CA 95470. 800/776-3256. Web www.meblo.com. This company carries some quality products for traveling with your pet in the car. The Deluxe Travelbed covers the entire backseat and acts as a barrier to keep your dog out of the front seat.

National Animal Poison Control Center. 1717 Thilo Rd, Suite #36, Urbana, IL 61802. 800/548-2423 for emergencies; 900/680-0000 for non-emergencies. Web www.napcc.aspca.org. Twenty-four-hour service for emergency calls; major credit cards are accepted. Be prepared to give relevant information regarding your pet, and if possible, the suspected poison. The 900 number should be used if you don't have a credit card and for non-emergency questions regarding poisons. The charge for all calls is $30.

National Dog Registry (Tattooing). Box 116, Woodstock, NY 12498. 914/679-BELL or 914/277-4485; 800/NDR-DOGS (548-2423). NDR members' dogs are registered with a tattooed number or with an implanted microchip. There is a one-time fee, which covers any pet you ever own. NDR has phones staffed 365 days a year, 24 hours a day. One of the benefits of this service is that if someone finds your pet, they have a number to call where someone will always answer the phone. The NDR was established in 1966 and currently has over 4 million registered pets.

Pet Affairs. 691 E 20th St, Building 111, Tucson, AZ 85719. 800/777-9192. This company sells a harness that converts to a seatbelt. The device clips into the seatbelt holder of your car.

Pet Assure. 10 South Morris St, Dover, NJ 07801. 888/789-PETS.   Web www.petassure.com. A membership savings program for pet owners. Members save 25 percent at the vet, an average of 50 percent off supplies and products and 10 to 50 percent off services such as training, grooming, boarding and pet-sitting. They also offer a lost-pet recovery program for members. Members can use any veterinarian in the network. There are currently approximately a thousand vets in over 30 US states in addition to vets overseas. Fees are lower if you register more than one pet. Discounts are available for groups and corporations for employees.

Pet Finders. 661 High St, Athol, NY 12810. 518/623-2166; 800/666-5678. Hrs: 24 hours a day. Web www.PetClubofAmerica.com or www.Pet-zone.com. Pet Finders keeps a medical history of your pet on file as well as your travel itinerary. Your pet will wear a tag with Pet Finders' 800 number. If someone finds your lost pet, they can call the number and Pet Finders can tell them if the animal needs any special medical care and how to find you. Also, if you lose your pet while traveling, Pet Finders will fax a description of your pet to every shelter, vet and boarding kennel in the area. There is a one-time data-entry fee and annual membership fees that are lowered if you register more than one pet.

Pet Pak, Inc. PO Box 982, Edison, NJ 08818-0982. 732/906-9200; 800/217-PETS. E-mail: SJCINC61@aol.com; web www.Petpak.com. This company sells pre-packed first-aid kits for dogs and cats.

RC Steele. 1989 Transit Way, Box 910, Brockport, NY 14420-0910. 800/872-3773. Catalog of wholesale pet- and animal-care supplies.

Roger's Visionary Pet Products. 4538 Saratoga Ave, San Diego, CA 92107. 800/364-4537. Web www.rogerspet.com. They have a nice product called *soft store* that is a convenient way to carry pet food and keep it fresh.

Tattoo-A-Pet International. 800/TAT-TOOS. Web www.Tattoo-a-pet.com. This company charges a one-time fee to register any pet(s) you have in your lifetime.

Their phones are staffed 365 days a year, 24 hours a day. Tattoo-a-pet has been in business for over 26 years and has more than 2 million registered pets.

US Department of Agriculture-APHIS. Animal Care Staff, 6505 Belcrest Rd, Hyattsville, MD 20782. 301/436-7833. Inquiries regarding airline reimbursements, pets lost in transport or mistreatment of animals by airline personnel should be directed here.

US Department of Transportation. Office of Consumer Affairs/I-25, 400 Seventh St SW, Washington, DC 20590. 202/366-2220. Inquiries regarding airline reimbursements or lost pets should be directed here.

Places to Visit with Your Pet

The American Kennel Club Library. 51 Madison Ave, New York, NY 10010-1603. 212/696-8200. E-mail info@AKC.org; web www.AKC.org. The AKC library is opened to the general public and has the most extensive collection of dog books and canine periodicals. There is also a beautiful collection of dog art adorning the walls of the AKC offices. In addition, canine travel tips are on view at the AKC website.

The Association of Pet Dog Trainers' Conference. PO Box 385, Davis, CA 95617. 800/PET-DOGS. E-mail apdtbod@aol.com; web www.apdt.com. Without a doubt one of the most fact-filled and enjoyable weekends with your dog will be found at the APDT conferences held every November. Dogs are welcome; there are many doggie activities and the conference topics cover just about every aspect of dog ownership. Venue changes yearly.

Camp Gone to the Dogs. Honey Loring, RR 1, Box 958, Putney, VT 05346. 802/387-5673. Your dog will love you forever if you take him here for a vacation. The activities are nonstop fun for both dogs and owners; including trick training, water sports, talent contests and dancing.

Dog Lovers Bookshop. 9 W 31st St, 2nd floor, New York, NY 10016. 212/594-3601. Hrs: noon-6 pm, Tues-Fri; or by appointment. Specializes in dog books, new and old. You will be greeted at the door by Houdine, the wire-haired dachshund, and your friendly dog is welcome.

The Dog Museum. Queeny Park, 1721 S Mason, St Louis MO 63131. 314/821-DOGS. Hrs: Tues-Sat, 9 am-5 pm; Sun, noon-5 pm. Museum of fine arts dedicated to the dog. A most wonderful place to visit for any dog-lover, but sadly your dog can't join you.

Whiz Kid Dog Camp. 4 Brookside Place, Westport, CT 06880. 203/226-9556; 203/222-7896 (fax). E-mail wizkid@netaxis.com. This camp for you and your dog is the perfect blend of vacation and education. There are over 50 outdoor and indoor activities including carting, puppy kindergarten, flyball and nutrition workshops held by some of the best dog professionals in the country.

William Secord Gallery. 52 E 76th St, New York, NY 10021. 212/249-0075. Hrs: Mon-Fri, 10 am-5 pm or by appointment. E-mail Wsecord@dogpainting.com; web www.dogpainting.com. Mr. Secord is the preeminent dealer of animal paintings in the US, specializing in 19th-century paintings of dogs. Works by artists such as Maud Earl, John Emms and Rosa Bonheur are permanently displayed. Also, two living masters are available for commissions of your pampered pet. The atmosphere is warm and inviting.

Index

Mobil Travel Guide

Looking for the Mobil Guides . . . ?

**Call toll-free 800/533-6478 around the clock
or use the order form below.**

Please check the guides you like to order:

☐ 0-679-03506-0
America's Best Hotels & Restaurants
$11.00 (Can $14.95)

☐ 0-679-03498-6
California and the West (Arizona, California, Nevada, Utah)
$15.95 (Can $21.95)

☐ 0-679-03500-1
Great Lakes (Illinois, Indiana, Michigan, Ohio, Wisconsin, Canada: Ontario)
$15.95 (Can $21.95)

☐ 0-679-03501-X
Mid-Atlantic (Delaware, District of Columbia, Maryland, New Jersey, North Carolina, Pennsylvania, South Carolina, Virginia, West Virginia)
$15.95 (Can $21.95)

☐ 0-679-03502-8
Northeast (Connecticut, Maine, Massachusetts, New Hampshire, New York, Rhode Island, Vermont, Canada: New Brunswick, Nova Scotia, Ontario, Prince Edward Island, Québec)
$15.95 (Can $21.95)

☐ 0-679-03503-6
Northwest and Great Plains (Idaho, Iowa, Minnesota, Montana, Nebraska, North Dakota, Oregon, South Dakota, Washington, Wyoming, Canada: Alberta, British Columbia, Manitoba)
$15.95 (Can $21.95)

☐ 0-679-03504-4
Southeast (Alabama, Florida, Georgia, Kentucky, Mississippi, Tennessee)
$15.95 (Can $21.95)

☐ 0-679-03505-2
Southwest & South Central (Arkansas, Colorado, Kansas, Louisiana, Missouri, New Mexico, Oklahoma, Texas)
$15.95 (Can $21.95)

☐ 0-679-03499-4
Major Cities (Detailed coverage of 45 major U.S. cities)
$17.95 (Can $25.00)

☐ 0-679-00047-X
Southern California (Includes California south of Lompoc, with Tijuana and Ensenada, Mexico)
$12.00 (Can $16.95)

☐ 0-679-00048-8
Florida
$12.00 (Can $16.95)

☐ 0-679-03548-6
On the Road with Your Pet (More than 3,000 Mobil-rated Lodgings that Welcome Travelers with Pets)
$12.00 (Can $16.95)

Total cost of book(s) ordered $_____

Shipping & Handling (please add $2 for first book, $.50 for each additional book) $_____

Add applicable sales tax (In Canada and in CA, CT, FL, IL, NJ, NY, TN and WA.) $_____

TOTAL AMOUNT ENCLOSED $_____

☐ My check is enclosed.

☐ Please charge my credit card.

☐ VISA ☐ MasterCard ☐ American Express

Credit Card # _____

Expiration _____

Signature _____

Please ship the books checked above to:

Name _____

Address _____

City _____ State _____ Zip _____

Please mail this form to: Mobil Travel Guides, Random House, 400 Hahn Rd., Westminster, MD 21157

Mobil Travel Guide.
On The Road With Your Pet.

ONE NIGHT FREE

One Free Night's Boarding Stay.
Advance reservations required.
Peak period restrictions may apply.
One offer per family per stay.
Must present at check-in to redeem offer.

OFFER EXPIRES APRIL 30, 1999

Budget.
Get out of the ordinary.™

15% OFF

Take 15% Off Weekly or Weekend Standard Rates.
Valid on economy through full-size cars.
For reservations call: **800-455-2848.**
Be sure to mention **BCD#:T445314.**

OFFER EXPIRES APRIL 30, 1999

≋ National Car Rental.

ONE FREE WEEKEND DAY
(With Purchase of Two Weekend Days)

Present this certificate at a National rental counter to
receive one free weekend day with the purchase of two
consecutive weekend days at applicable rate when using your
membership discount. Valid on a Compact through Full-size
4-door car at participating National locations in the U.S.
Reservations required.
Contact your Travel Agent or National at **1-800-CAR RENT®** .
Subject to terms and conditions on reverse side.
Discount #5708785 PC #013353-4 Type 7

OFFER EXPIRES APRIL 30, 1999

VETERINARY
PET INSURANCE
*Making the miracles of
veterinary medicine affordable™*

10% OFF

10% Discount Off the Premium of 12 Month Veterinary Pet Insurance Base Policies.

The discount does not apply to the Cancer
Endorsement or the Vaccination & Routine Care
Coverage Endorsement. No other discounts apply.

1-800-USA-PETS

OFFER EXPIRES APRIL 30, 1999

Please note: All offers may not be available in Canada. Call **(410) 825-3463** if you are unable to use an 800 number listed on the coupon. Read each coupon carefully before using. Discounts only apply to the items and terms specified in the offer at participating locations.

Best Friends
PET RESORT & SALON

Call 1-888-FOR-PETS
for a location nearest you.

Be sure to mention **BCD#T445314** when reserving an economy through full size car and present this certificate at participating U.S. Budget locations (except in the New York metro area) to receive your member savings discount. This offer is valid through April 30, 1999, requires a one day advance reservation, and is subject to vehicle availability. Vehicle must be returned to the original renting location except where intra/inter metro area drops-offs are permitted. Local age and rental requirements apply. Locations that rent to drivers under 25 may impose an age surcharge. Offer is not available with CorpRate, government or tour/wholesale rates, or with any other promotion. Refueling services, taxes, surcharges, and optional items like the Loss Damage Waiver are extra. Blackout dates may apply. Limit one certificate per rental.

Terms and Conditions. Valid for one weekend day with the purchase of two consecutive weekend days on car classes indicated on front at participating National locations in the U.S. (Not valid in Manhattan, NY.) • Subject to availability, blackout dates and capacity control.
• Weekend rate and time parameters, local rental and minimum rental day requirements apply.
• Cannot be used in multiples or with any other certificate, special discount or promotion.
• Standard rental qualifications apply. • Minimum rental age at most locations is 25.

In addition to rental charges, where applicable, renter is responsible for: Optional Loss Damage Waiver, up to $15.99 per day; a per mile charge in excess of mileage allowance; taxes; surcharges; additional charges if car is not returned within a prescribed rental period; drop charge and additional driver fee; optional refueling charge; optional insurance benefits.

RENTAL AGENT INSTRUCTIONS: 1. Rental Screen 1: • Key Promo Coup # from the front side. 2. Rental Screen 3: • Key discount # from the front side in "RATE RECAP #" field. • Key applicable rate for one weekend day in "DEP: ORIG" field. • Key 7 in "TYPE" field. 3. Write RA# and rental date below. 4. Retain certificate at rental. Send certificate to Headquarters, Attn: Travel Industry Billing.

RA# _____ Rental Date ___/___/___

VETERINARY
PET INSURANCE
*Making the miracles of
veterinary medicine affordable™*

PC-0017